200.00

MW00723542

The Sports Hall of Fame Encyclopedia

Baseball, Basketball, Football, Hockey, Soccer

Dave Blevins

Volume I: A–L

The Scarecrow Press, Inc.
Lanham, Maryland • Toronto • Plymouth, UK
2012

SCARECROW PRESS, INC.

Published in the United States of America
by Scarecrow Press, Inc.
A wholly owned subsidiary of The Rowman & Littlefield Publishing Group, Inc.
4501 Forbes Boulevard, Suite 200, Lanham, Maryland 20706
www.scarecrowpress.com

Estover Road
Plymouth PL6 7PY
United Kingdom

British Library Cataloguing in Publication Information Available

Library of Congress Cataloging-in-Publication Data

Blevins, David.
The sports hall of fame encyclopedia : baseball, basketball, football, hockey, soccer / Dave Blevins.
p. cm.
Includes bibliographical references and index.
ISBN 978-0-8108-6130-5 (cloth : alk. paper)
1. Athletes—United States—Biography—Dictionaries. 2. Athletes—Canada—Biography—Dictionaries. 3. Baseball players—United States—Biography—Dictionaries. 4. Basketball players—United States—Biography—Dictionaries. 5. Football players—United States—Biography—Dictionaries. 6. Hockey players—United States—Biography—Dictionaries. 7. Hockey players—Canada—Biography—Dictionaries. 8. Soccer players—United States—Biography—Dictionaries. I. Title.
GV697.A1B5534 2011
796.0922—dc22
[B]

2010034815

™ The paper used in this publication meets the minimum requirements of American National Standard for Information Sciences—Permanence of Paper for Printed Library Materials, ANSI/NISO Z39.48-1992.
Manufactured in the United States of America.

Contents

Abbreviations

AAFC	All-America Football Conference
AAU	Amateur Athletic Union
ABA	American Basketball Association
ABL	American Basketball League
AFC	American Football Conference
AFL	American Football League; Arena Football League
AHA	American Hockey Association
AHL	American Hockey League
AIAW	Association for Intercollegiate Athletics for Women
APFA	American Professional Football Association
APSL	American Professional Soccer League
ASHL	Alberta Senior Hockey League
ASL	American Soccer League
BAA	Basketball Association of America
CAHA	Canadian Amateur Hockey Association
CAHL	Canadian Amateur Hockey League
CBA	Continental Basketball Association
CBL	Central Basketball League
CCNY	City College of New York
CFL	Canadian Football League
CHL	Central Hockey League
CIAA	Central Intercollegiate Athletic Association
CISL	Continental Indoor Soccer League
CONCACAF	Confederation of North, Central American and Caribbean Association Football
CPFL	Continental Professional Football League
CPHL	Canadian Professional Hockey League; Central Professional Hockey League
CSL	Canadian Soccer League, Cosmopolitan Soccer League
EAHL	Eastern Amateur Hockey League
EBL	Eastern Basketball League
ECAHA	Eastern Canada Amateur Hockey Association
ECHA	Eastern Canada Hockey Association
ECHL	East Coast Hockey League
ECPSL	Eastern Canada Professional Soccer League
EHL	Eastern Hockey League
EPBL	Eastern Professional Basketball League
EPHL	Eastern Professional Hockey League
FAHL	Federal Amateur Hockey League
FIBA	Fédération Internationale de Basketball
FIFA	Fédération Internationale de Football Association
GASL	German American Soccer League
IBL	Interstate Basketball League

IHL	International Hockey League
IIHF	International Ice Hockey Federation
IPHL	International Professional Hockey League
ISL	International Soccer League
MBL	Metropolitan Basketball League
MHL	Manitoba Hockey League
MISL	Major Indoor Soccer League
MJHL	Manitoba Junior Hockey League
MLB	Major League Baseball
MLS	Major League Soccer
MPHL	Maritime Professional Hockey League
MSHL	Manitoba Senior Hockey League
MVP	Most Valuable Player
NABC	National Association of Basketball Coaches
NABBP	National Association of Base Ball Players
NAFL	National Association Football League
NAIA	National Association of Intercollegiate Athletics
NAPBBP	National Association of Professional Base Ball Players
NAPSL	North American Professional Soccer League
NASL	North American Soccer League
NBA	National Basketball Association
NBL	National Basketball League
NCAA	National Collegiate Athletic Association
NEPL	New England Professional League
NESL	New England Soccer League
NFC	National Football Conference
NFL	National Football League
NHA	National Hockey Association
NHL	National Hockey League
NISOA	National Intercollegiate Soccer Officials Association
NIT	National Invitation Tournament
NOHA	Northern Ontario Hockey Association
NPBL	National Professional Basketball League
NPSL	National Professional Soccer League
NSCAA	National Soccer Coaches Association of America
NSL	National Soccer League
NWBL	National Women's Basketball League
NYSL	New York State League
OHA	Ontario Hockey Association
OHL	Ontario Hockey League
ONDHL	Ontario National Defense Hockey League
OPHL	Ontario Professional Hockey League
PCHA	Pacific Coast Hockey Association
PCHL	Pacific Coast Hockey League
PCL	Pacific Coast League
QAHA	Quebec Amateur Hockey Association
QAHL	Quebec Amateur Hockey League
QJHL	Quebec Junior Hockey League
OMJHL	Ontario Major Junior Hockey League
QMJHL	Quebec Major Junior Hockey League
QSHL	Quebec Senior Hockey League
SEC	Southeastern Conference
SSHL	Saskatchewan Senior Hockey League
TBAHA	Thunder Bay Amateur Hockey Association
TBHL	Thunder Bay Hockey League
TBSHL	Thunder Bay Senior Hockey League

THL Toronto Hockey League
UFL United Football League
USAHA United States Amateur Hockey Association
USBL United States Basketball League
USFA United States Fastball Association
USFF United States Football Federation
USFL United States Football League
USHL United States Hockey League
USSF United States Soccer Federation
WABA Women's American Basketball Association
WBL Women's Basketball League, Women's Professional Basketball League
WCHL Western Canada Hockey League
WCJHL Western Canada Junior Hockey League
WCSHL Western Canada Senior Hockey League
WFL World Football League
WHA World Hockey Association
WHL Western Hockey League
WNBA Women's National Basketball Association
WPBL Women's Professional Basketball League
WPHL Western Pennsylvania Hockey League
WUSA Women's United Soccer Association
YMCA Young Men's Christian Association

Preface

This book contains more than 1,475 mini-biographies of the men, women, and teams that have been inducted into the five most popular halls of fame in North America, including the National Baseball Hall of Fame and Museum (Cooperstown, New York), Naismith Memorial Basketball Hall of Fame (Springfield, Massachusetts), Pro Football Hall of Fame (Canton, Ohio), Hockey Hall of Fame (Toronto, Ontario, Canada), and the National Soccer Hall of Fame and Museum (Oneonta, New York) as of 2010.

These biographies are comprehensive but, due to space limitations, do not cover every aspect of an inductee's life, but instead focus on the achievements and accomplishments in the sporting arena that enabled them to garner hall of fame induction. Each entry includes an overview of the inductee's career and their lifetime statistical accomplishments, where applicable.

Most of the information provided for each inductee comes directly from the appropriate hall of fame, while some additional sources were used, as indicated after the entry. In the gathering and editing of the information used to write each inductee's entry, there are bound to be contradictions and differences between multiple sources (such as birth date and place, statistical facts, specific dates of achievements, etc). Whenever differences existed, the information provided by the specific hall of fame was considered accurate and was used in the text.

This book also contains an appendix that lists inductees by year inducted. Additional appendixes are included for each specific hall of fame and history, inductee selection criteria, and voting procedures.

Chapter 1
1960 USA Men's Basketball Team to Averill

1960 USA Men's Basketball Team; inducted into the Naismith Memorial Basketball Hall of Fame in 2010 as a team; won the Olympic gold medal in Rome, Italy.

Consisting of all amateur players, the 1960 USA Men's Basketball Team went undefeated (8–0) and won a gold medal at the Olympic Games in Rome, Italy and won each of its games by an average of 42.4 points (the USA team averaged 101.9 points per game while holding opponents to 59.5 points per game). Ten players went on to the National Basketball Association and six team members have been inducted into the Naismith Memorial Basketball Hall of Fame, including four players (Walt Bellamy, Jerry Lucas, Oscar Robertson, Jerry West) and two coaches (Peter Newell, Dutch Lonborg). This 1960 team was inducted into the USA Olympic Hall of Fame in 1984. This team is considered to have the best roster of players until the 1992 "Dream Team."

The team finished first out of 16 teams, and consisted of players Jay Arnette, Walt Bellamy, Robert Boozer, Terry Dischinger, Burdette Haldorson, Darrall Imhoff, Allen Kelley, Lester Lane, Jerry Lucas, Oscar Robertson, Adrian Smith, and Jerry West.

Source: Naismith Memorial Basketball Hall of Fame

1992 USA Men's Basketball Olympic Team (The "Dream Team"); inducted into the Naismith Memorial Basketball Hall of Fame in 2010 as a team; won the Olympic gold medal in Barcelona, Spain.

Commonly referred to as the "Dream Team," the 1992 USA Men's Basketball Olympic Team went undefeated (8–0) at the Olympic Games in Barcelona, Spain to win the gold medal with an average margin of victory per game of 43.8 points (out of a field of 12 teams). Coached by a Hall of Famer, the late Chuck Daly, the "Dream Team" was the first squad made up primarily of NBA players, who were eligible to participate in international basketball competition (including the Olympics) for the first time because of a change in the Fédération Internationale de Basketball rules in 1989.

As of this writing, ten team players have been inducted into the Naismith Memorial Basketball Hall of Fame, including Charles Barkley, Larry Bird, Clyde Drexler, Patrick Ewing, Earvin "Magic" Johnson, Michael Jordan, Karl Malone, Scottie Pippen, David Robinson, and John Stockton. Hall of Fame coaches Mike Krzyzewski and Lenny Wilkens assisted Daly, while Chris Mullin and college star Christian Laettner (from Duke University) completed the roster. This team was inducted into the USA Olympic Hall of Fame in 2009.

Source: Naismith Memorial Basketball Hall of Fame

Aaron, Henry Louis "Hank" (born: February 5, 1934 in Mobile, Alabama); inducted into the National Baseball Hall of Fame and Museum in 1982 as a player; Position: Right Field; Uniform: #44; Bats: Right; Throws: Right; only player to hit at least 30 home runs in a season 15 times; first player to reach 3,000 hits and 500 home runs; retired as Major League Baseball's all-time home run king.

Coming from humble beginnings, Aaron (nicknamed "Hammerin' Hank" and "The Hammer") became one of baseball's biggest stars, and by the time he retired in 1976, he had become MLB's home run king. He passed Babe Ruth's magic number of 714 in 1974 and ended his career with 755. Aaron's career home run record was later surpassed on August 7, 2007 when the San Francisco Giants' Barry Bonds hit his home run number 756.

During his 23-year major league career (1954–1976), which began on April 13, 1954, Aaron played for the Milwaukee Braves (1954–1965), Atlanta Braves (1966–1974), and the Milwaukee Brewers (1975–1976). He was the National

League's Most Valuable Player in 1957, won the Lou Gehrig Memorial Award in 1970, and won three straight Gold Glove Awards (1958–1960). He played in two World Series, winning in 1957 and losing in 1958.

He led the National League in batting average twice (1956, 1959); home runs four times (1957, 1963, 1966–1967); runs batted in four times (1957, 1960, 1963, 1966); total bases eight times (1956–1957, 1959–1961, 1963, 1967, 1969); slugging percentage four times (1959, 1963, 1967, 1971); runs scored three times (1957, 1963, 1967); hits twice (1956, 1959); and doubles four times (1955–1956, 1961, 1965). Aaron is the only player to hit at least 30 home runs in a season 15 times, the only player to hit at least 20 home runs in a season 20 times, hit 40 home runs in a season eight times, and was the first player to reach 3,000 hits and 500 home runs.

Playing in the Louisiana Recreational League while attending Toulminville Grammar School (Mobile, Alabama), Aaron developed the unusual batting style that he used throughout his career, hitting with his left hand over his right. While at Central High School (Mobile), he played two years on the team and helped the squad win the Negro High School Championship both seasons. By age 15, he was playing with the semi-professional Pritchett Athletics for $3.00 a game. He also played for the independent Mobile Black Bears and at age 17, Aaron was offered a $200.00 a month contract to play for the Indianapolis Clowns of the Negro American League, one he accepted after graduating from high school.

In 1952, he was signed by the Milwaukee Braves and sent to the organization's Class C farm team, the Eau Clair Bears in the Northern League. Although he played in only 87 games, Aaron was selected to the All-Star team and named the league's Rookie of the Year, while hitting .336, scoring 89 runs, and powering nine home runs.

In 1953, the 6', 180-pound Aaron was promoted to the Braves' Jacksonville Tars Class A team, becoming the first black player in the South Atlantic League. He led the team to the league pennant, was named the league's MVP and won the batting championship with a .362 average.

During the winter, Aaron played in the Puerto Rican League and was moved to the outfield for the first time in his professional career. He later made his major league debut on April 13, 1954, going 0-for-5 against the St. Louis Cardinals. On April 15th, Aaron got his first major league hit, a single off Cardinal's pitcher Vic Raschi, and eight days later, on April 23, he hit his first home run, also off Raschi. His rookie season came to a sudden end on September 5 when he broke his ankle sliding into third base.

Recovering from his injury, Aaron returned to the Braves in 1955 and was named to the first of his 25 All-Star teams. In 1956, Aaron became the second youngest player ever to win the batting title, hitting .328. He was also the only batter in the league to have 200 hits and led the league in doubles. In 1957, the Braves won the league pennant as Aaron hit over 40 home runs for the first time (44). For the second season in a row, he hit a home run in every National League ballpark, which he would go on to do for eight straight years. He helped lead the Braves to a seven-game World Series victory over the New York Yankees, and at the end of the season, Aaron was named the National League's MVP at only 23 years of age.

After the success of his 1957 season, he began 1958 in a batting slump, although he did recover well enough to finish the year hitting .326 with 30 home runs and 95 RBIs, and helped the team win another pennant. After losing the Word Series to the Yankees, in 1959 Aaron became the second youngest player (at age 25) to collect 1,000 career hits in the major leagues. He ended the season winning another batting title (.355) and leading the league in hits, total bases, and slugging percentage.

Both Aaron and the team slumped in 1960 and for the first time in his career, he did not hit above .300. Although the team continued to slump into the 1961 season and attendance fell to just over one million, history was made on June 8, 1961, when Aaron, Eddie Mathews, Joe Adcock, and Frank Thomas hit consecutive home runs in the same inning (seventh) against the Cincinnati Reds, the first time the feat had ever been accomplished in the major leagues. Despite the power display (including another home run by Mathews and one by Warren Spahn), the game mirrored the team's downward spiral as the Reds would eventually win, 10–8. By the end of the season, his eighth in the majors, Aaron had hit career 253 home runs, while compiling a career batting average of .319.

While the Braves continued their downward spiral in 1962 (finishing in fifth place and attracting less than 800,000 fans), Aaron had a solid season, hitting .323, with 45 home runs and 128 RBIs. He reached two milestones in the 1963 season by hitting his 300th home run on April 19 and getting his 1,000th RBI on April 22nd. He collected his 2,000th hit on July 12, 1964 and in 1965 he and Matthews broke the major league record for home runs by teammates, surpassing Babe Ruth and Lou Gehrig. Eventually, as teammates, Aaron (442) and Mathews (421) would end with 863 home runs, while the Babe Ruth (434) / Lou Gehrig (349) combination ended with 783. After finishing the season in fifth place and having attracted just over 550,000 fans, the Braves moved to Atlanta.

Aaron's first year in Atlanta (1966) was notable. He became the eleventh player in major league history to hit 400 home runs; hit 44 home runs; and came to bat 603 times, a then National League record. As solid as 1966 had been, in 1967 he really excited the fans by reaching numerous milestones, such as getting his 2,500th hit (June 12); amassing 4,471 total career bases (June 17, sixth on the all-time National League list); hitting his eleventh grand slam (June 27, leading all active players); collecting his 1,500th career RBI (July 31); and his 8,050th official at-bat (August 1) made him the all-time Braves leader. After the season, he was named the team's MVP for the sixth time.

In 1968, Aaron hit his 500th home run and by the end of the season, he had garnered a career .314 batting average, then highest among active players. In 1969, the first season of divisional play, the Braves won their division, but lost in the league championship series to the "Miracle" New York Mets, eventual winners of that season's World Series.

In 1970, Aaron became only the ninth player to reach the 3,000-hit mark. In 1971, he hit his 600th home run and his first homer in the All-Star Game. While having less than 500 at bats in 1971, he was still able to hit 47 home runs and collect 118 RBIs. During the 1972 season, he hit his 647th home run to place him second on the all-time list, ahead of Willie Mays and behind Babe Ruth. The home run was a grand slam, which put him first on the all-time list, later to be passed by Willie McCovey. Later in the year, he hit home run 660 (setting a record for most by a player on the same team) and he also broke Stan Musial's record for total bases.

As Aaron began to approach Ruth's all-time home run record, he began to receive racially tinged hate mail and death threats, which amplified the closer he got to home run 714. He tied Ruth on April 4, 1974 against the Cincinnati Reds and broke the record four days later off the Los Angeles Dodgers' Al Downing in front of more than 53,000 fans at Atlanta's Fulton County Stadium.

After being traded to the Milwaukee Brewers in 1975, he broke Babe Ruth's all-time RBI record his first year with the new team. Retiring in 1976, Aaron returned to Atlanta as a team executive for the Braves, becoming one of the first blacks in professional baseball's upper-level management.

After retiring from the game, he wrote the autobiographical *I Had a Hammer: The Hank Aaron Story* and in February 1999, Major League Baseball announced the creation of the Hank Aaron Award, to be presented annually to the best hitters in the American and National Leagues. This was the first major award to be named after a former player still living at the time the award was created. Later in the year, he was ranked number five on *The Sporting News*' list of the 100 Greatest Baseball Players and was elected to the Major League Baseball All-Century Team.

In 2001, Aaron received the Presidential Citizens Medal from President Clinton and in 2002, he received the Presidential Medal of Freedom, the highest honor that can be bestowed on a private citizen, from President George W. Bush.

A statue of Aaron stands outside the front entrance of Turner Field, where the Braves currently play. His jersey number 44 has been retired by both the Atlanta Braves and the Milwaukee Brewers.

Hank Aaron's Career Statistics

YEAR	G	AB	R	H	2B	3B	HR	RBI	BB	SO	SB	AVG	SLG
1954	122	468	58	131	27	6	13	69	28	39	2	.280	.447
1955	153	602	105	189	37	9	27	106	49	61	3	.314	.540
1956	153	609	106	200	34	14	26	92	37	54	2	.328	.558
1957	151	615	118	198	27	6	44	132	57	58	1	.322	.600
1958	153	601	109	196	34	4	30	95	59	49	4	.326	.546
1959	154	629	116	223	46	7	39	123	51	54	8	.355	.636
1960	153	590	102	172	20	11	40	126	60	63	16	.292	.566
1961	155	603	115	197	39	10	34	120	56	64	21	.327	.594
1962	156	592	127	191	28	6	45	128	66	73	15	.323	.618
1963	161	631	121	201	29	4	44	130	78	94	31	.319	.586
1964	145	570	103	187	30	2	24	95	62	46	22	.328	.514
1965	150	570	109	181	40	1	32	89	60	81	24	.318	.560
1966	158	603	117	168	23	1	44	127	76	96	21	.279	.539
1967	155	600	113	184	37	3	39	109	63	97	17	.307	.573
1968	160	606	84	174	33	4	29	86	64	62	28	.287	.498
1969	147	547	100	164	30	3	44	97	87	47	9	.300	.607
1970	150	516	103	154	26	1	38	118	74	63	9	.298	.574
1971	139	495	95	162	22	3	47	118	71	58	1	.327	.669
1972	129	449	75	119	10	0	34	77	92	55	4	.265	.514
1973	120	392	84	118	12	1	40	96	68	51	1	.301	.643
1974	112	340	47	91	16	0	20	69	39	29	1	.268	.491
1975	137	465	45	109	16	2	12	60	70	51	0	.234	.355

YEAR	G	AB	R	H	2B	3B	HR	RBI	BB	SO	SB	AVG	SLG
1976	85	271	22	62	8	0	10	35	35	38	0	.229	.369
TOTALS	3,298	12,364	2,174	3,771	624	98	755	2,297	1,402	1,383	240	.305	.555

Sources: *Hank Aaron and the Home Run That Changed America* (Tom Stanton); *Hank Aaron: Brave in Every Way* (Peter Golenbock); *I Had a Hammer: The Hank Aaron* Story (Hank Aaron); Baseball-Reference.com; National Baseball Hall of Fame and Museum

Abbott, Senda Berenson (born: Senda Valvrojenski on March 19, 1868 in Vilna, Lithuania; died: February 16, 1954 in Santa Barbara, California); inducted into the Naismith Memorial Basketball Hall of Fame in 1985 as a contributor; often called the "Mother of Women's Basketball."

After emigrating from Lithuania to Boston, Massachusetts when she was seven years old, the family changed its name to Berenson. She attended the Girls' Latin School in Boston; later trained at the Boston Normal School of Gymnastics (1890–1892); and became the first Director of Physical Education at Smith College (Northampton, Massachusetts) in January 1892, where she stayed for 19 years. She began her tenure at Smith College just one month after the game of basketball had been invented by Dr. James Naismith at the International YMCA Training School in nearby Springfield.

After learning more about the game from Naismith, on March 21, 1893 she organized the first women's collegiate basketball contest (freshman against sophomores), and modified the rules to avoid the roughness of the men's game. Her primary changes were to use six players at a time; dividing the court into three areas; and assigning two players to each of the three zones, from which they were not allowed to roam. Players were allowed to dribble the ball only three times and could hold the ball for only a maximum of three seconds.

Her version of the game became popular with women's teams and Abbott's modified rules were first published in 1899. In 1901, she became editor of the *Women's Basketball Guide.*

In 1911, she married Herbert Abbott, an English professor at Smith, and left the school to assume control of the Physical Education Department at the Burnham School in Northampton, Massachusetts, where she stayed until 1921. In the meantime, she continued editing the *Women's Basketball Guide* until the 1916–1917 issue and organized the U.S. Women's Basketball Committee, serving as its chairwoman until 1917.

In 1985, Abbott and Margaret Wade were the first two women elected to the Naismith Memorial Basketball Hall of Fame. She was later inducted into the International Jewish Sports Hall of Fame in 1987 and the Women's Basketball Hall of Fame in 1999.

Sources: International Jewish Sports Hall of Fame; Naismith Memorial Basketball Hall of Fame; Women's Basketball Hall of Fame

Abdul-Jabbar, Kareem (born: Ferdinand Lewis Alcindor, Jr. on April 16, 1947 in Harlem, New York City, New York); inducted into the Naismith Memorial Basketball Hall of Fame in 1995 as a player; Position: Center; Uniform: #33; first man in NBA history to play 20 seasons.

Recognizable for his skyhook shot and dominant size (7'2", 267 pounds), Abdul-Jabbar retired as one of basketball's all-time greatest players. The first man to enjoy a 20-season NBA career (1969–1989), he played for the Milwaukee Bucks (1969–1975, winning a title in 1971) and the Los Angeles Lakers (1975–1989, where he led the team to five NBA championships (1980, 1982, 1985, 1987–1988).

When he retired in 1989 at age 42, Abdul-Jabbar ranked number one in nine NBA statistical categories: points scored (38,387); seasons played (20); playoff points scored (5,762); Most Valuable Player awards (six); minutes played (57,446); games played (1,560); field goals made (15,837); field goals attempted (28,307); and blocked shots (3,189). He led the NBA in scoring (per-game average; 1971–1972), rebounding (1976), and in blocked shots (1975–1976, 1979–1980); was a six-time NBA MVP (1971–1972, 1974, 1976–1977, 1980); named NBA Rookie of the Year (1970); a 10-time All-NBA First Team selection (1971–1974, 1976–1977, 1980–1981, 1984, 1986); NBA All-Defensive First Team (1974–1975, 1979–1981); NBA Finals MVP (1971, 1985); played in 18 NBA All-Star Games (1970–1977, 1979–1989); and was named to the NBA 35th Anniversary All-Time Team (1980) and to the NBA 50th Anniversary All-Time Team (1996).

Abdul-Jabbar attended Power Memorial High School (New York, New York) from 1962 to 1965; led the team to undefeated seasons as a sophomore and junior; and lost only one game as a senior. He finished his high school career with 2,067 points and 2,002 rebounds (both New York City high school records); was named All-City and All-American three straight years (1963–1965); and led his team to three straight New York City Catholic championships.

After high school, he attended the University of California at Los Angeles, and would eventually become the leader of one of the best college basketball teams ever assembled. In Abdul-Jabbar's first varsity game as a sophomore (freshmen were not allowed to play on varsity teams), he scored 56 points (a UCLA record) and finished the season averaging 29 points and 15.5 rebounds per game, leading the team to an undefeated 30–0 record. Guided by coach John Wooden, Abdul-Jabbar led the team to the first of seven consecutive national NCAA championships for the school.

After incurring an eye injury in his junior year, he often wore goggles on the court, a habit that he continued throughout his playing career. Abdul-Jabbar finished his college career winning three consecutive NCAA titles; was the school's all-time leading scorer (2,325 points, 26.4 per game); selected *The Sporting News* College Player of the Year three times (1967–1969); a three-time First Team All-American (1967–1969); a two-time National Player of the Year (1967, 1969); and was the first and only player to be named NCAA Tournament Most Outstanding Player three times (1967–1969).

After graduating from UCLA, Abdul-Jabbar was the number one draft pick of the Milwaukee Bucks in 1969. He was named NBA Rookie of the Year (1969–1970) and in his sophomore season, he was the league's top scorer (averaging 31.7 points per game) and won the first of his six Most Valuable Player Awards. In 1971, he led the Bucks to the franchise's only NBA championship.

A devout Muslim since his college days, Alcindor converted to Islam and legally changed his name to Kareem Abdul-Jabbar in the fall of 1971.

Traded to the Lakers in 1975, he won his fourth MVP Award, although the team finished the season with a 40–42 mark, and did not make the playoffs.

After retiring from the NBA, Abdul-Jabbar stayed active in basketball, became a writer, and appeared in several movies. As a player, he had gained the reputation of being moody and difficult to deal with, which hindered his chances of becoming a professional head coach.

Since 1998, he has worked as a volunteer coach at Alchesay High School on the Fort Apache Indian Reservation (Whiteriver, Arizona); was named an assistant coach of the NBA's Los Angeles Clippers in 2001; and in 2002, he accepted his first head coaching position with the Oklahoma Storm of the United States Basketball League. He later served as a scout for the New York Knicks, and in September 2005, Abdul-Jabbar returned to the Lakers as a special assistant to head coach Phil Jackson.

He has authored or co-authored several books, most of which deal with black history or minority struggles, including *Brothers in Arms: The Epic Story of the 761st Tank Battalion.*

Being a popular media attraction since his days at UCLA, he has appeared on numerous television programs, specials, and movies, including *Airplane!* and *Game of Death*, with Bruce Lee.

Kareem Abdul-Jabbar's Career Statistics

SEASON	TEAM	LG	G	MIN	FG	FT	TRB	AST	PTS
1969–1970	Milwaukee	NBA	82	3,534	938	485	1,190	337	2,361
1970–1971	Milwaukee	NBA	82	3,288	1,063	470	1,311	272	2,596
1971–1972	Milwaukee	NBA	81	3,583	1,159	504	1,346	370	2,822
1972–1973	Milwaukee	NBA	76	3,254	982	328	1,224	379	2,292
1973–1974	Milwaukee	NBA	81	3,548	948	295	1,178	386	2,191
1974–1975	Milwaukee	NBA	65	2,747	812	325	912	264	1,949
1975–1976	Los Angeles	NBA	82	3,379	914	447	1,383	413	2,275
1976–1977	Los Angeles	NBA	82	3,016	888	376	1,090	319	2,152
1977–1978	Los Angeles	NBA	62	2,265	663	274	801	269	1,600
1978–1979	Los Angeles	NBA	80	3,157	777	349	1,025	431	1,903
1979–1980	Los Angeles	NBA	82	3,143	835	364	886	371	2,034
1980–1981	Los Angeles	NBA	80	2,976	836	423	821	272	2,095
1981–1982	Los Angeles	NBA	76	2,677	753	312	659	225	1,818
1982–1983	Los Angeles	NBA	79	2,554	722	278	592	200	1,722
1983–1984	Los Angeles	NBA	80	2,622	716	285	587	211	1,717
1984–1985	Los Angeles	NBA	79	2,630	723	289	622	249	1,735
1985–1986	Los Angeles	NBA	79	2,629	755	336	478	280	1,846
1986–1987	Los Angeles	NBA	78	2,441	560	245	523	203	1,366

SEASON	TEAM	LG	G	MIN	FG	FT	TRB	AST	PTS
1987–1988	Los Angeles	NBA	80	2,308	480	205	478	135	1,165
1988–1989	Los Angeles	NBA	74	1,695	313	122	334	74	748
	TOTALS	NBA	1,560	57,446	15,837	6,712	17,440	5,660	38,387

Sources: Basketball-Reference.com; *From Lew Alcindor to Kareem Abdul-Jabbar* (James Haskins); *Kareem Abdu-Jabbar: Basketball Great (Black Americans of Achievement)* (R. Thomas Coburn); Naismith Memorial Basketball Hall of Fame

Abel, Sidney Gerald "Sid" (born: February 22, 1918 in Melville, Saskatchewan, Canada; died: February 8, 2000 in Farmington Hills, Michigan); inducted into the Hockey Hall of Fame in 1969 as a player; Position: Center-Left Wing; Uniform: #12; second player in Red Wings franchise history to win the Hart Memorial Trophy.

During his 13-year (1938–1954) NHL career, the 5'11", 170-pound Abel played for the Detroit Red Wings (1938–1943, 1945–1952) and the Chicago Black Hawks (1952–1954). He captured three Stanley Cup titles (1943, 1950, 1952); won the 1949 Hart Memorial Trophy as the NHL's MVP; was named Second-Team All-Star Left Wing in 1942; First-Team All-Star Center twice (1949–1950); and Second-Team All-Star Center in 1951.

Honing his skills in the minor leagues for several seasons, Abel played 15 games with the Red Wings during the 1938–1939 season. Needing more experience, he returned to the minor leagues, before rejoining Detroit in 1940. Rejoining Detroit after missing two seasons during World War II, he left the Red Wings in 1952 and played for Chicago until the end of his career.

In his second full NHL season (1941–1942), Abel averaged more than a point per game (49, 48) and was named a Second-Team All-Star. At age 24, he served as the team's captain when the squad won the Stanley Cup championship. In the 1948–1949 season, he led all Detroit scorers and became the second Red Wings player to win the Hart Memorial Trophy (Ebbie Goodfellow had been the first in 1940).

In 1949–1950, Abel set career highs with 34 goals and 69 points, while helping the team win another title. After winning his third Stanley Cup championship in 1952, he was traded to Chicago where he served as a player-coach before retiring.

Abel rejoined the Red Wings in the middle of the 1957–1958 season as the team's head coach and over his 10-year stint, he led the team to four Stanley Cup title series, losing them all (1961, 1963–1964, 1966). He also served as the team's general manager from 1962 to 1971.

He left the team in 1971 and was briefly a scout for the expansion Los Angeles Kings before becoming the general manager of the St. Louis Blues, a job he held until 1974. Abel went on to serve as the general manager of the Kansas City Scouts (now known as the New Jersey Devils) for two seasons (1974–1976), before returning to the Red Wings as a radio and television analyst (1976–1986).

His jersey number 12 has been retired by the Red Wings and in 1993 he was inducted into the Saskatchewan Sports Hall of Fame.

Sid Abel's Career Statistics

			REGULAR SEASON					PLAYOFFS				
SEASON	**TEAM**	**LEAGUE**	**GP**	**G**	**A**	**TP**	**PIM**	**GP**	**G**	**A**	**TP**	**PIM**
1936–1937	Melville Millionaires	S-SJHL										
1936–1937	Saskatoon Wesleys	N-SJHL						3	6	2	8	2
1936–1937	Saskatoon Wesleys	M-Cup	8	8	5	13	6					
1937–1938	Flin Flon Bombers	N-SSHL	23	12	16	28	13	8	4	4	8	17
1937–1938	Flin Flon Bombers	Al-Cup	7	6	1	7	4					
1938–1939	Detroit Red Wings	NHL	15	1	1	2	0	6	1	1	2	2
1938–1939	Pittsburgh Hornets	IAHL	41	22	24	46	27					
1939–1940	Detroit Red Wings	NHL	24	1	5	6	4	5	0	3	3	21
1939–1940	Indianapolis Capitols	IAHL	21	7	11	18	10					
1940–1941	Detroit Red Wings	NHL	47	11	22	33	29	9	2	2	4	2
1941–1942	Detroit Red Wings	NHL	48	18	31	49	45	12	4	2	6	8
1942–1943	Detroit Red Wings	NHL	49	18	24	42	33	10	5	8	13	4
1943–1944	Montreal RCAF	QSHL	7	5	4	9	12					
1943–1944	Montreal Canada Car	MCHL	2	1	0	1	4					

			REGULAR SEASON					PLAYOFFS				
SEASON	TEAM	LEAGUE	GP	G	A	TP	PIM	GP	G	A	TP	PIM
1944–1945	Montreal RCAF	MCHL	4	6	8	14	4					
1944–1945	Lachine Rapides	QPHL	2	2	2	4	0					
1944–1945	Kingston RCAF	Exhib.	2	2	1	3	0					
1945–1946	Detroit Red Wings	NHL	7	0	2	2	0	3	0	0	0	0
1946–1947	Detroit Red Wings	NHL	60	19	29	48	29	3	1	1	2	2
1947–1948	Detroit Red Wings	NHL	60	14	30	44	69	10	0	3	3	16
1948–1949	Detroit Red Wings	NHL	60	28	26	54	49	11	3	3	6	6
1949–1950	Detroit Red Wings	NHL	69	34	35	69	46	14	6	2	8	6
1950–1951	Detroit Red Wings	NHL	69	23	38	61	30	6	4	3	7	0
1951–1952	Detroit Red Wings	NHL	62	17	36	53	32	7	2	2	4	12
1952–1953	Chicago Black Hawks	NHL	39	5	4	9	6	1	0	0	0	0
1953–1954	Chicago Black Hawks	NHL	3	0	0	0	4					
	NHL TOTALS		612	189	283	472	376	97	28	30	58	79

Sources: Hockey Hall of Fame; Hockey-Reference.com; Saskatchewan Sports Hall of Fame

Abronzino, Umberto (born: November 16, 1920 in Sessa, Aurunca, Italy; died: July 1, 2006 in San Jose, California); inducted into the National Soccer Hall of Fame and Museum in 1971 as a builder; driving force behind the introduction of soccer to the San Francisco Bay Area in the 1950s.

In 1936, Abronzino began his playing career in Italy with the Lauro di Sessa team, before moving to the Hartford, Connecticut area in 1937, where he played and managed various Connecticut teams until 1952. He eventually moved to the San Francisco Bay Area in California and helped form the four-team Peninsula Soccer League in 1957, which currently includes more than 60 men's teams.

In 1959, he organized the Sons of Italy soccer team in San Jose, California and served as secretary-treasurer of the Peninsula Soccer Football League from 1961 into the 1970s. He helped develop youth soccer in the Bay Area; served as the financial secretary of the National Amateur Cup competitions; refereed games into the 1990s; and was named MasterCard Ambassador of Soccer, representing Italy, for the World Cup in 1994.

Abronzino has also been inducted into the California Soccer Association Hall of Fame (1964) and the California Youth Soccer Association Hall of Fame (1979).

Sources: California Soccer Association Hall of Fame; National Soccer Hall of Fame and Museum; *San Francisco Chronicle*, Sunday, July 9, 2006, page B6

Adams, Charles Francis (born: October 18, 1876 in Newport, Vermont; died: 1947); inducted into the Hockey Hall of Fame as a contributor in 1960; first owner of the Boston Bruins.

Adams focused on the growth of hockey in the northeast United States during the 1920s and helped sustain the National Hockey League during its early period of growth.

Before getting involved in hockey, he was a businessman and ran First National Stores, one of the early major grocery chains in the northeastern United States.

An avid sports fan, Adams regularly watched events at the 3,500-seat Boston Arena and his devotion to hockey began in 1924 when he watched the Stanley Cup final series between the Montreal Canadiens and Calgary Tigers. His intense interest in the game, and his financial resources, convinced the National Hockey League to award him a franchise in 1924. At the beginning of the 1924–1925 season, his Boston Bruins hosted the first NHL game in the United States, which was the impetus for the expansion of the sport in America.

Although the Bruins finished last in their first season with a 6–24 record, the team had undeniable fan support and the Boston Garden sold out every game. The Adams family would eventually own the team for most of the next fifty years.

In only three seasons, the Bruins made their first Stanley Cup playoff appearance in 1927, losing to the Ottawa Senators, and in 1929, Boston beat the New York Rangers to win the franchise's first Stanley Cup championship. Once the Bruins proved to be a successful NHL franchise, Adams realized that the Boston Arena was not adequate for continued growth or for attracting other New England-area sporting events. He gained financial support for the building of the Boston Garden, which originally seated over 10,000 fans. The Bruins played their first home game at the Garden on November 20, 1928, losing to the Montreal Canadiens, 1–0.

In addition to the Bruins, Adams and his family supported local baseball and horse racing franchises, and owned Major League Baseball's Boston Braves. Their contributions to hockey were recognized in 1974 when the NHL named one of its four new divisions after one of hockey's prominent families.

Source: Hockey Hall of Fame

Adams, John James "Jack" (born: June 14, 1895 in Fort William, Ontario, Canada; died: May 1, 1968); inducted into the Hockey Hall of Fame in 1959 as a player; Position: Center; only man to have his name on the Stanley Cup trophy as a player, coach, and general manager.

Although inducted into the Hockey Hall of Fame as a player, Adams spent most of his life as a coach and general manager with the Detroit Red Wings. He is the only man to have his name engraved on the Stanley Cup trophy as a player, coach, and general manager. After serving in the military during World War I, he joined the Toronto Arenas during the inaugural National Hockey League season (1917–1918) and won the league's first Stanley Cup title in five games over the Vancouver Millionaires.

During his seven-year NHL career, the 6', 200-pound Adams played for the Arenas (1917–1919), Toronto St. Pats (1922–1926), and the Ottawa Senators (1926–1927). He was named First-Team All–Star Coach twice (1937, 1943); Second-Team All-Star Coach in 1945; and won the Lester Patrick Trophy in 1966 for his contribution to hockey in the United States.

After two seasons with the Arenas, he left the NHL and played for the Millionaires in the Pacific Coast Hockey League for three seasons and led the team to the 1922 PCHL title, before losing the Stanley Cup championship to the Toronto St. Pats in five games. Adams then left the league, returned to the NHL, and played for the St. Pats for four years before finishing his NHL career with the Ottawa Senators in 1927, winning the Stanley Cup. He won a championship his first year in the league and in his last year in the league.

After retiring as a player, Adams coached the second-year Detroit Falcons. In 1932, the team changed its name to the Detroit Red Wings and in 1934 reached the Stanley Cup finals, losing to the Chicago Black Hawks in four games. In 1936, he led the team to its first-ever Stanley Cup title and they repeated as league champions the next season. After having early success, the team slumped for several years but bounced back to play for the Stanley Cup title six times in the 1940s, winning only a single championship during this streak in 1943. Adams coached his last Stanley Cup appearance team in 1945.

After leaving the coaching ranks, he became the team's general manager and oversaw the franchise as it rose to dynasty status after World War II, finishing in first place seven consecutive years (1948–1955) and winning four Stanley Cup titles (1950, 1952, 1954–1955). In recognition of his contributions to the game, the NHL created the Jack Adams Award, presented annually to the league's Coach of the Year.

Jack Adams' Career Statistics

			REGULAR SEASON					PLAYOFFS				
SEASON	**TEAM**	**LEAGUE**	**GP**	**G**	**A**	**TP**	**PIM**	**GP**	**G**	**A**	**TP**	**PIM**
1914–1915	Fort William Maple Leafs	NMHL						2	4	0	4	3
1915–1916	Calumet Miners	NMHL										
1916–1917	Peterborough 247th	OHA-Int.										
1917–1918	Sarnia Sailors	OHA-Sr.	6	15	0	15						
1917–1918	Toronto Arenas	NHL	8	0	0	0	31	2	1	0	1	6
1918–1919	Toronto Arenas	NHL	17	3	3	6	35					
1919–1920	Vancouver Millionaires	PCHA	22	9	6	15	18	2	0	0	0	0
1920–1921	Vancouver Millionaires	PCHA	24	17	12	29	60	2	3	0	3	0
1920–1921	Vancouver Millionaires	St-Cup						5	2	1	3	6
1921–1922	Vancouver Millionaires	PCHA	24	26	4	30	24	2	1	0	1	0
1921–1922	Vancouver Millionaires	West-P						2	0	0	0	12
1921–1922	Vancouver Millionaires	St-Cup						5	6	1	7	18
1922–1923	Toronto St. Pats	NHL	23	19	9	28	64					
1923–1924	Toronto St. Pats	NHL	22	14	4	18	51					
1924–1925	Toronto St. Pats	NHL	27	21	10	31	67	2	1	0	1	7
1925–1926	Toronto St. Pats	NHL	36	21	5	26	52					
1926–1927	Ottawa Senators	NHL	40	5	1	6	66	6	0	0	0	0
	NHL TOTALS		173	83	32	115	366	10	2	0	2	13

Sources: Hockey Hall of Fame; Hockey-Reference.com

Adams, Weston W., Sr. (born: August 9, 1904 in Springfield, Massachusetts; died: March 19, 1973 in Boston, Massachusetts); inducted into the Hockey Hall of Fame in 1972 as a builder; first director of the Boston Bruins.

After graduating from Harvard University (Cambridge, Massachusetts), Adams followed his father's path (hall of famer Charles) and began his life-long tenure with the National Hockey League's Boston Bruins by becoming the team's first director. In 1932, he became president of the Boston Tigers, the Bruins' farm team in the Canadian American Hockey League, and in 1936 he replaced his father as the Bruins' president.

As with most members of his family, Adams was involved in other local sports activities besides hockey and later served as the traveling secretary for Major League Baseball's Boston Braves.

Under his direction as president, the Bruins finished in first place four straight years (1938–1941) and won two Stanley Cup championships (1939, 1941). He later became the team's chairman of the board (1956) and served a second term as its president (1964–1969).

Source: Hockey Hall of Fame

Adderley, Herbert A. "Herb" (born: June 8, 1939 in Philadelphia, Pennsylvania); inducted into the Pro Football Hall of Fame in 1980 as a player; Position: Cornerback; played in four of the first six Super Bowls.

After being named an All-Big Ten selection at Michigan State University (East Lansing) as an offensive back, Adderley was a first-round pick (12th overall selection) of the Green Bay Packers in the 1961 National Football League Draft.

During his 12-year career (164 games), he played for the Packers (1961–1969) and the Dallas Cowboys (1970–1972); was voted all-NFL five times; played in seven NFL championship games, winning them all (1961–1962, 1965–1967, 1970–1971); and played in four of the first six Super Bowls, winning three rings (Super Bowl I (January 1967) and II (January 1968) with the Packers and Super Bowl VI (January 1972) with the Cowboys).

In Super Bowl II against the Oakland Raiders, Adderley had a 60-yard touchdown interception off a Daryle Lamonica pass, the only interception for a touchdown in the first 10 Super Bowls.

When it became obvious that he could never be a running back in the team's talent-laden backfield, Packer coach Vince Lombardi switched the 6'1", 205-pound Adderley to cornerback in his rookie year, and a hall-of-fame career was born.

He led the NFL in yards returned on interceptions twice (1965, 1969) and in touchdowns on interception returns twice (1962, 1965). Over his career, he totaled 48 interceptions (for 1,046 yards and seven touchdowns) and 120 kickoff returns (for 3,080 yards and two touchdowns). He was named to the NFL 1960s All-Decade Team; inducted into the Green Bay Packers Hall of Fame in 1981; and in 1999, Adderley was ranked number 45 on *The Sporting News*' list of the 100 Greatest Football Players.

Herb Adderley's Career Statistics

			INTERCEPTIONS				KICKOFF RETURNS			
YEAR	**TEAM**	**G**	**TOT**	**YDS**	**AVG**	**TD**	**TOT**	**YDS**	**AVG**	**TD**
1961	Green Bay	14	1	9	9.0	0	18	478	26.6	0
1962	Green Bay	14	7	132	18.9	1	15	418	27.9	1
1963	Green Bay	14	5	86	17.2	0	20	597	29.9	1
1964	Green Bay	13	4	56	14.0	0	19	508	26.7	0
1965	Green Bay	14	6	175	29.2	3	10	221	22.1	0
1966	Green Bay	14	4	125	31.3	1	14	320	22.9	0
1967	Green Bay	14	4	16	4.0	1	10	207	20.7	0
1968	Green Bay	14	3	27	9.0	0	14	331	23.6	0
1969	Green Bay	14	5	169	33.8	1	0	0	0.0	0
1970	Dallas	14	3	69	23.0	0	0	0	0.0	0
1971	Dallas	12	6	182	30.3	0	0	0	0.0	0
1972	Dallas	13	0	0	0.0	0	0	0	0.0	0
	TOTALS	164	48	1,046	21.8	7	120	3,080	25.7	2

Sources: Green Bay Packers Hall of Fame; Pro Football Hall of Fame; Pro-Football-Reference.com

Agoos, Jeffrey Alan "Jeff" (born: May 2, 1968 in Geneva, Switzerland); inducted into the National Soccer Hall of Fame and Museum in 2009 as a player; Position: Defender; International Caps (1988–2003): 134; International Goals: 4; won five MLS championships.

The 5'10" Agoos played for the U.S. National Team 15 years and won five championships in Major League Soccer's first eight seasons. The first of his international games was against Guatemala in 1988, and his last was against Wales in 2003. He played three games at the 2002 World Cup (held in Japan and Korea, eliminated in the quarterfinals); 26 games in World Cup qualifiers in 1996, 1997, 2000 and 2001; 1998 World Cup (France, failed to qualify); and the 2000 Olympic Games (Sydney, Australia; finishing in fourth place).

When MLS began operating in 1996, he joined D.C. United and won three league titles in the first four seasons (1996–1997, 1999). Agoos was traded to the San Jose Earthquakes in 2001, where he won two more league titles (2001, 2004). He retired in 2005 having played 244 MLS regular-season games in 10 seasons (D.C. United 1996–2000, Earthquakes, 2001–2004, New York/New Jersey MetroStars (2005)). He was chosen to Major League Soccer's All-Star Team three times (1997, 1999, 2001).

Agoos attended J.J. Pearce High School (Richardson, Texas), where he was a two-time *Parade* Magazine High School All-American, and led his team to the 1983 Texas State Championship. After high school, he went to the University of Virginia (Charlottesville, 1986, 1988–1990), where he was a four-time National Soccer Coaches Association of America All-American), before playing for the Maryland Bays (American Professional Soccer League, 1991); Dallas Sidekicks (Major Indoor Soccer League, 1991–1992); and SV Wehen Wiesbaden of the German third division (1994–1995).

Source: National Soccer Hall of Fame and Museum

Ahearn, Franklin Thomas "Frank" (born: May 10, 1886 in Ottawa, Ontario, Canada; died: November 17, 1962, location: unknown); inducted into the Hockey Hall of Fame in 1962 as a builder; owner of the Ottawa Senators; won four Stanley Cup championships.

Ahearn assumed control of his hometown National Hockey League's Ottawa Senators (first as a partner and later as sole owner) and led the team to four Stanley Cup championships (1920–1921, 1923, 1927). After a successful run in the 1920s, Ahearn, affected by the Depression, began selling off his best players in order to stay solvent.

As a young boy, he played organized hockey but realized that his talents were not as a player, but as a coach or manager and, as a teenager, Ahearn was the player-manager of the Ottawa Collegiate Institute (Ottawa, Ontario, Canada) team.

After being injured in World War I, he returned to Ottawa, where he managed and promoted numerous amateur hockey teams. After purchasing a share of the Ottawa Senators and winning three Stanley Cup titles, in 1924 he bought out majority owner Tommy Gorman and assumed complete control of the team, winning another Stanley Cup in 1927.

When the Depression hit the Senators, he suspended team operations for the 1931–1932 season. Trying to make a comeback, Ahearn returned the team to the NHL for the 1932–1933 season, finished last, lost more money, and was forced to move to St. Louis, where the team name was changed to the Eagles. Ottawa would not host another NHL team until 1992, with the creation of the "new" Ottawa Senators.

Sources: Hockey Hall of Fame; Hockey-Reference.com

Ahearne, John Francis "Bunny" (born: November 19, 1900 in Wexford, Ireland; died: April 11, 1985); inducted into the Hockey Hall of Fame in 1977 as a builder; former president of the British Ice Hockey Association.

Instrumental in bringing the sport to Great Britain, in 1934, Ahearne became manager of the National Team, and managed the team to three important wins in 1936: the Winter Olympics (Bavaria, Germany); the World Championship (counted from the Olympic win), and the European Championship (also counted from the Olympic win). He went on to lead the team to silver medals at both the 1937 (London, England) and 1938 (Prague, Czechoslovakia) European Championships.

Ahearne was Secretary of the British Ice Hockey Association (1934–1971) and served as its president from 1971 to 1982. He also was a member of the Council of the International Ice Hockey Federation; served as vice-president for three terms (1951–1957, 1960–1963, 1966–1969); and three terms as its president (1957–1960, 1963–1966, 1969–1975).

He was inducted into the International Ice Hockey Federation Hall of Fame in 1977 and the British Hall of Fame in 1986.

Sources: Hockey Hall of Fame; International Ice Hockey Federation Hall of Fame

Aikman, Troy Kenneth (born: November 21, 1966 in West Covina, California); inducted into the Pro Football Hall of Fame in 2006 as a player; Position: Quarterback; Uniform: #8; winningest starting quarterback of any decade in NFL history.

After failing to reach contract terms with Major League Baseball's New York Mets, Aikman went on to enjoy a 12-year National Football League career (1989–2000) with the Dallas Cowboys.

The number one pick in the 1989 NFL draft, he eventually led the Cowboys to three Super Bowl titles (1993–1994, 1996); was the winningest starting quarterback of any decade (90 of his 94 career wins came in the 1990s); posted 13 regular-season and four playoff 300–yard passing games; was named to six Pro Bowls (1991–1996); selected All-Pro in 1993; and was a two-time All-NFC Second Team choice (1994–1995).

Active in athletics at Henryetta (Oklahoma) High School, Aikman was named All-State in both football and baseball, and his high school eventually retired his jersey. After not coming to terms with the New York attended the University of Oklahoma (Norman) to play football for coach Barry Switzer. However, after breaking his leg in his very first game (against the University of Miami), he sat out the entire season and watched as his team won the 1985 NCAA title. Realizing that his pass-oriented skills would not fit well with Oklahoma's running game, Switzer helped Aikman transfer to the University of California at Los Angeles.

After sitting out one season, in adherence of the NCAA transfer rule, he went on to lead the Bruins to a 20–4 record; won the 1987 Aloha Bowl; won the 1989 Cotton Bowl; and finished his college career as the third-highest rated passer in NCAA history. During his relatively brief college career, Aikman was selected to *The Sporting News* College All-America second team (1987); was the Pacific 10 Conference Offensive Player of the Year (1987); Aloha Bowl MVP (1987); was selected to *The Sporting News* All-America team (1988); won the Henry R. "Red" Sanders Trophy in 1988 as the team's MVP; won the Davey O'Brien National Quarterback Award (1988); was named College Quarterback of the Year (1988); and was the Cotton Bowl MVP (1989).

Aikman was made the NFL's number one selection by new Cowboys' coach Jimmy Johnson, who had just been hired by team owner Jerry Jones to replace the legendary Tom Landry. Aikman became a starter in his rookie season and played to a record of 0–11, with nine touchdowns and 18 interceptions, as the team finished the season at 1–15. In 1990, Aikman led the Cowboys to a 7–7 record before suffering a season-ending injury. In his third season, the Cowboys finally made it to the playoffs and he was selected to the first of six consecutive Pro Bowls.

In 1992, the 6'4", 219-pound Aikman set career highs with 302 completions for 3,445 yards and 23 touchdown passes; led his team to a 52–17 win over the Buffalo Bills in Super Bowl XXVII (Pasadena, California); and was named Super Bowl MVP with 273 passing yards and four touchdown passes. Under Aikman, the Cowboys repeated as Super Bowl champions in 1993, beating the Bills again, 30–13. In 1994, Johnson was fired and Barry Switzer was hired, reuniting him with Aikman, as the Cowboys went on to fall short of being the first team to win three straight Super Bowls, losing to the San Francisco 49ers 38–28 in the NFC Championship game.

In 1995, Aikman threw for over 3,300 yards as the Cowboys went on to win a record-tying fifth Super Bowl (his third) in January 1996, beating the Pittsburgh Steelers. In 1997, Aikman became the first quarterback in Cowboys history to have three straight 3,000–yard seasons. However, for all of Aikman's offensive numbers, the team missed the playoffs and Switzer endured the first losing season of his coaching career, leading him to resign at the end of the season. During the remainder of Aikman's career, the Cowboys never repeated the team's earlier success and would not appear in another Super Bowl. He suffered a variety of injuries late in his career, and after suffering another in a series of concussions on December 10, 2000 in a game against the Washington Redskins, he ended his playing career.

Although having quit playing late in the previous season, Aikman did not officially retire until April 2001. He left the game as the Cowboys' all-time leading passer (32,942 yards) and his 61.5 percent completion rate is fourth best in NFL history. He retired holding numerous team records, including most passing attempts in a career (4,715); most passing attempts in a rookie season (293); most passing attempts in a game (57 against the Minnesota Vikings on November 26, 1998); most pass completions in a career (2,898); most pass completions in a rookie season (155); most pass completions in a game (34 against the New York Giants on October 5, 1997 and against the Minnesota Vikings on November 26, 1998); highest pass completion percentage in a career (61.5); highest pass completion percentage in a season (69.1 in 1993); most passing yards in a career (32,942); most passing yards in a rookie season (1,749); most passing yards in a game as a rookie (379 against the Arizona Cardinals on November 12, 1989); most seasons with 3,000 or more passing yards in a season (five; 1992–1993, 1995–1997); most games with 300 or more passing yards in a career (13); most touchdown passes in a career (165); most consecutive games with a touchdown pass (16, 1993–1994); most intercepted passes in a career (141); most consecutive pass attempts without an interception (216 in 1999); and most passing attempts in a game with no interceptions (57 against the Minnesota Vikings on November 26, 1998).

After retiring, Aikman began his broadcasting career in 2001 as an NFL color commentator for the Fox network. In September 2005, he was inducted into the Dallas Cowboys Ring of Honor with teammates Michael Irvin and Emmitt

Smith. He is also a joint owner of the National Association for Stock Car Auto Racing Nextel Cup racing team, Hall of Fame Racing, along with fellow former Cowboy quarterback, Roger Staubach.

Troy Aikman's Career Statistics

					PASSING					RUSHING			
YEAR	TEAM	G	ATT	COMP	YDS	TD	INT	RATING	NO	YDS	AVG	TD	F
1989	Dallas	11	293	155	1,749	9	18	55.7	38	302	7.9	0	6
1990	Dallas	15	399	226	2,579	11	18	66.6	40	172	4.3	1	5
1991	Dallas	12	363	237	2,754	11	10	86.7	16	5	0.3	1	4
1992	Dallas	16	473	302	3,445	23	14	89.5	37	105	2.8	1	4
1993	Dallas	14	392	271	3,100	15	6	99.0	32	125	3.9	0	7
1994	Dallas	14	361	233	2,676	13	12	84.9	30	62	2.1	1	2
1995	Dallas	16	432	280	3,304	16	7	93.6	21	32	1.5	1	5
1996	Dallas	15	465	296	3,126	12	13	80.1	35	42	1.2	1	6
1997	Dallas	16	518	292	3,283	19	12	78.0	25	79	3.2	0	6
1998	Dallas	11	315	187	2,330	12	5	88.5	22	69	3.1	2	3
1999	Dallas	14	442	263	2,964	17	12	81.1	21	10	0.5	1	8
2000	Dallas	11	262	156	1,632	7	14	64.3	10	13	1.3	0	2
	TOTALS	165	4,715	2,898	32,942	165	141	81.6	327	1,016	3.1	9	58

Sources: *101 Little Facts about Troy Aikman* (Sports Publishing, Inc.); Pro Football Hall of Fame; Pro-Football-Reference.com; *Sports Great Troy Aikman (Sports Great Books)* (Glen MacNow).

Aimi, Milton (born: March 29, 1926 in Brazil, South America); inducted into the National Soccer Hall of Fame and Museum in 1991 as a builder; first president of the Texas State Soccer Association.

A member of the Brazilian National Volleyball Team as a young man, Aimi played a major role as a soccer administrator in the early development of the game in Texas. In 1947, he founded the West Texas College soccer team and began playing for amateur teams in the Dallas-Fort Worth area. In 1952, he founded the Fort Worth International Soccer Club and later served as the first president of the Texas State Soccer Association.

Moving to Houston, Texas in 1967, Aimi was appointed Youth Commissioner for the South Texas region and was one of the founders of the Houston District Junior Soccer Association in 1968. He served as its president from 1972 to 1978, and in 1979, he was named the Association's Person of the Year.

In 1970, he helped form the Youth Soccer Referee Association, and in 1972, Aimi was elected president of the Texas State Soccer Association, a position he held until 2000. As president, he oversaw the Association's expansion from two to 20 leagues, with more than 339 senior teams, at the time the second largest Senior State Association in the United States.

Aimi was appointed to the National Referee Committee of the United States Soccer Federation (1979); was elected a vice president of the USSF twice (1982, 1988); and was inducted into the South Texas Youth Soccer Association Hall of Fame in 1992.

Sources: National Soccer Hall of Fame and Museum; South Texas Youth Soccer Association Hall of Fame

Akers, Michelle Anne (born: February 1, 1966 in Santa Clara, California); inducted into the National Soccer Hall of Fame and Museum in 2004 as a player; Position: Midfielder-Forward; International Caps (1985–2000): 153; International Goals: 105; first woman to win the Hermann Trophy; first American woman to play professional soccer.

The 5'10", 150-pound Akers was the most dominant player on the United States Women's National Team from 1985 until she retired in 2000. In 1999, she was named the Fédération Internationale de Football Association Women's Player of the Century as the top female soccer player in the world. In 2001, Akers and her teammates from the 1991 Women's World Championship squad were awarded the Medal of Honor from the National Soccer Hall of Fame.

After being named a three-time All-American at Shorecrest High School (Shoreline, Washington), she attended the University of Central Florida (Orlando), where she would go on to be named a four-time National Soccer Coaches Association of America All-American. She was the first woman to win the Hermann Trophy (1988) as the nation's top female soccer player; was the school's Athlete of the Year twice (1988–1989); the all-time leading scorer in UCF history; was elected to the school's hall of fame; had her #10 jersey retired; and was named to the Soccer America College Team of the Century. After graduation, she played three seasons for the Tyresco Club in Sweden, becoming the first American women to play professional soccer.

With the United States Women's National Team, Akers scored 105 goals in 153 appearances, at the time the second most goals scored in Women's National Team history. In 1985, she scored the first goal in team history against Denmark in a 2–2 draw in Jesolo, Italy. She gained worldwide attention at the FIFA World Championships for Women's Football (later renamed the FIFA Women's World Cup) in 1991 (played in China), when she scored 10 goals in only six games, including both goals in a 2–1 Finals win over Norway, giving the United States the gold medal.

She was the team leader of the U.S. Women's National Team at the 1999 FIFA Women's World Cup (Pasadena, California), leading the squad to its second World title. After the 1999 Finals, Akers retired and became a Founding Player of the Women's United Soccer Association in 2001, although she never played a competitive game in the league.

1996 was the first year that women's soccer was played in the Olympics and Akers was a member of the U.S. team that won the gold medal in Atlanta, Georgia. She was also named Most Valuable Player at the 1996 U.S. Women's Cup.

Akers was named U.S. Soccer' Female Athlete of the Year twice (1990–1991); won the Golden Boot Award (top goal scorer) at the 1991 FIFA Women's World Championship; was named Most Valuable Player of the 1994 CONCACAF Qualifying Championship (Montreal, Quebec, Canada); won the 1998 FIFA Order of Merit; and was selected to the 1999 Women's World Cup All-Star Team.

In 2004, Akers and fellow hall-of-famer Mia Hamm were the only two women, and the only two Americans, named to the FIFA 100, a list of the 125 greatest living soccer players, selected by Pelé and commissioned for the organization's 100th anniversary.

Since her retirement, she has continued to promote the game of soccer and has written several books, including *Standing Fast, Battles of a Champion*, which documents her battle with Epstein-Barr Virus (Chronic Fatigue Syndrome).

Michelle Akers' United States National Team Statistics

YEAR	MIN	G	GLS	AST	PTS	W–L–T
1985	180	2	2	0	4	0–1–1
1986	380	5	0	0	0	3–2–0
1987	450	9	3	2	8	5–4–0
1988	150	2	0	2	2	1–0–1
1990	420	6	9	0	18	6–0–0
1991	1926	26	39	7	85	22–3–1
1993	882	12	6	7	19	9–3–0
1994	521	12	11	7	29	11–1–0
1995	1202	18	15	5	35	14–2–2
1996	1244	17	7	3	17	15–0–2
1997	180	2	1	0	2	2–0–0
1998	932	15	5	3	13	14–1–0
1999	1336	20	6	1	13	16–2–2
2000	238	7	1	0	2	2–2–3
TOTALS	10,041	153	105	37	247	120–21–12

Source: National Soccer Hall of Fame and Museum

Alberto, Carlos (Torres) (born: July 17, 1944 in Rio de Janeiro, Brazil); inducted into the National Soccer Hall of Fame and Museum in 2003 as a player; Position: Defender; teammate of the legendary Pelé twice in his career, once in Brazil and again with the New York Cosmos.

After playing for Fluminense Futebol Clube (Rio de Janeiro) when he was 19, Alberto moved to Santos (São Paulo, Brazil) in 1966, where he became a teammate of the legendary Pelé. In 1970, he captained the Brazilian National Team that won the 1970 World Cup over Italy (hosted by Mexico). In 1974, he returned to Fluminense and helped the team capture two consecutive Campeonato Carioca championships. In 1977, he played for Clube de Regatas do Flamengo (Rio de Janeiro), before moving on to the New York Cosmos (North American Soccer League), where he was reunited with Pelé, and helped the Cosmos win back-to-back league titles (1977–1978). After spending one year with the California Surf, Alberto returned to the Cosmos in 1982, winning his third NASL title. He played his final NASL game on September 28, 1982 and left the league as a five-time NASL All-Star.

After retiring as a player, Alberto began his coaching career in 1983 with his old team Flamengo; went on to manage Fluminense in 1984; the Corinthians (São Paulo) for two seasons (1985–1986); Clube Náutico Capibaribe (Recife,

Brazil) for two seasons (1986–1987); the Miami Sharks of the American Soccer League (1987); Botafogo de Futebol e Regatas (Rio de Janeiro, 1993–1994, 1997–1999, 2002–2003); Fluminense (1994–1995); the Nigerian National Team (1995); Clube Atletico Mineriro (Belo Horizonte, Brazil) in 1998; Oman Football Association (2000); Desportiva Cabonfirense (Brazil) in 2001; Zamalek (Cairo, Egypt) in 2002; and the Paysandu Sport Clube (Belém, Brazil) in 2005.

Alberto was named by Pelé as one of the 125 greatest living footballers in March 2004 (as part of the FIFA 100 celebration).

Carlos Alberto's North American Soccer League Statistics

YEAR	TEAM	G	GLS	ASST	PTS
1977	New York Cosmos	4	0	2	2
1978	New York Cosmos	25	2	2	6
1979	New York Cosmos	28	2	6	10
1980	New York Cosmos	23	2	7	11
1981	California Surf	19	2	10	14
1982	New York Cosmos	20	0	5	5
	TOTALS	119	8	32	48

Source: National Soccer Hall of Fame and Museum

Alexander, Grover Cleveland "Pete" (born: February 26, 1887 in Elba, Nebraska; died: November 4, 1950 in St. Paul, Nebraska); inducted into the National Baseball Hall of Fame and Museum in 1938 as a player; Position: Pitcher; Bats: Right; Throws: Right; his 373 wins (third most in major league history) and 90 shutouts are both National League records; threw a still-MLB single-season record 16 shutouts in 1916.

A right-handed pitcher and one of the dominant throwers of his era, Alexander pitched for the Philadelphia Phillies (1911–1917, 1930), Chicago Cubs (1918–1926), and the St. Louis Cardinals (1926–1929). He pitched in three World Series (winning in 1926 and losing in 1915 and 1928).

Making his debut on April 15, 1911, over a 20-year career (1911–1930), the 6'1", 185-pound Alexander led the league in ERA four times (1915–1916, 1919–1920); wins six times (1911, 1914–1917, 1920); innings pitched seven times (1911–1912, 1914–1917, 1920); strikeouts six times (1912, 1914–1917, 1920); complete games six times (1911, 1914–1917, 1920); shutouts seven times (1911, 1913, 1915–1917, 1919, 1921); won 30 or more games three straight seasons (1915–1917); and won the pitcher's Triple Crown (leading the league in ERA, wins, and strikeouts) three times (1915–1916, 1920). He won 20 or more games in a season nine times and threw 90 shutouts (second most in MLB history).

In 1909, he began his professional minor league career with the Galesburg Boosters (Illinois) of the Central Association. Four days after pitching a no-hitter against the Pekin Celestials (Illinois) of the Illinois-Missouri League (July 23, 1909), he was hit in the head by a throw from the shortstop (while trying to break up a double play as a base runner) and was unconscious for two days, before waking up with double vision. Before fully recovering, he was sent to the Indianapolis Indians (American Association), where he was ineffective as a pitcher. The Indians gave up on him and sent him home, where he sat out a season before finally recovering.

When the Indians sold his contract to the Syracuse Chiefs (International League), he played for the team and won 29 games, including 15 shutouts. Major League Baseball's Philadelphia Phillies bought Alexander's contract in 1911 and he won 28 games his rookie season. He threw seven shutouts that year, including a 1–0 win over the legendary Cy Young.

Alexander recorded his first major league win on April 26, 1911, beating the Brooklyn Dodgers 10–3, and 12 days later, on May 8, he recorded his first shutout, again beating Brooklyn, 5–0. On June 5, 1911 in Pittsburgh, he was called for a balk against the Pirates, the only one he will have in his career.

Alexander's best seasons were in Philadelphia, during which he won 190 games (one-third of the team's total); won 30 or more games three straight years; and led the league in every major pitching statistic at least once. His 16 shutouts in 1916 is still an MLB single-season record.

On September 23, 1916, Alexander defeated the Cincinnati Reds twice (7–3 and 4–0) at Philadelphia. He again won two games on the same day on September 3, 1917, with 6–0 and 9–3 victories over the Brooklyn Dodgers.

Alexander was traded to the Chicago Cubs, and after spending most of the 1918 season serving in the military in France during World War I, he returned to the team and went on to win 128 games while playing for Chicago.

When it became apparent that he suffered from alcoholism, Alexander was traded to the St. Louis Cardinals in 1926. Although he had a mediocre 9–7 regular-season record, he surprised almost everyone when he won two games in that season's World Series against the New York Yankees. He saved the final game in the team's seven-game Series win when Babe Ruth was thrown out trying to steal second base.

Although he won 21 games in 1927, Alexander's career declined due to age and alcoholism. After pitching to a 25–20 record over the next three seasons, he retired from the major leagues in 1930, although he continued to pitch for numerous traveling teams until he was 51. From 1931 to 1935, the ironically clean-shaven Alexander managed and pitched for the barnstorming House of David club, a team made up of players whose religion forbid men to shave or cut their hair.

Alexander retired ranked third all time in wins (373, behind Cy Young and Walter Johnson); tenth in innings pitched; second in shutouts (90), and eighth in hits allowed (4,868). In 1999, he was ranked 12th on *The Sporting News*' list of the 100 Greatest Baseball Players, and was a nominee for the Major League Baseball All-Century Team.

Grover Alexander's Career Statistics

YEAR	W	L	PCT	SH	IP	H	R	ER	SO	BB	ERA
1911	28	13	.683	7	367	285	133		227	129	2.57
1912	19	17	.528	3	310	289	133	97	195	105	2.82
1913	22	8	.733	9	306	288	106	95	159	75	2.79
1914	27	15	.643	6	355	327	133	94	214	76	2.38
1915	31	10	.756	12	376	253	86	51	241	64	1.22
1916	33	12	.733	16	389	323	90	67	167	50	1.55
1917	30	13	.698	8	388	336	108	80	201	58	1.86
1918	2	1	.667	0	26	19	7	5	15	3	1.73
1919	16	11	.593	9	235	180	51	45	121	38	1.72
1920	27	14	.659	7	363	335	96	77	173	69	1.91
1921	15	13	.536	3	252	286	110	95	77	33	3.39
1922	16	13	.552	1	246	283	111	99	48	34	3.62
1923	22	12	.647	3	305	308	128	108	72	30	3.19
1924	12	5	.706	0	169	183	82	57	33	25	3.04
1925	15	11	.577	1	236	270	106	89	63	29	3.39
1926 (Cubs)	3	3	.500	0	52	55	26	20	12	7	3.46
1926 (Cardinals)	9	7	.563	2	148	136	57	48	35	24	2.92
1927	21	10	.677	2	268	261	94	75	48	38	2.52
1928	16	9	.640	1	244	262	107	91	59	37	3.36
1929	9	8	.529	0	132	149	65	57	33	23	3.89
1930	0	3	.000	0	22	40	24	22	6	6	9.00
TOTALS	373	208	.642	90	5,189	4,868	1,853	1,372	2,199	953	2.56

Sources: *Alexander the Great: The Story of Grover Cleveland Alexander* (Jerry Clark); Baseball-Reference.com; National Baseball Hall of Fame and Museum; *Ol' Pete: The Grover Cleveland Alexander Story* (Jack Kavanagh)

Allan, Sir Hugh Andrew Montagu (born: October 13, 1860 in Montreal, Quebec, Canada; died: September 26, 1951 in Montreal, Quebec, Canada); inducted into the Hockey Hall of Fame in 1945 as a builder; creator of the Allan Cup.

Allan was a Canadian banker and sportsman who donated the Allan Cup in 1908, a trophy symbolic of the best of men's amateur ice hockey in Canada. When the National Hockey League was created in 1917, many players who did not turn professional retired from the game, driving the amateur sport into decline. It quickly became apparent that amateur hockey needed a championship series to encourage players to continue their participation in the game. With the Stanley Cup designated for professional clubs, amateur hockey in Canada needed its own trophy to honor its best men's teams.

William Northey, a leader in amateur hockey in Montreal, persuaded his friend, Sir Montagu Allan, to donate a trophy that would represent the highest level of achievement for amateur teams across Canada. Allan, a former president of the Montreal Jockey Club and a horse owner who had won the Queen's Plate (Canada's most prestigious horse race) numerous times, rose to the challenge.

The Allan Cup was designed as a challenge trophy open to any senior amateur club which had won the championship of its league for that particular year. Initially, the cup was presented to the Victoria Hockey Club of Montreal and was to be defended by the champion of its league. As interest in the cup grew and more challenges were made, Victoria Hockey Club trustees arranged for regional elimination tournaments with the goal of bringing order to the challenge process.

The Ottawa Cliffsides were the first team to win the Allan Cup (1909) under the newly established procedures, but subsequently lost the trophy to the Queen's University team (Kingston, Ontario, Canada) that same year. Under the early rules, all challenges for the cup had to be approved by the trustees, but when the Canadian Amateur Hockey Association was formed in 1914, the Allan Cup became its senior amateur trophy. Rules for competition remained the same for 14 years until the Cup was donated to the CAHA, which developed its own rules for winning the trophy.

Winners of the Allan Cup routinely represented Canada at the World Hockey Championships and/or the Olympic Games. However, after the formation of the Canadian National Team in 1964, the Allan Cup became known solely as a national senior trophy. The annual competition for the Cup continues to the present day and Allan's contributions to the game were recognized in 1945 when he was elected as a charter member of the Hockey Hall of Fame in the builders category.

He studied at Bishop's College School (Lennoxville, Quebec, Canada) and then in Paris, France, before joining his father's shipping business, the Allan Line, where he would eventually become its chairman (1909–1912). He later became the last president of the Merchants' Bank of Canada (1920–1922) and oversaw its merger with the Bank of Montreal. Allan was named a knight bachelor by King Edward VII of the United Kingdom in 1906, and in 1907, he was decorated Commander of the Royal Victorian Order.

Source: Hockey Hall of Fame

Allen, Dr. Forrest Clare "Phog" (born: November 18, 1885 in Jamesport, Missouri; died: September 16, 1974 in Lawrence, Kansas); inducted into the Naismith Memorial Basketball Hall of Fame in 1959 as a coach; instrumental in making basketball an Olympic sport.

After playing forward on the basketball team at Independence (Missouri) High School, Allen attended the University of Kansas (Lawrence) from 1905 to 1907, where he played basketball for the game's founder, Dr. James Naismith, and was a two-time All-American (1904–1905). He acquired his nickname because of the sound of his voice, which sounded like a foghorn, later shortened to "Phog."

After leaving Kansas, Allen (often called the "Father of Basketball Coaching") began his 49-year college basketball coaching career at Baker University (Baldwin City, Kansas, 1908–1909), where he compiled a 46–2 (.958) record. He went on to coach at the Haskell Institute Indian School (Haskell Indian Nations University, Lawrence, Kansas) in 1907, compiling a record of 27–5 (.844), and at the Warrensburg (Missouri) Teachers College from 1913 to 1919, compiling a record of 107–7 (.939). Allen is most well-known for his 37-year career at his alma mater, the University of Kansas (1908–1909, 1920–1956), where he compiled a 591–219 (.730) record. He retired with an overall coaching record of 771–233 (.768).

He led Kansas to the 1923 Helms Foundation national championship and was a charter member of the Helms Foundation Hall of Fame; was instrumental in founding the National Association of Basketball Coaches in 1927 and was its first president; and played a pivotal role in getting basketball recognized as an official Olympic sport in 1936. In 1950, he was both the NABC National Coach of the Year and the Metropolitan New York Basketball Writers National Coach of the Year, and in 1952, he coached Kansas to the national championship and led the United States to a gold medal in the Olympic Games in Helsinki, Finland.

Allen retired as the all-time winningest coach in college basketball history. During his career, he wrote several books, including *My Basketball Bible* and *Better Basketball: Techniques, Tactics, Tales.*

In 1912, he became a Doctor of Osteopathy and gained a reputation for being able to quickly heal and rehabilitate injured athletes. Although often criticized by the medical profession for his techniques, many famous sports figures came to Allen for treatment, including Casey Stengel and Mickey Mantle.

In addition to his coaching innovations, Allen was also one of the game's first entrepreneurs, and marketed numerous basketball-related items, including shoes, basketballs, rulebooks, and medicine kits.

Source: Naismith Memorial Basketball Hall of Fame

Allen, George Herbert (born: April 29, 1918 in Detroit, Michigan; died: December 31, 1990 in Palos Verdes Estates, California); inducted into the Pro Football Hall of Fame in 2002 as a coach; never had a losing season in 12 years as a head coach in the National Football League.

After playing football at Lake Shore High School (Detroit, Michigan), Allen attended Alma College (Michigan) before transferring to Marquette University (Milwaukee, Wisconsin) as an officer trainee, where he played end on the school's football team. After graduating, he served on the athletic staff at the Farragut Navy Station (near Sandpoint, Idaho), before attending the University of Michigan (Ann Arbor), where he earned his master's degree in physical education in 1947. While at Michigan, Allen served as an assistant to coach Fritz Crisler.

In 1948, after leaving the University of Michigan, he started his coaching career at Morningside College (Sioux City, Iowa), where he compiled a 15–2–2 (.882) record over three seasons. From 1951 through 1956, he coached at Whittier College (California), compiling a record of 32–22–5 (.593).

In 1957, he left Whittier and began his National Football League career as an assistant to Sid Gillman with the Los Angeles Rams. The next season, he joined the Chicago Bears under George Halas as a defensive assistant and helped the team win the 1963 NFL Championship Game, 14–10 over the New York Giants.

Throughout his career, Allen gained a reputation for turning losing franchises into winning teams. Prior to his becoming head coach of the Rams in 1966, the team had endured seven consecutive losing seasons. In his first year, the Rams had a winning record of 8–6 and won their division the next season with an 11–1–2 record. The secret to his success was forming an offensive unit that could match in intensity the team's famed "Fearsome Foursome" defense of Deacon Jones, Lamar Lundy, Merlin Olsen, and Roosevelt "Rosey" Grier.

In 1971, he took over the Washington Redskins, a franchise that had experienced only one winning season in the previous 15 years. To address the team's weaknesses, Allen made numerous trades and abandoned future draft choices in order to acquire talent-laden veterans who could help him win immediately.

In his first year, the Redskins compiled a 9–4–1 record, and in 1972, the team played to an 11–3–0 mark and beat the Dallas Cowboys for the National Football Conference title, before losing to the Miami Dolphins in Super Bowl VII.

Allen was one of the first coaches to emphasize special teams and was known to focus on minute details, such as hiring a left-footed punter for practices before a game with a team that used a similar kicker. He conducted practices at the same time as upcoming games so that players could get used to the sun's position during all four quarters.

Allen was a two-time NFL Coach of the Year (1967, 1971); a National Football Conference Coach of the Year (1971); coached the 1967 and 1969 Los Angeles Rams to division championships and the 1972 Washington Redskins to the National Football Conference championship; and compiled a 12-year regular-season record of 116–47–5 (.712) and an overall record of 118–54–5 (.686), tenth best in NFL history when he retired.

George Allen's NFL Head Coaching Record

			REGULAR SEASON				**PLAYOFFS**		
YEAR	**TEAM**	**LG**	**W**	**L**	**T**	**WIN%**	**W**	**L**	**WIN%**
1966	Los Angeles	NFL	8	6	0	.571			
1967	Los Angeles	NFL	11	1	2	.917	0	1	.000
1968	Los Angeles	NFL	10	3	1	.769			
1969	Los Angeles	NFL	11	3	0	.786	0	1	.000
1970	Los Angeles	NFL	9	4	1	.692			
1971	Washington	NFL	9	4	1	.692	0	1	.000
1972	Washington	NFL	11	3	0	.786	2	1	.667
1973	Washington	NFL	10	4	0	.714	0	1	.000
1974	Washington	NFL	10	4	0	.714	0	1	.000
1975	Washington	NFL	8	6	0	.571			
1976	Washington	NFL	10	4	0	.714	0	1	.000
1977	Washington	NFL	9	5	0	.643			
	Los Angeles		49	17	4	.742	0	2	.000
	Washington		67	30	1	.691	2	5	.286
	TOTALS		116	47	5	.712	2	7	.222

Sources: Pro Football Hall of Fame; Pro-Football-Reference.com

Allen, Keith "Bingo" (born: August 21, 1923 in Saskatoon, Saskatchewan, Canada); inducted into the Hockey Hall of Fame in 1992 as a builder; a minor league and NHL player who would become one of the game's most influential general managers.

After a 13-year playing career, mainly in the minor leagues, Allen became one of the game's most successful general managers. His ability to judge talent helped the Philadelphia Flyers become one of the best National Hockey League teams of the 1970s and led to back-to-back Stanley Cup championships (1974–1975). In his very short 28-game NHL career, Allen played parts of two seasons with the Detroit Red Wings, and was a member of the 1954 Stanley Cup-winning team.

Beginning in 1956, Allen spent 10 years as the head coach and general manager of the Seattle Totems (Western Hockey League), where he led the team to the 1959 WHL title, and later became the first recipient of *The Hockey News*' Minor League Executive of the Year Award (1960).

The Philadelphia Flyers was an NHL expansion team (1967–1968) when the franchise hired Allen as its first coach. In his first year, he led the squad to the West Division Championship. Although he had early success as a coach, Allen knew he could be more effective in the team's front office and in December 1969, he was named the franchise's general manager. His player deals and trading acumen earned him the nickname "Keith the Thief" as he built the Flyers into a powerhouse team. Allen was credited with the Flyers becoming known as the "Broad Street Bullies," derived from the address of the team's arena.

During his 13 years as the team's general manager, the Flyers reached the Stanley Cup Finals four times (1974–1976, 1980); won back-to-back titles (1974–1975); compiled an overall 563–322–194 (.612) record; and he was named *The Hockey News*' NHL Executive of the Year (1980). Allen won the Lester Patrick Award for his outstanding contributions to hockey in the United States (1988) and was inducted into the Philadelphia Flyers Hall of Fame (1989).

Source: Hockey Hall of Fame

Allen, Marcus LeMarr (born: March 26, 1960 in San Diego, California); inducted into the Pro Football Hall of Fame in 2003 as a player; Position: Running Back; first college player to rush for more than 2,000 yards in a season; first player in NFL history to rush for more than 10,000 yards.

As a quarterback in his senior year at Abraham Lincoln High School (San Diego), Allen garnered a total of 3,098 yards (1,900 passing and 1,198 running), before attending the University of Southern California (Los Angeles). In 1981, he rushed for 2,342 yards, becoming the first college football player to break the 2,000-yard barrier. He ended the season by setting the NCAA record for rushing touchdowns (22) and winning the Heisman Trophy as the best player in college football.

Allen won the Walter Camp Award (1981) as the nation's top football player; was named Pacific-10 Conference Player of the Year (1981); was a two-time All-Pac 10 selection (1980–1981); and was inducted into the College Football Hall of Fame (2000).

After graduating in 1982, the 6'2", 210-pound Allen was the number one pick (10th overall selection) of the Oakland Raiders (before the team moved to Los Angeles) in the NFL Draft, and was named the league's Rookie of the Year. Over his 16-year, 222-game career, he played for the Los Angeles Raiders (1982–1992) and the Kansas City Chiefs (1993–1997); rushed for a then-record 123 touchdowns; carried the ball 3,022 times for 12,243 yards; and had 5,411 receiving yards. He played in Super Bowl XVIII (January 22, 1984); ran for a then-record 191 yards in a 38–9 win over the Washington Redskins; and was named the game's Most Valuable Player.

He was named American Football Conference Rookie of the Year (1982); Offensive Rookie of the Year (1982); NFL MVP (1985); NFL Offensive Player of the Year (1985); All-Pro Team twice (1982, 1985); six Pro Bowls (1983 1985–1988, 1994); and Comeback Player of the Year (1993).

He was the first player in NFL history to rush for more than 10,000 yards and when he retired in 1997, Allen held the single-season record for most rushing and receiving yards combined (2,314 in 1985). He led the Raiders in rushing yards seven consecutive seasons and the Chiefs four consecutive seasons.

Although he played in only one Super Bowl, he holds two game records, including longest run from scrimmage (74 yards) and highest average rushing yards (9.6). When he left the Raiders after the 1992 season, Allen held numerous team records, including most touchdowns in a career (95); most rushing attempts in a career (2,090); most rushing yards in a career (8,545); and most rushing touchdowns in a career (79).

He left the Chiefs after the 1997 season holding several team records, including most consecutive games scoring a touchdown (seven in 1993) and most rushing touchdowns in a career (44).

Marcus Allen's Career Statistics

			RUSHING				RECEIVING			
YEAR	**TEAM**	**G**	**NO**	**YDS**	**AVG**	**TD**	**NO**	**YDS**	**AVG**	**TD**
1982	Los Angeles	9	160	697	4.4	11	38	401	10.6	3
1983	Los Angeles	16	266	1,014	3.8	9	68	590	8.7	2
1984	Los Angeles	16	275	1,168	4.2	13	64	758	11.8	5
1985	Los Angeles	16	380	1,759	4.6	11	67	555	8.3	3
1986	Los Angeles	13	208	759	3.6	5	46	453	9.8	2
1987	Los Angeles	12	200	754	3.8	5	51	410	8.0	0

YEAR	TEAM	G	NO	RUSHING YDS	AVG	TD	NO	RECEIVING YDS	AVG	TD
1988	Los Angeles	15	223	831	3.7	7	34	303	8.9	1
1989	Los Angeles	8	69	293	4.2	2	20	191	9.6	0
1990	Los Angeles	16	179	682	3.8	12	15	189	12.6	1
1991	Los Angeles	8	63	287	4.6	2	15	131	8.7	0
1992	Los Angeles	16	67	301	4.5	2	28	277	9.9	1
1993	Kansas City	16	206	764	3.7	12	34	238	7.0	3
1994	Kansas City	13	189	709	3.8	7	42	349	8.3	0
1995	Kansas City	16	207	890	4.3	5	27	210	7.8	0
1996	Kansas City	16	206	830	4.0	9	27	270	10.0	0
1997	Kansas City	16	124	505	4.1	11	11	86	7.8	0
	TOTALS	222	3,022	12,243	4.1	123	587	5,411	9.2	21

Sources: College Football Hall of Fame, *Marcus: The Autobiography of Marcus Allen* (Marcus Allen with Carlton Stowers); Pro Football Hall of Fame; Pro-Football-Reference.com

Alonso, Julius Garcia (born: September 7, 1905 in Luanco, Asturias, Spain; died: January 24, 1988); inducted into the National Soccer Hall of Fame and Museum in 1972 as a builder; dedicated 70 years of his life to soccer as a player, manager, referee, league secretary, treasurer, and archivist.

Shortly after his birth, Alonso and his family moved to the United States and settled in Anmoore, West Virginia, where he eventually began playing soccer. In 1919, he returned to Spain, where he attended the Institute of Commerce and played for the Marino Football Club. In 1922, he played for the Madrid Football Club, before returning to the United States in 1924.

Over the next several years, Alonso formed both the Canton (Ohio) Sporting Club and the Donora (Pennsylvania) Spanish Football Club. In 1927, he studied electrical engineering at the Bliss Electrical School (Takoma Park) in Washington, D.C., and played for two soccer teams in the area, Blick's Acadians and Juventud Gallega.

In 1936, he became manager of the State Football Club in the Brooklyn League (New York) and then served as a referee-secretary of Brooklyn Hispano of the American Soccer League. During World War II, Alonso worked for the Defense Department before returning to Brooklyn Hispano in 1945.

In 1947, he began his long-term association with the American Soccer League, and at various times served as its vice president, secretary, business manager, and finally first executive secretary in 1967. He later served on both the U.S. Olympic and National Open Challenge Cup Committees.

Source: National Soccer Hall of Fame and Museum

Alston, Walter Emmons "Smokey" (born: December 1, 1911 in Venice, Ohio; died: October 1, 1984 in Oxford, Ohio); inducted into the National Baseball Hall of Fame and Museum in 1983 as a manager; played in only one major league game; led Brooklyn to its only World Series title (1955).

Hired in 1953 by Brooklyn Dodgers owner Walter O'Malley, Alston would go on to manage the team under 23 consecutive one-year contracts. After the team finished in second place his first season (1954), he led the Dodgers to the team's first World Series championship in 1955 (defeating Casey Stengel's New York Yankees in seven games). He followed the Dodgers when the franchise moved to Los Angeles, California in 1958 and by 1974 (at age 62), he had led the team to seven World Series, winning in 1955, 1959, 1963, and 1965.

Alston was named Manager of the Year six times by the Associated Press, five times by United Press International, and three times by *The Sporting News*; he managed seven winning All-Star Games; he was the first manager from the 1970s to be inducted into the National Baseball Hall of Fame and Museum; and his 2,040 regular-season wins is the seventh-highest in major league history.

As a pitcher, he earned the nickname "Smokey" because of his fastball at Darrtown (Ohio) High School. At Miami University (Oxford, Ohio), he captained both the baseball and basketball teams; graduated in 1932; and signed a professional contract with the St. Louis Cardinals, after which he was sent to the minor leagues. Leading the Mid-Atlantic League with 35 home runs in 1936, Alston was called up to the big leagues and played his only major league game for the Cardinals on September 27, 1936, when he replaced future hall-of-fame first baseman Johnny Mize, who had been ejected from the game (he struck out his only big-league at-bat and committed one error at first base). After the season, Alston was sent back to the minor leagues where he would play until 1947.

In 1940, he served as a player-manager for the Portsmouth (Ohio) Red Birds in the Mid-Atlantic League and led the circuit with 20 home runs, while managing the Red Birds to a sixth-place finish. Over the next two seasons, while still serving as a player-manager, Alston led the league in home runs and runs batted in. As a player, he was eventually promoted to the Rochester (New York) Red Wings of the International League, but was released in 1944.

Although his playing career had come to an end, Brooklyn Dodger President Branch Rickey, who had formerly served as a general manager with the St. Louis Cardinals, hired Alston as a player-manager for the Trenton (New Jersey) Packers of the Interstate League in 1944. This hiring marked the beginning of Alston's 33-year managerial career within the Dodgers organization.

After two years at Trenton, Alston was subsequently promoted to the Nashua Pride (New Hampshire) of the New England League, the Pueblo (Colorado) Dodgers of the Western League in 1947, and the St. Paul (Minnesota) Saints of the American Association from 1948 to 1949. After leading St. Paul to the Junior World Series in 1948 (losing to the Montreal Royals in five games), he advanced to Brooklyn's top minor league club, the Montreal Royals of the International League. During his four years with the Royals, the team never finished lower than second; won the Junior World Series in 1953 (after finishing second in 1950 and 1951); and in November 1953, Alston became a major league manager with the Dodgers.

He retired as the team's manager on September 29, 1976 and his uniform number 24 was retired by the Dodgers in June 1977.

Walter Alston's Managerial Career Statistics

YEAR	TEAM	W	L	WIN%
1954	Brooklyn	92	62	.597
1955	Brooklyn	98	55	.641
1956	Brooklyn	93	61	.604
1957	Brooklyn	84	70	.545
1958	Los Angeles	71	83	.461
1959	Los Angeles	88	68	.564
1960	Los Angeles	82	72	.532
1961	Los Angeles	89	65	.578
1962	Los Angeles	102	63	.618
1963	Los Angeles	99	63	.611
1964	Los Angeles	80	82	.494
1965	Los Angeles	97	65	.599
1966	Los Angeles	95	67	.586
1967	Los Angeles	73	89	.451
1968	Los Angeles	76	86	.469
1969	Los Angeles	85	77	.525
1970	Los Angeles	87	74	.540
1971	Los Angeles	89	73	.549
1972	Los Angeles	85	70	.548
1973	Los Angeles	95	66	.590
1974	Los Angeles	102	60	.630
1975	Los Angeles	88	74	.543
1976	Los Angeles	90	68	.570
	TOTALS	2,040	1,613	.558

Sources: Baseball-Reference.com; National Baseball Hall of Fame and Museum

Alworth, Lance Dwight (born: August 3, 1940 in Houston, Texas); inducted into the Pro Football Hall of Fame in 1978 as a player; Position: Flanker; Uniform: #19 (San Diego), #24 (Dallas); first San Diego Charger and the first original American Football League player inducted into the Pro Football Hall of Fame.

An All-American at the University of Arkansas (Fayetteville), Alworth was drafted by both the AFL's San Diego Chargers (round two, ninth overall pick) and the NFL's San Francisco 49ers (first round, eighth overall pick) in 1962. He signed with the Chargers and during his 11-year, 136-game career (1962–1972), Alworth played with San Diego (1962–1970) and the Dallas Cowboys (1971–1972).

Nicknamed "Bambi" for his running speed and elusiveness, the 6', 184-pound Alworth was named All-AFL seven straight seasons (1963–1969); was selected to the All-Time All-AFL Team; holds AFL records for most consecutive games with a reception (96) and most games with 200 or more receiving yards (five); and was the only AFL receiver to average more than 100 yards a game in three consecutive seasons (1964–1966).

His jersey number 19 was retired by the Chargers (only the second team jersey ever retired); in the AFL, he averaged more than 50 catches and 1,000 yards per season; played in the AFL's last seven All-Star games; and caught at least one pass in every AFL game he played. While with the Cowboys, Alworth caught the first touchdown pass in Super Bowl VI (January 16, 1972) to help beat the Miami Dolphins, 24–3.

He was named AFL MVP in 1963 by United Press International; was selected to the NFL 75th Anniversary All-Time Team; and was inducted into the Breitbard Hall of Fame in 1972, the San Diego Chargers Hall of Fame in 1977, and the College Football Hall of Fame in 1984.

At Brookhaven (Mississippi) High School, Alworth played basketball, baseball, football, and ran track. After declining professional baseball contracts from both the New York Yankees and the Pittsburgh Pirates, he accepted a football scholarship to the University of Arkansas, where he would play running back and lead the nation in punt return yardage in 1960 and 1961, the year he was named an All-American. He played in the 1960 Gator Bowl (beating Georgia Tech), the 1961 Cotton Bowl (losing to Duke), the 1962 Sugar Bowl (losing to Alabama), the 1962 Hula Bowl, and the 1962 College All- Star Game in Chicago, Illinois.

Lance Alworth's Career Statistics

			RECEIVING			
YEAR	**TEAM**	**G**	**NO**	**YDS**	**AVG**	**TD**
1962	San Diego	4	10	226	22.6	3
1963	San Diego	14	61	1,205	19.8	11
1964	San Diego	12	61	1,235	20.2	13
1965	San Diego	14	69	1,602	23.2	14
1966	San Diego	13	73	1,383	18.9	13
1967	San Diego	11	52	1,010	19.4	9
1968	San Diego	14	68	1,312	19.3	10
1969	San Diego	14	64	1,003	15.7	4
1970	San Diego	14	35	608	17.4	4
1971	Dallas	12	34	487	14.3	2
1972	Dallas	14	15	195	13.0	2
	TOTALS	136	542	10,266	18.9	85

Sources: College Football Hall of Fame; Pro Football Hall of Fame; Pro-Football-Reference.com; San Diego Chargers Hall of Fame

Anderson, George Lee "Sparky" (born: February 22, 1934 in Bridgewater, South Dakota); inducted into the National Baseball Hall of Fame and Museum in 2000 as a manager; upon retirement, he was the only manager in baseball history to have won a World Series championship in both the American and National Leagues; first manager to win 100 games in a season with two different teams; managed the longest game in organized baseball history not interrupted by a suspension of play.

In 1969, Anderson was hired as a coach for Major League Baseball's San Diego Padres; became the manager of the Cincinnati Reds in 1970; and won the National League pennant his first year before losing to the Baltimore Orioles in the World Series. During his 26-year major league managerial career with the Cincinnati Reds (1970–1978) and the Detroit Tigers (1979–1995), he won three World Series (1975–1976, 1984).

With the Reds, Anderson won more games (863) and compiled the best winning percentage (.596) of any manager in team history, and with the Tigers, he set managerial franchise records for most seasons (17), games (2,579), and wins (1,331).

In 1984, the Tigers began the season 35–5 (a still-major league record) and finished 104–58 and went on to beat the San Diego Padres in the World Series in five games, making him the first manager to win the World Series in both leagues. On September 23, 1984, when the Tigers beat the New York Yankees 4–1, Anderson became the first manager in Major League Baseball history to win 100 games in a season with two different clubs (he had previously led the Reds to three 100-win seasons). On June 29, 1986, when the Tigers beat the Milwaukee Brewers 9–5 in the first game of a doubleheader, the win marked Anderson as the first manager ever to win 600 games in each league.

During his career, Anderson earned the nickname "Captain Hook" because he was quick to pull his starting pitcher from the game and for his use of the team's bullpen.

He was named Manager of the Year twice (1984, 1987); retired with 2,194 wins (fourth all-time behind Connie Mack, John McGraw, and Tony La Russa); compiled 17 consecutive winning seasons (1972–1988); was inducted into the Cincinnati Reds Hall of Fame (2005); and in 2005, his jersey number 10 was retired by the Reds.

The 5'9", 170-pound Anderson grew up in Los Angeles, California and was a batboy for the University of Southern California (Los Angeles) Trojans. Bypassing college, he signed with the Brooklyn Dodgers directly out of high school and spent six years in the minor leagues, beginning in 1953. He was named Most Valuable Player of the 1958 Governor's Cup while playing with the Montreal Royals (International League) in his second season with the team, and the next season, he was called up to the Philadelphia Phillies and played one year (1959) as the team's starting second baseman.

Although Anderson's career began with him driving in the winning run in his first major league game (a 2–1 Phillies win over the Cincinnati Reds), his big league career did not last long as he hit only .218 (with no home runs and 34 RBIs) and his 119 total bases is the fewest ever for a player with 500 or more at bats. He was sent back to the minors in 1960 and played the next four seasons for the Triple-A Toronto Maple Leafs (International League), before realizing that his future in baseball was as a manager, not a player. He became the manager of the Maple Leafs in 1964 and went on to lead four different teams in the minor leagues over the next five seasons, winning four championships between 1964 and 1968.

After compiling an 80–72 record as the manager of the Maple Leafs in 1964, he quickly advanced through the managerial ranks until becoming a coach with the Padres in 1969. He was inducted into the Canadian Baseball Hall of Fame in 2007.

On June 14, 1966, Anderson managed the Miami Marlins (Florida State League) to a 4–3, 29-inning win over the St. Petersburg Cardinals. The contest ended at 2:29 a.m. and is the longest game in organized baseball history not interrupted by a suspension of play.

After leaving baseball, Anderson played himself in a movie, *Tiger Town*, and in several television shows, including *Arli$$* and *WKRP in Cincinnati*; became a motivational speaker; founded the non-profit CATCH (Caring Athletes Team for Children's & Henry Ford Hospitals) in 1987 (more commonly called "Sparky Anderson's Charity for Children"); and has written several books, including *They Call Me Sparky*, and the forward for the book, *Baseball For Dummies*.

Sparky Anderson's Managerial Career Statistics

YEAR	TEAM	LG	W	L	PCT
1970	Cincinnati	NL	102	60	.630
1971	Cincinnati	NL	79	83	.488
1972	Cincinnati	NL	95	59	.617
1973	Cincinnati	NL	99	63	.611
1974	Cincinnati	NL	98	64	.605
1975	Cincinnati	NL	108	54	.667
1976	Cincinnati	NL	102	60	.630
1977	Cincinnati	NL	88	74	.543
1978	Cincinnati	NL	92	69	.571
1979	Detroit	AL	56	50	.528
1980	Detroit	AL	84	78	.519
1981	Detroit	AL	60	49	.550
1982	Detroit	AL	83	79	.512
1983	Detroit	AL	92	70	.568
1984	Detroit	AL	104	58	.642
1985	Detroit	AL	84	77	.522
1986	Detroit	AL	87	75	.537
1987	Detroit	AL	98	64	.605
1988	Detroit	AL	88	74	.543
1989	Detroit	AL	59	103	.364
1990	Detroit	AL	79	83	.488
1991	Detroit	AL	84	78	.519
1992	Detroit	AL	75	87	.463
1993	Detroit	AL	85	77	.525

YEAR	TEAM	LG	W	L	PCT
1994	Detroit	AL	53	62	.461
1995	Detroit	AL	60	84	.417
	TOTALS		2,194	1,834	.545

Sources: Baseball-Reference.com; Canadian Baseball Hall of Fame, Cincinnati Reds Hall of Fame, National Baseball Hall of Fame and Museum

Anderson, Glenn (born: October 2, 1960 in Burnaby, British Columbia, Canada); inducted into the Hockey Hall of Fame in 2008 as a player; Position: Forward; won two Stanley Cup titles; played in four All-Star games.

After playing, but failing to medal, in the 1980 Winter Olympics (Lake Placid, New York) for the Canadian National Team, Anderson played 16 National Hockey League Seasons (1980–1996) with the Edmonton Oilers (1980–1991, 1996); Toronto Maple Leafs (1991–1994); New York Rangers (1994); and the St. Louis Blues (1994–1995, 1996), and played in four All-Star games (1984–1987).

The 5'11", 175-pound forward helped the Oilers win the 1990 Stanley Cup title in five games over the Boston Bruins. He was traded to the New York Rangers just before the 1994 playoffs and helped the team win that season's Stanley Cup championship in seven games over the Vancouver Canucks.

Glenn Anderson's Career Statistics

			REGULAR SEASON				PLAYOFFS			
SEASON	TEAM	LEAGUE	GP	G	A	TP	GP	G	A	TP
1977–1978	Bellingham Blazers	BCJHL	64	62	69	131				
1977–1978	New Westminster Bruins	WCJHL	1	0	1	1				
1978–1979	Seattle Breakers	WHL	2	0	1	1				
1978–1979	University of Denver	WCHA	40	26	29	55				
1979–1980	Seattle Breakers	WHL	7	5	5	10	2	0	1	1
1979–1980	Canada	Nat-Tm	49	21	21	42				
1979–1980	Canada	Olympics	6	2	2	4				
1980–1981	Edmonton Oilers	NHL	58	30	23	53	9	5	7	12
1981–1982	Edmonton Oilers	NHL	80	38	67	105	5	2	5	7
1982–1983	Edmonton Oilers	NHL	72	48	56	104	16	10	10	20
1983–1984	Edmonton Oilers	NHL	80	54	45	99	19	6	11	17
1984–1985	Canada	Can-Cup	8	1	4	5				
1984–1985	Edmonton Oilers	NHL	80	42	39	81	18	10	16	26
1985–1986	Edmonton Oilers	NHL	72	54	48	102	10	8	3	11
1986–1987	Edmonton Oilers	NHL	80	35	38	73	21	14	13	27
1986–1987	NHL All-Stars	RV-87	2	1	0	1				
1987–1988	Canada	Can-Cup	7	2	1	3				
1987–1988	Edmonton Oilers	NHL	80	38	50	88	19	9	16	25
1988–1989	Edmonton Oilers	NHL	79	16	48	64	7	1	2	3
1988–1989	Canada	WEC-A	6	2	2	4				
1989–1990	Edmonton Oilers	NHL	73	34	38	72	22	10	12	22
1990–1991	Edmonton Oilers	NHL	74	24	31	55	18	6	7	13
1991–1992	Toronto Maple Leafs	NHL	72	24	33	57				
1991–1992	Canada	WC-A	6	2	1	3				
1992–1993	Toronto Maple Leafs	NHL	76	22	43	65	21	7	11	18
1993–1994	Toronto Maple Leafs	NHL	73	17	18	35				
1993–1994	New York Rangers	NHL	12	4	2	6	23	3	3	6
1994–1995	Augsburger Panther	Germany	5	6	2	8				
1994–1995	Lukko Rauma	Finland	4	1	1	2				
1994–1995	Canada	Nat-Tm	26	11	8	19				
1994–1995	St. Louis Blues	NHL	36	12	14	26	6	1	1	2
1995–1996	Canada	Nat-Tm	11	4	4	8				
1995–1996	Augsburger Panther	Germany	9	5	3	8				
1995–1996	Edmonton Oilers	NHL	17	4	6	10				

			REGULAR SEASON				PLAYOFFS			
SEASON	**TEAM**	**LEAGUE**	**GP**	**G**	**A**	**TP**	**GP**	**G**	**A**	**TP**
1995–1996	St. Louis Blues	NHL	15	2	2	4	11	1	4	5
1996–1997	HC Bolzano	Alpenliga	2	0	1	1				
1996–1997	HC La Chaux-de-Fonds	Swiss	23	14	15	29				
	NHL TOTALS		1,129	498	601	1,099	225	93	121	214

Sources: Hockey Hall of Fame; Hockey-Reference.com

Anderson, W. Harold (born: September 11, 1902 in Akron, Ohio; died: June 13, 1967); inducted into the Naismith Memorial Basketball Hall of Fame in 1985 as a coach; one of the first college coaches to win 500 games; first coach to take two different teams to the NIT tournament.

Anderson attended Central High School (Akron, Ohio) from 1917 to 1920, before going to Otterbein College (Westerville, Ohio) from 1920 to 1924, where he was named All-State and All-Conference in basketball twice (1923–1924) and was voted the team's most valuable player in 1924.

After graduating from college, he began his coaching career at Wauseon (Ohio) High School (1925–1926), where he compiled a 24–5 record before moving on to Toledo (Ohio) Waite High School for eight seasons (1927–1934), compiling a 100–33 record. During his high school coaching career, Anderson won three city championships and appeared in the state finals twice. After gaining 10 years of coaching experience at the high school level, Anderson moved on to the University of Toledo (Ohio) for nine seasons (1934–1942) and Bowling Green State University (Ohio) for 22 years (1942–1963).

In 38 coaching seasons, Anderson compiled an overall 604–259 (.700) record at all levels; a 142–41 (.776) record at the University of Toledo (including a third-place finish in the 1942 NIT); a 362–185 (.662) record at Bowling Green (leading the team to six NIT and three NCAA tournaments); was the first coach to take two different teams to the NIT tournament; and served as president of the National Association of Basketball Coaches from 1962 to 1963.

Source: Naismith Memorial Basketball Hall of Fame

Anderson, William "Willie" (born: unknown; died: unknown); inducted into the National Soccer Hall of Fame and Museum in 1956 as a builder; involved with the Southern New York State Association, National League of New York, and the New York State Association his entire adult life.

Anderson served as president of both the Southern New York State Association and the National League of New York from 1952 to 1957. He was also a member of the Eastern New York State Soccer Association from 1962 to 1968.

Source: National Soccer Hall of Fame and Museum

Annis, Robert Joseph (born: September 5, 1928 in St, Louis, Missouri; died: March 31, 1995 in St. Louis, Missouri); inducted into the National Soccer Hall of Fame and Museum in 1995 as a player; Position: Halfback; International Caps (1948): 1; International Goals: 0; won two U.S. Open Cups; a member of the 1948 U.S. Olympic Team.

Annis played for St. Louis Simpkins-Ford (sponsored by the Joe Simpkins Ford Auto dealership that played in the St. Louis Major League) and helped the team win U.S. Open Cup titles in 1948 (beating New York Brookhattan) and in 1950 (defeating Fall River Ponta Delgada).

He was a member of the 1948 Olympic team (London, England) and played against the National Team of Israel in Philadelphia, Pennsylvania earlier in the year. After being eliminated from the Olympics in the first round (9–0 loss to Italy), he played against the Irish League All-Stars in Belfast, Northern Ireland. In 1950, he was a member of the U.S. team that played in the FIFA World Cup in Brazil, South America. Although the squad was eliminated early (after a 3–1 loss to Spain and a 5–2 loss to Chile), it was able to perform one of the great upsets in soccer history with a 1–0 win over England.

Annis also played for St. Louis Simpkins against Manchester United in 1950 and for the St. Louis Stars against Liverpool in 1953.

Source: National Soccer Hall of Fame and Museum

Anschutz, Philip Frederick (born: December 28, 1939 in Russell, Kansas); inducted into the National Soccer Hall of Fame and Museum in 2006 as a builder; owner of several Major League Soccer teams; financed the Home Depot Center soccer facility in California.

Best known in the sports world as the owner of several Major League Soccer teams, Anschutz played a key role in the growth of American soccer in the 1990s. After graduating from the University of Kansas (Lawrence) in 1961, he embarked on a highly successful business career that eventually encompassed oil and gas, real estate, railroads, newspapers, telecommunications, movie theaters, moviemaking, and sports.

He began his MLS participation as an investor of the Colorado Rapids in the league's inaugural season (1966), and eventually became involved with the Los Angeles Galaxy, the Chicago Fire, the San Jose Earthquakes, the MetroStars, and D.C. United.

Anschutz financed the building of the soccer complex at the Home Depot Center in Carson, California. While serving as the home of the Galaxy since its opening in 2003, the Center has hosted numerous events, including the 2003 Women's World Cup final and several U.S. National Team games. In 2005, it became the home of a second MLS team, Chivas USA. The Center also serves as the training facility for the U.S. Soccer Federation, USA Cycling, United States Track & Field, the United States Tennis Association, and is an official U.S. Olympic training site.

Anschutz's involvement with the National Team focused on having its games broadcast to as large an audience as possible. He helped negotiate the MLS' acquisition of English-language television rights to the World Cup and later financed the movie *The Game of Their Lives*, about the 1950 United States World Cup team.

In addition to his participation in soccer, he was also the majority owner of the NHL's Los Angeles Kings; a minority owner of the NBA's Los Angeles Clippers; developed the Staples Center, Los Angeles' primary indoor sports arena; and owned several professional hockey teams in Europe.

Anschutz graduated from Wichita (Kansas) High School East in 1957 and earned a business degree from the University of Kansas (Lawrence) in 1961.

Source: National Soccer Hall of Fame and Museum

Anson, Adrian Constantine "Cap" (born: April 11, 1852 in Marshalltown, Iowa; died: April 14, 1922 in Chicago, Illinois); inducted into the National Baseball Hall of Fame and Museum in 1939 as a player by the Veterans Committee; Position: First Base; Bats: Right; Throws: Right; first member of the 3,000-hit club.

Anson made his professional baseball debut on May 6, 1871 and played his entire 22-season Major League Baseball (National League) career (1876–1897) with the Chicago White Stockings/Colts, with his first National League game being on May 6, 1876. He also played for the Rockford Forest Citys (National Association of Professional Base Ball Players, 1871), the Philadelphia Athletics (National Association of Professional Base Ball Players, 1872–1875), and the New York Giants (National League, 1898). He played in both the 1885 pre-modern World Series (a 3–3–1 tie against the St. Louis Browns) and in the 1886 pre-modern World Series (losing to the Browns in six games).

He played at the major league level for 27 years, mainly at first base with the Chicago team in the National League; hit over .300 for 20 seasons; and accumulated over 3,081 hits, making him the first member of the 3,000-hit club. When he retired, Anson held numerous records, including games played, hits, at-bats, doubles, and runs scored. As a player-manager for Chicago, Anson collected more than 1,200 wins and five National League pennants.

Anson is known as the "first son" of Marshalltown. By the 1850s, enough people lived in the area to form several baseball teams, and by 1866, he played for a local team known as the "Stars." He later attended the University of Notre Dame (South Bend, Indiana), where he played first base on the school's team, while his brother, Sturgis, played center field. Not suited for college, after two years, Anson returned home for a short time before attending Iowa State University (Iowa City). Recognizing, once again, that college was not for him, after one semester Anson left and returned to Marshalltown, where he played third base on the town baseball team with his father (second base) and Sturgis (center field).

In 1871, he signed his first professional contract with the Rockford (Illinois) Forest Citys in the first year of the newly formed, nine-team National Association of Professional Base Ball Players. Thus, it can be argued, that the 6'1", 227-pound Anson was involved with major league professional baseball from its inception. Although he hit .325, the team finished in last place with a 4–21 record. Starting all 25 games in the team's inaugural season, he led the squad in hits, total bases, on-base percentage, doubles, and extra-base hits. When Rockford failed to make a profit its first season, the team folded and Anson moved on to the Philadelphia Athletics (National Association).

In his first season with Philadelphia, the team played to a 30–16 record and finished second behind the Boston Red Stockings. As the game became more established, its popularity grew, and more talented players entered the league, eventually raising the circuit's level of play. On July 16, 1874, Boston and Philadelphia went to the United Kingdom and participated in the first-ever international baseball exhibition. Organized by Albert Spalding, Boston manager Harry Wright, and baseball writer Henry Chadwick, the aim of the tour was to introduce baseball to England and Ireland, although many contemporaries felt the sport had derived from the English game of rounders. After an 11-day trip, the teams arrived in Liverpool, England, where they played their first exhibition game. The two teams traveled to Manchester, London, Sheffield, and Dublin (Ireland), and in addition to baseball, also played cricket against some of the local teams. Although a historic trip for professional baseball, the game was not well received in the United Kingdom and did not generate a profit.

After leaving the Athletics in 1875, Anson signed with the Chicago White Stockings (National League), where he played third base for Albert Spalding in 1876, the year the league was formed. In addition to Chicago, the league initially included the Boston Red Caps, Cincinnati Reds, Hartford Dark Blues, Louisville Grays, New York Mutuals, Philadelphia Athletics, and the St. Louis Brown Stockings.

Although the White Stockings did not do well in the league's early years, Anson was productive, hitting .337 in 1877; .341 in 1878; and .317 in 1879. He moved to first base, where he played for the rest of his career, and in 1879, he became the team's captain, earning the nickname "Cap." As Chicago's captain, he led the team to a 67–17 record in 1880, finishing 15 games ahead of the second-place Providence Grays. His 1881 season was the best of his playing career. While leading the team to a 56–28 record (nine games ahead of second-place Providence), Anson led the league with a .399 batting average, 137 hits, and 82 RBIs. As the White Stockings dominated the National League and won the pennant for a third straight season with a 55–29 record, Anson hit .362 (second in the league) and led the circuit with 83 RBIs.

After very poor showings in 1883 and 1884, the franchise completely remade the team with a new lineup in 1885, which included the "Chicago Stone Wall" infield with Anson at first, Fred Pfeffer at second, Ned Williamson at third, and Tom Burns at shortstop, currently considered one of the strongest in professional baseball history. With a new lineup, the team rebounded and finished the season in first place, two games ahead of the New York Giants. After finishing the 1885 season, the first pre-modern day World Series was played between the White Stockings and the St. Louis Browns of the American Association. In its early days, the World Series was viewed as an exhibition rather than a championship series. The first World Series ended in a 3–3–1 tie, with Anson hitting .423.

With a record of 90–34, Chicago went on to repeat as league champions in 1886, giving Anson his sixth championship as a player and fifth as a manager. The team once again faced the St. Louis Browns in the 1886 World Series, eventually losing four games to two. Chicago's dominance began to fade after the 1886 season as the franchise finished second or third over the next three seasons.

In 1890, baseball experienced its first major labor dispute when many players, upset at baseball's reserve clause (which basically made them slaves to management), left the National League and formed the Players' League. Although Anson was one of the few stars who stayed loyal to the National League, his White Stockings were severely affected by the player revolt and its lineup mainly consisted of rookies for the 1890 season. Since all league teams had been similarly weakened, Chicago managed to finish in second place, although Anson's personal offensive numbers declined significantly.

Although the Players' League folded after only one season, Anson felt personally betrayed by the player exodus and refused to allow former teammates to rejoin the White Stockings in 1891, in contrast to the attitude of the other teams in the league, which eagerly accepted the return of their stars. While many admired his stance, reality set in when the other teams began to flourish and Chicago fell in the standings while playing with an inferior lineup.

From 1892 to 1897, the White Stockings could not rise above fourth place and most of the blame and criticism for the team's lackluster performance fell on Anson, the team's leader and lone star. After the 1897 season, he was fired, after 27 seasons in the game (22 as the team's player-manager).

He returned briefly in 1898 to manage the New York Giants, but resigned after only three weeks. Anson was the first member of the 3,000-hit club, and as of this writing, is still third all-time in RBIs, seventh in hits, and eighth in runs scored.

In spite of his skills and contributions to baseball, Anson had a dark side and was one of the game's most ardent racists. His place in the sport as one of its greats allowed his racism to flourish and he played a major role in excluding black players from the major leagues. Although definitely not alone in his beliefs, his status in the game makes Anson a more important target for criticism since he had a chance to propose breaking the color line, but refused to do so. Due to the position he took, he is sometimes referred to as the "Father of Segregated Baseball."

For all his racism, Anson also understood the role that money played in the game. On August 10, 1883, the White Stockings were scheduled to play an exhibition game against the semi-professional Toledo Mud Hens of the American Association. This was a common practice in its day to allow both teams to generate extra revenue. When he realized that the Mudhens' catcher, Moses Walker, was black, Anson refused to allow Chicago to take the field until he received a guarantee that Walker would not be allowed to play. When the Mudhens, the home team, announced that its catcher would play, the team's manager informed Anson that if Chicago did not take the field, he would forfeit the team's share of the gate receipts. As so often happens in life, money won and Anson fielded his team, eventually winning the game.

However, this minor victory against the color line did not last long. On July 14, 1887, an exhibition game was scheduled between the Chicago White Stockings and the Newark Little Giants (International League). Anson refused to play if Newark's star black pitcher, George Stovey, was in the lineup. On this occasion, Anson refused to back down, and Stovey eventually left the game, which was won by Chicago. This incident is often cited as the moment when baseball's unofficial color line was established.

Shortly after this game, the International League, the National League, and the American Association adopted the policy of not signing black players, a ban that was eventually accepted by all major league teams. Although unofficial, and never included in any rule book, the major league color line existed until broken by Jackie Robinson in 1947.

After his playing days, Anson was elected Chicago's city clerk in 1905 and served one term. He then bought a semi-professional baseball team, renamed it Anson's Colts, and managed the squad for several seasons before it folded. He became a vaudeville performer, sometimes with his daughters, and appeared throughout New England and the Midwest, a career which lasted until 1921, one year before he died.

Anson was one of the original 26 members of the National Baseball Hall of Fame, having been voted in by the Hall's Centennial Commission (Veteran's Committee).

Cap Anson's Career Statistics

YEAR	TEAM	G	AB	R	H	2B	3B	HR	BB	SO	SB	AVG	SLG
1876	Chicago	66	321	63	110	13	6	2	12	8		.343	.439
1877	Chicago	47	200	36	67	20	1	0	9	3		.335	.445
1878	Chicago	59	256	54	86	12	2	0	13	1		.336	.398
1879	Chicago	49	221	41	90	22	1	0	2	2		.407	.516
1880	Chicago	84	346	52	117	22	1	1	14	12		.338	.416
1881	Chicago	84	343	67	137	25	7	1	26	4		.399	.522
1882	Chicago	82	348	69	126	30	8	1	20	7		.362	.503
1883	Chicago	98	413	69	127	33	6	0	18	9		.308	.416
1884	Chicago	111	471	108	159	32	5	21	29	13		.338	.561
1885	Chicago	112	464	100	144	35	6	7	34	13		.310	.457
1886	Chicago	125	504	117	187	34	11	10	55	19		.371	.542
1887	Chicago	122	532	107	224	33	13	7	60	18	27	.421	.571
1888	Chicago	134	515	101	177	17	13	12	47	24	28	.344	.497
1889	Chicago	134	518	99	177	30	6	7	86	19	27	.342	.463
1890	Chicago	139	504	102	157	17	4	7	113	23	29	.312	.403
1891	Chicago	136	537	82	158	25	9	8	75	29	21	.294	.419
1892	Chicago	147	561	62	154	23	9	1	67	30	15	.275	.353
1893	Chicago	101	381	70	123	25	3	0	68	12	13	.323	.404
1894	Chicago	83	347	87	137	26	6	5	40	15	17	.395	.548
1895	Chicago	122	476	88	161	23	6	2	55	23	16	.338	.424
1896	Chicago	106	403	72	135	17	3	2	49	10	28	.335	.407
1897	Chicago	112	423	66	128	16	3	3	60		16	.303	.376
	TOTALS	2,253	9,084	1,712	3,081	530	129	97	952	294	237	.339	.458

Sources: Baseball-Reference.com; *Cap Anson: The Grand Old Man of Baseball* (David L. Fleitz); National Baseball Hall of Fame and Museum

Aparicio, Luis Ernesto Montiel (born: April 29, 1934 in Maracaibo, Zulia, Venezuela); inducted into the National Baseball Hall of Fame and Museum in 1984 as a player; Position: Shortstop; Bats: Right; Throws: Right; first South American player inducted into the baseball hall of fame.

Nicknamed "Little Looey" (Little Louie), the 5'9" 160-pound Aparicio made his major league debut on April 17, 1956 and during his 18-year career played for the Chicago White Sox (1956–1962, 1968–1970), Baltimore Orioles (1963–1967), and the Boston Red Sox (1971–1973). He played in two World Series, beating the Los Angeles Dodgers in 1966 and losing to the Dodgers in 1959.

He played on 10 All-Star teams (1958–1964, 1970–1972); was the American League Rookie of the Year (1956); led the American League in stolen bases nine consecutive seasons (1956–1964); and won nine Gold Gloves (1958–1962, 1964, 1966, 1968, 1970).

Aparicio helped redefine the role of a shortstop. He was a great fielder, able to hit to all fields, and a superb base runner, skills that were not normally associated with the position. When he retired in 1973, he held major league career records (as a shortstop) for games played, double plays, and assists, as well as American League records for putouts and total chances by a shortstop.

The municipal stadium in Maracaibo has been renamed Estadio Luis Aparicio in his honor. While Aparicio had a .262 career batting average, he also tied the longest major league hitless streak for non-pitchers in the last 50 years by going 0 for 44 with the Boston Red Sox in 1971. He was the first player from South America inducted into the National Baseball Hall of Fame and Museum, and in 1999, he was a nominee for MLB's All-Century Team.

Luis Aparicio's Career Statistics

YEAR	TEAM	LG	G	AB	R	H	2B	3B	HR	RBI	BB	SO	AVG	SLG
1956	Chicago	AL	152	533	69	142	19	6	3	56	34	63	.266	.341
1957	Chicago	AL	143	575	82	148	22	6	3	41	52	55	.257	.332
1958	Chicago	AL	145	557	76	148	20	9	2	40	35	38	.266	.345
1959	Chicago	AL	152	612	98	157	18	5	6	51	53	40	.257	.332
1960	Chicago	AL	153	600	86	166	20	7	2	61	43	39	.277	.343
1961	Chicago	AL	156	625	90	170	24	4	6	45	38	33	.272	.352
1962	Chicago	AL	153	581	72	140	23	5	7	40	32	36	.241	.334
1963	Baltimore	AL	146	601	73	150	18	8	5	45	36	35	.250	.331
1964	Baltimore	AL	146	578	93	154	20	3	10	37	49	51	.266	.363
1965	Baltimore	AL	144	564	67	127	20	10	8	40	46	56	.225	.339
1966	Baltimore	AL	151	659	97	182	25	8	6	41	33	42	.276	.366
1967	Baltimore	AL	134	546	55	127	22	5	4	31	29	44	.233	.313
1968	Chicago	AL	155	622	55	164	24	4	4	36	33	43	.264	.334
1969	Chicago	AL	156	599	77	168	24	5	5	51	66	29	.280	.362
1970	Chicago	AL	146	552	86	173	29	3	5	43	53	34	.313	.404
1971	Boston	AL	125	491	56	114	23	0	4	45	35	43	.232	.303
1972	Boston	AL	110	436	47	112	26	3	3	39	26	28	.257	.351
1973	Boston	AL	132	499	56	135	17	1	0	49	43	33	.271	.309
	TOTALS		2,599	10,230	1,335	2,677	394	92	83	791	736	742	.262	.343

Sources: Baseball-Reference.com; National Baseball Hall of Fame and Museum

Appling, Lucius Benjamin "Luke" (born: April 2, 1907 in High Point, North Carolina; died: January 3, 1991 in Cumming, Georgia); inducted into the National Baseball Hall of Fame and Museum in 1964 as a player; Position: Shortstop; Bats: Right; Throws: Right; first Chicago White Sox player to win a batting title; voted the greatest White Sox player by Chicago fans.

Nicknamed "Old Aches and Pains," the 5'10", 183-pound Appling played his entire 20-year Major League Baseball career (1930–1950) with the Chicago White Sox (1930–1943, 1945–1950) and later managed the Kansas City Athletics for one season (1967) before the team moved to Oakland, California.

He was named to seven All-Star teams (1936, 1939–1941, 1943, 1946–1947); finished his career with 1,302 walks (at the time 25th in MLB history); won the American League batting title twice (1936, 1943); and was voted the White Sox greatest player by Chicago fans in a 1969 poll.

After two years at Oglethorpe University (Atlanta, Georgia), Appling left as a sophomore and signed a professional baseball contract with the Atlanta Crackers (Southern Association) in 1930; was sold to the Chicago Cubs late in the season; and wound up with the White Sox. In 1936, he led the American League with a .388 batting average, the first batting title won by a White Sox player, and went on to hit .300 or better for 15 seasons. Appling established major league shortstop records for games played and double plays, along with American League shortstop records for putouts and assists. All of these records would later be surpassed by Luis Aparicio.

Although he played almost every day during his career, Appling earned the nickname "Old Aches and Pains" due to his constant complaining about his physical ailments and the condition of the infield wherever the team played. After he retired, Appling became manager of the Memphis (Tennessee) Chicks of the Southern Association in 1951; was named Manager of the Year by *The Sporting News* in 1952; became the interim manager of the Kansas City Athletics in 1967; and the batting instructor for the Atlanta Braves in the 1980s.

Luke Appling's Career Statistics

YEAR	TEAM	LG	G	AB	R	H	2B	3B	HR	RBI	BB	SO	AVG	SLG
1930	Chicago	AL	6	26	2	8	2	0	0	2	0	0	.308	.385
1931	Chicago	AL	96	297	36	69	13	4	1	28	29	27	.232	.313
1932	Chicago	AL	139	489	66	134	20	10	3	63	40	36	.274	.374
1933	Chicago	AL	151	612	90	197	36	10	6	85	56	29	.322	.443
1934	Chicago	AL	118	452	75	137	28	6	2	61	59	27	.303	.405
1935	Chicago	AL	153	525	94	161	28	6	1	71	122	40	.307	.389
1936	Chicago	AL	138	526	111	204	31	7	6	128	85	25	.388	.508
1937	Chicago	AL	154	574	98	182	42	8	4	77	86	28	.317	.439
1938	Chicago	AL	81	294	41	89	14	0	0	44	42	17	.303	.350
1939	Chicago	AL	148	516	82	162	16	6	0	56	105	37	.314	.368
1940	Chicago	AL	150	566	96	197	27	13	0	79	69	35	.348	.442
1941	Chicago	AL	154	592	93	186	26	8	1	57	82	32	.314	.390
1942	Chicago	AL	142	543	78	142	26	4	3	53	63	23	.262	.341
1943	Chicago	AL	155	585	63	192	33	2	3	80	90	29	.328	.407
1945	Chicago	AL	18	57	12	21	2	2	1	10	12	7	.368	.526
1946	Chicago	AL	149	582	59	180	27	5	1	55	71	41	.309	.378
1947	Chicago	AL	139	503	67	154	29	0	8	49	64	28	.306	.412
1948	Chicago	AL	139	497	63	156	16	2	0	47	94	35	.314	.354
1949	Chicago	AL	142	492	82	148	21	5	5	58	121	24	.301	.394
1950	Chicago	AL	50	128	11	30	3	4	0	13	12	8	.234	.320
	TOTALS		2,422	8,856	1,319	2,749	440	102	45	1,116	1,302	528	.310	.398

Sources: Baseball-Reference.com; National Baseball Hall of Fame and Museum

Apps, Charles Joseph Sylvanus "Syl" (born: January 18, 1915 in Paris, Ontario, Canada; died: December 24, 1998 in Kingston, Ontario, Canada); inducted into the Hockey Hall of Fame in 1961 as a player; Position: Center; Uniform: #10; competed in the 1936 Summer Olympics in the pole vault; winner of the first Calder Trophy as the National Hockey League's Rookie of the Year; won three Stanley Cup titles.

At McMaster University (Hamilton, Ontario, Canada), Apps was captain of the football team and won two pole vault titles in track. He represented Canada, and finished sixth, at the 1936 Summer Olympics (Berlin, Germany). After the Olympics, he joined the National Hockey League's Toronto Maple Leafs, where he would play center his entire 10-year career (1936–1943, 1945–1948), interrupted by service with the Canadian Army during World War II.

In 1937, he won the inaugural Calder Trophy (now known as the Calder Memorial Trophy) as the NHL's Rookie of the Year; was named First All-Star Team Center twice (1939, 1942); Second All-Star Team Center three times (1938, 1941, 1943); and played the entire 1941–1942 season without receiving a single penalty, winning the Lady Byng Trophy for sportsmanship and gentlemanly conduct. He played in six Stanley Cup finals (winning in 1942, 1947–1948, and losing in 1938–1940), and retired with 201goals and 432 points.

In 1940, the 6', 185-pound Apps was named team captain, and two years later, he led the Leafs to a Stanley Cup championship over the Detroit Red Wings (1942) in seven games, after having lost the first three games of the series. A year later, he left the team to serve in the Canadian Army during World War II; was again named captain when he returned to the squad after his military service; and led the Leafs to two consecutive Stanley Cup championships (1947–1948). He retired after winning his third Stanley Cup title (1948), just after scoring 200 career goals, a feat that had only been accomplished previously by one other Leaf player, Charlie Conacher.

While still an active player, Apps ran for parliament in the 1940 federal election as a member of the National Government Party, but lost to George Ernest Wood of the Liberal Party by 138 votes. After retiring from the NHL, he served as the Ontario Athletic Commissioner in 1948 before again running for political office, serving as a Conservative Member of the Provincial Parliament in Ontario for 11 years (1963–1974). He was made a Member of the Order of Canada in 1977, and Apps is the only person to be inducted into the Hockey Hall of Fame, Canada's Sports Hall of Fame (1975), and the Canadian Amateur Athletics Hall of Fame.

Syl Apps' Career Statistics

SEASON	TEAM	LEAGUE	REGULAR SEASON G	G	A	TP	PLAYOFFS GP	G	A	TP
1930–1931	Paris Greens	OHA-Jr.	7	5	1	6				
1931–1935	McMaster University	OHA-Sr.								
1935–1936	Hamilton Tigers	OHA-Sr.	19	22	16	38	9	12	7	19
1935–1936	Toronto Dominions	OHA-Sr.	1	0	1	1				
1935–1936	Hamilton Tigers	Al-Cup	4	5	4	9				
1936–1937	Toronto Maple Leafs	NHL	48	16	29	45	2	0	1	1
1937–1938	Toronto Maple Leafs	NHL	47	21	29	50	7	1	4	5
1938–1939	Toronto Maple Leafs	NHL	44	15	25	40	10	2	6	8
1939–1940	Toronto Maple Leafs	NHL	27	13	17	30	10	5	2	7
1940–1941	Toronto Maple Leafs	NHL	41	20	24	44	7	3	2	5
1941–1942	Toronto Maple Leafs	NHL	38	18	23	41	13	5	9	14
1942–1943	Toronto Maple Leafs	NHL	29	23	17	40				
1943–1944	Toronto Army Daggers	OHA-Sr.	1	1	2	3				
1944–1945	Brockville Army	ONDHL								
1944–1945	Ottawa All-Stars	Exhib.	1	6	1	7				
1945–1946	Toronto Maple Leafs	NHL	40	24	16	40				
1946–1947	Toronto Maple Leafs	NHL	54	25	24	49	11	5	1	6
1947–1948	Toronto Maple Leafs	NHL	55	26	27	53	9	4	4	8
	NHL TOTALS		423	201	231	432	69	25	29	54

Sources: Canada's Sports Hall of Fame; Canadian Amateur Athletics Hall of Fame; Hockey Hall of Fame; Hockey-Reference.com

Arbour, Alger Joseph "Al" (born: November 1, 1932 in Sudbury, Ontario, Canada); inducted into the Hockey Hall of Fame in 1996 as a builder; won three Stanley Cup titles as a player; led the New York Islanders to the team's first Stanley Cup championship; guided the Islanders to four consecutive NHL titles.

After playing in the minor leagues, the 6', 180-pound Arbour began his 16-year NHL playing career with a brief appearance in 1953–1954 as a defenseman with the Detroit Red Wings, and would go on to become a successful player and coach. He played for the Red Wings for three more seasons (1955–1958); the Chicago Black Hawks for three seasons (1958–1961); the Toronto Maple Leafs for five seasons (1961–1966); and the St. Louis Blues (1967–1971) for four seasons, before retiring. He won three Stanley Cup championships during his playing career (1961 with the Chicago Black Hawks, and 1962 and 1964 with the Toronto Maple Leafs).

Arbour began his coaching career with the St. Louis Blues during the 1970–1971 season, after playing 22 games for the team that season. Two seasons later, he moved on to coach the expansion New York Islanders in 1972–1973, winning only 12 games in the franchise's inaugural season. Despite the team's slow start, in 1974–1975, Arbour led the Islanders to a victory over the New York Rangers in the team's very first post-season first-round series. The team went on to beat the Pittsburgh Penguins in the seventh game of the quarterfinals, becoming only the second franchise to win a best-of-seven series after being down 3–0 (the first being the Toronto Maple Leafs in the 1942 Stanley Cup). The dream season came to an end when the Islanders lost in the next series in seven games to the Philadelphia Flyers.

Proving the franchise's success was not a fluke, the Islanders enjoyed regular-season success over the next four years, but were never able to win the Stanley Cup, although Arbour won the Jack Adams Award as league Coach of the Year in 1979. Finally, in 1980, the team won its first championship over the Philadelphia Flyers in six games, the first of New York's four consecutive titles (giving Arbour a total of seven championships).

He retired from coaching in 1986 and became the team's Vice President of Player Development. When the team fell on hard times, Arbour reassumed coaching duties during the 1988–1989 season, and stayed on the bench until 1994. He retired with 781 regular-season coaching wins (739 with the Islanders); coached 1,606 games; and returned to the franchise's front office as Vice-President of Hockey Operations.

Al Arbour's Playing Statistics

SEASON	TEAM	LEAGUE	REGULAR SEASON G	G	A	TP	PIM	PLAYOFFS GP	G	A	TP	PIM
1949–1950	Windsor Spitfires	OHA-Jr.	3	0	0	0	0	1	0	0	0	0

SEASON	TEAM	LEAGUE	REGULAR SEASON G	G	A	TP	PIM	PLAYOFFS GP	G	A	TP	PIM
1949–1950	Detroit Hettche	IHL	33	14	8	22	10	3	0	0	0	4
1950–1951	Windsor Spitfires	OHA-Jr.	31	5	4	9	27					
1951–1952	Windsor Spitfires	OHA-Jr.	55	7	12	19	86					
1952–1953	Windsor Spitfires	OHA-Jr.	56	5	7	12	92					
1952–1953	Washington Lions	EAHL	4	0	2	2	0					
1952–1953	Edmonton Flyers	WHL	8	0	1	1	2	15	0	5	5	10
1953–1954	Detroit Red Wings	NHL	36	0	1	1	18					
1953–1954	Sherbrooke Saints	QHL	19	1	3	4	24	2	0	0	0	2
1954–1955	Edmonton Flyers	WHL	41	3	9	12	39					
1954–1955	Quebec Aces	QHL	20	4	5	9	55	4	0	0	0	2
1955–1956	Edmonton Flyers	WHL	70	5	14	19	109	3	0	0	0	4
1955–1956	Detroit Red Wings	NHL						4	0	1	1	0
1956–1957	Detroit Red Wings	NHL	44	1	6	7	38	5	0	0	0	6
1956–1957	Edmonton Flyers	WHL	24	2	3	5	24					
1957–1958	Detroit Red Wings	NHL	69	1	6	7	104	4	0	1	1	4
1958–1959	Chicago Black Hawks	NHL	70	2	10	12	86	6	1	2	3	26
1959–1960	Chicago Black Hawks	NHL	57	1	5	6	66	4	0	0	0	4
1960–1961	Chicago Black Hawks	NHL	53	3	2	5	40	7	0	0	0	2
1961–1962	Toronto Maple Leafs	NHL	52	1	5	6	68	8	0	0	0	6
1962–1963	Toronto Maple Leafs	NHL	4	1	0	1	4					
1962–1963	Rochester Americans	AHL	63	6	21	27	97	2	0	2	2	2
1963–1964	Toronto Maple Leafs	NHL	6	0	1	1	0	1	0	0	0	0
1963–1964	Rochester Americans	AHL	60	3	19	22	62	2	1	0	1	0
1964–1965	Rochester Americans	AHL	71	1	16	17	88	10	0	1	1	16
1964–1965	Toronto Maple Leafs	NHL						1	0	0	0	2
1965–1966	Toronto Maple Leafs	NHL	4	0	1	1	2					
1965–1966	Rochester Americans	AHL	59	2	11	13	86	12	0	2	2	8
1966–1967	Rochester Americans	AHL	71	3	19	22	48	13	0	1	1	16
1967–1968	St. Louis Blues	NHL	74	1	10	11	50	14	0	3	3	10
1968–1969	St. Louis Blues	NHL	67	1	6	7	50	12	0	0	0	10
1969–1970	St. Louis Blues	NHL	68	0	3	3	85	14	0	1	1	16
1970–1971	St. Louis Blues	NHL	22	0	2	2	6	6	0	0	0	6
	NHL TOTALS		626	12	58	70	617	86	1	8	9	92

Sources: Hockey Hall of Fame; Hockey-Reference.com

Archibald, Nathaniel "Nate" (born: September 2, 1948 in New York, New York); inducted into the Naismith Memorial Basketball Hall of Fame in 1991 as a player; Position: Guard; first player to lead the NBA in scoring and assists in the same season.

Nicknamed "Tiny," the 6'1", 150-pound Archibald was an All-City basketball star at DeWitt Clinton High School (Bronx, New York). After graduation, he attended Arizona Western College (Yuma, 1966–1967) and the University of Texas, El Paso (1967–1970), where he averaged more than 20 points a game as a junior and senior. After being named an Honorable Mention All-American and the Western Athletic Conference Most Valuable Player in 1970, Archibald was a second-round pick (19th overall selection) of the Cincinnati Royals in the 1970 National Basketball Association Draft and was with the team during its last two years of existence (1970–1972).

During his 13-year NBA career, Archibald played for the Royals, Kansas City Kings (1972–1976), New York Nets (1976–1977), Boston Celtics (1978–1983), and the Milwaukee Bucks (1983–1984). After the 1972 season, the Royals moved to Kansas City and became known as the Kansas City-Omaha Kings, and divided the franchise's home games between Kansas City, Missouri and Omaha, Nebraska. In the 1972–1973 season, Archibald became the first player to lead the NBA in scoring and assists (34.0 points and 11.4 assists per game) in the same season, remarkable feats while playing on a last-place team (Midwest Division).

After the 1976 season, he moved on to the New York Nets for one year (1976–1977), before signing with the Buffalo Braves in 1977. However, before he could play for his new team, Archibald suffered an Achilles tendon injury, which forced him to miss the entire season. He returned to the NBA the next year and played for five seasons with the Boston Celtics, before ending his career with the Milwaukee Bucks.

He was named to the All-NBA First-Team three times (1973, 1975–1976); the All-NBA Second-Team twice (1972, 1981); was a six-time All-Star (1973, 1975–1976, 1980–1982); NBA All-Star Game MVP (1981); won an NBA championship with the Boston Celtics (1981); and was named to the NBA 50th Anniversary All-Time Team (1996). He led the NBA in free throws made (three times) and free throw attempts (twice).

After retiring from the NBA, Archibald returned to New York City and worked as the athletic director at the Harlem Armory homeless shelter until it closed in 1991.

Nate Archibald's NBA Career Statistics

SEASON	TEAM	G	MP	FG	FT	TRB	AST	STL	BLK	PTS
1970–1971	Cincinnati	82	2,867	486	336	242	450			1,308
1971–1972	Cincinnati	76	3,272	734	677	222	701			2,145
1972–1973	Kansas City/Omaha	80	3,681	1,028	663	223	910			2,719
1973–1974	Kansas City/Omaha	35	1,272	222	173	85	266	56	7	617
1974–1975	Kansas City/Omaha	82	3,244	759	652	222	557	119	7	2,170
1975–1976	Kansas City	78	3,184	717	501	213	615	126	15	1,935
1976–1977	New York	34	1,277	250	197	80	254	59	11	697
1978–1979	Boston	69	1,662	259	242	103	324	55	6	760
1979–1980	Boston	80	2,864	383	361	197	671	106	10	1,131
1980–1981	Boston	80	2,820	382	342	176	618	75	18	1,106
1981–1982	Boston	68	2,167	308	236	116	541	52	3	858
1982–1983	Boston	66	1,811	235	220	91	409	38	4	695
1983–1984	Milwaukee	46	1,038	136	64	76	160	33	0	340
	TOTALS	876	31,159	5,899	4,664	2,046	6,476	719	81	16,481

Sources: Basketball-Reference.com; Naismith Memorial Basketball Hall of Fame

Ardizzone, John (born: January 16, 1909 in Vercelli, Italy; died: January 20, 1982 in San Francisco, California); inducted into the National Soccer Hall of Fame and Museum in 1971 as a builder; a soccer player, coach, manager, and administrator for more than 50 years.

After playing soccer as a young boy in Italy, Ardizzone built his hall-of-fame career by playing the game and serving as an administrator in the San Francisco, California Bay Area for over 50 years. Arriving in America at age 13, he and his family moved to the west coast, where he began his long association with the San Francisco Athletic Club, which won league championships in 1926 and 1928. In 1933, he left the Athletic Club and helped organize the Verdi Club Soccer Team, and as team captain, led the squad to the finals of the California State Cup.

Verdi was promoted to Division 1 in 1934 and won the championship, with Ardizzone setting a scoring record with 49 goals in 20 games. He also played for various San Francisco All-Star teams against the visiting English club in 1937 and the visiting Canadian club at the opening of the San Francisco World Fair in 1939.

Staying in the Bay Area, Ardizzone played for Teutonia in 1937, and helped the team win the title in 1940. He moved to Unione Española in 1941, and again won a title. Making his last appearance at the California State Cup final, he retired as a player in 1947. He went on to coach and manage the Lincoln School's (San Francisco) team and the Greek-American club, before serving as secretary of the San Francisco Soccer Football League from 1947 to 1954.

He also was a referee and served as president of the California Soccer Football Association (1954–1956); was one of its board members from 1957 to 1960; and served as its vice president from 1960 to 1966. He then returned to the San Francisco Soccer Football League and served as its secretary until his death in 1982.

Source: National Soccer Hall of Fame and Museum

Arena, Bruce (born: September 21, 1951 in Brooklyn, New York); inducted into the National Soccer Hall of Fame and Museum in 2010 as a builder; Position: Goalie; most successful National Team coach in the squad's history.

Currently the head coach of Major League Soccer's Los Angeles Galaxy, the 6' Arena attended H. Frank Carey High School (Franklin Square, New York) and played soccer for the school's team and for local squad Hota S.C. (Cosmopolitan Soccer League) in 1968. After high school, he went to Nassau Community College (Garden City, New York), where he played lacrosse and soccer. He was a two-time Honorable Mention All-American lacrosse player (1970–1971); an All-American soccer player; and was later inducted into the National Junior College Hall of Fame in 2008.

After two years at the community college, Arena transferred to Cornell University (Ithaca, New York), where he was both a 1972 Honorable Mention All-American and a 1973 Second-Team All-American lacrosse player. He also backstopped the school to the 1972 NCAA Men's Soccer Championship Final Four and was named Most Valuable Defensive Player in the tournament.

After graduating from college, he played one season with the Montreal Quebecois (National Lacrosse League) in 1975 and after the league folded, played soccer for the Tacoma Tides of the American Soccer League. In addition to playing for the team, Arena also coached the men's soccer team at the University of Puget Sound (Tacoma, Washington).

Internationally, he played only one game for the U.S. national soccer team in 1973 (a 2–0 loss to Israel) and also played for the national lacrosse team, which won the 1974 World Lacrosse Championship and finished runner-up in 1978.

In 1977, he returned to Cornell and became the school's assistant lacrosse coach. One year later, he moved on to the University of Virginia (Charlottesville) and coached both the lacrosse and soccer teams for seven years before focusing only on soccer, beginning in 1985. Arena eventually was the school's head coach for 18 years and won five national championships, including four straight (1991–1994), and finished with an overall record of 295–58–32 (.766). In addition to his coaching responsibilities, he worked as the Atlantic Coast Conference soccer coaches chairman and served two three-year terms on the NCAA Division I soccer committee (1989 to 1995).

In January 1996, Arena left the university to become coach of D.C. United (Major League Soccer, a new team in a new league) and also coached the U-23 National Team at the 1996 Summer Olympics (Atlanta, Georgia), where they finished with a 1–1–1 record. After the Olympics were over, he led United to the very first MLS Cup and helped the team win the 1996 U.S. Open Cup championship.

In 1997, United won its second MLS title and Arena was selected MLS Coach of the Year. In its third year, the team once again advanced to the MLS finals, but lost to the Chicago Fire. Although he lost the league title, Arena led United to the Confederation of North, Central American and Caribbean Association Football championship with a 1–0 win over Toluca on August 16, 1998. He followed United's COCCACAF championship with a victory over Brazilian club Vasco de Gama to win the Interamerican Cup title. Arena was also named the 1997 and 1998 MLS All-Star head coach.

In October 1998, Arena became the head coach of the U.S. National Team and became the most successful coach in team history with the most wins (71) and two Gold Cup championships (2002, 2005), but no FIFA World Cup titles. While he was coach of the National Team (1998–2006), the squad's FIFA world rankings increased from 19th to fourth.

After his National Team contract was not renewed, he became the head coach of the MLS' New York Red Bulls, where he stayed until November 2007, accumulating a 16–16–10 record. He was hired by the Galaxy in August 2008, where he still coaches, and was named MLS Coach of the Year in 2009.

Source: National Soccer Hall of Fame and Museum

Arizin, Paul Joseph (born: April 9, 1928 in Philadelphia, Pennsylvania; died: December 12, 2006 in Springfield, Pennsylvania); inducted into the Naismith Memorial Basketball Hall of Fame in 1978 as a player; Position: Forward-Guard; named to the NBA's 25th and 50th Anniversary teams; fastest player in NBA history to score 10,000 points.

When the 6'4", 190-pound Arizin entered the National Basketball Association in 1950, he introduced the jump shot; led the league in scoring in the 1951–1952 season; and played his entire 10-year NBA career (1950–1952, 1954–1962) with the Philadelphia Warriors.

He won an NBA title in 1956; was selected to the All-NBA First Team three times (1952, 1956–1957); All-NBA Second Team in 1959; was a 10-time NBA All-Star; All-Star MVP in 1952; and was named one of the 50 Greatest Players in NBA History in 1996.

Although Arizin did not play basketball at LaSalle High School (Philadelphia, Pennsylvania), he did play the game in intramural, church, and independent leagues throughout the city. After high school (1943–1946), he attended Villanova University (Pennsylvania, 1946–1950) and, as a walk-on, he earned a scholarship by making the school's basketball team as a sophomore. In his junior year, Arizin set a school single-game scoring record with 85 points (against the Philadelphia Naval Air Materials Center) and as a senior, he led the nation in scoring (25.3 points per game) and was named College Player of the Year (1950).

After college, he was a first-round pick in the 1950 NBA Draft of the Philadelphia Warriors, where he would play his entire career, only missing two seasons to military service with the U.S. Marines during the Korean War. As a rookie, Arizin averaged 17.2 points and 9.8 rebounds per game, offensive numbers that would normally earn a player Rookie of the Year honors, but the award would not come into existence until 1952.

In his second season, he led the league with 25.4 points per game; garnered 11.3 rebounds per game; and compiled a .448 field-goal percentage. In a triple-overtime game against the Minneapolis Lakers on December 21, 1951, he played for 63 minutes, a single-game record that stood for almost 40 years.

In his first season back to the NBA after returning from his Korean War service, Arizin averaged 21.0 points per game, second only to future hall-of-famer and teammate Neil Johnston. The next year (1955–1956), the Warriors had four of the league's top 20 scoring leaders (Arizin, Johnston, Joe Graboski, and Jack George) and won an NBA title.

Arizin won his second league scoring title the next season (25.6 points per game); collected 7.9 rebounds per game; shot .829 from the foul line; and was named to the All-NBA First Team. He averaged 20.7 points per game in the 1957–1958 season, and reached the 10,000-point mark the next year (1958–1959), faster than any other NBA player in history.

On December 1, 1961, he scored 33 points against the Los Angeles Lakers to become only the third player (at the time) in NBA history to reach the 15,000-point level. When the Warriors moved to San Francisco in 1962 (becoming the San Francisco Warriors), Arizin did not follow the team and decided to retire.

After leaving the NBA in 1962, he played three seasons (1962–1965) with the Camden Bullets of the Eastern Basketball League, and was named the league's Most Valuable Player in 1963.

Paul Arizin's NBA Career Statistics

SEASON	TEAM	G	MIN	REB	ASST	PTS	AVG
1950–1951	Philadelphia	65	N/A	640	138	1,121	17.2
1951–1952	Philadelphia	66	2,939	745	170	1,674	25.4
1954–1955	Philadelphia	72	2,953	675	210	1,512	21.0
1955–1956	Philadelphia	72	2,724	539	189	1,741	24.2
1956–1957	Philadelphia	71	2,767	561	150	1,817	25.6
1957–1958	Philadelphia	68	2,377	503	135	1,406	20.7
1958–1959	Philadelphia	70	2,799	637	119	1,851	26.4
1959–1960	Philadelphia	72	2,618	621	165	1,606	22.3
1960–1961	Philadelphia	79	2,935	681	188	1,832	23.2
1961–1962	Philadelphia	78	2,785	527	201	1,706	21.9
	TOTALS	713	24,897	6,129	2,764	16,266	22.8

Sources: Basketball-Reference.com; Naismith Memorial Basketball Hall of Fame

Armstrong, George Edward "Chief" (born: July 6, 1930 in Skead, Ontario, Canada); inducted into the Hockey Hall of Fame in 1975 as a player; Position: Center; Uniform: #10; won four Stanley Cup titles.

Nicknamed "Chief" because of his Native American heritage, Armstrong played professional hockey with the Pittsburgh Hornets (American Hockey League, 1950–1952) and 21 seasons with the National Hockey League's Toronto Maple Leafs (1949, 1951–1971). He served as the team's captain for 11 seasons; played in seven NHL All-Star games (1956–1957, 1959, 1962–1964, 1968); and played in six Stanley Cup championships, winning four (1962–1964, 1967) and losing two (1959–1960). When he retired, Armstrong held team records for most seasons played (21) and games played (1,187). He coached the Leafs for 47 games at the start of the 1988–1989 season (finishing with a 17–26–4 record) and his jersey #10 was retired by the team.

After retiring as a player, the 6', 204-pound Armstrong became a coach, and in 1975, he led the Toronto Marlboros (Ontario Hockey League) to the Memorial Cup championship.

George Armstrong's Career Statistics

			REGULAR SEASON				PLAYOFFS			
SEASON	TEAM	LEAGUE	G	GL	A	TP	GP	G	A	TP
1946–1947	Copper Cliff Jr. Redmen	NOJHA	9	6	5	11	5	0	1	1
1947–1948	Stratford Kroehlers	OHA-Jr.	36	33	40	73	2	1	0	1
1948–1949	Toronto Marlboros	OHA-Jr.	39	29	33	62	10	7	10	17
1948–1949	Toronto Marlboros	OHA-Sr.	3	0	0	0				
1948–1949	Toronto Marlboros	Al-Cup	10	2	5	7				
1949–1950	Toronto Marlboros	OHA-Sr.	45	64	51	115	3	0	0	0
1949–1950	Toronto Maple Leafs	NHL	2	0	0	0				
1949–1950	Toronto Marlboros	Al-Cup	17	19	19	38				

SEASON	TEAM	LEAGUE	REGULAR SEASON G	GL	A	TP	PLAYOFFS GP	G	A	TP
1950–1951	Pittsburgh Hornets	AHL	71	15	33	48	13	4	9	13
1951–1952	Toronto Maple Leafs	NHL	20	3	3	6	4	0	0	0
1951–1952	Pittsburgh Hornets	AHL	50	30	29	59				
1952–1953	Toronto Maple Leafs	NHL	52	14	11	25				
1953–1954	Toronto Maple Leafs	NHL	63	17	15	32	5	1	0	1
1954–1955	Toronto Maple Leafs	NHL	66	10	18	28	4	1	0	1
1955–1956	Toronto Maple Leafs	NHL	67	16	32	48	5	4	2	6
1956–1957	Toronto Maple Leafs	NHL	54	18	26	44				
1957–1958	Toronto Maple Leafs	NHL	59	17	25	42				
1958–1959	Toronto Maple Leafs	NHL	59	20	16	36	12	0	4	4
1959–1960	Toronto Maple Leafs	NHL	70	23	28	51	10	1	4	5
1960–1961	Toronto Maple Leafs	NHL	47	14	19	33	5	1	1	2
1961–1962	Toronto Maple Leafs	NHL	70	21	32	53	12	7	5	12
1962–1963	Toronto Maple Leafs	NHL	70	19	24	43	10	3	6	9
1963–1964	Toronto Maple Leafs	NHL	66	20	17	37	14	5	8	13
1964–1965	Toronto Maple Leafs	NHL	59	15	22	37	6	1	0	1
1965–1966	Toronto Maple Leafs	NHL	70	16	35	51	4	0	1	1
1966–1967	Toronto Maple Leafs	NHL	70	9	24	33	9	2	1	3
1967–1968	Toronto Maple Leafs	NHL	62	13	21	34				
1968–1969	Toronto Maple Leafs	NHL	53	11	16	27	4	0	0	0
1969–1970	Toronto Maple Leafs	NHL	49	13	15	28				
1970–1971	Toronto Maple Leafs	NHL	59	7	18	25	6	0	2	2
	NHL TOTALS		1187	296	417	713	110	26	34	60

Sources: Hockey Hall of Fame; Hockey-Reference.com

Armstrong, James (born: Carlisle, England; died: January 11, 1952 in Queens, New York); inducted into the National Soccer Hall of Fame and Museum in 1952 as a builder; secretary of both the American Soccer League and United States Football Association.

Armstrong was a teacher in Chester, Cheshire, England, where he also coached soccer, rugby, and cricket. He came to the United States as a young man; became secretary of the Brooklyn Soccer Club; and later served as manager of the New York Giants and the New York Americans, both of the American Soccer League.

He served as secretary of the American Soccer League (1924–1928); secretary of the United States Football Association (1931–1943); and attended the 1936 Summer Olympic Games (Berlin, Germany) serving as secretary to the United States team.

Source: National Soccer Hall of Fame and Museum

Armstrong, Neil (born: December 23, 1932 in Plympton, Ontario, Canada); inducted into the Hockey Hall of Fame in 1991 as an on-ice official; Position: Linesman; officiated in more games than Gordie Howe played.

Armstrong's 22-year National Hockey League career began in 1957, and he eventually refereed in 1,744 games, more than Gordie Howe played. On October 16, 1973, he officiated his 1,314th game, breaking the previous record for most games as a referee held by George Hayes. After retiring in 1978, he became a scout for the NHL's Montreal Canadiens. Armstrong earned the nickname "Ironman" by never missing a game during his entire career.

Before joining the NHL, he played minor league hockey in Galt (present day Cambridge, Ontario, Canada), and knowing that he did not have the skills to play in the NHL, he began officiating in local games, eventually earning his Ontario Hockey Association referee certification.

Source: Hockey Hall of Fame

Ashburn, Don Richard "Richie" (born: March 19, 1927 in Tilden, Nebraska; died: September 9, 1997 in New York, New York); inducted into the National Baseball Hall of Fame and Museum in 1995 as a player; Position: Center Field;

Uniform: #1; Bats: Left; Throws: Right; only rookie elected to the 1948 All-Star team; 86 percent of his career hits were singles.

Making his major league debut on April 20, 1948, the 5'10", 170-pound Ashburn played 15 seasons with the Philadelphia Phillies (1948–1959), Chicago Cubs (1960–1961), and the New York Mets (1962). He was a five-time All-Star (1948, 1951, 1953, 1958, 1962) and played in the 1950 World Series, losing to the New York Yankees.

Ashburn was one of the most consistent lead-off hitters in baseball history; hit over .300 in nine seasons; won the National League batting title twice (1955, 1958); led the National League in walks four times; accumulated more than 400 putouts nine times; and retired with 86 percent of his hits being singles. After retiring from the game, he became a broadcaster in 1963 and called Phillies games for more than 30 years, teaming up with the legendary Harry Kalas for 27 seasons. His broadcasting career ended suddenly when he died unexpectedly in his sleep after calling a Philadelphia Phillies–New York Mets game at Shea Stadium in New York.

Ashburn had speed on the base paths, but very little hitting power. True to form, his first home run of his career (May 29, 1948) was a leadoff inside-the-park hit. His hit against the Chicago Cubs on June 5, 1948 extended his consecutive game hitting streak to 23, at the time setting a modern-day National League record for a rookie.

In a remarkable coincidence, during a game between the Phillies and New York Giants (in Philadelphia) on August 17, 1957, Ashburn, while batting, hit spectator Alice Roth (wife of Earl Roth, the sports editor of the *Philadelphia Bulletin*) twice. One of his foul balls hit her in the stands and broke her nose. As she was leaving the stadium on a stretcher, another of Ashburn's foul balls hit her again.

Richie Ashburn's Career Statistics

YEAR	TEAM	G	AB	R	H	2B	3B	HR	RBI	BB	SO	SB	AVG	SLG
1948	Philadelphia	117	463	78	154	17	4	2	40	60	22	32	.333	.400
1949	Philadelphia	154	662	84	188	18	11	1	37	58	38	9	.284	.349
1950	Philadelphia	151	594	84	180	25	14	2	41	63	32	14	.303	.402
1951	Philadelphia	154	643	92	221	31	5	4	63	50	37	29	.344	.426
1952	Philadelphia	154	613	93	173	31	6	1	42	75	30	16	.282	.357
1953	Philadelphia	156	622	110	205	25	9	2	57	61	35	14	.330	.408
1954	Philadelphia	153	559	111	175	16	8	1	41	125	46	11	.313	.376
1955	Philadelphia	140	533	91	180	32	9	3	42	105	36	12	.338	.448
1956	Philadelphia	154	628	94	190	26	8	3	50	79	45	10	.303	.384
1957	Philadelphia	156	626	93	186	26	8	0	33	94	44	13	.297	.364
1958	Philadelphia	152	615	98	215	24	13	2	33	97	48	30	.350	.441
1959	Philadelphia	153	564	86	150	16	2	1	20	79	42	9	.266	.307
1960	Chicago	151	547	99	159	16	5	0	40	116	50	16	.291	.338
1961	Chicago	109	307	49	79	7	4	0	19	55	27	7	.257	.306
1962	New York	135	389	60	119	7	3	7	28	81	39	12	.306	.393
	TOTALS	2,189	8,365	1,322	2,574	317	109	29	586	1,198	571	234	.308	.382

Sources: Baseball-Reference.com; National Baseball Hall of Fame and Museum

Ashley, John George (born: March 5, 1930 in Galt, Ontario, Canada); inducted into the Hockey Hall of Fame in 1981 as an on-ice official; refereed every game seven in the Stanley Cup playoffs from 1964 to 1972.

Ashley lived in Preston, Ontario, Canada as a young boy and played Junior B hockey, before moving up to Junior A with the Toronto Marlies and the Guelph Biltmores, also located in Ontario. Never making it to the NHL as a player, he played in the minor leagues for three seasons with the Pittsburgh Hornets and the Syracuse Warriors, both of the American Hockey League. Realizing that he would probably never play in the NHL, Ashley retired, but applied for reinstatement after sitting out for one year.

He returned to the game and played three more seasons before finally giving up on his hopes of reaching the NHL. He then started his career as a referee in the Ontario Hockey Association, and two years later (1959), he signed an NHL contract. During his first year, he worked in the American Hockey League and the United States Hockey League, before being promoted to the NHL, where he would stay for 12 seasons and work every game seven of the Stanley Cup playoffs from 1964 to 1972.

Source: Hockey Hall of Fame

Atkins, Douglas Leon "Doug" (born: May 8, 1930 in Humboldt, Tennessee); inducted into the Pro Football Hall of Fame in 1982 as a player; Position: Defensive End-Tackle; Uniform: #91; attended the University of Tennessee on a basketball scholarship before becoming a star football player for the school.

At Humboldt (Tennessee) High School, Atkins was an All-State center on a basketball team that won 44 straight games. After graduation, he went to the University of Tennessee (Knoxville, 1950–1952) on a basketball scholarship, but was asked to join the football team due to his large size (6'8", 245 pounds). In his second year on the team (1950), he played defensive end on a squad that played to an 11–1 record and would go on to win the Cotton Bowl (January 1, 1951).

In his junior year, Atkins moved to defensive tackle as the team enjoyed an undefeated season (10–0) and won the 1951 national championship. In his senior year (1952), he won All-American honors as Tennessee led the nation in total defense. During his time at the school, the team appeared in three straight bowl games and recorded a 29–4–1 overall record.

Upon leaving Tennessee, Atkins was a first-round draft pick (11th overall selection) of the National Football League's Cleveland Browns in 1953, where he was moved to defensive end. During his 17-year (205 games) career (1953–1969), he played for the Cleveland Browns (1953–1954), Chicago Bears (1955–1966), and the New Orleans Saints (1967–1969); was named All-NFL four times; and played in eight Pro Bowls (1957–1963, 1965).

Atkins was named the 1958 Pro Bowl Most Valuable Player; was inducted into the College Football Hall of Fame in 1985; named to the NFL 1960s All-Decade Team; and his college jersey number 91 was retired by the University of Tennessee in 2005.

Sources: College Football Hall of Fame; Pro Football Hall of Fame

Auerbach, Arnold Jacob "Red" (born: September 20, 1917 in Brooklyn, New York; died: October 28, 2006 in Washington, D.C.); inducted into the Naismith Memorial Basketball Hall of Fame in 1969 as a coach; won 16 NBA titles (including eight straight) with the Boston Celtics as a coach, general manager, and club president; first coach in basketball history to win 1,000 games; first coach to draft an African-American player into the NBA.

Auerbach's basketball career began at Eastern District High School (Brooklyn, New York, 1932–1935), where he played for three seasons and was named All-Brooklyn Second Team in 1935 as a senior. After graduation, he attended Seth Low Junior College (part of Columbia University in Brooklyn, New York) one year (1936–1937) before moving on to George Washington University (Washington, D.C., 1937–1940).

After graduating from college, Auerbach began his coaching career at St. Albans Prep (Washington, D.C., 1940) and Roosevelt High School (Washington, D.C.) from 1941 to 1943. While coaching, he was able to play professional basketball with the Harrisburg Senators of the American Basketball League (1942–1943), but his playing career was cut short when he served with the U.S. Navy during World War II (1943–1945). While in the service, Auerbach served as the assistant basketball coach at the Norfolk Navy Base (Virginia).

Completing his military service and with his playing days over, he focused on coaching. Auerbach coached the Washington Capitols of the newly-formed Basketball Association of America (the precursor to the National Basketball Association) from 1946 to 1949. In 1949–1950, he was an assistant coach at Duke University (Durham, North Carolina) before taking over the Tri-Cities Blackhawks of the National Basketball League. When the National Basketball League merged with the Basketball Association of America to form the National Basketball Association, Auerbach led the Blackhawks to the playoffs in the NBA's inaugural season. Building on this early success, his legendary status would come from his years coaching the NBA's Boston Celtics from 1950 to 1966.

Auerbach led the Capitols to two division titles (1947, 1949); coached the Celtics to an amazing eight straight NBA championships (1959–1966) and nine titles overall; he would later win seven more championships with the Celtics as the team's general manager; was the first coach in history to win 1,000 games overall (1,037–548); was named NBA Coach of the Year (1965); coached in the NBA East-West All-Star Game 11 consecutive years (1957–1967), compiling a 7–4 record; was named the NBA 25th Anniversary All-Time team coach (1970); named the greatest coach in the history of the NBA by the Professional Basketball Writers Association of America (1980); and named NBA Executive of the Year (1980).

He wrote seven books, and his first, *Basketball for the Player, the Fan and the Coach*, (1971) has been translated into seven languages and is the largest-selling basketball book in print. Auerbach was inducted into the International Jewish Sports Hall of Fame in 1970; the Celtics retired jersey #2 in his honor (jersey #1 represented original team owner Walter Brown) in 1985; and the NBA Coach of the Year now receives the Red Auerbach Trophy. His NBA career coaching record of 938–479 (.662) currently ranks fifth all-time in NBA history.

After an extremely successful career in Boston, he was replaced as team president in 1997 by new coach Rick Pitino. However, after the team missed the playoffs the following three seasons, Auerbach returned to the Celtics as president in 2001, and in the 2001–2002 season, the team reached the Eastern Conference Finals before losing to the New Jersey Nets.

He was well-respected for his ability to judge player talent and to get the most from his players at all times. He was also known to readily complain to the referees over bad calls (in his judgment) against his team and for lighting up a cigar when his team had the game won, regardless of how much time was left to play.

In direct contrast to the times, Auerbach judged players on talent and desire, not for the color of their skin. He never hesitated to draft and play African-American players if they could help his teams; he was the first to draft an African-American player into the NBA (Chuck Cooper, 1950); and was the first coach to start five African-American players in a game (December 26, 1964 against the St. Louis Hawks, with Bill Russell, Satch Sanders, Willie Naulls, K.C. Jones, and Sam Jones).

When Auerbach retired from coaching in 1966 and became the team's general manager (after the Celtics had won the franchise's eighth consecutive championship), he again broke a racial barrier by naming future hall-of-famer Bill Russell as the team's player-coach, making him the first African-American coach in the NBA. His earlier trade for Russell (who had originally been drafted by the St. Louis Hawks) is considered one of the greatest NBA trades ever made, and Russell's joining Bob Cousy created the foundation for the Celtics dynasty.

Auerbach always coached from a team concept, not from an individual star-driven perspective. While he felt that individual honors were important and had a place in the game, to him, the team winning was the ultimate goal. Building a championship team and leading it to multiple titles was the driving concept behind Auerbach's success. With pride, he often emphasized the fact that during the nine championships he won as a coach, the team never had the league's top scorer, and in seven of the franchise's championship seasons, the Celtics did not have any player in the league's top 10 in scoring. These results were to him affirmation of the validity of the team concept over the player-driven performance.

His brother, Zang, a political cartoonist for the now closed *Washington Star*, designed the Celtics' famous logo.

Red Auerbach's Coaching Statistics

			REGULAR SEASON			POSTSEASON		
SEASON	**TEAM**	**LG**	**W**	**L**	**WIN%**	**W**	**L**	**WIN%**
1946–1947	Washington	BAA	49	11	.817	2	4	.333
1947–1948	Washington	BAA	28	20	.583			
1948–1949	Washington	BAA	38	22	.633	6	5	.545
1949–1950	Tri-Cities	NBA	28	29	.491	1	2	.333
1950–1951	Boston	NBA	39	30	.565	0	2	.000
1951–1952	Boston	NBA	39	27	.591	1	2	.333
1952–1953	Boston	NBA	46	25	.648	3	3	.500
1953–1954	Boston	NBA	42	30	.583	2	4	.333
1954–1955	Boston	NBA	36	36	.500	3	4	.429
1955–1956	Boston	NBA	39	33	.542	1	2	.333
1956–1957	Boston	NBA	44	28	.611	7	3	.700
1957–1958	Boston	NBA	49	23	.681	6	5	.545
1958–1959	Boston	NBA	52	20	.722	8	3	.727
1959–1960	Boston	NBA	59	16	.787	8	5	.615
1960–1961	Boston	NBA	57	22	.722	8	2	.800
1961–1962	Boston	NBA	60	20	.750	8	6	.571
1962–1963	Boston	NBA	58	22	.725	8	5	.615
1963–1964	Boston	NBA	59	21	.738	8	2	.800
1964–1965	Boston	NBA	62	18	.775	8	4	.667
1965–1966	Boston	NBA	54	26	.675	11	6	.647
3 SEASONS		BAA	115	53	.685	8	9	.471
17 SEASONS		NBA	823	426	.659	91	60	.603
20 SEASONS			938	479	.662	99	69	.589

Sources: Basketball-Reference.com; International Jewish Sports Hall of Fame; Naismith Memorial Basketball Hall of Fame

Auld, Andrew "Andy" (born: January 26, 1900 in Stevenston, North Ayrshire, Scotland; died: December 6, 1977 in Rhode Island); inducted into the National Soccer Hall of Fame and Museum in 1986 as a player; Position: Midfielder-Forward; International Caps (1926–1930): 5; International Goals: 2; was returning home to Scotland when he was convinced to play in the American Soccer League; a member of the 1930 U.S. World Cup team.

After playing soccer for the Stevenston Football Club from 1911 to 1913, Auld served in the military from 1913 to 1919 during World War I. When the war ended, he joined Ardeer Thistle (1919–1921), before moving on to the Parkhead Juniors in Glasgow (Scotland), where he played from 1921 to 1922.

After moving to the United States in 1923, he briefly lived in Gillespie, Illinois, but decided to return home. On his way back to Scotland, he visited a sister in Niagara Falls, New York, and was convinced to stay and play soccer for the local team. This decision soon led him to be signed by the Providence Clamdiggers (Gold Bugs) of the American Soccer League, forever changing his idea to return home.

Auld played for Providence from 1924 to 1930 and appeared in 277 games before the team moved to Fall River (Massachusetts) in 1931 to become the Fall River Football Club. He went on to play for the Pawtucket (Rhode Island) Rangers (ASL, 1932–1934) and the ASL's Portuguese Sport Club (Newark, New Jersey) from 1934 to 1935, before retiring as a player.

He was a member of the 1930 U.S. World Cup team that finished in third place in Uruguay (South America). Auld earned his first international cap (November 6, 1926) in a 6–1 win over Canada, by scoring his only two goals with the National Team. He did not play with the National Team again until the first game of the 1930 World Cup. He played two matches with the team until losing to Argentina in the semifinals. After the tournament, the U.S. team traveled to Brazil where Auld and his squad lost 4–3, marking his last game with the National Team.

He was inducted into the New England Soccer Hall of Fame in 1978.

Sources: National Soccer Hall of Fame and Museum; New England Soccer Hall of Fame

Auriemma, Geno (born: March 23, 1954 in Montella, Italy); inducted into the Naismith Memorial Basketball Hall of Fame in 2006 as a coach; first coach in women's basketball history to lead a team to five consecutive Final Four appearances in the NCAA tournament; won five NCAA titles at UConn.

Auriemma attended Montgomery County Community College (Blue Bell, Pennsylvania) and West Chester State College (West Chester, Pennsylvania) before beginning his coaching career as an assistant girl's coach at Bishop McDevitt High School (Wyncote, Pennsylvania, 1976–1978). He moved on to serve as the women's assistant basketball coach at St. Joseph's University (Philadelphia, Pennsylvania) from 1978 to 1979; was the assistant boy's coach at Bishop Kenrick High School (Norristown, Pennsylvania, 1979–1981); and served as the assistant women's coach at the University of Virginia (Charlottesville) from 1981 to 1985. After gaining almost 10 years of experience, in 1985, he accepted the head coaching position for the women's basketball team at the University of Connecticut (Storrs), where he has served 23 seasons as of this writing.

During his tenure at Connecticut, Auriemma has led the Huskies to seven NCAA championships (1995, 2000, 2002–2004, 2009–2010), 11 Final Four NCAA appearances, and four undefeated seasons (1995, 2002, 2009–2010). He has been named Naismith National Coach of the Year six times; Big East Coach of the Year nine times; and won 15 Big East regular-season and 14 Big East tournament titles. He has coached thirteen 30-win seasons, and his teams have made 20 consecutive NCAA tournament appearances.

Additionally, Auriemma served as the assistant coach of the United States gold medal-winning team in the 2000 Summer Olympics (Sydney, Australia); was head coach of the United States gold medal-winning team at the 2000 Junior World Cup Qualifying Tournament (Argentina); and head coach of the United States bronze medal-winning team at the 2001 FIBA Junior World Championship in the Czech Republic. He was an inaugural inductee into the New England Basketball Hall of Fame (2002) and is an inductee in the Women's Basketball Hall of Fame (2005).

Still active as a coach, as of this writing, Auriemma has compiled a 735–122 record (.858); was the first coach in women's basketball history to lead a team to five consecutive NCAA Final Four appearances (2000–2004); and the second fastest coach to reach the 500-win mark. In the 2003–2004 season, his Huskies became only the second women's basketball team in NCAA history to win three consecutive national titles (the other being Tennessee).

Auriemma led UConn to the school's first women's basketball national title in 1995 with a perfect 35–0 record, at the time, only the second Division I women's basketball team to go undefeated and win the national championship (following Texas in 1986). Additionally, UConn became the first unbeaten team in NCAA history to win 35 games in a season. In the 1990s, his teams won the second most number of games in Division I (290); ranked second in the nation in total winning percentage (.860) in the decade; and established a Big East record for conference victories (158).

With the school having only one winning women's basketball season in its 11-year history, since Auriemma has arrived the team has had 19 winning seasons. Four of his players (Rebecca Lobo, Jennifer Rizzotti, Kara Wolters, and

Sue Bird) have earned Associated Press National Player of the Year honors and have won both the Wade Trophy and the Honda Broderick Award as women's college basketball player of the year.

On December 21, 2010, the University of Connecticut women's basketball team won its 89th consecutive game (a 93–62 victory over Florida State University), surpassing the previous NCAA Division I record of the University of California at Los Angeles (men's basketball) under coach John Wooden.

Geno Auriemma's Coaching Record at Connecticut (as of this writing)

SEASON	Overall	Conference	Postseason
1985–1986	12–15	4–12	
1986–1987	14–13	9–7	
1987–1988	17–11	9–7	
1988–1989	24–6	13–2	NCAA 1st round
1989–1990	25–6	14–2	NCAA 2nd round
1990–1991	29–5	14–2	NCAA Final Four
1991–1992	23–11	13–5	NCAA 2nd round
1992–1993	18–11	12–6	NCAA 1st round
1993–1994	30–3	17–1	NCAA Elite 8
1994–1995	35–0	18–0	NCAA Champions
1995–1996	34–4	17–1	NCAA Final Four
1996–1997	33–1	18–0	NCAA Elite 8
1997–1998	34–3	17–1	NCAA Elite 8
1998–1999	29–5	17–1	NCAA Sweet 16
1999–2000	36–1	16–0	NCAA Champions
2000–2001	32–3	15–1	NCAA Final Four
2001–2002	39–0	16–0	NCAA Champions
2002–2003	37–1	16–0	NCAA Champions
2003–2004	31–4	14–2	NCAA Champions
2004–2005	25–8	13–2	NCAA Sweet 16
2005–2006	32–5	14–2	NCAA Elite 8
2006–2007	32–4	16–0	NCAA Elite 8
2007–2008	36–2	17–1	NCAA Final Four
2008–2009	39–0	16–0	NCAA Champions
2009–2010	39–0	16–0	NCAA Champions
TOTALS	735–122	371–55	

Sources: Basketball-Reference.com; Naismith Memorial Basketball Hall of Fame; New England Basketball Hall of Fame; Women's Basketball Hall of Fame

Averill, Howard Earl (born: May 21, 1902 in Snohomish, Washington; died: August 16, 1983 in Everett, Washington); inducted into the National Baseball Hall of Fame and Museum in 1975 as a player by the Veterans Committee; Position: Center Field; Uniform: #3; Bats: Left; Throws: Right; first American League player to hit a home run in his first major league at-bat; first major league player to hit four home runs in a doubleheader.

Known as the "Earl of Snohomish," the 5'9", 172-pound Averill made his major league debut on April 16, 1929 and played center field for the Cleveland Indians (1929–1939), Detroit Tigers (1939–1940), and eight games with the Boston Braves in 1941. During his 10-year Cleveland career, as of this writing, he remains the all-time team leader in total bases, runs batted in, runs scored, and triples.

In June 1939, Averill was traded to the Detroit Tigers and although he had limited playing time during his two seasons with the team, he helped the squad reach the 1940 World Series, eventually losing to the Cincinnati Reds in seven games. After playing only eight games with Boston, Averill retired in 1941.

He hit .300 or better in eight seasons; was elected to six All-Star teams (1933–1938); was the only American League outfielder to be named to each of the first six All-Star Games; and his uniform number 3 was retired by the Indians.

After playing for the San Francisco Seals of the Pacific Coast League for three seasons (1926–1928), Averill's contract was purchased by the Cleveland Indians. On Opening Day of the 1929 season, he became the first American League player to hit a home run in his initial big league at-bat (off Earl Whitehill of the Detroit Tigers). Averill finished his rookie season with 18 home runs (at the time, a team record) and a league-leading 388 putouts.

On September 17, 1930 against the Washington Senators, he hit three home runs in the first game and another in the second game to become the first major league player to hit four homers in a doubleheader, with his 11 RBIs that day setting an American League record.

Earl Averill's Career Statistics

YEAR	**TEAM**	**LG**	**G**	**AB**	**R**	**H**	**2B**	**3B**	**HR**	**RBI**	**SO**	**BB**	**AVG**
1929	Cleveland	AL	151	597	110	198	43	13	18	96	53	63	.332
1930	Cleveland	AL	139	534	102	181	33	8	19	119	48	56	.339
1931	Cleveland	AL	155	627	140	209	36	10	32	143	38	68	.333
1932	Cleveland	AL	153	631	116	198	37	14	32	124	40	75	.314
1933	Cleveland	AL	151	599	83	180	39	16	11	92	29	54	.301
1934	Cleveland	AL	154	598	128	187	48	6	31	113	44	99	.313
1935	Cleveland	AL	140	563	109	162	34	13	19	79	58	70	.288
1936	Cleveland	AL	152	614	136	232	39	15	28	126	35	65	.378
1937	Cleveland	AL	156	609	121	182	33	11	21	92	65	88	.299
1938	Cleveland	AL	134	482	101	159	27	15	14	93	48	81	.330
1939	Cleveland	AL	24	55	8	15	8		1	7	12	6	.273
1939	Detroit	AL	87	309	58	81	20	6	10	58	30	43	.262
1940	Detroit	AL	64	118	10	33	4	1	2	20	14	5	.280
1941	Boston	NL	8	17	2	2				2	4	1	.118
	TOTALS		1,668	6,353	1,224	2,019	401	128	238	1,164	518	774	.318

Sources: Baseball-Reference.com; National Baseball Hall of Fame and Museum

Chapter 2
Bachmeier to Butterfield

Bachmeier, Adolph (born: Romania); inducted into the National Soccer Hall of Fame and Museum in 2002 as a player-veteran; Position: Defender-Midfielder; International Caps (1959–1969): 15; International Goals: 0; first Chicago Kickers player inducted into the National Soccer Hall of Fame and Museum.

Bachmeier played on numerous Chicago-area soccer teams during the 1950s and 1960s, primarily with the Chicago Kickers of the National Soccer League. He played for the Chicago Mustangs in the inaugural North American Soccer League season in 1968, the same year he was captain of the United States National Team. He played 29 games for the Mustangs in 1968 and scored five goals.

He first played for the United States National Team against England in 1959 (an 8–1 loss) and for the last time against Haiti in 1969 (another loss). He played a total of 22 international games for the United States, including nine in the qualifying rounds of the 1966 and 1970 World Cups. In the qualifying rounds of the 1970 FIFA World Cup, he played in 1968 and 1969, and was the team's captain for all six games. Bachmeier also played in the 1963 Pan-American Games (São Paulo, Brazil), and in the qualifying rounds of the 1964 Olympic Games (Tokyo, Japan), in which the U.S. did not qualify.

In 1965, Bachmeier was named the Sepp Herberger German-American Illinois Soccer Player of the Year; won two National Amateur Cups with the Kickers (1966, 1968); played one season for the Chicago Mustangs of the North American Soccer League (1968); and then returned to the Kickers, where he won his third National Amateur Cup in 1970.

Source: National Soccer Hall of Fame

Badgro, Morris Hiram "Red" (born: December 1, 1902 in Orillia, Washington; died: July 13, 1998 in Kent, Washington); inducted into the Pro Football Hall of Fame in 1981 as a player; Position: End; scored the first touchdown in the inaugural 1933 NFL championship game; at the time of his induction, he was the oldest player ever elected to the Pro Football Hall of Fame; the 45-year span between his final NFL game and his induction into the hall of fame was a record.

The 6', 191-pound Badgro was a three-sport star at the University of Southern California (Los Angeles), where he played baseball, basketball, and football. After graduation, he played with the Red Grange-led New York Yankees (American Football League) for two seasons (1927–1928) before leaving the game to play professional baseball as an outfielder with Major League Baseball's St. Louis Browns (American League). After a two-season baseball career, he returned to the NFL with the New York Giants (1930–1935), before ending his career with the Brooklyn Dodgers (NFL) in 1936.

Badgro tied for the NFL pass-receiving title (16 in 1934); was a First- or Second-Team All-NFL selection four times (1930–1931, 1933–1934); scored the first touchdown in the inaugural 1933 NFL championship game (a 23–21 loss to the Chicago Bears); and at the time of his induction was the oldest player ever elected to the hall of fame (at age 78). The 45-year span between his final NFL game and his induction into the hall of fame was also a record for time elapsed.

After retiring from the NFL, Badgro worked in the movies as an extra with former teammate John Wayne, and eventually served as a coach at the University of Washington (Seattle). His nickname "Red" derived from the color of his hair.

Morris Badgro's NFL Statistics

YEAR	TEAM	G	REC	YDS	AVG	TD
1927	New York	12	N/A	N/A	N/A	1
1928	New York	1	N/A	N/A	N/A	0
1930	New York	17	N/A	N/A	N/A	3
1931	New York	13	N/A	N/A	N/A	0
1932	New York	12	6	106	17.7	0
1933	New York	12	9	176	19.6	2
1934	New York	13	16	206	12.9	1
1935	New York	5	1	13	13.0	0
1936	Brooklyn	9	3	59	19.7	0
	TOTALS	94	35	560	16.0	7

Sources: Pro Football Hall of Fame; Pro-Football-Reference.com

Bahr, Walter Alfred (born: April 1, 1927 in Philadelphia, Pennsylvania); inducted into the National Soccer Hall of Fame and Museum in 1976 as a player; Position: Half Back; International Caps (1948–1957): 18; International Goals: 1; won five ASL titles; captained the 1948 U.S. Olympic team.

One of the greatest American soccer players ever, Bahr began playing the game as a young boy, when he joined the Lighthouse Boys Club team in Philadelphia. At age 15, he played in an amateur status with the Philadelphia Nationals of the American Soccer League and helped the team win three ASL titles (1950–1951, 1953). He would later win two more league titles with the Uhrik Truckers (Philadelphia, 1955–1956).

In 1948, he captained the U.S. Olympic squad at the Summer Olympic Games in London, England (which was eliminated in the first round after a 9–0 loss to Italy). However, after he signed a professional contract, he was ineligible to play for the Olympic team again. In 1949, Bahr was a member of the U.S. World Cup team that qualified for the 1950 FIFA World Cup (in Brazil, South America), before being eliminated by Chile. One game before being eliminated, he led the squad to a historic 1–0 win over England, at the time one of the biggest upsets ever in World Cup play. Two years later, he was a member of the U.S. National Team that played against Scotland at Glasgow's Hampden Park.

Bahr often played with ASL All-Star squads against the world's best soccer teams, including the English (Liverpool) and the National Team of Israel (1948); Besiktas of Turkey and Jonkopping of Sweden (1950); A.I.K. Stockholm of Sweden (1951); and Rapid Vienna of Austria (1953), the Israeli Olympic team, Everton of England, Rapid Vienna of Austria (1956), and Hapoel of Tel Aviv (1957).

After retiring as a player, Bahr coached at Temple University (Philadelphia, Pennsylvania) from 1970 to 1973, and at Penn State University (University Park) from 1974 to 1988. He also coached two professional teams, the Philadelphia Ukrainians (ASL) and the Philadelphia Spartans (National Professional Soccer League), as well as coaching at Frankford High School (Philadelphia) for 17 years. He finished his coaching career with an overall record of 448–137–70 (.766); was named National Soccer Coaches Association of America Coach of the Year in 1979; led the Penn State team to the NCAA tournament 12 times; and was inducted into the NSCAA Hall of Fame in 1995.

Bahr was an All-American at Temple University in 1944; coached at the high school level for more than 20 years; began his coaching career at Swarthmore College (Pennsylvania) with the freshman team; and led Frankford High School to five city championships and six public league titles.

Sources: National Soccer Hall of Fame and Museum; NSCAA Hall of Fame; Temple University Athletics Hall of Fame

Bailey, Irvine Wallace "Ace" (born: July 3, 1903 in Bracebridge, Ontario, Canada; died: April 7, 1992 in Toronto, Ontario, Canada); inducted into the Hockey Hall of Fame in 1975 as a player; Position: Left Wing; Uniform: #6; played his entire eight-year NHL career with the Toronto Maple Leafs.

One of the game's most popular players, Bailey played his relatively brief eight-year National Hockey League career with the Toronto Maple Leafs (1926–1933) until forced to retire after suffering a severe head injury inflicted by Eddie Shore (Boston Bruins) in a game on December 12, 1933. Part of the proceeds from that season's All-Star game (played on February 14, 1934) were donated to his family to help pay for his medical expenses. Although he eventually recovered, Bailey never played hockey again, but continued to work for the team as a coach and in the front office. His #6 jersey is one of only two to have been permanently retired by the Maple Leafs.

The 5'10", 160-pound Bailey attended the University of Toronto (Ontario, Canada) and played two seasons (1924–1926) with the Peterborough Seniors (Ontario Hockey Association). He then played for the Toronto St. Pats and was with the team when the franchise became known as the Maple Leafs. He led the NHL in regular-season scoring in 1929.

Ace Bailey's Career Statistics

SEASON	TEAM	LEAGUE	REGULAR SEASON GP	GLS	ASST	TP	PLAYOFFS GP	G	A	TP
1918–1922	Bracebridge Bird Mill	OHA-Jr.								
1922–1923	Toronto St. Mary's	OHA-Jr.	4	2	1	3	4	2	1	3
1923–1924	Toronto St. Mary's	OHA-Jr.	8	10	0	10				
1924–1925	Peterborough Seniors	OHA-Sr.	8	5	0	5	2	3	0	3
1925–1926	Peterborough Seniors	OHA-Sr.	9	9	2	11	2	2	1	3
1925–1926	Peterborough Seniors	Al-Cup	6	2	2	4				
1926–1927	Toronto St. Pats/Maple Leafs	NHL	42	15	13	28				
1927–1928	Toronto Maple Leafs	NHL	43	9	3	12				
1928–1929	Toronto Maple Leafs	NHL	44	22	10	32	4	1	2	3
1929–1930	Toronto Maple Leafs	NHL	43	22	21	43				
1930–1931	Toronto Maple Leafs	NHL	40	23	19	42	2	1	1	2
1931–1932	Toronto Maple Leafs	NHL	41	8	5	13	7	1	0	1
1932–1933	Toronto Maple Leafs	NHL	47	10	8	18	8	0	1	1
1933–1934	Toronto Maple Leafs	NHL	13	2	3	5				
	NHL TOTALS		313	111	82	193	21	3	4	7

Sources: Hockey Hall of Fame; Hockey-Reference.com

Bain, Donald Henderson "Dan" (born: August 15, 1874 in Belleville, Ontario, Canada; died: August 15, 1962); inducted into the Hockey Hall of Fame in 1945 as a player; Position: Forward-Center; scored the first-ever overtime Stanley Cup-winning goal; won two Stanley Cup championships.

Bain was one of Manitoba's most talented amateur athletes, a Canadian businessman, and an avid sportsman. He played eight pre-NHL seasons (1895–1902) with the Winnipeg Victorias (Manitoba Hockey League) and won two Stanley Cup championships (1896, 1901). In the 1901 Stanley Cup challenge against the Montreal Shamrocks (Canadian Amateur Hockey League), Bain made history by registering the first-ever, overtime Stanley Cup-winning goal.

Also in 1901, he began using a home-made, wooden facemask to protect his broken nose, which earned him the nickname, the "Masked Man." Bain was chosen Canada's most outstanding athlete of the last half of the 19th century and was inducted into Canada's Sports Hall of Fame in 1971. He was also elected to the International Hockey Hall of Fame, the Manitoba Sports Hall of Fame (1981), and was one of the initial 12 players selected to the Hockey Hall of Fame when it was founded in 1945.

An all-round athlete, when he was 13, Bain won the Manitoba provincial roller skating championship; was named the province's All Round Gymnastic Champion at age 17; and took the 1903 Canadian Trapshooting title in Toronto.

He retired from hockey after the Victorias won their second Stanley Cup in 1901 and was later instrumental in establishing the Winter Club in Winnipeg (now known as the HMCS Chippewa) and the new Winter Club.

Donald Bain's Career Statistics

SEASON	TEAM	LEAGUE	G	GLS	AST	TP
1894–1895	Winnipeg Victorias	MNWHA				
1895–1896	Winnipeg Victorias	MNWHA				
1895–1896	Winnipeg Victorias	St-Cup	2	3	0	3
1896–1897	Winnipeg Victorias	MNWHA				
1897–1898	Winnipeg Victorias	MNWHA				
1898–1899	Winnipeg Victorias	MNWHA				
1898–1899	Winnipeg Victorias	St-Cup	1	0	0	0
1899–1900	Winnipeg Victorias	MNWHA				
1899–1900	Winnipeg Victorias	St-Cup	3	4	0	4
1900–1901	Winnipeg Victorias	MNWHA				
1900–1901	Winnipeg Victorias	St-Cup	2	3	0	3
1901–1902	Winnipeg Victorias	MNWHA				
1901–1902	Winnipeg Victorias	St-Cup	3	0	0	0

Sources: Canada's Sports Hall of Fame; Hockey Hall of Fame; Hockey-Reference.com; International Hockey Hall of Fame; Manitoba Sports Hall of Fame

Baker, Hobart Amery Hare "Hobey" (born: January 15, 1892 in Wissahickon (Bala Cynwyd), Pennsylvania; died: December 21, 1918 in Toul, France); inducted into the Hockey Hall of Fame in 1945 as a player; only man inducted into both the Hockey Hall of Fame and the College Football Hall of Fame; first American-born player elected to the International Hockey Hall of Fame.

The 5'10", 161-pound Baker attended St. Paul's School (a private, college-preparatory school in Concord, New Hampshire) for two years (1908–1910), where he was active in all sports. He then attended Princeton University (New Jersey) in 1910 and played baseball, football, and hockey. He led the school to an undefeated season (1911–1912) and to an intercollegiate championship.

In his senior season (1913–1914), he once again led the team to a hockey championship, while also serving as the captain of the school's football team. Baker was inducted into the College Football Hall of Fame in 1975, and is the only man inducted into both the College Football and Hockey halls of fame.

After graduating, he worked as a banker and played amateur hockey with the St. Nicholas Club (New York City) from 1915 to 1917. Baker refused to turn professional and was one of the few early hockey stars not born in Canada.

During World War I, he was a fighter pilot with the 103rd Aero Squadron and won the Croix de Guerre for bravery under fire. Shortly before he was to be discharged from the military, Baker died when a plane he was testing crashed in Toul, France.

The Hobey Baker Memorial Award is presented annually to the best college hockey player in the United States; the Hobey Baker Stick is awarded to players at his old prep school (St. Paul's); and the Princeton Tigers have named its hockey arena after him, Hobart Baker Memorial Rink. He has been inducted into the United States Hockey Hall of Fame (1973), was the first American-born player elected to the International Hockey Hall of Fame, and was a charter inductee into the Hockey Hall of Fame (1945). In 1987, sixty-nine years after his death, Baker was awarded the Lester Patrick Trophy to honor his contributions to the game in the United States.

Sources: College Football Hall of Fame; Hockey Hall of Fame; United States Hockey Hall of Fame

Baker, John Franklin "Frank" "Home Run" (born: March 13, 1886 in Trappe, Maryland; died: June 28, 1963 in Trappe, Maryland); inducted into the National Baseball Hall of Fame and Museum in 1955 as a player by the Veteran's Committee; Position: Third Base; Bats: Left; Throws: Right; led the American League in home runs four straight seasons.

One of the best third baseman of the pre-World War I era, Baker's Major League Baseball career began on September 21, 1908, and during his 13-year career, he played for the Philadelphia Athletics (1908–1914) and the New York Yankees (1916–1919, 1921–1922). He was part of the Athletics' so-called "$100,000 infield" (with Stuffy McInnis, Eddie Collins, and Jack Barry). When owner Connie Mack refused to raise his salary, Baker sat out the entire 1915 season and was eventually sold to the Yankees in 1916. He also did not play in the 1920 season when his wife fell ill and eventually died. During his career, he played in six World Series (winning in 1910–1911, 1913 and losing in 1914, 1921–1922).

In an era of singles hitters, the 5'11", 173-pound Baker gained a reputation as a slugger when he hit 11 home runs in 1911, leading the American League, and hitting two more during that season's World Series. He led the American League in home runs three times (1911, 1913–1914); twice led the league in runs batted in (1912–1913); had 100 or more RBIs three times; and scored 100 or more runs twice.

After retiring from the major leagues, Baker played and managed for the Easton Farmers (Eastern Shore League) for two seasons (1924–1925), where he discovered future hall-of-famer Jimmie Foxx.

Frank Baker's American League Career Statistics

YEAR	TEAM	G	AB	R	H	2B	3B	HR	RBI	BB	SO	SB	AVG	SLG
1908	Philadelphia	9	31	5	9	3	0	0	2	0	N/A	0	.290	.387
1909	Philadelphia	148	541	73	165	27	19	4	85	26	N/A	20	.305	.447
1910	Philadelphia	146	561	83	159	25	15	2	74	34	N/A	21	.283	.392
1911	Philadelphia	148	592	96	198	40	14	11	115	40	N/A	38	.334	.505
1912	Philadelphia	149	577	116	200	40	21	10	130	50	N/A	40	.347	.541
1913	Philadelphia	149	565	116	190	34	9	12	117	63	31	34	.336	.492

YEAR	TEAM	G	AB	R	H	2B	3B	HR	RBI	BB	SO	SB	AVG	SLG
1914	Philadelphia	150	570	84	182	23	10	9	89	53	37	19	.319	.442
1916	New York	100	360	46	97	23	2	10	52	36	30	15	.269	.428
1917	New York	146	553	57	156	24	2	6	71	48	27	18	.282	.365
1918	New York	126	504	65	154	24	5	6	62	38	13	8	.306	.409
1919	New York	141	567	70	166	22	1	10	83	44	18	13	.293	.388
1921	New York	94	330	46	97	16	2	9	71	26	12	8	.294	.436
1922	New York	69	234	30	65	12	3	7	36	15	14	1	.278	.444
	TOTALS	1,575	5,985	887	1,838	313	103	96	987	473	182	235	.307	.442

Sources: Baseball-Reference.com; National Baseball Hall of Fame and Museum

Balboa, Marcelo (born: August 8, 1967 in Chicago, Illinois); inducted into the National Soccer Hall of Fame and Museum in 2005; Position: Defender; International Caps (1988–2000): 128; International Goals: 13; one of only two players to win U.S. Soccer's Chevrolet Male Athlete of the Year award twice; first American player to acquire 100 Caps.

Balboa played with the U.S. National Team mainly through the 1990s and earned the nickname "Iron Man." He is one of only two players to win the U.S. Soccer's Chevrolet Male Athlete of the Year award twice (1992, 1994), and the Colorado Rapids (Major League Soccer) veteran was honored for scoring the MLS Goal of the Year in 2000 for his bicycle kick against the Columbus Crew.

He played soccer at San Diego State University (California) from 1988 to 1989, earning First-Team All-American honors in 1988 and Second-Team honors in 1989. He led the Aztecs to back-to-back NCAA appearances; a 29–8–7 overall record; and was inducted into the Aztec Hall of Fame in 1996. After leaving college, Balboa captained the U.S. National Team in the mid-1990s and was one of three American players to compete in three FIFA World Cups (1990 in Italy, 1994 in the United States, and 1998 in France).

In international competition, Balboa earned his first cap against Guatemala on January 10, 1988; scored his first international goal against Liechtenstein on May 30, 1990; played in all three games for the U.S. in the 1990 FIFA World Cup (losing all three and being eliminated in the first round); scored two goals in the 1991 CONCACAF Gold Cup; played every minute of every game for the United States team in the 1994 World Cup (eliminated in the Round of 16 after one tie and two losses); was the first U.S. player to acquire 100 caps (June 11, 1995); led the U.S. team to a third-place finish in the 1999 FIFA Confederations Cup; and has been honored with a star at the U.S. Soccer Star Plaza at Home Depot Center (Carson, California) in 2003.

The 6', 175-pound Balboa played in the American Professional Soccer League (1987–1992) with the San Diego Nomads (1987–1989), the San Francisco Bay Blackhawks (1990–1991), and the Colorado Foxes (1992–1993), and won a league title with Colorado in 1992. He played with León (Mexico) in 1994, and led the Mexican First Division team to the Mexican league playoffs in 1996; joined the Colorado Rapids in Major League Soccer in the league's inaugural year (1996), scoring seven goals in 18 games; led the Rapids to a second-place finish in the 1997 MLS Cup; was selected to the MLS All-Star team five seasons in a row (1996–2000); first defender in league history to score 20 goals and 20 assists (24 goals, 23 assists) in a career; and in 2002, he was traded to the New York/New Jersey MetroStars, where due to injuries he played for only five minutes the entire season before retiring.

After retiring as a player, he became a broadcaster; worked as an executive with the Colorado Rapids; and was named to the MLS All-Time Best XI team (2005).

Marcelo Balboa's Major League Soccer Statistics

YEAR	TEAM	G	MIN	GLS	ASST	PTS
1996	Colorado	18	1,525	7	2	17
1997	Colorado	28	2,520	2	3	7
1998	Colorado	26	2,290	5	5	15
1999	Colorado	27	2,430	1	2	4
2000	Colorado	28	2,495	4	5	13
2001	Colorado	24	2,119	5	6	16
2002	New York/New Jersey	1	5	0	0	0
	TOTALS	152	13,384	24	23	71

Marcelo Balboa's U.S. National Team Statistics

YEAR	G	MIN	GLS	ASST	PTS	W–L–T
1988	8	675	0	0	0	1–5–2
1989	4	360	0	0	0	1–2–1
1990	15	1,040	1	0	2	4–7–4
1991	15	1,350	2	1	5	5–4–6
1992	21	1,879	3	1	7	6–11–4
1993	10	707	0	0	0	2–2–6
1994	24	1,833	4	0	8	6–9–9
1995	6	466	1	0	2	6–11–4
1996	8	720	1	1	3	5–2–1
1997	10	900	0	1	1	3–1–6
1998	4	257	1	0	2	1–2–1
1999	2	180	0	0	0	2–0–0
2000	1	90	0	0	0	0–0–1
TOTALS	128	10,457	13	4	28	40–46–42

Sources: Aztec Hall of Fame; National Soccer Hall of Fame and Museum

Ballard, Howard "Harold" (born: July 30, 1903 in Toronto, Ontario, Canada; died: April 11, 1990 in Toronto, Ontario, Canada); inducted into the Hockey Hall of Fame in 1977 as a builder; led the Toronto National Sea Fleas to the 1932 Allan Cup.

Ballard enjoyed success with both amateur hockey teams and in the National Hockey League. He was a champion speed skater before turning to hockey, first as a player and then in various management roles. He led the Toronto National Sea Fleas (Toronto Mercantile League) to the Allan Cup championship in 1932, a feat that automatically qualified the team for the 1933 World Championships, where the team was upset by the United States, giving America its first world title.

After Ballard became the primary financial supporter of both the junior and senior Toronto Marlboro hockey clubs, the senior team won the 1950 Allan Cup, while the junior squad took back-to-back Memorial Cups (1955–1956). After he and his partners (Stafford Smythe and John Bassett, Sr.) bought the NHL's Toronto Maple Leafs from Conn Smythe in 1962, the franchise won three more Stanley Cup championships (1963–1964, 1967). After Bassett was bought out by the other two in 1970, and Smythe died in 1971, Ballard became the principal owner and chief executive of Maple Leaf Gardens Ltd. While he was the sole owner of the team (1971–1990), although the Leafs had very little on-ice success (no Stanley Cup appearances and no winning seasons from 1980 to 1992), the franchise continued to be economically viable and maintained its strong fan base.

Outside of hockey, Ballard owned the Hamilton Tiger-Cats (Canadian Football League) and led the team to the 1986 Grey Cup. He was inducted into the Canadian Football Hall of Fame in 1987.

Source: Hockey Hall of Fame

Bancroft, David James "Beauty" (born: April 20, 1891 in Sioux City, Iowa; died: October 9, 1972 in Superior, Wisconsin); inducted into the National Baseball Hall of Fame and Museum in 1971 as a player by the Veterans Committee; Position: Shortstop; Bats: Both; Throws: Right; holds the single-season record for most chances by a shortstop (984 in 1922).

Bancroft made his major league debut on April 14, 1915, and during his 16-year career, the 5'9", 160-pound shortstop played for the Philadelphia Phillies (1915–1920), New York Giants (1920–1923, 1930), Boston Braves (1924–1927 as a player-manager), and the Brooklyn Dodgers (1928–1929). He appeared in four World Series, winning two (1921–1922) and losing two (1915, 1923). As the player-manager of the Braves for four seasons, he led the team to an overall 249–363 (.407) record. Bancroft hit .300 or better five times and scored 100 or more runs in a season three times.

The switch-hitting Bancroft was a sure-handed fielder and a respectable lead-off hitter. His nickname "Beauty" derived from his habit of shouting the word after each good pitch to the opposing batter. He led National League shortstops in putouts four times; led the National League once in games played; and hit for the cycle (single, double, triple, home run) on June 1, 1921 as a New York Giant.

His induction into the hall of fame in 1971 by the Veterans Committee is considered by many to be one of the most controversial selections in the shrine's history. Critics felt he was inducted by friends on the Committee without regard to his playing production. It is often pointed out that many players with similar offensive numbers never have a chance of induction.

Dave Bancroft's National League Career Statistics

YEAR	TEAM	G	AB	R	H	2B	3B	HR	RBI	BB	SO	SB	AVG	SLG
1915	Philadelphia	153	563	85	143	18	2	7		77	62	15	.254	.330
1916	Philadelphia	142	477	53	101	10	0	3		74	57	15	.212	.252
1917	Philadelphia	127	478	56	116	22	5	4		44	42	14	.243	.335
1918	Philadelphia	125	499	69	132	19	4	0		54	36	11	.265	.319
1919	Philadelphia	92	335	45	91	13	7	0		31	30	8	.272	.352
1920	Philadelphia	42	171	23	51	7	2	0	5	9	12	1	.298	.363
1920	New York	108	442	79	132	29	7	0	31	33	32	7	.299	.396
1921	New York	153	606	121	193	26	15	6	67	66	23	17	.318	.441
1922	New York	156	651	117	209	41	5	4	60	79	27	16	.321	.418
1923	New York	107	444	80	135	33	3	1	31	62	23	8	.304	.399
1924	Boston	79	319	49	89	11	1	2	21	37	24	4	.279	.339
1925	Boston	128	479	75	153	29	8	2	49	64	22	7	.319	.426
1926	Boston	127	453	70	141	18	6	1	44	64	29	3	.311	.384
1927	Boston	111	375	44	91	13	4	1	31	43	36	5	.243	.307
1928	Brooklyn	149	515	47	127	19	5	0	51	59	20	7	.247	.303
1929	Brooklyn	104	358	35	99	11	3	1	44	29	11	7	.277	.332
1930	New York	10	17	0	1	1	0	0	0	2	1	0	.059	.118
	TOTALS	1,913	7,182	1,048	2,004	320	77	32	434	827	487	145	.279	.358

Dave Bancroft's National League Managerial Record

YEAR	TEAM	W	L	WIN%	FINISH
1924	Boston	53	100	.346	8th
1925	Boston	70	83	.458	5th
1926	Boston	66	86	.434	7th
1927	Boston	60	94	.390	7th
	TOTALS	249	363	.407	

Sources: Baseball-Reference.com; National Baseball Hall of Fame and Museum

Banks, Ernest "Ernie" (born: January 31, 1931 in Dallas, Texas); inducted into the National Baseball Hall of Fame and Museum in 1977 as a player; Position: Shortstop-First Base; Uniform: #14; Bats: Right; Throws: Right; Chicago Cubs' first black player; from 1955 to 1960, he hit more home runs than anyone in the major leagues; his uniform number was the first-ever retired by the Cubs; holds the major league single-season record for most grand slam home runs; Major League Baseball's first black manager.

Earning the moniker "Mr. Cub" for his outgoing demeanor and obvious love of the game, Banks made his major league debut on September 17, 1953 and played his entire 19-year career (1953–1971) with the Chicago Cubs. He was named to 11 All-Star teams (1955–1962, 1965, 1967, 1969); was the National League's Most Valuable Player twice (1958–1959); and won a Gold Glove at shortstop in 1960. Although remembered mostly as a shortstop, he actually played more games at first base, where he won the fielding title in 1969 and led the National League is assists five times. His two MVP awards are truly remarkable feats in light of the fact that the Cubs were rarely in pennant contention during his entire career. Banks also led the National League in home runs twice (1958, 1960) and RBIs twice (1958–1959).

Although he never appeared in a post-season game, the 6'1", 180-pound Banks was known for his ever-present smile and being a perennial fan favorite with his famous "let's play two" love for the game. His uniform number 14 was the first to be retired by the Cubs, and he was the all-time home run leader among shortstops until passed by Cal Ripken, Jr. of the Baltimore Orioles.

After retiring in 1971, Banks became a Cubs coach. On May 8, 1973, after Cubs manager Whitey Lockman was ejected from the game, Banks filled in as manager for the last few innings of a 12-inning, 3–2 win over the San Diego Padres, technically making him Major League Baseball's first black manager, predating Frank Robinson's hiring by almost two years.

Banks is the Cubs' all-time leader in games played (2,528); at-bats (9,421); total bases (4,706); and holds the major league single-season record for grand slam home runs (five in 1955). As a shortstop, he was the major league leader in fielding average (once), fewest errors (once), and was the National League leader in games played in a season (six times), extra base hits (four times), slugging percentage (once), total bases (once), and at-bats (once).

He had played two seasons (1950, 1953) with the Kansas City Monarchs (Negro American League), interrupted by two years of military service in the U.S. Army (1951–1952), before joining the Cubs as the team's first black player. In 1999, he was ranked number 38 on *The Sporting News*' list of the 100 Greatest Baseball Players, and was elected to the Major League Baseball All-Century Team.

Growing up in Dallas, Texas, Banks was a two-sport (baseball, football) star in high school, and at age 17, he played baseball with a Negro barnstorming team, before the legendary Cool Papa Bell signed him to the Kansas City Monarchs.

In 1955, he hit 44 home runs, the most ever by a shortstop up to that time. From 1955 to 1960, Banks hit more home runs than anyone in the major leagues, including Mickey Mantle, Willie Mays, and Hank Aaron. On June 2, 1961, he tied a major league record with three run-scoring sacrifice flies in one game in a 7–6 win over the Cincinnati Reds; on May 9, 1963, he became the first National League first baseman to register 22 putouts (and 23 chances) in one game in a 3–1 win over the Pittsburgh Pirates; on June 11, 1966, he tied a modern-day major league single-game record with three triples in an 8–2 win over the Houston Astros; and on May 12, 1970 at Wrigley Field in Chicago, Banks became the eighth member of the 500-home-run club.

Ernie Banks' Career Statistics

YEAR	TEAM	G	AB	R	H	2B	3B	HR	RBI	BB	SO	SB	AVG	SLG
1953	Chicago	10	35	3	11	1	1	2	6	4	5	0	.314	.571
1954	Chicago	154	593	70	163	19	7	19	79	40	50	6	.275	.427
1955	Chicago	154	596	98	176	29	9	44	117	45	72	9	.295	.596
1956	Chicago	139	538	82	160	25	8	28	85	52	62	6	.297	.530
1957	Chicago	156	594	113	169	34	6	43	102	70	85	8	.285	.579
1958	Chicago	154	617	119	193	23	11	47	129	52	87	4	.313	.614
1959	Chicago	155	589	97	179	25	6	45	143	64	72	2	.304	.596
1960	Chicago	156	597	94	162	32	7	41	117	71	69	1	.271	.554
1961	Chicago	138	511	75	142	22	4	29	80	54	75	1	.278	.507
1962	Chicago	154	610	87	164	20	6	37	104	30	71	5	.269	.503
1963	Chicago	130	432	41	98	20	1	18	64	39	73	0	.227	.403
1964	Chicago	157	591	67	156	29	6	23	95	36	84	1	.264	.450
1965	Chicago	163	612	79	162	25	3	28	106	55	64	3	.265	.453
1966	Chicago	141	511	52	139	23	7	15	75	29	59	0	.272	.432
1967	Chicago	151	573	68	158	26	4	23	95	27	93	2	.276	.455
1968	Chicago	150	552	71	136	27	0	32	83	27	67	2	.246	.469
1969	Chicago	155	565	60	143	19	2	23	106	42	101	0	.253	.416
1970	Chicago	72	222	25	56	6	2	12	44	20	33	0	.252	.459
1971	Chicago	39	83	4	16	2	0	3	6	6	14	0	.193	.325
	TOTALS	2,528	9,421	1,305	2,583	407	90	512	1,636	763	1,236	50	.274	.500

Sources: Baseball-Reference.com; *"Mr. Cub"* (Ernie Banks and Jim Enright); National Baseball Hall of Fame and Museum

Barber, William Charles "Bill" (born: July 11, 1952 in Callander, Ontario, Canada); inducted into the Hockey Hall of Fame in 1990 as a player; Position: Left Wing; Uniform: #7; helped the Philadelphia Flyers win the franchise's only two Stanley Cup championships.

After playing with the Kitchener Rangers (Ontario Hockey Association), the 6', 195-pound Barber was a first-round draft choice (seventh selection overall) of the Philadelphia Flyers in 1972, and played his entire 12-year NHL career (1972–1984) with the team. After playing just 11 games for the Richmond Robins (American Hockey League), he was called up by the Flyers and moved to left wing, where he scored 30 goals in 69 games during his rookie season.

Barber helped the Flyers win the franchise's only two Stanley Cups as of this writing (1974, becoming the first expansion team to win the championship, and 1975). He scored 20 or more goals in each of his 12 seasons and scored 40 or more goals five times during his 12-year career. On March 6, 1986, the Flyers retired his #7 jersey, and in March 1989 he was inducted into the Philadelphia Flyers Hall of Fame.

Barber was selected to seven All-Star teams (1975–1976, 1978–1982); named First-Team All-Star Left Wing once (1976); Second-Team All-Star Left Wing twice (1979, 1981); and won the team's Yanick Dupre Memorial Class Guy Award (1981).

After retiring as a player in 1984, he became the head coach of the minor league Hershey Bears (American Hockey League, 1984–1985). He left Hershey to become an assistant coach with the Philadelphia Flyers (1986–1988), before leaving the coaching ranks and serving in the team's front office. He returned to the AHL in mid-season (1995–1996) as head coach of the Hershey Bears, before serving as head coach of the AHL's Philadelphia Phantoms (1996–2000), leading the team to its first Calder Cup title in 1998. Barber returned to the NHL in the 2000–2001 season as head coach of the Flyers (winning the Jack Adams Award for Coach of the Year), before becoming the Director of Player Personnel with the Tampa Bay Lightning in 2002.

William Barber's Career Statistics

			REGULAR SEASON				PLAYOFFS			
SEASON	**TEAM**	**LEAGUE**	**GP**	**G**	**A**	**TP**	**GP**	**G**	**A**	**TP**
1967–1968	North Bay Trappers	NOJHA	34	18	35	53				
1968–1969	North Bay Trappers	NOJHA	48	32	38	70				
1969–1970	Kitchener Rangers	OHA-Jr.	54	37	49	86	8	5	10	15
1970–1971	Kitchener Rangers	OHA-Jr.	61	46	59	105	4	3	2	5
1971–1972	Kitchener Rangers	OMJHL	62	44	63	107	5	2	7	9
1972–1973	Philadelphia Flyers	NHL	69	30	34	64	11	3	2	5
1972–1973	Richmond Robins	AHL	11	9	5	14				
1973–1974	Philadelphia Flyers	NHL	75	34	35	69	17	3	6	9
1974–1975	Philadelphia Flyers	NHL	79	34	37	71	17	6	9	15
1975–1976	Philadelphia Flyers	NHL	80	50	62	112	16	6	7	13
1976–1977	Canada	Can-Cup	7	2	0	2				
1976–1977	Philadelphia Flyers	NHL	73	20	35	55	10	1	4	5
1977–1978	Philadelphia Flyers	NHL	80	41	31	72	12	6	3	9
1978–1979	Philadelphia Flyers	NHL	79	34	46	80	8	3	4	7
1978–1979	NHL All-Stars	Ch-Cup	3	0	1	1				
1979–1980	Philadelphia Flyers	NHL	79	40	32	72	19	12	9	21
1980–1981	Philadelphia Flyers	NHL	80	43	42	85	12	11	5	16
1981–1982	Philadelphia Flyers	NHL	80	45	44	89	4	1	5	6
1981–1982	Canada	WEC-A	10	8	1	9				
1982–1983	Philadelphia Flyers	NHL	66	27	33	60	3	1	1	2
1983–1984	Philadelphia Flyers	NHL	63	22	32	54				
1984–1985	Hershey Bears	AHL								
1985–1995	Philadelphia Flyers	NHLMGNT								
1995–1996	Hershey Bears	AHL								
1996–2000	Philadelphia Phantoms	AHL								
2000–2001	Philadelphia Flyers	NHL								
2002–2003	Tampa Bay Lightning	NHL								
	NHL TOTALS		903	420	463	883	129	53	55	108

William Barber's American Hockey League Coaching Record

SEASON	TEAM	W	L	OTL/T
1984–1985	Hershey Bears	6	9	1
1996–1997	Philadelphia Phantoms	49	18	13
1997–1998	Philadelphia Phantoms	47	21	12
1998–1999	Philadelphia Phantoms	44	31	5
	TOTALS	146	79	31

William Barber's National Hockey League Coaching Record

SEASON	TEAM	W	L	OTL/T
2000–2001	Philadelphia Flyers	31	13	10 (Qualified for NHL Playoffs; lost to Buffalo in six games)
2001–2002	Philadelphia Flyers	42	27	13 (Qualified for NHL Playoffs; lost to Ottawa in five games)
	TOTALS	73	40	23

Sources: Hockey Hall of Fame; Hockey-Reference.com; Philadelphia Flyers Hall of Fame

Barkley, Charles Wade (born: February 20, 1963 in Leeds, Alabama); inducted into the Naismith Memorial Basketball Hall of Fame in 2006 as a player; Position: Forward; Uniform: #34; one of four players in NBA history to score 20,000 points, 10,000 rebounds, and 4,000 assists.

Barkley attended Auburn University (Alabama) for three years, led the Southeastern Conference in rebounding, and was named All-SEC each year he was at the school. He left college to become the first-round draft choice (fifth selection overall) of the NBA's Philadelphia 76ers in 1984. During his 16-year career, he played for the 76ers (1984–1992), Phoenix Suns (1992–1996), and the Houston Rockets (1996–2000).

Known as "Sir Charles" and the "Round Mound of Rebound" (due to his weight sometimes reaching 300 pounds), the 6'6", 250-pound Barkley became one of four players in NBA history to score 20,000 points, 10,000 rebounds, and 4,000 assists (along with Kareem Abdul-Jabbar, Wilt Chamberlain, and Karl Malone).

He was named to 11 consecutive All-Star teams (1987–1997); named to the All-NBA First Team five times (1988–1991, 1993); All-NBA Second Team five times (1986–1987, 1992, 1994–1995); All-NBA Third Team in 1996; selected NBA Most Valuable Player in 1993; named one of the 50 Greatest Players in NBA history in 1996; and won two Olympic gold medals (1992, 1996).

After retiring from the NBA, Barkley became a highly successful and popular basketball commentator and analyst.

One of the greatest NBA players never to win a championship, Barkley led the 76ers to the playoffs each year he was with the team (except 1988 and 1992) and to the Eastern Conference Semifinals in 1990 and 1991, losing to the Chicago Bulls both times. While with the Suns, he helped lead the team to the 1993 NBA Finals, again losing to the Chicago Bulls.

He ranked #19 in *SLAM* magazine's Top 75 NBA Players of all time in 2003 and his Phoenix Suns #34 jersey was retired by the team in 2004.

Charles Barkley's Career Statistics

SEASON	TEAM	G	MIN	FG	3P	FT	REB	AST	STL	BLK	PTS
1984–1985	Philadelphia	60	2,347	427	1	293	703	155	95	80	1148
1985–1986	Philadelphia	80	2,952	595	17	396	1,026	312	173	125	1603
1986–1987	Philadelphia	62	2,740	557	21	429	994	331	119	104	1564
1987–1988	Philadelphia	80	3,170	753	44	714	951	254	100	103	2264
1988–1989	Philadelphia	79	3,088	700	35	602	986	325	126	67	2037
1989–1990	Philadelphia	79	3,085	706	20	557	909	307	148	50	1989
1990–1991	Philadelphia	67	2,498	665	44	475	680	284	110	33	1849
1991–1992	Philadelphia	75	2,881	622	32	454	830	308	136	44	1730
1992–1993	Phoenix	76	2,859	716	67	445	928	385	119	74	1944
1993–1994	Phoenix	65	2,298	518	48	318	727	296	101	37	1402
1994–1995	Phoenix	66	2,382	554	74	379	756	276	110	45	1561
1995–1996	Phoenix	71	2,632	580	49	440	821	262	114	56	1649
1996–1997	Houston	53	2,009	335	58	288	716	248	69	25	1016
1997–1998	Houston	41	2,243	361	18	296	794	217	71	28	1036

SEASON	TEAM	G	MIN	FG	3P	FT	REB	AST	STL	BLK	PTS
1998–1999	Houston	40	1,526	240	4	192	516	192	43	13	676
1999–2000	Houston	18	620	106	6	71	209	63	14	4	289
	TOTALS	1,012	39,330	8,435	538	2,020	12,546	4,215	1,648	888	23,757

Sources: Basketball-Reference.com; Naismith Memorial Basketball Hall of Fame

Barlick, Albert Joseph "Al" (born: April 2, 1915 in Springfield, Illinois; died: December 27, 1995 in Springfield, Illinois); inducted into the National Baseball Hall of Fame and Museum in 1989 as an umpire; sixth umpire to be inducted into the baseball hall of fame.

Known for his booming voice, animated hand signals, and an in-depth understanding of the rules, Barlick became a National League umpire in 1940, one of the youngest ever (age 25), and worked in the major leagues for 27 seasons. He served in seven All-Star games (1942, 1949, 1952, 1955–1956, 1966, 1970), the most of any umpire; seven World Series (1946, 1950–1951, 1954, 1958, 1962, 1967); and was named the National League Umpire of the Year twice (1961, 1970).

His umpiring career was interrupted during World War II when he served in the Coast Guard. After retiring as an umpire in 1972, he worked as a league consultant for 22 years.

Source: National Baseball Hall of Fame and Museum

Barlow, Thomas (born: July 9, 1896 in Trenton, New Jersey; died: September 26, 1983 in Lakehurst, New Jersey); inducted into the Naismith Memorial Basketball Hall of Fame in 1981 as a player; one of America's first professional basketball players.

After attending Rider Moore Stewart Business College (Trenton, New Jersey) for three years, Barlow became one of the first professional basketball players in America. During his career, he played for the Trenton Royal Bengals (Eastern League, 1915–1917); Philadelphia DeNeri (Eastern League, 1916–1918); Trenton Potters (Eastern League, 1919–1920); Patterson Silk Socks (Interstate League, 1919–1920); Wilkes-Barre Barons (Pennsylvania State League, 1919–1921); Trenton Royal Bengals II (Eastern League, 1920–1922); Trenton Tigers (Eastern League, 1922–1923); Philadelphia Holy Name (Philadelphia League, 1923–1924); and the Philadelphia Warriors (Philadelphia League/South Philadelphia Hebrew Association [later to be known as the American Basketball League], 1926–1932).

Large for his day (6'1", 195 pounds), Barlow played on more than 12 professional basketball teams (sometimes on several squads simultaneously) and is best known for his time with the Trenton Tigers and the Philadelphia Warriors, where he played under Hall of Fame coach Eddie Gottlieb.

Source: Naismith Memorial Basketball Hall of Fame

Barmore, Leon (born: June 3, 1944 in Ruston, Louisiana); inducted into the Naismith Memorial Basketball Hall of Fame in 2003 as a coach; fastest college women's basketball coach to reach 500 wins.

At Ruston (Louisiana) High School, Barmore was a three-year letter winner; two-time First-Team All-State selection (1961–1962); and won the Louisiana State Championship twice (1961–1962). After graduating from high school in 1962, he attended Louisiana Tech University (Ruston), where he earned three letters (1965–1967) and was a two-time First-Team All Gulf States Conference selection (1966–1967).

Graduating in 1967, Barmore began his coaching career at Bastrop (Louisiana) High School from 1967 to 1970; accumulated an 84–41 (.672) record; and led the school to first-place District finishes in 1969 and 1970, and to the Final Four in state competition. Leaving Bastrop, he coached at Ruston High School from 1971 to 1976; compiled a 148–49 (.751) record, and led the team to first-place District finishes five times (1971–1973, 1975–1976).

Leaving the high school ranks, Barmore became an assistant coach for the Louisiana Tech University women's basketball team (1977–1982), co-head coach (1982–1985), and eventually served as the school's head coach from 1985 to 2002. During his 25 years as head coach, he led Louisiana Tech to a 576–87 (.869) record (the best winning percentage in women's college basketball history at the time of his retirement) and was the fastest coach in women's basketball history to reach 500 wins.

As the team's head coach, he led the school to the 1988 NCAA Division I Women's Basketball Championship with a 32–2 record; guided the squad to five national championship games, nine Final Four appearances, and 20 straight NCAA appearances; compiled a 56–19 (.747) record in NCAA Tournament games (second best in history); and had thirteen 30-plus win seasons and nineteen 20-plus win seasons.

His overall head coach record is 808-177 (.820), and he was an assistant coach during Louisiana Tech's 54-game winning streak from 1980 to 1982. His teams were ranked in the Associated Press Top 25 for 179 consecutive weeks; ranked in the AP Top 10 in 18 different seasons; registered 13 regular-season conference titles in 15 years and compiled a 190–13 (.936) record in regular-season conference games; coached to a 35–3 (.921) record in conference tournament games; and compiled a 303–17 (.947) record at the Thomas Assembly Center (Louisiana Tech University's home court).

Barmore was named Naismith National Coach of the Year in 1988; the Women's Basketball Coaches Association Coach of the Year in 1996; the United States Basketball Writers Association National Coach of the Year twice (1990, 1996); United States Basketball Association Co-Coach of the Decade (1990); and was inducted into the Women's Basketball Hall of Fame in 2003.

Sources: Naismith Memorial Basketball Hall of Fame; Women's Basketball Hall of Fame

Barney, Lemuel Jackson Jr. "Lem" (born: September 8, 1945 in Gulfport, Mississippi); inducted into the Pro Football Hall of Fame in 1992 as a player; Position: Cornerback; named Defensive Rookie of the Year; selected to the Pro Bowl as a rookie.

Although Barney was a three-time All-Southwestern Athletic Conference selection and had 26 interceptions in three years at Jackson State University (Mississippi), he was a relatively unknown player entering the National Football League draft and became a second-round pick (34th selection overall) of the Detroit Lions, a team he would play for his entire 11-year (140 games) career (1967–1977). He was the NFL's Defensive Rookie of Year in 1967; selected to seven Pro Bowls (1967–1969, 1972–1973, 1975–1976); and was named to the NFL 1960s All-Decade Team.

Originally slotted to be a wide receiver, the Lions made the 6', 188-pound Barney a cornerback, where he excelled and was named to the Pro Bowl as a rookie. Barney also returned punts and kickoffs, and during his career, he would have one 98-yard kickoff return, a 94-yard field goal return, a 74-yard punt return, and a 71-yard interception runback. He served as the Lions' punter in 1967 and 1969; was named All-NFL twice (1968–1969); and selected All-NFC twice (1972, 1975).

Lem Barney's Career Statistics

				INTERCEPTIONS			FUMBLE RECOVERIES	
YEAR	TEAM	G	INT	YDS	AVG	TD	NO	YDS
1967	Detroit	14	10	232	23.2	3	0	0
1968	Detroit	14	7	82	11.7	0	5	0
1969	Detroit	13	8	126	15.8	0	2	25
1970	Detroit	13	7	168	24.0	2	0	0
1971	Detroit	9	3	78	26.0	1	2	0
1972	Detroit	14	3	88	29.3	0	1	20
1973	Detroit	14	4	130	32.5	0	3	0
1974	Detroit	13	4	61	15.3	0	0	0
1975	Detroit	10	5	23	4.6	0	1	74
1976	Detroit	14	2	62	31.0	1	1	0
1977	Detroit	12	3	27	9.0	0	2	49
	TOTALS	140	56	1,077	19.2	7	17	168

Sources: Pro Football Hall of Fame; Pro-Football-Reference.com

Barr, George (born: December 31, 1915 in Edinburgh, Scotland; died: April 11, 2000 in Syosset, New York); inducted into the National Soccer Hall of Fame and Museum in 1983 as a player; Position: Full Back; his first professional contract made him the youngest player in the American Soccer League.

Five years after moving to the United States, Barr signed his first professional contract with Brooklyn Celtic (Brooklyn St. Mary's Celtic) of the American Soccer League, making him the youngest player (age 17) in the league. In 1935, he moved on to New York Brookhattan; captained the team that won the U.S. Open Cup, the ASL championship, and the Lewis Cup in the 1944–1945 season; and stayed with the team until the end of the 1946–1947 season. Beginning in 1947, he played three seasons with Brooklyn Hispano (ASL), before retiring.

During his career, Barr played against numerous traveling teams, and during World War II, he served in the Southwest Pacific, where he captained the U. S. Army team in games played in Brisbane and Sydney, Australia.

He worked for J.C. Penney for almost 40 years, and after retiring as a player, Barr coached the Syosset Police Boys Club in the Long Island Junior League.

Source: National Soccer Hall of Fame and Museum

Barriskill, Joseph J. (born: 1889 in Belfast, Ireland; died: December 1981 in Paradise, California); inducted into the National Soccer Hall of Fame and Museum in 1953 as a builder; longtime official of both the New York Soccer Association and the U.S. Soccer Football Association.

As a young man, Barriskill first played soccer with Bensonhurst of the New York Field League, before playing with and managing the Crescent Club in Brooklyn, New York. As a Field League delegate, he attended the New York Soccer Association annual meetings, before becoming a state delegate to the U.S. Soccer Football Association. He was elected its vice president in 1932, and beginning in 1934, he served as its president for two years.

Barriskill was chairman of the National Challenge Cup Committee from 1928 to 1940; treasurer of the New York Soccer Association (1928 to 1948); and served as executive secretary of the USSFA from 1944 to 1950.

Source: National Soccer Hall of Fame and Museum

Barrow, Edward Grant "Ed" (born: May 10, 1868 in Springfield, Illinois; died: December 15, 1953 in Port Chester, New York); inducted into the National Baseball Hall of Fame and Museum in 1953 as an executive-pioneer by the Veterans Committee; credited with discovering future hall-of-famer Honus Wagner; president of the Eastern League; led the Boston Red Sox to the 1918 World Series title; built the New York Yankee dynasty teams from the 1920s to the 1940s.

After working as a newspaperman in Des Moines, Iowa, Barrow moved to Pittsburgh, Pennsylvania in 1890, and partnered with Harry Stevens to run concession stands at the Pittsburgh Pirates' Exposition Park. In 1894, he became general manager of the International League; managed the Paterson Silk Weavers (New Jersey) of the Atlantic League in 1895, where he signed Honus Wagner; and served as league president from 1897 to 1899.

In 1900, he became a minority owner of the Toronto Maple Leafs (Eastern League); served as the team's manager; and led the squad to a pennant in 1902. After enjoying minor league success, he managed Major League Baseball's Detroit Tigers for two seasons (1903–1904) and returned to the minor leagues as a manager for two more seasons, before leaving the game to become a businessman.

Barrow returned to baseball in 1910 as president of the Eastern League, before becoming manager of MLB's Boston Red Sox for three seasons (1918–1920). In his first year as the team's manager, he led the Red Sox to the franchise's fifth World Series title. After the Red Sox sold Babe Ruth to the Yankees in 1920, Barrow followed the legendary player and became the Yankees' general manager, where he built one of the game's great dynasty teams (winning 14 pennants and 10 World Series championships), before leaving in 1946.

Ironically, part of his success came from the fact that he signed numerous Boston players. When the Yankees won the franchise's first World Series in 1923, half of the team's starting lineup and five of its pitchers were former Red Sox players. Enjoying early success with the team, over the following seasons, Barrow would strengthen the Yankees teams by signing a continuing string of stars and future hall-of-famers, including Lou Gehrig, Tony Lazzeri, Lefty Gomez, and Joe DiMaggio.

Barrow was named *The Sporting News* Major League Executive of the Year twice (1937, 1941) and became the Yankees' chairman of the board in 1944, a position he held until 1946.

Edward Barrow's American League Managerial Record

YEAR	TEAM	W	L	WIN%	FINISH
1903	Detroit	65	71	.478	Fifth
1904	Detroit	32	46	.410	Seventh
1918	Boston	75	51	.595	First (won World Series)
1919	Boston	66	71	.482	Sixth
1920	Boston	72	81	.471	Fifth
	Detroit	97	117	.453	
	Boston	213	203	.512	
	TOTALS	310	320	.492	

Sources: Baseball-Reference.com; National Baseball Hall of Fame and Museum

Barry, Justin McCarthy "Sam" (born: December 17, 1892 in Aberdeen, South Dakota; died: September 25, 1950 in Berkeley, California); inducted into the Naismith Memorial Basketball Hall of Fame in 1979 as a coach; one of only three coaches to lead teams to both the NCAA basketball Final Four and the men's College Baseball World Series; his 40-game winning streak against UCLA still stands as the longest winning streak by any coach against a single opponent in the history of college basketball.

Barry attended Madison (Wisconsin) High School from 1908 to 1911, where he was a three-sport star (baseball, basketball, football); an All-State and All-Conference basketball guard (1911); and captain of the basketball team as a senior. After graduating from high school, he went to Lawrence College (Appleton, Wisconsin) from 1912 to 1916, and was captain of the basketball team in 1913, before completing his degree at the University of Wisconsin (Madison).

After graduating, he began his coaching career at his high school, before serving as a coach and athletic director at Knox College (Galesburg, Illinois) from 1918 to 1922, where he compiled a 36–19 (.655) record and won the Illinois Intercollegiate Conference twice (1919–1920). He also served as the school's football, baseball, and track coach, and led the school's football team to a 15–12–4 record from 1918 to 1921, including a perfect 8–0 season in 1919.

From 1922 to 1929, Barry coached at the University of Iowa (Iowa City); led the school to the 1923 Big Ten championship; and left with a 61–54 (.530) record. From 1923 to 1924, he also coached the school's baseball team.

He left Iowa to coach at the University of Southern California (Los Angeles) for 18 seasons (1930–1941, 1945–1950), where he compiled an overall 260–138 (.653) record. His USC teams won the Pacific Coast Conference championship three times (1930, 1935, 1940) and the Southern Division title eight times (1930, 1932–1936, 1939–1940). In addition to his basketball accomplishments, Barry also coached the school's baseball team (1930–1941, 1945–1950) and served as the school's head football coach in 1941. Before becoming the football head coach, he had served as an assistant coach on teams that claimed national championships in 1931, 1932, and 1939; seven Pacific Coast Conference titles; and five Rose Bowl appearances. At the time he took over the football team in 1941, Barry was serving as the head coach simultaneously for three sports.

He took a break from coaching when he served in the U.S. Navy during World War II, where he was in charge of physical and military training in the South Pacific, for which he would later receive a Naval Commendation from Secretary of the Navy James Forrestal. After leaving the Navy in 1945, he returned to USC and resumed his various coaching responsibilities, and led the USC baseball team to a College World Series championship in 1948 (becoming one of only three coaches to lead teams to both the NCAA basketball Final Four and the men's College Baseball World Series championship).

The strain of simultaneously coaching three sports at a major university took its toll on Barry, who died prematurely while scouting a USC football opponent (University of California, Berkeley) at a football game on September 23, 1950 in Berkeley.

Barry was instrumental in several basketball innovations, such as having the jump ball at center court after every free throw and basket made eliminated, which increased the speed and pace of the college game; creating the center line; adopting the 10-second rule; he helped invent the triangle offense; and was a national advocate of the delayed (or "slow-down" offense), which slows the game down so that the opposing team cannot score.

His 40-game winning streak against the University of California at Los Angeles (1932–1942, 1946) still stands as the longest winning streak by any coach against a single opponent in the history of college basketball. Barry was a charter member of the National Association of Basketball Coaches and has been inducted into the Helms Foundation Hall of Fame (Los Angeles, California) and the USC Athletic Hall of Fame (2007).

Sources: Naismith Memorial Basketball Hall of Fame; USC Athletic Hall of Fame

Barry, Martin A. "Marty" (born: December 8, 1904 in St. Gabriel, Quebec, Canada; died: August 20, 1969); inducted into the Hockey Hall of Fame in 1965 as a player; Position: Center; won back-to-back Stanley Cup titles with the Detroit Red Wings; first Detroit player to win the Lady Byng Trophy.

During his 12-year National Hockey League career (1927–1940), Barry played for the New York Americans (1927–1928), Boston Bruins (1929–1935), Detroit Red Wings (1935–1939, winning back-to-back Stanley Cup titles in 1936 and 1937), and the Montreal Canadiens (1939–1940).

Raised in Montreal, he was such a prolific scorer in local junior, senior, and minor league competition that he earned the nickname "Goal-a-Game Barry." After appearing in only nine games in 1927 for the Americans, he was sent to the Philadelphia Arrows (Can-Am League) and the New Haven Eagles (Can-Am League) to hone his skills, before he was drafted by the Boston Bruins and played with the team in the 1929–1930 season. While with the Bruins, the 6', 195-pound Barry had five consecutive 20-goal seasons (1931–1935) and was the NHL's second-highest scorer in the 1933–1934 season with 27 goals, behind Charlie Conacher's 32 (Toronto Maple Leafs).

After being traded to the Detroit Red Wings in 1935, he scored 40 points in the 1935–1936 season, second-highest in the league behind David "Sweeney" Schriner (New York Americans); scored a career-high 44 points the next season; was selected to the NHL First All-Star Team (1937); was the first Red Wing player to win the Lady Byng Trophy (1937) for gentlemanly conduct; and helped Detroit win back-to-back Stanley Cup titles (1936–1937), the first American team to win consecutive championships.

In 1939, he played with the Montreal Canadiens for his last NHL season, and retired in 1941 after playing two years in the minor leagues. After retiring, Barry coached the Halifax St. Mary's junior team in the 1940s and was inducted into the Detroit Red Wings Hall of Fame in 1944.

Martin Barry's Career Statistics

			REGULAR SEASON					PLAYOFFS				
SEASON	TEAM	LEAGUE	GP	G	A	TP	PIM	GP	G	A	TP	PIM
1924–1925	Montreal St. Anthony's	MCHL										
1924–1925	Montreal St. Ann's	ECHL	1	0	0	0	0					
1925–1926	Montreal St. Anthony's	MCHL										
1926–1927	Montreal Bell Telephone	MCHL										
1927–1928	New York Americans	NHL	9	1	0	1	2					
1927–1928	Philadelphia Arrows	Can-Am	33	11	3	14	70					
1928–1929	New Haven Eagles	Can-Am	35	19	10	29	54	2	0	1	1	2
1929–1930	Boston Bruins	NHL	44	18	15	33	34	6	3	3	6	14
1930–1931	Boston Bruins	NHL	44	20	11	31	26	5	1	1	2	4
1931–1932	Boston Bruins	NHL	48	21	17	38	22					
1932–1933	Boston Bruins	NHL	47	24	13	37	40	5	2	2	4	6
1933–1934	Boston Bruins	NHL	48	27	12	39	12					
1934–1935	Boston Bruins	NHL	48	20	20	40	33	4	0	0	0	2
1935–1936	Detroit Red Wings	NHL	48	21	19	40	16	7	2	4	6	6
1936–1937	Detroit Red Wings	NHL	47	17	27	44	6	10	4	7	11	2
1937–1938	Detroit Red Wings	NHL	48	9	20	29	34					
1938–1939	Detroit Red Wings	NHL	48	13	28	41	4	6	3	1	4	0
1939–1940	Montreal Canadiens	NHL	30	4	10	14	2					
1939–1940	Pittsburgh Hornets	IAHL	6	2	0	2	0	7	2	1	3	4
1940–1941	Minneapolis Millers	AHA	32	10	10	20	8	3	1	0	1	0
1941–1942	Minneapolis Millers	AHA										
	NHL TOTALS		509	195	192	387	231	43	15	18	33	34

Sources: Detroit Red Wings Hall of Fame; Hockey Hall of Fame; Hockey-Reference.com

Barry, Richard Francis Dennis III "Rick" (born: March 28, 1944 in Elizabeth, New Jersey); inducted into the Naismith Memorial Basketball Hall of Fame in 1987 as a player; Position: Forward; only player in basketball history to lead the NCAA, ABA, and the NBA in scoring.

After attending Roselle Park (New Jersey) High School (1957–1961), where he was a two-time All-State selection, Barry attended the University of Miami (Coral Gables, Florida) from 1961 to 1965, and became a star basketball player. He was named Associated Press First-Team All-America (1965); *The Sporting News* All-America Second Team (1965); a Consensus All-America (1965); and led the nation in scoring (37.4 points per game) as a senior. However, since the school was under NCAA probation, Miami did not participate in the NCAA tournament that year. During his college career, he averaged 29.8 points-per-game in 77 games, and is one of just two basketball players (along with Tim James) to have his jersey number retired by the school.

After college, the 6'7", 205-pound Barry entered the National Basketball Association as a first-round pick (second selection overall) of the San Francisco Warriors in the 1965 NBA draft, and was later named Rookie of the Year (1965–1966 season), averaging 25.7 points and 10.6 rebounds per game. During his 14-year career, Barry played for the Warriors (1965–1967), Oakland Oaks (American Basketball Association, 1968–1969), Washington Capitals (ABA, 1969–1970), New York Nets (ABA, 1970–1972), Golden State Warriors (1972–1978), and the Houston Rockets (1978–1979). He won an ABA title in 1969 with the Oaks and an NBA title in 1975 with the Warriors.

He was named to the ABA All-Star First Team all four years he played in the league (1969–1972); led the ABA in scoring in 1969, averaging 34.0 points per game; named to the All-NBA First Team five times (1966–1967, 1974–1976);

selected to the All-NBA Second Team in 1973; led the NBA in scoring (1967, 35.6 points-per-game); was the NBA Finals Most Valuable Player (1975 with the Golden State Warriors); the only player in basketball history to lead the NCAA, ABA, and NBA in scoring; and was named to the NBA 50th Anniversary All-Time Team (1996).

Using an underhanded free-throw style that was a throwback to the game's early days, he accumulated an .893 career free-throw percentage, second best in ABA/NBA history. However, for all his on-court success, Barry's abrasive personality and difficulty in dealing with fans and teammates alike, hindered his NBA coaching opportunities when he retired as a player.

In spite of his personality, his deep understanding of the sport and his ability to explain a game as it progressed to television viewers and radio listeners, made Barry a much sought after color commentator. After retiring as a player, he enjoyed a national radio and television career, before focusing his radio efforts to the San Francisco Bay Area.

In the early 1990s, Barry served as a coach for the Cedar Rapids Sharpshooters of the Global Basketball Association, before coaching the Fort Wayne Fury (Continental Basketball Association) to a 19–37 record in the 1993–1994 season.

Rick Barry's Career Statistics

SEASON	TEAM	LG	G	MIN	FG	3P	FT	REB	ASST	PTS
1965–1966	Warriors	NBA	80	2,990	745		569	850	173	2,059
1966–1967	Warriors	NBA	78	3,175	1,011		753	714	282	2,775
1968–1969	Oaks	ABA	35	1,361	392	3	403	329	136	1,190
1969–1970	Washington	ABA	52	1,849	517	8	400	363	178	1,442
1970–1971	New York	ABA	59	2,502	632	19	451	401	294	1,734
1971–1972	New York	ABA	80	3,616	902	73	641	602	327	2,518
1972–1973	Warriors	NBA	82	3,075	737		358	728	399	1,832
1973–1974	Warriors	NBA	80	2,918	796		417	540	484	2,009
1974–1975	Warriors	NBA	80	3,235	1,028		394	456	492	2,450
1975–1976	Warriors	NBA	81	3,122	707		287	496	496	1,701
1976–1977	Warriors	NBA	79	2,904	682		359	422	475	1,723
1977–1978	Warriors	NBA	82	3,024	760		378	449	446	1,898
1978–1979	Houston	NBA	80	2,566	461		160	277	502	1,082
1979–1980	Houston	NBA	72	1,816	325	73	143	236	268	866
	ABA	ABA	226	9,328	2,443	103	1,895	1,695	935	6,884
	NBA	NBA	794	28,825	7,252	73	3,818	5,168	4,017	18,395
	TOTALS		1,020	38,153	9,695	176	5,713	6,863	4,952	25,279

Sources: Basketball-Reference.com; Naismith Memorial Basketball Hall of Fame

Bathgate, Andrew James "Andy" (born: August 28, 1932 in Winnipeg, Manitoba, Canada); inducted into the Hockey Hall of Fame in 1978 as a player; Position: Right Wing-Center; won the Most Valuable Player award in both the Western Hockey League and the National Hockey League; won the 1964 Stanley Cup championship.

During his 23-year professional hockey career (1952–1975), the 6', 175-pound Bathgate played 17 NHL seasons with the New York Rangers (1952–1964), Toronto Maple Leafs (1964–1965), Detroit Red Wings (1965–1967), and the Pittsburgh Penguins (1967–1968, 1970–1971). He also played professionally with the Cleveland Barons (American Hockey League), after splitting the early part of his career between the Vancouver Canucks (Western Hockey League) and the New York Rangers.

He was named First-Team All-Star Right Wing twice (1959, 1962); Second-Team All-Star Right Wing twice (1958, 1963); and won the Hart Memorial Trophy in 1959 as the NHL's Most Valuable Player. He won a Stanley Cup championship in 1964 with the Toronto Maple Leafs, and in 1966, he helped the Red Wings reach the Stanley Cup finals before eventually losing to the Montreal Canadiens in six games.

Later in his career, he left the NHL and played briefly for the Vancouver Canucks and helped the team win back-to-back Lester Patrick Cup championships in the Western Hockey League (1969–1970). With the Canucks in the 1969–1970 season, he won the George Leader Cup as the MVP of the WHL, before returning to the Penguins.

After leaving the NHL for good, Bathgate served as a player-coach for the HC (Hockey Club) Ambri-Piotta in Switzerland for the 1971–1972 season and stayed with the team until 1973, when he became the coach of the Vancouver Blazers (World Hockey Association).

Andy Bathgate's Career Statistics

			REGULAR SEASON				PLAYOFFS			
SEASON	**TEAM**	**LEAGUE**	**GP**	**G**	**A**	**TP**	**GP**	**G**	**A**	**TP**
1948–1949	Winnipeg Black Hawks	MJHL	1	0	0	0				
1949–1950	Guelph Biltmores	OHA-Jr.	41	21	25	46	15	6	9	15
1949–1950	Guelph Biltmores	M-Cup	11	10	5	15				
1950–1951	Guelph Biltmores	OHA-Jr.	52	33	57	90	5	6	1	7
1951–1952	Guelph Biltmores	OHA-Jr.	34	27	50	77	11	6	10	16
1951–1952	Guelph Biltmores	M-Cup	12	8	12	20				
1952–1953	Guelph Biltmores	OHA-Jr.	2	2	1	3				
1952–1953	New York Rangers	NHL	18	0	1	1				
1952–1953	Vancouver Canucks	WHL	37	13	13	26	9	11	4	15
1953–1954	New York Rangers	NHL	20	2	2	4				
1953–1954	Vancouver Canucks	WHL	17	12	10	22				
1953–1954	Cleveland Barons	AHL	36	13	19	32	9	3	5	8
1954–1955	New York Rangers	NHL	70	20	20	40				
1955–1956	New York Rangers	NHL	70	19	47	66	5	1	2	3
1956–1957	New York Rangers	NHL	70	27	50	77	5	2	0	2
1957–1958	New York Rangers	NHL	65	30	48	78	6	5	3	8
1958–1959	New York Rangers	NHL	70	40	48	88				
1959–1960	New York Rangers	NHL	70	26	48	74				
1960–1961	New York Rangers	NHL	70	29	48	77				
1961–1962	New York Rangers	NHL	70	28	56	84	6	1	2	3
1962–1963	New York Rangers	NHL	70	35	46	81				
1963–1964	New York Rangers	NHL	56	16	43	59				
1963–1964	Toronto Maple Leafs	NHL	15	3	15	18	14	5	4	9
1964–1965	Toronto Maple Leafs	NHL	55	16	29	45	6	1	0	1
1965–1966	Detroit Red Wings	NHL	70	15	32	47	12	6	3	9
1966–1967	Detroit Red Wings	NHL	60	8	23	31				
1966–1967	Pittsburgh Hornets	AHL	6	4	6	10				
1967–1968	Pittsburgh Penguins	NHL	74	20	39	59				
1968–1969	Vancouver Canucks	WHL	71	37	36	73	8	3	5	8
1969–1970	Vancouver Canucks	WHL	72	40	68	108	16	7	5	12
1970–1971	Pittsburgh Penguins	NHL	76	15	29	44				
1971–1974	HC Ambri-Piotta	Swiss								
1974–1975	Vancouver Blazers	WHA	11	1	6	7				
	NHL TOTALS		1,069	349	624	973	54	21	14	35

Sources: Hockey Hall of Fame; Hockey-Reference.com

Battles, Clifford Franklin "Cliff" (born: May 1, 1910 in Akron, Ohio; died: April 28, 1981 in Clearwater, Florida); inducted into the Pro Football Hall of Fame in 1968 as a player; Position: Halfback; first player to rush for more than 100 yards in a game; first player to rush for more than 200 yards in a game.

After graduating from West Virginia Wesleyan College (Buckhannon, 1928–1931), the 6'1", 195-pound Battles played for the National Football League's Boston Braves/Redskins (1932–1936) and the Washington Redskins (1937, when the Boston team moved to Washington, D.C.). He led the NFL in rushing twice (1932 as a rookie, 1937); was an All-NFL choice five times (1932–1934, 1936–1937); was the first player to rush for more than 100 yards in a game (144, in the team's 7–7 tie with the Chicago Bears on October 30, 1932); and the first player to rush for 200 yards in a game (215, in a 21–20 win over the New York Giants on October 8, 1933).

In 1937, he teamed with future hall of fame quarterback Sammy Baugh to help the Redskins win the franchise's first NFL championship, a 28–21 win over the Chicago Bears. After winning the league title, Battles left the NFL and became an assistant coach at Columbia University (New York, New York).

Cliff Battles' NFL Statistics

			RUSHING				RECEIVING			
YEAR	TEAM	G	NO	YDS	AVG	TD	NO	YDS	AVG	TD
1932	Boston	8	148	576	3.9	3	4	60	15.0	1
1933	Boston	12	136	737	5.4	3	11	185	16.8	0
1934	Boston	12	96	480	5.0	6	5	95	19.0	1
1935	Boston	7	67	230	3.4	1	3	22	7.3	0
1936	Boston	11	176	614	3.5	5	6	103	17.2	1
1937	Washington	10	216	874	4.0	5	9	81	9.0	1
	TOTALS	60	839	3,511	4.2	23	38	546	14.4	4

Sources: Pro Football Hall of Fame; Pro-Football-Reference.com

Bauer, Father David (born: November 2, 1924 in Kitchener, Ontario, Canada; died: November 9, 1988 in Goderich, Ontario, Canada); inducted into the Hockey Hall of Fame in 1989 as a builder; helped the National Team win a bronze medal at the 1968 Winter Olympics.

Bauer and his brother, Robert, have both been inducted into the Hockey Hall of Fame. At age 16, Bauer attended St. Michael's College (Toronto, Ontario, Canada), before transferring to the University of Toronto (Ontario, Canada). While still a student, he played for the Oshawa Generals (Ontario Hockey Association Junior A league) and was on the team that won the 1944 Memorial Cup. After finishing his studies, Bauer abandoned his hockey playing career and became a priest in 1953.

Once ordained, he returned to St. Michael's College as a teacher and coach of the junior hockey team, and after leading the squad to the 1961 Memorial Cup, Bauer moved on to St. Mark's College at the University of British Columbia (Vancouver, Canada). While at St. Mark's, he was a driving force in the creation of the National Team (to be made up of top amateur players throughout Canada), which became a reality in 1962. The National Team finished fourth at the 1964 Winter Olympics (Innsbruck, Austria) and won a bronze medal at the 1968 Olympics (Grenoble, France).

An ardent believer that the National Team should never include professional players from the National Hockey League, Bauer conducted clinics throughout the world. When the Canadiens finished sixth at the 1980 Olympics (Lake Placid, New York), he served as the team's managing director. In 1981, he was named vice-president of Hockey Canada and chairman of the country's Olympic program, while still continuing to teach at St. Mark's.

Bauer received the Order of Canada (1967); had an arena named after him in Calgary which is used by the National Team; and a bursary was named in his honor at St. Michael's College (1987).

Source: Hockey Hall of Fame

Bauer, Robert Theodore "Bobby" (born: February 16, 1915 in Waterloo, Ontario, Canada; died: September 16, 1964 in Kitchener, Ontario, Canada); inducted into the Hockey Hall of Fame in 1996 as a player; Position: Left Wing; Uniform: #17; won two Stanley Cup titles.

The older brother of hall-of-famer Father David Bauer, Robert played hockey as a young boy before attending St. Michael's College (Toronto, Ontario, Canada). He eventually played for both the school's Junior B and Junior A teams, and helped the school win the 1934 Memorial Cup title.

During his more than 20-year playing career, Bauer spent nine seasons with the National Hockey League's Boston Bruins; won two Stanley Cup titles with the team (1939, 1941); and had his jersey #17 retired by the franchise.

The 5'7", 160-pound Bauer was selected to the NHL All-Star First-Team twice (1939, 1947); All-Star Second-Team four times (1939–1941, 1947); and won the Lady Byng Memorial Trophy for sportsmanship and gentlemanly conduct three times (1940–1941, 1947).

After retiring from the NHL in 1947, he returned to the Kitchener area and coached the Junior A Guelph Biltmore Madhatters of the Ontario Hockey Association. He later played senior hockey with the Kitchener-Waterloo Dutchmen (OHA), and led the team to three consecutive Allan Cups (1948–1950), losing them all. Moving into the team's front office, he was with the franchise as it won two Allan Cup championships (1953, 1955); a bronze medal at the 1956 Olympics (Cortina d'Ampezzo, Italy); and a silver medal at the 1960 Olympics (Squaw Valley, California).

Robert Bauer's Career Statistics

			REGULAR SEASON					PLAYOFFS				
SEASON	TEAM	LEAGUE	GP	G	A	TP	PIM	GP	G	A	TP	PIM
1930–1931	St. Michael's Buzzers	OHA-Jr.										

			REGULAR SEASON					PLAYOFFS				
SEASON	TEAM	LEAGUE	GP	G	A	TP	PIM	GP	G	A	TP	PIM
1931–1933	St. Michael's Majors	OHA-Jr.										
1933–1934	St. Michael's Majors	OHA-Jr.	10	4	2	6	0	2	0	1	1	0
1933–1934	St. Michael's Majors	M-Cup	13	10	5	15	0					
1934–1935	Toronto British Consols	TMHL	6	2	0	2	0	4	2	3	5	2
1934–1935	Kitchener Greenshirts	OHA-Jr.	11	12	6	18	0	3	1	2	3	2
1935–1936	Boston Cubs	Can-Am	48	15	13	28	8					
1936–1937	Boston Bruins	NHL	1	1	0	1	0	1	0	0	0	0
1936–1937	Providence Reds	IAHL	44	14	4	18	4	2	0	1	1	0
1937–1938	Boston Bruins	NHL	48	20	14	34	9	3	0	0	0	2
1938–1939	Boston Bruins	NHL	48	13	18	31	4	12	3	2	5	0
1939–1940	Boston Bruins	NHL	48	17	26	43	2	6	1	0	1	2
1940–1941	Boston Bruins	NHL	48	17	22	39	2	11	2	2	4	0
1941–1942	Boston Bruins	NHL	36	13	22	35	11					
1941–1942	Ottawa RCAF Flyers	QSHL						6	7	6	13	4
1941–1942	Ottawa RCAF Flyers	Al-Cup	5	3	6	9	0					
1942–1943	Halifax RCAF	NSDHL	7	12	8	20	0	5	7	5	12	0
1942–1943	Halifax RCAF	Al-Cup	7	2	5	7	0					
1944–1945	Toronto People's Credit	TIHL	1	1	0	1	0	8	5	5	8	2
1945–1946	Boston Bruins	NHL	39	11	10	21	4	10	4	3	7	2
1946–1947	Boston Bruins	NHL	58	30	24	54	4	5	1	1	2	0
1947–1948	Kitchener Dutchmen	OHA-Sr.	8	8	7	15	22	10	5	4	9	6
1948–1949	Kitchener Dutchmen	OHA-Sr.	31	17	21	38	13	12	4	4	8	0
1949–1950	Kitchener Dutchmen	OHA-Sr.	23	10	14	24	9	9	1	2	3	2
1951–1952	Kitchener Dutchmen	OHA-Sr.	37	8	10	18	14	1	0	1	1	0
1951–1952	Boston Bruins	NHL	1	1	1	2	0					
	NHL TOTALS		327	123	137	260	36	48	11	8	19	6

Sources: Hockey Hall of Fame; Hockey-Reference.com

Baugh, Samuel Adrian "Sammy" (born: March 17, 1914 in Temple, Texas; died: December 17, 2008 in Rotan, Texas); inducted into the Pro Football Hall of Fame in 1963 as a player; Position: Quarterback; Uniform: #33; won the very first Cotton Bowl; while leading the Washington Redskins to an NFL title in 1937, he also played shortstop in the St. Louis Cardinals' minor league organization; only player in NFL history to lead the league in single-season offensive, defensive, and special team categories.

Baugh was a two-time All-American quarterback at Texas Christian University (Fort Worth, 1934–1936), and as a junior, he led the team to a 10–1 regular-season record and a 3–2 win over Louisiana State University in the Sugar Bowl (January 1, 1936). The next season, he led TCU to a 16–6 win over Marquette in the very first Cotton Bowl ever played (January 1, 1937).

After college, Baugh was the number one draft choice (sixth pick overall) of the National Football League's Washington Redskins in the 1937 NFL Draft, and would play his entire 16-year career with the team. As a rookie, he led the NFL in passing and guided the Redskins to the NFL championship with a 28–21 win over the Chicago Bears. While playing for the Redskins in 1937, the 6'2", 182-pound Baugh was also a shortstop in Major League Baseball's St. Louis Cardinals' minor league organization. After playing minor league baseball for a few seasons, he left the game and focused on his professional football career.

Nicknamed "Slingin' Sammy," Baugh's passing ability changed the face of both college and professional football, which had been dominated by the running game. He was selected All-NFL seven times; was the NFL passing, punting, and interception leader in 1943; a six-time NFL passing leader; the game's top punter; and is the only player in NFL history to lead the league in single-season offensive, defensive, and special team categories.

His impact on the game led to the forward pass overtaking the running game as football's most effective offensive weapon, which was also very much a fan favorite. His best single-game performance came on November 23, 1947 when he passed for 355 yards and six touchdowns in a 45–21 win over the Chicago Cardinals.

After retiring from the NFL, Baugh coached at Hardin-Simmons University (Abilene, Texas) from 1955 to 1959, before becoming the first coach of the New York Titans (American Football League). His collegiate record was 23–28 (.451); he compiled a 14–14 record with the Titans; and his jersey #33 was retired by the Redskins.

Baugh was named to the 50th Anniversary Team by the NFL (1969); the 75th Anniversary Team by the NFL (1994); the third greatest NFL player of the 20th century by the Associated Press (1999); 1937 Cotton Bowl Most Valuable Player; NFL's 1940s All-Decade Team; College Football Hall of Fame in 1951; holds the record for most seasons leading the NFL in passing (six); and was among the 17 charter members to the Pro Football Hall of Fame in 1963.

Sammy Baugh's Career Statistics

						PASSING					RUSHING		
YEAR	**TEAM**	**G**	**ATT**	**COMP**	**PCT**	**YDS**	**TD**	**INT**	**RATING**	**NO**	**YDS**	**AVG**	**TD**
1937	Washington	11	171	81	47.4	1,127	8	14	50.5	86	240	2.8	1
1938	Washington	9	128	63	49.2	853	5	11	48.1	21	35	1.7	0
1939	Washington	9	96	53	55.2	518	6	9	52.3	14	46	3.3	0
1940	Washington	11	177	111	62.7	1,367	12	10	85.6	20	16	0.8	0
1941	Washington	11	193	106	54.9	1,236	10	19	52.2	27	14	0.5	0
1942	Washington	11	225	132	58.7	1,524	16	11	82.5	20	61	3.1	1
1943	Washington	10	239	133	55.6	1,754	23	19	78	19	-43	-2.3	0
1944	Washington	8	146	82	56.2	849	4	8	59.4	19	-38	-2.0	0
1945	Washington	8	182	128	70.3	1,669	11	4	109.9	19	-71	-3.7	0
1946	Washington	11	161	87	54	1,163	8	17	54.2	18	-76	-4.2	1
1947	Washington	12	354	210	59.3	2,938	25	15	92	25	47	1.9	2
1948	Washington	12	315	185	58.7	2,599	22	23	78.3	4	4	1.0	1
1949	Washington	12	255	145	56.9	1,903	18	14	81.2	13	67	5.2	2
1950	Washington	11	166	90	54.2	1,130	10	11	68.1	7	27	3.9	1
1951	Washington	12	154	67	43.5	1,104	7	17	43.8	11	-5	-0.5	0
1952	Washington	7	33	20	60.6	152	2	1	79.4	1	1	1.0	0
	TOTALS	165	2,995	1,693	56.5	21,886	187	203	72.2	324	325	1	9

			INTERCEPTIONS				FUMBLES		PUNTING		
YEAR	**TEAM**	**G**	**INT**	**YDS**	**AVG**	**TD**	**NO**	**YDS**	**NO**	**YDS**	**AVG**
1937	Washington	11	0	0	0.0	0	0	0	0	0	0.0
1938	Washington	9	0	0	0.0	0	0	0	0	0	0.0
1939	Washington	9	0	0	0.0	0	0	0	26	998	38.4
1940	Washington	11	3	84	28.0	0	0	0	35	1,799	51.4
1941	Washington	11	4	83	20.8	0	0	0	30	1,462	48.7
1942	Washington	11	5	77	15.4	0	0	0	37	1,785	48.2
1943	Washington	10	11	112	10.2	0	0	0	50	2,295	45.9
1944	Washington	8	4	21	5.3	0	0	0	44	1,787	40.6
1945	Washington	8	4	114	28.5	0	3	-12	33	1,429	43.3
1946	Washington	11	0	0	0.0	0	3	-5	33	1,488	45.1
1947	Washington	12	0	0	0.0	0	7	-5	35	1,528	43.7
1948	Washington	12	0	0	0.0	0	3	0	0	0	0.0
1949	Washington	12	0	0	0.0	0	1	2	1	53	53.0
1950	Washington	11	0	0	0.0	0	2	4	9	352	39.1
1951	Washington	12	0	0	0.0	0	2	0	4	221	55.3
1952	Washington	7	0	0	0.0	0	0	0	1	48	48.0
	TOTALS	165	31	491	15.8	0	21	-16	338	15,245	45.1

Sources: College Football Hall of Fame; Pro Football Hall of Fame; Pro-Football-Reference.com

Baylor, Elgin Gay (born: September 16, 1934 in Washington, D.C.); inducted into the Naismith Memorial Basketball Hall of Fame in 1977 as a player; Position: Forward; first NBA player to score more than 70 points in a game; first NBA player to finish in the top five in four categories: scoring, rebounding, assists, and free-throw percentage in a season.

Although Baylor was a high school sports star at both Phelps Vocational and Springarn High School (both in Washington, D.C.), he was not the academic type and dropped out of school for a while. He finally graduated in 1954 and went to the College of Idaho (Caldwell), but left after only one year to attend Seattle University (Washington) from

1955 to 1958. After sitting out one season to establish eligibility, Baylor became a consensus First-Team All-American (1958) and led the school to the 1958 NCAA championship game. Even though Seattle lost to Kentucky in the finals, he was named the tournament's Most Valuable Player.

He left college after his junior year and was the number one pick (first overall selection) in the 1958 National Basketball Association draft of the Minneapolis Lakers. He was named NBA Rookie of the Year in 1959; played his entire 14-year career with the Lakers; and retired early in 1972, the year the team won the NBA title without him on the roster.

In his rookie season, the 6'5", 225-pound Baylor finished fourth in the league in scoring (24.9 points per game); third in rebounding (15.0 per game); and eighth in assists (4.1 per game), while scoring 55 points in a single game, at the time the third-highest mark in NBA history.

Baylor was named to the All-NBA First Team 10 times (1959–1965, 1967–1969); an 11-time All-Star (1959–1965, 1967–1970); NBA All-Star Game Co-MVP (1959); he retired with the NBA Finals single-game record for most points (61, April 24, 1962 against the Boston Celtics); was the first NBA player to score more than 70 points in a game (71 on December 11, 1960 against the New York Knicks); was named to the NBA 35th Anniversary Team (1980); and to the NBA 50th Anniversary Team (1996).

After retiring as a player, Baylor joined the NBA's expansion New Orleans Jazz as an assistant coach during the team's inaugural 1974–1975 season. He was an assistant for two seasons before becoming the team's head coach in 1976 for three seasons (1976–1979).

At one point in his career, Baylor held the record for most points in a game, most points in a playoff game, and most points in one half of a playoff game. In the 1962–1963 season, he became the first NBA player to finish in the top five in four categories: scoring, rebounding, assists, and free-throw percentage.

In 1986, the NBA's Los Angeles Clippers hired Baylor to serve as the team's vice president of basketball operations, a job he still holds as of this writing.

Elgin Baylor's Career Statistics

SEASON	TEAM	G	MIN	FG	FT	REB	ASST	POINTS
1958–1959	Minneapolis	70	2,855	605	532	1,050	287	1,742
1959–1960	Minneapolis	70	2,873	755	564	1,150	243	2,074
1960–1961	Los Angeles	73	3,133	931	676	1,447	371	2,528
1961–1962	Los Angeles	48	2,129	680	476	892	222	1,836
1962–1963	Los Angeles	80	3,370	1,029	661	1,146	386	2,719
1963–1964	Los Angeles	78	3,164	756	471	936	347	1,983
1964–1965	Los Angeles	74	3,056	763	483	950	280	2,009
1965–1966	Los Angeles	65	1,975	415	249	621	224	1,079
1966–1967	Los Angeles	70	2,706	711	440	898	215	1,862
1967–1968	Los Angeles	77	3,029	757	488	941	355	2,002
1968–1969	Los Angeles	76	3,064	730	421	805	408	1,881
1969–1970	Los Angeles	54	2,213	511	276	559	292	1,298
1970–1971	Los Angeles	2	57	8	4	11	2	20
1971–1972	Los Angeles	9	239	42	22	57	18	106
	TOTALS	846	33,863	8,693	5,763	11,463	3,650	23,149

Elgin Baylor's NBA Coaching Record

SEASON	TEAM	W	L	WP%
1974–1975	New Orleans	0	1	.000
1976–1977	New Orleans	21	35	.375
1977–1978	New Orleans	39	43	.476
1978–1979	New Orleans	26	56	.317
	TOTALS	86	135	.389

Sources: Basketball-Reference.com; Naismith Memorial Basketball Hall of Fame

Beardsworth, Fred (born: 1889 in Leyland, Lancashire, England; died: October 10, 1964 in New Bedford, Massachusetts); inducted into the National Soccer Hall of Fame and Museum in 1965 as a player; Position: Half Back; won back-to-back American Cup medals.

Beardsworth grew up in England and began playing organized soccer in 1908 for the Farington Villa team in the Preston and District League. In 1909, he joined Leyland Town in the West Lancashire League and stayed with the team until he came to the United States in 1914.

While playing for Leyland, he won the Richardson Cup and the West Lancashire League championship in back-to-back seasons. After arriving in America, he played for New Bedford of the Southern New England League. In 1917, Beardsworth joined the Fall River Rovers (Southern New England Soccer League) and played in the 1918 U.S. Open Cup final, losing to Bethlehem Steel.

In 1919, he played for Robins Dry Dock (Brooklyn, New York, National Association Football League) and won back-to-back American Cup medals in 1920 and 1921. He retired from major league soccer competition in 1921 and began playing for the Booth Mill team of the New Bedford Industrial League, before finishing his career with the Saylesville Bleachery team in the Southern New England League.

After his playing days, Beardsworth became a teacher at the New Bedford Textile School (Massachusetts) in 1928 and was the school's soccer coach. He was awarded the Intercollegiate Athletic Award of Merit for his devoted service to the game in 1964.

Source: National Soccer Hall of Fame and Museum

Beckenbauer, Franz Anton (born: September 11, 1945 in Munich, West Germany); inducted into the National Soccer Hall of Fame and Museum in 1998 as a player; Position: Midfield; International Caps (1965–1977): 103; International Goals: 14; won three consecutive European Cups; only person to win the World Cup both as a captain and a coach.

One of the game's all-time great players, Beckenbauer began playing soccer at age nine with SC Munich (Germany) in 1954. He joined the Bayern Munich youth team in 1958 and made his debut with the squad in the Regionalliga Süd (Regional League South) playing left wing against FC St. Pauli on June 6, 1964. In his first season in the regional league, the team was promoted to the Bundesliga (Germany's highest-level football league).

While playing with Bayern, Beckenbauer won the German Cup in 1967, before becoming the team's captain in 1968 and leading the squad to its first league title. Nicknamed "der Kaiser" ("the Emperor"), he went on to lead Bayern to three consecutive European Cups (1974–1976). Internationally, Beckenbauer played in two World Cup Finals for West Germany (a 4–2 loss to England in 1966 and a 2–1 win over the Netherlands in 1974) and was named European Footballer of the Year twice (1972, 1976), before moving to the United States in 1977.

After arriving in America, he signed with the New York Cosmos (North American Soccer League) and teamed up with the legendary Pelé to help make the team one of the best and most famous soccer franchises in the world.

In his NASL debut (May 29, 1977) against the Tampa Bay Rowdies in Tampa, Florida, Beckenbauer scored a goal in his team's 4–2 loss. In his first season with New York, the Cosmos won Soccer Bowl '77, defeating the Seattle Sounders 2–1 in the Final, and would win the championship two more times (1978, 1980) before leaving the Cosmos in 1980 to play for Hamburg SV (Hamburg, Germany).

After two seasons with Hamburg, he returned to the Cosmos in 1983 for one final playing season. Retiring as a player, Beckenbauer became coach of the West German National Team and led the squad to the 1986 World Cup Final (hosted by Mexico), losing 3–2 to Argentina. Four years later, he again led the team to the World Cup Final (in Rome, Italy), and avenged the earlier loss by defeating Argentina 1–0 to win the title, becoming the only person to win the World Cup both as a captain and a coach.

After just over a year in a management role with Olympique Marseille (1990–1991), he coached Bayern for two short stints (December 1993 to June 1994, and April to May 1996), winning the Bundesliga title in 1994 and the Union of European Football Associations Cup in 1996. In 1994, he became club president and has served as chairman of the team's advisory board since 2002.

Beckenbauer made 424 Bundesliga appearances (scoring 44 goals); 78 European Cup appearances (scoring six goals); was a five-time German Championship winner (1969, 1972–1974, 1982); and four-time German Cup winner (1966–1967, 1969, 1971).

His international achievements include 103 caps (14 goals), with 50 caps as team captain; 1966 FIFA World Cup winner; 1972 European Championship winner; 1974 FIFA World Cup winner; and 1976 European Championship runner-up.

During his 66-game managerial career, he compiled a 34–13–19 record (.723) and won the 1990 FIFA World Cup; the 1994 German Championship; and the 1996 Union of European Football Associations Cup.

Beckenbauer was one of the charter members inducted into the International Football Hall of Fame.

Franz Beckenbauer's NASL Statistics

YEAR	TEAM	G	GLS	ASST	PTS
1977	New York Cosmos	15	4	5	13
1978	New York Cosmos	27	8	16	32
1979	New York Cosmos	12	1	6	8
1980	New York Cosmos	26	4	10	18
1983	New York Cosmos	25	2	10	14
	TOTALS	105	19	47	85

Sources: International Football Hall of Fame; National Soccer Hall of Fame and Museum

Beckley, Jacob Peter "Jake" (born: August 4, 1867 in Hannibal, Missouri; died: June 25, 1918 in Kansas City, Missouri); inducted into the National Baseball Hall of Fame and Museum in 1971 as a player by the Veterans Committee; Position: First Base; Bats: Left; Throws: Left; holds the major league career record for most putouts by a first baseman.

Nicknamed "Eagle Eye," Beckley made his major league debut on June 20, 1888 with the Pittsburgh Alleghenys, and during his 20-year career, he played for the Alleghenys / Pirates (1888–1889, 1891–1896), Pittsburgh Burghers (Players' League, 1890), New York Giants (1896–1897), Cincinnati Reds (1897–1903), and the St. Louis Cardinals (1904–1907). Decades after his last game, he still holds the major league career record for most putouts by a first baseman (23,709); ranks second to Eddie Murray in games played at first base (2,376); and retired as baseball's all-time leader in triples.

The 5'10", 200-pound Beckley hit .300 or better in 13 seasons, and after retiring as a player, he became a player-manager for the Kansas City Blues (American Association, 1908–1909); managed the Bartlesville (Oklahoma) Boosters (Western Association, 1910); and served as an umpire in the Federal League (1913).

In the spring of 1890, Beckley joined numerous players and left the National League to help form the Players' League. As he hit 22 triples that season to lead the league, his old team, the Alleghenys, finished in last place. When the Players' League folded after a single season, Beckley returned to the Alleghenys in 1891.

After leaving the major leagues, he signed with the Kansas City Blues of the American Association, and played three seasons and managed the team for one. In 1910, he played briefly for Bartlesville and Topeka, and for various semi-professional and amateur teams until retiring as a player for good. He later served as an assistant coach at William Jewell College (Liberty, Missouri).

Jake Beckley's Career Statistics

YEAR	TEAM	LG	G	AB	R	H	2B	3B	HR	BB	SO	SB	AVG	SLG
1888	Pittsburgh	NL	71	283	35	97	16	3	0	7	22	20	.343	.420
1889	Pittsburgh	NL	123	522	92	157	22	10	9	29	29	11	.301	.433
1890	Pittsburgh	PL	121	517	109	168	41	20	9	42	32	19	.325	.534
1891	Pittsburgh	NL	129	535	91	156	20	20	4	44	46	17	.292	.426
1892	Pittsburgh	NL	152	603	102	151	21	19	10	31	44	40	.250	.398
1893	Pittsburgh	NL	131	497	108	161	23	19	5	54	26	24	.324	.477
1894	Pittsburgh	NL	132	534	122	184	32	19	7	43	16	20	.345	.515
1895	Pittsburgh	NL	131	536	105	174	30	20	5	24	20	19	.325	.483
1896	Pittsburgh	NL	53	213	42	51	7	6	3	22	28	8	.239	.371
1896	New York	NL	46	182	37	55	8	4	6	9	7	11	.302	.489
1897	New York	NL	17	68	8	17	2	3	1	2		2	.250	.412
1897	Cincinnati	NL	97	369	76	125	17	8	7	18		20	.339	.485
1898	Cincinnati	NL	116	458	86	137	17	13	4	28		7	.299	.419
1899	Cincinnati	NL	135	519	87	173	23	18	3	40		18	.333	.464
1900	Cincinnati	NL	138	559	99	192	26	9	2	40		22	.343	.433
1901	Cincinnati	NL	140	590	80	177	39	13	3	28		6	.300	.425

YEAR	TEAM	LG	G	AB	R	H	2B	3B	HR	BB	SO	SB	AVG	SLG
1902	Cincinnati	NL	129	532	82	176	21	7	5	34		16	.331	.425
1903	Cincinnati	NL	120	459	85	150	29	10	2	42		23	.327	.447
1904	St. Louis	NL	142	551	72	179	22	9	1	35		17	.325	.403
1905	St. Louis	NL	134	514	48	147	20	10	1	30		12	.286	.370
1906	St. Louis	NL	87	320	29	79	16	6	0	13		3	.247	.334
1907	St. Louis	NL	32	115	6	24	3	0	0	1		0	.209	.235
	TOTALS		2,376	9,476	1,601	2,930	455	246	87	616	270	335	.309	.437

Sources: Baseball-Reference.com; National Baseball Hall of Fame and Museum

Beckman, John (born: October 22, 1895 in New York, New York; died: June 22, 1968 in Miami, Florida); inducted into the Naismith Memorial Basketball Hall of Fame in 1973 as a player; considered the "Babe Ruth of Basketball."

Although he never played college basketball, Beckman was a dominant player in the early 20th century and barnstormed with numerous professional basketball teams, and it was common for him to play for several teams simultaneously. During his 27-year career (1914–1941), he played for the Kingston Colonials (New York League, 1913–1914); Bridgeport Blue Ribbons (Interstate Basketball League, 1916–1917); Philadelphia DeNeri (Eastern Basketball League, 1915–1916, 1917–1918, 1920–1921); Reading Coal Barons (Eastern Basketball League, 1916–1917); Nanticoke Nans (Pennsylvania State League, 1917–1918, 1919–1921); Danbury Hatters (Connecticut League, 1917–1918); Jersey City Skeeters (Interstate League, 1917–1918, 1919–1920); Adams (New York State League, 1919–1920); New York Treat 'em Roughs (Interstate League, 1919–1920); Brooklyn Dodgers (Interstate League, 1919–1920); Stamford Companies (Connecticut League, 1920–1921); Thompsonville Big Harts (Interstate League, 1920–1921); Trenton Royal Bengals II (Eastern League, 1920–1921); Original Celtics (Eastern League, 1918–1919, 1921–1927, 1929); Atlantic City Celtics (Eastern League, 1922–1923); Baltimore Orioles (American Basketball League, 1926–1927); Chicago Bruins (American Basketball League, 1927–1928); Detroit Cardinals (American Basketball League, 1927–1928); Metropolitan Paterson Crescents (American Basketball League, 1927–1928); Cleveland Rosenblums (American Basketball League, 1928–1930); Rochester Centrals (American Basketball League, 1928–1929); and the Fort Wayne Hoosiers (American Basketball League, 1929–1930).

Nicknamed the "Iron Man," the 5'10" Beckman was considered the "Babe Ruth of Basketball," and became the sport's premier attraction. In 1926, he became player-coach with the Baltimore Orioles of the American Basketball League, and later played with Rochester and Cleveland, before returning to the Celtics for the 1929-1930 season, staying with the team until it disbanded in 1941.

Source: Naismith Memorial Basketball Hall of Fame

Bednarik, Charles Philip "Chuck" (born: May 1, 1925 in Bethlehem, Pennsylvania); inducted into the Pro Football Hall of Fame in 1967 as a player; Position: Center-Linebacker; Uniform: #60; first college offensive lineman to win the Maxwell Award; the last two-way, 60-minute players in the NFL.

After graduating from Liberty High School (Bethlehem, Pennsylvania), Bednarik enlisted in the United States Army Air Forces during World War II and flew over 30 combat missions, eventually winning the Air Medal. Leaving the military, he attended the University of Pennsylvania (Philadelphia) from 1945 to 1949, where he was an All-American center his last two seasons and was the first offensive lineman to win the Maxwell Award (1948, college football player of the year). He led the 1947 Quakers to an undefeated season (7–0–1, with a 7–7 tie against Army) and the Chuck Bednarik Award is presented annually to the nation's best college defensive player.

He was the number one overall pick of the Philadelphia Eagles in the 1949 National Football League Draft, and would play his entire 14-year (169 games) career (1949–1962) with the team. He was selected to nine All-NFL teams (1950–1957, 1960); played in eight Pro Bowls (1950–1954, 1956–1957, 1960, was named Most Valuable Player in the 1954 game); was named the NFL's all-time center in 1969; and was selected one of the NFL's 100 Greatest Players of All Time in 1999 by *The Sporting News*. He was league's last 60-minute, two-way players (center on offense and linebacker on defense).

One of Bednarik's most famous tackles came on November 27, 1960 against New York Giants' running star Frank Gifford. It was such a devastating and jarring hit that Gifford received a concussion and did not return to the NFL until 1962. Later in the same season, he made a game-saving tackle in the team's 17–13 NFL championship win over the Green Bay Packers.

The 6'3", 233-pound Bednarik was inducted into the College Football Hall of Fame in 1969; selected to the NFL 1950s All-Decade Team; named to the All-Time 50-Year NFL Team in 1970; to the 75th Anniversary NFL Two-Way Team; and his jersey #60 was retired by the Eagles.

During his career, Bednarik intercepted 20 passes, for 268 yards and one touchdown.

Sources: College Football Hall of Fame; Pro Football Hall of Fame

Bee, Clair Francis (born: March 2, 1896 in Grafton, West Virginia; died: May 20, 1983); inducted into the Naismith Memorial Basketball Hall of Fame in 1968 as a contributor; his college basketball teams won 95 percent of their games from 1931 to 1951, including 43 in a row from 1935 to 1937.

Bee attended Grafton (West Virginia) High School (1914–1916, 1919–1920) and Massanutten Military Academy (Woodstock, Virginia, 1916–1919), where he played football, basketball, and baseball. After graduating, he continued playing the three sports and received a bachelor's degree from Waynesburg College (Pennsylvania, 1922–1925) and master's degrees from both Rider College (Lawrenceville, New Jersey, 1931) and Rutgers University (New Jersey, 1932).

He began his basketball coaching career at Rider College (1929–1931), where he compiled a 53–7 record (.883), and his 1929–1930 team scored more than 1,000 points in a season for the first time in the school's history. He then became the head coach at Long Island University (New York, 1932–1943, 1946–1951), where he compiled a 359–80 record (.818) over 18 seasons and won 43 games in a row (1935–1937). He coached LIU to two undefeated seasons (1935–1936, 1938–1939) and seven NITs, winning two NIT championships (1939, 1941). Bee also coached the LIU football team until it was disbanded in 1940.

He then left the college ranks to coach the National Basketball Association's Baltimore Bullets (1952–1955), compiling a 33–115 record (.223) over three seasons.

Bee developed the 1–3–1 defense; the three-second rule (no offensive player could remain in the free throw lane, with or without the ball, for more than three seconds); and was instrumental in the NBA adopting the 24-second shot clock. He authored or co-authored more than 50 books on basketball (primarily as part of the Chip Hilton Sports Stories); was inducted into the Madison Square Garden Hall of Fame in 1967; and was elected to the LIU Sports Hall of Fame in 1975. The Clair Bee Coach of the Year Award (first presented in 1997) is given annually to a coach who makes an outstanding contribution to the game of college basketball.

Sources: Madison Square Garden Hall of Fame; Naismith Memorial Basketball Hall of Fame

Béliveau, Jean Arthur (born: August 31, 1931 in Trois-Rivières, Quebec, Canada); inducted into the Hockey Hall of Fame in 1972 as a player; Position: Center; Uniform: #4; won 10 Stanley Cup titles; fourth player in NHL history to score 500 goals and 1,000 points.

After more than five seasons in the junior and minor leagues, the 6'3", 205-pound Béliveau played his entire 20-year National Hockey League career (1950–1971) with the Montreal Canadiens; won 10 Stanley Cup championships (1956–1960, 1965–1966, 1968–1969, 1971); and retired as the all-time leading scorer in Stanley Cup history. Beliveau's name appears on the Stanley Cup a record 17 times, including seven times as an executive for the Canadiens.

He played in 14 NHL All-Star Games; was a First-Team All-Star Center six times and a Second-Team All-Star Center four times; was the longest-serving team captain in Canadiens' history; won the 1956 Art Ross Trophy as the league's regular-season scoring leader; won the Hart Memorial Trophy twice (1956, 1964) as the NHL's Most Valuable Player; and won the Conn Smythe Trophy in 1965 as the playoff's Most Valuable Player. In 1971, he became the fourth player in NHL history to score 500 goals and 1,000 points, and his jersey number four was retired by the team the same year. In 1998, he was ranked number seven on *The Hockey News'* list of the 100 Greatest Hockey Players.

After retiring as a player, Béliveau served as a team executive and official spokesman for the Canadiens until 1993. In 1981, he was named to the selection committee of the Hockey Hall of Fame; received the Loyola Medal in 1995 (from Loyola College in Montreal) for his contributions to Canadian hockey; was made a member of the National Order of Quebec and Companion of the Order of Canada (May 6, 1998), Canada's highest civilian award; added to Canada's Walk of Fame in 2001; and was honored with his portrait on a Canadian postage stamp in 2001.

Jean Béliveau's Career Statistics

			REGULAR SEASON				PLAYOFFS			
SEASON	**TEAM**	**LEAGUE**	**GP**	**G**	**A**	**TP**	**GP**	**G**	**A**	**TP**
1946–1947	Victoriaville Panthers	QIHA	30	47	21	68				

			REGULAR SEASON				PLAYOFFS			
SEASON	**TEAM**	**LEAGUE**	**GP**	**G**	**A**	**TP**	**GP**	**G**	**A**	**TP**
1947–1948	Victoriaville Tigers	QJHL	42	46	21	67				
1948–1949	Victoriaville Tigers	QJHL	42	48	27	75	4	4	2	6
1949–1950	Quebec Citadelles	QJHL	35	36	44	80	14	22	9	31
1950–1951	Quebec Citadelles	QJHL	46	61	63	124	22	23	31	54
1950–1951	Quebec Aces	QMHL	1	2	1	3				
1950–1951	Montreal Canadiens	NHL	2	1	1	2				
1951–1952	Quebec Aces	QMHL	59	45	38	83	15	14	10	24
1951–1952	Quebec Aces	Alx-Cup	5	9	2	11				
1952–1953	Quebec Aces	QMHL	57	50	39	89	19	14	15	29
1952–1953	Montreal Canadiens	NHL	3	5	0	5				
1953–1954	Montreal Canadiens	NHL	44	13	21	34	10	2	8	10
1954–1955	Montreal Canadiens	NHL	70	37	36	73	12	6	7	13
1955–1956	Montreal Canadiens	NHL	70	47	41	88	10	12	7	19
1956–1957	Montreal Canadiens	NHL	69	33	51	84	10	6	6	12
1957–1958	Montreal Canadiens	NHL	55	27	32	59	10	4	8	12
1958–1959	Montreal Canadiens	NHL	64	45	46	91	3	1	4	5
1959–1960	Montreal Canadiens	NHL	60	34	40	74	8	5	2	7
1960–1961	Montreal Canadiens	NHL	69	32	58	90	6	0	5	5
1961–1962	Montreal Canadiens	NHL	43	18	23	41	6	2	1	3
1962–1963	Montreal Canadiens	NHL	69	18	49	67	5	2	1	3
1963–1964	Montreal Canadiens	NHL	68	28	50	78	5	2	0	2
1964–1965	Montreal Canadiens	NHL	58	20	23	43	13	8	8	16
1965–1966	Montreal Canadiens	NHL	67	29	48	77	10	5	5	10
1966–1967	Montreal Canadiens	NHL	53	12	26	38	10	6	5	11
1967–1968	Montreal Canadiens	NHL	59	31	37	68	10	7	4	11
1968–1969	Montreal Canadiens	NHL	69	33	49	82	14	5	10	15
1969–1970	Montreal Canadiens	NHL	63	19	30	49				
1970–1971	Montreal Canadiens	NHL	70	25	51	76	20	6	16	22
	NHL TOTALS		1,125	507	712	1,219	162	79	97	176

Sources: Hockey Hall of Fame; Hockey-Reference.com

Bell, DeBenneville "Bert" (born: February 25, 1895 in Philadelphia, Pennsylvania; died: October 11, 1959 in Philadelphia, Pennsylvania); inducted into the Pro Football Hall of Fame in 1963 as a League Administrator-Owner; served as NFL Commissioner from 1946 to 1959.

While his father, John, served as the attorney general of Pennsylvania and his older brother, John, Jr., served briefly as governor of Pennsylvania (1947), Bell was a co-founder of the Frankford Yellow Jackets in 1924, one of the original National Football League teams whose name would be changed to the Philadelphia Eagles in 1933. Bell was the head coach of the Eagles (1936–1940); head coach of the Pittsburgh Steelers (1941); and served as NFL commissioner from 1946 until he died in 1959.

Bell attended the University of Pennsylvania (Philadelphia) and played quarterback for the Quakers' football team. His time at the school was interrupted by World War I when he served at a Mobile Hospital Unit in France. After the war, he resumed his studies, and after graduating served as the football backfield coach at his alma mater from 1920 to 1928. He later held the same job at Temple University (Philadelphia) for two years (1930–1931) before becoming co-owner of the Eagles in 1933. The next year he married Broadway actress Frances Upton and would go on to have three children.

Bell is credited with instituting the NFL Draft in 1935, which strengthened the league but did not help his Eagles, who lost a total of almost $100,000 by 1937. Bell became the team's sole owner in 1937 and briefly co-owned the Pittsburgh Steelers (with Art Rooney) until the team was sold to Alexis Thompson. In an unusual sports move, Bell and Thompson then traded franchises with Bell now owning the Steelers and Thompson owning the Eagles. The two teams briefly merged in 1943 due to the player shortage caused by World War II, and were known as the Phil-Pitt Steagles. Following the season, Thompson dissolved the merger and Bell's Steelers would go on to merge with the Chicago Cardinals.

In 1946, Bell was selected to replace Elmer Layden as NFL commissioner and he sold his ownership in the Steelers. As commissioner, he merged the NFL with the All-America Football Conference (bringing the Baltimore Colts, the Cleveland Browns, and the San Francisco 49ers into the NFL); negotiated the league's initial television broadcast deal; recognized the viability and authority of the NFL Players Association; dealt with competition from the Canadian Football League; and supposedly coined the phrase, "On any given Sunday, any team can beat any other team."

Shortly after being named commissioner, he had to deal with a gambling scandal that had tainted the 1946 NFL Championship game, won 24–14 by the Chicago Bears over the New York Giants. Responding to the controversy, Bell led the effort to create laws in most states that made it a crime for athletes not to report a bribe attempt. He was also known to personally develop league schedules for each team in each season.

Bell suffered a fatal heart attack on October 11, 1959 at Philadelphia's Franklin Field while watching a game between the team he had co-founded (the Eagles) and a team he had briefly co-owned during World War II (the Steelers). After his death, the NFL initiated the Bert Bell Benefit Bowl (more commonly referred to as the Playoff Bowl), which was established as a post-season contest for third place in the NFL. All 10 of its games (1961–1970) were played at the Orange Bowl in Miami, Florida, until players and coaches lost interest and the Bowl was discontinued after the 1970 season.

The Bert Bell Award (first awarded to Johnny Unitas in 1959) is presented annually to the NFL Player of the Year through the Maxwell Football Club (King of Prussia, Pennsylvania), an organization founded by Bell.

Source: Pro Football Hall of Fame

Bell, James Thomas "Cool Papa" (born: May 17, 1903 in Starkville, Mississippi; died: March 7, 1991 in St. Louis, Missouri); inducted into the National Baseball Hall of Fame and Museum in 1974 as a player by the Negro Leagues Committee; Position: Center Field; Bats: Both; Throws: Left; his hitting ability and speed revolutionized the way lead-off hitters and base runners played the game.

Born James Nicholson, in 1920 Bell and his family moved to St. Louis, Missouri, where he eventually played for the all-black semi-professional Compton Hill Cubs in the city league and for the East St. Louis Cubs across the river. He made his professional debut in 1922 and during his 20-year career, Bell played mostly center field for the St. Louis Stars (1922–1931), Detroit Wolves (1932), Kansas City Monarchs (1932, 1934), Homestead Grays (1932, 1943–1946), Pittsburgh Crawfords (1933–1938), Memphis Red Sox (1942), Chicago American Giants (1942), Detroit Senators (1947), and the Kansas City Stars (1948–1950). He also played for Santo Domingo (1937) and in the Mexican League (1938–1941).

Although he began his career as a pitcher, Bell's hitting ability dictated that he become an everyday player. A star in the Negro Leagues, he had speed on the bases, was an above-average lead-off hitter, and was an excellent defensive center fielder. One of the fastest runners in the Negro Leagues, Bell's hitting ability and speed revolutionized the way lead-off hitters and base runners played the game.

Before the team was disbanded during the Depression, in ten seasons, Bell led the St. Louis Stars to three league titles (1928, 1930–1931). In 1932, he joined the Detroit Wolves (East-West League), and when the team disbanded in midseason, he moved to the Kansas City Monarchs for the remainder of the year. In 1933, Bell played winter baseball in the Mexican League; after one season, he returned to the United States and joined the Pittsburgh Crawfords (Negro National League) in 1933; and helped lead the team to the league championship in 1935.

The 5'11", 150-pound Bell stayed with the team until 1937, before joining dictator Rafael Trujillo's All-Star team in Santo Domingo. He then toured Mexico with the Tampico, Torreon, Veracruz, and Monterrey clubs, and in the 90-game 1940 season, he led the Mexican League in runs scored (119), hits (167), triples (15), home runs (12), runs-batted-in (79), and slugging percentage (.685).

Bell returned to the United States in 1942 and played for the Chicago American Giants (Negro American League) and later the Homestead Grays (Negro National League), where he was a teammate with the legendary Josh Gibson. With the Homestead Grays, he won three straight league titles (1943–1945), before ending his playing career with the semi-professional Detroit Senators in 1946.

He coached and scouted for the Monarchs in the late 1940s and worked with several future stars, including Ernie Banks, Jackie Robinson, and Elston Howard. He was added to the St. Louis Walk of Fame in 1991 and was inducted into the Mississippi Sports Hall of Fame and Museum in 1995.

In 1999, Bell was ranked 66th on *The Sporting News*' list of Baseball's Greatest Players and was nominated as a finalist for the Major League Baseball All-Century Team.

Cool Papa Bell's Career Statistics

YEAR	TEAM	G	AB	H	2B	3B	HR	BA	SB
1922	St. Louis	22	60	25	3	1	3	.417	0
1923	St. Louis	34	74	22	5	1	1	.297	0
1924	St. Louis	59	216	67	15	1	0	.310	9
1925	St. Louis	89	362	128	29	7	11	.354	24
1926	St. Louis	85	370	134	24	7	15	.362	23
1927	St. Louis	93	401	128	18	3	5	.319	13
1928	St. Louis	72	310	103	16	6	4	.332	7
1929	St. Louis	89	359	112	25	6	4	.312	28
1930	St. Louis	62	264	93	17	6	7	.352	15
1931	St. Louis	19	68	20	0	1	0	.294	0
1932	Detroit	37	138	53	7	3	2	.384	3
1933	Pittsburgh	37	137	41	6	6	1	.299	6
1934	Pittsburgh	40	153	49	0	0	0	.320	5
1935	Pittsburgh	40	157	52	7	7	1	.331	7
1936	Pittsburgh	22	86	23	1	1	0	.267	1
1942	Chicago	14	51	19	3	0	0	.373	0
1943	Homestead Grays	44	178	70	6	5	6	.393	2
1944	Homestead Grays	30	114	40	5	2	2	.351	0
1945	Homestead Grays	27	103	25	6	0	1	.243	0
1946	Homestead Grays	25	86	37	1	1	0	.430	0
	TOTALS	940	3,687	1,241	194	64	63	.337	143

Sources: Baseball-Reference.com; National Baseball Hall of Fame and Museum

Bell, Robert Lee, Jr. "Bobby" (born: June 17, 1940 in Shelby, North Carolina); inducted into the Pro Football Hall of Fame in 1983 as a player; Position: Linebacker-Defensive End; Uniform: #78; first Kansas City Chiefs player inducted into the Pro Football Hall of Fame.

After graduating from Cleveland High School (Shelby High School) as a multi-sport star and an All-State prep quarterback, Bell enrolled at the University of Minnesota (Minneapolis), where he started his college career as a quarterback. He was soon moved to tackle and earned All-American status twice while winning the Outland Trophy in 1962 as the nation's most outstanding interior lineman. During Bell's tenure at the school, the team played to a 22–6–1 record (.786) and was in two Rose Bowls (a 1961 17–7 loss to the University of Washington and a 1962 21–3 win over the University of California at Los Angeles).

After college in 1963, he was both a second-round (16th selection overall) draft choice of the National Football League's Minnesota Vikings and a seventh-round (65th pick overall) selection of the American Football League's Kansas City Chiefs. He signed with Kansas City and played his entire 12-year (168 games) career with the team (AFL, 1963–1969; NFL [1970–1974]).

The 6'4", 228-pound Bell was an AFL All-Star six straight seasons (1964–1969); selected to the first three AFC-NFC Pro Bowls (1970–1972); played on two AFL Championship teams (a 31–7 win over the Buffalo Bills in 1966 and a 17–7 win over the Oakland Raiders in 1969); won a Super Bowl championship in January 1970 (a 23–7 win over the Minnesota Vikings in Super Bowl IV, after having lost to the Green Bay Packers in the very first Super Bowl ever played); and was named to the All-AFL team in 1970.

During his career, Bell scored nine defensive touchdowns; was the first Kansas City Chiefs player elected to the Pro Football Hall of Fame; inducted into the Kansas City Chiefs Hall of Fame in 1980; inducted into the North Carolina Sports Hall of Fame in 1987; elected to the College Football Hall of Fame in 1991; and his jersey #78 was retired by the Chiefs and the University of Minnesota.

Bobby Bell's Career Statistics

			INTERCEPTIONS				FUMBLES RECOVERED		
YEAR	TEAM	G	NO	YDS	AVG	TD	NO	YDS	TD
1963	Kansas City	14	1	20	20.0	0	1	0	0
1964	Kansas City	14	1	4	4.0	0	2	11	1
1965	Kansas City	14	4	73	18.3	1	2	4	0

YEAR	TEAM	G	INTERCEPTIONS NO	YDS	AVG	TD	FUMBLES RECOVERED NO	YDS	TD
1966	Kansas City	14	2	14	7.0	0	1	7	1
1967	Kansas City	14	4	82	20.5	1	2	0	0
1968	Kansas City	14	5	95	19.0	0	2	0	0
1969	Kansas City	14	0	0	0.0	0	3	0	0
1970	Kansas City	14	3	57	19.0	1	1	0	0
1971	Kansas City	14	1	26	26.0	1	0	0	0
1972	Kansas City	14	3	56	18.7	1	1	0	0
1973	Kansas City	14	1	24	24.0	0	0	0	0
1974	Kansas City	14	1	28	28.0	1	0	0	0
	TOTALS	168	26	479	18.4	6	15	22	2

Sources: College Football Hall of Fame; Kansas City Chiefs Hall of Fame; North Carolina Sports Hall of Fame; Pro Football Hall of Fame; Pro-Football-Reference.com

Bellamy, Walter Jones "Walt" (born: July 24, 1939 in New Bern, North Carolina); inducted into the Naismith Memorial Basketball Hall of Fame in 1993 as a player; Position: Center; one of only seven players to score more than 20,000 points and have more than 14,000 rebounds.

At J.T. Barber High School (New Bern, North Carolina), Bellamy was a three-year letter winner, a two-time All-State selection, and a two-time All-Conference choice. After graduating, he attended Indiana University (Bloomington, 1959–1961), where he averaged 20.6 points-per-game; was a two-time All-Big Ten selection (1960–1961); a two-time All-American (1960–1961); named to *The Sporting News* All-America Second Team (1961); and was a member of the gold medal-winning U.S. Olympic Team (Rome, Italy, 1960).

After leaving college, the 6'11", 245-pound Bellamy was the number one overall pick in the 1961 National Basketball Association draft by the Chicago Packers. During his 13-year career (and one game of a 14th season), the much-traveled center played for the Packers (1961–1962); Chicago Zephyrs (1962–1963); Baltimore Bullets (previously the Chicago Zephyrs) (1963–1965); New York Knicks (1965–1968); Detroit Pistons (1968–1970); Atlanta Hawks (1970–1974); and the New Orleans Jazz (1974). He was named NBA Rookie of the Year (1962) and was a four-time All-Star (1962–1965). During his career, Bellamy averaged 20.2 points and 13.7 rebounds per game, and is one of only seven players to score more than 20,000 points and have more than 14,000 rebounds.

Walt Bellamy's Career Statistics

SEASON	TEAM	G	MIN	FG	FT	REB	AST	PTS
1961–1962	Chicago	79	3,344	973	549	1,500	210	2,495
1962–1963	Chicago	80	3,306	840	553	1,309	233	2,233
1963–1964	Baltimore	80	3,394	811	537	1,361	126	2,159
1964–1965	Baltimore	80	3,301	733	515	1,166	191	1,981
1965–1966	Baltimore	8	268	56	40	102	18	152
1965–1966	New York	72	3,084	639	390	1,152	217	1,668
1966–1967	New York	79	3,010	565	369	1,064	206	1,499
1967–1968	New York	82	2,695	511	350	961	164	1,372
1968–1969	New York	35	1,136	204	125	385	77	533
1968–1969	Detroit	53	2,023	359	276	716	99	994
1969–1970	Detroit	56	1,173	210	140	397	55	560
1969–1970	Atlanta	23	855	141	75	310	88	357
1970–1971	Atlanta	82	2,908	433	336	1,060	230	1,202
1971–1972	Atlanta	82	3,187	593	340	1,049	262	1,526
1972–1973	Atlanta	74	2,802	455	283	964	179	1,193
1973–1974	Atlanta	77	2,440	389	233	740	189	1,011
1974–1975	New Orleans	1	14	2	2	5	0	6
	TOTALS	1,043	38,940	7,914	5,113	14,241	2,544	20,941

Sources: Basketball-Reference.com; Naismith Memorial Basketball Hall of Fame

Belov, Sergei (born: January 23, 1944 in Nashevoko, Russia); inducted into the Naismith Memorial Basketball Hall of Fame in 1992 as a player; first European and international player inducted into the basketball hall of fame.

The 6'3", 175-pound Belov played professional basketball for Uralmash (Sverdlovsk, Russia, 1964–1967), CSKA (Central Sports Club of the Army, 1968–1980), and the Russian National Team (1967–1980). He was the first international player elected to the Naismith Memorial Basketball Hall of Fame and helped the Russian National Team win an Olympic gold medal (1972 in Munich, Germany) and three bronze medals: 1968 in Mexico City, Mexico; 1976 in Montreal, Canada; and 1980 in Moscow, Russia.

He led the Russian National Team to four European Championships (1967 in Finland, 1969 in Italy, 1971 in West Germany, and 1979 in Italy); two World championships (1967, 1974); led the Central Sports Club of the Moscow Army to 11 Russian League championships (1969–1974, 1976–1980); the Spartakiada USSR squad to two European Cup titles (1969, 1971); and was a member of the USSR's silver medal-winning William Jones Cup team (1972).

Belov is considered the greatest international player of all time and is often referred to as the "Jerry West of Russia." In 1968, he became an Honored Master of Sports of the USSR; was named an Honored Trainer of Russia (1995); and was named President of the Russian Basketball Federation (1993–1998). In 1991, Federation Internationale de Basketball Amateur named him the "Best European Player Ever" and he was inducted into the FIBA Hall of Fame in 2007.

Source: Naismith Memorial Basketball Hall of Fame

Bench, Johnny Lee (born: December 7, 1947 in Oklahoma City, Oklahoma); inducted into the National Baseball Hall of Fame and Museum in 1989 as a player; Position: Catcher; Bats: Right; Throws: Right; Uniform: #5; a pioneer of the one-handed style of catching that is prevalent in today's game; first catcher to wear a protective helmet while behind the plate; first catcher to be named National League Rookie of the Year; one of the few professional baseball players ever to be a professional bowler.

After being a star baseball and basketball player at Binger (Oklahoma) High School, the 6'1", 208-pound Bench made his major league debut on August 28, 1967. He would play his entire 17-year career with the Cincinnati Reds (1967–1983), after being a second-round draft pick (36th selection overall) in 1965. During his career, he was named the 1968 National League Rookie of the Year (the first catcher to win the award); appeared in four World Series (winning in 1975 and 1976, while losing in 1970 and 1972); 1976 World Series Most Valuable Player; was a 14-time All-Star (1968–1980, 1983); National League Most Valuable Player twice (1970, 1972); and won 10 consecutive Gold Gloves (1968–1977).

Bench also won the Lou Gehrig Award in 1975 (given to the major league baseball player who best exemplifies the character of Lou Gehrig, both on and off the field); the Babe Ruth Award in 1976 (given to the World Series Most Valuable Player); and the Hutch Award in 1981 (given to the major league ballplayer that best exemplifies the fighting spirit and competitive desire of the late Fred Hutchinson, who died of cancer in the middle of the 1964 season).

Bench was a key member of the Reds' 1975 and 1976 world championship teams known as the "Big Red Machine." He led the National League in total bases (315) in 1974; twice in home runs (1970, 1972); in RBIs three times (1970, 1972, 1974); twice in extra base hits (1970, 1974); in sacrifice flies three times (1970, 1972–1973); in intentional walks (23) in 1972; and retired as the Reds' all-time leader in home runs (389), RBIs (1,376), sacrifice flies (90), and intentional walks (135).

Although a relatively durable catcher, by 1978, his years behind the plate began taking a toll on Bench's knees, and over the last three years of his career, he played mainly third base, first base, or in the outfield while catching only 13 games. He was inducted into the Cincinnati Reds Hall of Fame in 1986 and his jersey number five was retired by the team.

In 1999, he was ranked number 16 on *The Sporting News*' list of the 100 Greatest Baseball Players (the highest-ranking catcher), and was elected to the Major League Baseball All-Century Team. Beginning in 2000, the best collegiate catcher annually receives the Johnny Bench Award. After his playing days, Bench became a television and radio broadcaster, and was one of the few professional baseball players ever to be a professional bowler.

Johnny Bench's Career Statistics

YEAR	TEAM	LG	G	AB	R	H	2B	3B	HR	RBI	BB	SO	SB	AVG	SLG
1967	Cincinnati	NL	26	86	7	14	3	1	1	6	5	19	0	.163	.256
1968	Cincinnati	NL	154	564	67	155	40	2	15	82	31	96	1	.275	.433

YEAR	TEAM	LG	G	AB	R	H	2B	3B	HR	RBI	BB	SO	SB	AVG	SLG
1969	Cincinnati	NL	148	532	83	156	23	1	26	90	49	86	6	.293	.487
1970	Cincinnati	NL	158	605	97	177	35	4	45	148	54	102	5	.293	.587
1971	Cincinnati	NL	149	562	80	134	19	2	27	61	49	83	2	.238	.423
1972	Cincinnati	NL	147	538	87	145	22	2	40	125	100	84	6	.270	.541
1973	Cincinnati	NL	152	557	83	141	17	3	25	104	83	83	4	.253	.429
1974	Cincinnati	NL	160	621	108	174	38	2	33	129	80	90	5	.280	.507
1975	Cincinnati	NL	142	530	83	150	39	1	28	110	65	108	11	.283	.519
1976	Cincinnati	NL	135	465	62	109	24	1	16	74	81	95	13	.234	.394
1977	Cincinnati	NL	142	494	67	136	34	2	31	109	58	95	2	.275	.540
1978	Cincinnati	NL	120	393	52	102	17	1	23	73	50	83	4	.260	.483
1979	Cincinnati	NL	130	464	73	128	19	0	22	80	67	73	4	.276	.459
1980	Cincinnati	NL	114	360	52	90	12	0	24	68	41	64	4	.250	.483
1981	Cincinnati	NL	52	178	14	55	8	0	8	25	17	21	0	.309	.489
1982	Cincinnati	NL	119	399	44	103	16	0	13	38	37	58	1	.258	.396
1983	Cincinnati	NL	110	310	32	79	15	2	12	54	24	38	0	.255	.432
	TOTALS		2,158	7,658	1,091	2,048	381	24	389	1,376	891	1,278	68	.267	.476

Sources: Baseball-Reference.com; Johnny Bench Web Site (www.johnnybench.com); National Baseball Hall of Fame and Museum

Bender, Charles Albert "Chief" (born: May 5, 1884 in Brainerd, Minnesota; died: May 22, 1954 in Philadelphia, Pennsylvania); inducted into the National Baseball Hall of Fame and Museum by the Veterans Committee in 1953 as a player; Position: Pitcher; Bats: Right; Throws: Right; first American Indian inducted into the baseball hall of fame.

The son of a German father and a Chippewa Indian Tribe mother, Bender grew up on a reservation and went to a church-run school in Philadelphia when he was eight years old, before leaving the reservation for good at age 13 to attend the Carlisle Indian School (Carlisle, Pennsylvania).

Making his major league debut on April 20, 1903, the 6'2", 185-pound Bender pitched 16 seasons with the Philadelphia Athletics (1903–1914), Baltimore Terrapins (Federal League, 1915), Philadelphia Phillies (1916–1917), and the Chicago White Sox (1925).

He pitched in five World Series with the Athletics (winning in 1910, 1911, and 1913, while losing in 1905 and 1914); led the American League in winning percentage three times (1910–1911, 1914); and pitched a no-hitter on May 12, 1910 in a 4–0 win against the Cleveland Naps (Indians).

Bender left baseball in 1918 to work in the shipyards during World War I, and after the war, he returned to the game to coach for the Chicago White Sox, where he would later appear in one game in 1925.

In a doubleheader on October 5, 1905 against the Washington Senators, Bender won both games; had six hits; and accumulated eight runs batted in. In a game on May 8, 1906 against the Boston Americans (Pilgrims), he hit back-to-back inside-the-park home runs. In 1930, Bender coached baseball at the Naval Academy (Annapolis, Maryland) before signing with the New York Giants as a pitching coach.

Chief Bender's Career Statistics

YEAR	TEAM	LG	W	L	PCT	G	SH	IP	H	R	ER	SO	BB	ERA
1903	Philadelphia	AL	17	14	.548	36	2	270	239	115	92	127	65	3.07
1904	Philadelphia	AL	10	11	.476	29	4	204	167	90	65	149	59	2.87
1905	Philadelphia	AL	18	11	.621	35	4	229	193	103	72	142	90	2.83
1906	Philadelphia	AL	15	10	.600	36	0	238	208	98	67	159	48	2.53
1907	Philadelphia	AL	16	8	.667	33	4	219	185	67	50	112	34	2.05
1908	Philadelphia	AL	8	9	.471	18	2	139	121	48	27	85	21	1.75
1909	Philadelphia	AL	18	8	.692	34	5	250	196	68	46	161	45	1.66
1910	Philadelphia	AL	23	5	.821	30	3	250	182	63	44	155	47	1.58

YEAR	TEAM	LG	W	L	PCT	G	SH	IP	H	R	ER	SO	BB	ERA
1911	Philadelphia	AL	17	5	.773	31	2	216	198	66	52	114	58	2.17
1912	Philadelphia	AL	13	8	.619	27	1	171	169	63	52	90	33	2.74
1913	Philadelphia	AL	21	10	.677	48	2	237	208	78	58	135	59	2.51
1914	Philadelphia	AL	17	3	.850	28	7	179	159	49	45	107	55	2.26
1915	Baltimore	FL	4	16	.200	26	0	178	198	103	79	89	37	3.99
1916	Philadelphia	NL	7	7	.500	27	0	123	137	71	51	43	34	3.73
1917	Philadelphia	NL	8	2	.800	20	4	113	84	24	21	43	26	1.67
1925	Chicago	AL	0	0	.000	1	0	1	1	2	2	0	1	18.00
	TOTALS		212	127	.625	459	40	3,017	2,645	1,108	823	1,711	712	2.46

Sources: Baseball-Reference.com; National Baseball Hall of Fame and Museum

Benedict, Clinton S. "Benny" (born: September 25, 1894 in Ottawa, Ontario, Canada; died: November 12, 1976 in Ottawa, Ontario, Canada); inducted into the Hockey Hall of Fame in 1965 as a player; Position: Goalie; first goalie to win the Stanley Cup championship with two different NHL teams.

Benedict played professional hockey for 18 seasons (1912–1930) and spent most of 13 National Hockey League seasons split between the Ottawa Senators and the Montreal Maroons. He played amateur hockey for several seasons before turning professional with the NHL's Ottawa Senators for five seasons in the National Hockey Association (1912–1917), leading the team to a 1915 Stanley Cup challenge, eventually losing to the Vancouver Millionaires.

He was with the squad when the Senators became one of the founding teams of the National Hockey League (1917–1918), and on February 25, 1918, he recorded the second shutout in NHL history, an 8–0 win over the Montreal Canadiens.

For six of the seven seasons he was with Ottawa, Benedict led the NHL in wins; helped the franchise win three Stanley Cups in four seasons (1920–1921, 1923); and went on to win another title with the Montreal Maroons in 1926, becoming the first goalie to win the Stanley Cup with two different teams. In the 1919–1920 season, his 2.66 goals-against mark was 2.13 goals better than the league average, a defensive statistic that has never been equaled.

In 1924, he was sent to the Montreal Maroons; he won the Mappin Trophy in 1925 as the team's top player; and compiled four shutouts when Montreal won the Stanley Cup in 1926.

After retiring from the NHL, Benedict coached the Saint John Beavers of the Maritime Senior Hockey League, and in 1998, he was ranked number 77 on *The Hockey News*' list of the 100 Greatest Hockey Players.

Clinton Benedict's Career Statistics

			REGULAR SEASON						PLAYOFFS					
SEASON	TEAM	LEAGUE	GP	W	L	T	SO	AVG	GP	W	L	T	SO	AVG
1909–1910	Ottawa Stewartons	OCHL	7	5	2	0	0	3.00	1	0	1	0	0	2.00
1910–1911	Ottawa New Edinburghs	IPAHU	5	5	0	0	0	3.60	3	3	0	0	0	4.25
1910–1911	Ottawa New Edinburghs	OCHL	6	2	3	1	0	4.00						
1911–1912	Ottawa New Edinburghs	IPAHU	11	11	0	0	0	3.11	4	3	1	0	0	4.56
1912–1913	Ottawa Senators	NHA	10	7	2	1	1	3.49						
1913–1914	Ottawa Senators	NHA	9	5	3	0	0	3.67						
1914–1915	Ottawa Senators	NHA	20	14	6	0	0	3.14	2	1	1	0	1	0.50
1914–1915	Ottawa Senators	St-Cup							3	0	3	0	0	8.67
1915–1916	Ottawa Senators	NHA	24	13	11	0	1	2.99						
1916–1917	Ottawa Senators	NHA	18	14	4	0	1	2.72	2	1	1	0	0	3.50
1917–1918	Ottawa Senators	NHL	22	9	13	0	1	5.12						
1918–1919	Ottawa Senators	NHL	18	12	6	0	2	2.76	5	1	4	0	0	5.20
1919–1920	Ottawa Senators	NHL	24	19	5	0	5	2.66						
1919–1920	Ottawa Senators	St-Cup							5	3	2		1	2.20
1920–1921	Ottawa Senators	NHL	24	14	10	0	2	3.08	2	2	0	0	2	0.00
1920–1921	Ottawa Senators	St-Cup							5	3	2	0	0	2.40

			REGULAR SEASON						PLAYOFFS					
SEASON	TEAM	LEAGUE	GP	W	L	T	SO	AVG	GP	W	L	T	SO	AVG
1921–1922	Ottawa Senators	NHL	24	14	8	2	2	3.34	2	0	1	1	1	2.50
1922–1923	Ottawa Senators	NHL	24	14	9	1	4	2.18	2	1	1	0	1	1.00
1922–1923	Ottawa Senators	St-Cup							6	5	1	0	1	1.33
1923–1924	Ottawa Senators	NHL	22	15	7	0	3	1.99	2	0	2	0	0	2.50
1924–1925	Montreal Maroons	NHL	30	9	19	2	2	2.12						
1925–1926	Montreal Maroons	NHL	36	20	11	5	6	1.91	4	2	0	2	1	1.25
1925–1926	Montreal Maroons	St-Cup							4	3	1	0	3	0.75
1926–1927	Montreal Maroons	NHL	43	20	19	4	13	1.42	2	0	1	1	0	0.91
1927–1928	Montreal Maroons	NHL	44	24	14	6	7	1.70	9	5	3	1	4	0.86
1928–1929	Montreal Maroons	NHL	37	14	16	7	11	1.49						
1929–1930	Montreal Maroons	NHL	14	6	6	1	0	3.03						
1930–1931	Windsor Bulldogs	IHL	40	20	15	5	1	2.23						
	NHL TOTALS		362	190	143	28	58	2.32	28	11	12	5	9	1.86

Sources: Hockey Hall of Fame; Hockey-Reference.com

Bentley, Douglas Wagner "Doug" (born: September 3, 1916 in Delisle, Saskatchewan, Canada; died: November 24, 1972 in Saskatoon, Saskatchewan, Canada); inducted into the Hockey Hall of Fame in 1964 as a player; Position: Left Wing; in 1950, voted by the *Herald-American* as the top hockey player in Chicago for the first half of the century.

Bentley's 30-year hockey career began with the Delisle Tigers as a player and finished as a coach in the Western Hockey League. While most of his career was spent in the minors, he played in the National Hockey League for 13 seasons (1939–1954), beginning with the Chicago Black Hawks in 1939. Although relatively small (5'8", 145 pounds), six times in his career, Bentley scored 20 or more goals in a season, and in 1942–1943, he led the NHL in total points even though the Black Hawks did not qualify for the playoffs. During the season, the Bentley brothers (Douglas, Max [a fellow hall of famer], and Reggie) made history by being the first three brothers to play on the same team as a complete forward line.

At the start of the 1944–1945 season, the Hawks traveled to Canada to play an exhibition game. Upon the team's return to Chicago, Bentley was banned by Canadian officials from leaving the country and spent the entire season playing senior hockey for the Laura Beavers. He was eventually allowed to return to the United States the next year and resumed playing with the Black Hawks.

During his career, Bentley was selected First All-Star Team Left Wing three times (1943–1944, 1947); Second All-Star Team Center (1949); and won the Art Ross Trophy (as the league's regular-season scoring leader) in 1943. In 1950, he was voted by the *Herald-American* as the top hockey player in Chicago for the first half of the century.

Doug Bentley's Career Statistics

			REGULAR SEASON					PLAYOFFS				
SEASON	TEAM	LEAGUE	GP	G	A	TP	PIM	GP	G	A	TP	PIM
1932–1933	Delisle Tigers	SIHA										
1932–1933	Delisle Tigers	Al-Cup	2	0	0	0	0					
1933–1934	Saskatoon Wesleys	N-SJHL	4	3	3	6	0	9	3	1	4	8
1934–1935	Regina Victorias	S-SSHL	19	10	4	14	21	6	0	0	0	13
1935–1936	Moose Jaw Millers	S-SSHL	20	3	3	6	30					
1936–1937	Moose Jaw Millers	S-SSHL	24	18	19	37	49	3	3	0	3	4
1937–1938	Moose Jaw Millers	S-SSHL	21	25	18	43	20	6	6	8	14	6
1937–1938	Moose Jaw Millers	Al-Cup	4	3	2	5	8					
1938–1939	Drumheller Miners	ASHL	32	24	29	53	31	6	7	0	7	6
1939–1940	Chicago Black Hawks	NHL	39	12	7	19	12	2	0	0	0	0
1940–1941	Chicago Black Hawks	NHL	47	8	20	28	12	5	1	1	2	4
1941–1942	Chicago Black Hawks	NHL	38	12	14	26	11	3	0	1	1	4
1942–1943	Chicago Black Hawks	NHL	50	33	40	73	18					
1942–1943	San Diego Skyhawks	Exhib.										
1943–1944	Chicago Black Hawks	NHL	50	38	39	77	22	9	8	4	12	4
1944–1945	Laura Beavers	SIHA										
1945–1946	Chicago Black Hawks	NHL	36	19	21	40	16	4	0	2	2	0

SEASON	TEAM	LEAGUE	REGULAR SEASON GP	G	A	TP	PIM	PLAYOFFS GP	G	A	TP	PIM
1946–1947	Chicago Black Hawks	NHL	52	21	34	55	18					
1947–1948	Chicago Black Hawks	NHL	60	20	37	57	16					
1948–1949	Chicago Black Hawks	NHL	58	23	43	66	38					
1949–1950	Chicago Black Hawks	NHL	64	20	33	53	28					
1950–1951	Chicago Black Hawks	NHL	44	9	23	32	20					
1951–1952	Chicago Black Hawks	NHL	8	2	3	5	4					
1951–1952	Saskatoon Quakers	PCHL	35	11	14	25	12	13	6	6	12	4
1952–1953	Saskatoon Quakers	WHL	70	22	23	45	37	13	6	3	9	14
1953–1954	New York Rangers	NHL	20	2	10	12	2					
1953–1954	Saskatoon Quakers	WHL	42	8	13	21	18					
1954–1955	Saskatoon Quakers	WHL	61	14	23	37	52					
1955–1956	Saskatoon/Brandon	WHL	60	7	26	33	21					
1957–1958	Saskatoon/St. Paul Saints	WHL	19	11	16	27	0					
1958–1959	Saskatoon Quakers	WHL										
1959–1960	Saskatoon Quakers	WHL										
1960–1961	Saskatoon Quakers	WHL										
1961–1962	Los Angeles Blades	WHL	8	0	2	2	2					
	NHL TOTALS		566	219	324	543	217	23	9	8	17	12

Sources: Hockey Hall of Fame; Hockey-Reference.com

Bentley, Maxwell Herbert Lloyd "Max" (born: March 1, 1920 in Delisle, Saskatchewan, Canada; died: January 19, 1984 in Saskatchewan, Canada); inducted into the Hockey Hall of Fame in 1966 as a player; Position: Forward; led the Toronto Maple Leafs to three Stanley Cup titles in four seasons.

The 5'9", 158-pound Max Bentley was the youngest of the three brothers who played in the National Hockey League (along with fellow hall-of-famer Doug and Reggie), and went on to play 12 NHL seasons from 1940 to 1954. After several seasons in amateur hockey, the Chicago Black Hawks signed Bentley in 1940 and sent him to the Kansas City Americans of the American Hockey Association to develop his skills. However, injuries to the parent club forced Chicago to recall him after only five games.

In 1943, Bentley won the Lady Byng Trophy (for sportsmanship and gentlemanly conduct), and during the 1942–1943 season, the Bentley brothers (Douglas, Max, Reggie) made history by being the first three brothers to play on the same team as a complete forward line.

He won back-to-back Art Ross Trophies (as the league's regular-season scoring leader) in 1946 and 1947; a Hart Memorial Trophy as the NHL's Most Valuable Player in 1946; was named First-Team All-Star Center in 1946; and selected Second-Team All-Star Center in 1947. After being traded to the Toronto Maple Leafs in November 1947, he helped the team win three Stanley Cup titles in four seasons (1948–1949, 1951).

After injuries limited his playing time to only 36 games in the 1952–1953 season, Bentley was traded to the New York Rangers before he retired in 1954. When he retired, he had scored 245 goals and was second among active players only to Maurice Richard.

Max Bentley's Career Statistics

SEASON	TEAM	LEAGUE	REGULAR SEASON GP	G	A	TP	PIM	PLAYOFFS GP	G	A	TP	PIM
1935–1936	Rosetown Red Wings	SIHA										
1937–1938	Drumheller Miners	ASHL	26	28	15	43	10	5	7	1	8	2
1938–1939	Drumheller Miners	ASHL	32	29	24	53	16	6	5	3	8	6
1939–1940	Saskatoon Quakers	SSHL	31	37	14	51	4	4	1	1	2	2
1940–1941	Providence Reds	AHL	9	4	2	6	0					
1940–1941	Kansas City Americans	AHA	5	5	5	10	0					
1940–1941	Chicago Black Hawks	NHL	36	7	10	17	6	4	1	3	4	2
1941–1942	Chicago Black Hawks	NHL	39	13	17	30	2	3	2	0	2	0
1942–1943	Chicago Black Hawks	NHL	47	26	44	70	2					
1942–1943	Victoria Navy	NNDHL										

SEASON	TEAM	LEAGUE	REGULAR SEASON GP	G	A	TP	PIM	PLAYOFFS GP	G	A	TP	PIM
1942–1943	San Diego Skyhawks	Exhib.										
1943–1944	Calgary Currie Army	CNDHL	15	18	13	31	26	2	3	4	7	0
1944–1945	Calgary Currie Army	CNDHL	12	14	14	28	24	3	3	2	5	0
1945–1946	Chicago Black Hawks	NHL	47	31	30	61	6	4	1	0	1	4
1946–1947	Chicago Black Hawks	NHL	60	29	43	72	12					
1947–1948	Chicago Black Hawks	NHL	6	3	3	6	4					
1947–1948	Toronto Maple Leafs	NHL	53	23	25	48	10	9	4	7	11	0
1948–1949	Toronto Maple Leafs	NHL	60	19	22	41	18	9	4	3	7	2
1949–1950	Toronto Maple Leafs	NHL	69	23	18	41	14	7	3	3	6	0
1950–1951	Toronto Maple Leafs	NHL	67	21	41	62	34	11	2	11	13	4
1951–1952	Toronto Maple Leafs	NHL	69	24	17	41	40	4	1	0	1	2
1952–1953	Toronto Maple Leafs	NHL	36	12	11	23	16					
1953–1954	New York Rangers	NHL	57	14	18	32	15					
1954–1955	Saskatoon Quakers	WHL	40	24	17	41	23					
1955–1956	Saskatoon Quakers	WHL	10	2	2	4	20					
1956–1957	Saskatoon Quakers	SJHL										
1957–1958	Saskatoon Quakers	SJHL										
1958–1959	Saskatoon Quakers	WHL	26	6	12	18	2					
	NHL TOTALS		646	245	299	544	179	51	18	27	45	14

Sources: Hockey Hall of Fame; Hockey-Reference.com

Berling, Clay (born: November 25, 1930 in San Francisco, California); inducted into the National Soccer Hall of Fame and Museum in 1995 as a builder; founder and original publisher of *Soccer West*, renamed *Soccer America* in 1972.

Berling founded and served as president of the Two County Youth Soccer League in the San Francisco East Bay Area in 1967, and watched as the league grew from four to 30 teams in two years. In 1969, he helped create the California Youth Soccer Association, and in 1971 started a weekly newsletter called *Soccer West*. In 1972, when its focus expanded beyond the Bay Area, *Soccer West* was renamed *Soccer America*, and is still being published.

He also created and served as commissioner of the NorCal (Northern California) Soccer League (a semi-professional summer league), and served as vice-president and treasurer of the California Youth Soccer Association North from 1972 to 1977. In 1982, he was inducted into the California Youth Soccer Association Hall of Fame, and one year later was named Honorary All-American by the National Soccer Coaches Association of America.

In 1989, Berling became a member of the World Cup USA 1994 Founders Committee; in 1990, he received the Soccer Industry Council of America's Simon Sherman Industry Service Award; and from 1991 to 1994, he served on the World Cup San Francisco Bay Organizing Committee. As of this writing, Berling is Chairman of the Board of *Soccer America*, while his daughter serves as president and publisher of the magazine.

Sources: July 2006 issue of *Soccer America* magazine; National Soccer Hall of Fame and Museum

Bernabei, Raymond (born: November 26, 1925 in Indianola, Pennsylvania); inducted into the National Soccer Hall of Fame and Museum in 1978 as a player; Position: Full Back; an 11-time All-Star and inductee into the Western Pennsylvania Soccer Hall of Fame.

After being the leading scorer for the Indianola Indians, Bernabei played for the amateur Harmarville Hurricanes (Pittsburgh, Pennsylvania) from 1949 to 1963, and helped the squad win two National Open Cups (1952, 1956). He played in 10 West Penn finals and was named to 11 All-Star teams between 1949 and 1960.

In addition to playing the game, he also refereed at the high school, college, and professional levels for more than 40 years, including at two NCAA finals; served as president and executive director of the National Intercollegiate Soccer Officials Association; received the NISOA Honor Award in 1975; and was inducted into the Western Pennsylvania Soccer Hall of Fame.

Source: National Soccer Hall of Fame and Museum

Berra, Lawrence Peter "Yogi" (born: May 12, 1925 in St. Louis, Missouri); inducted into the National Baseball Hall of Fame and Museum in 1972 as a player; Position: Catcher; Bats: Left; Throws: Right; Uniform: #8; one of only four players to be named the Most Valuable Player of the American League three times; one of only six managers to lead both American and National League teams to the World Series.

Making his major league debut on September 22, 1946, the 5’7”, 185-pound Berra played 19 seasons for the New York Yankees (1946–1963) and four games with the New York Mets (1965). After his playing career ended, he would go on to manage the teams he had played for, the Yankees (1964, 1984–1985) and the New York Mets (1972–1975).

As a player, he appeared in 14 World Series (winning in 1947, 1949–1953, 1956, 1958, 1961–1962, and losing in 1955, 1957, 1960, and 1963). As a manager, he lost the 1964 World Series to the St. Louis Cardinals and won the 1973 National League Championship Series, before losing the World Series that season to the Oakland Athletics. During his career, Berra was named to 15 consecutive All-Star teams (1948–1962); American League Most Valuable Player three times (1951, 1954–1955); had more than 100 runs batted in four years in a row (1953–1956); caught Don Larsen’s perfect game in the 1956 World Series, the only one ever thrown in postseason play; and had his jersey number eight retired by the team in 1972.

Because he played on powerhouse Yankee teams, he was able to play in numerous World Series and set Series records for most games by a catcher (63); most hits (71); most times on a winning team (10); first in at bats; and first in doubles. He also hit the first pinch hit home run in World Series history (1947).

He received his nickname “Yogi” from a childhood friend, and years later, the Hanna-Barbera cartoon character Yogi Bear was named after him.

Although an undeniable baseball star, to most of today’s fans Berra is more well-known for his tendency to abuse the English language. So well-known are his “Yogiisms,” some of which are used in current AFLAC insurance commercials by Berra himself, that his legend lives on almost 50 years after he ended his playing career. Some of these “Yogiisms” include: “I never said half the things I really said”; “It ain’t over till it’s over”; “It’s like déjà vu all over again”; “When you get to a fork in the road, take it”; “Nobody goes there anymore, it's too crowded”; “We have a good time together, even when we’re not together”; “Slump? I ain’t in no slump. I just ain’t hitting”; “A nickel ain’t worth a dime anymore”; “If you don’t know where you’re going, you’ll wind up somewhere else”; and “Ninety percent of this game is mental, and the other half is physical.”

When signed by the Yankees, Berra was sent to the Norfolk Tars of the Class B Piedmont League, before his baseball career was interrupted by World War II, during which he served at the Normandy (France) invasion on D-Day at Omaha Beach (June 6, 1944). After later serving in North Africa and Italy, Berra returned to the United States after the war and resumed his baseball career with the Yankees’ New London (Connecticut) team, and was promoted to the Newark Bears of the AAA International League in 1946. At the end of the season, he was called up to the Yankees and never played in the minor leagues again.

Although Berra had an undisciplined swing, he rarely struck out and had only 12 strikeouts in 590 at-bats during the 1950 season. Early in his career, he gained a reputation as a talker behind the plate, a tactic used to distract the batter.

After his playing days, he was named the manager of the Yankees in 1964; won the American League pennant his rookie season; but was fired after losing to the St. Louis Cardinals in a seven-game World Series.

After leaving the Yankees, he joined the New York Mets as a player-coach and was named manager of the team after Gil Hodges died in 1971. In 1973, Berra led the team to the World Series, eventually losing to the Oakland Athletics in seven games. After leaving the Mets in 1975, he returned to the Yankees in 1976 as a coach, and was named the team’s manager in 1984, only to be fired 22 games into the 1985 season. In 1986, he joined the Houston Astros as a coach, where he stayed until retiring from baseball in 1992.

In 1972, while a manager with the Mets, he was elected to the National Baseball Hall of Fame and Museum; in 1999, he was ranked number 40 on *The Sporting News*’ list of the 100 Greatest Baseball Players; fan voting elected him to the Major League Baseball All-Century Team; he has been inducted into the St. Louis Walk of Fame; and received the Silver Buffalo Award, the Boy Scouts of America’s highest adult award.

On October 2, 1947, he became the first player to pinch hit a home run in World Series history (off the Brooklyn Dodgers’ Ralph Branca in the seventh inning); on September 26, 1954, he played his only major league game at third base; on October 5, 1956, he became the only player in World Series history to hit a grand slam in a losing cause; and on May 10, 1959, Berra set a new major league record for consecutive errorless games by a catcher (148).

Yogi Berra’s Career Statistics

YEAR	TEAM	LG	G	AB	R	H	2B	3B	HR	RBI	BB	SO	SB	AVG	SLG
1946	New York	AL	7	22	3	8	1	0	2	4	1	1	0	.364	.682
1947	New York	AL	83	293	41	82	15	3	11	54	13	12	0	.280	.464
1948	New York	AL	125	469	70	143	24	10	14	98	25	24	3	.305	.488

YEAR	TEAM	LG	G	AB	R	H	2B	3B	HR	RBI	BB	SO	SB	AVG	SLG
1949	New York	AL	116	415	59	115	20	2	20	91	22	25	2	.277	.480
1950	New York	AL	151	597	116	192	30	6	28	124	55	12	4	.322	.533
1951	New York	AL	141	547	92	161	19	4	27	88	44	20	5	.294	.492
1952	New York	AL	142	534	97	146	17	1	30	98	66	24	2	.273	.478
1953	New York	AL	137	503	80	149	23	5	27	108	50	32	0	.296	.523
1954	New York	AL	151	584	88	179	28	6	22	125	56	29	0	.307	.488
1955	New York	AL	147	541	84	147	20	3	27	108	60	20	1	.272	.470
1956	New York	AL	140	521	93	155	29	2	30	105	65	29	3	.298	.534
1957	New York	AL	134	482	74	121	14	2	24	82	57	25	1	.251	.438
1958	New York	AL	122	433	60	115	17	3	22	90	35	35	3	.266	.471
1959	New York	AL	131	472	64	134	25	1	19	69	43	38	1	.284	.462
1960	New York	AL	120	359	46	99	14	1	15	62	38	23	2	.276	.446
1961	New York	AL	119	395	62	107	11	0	22	61	35	28	2	.271	.466
1962	New York	AL	86	232	25	52	8	0	10	35	24	18	0	.224	.388
1963	New York	AL	64	147	20	43	6	0	8	28	15	17	1	.293	.497
1965	New York	NL	4	9	1	2	0	0	0	0	0	3	0	.222	.222
	TOTALS		2,120	7,555	1,175	2,150	321	49	358	1,430	704	415	30	.285	.482

Yogi Berra's Managerial Record

YEAR	TEAM	LG	W	L	WIN%	FINISH
1964	New York	AL	99	63	.611	1
1972	New York	NL	83	73	.532	3
1973	New York	NL	82	79	.509	1
1974	New York	NL	71	91	.438	5
1975	New York	NL	56	53	.514	3
1984	New York	AL	87	75	.537	3
1985	New York	AL	6	10	.375	2
	New York	AL	192	148	.565	
	New York	NL	292	296	.497	
	TOTALS		484	444	.522	

Sources: Baseball-Reference.com; National Baseball Hall of Fame and Museum; *Ten Rings: My Championship Seasons* (Yogi Berra with Dave Kaplan); Yogi Berra Web Site (www.yogiberra.com)

Berry, Raymond Emmett (born: February 27, 1933 in Corpus Christi, Texas); inducted into the Pro Football Hall of Fame in 1973 as a player; Position: End; Uniform: #82; a 20th-round draft pick who helped the Baltimore Colts win back-to-back NFL championships; as a coach, he led the New England Patriots to become the first team in NFL history ever to advance to the Super Bowl by winning three games on the road.

Although the team was coached by his father, Berry did not become a starter on the Paris (Texas) High School football team until his senior year. After graduation, he briefly attended Schreiner University (Kerrville, Texas) before transferring to Southern Methodist University (Dallas, Texas), where he would catch only 33 passes (for one touchdown) in three years with the team.

With an unremarkable college career, and for reasons that have never been made clear, the National Football League's Baltimore Colts selected the unknown 6'2", 187-pound Berry as a "future choice" in the 20th round (232nd pick overall) of the 1954 National Football League draft. As a no-name draft choice, he surprised everyone by making the Colts' practice squad and eventually became the team's starting end in 1957. He made the most of his implausible opportunity by leading the league in reception yards (800) on 47 catches, scoring six touchdowns. The next season, the Colts won the NFL championship as Berry had 56 receptions, with nine touchdowns and 794 yards, and he helped the team repeat as league champions in 1959.

Playing his entire 13-year career with the Colts (1955–1967), Berry was an All-NFL selection three times (1958–1960); named to six Pro Bowls (1958–1961, 1963–1964); and set the NFL title-game record (since surpassed) with 12 catches for 178 yards and one touchdown in the Colts' 23–17 1958 overtime win over the New York Giants.

While having productive seasons in 1959 and 1960, Berry underwent knee surgery that affected the rest of his career as his offensive numbers began to wane.

After retiring as a player, he became head coach of the New England Patriots in 1984; led the squad into the playoffs as a wild card team in his second season; and New England was the first franchise in NFL history ever to advance to the Super Bowl by winning three games on the road. The team's season ended with a thud when the Patriots lost to the Chicago Bears 46–10 in Super Bowl XX (January 1986), at the time the most lopsided defeat in Super Bowl history.

Berry resigned after the 1989 season, compiling an overall 51–41 (.554) record. His jersey number 82 was retired by the Colts; he was named to the NFL 1950s All-Decade Team; and he was selected to the NFL 75th Anniversary All-Time Team.

Raymond Berry's Career Statistics

YEAR	TEAM	G	NO	YDS	AVG	TD
1955	Baltimore	12	13	205	15.8	0
1956	Baltimore	12	37	601	16.2	2
1957	Baltimore	12	47	800	17.0	6
1958	Baltimore	12	56	794	14.2	9
1959	Baltimore	12	66	959	14.5	14
1960	Baltimore	12	74	1,298	17.5	10
1961	Baltimore	12	75	873	11.6	0
1962	Baltimore	14	51	687	13.5	3
1963	Baltimore	9	44	703	16.0	3
1964	Baltimore	12	43	663	15.4	6
1965	Baltimore	14	58	739	12.7	7
1966	Baltimore	14	56	786	14.0	7
1967	Baltimore	7	11	167	15.2	1
	TOTALS	154	631	9,275	14.7	68

Raymond Berry's Coaching Record

			REGULAR SEASON			POSTSEASON		
YEAR	TEAM	LG	W	L	Win%	W	L	Win%
1984	New England	NFL	4	4	.500			
1985	New England	NFL	11	5	.688	3	1	.750
1986	New England	NFL	11	5	.688	0	1	.000
1987	New England	NFL	8	7	.533			
1988	New England	NFL	9	7	.563			
1989	New England	NFL	5	11	.313			
	TOTALS		48	39	.552	3	2	.600

Sources: Pro Football Hall of Fame; Pro-Football-Reference.com

Best, John O. (born: April 10, 1912 in England; died: January 8, 1996 in Harbor City, California); inducted into the National Soccer Hall of Fame and Museum in 1982 as a builder; first U.S.-based referee to receive FIFA's "Special Award" for service in at least 20 international matches.

Best came to the United States in 1929 and played on numerous amateur teams in the Chicago, Illinois area from 1930 to 1936 before becoming a referee. He was the first Fédération Internationale de Football Association-certified referee from California; he served from 1948 to 1963; was a linesman at the 1948 Olympic Games (London, England); and served as a referee at the 1955 Pan American Games (Mexico).

Best officiated in numerous leagues around the world and was the first U.S.-based referee to receive FIFA's "Special Award" for service in at least 20 international matches and in various administrative functions.

In 1962, he was named Commissioner of the California Soccer Association-South; was instrumental in getting the California Soccer Association affiliated with the United States Soccer Football Association; and later served as vice-president of the USSFA twice (1967–1974, 1976–1979). Best won the Eddie Pearson Award in 1987 for his long-time contributions to the national referee development program, and recipients of the John O. Best Leadership and Service Award are selected for their leadership and service to the game of soccer.

Source: National Soccer Hall of Fame and Museum

Bethea, Elvin Lamont (born: March 1, 1946 in Trenton, New Jersey); inducted into the Pro Football Hall of Fame in 2003 as a player; Position: Defensive End; Uniform: #65; first player from North Carolina Agricultural and Technical State University to be inducted into the football hall of fame.

After graduating from Trenton (New Jersey) Central High School, the 6'2", 260-pound Bethea attended North Carolina Agricultural and Technical State University (Greensboro, North Carolina), where he played offensive guard and linebacker, and was named a *Pittsburgh Courier* All-American three years in a row. He was the first player from the school ever to be elected into the Pro Football Hall of Fame. At the end of his college career, he was a 1968 third-round draft pick (77th selection overall) of the American Football League's Houston Oilers, and would go on to play his entire 16-year career (1968–1983) with the team (1968–1969 in the AFL and 1970–1983 in the National Football League).

When he retired, Bethea held team records for most seasons played (16), most career regular-season games played (210), and most consecutive regular-season games played (135). Although not an official NFL statistic until 1982, his 105 career sacks total still ranks as the team's best, as does his single-season sack record of 16 (1973). Bethea was selected to eight Pro Bowls (1970, 1972–1976, 1979–1980); was All-AFL/AFC six times; All-AFL Second Team once (1969); and All-Pro Second Team four times (1973, 1975, 1978–1979).

His jersey number 65 was retired by the Oilers and he helped lead the team to back-to-back AFC championship games (1978–1979), eventually losing both times to the Pittsburgh Steelers.

Source: Pro Football Hall of Fame

Biasone, Danny (born: February 22, 1909 in Miglianico, Abruzzoi, Italy; died: May 25, 1992); inducted into the Naismith Memorial Basketball Hall of Fame in 2000 as a contributor; known as the "Father of the 24-Second Clock."

After moving to the United States as a boy, Biasone played basketball at Blodgett Vocational High School (Syracuse, New York), graduating in 1928. He was the founder and president of the Syracuse Nationals (now known as the Philadelphia 76ers) from 1946 to 1963, and led the team to the National Basketball Association Finals twice (1950, 1954), before finally winning the franchise's first title in 1955.

Although Biasone may not be well-known to the casual fan of the game, he is considered the "Father of the 24-Second Clock," which he introduced during the 1954–1955 NBA season. This innovation is credited with speeding up the game and increasing scoring as players were forced to shoot more often. The clock was later adopted at the college level (extended to 45 seconds) and is now used in international competition (30 seconds). Although he did not originate the idea of a shot clock, he strongly supported its adoption in professional basketball, and established the clock timing at 24 seconds, based on mathematical calculations he made after analyzing numerous games.

The impact of the 24-second clock was immediate. In the previous season, each NBA team averaged 79.5 points a game, while in the first year the clock was introduced, team scoring increased to 93.1 points a game.

Biasone won the John Bunn Award in 1982, which is presented annually by the Naismith Memorial Basketball Hall of Fame's Board of Trustees to an international or national figure who has contributed greatly to the game of basketball.

Source: Naismith Memorial Basketball Hall of Fame

Bickell, John Paris (born: September 26, 1884 in Toronto, Ontario, Canada; died: August 22, 1951 in New York, New York); inducted into the Hockey Hall of Fame in 1978 as a builder; a driving force behind the construction of the Maple Leaf Gardens.

A Toronto businessman, Bickell was a major supporter and financial contributor to professional hockey in his hometown and helped get the Maple Leaf Gardens arena built.

A successful mining executive, by the relatively young age of 23, he had started his own brokerage.

He became involved with hockey through his friend, Charlie Querrie, who was the managing director of the Toronto St. Pats (now known as the Maple Leafs), who eventually convinced Bickell to invest $25,000 to give the team financial stability. When Conn Smythe became the team's owner in 1927, he convinced Bickell to continue his financial support. In 1931, right in the middle of the Great Depression, Smythe began the construction of the Maple Leaf Gardens, and later acknowledged that the building would never have happened if not for Bickell's personal investment and his convincing others to provide money to the project.

When the arena was complete, Smythe appointed Bickell the first president of the Gardens, and later Chairman of the Board. With Bickell overseeing the Gardens and the team, the Maple Leafs won seven Stanley Cup championships between 1932 and 1951 (1932, 1942, 1945, 1947–1949, 1951).

He has been inducted into the Canadian Mining Hall of Fame.

Sources: Canadian Mining Hall of Fame; Hockey Hall of Fame

Bidwill, Charles W., Sr. (born: September 16, 1895 in Chicago, Illinois; died: April 19, 1947); inducted into the Pro Football Hall of Fame in 1967 as an owner-administrator; an early NFL executive who helped the league survive the Great Depression.

Bidwill purchased the Chicago Cardinals (now known as the Arizona Cardinals) in 1933, and his financial resources helped the National Football League survive the Great Depression, although he never had a profitable season with his Cardinals. He was the team's owner for 14 years (1933–1946), and months after he died, the franchise won its first NFL championship in 1947 (a 28–21 win over the Philadelphia Eagles).

A successful businessman in Chicago, Bidwill was vice-president of the Chicago Bears, before buying the Cardinals in 1933. When World War II depleted his team's roster, the Cardinals merged with the Pittsburgh Steelers for the 1944 NFL season (becoming known as Card-Pitt), finishing last with an 0–10 record.

Source: Pro Football Hall of Fame

Biletnikoff, Frederick S. "Fred" (born: February 23, 1943 in Erie, Pennsylvania); inducted into the Pro Football Hall of Fame in 1988 as a player; Position: Wide Receiver; Florida State University's very first football All-American selection.

Biletnikoff was a Florida State University (Tallahassee) All-American and caught four touchdown passes in the team's 36–19 Gator Bowl win over Oklahoma (January 2, 1965); was the school's first consensus All-American football player; and, after graduation, was a number two draft pick of the American Football League's Oakland Raiders, where he played his entire 14-year (190 games) AFL/NFL career (1965–1978; AFL 1965–1969, NFL 1970–1978).

The 6'1", 190-pound receiver had 40 or more catches per season for 10 straight years; was named All-AFL/AFC four times; was the 1971 NFL receiving champion (929 yards); played in two AFL All-Star games, four AFC-NFC Pro Bowls, eight AFL/AFC title games, two Super Bowls (winning Super Bowl XI (1977) after losing Super Bowl II (1968)); and was the Most Valuable Player in Super Bowl XI (a Raiders 32–14 win over the Minnesota Vikings on January 9, 1977).

After retiring as a player, Biletnikoff coached various teams, including the Montreal Alouettes (1980) of the Canadian Football League; Orange Glen High School (1982, Escondido, California); Palomar Junior College (1983, San Marcos, California); Diablo Valley Junior College (1984, Pleasant Hill, California); Oakland Invaders (1985, United States Football League); Arizona Wranglers (1986, United States Football League); Calgary Stampeders (1987–1988, Canadian Football League); and served as the wide receivers coach for the Oakland Raiders for 10 seasons, before retiring in January 2007.

He was inducted into the College Football Hall of Fame in 1991, and since 1994, the Fred Biletnikoff Award has been presented annually to the best wide receiver in college football.

After graduating from Technical Memorial High School (Erie, Pennsylvania), he attended FSU. In the school's 1965 Gator Bowl win, Biletnikoff had 13 catches for 192 yards and four touchdowns, all Gator Bowl records.

In 1987, *Southern Living* magazine named him to its 50-year All-Southern team; FSU retired his jersey number 25; and in 1999, he was ranked number 94 on *The Sporting News*' list of the 100 Greatest Football Players.

Fred Biletnikoff's Career Statistics

			RECEIVING			
YEAR	**TEAM**	**G**	**NO**	**YDS**	**AVG**	**TD**
1965	Oakland	14	24	331	13.8	0
1966	Oakland	10	17	272	16.0	3
1967	Oakland	14	40	876	21.9	5
1968	Oakland	14	61	1,037	17.0	6
1969	Oakland	14	54	837	15.5	12

RECEIVING

YEAR	TEAM	G	NO	YDS	AVG	TD
1970	Oakland	14	45	768	17.1	7
1971	Oakland	14	61	929	15.2	9
1972	Oakland	14	58	802	13.8	7
1973	Oakland	14	48	660	13.8	4
1974	Oakland	14	42	593	14.1	7
1975	Oakland	11	43	587	13.7	2
1976	Oakland	13	43	551	12.8	7
1977	Oakland	14	33	446	13.5	5
1978	Oakland	16	20	285	14.3	2
	TOTALS	190	589	8,974	15.2	76

Sources: College Football Hall of Fame; Pro Football Hall of Fame; Pro-Football-Reference.com

Bing, David "Dave" (born: November 24, 1943 in Washington, D.C.); inducted into the Naismith Memorial Basketball Hall of Fame in 1990 as a player; Position: Point Guard; Uniform: #21; first player to have his uniform number (22) retired at Syracuse University.

While attending Spingarn High School (Washington, D.C.) from 1959 to 1962, Bing was a three-year letter winner and won All-Inter High, All-Metro, and All-East honors, as well as All-American status in 1962. After high school, he went to Syracuse University (New York) from 1962 to 1966, where the 6'3", 185-pound Bing was named to *The Sporting News* All-America First Team (1966); was the Orangemen's first consensus All-American in 39 years (1966); was the nation's fifth leading scorer (1966, 28.4 points-per-game); led Syracuse in scoring all three years; was named Syracuse Athlete of the Year (1966); was the first player to have his uniform number (22) retired at the school; and was named to Syracuse University's All-Century team.

After graduating from Syracuse, Bing entered the National Basketball Association as the number one draft pick (first selection overall) of the Detroit Pistons, where he played from 1966 to 1975. During his 12-year career (1966–1978), Bing also played for the Washington Bullets (1975–1977) and the Boston Celtics (1977–1978); was named NBA Rookie of the Year in 1967; led the NBA in scoring in 1968; was named to the All-NBA First Team twice (1968, 1971); to the All-NBA Second Team once (1974); was an eight-time All-Star (1968–1969, 1971–1976); and was named Most Valuable Player of the 1976 All-Star Game.

Bing averaged more than 20 points per game in a season seven times; had his jersey number 21 retired by the Detroit Pistons; and was named to the NBA 50th Anniversary All-Time Team (1996).

Dave Bing's Career Statistics

SEASON	TEAM	G	MIN	FG	FT	TRB	AST	PTS
1966–1967	Detroit	80	2,762	664	273	359	330	1,601
1967–1968	Detroit	79	3,209	835	472	373	509	2,142
1968–1969	Detroit	77	3,039	678	444	382	546	1,800
1969–1970	Detroit	70	2,334	575	454	299	418	1,604
1970–1971	Detroit	82	3,065	799	615	364	408	2,213
1971–1972	Detroit	45	1,936	369	278	186	317	1,016
1972–1973	Detroit	82	3,361	692	456	298	637	1,840
1973–1974	Detroit	81	3,124	582	356	281	555	1,520
1974–1975	Detroit	79	3,222	578	343	286	610	1,499
1975–1976	Washington	82	2,945	497	332	237	492	1,326
1976–1977	Washington	64	1,516	271	136	143	275	678
1977–1978	Boston	80	2,256	422	244	212	300	1,088
	TOTALS	901	32,769	6,962	4,403	3,420	5,397	18,327

Sources: Basketball-Reference.com; Naismith Memorial Basketball Hall of Fame; Syracuse University Basketball (www.orangehoops.org)

Bird, Larry Joe (born: December 7, 1956 in West Baden, New Jersey); inducted into the Naismith Memorial Basketball Hall of Fame in 1998; Position: Forward; Uniform: #33; NBA Rookie of the Year; led the Boston Celtics to three NBA titles.

While playing basketball at Springs Valley High School (French Lick, Indiana) from 1970 to 1974, Bird led the school to the state sectional championship and, as a senior, averaged 30 points and 17 rebounds per game. He received a basketball scholarship to Indiana University (Bloomington), where he was to be coached by the legendary Bobby Knight. However, he was not prepared for the big college experience, and returned home to French Lick after only one month.

After briefly attending a local community college, he went to Indiana State University (Terre Haute) in 1975, where he would play for three years. While still in college, Bird was selected in the first round (sixth choice overall) of the 1978 National Basketball Association draft by the Boston Celtics. When he decided to complete his senior year, the team retained rights to him for the future.

During his collegiate career, Bird was named *The Sporting News* College Player of the Year (1979); won the Naismith Award as the top male college basketball player (1979); the John R. Wooden Award as the country's top male basketball player (1979); and was named to *The Sporting News* All-America First Team twice (1978–1979). He led Indiana State to the now-classic 1979 NCAA championship game (eventually losing to Michigan State, led by Earvin "Magic" Johnson); led Indiana State to an overall 81–13 record, including a 50–1 record at home; holds 30 Indiana State records, including most points (2,850), steals (240), and rebounds (1,247); graduated as the NCAA's fifth all-time leading scorer (30.3 points-per-game); and was a member of the gold medal-winning U.S. Team at the 1977 World University Games in Sofia, Bulgaria.

After graduating, the 6'9", 220-pound Bird joined the Celtics, where he played his entire career and quickly earned the nickname, "the Hick from French Lick." During his 13 seasons with Boston (1979–1992), he was named NBA Rookie of the Year in 1980, beating out his college rival "Magic" Johnson; won three Most Valuable Player awards (1984–1986); was named to the All-NBA First Team nine times (1980–1988); was named to the All-NBA Second Team once (1990); NBA All-Defensive Second Team twice (1982, 1984); was a 12-time All-Star (1980–1988, 1990–1992); an All-Star Game MVP once (1982); was the NBA Finals MVP twice (1984, 1986); won three NBA titles (1981, 1984, 1986); was named to the NBA 50th Anniversary All-Time Team (1996); and was a member of the gold medal-winning U.S. Olympic Team in 1992 (Barcelona, Spain).

Over a 12-year period, he teamed with future hall-of-famers Kevin McHale and Robert Parish to form one of the greatest frontlines in professional basketball history. Together, the three players compiled a 690–276 record (.714) and won nine Atlantic Division titles and five Eastern Conference championships. His jersey number 33 was retired by the Celtics.

After his playing days, Bird worked in the Celtics front office from 1992 to 1997, before being named head coach of the Indiana Pacers. He coached the team from 1997 to 2000; compiled a 147–67 (.687) record; won Coach of the Year honors in 1998; and led the team to its first NBA Finals appearance in 2000, eventually losing to the Los Angeles Lakers in six games. He was named Indiana Pacers President of Basketball Operations in July 2003.

Larry Bird's Career Statistics

SEASON	TEAM	G	MIN	FG	3P	FT	TRB	AST	STL	BLK	PTS
1979–1980	Boston	82	2,955	693	58	301	852	370	143	53	1,745
1980–1981	Boston	82	3,239	719	20	283	895	451	161	63	1,741
1981–1982	Boston	77	2,923	711	11	328	837	447	143	66	1,761
1982–1983	Boston	79	2,982	747	22	351	870	458	148	71	1,867
1983–1984	Boston	79	3,028	758	18	374	796	520	144	69	1,908
1984–1985	Boston	80	3,161	918	56	403	842	531	129	98	2,295
1985–1986	Boston	82	3,113	796	82	441	805	557	166	51	2,115
1986–1987	Boston	74	3,005	786	90	414	682	566	135	70	2,076
1987–1988	Boston	76	2,965	881	98	415	703	467	125	57	2,275
1988–1989	Boston	6	189	49	0	18	37	29	6	5	116
1989–1990	Boston	75	2,944	718	65	319	712	562	106	61	1,820
1990–1991	Boston	60	2,277	462	77	163	509	431	108	58	1,164
1991–1992	Boston	45	1,662	353	52	150	434	306	42	33	908
	TOTALS	897	34,443	8,591	649	3,960	8,974	5,695	1,556	755	21,791

Larry Bird's NBA Coaching Record

SEASON	TEAM	REGULAR SEASON W	L	WIN%	PLAYOFFS W	L	WIN%
1997–1998	Indiana	58	24	.707	10	6	.625
1998–1999	Indiana	33	17	.660	9	4	.692
1999–2000	Indiana	56	26	.683	13	10	.565
	TOTALS	147	67	.687	32	20	.615

Sources: Basketball-Reference.com; Larry Bird Web Site (www.larrybird.com); Naismith Memorial Basketball Hall of Fame

Blake, Hector "Toe" (born: August 21, 1912 in Victoria Mines, Ontario, Canada; died: May 17, 1995 in Montreal, Quebec, Canada); inducted into the Hockey Hall of Fame in 1966 as a player; Position: Left Wing; won five straight Stanley Cup championships in his first five years as coach of the Montreal Canadiens.

Before enjoying a highly successful coaching career, Blake played 14 National Hockey League seasons (1934–1948); scored 20 or more goals per season six times, and during the 1940s, he teamed with Maurice Richard and Elmer Lach to form the Punch Line, one of the most dynamic lines in league history.

After playing on numerous junior and senior teams, in 1935 Blake joined the NHL's Montreal Maroons for eight games just before the playoffs began. He was with the team as it won the Stanley Cup that season, but only appeared briefly in one game. Montreal returned him to the minor leagues after the postseason, where he played 33 games for the Providence Reds (Canadian-American Hockey League), before playing in 11 games for the NHL's Montreal Canadiens in 1936. Beginning with the 1936–1937 season, Blake was a full-time member of the team and played for the franchise for 12 more seasons.

The 5'10", 162-pound Blake scored a league-leading 47 points and won the Hart Memorial Trophy as the NHL's Most Valuable Player in 1939; won the Art Ross Trophy in 1939 as the league's regular-season scoring leader; was named NHL First All-Star Team Left Wing three times (1939–1940, 1945); was named Second All-Star Team Left Wing twice (1938, 1946); led the Canadiens as team captain to two Stanley Cup championships (1944, 1946); and won the Lady Byng Trophy for best sportsmanship in 1946.

After retiring in 1948, he became a minor league coach for various Canadiens' affiliates, before rejoining the team as a bench coach in 1955. Under Blake, Montreal won eight Stanley Cup championships in only 13 seasons (1956–1960, 1965–1966, 1968), including five in a row his first five years as the team's coach; he never had a losing season; and never failed to make the playoffs.

In 1982, Blake was presented the Order of Canada for his lifetime contributions to the game and to his country, and in 1998, he was ranked number 66 on *The Hockey News*' list of the 100 Greatest Hockey Players.

Toe Blake's Career Statistics

			REGULAR SEASON					PLAYOFFS				
SEASON	TEAM	LEAGUE	GP	G	A	TP	PIM	GP	G	A	TP	PIM
1929–1930	Cochrane Dunlops	NOJHA	7	3	0	3	4					
1930–1931	Sudbury Cub Wolves	NOJHA	6	3	1	4	12	2	0	0	0	6
1930–1931	Sudbury Industries	NOHA	8	7	1	8	10	3	1	1	2	4
1930–1931	Sudbury Cub Wolves	M-Cup	5	4	1	5	6					
1930–1931	Sudbury Wolves	Al-Cup	3	3	1	4	0					
1931–1932	Sudbury Cub Wolves	NOJHA	3	5	0	5	4					
1931–1932	Falconbridge Falcons	NOHA	10	8	1	9	18	2	1	0	1	2
1932–1933	Hamilton Tigers	OHA-Sr.	22	9	4	13	26	2	0	0	0	2
1933–1934	Hamilton Tigers	OHA-Sr.	23	19	14	33	28	4	3	4	7	4
1933–1934	Hamilton Tigers	Al-Cup	8	5	2	7	4					
1934–1935	Hamilton Tigers	OHA-Sr.	18	15	11	26	48					
1934–1935	Montreal Maroons	NHL	8	0	0	0	0	1	0	0	0	0
1935–1936	Providence Reds	Can-Am	33	12	11	23	65	7	2	3	5	2
1935–1936	Montreal Canadiens	NHL	11	1	2	3	28					
1936–1937	Montreal Canadiens	NHL	43	10	12	22	12	5	1	0	1	0
1937–1938	Montreal Canadiens	NHL	43	17	16	33	33	3	3	1	4	2
1938–1939	Montreal Canadiens	NHL	48	24	23	47	10	3	1	1	2	2

			REGULAR SEASON					PLAYOFFS				
SEASON	**TEAM**	**LEAGUE**	**GP**	**G**	**A**	**TP**	**PIM**	**GP**	**G**	**A**	**TP**	**PIM**
1939–1940	Montreal Canadiens	NHL	48	17	19	36	48					
1940–1941	Montreal Canadiens	NHL	48	12	20	32	49	3	0	3	3	5
1941–1942	Montreal Canadiens	NHL	48	17	28	45	19	3	0	3	3	2
1942–1943	Montreal Canadiens	NHL	48	23	36	59	26	5	4	3	7	0
1943–1944	Montreal Canadiens	NHL	41	26	33	59	10	9	7	11	18	2
1944–1945	Montreal Canadiens	NHL	49	29	38	67	25	6	0	2	2	5
1945–1946	Montreal Canadiens	NHL	50	29	21	50	2	9	7	6	13	5
1946–1947	Montreal Canadiens	NHL	60	21	29	50	6	11	2	7	9	0
1947–1948	Montreal Canadiens	NHL	32	9	15	24	4					
1948–1949	Buffalo Bisons	AHL	18	1	3	4	0					
1949–1950	Valleyfield Braves	QSHL	43	12	15	27	15	3	0	1	1	0
1950–1951	Valleyfield Braves	QMHL										
1950–1951	Valleyfield Braves	Alx-Cup	1	0	0	0	0					
	NHL TOTALS		577	235	292	527	272	58	25	37	62	23

Sources: Hockey Hall of Fame; Hockey-Reference.com

Blanda, George Frederick (born: September 17, 1927 in Youngwood, Pennsylvania); inducted into the Pro Football Hall of Fame in 1981 as a player; Position: Quarterback-Kicker; played more seasons in the National Football League than any other player; first player to score 2,000 points.

In his record-setting 26-season National Football League career (1949–1975, more seasons than any other player), the 6'2", 215-pound Blanda played for the Chicago Bears (1949, 1950–1958), Baltimore Colts (1950), Houston Oilers (1960–1966), and the Oakland Raiders (1967–1975). Playing until he was 48, in Blanda's 340-game career, he scored a then-record 2,002 points; on November 19, 1961, he threw seven touchdowns in a 49–13 win over the New York Titans; passed for 36 touchdowns in 1961, a single-season record that would last 23 seasons until surpassed by Dan Marino's 48 touchdown passes in 1984; and was both 1961 American Football League and 1970 American Football Conference Player of the Year.

In 1970, he became the oldest quarterback to play in a title game. Although the Raiders lost 27–17 to the Baltimore Colts, Blanda accounted for all of the team's points with two touchdown passes and a field goal.

His career was interrupted for one season in 1959 when Blanda retired instead of becoming a full-time kicker for the Bears, which was the only role coach George Halas wanted him to play. His brief absence from the game ended in 1960 when he was signed by the AFL's Oilers, where he led the team to the league's first two AFL titles and was named AFL Player of the Year for 1961.

Blanda is one of only 20 players to play the entire 10 years of the AFL's existence; one of only three players to compete in every AFL game his team played; and is a member of the All-Time All-AFL Team.

He was a four-time AFL All-Star (1961–1963, 1967); was inducted into the University of Kentucky Hall of Fame in 1998; and in 1999, was ranked number 98 on *The Sporting News*' list of the 100 Greatest Football Players. He still holds numerous NFL records, including most seasons played (26); most extra points made (943) and attempted (959); most interceptions thrown in a single season (42 in 1962); and most interceptions thrown in a career (277).

George Blanda's Career Statistics

					PASSING					RUSHING		
YEAR	**TEAM**	**G**	**ATT**	**COMP**	**YDS**	**TD**	**INT**	**RATING**	**NO**	**YDS**	**AVG**	**TD**
1949	Chicago	12	21	9	197	0	5	37.3	2	9	4.5	1
1950	Baltimore/Chicago	12	1	0	0	0	0	39.6	0	0	0.0	0
1951	Chicago	12	0	0	0	0	0	0.0	0	0	0.0	0
1952	Chicago	12	131	47	664	8	11	38.5	20	104	5.2	1
1953	Chicago	12	362	169	2,164	14	23	52.3	24	62	2.6	0
1954	Chicago	8	281	131	1,929	15	17	62.1	19	41	2.2	0
1955	Chicago	12	97	42	459	4	7	41.6	15	54	3.6	2
1956	Chicago	12	69	37	439	7	4	82.9	6	47	7.8	0
1957	Chicago	12	19	8	65	0	3	11.8	5	–5	–1.0	1
1958	Chicago	12	7	2	19	0	0	39.6	0	0	0.0	0

YEAR	TEAM	G	ATT	COMP	PASSING YDS	TD	INT	RATING	NO	RUSHING YDS	AVG	TD
1960	Houston	14	363	169	2,413	24	22	65.4	16	16	1.0	4
1961	Houston	14	362	187	3,330	36	22	91.3	7	12	1.7	0
1962	Houston	14	418	197	2,810	27	42	51.3	3	6	2.0	0
1963	Houston	14	423	224	3,003	24	25	70.1	4	1	0.3	0
1964	Houston	14	505	262	3,287	17	27	61.4	4	–2	–0.5	0
1965	Houston	14	442	186	2,542	20	30	47.9	4	–6	–1.5	0
1966	Houston	14	271	122	1,764	17	21	55.3	3	1	0.3	0
1967	Oakland	14	38	15	285	3	3	59.6	0	0	0.0	0
1968	Oakland	14	49	30	522	6	2	120.1	0	0	0.0	0
1969	Oakland	14	13	6	73	2	1	71.5	1	0	0.0	0
1970	Oakland	14	55	29	461	6	5	79.4	2	4	2.0	0
1971	Oakland	14	58	32	378	4	6	58.6	0	0	0.0	0
1972	Oakland	14	15	5	77	1	0	73.5	0	0	0.0	0
1973	Oakland	14	0	0	0	0	0	0.0	0	0	0.0	0
1974	Oakland	14	4	1	28	1	0	95.8	0	0	0.0	0
1975	Oakland	14	3	1	11	0	1	5.6	0	0	0.0	0
	TOTALS	340	4,007	1,911	26,920	236	277	60.6	135	344	2.5	9

YEAR	TEAM	G	FG	FGA	KICKING XK	XKA	PTS
1949	Chicago	12	7	15	0	0	27
1950	Baltimore/Chicago	12	6	15	0	0	18
1951	Chicago	12	6	17	26	26	44
1952	Chicago	12	6	25	30	30	54
1953	Chicago	12	7	20	27	27	48
1954	Chicago	8	8	16	23	23	47
1955	Chicago	12	11	16	37	37	82
1956	Chicago	12	12	28	45	47	81
1957	Chicago	12	14	26	23	23	71
1958	Chicago	12	11	23	36	37	69
1960	Houston	14	15	32	46	47	115
1961	Houston	14	16	29	64	65	112
1962	Houston	14	11	26	48	49	81
1963	Houston	14	9	24	39	39	66
1964	Houston	14	13	29	37	38	76
1965	Houston	14	11	21	28	28	61
1966	Houston	14	16	30	39	40	87
1967	Oakland	14	20	30	56	57	116
1968	Oakland	14	21	34	54	54	117
1969	Oakland	14	20	37	45	45	105
1970	Oakland	14	16	29	36	36	84
1971	Oakland	14	15	22	41	42	86
1972	Oakland	14	17	26	44	44	95
1973	Oakland	14	23	33	31	31	100
1974	Oakland	14	11	17	44	46	77
1975	Oakland	14	13	21	44	48	83
	TOTALS	340	335	641	943	959	2,002

Sources: *Blanda—Alive and Kicking* (Wells Twombly); Pro Football Hall of Fame; Pro-Football-Reference.com

Blazejowski, Carol (born: September 29, 1956 in Elizabeth, New Jersey); inducted into the Naismith Memorial Basketball Hall of Fame in 1994 as a player; Position: Forward; inducted into the inaugural class of the Women's Basketball Hall of Fame.

Nicknamed "The Blaze," Blazejowski's basketball career started when she was a senior (the first year the school had a varsity girl's team) at Cranford (New Jersey) High School (1970–1974), where she was named team captain; averaged 25 points a game; and was selected All-State in 1974.

After graduating, the 5'10", forward attended Montclair State University (New Jersey) from 1974 to 1978, where she scored 3,199 points (at the time, second only to Pete Maravich in all-time scoring among male or female college players); was the first-ever recipient of the Wade Trophy as the 1978 Women's Basketball Player of the Year; a three-time All-America selection (1976–1978); was named Converse Women's Player of the Year (1977); holds single-season (1,235 points, 38.6 points-per-game) and career (31.7 points-per-game) NCAA scoring records; led Montclair State to the 1976 Association for Intercollegiate Athletics for Women Final Four; was a member of the first-ever U.S. Women's gold medal-winning 1979 World University Team (Seoul, South Korea); the silver medal-winning 1979 Pan American Team (San Juan, Puerto Rico); and the 1980 Olympic Team that did not participate in the XXII Olympics in Moscow, Russia due to President Carter's boycott.

After college, Blazejowski played two seasons of Amateur Athletic Union basketball with the Allentown (Pennsylvania) Crestettes and, after her Olympic hopes faded when the U.S. boycotted the 1980 Games in Moscow, she turned professional with the New Jersey Gems (Women's Professional Basketball League) in the 1980–1981 season. She led the team to the league's inaugural playoffs; was the league's top scorer (1,067 points, 29.6 points-per-game); was selected to the All-Star team; and named the WBL's Most Valuable Player.

Due to financial troubles, the WBL lasted only one season, ending Blazejowski's playing career.

After working in the National Basketball Association's front office for six years, she was named Vice President and General Manager of the Women's National Basketball Association's New York Liberty in January 1997.

In 1994, she was inducted into the National Polish-American Sports Hall of Fame, and in 1999, she was part of the inaugural class inducted into the Women's Basketball Hall of Fame.

Sources: Basketball-Reference.com; Naismith Memorial Basketball Hall of Fame; National Polish-American Sports Hall of Fame

Blood, Ernest A. (born: October 4, 1872 in Manchester, New Hampshire; died: February 5, 1955); inducted into the Naismith Memorial Basketball Hall of Fame in 1960 as a coach; considered basketball's first great coach.

The 5'6", 175-pound Blood is considered basketball's first great coach. His career began as a high school coach at Potsdam (New York) State Normal and Training High School (now Potsdam State University) from 1906 to 1915, where he accumulated a 72–2 (.973) record. While overseeing the high school team, he briefly coached at Clarkson University (Potsdam).

He coached at Passaic (New Jersey) High School from 1915 to 1924 and compiled an unbelievable 200–1 (.995) record, while winning seven state championships. He coached the so-called Passaic High School "Wonder Teams" to a high school record 159-game winning streak through five-and-one-half seasons, thought to be the longest winning streak in basketball history. His 1921–1922 team won 33 straight games and outscored their opponents by 2,293–612 points.

After leaving Passaic, Blood spent 26 seasons coaching at St. Benedicts Prep (Newark, New Jersey) from 1925–1950, leaving the school with a 421–128 (.767) record after leading his teams to five prep school state championships. While at St. Benedicts, he also coached for one season (1925–1926) at the U.S. Military Academy at West Point (New York), compiling a 16–2 (.889) record.

Source: Naismith Memorial Basketball Hall of Fame

Blount, Melvin Cornell "Mel" (born: April 10, 1948 in Vidalia, Georgia); inducted into the Pro Football Hall of Fame in 1989 as a player; Position: Cornerback; his style of play led the NFL to create the "illegal use of hands" penalty.

With speed and strength, Blount played a major role in the Pittsburgh Steelers' dominance of the National Football League in the 1970s. A third-round draft pick (53rd overall selection) in 1970, he played his entire 14-year NFL career (1970–1983) with the Steelers.

A Pro Scouts All-American as both a safety and cornerback at Southern University (Baton Rouge, Louisiana), the 6'3", 205-pound cornerback was an All-Pro four times (1975–1977, 1981); named NFL Defensive Most Valuable Player in 1975 by the Associated Press; played in and won four Super Bowls (IX (1975), X (1976), XIII (1970), XIV (1980)); and was named to five Pro Bowls (1975–1976, 1978–1979, 1981 and was the Pro Bowl MVP in 1976).

Becoming a starter in 1972, Blount did not allow a single touchdown at right cornerback and his aggressive style of play eventually led to NFL rule changes (introducing as a penalty "illegal use of hands") that made it more difficult to closely cover receivers (commonly referred to as the "Mel Blount Rule"). He had at least one interception in each season he played and led the league with 11 in 1975.

After retiring as a player, Blount became the Director of Player Relations for the NFL (1983–1990) and founded the Mel Blount Youth Home, a shelter and Christian mission for victims of child abuse and neglect in Vidalia in 1983. In 1989, he opened a second youth home in Claysville, Pennsylvania.

He was inducted into the Louisiana Sports Hall of Fame in 1989 and into the Georgia Sports Hall of Fame in 1990. Blount was selected to the NFL 1980s All-Decade Team; named to the NFL's 75th Anniversary All-Time team in 1994; and in 1999, he was ranked number 36 on *The Sporting News*' list of the 100 Greatest Football Players.

Mel Blount's Career Statistics

YEAR	TEAM	G	INT	YDS	AVG	TD	FUM REC	YDS	TD
1970	Pittsburgh	14	1	4	4.0	0	1	0	0
1971	Pittsburgh	14	2	16	8.0	0	0	0	0
1972	Pittsburgh	14	3	75	25.0	0	2	35	1
1973	Pittsburgh	14	4	82	20.5	0	2	0	0
1974	Pittsburgh	13	2	74	37.0	1	3	5	0
1975	Pittsburgh	14	11	121	11.0	0	0	0	0
1976	Pittsburgh	14	6	75	12.5	0	1	0	0
1977	Pittsburgh	14	6	65	10.8	0	1	15	0
1978	Pittsburgh	16	4	55	13.8	0	0	0	0
1979	Pittsburgh	16	3	1	0.3	0	1	15	0
1980	Pittsburgh	16	4	28	7.0	0	1	32	0
1981	Pittsburgh	16	6	106	17.7	1	0	0	0
1982	Pittsburgh	9	1	2	2.0	0	0	0	0
1983	Pittsburgh	16	4	32	8.0	0	1	3	1
	TOTALS	200	57	736	12.9	2	13	105	2

Sources: Pro Football Hall of Fame; Pro-Football-Reference.com

Boeheim, James Arthur "Jim" (born: November 17, 1944 in Lyons, New York); inducted into the Naismith Memorial Basketball Hall of Fame in 2005 as a coach; associated with Syracuse University his entire basketball career; led the school to its first NCAA championship.

Boeheim enrolled at Syracuse University (New York) in 1962, and has been associated with his alma mater ever since. A walk-on freshman who played guard, he eventually served as team co-captain in his senior year with fellow hall-of-famer Dave Bing; helped lead the school to a 22–6 record; and led the squad to its second NCAA tournament appearance in 1966. In 1976, he was appointed head coach after serving as an assistant, never having coached at any other school.

By the time of his hall of fame induction, Boeheim had led Syracuse to its first NCAA championship (2003); three NCAA Final Four appearances (1987, 1996, 2003); and more than 700 wins (the 18th coach in Division I history to do so). The winningest coach in Big East Conference history (he is still active as of this writing and has compiled an overall 829–293 (.739) record), he has also served on seven different USA Basketball coaching staffs that have combined to win seven medals, including three gold, in international competition. He has been named Big East Conference Coach of the Year four times (1984, 1991, 2000, 2010) and USA Basketball National Coach of the Year in 2001. In 2001, he helped lead the USA Basketball Young Men's Team to a gold medal at the World Championship in Japan.

In his 34 seasons at Syracuse (and still counting), Boeheim's teams have had thirty-two 20-win seasons; have never finished with a losing record; have won eight Big East titles (1980, 1986–1987, 1990, 1998, 2000, 2003, 2010); five Big East Tournaments (1981, 1988, 1992, 2005–2006); and have been to 27 NCAA Tournaments. In February 2002, the basketball court at the Carrier Dome (on the Syracuse campus) was renamed Jim Boeheim Court; on January 25, 2007, he coached his 1000th career game; and on March 19, 2007, Boeheim won his 750th game (against San Diego State).

Boeheim graduated from Lyons (New York) Central High School in 1962 before attending Syracuse. He later attended graduate school while playing minor league basketball on the weekends. In 1969, he began coaching the freshman basketball and golf teams at Syracuse, and eventually became an assistant to head basketball coach Roy Danforth. After the Orange reached the school's first NCAA Final Four, Danforth moved on to Tulane and Boeheim became head basketball coach.

He is one of four Big East coaches to be inducted into the basketball hall of fame (along with John Thompson of Georgetown, Lou Carnesecca of St. John's, and Jim Calhoun of Connecticut); was named District II Coach of the Year by the National Association of Basketball Coaches 10 times; in 2004, he received the Clair Bee Award for his contributions to basketball; and also in 2004, he received Syracuse University's Arents Award, the University's highest alumni honor.

Jim Boeheim's Coaching Statistics

SEASON	W	L	WIN%	POSTSEASON
1976–1977	26	4	.867	Lost in NCAA Sweet 16
1977–1978	22	6	.786	Lost in NCAA First Round
1978–1979	26	4	.867	Lost in NCAA Sweet 16
1979–1980	26	4	.867	Lost in NCAA Sweet 16
1980–1981	22	12	.647	Lost in NIT Final
1981–1982	16	13	.552	Lost in NIT Second Round
1982–1983	21	10	.677	Lost in NCAA Second Round
1983–1984	23	9	.719	Lost in NCAA Sweet 16
1984–1985	22	9	.710	Lost in NCAA Second Round
1985–1986	26	6	.813	Lost in NCAA Second Round
1986–1987	31	7	.816	Lost in NCAA Championship Game
1987–1988	26	9	.743	Lost in NCAA Second Round
1988–1989	30	8	.789	Lost in NCAA Regional Final
1989–1990	26	7	.788	Lost in NCAA Sweet 16
1990–1991	26	6	.813	Lost in NCAA First Round
1991–1992	22	10	.688	Lost in NCAA Second Round
1992–1993	20	9	.690	No Postseason (NCAA Violations)
1993–1994	23	7	.767	Lost in NCAA Sweet 16
1994–1995	20	10	.667	Lost in NCAA Second Round
1995–1996	29	9	.763	Lost in NCAA Championship Game
1996–1997	19	13	.594	Lost in NIT First Round
1997–1998	26	9	.743	Lost in NCAA Sweet 16
1998–1999	21	12	.636	Lost in NCAA First Round
1999–2000	26	6	.813	Lost in NCAA Sweet 16
2000–2001	25	9	.735	Lost in NCAA Second Round
2001–2002	23	13	.639	Lost in NIT Semi–Finals
2002–2003	30	5	.857	National Champions
2003–2004	23	8	.742	Lost in NCAA Sweet 16
2004–2005	27	7	.794	Lost in NCAA First Round
2005–2006	23	12	.657	Lost in NCAA First Round
2006–2007	24	11	.686	Lost in NIT Quarter–Finals
2007–2008	21	14	.600	Lost in NIT Quarter–Finals
2008–2009	28	10	.737	Lost in NCAA Sweet 16
2009–2010	30	5	.857	Lost in NCAA Sweet 16
TOTALS	829	293	.739	

Source: Naismith Memorial Basketball Hall of Fame

Boggs, Wade Anthony (born: June 15, 1958 in Omaha, Nebraska); inducted into the National Baseball Hall of Fame and Museum in 2005 as a player; Position: Third Base; Bats: Left; Throws: Right; Uniform: #26 (with the Red Sox); only player to hit a home run for his 3,000th career hit.

Drafted out of high school in the seventh round (166th overall pick) of the 1976 Amateur Draft by the Boston Red Sox, the 6'2", 197-pound Boggs made his major league debut on April 10, 1982 and would go on to have an 18-year career with the Red Sox (1982–1992), New York Yankees (1993–1997), and Tampa Bay Devil Rays (1998–1999). He played in two World Series (winning in 1996 and losing in 1986); made 12 straight All-Star appearances (1985–1996, second only to Brooks Robinson in number of consecutive appearances by a third baseman); and won two Gold Gloves (1994–1995).

Boggs won five batting titles (1983, 1985–1988); had 200 or more hits in seven consecutive seasons (1983–1989, an American League record for the 20th century); accumulated 100 or more walks four straight seasons (1986–1989);

scored at least 100 runs every season from 1983 to 1989; and is a member of the 3,000-hit club (the only member ever to hit a home-run for his 3,000th hit).

He won the Silver Slugger Award eight times (1983, 1986–1989, 1991, 1993–1994); led the American League in hits (1985); led the league in doubles twice (1988–1989); was the league on-base percentage leader six times (1983, 1985–1989; and led the league in runs scored twice (1988–1989).

Although the Red Sox have not yet retired his uniform number, he was inducted into the Boston Red Sox Hall of Fame in 2004. The Tampa Bay Devil Rays retired the uniform number he used with the team (#12) in April 2000.

Boggs also pitched a few innings in the major leagues and had one shutout inning while pitching for the Yankees against the Anaheim Angels in 1997. He played in the longest game in professional baseball history as a member of the Pawtucket Red Sox on April 18, 1981 against the Rochester Red Wings, both teams from the AAA International League. The game began on Saturday (April 18) at Pawtucket's McCoy Stadium, and continued through the night and into Easter morning before finally being suspended at 4:09 a.m. at the end of the 32nd inning. The game resumed on Tuesday, June 23 (the next time the Red Wings were in town) and took just one inning and 18 minutes before the Red Sox won the game in the bottom of the 33rd inning.

In 1999, Boggs ranked number 95 on *The Sporting News*' list of the 100 Greatest Baseball Players and was a nominee for the Major League Baseball All-Century Team. After retiring as a player, Boggs became the baseball coach at Gaither High School in Tampa, Florida.

During his career, Boggs reached base safely in 80% of his games. Not known as a power hitter, he set an American League record in 1985 with 187 singles (78% of his hits), a mark since tied by Ichiro Suzuki. Although age and injuries slowed him down, his first Gold Glove in 1994 made him the oldest first-time recipient (age 36) of that honor since the award was introduced in 1957.

On September 25, 1989, he went 4-for-5 in a win over the New York Yankees to become the first player in major league history to have both 200 hits and 100 walks in four consecutive seasons. After being traded to Tampa Bay, Boggs hit the first home run in the expansion Devil Rays history on March 31, 1998 against the Detroit Tigers.

Wade Boggs' Career Statistics

YEAR	TEAM	LG	G	AB	R	H	2B	3B	HR	RBI	BB	SO	SB	AVG	SLG
1982	Boston	AL	104	338	51	118	14	1	5	44	35	21	1	.349	.441
1983	Boston	AL	153	582	100	210	44	7	5	74	92	36	3	.361	.486
1984	Boston	AL	158	625	109	203	31	4	6	55	89	44	3	.325	.416
1985	Boston	AL	161	653	107	240	42	3	8	78	96	61	2	.368	.478
1986	Boston	AL	149	580	107	207	47	2	8	71	105	44	0	.357	.486
1987	Boston	AL	147	551	108	200	40	6	24	89	105	48	1	.363	.588
1988	Boston	AL	155	584	128	214	45	6	5	58	125	34	2	.366	.490
1989	Boston	AL	156	621	113	205	51	7	3	54	107	51	2	.330	.449
1990	Boston	AL	155	619	89	187	44	5	6	63	87	68	0	.302	.418
1991	Boston	AL	144	546	93	181	42	2	8	51	89	32	1	.332	.460
1992	Boston	AL	143	514	62	133	22	4	7	50	74	31	1	.259	.358
1993	New York	AL	143	560	83	169	26	1	21	59	74	49	0	.302	.464
1994	New York	AL	97	366	61	125	19	1	11	55	61	29	2	.342	.489
1995	New York	AL	126	460	76	149	22	4	5	63	74	50	1	.324	.422
1996	New York	AL	132	501	80	156	29	2	2	41	67	32	1	.311	.389
1997	New York	AL	104	353	55	103	23	1	4	28	48	38	0	.292	.397
1998	Tampa Bay	AL	123	435	51	122	23	4	7	52	46	54	3	.280	.400
1999	Tampa Bay	AL	90	292	40	88	14	1	2	29	38	23	1	.301	.377
	TOTALS		2,440	9,180	1,513	3,010	578	61	137	1,014	1,412	745	24	.328	.449

Sources: Baseball-Reference.com; National Baseball Hall of Fame and Museum

Bogićević, Vladislav "Bogie" (born: November 7, 1950 in Belgrade, Yugoslavia); inducted into the National Soccer Hall of Fame and Museum in 2002 as a player; Position: Midfielder; a seven-time NASL All-Star.

Bogićević was the driving force behind some of the New York Cosmos' greatest teams, and is considered one of the best midfielders in North American Soccer League history. He played for the Cosmos from 1978 to 1984 and helped lead the team to NASL championships in 1978 and 1982. Earlier in his career, he had won five First Division titles during his 13 seasons with Red Star Belgrade (Yugoslavia).

In his seven-year NASL career, Bogićević played in 236 games (203 regular season, 33 playoffs); scored 39 career goals (regular season and playoffs); garnered 166 assists (leading the league for three consecutive years, 1981–1983); and was named to All-Star teams each year he was in the league (First-Team All-Star in 1980–1984 and Second-Team

All-Star in 1978–1979). Before joining the Cosmos, he had appeared in 23 games for Yugoslavia and had represented his country at the 1974 FIFA World Cup in West Germany.

After retiring from the game as a player, Bogićević was hired by the Confederation of North, Central American and Caribbean Association Football to promote soccer throughout the United States, before leaving the game for a few years. Returning to soccer in 1994, he coached the Iranian club Persepolis F.C. (Tehran), and in July 1995, Bogićević became coach of the A-League's New York Centaurs (New York City), which would finish last in its division.

During the 1998 World Cup in France, he served as a scout for his National Team and in 2000, he signed a two-year deal with Yugoslav FA, becoming the team's head coach in 2001. His contract expired in the summer of 2002 and he went on to coach the Portuguese first-division team Belenenses (Belém, Lisbon) during the 2003–2004 season, but was fired in January 2004.

Vladislav Bogićević's NASL Statistics

YEAR	TEAM	G	GLS	ASST	PTS
1978	New York	30	10	17	37
1979	New York	25	1	23	25
1980	New York	32	5	19	29
1981	New York	31	1	22	24
1982	New York	31	4	24	32
1983	New York	30	7	29	43
1984	New York	24	3	13	19
		G	**GLS**	**ASST**	**PTS**
	TOTALS	203	31	147	209

Source: National Soccer Hall of Fame and Museum

Boivin, Leo Joseph (born: August 2, 1932 in Prescott, Ontario, Canada); inducted into the Hockey Hall of Fame in 1986 as a player; Position: Defense; played for the Memorial Cup each of his three seasons in juniors.

After playing for the Memorial Cup all three years in juniors (1948–1951), Boivin began his professional career in the 1951–1952 season with the Pittsburgh Hornets of the American Hockey League, before joining the Toronto Maple Leafs. Making his National Hockey League debut on March 8, 1952, Boivin played 19 seasons (1951–1970) in the NHL for the Leafs (1952–1954), the Boston Bruins (1954–1966), Detroit Red Wings (1966–1967), Pittsburgh Penguins (1967–1969), and the Minnesota North Stars (1969–1970).

Nicknamed "Fireplug" because of his compact size (5'7", 177 pounds), Boivin was captain of the Bruins during four of his 12 years with the club; led the team to back-to-back Stanley Cup finals, eventually losing both series (1958–1959); and played in three NHL All-Star games (1961–1962, 1964).

After retiring, he stayed in the game as a scout; served as an interim coach with the NHL's St. Louis Blues during the 1975–1976 and 1977–1978 seasons; and coached the Ottawa 67s (Ontario Hockey League) briefly before resuming his scouting duties.

Leo Boivin's Career Statistics

			REGULAR SEASON					PLAYOFFS				
SEASON	**TEAM**	**LEAGUE**	**GP**	**G**	**A**	**TP**	**PIM**	**GP**	**G**	**A**	**TP**	**PIM**
1948–1949	Inkerman Rockets	OVJHL										
1948–1949	Inkerman Rockets	M-Cup	4	2	0	2	0					
1949–1950	Port Arthur Bruins	TBJHL	18	4	4	8	32	5	0	3	3	10
1949–1950	Port Arthur Bruins	M-Cup	16	6	4	10	12					
1950–1951	Port Arthur Bruins	TBJHL	20	16	11	27	37	13	3	6	9	28
1950–1951	Port Arthur Bruins	M-Cup	7	1	3	4	16					
1951–1952	Toronto Maple Leafs	NHL	2	0	1	1	0					
1951–1952	Pittsburgh Hornets	AHL	30	2	3	5	32	10	0	1	1	16
1952–1953	Toronto Maple Leafs	NHL	70	2	13	15	97					
1953–1954	Toronto Maple Leafs	NHL	58	1	6	7	81	5	0	0	0	2
1954–1955	Toronto Maple Leafs	NHL	7	0	0	0	8					
1954–1955	Boston Bruins	NHL	59	6	11	17	105	5	0	1	1	4

SEASON	TEAM	LEAGUE	REGULAR SEASON GP	G	A	TP	PIM	PLAYOFFS GP	G	A	TP	PIM
1955–1956	Boston Bruins	NHL	68	4	16	20	80					
1956–1957	Boston Bruins	NHL	55	2	8	10	55	10	2	3	5	12
1957–1958	Boston Bruins	NHL	33	0	4	4	54	12	0	3	3	21
1958–1959	Boston Bruins	NHL	70	5	16	21	94	7	1	2	3	4
1959–1960	Boston Bruins	NHL	70	4	21	25	66					
1960–1961	Boston Bruins	NHL	57	6	17	23	50					
1961–1962	Boston Bruins	NHL	65	5	18	23	70					
1962–1963	Boston Bruins	NHL	62	2	24	26	48					
1963–1964	Boston Bruins	NHL	65	10	14	24	42					
1964–1965	Boston Bruins	NHL	67	3	10	13	68					
1965–1966	Boston Bruins	NHL	46	0	5	5	34					
1965–1966	Detroit Red Wings	NHL	16	0	5	5	16	12	0	1	1	16
1966–1967	Detroit Red Wings	NHL	69	4	17	21	78					
1967–1968	Pittsburgh Penguins	NHL	73	9	13	22	74					
1968–1969	Pittsburgh Penguins	NHL	41	5	13	18	26					
1968–1969	Minnesota North Stars	NHL	28	1	6	7	16					
1969–1970	Minnesota North Stars	NHL	69	3	12	15	30	3	0	0	0	0
	NHL TOTALS		1,150	72	250	322	1,192	54	3	10	13	59

Sources: Hockey Hall of Fame; Hockey-Reference.com

Bookie, Michael (born: September 12, 1904 in Pittsburgh, Pennsylvania; died: October 12, 1944 in Camp Eglin, Florida); inducted into the National Soccer Hall of Fame and Museum in 1986 as a player; Position: Inside Forward; International Caps (1930): 1; International Goals: 0; selected to the 1930 U.S. World Cup team.

Bookie played semi-professional baseball as a shortstop in Pittsburgh before focusing on soccer with teams in Jeannette and Vestaburg (both in Western Pennsylvania). In the 1924–1925 season, he played for the Boston Wonder Workers of the American Soccer League before moving on to the New Bedford (Massachusetts) Whalers the next season (also in the ASL).

In the 1926–1927 season, Bookie played for Cleveland (Ohio) Slavia in the Mid-West Professional League. In 1927, he played for both the Cleveland All-Stars against the touring National club of Montevideo (Uruguay) and for the Cleveland Hungarians against Vienna Hakoah.

In 1929, he played for the Ohio All-Stars against the English club Preston North End and scored his team's only goal in a 5–1 loss. In 1930, Bookie played for Cleveland Bruells against the Scottish club Kilmarnock and was also selected to the 1930 U.S. World Cup team, but did not play.

After the World Cup was over, he played against Montevideo's National Team, Santos in Brazil, and the Brazilian National Team in Rio de Janeiro. He continued to play for various teams in Cleveland before finishing his career with Pittsburgh Curry.

Source: National Soccer Hall of Fame and Museum

Boon, Richard "Rich" "Dickie" (born: January 10, 1878 in Belleville, Ontario, Canada; died: May 3, 1961); inducted into the Hockey Hall of Fame in 1952 as a player; Position: Defense; first player to use the poke-check; his MAAA team was the last amateur club to win the Stanley Cup.

Boon began playing organized hockey in 1894 in Montreal before moving on to the Monarch Hockey Club in 1897, and would go on to play six pre-National Hockey League seasons from 1899 to 1906. In 1900, he joined the Montreal Amateur Athletic Association Junior Hockey Club and was promoted to the senior team the following year (Canadian Amateur Hockey League).

He is credited with being the first player to use the poke-check, a move in which a defender uses the blade of the stick to push the puck off the stick of an opponent. He was on the MAAA team that won the Stanley Cup in 1902 over the Winnipeg Victorias, the last amateur club to win the Cup.

When professional players began to take over the game, Boon retired as a player in 1905. Although he never played professionally, he was a co-founder of the Montreal Wanderers, Montreal's first professional hockey team. As manager of the team from 1906 to 1916, he led the Wanderers to three Stanley Cup championships in four years (1907–1908, 1910).

Richard Boon's Career Statistics

			REGULAR SEASON					PLAYOFFS				
SEASON	TEAM	LEAGUE	GP	G	A	TP	PIM	GP	G	A	TP	PIM
1899–1900	Montreal AAA	CAHL	8	2	0	2						
1900–1901	Montreal AAA	CAHL	7	3	0	3						
1901–1902	Montreal AAA	CAHL	8	2	0	2	6	3	0	0	0	0
1902–1903	Montreal AAA	CAHL	7	3	0	3	6	4	0	0	0	10
1903–1904	Montreal Wanderers	FAHL	4	0	0	0	0					
1904–1905	Montreal Wanderers	FAHL	8	0	0	0	6					
1905–1906	Montreal Wanderers	ECAHA										

Sources: Hockey Hall of Fame; Hockey-Reference.com

Booth, Joseph (born: unknown date in Bradford, England; died: August 1947 in Bridgeport, Connecticut); inducted into the National Soccer Hall of Fame and Museum in 1952 as a builder; served as secretary of the Connecticut State Association for 25 years.

After serving six years as president of the Bradford and District Football Association, Booth left his native England in 1910 and moved to Bridgeport, Connecticut, where he eventually served as secretary of the Connecticut State League in 1913. In 1914, he organized the Connecticut State Association and served as the organization's secretary for 25 years.

Also in 1914, Booth organized multiple organizations, including the Connecticut Junior League, the Bridgeport Public Schools League, the Eastern League, and the Connecticut Referees Association. In 1915, he organized the Connecticut State Amateur League, and in 1924, he founded the Connecticut State Football Players Protective Association, and served as secretary for both groups.

He also served as the third vice president of the United States Football Association (1920–1923); was chairman and secretary of the National Soccer Football Writers Association; and was a member of the USFA National Challenge Cup Commission.

Source: National Soccer Hall of Fame and Museum

Borghi, Frank (born: April 9, 1925 in St. Louis, Missouri); inducted into the National Soccer Hall of Fame and Museum in 1976 as a player; Position: Goalkeeper; International Caps (1949–1954): 9; International Goals: 0; shut out England in the 1950 World Cup (a 1–0 U.S. win) in one of the greatest upsets of World Cup play.

Before playing soccer, Borghi served in the U.S. Army during World War II, and after the war, he played two years of professional baseball with the Carthage (Missouri) Cardinals of the Kansas-Oklahoma-Missouri League. After deciding to focus on soccer, he played on numerous teams in the St. Louis area, including the Schumakers, Simpkins-Ford, and St. Ambrose.

Although he won two U.S. Open Cup medals with Simpkins-Ford (1948, 1950), he is best remembered for his play in the 1950 FIFA World Cup (in Belo Horizonte, Brazil) where, as a goalkeeper, he shut out England in one of the most famous upsets (a 1–0 U.S. win) in World Cup play.

Prior to the 1950 World Cup, Borghi played four games for the United States in the qualifying rounds and all three games in the finals. Also in 1950, he played for Simpkins-Ford against Manchester United and for the U.S. Stars against the Turkish club Besiktas in St. Louis.

He has been inducted into the St. Louis Soccer Hall of Fame and the Spanish Society Hall of Fame, and was named Most Valuable Player in 1955 by the Missouri Soccer Commission.

Source: National Soccer Hall of Fame and Museum

Borgmann, Bernard, Sr. "Bennie" (born: November 22, 1900 in Haledon, New Jersey; died: November 11, 1978 in Hawthorne, New Jersey); inducted into the Naismith Memorial Basketball Hall of Fame in 1961 as a player; Position: Forward; played in almost 3,000 basketball and 2,000 baseball games.

The 5'8", 170-pound Borgmann began his two-sport career at Clifton (New Jersey) High School (1913–1917), where he was a basketball forward and a baseball shortstop. While playing basketball, it was common for him to score more than 30 percent of his team's total points. As a shortstop, he played for several years in the Boston Red Sox farm system before breaking into the major leagues in 1932 with the St. Louis Cardinals.

During his career, he was an active athlete for almost 50 years, and also served as a manager, scout, and coach.

During his professional basketball career, which lasted from 1918 to 1942, he played for numerous teams and leagues, including the Kingston (New York) Colonels of the Metropolitan Basketball League (1921–1923, winners of the First World Championship); the Fort Wayne (Indiana) Hoosiers of the American Basketball League (1926–1930); the ABL's Chicago Bruins (1930–1931); the Original Celtics (Eastern Basketball League in New York, 1930–1931); the Brooklyn (New York) Americans of the American Basketball League (1932–1933); and the Newark (New Jersey) Mules of the ABL (1934–1935).

Borgmann also played for the Interstate League's Paterson (New Jersey) Silk Socks (1919–1920); the Metropolitan League's Paterson (New Jersey) Powers Brothers Five (1921–1922); the Interstate League's Springfield (New York) Gunners (1921–1923); the Paterson (New Jersey) Legionnaires of the Metropolitan Basketball League (1922–1923, 1926–1927); the Cohoes Cohosiers (New York) of the New York League (1924–1926); the Paterson (New Jersey) Crescents of the American Basketball League (1929–1931); the Interstate League's Long Island Pro-Imps (1931–1932); the Bridgeton (New Jersey) Gems of the Eastern League (1931–1933); the ABL's New Britain (Connecticut) Jackaways (1934–1935); the Passaic (New Jersey) Reds of the ABL (1935–1936); the Paterson (New Jersey) Panthers of the ABL (1935–1936); the Trenton (New Jersey) Moose (1935–1936); and the ABL's Jersey City Reds (1938–1940).

During his career, he coached the Syracuse Chiefs; at Muhlenberg College (Allentown, Pennsylvania); and at St. Michael's College (Winooski, Vermont). Borgmann was basketball's leading scorer in the 1920s and won 15 scoring titles with various leagues (1922–1935).

Source: Naismith Memorial Basketball Hall of Fame

Bossy, Michael Dean "Mike" (born: January 22, 1957 in Montreal, Quebec, Canada); inducted into the Hockey Hall of Fame in 1991 as a player; Position: Right Wing; Uniform: #22; scored 50 or more goals in nine of his 10 NHL seasons; NHL Rookie of the Year.

Bossy began his junior career in the 1972–1973 season with the Laval Nationals of the Quebec Major Junior Hockey League, and after four seasons, he was selected in the first round (15th overall pick) of the 1977 Amateur Draft by the New York Islanders, where he would play his entire 10-year National Hockey League career (1977–1987).

In his first season with the Islanders, he scored a then rookie record 53 goals (and a total of 92 points), winning the Calder Memorial Trophy as the league's Rookie of the Year. He would go on to score 50 or more goals nine times (a record he shares with Wayne Gretzky) and scored 50 or more goals nine consecutive years, an NHL record; scored 50 goals in his first 50 games during the 1980–1981 season (only the second player to do so after Maurice Richard); appeared in five Stanley Cups and won four straight (1980–1983); and had his jersey number 22 retired by the team in March 1992. He and Gretzky are the only two players to have scored 60 or more goals in five seasons. Bossy recorded nine hat tricks in the 1980–1981 season, an NHL record that lasted only one season until broken by Wayne Gretzky, who had ten.

The 6', 185-pound Bossy won the Conn Smythe Trophy as the Stanley Cup playoff Most Valuable Player in 1982; the Lady Byng Memorial Trophy (for sportsmanship) three times (1983–1984, 1986); was named to the First All-Star Team five times (1981–1984, 1986); to the Second All-Star Team three times (1978–1979, 1985); and is the only player to score 17 goals in three straight playoffs (1981–1983).

His .762 goals per game in the regular season ranks as the best in NHL history, and his .659 goals per game in the playoffs ranks second to Mario Lemieux (.710).

After injuries and poor health forced him to retire in 1987 at the relatively young age of 30, Bossy became a television broadcaster for the Quebec Nordiques until 1990. In 2006, he returned to the Islanders organization to work in the front office.

In 1998, he was ranked number 20 on *The Hockey News*' list of the 100 Greatest Hockey Players, and in 2007 he was inducted into the Nassau County Sports Hall of Fame.

Mike Bossy's Career Statistics

			REGULAR SEASON						PLAYOFFS				
SEASON	**TEAM**	**LEAGUE**	**GP**	**G**	**A**	**TP**	**PIM**	**+/–**	**GP**	**G**	**A**	**TP**	**PIM**
1972–1973	Montreal-Bourassa	QAAA											
1972–1973	Laval Nationals	QMJHL	4	1	2	3	0						
1973–1974	Laval Nationals	QMJHL	68	70	48	118	45		11	6	16	22	2
1974–1975	Laval Nationals	QMJHL	67	84	65	149	42		16	18	20	38	2
1975–1976	Laval Nationals	QMJHL	64	79	57	136	25						
1976–1977	Laval Nationals	QMJHL	61	75	51	126	12		7	5	5	10	12

SEASON	TEAM	LEAGUE	REGULAR SEASON GP	G	A	TP	PIM	+/–	PLAYOFFS GP	G	A	TP	PIM
1977–1978	New York Islanders	NHL	73	53	38	91	6	+31	7	2	2	4	2
1978–1979	New York Islanders	NHL	80	69	57	126	25	+63	10	6	2	8	2
1978–1979	NHL All-Stars	Ch-Cup	3	2	2	4	0						
1979–1980	New York Islanders	NHL	75	51	41	92	12	+28	16	10	13	23	8
1980–1981	New York Islanders	NHL	79	68	51	119	32	+37	18	17	18	35	4
1981–1982	Canada	Can-Cup	7	8	3	11	2						
1981–1982	New York Islanders	NHL	80	64	83	147	22	+69	19	17	10	27	0
1982–1983	New York Islanders	NHL	79	60	58	118	20	+27	19	17	9	26	10
1983–1984	New York Islanders	NHL	67	51	67	118	8	+66	21	8	10	18	4
1984–1985	Canada	Can-Cup	8	5	4	9	2						
1984–1985	New York Islanders	NHL	76	58	59	117	38	+37	10	5	6	11	4
1985–1986	New York Islanders	NHL	80	61	62	123	14	+30	3	1	2	3	4
1986–1987	New York Islanders	NHL	63	38	37	75	33	–7	6	2	3	5	0
	NHL TOTALS		752	573	553	1126	210		129	85	75	160	38

Sources: Hockey Hall of Fame; Hockey-Reference.com

Bottomley, James Leroy "Jim" (born: April 23, 1900 in Oglesby, Illinois; died: December 11, 1959 in St. Louis, Missouri); inducted into the National Baseball Hall of Fame and Museum in 1974 as a player by the Veterans Committee; Position; First Base; Bats: Left; Throws: Right; first Most Valuable Player to emerge from his team's own farm system; set a single-season record for most unassisted double plays by a first baseman (eight in 1936).

Making his major league debut on August 18, 1922, Bottomley played 16 years (1922–1937) with the St. Louis Cardinals (1922–1932), Cincinnati Reds (1933–1935), and St. Louis Browns (1936–1937). The 6', 180-pound first baseman played in four World Series (winning in 1926 and 1931, while losing in 1928, and 1930), and was named the National League Most Valuable Player in 1928, becoming the first MVP to emerge from a team's own farm system (a newly-developed idea by the early 1920s).

Bottomley hit .300 or better per season nine times and set a single-season record for most unassisted double plays by a first baseman with eight (1936). On September 16, 1924, against the Brooklyn Robins/Dodgers, he drove in a then-record 12 runs (two home runs, one double, and three singles), and twice in his career he collected six hits in six at bats (September 16, 1924 and August 5, 1931).

After playing just over one season with the St. Louis Browns, Bottomley retired in the middle of the 1937 season, and took over as manager from Rogers Hornsby, who had been fired for betting on horses. The team did not improve under his leadership as the Browns finished in last place, ending his half-season managerial career with a 21–56 (.273) record.

Jim Bottomley's Career Statistics

YEAR	TEAM	LG	G	AB	R	H	2B	3B	HR	RBI	BB	SO	SB	AVG	SLG
1922	St. Louis	NL	37	151	29	49	8	5	5	35	6	13	3	.325	.543
1923	St. Louis	NL	134	523	79	194	34	14	8	94	45	44	4	.371	.535
1924	St. Louis	NL	137	528	87	167	31	12	14	111	35	35	5	.316	.500
1925	St. Louis	NL	153	619	92	227	44	12	21	128	47	36	3	.367	.578
1926	St. Louis	NL	154	603	98	180	40	14	19	120	58	52	4	.299	.506
1927	St. Louis	NL	152	574	95	174	31	15	19	124	74	49	8	.303	.509
1928	St. Louis	NL	149	576	123	187	42	20	31	136	71	54	10	.325	.628
1929	St. Louis	NL	146	560	108	176	31	12	29	137	70	54	3	.314	.568
1930	St. Louis	NL	131	487	92	148	33	7	15	97	44	36	5	.304	.493
1931	St. Louis	NL	108	382	73	133	34	5	9	75	34	24	3	.348	.534
1932	St. Louis	NL	91	311	45	92	16	3	11	48	25	32	2	.296	.473
1933	Cincinnati	NL	145	549	57	137	23	9	13	83	42	28	3	.250	.395
1934	Cincinnati	NL	142	556	72	158	31	11	11	78	33	40	1	.284	.439
1935	Cincinnati	NL	107	399	44	103	21	1	1	49	18	24	3	.258	.323
1936	St. Louis	AL	140	544	72	162	39	11	12	95	44	55	0	.298	.476

YEAR	TEAM	LG	G	AB	R	H	2B	3B	HR	RBI	BB	SO	SB	AVG	SLG
1937	St. Louis	AL	65	109	11	26	7	0	1	12	18	15	1	.239	.330
	TOTALS		1,991	7,471	1,177	2,313	465	151	219	1,422	664	591	58	.310	.500

Sources: Baseball-Reference.com; National Baseball Hall of Fame

Bouchard, Emile "Butch" (born: September 11, 1920 in Montreal, Quebec, Canada); inducted into the Hockey Hall of Fame in 1966 as a player; Position: Defenseman; the Quebec Major Junior Hockey League's Defenseman of the Year Trophy is named in his honor

After playing in the juniors for parts of four seasons, Bouchard signed with the Montreal Canadiens in 1941 and was sent to the Providence Reds in the American Hockey League for 12 games, before being called up to the National Hockey League, where he spent his entire 15-year career with the Montreal Canadiens (1941–1956).

The 6'2", 205-pound Bouchard was named First All-Star Team Defense three times (1945–1947) and to the Second All-Star Team in 1944. The Quebec Major Junior Hockey League's Defenseman of the Year Trophy is named in his honor.

After retiring as a player, Bouchard developed amateur hockey leagues and players in the Montreal area, and prior to the 1968–1969 season, he was named president of the Metropolitan Junior A Hockey League.

Emile Bouchard's Career Statistics

			REGULAR SEASON					PLAYOFFS				
SEASON	TEAM	LEAGUE	GP	G	A	TP	PIM	GP	G	A	TP	PIM
1937–1938	Verdun Jr. Maple Leafs	MCJHL	2	0	0	0	2	2	0	0	0	2
1937–1938	Verdun Jr. Maple Leafs	M-Cup	5	2	1	3	8					
1938–1939	Verdun Jr. Maple Leafs	MCJHL	9	1	1	2	20	3	0	0	0	0
1938–1939	Verdun Jr. Maple Leafs	M-Cup	7	0	2	2	12					
1939–1940	Verdun Jr. Maple Leafs	MCJHL										
1940–1941	Montreal Jr. Canadiens	QJHL	31	2	8	10	60					
1940–1941	Providence Reds	AHL	12	3	1	4	8	3	0	1	1	8
1941–1942	Montreal Canadiens	NHL	44	0	6	6	38	3	1	1	2	0
1942–1943	Montreal Canadiens	NHL	45	2	16	18	47	5	0	1	1	4
1943–1944	Montreal Canadiens	NHL	39	5	14	19	52	9	1	3	4	4
1944–1945	Montreal Canadiens	NHL	50	11	23	34	34	6	3	4	7	4
1945–1946	Montreal Canadiens	NHL	45	7	10	17	52	9	2	1	3	17
1946–1947	Montreal Canadiens	NHL	60	5	7	12	60	11	0	3	3	21
1947–1948	Montreal Canadiens	NHL	60	4	6	10	78					
1948–1949	Montreal Canadiens	NHL	27	3	3	6	42	7	0	0	0	6
1949–1950	Montreal Canadiens	NHL	69	1	7	8	88	5	0	2	2	2
1950–1951	Montreal Canadiens	NHL	52	3	10	13	80	11	1	1	2	2
1951–1952	Montreal Canadiens	NHL	60	3	9	12	45	11	0	2	2	14
1952–1953	Montreal Canadiens	NHL	58	2	8	10	55	12	1	1	2	6
1953–1954	Montreal Canadiens	NHL	70	1	10	11	89	11	2	1	3	4
1954–1955	Montreal Canadiens	NHL	70	2	15	17	81	12	0	1	1	37
1955–1956	Montreal Canadiens	NHL	36	0	0	0	22	1	0	0	0	0
	NHL TOTALS		785	49	144	193	863	113	11	21	32	121

Sources: Hockey Hall of Fame; Hockey-Reference.com

Boucher, Francois X. "Frank" (born: October 7, 1901 in Ottawa, Ontario, Canada; died: December 12, 1977 in Kemptville, Ontario, Canada); inducted into the Hockey Hall of Fame in 1958 as a player; Position: Center-Forward; Uniform: #7; won two Stanley Cup titles as a player and one as a coach.

Boucher played 18 professional hockey seasons (1921–1944), including 14 years in the National Hockey League with the Ottawa Senators (1921–1922) and the New York Rangers (1926–1938, 1943–1944). He won the Lady Byng Trophy (sportsmanship and gentlemanly conduct) seven out of eight seasons (1928–1931, 1933–1935).

The 5'9", 185-pound Boucher began playing hockey at age eight, and worked his way through juniors and seniors, before joining the professional ranks in 1921 with the NHL's Ottawa Senators. After one season with the Senators, his contract was sold to the Vancouver Maroons (Pacific Coast Hockey Association), where he was selected to league All-Star teams for three consecutive years (1923–1925).

When the PCHA folded in 1926, his contract was sold to the NHL expansion New York Rangers, a team with which he would become associated for 25 years. He helped the Rangers win the franchise's first Stanley Cup championship in its second year of existence (1928), and led New York to its second title in 1933. Boucher retired during the 1937–1938 season, but returned briefly for 15 games in the 1943–1944 season when the Rangers' roster was depleted due to players serving in the military during World War II.

After his first retirement, Boucher coached the New York Rovers (the Rangers' minor league team in the Eastern Amateur Hockey League) and led the squad to the league championship in 1939, before rejoining the NHL Rangers as a coach. He led the Rangers to the 1940 Stanley Cup title; coached the team for the next 10 seasons; and added the title of general manager to his responsibilities during the 1946–1947 season. In 1949, Boucher resigned as the team's coach to focus on being the franchise's general manger, a position he held until 1955.

While with the Rangers, he served as chairman of the NHL rules committee for 15 years, and after leaving the NHL, Boucher served as commissioner of the Saskatchewan Junior Hockey League from 1959 to 1967.

Boucher was selected First All-Star Team Center three times (1933–1935); Second All-Star Team Center in 1931; named First All-Star Team Coach in 1942; and Second All-Star Team Coach in 1940. Boucher was inducted into the Ottawa Sports Hall of Fame in 1966; into the Canadian Sports Hall of Fame in 1975; and in 1998, he was ranked number 61 on *The Hockey News*' list of the 100 Greatest Hockey Players. After he died, he was awarded the Lester Patrick Trophy in 1993 for his lifetime contribution to the game in the United States.

One of Boucher's brothers, George, played on the Ottawa Senators' dynasty teams of the 1920s; won four Stanley Cup championships; and was inducted into the Hockey Hall of Fame in 1960.

Frank Boucher's Career Statistics

			REGULAR SEASON					PLAYOFFS				
SEASON	**TEAM**	**LEAGUE**	**GP**	**G**	**A**	**TP**	**PIM**	**GP**	**G**	**A**	**TP**	**PIM**
1916–1917	Ottawa New Edinburghs	OCJHL	9	11	0	11		2	6	0	6	
1917–1918	Ottawa New Edinburghs	OCJHL	4	1	0	1	0					
1917–1918	Ottawa Munitions	OCHL	1	0	0	0	0	1	0	0	0	0
1918–1919	Ottawa New Edinburghs	OCHL	7	1	2	3	5					
1919–1920	Lethbridge Vets	ASHL										
1919–1920	Lethbridge Vets	Al-Cup	1	1	0	1	0					
1920–1921	Banff	RMSHL										
1921–1922	Ottawa Senators	NHL	24	8	2	10	4	1	0	0	0	0
1922–1923	Vancouver Maroons	PCHA	29	11	9	20	2	2	0	1	1	2
1922–1923	Vancouver Maroons	St-Cup						4	2	0	2	0
1923–1924	Vancouver Maroons	PCHA	28	15	5	20	10	2	1	0	1	0
1923–1924	Vancouver Millionaires	West-P						3	1	0	1	0
1923–1924	Vancouver Maroons	St-Cup						2	1	1	2	2
1924–1925	Vancouver Maroons	WCHL	27	16	12	28	6					
1925–1926	Vancouver Maroons	WHL	29	15	7	22	14					
1926–1927	New York Rangers	NHL	44	13	15	28	17	2	0	0	0	4
1927–1928	New York Rangers	NHL	44	23	12	35	15	9	7	3	10	2
1928–1929	New York Rangers	NHL	44	10	16	26	8	6	1	0	1	0
1929–1930	New York Rangers	NHL	42	26	36	62	16	3	1	1	2	0
1930–1931	New York Rangers	NHL	44	12	27	39	20	4	0	2	2	0
1931–1932	New York Rangers	NHL	48	12	23	35	18	7	3	6	9	0
1932–1933	New York Rangers	NHL	46	7	28	35	4	8	2	2	4	6
1933–1934	New York Rangers	NHL	48	14	30	44	4	2	0	0	0	0
1934–1935	New York Rangers	NHL	48	13	32	45	2	4	0	3	3	0
1935–1936	New York Rangers	NHL	48	11	18	29	2					
1936–1937	New York Rangers	NHL	44	7	13	20	5	9	2	3	5	0
1937–1938	New York Rangers	NHL	18	0	1	1	2					
1938–1939	New York Rovers	EAHL										
1939–1943	New York Rangers	NHLMGNT										
1943–1944	New York Rangers	NHL	15	4	10	14	2					
1944–1955	New York Rangers	NHLMGNT										

SEASON	TEAM	LEAGUE	REGULAR SEASON GP	G	A	TP	PIM	PLAYOFFS GP	G	A	TP	PIM
	NHL TOTALS		557	160	263	423	119	55	16	20	36	12

Sources: Canadian Sports Hall of Fame; Hockey Hall of Fame; Hockey-Reference.com; Ottawa Sports Hall of Fame

Boucher, George "Buck" (born: August 19, 1896 in Ottawa, Ontario, Canada; died: October 17, 1960); inducted into the Hockey Hall of Fame in 1960 as a player; Position: Forward; won four Stanley Cup championships.

A member of one of hockey's best-known families (his younger brother Frank was inducted into the Hockey Hall of Fame in 1958, while brothers Billy, Bob, and Joe also played in the NHL), Boucher's career lasted 17 seasons (in both the National Hockey Association and the National Hockey League) with the Ottawa Senators (1915–1929), Montreal Maroons (1929–1931), and the Chicago Black Hawks (1931–1932).

He was a member of the Senators when the team became one of the founding franchises of the National Hockey League in 1917. The 5'9", 169-pound Boucher eventually helped the Senators win four Stanley Cup championships (1920–1921, 1923, 1927).

After playing one season with the Black Hawks, he retired from the NHL; played nine games with the Boston Cubs of the Canadian-American Hockey League; and ended his professional career in 1932. The next season, Boucher led the Cubs to the league championship as the team's coach, before returning to the NHL to coach the Senators to a last-place finish in the 1933–1934 season. He continued as the team's coach when the franchise moved to St. Louis (and became the Eagles) in 1934, but lost his job when the team disbanded in 1935. After coaching for five more years in the minor leagues, Boucher retired from the game.

After being away from the game for five years, he returned to coach the Ottawa Senators (Quebec Senior Hockey League) and led the team to the 1949 Allan Cup championship. He helped train the Canadian team (Ottawa Royal Canadian Air Force Flyers) to a gold medal at the 1948 Winter Olympics (St. Moritz, Switzerland).

Buck Boucher's Career Statistics

SEASON	TEAM	LEAGUE	REGULAR SEASON GP	G	A	TP	PIM	PLAYOFFS GP	G	A	TP	PIM
1913–1914	Ottawa New Edinburghs	Exhib.	5	1	0	1						
1914–1915	Ottawa New Edinburghs	OCHL	15	12	0	12		1	0	0	0	
1914–1915	Ottawa Royal Canadians	OCHL	4	6	0	6		2	2	0	2	
1915–1916	Ottawa Royal Canadians	OCHL										
1915–1916	Montreal La Casquette	MCHL	1	1	0	1	0					
1915–1916	Ottawa Senators	NHA	19	9	1	10	62					
1916–1917	Ottawa Senators	NHA	18	10	5	15	27	2	1	0	1	8
1917–1918	Ottawa Senators	NHL	21	9	8	17	46					
1918–1919	Ottawa Senators	NHL	17	3	2	5	29	5	2	0	2	9
1919–1920	Ottawa Senators	NHL	22	9	8	17	55					
1919–1920	Ottawa Senators	St-Cup						5	2	0	2	2
1920–1921	Ottawa Senators	NHL	23	11	8	19	53	2	3	0	3	10
1920–1921	Ottawa Senators	St-Cup						5	2	0	2	9
1921–1922	Ottawa Senators	NHL	23	13	12	25	12	2	0	0	0	4
1922–1923	Ottawa Senators	NHL	24	14	9	23	58	2	0	1	1	2
1922–1923	Ottawa Senators	St-Cup						6	2	1	3	6
1923–1924	Ottawa Senators	NHL	21	13	10	23	38	2	0	1	1	4
1924–1925	Ottawa Senators	NHL	28	15	5	20	95					
1925–1926	Ottawa Senators	NHL	36	8	4	12	64	2	0	0	0	10
1926–1927	Ottawa Senators	NHL	40	8	3	11	115	6	0	0	0	43
1927–1928	Ottawa Senators	NHL	43	7	5	12	78	2	0	0	0	4
1928–1929	Ottawa Senators	NHL	29	3	1	4	60					
1928–1929	Montreal Maroons	NHL	12	1	1	2	10					
1929–1930	Montreal Maroons	NHL	37	2	6	8	50	3	0	0	0	2
1930–1931	Montreal Maroons	NHL	30	0	0	0	25					
1931–1932	Chicago Black Hawks	NHL	43	1	5	6	50	2	0	1	1	0
1932–1933	Boston Cubs	Can-Am	9	0	0	0	8					

SEASON	TEAM	LEAGUE	REGULAR SEASON GP	G	A	TP	PIM	PLAYOFFS GP	G	A	TP	PIM
1933–1934	Ottawa Senators	NHLMGNT										
	NHL TOTALS		449	117	87	204	838	28	5	3	8	88

Sources: Hockey Hall of Fame; Hockey-Reference.com

Boudreau, Louis "Lou" (born: July 17, 1917 in Harvey, Illinois; died: August 10, 2001 in Frankfort, Illinois); inducted into the National Baseball Hall of Fame and Museum in 1970 as a player; Position: Shortstop; Bats: Right; Throws: Right; Uniform: #5; was part of a unique move when he became manager of the Cubs and was replaced in the broadcast booth by the then-current Cubs manager, Charlie Grimm; youngest manager ever (age 24) in the major leagues.

Making his major league debut on September 9, 1938, the 5'11", 185-pound Boudreau played 15 seasons (1938–1952) with the Cleveland Indians (1938–1950) and Boston Red Sox (1951–1952). He appeared in eight All-Star games (1940–1945, 1947–1948); led the Indians to the 1948 World Series championship; and was named the American League Most Valuable Player (1948). He was a player-manager for the Indians from 1942 to 1950; was the 1949 All-Star game manager; a player-manager for the Red Sox in 1952; and after retiring as a player, managed the Red Sox until 1954.

Boudreau led American League shortstops in fielding eight times; won the 1944 league batting title (.327); and led the league in doubles three times (1941, 1944, 1947). After three dismal seasons as the manager of the Kansas City Athletics (1955–1957), he became a radio color commentator for the Chicago Cubs.

On July 14, 1946, he hit four consecutive doubles in one game against the Boston Red Sox, tying the major league record; in 1948, he struck out only nine times in 560 at bats; and his number 5 jersey was retired by the Cleveland Indians in 1970.

Early in the 1960 season, Cubs owner Philip Wrigley convinced Boudreau to leave the broadcast booth to manage the team, and replaced him in the booth with then-current team manager Charlie Grimm. After this one-season move did not work for either man, Grimm retired from the game and Boudreau returned to the broadcast booth, where he stayed for 30 years. In addition to his playing days and broadcasting career, Boudreau managed the Cleveland Indians (1942–1950), Boston Red Sox (1952–1954), Kansas City Athletics (1955–1957), and Chicago Cubs (1960) to an overall 1,162–1,224 (.487) record.

He hit .300 or better in a season four times (1944–1945, 1947–1948) and won the American League batting title in 1944 (.327) as a player-manager with the Indians. As a manager, he created the Ted Williams defensive shift (moving all but one infield player to the right side of the field) and converted Bob Lemon from an infielder to a hall-of-fame pitcher.

Boudreau played on the Indians' team that stopped Joe DiMaggio's 56-game hitting streak, when he fielded a ground ball and threw DiMaggio out at first base in his last at-bat of the game.

As a young man, he was also a basketball star and led his University of Illinois (Urbana-Champaign) team to the Big Ten title in 1937 and earned All-American honors in 1938. He also served as captain of both the baseball and basketball teams. When he signed a contract to play baseball for the Indians, he was deemed ineligible for college athletics, and appeared in one major league game for Cleveland as a pinch-hitter in 1938. He also played professional basketball briefly with the Hammond Ciesar All-Americans of the National Basketball League.

After having played in one game with the Indians in 1938, Boudreau was sent to the minor league Buffalo Bisons of the International League in 1939, and was called up to the major league in the second half of the season. He joined the Indians full-time in 1940 and was named to the All-Star team. In 1942 (at age 24), he was named player-manager of the Indians, making him the youngest man ever to manage a major league team from the beginning of a season.

Before attending the University of Illinois, Boudreau excelled at both baseball and basketball at Thornton Township High School (Harvey, Illinois).

Lou Boudreau's Career Statistics

YEAR	TEAM	LG	G	AB	R	H	2B	3B	HR	RBI	BB	SO	SB	AVG	SLG
1938	Cleveland	AL	1	1	0	0	0	0	0	0	1	0	0	.000	.000
1939	Cleveland	AL	53	225	42	58	15	4	0	19	28	24	2	.258	.360
1940	Cleveland	AL	155	627	97	185	46	10	9	101	73	39	6	.295	.443
1941	Cleveland	AL	148	579	95	149	45	8	10	56	85	57	9	.257	.415
1942	Cleveland	AL	147	506	57	143	18	10	2	58	75	39	7	.283	.370
1943	Cleveland	AL	152	539	69	154	32	7	3	67	90	31	4	.286	.388

YEAR	TEAM	LG	G	AB	R	H	2B	3B	HR	RBI	BB	SO	SB	AVG	SLG
1944	Cleveland	AL	150	584	91	191	45	5	3	67	73	39	11	.327	.437
1945	Cleveland	AL	97	345	50	106	24	1	3	48	35	20	0	.307	.409
1946	Cleveland	AL	140	515	51	151	30	6	6	62	40	14	6	.293	.410
1947	Cleveland	AL	150	538	79	165	45	3	4	67	67	10	1	.307	.424
1948	Cleveland	AL	152	560	116	199	34	6	18	106	98	9	3	.355	.534
1949	Cleveland	AL	134	475	53	135	20	3	4	60	70	10	0	.284	.364
1950	Cleveland	AL	81	260	23	70	13	2	1	29	31	5	1	.269	.346
1951	Boston	AL	82	273	37	73	18	1	5	47	30	12	1	.267	.396
1952	Boston	AL	4	2	1	0	0	0	0	2	0	0	0	.000	.000
	TOTALS		1,646	6,029	861	1,779	385	66	68	789	796	309	51	.295	.415

Lou Boudreau's Managerial Record

YEAR	TEAM	W	L	WIN%
1942	Cleveland	75	79	.487
1943	Cleveland	82	71	.536
1944	Cleveland	72	82	.468
1945	Cleveland	73	72	.503
1946	Cleveland	68	86	.442
1947	Cleveland	80	74	.519
1948	Cleveland	97	58	.626
1949	Cleveland	89	65	.578
1950	Cleveland	92	62	.597
1952	Boston	76	78	.494
1953	Boston	84	69	.549
1954	Boston	69	85	.448
1955	Kansas City	63	91	.409
1956	Kansas City	52	102	.338
1957	Kansas City	36	67	.350
1960	Chicago	54	83	.394
	TOTALS	1,162	1,224	.487

Sources: Baseball-Reference.com; National Baseball Hall of Fame and Museum

Boulos, John "Frenchy" "Pocket Rocket" (born: June 7, 1921 in Haiti; died: January 16, 2002 in Brooklyn, New York); inducted into the National Soccer Hall of Fame and Museum in 1980 as a player; Position: Forward; won championships at every level of play.

Boulos attended the St. Louis De Gonzagne School in Haiti before moving to the United States in 1930, where he began playing soccer at the Manual Training School in Brooklyn, New York. He helped lead the team to the New York City championship; was the city's leading scorer; and was named Most Valuable Player. He then played for the Bay Ridge Hearts (Brooklyn) and continued his scoring prowess.

Leaving the junior ranks, Boulos signed with Segura of the Metropolitan League, before moving up to the American Soccer League, playing for Brooklyn Hispano.

In 1942, he joined the U.S. Army Air Force during World War II and was assigned to India, where he continued to play soccer. He organized an American soccer team known as the Eagles and competed in the British Military League, winning one championship.

After the war, Boulos rejoined Hispano for the 1946–1947 season, and played with the team for three years before joining New York Hakoah (New York, New York) of the American Soccer League for the 1949–1950 season. He left the ASL in 1953 to play for Lithuanian Sport (Brooklyn) in the German-American League; won the league championship his first season; and won the New York State Cup in 1954.

He played for the New York Stars against both the English club Liverpool in 1946 and the Israeli club Hapoel Tel Aviv in 1947. Boulos played for the American Soccer League All-Stars against the Turkish club Besiktas in 1950; a team representing the English F.A. in 1951; and the Young Boys club of Bern, Switzerland in 1953.

Source: National Soccer Hall of Fame and Museum

Bourque, Raymond "Ray" (born: December 28, 1960 in Montreal, Quebec, Canada); inducted into the Hockey Hall of Fame in 2004 as a player; Position: Defense; Uniform: #7, 77; first non-goaltender to win the Calder Trophy and a spot on the First All-Star Team in the same season; won a Stanley Cup title in his last season; his jersey #77 has been retired by both the Boston Bruins and Colorado Avalanche.

After being chosen in the first round (eighth overall selection) of the 1979 National Hockey League Draft by the Boston Bruins, Bourque played 22 seasons in the NHL with the Bruins (1979–2000) and the Colorado Avalanche (2000–2001). In his rookie NHL season, Bourque scored 65 points (17 goals, 48 assists), the most for a rookie defenseman in NHL history at the time. He won the Calder Trophy as the NHL's Rookie of the Year and a spot on the First All-Star Team, becoming the first non-goaltender to win both honors in the same season.

During his 20 seasons with the Bruins, 12 as team captain, the 5'11", 220-pound Bourque was named to 19 All-Star Teams, 13 on the First Team (1980, 1982, 1984–1985, 1987–1988, 1990–1994, 1996, 2001) and six on the Second Team (1981, 1983, 1986, 1989, 1995, 1999); won the James Norris Memorial Trophy as the league's best defenseman five times (1987–1988, 1990–1991, 1994); the King Clancy Memorial Trophy for leadership in 1992; and the Lester Patrick Trophy for his contributions to hockey in the United States in 2003. He appeared in the Stanley Cup finals three times (winning in 2001 and losing in 1988 and 1990).

Bourque wore jersey #7 for his first eight seasons with the Bruins until it was retired by the team to honor Phil Esposito, after which, he switched to jersey #77. He played for the Avalanche for just over one season, and retired in 2001, after winning his only Stanley Cup title. He represented Canada in three Canada Cup tournaments (1981, 1984, 1997) and in the 1998 Winter Olympics in Nagano, Japan, failing to win a medal.

His jersey #77 has been retired by both the Boston Bruins and Colorado Avalanche; he was only the sixth defenseman in NHL history to score 30 goals in a season (1984); third defenseman in NHL history to score 1,000 points (1992); and in 1998, he was ranked number 14 on *The Hockey News*' list of the 100 Greatest Hockey Players.

Ray Bourque's Career Statistics

			REGULAR SEASON						PLAYOFFS				
SEASON	**TEAM**	**LEAGUE**	**GP**	**G**	**A**	**TP**	**PIM**	**+/–**	**GP**	**G**	**A**	**TP**	**PIM**
1976–1977	Sorel Eperviers	QMJHL	69	12	36	48	61						
1977–1978	Verdun Eperviers	QMJHL	72	22	57	79	90		4	2	1	3	0
1978–1979	Verdun Eperviers	QMJHL	63	22	71	93	44		11	3	16	19	18
1979–1980	Boston Bruins	NHL	80	17	48	65	73	+52	10	2	9	11	27
1980–1981	Boston Bruins	NHL	67	27	29	56	96	+29	3	0	1	1	2
1981–1982	Canada	Can-Cup	7	1	4	5	6						
1981–1982	Boston Bruins	NHL	65	17	49	66	51	+22	9	1	5	6	16
1982–1983	Boston Bruins	NHL	65	22	51	73	20	+49	17	8	15	23	10
1983–1984	Boston Bruins	NHL	78	31	65	96	57	+51	3	0	2	2	0
1984–1985	Canada	Can-Cup	8	0	4	4	8						
1984–1985	Boston Bruins	NHL	73	20	66	86	53	+30	5	0	3	3	4
1985–1986	Boston Bruins	NHL	74	19	58	77	68	+17	3	0	0	0	0
1986–1987	Boston Bruins	NHL	78	23	72	95	36	+44	4	1	2	3	0
1986–1987	NHL All-Stars	RV-87	2	1	0	1	2						
1987–1988	Canada	Can-Cup	9	2	6	8	10						
1987–1988	Boston Bruins	NHL	78	17	64	81	72	+34	23	3	18	21	26
1988–1989	Boston Bruins	NHL	60	18	43	61	52	+20	10	0	4	4	6
1989–1990	Boston Bruins	NHL	76	19	65	84	50	+31	17	5	12	17	16
1990–1991	Boston Bruins	NHL	76	21	73	94	75	+33	19	7	18	25	12
1991–1992	Boston Bruins	NHL	80	21	60	81	56	+11	12	3	6	9	12
1992–1993	Boston Bruins	NHL	78	19	63	82	40	+38	4	1	0	1	2
1993–1994	Boston Bruins	NHL	72	20	71	91	58	+26	13	2	8	10	0
1994–1995	Boston Bruins	NHL	46	12	31	43	20	+3	5	0	3	3	0
1995–1996	Boston Bruins	NHL	82	20	62	82	58	+31	5	1	6	7	2
1996–1997	Boston Bruins	NHL	62	19	31	50	18	–11					
1997–1998	Boston Bruins	NHL	82	13	35	48	80	+2	6	1	4	5	2
1997–1998	Canada	Olympics	6	1	2	3	4						
1998–1999	Boston Bruins	NHL	81	10	47	57	34	–7	12	1	9	10	14
1999–2000	Boston Bruins	NHL	65	10	28	38	20	–11					

SEASON	TEAM	LEAGUE	REGULAR SEASON GP	G	A	TP	PIM	+/–	PLAYOFFS GP	G	A	TP	PIM
1999–2000	Colorado Avalanche	NHL	14	8	6	14	6	+9	13	1	8	9	8
2000–2001	Colorado Avalanche	NHL	80	7	52	59	48	+25	21	4	6	10	12
	NHL TOTALS		1,612	410	1,169	1,579	1,141		214	41	139	180	171

Sources: Hockey Hall of Fame; Hockey-Reference.com

Bower, John William "Johnny" (born: November 8, 1924 in Prince Albert, Saskatchewan, Canada); inducted into the Hockey Hall of Fame in 1976 as a player; Position: Goalie; Uniform: #1; won three Calder Cup titles; won four Stanley Cup championships.

During his 25-year professional hockey career, Bower played for the Cleveland Barons (American Hockey League, 1945–1953, 1957–1958); New York Rangers (National Hockey League, 1953–1955); Providence Reds (AHL, 1955–1957); and the Toronto Maple Leafs (1958–1970). Before starting his professional hockey career, he had served in the army during World War II.

After playing one full NHL season with New York (1953–1954), Bower spent the next four seasons between the NHL, the American Hockey League, and the Western Hockey League. During 14 seasons in the minors, he won the Les Cunningham Award as the AHL's Most Valuable Player three straight years (1956–1958); the Hap Holmes Award as the league's best goalie three times (1952, 1957–1958); and led his teams to three Calder Cup titles (1951 and 1953 with the Barons and in 1956 with the Providence Reds). The 5'11", 189-pound Bower rejoined the NHL full-time in the 1958–1959 season with the Toronto Maple Leafs. Never wearing a mask in his career, Bower played with Toronto for 12 seasons before retiring in 1970.

He led the Leafs to the Stanley Cup finals his first two seasons with the team (1959–1960), losing both times to the Montreal Canadiens. Bower eventually led the franchise to three straight titles (1962–1964), and as a 43-year-old goalie, guided the team to the 1967 Stanley Cup championship.

After retiring in 1970 as the oldest goalie ever to play in the NHL, Bower stayed with the Leafs as a scout and goalie coach from 1976 to 1978. He won the Vezina Trophy as the league's best goalie twice (1961, 1965) and was named First All-Star Team Goalie in 1961. In 1969, he became the oldest goalie ever to appear in a Stanley Cup playoff game.

In 1998, he was ranked number 87 on *The Hockey News*' list of the 100 Greatest Hockey Players; was inducted into the Etobicoke Sports Hall of Fame in 1994 and into the American Hockey League Hall of Fame in 2006; and received a star on Canada's Walk of Fame in 2007.

Johnny Bower's Career Statistics

SEASON	TEAM	LEAGUE	REGULAR SEASON GP	W	L	T	SO	AVG	PLAYOFFS GP	W	L	SO	AVG
1944–1945	Prince Albert Black Hawks	SJHL	10	5	4	1	0	2.57					
1944–1945	Laura Beavers	SIHA							1	1	0	0	3.00
1944–1945	Prince Albert Black Hawks	M-Cup	3	0	3	0	0	7.67					
1945–1946	Cleveland Barons	AHL	41	18	17	6	4	3.90					
1945–1946	Providence Reds	AHL	1	0	1	0	0	5.00					
1946–1947	Cleveland Barons	AHL	40	22	11	7	3	3.10					
1947–1948	Cleveland Barons	AHL	31	18	6	6	1	2.65					
1948–1949	Cleveland Barons	AHL	37	23	9	5	3	3.43	5	2	3	0	4.19
1949–1950	Cleveland Barons	AHL	61	38	15	8	5	3.30	9	4	5	0	2.96
1950–1951	Cleveland Barons	AHL	70	44	21	5	5	2.99	11	8	3	0	2.73
1951–1952	Cleveland Barons	AHL	68	44	19	5	3	2.41	5	2	3	0	3.40
1952–1953	Cleveland Barons	AHL	61	40	19	2	6	2.53	11	7	4	4	1.69
1953–1954	New York Rangers	NHL	70	29	31	10	5	2.60					
1954–1955	New York Rangers	NHL	5	2	2	1	0	2.60					
1954–1955	Vancouver Canucks	WHL	63	30	25	8	7	2.71	5	1	4	0	3.20
1955–1956	Providence Reds	AHL	61	45	14	2	3	2.81	9	7	2	0	2.56
1956–1957	New York Rangers	NHL	2	0	2	0	0	3.00					
1956–1957	Providence Reds	AHL	57	30	19	8	4	2.37	5	1	4	0	3.00
1957–1958	Cleveland Barons	AHL	64	37	23	3	8	2.17					

				REGULAR SEASON						PLAYOFFS			
SEASON	TEAM	LEAGUE	GP	W	L	T	SO	AVG	GP	W	L	SO	AVG
1958–1959	Toronto Maple Leafs	NHL	39	15	17	7	3	2.72	12	5	7	0	3.06
1959–1960	Toronto Maple Leafs	NHL	66	34	24	8	5	2.68	10	4	6	0	2.88
1960–1961	Toronto Maple Leafs	NHL	58	33	15	10	2	2.50	3	0	3	0	2.67
1961–1962	Toronto Maple Leafs	NHL	59	31	18	10	2	2.56	10	6	3	0	2.07
1962–1963	Toronto Maple Leafs	NHL	42	20	15	7	1	2.60	10	8	2	2	1.60
1963–1964	Toronto Maple Leafs	NHL	51	24	16	11	5	2.11	14	8	6	2	2.12
1964–1965	Toronto Maple Leafs	NHL	34	13	13	8	3	2.38	5	2	3	0	2.43
1965–1966	Toronto Maple Leafs	NHL	35	18	10	5	3	2.25	2	0	2	0	4.00
1966–1967	Toronto Maple Leafs	NHL	27	12	9	3	2	2.64	4	2	0	1	1.64
1967–1968	Toronto Maple Leafs	NHL	43	14	18	7	4	2.25					
1968–1969	Toronto Maple Leafs	NHL	20	5	4	3	2	2.85	4	0	2	0	4.29
1969–1970	Toronto Maple Leafs	NHL	1	0	1	0	0	5.00					
	NHL TOTALS		552	250	195	90	37	2.51	74	35	34	5	2.47

Sources: American Hockey League Hall of Fame; Hockey Hall of Fame; Hockey-Reference.com

Bowie, Russell "Dubbie" (born: August 24, 1880 in Montreal, Quebec, Canada; died: April 9, 1959); inducted into the Hockey Hall of Fame in 1945 as a player; Position: Center-Forward; one of the original inductees into the Hockey Hall of Fame.

Active in the pre-National Hockey League era, Bowie played 10 amateur seasons (1898–1908) with the Montreal Victorias in both the Canadian Amateur Hockey League/Association and the Eastern Canada Amateur Hockey Association. In 1898, he won a Stanley Cup championship with the Victorias and retired from the game in 1909 when the professional National Hockey Association was formed.

After retiring as an amateur player, Bowie served as a referee in the professional NHA.

Russell Bowie's Career Statistics

			REGULAR SEASON					PLAYOFFS				
SEASON	TEAM	LEAGUE	GP	G	A	TP	PIM	GP	G	A	TP	PIM
1892–1893	Montreal St. John's	QAHA										
1893–1894	Montreal Tuckers	QAHA										
1894–1895	Montreal Comets	MCJHL										
1894–1895	Montreal Tuckers	QAHA										
1895–1896	Montreal Comets	MCJHL										
1895–1896	Montreal Tuckers	QAHA										
1896–1897	Montreal Comets	MCJHL										
1896–1897	Montreal Victorias	MCJHL										
1897–1899	Montreal Victorias-2	QAHA-I										
1898–1899	Montreal Victorias	CAHL	7	11	0	11		2	1	0	1	
1899–1900	Montreal Victorias	CAHL	7	15	0	15						
1900–1901	Montreal Victorias	CAHL	7	24	0	24						
1901–1902	Montreal Victorias	CAHL	7	13	0	13						
1902–1903	Montreal Victorias	CAHL	7	22	0	22		2	0	0	0	3
1903–1904	Montreal Victorias	CAHL	8	27	0	27						
1904–1905	Montreal Victorias	ECAHA	8	26	0	26						
1905–1906	Montreal Victorias	ECAHA	9	30	0	30	8					
1906–1907	Montreal Victorias	ECAHA	10	38	0	38	13					
1907–1908	Montreal Victorias	ECAHA	10	31	0	31	22					
1908–1909	Montreal Victorias	IPAHU	5	21	0	21	19					
1909–1910	Montreal Victorias	IPAHU	3	6	0	6		2	5	0	5	8

Sources: Hockey Hall of Fame; Hockey-Reference.com

Bowman, William Scott "Scotty" (born: September 18, 1933 in Montreal, Quebec, Canada); inducted into the Hockey Hall of Fame in 1991 as a builder; led the Montreal Canadiens to at least 45 wins in each of his eight seasons as the team's coach; won a total of nine Stanley Cup titles.

As a coach for 27 years, Bowman never had a losing record in any full season. After a head injury ended his playing days, he became a coach with the Ottawa Jr. Canadiens in the Quebec Junior Hockey League in 1956, and later led the team to the 1958 Memorial Cup title.

After working in the minors for years, Bowman joined the National Hockey League as a coach with the St. Louis Blues in the 1967–1968 season and led the team to three straight Stanley Cup appearances (losing to the Montreal Canadiens in 1968 and 1969 and to the Boston Bruins in 1970). In 1971, he was hired by the Canadiens and would eventually win at least 45 games in each of his eight years as coach and lead the team to five Stanley Cup championships (1973, 1976–1979).

He left the Canadiens in 1979 to become coach and general manager of the Buffalo Sabres; left the NHL in 1987; later returned to the league as Director of Player Development for the Pittsburgh Penguins; became the team's coach in 1991 after being inducted into the Hockey Hall of Fame; and led the franchise to a Stanley Cup title in 1992.

In 1993, Bowman left Pittsburgh to coach the Detroit Red Wings, and led the team into the Stanley Cup playoffs, before eventually being eliminated by the San Jose Sharks. In 1995, he led the Red Wings into the Stanley Cup finals (the team's first appearance in 29 seasons), eventually losing to the New Jersey Devils in a four-game sweep. On December 5, 1995, Bowman made personal history when he coached his NHL-record 1,607th game, a 5–3 win over the Philadelphia Flyers.

In 1997, he led Detroit to the franchise's first Stanley Cup title in 42 years, and they repeated as league champions in 1998. On February 8, 1997, Bowman won his 1,000th regular-season game (6–5 in overtime against the Pittsburgh Penguins). After leading the Red Wings to another Stanley Cup championship in 2002 (his ninth title), Bowman announced his retirement as his players were celebrating on the ice.

He retired as the winningest coach in NHL regular-season history (1,244 victories, .654 winning percentage); his nine Stanley Cup championships as a coach rank first all-time; he is the only coach in the big four North American professional sports leagues (Major League Baseball, National Basketball Association, National Football League, National Hockey League) to win championships with three different teams; and he was a two-time Jack Adams Award winner (1977, 1996) as the NHL Coach of the Year.

Scotty Bowman's NHL Coaching Record

SEASON	TEAM	G	W	L	T	WIN%
1967–1968	St. Louis Blues	58	23	21	14	.517
1968–1969	St. Louis Blues	76	37	25	14	.579
1969–1970	St. Louis Blues	76	37	27	12	.566
1970–1971	St. Louis Blues	28	13	10	5	.554
1971–1972	Montreal Canadiens	78	46	16	16	.692
1972–1973	Montreal Canadiens	78	52	10	16	.769
1973–1974	Montreal Canadiens	78	45	24	9	.635
1974–1975	Montreal Canadiens	80	47	14	19	.706
1975–1976	Montreal Canadiens	80	58	11	11	.794
1976–1977	Montreal Canadiens	80	60	8	12	.825
1977–1978	Montreal Canadiens	80	59	10	11	.806
1978–1979	Montreal Canadiens	80	52	17	11	.719
1979–1980	Buffalo Sabres	80	47	17	16	.688
1981–1982	Buffalo Sabres	35	18	10	7	.614
1982–1983	Buffalo Sabres	80	38	29	13	.556
1983–1984	Buffalo Sabres	80	48	25	7	.644
1984–1985	Buffalo Sabres	80	38	28	14	.563
1985–1986	Buffalo Sabres	37	18	18	1	.500
1986–1987	Buffalo Sabres	12	3	7	2	.333
1991–1992	Pittsburgh Penguins	80	39	32	9	.544
1992–1993	Pittsburgh Penguins	84	56	21	7	.708
1993–1994	Detroit Red Wings	84	46	30	8	.595
1994–1995	Detroit Red Wings	48	33	11	4	.729
1995–1996	Detroit Red Wings	82	62	13	7	.799

SEASON	TEAM	G	W	L	T	WIN%
1996–1997	Detroit Red Wings	82	38	26	18	.573
1997–1998	Detroit Red Wings	82	44	23	15	.628
1998–1999	Detroit Red Wings	77	39	31	7	.552
1999–2000	Detroit Red Wings	82	48	24	10	.646
2000–2001	Detroit Red Wings	82	49	24	9	.652
2001–2002	Detroit Red Wings	82	51	21	10	.683
	NHL TOTALS	2,141	1,244	583	314	.654

Scotty Bowman's NHL Playoff Record

SEASON	TEAM	G	W	L	T	WIN%
1967–1968	St. Louis Blues	18	8	10	0	.444
1968–1969	St. Louis Blues	12	8	4	0	.667
1969–1970	St. Louis Blues	16	8	8	0	.500
1970–1971	St. Louis Blues	6	2	4	0	.333
1971–1972	Montreal Canadiens	6	2	4	0	.333
1972–1973	Montreal Canadiens	17	12	5	0	.706
1973–1974	Montreal Canadiens	6	2	4	0	.333
1974–1975	Montreal Canadiens	11	6	5	0	.545
1975–1976	Montreal Canadiens	13	12	1	0	.923
1976–1977	Montreal Canadiens	14	12	2	0	.857
1977–1978	Montreal Canadiens	15	12	3	0	.800
1978–1979	Montreal Canadiens	16	12	4	0	.750
1979–1980	Buffalo Sabres	14	9	5	0	.643
1981–1982	Buffalo Sabres	4	1	3	0	.250
1982–1983	Buffalo Sabres	10	6	4	0	.600
1983–1984	Buffalo Sabres	3	0	3	0	.000
1984–1985	Buffalo Sabres	5	2	3	0	.400
1991–1992	Pittsburgh Penguins	21	16	5	0	.762
1992–1993	Pittsburgh Penguins	12	7	5	0	.583
1993–1994	Detroit Red Wings	7	3	4	0	.429
1994–1995	Detroit Red Wings	18	12	6	0	.667
1995–1996	Detroit Red Wings	19	10	9	0	.526
1996–1997	Detroit Red Wings	20	16	4	0	.800
1997–1998	Detroit Red Wings	22	16	6	0	.727
1998–1999	Detroit Red Wings	10	6	4	0	.600
1999–2000	Detroit Red Wings	9	5	4	0	.556
2000–2001	Detroit Red Wings	6	2	4	0	.333
2001–2002	Detroit Red Wings	23	16	7	0	.696
	NHL TOTALS	353	223	130	0	.632

Sources: Hockey Hall of Fame; Hockey-Reference.com

Boxer, Matthew (born: 1913 in Irkutsk, Siberia, Russia: died: January 19, 1992 in Burlingame, California); inducted into the National Soccer Hall of Fame and Museum in 1961 as a builder; president of the San Francisco Football Association; Junior Soccer Commissioner for the United States Soccer Football Association.

As a young boy, Boxer played soccer in China before he and his family moved to the United States and settled in San Francisco, California. He played for Polytechnic High School (San Francisco) and the Mercury and French clubs, and in 1938, he played for the San Francisco All-Stars against the Los Angeles All-Stars.

After he quit playing soccer, Boxer coached at Polytechnic, before becoming president of the San Francisco Football Association. During his career, he served in a variety of administrative positions in the San Francisco area, and arranged for many foreign teams to play in the Bay Area, including Hapoel, Plymouth Argyle, Glasgow Celtic, Manchester City, and Dundee. He also helped secure San Francisco City Council financial support for the building of a soccer stadium with dressing rooms. In 1958, he was named Junior Soccer Commissioner for the United States Soccer Football Association.

Source: National Soccer Hall of Fame and Museum

Bradley, Gordon (born: November 23, 1938 in Sunderland, England); inducted into the National Soccer Hall of Fame and Museum in 1996 as a builder; International Caps (1973): 1, Goals: 0; only person in the history of the game to have coached soccer superstars Pelé, Franz Beckenbauer, and Johan Cruyff; won two NASL championships.

Bradley began playing soccer at the relatively advanced age of 16, but a serious knee injury kept him out of the game for two years. He recovered and played for Carlisle United, where he made 130 Football League appearances and scored three goals between 1957 and 1960.

After moving to Canada in 1963, he played for Toronto Roma in the Eastern Canada Professional Soccer League; stayed with the team for two seasons; and played for Toronto City in 1965, before moving to the United States. Originally signed by the New York Generals of the North American Soccer League as a player and assistant coach, Bradley stayed in the United States, and was a longtime coach in the NASL.

When the Generals folded at the end of the 1968 season, he played for the Baltimore Bays (also of the NASL), before returning to New York in 1971 to become the first player signed by the New York Cosmos of the NASL. In addition to his playing responsibilities, he was also head coach and vice president of the team from 1971 to 1977, and helped lead the franchise to two league championships (1972, 1977). In 1973, while still with the Cosmos, he coached the U.S. Men's National Team and made an international appearance against Israel in Beersheba.

In the late 1970s, Bradley moved to the Washington, D.C. area to become head coach and vice president of the NASL's Washington Diplomats. During his time with the Cosmos and the Diplomats, he coached three of the greatest soccer players of all time: Pelé, Franz Beckenbauer, and Johan Cruyff, the only person in the history of soccer to have coached each of these international superstars.

Bradley served as head coach of George Mason University's (Fairfax, Virginia) soccer team from 1985 to 2000, and led the Patriots to an overall record of 183–113–35 (.606). He led the team to six NCAA appearances and moved on to the second round three times. He was inducted into the Eastern New York Youth Soccer Hall of Fame (1997) and to the Mason Men's Soccer Hall of Fame (2006). He currently works as a television commentator of DC United's Major League Soccer games.

Gordon Bradley's North American Soccer League Statistics

YEAR	TEAM	G	GLS	ASST	PTS
1968	New York Generals	27	0	0	0
1969	Baltimore Bays	6	0	0	0
1971	New York Cosmos	18	0	0	0
1972	New York Cosmos	12	0	1	1
1973	New York Cosmos	9	0	0	0
1974	New York Cosmos	8	0	0	0
1975	New York Cosmos	1	0	0	0
	TOTALS	81	0	1	1

Source: National Soccer Hall of Fame and Museum

Bradley, William Warren "Bill" (born: July 28, 1943 in Crystal City, Missouri); inducted into the Naismith Memorial Basketball Hall of Fame in 1983 as a player; Position: Forward; Uniform: #24; first college basketball player to win the Sullivan Award as the country's top amateur athlete.

Bradley was a basketball star since his high school playing days at Crystal City (Missouri) High School from 1957 to 1961, where he scored 3,068 points and averaged 27.4 points-per-game in his 112-game high school career. He was a four-year letter winner; a two-time *Parade* All-American; a two-time All-State selection; a three-time All-Conference selection; led his team into the Missouri State Final Four three times; and was recruited by more than 70 colleges.

After high school, he went to Princeton University (New Jersey) from 1961 to 1965, and had to pay his own tuition, since at the time, Ivy League schools did not offer scholarships. He was named Associated Press, United Press International, and United States Basketball Writers Association Player of the Year (1965); was a consensus First Team All-American twice (1964–1965); a First Team All-Academic (1965); led the team to the 1965 NCAA Final Four, where he scored a record 58 points against Wichita State; was an All-Ivy League selection three times (1963–1965); NCAA Tournament MVP (1965); averaged 30.2 points-per-game (total of 2,503 points) in three college seasons; was a member of the gold medal-winning U.S. Olympic Team (1964, Tokyo, Japan); was a Rhodes Scholar at Oxford (1964); and received the Sullivan Award as the top amateur athlete in the country (1965), the first basketball player to win the honor. The Princeton Tigers won the Ivy League championship in each of his three varsity seasons.

As a freshman, Bradley made 57 consecutive free throws, a feat that has been unmatched by any other player, college or professional. As a sophomore, he led the league in rebounds, field goals, free throws, and total points; in his junior year, he scored 51 points against Harvard, more than the entire opposing team had scored before he was taken out of the game; and in his senior year, Bradley led Princeton to the highest national ranking it had ever achieved in basketball, third behind UCLA and Michigan.

After graduating from Princeton, the 6'5", 205-pound Bradley played professional basketball for Olympia Simmenthal in Italy for one season (1965–1966), before returning to the United States and enjoying a 10-year National Basketball Association career (1967–1977) with the New York Knicks. He helped the Knicks win two NBA titles (1970, 1973) and his jersey #24 was retired by the team in 1984.

In 1976, he wrote *Life on the Run*, which chronicled his experiences in the NBA, and after retiring as a player, he was elected to the United States Senate as a Democrat from New Jersey in 1979, and served three terms before leaving the Senate in 1997.

Bill Bradley's Career Statistics

YEAR	TEAM	G	MIN	FG	FT	REB	AST	PTS
1967–1968	New York	45	874	142	76	113	137	360
1968–1969	New York	82	2,413	407	206	350	302	1,020
1969–1970	New York	67	2,098	413	145	239	268	971
1970–1971	New York	78	2,300	413	144	260	280	970
1971–1972	New York	78	2,780	504	169	250	315	1,177
1972–1973	New York	82	2,998	575	169	301	367	1,319
1973–1974	New York	82	2,813	502	146	253	242	1,150
1974–1975	New York	79	2,787	452	144	251	247	1,048
1975–1976	New York	82	2,709	392	130	234	247	914
1976–1977	New York	67	1,027	127	34	103	128	288
	TOTALS	742	22,799	3,927	1,363	2,354	2,533	9,217

Sources: Basketball-Reference.com; Naismith Memorial Basketball Hall of Fame

Bradshaw, Terry Paxton (born: September 2, 1948 in Shreveport, Louisiana); inducted into the Pro Football Hall of Fame in 1989 as a player; Position: Quarterback; Uniform: #12; won four Super Bowl championships; threw the pass to Franco Harris that has become known as the "Immaculate Reception."

A star at Louisiana Tech University (Ruston, Louisiana), Bradshaw was the first player selected in the 1970 National Football League draft and had a 14-year career (1970–1983) with the Pittsburgh Steelers. Although the 6'3", 215-pound quarterback was known for calling his own plays, he was often publicly perceived as not being too bright, a criticism that Bradshaw ignored throughout his career, willing to let his on-field success do the talking for him.

During his career, he led the team to eight American Football Conference titles and four Super Bowl championships in six seasons (SB IX in 1975, SB X in 1976, SB XIII in 1979, and SB XIV in 1980); was named Most Valuable Player in Super Bowl XIII and XIV, and when he retired, Bradshaw held Super Bowl records for touchdowns (nine) and total yards (932). He passed for more than 27,000 career yards; was named NFL MVP in 1978, and was selected to three Pro Bowls. Bradshaw never led the NFL in passing and threw only two more career touchdowns (212) than interceptions (210).

On December 23, 1972, in an American Football Conference Divisional Playoff Game against the Oakland Raiders at Three Rivers Stadium (Pittsburgh, Pennsylvania), he threw the pass to Franco Harris that has become known as the "Immaculate Reception," considered one of the most famous (and controversial) plays in NFL history. At the time, the Steelers trailed the Oakland Raiders 7–6 and were facing fourth-and-10 on the team's own 40-yard line with 22 seconds left in the game and no time-outs available. The original play called for a pass to Barry Pearson, but when he could not get open, Bradshaw threw the ball toward fullback John Fuqua. Reacting to the throw, Raiders' safety Jack Tatum hit Fuqua as the ball arrived, knocking Fuqua to the ground, and sending the ball backwards, where it was caught by Steelers' running back Franco Harris, who ran the ball for a touchdown, giving the Steelers the win, 13–7.

Bradshaw attended Woodlawn High School (Shreveport, Louisiana) and led the Knights to the AAA High School Championship game, losing to the Sulphur Tors 12–9. While a senior at Woodlawn, he set a national record for throwing the javelin 244 feet and 11–3/4 inches, which led to his receiving more than 200 college track and field scholarship offers. He decided to attend Louisiana Tech; as a junior, his 2,890 total yards ranked first in the NCAA; and he led his team to a 33–13 win over Akron in the 1968 Grantland Rice Bowl.

Since retiring from the NFL, Bradshaw has been a long-time television broadcaster (currently with FOX NFL Sunday); appears in numerous television commercials and programs; has acted in movies (*Hooper* and *Cannonball Run* with Burt Reynolds and *Failure to Launch* with Sarah Jessica Parker); has written or co-written five books; recorded six country/western/gospel albums; and is active in NASCAR with FitzBradshaw Racing.

In 2006, he was inducted into the College Football Hall of Fame.

Terry Bradshaw's Career Statistics

					PASSING					RUSHING			
YEAR	TEAM	G	ATT	COMP	PCT	YDS	TD	INT	RATING	NO	YDS	AVG	TD
1970	Pittsburgh	13	218	83	38.1	1,410	6	24	30.4	32	233	7.3	1
1971	Pittsburgh	14	373	203	54.4	2,259	13	22	59.7	53	247	4.7	5
1972	Pittsburgh	14	308	147	47.7	1,887	12	12	64.1	58	346	6.0	7
1973	Pittsburgh	10	180	89	49.4	1,183	10	15	54.5	34	145	4.3	3
1974	Pittsburgh	8	148	67	45.3	785	7	8	55.2	34	224	6.6	2
1975	Pittsburgh	14	286	165	57.7	2,055	18	9	88.0	35	210	6.0	3
1976	Pittsburgh	10	192	92	47.9	1,177	10	9	65.4	31	219	7.1	3
1977	Pittsburgh	14	314	162	51.6	2,523	17	19	71.4	31	171	5.5	3
1978	Pittsburgh	16	368	207	56.3	2,915	28	20	84.7	32	93	2.9	1
1979	Pittsburgh	16	472	259	54.9	3,724	26	25	77.0	21	83	4.0	0
1980	Pittsburgh	15	424	218	51.4	3,339	24	22	75.0	36	111	3.1	2
1981	Pittsburgh	14	370	201	54.3	2,887	22	14	83.9	38	162	4.3	2
1982	Pittsburgh	9	240	127	52.9	1,768	17	11	81.4	8	10	1.3	0
1983	Pittsburgh	1	8	5	62.5	77	2	0	133.9	1	3	3.0	0
	TOTALS	168	3,901	2,025	51.9	27,989	212	210	70.9	444	2,257	5.1	32

Sources: College Football Hall of Fame; Pro Football Hall of Fame; Pro-Football-Reference.com

Brennan, Joseph R. (born: November 15, 1900 in Brooklyn, New York; died: May 10, 1989); inducted into the Naismith Memorial Basketball Hall of Fame in 1974 as a player; won five league championships as a player and compiled an overall 176–53 (.769) record as a coach.

Brennan played high school basketball at St. Augustine's Academy (Brooklyn, New York) from 1915 to 1919, where he was a four-year letter winner and the team captain as a senior. Deciding to forgo college, his professional career began with the Albany Senators of the New York League (1920–1921, 1922–1924).

During his 17-year professional career, Brennan played for many of the game's early startup teams and leagues, including the Plymouth Shawnees of the Pennsylvania Basketball League (1920–1921); Trenton (New Jersey) Royal Bengals II of the Eastern Basketball League (1920–1921); Wilkes-Barre (Pennsylvania) Barons I of the Eastern Basketball League (1920–22); Brooklyn (New York) Dodgers of the Metropolitan Basketball League (1921–1923); Springfield (New York) Gunners of the Interstate Basketball League (1921–1923); Brooklyn (New York) Visitations of the Metropolitan Basketball League (1923–1931) and of the American Basketball League 1934–1935); Holyoke (Massachusetts) Reds of the Interstate Basketball League (1921–1922); Troy (New York) Trojans II of the New York Basketball League (1922–1923); Amsterdam (New York) Flashes of the New York Basketball League (1922–23); Philadelphia (Pennsylvania) Jaspers of the Eastern Basketball League (1922–1923); Gloversville (New York) Wonder Workers of the New York Basketball League (1923–1924); Philadelphia (Pennsylvania) Kay of the Philadelphia Basketball League (1924–1925); Philadelphia (Pennsylvania) Cathedral of the Eastern Basketball League (1924–1925); Philadelphia (Pennsylvania) Cranes of the Eastern Basketball League (1925–1926); Trenton (New Jersey) Royal Bengals III of the Metropolitan Basketball League (1925–1926); and the Paterson (New Jersey) Crescents II of the Metropolitan Basketball League (1927–1928).

The 5'11", 175-pound Brennan led the Metropolitan Basketball League in scoring in 1922; led the Brooklyn Dodgers to the Metropolitan Basketball League championship in 1922 and 1923; and led the Brooklyn Visitations to the Metropolitan Basketball League / American Basketball League championship in 1929, 1931, and 1935.

After retiring as a player, he began his college coaching career with the Manhattan College (New York) freshman team from 1936 to 1938, before moving on to St. Francis College (Brooklyn, New York) from 1941 to 1948. With

Manhattan College, he compiled an 80–7 record and a 96–46 record with St. Francis, for an overall mark of 176–53 (.769).

Source: Naismith Memorial Basketball Hall of Fame

Bresnahan, Roger Philip (born: June 11, 1879 in Toledo, Ohio; died: December 4, 1944 in Toledo, Ohio); inducted into the National Baseball Hall of Fame and Museum in 1945 as a player by the Veterans Committee; Position: Catcher; Bats: Right; Throws: Right; first catcher inducted into the baseball hall of fame.

Bresnahan made his major league debut on August 27, 1897 with the Washington Senators, and during his 17-year career, he played for the Chicago Orphans (1900); Baltimore Orioles (1901–1902); New York Giants (1902–1908); was a player-manager with the St. Louis Cardinals (1909–1912); and ended his career as a player with the Chicago Cubs (1913–1915, serving as a player-manager his last year with the team). He was on the Giants team that won the 1905 World Series. After retiring as a player, he became owner-manager of the Toledo Mud Hens from 1916 to 1923, before going on to coach the New York Giants (1925–1928) and Detroit Tigers (1930–1931).

While primarily a catcher, Bresnahan played all nine positions at one time or another during his professional career. He introduced the shin guard and experimented with a protective helmet after being beaned during a game against the Cincinnati Reds. The 5’9”, 200-pound Bresnahan was the first catcher to be inducted into the hall of fame.

His major league debut was as a pitcher, and in his first big-league game, he threw a six-hit shutout in a 3-0 win over the St. Louis Browns. He continued to pitch for the next four seasons and three teams but, never able to perform consistently, tried playing various positions until made a catcher by John McGraw while with the Baltimore Orioles.

He hit two inside-the-park home runs in the same game twice in his career (May 30, 1902 with Baltimore against the Cleveland Blues and on June 6, 1904 with the Giants against the Pittsburgh Pirates). On July 1, 1903, while playing center field for the Giants, Bresnahan started a triple play against the St. Louis Cardinals. With the bases loaded he caught a line drive for an out, his throw to home held the runner at third base, the catcher threw to second base to get the runner off the bag, and the return throw home caught the runner trying to score from third.

Roger Bresnahan’s Career Statistics

YEAR	TEAM	LG	G	AB	R	H	2B	3B	HR	BB	SO	SB	AVG	SLG
1897	Washington	NL	7	18	2	6	0	0	0	1		0	.333	.333
1900	Chicago	NL	1	2	0	0	0	0	0	0		0	.000	.000
1901	Baltimore	AL	86	293	40	77	9	9	1	23		10	.263	.365
1902	Baltimore	AL	66	234	31	64	9	6	4	21		11	.274	.415
1902	New York	NL	50	178	16	52	13	3	1	16		6	.292	.416
1903	New York	NL	112	406	87	142	30	8	4	61		34	.350	.493
1904	New York	NL	109	402	81	114	22	7	5	58		13	.284	.410
1905	New York	NL	104	331	58	100	18	3	0	50		11	.302	.375
1906	New York	NL	124	405	69	114	22	4	0	81		25	.281	.356
1907	New York	NL	110	328	57	83	9	7	4	61		15	.253	.360
1908	New York	NL	140	449	70	127	25	3	1	83		14	.283	.359
1909	Saint Louis	NL	72	234	27	57	4	1	0	46		11	.244	.269
1910	Saint Louis	NL	88	234	35	65	15	3	0	55	17	13	.278	.368
1911	Saint Louis	NL	81	227	22	63	17	8	3	45	19	4	.278	.463
1912	Saint Louis	NL	48	108	8	36	7	2	1	14	9	4	.333	.463
1913	Chicago	NL	69	162	20	37	5	2	1	21	11	7	.228	.302
1914	Chicago	NL	86	248	42	69	10	4	0	49	20	14	.278	.351
1915	Chicago	NL	77	221	19	45	8	1	1	29	23	19	.204	.262
	TOTALS		1,430	4,480	684	1,251	223	71	26	714	99	211	.279	.378

Roger Bresnahan’s Career Managerial Record

YEAR	TEAM	W	L	WIN%	FINISH

YEAR	TEAM	W	L	WIN%	FINISH
1909	St. Louis	54	98	.355	7 (Player-Manager)
1910	St .Louis	63	90	.412	7 (Player-Manager)
1911	St. Louis	75	74	.503	5 (Player-Manager)
1912	St. Louis	63	90	.412	6 (Player-manager)
1915	Chicago	73	80	.477	4 (Player-Manager)
	TOTALS	328	432	.432	

Sources: Baseball-Reference.com; National Baseball Hall of Fame and Museum

Brett, George Howard (born: May 15, 1953 in Glen Dale, West Virginia); inducted into the National Baseball Hall of Fame and Museum in 1999 as a player; Position: Third Base; Bats: Left; Throws: Right; Uniform: #5; first Kansas City Royal inducted into the hall of fame; first player in baseball history to win batting titles in three different decades.

After being born in West Virginia, Brett and his family moved to El Segundo, California, where he eventually graduated from El Segundo High School in 1971, and was picked by the Kansas City Royals in the second round of the 1971 draft (29th overall selection).

Making his major league debut on August 2, 1973, Brett played his entire 21-year career with the Royals (1973–1993); led the Royals to two World Series (winning in 1985 and losing in 1980); was named to 12 All-Star teams (1976–1986, 1988); won the American League Most Valuable Player Award in 1980; and won a Gold Glove in 1985.

The 6', 200-pound Brett was the first player in major league history to accumulate 3,000 hits, 300 home runs, 600 doubles, 100 triples, 1,500 RBIs, and 200 stolen bases. He won three batting titles (1976, 1980, 1990) and his .390 average in 1980 was the highest in major league baseball since Ted Williams hit .406 in 1941. While his primary position was third base, during his career, Brett also played first base, shortstop, and in the outfield; and was the first Royal inducted into the baseball hall of fame.

Although a great major league hitter, it took Brett some time to establish himself. In three minor league seasons, he averaged only .281 and led the California League (while with the San Jose Bees) in errors at third base in his second professional season. In 1971, he played for the Billings (Montana) Mustangs (Rookie League), and moved to the San Jose (California) Bees (A level) in 1972, before finally reaching the AAA level in 1973 with the Omaha (Nebraska) Royals.

During his first trip to the major leagues in 1973, Brett hit only .125, and in his first full season with the team (1974), he hit only two home runs and 47 runs batted in. He gradually adapted to the majors, and in 1975, he led the American League in hits and triples. In 1979, he became only the sixth player in history to collect 20 or more doubles, triples, and home runs in the same season. In 1980, his .390 batting average was the highest ever for a third baseman; he established a Royals record by hitting in 30 consecutive games (July 18 to August 18); and he became one of the few hitters over a full season to have more RBIs (118) than games played (117).

On July 24, 1983, Brett was involved in one of baseball's greatest-ever tirades caught on tape, the so-called "pine tar" incident. With the Royals playing the New York Yankees in Yankee Stadium, he hit a ninth-inning, two-out home run to give Kansas City a 5–4 lead. When Brett returned to the dugout, Yankee manager Billy Martin protested to home plate umpire Tim McClelland that there was too much pine tar on Brett's bat. After measuring the amount of pine tar used, the umpire called Brett out, triggering one of the game's great tirades. After being restrained by his coaches and teammates, he was eventually ejected from the game and his home run disallowed, leading to a 4–3 Yankee win. While the tirade is well-known to all baseball fans, few realize that the story does not end there.

After reviewing the situation, American League president Lee McPhail overturned the umpire's decision and reinstated Brett's home run. Although ruling that Brett did indeed have too much pine tar on his bat, the league president reasoned that games should be won and lost on the playing field and not through technical rules infractions. He also decided that the bat should have been removed from the game, but that the player should not have been called out. McPhail ordered the game resumed on August 18, with the Royals leading 5–4. The Yankees failed to score in the bottom of the ninth inning and the Royals preserved the team's win. While the incident is famous in baseball lore, the results of the game had no bearing on the pennant race. The "pine tar" bat is on display in the baseball hall of fame.

After receiving a unique lifetime contract from the Royals in the early 1980s, Brett responded with a great year in 1985, hitting .335 with 112 runs batted in and a career-high 30 home runs, and leading the team to its first and, as of this writing, only World Series title. He won another batting title in 1990, making him the first player in baseball history to win batting titles in three different decades and the third-oldest ever (behind Ted Williams and Honus Wagner).

On September 30, 1992, in the team's last road game (against the California Angels), Brett got four hits in four at-bats to reach the 3,000-hit mark, becoming the first player ever to collect four hits in a game to reach that level. Although a great moment, it ended on an embarrassing note. While at first base after his fourth hit, he was enjoying the achievement with first baseman Wally Joyner when he was picked off by pitcher Tim Fortugno, who had just given up Brett's historic hit.

After getting a hit in his last at-bat in Arlington Stadium against the Texas Rangers, Brett retired after the 1993 season. Interestingly, his last game was also the final career game for Rangers' pitching great Nolan Ryan. The two players ended their careers on the same day and, five years later, they would both be inducted into the baseball hall of fame on their first ballot of eligibility.

During his career, Brett collected three or more hits in six consecutive games (May 8–13, 1976), setting a major league record; hit for the cycle twice (May 28, 1979 and July 25, 1990); and joined Ty Cobb as the only players to lead their league in hits and triples three times. His 3,154 career hits are the most by any third baseman in major league history, and he was elected to the hall of fame with the fourth-highest voting percentage in baseball history (98.2%), higher than Babe Ruth, Hank Aaron, Willie Mays, Stan Musial, Ted Williams, and Joe DiMaggio. In 1999, he was ranked number 55 on *The Sporting News*' list of the 100 Greatest Baseball Players, and was nominated as a finalist for the Major League Baseball All-Century Team. After retiring as a player, Brett moved into the Royals front office as the team's vice-president in charge of baseball operations, and also serves as a part-time coach and hitting instructor in spring training.

George Brett's Career Statistics

YEAR	TEAM	G	AB	R	H	2B	3B	HR	RBI	BB	SO	SB	AVG	SLG
1973	Kansas City	13	40	2	5	2	0	0	0	0	5	0	.125	.175
1974	Kansas City	133	457	49	129	21	5	2	47	21	38	8	.282	.363
1975	Kansas City	159	634	84	195	35	13	11	89	46	49	13	.308	.456
1976	Kansas City	159	645	94	215	34	14	7	67	49	36	21	.333	.462
1977	Kansas City	139	564	105	176	32	13	22	88	55	24	14	.312	.532
1978	Kansas City	128	510	79	150	45	8	9	62	39	35	23	.294	.467
1979	Kansas City	154	645	119	212	42	20	23	107	51	36	17	.329	.563
1980	Kansas City	117	449	87	175	33	9	24	118	58	22	15	.390	.664
1981	Kansas City	89	347	42	109	27	7	6	43	27	23	14	.314	.484
1982	Kansas City	144	552	101	166	32	9	21	82	71	51	6	.301	.505
1983	Kansas City	123	464	90	144	38	2	25	93	57	39	0	.310	.563
1984	Kansas City	104	377	42	107	21	3	13	69	38	37	0	.284	.459
1985	Kansas City	155	550	108	184	38	5	30	112	103	49	9	.335	.585
1986	Kansas City	124	441	70	128	28	4	16	73	80	45	1	.290	.481
1987	Kansas City	115	427	71	124	18	2	22	78	72	47	6	.290	.496
1988	Kansas City	157	589	90	180	42	3	24	103	82	51	14	.306	.509
1989	Kansas City	124	457	67	129	26	3	12	80	59	47	14	.282	.431
1990	Kansas City	142	544	82	179	45	7	14	87	56	63	9	.329	.515
1991	Kansas City	131	505	77	129	40	2	10	61	58	75	2	.255	.402
1992	Kansas City	152	592	55	169	35	5	7	61	35	69	8	.285	.397
1993	Kansas City	145	560	69	149	31	3	19	75	39	67	7	.266	.434
	TOTALS	2,707	10,349	1,583	3,154	665	137	317	1,595	1,096	908	201	.305	.487

Sources: Baseball-Reference.com; National Baseball Hall of Fame and Museum

Briggs, Lawrence E. (born: June 23, 1903 in Rockland, Massachusetts; died: December 20, 1970); inducted into the National Soccer Hall of Fame and Museum in 1978 as a coach; University of Massachusetts' first-ever soccer coach; known as the "Father of the NISOA."

After graduating from the University of Massachusetts (Amherst) in 1927, Briggs became a professor of physical education and the school's first soccer coach, a position he held for 37 years. He was a founding member of the New England Intercollegiate Soccer League and served as the group's secretary for four years; joined the National Soccer Coaches Association of America in its founding year and served as its president in 1947; was a driving force behind the creation of the National Intercollegiate Soccer Officials of America; and is often referred to as the "Father of NISOA."

In addition to his coaching career, in 1942 Briggs helped form the Pioneer Valley Intercollegiate Soccer Officials Association and served as the group's secretary-treasurer from 1947 to 1959; was awarded the NSCAA Honor Award in 1953; coordinated the New England Regional Clinics for Coaches and Referees in 1955; formed the New England ISOA in 1957; won the 1967 NISOA Honor Award; and was inducted into the NISOA Hall of Fame in 2001.

Source: National Soccer Hall of Fame and Museum

Brimsek, Francis Charles "Frank" (born: September 26, 1913 in Eveleth, Minnesota; died: November 11, 1998 in Virginia, Minnesota); inducted into the Hockey Hall of Fame in 1966 as a player; Position: Goaltender; Uniform: #1; first American inducted into the Hockey Hall of Fame.

Brimsek played in the National Hockey League for 10 seasons (1938–1950, with a two-year gap for military service during World War II) with the Boston Bruins (1938–1943, 1945–1949) and the Chicago Black Hawks (1949–1950). One of the greatest American hockey players in an era when the game was dominated by Canadians, during his career, Brimsek registered 40 shutouts and won 252 regular-season games. He twice led all goalies in shutouts, goals-against average, and wins, and helped the Bruins win two Stanley Cup championships (1939, 1941).

After several seasons in the minors, the 5'9", 170-pound Brimsek joined the Providence Reds of the American Hockey League for the 1937–1938 season, and was signed to his rookie NHL season early in 1938 by the Bruins, where he led the league with 10 shutouts and a 1.56 goals-against mark. He also recorded two shutout streaks of more than 200 minutes each; won the Calder Trophy as the NHL's Rookie of the Year; and helped the Bruins win the Stanley Cup.

After winning his second Cup in 1941, he joined the military in 1943, where he stayed for two years and played for the Coast Guard Cutters.

After the war, he returned to the Bruins for the 1945–1946 season; was named to the Second All-Star Team; and played three more seasons with Boston before joining the Chicago Black Hawks in September 1949. After only one season with the team, Brimsek retired, having compiled nine 20-win seasons and more than 31,000 minutes of ice time. He was named to the First All-Star Team twice (1939, 1942); won the Vezina Trophy as the league's best goalie twice (1939, 1942); and was named to the Second All-Star Team six times (1940–1941, 1943, 1946–1948).

He was the first American inducted into the Hockey Hall of Fame; inducted into the United States Hockey Hall of Fame in 1973; and in 1998, he was ranked number 67 on *The Hockey News*' list of the 100 Greatest Hockey Players.

Frank Brimsek's Career Statistics

			REGULAR SEASON						PLAYOFFS					
SEASON	TEAM	LEAGUE	G	W	L	T	SO	AVG	G	W	L	T	SO	AVG
1934–1935	Eveleth Rangers	USJHA												
1934–1935	Pittsburgh Yellowjackets	X-Games	16	14	2	0	1	2.44						
1935–1936	Pittsburgh Yellowjackets	EAHL	38	20	16	2	8	1.95	8	4	3	1	2	2.36
1936–1937	Pittsburgh Yellowjackets	EAHL	47	19	23	5	3	3.02						
1937–1938	Providence Reds	IAHL	48	25	16	7	5	1.75	7	5	2	0	0	1.86
1937–1938	New Haven Eagles	IAHL							1	0	1	0	0	1.94
1938–1939	Providence Reds	IAHL	9	5	2	2	0	1.89						
1938–1939	Boston Bruins	NHL	43	33	9	1	10	1.56	12	8	4		1	1.25
1939–1940	Boston Bruins	NHL	48	31	12	5	6	1.99	6	2	4		0	2.50
1940–1941	Boston Bruins	NHL	48	27	8	13	6	2.01	11	8	3		1	2.04
1941–1942	Boston Bruins	NHL	47	24	17	6	3	2.35	5	2	3		0	3.13
1942–1943	Boston Bruins	NHL	50	24	17	9	1	3.52	9	4	5		0	3.54
1943–1944	Coast Guard Cutters	X-Games	27	19	6	2	1	3.07	5	4	0	0	1	0.80
1945–1946	Boston Bruins	NHL	34	16	14	4	2	3.26	10	5	5		0	2.67
1946–1947	Boston Bruins	NHL	60	26	23	11	3	2.92	5	1	4		0	2.80
1947–1948	Boston Bruins	NHL	60	23	24	13	3	2.80	5	1	4		0	3.79
1948–1949	Boston Bruins	NHL	54	26	20	8	1	2.72	5	1	4		0	3.04
1949–1950	Chicago Black Hawks	NHL	70	22	38	10	5	3.49						
	NHL TOTALS		514	252	182	80	40	2.70	68	32	36		2	2.54

Sources: Hockey Hall of Fame; Hockey-Reference.com

Brittan, Harold Pemberton (born: November 11, 1894 in Derby, England; died: April 1964 in New York); inducted into the National Soccer Hall of Fame and Museum in 1951 as a player; Position: Center Forward; won the initial ASL championship.

An outstanding player in the early days of the original American Soccer League, Brittan came to the United States from the London soccer club in Chelsea (English First Division) after serving during World War I with the British Army. He joined Bethlehem (Pennsylvania) Steel (of the National Association Football League) late in the 1919–1920 season; became the team's starting center forward in the 1920–1921 season; was one of the league's top scorers; and led Bethlehem to the league championship.

When the NAFBL began experiencing financial difficulties, several of the league's teams left and helped create the first American Soccer League. The owners of the Bethlehem Steel team (Edgar and W. Luther Lewis) moved the squad to Philadelphia; competed in the ASL as the Philadelphia Field Club; and led the team to the league's initial title with Brittan as the ASL's top scorer. When on-field success did not translate into a profitable season, Brittan was sold to the Fall River (Massachusetts) Marksmen in 1922; was named player-coach by team owner Sam Mark; and helped the franchise win three straight ASL championships (1924–1926) and the 1924 U.S. Open Cup.

Although still playing well, Brittan was released by the Marksmen after the 1926 season and signed with the New Bedford Whalers (Massachusetts) as a player-coach, where he stayed briefly before retiring from the game later in 1926. After being out of the game for a year, he returned to the Marksmen in 1927 and led the team to the U.S. Open Cup title. He played one more year (scoring 16 goals in 28 games) before retiring for good after the 1927–1928 season to focus on his business interests. He retired with the Marksmen team record of 135 goals in 168 games.

Source: National Soccer Hall of Fame and Museum

Broadbent, Harry L. "Punch" (born: July 13, 1892 in Ottawa, Ontario, Canada; died: March 6, 1971 in Ottawa, Ontario, Canada); inducted into the Hockey Hall of Fame in 1962 as a player; Position: Right Wing; scored at least one goal in a still-NHL record 16 consecutive games; won four Stanley Cup titles.

Broadbent played 14 professional seasons in the National Hockey Association and National Hockey League with the Ottawa Senators (1912–1915, 1918–1924, 1927–1928), Montreal Maroons (1924–1927), and the New York Americans (1928–1929). He won four Stanley Cup championships (1920–1921, 1923, 1926) and the Art Ross Trophy as the NHL's leading scorer in 1922.

He started his hockey career in local leagues before joining the Ottawa Senators in 1912 when the team played in the pre-NHL National Hockey Association.

In 1915, Broadbent left professional hockey to serve in the military in World War I, eventually winning the Military Medal for heroism. When he returned to the Senators for the 1918–1919 season, the team was part of the newly-formed National Hockey League. In the 1921–1922 season, he scored 32 goals in the 24-game schedule, with a still-NHL record of 16 consecutive games with at least one goal. During his time with the team, he led the Senators to three Stanley Cup titles in four seasons (1920–1921, 1923).

Broadbent was traded to the expansion Montreal Maroons before the 1924–1925 season and led the team to a Stanley Cup title in 1926. He returned to the Senators for one year (1927–1928) and played for the New York Americans for one season before retiring in 1929.

Punch Broadbent's Career Statistics

			REGULAR SEASON					PLAYOFFS				
SEASON	**TEAM**	**LEAGUE**	**GP**	**G**	**A**	**TP**	**PIM**	**GP**	**G**	**A**	**TP**	**PIM**
1908–1909	Ottawa Emmetts	OCHL	6	14	0	14	6	2	1	0	1	0
1909–1910	Ottawa Seconds	OCHL	2	3	0	3	5					
1909–1910	Hull Volants	LOVHL	1	0	0	0	0					
1909–1910	Ottawa Cliffsides	IPAHU						3	1	0	1	6
1910–1911	Ottawa Cliffsides	OCHL	2	2	0	2	6					
1910–1911	Ottawa Cliffsides	IPAHU	6	14	0	14	18	1	0	0	0	3
1911–1912	Ottawa New Edinburghs	IPAHU	10	20	0	20	39	4	7	0	7	0
1912–1913	Ottawa Senators	NHA	20	20	0	20	15					
1913–1914	Ottawa Senators	NHA	17	6	7	13	61					
1914–1915	Ottawa Senators	NHA	20	24	3	27	115	5	3	0	3	
1918–1919	Ottawa Senators	NHL	8	4	3	7	12	5	2	2	4	28
1919–1920	Ottawa Senators	NHL	21	19	6	25	40					

SEASON	TEAM	LEAGUE	REGULAR SEASON GP	G	A	TP	PIM	PLAYOFFS GP	G	A	TP	PIM
1919–1920	Ottawa Senators	St-Cup						4	0	0	0	3
1920–1921	Ottawa Senators	NHL	9	4	1	5	10	2	0	2	2	4
1920–1921	Ottawa Senators	St-Cup						4	2	0	2	0
1921–1922	Ottawa Senators	NHL	24	32	14	46	28	2	0	1	1	8
1922–1923	Ottawa Senators	NHL	24	14	1	15	34	2	0	0	0	2
1922–1923	Ottawa Senators	St-Cup						6	6	1	7	10
1923–1924	Ottawa Senators	NHL	22	9	4	13	44	2	0	0	0	2
1924–1925	Montreal Maroons	NHL	30	14	6	20	75					
1925–1926	Montreal Maroons	NHL	36	12	5	17	112	4	2	1	3	14
1925–1926	Montreal Maroons	St-Cup						4	1	0	1	22
1926–1927	Montreal Maroons	NHL	42	9	5	14	88	2	0	0	0	0
1927–1928	Ottawa Senators	NHL	43	3	2	5	62	2	0	0	0	0
1928–1929	New York Americans	NHL	44	1	4	5	59	2	0	0	0	2
	NHL TOTALS		303	121	51	172	564	23	4	6	10	60

Sources: Hockey Hall of Fame; Hockey-Reference.com

Brock, John (born: February 4, 1885 in Stamford, Connecticut; died: April 1953); inducted into the National Soccer Hall of Fame and Museum in 1950 as a builder; first soccer coach at Springfield College and led the school to two national championships.

In 1906, Brock became the coach of the first-ever soccer team at Springfield College (Massachusetts). Graduating in 1910, he returned to the college in 1920 as a member of the physical education department and became the school's varsity coach in 1929. During his years at the school, he led the Maroons to two National Championships and the New England Intercollegiate title four times.

He retired before World War II, but returned to coach the Maroons for two years (1946–1947), leading his teams to back-to-back undefeated seasons, while being named two-time national champions by the Soccer Coaches Association.

Source: National Soccer Hall of Fame and Museum

Brock, Louis Clark "Lou" (born: June 18, 1939 in El Dorado, Arkansas); inducted into the National Baseball Hall of Fame and Museum in 1985 as a player; Position: Left Field; Bats: Left; Throws: Left; Uniform: #20; oldest player to steal more than 100 bases in a season; first player to steal 50 bases and hit 20 home runs in the same season; only baseball player to have an award named in his honor while still active.

Brock did not begin playing baseball until he was 13 years old at Union High School (Mer Rouge, Louisiana), where he played basketball and eventually joined the school's baseball team as a left-handed pitcher. After high school, he attended Southern University and A&M College (Baton Rouge, Louisiana), but poor grades eventually cost him his scholarship. Hanging around the team during semester break, Brock began retrieving balls, and was eventually allowed to take batting practice. Seizing the opportunity, Brock hit three of the balls over the fence; was offered a baseball scholarship; and was switched from pitcher to outfielder to take advantage of his offensive power.

He helped the school win the 1959 NAIA World Series Championship; played on the 1959 Pan American Games team (Chicago, Illinois); and signed with the Chicago Cubs in 1961, who sent him to the St. Cloud Rox (Northern League).

After leading the Northern League in hits, runs, doubles, and batting average, Brock was called up to the Chicago Cubs to finish the 1961 season, making his debut on September 10, 1961. During his 19-year career, the 5'11", 170-pound Brock played for the Cubs (1961–1964) and the St. Louis Cardinals (1964–1979); appeared in three World Series (winning in 1964 and 1967, while losing in 1968); and was a six-time All-Star (1967, 1971–1972, 1974–1975, 1979).

A slow major league start and a consistently low batting average eventually forced the Cubs to use him solely as a pinch hitter. Brock was traded to the Cardinals in the middle of the 1964 season and was on the team when it won the World Series. With the Cardinals, Brock's offensive numbers began to improve and he helped the team win the 1967 World Series by stealing 14 bases, setting a new record. In 1967, he became the first player to steal 50 bases and hit 20 home runs in the same season, and would go on to lead the National League in stolen bases from 1971 to 1974. In 1974, he broke Maury Wills' single-season stolen base record with 118, which was later surpassed in 1982 by Rickey Henderson's 130. In that season, he became the oldest player to steal more than 100 bases; in 1977, Brock broke Ty

Cobb's career stolen base record of 892 (and would finish his career with a then-record 938); and in 1979, he joined the 3,000-hit club.

He scored 90 or more runs in 10 seasons; hit .300 or better eight times; won eight stolen-base titles; was named as one of the Top 100 Players in the Century; and was the only baseball player to have an award named in his honor while still an active player. The Lou Brock Award is awarded to the National League's stolen base leader.

After retiring as a player, Brock became an ordained minister and elder at the Abundant Life Fellowship Church in St. Louis and also worked as a spring training instructor for the Cardinals. In 2002, he received the Horatio Alger Association of Distinguished Americans Award and has been inducted into the Arkansas, Louisiana, and Missouri Sports halls of hame. Brock won *The Sporting News* Player of the Year award in 1974; the Jackie Robinson "Ebony" Award in 1975; the Roberto Clemente Award in 1975; led the National League in at-bats and bases stolen in 1967; led the National League in doubles, triples and bases stolen in 1968; and established a record of 12 straight seasons with more than 50 steals.

Lou Brock's Career Statistics

YEAR	TEAM	G	AB	R	H	2B	3B	HR	RBI	BB	SO	SB	AVG	SLG
1961	Chicago	4	11	1	1	0	0	0	0	1	3	0	.091	.091
1962	Chicago	123	434	73	114	24	7	9	35	35	96	16	.263	.412
1963	Chicago	148	547	79	141	19	11	9	37	31	122	24	.258	.382
1964	Chicago	52	215	30	54	9	2	2	14	13	40	10	.251	.340
1964	St. Louis	103	419	81	146	21	9	12	44	27	87	33	.348	.527
1965	St. Louis	155	631	107	182	35	8	16	69	45	116	63	.288	.445
1966	St. Louis	156	643	94	183	24	12	15	46	31	134	74	.285	.429
1967	St. Louis	159	689	113	206	32	12	21	76	24	109	52	.299	.472
1968	St. Louis	159	660	92	184	46	14	6	51	46	124	62	.279	.418
1969	St. Louis	157	655	97	195	33	10	12	47	50	115	53	.298	.434
1970	St. Louis	155	664	114	202	29	5	13	57	60	99	51	.304	.422
1971	St. Louis	157	640	126	200	37	7	7	61	76	107	64	.313	.425
1972	St. Louis	153	621	81	193	26	8	3	42	47	93	63	.311	.393
1973	St. Louis	160	650	110	193	29	8	7	63	71	112	70	.297	.398
1974	St. Louis	153	635	105	194	25	7	3	48	61	88	118	.306	.381
1975	St. Louis	136	528	78	163	27	6	3	47	38	64	56	.309	.400
1976	St. Louis	133	498	73	150	24	5	4	67	35	75	56	.301	.394
1977	St. Louis	141	489	69	133	22	6	2	46	30	74	35	.272	.354
1978	St. Louis	92	298	31	66	9	0	0	12	17	29	17	.221	.252
1979	St. Louis	120	405	56	123	15	4	5	38	23	43	21	.304	.398
	TOTALS	2,616	10,332	1,610	3,023	486	141	149	900	761	1,730	938	.293	.410

Sources: Baseball-Reference.com; Lou Brock Web Site (National Baseball Hall of Fame and Museum)

Broda, Walter Edward "Turk" (born: May 15, 1914 in Brandon, Manitoba, Canada; died: October 17, 1972); inducted into the Hockey Hall of Fame in 1967 as a player; Position: Goalie; Uniform: #1; won five Stanley Cup championships.

Before playing his entire 14-season National Hockey League career (1936–1952) with the Toronto Maple Leafs, Broda began his professional playing days with the Detroit Olympics, the minor league affiliate of the Detroit Red Wings (of the International Hockey League) in the 1935–1936 season.

He was a member of the 1942 Stanley Cup-winning team that had come back from a 3–0 finals deficit to win four in a row to claim the championship. In 1943, he joined the army during World War II and was sent to England for two years, primarily to play hockey.

After leaving the military in 1945, the 5'9", 180-pound Broda returned to the Leafs and helped the team win the Stanley Cup four times in five seasons, including three years in a row (1947–1949, 1951); led the league in shutouts twice; and retired after playing only one game in the 1951–1952 season. Broda was selected to the First All-Star Team twice (1941, 1948); to the Second All-Star Team in 1942; and won the Vezina Trophy as the league's best goalie twice (1941, 1948).

Turk Broda's Career Statistics

			REGULAR SEASON						PLAYOFFS				
SEASON	TEAM	LEAGUE	GP	W	L	T	SO	AVG	GP	W	L	SO	AVG
1931–1932	Brandon Athletics	MAHA											
1932–1933	Brandon Native Sons	MJHL											
1932–1933	Brandon Native Sons	M-Cup	7	2	2	3	0	1.17					
1933–1934	Winnipeg Monarchs	MJHL	12	1	11	0	0	4.25	3	1	2	0	4.00
1933–1934	Winnipeg Monarchs	MHL-Sr.	1	0	1	0	0	6.00					
1933–1934	St. Michael's Majors	M-Cup											
1934–1935	Detroit Farm Crest	MOHL	2	1	1	0	0	2.00					
1935–1936	Detroit Olympics	IHL	47	26	18	3	6	2.10	6	6	0	1	1.32
1936–1937	Toronto Maple Leafs	NHL	45	22	19	4	3	2.30	2	0	2	0	2.26
1937–1938	Toronto Maple Leafs	NHL	48	24	15	9	6	2.56	7	4	3	1	1.73
1938–1939	Toronto Maple Leafs	NHL	48	19	20	9	8	2.15	10	5	5	2	1.94
1939–1940	Toronto Maple Leafs	NHL	47	25	17	5	4	2.23	10	6	4	1	1.74
1940–1941	Toronto Maple Leafs	NHL	48	28	14	6	5	2.00	7	3	4	0	2.05
1941–1942	Toronto Maple Leafs	NHL	48	27	18	3	6	2.76	13	8	5	1	2.38
1942–1943	Toronto Maple Leafs	NHL	50	22	19	9	1	3.18	6	2	4	0	2.73
1942–1943	Victoria Navy	NNDHL											
1942–1943	San Diego Skyhawks	X-Games											
1945–1946	Toronto Maple Leafs	NHL	15	6	6	3	0	3.53					
1946–1947	Toronto Maple Leafs	NHL	60	31	19	10	4	2.87	11	8	3	1	2.38
1947–1948	Toronto Maple Leafs	NHL	60	32	15	13	5	2.38	9	8	1	1	2.15
1948–1949	Toronto Maple Leafs	NHL	60	22	25	13	5	2.68	9	8	1	1	1.57
1949–1950	Toronto Maple Leafs	NHL	68	30	25	12	9	2.48	7	3	4	3	1.33
1950–1951	Toronto Maple Leafs	NHL	31	14	11	5	6	2.23	8	5	1	2	1.10
1951–1952	Toronto Maple Leafs	NHL	1	0	1	0	0	6.00	2	0	2	0	3.50
	NHL TOTALS		629	302	224	101	62	2.53	101	60	39	13	1.98

Sources: Hockey Hall of Fame; Hockey-Reference.com

Brooks, Herbert Paul "Herb" (born: August 5, 1937 in St. Paul, Minnesota; died: August 11, 2003 in Forest Lake, Minnesota); inducted into the Hockey Hall of Fame in 2006 as a coach-builder; coached the 1980 U.S. Olympic hockey squad to it's "Miracle on Ice" win over the Russian National Team.

Best known as the coach that led the United Stated hockey team to an upset win over the Russian National Team in the 1980 Winter Olympics at Lake Placid, New York, Brooks played hockey as a kid and had led Johnson High School (St. Paul, Minnesota) to the state hockey championship in 1955. After high school, he played for the University of Minnesota (Minneapolis-St. Paul) from 1955 to 1959, and after graduating, he eventually played for the 1964 (Innsbruck, Austria, failing to medal) and 1968 (Grenoble, France, failing to medal) U.S. Olympic teams and for the National Team five times (1961, 1962, 1965, 1967, 1970).

In 1972, Brooks became the hockey coach at his alma mater and led the school to three NCAA Division I championships (1974, 1976, 1979) and back-to-back Western Collegiate Hockey Association championships in 1974 and 1975. He was named WCHA Coach of the Year in 1974; finished his collegiate coaching career with a record of 175–101–20 (.634); and left the school in 1979 to become general manager and head coach of the U. S. National Team.

While he did lead the U.S. to a 4–3 upset over the Soviet Union in a game often referred to in the United States as the "Miracle on Ice," many hockey fans and historians do not regard the win as a major upset since the Russian team was not as strong as past squads. However, contrary to what many fans think, that win did not give the U.S. team the gold medal, although it allowed the squad to advance and play Finland. The team's 4–2 win over Finland is the victory that gave the U.S. the gold medal. In 1980, Brooks and the Olympic team were awarded the Lester Patrick Trophy for contributions to hockey in the United States, and in 2002, he would again win the award as an individual.

After winning the Olympic gold medal, Brooks coached Davos of the Swiss League in the 1980–1981 season, before returning to the United States to coach the National Hockey League's New York Rangers. In his first season with the team (1981–1982), he led the squad to a 39–27–14 record; was named *The Sporting News*' Coach of the Year; and went on to win 100 games faster than any other coach in franchise history.

Brooks left the NHL to coach at St. Cloud State University (Minnesota) from 1986 to 1987, before returning to the NHL as coach of the Minnesota North Stars (1987–1988), becoming the first native of the state to lead the team. After the squad won only 19 games, Brooks was fired and did not return to the NHL until the 1992–1993 season with the New Jersey Devils, where he stayed for one year.

After coaching the French Olympic team in 1998 (failing to medal at Nagano, Japan), he returned to the NHL with the Pittsburgh Penguins for the 1999–2000 season, before leaving the league for good with an overall 219–222–66 (.497) record. In 2002, Brooks coached the U. S. Olympic team to a silver medal at Salt Lake City, Utah; before retiring from the game.

He was inducted into the United States Hockey Hall of Fame in 1990 and to the International Ice Hockey Federation Hall of Fame in 1999.

Source: Hockey Hall of Fame

Brouthers, Dennis Joseph "Dan" (born: May 8, 1858 in Sylvan Lake, New York; died: August 2, 1932 in East Orange, New Jersey); inducted into the National Baseball Hall of Fame and Museum in 1945 as a player by the Veterans Committee; Position: First Base; Bats: Left; Throws: Left; considered the first great slugger in professional baseball; participated in baseball's only 20th-century quadruple header.

Brouthers made his major league debut on June 23, 1879 and played 19 seasons (1879–1904) with the Troy (New York) Trojans (1879–1880); Buffalo (New York) Bisons (1881–1885); Detroit (Michigan) Wolverines (1886–1888); Boston (Massachusetts) Beaneaters (1889); Boston (Massachusetts) Red Stockings (Players' League, 1890–1891); Brooklyn (New York) Grooms (1892–1893); Baltimore Orioles (1894–1895); Louisville (Kentucky) Colonels (1895); Philadelphia Phillies (1896); and the New York Giants (1904).

The first great slugger in professional baseball, the 6'2", 207-pound Brouthers won five batting titles (more than any other 19th-century player); led his league in slugging percentage seven times; led his league in hits three times; hit over 100 home runs before 1900; and his .349 career batting average still ranks in baseball's all-time top ten.

He played in the single-season Players' League in 1890 and led Boston to the league championship, before signing with Boston's American Association team in 1891, where he won his fourth batting title. Back in the National League with Brooklyn in 1892, he led the league in hitting (.335) and hits (197).

On September 3, 1903, Brouthers was a member of the Poughkeepsie Colts (Class C, Hudson River League) that participated in baseball's only 20th-century quadruple header. After a series of rainouts, the team was forced to play four games in one day and would lose all four to the Hudson Marines.

Dan Brouthers' Career Statistics

YEAR	TEAM	LG	G	AB	R	H	2B	3B	HR	BB	SO	SB	AVG	SLG
1879	Troy	NL	39	168	17	46	13	1	4	1	18		.274	.435
1880	Troy	NL	3	13	0	2	0	0	0	1	0		.154	.154
1881	Buffalo	NL	65	270	60	86	15	7	8	18	22		.319	.515
1882	Buffalo	NL	84	351	71	129	25	11	6	21	7		.368	.553
1883	Buffalo	NL	97	420	83	156	39	17	3	16	17		.371	.567
1884	Buffalo	NL	90	381	80	124	22	16	14	33	20		.325	.577
1885	Buffalo	NL	98	407	87	146	27	13	7	34	10		.359	.541
1886	Detroit	NL	121	489	139	181	41	16	11	66	16		.370	.587
1887	Detroit	NL	122	570	153	239	35	20	12	71	9	34	.419	.614
1888	Detroit	NL	129	522	118	160	35	13	9	68	13	34	.307	.475
1889	Boston	NL	126	485	105	181	25	8	7	66	6	22	.373	.501
1890	Boston	PL	123	464	116	160	32	9	1	99	17	26	.345	.459
1891	Boston	AA	123	458	111	160	26	20	5	87	20	33	.349	.526
1892	Brooklyn	NL	152	588	121	197	33	20	5	84	30	36	.335	.485
1893	Brooklyn	NL	75	267	53	93	21	11	2	52	10	8	.348	.532
1894	Baltimore	NL	123	528	137	182	33	25	9	67	9	40	.345	.553
1895	Baltimore	NL	5	23	2	6	2	0	0	1	1	0	.261	.348
1895	Louisville	NL	24	98	13	29	10	1	2	11	2	1	.296	.480
1896	Philadelphia	NL	57	218	41	72	15	3	1	44	11	8	.330	.440
1904	New York	NL	2	5	0	0	0	0	0	0	0	0	.000	.000
	TOTALS		1,658	6,725	1,507	2,349	449	211	106	840	238	242	.349	.526

Sources: Baseball-Reference.com; National Baseball Hall of Fame and Museum

Brown, Andrew M. (born: 1870 in Paisley, Scotland; died: August 10, 1948 in Revenna, Ohio); inducted into the National Soccer Hall of Fame and Museum in 1950 as a builder; a driving force behind the creation of the United States Soccer Football Association.

Brown moved to the United States at age 20 and played soccer in the Philadelphia, Pennsylvania area, before eventually becoming a delegate to the American Amateur Association, the organization that controlled soccer in the eastern United States and sponsor of the American Challenge Cup. In 1913, he both served as president of the American Football Association and helped form the United States Soccer Football Association.

He was an honorary secretary of the USSFA in 1925 and 1926; the organization's president in 1927 and 1928; and later was the acting president of the New York State Association. In 1928, when the Fédération Internationale de Football Association threatened to expel the USSFA for allowing foreign professional players to play, Brown was sent to Helsinki, Finland and was able to help resolve the problem.

He later attended the Barcelona (Spain) Congress of FIFA and served as a goodwill ambassador to the Dominion of Canada annual meeting in 1948.

Source: National Soccer Hall of Fame and Museum

Brown, David R. "Davey" (born: November 18, 1898 in East Newark, New Jersey; died: September 17, 1970 in Kearny, New Jersey); inducted into the National Soccer Hall of Fame and Museum in 1951 as a player; Position: Center Forward-Winger; International Caps (1925–1926): 3; International Goals: 4; scored a career 189 goals in the American Soccer League.

One of the best center forwards ever born in the United States, Brown was relatively small (5'3") for a position usually dominated by big men. After having an amateur career with a series of New Jersey-area teams, he played professionally with the West Hudson Athletic Association entry in the 1917–1918 National Association Foot Ball League season. When West Hudson withdrew from the NAFBL after only one year, Brown played for the Paterson Football Club (also in the NAFLB). After two seasons, the team withdrew from the league and Brown moved on to the Erie Athletic Association squad for the 1920–1921 NAFBL season.

In 1921, Erie joined the newly-established American Soccer League and changed its name to the Harrison Erie Soccer Club. Brown stayed with the team through 1923; played one year each with the Newark Skeeters and the Harrison (New Jersey) Soccer Club, before joining the ASL's New York Giants, where he cemented his reputation.

After making three appearances for the United States National Team, all against Canada (twice in 1925 and once in 1926), Brown played the 1926–1927 ASL season with the Giants; led the league in scoring (52 goals in 38 games); and would go on to garner a career total of 189 ASL goals.

Source: National Soccer Hall of Fame and Museum

Brown, George (born: August 19, 1935 in Ealing, England); inducted into the National Soccer Hall of Fame and Museum in 1995 as a player; Position: Outside Right; International Caps (1957): 1; International Goals: 0; won a bronze medal in the 1959 Pan American Games.

The Brown family moved to the United States in 1948 and settled in Greenwich, Connecticut, where he played on the Greenwich High School soccer team, graduating in 1952. In 1955, he returned to coach at the school and led the team to a County Championship that year, the same year he became a United States citizen.

The 5'4", 140-pound Brown's soccer career had begun in 1950 with Greenport United in the Connecticut State Amateur League (where he played alongside his father, James, who is also a soccer hall of fame inductee), and was on the team that won the league championship in 1951. In 1953, he signed with the German Hungarians of the German American Soccer League, where he played the next three seasons and helped the team win three consecutive league championships and the 1956 New York State Cup. He was voted league Most Valuable Player in 1953 and was selected to the GASL All-Star team, which went on to play a variety of international traveling teams, such as Rot-Weiss Essen (Essen, Nordrhein-Westfalen, Germany), Sochaux (France), and Nurnberg Football Club (Germany).

In 1957, he returned to the ASL with the Polish Falcons (Elizabeth, New Jersey) and was again named to the All-Star team that played against Hapoel Tel Aviv (Israel); Maccabi Tel Aviv (Israel); Norkopping (Sweden); and First Vienna Football Club (Austria). Also in 1957, he played on the United States World Cup Qualifier team against Mexico and was the ASL's top scorer (13). Brown was a member of the United States team that won the bronze medal in the 1959 Pan American Games (Chicago, Illinois).

He then served for two years in the U.S. Army, and when he left the military in 1961, Brown attended the University of Bridgeport (Connecticut) on a soccer scholarship, but was not allowed to play in any games because the NCAA barred professional players. The school allowed him to earn his scholarship by coaching freshman soccer and varsity tennis until 1963.

After retiring as a player, Brown coached numerous youth teams throughout the United States, Canada, and the Middle East. In 1993 his girls' team at Cabot High School (Nova Scotia, Canada) won the Provincial Championship.

He was also inducted into the Connecticut Soccer Hall of Fame in 2002 and currently serves on the National Soccer Hall of Fame's Board of Directors.

Source: National Soccer Hall of Fame and Museum

Brown, George V. (born: October, 21, 1880 in Boston, Massachusetts; died: October 17, 1937 in Hopkinton, Massachusetts); inducted into the Hockey Hall of Fame in 1961 as a builder; promoted the early popularity of hockey in the northeastern United States; was a co-founder of the Boston Marathon.

A longtime supporter of college and high school hockey, Brown helped introduce the sport to numerous universities in the area. In 1910, when the Boston Arena was built, he organized a hockey team that eventually sparked amateur hockey competition in the northeastern United States. He expanded the sport's popularity by organizing exhibition games with numerous Canadian teams.

When the Boston Arena was destroyed by fire in 1918, he established the corporation that built a new facility and served as the manager of the building while continuing to operate the Boston Athletic Association hockey team. The popularity of the sport in the Arena helped convince the National Hockey League to establish a professional team in the area. Brown also helped organize the U.S. Olympic team that won the silver medal at the 1924 Games in Chamonix, France.

After the Bruins entered the NHL and moved into the new Boston Garden in 1928, Brown helped establish the Can-Am (Canadian-American) League and the league's Boston Cubs often played before the Bruins' games at the Garden. Although primarily associated with hockey throughout his life, he was also very interested in international track and field, which led him to become one of the co-founders of the Boston Marathon.

He was inducted into the United States Hockey Hall of Fame in 1973.

Source: Hockey Hall of Fame

Brown, Hubert Jude "Hubie" (born: September 25, 1933 in Elizabeth, New Jersey); inducted into the Naismith Memorial Basketball Hall of Fame in 2005 as a coach; won two NBA Coach of the Year awards, 26 years apart.

After honing his coaching skills in high school and college, and with two seasons as a National Basketball Association assistant with the Milwaukee Bucks, Brown became the head coach of the American Basketball Association's Kentucky Colonels from 1974 to 1976, and led the Colonels to the franchise's only championship in 1975.

He was named NBA Coach of the Year twice (1978 with the Atlanta Hawks and 26 years later with the Memphis Grizzlies in 2004) and was the Curt Gowdy Media Award winner in 2000. In addition to coaching, Brown has worked as a television analyst and has conducted clinics around the world.

He played basketball at Saint Mary of the Assumption High School (Elizabeth, New Jersey), graduated in 1952, and went to Niagara University (Lewiston, New York), graduating in 1955 with a degree in education. After college, Brown joined the U.S. Army and, after leaving the military in 1958, he played briefly with the Rochester Colonels (Eastern Professional Basketball League) before the team folded after eight games.

Brown's coaching career had begun in 1955 at St. Mary's High School (Little Falls, New York), where he coached both basketball and baseball, before entering the military. He spent a total of nine seasons coaching at the high school level (including Cranford (New Jersey) High School and Fair Lawn (New Jersey) High School), before becoming an assistant coach for one season at the College of William and Mary (Williamsburg, Virginia) in 1968. He then became an assistant coach at Duke University (Durham, North Carolina), where he stayed until 1972, before joining the NBA as an assistant coach for the Milwaukee Bucks.

Two seasons later, Brown became the head coach of the Kentucky Colonels, and led the team to the ABA championship in 1975 before the Colonels folded after the 1976 ABA-NBA merger. He then rejoined the NBA as head coach of the Atlanta Hawks, winning his first Coach of the Year Award by leading the team to a .500 record. In 1982, he left Atlanta to coach the New York Knicks, replacing Red Holzman, where he stayed until 16 games into the 1986–1987 season.

He then became a television broadcaster for national and local games and joined TNT in the early 1990s, where he stayed until 2002 when he returned to the NBA (after 16 seasons) as head coach of the Memphis Grizzlies, becoming the oldest coach in the league at age 69. In the 2003–2004 season, he led the Grizzlies to the franchise's first-ever playoff appearance and won his second NBA Coach of the Year award 26 years after his first one.

After resigning from the Grizzlies on Thanksgiving (November 25, 2004), he returned to the broadcast booth with ABC as an analyst, a job he still holds as of this writing.

Hubie Brown's Coaching Record

		REGULAR SEASON			PLAYOFFS		
YEAR	**TEAM**	**W**	**L**	**WIN%**	**W**	**L**	**WIN%**
1976	Atlanta	31	51	.378	0	0	.000
1977	Atlanta	41	41	.500	0	2	.000
1978	Atlanta	46	36	.561	5	4	.556
1979	Atlanta	50	32	.610	1	4	.200
1980	Atlanta	31	48	.392	0	0	.000
1982	New York	44	38	.537	2	4	.333
1983	New York	47	35	.573	6	6	.500
1984	New York	24	58	.293	0	0	.000
1985	New York	23	59	.280	0	0	.000
1986	New York	4	12	.250	0	0	.000
2002	Memphis	28	46	.378	0	0	.000
2003	Memphis	50	32	.610	0	4	.000
2004	Memphis	5	7	.417	0	0	.000
	TOTALS	424	495	.461	14	24	.368

Sources: Basketball-Reference.com; Naismith Memorial Basketball Hall of Fame

Brown, James (born: December 31, 1908 in Kilmarnock, Scotland; died: November 9, 1994 in Berkeley Heights, New Jersey); inducted into the National Soccer Hall of Fame and Museum as a player in 1986; Position: Outside Right; International Caps (1930): 4; International Goals: 1; played on America's very first U.S. World Cup squad (1930) and scored the team's only goal in the semifinal match; established and served as president of the Connecticut State Amateur League.

After leaving school at age 13 and working in the shipyards, Brown moved to the United States when he was 19, where he played soccer for the Bayonne (New Jersey) Rovers and then for the Newark (New Jersey) Skeeters in the American and Eastern Soccer Leagues during the 1928–1929 season.

Early in 1930, Brown signed with the New York Giants of the Atlantic Soccer League, where his performance won him a spot on the very first United States World Cup team. He played in all three games in Montevideo, Uruguay in 1930 and scored the only U.S. goal in the semifinal match against Argentina. After the World Cup, he returned to the New York Giants, which by now had been sold and renamed the New York Soccer Club, before joining the Brooklyn Wanderers of the American Soccer League in 1931.

In 1932, he moved to England and played 40 games for Manchester United (Football Association Premier League) and scored a total of 17 goals for the team, before transferring to Brentford in 1935. He would later score 148 goals in 150 games playing for Guilford City (Southern League), before ending his playing career with Clyde (Scottish First Division) in 1939.

In 1948, he returned to the United States to become the soccer coach at Greenwich (Connecticut) High School. In 1950, he established the Connecticut State Amateur League; served as the group's president; and later in the same year formed the Greenport United team of the CSAL. He came out of retirement at the age of 42 to play alongside his son George (also a soccer hall of fame inductee) for two seasons, winning the league championship in 1951.

Brown later coached the Brunswick School (Greenwich, Connecticut) soccer team for 22 years as well as the Elizabeth (New Jersey) Polish Falcons of the American Soccer League in 1957 and 1958. He was inducted into the Connecticut State Hall of Fame in 2000, and he and his son are the only father and son to be inducted into the National Soccer Hall of Fame and Museum as players.

Source: National Soccer Hall of Fame and Museum

Brown, James Nathaniel "Jim" (born: February 17, 1936 in St. Simons Island, Georgia); inducted into the Pro Football Hall of Fame in 1971 as a player; Position: Fullback; Uniform: #32; only person inducted into the halls of fame for professional football, college football, and lacrosse; scored a single-game college record 43 points in 1956; first NFL player to run for more than a mile (1,863 yards) in a single season; established a still-NFL career record of 5.2 yards per carry.

Using his speed and power, Brown is considered by many to be the greatest running back ever to play in the National Football League. He played his entire nine-year NFL career (1957–1965) with the Cleveland Browns; led the league in rushing eight of his nine seasons (not winning the rushing title in 1962); selected All-NFL eight times; NFL's Rookie of the Year in 1957; NFL's Most Valuable Player twice (1958, 1965); played in nine straight Pro Bowls; and appeared in three championship games (pre-Super Bowl, winning in 1964 and losing in 1957 and 1965).

Raised by his great-grandmother early in life, when he was eight, he moved to New York to live with his mother. At Manhasset (New York) High School, Brown was an all-around athlete and earned 13 letters playing football, basketball, baseball, lacrosse, and track. Despite being named a First Team All-American in both football and lacrosse, he was not offered an athletic scholarship, but was able to attend Syracuse University (New York) in 1954, thanks to a local benefactor paying for his first year. Given a chance to display his athletic talents, by the time he finished college in 1957, Brown had earned a scholarship and All-American honors in both football and lacrosse.

Brown was athletically productive in his college years. As a sophomore, he was the second leading rusher on the football team and was the basketball team's high scorer, averaging 15 points per game; as a junior, he rushed for 666 yards (5.2 yards per carry), averaged 11.3 points per game in basketball, and was named a Second Team All-American in lacrosse; and as a senior, Brown was named First Team All-American in both football (986 yards, 6.2 yards per carry) and lacrosse (scoring 43 goals in 10 games to tie for the national scoring championship).

In his final regular-season football game, a 61–7 win over Colgate on November 17, 1956, Brown rushed for 197 yards, scored six touchdowns, and kicked seven extra points, scoring 43 total points (a college single-game record).

The 6'2", 232-pound Brown was a first-round draft pick of the Cleveland Browns (sixth selection overall) in 1957, and won the NFL Rookie of the Year award by leading all rushers with 942 yards. In addition to being an explosive runner with power, he also caught passes, returned kickoffs, and threw three touchdown passes in his career. In 1963, after coach Blanton Collier replaced Paul Brown, Brown became the first running back to run for more than a mile (1,863 yards). In 1964, he led the NFL with 1,446 yards as the Browns went on to win the NFL championship with a 27–0 victory over the Baltimore Colts. In his last season (1965), he won his second MVP award; led the league in rushing with 1,544 yards; and scored 21 touchdowns (17 rushing), before losing the Championship Game 23–12 to the Green Bay Packers.

In 1966, at the relatively young age of 30 and still in his prime, Brown retired from football, having never missed a single game in nine seasons, and amassing a still-NFL record of 5.2 yards per carry. He ran for at least 100 yards in 58 of his 118 regular-season games; ran for 237 yards in a game twice; scored five touchdowns in a game once; scored four touchdowns in a game four times; and rushed for more than 1,000 yards in seven of his nine seasons.

After working on the movie *The Dirty Dozen* prior to announcing his retirement, Brown appeared in more than 30 movies, including *Ice Station Zebra* and *Mars Attacks*, and numerous television shows. At the time he retired from the game, no player had ever run for as many yards (12,312) or scored more touchdowns (106). He is the only person to be inducted into the Pro Football Hall of Fame, the National Lacrosse Hall of Fame (1983), and the College Football Hall of Fame (1995).

In 1999, Brown was named the greatest football player ever by *The Sporting News*, and in 2006, he was named by the Cable News Network as the greatest college athlete of all time.

For all his sports-related, on-field accomplishments, Brown's life has not been focused solely on athletics. He is, and always has been, very involved in social causes and minority issues. In the 1960s, Brown helped form the Negro Industrial Economic Union to assist black-owned businesses and in 1988, he created the Amer-I-Can program, an effort to address the issues and futures of gang members.

Jim Brown's Career Statistics

				RUSHING				RECEIVING		
YEAR	**TEAM**	**G**	**NO**	**YDS**	**AVG**	**TD**	**NO**	**YDS**	**AVG**	**TD**
1957	Cleveland	12	202	942	4.7	9	16	55	3.4	1
1958	Cleveland	12	257	1,527	5.9	17	16	138	8.6	1
1959	Cleveland	12	290	1,329	4.6	14	24	190	7.9	0
1960	Cleveland	12	215	1,257	5.8	9	19	204	10.7	2
1961	Cleveland	14	305	1,408	4.6	8	46	459	10.0	2
1963	Cleveland	14	291	1,863	6.4	12	24	268	11.2	3
1964	Cleveland	14	280	1,446	5.2	7	36	340	9.4	2

			RUSHING				RECEIVING			
YEAR	TEAM	G	NO	YDS	AVG	TD	NO	YDS	AVG	TD
1965	Cleveland	14	289	1,544	5.3	17	34	328	9.6	4
	TOTALS	118	2,359	12,312	5.2	106	262	2,499	9.5	20

Sources: Pro Football Hall of Fame; Pro-Football-Reference.com

Brown, Lawrence Harvey "Larry" (born: September 14, 1940 in Brooklyn, New York); inducted into the Naismith Memorial Basketball Hall of Fame in 2002 as a coach; only coach in NBA history to lead seven different teams into the playoffs; won an Olympic gold medal as a player in 1964; first coach to win both a college national championship and an NBA title; only person in North American major professional sports history to coach nine different teams.

Brown has been a successful college and professional basketball coach for more than 30 years; has won more than 1,300 professional games in the American Basketball Association and the National Basketball Association; and is the only coach in NBA history to lead seven different teams into the playoffs. Through the 2010 season, Brown had compiled an overall coaching record of 1,318–992 (.571), 229–107 (.682) with the ABA and 1,089–885 (.552) in the NBA.

After Brown graduated from Long Beach (New York) High School in 1959, he attended the University of North Carolina (Chapel Hill), graduating in 1963. He was named to the All-Atlantic Coast Conference team in his senior year; averaged 11.8 points and 2.3 rebounds in 56 college games; and was a member of the 1964 gold medal-winning U.S. Olympic team (Tokyo, Japan).

After college, the 5'9", 160-pound Brown played for the Akron (Ohio) Wingfoots in the Amateur Athletic Union for the 1964–1965 season, and won the Most Valuable Player award in the 1964 AAU Tournament.

Brown then took a break as a player and served as an assistant coach at his alma mater for two seasons (1965–1967). After his short coaching stint, he returned to the ABA as a player for five teams in five seasons (New Orleans Buccaneers (1967–1968); Oakland Oaks (1968–1969); Washington Capitols (1969–1970); Virginia Squires (1970–1971); and the Denver Nuggets (1971–1972)); was named to the ABA All-Star team three times (1968–1970); was the All-Star MVP in 1968; won a championship with the Oaks (1969); and holds the league's single-game record for assists (23) against the Pittsburgh Condors (February 20, 1972).

After retiring as a player, he began his head coaching career in the ABA with the Carolina Cougars for two seasons (1972–1974, compiling a 104–64 record) and then with the Denver Nuggets for two seasons (1974–1976, compiling a 125–43 record). His overall ABA coaching record was 229–107 (.682) and he was named ABA Coach of the Year three times (1973, 1975–1976). Moving to the NBA after the ABA/NBA merger, Brown stayed with the Nuggets for three more seasons (1976–1979), compiling a record of 126–91.

He then took a break from the professional ranks to become head coach of the UCLA Bruins (Los Angeles, California) for two seasons (1979–1981), compiling a 42–17 record and leading the team to the 1980 NCAA Finals, losing to Louisville 59–54 in the title game. Brown then returned to the NBA as a coach with the New Jersey Nets for two seasons (1981–1983) and compiled a 91–67 record before, once again, leaving the professional game to return to the college ranks as the head coach at the University of Kansas (Lawrence) for five years (1983–1988). He was named Big Eight Conference Coach of the Year in 1986; left with a 135–33 record; and led the Jayhawks to the 1988 NCAA championship.

The much-traveled Brown then returned to the NBA with the San Antonio Spurs for three seasons (1988–1992); Los Angeles Clippers for one season (1992–1993); Indiana Pacers for four seasons (1993–1997); Philadelphia 76ers for five years (1997–2003, led the team to the NBA Finals for the first time in 18 years, and was named Coach of the Year in 2001); Detroit Pistons for two seasons (2003–2005, leading the team to the 2004 Championship); and the New York Knicks for one year (2005–2006). In 2008, he was hired as the head coach of the NBA's Charlotte Bobcats, making him the only person in North American major professional sports history to coach nine different teams.

He was the 11th NBA coach to win 700 games and ranks fourth on the all-time NBA wins list as of this writing.

Brown was named the 1999 USA Basketball National Coach of the Year; served as an assistant coach for the 2000 Olympic Games in Sydney, Australia; compiled a winning record in 27 of 31 seasons at both the professional and collegiate levels; was the first coach to win both a college national championship and an NBA title; and was inducted into the International Jewish Sports Hall of Fame in 1990.

Larry Brown's Professional Career Coaching Statistics

			REGULAR SEASON			PLAYOFFS		
SEASON	TEAM	LG	W	L	WIN%	W	L	WIN%

			REGULAR SEASON			PLAYOFFS		
SEASON	TEAM	LG	W	L	WIN%	W	L	WIN%
1972–1973	Carolina	ABA	57	27	.679	7	5	.583
1973–1974	Carolina	ABA	47	37	.560	0	4	.000
1974–1975	Denver	ABA	65	19	.774	7	6	.538
1975–1976	Denver	ABA	60	24	.714	6	7	.462
1976–1977	Denver	NBA	50	32	.610	2	4	.333
1977–1978	Denver	NBA	48	34	.585	6	7	.462
1978–1979	Denver	NBA	28	25	.528			
1981–1982	New Jersey	NBA	44	38	.537	0	2	.000
1982–1983	New Jersey	NBA	47	29	.618			
1988–1989	San Antonio	NBA	21	61	.256			
1989–1990	San Antonio	NBA	56	26	.683	6	4	.600
1990–1991	San Antonio	NBA	55	27	.671	1	3	.250
1991–1992	San Antonio	NBA	21	17	.553			
1991–1992	Los Angeles	NBA	23	12	.657	2	3	.400
1992–1993	Los Angeles	NBA	41	41	.500	2	3	.400
1993–1994	Indiana	NBA	47	35	.573	10	6	.625
1994–1995	Indiana	NBA	52	30	.634	10	7	.588
1995–1996	Indiana	NBA	52	30	.634	2	3	.400
1996–1997	Indiana	NBA	39	43	.476			
1997–1998	Philadelphia	NBA	31	51	.378			
1998–1999	Philadelphia	NBA	28	22	.560	3	5	.375
1999–2000	Philadelphia	NBA	49	33	.598	5	5	.500
2000–2001	Philadelphia	NBA	56	26	.683	12	11	.522
2001–2002	Philadelphia	NBA	43	39	.524	2	3	.400
2002–2003	Philadelphia	NBA	48	34	.585	6	6	.500
2003–2004	Detroit	NBA	54	28	.659	16	7	.696
2004–2005	Detroit	NBA	54	28	.659	15	10	.600
2005–2006	New York	NBA	23	59	.280			
2008–2009	Charlotte	NBA	35	47	.427			
2009–2010	Charlotte	NBA	44	38	.537	0	4	.000
	4 SEASONS	ABA	229	107	.682	20	22	.476
	25 SEASONS	NBA	1,089	885	.552	100	93	.518
	TOTALS		1,318	992	.571	120	115	.511

Sources: Basketball-Reference.com; Naismith Memorial Basketball Hall of Fame

Brown, Mordecai Peter Centennial "Three Finger" (born: October 19, 1876 in Nyesville, Indiana; died: February 14, 1948 in Terre Haute, Indiana); inducted into the National Baseball Hall of Fame and Museum in 1949 as a player by the Veterans Committee; Position: Pitcher; Bats: Both; Throws: Right; considered major league baseball's first "swing man" for his ability to alternate between the starting rotation and pitching out of the bullpen; holds the major league single-season record for the lowest ERA by a right-hander (1.04 in 1906).

Making his major league debut on April 19, 1903, the 5'10", 175-pound Brown had a 14-year career (1903–1916) with the St. Louis Cardinals (1903), Chicago Cubs (1904–1912, 1916), Cincinnati Reds (1913), Brooklyn Tip-Tops (1914, Federal League), St. Louis Terriers (1914, player-manager, Federal League), and the Chicago Whales (1915, Federal League). He would play in four World Series, all with the Cubs (winning in 1907 and 1908, while losing in 1906 and 1910).

Nicknamed "Three Finger" because of a farm-machinery accident he had as a boy, Brown was one of the game's best pitchers in the early 20th century; won 20 or more games in a season six times; and as player-manager with the Terriers in 1914, compiled a 50–63 record (.442).

His baseball career started in 1901 when he began playing for the Terre Haute (Indiana) Hottentots of the Three-I League (Illinois-Indiana-Iowa League). After pitching for two seasons and compiling a record of 50–23, Brown signed with the National League's St. Louis Cardinals in 1903, where he played for one season before being traded to the Chicago Cubs.

He is considered baseball's first "swing man" for his ability to perform as both a starting pitcher and as a reliever. After the team lost the 1906 World Series, he helped the Cubs win the championship the next year by throwing a shutout for the final win against the Detroit Tigers. The Cubs repeated as World Series champions in 1908, again against Detroit, with Brown winning two games and throwing 11 scoreless innings.

From 1908 to 1911, Brown led the league in saves (32) and compiled a .703 won-loss record (102–43). After pitching two losing seasons in 1912 and 1913, Brown was one of the many stars who left the National League and played in the short-lived Federal League, leading the Chicago Whales to a league title in 1915.

Brown played at the same time as legendary fellow hall-of-famer Christy Mathewson of the New York Giants. Their pitching duels were fan favorites (Brown won 13 of the 24) and, in one of baseball's great ironies, they faced each other in what turned out to be each pitcher's last major league game (September 4, 1916), won by Mathewson, 10 to 8.

After his major league career ended in 1916, he played four more years in the minor leagues before finally retiring as a player in 1920. He was the National League ERA leader in 1906; the league wins leader in 1909; and led the league in games pitched twice (1909, 1911), in innings pitched (1909), in complete games twice (1909–1910), and in shutouts twice (1906, 1910). Brown won 15 or more games nine times; won 20 or more games six times; won 25 or more games four times; and holds the major league record for the lowest single-season ERA by a right-hander (1.04 in 1906).

He was inducted into the Indiana Baseball Hall of Fame in 1979.

Mordecai Brown's Career Statistics

YEAR	TEAM	LG	W	L	PCT	SH	IP	H	R	ER	SO	BB	ERA
1903	Saint Louis	NL	9	13	.409	1	201	231	105	58	83	59	2.60
1904	Chicago	NL	15	10	.600	4	212	155	74	44	81	50	1.87
1905	Chicago	NL	18	12	.600	4	249	219	89	60	89	44	2.17
1906	Chicago	NL	26	6	.813	9	277	198	56	32	144	61	1.04
1907	Chicago	NL	20	6	.769	6	233	180	51	36	107	40	1.40
1908	Chicago	NL	29	9	.763	9	312	214	64	51	123	49	1.47
1909	Chicago	NL	27	9	.750	8	343	246	78	50	172	53	1.31
1910	Chicago	NL	25	14	.641	6	295	256	95	61	143	64	1.86
1911	Chicago	NL	21	11	.656	0	270	267	110	84	129	55	2.80
1912	Chicago	NL	5	6	.455	2	89	92	35	26	34	20	2.63
1913	Cincinnati	NL	11	12	.478	1	173	174	79	56	41	44	2.91
1914	Saint Louis	FL	12	6	.667	2	175	172	73	64	81	43	3.29
1914	Brooklyn	FL	2	5	.286	0	58	63	33	27	32	18	4.19
1915	Chicago	FL	17	8	.680	3	236	189	75	55	95	64	2.10
1916	Chicago	NL	2	3	.400	0	48	52	27	21	21	9	3.94
	TOTALS		239	130	.648	55	3,171	2,708	1,044	725	1,375	673	2.06

Sources: Baseball-Reference.com; Indiana Baseball Hall of Fame (www.indbaseballhalloffame.org); National Baseball Hall of Fame and Museum

Brown, Paul Eugene (born: September 7, 1908 in Norwalk, Ohio; died: August 5, 1991); inducted into the Pro Football Hall of Fame in 1967 as a coach; helped create the All-America Football Conference; won seven league championships.

A successful football coach at all levels (high school, college, military, and professional), Brown was a driving force behind making the National Football League a stronger entity. He helped create the All-America Football Conference, which lasted four years (1946–1949), with his Cleveland Browns winning all four AAFC Championships. The success and popularity of the AAFC led to its merger with the National Football League after the 1949 season. He led the Browns to a total AAFC/NFL record of 167–53–8 (1946–1962); four AAFC titles; and three NFL Championships (1950, 1954–1955).

Brown was the first coach to hire a full-time staff on a year-round basis; create a system for scouting college talent on a scale never before seen in the professional ranks; use playbooks; film practices and games for future study and creating game-day scenarios; and keep his players together at a hotel the night before both home and road games.

Brown also started calling plays from the sideline by sending alternate players into the game; developed detailed pass patterns for the offense; and created defensive schemes to match his opponents' offense. He also introduced face masks for helmets; experimented with helmet radios (decades before they became a standard part of the game); and created complex offensive schemes, which eventually led to the so-called "West Coast Offense" made famous by Brown's protégé, Bill Walsh, with the San Francisco 49ers.

Brown built a football dynasty in Cleveland starting with his years in the AAFC, in which the team only lost four games in four seasons. When the Browns joined the NFL after the AAFC/NFL merger, the team continued its domination and played in the next six championship games, winning the title in 1950, 1954, and 1955.

Brown graduated from Washington High School (Massillon, Ohio) in 1925, having played varsity football. When he entered Ohio State University (Columbus), he realized that he was too small (145 pounds) to play for a major college football program, so Brown transferred to Miami University (Oxford, Ohio). After missing one year of eligibility, he played football for two years and was named to the All-Ohio Small College Second Team by the Associated Press in 1928. He graduated from Miami in 1930 with a bachelor's degree in Education and in 1940, he received a master's degree in Education from Ohio State University (Columbus).

Brown's coaching career had begun earlier in 1930 when he was hired as a teacher-coach at the Naval Academy's preparatory Severn School (Severna Park, Maryland), where he compiled a two-season record of 16–1–1. In 1932, he became the head football coach at his old high, where he stayed for nine years; compiled a record of 80–8–2; and won six consecutive Ohio state high school football championships (1935–1940).

Following his high school success, Brown moved on to become the head coach of the Ohio State Buckeyes (Columbus) in January 1941; compiled a record of 18–8–1 during his three seasons; and led the school to its first National Championship in his second year (1942).

He served in the U.S. Navy during World War II and in April 1944, Brown was assigned to the Great Lakes Naval Station (North Chicago, Illinois) as head coach of its Bluejacket football team, which competed against other service teams and college programs in the area. He ended his two year stint with a record of 15–5–2.

In February 1945, while still in the U.S. Navy, Brown was named head coach of the Cleveland franchise of the newly created AAFC, which he joined as soon as his military service was completed. His popularity led the team to be named the Cleveland Browns. He switched Otto Graham from tailback to quarterback, creating a hall-of-fame career for the player who would lead the Browns to the title game in each of his 10 seasons (AAFC and NFL) with the team (1946–1955), winning seven titles and losing three. In a much riskier move for the times, Brown ignored the game's "unofficial agreement" barring African-American players from the league by adding future hall-of-famers Marion Motley and Bill Willis to his squad.

On occasion, Brown was an overly proud man who did not respond well to criticism. When his game plan ("all the team does is pass") was challenged after a 35–10 win over the Philadelphia Eagles in 1950, he responded by setting a still-NFL record by throwing no passes the next time the teams met later in the season, with the Browns still winning 13–7.

After Brown was fired in January 1963 by team owner Art Modell, he stayed out of football and never attended a Browns game. In September 1967, he returned to professional football as part-owner of the Cincinnati Bengals (American Football League), which would later join the NFL after the NFL-AFL merger in 1970. He coached the Bengals for eight seasons (1968–1975) and led the team to three playoff appearances. After retiring as its coach in 1976, Brown stayed with the team for 15 years as president, and watched the Bengals make two trips to the Super Bowl, losing both times to the San Francisco 49ers (SB XVI in 1982 and SB XXIII in 1989).

He was named *The Sporting News* NFL Coach of the Year three times (1949, 1951, 1953); United Press International Coach of the Year three times (1957, 1969–1970); retired with an overall career coaching record of 170–108–6 (.612); and Paul Brown Stadium (Cincinnati, Ohio) was named in his honor.

Paul Brown's Coaching Record

		REGULAR SEASON				**PLAYOFFS**		
YEAR	**TEAM**	**W**	**L**	**T**	**WIN%**	**W**	**L**	**WIN%**
1950	Cleveland	10	2	0	.833	2	0	1.000
1951	Cleveland	11	1	0	.917	0	1	.000
1952	Cleveland	8	4	0	.667	0	1	.000
1953	Cleveland	11	1	0	.917	0	1	.000
1954	Cleveland	9	3	0	.750	1	0	1.000
1955	Cleveland	9	2	1	.750	1	0	1.000
1956	Cleveland	5	7	0	.417	0	0	
1957	Cleveland	9	2	1	.750	0	1	.000
1958	Cleveland	9	3	0	.750	0	1	.000

YEAR	TEAM	REGULAR SEASON W	L	T	WIN%	PLAYOFFS W	L	WIN%
1959	Cleveland	7	5	0	.583	0	0	
1960	Cleveland	8	3	1	.667	0	0	
1961	Cleveland	8	5	1	.571	0	0	
1962	Cleveland	7	6	1	.500	0	0	
1968	Cincinnati	3	11	0	.214	0	0	
1969	Cincinnati	4	9	1	.286	0	0	
1970	Cincinnati	8	6	0	.571	0	1	.000
1971	Cincinnati	4	10	0	.286	0	0	
1972	Cincinnati	8	6	0	.571	0	0	
1973	Cincinnati	10	4	0	.714	0	1	.000
1974	Cincinnati	7	7	0	.500	0	0	
1975	Cincinnati	11	3	0	.786	0	1	.000
	TOTALS	166	100	6	.610	4	8	.333

Sources: Pro Football Hall of Fame; Pro-Football-Reference.com

Brown, Raymond "Ray" (born: February 23, 1908 in Alger, Ohio; died: February 8, 1965 in Dayton, Ohio); inducted into the National Baseball Hall of Fame and Museum in 2006 as a player by the Negro Leagues Committee; Position: Pitcher; Bats: Both; Throws: Right; threw a one-hitter in the 1944 Negro League World Series.

Brown pitched primarily for the Homestead Grays of the Negro National League from 1932 to 1945, during the team's dynasty years when the Grays won eight pennants between 1937 and 1945. An all-around athlete, he often played the outfield and pinch hit when he was not on the mound. He was named to the East-West All-Star team twice during his 19-year career and threw a one-hitter in the 1944 Negro League World Series against the Birmingham Black Barons.

After leaving the Grays, Brown played in Mexico (1946–1949) and for the Canadian Provincial League (1950–1953), leading Sherbrooke (Nova Scotia, Canada) to a title in 1951.

According to existing Negro League records, which cannot be fully verified, the 6'1", 195-pound Brown had a 109–30 (.762) pitching record with the Grays, fifth on the league's all-time win list.

Source: National Baseball Hall of Fame and Museum

Brown, Robert Stanford "Bob" "Boomer" (born: December 8, 1941 in Cleveland, Ohio); inducted into the Pro Football Hall of Fame in 2004 as a player; Position: Offensive Tackle; named to the 1960s All-Decade Team.

During his 10-year (126 games) National Football League career (1964–1973), Brown played for the Philadelphia Eagles (1964–1968), Los Angeles Rams (1969–1970), and the Oakland Raiders (1971–1973). He was named to the All-NFL Second Team six times (1964–1965, 1967–1968, 1971–1972); All-NFL seven times (1965–1966, 1968–1972); named to the All-Pro Second Team in 1968 and to the All-Pro team in 1969; All-AFC in 1970; All-AFC Second Team in 1971; All-AFC in 1971 and 1972; named to the Pro Bowl six times (1966–1967, 1969–1972); and was named to the 1960s All-Decade Team.

After attending East Technical High School (Cleveland, Ohio), Brown became an All-American guard at the University of Nebraska (Lincoln); was voted college football's Lineman of the Year in 1963 by the Washington D.C. Touchdown Club; and was inducted into the College Football Hall of Fame in 1993. After college, in 1964, the 6'4", 280-pound Brown was drafted in the first round by both the NFL's Eagles (second overall selection) and the Denver Broncos (first overall selection) of the American Football League.

Sources: College Football Hall of Fame; Pro Football Hall of Fame; Pro-Football-Reference.com

Brown, Roosevelt, Jr. "Rosey" (born: October 20, 1932 in Charlottesville, Virginia; died: June 9, 2004 in Mansfield Township, New Jersey); inducted into the Pro Football Hall of Fame in 1975 as a player; Position: Offensive Tackle; second player to be elected to the football hall of fame as an offensive lineman.

Brown played his entire 13-year, 162-game career (1953–1965) with the National Football League's New York Giants, was named All-NFL for eight consecutive years (1956–1963); played in nine Pro Bowls (1955–1960, 1962, 1964–1965); and was named the NFL's Lineman of the Year in 1956. Before playing in the NFL, Brown had attended Morgan State University (Baltimore, Maryland) and was twice named to the Black All-American Team (1951–1952).

He was drafted by the Giants in the 27th round (321st selection overall) in 1953, and at age 20 became a starter. While he was with the team, the Giants won their division six times and one NFL title in 1956, in which Brown was named Lineman of the Game. He was only the second offensive lineman to be elected to the hall of fame.

During his career, the 6'3", 255-pound Brown pass blocked for hall of fame quarterback Y.A. Tittle, and run blocked for hall of fame running back Frank Gifford. After retiring as a player, in 1966, he became the Giants' assistant offensive line coach; was promoted to offensive line coach in 1969; and later served in the team's scouting department. He was named to the NFL 1950s All-Decade Team and to the NFL 75th Anniversary All-Time Team.

Source: Pro Football Hall of Fame

Brown, Walter A. (born: February 10, 1905 in Boston (Hopkinton), Massachusetts; died: September 7, 1964); inducted into the Hockey Hall of Fame in 1962 as a builder; inducted into the Naismith Memorial Basketball Hall of Fame in 1965 as a contributor; won two World Championship medals (hockey); won a bronze medal at the 1936 Olympics (hockey); original owner of the Boston Celtics; established the Basketball Association of America and helped create the National Basketball Association.

The son of fellow hall-of-famer, George V., Brown succeeded his father as manager of the Boston Garden in 1937. He had attended high school at Boston Latin (Boston, Massachusetts) from 1922 to 1923 and then Philips Exeter (New Hampshire) Academy from 1923 to 1926.

Brown coached the amateur Boston Olympics of the Eastern Hockey League to five league titles between 1930 and 1940, including the United States' first-ever World Championship in 1933. He also led the United States to the silver medal at the 1931 (Krynica, Poland) and 1934 (Milan, Italy) World Championships and a bronze medal at the 1936 Olympics (Garmisch–Partenkirchen, Germany).

After succeeding his father as manager of the Boston Garden (he would serve as its president from 1937 to 1964), Brown established the Basketball Association of America in 1946; was instrumental in merging the BAA and the National Basketball League to form the National Basketball Association in 1949; and became the original owner of the Boston Celtics in 1945.

He became president of the National Hockey League's Boston Bruins in 1951; served as the International Ice Hockey Federation's vice president twice and president from 1954 to 1957; and in 1960, he was the chairman of the United States squad that won the gold medal at the Squaw Valley (California) Olympics.

Brown has been inducted into both the hockey and basketball halls of fame; worked on the Hockey Hall of Fame Governing Committee; and served as chairman of the Naismith Memorial Basketball Hall of Fame.

After his death in 1964, the annual Walter Brown Award was established in his honor to recognize the top American-born player attending a New England-area college. Also in his memory, the NBA has named its championship trophy after him.

Sources: Hockey Hall of Fame; Naismith Memorial Basketball Hall of Fame

Brown, Willard Jessie (born: June 26, 1915 in Shreveport, Louisiana; died: August 4, 1996 in Houston, Texas); inducted into the National Baseball Hall of Fame and Museum in 2006 as a player by the Negro Leagues Committee; Position: Center Field; Bats: Right; Throws: Right; first black player to hit a home run in the American League.

Before making his major league debut on July 19, 1947, Brown had been a star in the Negro Leagues, and had played for the Monroe (Louisiana) Monarchs (1934–1935) and the Kansas City (Missouri) Monarchs (1937–1952). He was signed as a free agent by major league baseball's St. Louis Browns of the American League for one month in 1947 (July to August). Called "Home Run" Brown by legendary player Josh Gibson, he was named to the Negro Leagues All-Star team seven times (1937, 1939–1942, 1946, 1950). Brown also played in the Puerto Rican Winter League and ended his career hitting 35 home runs in the Texas League in 1954.

He was a member of the Kansas City Monarchs teams that won six pennants between 1937 and 1946; left baseball for two seasons and served in the Army during World War II; won two Triple Crown titles; and hit over .400 twice.

Brown started his professional career as a shortstop for the Monroe Monarchs, before signing with the Kansas City Monarchs and played in the 1942 and 1946 Negro League World Series (beating the Homestead Grays in 1942 and losing to the Newark Eagles in 1946).

At 5'11", 195 pounds, he was a star in the Puerto Rican Winter League; won three home run and three batting titles from 1946 through 1950; and in the 1947–1948 season, he won the Triple Crown, hitting .432 with 27 home runs and 86 RBIs in 60 games.

While leading the Negro National League with a .372 average in 1947, the 34-year-old Brown signed with Major League Baseball's St. Louis Browns, but returned to the Monarchs one month later after hitting only .179 with the

Browns. Although only in the majors for a brief time, he was involved in two memorable events. On July 20, 1947, he and second baseman Hank Thompson took the field for the Browns against the Boston Red Sox, marking the first time two black players appeared in the same major-league lineup. On August 13, 1947, Brown became the first black player to hit a home run in the American League when he pinch-hit an inside-the-park homer in a 6–5 win over the Detroit Tigers.

Source: National Baseball Hall of Fame and Museum

Brown, William Ferdie "Willie" (born: December 2, 1940 in Yazoo City, Mississippi); inducted into the Pro Football Hall of Fame in 1984 as a player; Position: Cornerback; Uniform: #24; established a then-record 75-yard interception for a touchdown in Super Bowl XI.

During his 16-year, 204-game career, Brown played for the Denver Broncos (1963–1966) of the American Football League and the Oakland Raiders (1967–1978) of the AFL/National Football League. After playing defensive end at Grambling State University (Louisiana), the 6'1", 195-pound Brown was not drafted by any NFL team and signed as a free agent with the Houston Oilers, but was cut by the team before the end of camp.

He was then signed by Denver; became a starter halfway through his rookie year; and was named All-AFL in his second season. Brown was named All-AFL/AFC seven times; All-Time AFL team in 1969; played in five All-Star games (1964–1965, 1967–1969), four AFC-NFC Pro Bowls (1970–1973), and nine AFL/AFC titles games; and participated in two Super Bowls (winning in SB XI in 1977 and losing in SB II in 1968). He retired with 54 interceptions for 472 yards and two touchdowns.

In 1967, he was traded to the AFL's Oakland Raiders and served as defensive captain for 10 of his 12 seasons with the team. In Super Bowl XI against the Minnesota Vikings (1977), Brown intercepted a Fran Tarkenton pass and returned it for a then-Super Bowl record 75 yards for a touchdown, a mark that stood for 29 seasons until broken by the Seattle Seahawk's Kelly Herndon's 76-yard interception in Super Bowl XL in 2006.

When he retired after the 1978 season, Brown's 39 interceptions tied him for the club record; he was named to the AFL All-Time Team; and to the NFL 1970s All-Decade Team. He worked for the Raiders from 1979 to 1988 as a defensive backfield coach, and later served as head coach at Long Beach State (California) in 1991 and at Jordan High School (Los Angeles, California) in 1994. Brown was inducted into the Louisiana Sports Hall of Fame in 1992; the Mississippi Sports Hall of Fame in 1994; and, in 1995, he returned to the Raiders as the Director of Staff Development.

Source: Pro Football Hall of Fame

Buchanan, Junious "Buck" (born: September 10, 1940 in Gainesville, Alabama; died: July 16, 1992); inducted into the Pro Football Hall of Fame in 1990 as a player; Position: Defensive Right Tackle; Uniform: #86; first player selected in the 1963 AFL draft.

A star player at Grambling State University (Louisiana), Buchanan was selected a National Association of Intercollegiate Athletics All-American in 1962. After college, he spent his entire 13-year (182 games) National Football League career (1963–1975) with the Kansas City Chiefs, after being the first player selected in the 1963 American Football League Draft. Also in 1963, he had been selected in the 19th round (265th pick overall) in the National Football League draft by the New York Giants.

The 6'7", 270-pound Buchanan only missed one game in his entire career; was a four-time All-AFL selection; named All-AFC in 1970 and 1971; led the defensive unit in two Super Bowls (winning in Super Bowl IV in 1970 and losing Super Bowl I in 1967); played in six AFL All-Star games (1964–1969); and was named to two AFC-NFC Pro Bowls.

Named in his honor, the Buck Buchanan Award is presented annually to the nation's most outstanding defensive player in the NCAA Division I Football Championship Subdivision. In addition to the football hall of fame, he has been inducted into the NAIA and Kansas City Chiefs halls of fame. His uniform number 86 was retired by the Chiefs in 1992.

Buchanan attended A.H. Parker High School (Birmingham, Alabama), lettering in football and basketball. At Grambling, he lettered in football, and was inducted into the College Football Hall of Fame in 1996. In 1999, he was ranked number 67 on *The Sporting News*' list of the 100 Greatest Football Players.

Sources: College Football Hall of Fame; Pro Football Hall of Fame

Buckland, Frank (born: May 23, 1902 in Gravenhurst, Ontario, Canada; died: June 23, 1991); inducted into the Hockey Hall of Fame in 1975 as a builder; president and treasurer of the Ontario Hockey Association.

Buckland grew up in Guelph (Ontario, Canada) and after graduating from the University of Toronto (Ontario, Canada), he moved to Peterborough (Ontario, Canada), where he coached junior and senior teams between 1932 and 1940.

Beginning in 1955, he served as president of the Ontario Hockey Association for two years and, in 1961, began serving as the organization's treasurer, a position he would hold for 15 years.

The Canadian Amateur Hockey Association presented him the CAHA Meritorious Award; the OHA presented him with its Gold Stick Award; in 1973, he was named a Life Member of that organization; and in 1974, the Province of Ontario presented him with its Sports Achievement Award.

Source: Hockey Hall of Fame

Bucyk, John Paul "Chief" (born: May 12, 1935 in Edmonton, Alberta, Canada); inducted into the Hockey Hall of Fame in 1981 as a player; Position: Left Wing; Uniform: #9; oldest player to score more than 50 goals in a season; oldest player to score 50 or more goals in a season for the first time in a career.

Bucyk played 23 National Hockey League seasons with the Detroit Red Wings (1955–1957) and the Boston Bruins (1957–1978); was named to the Second All-Star team in 1968 and the First All-Star team in 1971; won the Lady Byng Memorial Trophy for sportsmanship twice (1971, 1974); won the Lester Patrick Trophy in 1977 for his contributions to hockey in the United States; and played in seven All-Star Games (1955, 1963–1965, 1968, 1970–1971).

Before embarking on his 21-season stay with the Bruins in 1957, he had spent almost five years moving back and forth from the minor leagues and the NHL's Red Wings.

The 6', 215-pound Bucyk set numerous Bruins records (some of which have since been surpassed), including most seasons played (21), most games played (1,436), most goals scored (545), most assists (794), and most points scored (1,339). By the time he retired, Bucyk was the fourth-leading scorer in NHL history and had been on six Bruins' teams that played in the Stanley Cup finals (winning in 1970 and 1972, while losing in 1958, 1974, 1977, and 1978).

Contrary to the nature of sports numbers, his offensive statistics increased as he got older. Over a 10-year span (1967–1977), Bucyk scored 20 or more goals per season.

He served as an assistant coach in his last years with the team; worked in the Bruins' public relations office after he retired as a player; and later provided radio color commentary for Bruins' games. The Bruins retired his jersey number nine and his 545 goals as a Bruin are the most in franchise history.

In the 1970–1971 season, Bucyk became both the oldest player to score more than 50 goals in a season and the oldest player to score 50 or more goals for the first time in a career. In 1998, he was ranked number 45 on *The Hockey News*' list of the 100 Greatest Hockey Players.

Johnny Bucyk's Career Statistics

			REGULAR SEASON					PLAYOFFS				
SEASON	**TEAM**	**LEAGUE**	**GP**	**G**	**A**	**TP**	**PIM**	**GP**	**G**	**A**	**TP**	**PIM**
1951–1952	Edmonton Maple Leafs	AJHL										
1951–1952	Edmonton Oil Kings	WCJHL						1	0	0	0	0
1952–1953	Edmonton Oil Kings	WCJHL	39	19	12	31	24	12	5	1	6	14
1953–1954	Edmonton Oil Kings	WCJHL	33	29	38	67	38	21	28	17	45	30
1953–1954	Edmonton Flyers	WHL	2	2	0	2	2					
1953–1954	Edmonton Oil Kings	M-Cup	14	14	10	24	10					
1954–1955	Edmonton Flyers	WHL	70	30	58	88	57	9	1	6	7	7
1954–1955	Edmonton Flyers	Ed-Cup	7	2	3	5	22					
1955–1956	Detroit Red Wings	NHL	38	1	8	9	20	10	1	1	2	8
1955–1956	Edmonton Flyers	WHL	6	0	0	0	9					
1956–1957	Detroit Red Wings	NHL	66	10	11	21	41	5	0	1	1	0
1957–1958	Boston Bruins	NHL	68	21	31	52	57	12	0	4	4	16
1958–1959	Boston Bruins	NHL	69	24	36	60	36	7	2	4	6	6
1959–1960	Boston Bruins	NHL	56	16	36	52	26					
1960–1961	Boston Bruins	NHL	70	19	20	39	48					
1961–1962	Boston Bruins	NHL	67	20	40	60	32					
1962–1963	Boston Bruins	NHL	69	27	39	66	36					
1963–1964	Boston Bruins	NHL	62	18	36	54	36					

SEASON	TEAM	LEAGUE	REGULAR SEASON GP	G	A	TP	PIM	PLAYOFFS GP	G	A	TP	PIM
1964–1965	Boston Bruins	NHL	68	26	29	55	24					
1965–1966	Boston Bruins	NHL	63	27	30	57	12					
1966–1967	Boston Bruins	NHL	59	18	30	48	12					
1967–1968	Boston Bruins	NHL	72	30	39	69	8	3	0	2	2	0
1968–1969	Boston Bruins	NHL	70	24	42	66	18	10	5	6	11	0
1969–1970	Boston Bruins	NHL	76	31	38	69	13	14	11	8	19	2
1970–1971	Boston Bruins	NHL	78	51	65	116	8	7	2	5	7	0
1971–1972	Boston Bruins	NHL	78	32	51	83	4	15	9	11	20	6
1972–1973	Boston Bruins	NHL	78	40	53	93	12	5	0	3	3	0
1973–1974	Boston Bruins	NHL	76	31	44	75	8	16	8	10	18	4
1974–1975	Boston Bruins	NHL	78	29	52	81	10	3	1	0	1	0
1975–1976	Boston Bruins	NHL	77	36	47	83	20	12	2	7	9	0
1976–1977	Boston Bruins	NHL	49	20	23	43	12	5	0	0	0	0
1977–1978	Boston Bruins	NHL	53	5	13	18	4					
	NHL TOTALS		1,540	556	813	1,369	497	124	41	62	103	42

Sources: Hockey Hall of Fame; Hockey-Reference.com

Buffalo Germans; inducted into the Naismith Memorial Basketball Hall of Fame in 1961 as a team; one of only four teams inducted into the basketball hall of fame.

Considered basketball's first great team, the Buffalo Germans got their start at the Young Men's Christian Association (Buffalo, New York) in 1895, and the history of the team can be traced directly back to the game's inventor, Dr. James Naismith. Fred W. Burkhardt, one of Naismith's original players who had participated in the very first established basketball game, would go on to become the physical director at the Genesee Street YMCA in Buffalo in 1895. He manned the team with those who regularly played at the facility; served as the squad's coach; and called them the Buffalo Germans.

As inductees into the basketball hall of fame, the team consisted of Burkhardt, Philip Dischinger, Henry J. Faust, Alfred A. Heerdt, Edward Linneborn, John I. Maier, Albert W. Manweiler, Edward C. Miller, Harry J. Miller, Charles P. Monahan, George L. Redlein, Dr. Edmund Reimann, Williams C. Rhode, and George Schell.

In 1898, the Germans entered the local area men's league and by 1900 had accumulated a 48–4 record. The team won the 1901 Pan American championship (held in Buffalo, New York) and the 1904 Olympic title in St. Louis, Missouri, where basketball was played as a demonstration sport.

The Germans won 111 straight games over three seasons (beginning in 1908); defeated opponents by more than 30 points a game; went undefeated in five of their first 18 seasons; and disbanded in 1929, having compiled an overall 792–86 (.902) record.

In 1992, the Buffalo Germans was inducted into the Greater Buffalo Sports Hall of Fame.

Sources: Greater Buffalo Sports Hall of Fame; Naismith Memorial Basketball Hall of Fame

Bulkeley, Morgan Gardner (born; December 26, 1837 in East Haddam, Connecticut; died: November 6, 1922 in Hartford, Connecticut); inducted into the National Baseball Hall of Fame and Museum in 1937 as a pioneer-executive by the Veterans Committee; first president of the National League.

As a teenager, Bulkeley swept floors at the Aetna Insurance Company, which had been founded by his father, and eventually, he became the company's president. He was already a successful businessman when he became involved in professional baseball as president of the National Association's Hartford (Connecticut) Dark Blues in 1874 and 1875. When the National League was formed in 1876, Bulkeley served as its first president, and helped enhance the image of the game by addressing its most pressing problems of the day: illegal gambling, drinking in the stands, and fan rowdiness. After serving as league president for only one season, he returned to the business world and eventually began a successful political career.

He would later serve as the mayor of Hartford (1880–1888); governor of Connecticut (1889–1893), and senator from Connecticut (1905–1911). Bulkeley had earlier served in the Civil War with the 13th New York Volunteers as a private in the Union Army under General George B. McClellan. After the war, he returned to his business interests and when his father died in 1872, he moved to Hartford and helped form the United States Bank of Hartford (serving as its first president) and took over the Aetna Insurance Company.

Bulkeley was one of the seven members of the Mills Commission formed by Albert Spalding that gave credence (which has basically been discredited over the years) to the myth that Abner Doubleday invented baseball.

Source: National Baseball Hall of Fame

Bunn, John William (born: September 26, 1898 in Wellston, Ohio; died: August 13, 1979); inducted into the Naismith Memorial Basketball Hall of Fame in 1964 as a contributor; first athlete to win ten letters at the University of Kansas; first chairman of the Naismith Memorial Basketball Hall of Fame Committee.

Through his work as a coach, teacher, and writer, Bunn was a national and international authority on the game of basketball. He was the first athlete to win ten letters at the University of Kansas (Lawrence, 1917–1921) and played basketball for legendary coach "Phog" Allen at a time when the sport's inventor, Dr. James Naismith, was a professor of physical education at the school. After graduating, Bunn served as Allen's assistant for nine years, before becoming head basketball coach at Stanford University (Palo Alto, California) in 1930.

In eight seasons at Stanford, he led the Cardinals to national prominence by playing a coast-to-coast schedule, including a 45–31 win over Long Island University at New York's Madison Square Garden in December 1936, which marked the very first time a west coast team had played in New York. This team also won the 1937 Helms Foundation national championship, and under Bunn, Stanford won three consecutive Pacific Coast Conference championships (1936–1938). He left the school having compiled a 107–81 (.569) record.

He took a break from coaching in 1939 to become a college administrator, but returned to the game as Director of Athletics and head coach at Springfield College (Massachusetts) from 1946 to 1956, eventually compiling an overall 139–130 (.517) record. While at Springfield, Bunn became the first chairman of the Naismith Memorial Basketball Hall of Fame Committee, serving until 1963.

In 1956, Bunn became the head coach at Colorado State College (Greeley), where he stayed until 1963, compiling a 75–95 (.441) record, before retiring with an overall coaching record of 321–306 (.512).

He was responsible for numerous rule changes, the most significant being the elimination of the center jump following a field goal, which sped up the game significantly. From 1959 to 1967, he was editor of the *NCAA Basketball Guide*; an official rules interpreter; and wrote six books on coaching, officiating, and team play.

Often referred to as the "American Ambassador of Basketball," he conducted international clinics in Japan, Korea, France, and Germany, and the John Bunn Award, named in his honor, is presented annually (since 1973) to a national or international figure who has contributed greatly to the game of basketball.

Bunn earned three letters each in football, basketball, baseball, and track while attending Humboldt (Kansas) High School from 1912 to 1916; earned a bachelor's degree in 1921 and a master's degree in 1936, both from the University of Kansas; was president of the National Association of Basketball Coaches (1949–1950); and won the NABC Metropolitan Award in 1961, which is presented annually for continued outstanding service to college basketball.

Source: Naismith Memorial Basketball Hall of Fame

Bunning, James Paul David "Jim" (born: October 23, 1931 in Southgate, Kentucky); inducted into the National Baseball Hall of Fame and Museum in 1996 as a player by the Veterans Committee; Position: Pitcher; Bats: Right; Throws: Right; Uniform: #14; first pitcher to record 100 wins and 1,000 strikeouts in both the American and National leagues.

Making his major league debut on July 20, 1955, Bunning played 17 major league seasons (1955–1971) with the Detroit Tigers (1955–1963), Philadelphia Phillies (1964–1967, 1970–1971), Pittsburgh Pirates (1968–1969), and Los Angeles Dodgers (1969). He was named to seven All-Star teams (1957, 1959, 1961–1964, 1966); was the first pitcher to record 100 wins and 1,000 strikeouts in both the American and National leagues; and the first pitcher to throw no-hitters in both leagues, including a perfect game on Father's Day in 1964, the first in the National League since 1880. Bunning led the American League in wins (20) in 1957; led the American League in strikeouts twice (201 in 1959, 201 in 1960); and led the National League in strikeouts in 1967 (253).

He graduated from St. Xavier High School (Cincinnati, Ohio) in 1949 and later received a bachelor's degree in economics from Xavier University (Cincinnati, Ohio).

When he won 17 games in 1967, the 6'3", 195-pound Bunning set a major league record with five 1–0 losses.

After retiring as a player, Bunning managed in the minors for five years before entering Kentucky politics as a Republican. In 1977, he served on the Fort Thomas, Kentucky city council and two years later (1979) won a seat in the Kentucky State Senate. He later served in the U.S. House of Representatives (1987–1999); and currently serves in the U.S. Senate (1999 to present).

On August 2, 1959, in the ninth inning, Bunning struck out three Boston Red Sox batters on nine straight pitches in a 5–4 Tigers loss, making him the first pitcher to accomplish this nine-pitch feat since Lefty Grove in 1928. On June 21, 1964, Father's Day, at Shea Stadium, Bunning threw a perfect game, as the Phillies beats the New York Mets 6–0. This victory made him the first pitcher to win no-hitters in both leagues, his first had come on July 20, 1958 as a Tiger in a 3–0 win over the Boston Red Sox.

Somewhat surprisingly, considering both his 100 wins and no-hitters in both leagues, Bunning was never voted into the baseball hall of fame by sportswriters. In fact, the voting for induction (requiring 75%) over his 15-year eligibility was almost never very close, although he was nearly inducted in 1988 when he received 317 votes (74.2%).

Jim Bunning's Career Statistics

YEAR	TEAM	LG	W	L	PCT	G	SH	SV	IP	H	R	ER	SO	BB	ERA
1955	Detroit	AL	3	5	.375	15	0		51	59	38	36	37	32	6.35
1956	Detroit	AL	5	1	.833	15	0		53	55	24	22	34	28	3.74
1957	Detroit	AL	20	8	.714	45	1		267	214	91	80	182	72	2.70
1958	Detroit	AL	14	12	.538	35	3		220	188	96	86	177	79	3.52
1959	Detroit	AL	17	13	.567	40	1		250	220	111	108	201	75	3.89
1960	Detroit	AL	11	14	.440	36	3		252	217	92	78	201	64	2.79
1961	Detroit	AL	17	11	.607	38	4		268	232	113	95	194	71	3.19
1962	Detroit	AL	19	10	.655	41	2		258	262	112	103	184	74	3.59
1963	Detroit	AL	12	13	.480	39	2		248	245	119	107	196	69	3.88
1964	Philadelphia	NL	19	8	.704	41	5		284	248	99	83	219	46	2.63
1965	Philadelphia	NL	19	9	.679	39	7		291	253	92	84	268	62	2.60
1966	Philadelphia	NL	19	14	.576	43	5		314	260	91	84	252	55	2.41
1967	Philadelphia	NL	17	15	.531	40	6		302	241	94	77	253	73	2.29
1968	Pittsburgh	NL	4	14	.222	27	1		160	168	75	69	95	48	3.88
1969	Pittsburgh	NL	10	9	.526	25	0	0	156	147	74	66	124	49	3.81
1969	Los Angeles	NL	3	1	.750	9	0	0	56	65	23	21	33	10	3.38
1970	Philadelphia	NL	10	15	.400	34	0	0	219	233	111	100	147	56	4.11
1971	Philadelphia	NL	5	12	.294	29	0	1	110	126	72	67	58	37	5.48
	TOTALS		224	184	.549	591	40	1	3,759	3,433	1,527	1,366	2,855	1,000	3.27

Sources: Baseball-Reference.com; National Baseball Hall of Fame and Museum

Buoniconti, Nicholas Anthony "Nick" (born: December 15, 1940 in Springfield, Massachusetts); inducted into the Pro Football Hall of Fame in 2001 as a player; Position: Linebacker; played in three consecutive Super Bowls; a member of the Miami Dolphins 1972 undefeated team.

Buoniconti had a 14-year professional football career (1962–1976) with the Boston Patriots (1962–1968) and the Miami Dolphins (1969–1974). After graduating from the University of Notre Dame (South Bend, Indiana) in 1962, the 5'11", 220-pound linebacker was selected in the 13th round (102nd choice overall) of the 1962 American Football League Draft.

He played in six AFL All-Star games (1963–1967, 1969) and, after the AFL-National Football League merger, was selected to two Pro Bowls (1972–1973). A mainstay in Miami's famed "No-Name Defense," he played in three consecutive Super Bowls (losing in SB VI in 1972, winning SB VII in 1973 after the team's NFL-record undefeated 1972 season, and winning in SB VIII in 1974); was named to the First Team All-AFL/AFC eight times; and was selected to the All-Time AFL Team in 1969. He was also named to the Dolphins' Silver Anniversary Team.

Although Buoniconti had played both guard and linebacker at Notre Dame, he was considered too small to play in the professional ranks. After graduation, he was not selected until deep in the draft, but eventually helped the Patriots win the 1963 AFL Eastern Division title.

Although Buoniconti received a law degree while playing with the Patriots, he was never a practicing attorney. After retiring as a player, he served briefly as President of the U.S. Tobacco Company during the late 1970s and early

1980s, and was often criticized for deriding studies which indicated that smokeless tobacco caused cancer of the mouth as well as other types of cancers.

In 1985, after his son, Marc, suffered a paralyzing spinal cord injury in a college football game, Buoniconti became the public face for the group that eventually founded the Miami Project to Cure Paralysis, which has grown to become one of the world's leading neurological research centers.

Nick Buoniconti's Career Statistics

			INTERCEPTIONS				FUMBLES RECOVERED		
YEAR	**TEAM**	**G**	**NO**	**YDS**	**AVG**	**TD**	**NO**	**YDS**	**TD**
1962	Boston	14	2	3	1.5	0	0	0	0
1963	Boston	14	3	42	14.0	0	3	7	1
1964	Boston	14	5	75	15.0	0	0	0	0
1965	Boston	14	3	31	10.3	0	0	0	0
1966	Boston	14	4	43	10.8	0	1	0	0
1967	Boston	13	4	7	1.8	0	2	0	0
1968	Boston	8	3	22	7.3	0	0	0	0
1969	Miami	13	3	27	9.0	0	1	0	0
1970	Miami	14	0	0	0.0	0	0	0	0
1971	Miami	14	1	16	16.0	0	0	0	0
1972	Miami	14	2	17	8.5	0	0	0	0
1973	Miami	13	0	0	0.0	0	3	13	1
1974	Miami	13	2	29	14.5	0	0	0	0
1976	Miami	11	0	0	0.00	0	0	0	0
	TOTALS	183	32	312	9.8	0	10	20	2

.*Sources*: Pro Football Hall of Fame; Pro-Football-Reference.com

Burch, William "Billy" (born: November 20, 1900 in Yonkers, New York; died: December 30, 1950); inducted into the Hockey Hall of Fame in 1974 as a player; Position: Forward; the second player in NHL history to win both the Hart and Lady Byng trophies.

Burch played 11 National Hockey League seasons (1922–1933) with the Hamilton Tigers (1922–1925), New York Americans (1925–1932), Boston Bruins (1932–1933), and the Chicago Black Hawks (1932–1933).

In 1925, he won the Hart Trophy as the NHL's Most Valuable Player, and two years later, he won the Lady Byng Trophy for sportsmanship, becoming only the second player to win both awards. In 1926, the Tigers moved to New York and were renamed the New York Americans, and when he retired, Burch was the last active player who had played for the Hamilton Tigers.

Billy Burch's Career Statistics

			REGULAR SEASON					PLAYOFFS				
SEASON	**TEAM**	**LEAGUE**	**GP**	**G**	**A**	**TP**	**PIM**	**GP**	**G**	**A**	**TP**	**PIM**
1918–1919	Parkdale Canoe Club	OHA-Jr.										
1919–1920	Toronto Canoe Club	OHA-Jr.						12	42	12	54	
1920–1921	Toronto Aura Lee	OHA-Sr.	10	12	2	14						
1921–1922	Toronto Aura Lee	OHA-Jr.	9	13	10	23		2	2	1	3	
1922–1923	New Haven Westminsters	USAHA		4	0	4						
1922–1923	Hamilton Tigers	NHL	10	6	3	9	4					
1923–1924	Hamilton Tigers	NHL	24	16	6	22	6					
1924–1925	Hamilton Tigers	NHL	27	20	7	27	10					
1925–1926	New York Americans	NHL	36	22	3	25	33					
1926–1927	New York Americans	NHL	43	19	8	27	40					
1927–1928	New York Americans	NHL	32	10	2	12	34					
1928–1929	New York Americans	NHL	44	11	5	16	45	2	0	0	0	0
1929–1930	New York Americans	NHL	35	7	3	10	22					

SEASON	TEAM	LEAGUE	REGULAR SEASON GP	G	A	TP	PIM	PLAYOFFS GP	G	A	TP	PIM
1930–1931	New York Americans	NHL	44	14	8	22	35					
1931–1932	New York Americans	NHL	48	7	15	22	20					
1932–1933	Boston Bruins	NHL	23	3	1	4	4					
1932–1933	Chicago Black Hawks	NHL	24	2	0	2	2					
	NHL TOTALS		390	137	61	198	255	2	0	0	0	0

Sources: Hockey Hall of Fame; Hockey-Reference.com

Burkett, Jesse Cail (born: December 4, 1868 in Wheeling, West Virginia; died: May 27, 1953 in Worcester, Massachusetts); inducted into the National Baseball Hall of Fame and Museum in 1946 as a player by the Veterans Committee; Position: Left Field; Bats: Left; Throws: Left; first player born in West Virginia to be elected to the baseball hall of fame.

Making his major league debut on April 22, 1890, Burkett played 16 seasons (1890–1905) for the New York Giants (1890), Cleveland Spiders (1891–1898), St. Louis Perfectos/Cardinals (1899–1901), St. Louis Browns (1902–1904), and the Boston Red Sox (1905). He hit over .400 three times (joining Ty Cobb and Rogers Hornsby as the only players to accomplish this feat); accumulated 200 or more hits in a season six times; and his 2,872 career hits were, at the time, second-most only to Cap Anson.

The 5’8”, 155-pound Burkett started his baseball career as a pitcher and once won 39 games with Worcester (Massachusetts) of the minor league Atlantic Association. He was the National League hitting champion three times (1895–1896, 1901); led the league in runs scored twice (1896, 1901); led the league in hits three times (1895–1896, 1901); and led the league in doubles in 1894.

Burkett began his professional career in 1888 with the Scranton Miners (Central League) as a pitcher and won 27 games. The next season, he moved up to Worcester; compiled a 39–6 record; and hit .280, while also playing second base.

After his playing days, he became owner, manager, and outfielder of the Worcester Busters (New England League); won the league batting title his first season; and his team would go on to win four straight pennants from 1906 to 1909. After playing his last professional game in 1916 (at age 47), Burkett coached at Holy Cross College (Worcester, Massachusetts) for four years. He later coached Major League Baseball’s New York Giants and went on to manage various teams in the New England area until 1933.

He was inducted into the Wheeling Hall of Fame in 1982.

Jesse Burkett’s Career Statistics

YEAR	TEAM	LG	G	AB	R	H	2B	3B	HR	BB	SO	SB	AVG	SLG
1890	New York	NL	101	401	67	124	22	12	4	33	52	14	.309	.454
1891	Cleveland	NL	40	166	30	45	7	4	0	23	19	2	.271	.361
1892	Cleveland	NL	145	605	117	168	15	14	6	67	59	36	.278	.379
1893	Cleveland	NL	124	480	144	179	23	15	6	98	23	39	.373	.521
1894	Cleveland	NL	124	518	134	185	25	15	8	84	27	32	.357	.510
1895	Cleveland	NL	132	555	149	235	21	15	5	74	31	47	.423	.542
1896	Cleveland	NL	133	585	159	240	26	16	6	49	19	32	.410	.540
1897	Cleveland	NL	128	519	128	199	28	8	2	76		27	.383	.480
1898	Cleveland	NL	148	624	115	215	18	9	0	69		20	.345	.402
1899	Saint Louis	NL	138	567	115	228	17	10	7	67		22	.402	.504
1900	Saint Louis	NL	142	560	88	202	14	12	7	62		31	.361	.466
1901	Saint Louis	NL	142	597	139	228	21	17	10	59		27	.382	.524
1902	Saint Louis	AL	137	549	99	168	29	9	5	71		22	.306	.419
1903	Saint Louis	AL	133	514	74	152	20	7	3	52		16	.296	.379
1904	Saint Louis	AL	147	576	72	157	15	9	2	78		12	.273	.340
1905	Boston	AL	148	573	78	147	13	13	4	67		13	.257	.346
	TOTALS		2,062	8,389	1,708	2,872	314	185	75	1,029	230	392	.342	.451

Sources: Baseball-Reference.com; National Baseball Hall of Fame; Wheeling Hall of Fame

Bush, Walter L., Jr. (born: September 25, 1929 in Minneapolis, Minnesota); inducted into the Hockey Hall of Fame in 2000 as a builder; helped create the Central Hockey League; brought the NHL to Minnesota.

Bush helped bring the National Hockey League to Minnesota (North Stars) by guaranteeing that the Metropolitan Sports Center (Bloomington) would be ready for the start of the 1967–1968 NHL season.

In 1955, Bush helped create the Central Hockey League; served as its president for three years; and briefly owned, managed, and coached the Minneapolis Bruins of the CHL.

He played hockey at Dartmouth College (Hanover, New Hampshire); received a law degree from the University of Minnesota (Minneapolis); and, by his late twenties, Bush had stopped playing the game to concentrate more on the administrative side of the game.

In 1959, he was named general manager of the U.S. National Team; was later elected a director of the Amateur Hockey Association of the United States; and became the organization's president in 1986. Also in 1986, Bush was elected to the International Ice Hockey Federation Council and later became the IIHF's vice-president.

He served as a director of the United States Hockey Hall of Fame in Eveleth, Minnesota; in 1972, he was the first U.S.-born official named to the Board of Directors of the Hockey Hall of Fame in Toronto, Canada; and he later became chairman of the IIHF's Women's Hall of Fame.

In 1973, Bush was awarded the Lester Patrick Trophy by the NHL and USA Hockey for his contribution to hockey in the United States, and he has been inducted into the United States Hockey (1980), the Minnesota Sports (1989), and the Breck Military Academy halls of fame.

Sources: Hockey Hall of Fame; United States Hockey Hall of Fame

Buss, Gerald Hatten "Jerry" Dr. (born: January 27, 1934 in Salt Lake City, Utah); inducted into the Naismith Memorial Basketball Hall of Fame in 2010 as a contributor; has owned the Los Angeles Lakers since 1979.

Having built one of the most successful sports franchises in history, Buss is the third Laker to enter the Basketball Hall of Fame as a contributor (after Chick Hearn and Pete Newell). Under his leadership since 1979, the team has made 16 trips to the NBA Finals and has won 10 Championships.

In addition to his success with the Lakers, Buss owned the Los Angeles Sparks of the WNBA from 1996 to 2006, winning two championships (2001–2002); was the first NBA team owner of a D-League franchise (Los Angeles D-Fenders in 2006); and has also served two terms as Chairman of the NBA Board of Governors.

He is credited with introducing the Laker Girls cheering squad.

He attended the University of Wyoming (Laramie), graduating in 1953, before earning his doctorate at the University of Southern California (Los Angeles).

Before becoming a sports owner, Buss worked as a chemist for the Bureau of Mines (now the Mine Safety and Health Administration); in the aerospace industry; was on the faculty of USC's chemistry department, and made his fortune in real estate.

His first foray into sports was as the owner of World Team Tennis. He then purchased the Los Angeles Lakers (NBA); the Los Angeles Kings (NHL), the Los Angeles Forum, the Los Angeles Lazers (Major Indoor Soccer League), and the WNBA's Los Angeles Sparks.

Source: Naismith Memorial Basketball Hall of Fame

Butkus, Richard Marvin "Dick" (born: December 9, 1942 in Chicago, Illinois); inducted into the Pro Football Hall of Fame in 1979 as a player; Position: Middle Linebacker; Uniform: #51; holds the Chicago Bears' record with 49 takeaways.

A two-time All-American at the University of Illinois (Urbana-Champaign), the 6'3", 245-pound Butkus played his entire nine-year (1965–1973) National Football League career with the Chicago Bears. He was the team's first-round draft pick in 1965 (third selection overall); garnered 22 career interceptions and 27 career fumble recoveries (for a combined Chicago Bears' record of 49 takeaways); was selected All-NFL six times (including his rookie year); and played in eight straight Pro Bowls (1966–1973). Butkus was named 1969 NFL Defensive Player of the Year; 1970 NFL Defensive Player of the Year; selected to the NFL 1960s All-Decade Team; to the NFL 1970s All-Decade Team; and to the NFL 75th Anniversary team.

While in college, Butkus won the *Chicago Tribune* Silver Football in 1963 as the Big Ten Most Valuable Player, and was named the American Football Coaches Association's Player of the Year in 1964.

After graduating, he signed with the Bears and earned a name for himself right away in his NFL debut with 11 unassisted tackles against the San Francisco 49ers. He finished his rookie year as the team leader in pass interceptions and fumble recoveries.

When knee injuries ended his career early, Butkus began making commercials; acting on television and in the movies; and running the Dick Butkus Football Network, which broadcasts football games on radio and television. The Dick Butkus Award, started in 1985, is presented annually by the Downtown Athletic Club of Orlando (Florida) to the top linebacker in college football.

He was inducted into the College Football Hall of Fame in 1983 and is one of only two players to have a uniform number (#50) retired by the University of Illinois. Butkus was selected to the Walter Camp All-Century team in 1990; named the sixth-best college football player ever by *College Football News* in 2000; selected the 70th greatest athlete of the 20th century by ESPN, the ninth best player in league history by *The Sporting News*, and the fifth best by the Associated Press; and the NFL named him to its All-Time team in 2000. The Bears retired his jersey #51 in October 1994.

In 2006, he teamed up with the Taylor Hooton Foundation to lead a nationwide anti-steroid campaign ("Mean and Clean Campaign for Steroid-Free Sports") directed at high school athletes with Butkus as spokesperson.

Dick Butkus' Career Statistics

			INTERCEPTIONS				FUMBLES RECOVERED		
YEAR	**TEAM**	**G**	**INT**	**YDS**	**AVG**	**TD**	**NO**	**YDS**	**TD**
1965	Chicago	14	5	84	16.8	0	7	11	0
1966	Chicago	14	1	3	3.0	0	4	0	0
1967	Chicago	14	1	24	24.0	0	3	0	0
1968	Chicago	13	3	14	4.7	0	1	0	0
1969	Chicago	13	2	13	6.5	0	2	0	0
1970	Chicago	14	3	0	0.0	0	2	0	0
1971	Chicago	14	4	9	2.3	0	3	0	0
1972	Chicago	14	2	19	9.5	0	4	11	0
1973	Chicago	9	1	0	0.0	0	1	0	1
	TOTALS	119	22	166	7.5	0	27	22	1

Sources: Dick Butkus Web Page (www.dickbutkus.com); Pro Football Hall of Fame; Pro-Football-Reference.com

Butterfield, Jack A. (born: August 1, 1919 in Regina, Saskatchewan, Canada); inducted into the Hockey Hall of Fame in 1980 as a builder; president of the American Hockey League for 28 years.

Butterfield helped the American Hockey League survive against financial and competitive threats from both the expansion of the National Hockey League and the emergence of the World Hockey Association in the late 1960s and early 1970s.

He played amateur hockey as a young man, but his career came to an end when he suffered a broken back while serving with the Royal Canadian Air Force in World War II.

After the war, Butterfield began his administrative career in the AHL, working in public relations, before serving as business manager for the Fort Worth (Texas) Rangers of the United States Hockey League and the Oakland (California) Oaks of the Pacific Coast League. He returned to the AHL with the Springfield (Massachusetts) Indians in a variety of positions, eventually serving as the team's general manager. He was general manager when the Indians won three straight Calder Cup championships (1960–1962).

In 1966, he became president of the AHL, a job he held for 28 years (1994). As league president, Butterfield helped structure the Joint Affiliation Agreement with the NHL, which ensured that the AHL would serve as the NHL's minor league. He also sought financial support for struggling teams and created the annual schedule. After retiring as the AHL's president, he served on the league's Board of Directors.

The Jack A. Butterfield Trophy is presented annually to the AHL's Most Valuable Player in the Calder Cup playoffs. He was one of the first inductees of the AHL's Hall of Fame in 2006.

Sources: American Hockey League Hall of Fame; Hockey Hall of Fame

Chapter 3
Cahill to Cuyler

Cahill, Thomas W. (born: December 25, 1864 in New York, New York; died: September 29, 1951 in South Orange, New Jersey); inducted into the National Soccer Hall of Fame and Museum in 1950 as an administrator; helped form the American Amateur Football Association, the United States Football Association, and the American Soccer League.

Cahill moved with his family to St. Louis, Missouri in 1871 and played hockey in the city school's system and later, at St. Louis University (Missouri). He would eventually become one of the charter members of the Missouri Athletic Club, and in 1890, he organized the semi-professional Missouri-Illinois Trolley League (baseball).

Destined to become one of the most important administrators in the early history of the game, as a young man, Cahill played soccer with the St. Louis Shamrocks of the St. Louis Soccer League.

He helped form the American Amateur Football Association in 1912 and the United States Football Association (today's United States Soccer Federation) in 1913, and became its first executive secretary, a position he held for three terms (1913–1921, 1923–1924, 1928).

In 1916, Cahill became coach of the U.S. National Team and took the squad to Scandinavia, leading the U.S. into its first international play. He returned to Scandinavia for more international matches in 1919 (Bethlehem [Pennsylvania] Steel team) and in 1921 (St. Louis All-Star team). Also in 1921, he helped create the original American Soccer League (America's first professional soccer league), and served as the organization's secretary in its early years.

In 1928, while executive secretary of the USFA, Cahill oversaw the infamous "Soccer War" between the USFA and the American Soccer League. The long-running conflict led him to propose separate organizations to run amateur and professional soccer leagues under a unified USFA organization.

Source: National Soccer Hall of Fame and Museum

Calder, Frank (born: November 17, 1877 in Bristol, England; died: February 4, 1943 in Montreal, Quebec, Canada); inducted into the Hockey Hall of Fame in 1947 as a builder; first president of the National Hockey League.

Calder immigrated to Canada in the early 1900s to teach in Montreal. A few years later, he changed careers and became a sportswriter with the *Montreal Witness*, and later, a sports editor with the *Montreal Herald* and the *Daily Telegraph*. He was one of the founders of the Montreal School Rugby League, and served as secretary of the Montreal and district football league.

He was secretary-treasurer of the National Hockey Association when the NHA folded and the National Hockey League was created in 1917. Calder became the new league's first president, and stayed on the job for 25 years, until 1943. As NHL president, he oversaw the expansion of the league in both Canada and into the United States; helped the league survive through World War I, the Great Depression, and World War II; and constantly monitored each team's financial stability to ensure its continued existence.

Since 1933, Calder had personally purchased a trophy and presented it annually to the NHL's Rookie of the Year. After he died in 1943, the NHL continued his tradition and established the Calder Memorial Trophy. Another trophy named in his honor, the Calder Cup, is presented annually to the American Hockey League championship team.

Source: Hockey Hall of Fame

Calhoun, James A. "Jim" (born: May 10, 1942 in Braintree, Massachusetts); inducted into the Naismith Memorial Basketball Hall of Fame in 2005 as a coach; first coach in NCAA history to win at least 250 games at two different Division I schools; only coach in the history of the Big East Conference to have been named Conference Coach of the Year four times.

Having worked in the New England area his entire college coaching career, which began in 1972, Calhoun transformed Northeastern University (Boston, Massachusetts) and the University of Connecticut (Storrs) basketball into powerhouse college programs. During his 14 seasons (1972–1986) at Northeastern, he upgraded the school's program from Division II status and built it into a perennial NCAA Division I tournament team. Starting in 1986, he elevated Connecticut from regional contender to two-time NCAA national champion (1999, 2004), turning the school into one of the nation's elite college basketball programs. He won an NIT Championship in 1980 with Connecticut; was selected National Coach of the Year in 1990; and was the only coach to be named Big East Conference Coach of the Year four times (1990, 1994, 1996, 1998).

He played basketball, football, and baseball at Braintree High School, and his hometown later named one of its outdoor courts "Calhoun Park." After briefly attending Lowell State (now known as the University of Massachusetts, Lowell), he returned home to take care of family problems. Eighteen months later, Calhoun went to American International College (Springfield, Massachusetts) on a basketball scholarship; was the team's top scorer as a junior and senior; its captain as a senior, graduated in 1969 as the fourth-highest all-time scorer at AIC; and was named a Little All-American.

He started his coaching career as an assistant at his alma mater, and served as a head coach at three local-area high schools before being hired by Northeastern in 1972. He led the Huskies to the NCAA tournament in five of his last six seasons at the school, and in 1986 he was hired as the men's head basketball coach at Connecticut. He led the team to the 1988 NIT championship, and since the NCAA tournament expanded to 64 teams, UConn is one of only four schools to win two national titles (along with Duke, Kentucky, and North Carolina).

Calhoun began his coaching career at Old Lyme (Connecticut) High School in 1968 and, after finishing 3–16, he returned to Massachusetts and coached at Westport High School. After one year, he moved to Dedham (Massachusetts) High School and, after leading the team to a 21–1 record in 1972, he was hired by Northeastern.

At Northeastern, he compiled a 75–19 tournament record; won six regional Coach of the Year awards; and is the school's all-time winningest coach (248–137, .644).

At UConn, he finished his first year with a 9–19 record; won the 1988 NIT title; and was a national Coach of the Year in 1990 after leading the Huskies to the school's first-ever Big East championship, the NCAA Tournament Elite Eight, and a 31–6 record. While Calhoun has been at UConn, the Huskies thus far have won 16 league titles; won or shared nine conference titles (1990, 1994–1996, 1998–1999, 2002, 2005–2006); and won six Big East Tournament championships (1990, 1996, 1998–1999, 2002, 2004).

On March 15, 2005, he won his 700th game (over Georgetown) and is the first coach in NCAA history to win at least 250 games at two different Division I schools. In 35 seasons as a head coach on the NCAA Division I collegiate level (he is still active), Calhoun has compiled an overall record of 823–358 (.697), including a 248–137 record at Northeastern and a 575–221 mark at Connecticut.

In the June 2006 National Basketball Association Draft, UConn became the first college in the history of the NBA to have five players (sophomore Rudy Gay, senior Hilton Armstrong, junior Marcus Williams, junior Josh Boone, and senior Denham Brown) selected in the first two rounds of the draft, and for the first time in school history, the Huskies had four players selected in the first round (Gay, Armstrong, Williams, Boone). UConn became only the third school in NBA history to have four players selected in the first round of the draft, along with Duke (1999) and North Carolina (2005).

He was inducted into the Northeastern University Sports Hall of Fame in 1985.

Jim Calhoun's Coaching Record

Northeastern University (America East Conference / North Atlantic Conference) (1972–1986)

SEASON	SCHOOL	W-L RECORD	WIN%	CONFERENCE W-L RECORD	WIN%	POSTSEASON
1972–1973	Northeastern	19–7	.731			
1973–1974	Northeastern	12–11	.522			
1974–1975	Northeastern	12–12	.500			
1975–1976	Northeastern	12–13	.480			
1976–1977	Northeastern	12–14	.462			
1977–1978	Northeastern	14–12	.538			
1978–1979	Northeastern	13–13	.500			
1979–1980	Northeastern	19–8	.704	19–7	.731	

SEASON	SCHOOL	W-L RECORD	WIN%	CONFERENCE W-L RECORD	WIN%	POSTSEASON
1980–1981	Northeastern	24–6	.800	21–5	.808	NCAA Second Round
1981–1982	Northeastern	23–7	.767	8–1	.889	NCAA Second Round
1982–1983	Northeastern	13–15	.464	4–6	.400	
1983–1984	Northeastern	27–5	.844	14–0	1.000	NCAA First Round
1984–1985	Northeastern	22–9	.710	13–3	.813	NCAA First Round
1985–1986	Northeastern	26–5	.839	16–2	.889	NCAA First Round
	TOTALS	248–137	.644	95–24	.798	

University of Connecticut (Big East Conference) (1986–2010)

SEASON	SCHOOL	W-L RECORD	WIN%	CONFERENCE RECORD	WIN%	POSTSEASON
1986–1987	Connecticut	9–19	.321	3–13	.188	
1987–1988	Connecticut	20–14	.588	4–12	.250	NIT Champions
1988–1989	Connecticut	18–13	.581	6–10	.375	NIT Quarterfinals
1989–1990	Connecticut	31–6	.838	12–4	.750	NCAA Elite Eight
1990–1991	Connecticut	20–11	.645	9–7	.563	NCAA Sweet Sixteen
1991–1992	Connecticut	20–10	.667	10–8	.556	NCAA Second Round
1992–1993	Connecticut	15–13	.536	9–9	.500	NIT First Round
1993–1994	Connecticut	29–5	.853	16–2	.889	NCAA Sweet Sixteen
1994–1995	Connecticut	28–5	.848	16–2	.889	NCAA Elite Eight
1995–1996	Connecticut	30–2	.938	17–1	.944	NCAA Sweet Sixteen
1996–1997	Connecticut	18–15	.545	7–11	.389	NIT Third Round
1997–1998	Connecticut	32–5	.865	15–3	.833	NCAA Elite Eight
1998–1999	Connecticut	34–2	.944	16–2	.889	NCAA Champion
1999–2000	Connecticut	25–10	.714	10–6	.625	NCAA Second Round
2000–2001	Connecticut	20–12	.625	8–8	.500	NIT Second Round
2001–2002	Connecticut	27–7	.794	13–3	.813	NCAA Elite Eight
2002–2003	Connecticut	23–10	.697	10–6	.625	NCAA Sweet Sixteen
2003–2004	Connecticut	33–6	.846	12–4	.750	NCAA Champion
2004–2005	Connecticut	23–8	.742	13–3	.813	NCAA Second Round
2005–2006	Connecticut	30–4	.882	14–2	.875	NCAA Elite Eight
2006–2007	Connecticut	17–14	.548	6–10	.375	
2007–2008	Connecticut	24–9	.558	13–5	.722	NCAA First Round
2008–2009	Connecticut	31–5	.727	15–3	.833	NCAA Final Four
2009–2010	Connecticut	18–16	.529	7–11	.389	NIT Second Round
	TOTALS	575–221	.722	261–145	.643	
	CAREER TOTALS	823–358	.697	356–169	.678	

Source: Naismith Memorial Basketball Hall of Fame

Caligiuri, Paul David (born: May 9, 1964 in Westminster, California); inducted into the National Soccer Hall of Fame and Museum in 2004 as a player; Position: Midfielder-Defender; Uniform: #20; International Caps (1984–1997): 110; International Goals: 5; scored the "Goal Heard Round the World" in November 1989; first American-born player to play in Germany's top division.

In addition to being a member of the United States Men's National Team, Caligiuri was one of the first American-born players to play professional soccer outside the United States. He earned his first international cap against El Salvador in 1984 while he was still playing at the University of California at Los Angeles. He went on to accrue 110 caps and scored five goals, the most well-known of which was against Trinidad & Tobago on November 19, 1989 in a 1–0 win that sent the United States to its first FIFA World Cup in 40 years, and is now known as the "Goal Heard Round the World."

After graduating from Walnut (California) High School, Caligiuri attended UCLA from 1982 to 1985; captained the 1985 UCLA Bruins to the NCAA Division I Men's National Soccer Championship; and was a two-time National Soccer Coaches Association of America All-American. After graduating from UCLA, he played for the San Diego Nomads of the Western Soccer Alliance for a single season (1986); was named the league's most valuable player; and was selected 1986 U.S. Soccer Athlete of the Year. He played in the 1986 World Cup qualifiers; the 1988 Summer Olympic Games (Seoul, South Korea, failed to medal); and in two World Cups for the Men's National Team (1990, 1994).

Caligiuri began his professional career with SV Meppen Bundesliga 2nd Division (Germany), where he played from 1987 to 1989. He later became the first American-born player to play in Germany's top division when he went to East Germany for the 1990–1991 season and played for FC Hansa Rostock, which won the East German title that year. After one season, he transferred to FC Freiburg (now known as German Bundesliga), and later played at Hamburg and St. Pauli, before continuing his professional career in the United States.

On May 4, 1995, the 5'10" Caligiuri signed with the Los Angeles Salsa of the American Professional Soccer League, and donated his entire salary to the victims of the Oklahoma City bombing. In August, the Salsa loaned him to Bundesliga club FC St. Pauli, where he appeared in 14 games. In January 1996, the team decided not to renew his contract and he returned to America and signed with the newly formed Columbus (Ohio) Crew of Major League Soccer.

After one season, he moved to the Los Angeles (California) Galaxy (MLS), where he finished his professional career by winning the 2001 U.S. Open Cup. In 2002, he was inducted into the American Youth Soccer Organization Hall of Fame and was named the head coach of the California State Polytechnic University (Pomona) Broncos men's and women's soccer programs.

Paul Caligiuri's U.S. National Team Statistics

YEAR	G	MIN	G	ASST	PTS	W–L–T
1984	6	540	0	0	0	2–2–2
1985	8	560	1	0	2	2–3–3
1986	2	180	0	0	0	0–0–2
1989	5	405	1	0	2	3–2–0
1990	16	1,150	2	1	5	4–11–1
1991	8	720	0	0	0	6–0–2
1992	7	509	0	1	1	3–2–2
1993	15	1,075	0	0	0	2–4–9
1994	20	1,420	0	2	2	4–7–9
1995	14	1,250	1	0	2	5–5–4
1996	8	454	0	0	0	6–1–1
1997	1	90	0	0	0	1–0–0
TOTALS	110	8,272	5	4	14	39–37–34

Paul Caligiuri's Major League Soccer Statistics

YEAR	TEAM	G	MIN	G	ASST	PTS
1996	Columbus	22	1,869	3	2	8
1997	Los Angeles	16	1,406	1	2	4
1998	Los Angeles	18	1,293	1	1	3
1999	Los Angeles	27	2,275	1	1	3
2000	Los Angeles	28	2,212	3	4	10
2001	Los Angeles	24	1,854	0	4	4
TOTALS		135	10,909	9	14	32

Source: National Soccer Hall of Fame and Museum

Cameron, Harold Hugh "Harry" (born: February 6, 1890 in Pembroke, Ontario, Canada; died: October 20, 1953); inducted into the Hockey Hall of Fame in 1962 as a player; Position: Forward; member of the first National Hockey League team to win the Stanley Cup; first player to achieve the "Gordie Howe hat trick."

Cameron played 14 seasons of professional hockey from 1912 to 1926. He joined the Toronto Blueshirts of the National Hockey Association for the 1912–1913 season; won the Stanley Cup in 1914; stayed with the team when it became the Arenas of the newly formed National Hockey League in 1917; and won the Stanley Cup again in 1918, the first NHL team to win the championship.

Cameron played briefly for the Ottawa Senators and the Montreal Wanderers before returning to Toronto (which had since changed its name to the St. Patricks [Pats, now known as the Maple Leafs]), and led the team to another Stanley Cup title in 1922. In 1923, he became the player-manager of the Saskatoon Sheiks/Crescents of the Western Canada

Hockey League/Western Hockey League, where he continued to play until 1933, before becoming a full-time coach with the Saskatoon Standards in senior hockey.

On December 26, 1917, Cameron became the first player to achieve what is now called the "Gordie Howe hat trick," wherein a player accomplishes the following feats in a single game: scores a goal, gets an assist, and participates in a fight. It is named after legendary hockey player Gordie Howe, who was known for both his scoring ability and his on-ice scuffles.

Harry Cameron's Career Statistics

			REGULAR SEASON					PLAYOFFS				
SEASON	**TEAM**	**LEAGUE**	**GP**	**G**	**A**	**TP**	**PIM**	**GP**	**G**	**A**	**TP**	**PIM**
1908–1909	Pembroke Debaters	UOVHL	6	13	0	13						
1909–1910	Pembroke Debaters	UOVHL	8	17	0	17						
1910–1911	Pembroke Debaters	UOVHL	6	9	1	10	8	2	4	4	8	0
1911–1912	Port Arthur Lake City	NOHL	15	6	0	6	48	2	2	0	2	0
1912–1913	Toronto Blueshirts	NHA	20	9	0	9	20					
1913–1914	Toronto Blueshirts	NHA	19	15	4	19	22	2	0	2	2	6
1913–1914	Toronto Blueshirts	St-Cup						3	1	0	1	4
1914–1915	Toronto Blueshirts	NHA	17	12	8	20	43					
1915–1916	Toronto Blueshirts	NHA	24	8	3	11	70					
1916–1917	Toronto 228th Battalion	NHA	14	8	4	12	20					
1916–1917	Montreal Wanderers	NHA	6	1	1	2	9					
1917–1918	Toronto Arenas	NHL	21	17	10	27	28	2	1	2	3	0
1917–1918	Toronto Arenas	St-Cup						5	3	1	4	12
1918–1919	Toronto Arenas	NHL	7	6	2	8	9					
1918–1919	Ottawa Senators	NHL	7	5	1	6	26	5	4	0	4	6
1919–1920	Toronto St. Pats	NHL	7	3	0	3	6					
1919–1920	Montreal Canadiens	NHL	16	12	5	17	36					
1920–1921	Toronto St. Pats	NHL	24	18	9	27	35	2	0	0	0	2
1921–1922	Toronto St. Pats	NHL	24	18	17	35	22	2	0	2	2	8
1921–1922	Toronto St. Pats	St-Cup						4	0	2	2	14
1922–1923	Toronto St. Pats	NHL	22	9	7	16	27					
1923–1924	Saskatoon Crescents	WCHL	29	10	10	20	16					
1924–1925	Saskatoon Crescents	WCHL	28	13	7	20	21	2	1	0	1	0
1925–1926	Saskatoon Crescents	WHL	30	9	3	12	12	2	0	0	0	0
1926–1927	Saskatoon Sheiks	PrHL	31	26	19	45	20	4	1	0	1	4
1927–1928	Minneapolis Millers	AHA	19	2	3	5	32					
1928–1929	St. Louis Flyers	AHA	34	14	3	17	30					
1929–1930	St. Louis Flyers	AHA	46	14	6	20	34					
1930–1931	St. Louis Flyers	AHA	37	4	3	7	30					
1932–1933	Saskatoon Crescents	WCHL	9	0	0	0	4					
	NHL TOTALS		128	88	51	139	189	11	5	4	9	16

Sources: Hockey Hall of Fame; Hockey-Reference.com

Campanella, Roy (born: November 19, 1921 in Philadelphia, Pennsylvania; died: June 26, 1993 in Woodland Hills, California); inducted into the National Baseball Hall of Fame and Museum in 1969 as a player; Position: Catcher; Bats: Right; Throws: Right; Uniform: #39; first catcher to break Major League Baseball's color line; his last game was also the last major league game ever played at Brooklyn's Ebbets Field; second African-American player to be inducted into the baseball hall of fame.

Making his major league debut on April 20, 1948 Campanella played his entire 10-year career with the Brooklyn Dodgers (1948–1957); appeared in five World Series, all against the New York Yankees (winning in 1955 and losing in 1949, 1952–1953, and 1956); was an eight-time All-Star (1949–1956); and was named the National League Most Valuable Player three times (1951, 1953 [setting a then single-season record for catchers with 41 home runs], 1955).

Before signing with the Dodgers, Campanella was a star catcher with the Baltimore Elite Giants (Negro National League) for seven seasons (1937–1942, 1944–1945). His major league career ended prematurely when he was badly injured in an automobile accident prior to the 1958 season that temporarily left him paralyzed. Although he would later regain partial use of his hands and legs, his career was over and he spent the rest of his life in a wheelchair. His last game, September 29, 1957, was also the last major league game ever played at Brooklyn's Ebbets Field.

Nicknamed "Campy," the 5'8", 200-pound catcher led the National League with 142 RBIs in 1953.

Born in Philadelphia to a black mother and an Italian father, Campanella began playing baseball in 1937 with the Bacharach Giants, a local semi-professional team. At age 15, when he signed with the Baltimore Elite Giants (Negro National League), he was still in school and could only play on the weekends. He left school at age 16 and joined the team full-time, becoming a starter in 1939. He was voted Most Valuable Player in the 1941 East-West All-Star game; left the team briefly to play in the Mexican League (1942–1943); rejoined the Giants in 1944; and led the Negro National League in doubles in 1944 and in RBIs in 1945.

When Campanella became one of five black players signed by Major League Baseball's Brooklyn Dodgers before the 1946 season, he was sent to the organization's Class-B farm team in Nashua, New Hampshire of the Eastern League (New England League). After winning the MVP award, he was promoted to the Montreal Royals of the AAA-level International League for the 1947 season, before joining the Dodgers the next year.

On May 7, 1959, the Dodgers (who by now had moved to Los Angeles, California) honored him with "Roy Campanella Night" at the Los Angeles Memorial Coliseum. For the event, the New York Yankees made a special trip to Los Angeles and played an exhibition game against the Dodgers. The attendance mark of more than 93,000 is still the largest crowd ever to attend a Major League Baseball game.

Campanella was the second African-American player to be inducted into the hall of fame, after Jackie Robinson. In June 1972, the Dodgers retired his uniform number 39, along with Jackie Robinson's #42 and Sandy Koufax's #32.

After his playing career, Campanella remained involved with the Dodgers in a variety of community relations roles and as an advisor to the franchise's catchers. In 1999, he was ranked number 50 on *The Sporting News*' list of the 100 Greatest Baseball Players, and was a nominee for the Major League Baseball All-Century Team. In 2006, he was featured on a United States postage stamp, one of four honoring baseball sluggers (including Mickey Mantle, Hank Greenberg, and Mel Ott).

On September 21, 1952, Campanella hit the last-ever home run at Braves Field in an 8–2 Dodger win over the Boston Braves, before the franchise moved to Milwaukee. In September 2006, the Los Angeles Dodgers created the annual Roy Campanella Award, which is voted among the club's players and coaches and given to the Dodger who best exemplifies his spirit and leadership.

Roy Campanella's National League Career Statistics

Year	Team	G	AB	R	H	2B	3B	HR	RBI	BB	SO	SB	AVG	SLG
1948	Brooklyn	83	279	32	72	11	3	9	45	36	45	3	.258	.416
1949	Brooklyn	130	436	65	125	22	2	22	82	67	36	3	.287	.498
1950	Brooklyn	126	437	70	123	19	3	31	89	55	51	1	.281	.551
1951	Brooklyn	143	505	90	164	33	1	33	108	53	51	1	.325	.590
1952	Brooklyn	128	468	73	126	18	1	22	97	57	59	8	.269	.453
1953	Brooklyn	144	519	103	162	26	3	41	142	67	58	4	.312	.611
1954	Brooklyn	111	397	43	82	14	3	19	51	42	49	1	.207	.401
1955	Brooklyn	123	446	81	142	20	1	32	107	56	41	2	.318	.583
1956	Brooklyn	124	388	39	85	6	1	20	73	66	61	1	.219	.394
1957	Brooklyn	103	330	31	80	9	0	13	62	34	50	1	.242	.388
	TOTALS	1,215	4,205	627	1,161	178	18	242	856	533	501	25	.276	.500

Sources: Baseball-Reference.com; National Baseball Hall of Fame and Museum; Roy Campanella Web Site (www.roycampanella.com)

Campbell, Angus Daniel (born: March 19, 1884 in Stayner, Ontario, Canada; died: 1976); inducted into the Hockey Hall of Fame in 1964 as a builder; founder of the Northern Ontario Hockey Association.

A mining engineer by trade, Campbell formed and organized the Northern Ontario Hockey Association. He graduated from the University of Toronto (Canada) with a bachelor of science degree and then a master's in mining engineering. While at the university, he played hockey and lacrosse, and while working in the summer near Cobalt (northern Ontario), he played on a team that won the Temiskaming Hockey League championship.

After his playing days, Campbell decided to focus on administration began improving the sport's organization in the northern Ontario area. In October 1919, he helped form the Northern Ontario Hockey Association; instituted its affiliation with the Ontario Hockey Association; and served in executive positions within both organizations. For his efforts, the OHA presented him with its Gold Stick Award and the NOHA made him a lifetime member.

The Angus Campbell Merit Award is presented annually by the NOHA to an individual for outstanding service to the game other than as a player.

Source: Hockey Hall of Fame

Campbell, Clarence Sutherland (born: July 9, 1905 in Fleming, Saskatchewan, Canada; died: June 24, 1984 in Montreal, Quebec, Canada); inducted into the Hockey Hall of Fame in 1966 as a builder; former president of the National Hockey League.

A major influence in professional hockey, Campbell served as president of the National Hockey League for 31 years (1946–1977). Earlier in life (1924), he had graduated from the University of Alberta (Canada) with a degree in law and earned a Rhodes Scholarship to Oxford University (Oxfordshire, England). While based in England, he refereed hockey and lacrosse matches in Europe.

After six years at Oxford, Campbell returned to Canada during the Great Depression and worked for an Edmonton law firm, while refereeing in the Canadian Amateur Hockey Association. He was hired by NHL president Frank Calder at the start of the 1936 season and quickly became one of the league's best officials. After only one year, he was chosen to work the Stanley Cup semifinals series between the Detroit Red Wings and the Montreal Canadiens.

In 1940, he enlisted in the Canadian Army during World War II and rose to the rank of Lieutenant Colonel before leaving the military in 1945; commanded the 4th Armored Division; and eventually was promoted to the rank of lieutenant colonel by 1945. After the war, Campbell was the prosecution lawyer for the Canadian War Crimes Commission at the Nuremberg trial of Nazi Kurt Meyer. For this work, he received the Order of the British Empire and made King's Counsel.

He returned to Canada in 1946 and worked as an assistant to NHL president Mervyn Dutton, who he replaced when Dutton resigned a few months later. As league president, Campbell increased the number of regular-season games from 50 to 70; instituted the All-Star Game; and created the NHL Pension Plan.

In the early 1950s, he inaugurated the Inter-League Draft, which allowed weak and underperforming teams access to young talent controlled by the richer clubs. Campbell oversaw the league's tripling in size from 1967 to 1975; led the NHL expansion throughout North America; resisted the inroads sought by the World Hockey Association; and refused to allow players not under contract to NHL teams to participate in the 1972 Summit Series between Canada and the USSR.

While still active as the league's president, Campbell was inducted into the Hockey Hall of Fame; had one of the league's conferences named after him (now known as the Western Conference); and the Clarence S. Campbell Bowl is presented annually to the winner of the Western Conference. He also served as a Stanley Cup trustee from 1979 to 1984.

Source: Hockey Hall of Fame

Campbell, Earl Christian (born: March 29, 1955 in Tyler, Texas); inducted into the Pro Football Hall of Fame in 1991 as a player; Position: Running Back; Uniform: #34; first player at the University of Texas to win the Heisman Trophy; first player taken in the 1978 NFL draft.

The powerfully built 5'11", 232-pound Campbell played a relatively short eight seasons (1978–1985, 115 games) in the National Football League with the Houston Oilers (1978–1984) and the New Orleans Saints (1984–1985). He was an All-American at the University of Texas (Austin, 1974–1977); a Heisman Trophy winner in 1977; first player selected All-Southwest Conference four times; and the first player taken in the 1978 NFL draft. He is one of only two players (along with quarterback Brett Favre) to receive some form of the NFL Most Valuable Player Award in three consecutive regular seasons, and he is the only player to do so in his first three seasons as a professional (1978–1980). He was a five-time Pro Bowl selection (1978–1981, 1983); was ranked 35 on the NFL's 100 Greatest Players of All-Time; and was inducted into the College Football Hall of Fame in 1990.

At Dogan Junior High School (Tyler, Texas), he was a lineman on both offense and defense, but did not focus on football when he first went to John Tyler High School (Tyler, Texas) in 1969. A poor student, his football career as a freshman started slowly, but he was eventually named an All-American middle linebacker as a junior. In his senior year (1972–1973), Campbell became a full-time running back and also played outside linebacker on defense; led the team to an undefeated season; and helped the school win the state championship by running for more than 200 yards in a 21–14 win over Austin Reagan High School. He was again named an All-American, his first time as a running back, and gained 2,224 yards as a senior (225 yards a game).

After high school, he went to the University of Texas to play for legendary coach Darrell Royal for the 1974 season, where as a freshman, he won the Southwest Conference Newcomer of the Year Award by rushing for 928 yards. In his sophomore year (1975), he led the team to a 38–21 win over the Colorado Buffaloes; was named Bluebonnet Offensive Player of the Game; and was selected to both All-Southwest Conference and All-American teams.

After suffering a hamstring injury in practice before the start of his junior year, his offensive numbers declined significantly as the team finished the year with an unexpected 5–5–1 record, the school's worst season since 1956. The team's poor performance led to the resignation of coach Royal and the hiring of Fred Akers for Campbell's senior year (1977).

With a new coach, the team rebounded to an 11–1 record; was ranked third in the country; Campbell was named college's Best Running Back; he became the first player from the University of Texas to win the Heisman Trophy; and ended his college career with 4,443 yards and 41 touchdowns.

In the 1978 National Football League Draft, Campbell was picked as the number one selection by the Houston Oilers under coach Bum Phillips. His transition from the college game to the pros did not appear to be a problem as he won the NFL's rushing title (1,450 yards and 13 touchdowns); was named Rookie of the Year; named Most Valuable Player; and was selected All-Pro. He repeated his success the next two seasons and would again win the rushing title; be named the MVP; and selected All-Pro. Nicknamed the "Tyler Rose," he missed only six games due to injury.

In Campbell's rookie year, the Oilers finished the regular season with a 10–6 record, and beat the Miami Dolphins and the New England Patriots in the playoffs before losing to the Pittsburgh Steelers (in the famous "Ice Bowl") in the AFC Championship game. After the season, Campbell returned to the University of Texas and graduated with a Bachelor's Degree in Speech Communications. In 1979, the team improved its record to 12–4, again won its first two playoff games (against the Denver Broncos and the San Diego Chargers) before once more losing to the Steelers in the title game. He would never again get so close to playing in the Super Bowl.

In 1980, he rushed for 1,934 yards (at the time second only to 0. J. Simpson's 2,003 yards in 1973) and ran for 200 or more yards in four games. The Oilers finished the season with an 11–5 record, but after losing its first playoff game to the Oakland Raiders, Phillips was fired. Although the team's fortunes did not improve, Campbell continued to generate positive offensive numbers. In 1981, he won his fourth consecutive American Football Conference rushing title, and the Texas State Legislature proclaimed Earl Campbell an Official State Hero of Texas (joining Stephen F. Austin, Davy Crockett, and Sam Houston).

He was traded to the New Orleans Saints during the 1984 season, where he reteamed with Bum Phillips, who had been hired as the team's head coach. After two mediocre seasons, Campbell retired in 1986, and began to enjoy his celebrity life in Houston by participating in golfing events and charitable activities.

An avid cook, in 1990, Campbell and his business partners began selling his spicy sausage through Scholz's, and eventually, inked a deal with the Appletree Food Stores under the name Earl Campbell Foods. He and his partners later opened a restaurant in Austin, called Earl Campbell's.

In 1999, he was ranked number 33 on *The Sporting News*' list of the 100 Greatest Football Players, the highest-ranked player from the Houston Oilers franchise.

Earl Campbell's Career Statistics

			RUSHING				RECEIVING			
YEAR	TEAM	G	NO	YDS	AVG	TD	NO	YDS	AVG	TD
1978	Houston	15	302	1,450	4.8	13	12	48	4.0	0
1979	Houston	16	368	1,697	4.6	19	16	94	5.9	0
1980	Houston	15	373	1,934	5.2	13	11	47	4.3	0
1981	Houston	16	361	1,376	3.8	10	36	156	4.3	0
1982	Houston	9	157	538	3.4	2	18	130	7.2	0
1983	Houston	14	322	1,301	4.0	12	19	216	11.4	0
1984	Houston/New Orleans	14	146	468	3.2	4	3	27	9.0	0
1985	New Orleans	16	158	643	4.1	1	6	88	14.7	0
	TOTALS	115	2,187	9,407	4.3	74	121	806	6.66	0

Sources: College Football Hall of Fame; Earl Campbell Web Site (www.earlcampbell.com); Pro Football Hall of Fame; Pro-Football-Reference.com

Canadeo, Anthony Robert "Tony" (born: May 5, 1919 in Chicago, Illinois; died: November 29, 2003 in Green Bay, Wisconsin); inducted into the Pro Football Hall of Fame in 1974 as a player; Position: Halfback; Uniform: #3; third back to run for more than 1,000 yards in a season.

The relatively small Canadeo (5'11", 190 pounds) entered the National Football League as a ninth-round (77th selection overall) draft pick out of Gonzaga University (Seattle, Washington), and played his entire 11-season (116 games) NFL career with the Green Bay Packers (1941–1944, 1946–1952). He was the third back to run for 1,000 or more yards in a season (1949), and was named All-NFL twice (1943, 1949). A versatile player, he played offense and defense; ran with the ball; threw and caught passes; returned punts and kickoffs, punted; and intercepted nine passes. He accumulated 8,667 all-purpose yards, averaging almost 75 yards in each of his 116 NFL games.

After World War II briefly interrupted his career, Canadeo returned to the Packers in 1946, but was no longer an all-purpose player, instead working almost exclusively as a running back.

As of this writing, he is one of only five Green Bay Packers to have his number retired (joining Reggie White, Bart Starr, Ray Nitschke, and Don Hutson). He was the first Packer to rush for 1,000 yards in a season and was selected to the NFL 1940s All-Decade Team.

Tony Canadeo's Career Statistics

			RUSHING				RECEIVING			
YEAR	TEAM	G	NO	YDS	AVG	TD	NO	YDS	AVG	TD
1941	Green Bay	9	43	137	3.2	3	0	0	0.0	0
1942	Green Bay	11	89	272	3.1	3	10	66	6.6	0
1943	Green Bay	10	94	489	5.2	3	3	31	10.3	2
1944	Green Bay	3	31	149	4.8	0	1	12	12.0	0
1946	Green Bay	11	122	476	3.9	0	2	25	12.5	0
1947	Green Bay	12	103	464	4.5	2	0	0	0.0	0
1948	Green Bay	12	123	589	4.8	4	9	81	9.0	0
1949	Green Bay	12	208	1,052	5.1	4	3	–2	–0.7	0
1950	Green Bay	12	93	247	2.7	4	10	54	5.4	0
1951	Green Bay	12	54	131	2.4	1	22	226	10.3	2
1952	Green Bay	12	65	191	2.9	2	9	86	9.6	1
	TOTALS	116	1,025	4,197	4.1	26	69	579	8.4	5

			PUNT RETURNS				KICKOFF RETURNS			
YEAR	TEAM	G	NO	YDS	AVG	TD	NO	YDS	AVG	TD
1941	Green Bay	9	4	26	6.5	0	4	110	27.5	0
1942	Green Bay	11	7	76	10.9	0	6	137	22.8	0
1943	Green Bay	10	8	93	11.6	0	10	242	24.2	0
1944	Green Bay	3	1	4	4.0	0	1	12	12.0	0
1946	Green Bay	11	6	76	12.7	0	6	163	27.2	0
1947	Green Bay	12	10	111	11.1	0	15	312	20.8	0
1948	Green Bay	12	4	55	13.8	0	9	166	18.4	0
1949	Green Bay	12	0	0	0.0	0	2	20	10.0	0
1950	Green Bay	12	5	68	13.6	0	16	411	25.7	0
1951	Green Bay	12	0	0	0.0	0	4	101	25.3	0
1952	Green Bay	12	1	4	4.0	0	2	62	31.0	0
	TOTALS	116	46	513	11.2	0	75	1,736	23.1	0

Sources: Pro Football Hall of Fame; Pro-Football-Reference.com

Cann, Howard G. (born: October 11, 1895 in Bridgeport, Connecticut; died: December 18, 1992 in Dobbs Ferry, New York); inducted into the Naismith Memorial Basketball Hall of Fame in 1968 as a coach; competed in the 1920 Summer Olympics; coached New York University in the first-ever college basketball game played at Madison Square Garden.

Cann attended the High School of Commerce (New York, New York) from 1909 to 1913 and was a three-sport star (basketball, football, track) each of his four years. After high school, he attended Dartmouth College (Hanover, New Hampshire) from 1913 to 1914, before moving on to New York University (New York) from 1914 to 1920.

While at NYU, Cann played basketball, football, and track and earned four letters in each sport. He was the Helm's Athletic Foundation Player of the Year (1920); led the team to the Amateur Athletic Union national basketball championship (1920); and was a member of the 1920 U.S. Olympic shot-put team (finishing eight in Antwerp, Belgium).

After college, the 6'4", 217-pound Cann briefly played professional basketball with the Mohawk Indians (1921–1922) of the New York League, before returning to NYU as the school's basketball coach (1923–1958), where he compiled a 409–232 (.638) record, including an undefeated season in 1933–1934.

His 1934–1935 team played the first basketball game in Madison Square Garden against Notre Dame on December 29, 1934; he coached NYU to the NCAA Finals in 1945 and to the NIT Finals in 1948; named National Coach of the Year by the Metropolitan Basketball Association in 1947; and won the National Association of Basketball Coaches Merit Award in 1967.

While playing at NYU, Cann was the leading scorer on the NYU men's basketball team as a freshman in 1914, and served as captain of the 1916–1917 football team. He left college to serve in the Navy during World War I. After the war, Cann returned to NYU in 1919; led the school basketball team to an AAU National Championship title; and was named the Helms Athletic Foundation Player of the Year. As a member of the track and field team, he won the shot put competitions at both the Penn Relays and the IC4A Middle Atlantic States event.

Three years after graduating from NYU, Cann returned to the school as the men's basketball coach, a job he held for 35 years (1923–1958), and led the 1944–1945 team to the final game of the NCAA tournament, eventually losing to Oklahoma State University. After being named National Coach of the Year in 1947, he led the team to the NIT final the next year, losing to Saint Louis University.

Source: Naismith Memorial Basketball Hall of Fame

Caraffi, Ralph (born: January 19, 1901 in Dunlevy, Pennsylvania; died: January 1978 in Cleveland, Ohio); inducted into the National Soccer Hall of Fame and Museum in 1959 as a player; Position: Midfielder; played in the inaugural season of the first American Soccer League.

Caraffi played soccer in Pennsylvania, Massachusetts, and Ohio during a career that began in 1915. At age 15, he played for the Vestaburg club of Pennsylvania for two years (1915–1917), before moving on to the Fall River (Massachusetts) Rovers from 1919 to 1921.

In 1921, when the Fall River (Massachusetts) United club was formed to play in the newly created American Soccer League, Caraffi played the initial season with the team. He then left the squad; moved to the Cleveland, Ohio area; and played for the American Hungarians from 1926 to 1929. He then played for the Cleveland Bruell Insurance team from 1929 to 1934, and was on the 1930 team that played in the National Open Cup Final, losing to the Fall River Marksmen.

Caraffi played for the U.S. Army team in Europe; became a coach from 1935 to 1938 with the youth teams run by Bartunek Clothes; and was a referee from 1954–1957.

He was inducted into the Greater Cleveland Sports Hall of Fame in June 1992.

Source: National Soccer Hall of Fame and Museum

Carenza, Joseph S., Sr. (born: St. Louis, Missouri; died: October 6, 1981 in St. Louis, Missouri); inducted into the National Soccer Hall of Fame and Museum in 1982 as a player; Position: Center Half; founder and first coach of Washington University's men's soccer team.

Carenza was a soccer player and administrator for many years in the St. Louis, Missouri area. After serving in the Navy during World War II, he played for St. Margaret's Senior Catholic Youth Council, and in the late 1940s, he advanced to the St. Louis Major League and played for numerous teams, including the Steamfitters and Patterson Ford.

He was a member of the St. Louis Zenthoefers team that upset Germany's Eintract Frankfurt 2–1 in St. Louis in 1951; played for the St. Louis All-Stars against Liverpool (England) in 1953; and joined St. Louis Kutis in 1954 as a player-coach, winning National Amateur Cup championships in 1956 and 1957, and the National Open Cup title in 1957, before joining St. Louis Simpkins-Ford in 1958.

Carenza was selected to numerous St. Louis All-Star teams, and coached the first-ever Washington University (St. Louis, Missouri) men's soccer team, from 1959 to 1964, compiling an overall record of 31–17–6 (.630). He served as director of the Khoury League soccer program before becoming executive secretary of the Catholic Youth Council in 1967.

He has been inducted into the Soccer Old Timers Hall of Fame, St. Louis Soccer Hall of Fame, and the Washington University Sports Hall of Fame.

Sources: National Soccer Hall of Fame and Museum; Washington University Sports Hall of Fame

Carew, Rodney Cline "Rod" (born: October 1, 1945 in Gatun, Panama); inducted into the National Baseball Hall of Fame and Museum in 1991 as a player; Position: Second Base; Bats: Left; Throws: Right; Uniform: #29; American

League Rookie of the Year in 1967; fourth player in baseball history (and the first in the American League) to win a batting title without hitting a home run; first Minnesota Twins player to ever hit for the cycle; a member of the 3,000-hit club.

Making his major league debut on April 11, 1967, Carew had a 19-year career (1967–1985) with the Minnesota Twins (1967–1978) and the California Angels (1979–1985). He played in the American League Championship Series four times (1969–1970, 1979, 1982); was selected to 18 consecutive All-Star teams (1967–1984); was the American League Rookie of the Year in 1967; and was the AL Most Valuable Player in 1977.

A great bunter and pinpoint hitter, Carew's seven batting titles (1969, 1972–1975, 1977–1978) are surpassed only by Ty Cobb, Tony Gwynn, and Honus Wagner, and equaled only by Rogers Hornsby and Stan Musial. He hit over .300 for 15 consecutive seasons (1969–1983), and in 1969, he stole home seven times, a single-season total surpassed only by Ty Cobb.

Born on a train in the Panama Canal Zone, Carew and his mother moved to New York when he was 17. After signing with the Minnesota Twins after graduating from high school in 1964, he played three minor league seasons (1964 with the Melbourne Twins in the Cocoa Rookie League, 1965 with the Orlando Twins of the Florida State League, 1966 with the Wilson Tobs of the Carolina League) before entering the major leagues in 1967. Carew got his first major league hit on Opening Day off Dave McNally of the Baltimore Orioles and became the 16th player to join the 3,000-hit club on August 4, 1985 with a hit off Frank Viola of the Minnesota Twins.

In 1972, he became the fourth player in MLB history (and the first in the American League) to win a batting title without hitting a home run. In his 1977 MVP season, Carew's .388 batting average was 50 points higher than the next-best average (Dave Parker's .338 in the National League), the largest margin in MLB history.

On May 18, 1969, the 6', 182-pound Carew stole three bases in one inning in a Twins' 8–2 loss to the Detroit Tigers, tying a major league record. On May 20, 1970, in a 10–5 win over the Kansas City Royals, Carew hit for the cycle, the first Minnesota Twins player ever to do so.

In 1975, Carew became a first baseman, and in 1979, he was traded to the Angels and helped the team win its first-ever division title.

After retiring as a player, Carew served as a batting coach for the Angels and the Milwaukee Brewers. In 1999, he was ranked number 61 on *The Sporting News*' list of the 100 Greatest Baseball Players, and was a finalist for the Major League Baseball All-Century Team.

On January 19, 2004, Panama City, Panama's National Stadium was renamed Rod Carew Stadium, and in 2005, Carew was named the second baseman on the Major League Baseball Latino Legends Team. His number 29 has been retired by both the Minnesota Twins and the Los Angeles Angels of Anaheim (previously known as the California Angels).

Rod Carew's Career Statistics

YEAR	TEAM	G	AB	R	H	2B	3B	HR	RBI	BB	SO	SB	AVG	SLG
1967	Minnesota	137	514	66	150	22	7	8	51	37	91	5	.292	.409
1968	Minnesota	127	461	46	126	27	2	1	42	26	71	12	.273	.347
1969	Minnesota	123	458	79	152	30	4	8	56	37	72	19	.332	.467
1970	Minnesota	51	191	27	70	12	3	4	28	11	28	4	.366	.524
1971	Minnesota	147	577	88	177	16	10	2	48	45	81	6	.307	.380
1972	Minnesota	142	535	61	170	21	6	0	51	43	60	12	.318	.379
1973	Minnesota	149	580	98	203	30	11	6	62	62	55	41	.350	.471
1974	Minnesota	153	599	86	218	30	5	3	55	74	49	38	.364	.446
1975	Minnesota	143	535	89	192	24	4	14	80	64	40	35	.359	.497
1976	Minnesota	156	605	97	200	29	12	9	90	67	52	49	.331	.463
1977	Minnesota	155	616	128	239	38	16	14	100	69	55	23	.388	.570
1978	Minnesota	152	564	85	188	26	10	5	70	78	62	27	.333	.441
1979	California	110	409	78	130	15	3	3	44	73	46	18	.318	.391
1980	California	144	540	74	179	34	7	3	59	59	38	23	.331	.437
1981	California	93	364	57	111	17	1	2	21	45	45	16	.305	.374
1982	California	138	523	88	167	25	5	3	44	67	49	10	.319	.403
1983	California	129	472	66	160	24	2	2	44	57	48	6	.339	.411
1984	California	93	329	42	97	8	1	3	31	40	39	4	.295	.353
1985	California	127	443	69	124	17	3	2	39	64	47	5	.280	.345

YEAR	TEAM	G	AB	R	H	2B	3B	HR	RBI	BB	SO	SB	AVG	SLG
	TOTALS	2,469	9,315	1,424	3,053	445	112	92	1,015	1,018	1,028	353	.328	.429

Sources: Baseball-Reference.com; National Baseball Hall of Fame and Museum; Rod Carew Web Site (www.rodcarew.com)

Carey, Max George (born: January 11, 1890 in Terre Haute, Indiana; died: May 30, 1976 in Miami, Florida); inducted into the National Baseball Hall of Fame and Museum in 1961 as a player by the Veterans Committee; Position: Center Field; Bats: Both; Throws: Right; Uniform: #22; only outfielder to accumulate more than 400 putouts a season six times; held the National League record with 738 stolen bases (until surpassed by Lou Brock); stole home 133 times; his career total of 339 outfield assists is the modern-day National League record.

Making his major league debut on October 3, 1910, Carey enjoyed a 20-year playing career (1910–1929) with the Pittsburgh Pirates (1910–1926) and the Brooklyn Robins/Dodgers (1926–1929). He played on the 1925 World Series-winning team that defeated the Washington Senators in seven games.

After retiring as a player, he managed the Dodgers from 1932 to 1933, compiling a 146–161 (.476) record, before being replaced by Casey Stengel.

Although he hit over .300 six times in his career, the 5'11", 170-pound Carey was more well known as an outstanding defensive outfielder and base stealer, leading the National League and/or the Major Leagues in steals in 10 seasons (1913–1914, 1916–1918, 1920, 1922–1925). In 1922, he stole 51 bases in 53 attempts, and in 1925, he hit .343 in the regular season and .458 in the World Series. He finished his career stealing home 33 times, a National League record until surpassed by Lou Brock in 1974. Carey led the National League in runs scored in 1913 (99); in triples twice (1914, 1917); and led the Major Leagues in triples in 1923 (19). In 1922, he stole 31 consecutive bases without being thrown out, a record that stood until broken by Davey Lopes in 1975.

The best-fielding center fielder of his time, for nine of his 17 seasons with Pittsburgh Carey led the league in putouts and total chances, and his career totals are exceeded only by Willie Mays and Tris Speaker for putouts, and by Speaker, Mays, and Ty Cobb for total chances. He led the league in outfield assists four times, and his lifetime total of 339 is the modern-day National League record.

On July 25, 1913, Carey scored five runs in a 12–2 win against the Philadelphia Phillies without getting a hit, reaching first on an error and four walks. During the game, he stole four bases and advanced twice on wild pitches. On July 25, 1921 against the New York Giants, he caught 11 fly ball outs, tying with three other National League players for most putouts in a game. On June 22, 1925 in a 24–6 win over the St. Louis Cardinals, he had two hits in an inning twice (first, eighth).

Carey was a baseball and track star at Concordia Theological Seminary (Fort Wayne, Indiana), but turned full-time to baseball when he could no longer pay for his education. He was born Maximillian Carnarius, but adopted the name "Max Carey" when he played his first professional baseball game in 1909 in order to retain his amateur status at Concordia. The name stuck when he finally played professionally full-time.

After retiring as a player, he scouted for the Pittsburgh Pirates in 1930 and managed the Dodgers to third- and sixth-place finishes in 1932 and 1933. He later managed both the Milwaukee Chicks and the Fort Wayne Daisies of the All-American Girls Professional Baseball League, and scouted and managed in the minor leagues until 1956.

He was inducted into the Indiana Baseball Hall of Fame in 1979.

Max Carey's National League Career Statistics

YEAR	TEAM	G	AB	R	H	2B	3B	HR	RBI	BB	SO	SB	AVG	SLG
1910	Pittsburgh	2	6	2	3	0	1	0	2	2	1	0	.500	.833
1911	Pittsburgh	129	427	77	110	15	10	5	43	44	75	27	.258	.375
1912	Pittsburgh	150	587	114	177	23	8	5	66	61	79	45	.302	.394
1913	Pittsburgh	154	620	99	172	23	10	5	49	55	67	61	.277	.371
1914	Pittsburgh	156	593	76	144	25	17	1	31	59	56	38	.243	.347
1915	Pittsburgh	140	564	76	143	26	5	3	27	57	58	36	.254	.333
1916	Pittsburgh	154	599	90	158	23	11	7	42	59	58	63	.264	.374
1917	Pittsburgh	155	588	82	174	21	12	1	51	58	38	46	.296	.378
1918	Pittsburgh	126	468	70	128	14	6	3	48	62	25	58	.274	.348
1919	Pittsburgh	66	244	41	75	10	2	0	9	25	24	18	.307	.365

YEAR	TEAM	G	AB	R	H	2B	3B	HR	RBI	BB	SO	SB	AVG	SLG
1920	Pittsburgh	130	485	74	140	18	4	1	35	59	31	52	.289	.348
1921	Pittsburgh	140	521	85	161	34	4	7	56	70	30	37	.309	.430
1922	Pittsburgh	155	629	140	207	28	12	10	70	80	26	51	.329	.459
1923	Pittsburgh	153	610	120	188	32	19	6	63	73	28	51	.308	.452
1924	Pittsburgh	149	599	113	178	30	9	8	55	58	17	49	.297	.417
1925	Pittsburgh	133	542	109	186	39	13	5	44	66	19	46	.343	.491
1926	Pittsburgh	86	324	46	72	14	5	0	28	30	14	10	.222	.296
1926	Brooklyn	27	100	18	26	3	1	0	7	8	5	0	.260	.310
1927	Brooklyn	144	538	70	143	30	10	1	54	64	18	32	.266	.364
1928	Brooklyn	108	296	41	73	11	0	2	19	47	24	18	.247	.304
1929	Brooklyn	19	23	2	7	0	0	0	1	3	2	0	.304	.304
	TOTALS	2,476	9,363	1,545	2,665	419	159	70	800	1,040	695	738	.285	.386

Max Carey's Managerial Record

YEAR	TEAM	LG	G	W	L	WIN%	FINISH
1932	Brooklyn	NL	154	81	73	.526	3
1933	Brooklyn	NL	153	65	88	.425	6
	TOTALS		307	146	161	.476	

Sources: Baseball-Reference.com; Indiana Baseball Hall of Fame; National Baseball Hall of Fame and Museum

Carlson, Henry Clifford "Doc" (born: July 4, 1894 in Murray City, Ohio; died: November 1, 1964 in Ligonier, Pennsylvania); inducted into the Naismith Memorial Basketball Hall of Fame in 1959 as a coach; first college coach to take an eastern team to the west coast; created the Figure 8 offense.

Carlson went to high school at the Bellefonte (Pennsylvania) Academy from 1910 to 1914, and earned two varsity letters each in football, baseball, and basketball. He attended the University of Pittsburgh (Pennsylvania) from 1914 to 1918, and earned three letters in basketball, two in baseball, and four in football. He was an All-American football player and captain for legendary coach Pop Warner's undefeated 1917 team.

After graduating, he stayed at the school and earned his medical degree, and in 1921, he played professional football for the National Football League's Cleveland Bulldogs (later to become the Cleveland Indians, then the Browns). While a practicing physician for the Carnegie Steel Company, Carlson started his basketball coaching career at his alma mater in 1922, a position he held until 1958, compiling a 369–247 (.599) record. He led the Panthers to a perfect 21–0 record and the national championship in 1928, and won another "unofficial" national championship in 1930 (both selections were made by the Helms Athletic Foundation).

In 1931, Carlson was the first coach to take an eastern team westward, winning at the University of Kansas, the University of Colorado, Stanford University, and the University of Southern California. He created the Figure 8 (the first patterned offense), which was later copied and used by numerous college coaches. He became the school's director of student health services in 1932 and served in that capacity until retiring.

Source: Naismith Memorial Basketball Hall of Fame

Carlton, Steven Norman "Lefty" (born: December 22, 1944 in Miami, Florida); inducted into the National Baseball Hall of Fame and Museum in 1994 as a player; Position: Pitcher; Bats: Left; Throws: Left; Uniform: #32; first pitcher to win four Cy Young awards; threw a modern-day National League record six career one-hitters; won 45% of his team's total victories in 1972; picked off 144 runners, the most in Major League Baseball history.

Making his major league debut on April 12, 1965 the 6'4", 210-pound Carlton enjoyed a 23-year pitching career (1965–1988) with the St. Louis Cardinals (1965–1971), Philadelphia Phillies (1972–1986), Chicago White Sox (1986), San Francisco Giants (1986), Cleveland Indians (1987), and the Minnesota Twins (1987–1988), and pitched in four World Series (winning in 1967 and 1980, while losing in 1968 and 1983). Although he played for the Minnesota Twins during the 1987 regular season, he was not on the playoff roster and did not play in the team's World Series title win.

Carlton was named to 10 All-Star Teams (1968–1969, 1971–1972, 1974, 1977, 1979–1982); won a Gold Glove in 1981; and was the first pitcher to win four Cy Young Awards (1972, 1977, 1980, 1982). He won 329 games in his career (second only to Warren Spahn among left-handed pitchers), and his 4,136 strikeouts are third all-time only to Nolan Ryan and Randy Johnson. He led the National League in ERA in 1972 (1.97); led the league in wins four times (1972, 1977, 1980, 1982); and led the league in strikeouts five times (1972, 1974, 1980, 1982–1983).

Nicknamed "Lefty," Carlton recorded 19 strikeouts in a game once (September 15, 1969, ironically losing to the New York Mets 4–3) and won 20 or more games in a season six times. In a remarkable 1972 season, he won 27 games (while losing only 10) for the last-place Phillies, who as a team won only a total of 59 games. He accounted for an unheard of 45.76% of his team's wins. In that season, he led the league in wins, earned run average (1.97), strikeouts (310, only the second left-hander ever to reach 300), and complete games, winning his first Cy Young Award.

On April 29, 1981, Carlton became the first left-handed pitcher in major league history (and the sixth overall) to record 3,000 career strikeouts. In 1983, he signed a four-year, $4.15 million contract with the Phillies that made him the highest-paid pitcher in baseball history up to that time.

Although he never threw a no-hitter, Carlton's six career one-hitters are a modern-day National League record. After the Phillies released him in 1986, Carlton briefly pitched for four more teams before finally retiring in 1988. In his career, Carlton picked off 144 base runners, the most in MLB history since pickoff records began being collected in 1957. Jerry Koosman is second all-time with 82.

The Phillies retired Carlton's number 32; in 1999, he ranked number 30 on *The Sporting News*' list of the 100 Greatest Baseball Players; and he was a nominee for the Major League Baseball All-Century Team.

Steve Carlton's Career Statistics

YEAR	TEAM	LG	W	L	PCT	G	SH	IP	H	R	ER	SO	BB	ERA
1965	Saint Louis	NL	0	0	.000	15	0	25	27	7	7	21	8	2.52
1966	Saint Louis	NL	3	3	.500	9	1	52	56	22	18	25	18	3.12
1967	Saint Louis	NL	14	9	.609	30	2	193	173	71	64	168	62	2.98
1968	Saint Louis	NL	13	11	.542	34	5	232	214	87	77	162	61	2.99
1969	Saint Louis	NL	17	11	.607	31	2	236	185	66	57	210	93	2.17
1970	Saint Louis	NL	10	19	.345	34	2	254	239	123	105	193	109	3.72
1971	Saint Louis	NL	20	9	.690	37	4	273	275	120	108	172	98	3.56
1972	Philadelphia	NL	27	10	.730	41	8	346	257	84	76	310	87	1.98
1973	Philadelphia	NL	13	20	.394	40	3	293	293	146	127	223	113	3.90
1974	Philadelphia	NL	16	13	.552	39	1	291	249	118	104	240	136	3.22
1975	Philadelphia	NL	15	14	.517	37	3	255	217	116	101	192	104	3.56
1976	Philadelphia	NL	20	7	.741	35	2	253	224	94	88	195	72	3.13
1977	Philadelphia	NL	23	10	.697	36	2	283	229	99	83	198	89	2.64
1978	Philadelphia	NL	16	13	.552	34	3	247	228	91	78	161	63	2.84
1979	Philadelphia	NL	18	11	.621	35	4	251	202	112	101	213	89	3.62
1980	Philadelphia	NL	24	9	.727	38	3	304	243	87	79	286	90	2.34
1981	Philadelphia	NL	13	4	.765	24	1	190	152	59	51	179	62	2.42
1982	Philadelphia	NL	23	11	.676	38	6	295.2	253	114	102	286	86	3.10
1983	Philadelphia	NL	15	16	.484	37	3	283.2	277	117	98	275	84	3.11
1984	Philadelphia	NL	13	7	.650	33	0	229	214	104	91	163	79	3.58
1985	Philadelphia	NL	1	8	.111	16	0	92	84	43	34	48	53	3.33
1986	Philadelphia	NL	4	8	.333	16	0	83	102	70	57	62	45	6.18
1986	San Francisco	NL	1	3	.250	6	0	30	36	20	17	18	16	5.10
1986	Chicago	AL	4	3	.571	10	0	63.1	58	30	26	40	25	3.69
1987	Cleveland	AL	5	9	.357	23	0	109	111	76	65	71	63	5.37
1987	Minnesota	AL	1	5	.167	9	0	43	54	35	32	20	23	6.70
1988	Minnesota	AL	0	1	.000	4	0	9.2	20	19	18	5	5	16.76
	TOTALS		329	244	.574	741	55	5,216	4,672	2,130	1,864	4,136	1,833	3.22

Sources: Baseball-Reference.com; National Baseball Hall of Fame and Museum; Steve Carlton Web Site (www.stevecarlton.com)

Carnesecca, Louis P. "Lou" (born: January 5, 1925 in New York, New York); inducted into the Naismith Memorial Basketball Hall of Fame in 1992 as a coach; led all of his teams into postseason competition; 30th college coach in history to win 500 games.

Carnesecca attended high school at St. Ann's Academy (New York, New York) from 1939 to 1943, where he played basketball for two years. After graduation, he joined the Coast Guard during World War II and served from 1943 to 1946. After the war, he returned to New York City and attended St. John's University from 1946 to 1950.

He coached two stints at his alma mater (1957–1970, 1973–1992), compiling an overall 526–200 (.725) record. He led each of his Redmen teams into postseason competition, including 18 NCAA tournaments (advancing to the Final Four in 1985) and six NIT appearances (winning the NIT championship in 1989). He compiled a 40–34 postseason record; his teams had eighteen 20-win seasons; and averaged 22 wins a year.

His teams won 17 Lapchick Memorial Tournament Championships and a record eight Eastern College Athletic Conference Holiday Festival titles. On February 2, 1991, Carnesecca became the 30th coach in history to win 500 games; was voted National Coach of the Year by the United States Basketball Writers Association and the National Association of Basketball Coaches twice (1983, 1985); named Big East Conference Coach of the Year three times (1983, 1985–1986); Kodak NIT Man of the Year in 1985; Metropolitan Coach of the Year five times (1970, 1978, 1983, 1985–1986); and has been inducted into the New York City Sports Hall of Fame.

Carnesecca took a three-season break from college basketball to coach the New York Nets of the American Basketball Association from 1970 to 1973. He led the Nets to the 1972 Finals (losing to the Indiana Pacers in six games) and compiled a 114–138 (.452) record.

Carnesecca Arena (formerly Alumni Hall) is a 6,008-seat multi-purpose arena in Queens County, New York that was built in 1961 and renamed in his honor in November 2004. It is home to the St. John's University Red Storm women's basketball team, and occasionally hosts the men's team.

Source: Naismith Memorial Basketball Hall of Fame

Carnevale, Bernard L. "Ben" (born: October 30, 1915 in Raritan, New Jersey); inducted into the Naismith Memorial Basketball Hall of Fame in 1970 as a coach; coached at the U.S. Naval Academy for 20 seasons.

While at Somerville (New Jersey) High School from 1930 to 1934, Carnevale played basketball; was selected All-County in 1934; and was an Honorable Mention All-State in 1934. After graduation, he attended New York University (New York) from 1934 to 1938, where he played basketball under legendary hall-of-fame coach Howard Cann, and was selected team captain and All-District in 1938.

After college, Carnevale played professional basketball with the Jersey Reds (North Bergen, New Jersey) of the American Basketball League from 1938 to 1940, and won the 1939 league championship when the team became known as the New York Jewels.

He began his coaching career in 1939 at Cranford (New Jersey) High School; compiled a record of 75–20 (.789); lost in the state semifinals (1942); won the New Jersey Sectional Tournament, before losing in the state finals (1943); and left after the end of the 1942–1943 season.

After serving briefly in the Navy during World War II, Carnevale left the military and served as the head basketball coach at the University of North Carolina (Chapel Hill) from 1944 to 1946, before coaching at the U.S. Naval Academy (Annapolis, Maryland) for 20 seasons (1947–1967). While compiling a 51–11 (.823) record at Chapel Hill, he led the Tar Heels to the 1945 and 1946 Southern Conference championship and to the 1946 NCAA tournament finals, eventually losing to Oklahoma A&M.

While coaching at the Naval Academy, Carnevale compiled a 257–160 (.616) record; was named College Coach of the Year in 1947; and led five of his teams to the NCAA tournament and two other teams to NIT appearances. He also served as president of the National Association of Basketball Coaches from 1965 to 1966.

After leaving the Academy in 1967, Carnevale became the athletic director at NYU and would go on to serve in the same position at the College of William and Mary (Williamsburg, Virginia) from 1973 until retiring in 1981.

Source: Naismith Memorial Basketball Hall of Fame

Carr, Joseph F. "Joe" (born: October 23, 1879 in Columbus, Ohio; died: May 20, 1939); inducted into the Pro Football Hall of Fame in 1963 as an administrator; served as NFL president from 1921 to 1939.

Carr was a sportswriter and promoter who founded the Columbus (Ohio) Panhandles in 1904 (American Professional Football Association), which later became one of the charter teams of the National Football League. He helped form the NFL and served as the league's president (commissioner) from 1921 to 1939, succeeding the legendary Jim Thorpe. As president of the league, he was a strict enforcer of the rules; introduced the idea of standard player contracts; banned the use of college players (it was a common practice at the time for college players to enter the NFL under assumed names); and attracted financially stable investors as team owners.

He was one of the first league executives to recognize that if the NFL wanted to thrive, it had to expand into large cities with substantial fan bases. Focusing on New York, he worked with investors and city officials to form the New York Giants in 1925. His idea proved to be on-track when more than 70,000 fans attended a 1925 game between the Giants and the Chicago Bears, led by the legendary Red Grange.

Using his administrative talents beyond professional football, Carr also served as president of both the American Basketball League (1925–1928) and the minor league Columbus Senators baseball team (American Association, 1926–1931), all while running the NFL. He was inducted into the Helms Foundation Hall of Fame in 1950 and is the only non-player inducted into both the Helms and Pro Football halls of fame.

The NFL's original Most Valuable Player Award was named for Carr in 1938.

Source: Pro Football Hall of Fame

Carril, Peter J. "Pete" (born: July 10, 1930 in Bethlehem, Pennsylvania); inducted into the Naismith Memorial Basketball Hall of Fame in 1997 as a coach; coached at Princeton University for 29 seasons and had only one losing year; only Division I coach to record more than 500 wins without ever providing athletic scholarships.

Carril attended Liberty High School (Bethlehem, Pennsylvania) from 1944 to 1948; played on the school's basketball team; and was selected All-State in 1948. After high school, he went to Lafayette College (Easton, Pennsylvania) from 1948 to 1952; was a four-year letter winner; and earned All-State and Little All-America honors in 1952.

His coaching career started in 1959 at Reading (Pennsylvania) High School, where he stayed until 1966, compiling a 145–42 (.775) record. He then moved to Lehigh University (Bethlehem, Pennsylvania) from 1966 to 1967, before coaching 29 seasons at Princeton University (New Jersey) from 1967 to 1997. His overall college coaching record was 525–273 (.658) (11–12 at Lehigh, 514–261 at Princeton), including only one losing season at Princeton.

Carril led Princeton to 13 Ivy League championships and 13 postseason tournaments (11 NCAA, two NIT); posted 10 seasons with 20 or more wins; led the nation in defensive points allowed in 14 seasons; and ended his career as the only Division I coach to record 500 or more wins without ever providing athletic scholarships. He led Princeton to the NIT title over Providence College in 1975, the Ivy League's only NIT title.

Leaving the college ranks, Carril joined the National Basketball Association in 1997 as an assistant coach with the Sacramento Kings, a job he held until retiring in 2006.

Source: Naismith Memorial Basketball Hall of Fame

Carson, Harry Donald (born: November 26, 1953 in Florence, South Carolina); inducted into the Pro Football Hall of Fame in 2006 as a player; Position: Linebacker; played on the winning team in Super Bowl XXI; has been inducted into more than 10 sports-related halls of fame.

Carson was a 1976 fourth-round draft pick (105th selection overall) of the New York Giants out of South Carolina State University (Orangeburg) and would play his entire 13-year National Football League career (1976–1988) with the team, 10 seasons as captain. He became a starting middle linebacker halfway through his rookie season and was named to the All-NFL Rookie Team; he led the Giants in tackles five times; and had 14 career fumble recoveries. Although he played defensive end in college, once Carson joined the Giants, he was moved to the middle linebacker position.

The 6'2", 237-pound Carson was named to the Pro Bowl nine times (1979–1980, 1982–1988); named First- or Second-Team All-Pro six times (1978, 1981–1982, 1984–1986); named First- or Second-Team All-NFC six times (1978–1979, 1981–1982, 1985–1986); and was on the winning team in Super Bowl XXI in 1987 with a 39–20 win over the Denver Broncos. He was rated the #1 "Inside Linebacker" in NFL history by *Pro Football Weekly*.

Carson attended Wilson Senior and McClenaghan high schools in Florence, South Carolina, before going to South Carolina State University (Orangeburg), where he earned a Bachelor of Science Degree in Education. He was a two-time captain on the school's football team; never missed a game during his four seasons as a defensive lineman for the Bulldogs; and had 114 tackles and 17 quarterback sacks in his senior year. Carson was named to the Kodak All-American Football Team; NAIA All-American Team; All-State (South Carolina); All Mid-Eastern Athletic Conference; and Mid-Eastern Athletic Conference Defensive Player of the Year twice.

After retiring from professional football, he became a sports broadcaster; co-hosted CNN's "NFL Preview"; appeared on WCBS as a broadcast analyst; and worked for ABC Sports as well as for the Madison Square Garden Network.

He is currently CEO and President of Harry Carson Inc., a sports consulting and promotion company that consults with media outlets, educational sources, and corporations on sports as well as non-sports related issues. He also serves as executive director of the Fritz Pollard Alliance, an organization dedicated to creating racial diversity within non-player roles in the National Football League.

Carson has been inducted into numerous sports shrines, including the Wilson High School Alumni Hall of Fame; South Carolina State University Athletic Hall of Fame; Mid-Eastern Athletic Conference Hall of Fame; Florence, South Carolina Athletic Hall of Fame; South Carolina Athletic Hall of Fame; the Sports Hall of Fame of New Jersey; New Jersey Sportswriter's Hall of Fame; Black College Alumni Hall of Fame; College Football Hall of Fame (Division II); and the College Football Hall of Fame. He has also been named to the Sheridan Broadcasting Network 100 Year Anniversary Black College All-American Team and is a member of the All Division II College Football Team of the Quarter Century (1975–1999).

Sources: College Football Hall of Fame; Harry Carson Web Site (www.harrycarson.com); Pro Football Hall of Fame; Pro-Football-Reference.com

Carter, Gary Edmund (born: April 8, 1954 in Culver City, California); inducted into the National Baseball Hall of Fame and Museum in 2003 as a player; Position: Catcher; Bats: Right; Throws: Right; Uniform: #8; in its 1961 inaugural year, Carter was the seven-year-old national champion of the "Punt, Pass and Kick" contest; only member of the baseball hall of fame to sport a Montreal Expos cap on his plaque.

Making his debut on September 16, 1974, Carter would go on to play 19 major league seasons (1974–1992) with the Montreal Expos (1974–1984, 1992), New York Mets (1985–1989), San Francisco Giants (1990), and Los Angeles Dodgers (1991). He was named to 11 All-Star Teams (1976, 1979–1988); was the All-Star Game MVP twice (1981, 1984); won three Gold Glove Awards (1980–1982); won five Silver Slugger awards (1981–1982, 1984–1986); and was on the Mets team that won the 1986 World Series, defeating the Boston Red Sox in seven games.

The 6'2", 215-pound Carter, known as "The Kid," was drafted by the Montreal Expos in the third round of the 1972 amateur draft (53rd overall selection) and quickly gained a reputation as a durable catcher and clutch hitter.

At Sunny Hills High School (Fullerton, California), he was an All-American quarterback; captain of his baseball, football, and basketball teams; and a member of the National Honor Society. Although an outfielder in high school, the Expos converted him to a catcher, and in 1975, Carter was named *The Sporting News* Rookie of the Year.

He became a full-time catcher in 1977, and on April 20th of that year, hit home runs in three consecutive at-bats in an 8–6 loss to the Pittsburgh Pirates (a feat he would repeat on September 3, 1985 in an 8–3 win over the San Diego Padres). Between 1977 and 1982, Carter led the National League in most chances six times, in putouts five times, assists four times, and double plays three times.

In the 1986 World Series, he hit two home runs in game four and a timely single in the 10th inning of game six, which helped the Mets rally to win the game after the Red Sox had been one out away from winning the World Series. The Mets' rally forced a seventh game, which the team eventually won 8–5, giving them the series title.

In 2001, Carter was inducted into the New York Mets Hall of Fame, and in 2003, he was inducted into the Canadian Baseball Hall of Fame. After his playing career ended, he managed the Gulf Coast Mets (Gulf Coast League) minor league team in 2005, before being promoted to the A-level St. Lucie Mets (Florida State League) for the 2006 season.

Carter is the only member of the baseball hall of fame to sport an Expos cap on his plaque.

In its 1961 inaugural year, Carter was the seven-year-old national champion of the "Punt, Pass and Kick" contest.

Gary Carter's Career Statistics

YEAR	TEAM	G	AB	R	H	2B	3B	HR	RBI	BB	SO	SB	AVG	SLG
1974	Montreal	9	27	5	11	0	1	1	6	1	2	2	.407	.593
1975	Montreal	144	503	58	136	20	1	17	68	72	83	5	.270	.416
1976	Montreal	91	311	31	68	8	1	6	38	30	43	0	.219	.309
1977	Montreal	154	522	86	148	29	2	31	84	58	103	5	.284	.525
1978	Montreal	157	533	76	136	27	1	20	72	62	70	10	.255	.422
1979	Montreal	141	505	74	143	26	5	22	75	40	62	3	.283	.485
1980	Montreal	154	549	76	145	25	5	29	101	58	78	3	.264	.486
1981	Montreal	100	374	48	94	20	2	16	68	35	35	1	.251	.444
1982	Montreal	154	557	91	163	32	1	29	97	78	64	2	.293	.510
1983	Montreal	145	541	63	146	37	3	17	79	51	57	1	.270	.444

YEAR	TEAM	G	AB	R	H	2B	3B	HR	RBI	BB	SO	SB	AVG	SLG
1984	Montreal	159	596	75	175	32	1	27	106	64	57	2	.294	.487
1985	New York	149	555	83	156	17	1	32	100	69	46	1	.281	.488
1986	New York	132	490	81	125	14	2	24	105	62	63	1	.255	.439
1987	New York	139	523	55	123	18	2	20	83	42	73	0	.235	.392
1988	New York	130	455	39	110	16	2	11	46	34	52	0	.242	.358
1989	New York	50	153	14	28	8	0	2	15	12	15	0	.183	.275
1990	San Francisco	92	244	24	62	10	0	9	27	25	31	1	.254	.406
1991	Los Angeles	101	248	22	61	14	0	6	26	22	26	2	.246	.375
1992	Montreal	95	285	24	62	18	1	5	29	33	37	0	.218	.340
	TOTALS	2,296	7,971	1,025	2,092	371	31	324	1,225	848	997	39	.262	.439

Sources: Baseball-Reference.com; National Baseball Hall of Fame and Museum

Cartwright, Alexander Joy (born: April 17, 1820 in New York, New York; died: July 12, 1892 in Honolulu, Hawaii); inducted into the National Baseball Hall of Fame and Museum as a pioneer-executive in 1938 by the Veterans Committee; often called the "Father of Modern Baseball."

In contrast to the Abner Doubleday legend, many baseball historians often refer to Cartwright as the true "Father of Modern Baseball." He was a founding and influential member of the Knickerbocker Base Ball Club of New York City, considered baseball's first organized team.

He played a key role in formalizing and publishing some of the game's early field layout and rules, including identifying foul territory; specifying the distance between bases; defining that an inning consists of three outs; eliminating the practice of retiring runners by throwing batted baseballs at them; and mandating the addition of an umpire.

Cartwright was a member of the New York Knickerbockers Fire Fighting Brigade in 1842, and from 1843 to 1845, he worked as a bank teller. While working at the Knickerbockers fire station, Cartwright became involved in playing town ball (an early version of baseball, often called rounders) on a vacant lot in Manhattan, and in 1845, the team began playing its games at Elysian Fields in Hoboken, New Jersey. He organized the team on September 23, 1845; called it the Knickerbockers in honor of the fire station where he worked; began charging admission to fans; and established 20 basic rules, most of which are still in use today. Up to the time of his involvement, the game had been played basically by local rules in the surrounding area and baseball's structure was often haphazard.

Other rules of his included having four bases laid out in a square pattern; bases being 90 feet apart; balls hit outside of first or third base were foul; each team plays the same number of innings; the batter (then called the striker) must swing and miss three times to strike out; and a batter must be tagged or forced at a base to be out. Some of the major differences between Cartwright's rules and those of today's game include foul balls were not considered strikes; there were no called strikes; the game continued until one team scored 21 runs (then called aces) as long as both teams played an equal number of innings; the ball was thrown underhanded; and a batter was out if the ball was caught in the air or on the first bounce.

When the Knickerbockers moved to New Jersey, for a variety of reasons many players refused to follow the team and stayed in New York, creating their own club called the New York Nine. The first documented game, using Cartwright's 20 rules, between these teams was played on June 19, 1846 at Elysian Fields, with the New York Nine winning 23–1. Although there is no documented historical proof, the lopsided score is usually attributed to the fact that most of the best players stayed in New York and played for the New York Nine.

As the rules of the game became more formalized and standard, its popularity spread throughout the country as players migrated to the south and the west. Cartwright's rules became part of the National Association of Baseball Players Rules in 1860, which have slowly evolved into today's game.

At the height of the California gold rush, Cartwright headed west in 1849 to seek his fortune, and introduced the game of baseball to various cities and towns as he traveled. After arriving in California, he became ill, abandoned his dreams of riches, and moved to Honolulu, Hawaii, where he introduced the game to a whole new fan base.

He became a successful businessman in Honolulu; founded the library and fire department (serving as its chief for 10 years); and had a street named in his honor, as well as a ballpark. He also created the first baseball league in Hawaii using teams scattered throughout the islands.

Sources: National Baseball Hall of Fame and Museum; *The Man Who Invented Baseball* (Harold Peterson)

Case, Everett N. (born: June 21, 1900 in Anderson, Indiana; died: April 30, 1966); inducted into the Naismith Memorial Basketball Hall of Fame in 1982 as a coach; won four state basketball championships at Frankfort High School; coached at North Carolina State University for 18 seasons, compiling a .739 won-loss record; credited with starting the tradition of cutting down the hoop nets after winning a tournament.

After attending Anderson (Indiana) High School from 1913 to 1917, Case went to the University of Wisconsin (Madison) from 1919 to 1923. While still in college, he began his coaching career at Columbus (Indiana) High School from 1920 to 1921, where he compiled a 20–10 record. He then moved on to Smithfield (Indiana) High School (1921–1922) and compiled a 32–6 record, before establishing himself with two stints at Frankfort (Indiana) High School (1922–1931, 1935–1942), compiling an overall 385–99–1 record. As a high school basketball coach, Case compiled a 467–124–1 (.789) record and won four state championships (1925, 1929, 1936, 1939) at Frankfort. Frankfort's Case Arena is named in his honor.

In 1946, Case left the high school ranks to become head coach at North Carolina State University (Raleigh) from 1946 to 1965, eventually compiling a 379–134 (.739) record. He led the Wolfpack to six straight Southern Conference titles (1947–1952); four Atlantic Coast Conference titles (1954–1956, 1959); seven Dixie Classic titles (1949–1952, 1954–1955, 1958); was named Atlantic Coast Conference Coach of the Year three times (1954–1955, 1958); finished third in the NIT (1947) and NCAA Tournament (1950); and won 20 or more games 10 times and 30 games once (1951).

His teams were known for ball handling and quick, offensive-minded schemes. Case is credited with starting the tradition of cutting down the hoop nets after winning a tournament. He also was the first coach to use player introductions and the "noise-meter."

In 1941, he enlisted in the U.S. Navy during World War II and served as the assistant athletic director and director of basketball operations at St. Mary's College (Moraga, California). He also served as the athletic director at the Alameda (California) Naval Air Station. In 1943, while still in the military, Lieutenant Commander Case served as athletic director of the navy flight preparatory school at DePauw University (Greencastle, Indiana).

After leaving the military, he began an 18-year career at North Carolina State University; is often credited with turning North Carolina into a "basketball state"; was inducted into the North Carolina Sports Hall of Fame in 1964; and into the Raleigh Hall of Fame in 2005.

A blemish on his career came in 1956 when the NCAA put the school on four years probation over the charge that Case had paid Louisiana high school star Jackie Moreland cash and gifts to lure him to the school and away from Kentucky. Although Case always insisted he was innocent, the probation was upheld. As the program was coming off the penalty, in 1960 the school was again hit with probation for a point-shaving scandal that caused the cancellation of the Dixie Classic.

North Carolina State University's main athletic office is named in his honor.

Sources: Naismith Memorial Basketball Hall of Fame; Raleigh Hall of Fame

Casper, David John "Dave" (born: February 2, 1952 in Bemidji, Minnesota); inducted into the Pro Football Hall of Fame in 2002 as a player; Position: Tight End; Uniform: #87; member of the Super Bowl XI winning team; scored a game-winning touchdown on a play known as "The Holy Roller" in NFL lore.

A second-round draft pick (45th selection overall) of the Oakland Raiders in 1974 out of the University of Notre Dame (South Bend, Indiana), Casper played 11 NFL seasons (147 games, 1974–1984) with the Oakland/Los Angeles Raiders (1974–1980, 1984), Houston Oilers (1980–1983), and the Minnesota Vikings (1983). The 6'4", 220-pound Casper was named All-Pro and All-AFC four consecutive years (1976–1979) and selected to five Pro Bowls (1976–1980).

While at Notre Dame, he was an Honorable Mention All-American as an offensive tackle in 1972 and an All-American tight end in 1973.

Casper became a starter in 1976 and caught the first touchdown pass in Super Bowl XI (1977) in a 32–14 win over the Minnesota Vikings.

Early in the 1977 season, Casper was involved in a play that will forever be remembered as "The Holy Roller" in NFL lore. With the Raiders down six points to the San Diego Chargers and 10 seconds remaining in the game, Oakland quarterback Ken Stabler fumbled the ball, which rolled to the Chargers' 11 yard line, before running back Pete Banaszak knocked it toward the goal line. At the five-yard-line, Casper kicked the ball before falling on it in the end zone for the game-winning touchdown in a 21–20 win. As a result of this play, the NFL instituted a rule making it illegal for a team to advance the ball on its own fumble on fourth down or in the last two minutes of a game.

In the middle of the 1980 season, Casper was traded to the Houston Oilers, where he was reunited with Stabler, who had been traded to the team at the start of the season, and was eventually named to his fifth Pro Bowl. In 1984, after playing briefly with the Minnesota Vikings, he retired.

An all-round athlete, Casper played football, golf, baseball, and basketball at St. Edward High School (Elgin, Illinois) and Chilton (Wisconsin) High School. As a senior, his Chilton football team went undefeated and did not allow any team to score during the entire season. Four years later, in 1973, he captained Notre Dame's unbeaten national championship team that defeated Alabama 24–23 in the Sugar Bowl.

Dave Casper's Career Statistics

			RECEIVING			
YEAR	TEAM	G	NO	YDS	AVG	TD
1974	Oakland	14	4	26	6.5	3
1975	Oakland	14	5	71	14.2	1
1976	Oakland	13	53	691	13.0	10
1977	Oakland	14	48	584	12.2	6
1978	Oakland	16	62	852	13.7	9
1979	Oakland	15	57	771	13.5	3
1980	Oakland/Houston	16	56	796	14.2	4
1981	Houston	16	33	572	17.3	8
1982	Houston	9	36	573	15.9	6
1983	Houston/Minnesota	13	20	251	12.6	0
1984	Los Angeles	7	4	29	7.3	2
	TOTALS	147	378	5,216	13.8	52

Sources: Pro Football Hall of Fame; Pro-Football-Reference.com

Cattarinich, Joseph (born: November 13, 1881 in Levis, Quebec, Canada; died: December 7, 1938); inducted into the Hockey Hall of Fame in 1977 as a builder; helped the Montreal Canadiens win three Stanley Cup titles.

As a young man, Cattarinich played hockey prior to the creation of the National Hockey League and was the first-ever goaltender of the professional Le Canadien club, which eventually evolved into the NHL's Montreal Canadiens.

In November 1921, he and business partners Leo Dandurand and Louis Letourneau purchased the Montreal Canadiens from the widow of former owner George Kennedy, and led the team to three Stanley Cup championships (1924, 1930–1931). When Letourneau retired in 1931, the other two partners led the team through the Great Depression, before they ran out of money and were forced to sell the franchise in 1935 to J. Ernest Savard, Maurice Forget, and Louis Gélinas.

In addition to his business interests and his hockey team, Cattarinich was an avid horse breeder. He operated the Arlington Park racetrack in Arlington Heights, Illinois before moving on to oversee the Jefferson Downs facility in New Orleans, Louisiana.

Source: Hockey Hall of Fame

Cepeda, Orlando Manuel (born: Orlando Manuel Cepeda Pennes on September 17, 1937 in Ponce, Puerto Rico); inducted into the National Baseball Hall of Fame and Museum in 1999 as a player by the Veterans Committee; Position: First Base; Bats: Right; Throws: Right; Uniform: #30; first-ever designated hitter for the Boston Red Sox; second Puerto Rican elected to the baseball hall of fame; only player in baseball history to win Rookie of the Year and Most Valuable Player awards unanimously; first player in National League history to hit more than 40 home runs and have less than 40 walks in a single season.

Cepeda made his major league debut on April 15, 1958 with the San Francisco Giants (the team's first regular-season game in San Francisco) and would go on to play 17 major league seasons (1958–1974) with the Giants (1958–1966), St. Louis Cardinals (1966–1968), Atlanta Braves (1969–1972), Oakland A's (1972), Boston Red Sox (1973), and the Kansas City Royals (1974). He played in three World Series (winning in 1967 and losing in 1962 and 1968); was the 1958 National League Rookie of the Year; the 1967 National League Most Valuable Player; and was a seven-time National League All-Star (1959–1964, 1967).

Nicknamed "Baby Bull," the 6'2", 210-pound Cepeda was the first-ever designated hitter for the Boston Red Sox.

After retiring from the game, Cepeda was caught picking up a marijuana shipment at the San Juan, Puerto Rico airport. His arrest, conviction, and time served in prison were negative factors that kept him out of the baseball hall of fame during his initial 15-year eligibility period. It would take 25 years after his last game before he would be inducted into the hall of fame via the Veterans Committee. He was the second Puerto Rican native to be selected, after Roberto Clemente. The Giants retired his jersey number 30 in 1999.

In his first major league game, Cepeda hit a home run in an 8–0 Giants win over the Los Angeles Dodgers. During his career, he hit over .300 ten times and had 25 or more home runs in eight seasons. In 1961, he moved to first base; led the National League in home runs and RBIs; and became the first player in National League history with more than 40 home runs and less than 40 walks.

On October 12, 1963, he participated in the first and only Hispanic-American Major League All-Star Game, in which the National League beat the American League 5–2 at the Polo Grounds; on January 18, 1973, he was signed by the Boston Red Sox, making him the first player signed by a team specifically as a designated hitter; and on August 8, 1973, he tied the major league record with four doubles in a 9–4 win over the Kansas City Royals.

Cepeda led the league in doubles (38) in 1958; in sacrifice flies twice (nine in both 1958 and 1966); in home runs (46) and at bats per home run (12.7) in 1961; and in RBIs twice (142 in 1961 and 111 in 1967). He was the second National League player (following Carl Hubbell) to win the MVP unanimously; is the only player in baseball history to win Rookie of the Year and Most Valuable Player awards unanimously; and was the first Latin player to win the home run and RBI titles.

He was the first Puerto Rican to be selected to an All-Star team (1959) and is the only Puerto Rican to be selected for the All-Star Game in two different positions (first base, left field). In his first seven seasons, Cepeda had more home runs than Eddie Mathews, Frank Robinson, Ernie Banks, Ted Williams, Mark McGwire, and Hank Aaron had in their first seven seasons.

Cepeda is one of eleven players who hit .300 or better with 30 or more home runs in four consecutive seasons, joining Babe Ruth, Hack Wilson, Lou Gehrig, Chuck Klein, Jimmie Foxx, Joe DiMaggio, Hank Greenberg, Mickey Mantle, Ted Kluszewski, and Albert Pujols. He was the first player to win the Designated Hitter of the Year Award (1973).

In 1956, while playing with the St. Cloud Rox, a Class "C" minor league club in the Northern League, he won the triple crown; in 2006, the Society for American Baseball Research approved a chapter for Puerto Rico, the first in Latin America, and named it after Cepeda; in 2001, he won the Ernie Banks Positive Image Lifetime Achievement Award; and he was inducted into the Bay Area Sports Hall of Fame in 1990.

Orlando Cepeda's Career Statistics

YEAR	TEAM	LG	G	AB	R	H	2B	3B	HR	RBI	BB	SO	SB	AVG	SLG
1958	San Francisco	NL	148	603	88	188	38	4	25	96	29	84	15	.312	.512
1959	San Francisco	NL	151	605	92	192	35	4	27	105	33	100	23	.317	.522
1960	San Francisco	NL	151	569	81	169	36	3	24	96	34	91	15	.297	.497
1961	San Francisco	NL	152	585	105	182	28	4	46	142	39	91	12	.311	.609
1962	San Francisco	NL	162	625	105	191	26	1	35	114	37	97	10	.306	.518
1963	San Francisco	NL	156	579	100	183	33	4	34	97	37	70	8	.316	.563
1964	San Francisco	NL	142	529	75	161	27	2	31	97	43	83	9	.304	.539
1965	San Francisco	NL	33	34	1	6	1	0	1	5	3	9	0	.176	.294
1966	San Francisco	NL	19	49	5	14	2	0	3	15	4	11	0	.286	.510
1966	Saint Louis	NL	123	452	65	137	24	0	17	58	34	68	9	.303	.469
1967	Saint Louis	NL	151	563	91	183	37	0	25	111	62	75	11	.325	.524
1968	Saint Louis	NL	157	600	71	149	26	2	16	73	43	96	8	.248	.378
1969	Atlanta	NL	154	573	74	147	28	2	22	88	55	76	12	.257	.428
1970	Atlanta	NL	148	567	87	173	33	0	34	111	47	75	6	.305	.543
1971	Atlanta	NL	71	250	31	69	10	1	14	44	22	29	3	.276	.492
1972	Atlanta	NL	28	84	6	25	3	0	4	9	7	17	0	.298	.476
1972	Oakland	AL	3	3	0	0	0	0	0	0	0	0	0	.000	.000
1973	Boston	AL	142	550	51	159	25	0	20	86	50	81	0	.289	.444
1974	Kansas City	AL	33	107	3	23	5	0	1	18	9	16	1	.215	.290
	TOTALS		2,124	7,927	1,131	2,351	417	27	379	1,365	588	1,169	142	.297	.499

Sources: *Baby Bull: From Hardball to Hard Time and Back* (Orlando Cepeda with Herb Fagen); Baseball-Reference.com; National Baseball Hall of Fame and Museum

Cervi, Alfred Nicholas (born: February 12, 1917 in Buffalo, New York); inducted into the Naismith Memorial Basketball Hall of Fame in 1985 as a player; Position: Forward-Guard; Uniform: #15; joined the professional ranks without ever playing a single basketball game in college; won an NBL championship as a player and won an NBA title as a coach.

Cervi attended East High School (Buffalo, New York) and was selected All-City as a sophomore, the only year he played on the team. He left school in his junior year to work in the family business and, without ever playing a game of college basketball, he began his professional career with the National Basketball League's Buffalo (New York) Bisons from 1937 to 1938 before moving on to the Syracuse (New York) Reds of the Independent League from 1939 to 1940.

He joined the Army Air Force during World War II and served five years in the military, before returning to the NBL and playing for the Rochester (New York) Royals (1945–1948, the team would eventually become the Sacramento Kings of the NBA); Syracuse (New York) Nationals (1948–1949); and then stayed with the Nationals when the team joined the National Basketball Association (1949–1953).

Cervi led the Royals to the 1946 NBL Championship in a three-game sweep over the Sheboygan (Wisconsin) Redskins; was selected to the All-NBL Second Team in 1946; led the NBL in scoring in 1947; selected to the All-NBL First Team three consecutive years (1947–1949); was NBL Coach of the Year in 1949; and was named to the All-NBA Second Team in 1950.

The 5'11", 185-pound Cervi began his professional coaching career as a player-coach for the NBL/NBA Syracuse Nationals (1948–1956), before becoming head coach of the NBA's Philadelphia Warriors (1957–1958). He compiled an overall coaching record of 366–264 (.581, 210–120 as a player-coach), 330–216 at Syracuse and 36–48 at Philadelphia. He retired from playing in 1953 and coached the Dolph Schayes-led Syracuse Nationals to the 1955 NBA title.

Alfred Cervi's NBA Career Statistics

SEASON	TEAM	G	MIN	FG	FT	TRB	ASST	PTS
1949–1950	Syracuse	56		143	287		264	573
1950–1951	Syracuse	53		132	194	152	208	458
1951–1952	Syracuse	55	850	99	219	87	148	417
1952–1953	Syracuse	38	301	31	81	22	28	143
	TOTALS	202	1,151	405	781	261	648	1,591

Alfred Cervi's NBA Coaching Record

		REGULAR SEASON			PLAYOFFS		
SEASON	TEAM	W	L	WIN%	W	L	WIN%
1949–1950	Syracuse	51	13	.797	6	5	.545
1950–1951	Syracuse	32	34	.485	4	3	.571
1951–1952	Syracuse	40	26	.606	3	4	.429
1952–1953	Syracuse	47	24	.662	0	2	.000
1953–1954	Syracuse	42	30	.583	9	4	.692
1954–1955	Syracuse	43	29	.597	7	4	.636
1955–1956	Syracuse	35	37	.486	5	4	.556
1956–1957	Syracuse	4	8	.333			
1957–1958	Philadelphia	32	40	.444			
	TOTALS	326	241	.575	34	26	.567

Sources: Basketball-Reference.com; Naismith Memorial Basketball Hall of Fame

Chacurian, Efrain "Chico" (born: February 22, 1924 in Cordoba, Argentina); inducted into the National Soccer Hall of Fame and Museum in 1992 as a player; Position: Forward; International Caps (1953–1954): 4; International Goals: 1; first Hispanic inducted into the soccer hall of fame.

Chacurian's first professional contract was in 1939 with the Racing Club of Buenos Aires (Argentine First Division). In 1947, he moved to the United States; played with the Armenian Club of the New York Eastern District League; helped the team win the championship; and was voted the league's Most Valuable Player.

In 1949 he signed with Brooklyn (New York) Hispano of the American Soccer League and played for the league's All-Star team against the Scottish and Inter-Milan teams. In the same year, he played for the New York Stars against Belfast Celtic and Inter-Milan again.

Chacurian later moved to Connecticut and played for Bridgeport City, a club he would later coach. He played for the U.S. National Team four times, making his debut against England in New York in 1953, and then played against Mexico (twice) and Haiti in the World Cup qualifying round in 1954.

After retiring as a player, in 1965 he coached for 10 years at Southern Connecticut State College (New Haven) before moving to Yale University (New Haven, Connecticut) as the school's freshman coach and leading the team to an undefeated season. From 1976 to 1979, Chacurian also coached the women's team. He moved on to become regional head coach for U.S. Soccer's Olympic Development Program. As a coach, he won five semi-professional championships from 1974 to 1980 with the Bridgeport (Connecticut) Vasco da Gama team.

Source: National Soccer Hall of Fame and Museum

Chadwick, Bill (born: October 10, 1915 in New York, New York); inducted into the Hockey Hall of Fame in 1964 as an on-ice official; invented hand signals to explain to fans what foul or infraction had been committed.

Chadwick was one of the game's first hockey officials born in the United States. While trying out for the U.S. National Team in 1935, he suffered an on-ice eye injury that basically ended his playing career. Eastern League president Tommy Lockhart asked him to substitute for a referee who had taken ill, and in only two years (age 24), he was officiating in the National Hockey League, where he stayed until 1955.

Chadwick invented hand signals so that the fans would know what infraction had occurred, which led to them being able to better follow the flow of the game. He refereed in every playoff series from 1939 to 1955, and retired having officiated more than 1,000 games.

After retiring, he began doing radio work for the New York Rangers in 1965, and was inducted into the United States Hockey Hall of Fame in 1974.

Source: Hockey Hall of Fame

Chadwick, Henry (born: October 5, 1824 in Exeter, England; died: April 20, 1908 in Brooklyn, New York); inducted into the National Baseball Hall of Fame and Museum in 1938 as a pioneer-executive by the Veterans Committee; credited with writing the first comprehensive baseball rule book; developed the box score; only writer inducted into the baseball hall of fame proper, as opposed to the Writers Wing.

Although he never played baseball or was an executive at the professional level, Chadwick was an early influential force in the game and is sometimes referred to as the "Father of Base Ball." He was a sportswriter, statistician, and historian; developed the modern box score; introduced statistics (such as batting average and earned run average); wrote numerous instruction manuals; edited multiple baseball guides; wrote the first comprehensive baseball rule book; and reported on baseball games for local newspapers. He also served on the game's early rules committee, and in 1868, he wrote the first hardcover book on the game, *The Game of Base Ball*.

His statistical formulas made it possible for players to be rated and to be ranked from top to bottom. This made it easier for fans to understand a particular player's contributions to the game.

In 1867, Chadwick accompanied the National Base Ball Club of Washington, D.C. on the team's inaugural national tour as official scorer, and in 1874, he was instrumental in organizing a similar tour of England, which included games of both baseball and cricket.

In spite of a longtime friendship with early baseball pioneer Albert Spalding, Chadwick ardently opposed Spalding's attempts to have Abner Doubleday declared the inventor of the game of baseball. He wrote numerous articles debunking the myth and presenting to the public research into the early game and its origins, focusing on baseball basically being derived from the English game of crickets or rounders, a game he had played as a boy in England.

In addition to baseball, Chadwick wrote articles and books about numerous other sports and games, including yachting, billiards, and chess. As an inductee, he is the only writer elected to the hall of fame proper, as opposed to the Writers Wing.

Sources: Henry Chadwick Web Site (www.henrychadwick.com); National Baseball Hall of Fame and Museum

Chamberlain, Wilton Norman "Wilt" (born: August 21, 1936 in Philadelphia, Pennsylvania; died: October 12, 1999 in Los Angeles, California); inducted into the Naismith Memorial Basketball Hall of Fame in 1979 as a player; Position: Center; Uniform: #13; first player in NBA history named MVP and Rookie of the Year in the same season; only NBA player to score 100 points in a single game.

One of nine children, Chamberlain was a basketball legend at all three levels of play: high school, college, and professional. At Overbrook (Pennsylvania) High School (1951–1955), he was selected All-American in 1955; scored 90 points, including 60 points in 12 minutes, against Roxborough High School (Philadelphia, Pennsylvania); led the school to back-to-back city championships (1954–1955); scored 800 points in his first 16 games during the 1955 season; and scored a total of 2,252 points in his high school career. He was also a star on the track and field team as a high-jumper, long-jumper, 440- and 880-yard runner, and shot-putter.

After high school, Chamberlain went to the University of Kansas (Lawrence) from 1955 to 1958 but, due to NCAA rules, was not allowed to play varsity basketball as a freshman. Once he began to play varsity ball, he quickly made his presence known. He was a unanimous First-Team All-American twice (1957–1958); named *The Sporting News* First-Team All-American (1958); in 48 varsity games, he scored 1,433 points (29.9 points-per-game) and grabbed 877 rebounds (18.3 per game); scored 52 points against Northwestern in 1957 and grabbed 36 rebounds against Iowa in 1958; was the NCAA Tournament MVP in 1957; led the Jayhawks to the 1957 NCAA championship game (which ended in a 54–53 triple overtime loss to North Carolina); and led the school to Big Seven championships twice (1957–1958).

As in high school, Chamberlain also participated in track and field, winning the high jump in the Big Eight championships three straight years.

During his senior year, it was determined that he was ineligible for the National Basketball Association draft since he had only played two seasons in college. To wait for his eligibility, Chamberlain left school and played for the Harlem Globetrotters for one year (1958–1959).

Leaving the Globetrotters, he began his 14-year National Basketball Association career after being selected third overall in the 1959 NBA draft by the Philadelphia Warriors. The 7'1", 275-pound center played with the Warriors (1959–1962) and stayed with the team when it moved to San Francisco (1963–1964). He left to play for the Philadelphia 76ers (1964–1968) and ended his career with the Los Angeles Lakers (1968–1973). He was named NBA Rookie of the Year in 1960; NBA Most Valuable Player four times (1960, 1966–1968); first player in NBA history to be named Rookie of the Year and MVP in the same season; named to the All-NBA First-Team eight times (1960–1962, 1964–1968); All-NBA Second-Team three times (1963, 1965, 1972); NBA All-Defensive First-Team twice (1972–1973); NBA Finals MVP (1972); holds the NBA Finals record for most rebounds (41, April 5, 1967 against the Boston Celtics); 1960 NBA All-Star Game MVP; a 13-time NBA All-Star (1960–1969, 1971–1973); and won NBA championships with the Philadelphia 76ers (1967) and Los Angeles Lakers (1972).

Nicknamed "Wilt the Stilt," Chamberlain scored 31,419 points (30.1 per game) in 1,045 games (all-time NBA leader when he retired, currently second behind Kareem Abdul-Jabbar); led the NBA in scoring seven straight years (1960–1966), including a career-high 50.4 points-per-game in 1962; holds single-game record for points in one game (100, March 2, 1962 against the New York Knicks in Hershey, Pennsylvania); scored 50 or more points in a game 118 times; scored 50 or more points 45 times in the 1961–1962 season, including seven consecutive games (December 16–29, 1961); scored 40 points or more in a game 271 times; holds single-game record for most points by a rookie (58, January 25, 1960 against the Detroit Pistons); led the NBA in field goal percentage eight times (1961, 1963, 1965–1969, 1972); holds the record for most free throws attempted (11,862); grabbed 23,924 rebounds (22.9 per game), best in league history in both number and per game average; holds single-season records for most minutes (3,338, 41.7 per game), most points (4,029), points per game (50.4), field goals made (1,597) and field goals attempted (3,159), all in 1962; led the NBA in minutes played seven times (1961–1964, 1966–1968); and was named to the NBA 35th Anniversary All-Time Team (1980) and to the NBA 50th Anniversary All-Time Team (1996).

The 36 field goals and 28 free throws made by Chamberlain in his 100-point game are still NBA regular-season, single-game records, as is the 59 points he scored in the second half.. He is the only player to grab more than 2,000 rebounds in a single season (2,149 rebounds in the 1960–1961 season and 2,052 in the 1961–1962 season).

In the 1971–1972 season, Chamberlain grabbed 1,572 rebounds while his teammate, forward Happy Hairston, nabbed 1,045. This marks the only time that teammates on any NBA team have grabbed more than 1,000 rebounds each in the same season.

Chamberlain's on-court battles with the legendary Bill Russell have become basketball lore. Although he often received hard fouls because of his large size, he rarely retaliated, and throughout his entire career, Chamberlain never fouled out of a game.

After he retired from the NBA, Chamberlain coached the American Basketball Association's San Diego Conquistadors for a year (1973–1974); began an acting career by starring with Arnold Schwarzenegger in the movie, *Conan the Destroyer*; and wrote four books, including *A View from Above* (1991), in which he claimed to have had sex with almost 20,000 women.

His jersey #13 has been retired by five different teams, including the Golden State Warriors, Harlem Globetrotters, Los Angeles Lakers, Philadelphia 76ers, and the University of Kansas men's basketball program.

Wilt Chamberlain's Career Statistics

SEASON	TEAM	G	MIN	FG	FT	TRB	AST	POINTS
1959–1960	Philadelphia	72	3,338	1,065	577	1,941	168	2,707
1960–1961	Philadelphia	79	3,773	1,251	531	2,149	148	3,033
1961–1962	Philadelphia	80	3,882	1,597	835	2,052	192	4,029
1962–1963	San Francisco	80	3,806	1,463	660	1,946	275	3,586
1963–1964	San Francisco	80	3,689	1,204	540	1,787	403	2,948
1964–1965	San Francisco	38	1,743	636	208	893	117	1,480
1964–1965	Philadelphia	35	1,558	427	200	780	133	1,054

SEASON	TEAM	G	MIN	FG	FT	TRB	AST	POINTS
1965–1966	Philadelphia	79	3,737	1,074	501	1,943	414	2,649
1966–1967	Philadelphia	81	3,682	785	386	1,957	630	1,956
1967–1968	Philadelphia	82	3,836	819	354	1,952	702	1,992
1968–1969	Los Angeles	81	3,669	641	382	1,712	366	1,664
1969–1970	Los Angeles	12	505	129	70	221	49	328
1970–1971	Los Angeles	82	3,630	668	360	1,493	352	1,696
1971–1972	Los Angeles	82	3,469	496	221	1,572	329	1,213
1972–1973	Los Angeles	82	3,542	426	232	1,526	365	1,084
	TOTALS	1,045	47,859	12,681	6,057	23,924	4,643	31,419

Sources: Basketball-Reference.com; Naismith Memorial Basketball Hall of Fame; *Wilt* (Wilt Chamberlain and David Shaw); *Wilt, 1962: The Night of 100 Points and the Dawn of a New Era* (Gary M. Pomerantz)

Chamberlin, Berlin Guy (born: January 16, 1894 in Blue Springs, Nebraska; died: April 4, 1967 in Lincoln, Nebraska); inducted into the Pro Football Hall of Fame in 1965 as a player; Position: End; of all NFL coaches with 50 or more wins, his .759 winning percentage (58–16–7) ranks as the best; as a coach, he won three straight NFL championships.

Chamberlin was a two-time All-American at the University of Nebraska (Lincoln) and one of the premier ends and coaches in the early days of the National Football League. After playing for the pre-NFL Canton (Ohio) Bulldogs in 1919, he joined the NFL and enjoyed an eight-year (92-games) career with the Chicago (Illinois) Staleys (1921), Canton (Ohio) Bulldogs (1922–1923), Cleveland (Ohio) Bulldogs (1924), Frankford (Philadelphia) Yellow Jackets (1925–1926), and the Chicago (Illinois) Cardinals (1927–1928). He was a player-coach for four NFL championship teams (1922–1923 Canton Bulldogs, 1924 Cleveland Bulldogs, and the 1926 Frankford Yellow Jackets). His six-year coaching record (five years as a player-coach) of 58–16–7 (.759) is the league's all-time best for coaches with at least 50 wins.

The 6'2", 196-pound Chamberlin was a durable 60-minute player and coached the Bulldogs to back-to-back undefeated seasons (1922–1923), the league's first two-time champion. When the Bulldogs were sold to owners in Cleveland, he moved with the team and led the squad to the 1924 championship.

In 1925, he joined the Yellow Jackets and in 1926 led the team to his fourth NFL title, before retiring after the 1928 season. Chamberlin was inducted into the College Football Hall of Fame in 1962 and was named to the NFL 1920s All-Decade Team.

Source: Pro Football Hall of Fame

Chance, Frank Leroy (born: September 9, 1877 in Fresno, California; died: September 15, 1924 in Los Angeles, California); inducted into the National Baseball Hall of Fame and Museum in 1946 as a player by the Veterans Committee; Position: First Base; Bats: Right; Throws: Right; first player ejected from a World Series game; holds the major league record of being hit by a pitch four times in a doubleheader.

Making his major league debut on April 29, 1898, Chance played 17 seasons for the Chicago Cubs (originally called the Chicago Orphans until the 1902 season, 1898–1912) and the New York Yankees (1913–1914). He was a player-manager with the Cubs (1905–1912); a player-manager with the Yankees (1913–1914); and a manager with the Boston Red Sox (1923). He played in four World Series (winning in 1907 and 1908, while losing in 1906 and 1910). In the 1910 Fall Classic, Chance became the first player ejected from a World Series game following an argument with future hall-of-fame umpire Tom Connolly in game three (October 10, 1910).

While many baseball fans may not be familiar with the details of Chance's career, his name is well-known as the first baseman in the Tinker-to-Evers-to-Chance double-play combination made famous in the 1910 poem "Baseball's Sad Lexicon" by Franklin Pierce Adams of the *New York Evening Mail* (Joe Tinker played shortstop for the Cubs while Johnny Evers played second base).

The 6', 190-pound Chance guided the Cubs' dynasty in the early 1900s, winning four pennants in five years (1906–1910). He led the Cubs to 116 wins in the 1906 season, a record later tied by the 2001 Seattle Mariners.

Chance led the National League with 67 stolen bases in 1903, and with 57 in 1906, and hit .300 or better four times. In seven seasons with the Cubs, he won at least 100 games, and his .664 winning percentage (768–389) ranks as the best in team history.

After bad health forced him out of the game, he recuperated and came back to baseball as the owner and manager of the Los Angeles Angels of the Pacific Coast League from 1916 to 1917. He returned to the majors in 1923 to manage the Boston Red Sox before his health problems forced him out of the game for good.

On September 1, 1902, Tinker, Evers, and Chance appeared in the lineup together for the first time, but not at the positions for which they would later become more well known (Tinker played third base, Evers played shortstop, and Chance played first base). On September 13, 1902, the trio played their first game in the more famous shortstop-second base-first base lineup, and two days later, they pulled off their first double play in a 6–3 win over the Cincinnati Reds.

On May 30, 1904, during a doubleheader against the Cincinnati Reds, Chance sets a record by being hit by a pitch four times (three times by Jack Harper in the first game and once by Win Kellum in the second game). On June 24, 1905, in an 18-inning game against the St. Louis Cardinals, Chance recorded 27 putouts and two assists.

For the only time in baseball history, on April 28, 1906, two managers stole home on the same day. Chance stole his in the ninth inning to give the Cubs a 1–0 win over the Reds, while Fred Clarke stole home in the Pittsburgh Pirates' 10–1 win over the St. Louis Cardinals.

Chance was inducted into the baseball hall of fame in 1946 along with Joe Tinker and Johnny Evers.

Frank Chance's Career Statistics

YEAR	TEAM	LG	G	AB	R	H	2B	3B	HR	BB	SO	SB	AVG	SLG
1898	Chicago	NL	42	146	32	42	2	3	1	7		5	.288	.363
1899	Chicago	NL	57	190	36	55	6	2	1	15		11	.289	.358
1900	Chicago	NL	48	151	26	46	8	4	0	15		9	.305	.411
1901	Chicago	NL	63	228	37	66	11	4	0	29		30	.289	.373
1902	Chicago	NL	67	236	40	67	8	4	1	35		28	.284	.364
1903	Chicago	NL	125	441	83	144	24	10	2	78		67	.327	.440
1904	Chicago	NL	124	451	89	140	16	10	6	36		42	.310	.430
1905	Chicago	NL	118	392	92	124	16	12	2	78		38	.316	.434
1906	Chicago	NL	136	474	103	151	24	10	3	70		57	.319	.430
1907	Chicago	NL	111	382	58	112	19	2	1	51		35	.293	.361
1908	Chicago	NL	129	452	65	123	27	4	2	37		27	.272	.363
1909	Chicago	NL	93	324	53	88	16	4	0	30		29	.272	.346
1910	Chicago	NL	88	295	54	88	12	8	0	37	15	16	.298	.393
1911	Chicago	NL	31	88	23	21	6	3	1	25	13	9	.239	.409
1912	Chicago	NL	2	5	2	1	0	0	0	3	0	1	.200	.200
1913	New York	AL	11	24	3	5	0	0	0	8	1	1	.208	.208
1914	New York	AL	1	0	0	0	0	0	0	0	0	0	.000	.000
	TOTALS		1,246	4,279	796	1,273	195	80	20	554	29	405	.297	.394

Sources: Baseball-Reference.com; National Baseball Hall of Fame and Museum

Chancellor, Van (born: September 27, 1943 in Louisville, Mississippi); inducted into the Naismith Memorial Basketball Hall of Fame in 2007 as a coach; coached the 2004 Olympic women's gold-medal winning team; first coach and general manager of the WNBA's Houston Comets; named WNBA Coach of the Year three times.

After having coached women's teams in college, in the Olympics, and in the Women's National Basketball Association, in April 2007, Chancellor was hired as the head coach of the women's basketball team at Louisiana State University (Baton Rouge). He had earlier coached at the University of Mississippi (Oxford) from 1978 to 1997; compiled a 439–154 (.740) record; and led the Lady Rebels to the NCAA Tournament 14 times, including 11 consecutive years (1982–1992). Chancellor's teams had fifteen 20-win seasons, including a school-record 31 wins in 1978–1979; he led the team to the NCAA Elite Eight four times; never had a losing season at Ole Miss; and his 1991–1992 team won the program's first-ever Southeastern Conference championship.

Similarly successful with the National Team, Chancellor coached the undefeated United States women's gold medal-winning team at the 2004 Summer Olympic Games in Athens, Greece, and has an unblemished (38–0) record in international competition.

In 1997, he became the first head coach and general manager of the Houston Comets in the inaugural WNBA season; led the team to the league's first four championships (1997–2000); and was the only franchise to make the playoffs in each of the first seven seasons of the new league. His 1998 team still holds the record for the highest winning percentage in the history of NBA and WNBA basketball (27–3, .900 winning percentage). In his 10 years with the team (1997–

2006), Chancellor led the Comets to a 211–111 (.655) regular-season record; a 20–14 (.588) playoff record; and was named WNBA Coach of the Year three straight seasons (1997–1999). He was inducted into the Women's Basketball Hall of Fame in 2001.

He was named Southeastern Conference Coach of the Year three times (1987, 1990, 1992); coach of the WNBA Western Conference All-Stars three times (1999–2001); coach of the WNBA's All-Decade Team (2006); and was a two-time USA Basketball National Coach of the Year (2002, 2004).

Chancellor played two years of basketball at East Central Junior College (Decatur, Mississippi), before transferring to Mississippi State University (Starkville), where he earned a bachelor's degree in mathematics and physical education in 1965. During his senior year at Mississippi State, he served as head coach of the boy's basketball team at Noxapater (Louisville, Mississippi) High School, and after graduation, he went on to coach boy's and girl's basketball at Horn Lake (Mississippi) High School and Harrison Central High School (Gulfport, Mississippi).

In addition to leading the women's USA team to a gold medal at the 2004 Summer Olympics, Chancellor guided the squad to a first-place finish at the 2002 Opals World Challenge (Sydney, Australia) and to a gold medal at the 2002 FIBA World Championships (China).

Van Chancellor's USA Basketball Head Coaching Record

EVENT	**W-L**	**FINISH**
2002 FIBA World Championship	9–0	Gold
2002 Opals World Challenge	4–0	1st Place
2002 WBCA All-Star Challenge	1–0	N/A
Pre-Olympic Exhibition Games	16–0	N/A
2004 Olympics	8–0	Gold
TOTALS	38–0	(1.000)

Van Chancellor's Mississippi Head Coaching Record

SEASON	**RECORD**	**WIN %**	**POSTSEASON**
1978–1979	31–9	.775	AIAW State Tournament Champions Third Place Region III
1979–1980	23–14	.622	AIAW State Tournament
1980–1981	14–12	.538	AIAW State Tournament
1981–1982	27–5	.844	NCAA First Round
1982–1983	26–6	.813	NCAA Second Round
1983–1984	24–6	.800	NCAA Second Round
1984–1985	29–3	.906	NCAA Elite Eight
1985–1986	24–8	.750	NCAA Elite Eight
1986–1987	25–5	.833	NCAA Sweet Sixteen
1987–1988	24–7	.774	NCAA Sweet Sixteen
1988–1989	23–8	.742	NCAA Elite Eight
1989–1990	22–10	.688	NCAA Sweet Sixteen
1990–1991	20–9	.690	NCAA First Round
1991–1992	29–3	.906	NCAA Elite Eight
1992–1993	19–10	.655	
1993–1994	24–9	.727	NCAA Second Round
1994–1995	21–8	.724	NCAA First Round
1995–1996	18–11	.621	NCAA First Round
1996–1997	16–11	.593	
TOTALS	439–154	.740	14 NCAA Tournaments; 3 AIAW State Tournaments

Van Chancellor's WNBA Statistics (Houston Comets)

SEASON	**W**	**L**	**WIN %**	**PLAYOFF RESULTS**
1997	18	10	.643	Won WNBA Title
1998	27	3	.900	Won WNBA Title
1999	26	6	.813	Won WNBA Title
2000	27	5	.844	Won WNBA Title

SEASON	W	L	WIN %	PLAYOFF RESULTS
2001	19	13	.594	Eliminated in First Round
2002	24	8	.750	Eliminated in First Round
2003	20	14	.588	Eliminated in First Round
2004	13	21	.382	
2005	19	15	.559	Eliminated in Conference Final
2006	18	16	.529	Eliminated in First Round
TOTALS	211	111	.655	
PLAYOFFS	20	14	.588	

Source: Naismith Memorial Basketball Hall of Fame

Chandler, Albert Benjamin "Happy" (born: July 14, 1898 in Corydon, Kentucky; died: June 15, 1991 in Versailles, Kentucky); inducted into the National Baseball Hall of Fame and Museum in 1982 as a pioneer-executive by the Veterans Committee; Major League Baseball's second commissioner.

Often referred to as "A.B.," Chandler was a Lt. Governor and Governor of Kentucky; a U.S. Senator from Kentucky; and served as Major League Baseball's second commissioner for six years (1945–1951) after the death of Kenesaw Mountain Landis in 1945. Still serving as a U.S. Senator during the first six months of his tenure as commissioner, he suspended for five years all players who had left MLB to play in the Mexican League (although he allowed them to return in 1949), and approved Brooklyn Dodgers' president Branch Rickey signing Jackie Robinson in 1945 and integrating major league baseball in 1947.

In stark contrast to the stern Landis, Chandler had a jovial personality and an obvious love of the game. He was a player's commissioner; suspended Brooklyn Dodgers manager Leo Durocher for associating with gamblers; and was the first to put six umpires on the field for the World Series.

On February 1, 1947, Chandler announced Major League Baseball's first pension plan for players, which would later be expanded to include coaches and trainers. Originally funded by both teams (80%) and players (20%), this modest start has evolved over the years into the pension plan in place today. On November 8, 1950, Chandler and player representatives agreed on the revenue split of television and radio rights from the World Series, a basis for future deals.

Chandler graduated from Transylvania University (Lexington, Kentucky) in 1921 and the University of Kentucky College of Law (Lexington) before beginning a political career as a Democrat. He began serving as a Kentucky state senator in 1929, and was Governor from 1935 to 1939, but resigned the office to be appointed U.S. Senator in 1939. He was later elected to the Senate in 1940 to fill out the term and was re-elected in 1942, during which time he was elected the commissioner of Major League Baseball. After leaving the commissioner's office in 1951, Chandler again served as governor of Kentucky from 1955 to 1959.

In 1957, Chandler was inducted into the Kentucky Sports Hall of Fame, and in 1965, he served as the acting commissioner of the Continental Professional Football League.

Source: National Baseball Hall of Fame and Museum

Chaney, John (born: January 21, 1932 in Jacksonville, Florida); inducted into the Naismith Memorial Basketball Hall of Fame in 2001 as a coach; first African-American coach to win 700 college games.

Chaney's basketball career began at Benjamin Franklin High School (Philadelphia, Pennsylvania, 1948–1951), where he was named Philadelphia Public League Player of the Year in 1951. He then attended Bethune-Cookman College (Daytona Beach, Florida) from 1951 to 1955, where he was named a National Association of Intercollegiate Athletics All-American in 1953 and Most Valuable Player of the 1953 NAIA Championships.

After graduating from college, Chaney played for the Sunbury (Pennsylvania) Mercuries of the Eastern Professional Basketball League (today's Continental Basketball Association); was a two-time league Most Valuable Player; a seven-time All-Star; and was the All-Star Game MVP twice (1959–1960).

He left Sunbury to become the player-coach of the Williamsport (Pennsylvania) Billies of the EPBL from 1963 to 1966. During this time, Chaney also served as the head basketball coach at Sayre (Pennsylvania) Junior High School. In 1966, he retired as a professional player; left Sayre Junior High School; and became the head coach at Simon Gratz High School (Philadelphia, Pennsylvania), where he served until 1972.

In 1972, he left the high school ranks to become the head coach at Cheyney State College (now called Cheyney University of Pennsylvania) from 1972 to 1982, where he compiled a 225–59 (.792) record. His teams appeared in eight national championship tournaments and won the NCAA Division II title in 1978.

For all his earlier success, Chaney made a name for himself as head coach for 24 seasons at Temple University (Philadelphia, Pennsylvania) from 1982 to 2006, where he compiled a 499–238 (.677) record; led the Owls to fifteen 20-win seasons; and guided the team to 22 post-season appearances. He compiled an overall college record of 724–297 (.709); took his teams to 30 post-season tournaments; as of this writing, he ranks fourth among winningest Division I men's coaches; and he was the first African-American coach to win 700 games.

He led the Temple Owls to eight NCAA Division II tournaments (1973–1974, 1976–1980, 1982); named Division II National Coach of the Year (1978); and received the State of Pennsylvania Distinguished Faculty Award in 1979.

Chaney compiled a 327–108 (.752) Atlantic 10 Conference regular-season record; was named Atlantic 10 Conference Coach of the Year five times (1984–1985, 1987–1988, 2000); named the United States Basketball Writers Association National Coach of the Year twice (1987–1988); in 1988, he was named National Coach of the Year by the Associated Press, United Press International, CNN/USA Today, Kodak-NABC, Chevrolet, and the Black Coaches Association; and in 1993, he was named Eastern Basketball Coach of the Year.

On December 20, 2004, he became the fifth then-active coach and 19th all-time to coach in 1,000 games.

Source: Naismith Memorial Basketball Hall of Fame

Charleston, Oscar McKinley (born: October 14, 1896 in Indianapolis, Indiana; died: October 5, 1954 in Philadelphia, Pennsylvania); inducted into the National Baseball Hall of Fame and Museum in 1976 by the Negro Leagues Committee; Position: Center Field; Bats: Left; Throws: Left; helped the ABCs win the 1916 Black World Series.

One of the best all-round athletes ever to play in the Negro Leagues, Charleston hit for both average and power; had speed on the bases; and altered the defensive play of the center field position. In 1921, he hit .434 while leading the Negro National League in doubles, triples, home runs, and stolen bases. During a 40-year career, Charleston played and/or managed for the Indianapolis (Indiana) ABCs (Negro National League, 1915–1918, 1920, 1922–1923); New York (New York) Lincoln Stars (Negro National League, 1915–1916); Bowser's ABCs (Indianapolis, Indiana) (Negro National League, 1916); Chicago (Illinois) American Giants (Negro National League, 1919); St. Louis (Missouri) Giants (Negro National League, 1921); Harrisburg (Pennsylvania) Giants (Eastern Colored League, 1924–1927); Hilldale Daisies (Darby, Pennsylvania) (Eastern Colored League, 1928–1929); Homestead (Pennsylvania) Grays (Negro National League, 1930–1931); Pittsburgh (Pennsylvania) Crawfords (Independent/Negro National League, 1932–1938); Toledo (Ohio) Crawfords (Negro American League, 1939); Indianapolis (Indiana) Crawfords (Negro American League, 1940); Philadelphia (Pennsylvania) Stars (Negro National League, 1941, 1942–1944, 1946–1950); Brooklyn (New York) Brown Dodgers (United States Baseball League, 1945); and Indianapolis (Indiana) Clowns (Negro American League, 1954). He also served as a player-manager for the Pittsburgh Crawfords (1932–1938) and the Philadelphia Stars (1941, 1942–1944, 1946–1950).

Having grown up in Indianapolis, Indiana, Charleston served as a batboy for the local ABCs Negro League team. After joining the Army at age 15 and serving in the Philippines, he left the military and began his long-time professional baseball career with the ABCs in 1915. He helped lead the team to its 1916 Black World Series win over the Chicago American Giants, hitting .360 and appearing in seven of the 10 games played.

From 1922 to 1925, he was player-manager for the Eastern Colored League's Harrisburg Giants, and later helped the Grays win a 10-game Eastern Championship Series over the New York Lincoln Giants in 1930.

In 1932, Charleston was a player-manager of the Pittsburgh Crawfords (then an independent team, later to join the National Negro Association), considered one of the best Negro League teams ever with a roster that included future hall of famers Josh Gibson, Satchel Paige, and Judy Johnson.

In 1999, he was ranked #67 on *The Sporting News*' list of the 100 Greatest Baseball Players (one of only five players from the pre-1947 Negro Leagues to make the list) and was nominated as a finalist for the Major League Baseball All-Century Team.

Source: National Baseball Hall of Fame and Museum

Cheevers, Gerald Michael "Gerry" (born: December 7, 1940 in St. Catharines, Ontario, Canada); inducted into the Hockey Hall of Fame in 1985 as a player; Position: Goalie; Uniform: #30 (Boston); known for his trademark of painting stitches on his mask to indicate where a puck had hit him.

Cheevers anchored the Boston Bruins team that won the Stanley Cup in 1970 and 1972. His 24-year playing career begin in 1956 when he signed with the National Hockey League's Toronto Maple Leafs and was sent to the St. Michael's Majors in the Ontario Junior League, where he played for five years. His NHL career lasted 13 seasons with the Toronto Maple Leafs (1961–1962) and the Boston Bruins (1965–1972, 1975–1980).

Although he played two games for the Leafs in the 1961–1962 season and seven games with the Bruins during the 1965–1966 season, the 5'11", 185-pound Cheevers normally played for numerous minor league teams until finally becoming a full-time NHL player with Boston in the 1966–1967 season. During the 1968–1969 season, he began what was to be his trademark, painting stitches on his mask to indicate where a puck had hit him.

In 1972, immediately after winning his second Stanley Cup championship with the Bruins, Cheevers joined a group of players and left the NHL to play in the newly-formed World Hockey Association with the Cleveland Crusaders. After three years, he returned to the NHL with the Bruins for most of the next four seasons before retiring as a player. He then became the Bruins' head coach, a position he held for five seasons, before joining the team's scouting staff.

Cheevers won the Harry (Hap) Holmes Memorial Award in 1965 as the American Hockey League's goalie with the best goals against average; set a record during the 1971–1972 season by going undefeated in 33 consecutive games; won the Ben Hatskin Award for best goaltender. In 1974 and in 1979, he played for the NHL All-Stars in the Challenge Cup against Team Soviet Union.

Gerry Cheevers' Career Statistics

			REGULAR SEASON						PLAYOFFS				
SEASON	**TEAM**	**LEAGUE**	**GP**	**W**	**L**	**T**	**SO**	**AVG**	**GP**	**W**	**L**	**SO**	**AVG**
1956–1957	St. Michael's Midget Majors	THL											
1956–1957	St. Michael's Majors	OHA-Jr.	1				0	4.00					
1957–1958	St. Michael's Majors	OHA-Jr.	1	1	0	0	0	3.00					
1958–1959	St. Michael's Buzzers	OHA-B											
1958–1959	St. Michael's Majors	OHA-Jr.	6				0	4.67					
1959–1960	St. Michael's Majors	OHA-Jr.	36	18	13	5	5	3.08	10			0	3.30
1960–1961	St. Michael's Majors	OHA-Jr.	30	12	20	5	2	3.18	20			1	2.60
1960–1961	St. Michael's Majors	M-Cup	9	7	2	0	1	2.33					
1961–1962	Pittsburgh Hornets	AHL	5	2	2	1	0	4.20					
1961–1962	Sault Ste. Marie Greyhounds	EPHL	29	13	13	3	1	3.55					
1961–1962	Toronto Maple Leafs	NHL	2	1	1	0	0	3.00					
1961–1962	Rochester Americans	AHL	19	9	9	1	1	3.63	2	2	0	0	4.00
1962–1963	Rochester Americans	AHL	19	7	9	3	1	3.95					
1962–1963	Sudbury Wolves	EPHL	51	17	24	10	4	4.15	8	4	4	1	3.59
1963–1964	Rochester Americans	AHL	66	38	25	2	3	2.84	2	0	2	0	4.00
1964–1965	Rochester Americans	AHL	72	48	21	3	5	2.68	10	8	2	0	2.34
1965–1966	Boston Bruins	NHL	7	0	4	1	0	6.00					
1965–1966	Oklahoma City Blazers	CPHL	30	16	9	5	3	2.49	9	8	1	0	2.11
1966–1967	Boston Bruins	NHL	22	5	10	6	1	3.33					
1966–1967	Oklahoma City Blazers	CPHL	26	14	6	5	1	2.80	11	8	3	1	2.57
1967–1968	Boston Bruins	NHL	47	23	17	5	3	2.83	4	0	4	0	3.75
1968–1969	Boston Bruins	NHL	52	28	12	12	3	2.80	9	6	3	3	1.68
1969–1970	Boston Bruins	NHL	41	24	8	8	4	2.72	13	12	1	0	2.23
1970–1971	Boston Bruins	NHL	40	27	8	5	3	2.73	6	3	3	0	3.50
1971–1972	Boston Bruins	NHL	41	27	5	8	2	2.50	8	6	2	2	2.61
1972–1973	Cleveland Crusaders	WHA	52	32	20	0	5	2.84	9	5	4	0	2.41
1973–1974	Cleveland Crusaders	WHA	59	30	20	6	4	3.03	5	1	4	0	3.56
1974–1975	Canada	Summit-74	7	1	3	3	0	3.43					
1974–1975	Cleveland Crusaders	WHA	52	26	24	2	4	3.26	5	1	4	0	4.60
1975–1976	Cleveland Crusaders	WHA	28	11	14	1	1	3.63					
1975–1976	Boston Bruins	NHL	15	8	2	5	1	2.73	6	2	4	1	2.14
1976–1977	Canada	Can-Cup											
1976–1977	Boston Bruins	NHL	45	30	10	5	3	3.04	14	8	5	1	3.08
1977–1978	Boston Bruins	NHL	21	10	5	2	1	2.65	12	8	4	1	2.87
1978–1979	Boston Bruins	NHL	43	23	9	10	1	3.16	6	4	2	0	2.50
1978–1979	NHL All-Stars	Ch-Cup	1	0	1	0	0	6.00					
1979–1980	Boston Bruins	NHL	42	24	11	7	4	2.81	10	4	6	0	3.10
1980–1984	Boston Bruins	NHLMGNT											
	NHL TOTALS		418	230	102	74	26	2.89	88	53	34	8	2.69

Sources: Hockey Hall of Fame; Hockey-Reference.com

Chesbro, John Dwight "Jack" (born: June 5, 1874 in North Adams, Massachusetts; died: November 6, 1931 in Conway, Massachusetts); inducted into the National Baseball Hall of Fame and Museum in 1946 as a player by the Veterans Committee; Position: Pitcher; Bats: Right; Throws: Right; holds the modern-day major league record for most wins in a season with 41; only pitcher to lead both leagues in winning percentage (.824 in 1902, .774 in 1904).

Making his major league debut on July 12, 1899, the 5'9", 180-pound Chesbro played 11 seasons for the Pittsburgh Pirates (1899–1902), New York Highlanders/New York Yankees (1903–1909), and Boston Red Sox (1909). His 1904 season rates as one of the best pitching performances ever. He completed 48 of the 51 games he started; won 41 (still a modern-day major league record); finished the season with a 41–12 record; and threw 455 innings. From 1901 to 1906, he won 154 games; led the league in winning percentage three times; led the league in wins, appearances, and games started twice; and led the league in complete games, innings, and shutouts once each.

On April 22, 1903, Chesbro pitched the very first game in the history of the New York Yankees, then known as the Highlanders (a 3–1 loss to the Washington Senators), and was a member of two pennant-winning teams (in 1901 and 1902 with the Pirates). On July 4, 1904, he won his 14th game in a row, an American League record until Walter Johnson won 16 straight in 1912. Chesbro is the only pitcher to lead both leagues in winning percentage (.824 in 1902 [28–6] and .774 in 1904 [41–12]).

Jack Chesbro's Career Statistics

YEAR	TEAM	LG	W	L	PCT	G	SH	IP	H	R	SO	BB
1899	Pittsburgh	NL	6	9	.400	19	0	149	165	99	28	59
1900	Pittsburgh	NL	15	13	.536	32	3	216	220	123	56	79
1901	Pittsburgh	NL	21	10	.677	36	6	288	261	104	129	52
1902	Pittsburgh	NL	28	6	.824	35	8	286	242	81	136	62
1903	New York	AL	21	15	.583	40	1	325	300	140	147	74
1904	New York	AL	41	12	.774	55	6	455	338	128	239	88
1905	New York	AL	19	15	.559	41	3	303	262	125	156	71
1906	New York	AL	23	17	.575	49	4	325	314	138	152	75
1907	New York	AL	10	10	.500	30	1	206	192	83	78	46
1908	New York	AL	14	20	.412	45	3	289	276	135	124	67
1909	New York	AL	0	4	.000	9	0	50	70	47	17	13
1909	Boston	AL	0	1	.000	1	0	6	7	4	3	4
	TOTALS		198	132	.600	392	35	2,898	2,647	1,207	1,265	690

Sources: Baseball-Reference.com; National Baseball Hall of Fame and Museum

Chesney, Stanley (born: January 19, 1910 in Bayonne, New Jersey; died: January 1978 in Cleveland, Ohio); inducted into the National Soccer Hall of Fame and Museum in 1966 as a player; Position: Goalkeeper; one of the game's greatest American-born goalies.

Chesney began playing soccer at age 17 with the Bayonne Rovers, but it was with the New York Americans of the American Soccer League that he established his reputation as one of the game's greatest American-born goalkeepers. He played for the Americans 17 seasons and was a member of the team that reached the U.S. Open Cup final in 1933, only to lose to St. Louis Stix, Baer and Fuller of the St. Louis Soccer League.

He helped the Americans win the ASL title in 1936 and the U.S. Open Cup in 1937.

Although he participated in many games against foreign touring teams, Chesney never played for the United States in a full international game. His international competition included the Metropolitan All-Stars against Kladno of Czechoslovakia (1934); the Eastern United States against the Scottish Football Association (1935); the ASL against Maccabi Tel Aviv (1936); the ASL and a U.S. team against Charlton Athletic (1937); the New York Americans against Atlante of Mexico (1940); the ASL against Botafogo of Brazil (1940); and the New York Americans against Puentes Grandes of Cuba (1940).

Source: National Soccer Hall of Fame and Museum

Child, Paul (born: December 8, 1952 in Birmingham, England); inducted into the National Soccer Hall of Fame and Museum in 2003 as a player; Position: Forward; International Caps (1973): 2; International Goals: 0; scored 102 goals in 241 NASL games.

One of the top goal scorers in North American Soccer League history, the 6'1" Child originally joined the NASL's Atlanta Chiefs in 1972, on loan from Aston Villa (English Football Club). He would go on to play for five NASL teams, three of them in Atlanta, and on two United States teams in international competition, against Canada and Poland, both in 1973.

Playing his first NASL game on May 6, 1972, Child scored eight goals in his first season, three of them in one game against the Dallas Tornado. In 1973, the Atlanta team changed owners and became known as the Apollos. The next year, he was traded to the San Jose Earthquakes, where he would play six seasons. In 1980, he played for the Memphis Rogues and when the team moved to Calgary, Canada the next season, Child returned to play in Atlanta for the Chiefs.

In his 10 NASL seasons, he scored 102 goals in 241 games, and was named to the league's First All-Star Team twice (1972, 1974). After retiring as a player, he coached the Pittsburgh Riverhounds of the A-League.

After playing for the Atlanta Chiefs in his last NASL season (1981), Child left the league and focused on his indoor career with the Pittsburgh Spirit of the Major Indoor Soccer League, where he would go on to score 140 goals in 133 games. In 1983, he returned to outdoor soccer with the Carolina Lightnin' of the American Soccer League for one season. After the Spirit ceased operations in 1986, Child played with the Baltimore Blast for one year before joining the Los Angeles Lazers for the 1987–1988 MISL season. Although he was not an American citizen, he earned two caps in 1973 with the U.S. National Team, a 2–0 win over Canada and a 1–0 win over Poland, both in August.

In 1995, Child became the head coach of the Detroit Neon of the Continental Indoor Soccer League, and he stayed with the team until it folded after the 1997 season. In October 1998, he was hired by the A-League's Pittsburgh Riverhounds as director of youth development and the team's assistant coach. In 2001, he served as the team's interim head coach until 2002, and later returned to the team as an assistant coach in 2005.

Source: National Soccer Hall of Fame and Museum

Chinaglia, Giorgio (born: January 24, 1947 in Carrera, Italy); inducted into the National Soccer Hall of Fame and Museum in 2000 as a player; Position: Forward; International Caps (1972–1974): 14; International Goals: 4; led the North American Soccer League in scoring four times and won four league championships.

By the time he retired after eight North American Soccer League seasons (1976–1983), Chinaglia had become one of the most prolific goal scorers in league history. Before playing in the NASL with the New York Cosmos, he had played seven seasons for Lazio in the Italian Serie A, and for Italy 14 times, including appearances in the 1974 World Cup.

In his eight NASL seasons, Chinaglia scored 242 goals in 254 games (including postseason), second only to Archie Stark's 253 goals in first division professional soccer in the United States. He led the NASL in scoring four times (1978–1980, 1982); had 124 assists (including postseason), with 37 in 1980; and was on Cosmos teams that won four NASL championships (1977–1978, 1980, 1982). He scored 24 or more goals in six straight seasons (1978–1983); was a First Team All-Star six times (1976, 1978–1982); and was named the league's Most Valuable Player in 1981. His international career included stints with Massese and Internapoli in Italy, after beginning his career with Welsh club Swansea Town in 1964.

After playing for Cardiff Schools (in Italy), Chinaglia began his professional career with Swansea Town in the 1964–1965 season in a 2–2 tie at Rotherham United on October 14, 1964, in the League Cup Third Round. His only other appearance that season was a 0–0 draw at home against Portsmouth on February 13, 1965. In the next season, he only played four more times for Swansea and scored his only goal in a 2–1 loss at Bournemouth on August 24, 1965.

Chinaglia would later play in his native Italy for Massese, Internapoli, and Lazio, where he would make his mark in seven seasons with the team. In 1974, he led Lazio to the team's first-ever championship, and was the league's top scorer. He also played for Italy in the 1974 FIFA World Cup (played in West Germany, eliminated in first round).

In 1976, Chinaglia moved to the United States and played for the New York Cosmos of the NASL, and was considered the first great European player to leave his original team to join the NASL in the prime of his career. A controversial move on his part, he was never known as a fan-friendly player, and many criticized his move to the United States, believing he should have stayed in Italy to help the nation win the FIFA World Cup.

Giorgio Chinaglia's North American Soccer League Statistics

YEAR	TEAM	G	GLS	ASST	PTS
1976	New York Cosmos	19	19	11	49
1977	New York Cosmos	24	15	18	38
1978	New York Cosmos	30	34	11	79
1979	New York Cosmos	27	26	5	57
1980	New York Cosmos	32	32	13	77
1981	New York Cosmos	32	29	16	74
1982	New York Cosmos	32	20	15	55
1983	New York Cosmos	17	18	2	38
	TOTALS	213	193	81	467

Source: National Soccer Hall of Fame and Museum

Christiansen, Jack Leroy (born: December 20, 1928 in Sublette, Kansas; died: June 29, 1986); inducted into the Pro Football Hall of Fame in 1970 as a player; Position: Defensive Back; won three NFL championships; served as head coach of both the NFL's San Francisco 49ers and Stanford University.

Relatively small for his time (6'1", 160 pounds), Christiansen attended Colorado State University (Fort Collins) to be a sprinter on the track team. As a sophomore, he joined the school's football team and for the next three seasons was the squad's kickoff and return man, as well as a premier defensive player.

After college, he was a sixth-round draft choice (69th selection overall) of the Detroit Lions, where he would play his entire, relatively-brief eight-year career (1951–1958). In his rookie year, Christiansen scored four touchdowns on punt returns (47 and 69 yards against the Los Angeles Rams; 71 and 89 yards against the Green Bay Packers).

He was named All-NFL six straight years (1952–1957); played in five consecutive Pro Bowls (1954–1958); was the NFL's interception leader in 1953 and co-leader in 1957; and was a member of Lions teams that won four divisional and three NFL / world championships (1952–1953, 1957), pre-Super Bowl.

After retiring as a player, Christiansen served as defensive backs coach for the San Francisco 49ers from 1959 to 1963, before becoming the team's head coach until 1967 (he left the 49ers after compiling a record of 26–38–3). After working briefly at his alma mater, he became a coaching assistant at Stanford University (Palo Alto, California) in April 1968, and helped the Indians (the team's nickname at the time) to consecutive Rose Bowl upsets of Ohio State University (27–17 in 1971) and the University of Michigan (13–12 in 1972). After four years with the team, he was named head coach in January 1972 and stayed until 1976, compiling a record of 30–22–3.

After being fired from Stanford, Christiansen returned to the professional ranks in 1977 with the Kansas City Chiefs, and in 1978, he was hired by the Seattle Seahawks as the team's defensive backs coach, where he served for five seasons. After the strike-shortened 1982 NFL season, Christiansen's last coaching job came with the Atlanta Falcons in 1983, before he was forced to resign in 1984 due to ill health.

Six weeks before his death, he was inducted into the Michigan Sports Hall of Fame in recognition of his career with the Lions, and in 1972 *Football Digest* selected Christiansen as one of the all-time top 25 players in the NFL. In 1999, he was ranked number 86 on *The Sporting News*' list of the 100 Greatest Football Players.

Jack Christiansen's Career Statistics

			PUNT RETURNS				KICKOFF RETURNS			
YEAR	TEAM	G	NO	YDS	AVG	TD	NO	YDS	AVG	TD
1951	Detroit	12	18	343	19.1	4	11	270	24.5	0
1952	Detroit	11	15	322	21.5	2	16	409	25.6	0
1953	Detroit	12	8	22	2.8	0	10	183	18.3	0
1954	Detroit	11	23	225	9.8	1	5	102	20.4	0
1955	Detroit	9	12	87	7.3	0	7	169	24.1	0
1956	Detroit	12	6	73	12.2	1	6	116	19.3	0
1957	Detroit	12	3	12	4.0	0	4	80	20.0	0
1958	Detroit	10	0	0	0.0	0	0	0	0.0	0
	TOTALS	89	85	1,084	12.8	8	59	1,329	22.5	0

			DEFENSE					
YEAR	TEAM	G	INT	YDS	AVG	TD	FUMREC	YDS
1951	Detroit	12	2	53	26.5	0	1	52

DEFENSE

YEAR	TEAM	G	INT	YDS	AVG	TD	FUMREC	YDS
1952	Detroit	11	2	47	23.5	0	1	0
1953	Detroit	12	12	238	19.8	1	3	0
1954	Detroit	11	8	84	10.5	1	0	0
1955	Detroit	9	3	49	16.3	0	2	36
1956	Detroit	12	8	109	13.6	0	0	0
1957	Detroit	12	10	137	13.7	1	0	0
1958	Detroit	10	1	0	0.0	0	0	0
	TOTALS	89	46	717	15.6	3	7	88

Sources: Pro Football Hall of Fame; Pro-Reference.com

Chylak, Nestor George, Jr. (born: May 11, 1922 in Olyphant, Pennsylvania; died: February 17, 1982 in Dunmore, Pennsylvania); inducted into the National Baseball Hall of Fame and Museum in 1999 as an umpire by the Veterans Committee; worked the first-ever League Championship Series (1969) and the first-ever game played in Toronto (1977).

Chylak enjoyed a 25-year umpiring career in the American League (1954–1978). The longtime crew chief worked six All-Star games (1957, 1960 (both games), 1964, 1973, 1978), three League Championship Series, including the first one ever played (1969, 1972–1973), and five World Series (1957, 1960, 1966, 1971, 1977).

After attending the University of Scranton (Pennsylvania), he served in the United States Army during World War II; fought in the Battle of the Bulge (Ardennes Mountains region of Belgium, France, and Luxembourg); and was awarded the Silver Star and Purple Heart for his military service. After the war, Chylak began umpiring amateur baseball in 1946; began working in the minor leagues in 1947; and eventually was promoted to the American League seven years later. After retiring as an active on-field official in 1978, he served as an assistant league supervisor of umpires.

Chylak worked Sandy Koufax's final game in the 1966 World Series; served as crew chief for the infamous "10-cent Beer Night" promotion in Cleveland on June 4, 1974, that ultimately resulted in a forfeit to the visiting Texas Rangers due to unruly fans and him being hit over the head with a chair; and worked the first-ever major league game played in Toronto (during a snowstorm in 1977 at Exhibition Stadium). As an assistant league supervisor, Chylak was in the umpires' dressing room at Comiskey Park (Chicago) on "Disco Demolition Night," a July 12, 1979 doubleheader between the Detroit Tigers and Chicago White Sox. In between games of the doubleheader, when unruly fans began to blow up disco records on the field and caused a riot, Chylak told White Sox owner Bill Veeck that the second game could not be played and it was forfeited to Detroit.

Source: National Baseball Hall of Fame and Museum

Chynoweth, Ed (born: December 14, 1940 in Dodsland, Saskatchewan, Canada; died: April 22, 2008 in Calgary, Alberta, Canada); inducted into the Hockey Hall of Fame in 2008 as a builder; president of the Western Hockey League.

Chynoweth first served as president of the Saskatoon Minor Hockey Association, before becoming an assistant general manager of the Saskatoon Blades of the Western Canada Hockey League (1971–1972). In November 1972, he became the first full-time president of the Western Canada Hockey League (now known as the Western Hockey League), a job he held until 1996, with a one-year break. During the 1979–1980 season, Chynoweth took a break as president to serve as the owner and general manager of the WHL's Calgary Wranglers for one year before resuming the duties as the league's president.

In 1973–1974, he played a key role in forming the Canadian Major Junior Hockey League (now known as the Canadian Hockey League) by forming a partnership between the WHL, the Ontario Hockey League, and the Quebec Major Junior Hockey League. Chynoweth became the first president of the CMJHL in 1975–1976, a job he held until June 1995, all the while still acting as president of the WHL.

In August 1995, Chynoweth was named president and general manager of the newly-created Edmonton Ice, which joined the WHL for the 1996–1997 season. When the franchise relocated to Cranbrook, British Columbia in 1998 and was renamed the Kootenay Ice, he stayed with the team in his management positions and helped the squad win the Memorial Cup in 2002. He was the team's president until his death in 2008 and also served two terms as the WHL's chairman of the board (1996–1998, 2004–2007).

He was appointed to the Federal Government Commission of Fair Play in 1986 and 1987; served on the Hockey Hall of Fame's Selection Committee from 1990 until 2008; received the CMJHL Distinguished Service Award twice (1977, 1983); was awarded the CAHA Order of Merit for service to Canadian Amateur Hockey; in 1996, the CHL named its award for the top scorer in the Memorial Cup tournament the Ed Chynoweth Trophy; the WHL Championship

Trophy was renamed the Ed Chynoweth Cup in May 2007; and he was inducted into the Alberta Sports Hall of Fame in 2000.

Source: Hockey Hall of Fame

Chyzowych, Walter (born: April 20, 1937 in Sambir (Litovyska), Ukraine; died: September 2, 1994 in Raleigh-Durham, North Carolina); inducted into the National Soccer Hall of Fame and Museum in 1997 as a builder; International Caps (1964–1965): 3; International Goals: 0; named American Soccer League Most Valuable Player in 1966; won two league titles.

In 1943, Chyzowych and his family moved to West Germany prior to the Soviet reoccupation of the Ukraine during the war. After five years in Germany, the family immigrated to the United States and settled in the Philadelphia, Pennsylvania area in 1949.

He was a First Team All-American at Temple University (Philadelphia, Pennsylvania) twice (1959–1960), where he played soccer from 1957 to 1961, setting a record for career goals (25). He played at the professional level in the American Soccer League from 1958 to 1974 with the Philadelphia Ukrainian Nationals and Newark Sitch. He was named to six All-Star teams; was the league's Most Valuable Player in 1966; won two league titles (in 1966 with the Sitch and in 1971 with the Nationals); and won two U.S. Open titles with the Nationals (1963–1964).

He played for Toronto City of the Eastern Canada Professional Soccer League from 1961 to 1964 (winning the league title his last season with the team) and for the Philadelphia Spartans of the National Professional Soccer League in 1967. He played for the United States National Team twice in World Cup qualifying against England in 1964 and Honduras in 1965. Chyzowych began his coaching career, while still a player, with Philadelphia Textile from 1961 to 1963 and from 1966 to 1975. He led the team to three NCAA quarterfinals and was named National Soccer Coaches Association of America Coach of the Year in 1975. He was also a player-coach for the Philadelphia Ukrainians and Inter clubs from 1971 to 1975.

Chyzowych served as director of coaching for the U.S. Soccer Federation from 1975 to 1981, and as head coach for the National, Olympic, and Youth teams. He led the youth team to its first-ever appearance in the finals in 1981 and the Olympic team's second qualification in 1980. He coached the National Team from 1976 to 1980, including the qualification rounds for the 1978 and 1982 World Cups, and a 2–0 upset of Hungary in 1979.

He coached professional indoor soccer with the Philadelphia Fever of the Major Indoor Soccer League from 1981 to 1982 and in 1986, he was named head coach at Wake Forest University (Winston-Salem, North Carolina), where he led the team to four NCAA bids and one national championship.

Chyzowych worked as a television analyst and was part of the broadcast team during the 1977 Soccer Bowl, which was Pelé's last professional game. He has been inducted into the Philadelphia Textile, Temple Pennsylvania Sports, and Eastern Pennsylvania halls of fame; was named South region coach of the year in 1989; named one of *Soccer America*'s Twenty Men of Influence in American Soccer; inducted into the NSCAA Hall of Fame in 1997; and has been inducted into the U.S. Soccer Federation Hall of Fame, which also established the Walter Chyzowych Soccer Scholarship Fund.

He wrote *The Official Soccer Book of the United States Soccer Federation* and *The World Cup*, and co-authored *One-on-One: Moves and Tricks of the Soccer Stars (The Skills Book of the United States Soccer Federation)* with Ole Anderson.

Source: National Soccer Hall of Fame and Museum

Ciccarelli, Dino (born: February 8, 1960 in Sarnia, Ontario, Canada); inducted into the Hockey Hall of Fame in 2010 as a player; Position: Right Wing; considered one of the best players in league history never to have won a Stanley Cup title.

The 5'10", 180-pound Ciccarelli (a right-handed shooter) was a star with the London Knights (Ontario Major Junior Hockey League), where he played for four years (1976–1980), and had his jersey number 8 retired by the team. In 1979, as a free agent, he signed with the NHL's Minnesota North Stars and joined the team during the 1980–1981 season, falling to the New York Islanders in the Stanley Cup Championship.

In 19 NHL seasons, he played for the Minnesota North Stars (1980–1989); Washington Capitals (1989–1992); Detroit Red Wings (1992–1996); Tampa Bay Lightning (1996–1997); and the Florida Panthers (1998–1999). After nine seasons with the North Stars (where he had accumulated 651 points, the fourth most in team history), Ciccarelli was traded to the Washington Capitals and in 1992, he was traded to the Red Wings and helped the team reach the 1995 Stanley Cup, eventually falling to the New Jersey Devils in four games.

In both 1995 and 1996, the Red Wings finished with the best overall record in the NHL, winning the President's Trophy. In August 1996, Ciccarelli was traded to the Tampa Bay Lightning, before being traded to the Florida Panthers in January 1998, where he scored his 600th career goal in his 18th NHL season. He retired in August 1999, ranked ninth in NHL history in goals scored. He is often considered one of the best players in league history never to have won a Stanley Cup title, and played in four NHL All-Star Games (1982–1983, 1989, 1997).

Dino Ciccarelli's Career Statistics

			REGULAR SEASON					PLAYOFFS				
SEASON	**TEAM**	**LEAGUE**	**GP**	**G**	**A**	**TP**	**PIM**	**GP**	**G**	**A**	**TP**	**PIM**
1974–1975	Sarnia Army Vets	Minor-ON										
1975–1976	Sarnia Bees	OHA-B	40	45	43	88						
1976–1977	London Knights	OMJHL	66	39	43	82	45	20	11	13	24	14
1977–1978	London Knights	OMJHL	68	72	70	142	49	9	6	10	16	6
1978–1979	London Knights	OMJHL	30	8	11	19	35	7	3	5	8	0
1979–1980	London Knights	OMJHL	62	50	53	103	72	5	2	6	8	15
1979–1980	Canada	WJC-A	5	5	1	6	2					
1979–1980	Oklahoma City Stars	CHL	6	3	2	5	0					
1980–1981	Minnesota North Stars	NHL	32	18	12	30	29	19	14	7	21	25
1980–1981	Oklahoma City Stars	CHL	48	32	25	57	45					
1981–1982	Minnesota North Stars	NHL	76	55	51	106	138	4	3	1	4	2
1981–1982	Canada	WEC-A	9	2	1	3	0					
1982–1983	Minnesota North Stars	NHL	77	37	38	75	94	9	4	6	10	11
1983–1984	Minnesota North Stars	NHL	79	38	33	71	58	16	4	5	9	27
1984–1985	Minnesota North Stars	NHL	51	15	17	32	41	9	3	3	6	8
1985–1986	Minnesota North Stars	NHL	75	44	45	89	51	5	0	1	1	6
1986–1987	Minnesota North Stars	NHL	80	52	51	103	88					
1986–1987	Canada	WEC-A	10	4	2	6	2					
1987–1988	Minnesota North Stars	NHL	67	41	45	86	79					
1988–1989	Minnesota North Stars	NHL	65	32	27	59	64					
1988–1989	Washington Capitals	NHL	11	12	3	15	12	6	3	3	6	12
1989–1990	Washington Capitals	Fr-Tour	3	3	0	3	2					
1989–1990	Washington Capitals	NHL	80	41	38	79	122	8	8	3	11	6
1990–1991	Washington Capitals	NHL	54	21	18	39	66	11	5	4	9	22
1991–1992	Washington Capitals	NHL	78	38	38	76	78	7	5	4	9	14
1992–1993	Detroit Red Wings	NHL	82	41	56	97	81	7	4	2	6	16
1993–1994	Detroit Red Wings	NHL	66	28	29	57	73	7	5	2	7	14
1994–1995	Detroit Red Wings	NHL	42	16	27	43	39	16	9	2	11	22
1995–1996	Detroit Red Wings	NHL	64	22	21	43	99	17	6	2	8	26
1996–1997	Tampa Bay Lightning	NHL	77	35	25	60	116					
1997–1998	Tampa Bay Lightning	NHL	34	11	6	17	42					
1997–1998	Florida Panthers	NHL	28	5	11	16	28					
1998–1999	Florida Panthers	NHL	14	6	1	7	27					
	NHL TOTALS		1,232	608	592	1,200	1,425	141	73	45	118	211

Sources: Hockey Hall of Fame; Hockey-Reference.com

Clancy, Francis Michael "King" (born: February 25, 1903 in Ottawa, Ontario, Canada; died: November 8, 1986 in Toronto, Ontario, Canada); inducted into the Hockey Hall of Fame in 1958 as a player; Position: Defenseman; Uniform: #7; joined the NHL as the youngest player in the league at the time; won three Stanley Cup titles as a player and one AHL Calder Cup as a coach.

A legendary name in the hockey world, Clancy played 16 National Hockey League seasons with the Ottawa Senators (1921–1930) and the Toronto Maple Leafs (1930–1937). After retiring as a player, he stayed involved with the game as a referee, coach, and executive. After playing at the junior and senior level for four years, he debuted as the youngest player in the NHL on December 17, 1921.

After the 5'7", 150-pound Clancy helped the Senators win two Stanley Cup titles (1923, 1927), he was traded to Toronto in 1930 and led the team to its first-ever Stanley Cup championship in 1932 (the team's first year at Maple Leaf Gardens).

Clancy was named to the NHL First All-Star Team Defense twice (1931, 1934) and to the Second All-Star Team Defense twice (1932, 1933), and participated in the Ace Bailey benefit game in 1934.

After retiring as a player in 1936, he coached the Montreal Maroons (NHL) for one month during the 1937–1938 season, before becoming an NHL referee. After 11 seasons, Clancy quit being a referee to coach the Cincinnati Mohawks (the American Hockey League affiliate of the Montreal Canadiens) for the 1949–1950 season, and was named the AHL's All-Star coach. After finishing in last place his two years with the team, he became the head coach of the AHL's Pittsburgh Hornets (a Maple Leafs affiliate) for the 1951–1952 season, and led the team to its first-ever Calder Cup as AHL champions.

In 1953, Clancy rejoined the Leafs as coach for three years; in 1956, he left coaching and became the team's assistant general manager; and was in the front office as the franchise won four Stanley Cup titles in the 1960s (1962–1964, 1967). The King Clancy Memorial Trophy is an annual award presented to the player who best exemplifies leadership qualities on and off the ice while making a significant contribution to his community.

Clancy played in four NHL All-Star games (1931–1934); was inducted into Canada's Sports Hall of Fame in 1975; and in 1998, he was ranked number 52 on *The Hockey News*' list of the 100 Greatest Hockey Players.

King Clancy's Career Statistics

			REGULAR SEASON					PLAYOFFS				
SEASON	**TEAM**	**LEAGUE**	**GP**	**G**	**A**	**TP**	**PIM**	**GP**	**G**	**A**	**TP**	**PIM**
1916–1917	Ottawa Sandy Hill	OCJHL	4	3	0	3						
1916–1917	St. Joseph's (Ottawa)	High-ON						2	3	0	3	
1917–1918	Ottawa Munitions	OCJHL	4	2	0	2						
1917–1918	Ottawa Collegiate	High-ON						2	3	0	3	
1918–1919	Ottawa St. Brigid's	OCHL	8	0	1	1	3	1	0	0	0	6
1919–1920	Ottawa St. Brigid's	OCHL	8	1	0	1						
1920–1921	Ottawa St. Brigid's	OCHL	11	6	0	6		6	5	1	6	12
1921–1922	Ottawa Senators	NHL	24	4	6	10	21	2	0	0	0	2
1922–1923	Ottawa Senators	NHL	24	3	2	5	20	2	0	0	0	0
1922–1923	Ottawa Senators	St-Cup						6	1	0	1	4
1923–1924	Ottawa Senators	NHL	24	8	8	16	26	2	0	0	0	6
1924–1925	Ottawa Senators	NHL	29	14	7	21	61					
1925–1926	Ottawa Senators	NHL	35	8	4	12	80	2	1	0	1	4
1926–1927	Ottawa Senators	NHL	43	9	10	19	78	6	1	1	2	14
1927–1928	Ottawa Senators	NHL	39	8	7	15	73	2	0	0	0	6
1928–1929	Ottawa Senators	NHL	44	13	2	15	89					
1929–1930	Ottawa Senators	NHL	44	17	23	40	83	2	0	1	1	2
1930–1931	Toronto Maple Leafs	NHL	44	7	14	21	63	2	1	0	1	0
1931–1932	Toronto Maple Leafs	NHL	48	10	9	19	61	7	2	1	3	14
1932–1933	Toronto Maple Leafs	NHL	48	13	12	25	79	9	0	3	3	14
1933–1934	Toronto Maple Leafs	NHL	46	11	17	28	62	3	0	0	0	8
1934–1935	Toronto Maple Leafs	NHL	47	5	16	21	53	7	1	0	1	8
1935–1936	Toronto Maple Leafs	NHL	47	5	10	15	61	9	2	2	4	10
1936–1937	Toronto Maple Leafs	NHL	6	1	0	1	4					
1937–1938	Montreal Maroons	NHLMGNT										
	NHL TOTALS		592	136	147	283	914	55	8	8	16	88

Sources: Hockey Hall of Fame; Hockey-Reference.com

Clapper, Aubrey Victor "Dit" (born: February 9, 1907 in Newmarket, Ontario, Canada; died: January 21, 1978 in Newmarket, Ontario, Canada); inducted into the Hockey Hall of Fame as a player in 1947; Position: Defenseman-Forward; Uniform: #5; first 20-season player in NHL history.

After playing one year with the Boston Tigers of the Canadian-American League, Clapper became the National Hockey League's first 20-season player in league history and played his entire career (1927–1947) with the Boston Bruins. While playing Right Wing, he scored a goal in the team's first-ever Stanley Cup championship in the 1929 three-game series win over the New York Rangers. He would go on to win two more titles (1939, 1941).

In the 1929–1930 season, the Bruins played to a 38–5–1 regular-season record, while Clapper scored 41 goals in 44 games. After being selected Right Wing on the NHL Second All-Star Team twice (1931, 1935), he once again became a defenseman in 1937; was named to the NHL First All-Star Team three consecutive seasons (1939–1941); on January 8,

1941, he scored his 200th career goal at Maple Leaf Gardens; and helped Boston win the team's third Stanley Cup trophy in a four-game sweep of the Detroit Red Wings.

In 1944, the 6'2", 200-pound Clapper was chosen to the NHL Second All-Star Team, and in the 1945–1946 season, as player-coach, he led the Bruins to the Stanley Cup finals, losing in five games to the Montreal Canadiens. He retired six games into the 1946–1947 season, and the team retired his jersey in February 1947.

He was inducted into the Canadian Sports Hall of Fame in 1975; in 1998, he was ranked number 41 on *The Hockey News*' list of the 100 Greatest Hockey Players; and the hall of fame selection committee waived the customary three-year waiting period and inducted him into the Hockey Hall of Fame the night he retired.

Dit Clapper's Career Statistics

			REGULAR SEASON					PLAYOFFS				
SEASON	**TEAM**	**LEAGUE**	**GP**	**G**	**A**	**TP**	**PIM**	**GP**	**G**	**A**	**TP**	**PIM**
1925–1926	Toronto Parkdale	OHA-Jr.	2	0	0	0	0					
1925–1926	Toronto Parkdale	M-Cup	5	1	0	1						
1926–1927	Boston Tigers	Can-Am	29	6	1	7	57					
1927–1928	Boston Bruins	NHL	40	4	1	5	20	2	0	0	0	2
1928–1929	Boston Bruins	NHL	40	9	2	11	48	5	1	0	1	0
1929–1930	Boston Bruins	NHL	44	41	20	61	48	6	4	0	4	4
1930–1931	Boston Bruins	NHL	43	22	8	30	50	5	2	4	6	4
1931–1932	Boston Bruins	NHL	48	17	22	39	21					
1932–1933	Boston Bruins	NHL	48	14	14	28	42	5	1	1	2	2
1933–1934	Boston Bruins	NHL	48	10	12	22	6					
1934–1935	Boston Bruins	NHL	48	21	16	37	21	3	1	0	1	0
1935–1936	Boston Bruins	NHL	44	12	13	25	14	2	0	1	1	0
1936–1937	Boston Bruins	NHL	48	17	8	25	25	3	2	0	2	5
1937–1938	Boston Bruins	NHL	46	6	9	15	24	3	0	0	0	12
1938–1939	Boston Bruins	NHL	42	13	13	26	22	12	0	1	1	6
1939–1940	Boston Bruins	NHL	44	10	18	28	25	5	0	2	2	2
1940–1941	Boston Bruins	NHL	48	8	18	26	24	11	0	5	5	4
1941–1942	Boston Bruins	NHL	32	3	12	15	31					
1942–1943	Boston Bruins	NHL	38	5	18	23	12	9	2	3	5	9
1943–1944	Boston Bruins	NHL	50	6	25	31	13					
1944–1945	Boston Bruins	NHL	46	8	14	22	16	7	0	0	0	0
1945–1946	Boston Bruins	NHL	30	2	3	5	0	4	0	0	0	0
1946–1947	Boston Bruins	NHL	6	0	0	0	0					
1947–1948	Boston Bruins	NHLMGNT										
	NHL TOTALS		833	228	246	474	462	82	13	17	30	50

Sources: Hockey Hall of Fame; Hockey-Reference.com

Clark, Earl Harry "Dutch" (born: October 11, 1906 in Fowler, Colorado; died: August 5, 1978 in Cañon City, Colorado); inducted into the Pro Football Hall of Fame in 1963 as a player; Position: Quarterback-Tailback; the NFL's last dropkicking specialist; first football player to be named an All-American from Colorado College.

Although Clark was the first football player from Colorado College (Colorado Springs, Colorado) to earn All-American honors (1929), he did not play professional football until two years after he graduated. His professional career began in 1931 with the Portsmouth (Ohio) Spartans, an early National Football League team, that later moved to Detroit in 1933 and was renamed the Lions. On September 24, 1930, the Spartans beat the Brooklyn Dodgers at home (in University Stadium) in the first-ever NFL night game (played in front of portable lights), and with a 6–1–4 record at the end of the 1932 season, the Spartans were tied with the Chicago Bears, the first time in NFL history that two teams were tied for the lead. The league arranged for its first playoff game to decide its champion, won by the Bears 9–0.

Clark left the Spartans in 1933 and became the head football coach at the Colorado School of Mines (Golden, Colorado). After coaching only one college season, he returned to the NFL as a player when the Spartans moved to Detroit, where he played through the 1938 season. The 6', 185-pound Clark was the NFL's last dropkicking specialist; named All-NFL in six of his seven seasons; was the league's leading scorer three times; and led the Lions to the 1935 title. After retiring as a player, Clark became the Lions' head coach for two seasons (1937–1938), before coaching the Cleveland Rams for four seasons (1939–1942).

Although he played tailback, he was designated as the team's quarterback because he called the plays, and was named to the NFL 1930s All-Decade Team.

Dutch Clark's Career Statistics

			PASSING							RUSHING			
YEAR	TEAM	G	ATT	COMP	PCT	YDS	TD	INT	RATING	NO	YDS	AVG	TD
1931	Portsmouth	11	0	0	0.0	0	1	0	0.0	0	0	0.0	9
1932	Portsmouth	11	52	17	32.7	272	2	8	24.4	137	461	3.4	3
1934	Detroit	12	50	23	46.0	383	0	3	47.3	123	763	6.2	8
1935	Detroit	12	26	11	42.3	133	2	4	44.7	120	427	3.6	4
1936	Detroit	12	71	38	53.5	467	4	6	57.7	123	628	5.1	7
1937	Detroit	11	39	19	48.7	202	1	3	40.8	96	468	4.9	5
1938	Detroit	6	12	6	50.0	50	1	2	49.3	7	25	3.6	0
	TOTALS	75	250	114	45.6	1,507	11	26	40.3	606	2,772	4.6	36

Sources: Pro Football Hall of Fame; Pro-Football-Reference.com

Clarke, Fred Clifford (born: October 3, 1872 in Winterset, Iowa; died: August 14, 1960 in Winfield, Kansas); inducted into the National Baseball Hall of Fame and Museum in 1945 as a player by the Veterans Committee; Position: Left Field; Bats: Left; Throws: Right; managed the 1902 Pirates to only 36 losses, set a major league record by going five-for-five in his first major league game; Pittsburgh's most successful manager in both wins and winning percentage.

Making his major league debut on June 30, 1894, Clarke enjoyed a 21-year National League career as a player and manager with the Louisville Colonels (1894–1899) and the Pittsburgh Pirates (1900–1911, 1913–1915). He served as player-manager with the Louisville Colonels (1897–1899) and the Pittsburgh Pirates (1900–1915); led his teams to four National League pennants (1901–1903, 1909); and played in two World Series (winning in 1909 and losing in 1903).

He managed the 1902 Pirates to only 36 losses, a modern-era record shared with Frank Chance of the 1906 Chicago Cubs. He went 5-for-5 in his first major league game (a major league record) and hit over .300 in 11 seasons. In 1903, he led the league in doubles and slugging average; helped the Pirates advance to the first modern World Series (losing to the Boston Americans); was a full-time player-manager in 16 of his 19 seasons; and finished his career with 2,703 hits and 1,602 managerial wins.

After the 1899 season, the 5'11", 165-pound Clarke was one of many players who went to Pittsburgh when the Colonels merged with the Pirates. With the Pittsburgh roster containing the best players from both teams, the Pirates won 859 games between 1901 and 1909 (.634). In 1909, Clarke led Pittsburgh to a club-record 110 wins and hit two home runs against the Detroit Tigers in the World Series, which the Pirates won in seven games.

When he retired after the 1915 season, Clarke was the oldest active player in major league baseball. He was Pittsburgh's most successful manager in both wins (1,422) and winning percentage (.595), and ranked among the all-time club leaders in games, at-bats, hits, triples, and stolen bases. Years after retiring, he returned to the Pirates as a coach, and later served as the team's vice president and assistant manager.

He played baseball with local teams in Des Moines, Iowa and Hastings, Nebraska, before joining the Southern League when he was 21 and playing for the Montgomery (Alabama) Lambs/Colts and the Savannah (Georgia) Modocs. After a brief time in the minor leagues, Clark signed with the Colonels in 1894.

Clarke was one of the first 10 men elected into the baseball hall of fame by the Veterans Committee (at the time known as the Old-Timers Committee), and was one of the 24 original inductees into the Iowa Sports Hall of Fame in 1951.

April 28, 1906 marks the only time in major league history that two managers stole home on the same day. Chicago Cubs manager Frank Chance stole home in the ninth inning to give his team a 1–0 win over the Cincinnati Reds, while Clarke stole home in the Pirates' 10–1 win over the St. Louis Cardinals. On May 6, 1906, during a 5–1 loss to the Chicago Cubs, the Pirates' ground crew used a tarp to cover the entire infield, the first time a major league team had done this. Up to that point, only selected areas of the field (pitcher's mound and bases) would be covered during bad weather. In June 1906, Clarke filed for a patent for a "diamond cover," which was eventually approved in February 1911. On August 23, 1910, in a 6–2 win over the Philadelphia Phillies, Clarke recorded four assists from the outfield in one game, tying a major league record.

Fred Clarke's Career Statistics

YEAR	TEAM	G	AB	R	H	2B	3B	HR	RBI	BB	SO	SB	AVG	SLG
1894	Louisville	76	316	55	87	10	5	7	48	25	27	24	.275	.405
1895	Louisville	132	556	94	197	23	4	4	82	34	24	36	.354	.432
1896	Louisville	131	517	93	169	13	18	9	79	43	34	32	.327	.474
1897	Louisville	129	525	122	213	28	15	6	67	45		60	.406	.550
1898	Louisville	147	598	115	190	24	11	3	47	48		66	.318	.410
1899	Louisville	147	601	124	209	21	11	5	70	49		47	.348	.444
1900	Pittsburgh	103	398	85	112	14	12	3	32	51		18	.281	.399
1901	Pittsburgh	128	525	118	166	26	14	6	60	51		22	.316	.453
1902	Pittsburgh	114	461	104	148	27	14	2	53	51		34	.321	.453
1903	Pittsburgh	104	427	88	150	32	15	5	70	41		21	.351	.532
1904	Pittsburgh	72	278	51	85	7	11	0	25	22		11	.306	.410
1905	Pittsburgh	141	525	95	157	18	15	2	51	55		24	.299	.402
1906	Pittsburgh	118	417	69	129	14	13	1	39	40		18	.309	.412
1907	Pittsburgh	148	501	97	145	18	13	2	59	68		37	.289	.389
1908	Pittsburgh	151	551	83	146	18	15	2	53	65		24	.265	.363
1909	Pittsburgh	152	550	97	158	16	11	3	68	80		31	.287	.373
1910	Pittsburgh	123	429	57	113	23	9	2	63	53	23	12	.263	.373
1911	Pittsburgh	110	392	73	127	25	13	5	49	53	27	10	.324	.492
1913	Pittsburgh	9	13	0	1	1	0	0	0	0	0	0	.077	.154
1914	Pittsburgh	2	2	0	0	0	0	0	0	0	0	0	.000	.000
1915	Pittsburgh	1	2	0	1	0	0	0	0	0	0	0	.500	.500
	TOTALS	2,238	8,584	1,620	2,703	358	219	67	1,015	874	135	527	.315	.431

Fred Clarke's Managerial Record

YEAR	TEAM	W	L	WIN%	FINISH
1897	Louisville	35	54	.393	11 (Player-Manager)
1898	Louisville	70	81	.464	9 (Player-Manager)
1899	Louisville	75	77	.493	9 (Player-Manager)
1900	Pittsburgh	79	60	.568	2 (Player-Manager)
1901	Pittsburgh	90	49	.647	1 (Player-Manager)
1902	Pittsburgh	103	36	.741	1 (Player-Manager)
1903	Pittsburgh	91	49	.650	1 (Player-Manager)
1904	Pittsburgh	87	66	.569	4 (Player-Manager)
1905	Pittsburgh	96	57	.627	2 (Player-Manager)
1906	Pittsburgh	93	60	.608	3 (Player-Manager)
1907	Pittsburgh	91	63	.591	2 (Player-Manager)
1908	Pittsburgh	98	56	.636	2 (Player-Manager)
1909	Pittsburgh	110	42	.724	1 (Player-Manager)
1910	Pittsburgh	86	67	.562	3 (Player-Manager)
1911	Pittsburgh	85	69	.552	3 (Player-Manager)
1912	Pittsburgh	93	58	.616	2
1913	Pittsburgh	78	71	.523	4 (Player-Manager)
1914	Pittsburgh	69	85	.448	7 (Player-Manager)
1915	Pittsburgh	73	81	.474	5 (Player-Manager)
	Louisville	180	212	.459	
	Pittsburgh	1,422	969	.595	
	TOTALS	1,602	1,181	.576	

Sources: Baseball-Reference.com; National Baseball Hall of Fame

Clarke, Robert Earle "Bobby" (born: August 13, 1949 in Flin Flon, Manitoba, Canada); inducted into the Hockey Hall of Fame in 1987 as a player; Position: Center-Forward; Uniform: #16; first Philadelphia Flyers player to ever win the

Bill Masterton Memorial Trophy; first player from an expansion team to score more than 100 points in a season; led the Flyers to the first Stanley Cup title ever won by an expansion team.

After playing two seasons with his hometown Flin Flon Bombers of the Western Canada Junior Hockey League, Clarke would go on to play his entire 15-year National Hockey League career with the Philadelphia Flyers (1969–1984), after being the expansion team's second round pick (17th overall selection) in the 1969 league draft.

Although initially hampered by diabetic seizures that limited his playing time, Clarke learned to control the disease, and in his third NHL season, he scored 81 points (35 goals, 46 assists), highest in club history at that time. He was the first Flyers' player to win the Bill Masterton Memorial Trophy (1972) for perseverance, sportsmanship, and dedication to ice hockey; won the Hart Memorial Trophy as the NHL's Most Valuable Player three times (1973, 1975–1976); was awarded the Lester B. Pearson Award in 1973 as the league's Most Outstanding Player as judged by the members of the NHL Players Association; selected First All-Star Team Center twice (1975–1976) and Second All-Star Center twice (1973–1974); won the Lester Patrick Trophy in 1980 for his contributions to hockey in the United States; and won the Frank J. Selke Trophy in 1983 as the league's best defensive forward.

Clarke played for Team Canada in the 1972 Summit Series against the Russian team, which the Canadiens eventually won 4–3–1. He would go on to play internationally twice more for Canada, as captain of the team that won the gold medal at the 1976 Canada Cup and for the team that won the bronze medal at the 1982 World Championships (in Finland).

In the 1972–1973 season, Clarke became the first player from an expansion team to score more than 100 points in a season (104, with 37 goals and 67 assists). As the youngest captain (23) ever in the NHL up to that time, of a Flyers team known as the "Broad Street Bullies" for its rough and tumble playing style, he led the squad to back-to-back Stanley Cup championships (1974–1975), the first expansion team to win the title.

The 5'10", 176-pound Clarke played in eight All-Star Games (1970–1975, 1977–1978); retired as the Flyers' record holder for most games played (1,144), most assists (852), and most points (1,210); and still holds the team record for most assists in a season (89) twice (1975–1976). He served as a player-assistant coach from 1979 to 1982, and after retiring from the NHL, Clarke became the team's general manager in 1984, but was unable to lead the team to another Stanley Cup title.

He left the Flyers in 1990 to become general manager of the Minnesota North Stars, and helped guide the team to the 1991 Stanley Cup finals, before losing to the Pittsburgh Penguins in six games. After serving briefly as the Flyers' Senior Vice President (1992–1993), Clarke became the Florida Panthers' first-ever general manager in 1993, and put together a team that set NHL records for wins and points by an expansion team. He left Florida after only one season to once again serve as the general manager in Philadelphia.

In 1998, Clarke served as general manager of the Canadian Olympic hockey team, and assembled the first-ever squad that was comprised of the best players from the NHL. Although the team was made up of NHL stars, Canada finished a surprising fourth at the Olympics (held in Nagano, Japan).

The Flyers retired his number 16 in 1984; he was inducted into the Philadelphia Flyers Hall of Fame in 1988; in 1998, Clarke was ranked 23 on *The Hockey News*' list of the 100 Greatest Hockey Players; and he was inducted into Canada's Sports Hall of Fame in 2005.

The Bob Clarke Trophy is awarded annually to the top scorer in the Western Hockey League, and the Bobby Clarke Trophy is presented annually to the Team MVP of the Philadelphia Flyers. He was made an Officer of the Order of Canada in 1981.

Bobby Clarke's Career Statistics

			REGULAR SEASON					PLAYOFFS				
SEASON	**TEAM**	**LEAGUE**	**GP**	**G**	**A**	**TP**	**PIM**	**GP**	**G**	**A**	**TP**	**PIM**
1965–1966	Flin Flon Midget Bombers	MAHA										
1965–1966	Flin Flon Bombers	SJHL	4	4	3	7	0					
1966–1967	Flin Flon Bombers	MJHL	45	71	112	183	123	14	10	18	28	51
1966–1967	Flin Flon Bombers	M-Cup	6	2	5	7	49					
1967–1968	Flin Flon Bombers	WCJHL	59	51	117	168	148	15	4	10	14	2
1968–1969	Flin Flon Bombers	WCJHL	58	51	86	137	123	18	9	16	25	
1969–1970	Philadelphia Flyers	NHL	76	15	31	46	68					
1970–1971	Philadelphia Flyers	NHL	77	27	36	63	78	4	0	0	0	2
1971–1972	Philadelphia Flyers	NHL	78	35	46	81	87					
1972–1973	Canada	Summit-72	8	2	4	6	18					
1972–1973	Philadelphia Flyers	NHL	78	37	67	104	80	11	2	6	8	6

SEASON	TEAM	LEAGUE	REGULAR SEASON GP	G	A	TP	PIM	PLAYOFFS GP	G	A	TP	PIM
1973–1974	Philadelphia Flyers	NHL	77	35	52	87	113	17	5	11	16	42
1974–1975	Philadelphia Flyers	NHL	80	27	89	116	125	17	4	12	16	16
1975–1976	Philadelphia Flyers	NHL	76	30	89	119	136	16	2	14	16	28
1976–1977	Canada	Can-Cup	6	1	2	3	0					
1976–1977	Philadelphia Flyers	NHL	80	27	63	90	71	10	5	5	10	8
1977–1978	Philadelphia Flyers	NHL	71	21	68	89	83	12	4	7	11	8
1978–1979	Philadelphia Flyers	NHL	80	16	57	73	68	8	2	4	6	8
1978–1979	NHL All-Stars	Ch-Cup	3	0	1	1	0					
1979–1980	Philadelphia Flyers	NHL	76	12	57	69	65	19	8	12	20	16
1980–1981	Philadelphia Flyers	NHL	80	19	46	65	140	12	3	3	6	6
1981–1982	Philadelphia Flyers	NHL	62	17	46	63	154	4	4	2	6	4
1981–1982	Canada	WEC-A	9	0	1	1	6					
1982–1983	Philadelphia Flyers	NHL	80	23	62	85	115	3	1	0	1	2
1983–1984	Philadelphia Flyers	NHL	73	17	43	60	70	3	2	1	3	6
1984–1990	Philadelphia Flyers	NHLMGNT										
1990–1992	Minnesota North Stars	NHLMGNT										
1992–1993	Philadelphia Flyers	NHLMGNT										
1993–1994	Florida Panthers	NHLMGNT										
1994–2000	Philadelphia Flyers	NHLMGNT										
	NHL TOTALS		1,144	358	852	1,210	1,453	136	42	77	119	152

Sources: Hockey Hall of Fame; Hockey-Reference.com

Clarkson, John Gibson (born: July 1, 1861 in Cambridge, Massachusetts; died: February 4, 1909 in Belmont, Massachusetts); inducted into the National Baseball Hall of Fame and Museum in 1963 as a player by the Veterans Committee; Position: Pitcher; Bats: Right; Throws: Right; first pitcher in major league history to strike out three batters on nine pitches; retired as the winningest pitcher in National League history.

Making his major league debut on May 2, 1882, Clarkson had a 12-year National League career with the Worcester Ruby Legs (1882), Chicago White Stockings (1884–1887, later to be called the Cubs), Boston Beaneaters (1888–1892, later to be called the Braves), and the Cleveland Spiders (1892–1894). He appeared in two pre-1903 World Series (tying the St. Louis Browns 3–3–1 in 1885 and losing to the Browns 4–2 in 1886).

In only 12 seasons, the 5'10", 155-pound Clarkson compiled a 327–177 (.649) career record; won 53 games in leading the Chicago White Stockings to the 1885 National League pennant; twice threw more than 600 innings in a season; and won 30 or more games six times (second most only to Kid Nichols' seven seasons). At the time Clarkson retired from the game, he was the winningest pitcher in National League history.

Pitching in the 19th century, an era of two-man pitching staffs, Clarkson led the National League in wins, appearances, starts, complete games, and innings three times (1885, 1887, 1889); in earned run average in 1889; and in strikeouts four times (1885–1887, 1889). He accounted for 53 of Chicago's 87 wins in 1885 (60.9%) and 49 of Boston's 83 wins in 1889 (59%). His win totals in those two years rank second and fourth on the all-time single-season list. On July 27, 1885, he threw the only no-hitter of his career, a 4–0 win over the Providence Grays.

Together with his pitching brothers (Dad and Walter), Clarkson shares third place for most career wins by brothers, behind the Niekros and Perrys.

He won the National League pitching Triple Crown in 1889 (leading the league in wins, earned run average, and strikeouts); currently ranks 12th on the all-time Major League Baseball wins list; league ERA champion in 1889; and his 53 wins in 1885 is second most in Major League Baseball history. Clarkson was an above-average hitting pitcher. His 24 career home runs ranks seventh on the all-time home run list for pitchers, and he also had 232 career RBIs and scored 254 runs.

After playing semi-professional baseball for several years, Clarkson signed with the Worcester Ruby Legs of the National League in 1882. He played in three games for the team and finished with a 1–2 record in 24 innings. When Worcester folded after the season, he pitched in the minor leagues for two seasons, before returning to the majors for good with the Chicago White Stockings, managed by hall-of-famer Cap Anson.

John Clarkson's National League Career Statistics

YEAR	TEAM	W	L	PCT	G	SH	IP	H	R	SO	BB
1882	Worcester	1	2	.333	3	0	24	49	31	3	2

YEAR	TEAM	W	L	PCT	G	SH	IP	H	R	SO	BB
1884	Chicago	10	4	.714	14	0	118	94	64	102	25
1885	Chicago	53	16	.768	70	10	623	497	255	318	97
1886	Chicago	35	17	.673	55	3	467	419	246	340	86
1887	Chicago	37	21	.638	60	2	523	513	283	237	92
1888	Boston	33	19	.635	54	3	483	448	247	223	119
1889	Boston	49	19	.721	73	8	620	589	280	284	203
1890	Boston	26	18	.591	44	2	383	370	186	138	140
1891	Boston	34	18	.654	55	3	461	435	244	141	154
1892	Boston	8	7	.533	16	4	146	115	65	48	60
1892	Cleveland	17	10	.630	29	1	243	235	132	91	72
1893	Cleveland	16	18	.471	36	0	295	358	240	62	95
1894	Cleveland	8	8	.500	22	1	151	173	109	28	46
	TOTALS	327	177	.649	531	37	4,537	4,295	2,382	2,015	1,191

Sources: Baseball-Reference.com; National Baseball Hall of Fame and Museum

Clavijo, Fernando (born: January 23, 1957 in Maldonado, Uruguay); inducted into the National Soccer Hall of Fame and Museum in 2005 as a player; Position: Defender; International Caps (1990–1994): 61; International Goals: 0; played in the American Soccer League, Major Indoor Soccer League, North American Soccer League, and for the U.S. Men's National Team.

Clavijo began his professional career at age 16 in his native Uruguay, where he played for the national junior team and then for Atletico Atenas in the Uruguyan Second Division. He came to the United States in 1979 to play for the New York Apollos of the American Soccer League, and played two more seasons in the ASL with New York United. In his ASL career, Clavijo appeared in 66 games and scored five goals.

Leaving the ASL, he began playing indoor soccer in 1981 with the New York Arrows of the Major Indoor Soccer League, which marked the beginning of his 10-season MISL career. After two seasons, he moved to the San Diego Sockers and stayed with the team until the end of the 1987–1988 season. While with San Diego, his teams won four championships (one in the North American Soccer League [1984] and three in the MISL [1985–1986, 1988]). He spent the 1988–1989 season with the Los Angeles Lazers before moving on to the St. Louis Storm for three seasons. He was named to the league All-Star team each of his 10 seasons.

In the final years of the North American Soccer League, Clavijo played with the Golden Bay Earthquakes during the 1983 and 1984 seasons; appeared in 40 games; scored one goal; and was named to the league's 1984 All-Star team.

After the 5'10" Clavijo became a U.S. citizen in 1987, he was selected to the U.S. Men's National Team; made his debut against the Soviet Union on November 21, 1990; and would go on to play in 61 international games. He was a member of the 1994 Fédération Internationale de Football Association World Cup team at the age of 37, the oldest member on the squad, and retired from the team after the World Cup (which was hosted by the United States).

After retiring as a player, he coached the Seattle Sea Dogs of the Continental Indoor Soccer League and in three seasons (1994–1997) led the team to an overall 27–7 record, before coaching the Florida Thundercats (1998–1999) of the National Professional Soccer League. In 1998, Clavijo began coaching outdoor teams as an assistant coach for the U.S. Project-40 team and also spent part of the year as head coach of the U.S. National Futsal Team. Also in 1998, he was named assistant coach of the Nigerian National Team in the World Cup finals, held in France.

In 2000, Clavijo was named head coach of the New England Revolution of Major League Soccer; spent three seasons at New England (2000–2002); and led the team to the finals of the Lamar Hunt U.S. Open Cup in 2001. He later coached the Haitian National Team (2003–2005) and in 2004, he led the squad into FIFA World Cup qualifying rounds. After the team was eliminated, Clavijo was hired as the head coach of the Colorado Rapids (of the MLS) in December 2004.

Fernando Clavijo's MISL Career Statistics

YEAR	TEAM	G	GLS	ASST	PTS
1981–1982	New York	22	2	2	4
1982–1983	New York	43	9	11	20

YEAR	TEAM	G	GLS	ASST	PTS
1984–1985	San Diego	39	5	4	9
1985–1986	San Diego	47	17	9	26
1986–1987	San Diego	50	16	12	28
1987–1988	San Diego	51	11	16	27
1988–1989	Los Angeles	46	10	17	29
1989–1990	St. Louis	52	17	18	35
1990–1991	St. Louis	47	15	23	38
1991–1992	St. Louis	37	9	19	28
	TOTALS	434	111	131	242

Fernando Clavijo's NASL Career Statistics

YEAR	TEAM	G	GLS	ASST	PTS
1983	Golden Bay	21	0	1	1
1984	Golden Bay	19	1	1	3
	TOTALS	40	1	2	4

Fernando Clavijo's U.S. National Team Statistics

YEAR	G	MIN	GLS	ASST	PTS	W–L–T
1990	1	90	0	0	0	0–0–1
1991	14	1,195	0	0	0	7–4–3
1992	15	1,160	0	1	1	4–8–3
1993	23	2,029	0	0	0	6–8–9
1994	8	591	0	0	0	2–4–2
Totals	61	5,332	0	1	1	19–24–18

Source: National Soccer Hall of Fame and Museum

Cleghorn, Sprague Horace (born: March 11, 1890 in Montreal, Quebec, Canada; died: July 12, 1956 in Montreal, Quebec, Canada); inducted into the Hockey Hall of Fame in 1958 as a player; Position: Forward-Defenseman; among league leaders in penalty minutes in nine of the NHL's first 10 seasons; won three Stanley Cup championships.

Cleghorn made his professional debut with the Renfrew (Ontario) Millionaires of the National Hockey Association in the 1910–1911 season, and would go on to play professionally for 17 years, until 1928. His aggressive playing style eventually labeled him as one of the dirtiest players in the game, and he ranked among league leaders in penalty minutes for nine of the first ten seasons of the NHL's history.

While attending Westmount Academy (Montreal), from 1906 to 1909, he played with several amateur teams in the city before joining the New York Wanderers of the United State Amateur Hockey Association for the 1909–1910 season. After one season, he played for the Montreal Wanderers of the NHA until 1917, and one year with the Toronto Arenas, before joining the National Hockey League's Ottawa Senators in 1918, where he helped the team win back-to-back Stanley Cup titles in 1920 and 1921.

After the 1921 championship win, Cleghorn served as team captain for the Montreal Canadiens; stayed with the team until 1925; and helped the franchise win the 1924 Stanley Cup (his third). He joined the Boston Bruins in 1925 and stayed with the team until retiring in 1928.

Leaving the game as a player, he managed in the Can-Am League and the International-American Hockey League (later renamed the American Hockey League), and served as a coach in his only NHL season (1931–1932), leading the Montreal Maroons to the Stanley Cup semifinals.

In 1998, forty years after being inducted into the Hockey Hall of Fame, Cleghorn was ranked number 88 on *The Hockey News*' list of the 100 Greatest Hockey Players.

Sprague Cleghorn's Career Statistics

			REGULAR SEASON					PLAYOFFS				
SEASON	TEAM	LEAGUE	GP	G	A	TP	PIM	GP	G	A	TP	PIM
1908–1909	Montreal Canadian Rubber	MCHL	3	1	0	1	10					

			REGULAR SEASON					PLAYOFFS				
SEASON	**TEAM**	**LEAGUE**	**GP**	**G**	**A**	**TP**	**PIM**	**GP**	**G**	**A**	**TP**	**PIM**
1909–1910	New York Wanderers	USAHA	8	7	0	7						
1910–1911	Renfrew Hockey Club	NHA	12	5	0	5	27					
1911–1912	Montreal Wanderers	NHA	18	9	0	9	40					
1911–1912	NHA All-Stars	Exhibition.	3	1	0	1	10					
1912–1913	Montreal Wanderers	NHA	19	12	0	12	46					
1913–1914	Montreal Wanderers	NHA	20	12	8	20	17					
1914–1915	Montreal Wanderers	NHA	19	21	12	33	51	2	0	0	0	17
1915–1916	Montreal Wanderers	NHA	8	9	4	13	22					
1916–1917	Montreal Wanderers	NHA	19	16	9	25	62					
1918–1919	Ottawa Senators	NHL	18	7	6	13	27	5	2	1	3	9
1919–1920	Ottawa Senators	NHL	21	16	5	21	85					
1919–1920	Ottawa Senators	St-Cup						5	0	1	1	4
1920–1921	Toronto St. Pats	NHL	13	3	5	8	31	1	0	0	0	0
1920–1921	Ottawa Senators	St-Cup						5	1	2	3	38
1921–1922	Montreal Canadiens	NHL	24	17	9	26	80					
1922–1923	Montreal Canadiens	NHL	24	9	8	17	34	1	0	0	0	7
1923–1924	Montreal Canadiens	NHL	23	8	4	12	45	2	0	0	0	0
1923–1924	Montreal Canadiens	St-Cup						4	2	1	3	2
1924–1925	Montreal Canadiens	NHL	27	8	10	18	89	2	1	2	3	2
1924–1925	Montreal Canadiens	St-Cup						4	0	0	0	2
1925–1926	Boston Bruins	NHL	28	6	5	11	49					
1926–1927	Boston Bruins	NHL	44	7	1	8	84	8	1	0	1	8
1927–1928	Boston Bruins	NHL	37	2	2	4	14	2	0	0	0	0
1928–1929	Newark Bulldogs	Can-Am	3	0	0	0	0					
1929–1930	Providence Reds	Can-Am										
	NHL TOTALS		259	83	55	138	538	21	4	3	7	26

Sources: Hockey Hall of Fame; Hockey-Reference.com

Clemente, Roberto Walker (born: Roberto Clemente Walker on August 18, 1934 in Carolina, Puerto Rico; died: December 31, 1972 in the Caribbean); inducted into the National Baseball Hall of Fame and Museum in 1973 as a player; Position: Right Field; Bats: Right; Throws: Right; Uniform: #21; accumulated his 3,000th hit in his last regular-season at-bat; only player to have ever scored a walk-off inside-the-park grand slam.

Making his major league debut on April 17, 1955, Clemente enjoyed a great career, but his life ended prematurely on New Year's Eve 1972 in a plane crash in the Caribbean while he was helping deliver relief supplies to Nicaraguan earthquake victims. His body was never recovered. He played his entire 18-year career with the Pittsburgh Pirates (1955–1972); appeared in two World Series (winning in 1960 and 1971); was a 12-time All-Star (1960–1967, 1969–1972); National League Most Valuable Player in 1966; a 12-time Gold Glove winner (1961–1972); won four batting titles (1961, 1964–1965, 1967); and accumulated exactly 3,000 hits.

The youngest of four children and a natural athlete as a young boy, Clemente played baseball for the Juncos Double A Club and the Santurce Crabbers in the Puerto Rican Winter League, before signing with the Brooklyn Dodgers. He played for the team's AAA affiliate, the Montreal Royals of the International League, until the Pittsburgh Pirates made him the number one pick of the 1954 Draft, and the 5'11", 175-pound Clemente entered the major leagues in 1955.

His life ended months after he had collected his 3,000th major league hit in his last regular-season at-bat (September 30, 1972). The 300-acre sports complex, Roberto Clemente Sports City, is located in Carolina, Puerto Rico and includes a 12-foot statue of Clemente at its entrance.

Although Clemente often stated that he was hurt and could not play, he appeared in 140 or more games for eight straight seasons (1960–1967). Due to the nature of his death while involved in humanitarian efforts, the National Baseball Hall of Fame and Museum waived the five-year mandatory waiting period for hall of fame eligibility and inducted him in 1973.

On October 12, 1963, Clemente appeared in the first and last Hispanic-American Major League All-Star Game, won by the National League 5–2 at the Polo Grounds (New York). On September 1, 1971, the Pirates started what is believed to be the first all-black lineup (including several Latinos) in major league history, in a 10–7 win over the Philadelphia Phillies, which included Rennie Stennett at second base, Gene Clines in center field, Roberto Clemente in right field, Willie Stargell in left field, Manny Sanguillen at catcher, Dave Cash at third base, Al Oliver at first base, Jackie Hernandez at shortstop, and Dock Ellis as the team's pitcher. On October 14, 1971, Clemente hit safely in his 12th straight World Series game. The game is noteworthy for being the last weekday day game ever played in the World Series.

Clemente's uniform number was retired in April 1973, and in July 1994, the Pirates unveiled a statue of him outside Three Rivers Stadium. In October 2001, Arizona pitcher Curt Schilling was selected the first winner of the newly created annual Roberto Clemente Award for his contributions to the game both on and off the field.

Clemente was awarded the Congressional Gold Medal in 1973 and the Presidential Medal of Freedom in 2002; in 2003, he was inducted into the U.S. Marine Corps Sports Hall of Fame; and on October 26, 2005, he was named a member of Major League Baseball's Latino Legends Team.

In August 1984, the United States Postal Service issued a stamp honoring Clemente; in 1999, he ranked number 20 on *The Sporting News*' list of the 100 Greatest Baseball Players, the highest-ranked Latino player; and later that year, he was nominated as a finalist for the Major League Baseball All-Century Team. Clemente shares the record for most Gold Glove Awards among outfielders (12) with Willie Mays; is the only player to have ever scored a walk-off inside-the-park grand slam (July 25, 1956 in a 9–8 win over the Chicago Cubs); and is one of four players to have won 10 or more Gold Gloves while accumulating a lifetime batting average of .300 or better.

Roberto Clemente's Career Statistics

YEAR	TEAM	G	AB	R	H	2B	3B	HR	RBI	BB	SO	SB	AVG	SLG
1955	Pittsburgh	124	474	48	121	23	11	5	47	18	60	2	.255	.382
1956	Pittsburgh	147	543	66	169	30	7	7	60	13	58	6	.311	.431
1957	Pittsburgh	111	451	42	114	17	7	4	30	23	45	0	.253	.348
1958	Pittsburgh	140	519	69	150	24	10	6	50	31	41	8	.289	.408
1959	Pittsburgh	105	432	60	128	17	7	4	50	15	51	2	.296	.396
1960	Pittsburgh	144	570	89	179	22	6	16	94	39	72	4	.314	.458
1961	Pittsburgh	146	572	100	201	30	10	23	89	35	59	4	.351	.559
1962	Pittsburgh	144	538	95	168	28	9	10	74	35	73	6	.312	.454
1963	Pittsburgh	152	600	77	192	23	8	17	76	31	64	12	.320	.470
1964	Pittsburgh	155	622	95	211	40	7	12	87	51	87	5	.339	.484
1965	Pittsburgh	152	589	91	194	21	14	10	65	43	78	8	.329	.463
1966	Pittsburgh	154	638	105	202	31	11	29	119	46	109	7	.317	.536
1967	Pittsburgh	147	585	103	209	26	10	23	110	41	103	9	.357	.554
1968	Pittsburgh	132	502	74	146	18	12	18	57	51	77	2	.291	.482
1969	Pittsburgh	138	507	87	175	20	12	19	91	56	73	4	.345	.544
1970	Pittsburgh	108	412	65	145	22	10	14	60	38	66	3	.352	.556
1971	Pittsburgh	132	522	82	178	29	8	13	86	26	65	1	.341	.502
1972	Pittsburgh	102	378	68	118	19	7	10	60	29	49	0	.312	.479
	TOTALS	2,433	9,454	1,416	3,000	440	166	240	1,305	621	1,230	83	.317	.475

Sources: Baseball-Reference.com; *Clemente: The Passion and Grace of Baseball's Last Hero* (David Maraniss); National Baseball Hall of Fame and Museum

Cobb, Tyrus Raymond "Ty" (born: December 18, 1886 in Narrows, Georgia; died: July 17, 1961 in Atlanta, Georgia); inducted into the National Baseball Hall of Fame and Museum in 1936 as a player; Position: Center Field; Bats: Left; Throws: Right; his .367 lifetime batting average is the highest in Major League Baseball history; leading vote-getter (222) as part of the first class to be inducted into the then-new National Baseball Hall of Fame; only player in the 20th century to lead the league in home runs without hitting one out of the park (1909); only player ever to win a quadruple crown (1909); youngest player (age 34) in Major League Baseball history to accumulate 3,000 hits.

Simultaneously regarded as one of the most hated men in the game and one of Major League Baseball's greatest players, Cobb made his American League debut on August 30, 1905 and played 24 seasons with the Detroit Tigers (1905–1926) and the Philadelphia Athletics (1927–1928); appeared in three World Series, losing them all (1907–1909); and was named the American League Most Valuable Player in 1911.

He retired with a .367 lifetime batting average (the highest in MLB history); 4,191 hits (second only to Pete Rose); 12 batting titles; 23 straight seasons in which he hit over .300; and three .400 seasons. In 1907, he became the youngest player ever to win a batting title, his first of nine in a row, and he won a Triple Crown in 1909. The 6'1", 175-pound center fielder had 30 outfield assists in 1907; led the league in assists in 1908; and finished his career second all-time in assists and double plays among outfielders.

Nicknamed "The Georgia Peach," on May 5, 1925 (in a 14–8 win over the St. Louis Browns), Cobb compiled 16 total bases (three home runs, a double, and two singles), a then single-game American League record. His offensive accomplishments were, at times, almost overshadowed by his fierce competitiveness, mean spirit, and prejudice. He was known to sharpen his spikes in plain view of opposing players and was feared for his "spikes up" slides into the bases.

Additionally, Cobb was not impressed with one of the game's icons, Babe Ruth. He personally did not like the Yankee great, thought he was not a very good ballplayer, and was not impressed with his home run ability, feeling that homers were an overrated part of the game. In an attempt to embarrass Ruth, in the May 5, 1925 game where he compiled 16 total bases, Cobb copied Ruth's batting style and proceeded to hit three home runs. To emphasize his point, the next day Cobb repeated the style and hit two more home runs before reverting to his natural batting stance. While he may have proven his point, Cobb's actions did not alter the status of either player: Ruth was still adored and Cobb was still hated.

In 1911, Cobb set an American League record by hitting in 41 straight games, and won another batting title with an average of .420 to runner-up Joe Jackson's .408. In 1912, one of his recurring fights led to the game's first strike. In a May 15 contest against the New York Highlanders, Cobb was angered at the constant fan insults and reacted by going into the stands and beating up one of the fans sitting behind the Tigers' dugout. When Cobb was suspended, to the surprise of almost everyone, his teammates (who did not care for Cobb either) rallied behind him and said that they would not play until Cobb was reinstated. When the players did not play the next day in Philadelphia, team owner Frank Navin was forced to use amateur players and suffered an embarrassing 24–2 loss. Cobb then persuaded his teammates to end their strike and he was reinstated shortly thereafter.

While one of the game's great all-time hitters, he was also an outstanding base runner and one of baseball's great base stealers until surpassed 50 years later by the St. Louis Cardinals' Lou Brock.

Fans and players were caught off guard when both Cobb and Indians player-manager Tris Speaker retired after the 1926 season for no apparent reason. It was made public on the day after Christmas that both men had been accused by player Dutch Leonard of fixing a game on September 24, 1919. Leonard claimed that the two men agreed to let Detroit win the game to ensure that the Tigers would finish the season in third place (which, in those days, meant the players would be awarded bonus money). Although league president Ban Johnson forced the two stars to quit, Commissioner Kenesaw Mountain Landis eventually cleared and reinstated both players. Cobb returned to the game with the Philadelphia Athletics for two seasons before retiring in 1928.

Unlike many players of his time, Cobb had been smart with his money and had invested wisely (he also owned a large amount of Coca-Cola stock), making him one of the richest men in the game. Even though he was undoubtedly one of the most hated men ever to play the game, his skills were too strong for anyone to ignore, and he received 222 of a possible 226 votes (seven more than Babe Ruth and Honus Wagner) to become the leading vote-getter as part of the first class to be inducted into the newly created National Baseball Hall of Fame and Museum.

On April 26, 1904, Cobb made his professional debut for the Augusta Tourists (South Atlantic League). Barely 16 months later, on August 9, 1905, mistaking her husband for a burglar (as the story goes), Cobb's mother shot and killed him. Three short weeks later, in his major league debut on August 30, 1905, Cobb hit a double in his first at-bat. His first home run (September 23, 1905) was an inside-the-park hit off the Washington Senators' Cy Falkenberg.

In a doubleheader on July 15, 1909, Cobb hit two inside-the-park home runs (one in each game) to lead the Tigers in a sweep of the Boston Nationals, 9–5 and 7–0. On July 22, 1909, for the first of four times in his career, Cobb stole second base, third base, and home in the same inning (in the seventh inning against Boston Red Sox pitcher Harry Wolter). On September 13, 1909, he clinched the American League home run title with his ninth, an inside-the-park hit against the St. Louis Browns. All of his home runs that season were of the inside-the-park variety, and he is the only player in the 20th century to lead the league in home runs without hitting one out of the park. In 1909, Cobb won the Triple Crown (leading the league in home runs, runs batted in, and batting average), and his 76 stolen bases makes him the only player ever to win a quadruple crown.

Cobb's single against the Cleveland Naps on June 20, 1911 gave him a consecutive hitting streak of 30 games, setting a new American League record. He would go on to hit in 40 straight games before the streak would end on July 4, 1911 against the Chicago White Sox. His American League record would stand until George Sisler of the St. Louis Browns hit in 41 straight games in 1922. After the 1911 season, Cobb was the unanimous choice for American League Most Valuable Player in the first year that the award was determined by a formal voting system.

In July 1912, Cobb set the American League and tied the Major League record for most hits in a month with 67. He repeated the feat in July 1922 and was the league record holder until August 1923 when Tris Speaker of the Indians also collected 67 hits. This record still stands today. In the 1915 season, Cobb stole 96 bases, a record that would stand until 1962 when Maury Wills of the Los Angeles Dodgers stole 104. At age 34, Cobb was the youngest player ever to accumulate 3,000 hits (a single off Boston Red Sox pitcher Elmer Myers on August 19, 1921).

Ty Cobb's Career Statistics

YEAR	TEAM	G	AB	R	H	2B	3B	HR	RBI	BB	SO	SB	AVG	SLG
1905	Detroit	41	150	19	36	6	0	1	15	10		2	.240	.300
1906	Detroit	98	350	45	112	13	7	1	34	19		23	.320	.406
1907	Detroit	150	605	97	212	29	15	5	119	24		49	.350	.473
1908	Detroit	150	581	88	188	36	20	4	108	34		39	.324	.475
1909	Detroit	156	573	116	216	33	10	9	107	48		76	.377	.517
1910	Detroit	140	509	106	196	36	13	8	91	64		65	.385	.554
1911	Detroit	146	591	147	248	47	24	8	127	44		83	.420	.621
1912	Detroit	140	553	119	227	30	23	7	83	43		61	.410	.586
1913	Detroit	122	428	70	167	18	16	4	67	58	31	52	.390	.535
1914	Detroit	97	345	69	127	22	11	2	57	57	22	35	.368	.513
1915	Detroit	156	563	144	208	31	13	3	99	118	43	96	.369	.487
1916	Detroit	145	542	113	201	31	10	5	68	78	39	68	.371	.493
1917	Detroit	152	588	107	225	44	23	6	102	61	34	55	.383	.566
1918	Detroit	111	421	83	161	19	14	3	64	41	21	34	.382	.515
1919	Detroit	124	497	92	191	36	13	1	70	38	22	28	.384	.515
1920	Detroit	112	428	86	143	28	8	2	63	58	28	14	.334	.451
1921	Detroit	128	507	124	197	37	16	12	101	56	19	22	.389	.596
1922	Detroit	137	526	99	211	42	16	4	99	55	24	9	.401	.565
1923	Detroit	145	556	103	189	40	7	6	88	66	14	9	.340	.469
1924	Detroit	155	625	115	211	38	10	4	78	85	18	23	.338	.450
1925	Detroit	121	415	97	157	31	12	12	102	65	12	13	.378	.598
1926	Detroit	79	233	48	79	18	5	4	62	26	2	9	.339	.511
1927	Philadelphia	133	490	104	175	32	7	5	93	67	12	22	.357	.482
1928	Philadelphia	95	353	54	114	27	4	1	40	34	16	5	.323	.431
	TOTALS	3,033	11,429	2,245	4,191	724	297	117	1,937	1,249	357	892	.367	.513

Sources: Baseball-Reference.com; *Cobb* (Al Stump); National Baseball Hall of Fame and Museum

Cochrane, Gordon Stanley "Mickey" (born: April 6, 1903 in Bridgewater, Massachusetts; died: June 28, 1962 in Lake Forest, Illinois); inducted into the National Baseball Hall of Fame and Museum in 1947 as a player; Position: Catcher; Bats: Left; Throws: Right; Uniform: #2; appeared in five World Series; was a two-time American League Most Valuable Player.

Making his major league debut on April 14, 1925, Cochrane enjoyed a 13-year American League career with the Philadelphia Athletics (1925–1933) and the Detroit Tigers (1934–1937), where he was a player-manager from 1934 until 1937 and the team's manager in 1938. He appeared in five World Series (winning three times [1929–1930, 1935] and losing twice [1931, 1934]); played on two All-Star Teams (1934–1935); and was the American League Most Valuable Player twice (1928, 1934).

One of the game's best catchers in the 1920s and 1930s, Cochrane was the leader of the Athletics' World Series teams, and as a player-manager for the Tigers, he led Detroit to two World Series. Cochrane's last major league at-bat was a home-run, and his career ended prematurely when he was beaned in 1937. New York Yankees hall of famer Mickey Mantle was named after Cochrane.

After graduating from Boston University (Massachusetts) as a five-sport star, Cochrane joined the Athletics in 1925 and quickly established himself as one of the game's best offensive catchers. His temper and willingness to destroy locker rooms after losses, made it appear natural that he would become close friends with the legendary Ty Cobb, who shared these same traits. Cobb provided financial support to Cochrane after his playing career, and the catcher was one of only two players (along with Ray Schalk) who attended Cobb's funeral.

The 5'11", 180-pound Cochrane was sold to the Tigers when Philadelphia owner Connie Mack began reducing team payroll. Cochrane led Detroit to back-to-back World Series appearances in 1934 and 1935, and helped the franchise win its first championship in 1935.

At the relatively young age of 34, Cochrane's career came to a sudden end when he was beaned by New York Yankees pitcher Bump Hadley on May 25, 1937. He retired as a player but continued as manager with the Tigers, compiling a .582 (348–250) winning percentage.

Although he had suffered a head injury, Cochrane was able to serve in the United States Navy during World War II, where he managed the Great Lakes Naval Academy (Illinois) baseball team to 33 consecutive wins at one point. His team included such major league stars as Johnny Mize, Schoolboy Rowe, and Virgil Trucks.

When the Athletics left Philadelphia in 1954 without retiring Cochrane's uniform number, the Philadelphia Phillies honored Cochrane by adding him to the Philadelphia Baseball Wall of Fame at Veterans Stadium.

In 1999, he ranked number 65 on *The Sporting News*' list of the 100 Greatest Baseball Players, and was a nominee for the Major League Baseball All-Century Team. In his major league debut, Cochrane caught pitcher Lefty Grove, who was also making his major league debut. As of this writing, this is the only time that two future hall of famers debuted as a battery.

Five weeks into his major league career, Cochrane hit three home runs in one game (May 21, 1925) and would eventually hit for the cycle twice in his career (July 22, 1932 and August 2, 1933). He hit .300 or better nine times and scored 100 or more runs four times.

Mickey Cochrane's Career Statistics

YEAR	TEAM	G	AB	R	H	2B	3B	HR	RBI	BB	SO	SB	AVG	SLG
1925	Philadelphia	134	420	69	139	21	5	6	55	44	19	7	.331	.448
1926	Philadelphia	120	370	50	101	8	9	8	47	56	15	5	.273	.408
1927	Philadelphia	126	432	80	146	20	6	12	80	50	7	9	.338	.495
1928	Philadelphia	131	468	92	137	26	12	10	57	76	25	7	.293	.464
1929	Philadelphia	135	514	113	170	37	8	7	95	69	8	7	.331	.475
1930	Philadelphia	130	487	110	174	42	5	10	85	55	18	5	.357	.526
1931	Philadelphia	122	459	87	160	31	6	17	89	56	21	2	.349	.553
1932	Philadelphia	139	518	118	152	35	4	23	112	100	22	0	.293	.510
1933	Philadelphia	130	429	104	138	30	4	15	60	106	22	8	.322	.515
1934	Detroit	129	437	74	140	32	1	2	76	78	26	8	.320	.412
1935	Detroit	115	411	93	131	33	3	5	47	96	15	5	.319	.450
1936	Detroit	44	126	24	34	8	0	2	17	46	15	1	.270	.381
1937	Detroit	27	98	27	30	10	1	2	12	25	4	0	.306	.490
	TOTALS	1,482	5,169	1,041	1,652	333	64	119	832	857	217	64	.320	.478

Mickey Cochrane's Managerial Record (Detroit Tigers)

YEAR	W	L	WIN%	FINISH
1934	101	53	.656	First
1935	93	58	.616	First (won World Series)
1936	65	55	.542	Second
1937	42	33	.560	Second
1938	47	51	.480	Fourth
TOTALS	348	250	.582	

Sources: Baseball-Reference.com; National Baseball Hall of Fame and Museum

Coffey, Paul Douglas (born: June 1, 1961 in Weston, Ontario, Canada); inducted into the Hockey Hall of Fame in 2004 as a player; Position: Defenseman; Uniform: #7; helped lead the Edmonton Oilers and the Pittsburgh Penguins to Stanley Cup titles; retired as the highest scoring defenseman in NHL playoff history.

A first-round pick (sixth overall selection) in the 1979 NHL Draft by the Edmonton Oilers, Coffey played 21 National Hockey League seasons (1980–2001) for the Edmonton Oilers (1980–1987), Pittsburgh Penguins (1987–1992), Los Angeles Kings (1992–1993), Detroit Red Wings (1992–1996), Hartford Whalers (1996–1997), Philadelphia Flyers (1996–1998), Chicago Black Hawks (1998), Carolina Hurricanes (1998–2000), and the Boston Bruins (2000).

After playing junior level hockey for three seasons, Coffey joined the NHL and, in his sophomore season, led all defensemen with 89 points and was chosen to the NHL's Second All-Star Team. In the 1983–1984 season, he scored 126 points, second in the league only to teammate Wayne Gretzky, and helped the team win its first Stanley Cup championship (the first of three he would win with the team). When the team repeated as Stanley Cup champions the next season, Coffey won the James Norris Memorial Trophy as the NHL's best defenseman (an award he would win again in 1986); was selected to the First All-Star Team; and finished third in league scoring with 138 points (48 goals and 90 assists).

He was traded to the Pittsburgh Penguins before the 1987–1988 season; scored more than 100 points in back-to-back seasons (1989–1990); and helped the franchise win its first Stanley Cup title in 1991. After playing briefly with the Los Angeles Kings (1992–1993), the much-traveled, 6', 200-pound Coffey was traded to the Detroit Red Wings, where he won his second Norris Trophy in 1995.

He stayed with the Red Wings until October 1996 when he was traded to the Hartford Whalers, before finishing the season with the Philadelphia Flyers. In the summer of 1998, Coffey was traded to the Chicago Black Hawks, but after only 10 games, he was traded to the Carolina Hurricanes, where he stayed until the end of the 2000 season. He then was traded to the Boston Bruins for the 2000–2001 season, but retired after playing only 18 games.

Coffey was named to either the First or Second All-Star Team eight times (1982–1986, 1989–1990, 1995); won the Norris Trophy three times (1985–1986, 1995); appeared in 14 NHL All-Star Games (1982–1986, 1988–1994, 1996–1997); and represented Canada at four Canada/World Cup tournaments. He retired as the highest scoring defenseman in NHL playoff history; in 2005, the Oilers retired his uniform number 7; and in 1998, he was ranked number 28 on *The Hockey News*' list of the 100 Greatest Hockey Players.

Some of his NHL records include most goals in one season by a defenseman (48, 1985–1986); longest point-scoring streak by a defenseman (28 games, 1985–1986); most goals by a defenseman in one playoff year (12, 1985); most assists by a defenseman in one playoff year (25, 1985); and most points by a defenseman in one playoff year (37, 1985).

Paul Coffey's Career Statistics

			REGULAR SEASON					PLAYOFFS				
SEASON	TEAM	LEAGUE	GP	G	A	TP	PIM	GP	G	A	TP	PIM
1977–1978	North York Rangers	OPJHL	50	14	33	47	64					
1977–1978	Kingston Canadians	OMJHL	8	2	2	4	11	5	0	0	0	0
1978–1979	Sault Ste. Marie Greyhounds	OMJHL	68	17	72	89	103					
1979–1980	Sault Ste. Marie Greyhounds	OMJHL	23	10	21	31	63					
1979–1980	Kitchener Rangers	OMJHL	52	19	52	71	130					
1980–1981	Edmonton Oilers	NHL	74	9	23	32	130	9	4	3	7	22
1981–1982	Edmonton Oilers	NHL	80	29	60	89	106	5	1	1	2	6
1982–1983	Edmonton Oilers	NHL	80	29	67	96	87	16	7	7	14	14
1983–1984	Edmonton Oilers	NHL	80	40	86	126	104	19	8	14	22	21
1984–1985	Canada	Can-Cup	8	3	8	11	4					
1984–1985	Edmonton Oilers	NHL	80	37	84	121	97	18	12	25	37	44
1985–1986	Edmonton Oilers	NHL	79	48	90	138	120	10	1	9	10	30
1986–1987	Edmonton Oilers	NHL	59	17	50	67	49	17	3	8	11	30
1987–1988	Canada	Can-Cup	9	2	4	6	0					
1987–1988	Pittsburgh Penguins	NHL	46	15	52	67	93					
1988–1989	Pittsburgh Penguins	NHL	75	30	83	113	195	11	2	13	15	31
1989–1990	Pittsburgh Penguins	NHL	80	29	74	103	95					
1989–1990	Canada	WEC-A	10	1	6	7	10					
1990–1991	Pittsburgh Penguins	NHL	76	24	69	93	128	12	2	9	11	6
1991–1992	Canada	Can-Cup	8	1	6	7	8					
1991–1992	Pittsburgh Penguins	NHL	54	10	54	64	62					
1991–1992	Los Angeles Kings	NHL	10	1	4	5	25	6	4	3	7	2
1992–1993	Los Angeles Kings	NHL	50	8	49	57	50					
1992–1993	Detroit Red Wings	NHL	30	4	26	30	27	7	2	9	11	2
1993–1994	Detroit Red Wings	NHL	80	14	63	77	106	7	1	6	7	8
1994–1995	Detroit Red Wings	NHL	45	14	44	58	72	18	6	12	18	10

SEASON	TEAM	LEAGUE	REGULAR SEASON GP	G	A	TP	PIM	PLAYOFFS GP	G	A	TP	PIM
1995–1996	Detroit Red Wings	NHL	76	14	60	74	90	17	5	9	14	30
1996–1997	Canada	W-Cup	8	0	7	7	12					
1996–1997	Hartford Whalers	NHL	20	3	5	8	18					
1996–1997	Philadelphia Flyers	NHL	37	6	20	26	20	17	1	8	9	6
1997–1998	Philadelphia Flyers	NHL	57	2	27	29	30					
1998–1999	Chicago Black Hawks	NHL	10	0	4	4	0					
1998–1999	Carolina Hurricanes	NHL	44	2	8	10	28	5	0	1	1	2
1999–2000	Carolina Hurricanes	NHL	69	11	29	40	40					
2000–2001	Boston Bruins	NHL	18	0	4	4	30					
	NHL TOTALS		1,409	396	1,135	1,531	1,802	194	59	137	196	264

Sources: Hockey Hall of Fame; Hockey-Reference.com

Colangelo, Jerry (born: November 20, 1939 in Chicago Heights, Illinois); inducted into the Naismith Memorial Basketball Hall of Fame in 2004 as a contributor; played professional basketball for one season and later led the NBA's Phoenix Suns to the team's first playoff appearance.

Colangelo's basketball career began at Bloom Township High School (Chicago Heights, Illinois), where he played from 1954 to 1957; he was selected First Team All-State in 1957; and led the school to two straight State Championship appearances. After high school, he attended the University of Kansas (Lawrence) from 1957 to 1958, before moving on to, and graduating from, the University of Illinois (Urbana-Champaign, 1959–1962). While in college, he was named to the All Big Ten Conference team twice (1961–1962).

After college, Colangelo played professional basketball for Michigan of the North American Basketball League from 1962 to 1963, before joining the National Basketball Association's Phoenix Suns in 1968 as the expansion team's first general manager, a job he would hold until 1987. He coached the team twice (1969–1970, 1972–1973); compiled an overall 59–60 record; and led the Suns to the franchise's first playoff appearance in 1970. In 1987, he was promoted to president and chief executive officer of the team, and in 1999, he was named the Suns' CEO and Chairman, a position he still holds as of this writing. Colangelo also serves as president and CEO of the Women's National Basketball Association's Phoenix Mercury, and has served on the NBA's Board of Governors since 1968.

He has been named *The Sporting News* NBA Executive of the Year four times (1976, 1981, 1989, 1993) and was inducted into the Illinois Basketball Hall of Fame in 1995.

In addition to his basketball-related responsibilities, Colangelo also served as chairman and CEO of Major League Baseball's Arizona Diamondbacks from 1995 to 2004 (leading the team to a World Series title in 2001 over the New York Yankees); was a part-owner of the Arizona Rattlers of the Arena Football League; and played a major role in relocating the National Hockey League's Winnipeg Jets to Phoenix as the Phoenix Coyotes.

In 2005, Colangelo was named managing director of the USA Basketball Men's Senior National Team, and he has been named by the *Arizona Republic* as the Most Influential Sports Figure in the state of Arizona for the 20th century.

Source: Naismith Memorial Basketball Hall of Fame

Coll, John "Jock" (born: 1893 in Downpatrick, Northern Ireland; died: Glasgow, Scotland); inducted into the National Soccer Hall of Fame and Museum in 1986 as a builder; a trainer with the 1930 U.S. World Cup team.

At age eight, Coll and his parents left Ireland and moved to Glasgow, where he grew up. His first soccer job came in 1912 when he became a trainer for the Springburn White Rose soccer team. He then became a trainer for the Townhead Benburbs, and in 1915, he moved to the Parkhead team, one of the leading junior clubs in Scotland.

In addition to soccer, Coll served as the trainer for the Maryhill Harriers relay team; the Irish athletic team that competed against England and Scotland in Glasgow in 1922; and served as the trainer of the United Scottish Amateur Boxing Association.

In December 1922, Coll came to the United States as a trainer for the New York Football Club in the American Soccer League, before joining the Scullin Steel team of St. Louis that went to the U.S. Open Cup in 1923. The following season, he worked with the New York Giants of the ASL and then the Chicago Bricklayers, before settling with the Brooklyn Wanderers (of the ASL) for seven seasons. Coll was also the trainer of the 1930 U.S. World Cup team.

Source: National Soccer Hall of Fame and Museum

Collins, Edward Throwbridge, Sr. "Eddie" (born: May 2, 1887 in Millerton, New York; died: March 25, 1951 in Boston, Massachusetts); inducted into the National Baseball Hall of Fame and Museum in 1939 as a player; Position: Second Base; Bats: Left; Throws: Right; only American League player to steal six bases in a single game, a feat he accomplished twice in a span of less than two weeks (September 11 and 22, 1912).

Making his major league debut on September 17, 1906, Collins played his 25-year American League career (a 20th century record for a position player) with the Philadelphia Athletics (1906–1914, 1927–1930) and the Chicago White Sox (1915–1926), as well as serving as the White Sox player-manager from 1924 to 1926 (compiling a 160–147, .521 record). He appeared in six World Series, winning four times (1910–1911, 1913, 1917) and losing twice (1914, 1919).

The 5'9", 175-pound Collins hit over .340 ten times in his career, and is a member of the 3,000-hit club. Although Collins never won a batting title, he led the American League in stolen bases four times and in runs scored three consecutive seasons (1912–1914).

He was the captain of the Columbia University (New York, New York) baseball team from 1904 to 1906, but was barred from playing his senior year because he had used the name "Eddie Sullivan" in order to play professional baseball with the Philadelphia Athletics. Despite his ineligibility to play, Collins was named Columbia's coach; stayed at the university to earn his degree; and was one of the charter members (2006) of the Columbia Athletics Hall of Fame.

In 1918, Collins joined the U.S. Marines during World War I, but was back in the major leagues the next season on another pennant-winning team, the infamous 1919 Chicago "Black Sox." As one of the so-called "Clean Sox," although he never forgave the eight players who had conspired to throw the World Series, he always insisted that the 1919 team was the greatest he had ever played on.

When Tom Yawkey purchased the Boston Red Sox in 1933, he brought in Collins, a long-time friend, as the team's part-owner and general manager. Collins began rebuilding a franchise that had never fully recovered from the sale of the team's stars to the New York Yankees a decade earlier by former owner Harry Frazee.

On August 4, 1909, umpire Tim Hurst caused a riot within the stadium by spitting in the face of Collins, who had questioned a call. Under police guard, Hurst was ushered off the field and was later banned from the game. On May 6, 1911, Collins hit the first-ever home run at Griffith Stadium (home of the Washington Nationals), although Philadelphia would go on to lose the game 7–6. Collins got his 3,000th hit in a 12–7 win over the Detroit Tigers on June 3, 1925; in 1999, he was ranked number 24 on *The Sporting News*' list of the 100 Greatest Baseball Players; and he was a nominee for the Major League Baseball All-Century Team.

Collins is ranked seventh all-time in career stolen bases (744); is the all-time leader in sacrifice hits (512); led the major leagues in stolen bases (1910); led the major leagues in runs scored three straight seasons (1912–1914); was the American League Most Valuable Player in 1914; and led the American League in stolen bases four times (1910, 1919, 1923–1924).

Eddie Collins' Career Statistics

YEAR	TEAM	G	AB	R	H	2B	3B	HR	RBI	BB	SO	SB	AVG	SLG
1906	Philadelphia	6	17	1	4	0	0	0	0	0		1	.235	.235
1907	Philadelphia	14	23	0	6	0	1	0	2	0		0	.261	.348
1908	Philadelphia	102	330	39	90	18	7	1	40	16		8	.273	.379
1909	Philadelphia	153	572	104	198	30	10	3	56	62		67	.346	.449
1910	Philadelphia	153	581	81	188	16	15	3	81	49		81	.324	.418
1911	Philadelphia	132	493	92	180	22	13	3	73	62		38	.365	.481
1912	Philadelphia	153	543	137	189	25	11	0	64	101		63	.348	.435
1913	Philadelphia	148	534	125	184	23	13	3	73	85	37	55	.345	.453
1914	Philadelphia	152	526	122	181	23	14	2	85	97	31	58	.344	.452
1915	Chicago	155	521	118	173	22	10	4	77	119	27	46	.332	.436
1916	Chicago	155	545	87	168	14	17	0	52	86	36	40	.308	.396
1917	Chicago	156	564	91	163	18	12	0	67	89	16	53	.289	.363
1918	Chicago	97	330	51	91	8	2	2	30	73	13	22	.276	.330
1919	Chicago	140	518	87	165	19	7	4	80	68	27	33	.319	.405
1920	Chicago	153	602	117	224	38	13	3	76	69	19	19	.372	.493
1921	Chicago	139	526	79	177	20	10	2	58	66	11	12	.337	.424
1922	Chicago	154	598	92	194	20	12	1	69	73	16	20	.324	.403

YEAR	TEAM	G	AB	R	H	2B	3B	HR	RBI	BB	SO	SB	AVG	SLG
1923	Chicago	145	505	89	182	22	5	5	67	84	8	47	.360	.453
1924	Chicago	152	556	108	194	27	7	6	86	89	16	42	.349	.455
1925	Chicago	118	425	80	147	26	3	3	80	87	8	19	.346	.442
1926	Chicago	106	375	66	129	32	4	1	62	62	8	13	.344	.459
1927	Philadelphia	95	225	50	76	12	1	1	15	60	9	6	.338	.413
1928	Philadelphia	36	33	3	10	3	0	0	7	4	4	0	.303	.394
1929	Philadelphia	9	7	0	0	0	0	0	0	2	0	0	.000	.000
1930	Philadelphia	3	2	1	1	0	0	0	0	0	0	0	.500	.500
	TOTALS	2,826	9,951	1,820	3,314	438	187	47	1,300	1,503	286	743	.333	.429

Eddie Collins' Managerial Record (Player-Manager with Chicago)

YEAR	W	L	WIN%	FINISH
1924	14	13	.519	Sixth
1925	79	75	.513	Fifth
1926	81	72	.529	Fifth
TOTALS	174	160	.521	

Sources: Baseball-Reference.com; National Baseball Hall of Fame and Museum

Collins, George Matthew (born: 1888 in Rothesay, Bute, Scotland; died: June 30, 1950 in Boston, Massachusetts); inducted into the National Soccer Hall of Fame and Museum in 1951 as a builder; helped create the Amateur Cup; manager of the 1924 U.S. Olympic team.

As a schoolboy, Collins played soccer in Scotland, before moving to the United States in 1907, where he played for the Boston Rovers and Charlestown as a winger and a halfback. He organized the Massachusetts State Association and served as its secretary for nine years. As a delegate to the United States Football Association, he assisted in creating the Amateur Cup competition, but is best known as the manager of the 1924 U.S. Olympic team that was eliminated in the second round at the Paris (France) Olympics. Collins was the third vice-president of the United States Soccer Football Association (1916–1917), and was the soccer writer for the *Boston Globe* from 1914 until his death in Boston at the age of 62.

Source: National Soccer Hall of Fame and Museum

Collins, James Joseph "Jimmy" (born: January 16, 1870 in Buffalo, New York; died: March 6, 1943 in Buffalo, New York); inducted into the National Baseball Hall of Fame and Museum in 1945 as a player by the Veterans Committee; Position: Third Base; Bats: Right; Throws: Right; first player selected to the baseball hall of fame as a third baseman; set the National League single-season record for most chances at third base (601).

Making his major league debut on April 19, 1895, Collins played his 14-year career with the Louisville Colonels (1895), Boston Beaneaters (1895–1900), Boston Pilgrims / Red Sox (1901–1907), and the Philadelphia Athletics (1907–1908). He also managed the Boston Americans / Somersets / Pilgrims from 1901 to 1906. Collins played in, and won, the first "modern" World Series (1903, beating the Pittsburgh Pirates in eight games).

A great defensive player with a good bat, the 5'9", 178-pound Collins led the National League in home runs with 15 in 1898; hit .300 or better five times; was Boston's player-manager for its first six seasons in the newly created American League; and led his club to the first modern World Series title in 1903.

Until Pie Traynor came along in the 1920s, Collins was considered baseball's greatest third baseman. Playing at the turn of the century, when the bunt was a big part of the game, Collins was the best at fielding them. His 601 chances at third base in 1899 remain a National League single-season record. He led his league's third basemen in putouts five times, assists four times, double plays twice, and still stands second all-time in career putouts at his position. He had 100 or more runs batted in twice, and scored 100 or more runs four times.

Jimmy Collins' Career Statistics

YEAR	TEAM	LG	G	AB	R	H	2B	3B	HR	BB	SO	SB	AVG	SLG

YEAR	TEAM	LG	G	AB	R	H	2B	3B	HR	BB	SO	SB	AVG	SLG
1895	Boston	NL	11	38	10	8	3	0	1	4	4	0	.211	.368
1895	Louisville	NL	93	372	65	106	12	8	6	33	16	14	.285	.409
1896	Boston	NL	83	303	52	91	7	6	1	30	12	10	.300	.373
1897	Boston	NL	133	529	102	183	25	11	6	41		16	.346	.469
1898	Boston	NL	152	600	106	202	34	4	15	40		10	.337	.482
1899	Boston	NL	151	597	98	164	26	13	5	40		12	.275	.387
1900	Boston	NL	142	585	104	175	20	6	6	34		23	.299	.385
1901	Boston	AL	138	563	109	185	42	16	6	34		19	.329	.492
1902	Boston	AL	105	425	71	138	21	10	6	24		18	.325	.464
1903	Boston	AL	130	541	87	160	34	17	5	24		23	.296	.449
1904	Boston	AL	156	633	85	168	32	13	3	27		19	.265	.371
1905	Boston	AL	131	508	66	140	25	5	4	37		18	.276	.368
1906	Boston	AL	37	142	17	39	8	4	1	4		1	.275	.408
1907	Boston	AL	41	158	13	46	8	0	0	10		4	.291	.342
1907	Philadelphia	AL	101	364	38	99	22	0	0	24		4	.272	.332
1908	Philadelphia	AL	115	433	34	94	14	3	0	20		5	.217	.263
	TOTALS		1,719	6,791	1,057	1,998	333	116	65	426	32	196	.294	.406

Jimmy Collins' Managerial Record (Player-Manager with Boston)

YEAR	W	L	WIN%	FINISH
1901	79	57	.581	Second
1902	77	60	.562	Third
1903	91	47	.659	First (won the World Series)
1904	95	59	.617	First (won league pennant)
1905	78	74	.513	Fourth
1906	35	79	.307	Eighth
TOTALS	455	376	.548	

Sources: Baseball-Reference.com; National Baseball Hall of Fame and Museum

Collins, Peter (born: Ireland); inducted into the National Soccer Hall of Fame and Museum in 1998 as a builder; served as president of the Long Island Junior Soccer League.

For more than 20 years, Collins served as president of the Long Island Junior Soccer League, during which time he built the league from 300 to more than 1,200 teams. He also helped establish the Long Island Soccer Park; created the Long Island Junior Soccer League's Esteemed Sportsman's Program in 1980 to counter negative influences in sports; and organized Liberty Cup sister tournaments in Russia, Ireland, and Italy. He was elected as a member of the LIJSL Board of Directors in 1974; elected president of the league in 1997; and coached the Long Island Minutemen to the McGuire Cup Finals in 1978.

Source: National Soccer Hall of Fame and Museum

Colombo, Charles Martin (born: July 20, 1920 in St. Louis, Missouri; died: May 7, 1986 in St. Louis, Missouri); inducted into the National Soccer Hall of Fame and Museum in 1976 as a player; Position: Center Half; International Caps (1948–1952): 11; International Goals: 0; won two U.S. Open Cup titles with St. Louis Simpkins-Ford.

Colombo won U.S. Open Cup medals with Simpkins-Ford in 1948 and 1950, and was known to always wear gloves, regardless of the weather. His greatest claim to fame was his rugby-style tackle of Stan Mortensen during the U.S. 1–0 upset win over England in the 1950 FIFA World Cup. He continued to play locally for the Simpkins club, and in later years, Colombo coached the St. Louis Ambrose team. Between 1948 and 1952, he earned 11 international caps as center half for the United States Men's National Soccer Team.

Source: National Soccer Hall of Fame and Museum

Colville, Neil McNeil "Frosty" (born: August 4, 1914 in Edmonton, Alberta, Canada; died: December 26, 1987 in Richmond, British Columbia, Canada); inducted into the Hockey Hall of Fame in 1967 as a player; Position: Center; first player named to NHL All-Star teams both as a forward and a defenseman.

Colville played his entire 12-season National Hockey League career (1935–1949) with the New York Rangers. Prior to joining the NHL, he played three seasons of junior hockey in and around Edmonton before moving into the New York Rangers' organization.

The 5'11", 180-pound Colville helped the Rangers win the Stanley Cup in 1940 (in six games over the Toronto Maple Leafs), before joining the military during World War II in 1942. From 1942 to 1945, he served with the Canadian Armed Forces and was stationed in Ottawa, where he captained the 1942–1943 Allan Cup-winning Ottawa Commandos.

After the war, Colville returned to the NHL, and was the first player named to All-Star teams both as a forward and a defenseman. He retired in 1949; coached at New Haven (Connecticut) for one season; and returned to the NHL as the league's youngest coach (36) of the Rangers, where he served for just over a season. He later served on the NHL's Selection Committee from 1975 until 1984.

Neil Colville's Career Statistics

			REGULAR SEASON					PLAYOFFS				
SEASON	**TEAM**	**LEAGUE**	**GP**	**G**	**A**	**TP**	**PIM**	**GP**	**G**	**A**	**TP**	**PIM**
1929–1930	Edmonton Enarcos	EJrHL	12	1	0	1						
1930–1931	Edmonton Canadians	EJrHL	13	2	0	2	8					
1931–1932	Edmonton Poolers	EJrHL	11	7	3	10		4	2	1	3	0
1931–1932	Edmonton Poolers	M-Cup	5	2	0	2	2					
1932–1933	Edmonton Athletic Club	EJrHL	11				10	3	0	0	0	2
1933–1934	Edmonton Athletic Club	EJrHL	9	14	4	18	13	2	4	2	6	5
1933–1934	Edmonton Athletic Club	M-Cup	12	15	6	21	4					
1934–1935	New York Crescents	EAHL	21	24	11	35	16	8	8	4	12	2
1935–1936	New York Rangers	NHL	1	0	0	0	0					
1935–1936	Philadelphia Ramblers	Can-Am	35	15	16	31	8	4	0	2	2	0
1936–1937	New York Rangers	NHL	45	10	18	28	33	9	3	3	6	0
1937–1938	New York Rangers	NHL	45	17	19	36	11	3	0	1	1	0
1938–1939	New York Rangers	NHL	47	18	19	37	12	7	0	2	2	2
1939–1940	New York Rangers	NHL	48	19	19	38	22	12	2	7	9	18
1940–1941	New York Rangers	NHL	48	14	28	42	28	3	1	1	2	0
1941–1942	New York Rangers	NHL	48	8	25	33	37	6	0	5	5	6
1942–1943	Ottawa Commandos	QSHL	22	12	30	42	32					
1942–1943	Ottawa Army	OCHL	12	11	12	23	6					
1942–1943	Ottawa Commandos	Al-Cup	12	14	14	28	17					
1944–1945	New York Rangers	NHL	4	0	1	1	2					
1944–1945	Winnipeg RCAF	WNDHL	6	5	4	9	4					
1944–1945	Ottawa Commandos	QSHL	2	0	0	0	0					
1944–1945	Quebec Aces	QSHL	5	1	2	3	0	7	2	5	7	4
1944–1945	Quebec Aces	Al-Cup	3	0	3	3	0					
1945–1946	New York Rangers	NHL	49	5	4	9	25					
1946–1947	New York Rangers	NHL	60	4	16	20	16					
1947–1948	New York Rangers	NHL	55	4	12	16	25	6	1	0	1	6
1948–1949	New York Rangers	NHL	14	0	5	5	2					
1948–1949	New Haven Ramblers	AHL	11	0	3	3	8					
1949–1950	New Haven Ramblers	AHL	17	3	4	7	13					
	NHL TOTALS		464	99	166	265	213	46	7	19	26	32

Sources: Hockey Hall of Fame; Hockey-Reference.com

Combs, Earle Bryan (born: May 14, 1899 in Pebworth, Kentucky; died: July 21, 1976 in Richmond, Kentucky); inducted into the National Baseball Hall of Fame and Museum in 1970 as a player by the Veterans Committee; Position: Center Field; Bats: Left; Throws: Right; Uniform: #1; first member of the New York Yankees to wear uniform number

1; was the leadoff hitter in the famous "Murderers' Row" Yankee lineup; won three World Series titles as a player and six as a coach.

Making his major league debut on April 16, 1924, Combs played his entire 12-year American League career with the New York Yankees (1924–1935), and appeared in four World Series (winning in 1927–1928, 1932 and losing in 1926).

Known as the "Kentucky Colonel," the 6', 185-pound Combs led the American League in triples three times and putouts twice, and had his career shortened by two serious collisions, with an outfield wall in St. Louis (July 24, 1934) and with teammate Red Rolfe on August 25, 1935.

He left the Yankees to serve in World War II and, after the war, returned to the major leagues to coach the St. Louis Browns, Boston Red Sox, and the Philadelphia Phillies.

In 1917, Combs attended Eastern State Normal School (now known as Eastern Kentucky University in Richmond) and earned his teaching certificate in 1919. He played on the school's baseball team and with semi-professional teams in the area during the summers.

While playing with the Lexington Reds of the Blue Grass League, Combs signed with the Louisville Colonels of the American Association and in 1922 and 1923, he played for legendary manager Joe McCarthy. After hitting .344 in 1922 and .380 in 1923 for Louisville, the Yankees signed him for the 1924 major league season, and in 1925, he became the team's leadoff hitter in the famed "Murderers Row" Yankee lineup, a position he held for the rest of his career.

In 1927, he led the American League in at-bats (648), hits (231) and triples (23), and scored the winning run in the World Series in New York's four-game sweep of the Pittsburgh Pirates. Combs hit over .300 per season nine times and had 200 or more hits in a season three times.

His career was cut short on July 24, 1934 when he crashed into the Sportsman's Park (St. Louis) outfield wall in a game against the St. Louis Browns while chasing a fly ball. He suffered a fractured skull, broken shoulder, and damaged knee. Combs eventually returned to the Yankees in 1935, but retired after the season when he suffered another injury.

In 1936, he was signed by the Yankees as a coach and helped train his replacement, future hall-of-famer Joe DiMaggio, who coincidentally retired with the exact same lifetime batting average as Combs (.325). Combs continued working as a Yankee coach until 1944 (winning six more World Series titles with the team), before coaching with the St. Louis Browns in 1947, the Boston Red Sox from 1948 to 1952, and the Philadelphia Phillies in 1954.

After retiring from baseball, Combs returned to Kentucky and served as the state's banking commissioner during Governor A.B. Chandler's second administration (1955–1959); served on Eastern Kentucky University's Board of Regents from 1956 until 1975; and was inducted as a charter member into the Eastern Kentucky University Athletics Hall of Fame in 2006.

Earle Combs' Career Statistics

YEAR	TEAM	G	AB	R	H	2B	3B	HR	RBI	BB	SO	SB	AVG	SLG
1924	New York	24	35	10	14	5	0	0	2	4	2	0	.400	.543
1925	New York	150	593	117	203	36	13	3	61	66	43	12	.342	.462
1926	New York	145	606	113	181	31	12	8	55	47	23	8	.299	.429
1927	New York	152	648	137	231	36	23	6	64	63	31	15	.356	.511
1928	New York	149	626	118	194	33	21	7	56	77	33	10	.310	.463
1929	New York	142	586	119	202	33	15	3	65	70	32	11	.345	.468
1930	New York	137	532	129	183	30	22	7	82	74	26	16	.344	.523
1931	New York	138	563	120	179	31	13	5	58	68	34	11	.318	.446
1932	New York	143	591	143	190	32	10	9	65	81	16	3	.321	.455
1933	New York	122	417	86	125	22	16	5	60	47	19	6	.300	.465
1934	New York	63	251	47	80	13	5	2	25	40	9	3	.319	.434
1935	New York	89	298	47	84	7	4	3	35	36	10	1	.282	.362
	TOTALS	1,454	5,746	1,186	1,866	309	154	58	628	673	278	96	.325	.462

Sources: Baseball-Reference.com; Earle Combs Web Site (www.earlecombs.com); National Baseball Hall of Fame and Museum

Comiskey, Charles Albert "Commy" (born: August 15, 1859 in Chicago, Illinois; died: October 26, 1931 in Eagle River, Wisconsin); inducted into the National Baseball Hall of Fame and Museum in 1939 as a pioneer-executive by the Veterans Committee; Position: First Base; Bats: Right; Throws: Right; first player to position himself off and behind the bag as a first baseman.

With more than 50 years of his life dedicated to baseball, Comiskey served as a player, manager, and owner. Making his major league playing debut on May 2, 1882, he was a player-manager for the St. Louis Browns (Brown Stockings, 1882–1889, 1891), Chicago Pirates (1890), and the Cincinnati Reds (1892–1894), and compiled a career managerial record of .608 (840–541). Comiskey played in four World Series, all against the Chicago White Stockings (tied in 1885; beat the White Stockings in 1886; and lost in 1887 and 1888).

He became a player-manager with the American Association's Browns at age 24, and led the team to four consecutive pennants (1885–1888). Although Comiskey started his career as a pitcher, he later moved to first base and is credited with being the first player to position himself off and well behind the bag as a first baseman, a practice that is commonly used in today's game. He was one of the founders of the American League in 1901 and owned the Chicago White Sox for 31 years, winning five pennants. In 1910, he built Comiskey Park, which stood for 80 years.

For all his accomplishments, unfortunately, his name is also linked to one of baseball's most infamous scandals when eight players of his 1919 White Sox team (forever known as the "Black Sox") were accused of throwing the World Series to the Cincinnati Reds in return for payoffs from gamblers. Although the players were eventually cleared of all wrongdoing within the legal system, the scandal forced baseball to create the position of Commissioner and the owners turned to Kenesaw Mountain Landis to help save the game. One of the new commissioner's first acts was to ban from the game for life the eight players accused in the "Black Sox" scandal (Eddie Cicotte, Oscar "Happy" Felsch, Arnold "Chick" Gandil, "Shoeless" Joe Jackson, Fred McMullin, Charles "Swede" Risberg, George "Buck" Weaver, and Claude "Lefty" Williams).

Many historians feel that Comiskey (often called "The Old Roman") was indirectly responsible for the scandal because of his famously conservative (some would say cheap) spending habits, which angered the players and made them more receptive to accepting bribes from gamblers. Although he arguably had the best team ever assembled, he paid his players as little as possible, and often boasted that he had the lowest payroll in the major leagues. Although never proven, it was rumored that he took steps to ensure that players could not reach contract-specified bonus levels, such as not allowing pitchers to play when they neared bonus levels in games won.

Additionally, he forced players to pay to launder their own uniforms. The team's dirty uniforms are what led to the nickname the "Black Sox." Contrary to popular belief, the nickname was given to the team long before the scandal of the 1919 World Series. Many historians assert that the players participated in the scheme not only to make money but to embarrass their owner.

From his start with the Dubuque Rabbits (Northwestern League), Comiskey was promoted to the major leagues in 1882 with the St. Louis Browns of the American Association. He would go on to play for the Browns (1882–1889, 1891), the Chicago Pirates (Players' League, 1890), and the National League's Cincinnati Reds (1892–1894). After 13 years as a player, he left the major leagues in 1894 and purchased the Sioux City (Iowa) Cornhuskers of the Western League, and moved the team to Saint Paul, Minnesota (as the Saint Paul Saints) in 1895. After five seasons of sharing the Twin Cities area with the Minneapolis Millers (also of the Western League), he moved the team to Chicago, joined the newly created American League (which was basically the Western League renamed), and the team became known as the White Stockings (later the White Sox).

Charles Comiskey's Career Playing Statistics

YEAR	TEAM	G	AB	RUNS	HITS	HR	RBI	AVG
1882	St. Louis	78	329	58	80	1	45	.243
1883	St. Louis	96	401	87	118	2	64	.294
1884	St. Louis	108	460	76	109	2	84	.237
1885	St. Louis	83	340	68	87	2	44	.256
1886	St. Louis	131	578	95	147	3	76	.254
1887	St. Louis	125	538	139	180	4	103	.335
1888	St. Louis	137	576	102	157	6	83	.273
1889	St. Louis	137	587	105	168	3	102	.286
1890	Chicago	88	377	53	92	0	59	.244
1891	St. Louis	141	580	86	152	3	93	.262
1892	Cincinnati	141	551	61	125	3	71	.227
1893	Cincinnati	64	259	38	57	0	26	.220

YEAR	TEAM	G	AB	RUNS	HITS	HR	RBI	AVG
1894	Cincinnati	61	220	26	58	0	33	.264
	TOTALS	1,390	5,796	994	1,530	29	883	.264

Charles Comiskey's Managerial Record (Player-Manager)

YEAR	TEAM	W	L	WIN%	FINISH
1883	St. Louis	12	7	.632	Second
1884	St. Louis	16	7	.696	Fourth
1885	St. Louis	79	33	.705	First
1886	St. Louis	93	46	.669	First (won World Series)
1887	St. Louis	95	40	.704	First
1888	St. Louis	92	43	.681	First
1889	St. Louis	90	45	.667	Second
1890	Chicago	75	62	.547	Fourth
1891	St. Louis	86	52	.623	Second
1892	Cincinnati	44	31	.587	Fourth (First Half)
1892	Cincinnati	38	37	.507	Eighth (Second Half)
1893	Cincinnati	65	63	.508	Sixth
1894	Cincinnati	55	75	.423	Tenth
	St. Louis	563	273	.673	
	Chicago	75	62	.547	
	Cincinnati	202	206	.495	
	TOTALS	840	541	.608	

Sources: Baseball-Reference.com; National Baseball Hall of Fame and Museum

Commander, Colin (born: November 28, 1905 in Sheffield, Yorkshire, England; died: September 14, 1990 in Ohio); inducted into the National Soccer Hall of Fame and Museum in 1967 as a builder; served as the National Cups Commissioner of the United States Soccer Football Association from 1950 to 1957.

Commander immigrated to the United States in 1921 and moved to the Cleveland, Ohio area. Beginning in 1922, he participated in various soccer leagues until a knee injury ended his playing career in 1939. He played on three league championship teams (1927–1928, 1931) and won the Ohio State Championship twice (1929–1930).

In the 1945–1946 season, Commander was the secretary and business manager of the Cleveland Americans, who reached the U.S. Open Cup final before losing the two-game playoff to New York Brookhattan. The following year, the team reached the Eastern semi-final of the National Amateur Cup, and in 1948, Commander became secretary of the Cleveland Soccer League, before becoming secretary of the state association, a position he held from 1948 into the 1960s. He organized the Ohio State Championship in 1950, and served as National Cups Commissioner of the United States Soccer Football Association from 1950 to 1957. He would later become secretary and a member of the executive board of the Erie Amateur Athletic Union.

Source: National Soccer Hall of Fame and Museum

Conacher, Charles William "Charlie" (born: December 20, 1909 in Toronto, Ontario, Canada; died: December 30, 1967 in Toronto, Ontario, Canada); inducted into the Hockey Hall of Fame in 1961 as a player; Position: Right Wing; won the Memorial Cup in 1929 as a player and in 1944 as a coach; won the Stanley Cup in 1932.

Conacher played 12 National Hockey League seasons (1929–1941) with the Toronto Maple Leafs (1929–1937), Detroit Red Wings (1938–1939), and the New York Americans (1939–1941). Known in his day for having the hardest shot in hockey, he was a member of the Toronto Maple Leafs' "Kid Line" of the 1930s (along with Harvey "Busher" Jackson and center Joe Primeau).

Of Conacher's 10 siblings, older brother Lionel and younger brother Roy have also been inducted into the Hockey Hall of Fame. The 6'1", 200-pound Conacher led or tied for the league lead in goal scoring five times between 1930 and 1936; was a Second-Team All-Star in his second and third years in the league; a First-Team selection for three consecutive seasons (1934–1946); helped the Leafs win the Stanley Cup in 1932; and played on three Stanley Cup runner-up teams (1933, 1935–1936).

After playing nine seasons with Toronto, he was sold to the Detroit Red Wings, where he played for one year before ending his career with the New York Americans. After retiring as a player in 1941, Conacher coached the Oshawa Generals of the Ontario Hockey League to a Memorial Cup championship in 1944.

He was inducted into Canada's Sports Hall of Fame in 1975, and in 1998, he was ranked number 36 on *The Hockey News*' list of the 100 Greatest Hockey Players.

Charlie Conacher's Career Statistics

			REGULAR SEASON					PLAYOFFS				
SEASON	**TEAM**	**LEAGUE**	**GP**	**G**	**A**	**TP**	**PIM**	**GP**	**G**	**A**	**TP**	**PIM**
1926–1927	North Toronto Juniors	OHA-Jr.	9	9	1	10		1	0	0	0	0
1926–1927	North Toronto Rangers	OHA-Sr.	2	1	0	1	2					
1927–1928	Toronto Marlboros	OHA-Jr.	9	11	0	11		2	1	0	1	
1927–1928	Toronto Marlboros	OHA-Sr.	1	2	0	2	0					
1927–1928	Toronto Marlboros	M-Cup	11	15	3	18						
1928–1929	Toronto Marlboros	OHA-Jr.	8	18	3	21		2	7	0	7	
1928–1929	Toronto Marlboros	M-Cup	15	28	8	36	12					
1929–1930	Toronto Maple Leafs	NHL	38	20	9	29	48					
1930–1931	Toronto Maple Leafs	NHL	37	31	12	43	78	2	0	1	1	0
1931–1932	Toronto Maple Leafs	NHL	44	34	14	48	66	7	6	2	8	6
1932–1933	Toronto Maple Leafs	NHL	40	14	19	33	64	9	1	1	2	10
1933–1934	Toronto Maple Leafs	NHL	42	32	20	52	38	5	3	2	5	0
1934–1935	Toronto Maple Leafs	NHL	47	36	21	57	24	7	1	4	5	6
1935–1936	Toronto Maple Leafs	NHL	44	23	15	38	74	9	3	2	5	12
1936–1937	Toronto Maple Leafs	NHL	15	3	5	8	13	2	0	0	0	5
1937–1938	Toronto Maple Leafs	NHL	19	7	9	16	6					
1938–1939	Detroit Red Wings	NHL	40	8	15	23	39	5	2	5	7	2
1939–1940	New York Americans	NHL	47	10	18	28	41	3	1	1	2	8
1940–1941	New York Americans	NHL	46	7	16	23	32					
	NHL TOTALS		459	225	173	398	523	49	17	18	35	49

Sources: Hockey Hall of Fame; Hockey-Reference.com

Conacher, Lionel Pretoria (born: May 29, 1900 in Toronto, Ontario, Canada; died: May 26, 1954 in Ottawa, Ontario, Canada); inducted into the Hockey Hall of Fame in 1994 as a player; won the Memorial Cup in 1920; won Stanley Cup championships in 1934 and 1935; named Canada's top male athlete of the half-century; a charter member of the Canadian Sports, Canadian Football, and Canadian Lacrosse halls of fame.

Conacher played 12 National Hockey League seasons with the Pittsburgh Pirates (1925–1926), New York Americans (1926–1930), Montreal Maroons (1930–1933, 1934–1937), and the Chicago Black Hawks (1933–1934). Nicknamed "The Big Train," the 6', 195-pound Conacher was named Canada's top male athlete of the half-century in 1950.

While playing junior and senior hockey for 10 seasons (and winning the Memorial Cup in 1920 with the Toronto Canoe Club), he won a semi-professional baseball league championship for Toronto in 1920, and in 1921, he scored two touchdowns to lead the Toronto Argonauts (Canadian Football League) to victory in the Grey Cup.

Conacher accepted an athletic scholarship from the Bellefonte Academy (Pittsburgh, Pennsylvania) and eventually led the Yellow Jackets to consecutive (1924–1925) United States Amateur Hockey Association titles. In the 1925–1926 season, he decided to play professional hockey with the Yellow Jackets when the team entered the National Hockey League as an expansion franchise and changed its name to the Pirates. He was the squad's captain and scored the first goal in team history against the Boston Bruins on November 26, 1925.

Early in the 1926–1927 season, Conacher was traded to the New York Americans, where he played four seasons and served as the squad's player-coach in the 1929–1930 season. His joined the Montreal Maroons in 1930, and two years later, he scored a career-high 28 points during the 1932–1933 season.

In the 1933–1934 season, Conacher played for the Chicago Black Hawks and helped the franchise win its first-ever Stanley Cup title in 1934. After only one season in Chicago, he left the team and returned to the Maroons for three seasons, winning another Stanley Cup championship in 1935, before retiring in 1937.

One of 10 siblings, he is the older brother of Charles and Roy, both of whom have also been inducted into the Hockey Hall of Fame. Conacher is a charter member of the Canadian Sports Hall of Fame (1955), the Canadian Football Hall of Fame and Museum (1963), and the Canadian Lacrosse Hall of Fame and Museum (1966).

After retiring as a player, he was elected to the Ontario Legislature as a Liberal Member of the Provincial Parliament (MPP) from the Toronto section of Bracondale, and served from October 1937 to June 1943. In 1949, he was elected as a Liberal Member of Parliament in the Toronto area of Trinity and was re-elected in 1953. He continued to serve until his death in May 1954.

The Lionel Conacher Award is presented annually to Canada's male athlete of the year. The award, first given in 1932, is voted upon by members of the Canadian media.

Lionel Conacher's Career Statistics

			REGULAR SEASON					**PLAYOFFS**				
SEASON	**TEAM**	**LEAGUE**	**GP**	**G**	**A**	**TP**	**PIM**	**GP**	**G**	**A**	**TP**	**PIM**
1916–1917	Toronto Century Rovers	OMHA										
1917–1918	Toronto Aura Lee	OHA-Jr.										
1918–1919	Parkdale Canoe Club	OHA-Jr.										
1919–1920	Toronto Canoe Club	OHA-Jr.						12	21	9	30	
1920–1921	Toronto Aura Lee	OHA-Sr.	10	3	2	5						
1921–1922	Toronto Aura Lee	OHA-Sr.	20	7	2	9		2	2	0	2	0
1922–1923	North Toronto A.A.	OHA-Int.						6	12	4	16	
1923–1924	Pittsburgh Yellowjackets	USAHA	20	12	4	16		13	6	3	9	
1924–1925	Pittsburgh Yellowjackets	USAHA	40	14	0	14		8	5	0	5	
1925–1926	Pittsburgh Pirates	NHL	33	9	4	13	64	2	0	0	0	0
1926–1927	Pittsburgh Pirates	NHL	9	0	0	0	12					
1926–1927	New York Americans	NHL	30	8	9	17	81					
1927–1928	New York Americans	NHL	35	11	6	17	82					
1928–1929	New York Americans	NHL	44	5	2	7	132	2	0	0	0	10
1929–1930	New York Americans	NHL	40	4	6	10	73					
1930–1931	Montreal Maroons	NHL	36	4	3	7	57	2	0	0	0	2
1931–1932	Montreal Maroons	NHL	45	7	9	16	60	4	0	0	0	2
1932–1933	Montreal Maroons	NHL	47	7	21	28	61	2	0	1	1	0
1933–1934	Chicago Black Hawks	NHL	48	10	13	23	87	8	2	0	2	4
1934–1935	Montreal Maroons	NHL	38	2	6	8	44	7	0	0	0	14
1935–1936	Montreal Maroons	NHL	46	7	7	14	65	3	0	0	0	0
1936–1937	Montreal Maroons	NHL	47	6	19	25	64	5	0	1	1	2
	NHL TOTALS		498	80	105	185	882	35	2	2	4	34

Sources: Canadian Football Hall of Fame and Museum; Canadian Lacrosse Hall of Fame and Museum; Canadian Sports Hall of Fame; Hockey Hall of Fame; Hockey-Reference.com

Conacher, Roy Gordon (born: October 5, 1916 in Toronto, Ontario, Canada; died: December 29, 1984 in Victoria, British Columbia, Canada); inducted into the Hockey Hall of Fame as a player in 1998; won the Memorial Cup in 1936; first rookie to lead the NHL in scoring for a single season; scored the winning goal in the 1939 Stanley Cup championship.

The youngest of 10 siblings, two of his brothers (Lionel and Charles), have also been inducted into the Hockey Hall of Fame. Conacher played 11 seasons in the National Hockey League with the Boston Bruins (1938–1942, 1945–1946), Detroit Red Wings (1946–1947), and the Chicago Black Hawks (1947–1952). He led the NHL with 26 goals in 47 games his rookie season.

After five seasons in the bantam and junior levels (including a Memorial Cup title in 1936 with the West Toronto Nationals [Ontario Hockey Association]), he joined the National Hockey League in 1938 (age 22); led the NHL in scoring as a rookie; and scored the goal that won his team's 1939 Stanley Cup championship. He was among the NHL's top 10 scorers his first four years in the league, and won another championship in 1941.

His hockey career was interrupted during World War II when he served in the Royal Canadian Air Force. After the war, Conacher returned to the Bruins and played four games, before he was traded to the Detroit Red Wings during the 1946–1947 season. Playing only one season in Detroit, he moved on to the Chicago Black Hawks, by then being coached by his brother, Charles.

In 1949, Conacher won the Art Ross Trophy as the NHL's leading scorer with 68 points (26 goals, 42 assists), and was selected to the NHL's First All-Star Team. He retired 12 games into the 1951–1952 season.

Roy Conacher's Career Statistics

			REGULAR SEASON					PLAYOFFS				
SEASON	TEAM	LEAGUE	GP	G	A	TP	PIM	GP	G	A	TP	PIM
1933–1934	West Toronto Nationals	OHA-Jr.	6	0	1	1	0					
1934–1935	West Toronto Nationals	OHA-Jr.	9	4	3	7	8					
1935–1936	West Toronto Nationals	OHA-Jr.	10	12	3	15	11	5	4	2	6	4
1935–1936	West Toronto Nationals	M-Cup	12	8	5	13	11					
1936–1937	Toronto Dominions	OHA-Sr.	8	3	3	6	4	1	0	0	0	0
1936–1937	Toronto Dominions	Al-Cup	3	3	0	3	2					
1937–1938	Kirkland Lake Hargreaves	NOHA	14	12	11	23	2	1	1	0	1	0
1938–1939	Boston Bruins	NHL	47	26	11	37	12	12	6	4	10	12
1939–1940	Boston Bruins	NHL	31	18	12	30	9	6	2	1	3	0
1940–1941	Boston Bruins	NHL	41	24	14	38	7	11	1	5	6	0
1941–1942	Boston Bruins	NHL	43	24	13	37	12	5	2	1	3	0
1942–1943	Saskatoon RCAF	SSHL	20	13	8	21	2	3	2	2	4	0
1943–1944	Dartmouth RCAF	NSDHL	3	9	2	11	4					
1944–1945	Dartmouth RCAF	NSDHL	4	1	2	3	0					
1944–1945	Millward-St. George RCAF	Britain										
1945–1946	Boston Bruins	NHL	4	2	1	3	0	3	0	0	0	0
1946–1947	Detroit Red Wings	NHL	60	30	24	54	6	5	4	4	8	2
1947–1948	Chicago Black Hawks	NHL	52	22	27	49	4					
1948–1949	Chicago Black Hawks	NHL	60	26	42	68	8					
1949–1950	Chicago Black Hawks	NHL	70	25	31	56	16					
1950–1951	Chicago Black Hawks	NHL	70	26	24	50	16					
1951–1952	Chicago Black Hawks	NHL	12	3	1	4	0					
	NHL TOTALS		490	226	200	426	90	42	15	15	30	14

Sources: Hockey Hall of Fame; Hockey-Reference.com

Conlan, John Bertrand "Jocko" (born: December 6, 1899 in Chicago, Illinois; died: April 16, 1989 in Scottsdale, Arizona); inducted into the National Baseball Hall of Fame and Museum as an umpire in 1974 by the Veterans Committee; Position: Center Fielder; Bats: Left; Throws: Left; fourth umpire chosen for hall of fame induction and was the only one of the eight umpires elected to the hall of fame to have played in the major leagues.

Ten years before starting a professional baseball career, Conlan had been a licensed New York state boxing referee. He later had a short-lived baseball playing career before he turned to umpiring. The 165-pound outfielder made his major league debut on July 6, 1934 (age 34) with the Chicago White Sox, and played his last game on September 29, 1935, compiling a career batting average of .263 with 31 RBIs.

Conlan's career began unexpectedly when Red Ormsby was overcome by heat while umpiring a 1935 game between the White Sox and St. Louis Browns. For reasons that are not totally clear, Conlan was asked to fill in and became a full-time official in the minor leagues the next season.

He was known for wearing a polka-dot tie and for being the last National League umpire to wear an outside chest protector. Conlan umpired in the National League from 1941 to 1964 (and served as a substitute for 17 games in 1965); officiated in five World Series (1945, 1950, 1954, 1957, 1961); and worked six All-Star games (1943, 1947, 1950, 1953, 1958, 1962).

Conlan umpired in the playoff series to decide the National League's regular-season champion three times (1951, 1959, 1962); was the home plate umpire when Gil Hodges hit four home runs on August 31, 1950; and he umpired in the April 30, 1961 game when future hall of famer Willie Mays hit four home runs. He was the fourth umpire chosen for hall of fame induction, and was the only one of the eight umpires elected to have played in the major leagues.

Source: National Baseball Hall of Fame and Museum

Connell, Alexander "Alex" (born: February 8, 1902 in Ottawa, Ontario, Canada; died: May 10, 1958); inducted into the Hockey Hall of Fame in 1958 as a player; Position: Goaltender; holds the NHL record for the longest shutout time (461:29); his 1.99 career goals against average is the all-time record among goaltenders of his era; won two Stanley Cup championships.

Connell played 12 seasons in the National Hockey League with the Ottawa Senators (1924–1931, 1932–1933), Detroit Falcons (1931–1932), New York Americans (1933–1934), and the Montreal Maroons (1934–1935, 1936–1937).

Connell was a well-rounded athlete; a baseball catcher in the Interprovincial League; played lacrosse for the Eastern Canadian champion Ottawa team in the 1920s; and played football with St. Brigid's of the Ottawa City League.

After playing amateur and junior level hockey for seven years, Connell turned professional with the National Hockey League's Ottawa Senators in the 1924–1925 season and helped the team win a Stanly Cup championship in 1927 over the Boston Bruins.

During the 1927–1928 season, Connell established the NHL's record for longest shutout time (461 minutes, 29 seconds) by recording six consecutive shutouts (January 31 to February 18, 1928), a record that still stands today.

He briefly retired from hockey in 1933; returned for one game during the 1933–1934 season as a substitute goaltender for the New York Americans; and returned to the NHL full-time, winning his second Stanley Cup title as a member of the Montreal Maroons in 1935. He retired once again; did not play during the 1935–1936 season; but returned to the Maroons for 27 games in the 1936–1937 season, before retiring for good. His 1.99 career goals against average (regular season and playoffs) is the all-time record among goaltenders of his era.

Alex Connell's Career Statistics

			REGULAR SEASON						PLAYOFFS					
SEASON	TEAM	LEAGUE	GP	W	L	T	SO	AVG	GP	W	L	T	SO	AVG
1917–1918	Kingston Frontenacs	OHA-Jr.	4	4	0	0	0	2.75	4	3	1	0	0	4.50
1918–1919	Kingston Frontenacs	OHA-Jr.	5	3	2	0	0	4.72	4	0	1	3	0	5.00
1919–1920	Ottawa Cliffsides	OCHL	7	4	3	0	2	1.12						
1920–1921	Ottawa St. Brigid's	OCHL	11	8	2	1	2	1.09	8	6	1	1	1	1.62
1921–1922	Ottawa Gunners	OCHL	14	10	3	1	5	1.26	6	5	1	0	0	2.83
1922–1923	Ottawa St. Brigid's	OCHL	17	8	8	1	4	1.43						
1923–1924	Ottawa St. Brigid's	OCHL	12	8	4	0	5	1.14						
1924–1925	Ottawa Senators	NHL	30	17	12	1	7	2.14						
1925–1926	Ottawa Senators	NHL	36	24	8	4	15	1.12	2	0	1	1	0	1.00
1926–1927	Ottawa Senators	NHL	44	30	10	4	13	1.49	6	3	0	3	2	0.60
1927–1928	Ottawa Senators	NHL	44	20	14	10	15	1.24	2	0	2	0	0	1.50
1928–1929	Ottawa Senators	NHL	44	14	17	13	7	1.43						
1929–1930	Ottawa Senators	NHL	44	21	15	8	3	2.55	2	0	1	1	0	3.00
1930–1931	Ottawa Senators	NHL	36	10	22	4	3	3.01						
1931–1932	Detroit Falcons	NHL	48	18	20	10	6	2.12	2	0	1	1	0	1.50
1932–1933	Ottawa Senators	NHL	15	4	8	2	1	2.56						
1933–1934	New York Americans	NHL	1	1	0	0	0	3.00						
1934–1935	Montreal Maroons	NHL	48	24	19	5	9	1.86	7	5	0	2	2	1.12
1936–1937	Montreal Maroons	NHL	27	10	11	6	2	2.21						
	NHL TOTALS		417	193	156	67	81	1.91	21	8	5	8	4	1.19

Sources: Hockey Hall of Fame; Hockey-Reference.com

Connolly, Thomas Henry "Tommy" (born: December 31, 1870 in Manchester, England; died: April 28, 1961 in Natick, Massachusetts); inducted into the National Baseball Hall of Fame and Museum as an umpire in 1953 by the Veterans Committee; served as the only umpire in the very first American League game ever played; worked in the first modern-day World Series; served as the American League's first-ever supervisor of officials.

While living in England, Connolly played cricket as a boy and did not even see his first baseball game until his family immigrated to the United States in 1885. While umpiring local YMCA games, he signed with the New England League, where he worked from 1894 to 1897.

In 1898, he was promoted to the major leagues and worked in the National League briefly, but disagreed with the league's policy of not supporting umpires' on-field decisions. He resigned in the middle of the 1900 season, and in 1901, Connolly signed with the newly formed American League, whose president, Ban Johnson, provided strong support for umpires. He was the sole umpire in the first American League game ever played on April 24, 1901, and would work in the league for 31 years.

Connolly umpired in the first modern-day World Series (1903) and would go on to work in seven more (1908, 1910–1911, 1913, 1916, 1920, 1924). After having ejected 10 players from games in his first season, he once worked 10 consecutive seasons without ejecting a player. He also umpired in the first games ever played at Fenway Park (Boston), Comiskey Park (Chicago), Shibe Park (Philadelphia), and Yankee Stadium (New York).

He was not afraid to stand up to the most intense players, coaches, and managers of his time. On September 11, 1912, he called Ty Cobb out for stepping across home plate while batting, after Cobb had hit an RBI triple on the third pitch of an intentional walk. He was later the home-plate umpire for Addie Joss' perfect game on October 2, 1908, one of four no-hitters in which he called balls and strikes. The last player Connolly ejected from a game was Babe Ruth (1922) as the star tried to enter the stands to confront a heckler.

On May 2, 1901, in a game threatened by bad weather, the Detroit Tigers scored five runs in the top of the ninth inning to take a 7–5 lead over the Chicago White Sox (White Stockings). Once rain began to fall in the bottom of the inning, Sox manager Clark Griffith ordered his players to stall the game, hoping the ninth inning would be erased by rain and Chicago would win the game based on the score at the end of the eighth inning. After Griffith failed to heed several warnings, Connolly forfeited the game to Detroit, the first-ever forfeit in the American League.

Chicago Cubs' player-manager Frank Chance became the first player ever ejected from a World Series game on October 20, 1910 when he and Connolly argued a home run call on a ball hit by the Philadelphia Athletics' Danny Murphy, which Chance argued should have been a ground rule double since it had hit an outfield sign. On August 28, 1918, Tris Speaker was suspended for the remainder of the season because of his assault on Connolly following a dispute at home plate in a game in Philadelphia.

In 1931, American League president Will Harridge removed Connolly from active field duty and assigned him as the league's first supervisor of umpires. He served in that capacity until 1954 and became known as one of the game's foremost experts on baseball rules.

Connolly was one of the first two umpires inducted into the hall of fame (along with the National League's Bill Klem), and they are the only two umpires in major league history to work in five decades. Connolly's record of 31 years umpiring American League games was broken by Larry Barnett in 1999.

Source: National Baseball Hall of Fame and Museum

Connor, George Leo (born: January 21, 1925 in Chicago, Illinois; died: March 31, 2003 in Chicago, Illinois); inducted into the Pro Football Hall of Fame in 1975 as a player; Position: Tackle-Linebacker; was named All-NFL at three positions: offensive tackle, defensive tackle, and linebacker; first-ever winner of the Outland Trophy.

After attaining All-American status at both the College of the Holy Cross (Worcester, Massachusetts, 1942–1943) and the University of Notre Dame (South Bend, Indiana, 1946–1947), Connor went on to enjoy an eight-year National Football League career with the Chicago Bears from 1948 to 1955. He was named All-NFL at three positions (offensive tackle, defensive tackle, and linebacker); named All-NFL five times; was a two-way performer during his entire career; and played in four Pro Bowl games (1950–1953).

The 6'3", 240-pound Connor was inducted into the College Football Hall of Fame in 1963, and while at Notre Dame, he never played in a losing game (the team went 8–0–1 in 1946 and a perfect 9–0 in 1947). In 1946, he was the first-ever winner of the Outland Trophy as the nation's best interior lineman, and was Notre Dame's team captain in 1947.

George Connor's Career Statistics

			DEFENSE						
YEAR	**TEAM**	**G**	**INT**	**YDS**	**AVG**	**TD**	**FUMREC**	**YDS**	**TD**
1948	Chicago Bears	11	0	0	0.0	0	2	0	0
1949	Chicago Bears	12	0	0	0.0	0	2	0	0
1950	Chicago Bears	11	1	8	8.0	0	0	0	0
1951	Chicago Bears	12	2	21	10.5	0	0	0	0
1952	Chicago Bears	12	2	31	15.5	0	2	14	0
1953	Chicago Bears	12	0	0	0.0	0	1	0	0
1954	Chicago Bears	8	1	6	6.0	0	1	6	0
1955	Chicago Bears	12	1	0	0.0	0	2	53	1
	TOTALS	90	7	66	9.4	0	10	73	1

Sources: College Football Hall of Fame; Pro Football Hall of Fame; Pro-Football-Reference.com

Connor, Roger (born: July 1, 1857 in Waterbury, Connecticut; died: January 4, 1931 in Waterbury, Connecticut); inducted into the National Baseball Hall of Fame and Museum in 1976 as a player by the Veterans Committee; Position: First Base; Bats: Left; Throws: Left; 19th century home run king; hit the first grand slam in major league history.

Making his major league debut on May 1, 1880, the 6'3", 220-pound Connor enjoyed an 18-year career with the Troy Trojans (1880–1882), New York Gothams / Giants (1883–1889, 1891, 1893–1894), New York Giants (Players' League, 1890), Philadelphia Phillies (1892), and the St. Louis Browns (1894–1897). He was a player-manager for the Browns in 1896. Due to his relatively large size, Connor was the impetus for the Gothams earning the nickname "Giants," which evolved into the team's official name.

Connor was the 19th century's home run king. His 138 career home runs set the major league record until surpassed by the legendary Babe Ruth in 1921. He hit 10 or more home runs in a season seven times (a 19th century record); hit three home runs in one game (May 9, 1888); and was the first player to hit an over-the-wall home run at the Polo Grounds (home field of the New York Giants). He hit .300 or better in 12 seasons; got six hits in six at bats in a game on June 1, 1895 in a 23–2 win over the Giants; and on September 10, 1881, with the Troy Trojans trailing in the bottom of the ninth inning with two outs, he won the game 8–7 against the Worcester Ruby Legs by hitting the first grand slam in major league history.

After retiring as a player in 1897, Connor managed several minor league teams, and lived to see his career home run record fall to Babe Ruth.

Roger Connor's Career Statistics

YEAR	TEAM	LG	G	AB	R	H	2B	3B	HR	BB	SO	SB	AVG	SLG
1880	Troy	NL	83	340	53	113	17	10	3	13	21		.332	.468
1881	Troy	NL	84	361	54	104	17	6	2	15	20		.288	.385
1882	Troy	NL	79	339	63	111	22	17	4	13	20		.327	.528
1883	New York	NL	96	401	80	145	28	14	1	25	16		.362	.509
1884	New York	NL	112	462	93	146	27	4	4	38	32		.316	.418
1885	New York	NL	110	455	102	169	23	15	1	51	8		.371	.495
1886	New York	NL	118	485	105	172	30	19	7	41	15		.355	.538
1887	New York	NL	127	546	113	209	26	22	17	75	50	43	.383	.604
1888	New York	NL	134	481	98	140	15	17	14	73	44	27	.291	.480
1889	New York	NL	131	496	117	157	32	17	13	93	46	21	.317	.528
1890	New York	PL	123	484	134	180	25	15	14	88	32	23	.372	.572
1891	New York	NL	129	477	110	140	27	12	7	83	39	32	.294	.444
1892	Philadelphia	NL	153	558	122	159	31	11	12	116	39	20	.285	.444
1893	New York	NL	135	490	111	158	25	8	11	91	26	29	.322	.473
1894	New York	NL	22	82	10	24	7	0	1	8	0	2	.293	.415
1894	St. Louis	NL	99	380	83	121	27	26	7	51	17	13	.318	.582
1895	St. Louis	NL	104	402	78	131	28	7	8	63	10	8	.326	.490
1896	St. Louis	NL	126	485	68	137	19	6	11	52	14	14	.282	.414
1897	St. Louis	NL	22	83	13	19	3	1	1	13		3	.229	.325
	TOTALS		1,987	7,807	1,607	2,535	429	227	138	1,002	449	235	.325	.491

Sources: Baseball-Reference.com; National Baseball Hall of Fame and Museum

Conradt, Jody (born: May 13, 1941 in Goldthwaite, Texas); inducted into the Naismith Memorial Basketball Hall of Fame in 1998 as a coach; second woman inducted into the hall of fame as a coach; led Texas to the NCAA title with a 34–0 record (the first women's team in Division I history to go undefeated).

After attending Goldthwaite High School from 1955 to 1959 (where she averaged 40 points a game in her four-year career), Conradt went to Baylor University (Waco, Texas) from 1959 to 1963, and played on the university's inaugural varsity women's basketball team, eventually earning four letters while averaging 20 point a game.

After graduating from Baylor, she became a teacher and basketball coach at Waco (Texas) Midway High School, before returning to her alma mater to earn a master's degree in 1969. Her head coaching career began at Sam Houston

State University (Huntsville, Texas, 1969–1973), where she compiled a 74–23 (.763) record, before moving on to the University of Texas, Arlington (1973–1976), compiling a 43–39 (.524) record.

Conradt is best known for her 30-year career at the University of Texas-Austin, where she coached from 1976 to 2007, compiling a 752–216 (.777) record. She won her 800th college game on January 22, 2003 when the Lady Longhorns defeated Texas Tech 69–58. At the time, this win made her the second winningest coach in women's basketball history (behind Tennessee's Pat Summitt). Her 700th win (an 89–86 victory over Northwestern on December 18, 1997) had made her the eighth collegiate basketball coach in history (male or female) and the first female coach to reach the 700-win mark. She is the second woman (after Margaret Wade) to be inducted into the basketball hall of fame.

Conradt compiled an overall record of 869–278 (.758); has been selected National Coach of the Year four times (1980, 1984, 1986, 1997); and in 1997, she was the first-ever winner of the John and Nellie Wooden Award as the women's basketball national Coach of the Year. She led the University of Texas to 27 national post-season tournaments; 20 NCAA Tournaments; and three NCAA Final Four appearances (1986–1987, 2003), winning a national championship in 1986. She is a five-time Southwestern Conference Coach of the Year (1984–1985, 1987–1988, 1996); won the first-ever Big 12 Conference regular season title (15–1, in 2002–2003); and was named Big 12 Conference Coach of the Year in 2003.

She coached Texas to 10 regular-season Southwest Conference titles and nine post-season championships; led the school to the 1986 NCAA title with a 34–0 record (the first women's team in Division I history to go undefeated); has compiled ten 30-win or better seasons; led Texas to 20 or more wins per season 26 times; and led the Lady Longhorns to a 183-game winning streak against Southwest Conference teams during a 12-year stretch (1978–1990).

Conradt has been inducted into the Texas Women's Hall of Fame (1986); the International Women's Sports Hall of Fame (1995); Texas Sports Hall of Fame (1998); was part of the inaugural 1999 class of the Women's Basketball Hall of Fame (Knoxville, Tennessee); was one of seven finalists for the Naismith Women's Basketball Coach of the Century; and in 2003, and was inducted into the International Scholar-Athlete Hall of Fame (at the Institute for International Sport in Providence, Rhode Island).

Jody Conradt's Coaching Statistics
(Sam Houston State University)

YEAR	RECORD
1969–1970	17–2
1970–1971	18–7
1971–1972	19–7
1972–1973	20–7
TOTALS	74–23 (.763)

Jody Conradt's Coaching Statistics
(University of Texas, Arlington)

YEAR	RECORD
1973–1974	9–14
1974–1975	11–14
1975–1976	23–11
TOTALS	43–39 (.524)

Jody Conradt's Coaching Statistics (University of Texas, Austin)

YEAR	REG SEASON	CONF	FINISH	POSTSEASON
1976–1977	36–10			3rd AIAW
1977–1978	29–10			5th AIAW
1978–1979	37–4			3rd AIAW
1979–1980	33–4			5th AIAW
1980–1981	28–8			9th AIAW
1981–1982	35–4			2nd AIAW
1982–1983	30–3	8–0	1st	2nd NCAA Midwest Regional
1983–1984	32–3	16–0	1st	2nd NCAA Midwest Regional

YEAR	REG SEASON	CONF	FINISH	POSTSEASON
1984–1985	28–3	16–0	1st	3rd NCAA Mideast Regional
1985–1986	34–0	16–0	1st	1st NCAA National Champions
1986–1987	31–2	16–0	1st	NCAA Final Four
1987–1988	32–3	16–0	1st	NCAA Round Two
1988–1989	27–5	16–0	1st	NCAA Round Two
1989–1990	27–5	15–1	T1st	NCAA Round Two
1990–1991	21–9	14–2	2nd	NCAA Round Two
1991–1992	21–10	13–4	2nd	NCAA Round One
1992–1993	22–8	15–2	T1st	NCAA Round One
1993–1994	22–9	13–4	3rd	NCAA Round One
1994–1995	12–16	7–7	T4th	
1995–1996	21–9	13–1	T1st	NCAA Round Two
1996–1997	22–8	12–4	T2nd	NCAA Round Two
1997–1998	12–15	7–9	7th	
1998–1999	16–12	10–6	4th	NCAA Round One
1999–2000	21–13	9–7	6th	NCAA Round One
2000–2001	20–13	7–9	7th	NCAA Round One
2001–2002	22–10	10–6	5th	NCAA Sweet Sixteen
2002–2003	29–6	15–1	1st	NCAA Final Four
2003–2004	30–5	14–2	T1st	NCAA Sweet Sixteen
2004–2005	22–9	13–3	2nd	
2005–2006	13–15	7–9	T8th	
2006–2007	18–14	6–10	T7th	
TOTALS	752–216 (.777)			

Source: Naismith Memorial Basketball Hall of Fame

Conzelman, James Gleason "Jimmy" (born: March 6, 1898 in St. Louis, Missouri; died: July 31, 1970 in St. Louis, Missouri); inducted into the Pro Football Hall of Fame in 1964 as a coach-owner; Position: Quarterback; Uniform: #1; won the NFL title in 1928 as a player-coach and the 1947 NFL title as a coach.

Before suffering a career-ending knee injury, Conzelman played 10 seasons (102 games) in the National Football League as a player-coach (quarterback) with the Decatur Staleys (1920), Rock Island Independents (1921–1922), Milwaukee Badgers (1922–1924), Detroit Panthers (1925–1926), and the Providence Steam Roller (1927–1929). After retiring as a player, he stayed in the NFL as a coach with Providence (1930) and six years as head coach of the Chicago Cardinals (1940–1942, 1946–1948), leading the team to the 1947 and 1948 divisional championship and the 1947 NFL title.

The 6', 175-pound Conzelman was a halfback at Washington University (St. Louis, Missouri) and began his post-college career as a member of the Great Lakes Navy team (North Chicago, Illinois) that won the 1919 Rose Bowl.

After a single season with the Staleys, he joined the Rock Island Independents, where he began his career as a player-coach. He stayed with the team for seven games of the 1922 season before moving to the Milwaukee Badgers for the remainder of the year and for the entire 1923 and 1924 seasons. When offered a franchise in Detroit in 1925, Conzelman became an NFL owner of the Panthers, which folded after the 1926 season.

In 1927, Conzelman joined the Providence Steam Roller as the team's player-coach, and led the squad to the 1928 NFL title. He left the league in 1930 and eventually became head coach of his alma mater from 1934 through 1939, compiling a 32–16–2 record. He was voted to the NFL 1920s All-Decade Team.

In 1940, he returned to the NFL as a coach with the Chicago Cardinals, but after three seasons, he once again left the league to become an executive with Major League Baseball's St. Louis Browns. In 1946, he returned to the Cardinals and led the team to two divisional championships (1947–1948) and the NFL title in 1947. Conzelman retired from professional football after the 1948 season.

Jimmy Conzelman's Coaching Statistics

YEAR	TEAM	W	L	T	WIN%
1921	Rock Island	4	1	0	.800
1922	Rock Island	4	2	1	.667
1922	Milwaukee	0	3	0	.000

YEAR	TEAM	W	L	T	WIN%
1923	Milwaukee	7	2	3	.778
1925	Detroit	8	2	2	.800
1926	Detroit	4	6	2	.400
1927	Providence	8	5	1	.615
1928	Providence	8	1	2	.889
1929	Providence	4	6	2	.400
1930	Providence	6	4	1	.600
1940	Chicago	2	7	2	.222
1941	Chicago	3	7	1	.300
1942	Chicago	3	8	0	.273
1946	Chicago	6	5	0	.545
1947	Chicago	9	3	0	.750
1948	Chicago	11	1	0	.917
	Rock Island	8	3	1	.727
	Milwaukee	7	5	3	.467
	Detroit	12	8	4	.500
	Providence	26	16	6	.542
	Chicago	34	31	3	.500
	TOTALS	87	63	17	.572

Sources: Pro Football Hall of Fame; Pro-Football-Reference.com

Cook, Frederick Joseph "Bun" (born: September 18, 1903 in Kingston, Ontario, Canada; died: March 19, 1988); inducted into the Hockey Hall of Fame in 1995 as a player; Position: Left Wing; won seven Calder Cup titles as a coach.

Cook scored 302 points (158 goals and 144 assists) in an 11-year, 473-game National Hockey League career with the New York Rangers (1926–1936) and Boston Bruins (1936–1937). He and his hall of fame brother, Bill, lined up on either side of center Frank Boucher (also a hall of famer) to form the "Bread Line," one of the most famous forward units in NHL history. Cook has been credited with introducing and perfecting the drop pass.

In 1926, the Cook brothers and Boucher were among a group of players who joined the expansion New York Rangers, and all three helped the team win the franchise's first Stanley Cup championship in 1928 in five games over the Montreal Maroons. Cook scored a career-high 24 goals in the 1929–1930 season; was selected to the NHL Second All-Star Team the next season; and helped the team win its second Stanley Cup title in 1933.

In 1936, he played for the Boston Bruins for one season before retiring from the NHL and embarking on a legendary coaching career in the American Hockey League. As a rookie coach in the 1937–1938 season, he led the Providence Reds to the American Hockey League's Calder Cup championship, and they repeated as champions in 1939–1940. In 1943, he became coach of the Cleveland Barons (also of the AHL) and led the team to five Calder Cup titles (1945, 1948, 1951, 1953–1954), before retiring from the minor leagues in 1956.

Frederick Cook's Career Statistics

			REGULAR SEASON					PLAYOFFS				
SEASON	TEAM	LEAGUE	GP	G	A	TP	PIM	GP	G	A	TP	PIM
1921–1922	Sault Ste. Marie Greyhounds	NOHA	3	2	1	3	2					
1922–1923	Sault Ste. Marie Greyhounds	NOHA	8	2	3	5	10	2	0	2	2	0
1922–1923	Sault Ste. Marie Greyhounds	Al-Cup	3	2	0	2	4					
1923–1924	Sault Ste. Marie Greyhounds	NOHA	8	3	3	6	10	7	1	0	1	8
1924–1925	Saskatoon Crescents	WCHL	28	17	4	21	44	2	0	1	1	0
1925–1926	Saskatoon Crescents	WHL	30	8	4	12	22	2	0	0	0	0
1926–1927	New York Rangers	NHL	44	14	9	23	42	2	0	0	0	6
1927–1928	New York Rangers	NHL	44	14	14	28	45	9	2	1	3	10
1928–1929	New York Rangers	NHL	43	13	5	18	70	6	1	0	1	12
1929–1930	New York Rangers	NHL	43	24	18	42	55	4	2	0	2	2
1930–1931	New York Rangers	NHL	44	18	17	35	72	4	0	0	0	2
1931–1932	New York Rangers	NHL	45	14	20	34	43	7	6	2	8	12
1932–1933	New York Rangers	NHL	48	22	15	37	35	8	2	0	2	4
1933–1934	New York Rangers	NHL	48	18	15	33	36	2	0	0	0	2
1934–1935	New York Rangers	NHL	48	13	21	34	26	4	2	0	2	0

SEASON	TEAM	LEAGUE	REGULAR SEASON GP	G	A	TP	PIM	PLAYOFFS GP	G	A	TP	PIM
1935–1936	New York Rangers	NHL	26	4	5	9	12					
1936–1937	Boston Bruins	NHL	40	4	5	9	8					
1937–1938	Providence Reds	IAHL	19	0	1	1	4	4	0	0	0	2
1938–1939	Providence Reds	IAHL	11	1	3	4	4					
1939–1940	Providence Reds	IAHL	1	0	0	0	0	2	0	0	0	0
1940–1941	Providence Reds	AHL	1	0	0	0	0					
1941–1942	Providence Reds	AHL	2	0	1	1	0					
1942–1943	Providence Reds	AHL	3	1	1	2	4					
	NHL TOTALS		473	158	144	302	444	46	15	3	18	50

Frederick Cook's AHL Coaching Record

SEASON	TEAM	REGULAR SEASON G	W	L	T	PTS	PCT	PLAYOFFS G	W	L	PCT	FINISH
1937–1938	Providence Reds	48	25	16	7	57	.594	7	5	2	.714	Won Calder Cup
1938–1939	Providence Reds	54	21	22	11	53	.491	5	2	3	.400	Lost semifinal
1939–1940	Providence Reds	54	27	19	8	62	.574	8	6	2	.750	Won Calder Cup
1940–1941	Providence Reds	56	31	21	4	66	.589	4	1	3	.250	Lost semifinal
1941–1942	Providence Reds	56	17	32	7	41	.366					
1942–1943	Providence Reds	56	27	27	2	56	.500	2	0	2	.000	Lost quarterfinal
1943–1944	Cleveland Barons	54	33	14	7	73	.676	11	4	7	.364	Lost Final
1944–1945	Cleveland Barons	60	34	16	10	78	.650	12	8	4	.667	Won Calder Cup
1945–1946	Cleveland Barons	62	28	26	8	64	.516	12	7	5	.583	Lost Final
1946–1947	Cleveland Barons	64	38	18	8	84	.656	4	0	4	.000	Lost semifinal
1947–1948	Cleveland Barons	68	43	13	12	98	.721	9	8	1	.889	Won Calder Cup
1948–1949	Cleveland Barons	68	41	21	6	88	.647	5	2	3	.400	Lost semifinal
1949–1950	Cleveland Barons	70	45	15	10	100	.714	9	4	5	.444	Lost Final
1950–1951	Cleveland Barons	71	44	22	5	93	.655	11	8	3	.727	Won Calder Cup
1951–1952	Cleveland Barons	68	44	19	5	93	.684	5	2	3	.400	Lost quarterfinal
1952–1953	Cleveland Barons	64	42	20	2	86	.672	11	7	4	.636	Won Calder Cup
1953–1954	Cleveland Barons	70	38	32	0	76	.543	9	7	2	.778	Won Calder Cup
1954–1955	Cleveland Barons	64	32	29	3	67	.523	4	1	3	.250	Lost semifinal
1955–1956	Cleveland Barons	64	26	31	7	59	.461	8	3	5	.375	Lost Final
	TOTALS	1,171	636	413	122	1,394	.595	136	75	61	.551	

Sources: Hockey Hall of Fame; Hockey-Reference.com

Cook, William Osser (born: October 9, 1896 in Brantford, Ontario, Canada; died: April 6, 1986 in Kingston, Ontario, Canada); inducted into the Hockey Hall of Fame in 1952 as a player; Position: Right Wing; won two Stanley Cup titles; first player signed by the NHL's New York Rangers and scored the franchise's first-ever NHL goal; scored the first-ever NHL Stanley Cup-winning overtime goal.

Cook had a 16-year professional hockey career (1921–1937), including 11 seasons with the National Hockey League's New York Rangers (1926–1937). He was part of the Rangers' "Bread Line," which included his brother (and future hall of famer) Fred and future hall of famer Frank Boucher, which led the Rangers to Stanley Cup titles in 1928 (the franchise's first) and 1933.

After serving in World War I and playing junior hockey for several years, Cook made his professional debut in the 1921–1922 season with the Saskatoon Sheiks (Western Canada Hockey League). During his five years with the team (known as the Crescents starting with the 1923–1924 season), he won the league's scoring title twice and scored 31 goals in 30 games during his last season (1925–1926, in what by now was known as the Western Hockey League). When the WHL folded, Cook became the first-ever player signed by the NHL's expansion New York Rangers for the 1926–1927 season; was the team's first captain; and scored the franchise's first-ever goal on November 16, 1926 in a 1–0 win over the Montreal Maroons. The "Bread Line" led New York to its first Stanley Cup title in 1928 by scoring all of the team's goals in a five-game series against the Montreal Maroons. After losing in the finals for two seasons (1929, 1932), the team won its second Cup championship in 1933 (in four games over the Toronto Maple Leafs), during which Cook ended the series by scoring the first-ever NHL Stanley Cup-winning overtime goal.

Cook led the NHL twice in scoring (1927, 1933), was selected NHL First All-Star Team Right Wing three times (1931–1933), and Second Team once (1934).

After retiring from the NHL in 1937, he coached the American Hockey League's Cleveland Barons for six seasons and led the team to Calder Cup titles twice (1939, 1941); in 1950, he led the Minneapolis Millers (United States Hockey League) to the Paul W. Loudon Trophy; and in 1951, he began a two-season stint as the coach of the NHL's Rangers before retiring from the game for good.

Cook was inducted into the Canadian Sports Hall of Fame in 1975, and in 1998, he was ranked number 44 on *The Hockey News*' list of the 100 Greatest Hockey Players, making him the highest-ranked player to have played a majority of his career with the Rangers.

William Cook's Career Statistics

			REGULAR SEASON					PLAYOFFS				
SEASON	TEAM	LEAGUE	GP	G	A	TP	PIM	GP	G	A	TP	PIM
1913	Kingston Frontenacs	OHA-Jr.										
1914–1915	Kingston Frontenacs	OHA-Sr.										
1919–1920	Kingston Frontenacs	OHA-Sr.										
1920–1921	Sault Ste. Marie Greyhounds	NOHA	9	12	7	19	48	5	5	1	6	
1920–1921	Sault Ste. Marie Greyhounds	NMHL	12	12	6	18						
1921–1922	Sault Ste. Marie Greyhounds	NMHL	12	20	8	28						
1921–1922	Sault Ste. Marie Greyhounds	NOHA	8	7	5	12	38	2	1	1	2	2
1922–1923	Saskatoon Sheiks	WCHL	30	9	16	25	19					
1923–1924	Saskatoon Crescents	WCHL	30	26	14	40	20					
1924–1925	Saskatoon Crescents	WCHL	27	22	10	32	79	2	0	0	0	4
1925–1926	Saskatoon Crescents	WHL	30	31	13	44	26	2	2	0	2	26
1926–1927	New York Rangers	NHL	44	33	4	37	58	2	1	0	1	6
1927–1928	New York Rangers	NHL	43	18	6	24	42	9	2	3	5	26
1928–1929	New York Rangers	NHL	43	15	8	23	41	6	0	0	0	6
1929–1930	New York Rangers	NHL	44	29	30	59	56	4	0	1	1	11
1930–1931	New York Rangers	NHL	43	30	12	42	39	4	3	0	3	4
1931–1932	New York Rangers	NHL	48	34	14	48	33	7	3	3	6	2
1932–1933	New York Rangers	NHL	48	28	22	50	51	8	3	2	5	4
1933–1934	New York Rangers	NHL	48	13	13	26	21	2	0	0	0	2
1934–1935	New York Rangers	NHL	48	21	15	36	23	4	1	2	3	7
1935–1936	New York Rangers	NHL	44	7	10	17	16					
1936–1937	New York Rangers	NHL	21	1	4	5	6					
1937–1938	Cleveland Barons	IAHL	5	0	0	0	5	1	0	0	0	0
	NHL TOTALS		474	229	138	367	386	46	13	11	24	68

Sources: Hockey Hall of Fame; Hockey-Reference.com

Coombes, Geoff "Jeff" (born: April 23, 1919 in Lincoln, England; died: December 5, 2002 in Rockledge, Florida); inducted into the National Soccer Hall of Fame and Museum in 1976 as a player; Position: Forward-Half Back; a member of the 1950 U.S. Men's National Team.

Growing up in High Wycombe, Buckinghamshire, England, Coombes played rugby and soccer in school and for local leagues. He and his family moved to the United States in 1935, and by 1939, he was on the Michigan All-Star team that played against the touring Scottish F.A. team, scoring Michigan's only goal in a 7–1 loss.

After serving in World War II, in 1946 he was a member of the Chicago Vikings team that won the U.S. Open Cup, and later that year, Coombes played for the Detroit Wolverines of the North American Professional Soccer League. In 1950, he was selected to the U.S. Men's National Team for the FIFA World Cup finals in Brazil, but never played in any games.

Coombes was inducted, along with the rest of the 1950 U.S. World Cup team, into the National Soccer Hall of Fame and Museum in 1976.

Source: National Soccer Hall of Fame and Museum

Cooper, Andrew Lewis "Andy" (born: April 24, 1898 in Waco, Texas; died: June 3, 1941 in Waco, Texas); inducted into the National Baseball Hall of Fame and Museum in 2006 as a player by the Negro Leagues Committee; Position: Pitcher; Bats: Right; Throws: Left; helped the Monarchs win the Negro National League pennant in 1929; holds the Negro League career record for saves (29).

Often ranked second only to Bill Foster among Negro League left-handed pitchers, the 6'2", 220-pound Cooper played for the Detroit Stars (Negro National League, 1920–1927) and the Kansas City Monarchs (Negro National League, 1928–1941). He won twice as many games as he lost and helped the Monarchs win the Negro National League pennant in 1929. As a player-manager, Cooper managed the Monarchs to three league titles between 1937 and 1940, and holds the Negro League career record for saves with 29.

His career statistics in the Negro Leagues include a record of 118–57 (.674), with 1,455 innings pitched, 1,330 hits, 263 walks, and 476 strikeouts. Playing in the California Winter League, Cooper pitched in 43 games over six seasons and compiled a record of 22–6 (.786).

Source: National Baseball Hall of Fame and Museum

Cooper, Charles "Tarzan" (born: August 30, 1907 in Newark, Delaware; died: December 19, 1980 in Philadelphia, Pennsylvania); inducted into the Naismith Memorial Basketball Hall of Fame in 1977 as a player; Position: Center; led the Rens to the 1939 World Professional Tournament title.

Cooper was a basketball star at Central High School (Philadelphia, Pennsylvania) from 1921 to 1925, before bypassing college to enter the professional ranks. His 20-year career started in 1924 with the Philadelphia Panthers of the Independent League. Staying within the league, he would go on to play for the Philadelphia Giants (1926–1929), New York Renaissance (an all-black team known as the Rens, 1929–1941), Long Island Grumman Hellcats (1941–1942), and the Washington Bears (1941–1944).

The 6'4", 215-pound Cooper led the Rens to 1,303 wins in 1,506 games (.865 record), including a streak of 88 straight victories (1932–1933). He led the team to the 1939 World Professional Tournament title and was the captain of the Bears team that won the title again in 1943.

Source: Naismith Memorial Basketball Hall of Fame

Cooper-Dyke, Cynthia Lynne (born: April 14, 1963) in Chicago, Illinois); inducted into the Naismith Memorial Basketball Hall of Fame in 2010 as a player; Position: Guard; won two NCAA Championships and four WNBA titles.

After going to Locke High School (Los Angeles, California), the 5'10" Cooper-Dyke attended the University of Southern California (Los Angeles, 1982–1986), where she won two NCAA Championships (1983–1984). After college, she joined the Houston Comets (1997–2000, 2003) of the Women's National Basketball Association, where she won four titles (1997–2000); named Finals MVP each time the Comets won a title; and was named regular-season Most Valuable Player twice (1997 and 1998).

She was the first player in WNBA history to score 500, 1,000, 2,000, and 2,500 career points. Cooper scored 30 or more points 16 times; had a 92-game double-figure scoring streak (1997–2000); and went on to coach the WNBA's Phoenix Mercury for just over a season.

While participating with USA Basketball, she won two Olympic medals (gold in 1988 [Seoul, South Korea] and bronze in 1992 [Barcelona, Spain]); a gold medal at the 1987 Pan American Games (Indianapolis, Indiana); and a gold medal at the 1990 Fédération Internationale de Basketball tournament in Malaysia.

After college and prior to joining the WNBA, Cooper played for several teams in Europe, including Segovia (Spain, 1986–1987); Parma (Italy, 1987–1994); and Alcamo (Italy, 1994–1996). In 1987, she was the Most Valuable Player of the European All-Star team and was twice named to the All-Star team of the Italian leagues (1996–1997).

In May 2005, Cooper was named the head coach of the women's basketball team at Prairie View A&M University (Prairie View, Texas), where she stayed until 2010. In her second season as coach, she led the Panthers to the Southwestern Athletic Conference title and to the school's first-ever Women's NCAA Tournament.

She was inducted into the Women's Basketball Hall of Fame in 2009 and in May 2010, she became the head coach of the women's basketball team at the University of North Carolina, Wilmington.

In 2000, she published her autobiography, *She Got Game: My Personal Odyssey*.

Cynthia Cooper-Dyke's WNBA Career Statistics

YEAR	TEAM	G	MP	FG	3P	FT	TRB	AST	STL	BLK	PTS
1997	Houston	28	982	191	67	172	111	131	59	6	621
1998	Houston	30	1,051	203	64	210	110	131	48	11	680
1999	Houston	31	1,101	212	58	204	87	162	43	11	686
2000	Houston	31	1,085	180	43	147	85	156	39	6	550
2003	Houston	4	144	16	7	25	10	22	4	1	64

YEAR	TEAM	G	MP	FG	3P	FT	TRB	AST	STL	BLK	PTS
	TOTALS	124	4,363	802	239	758	403	602	193	35	2,601

Sources: Naismith Memorial Basketball Hall of Fame; WNBA.com

Cordery, Ted (born: June 15, 1917 in San Francisco, California; died: June 1, 1996 in San Francisco, California); inducted into the National Soccer Hall of Fame and Museum in 1975 as a builder; served as secretary of the California Soccer Association.

Cordery began his soccer career in 1932 at Aptos (California) Junior High School and was on the team that won the city championship that same year. In 1934, he joined the San Francisco Rovers (San Francisco Soccer Football League); played for almost 20 years as the team won the California State Championship twice (1937, 1950); and was on the team as it won the San Francisco League title each season from 1934 to 1941.

After the team folded in 1954, Cordery went on to play for the Mercury Soccer Club for one season; in 1955, he played for the Olympic Club (San Francisco); and spent his last two playing seasons with the Viking Soccer Club.

After retiring as a player, he was elected secretary of the California Soccer Association, a position he held for 20 years. He also served as the California delegate to various United States Soccer Football Association conventions, National Junior Cup Commissioner and National Cup Coordinator, and was a member of the Rules and Revisions Committee for two years.

Source: National Soccer Hall of Fame and Museum

Ćosić, Krešimir (born: November 26, 1948 in Zagreb, Croatia; died: May 25, 1995 in Baltimore, Maryland); inducted into the Naismith Memorial Basketball Hall of Fame in 1996 as a player; his decision to attend Brigham Young University paved the way for international basketball players to come to America to play at the collegiate level.

The 6'11" Ćosić came to the United States specifically to play college basketball at Brigham Young University (Provo, Utah) from 1971 to 1973; became the first foreign-born player to earn All-American honors from United Press International (1972–1973); and was named to the All-Western Athletic Conference First-Team three times (1971–1973). He was named to the WAC All-Decade Team in 1974; played in the East-West College All-Star Game (1973); led BYU in scoring as a junior (22.3 points per game) and as a senior (20.2 points per game); and led the school to WAC titles and the NCAA Regional Finals twice (1971–1972). His decision to attend BYU paved the way for other international basketball players to come to America to play at the collegiate level.

Refusing to play professionally (having been drafted by both the Los Angeles Lakers of the National Basketball Association and the Carolina Cougars of the American Basketball Association), he returned to Yugoslavia in 1973; represented his country in four Olympic Games (1968, 1972, 1976, and in Moscow, Russia in 1980 Russia when he led his team to the gold medal); and led Yugoslavia to two World Championship gold medals (1970 in Yugoslavia and 1978 in the Philippines).

After retiring as a player, Ćosić coached the Yugoslav team to a silver medal in the 1988 Olympics in Seoul, South Korea, and was only the third international player ever elected to the Naismith Memorial Basketball Hall of Fame.

When his basketball career ended, he served in the United States as a diplomat at the Croatian Embassy in Washington, D.C., and in 2006, he became the second men's basketball player to have his jersey (#11) retired by BYU (following Danny Ainge).

Internationally, Ćosić played for KK Zadar (1964–1969, 1973–1975) and KK Cibona (1980–1983). He led Cibona to a gold medal (1980) and Zadar to two silver medals (1968, 1976); guided Cibona to a pair of World Championship gold medals (1970, 1978) and three European titles; earned First-Team All-European honors seven times; played for two-time Italian champions Virtus Bologna (1979–1980); and led Virtus Bologna to a third place finish in the European Cup of Champions (1980).

Source: Naismith Memorial Basketball Hall of Fame

Costello, Murray (born: February 24, 1934 in South Porcupine, Ontario, Canada); inducted into the Hockey Hall of Fame in 2005 as a builder; Position: Forward; served as president of the Canadian Amateur Hockey Association from 1979 to 1998.

Although an accomplished player, Costello's contributions to hockey are best known as a builder and executive. After three years of junior play with St. Michael's College (Toronto, Ontario), he was signed by the Chicago Black Hawks of the National Hockey League and made his professional debut during the 1953–1954 season.

The 6'3", 190-pound Costello was traded to the Boston Bruins the next season, and after just over a season in Boston, he was sent to the Detroit Red Wings. After being sent to the Edmonton Flyers (Western Hockey League) in 1956, Costello regained his amateur status and finished his playing career with the Windsor Bulldogs (Ontario Hockey Association Senior League).

After his playing career, Costello worked in the front office of the Seattle Totems (Western Hockey League), and guided the team to back-to-back championships in 1967 and 1968. He later served as president of the Canadian Amateur Hockey Association (now known as Hockey Canada) from 1979 to 1998.

Costello served on the Hockey Hall of Fame Board of Directors, and was a member of its Selection Committee.

Murray Costello's Career Statistics

			REGULAR SEASON					PLAYOFFS				
SEASON	TEAM	LEAGUE	GP	G	A	TP	PIM	GP	G	A	TP	PIM
1950–1951	St. Michael's Majors	OHA-Jr.	50	18	16	34	24					
1951–1952	St. Michael's Majors	OHA-Jr.	51	16	27	43	18	8	5	8	13	4
1952–1953	St. Michael's Majors	OHA-Jr.	51	30	28	58	38	17	7	8	15	13
1953–1954	Galt Black Hawks	OHA-Jr.	3	1	0	1	0					
1953–1954	Chicago Black Hawks	NHL	40	3	2	5	6					
1953–1954	Hershey Bears	AHL	26	7	13	20	10	11	4	4	8	9
1954–1955	Boston Bruins	NHL	54	4	11	15	25	1	0	0	0	2
1955–1956	Boston Bruins	NHL	41	6	6	12	19					
1955–1956	Detroit Red Wings	NHL	24	0	0	0	4	4	0	0	0	0
1956–1957	Detroit Red Wings	NHL	3	0	0	0	0					
1956–1957	Edmonton Flyers	WHL	65	19	26	45	37	7	0	2	2	12
1958–1959	Windsor Bulldogs	OHA-Sr.	35	14	20	34	26					
1959–1960	Windsor Bulldogs	OHA-Sr.	43	18	20	38	23	17	5	7	12	12
	NHL TOTALS		162	13	19	32	54	5	0	0	0	2

Sources: Hockey Hall of Fame; Hockey-Reference.com

Coulter, Arthur Edmund "Art" (born: May 31, 1909 in Winnipeg, Manitoba, Canada; died: October 14, 2000 in Mobile, Alabama); inducted into the Hockey Hall of Fame as a player in 1974; Position: Defenseman; won two Stanley Cup titles.

During Coulter's 465-game, 11-year National Hockey League career, he played for the Chicago Black Hawks (1931–1936) and the New York Rangers (1936–1942). His professional career began in 1929 with the Philadelphia Arrows (Can-Am League), and in the 1930–1931 season, he led the league in penalty minutes.

He helped Chicago win its first Stanley Cup title in 1934; was named to the NHL Second All-Star team in 1935; was traded to the New York Rangers in 1936 and became the team's captain in 1937; selected to three consecutive Second All-Star teams (1938–1940); and helped the franchise win its third Stanley Cup title in 1940.

Coulter joined the Canadian Armed Forces during World War II; spent two seasons with the Coast Guard Clippers (Eastern League); and was named to the league's First All-Star team in 1943.

Art Coulter's Career Statistics

			REGULAR SEASON					PLAYOFFS				
SEASON	TEAM	LEAGUE	GP	G	A	TP	PIM	GP	G	A	TP	PIM
1924–1925	Winnipeg Pilgrims	WJrHL										
1925–1926	Winnipeg Pilgrims	WJrHL	9	3	1	4	10					
1926–1927	Winnipeg Pilgrims	WJrHL	5	3	2	5	6					
1929–1930	Philadelphia Arrows	Can-Am	35	2	2	4	40	2	0	0	0	2
1930–1931	Philadelphia Arrows	Can-Am	40	4	8	12	109					
1931–1932	Philadelphia Arrows	Can-Am	26	9	4	13	42					
1931–1932	Chicago Black Hawks	NHL	13	0	1	1	23	2	1	0	1	0
1932–1933	Chicago Black Hawks	NHL	46	3	2	5	53					
1933–1934	Chicago Black Hawks	NHL	46	5	2	7	39	8	1	0	1	10
1934–1935	Chicago Black Hawks	NHL	48	4	8	12	68	2	0	0	0	5

SEASON	TEAM	LEAGUE	REGULAR SEASON GP	G	A	TP	PIM	PLAYOFFS GP	G	A	TP	PIM
1935–1936	Chicago Black Hawks	NHL	25	0	2	2	18					
1935–1936	New York Rangers	NHL	23	1	5	6	26					
1936–1937	New York Rangers	NHL	47	1	5	6	27	9	0	3	3	15
1937–1938	New York Rangers	NHL	43	5	10	15	90					
1938–1939	New York Rangers	NHL	44	4	8	12	58	7	1	1	2	6
1939–1940	New York Rangers	NHL	48	1	9	10	68	12	1	0	1	21
1940–1941	New York Rangers	NHL	35	5	14	19	42	3	0	0	0	0
1941–1942	New York Rangers	NHL	47	1	16	17	31	6	0	1	1	4
1942–1943	Coast Guard Clippers	EAHL	37	13	20	33	32	10	4	1	5	8
1943–1944	Coast Guard Clippers	Exhib.	26	10	13	23	10	12	6	8	14	8
	NHL TOTALS		465	30	82	112	543	49	4	5	9	61

Sources: Hockey Hall of Fame; Hockey-Reference.com

Cournoyer, Yvan Serge "Roadrunner" (born: November 22, 1943 in Drummondville, Quebec, Canada); inducted into the Hockey Hall of Fame in 1982 as a player; Position: Forward; Uniform: #12; won 10 Stanley Cup titles.

Cournoyer played his entire 16-season National Hockey League career (1963–1979) with the Montreal Canadiens; won 10 Stanley Cup titles (1965–1966, 1968–1969, 1971, 1973, 1976–1979); and was the team's captain.

Due to his relatively small size (5'7", 172 pounds), he rarely played during his first four years with the Canadiens, although he was on teams that won three Stanley Cup titles. Beginning in his fourth season, Cournoyer began playing in more games; scored 43 points in the 1968–1969 season; was named to the NHL's Second All-Star Team for the first of his four times (1969, 1971–1973); and won the Conn Smythe Trophy in 1973 as the MVP of the Stanley Cup playoffs.

Cournoyer scored three goals for Canada in the 1972 Summit Series, and eventually retired 15 games into the 1978–1979 season after winning 10 Stanley Cup championships. In 1998, he was ranked number 98 on *The Hockey News*' list of the 100 Greatest Hockey Players, and in November 2005, the Canadiens retired his uniform number 12.

Yvan Cournoyer's Career Statistics

SEASON	TEAM	LEAGUE	REGULAR SEASON GP	G	A	TP	PIM	+/–	PLAYOFFS GP	G	A	TP	PIM
1960–1961	Lachine Maroons	MMJHL	42	37	31	68							
1961–1962	Montreal Jr. Canadiens	OHA-Jr.	35	15	16	31	8		6	4	4	8	0
1962–1963	Montreal Jr. Canadiens	OHA-Jr.	36	37	27	64	24		10	3	4	7	6
1963–1964	Montreal Jr. Canadiens	OHA-Jr.	53	63	48	111	30		17	19	8	27	15
1963–1964	Montreal Canadiens	NHL	5	4	0	4	0						
1964–1965	Montreal Canadiens	NHL	55	7	10	17	10		12	3	1	4	0
1964–1965	Quebec Aces	AHL	7	2	1	3	0						
1965–1966	Montreal Canadiens	NHL	65	18	11	29	8		10	2	3	5	2
1966–1967	Montreal Canadiens	NHL	69	25	15	40	14		10	2	3	5	6
1967–1968	Montreal Canadiens	NHL	64	28	32	60	23	+19	13	6	8	14	4
1968–1969	Montreal Canadiens	NHL	76	43	44	87	31	+19	14	4	7	11	5
1969–1970	Montreal Canadiens	NHL	72	27	36	63	23	+1					
1970–1971	Montreal Canadiens	NHL	65	37	36	73	21	+20	20	10	12	22	6
1971–1972	Montreal Canadiens	NHL	73	47	36	83	15	+23	6	2	1	3	2
1972–1973	Canada	Summit-72	8	3	2	5	2						
1972–1973	Montreal Canadiens	NHL	67	40	39	79	18	+50	17	15	10	25	2
1973–1974	Montreal Canadiens	NHL	67	40	33	73	18	+16	6	5	2	7	2
1974–1975	Montreal Canadiens	NHL	76	29	45	74	32	+16	11	5	6	11	4
1975–1976	Montreal Canadiens	NHL	71	32	36	68	20	+37	13	3	6	9	4
1976–1977	Montreal Canadiens	NHL	60	25	28	53	8	+27					
1977–1978	Montreal Canadiens	NHL	68	24	29	53	12	+39	15	7	4	11	10
1978–1979	Montreal Canadiens	NHL	15	2	5	7	2	+5					
	NHL TOTALS		968	428	435	863	255		147	64	63	127	47

Sources: Hockey Hall of Fame; Hockey-Reference.com

Cousy, Robert Joseph "Bob" (born: August 9, 1928 in New York, New York); inducted into the Naismith Memorial Basketball Hall of Fame as a player in 1971; Position: Guard; Uniform: #14; won six NBA titles; holds the NBA record for most assists in one half; holds the NBA record for most free throws in an NBA game.

At Andrew Jackson High School (Queens, New York, 1942–1946), Cousy was a three-year letter winner and was selected All-Metropolitan in 1946. At the College of the Holy Cross (Worcester, Massachusetts, 1946 to 1950), he helped lead the team to the NCAA championship (1947); was selected *The Sporting News*' Second-Team All-American (1949); *The Sporting News'* First-Team All-American (1950); was a two-time All-Conference and All-New England selection (1949–1950); and was the team's Most Valuable Player and leading scorer (1949–1950).

After college, he was drafted in 1950 by the National Basketball League/National Basketball Association Tri-Cities Blackhawks, but was then traded to the Chicago Stags. After the team folded, Cousy was signed by the Boston Celtics, where he stayed from 1950 until 1963. After coaching in college, he returned to the NBA briefly to play for the Cincinnati Royals (1969–1970), before becoming an NBA coach.

At 6'1", 175 pounds, Cousy was named NBA MVP in 1957; selected to the All-NBA First Team 10 times (1952–1961); All-NBA Second Team twice (1962–1963); was a two-time All-Star Game MVP (1954, 1957); a 13-time All-Star (1951–1963); and won six NBA championships (1957, 1959–1963). He led the NBA in assists from 1953 to 1960; holds the NBA record for most assists in one half (19, February 27, 1959 against the Minneapolis Lakers); and was selected to the NBA 25th Anniversary All-Time Team (1970), the NBA 35th Anniversary All-Time Team (1980), and the NBA 50th Anniversary All-Time Team (1996).

After leaving the Celtics in 1963, Cousy coached at Boston College (Massachusetts, 1963–1969); compiled a 117–38 (.755) record; was named New England Coach of the Year twice (1968–1969); led the school to three NIT's (including the 1969 finals); and coached his teams in two NCAA Tournaments (including the 1967 Eastern Regional Finals).

Leaving the college ranks, Cousy returned to the NBA as a player-coach with the Cincinnati Royals in 1969 (becoming the league's oldest player ever at age 41), and after one year of playing, stayed on as the team's coach until 1972. He moved on to coach the Kansas City-Omaha Kings from 1972 to 1974, before retiring with an overall 141–209 (.403) coaching record in five professional seasons.

He retired as the Celtics' all-time leader in assists (6,955) and still holds the NBA record for most free throws in an NBA game (making 30 free throws in 32 attempts in a playoff game on March 21, 1953 against the Syracuse Nationals).

After retiring, Cousy served as the Commissioner of the American Soccer League in the late 1970s; made a cameo appearance in the 1994 movie, *Blue Chips* (with Nick Nolte); and has worked in a variety of positions within the Celtics organization. In October 1963, his jersey number 14 was retired by the Celtics, and in 1996, Cousy was chosen as one of the NBA's 50 greatest players of all time.

Bob Cousy's NBA Career Statistics

SEASON	TEAM	G	MIN	FG	FT	TRB	AST	POINTS
1950–1951	Boston	69		401	276	474	341	1,078
1951–1952	Boston	66	2,681	512	409	421	441	1,433
1952–1953	Boston	71	2,945	464	479	449	547	1,407
1953–1954	Boston	72	2,857	486	411	394	518	1,383
1954–1955	Boston	71	2,747	522	460	424	557	1,504
1955–1956	Boston	72	2,767	440	476	492	642	1,356
1956–1957	Boston	64	2,364	478	363	309	478	1,319
1957–1958	Boston	65	2,222	445	277	322	463	1,167
1958–1959	Boston	65	2,403	484	329	359	557	1,297
1959–1960	Boston	75	2,588	568	319	352	715	1,455
1960–1961	Boston	76	2,468	513	352	331	587	1,378
1961–1962	Boston	75	2,116	462	251	261	584	1,175
1962–1963	Boston	76	1,975	392	219	193	515	1,003
1969–1970	Cincinnati	7	34	1	3	5	10	5
	TOTALS	924	30,167	6,168	4,624	4,786	6,955	16,960

Bob Cousy's NBA Coaching Record

SEASON	TEAM	W	L	WIN%
1969–1970	Cincinnati	36	46	.439
1970–1971	Cincinnati	33	49	.402
1971–1972	Cincinnati	30	52	.366
1972–1973	Kansas City-Omaha	36	46	.439
1973–1974	Kansas City-Omaha	6	16	.273
	TOTALS	141	209	.403

Sources: Basketball-Reference.com; Naismith Memorial Basketball Hall of Fame

Coveleski, Stanley Anthony "Stan" (born: July 13, 1889 in Shamokin, Pennsylvania; died: March 20, 1984 in South Bend, Indiana); inducted into the National Baseball Hall of Fame and Museum in 1969 as a player by the Veterans Committee; Position: Pitcher; Bats: Right; Throws: Right; pitched a 19-inning complete game win over the New York Yankees in 1918.

Making his major league debut on September 10, 1912, Coveleski enjoyed a 14-year American League career with the Philadelphia Athletics (1912), Cleveland Indians (1916–1924), Washington Senators (1925–1927), and New York Yankees (1928). He played in two World Series (winning in 1920 and losing in 1925).

Although Coveleski pitched a three-hit shutout against the Detroit Tigers in his first start with the Athletics in 1912, he only played in five games for the team before being sent to the minor leagues (Pacific Coast League). He returned to the majors when his contract was bought by the Indians, and he would go on to become a five-time 20-game winner with Cleveland and Washington. On May 24, 1918, he pitched a 19-inning complete game 3–2 win over the New York Yankees, and in the 1920 World Series, he pitched three complete-game wins against the Brooklyn Robins, while only allowing two runs (an earned run average of 0.67).

The 5'11", 165-pound pitcher was best known for his spitball and was one of 17 pitchers allowed to continue throwing the pitch when it was outlawed in 1920. He is still one of the top 100 winning pitchers in major league history; in 1976, he was inducted into the National Polish-American Sports Hall of Fame and Museum; and the minor league baseball stadium in South Bend, Indiana is named in his honor.

Stan Coveleski's Career Statistics

YEAR	TEAM	LG	W	L	PCT	G	SH	IP	H	R	ER	SO	BB	ERA
1912	Philadelphia	AL	2	1	.667	5	1	21	18	9		9	4	
1916	Cleveland	AL	15	13	.536	45	1	232	247	100	88	76	58	3.41
1917	Cleveland	AL	19	14	.576	45	9	298	202	78	60	133	94	1.81
1918	Cleveland	AL	22	13	.629	38	2	311	261	91	63	87	76	1.82
1919	Cleveland	AL	24	12	.667	43	4	296	286	99	83	118	60	2.52
1920	Cleveland	AL	24	14	.632	41	3	315	284	110	87	133	65	2.49
1921	Cleveland	AL	23	13	.639	43	2	315	341	137	118	99	84	3.37
1922	Cleveland	AL	17	14	.548	35	3	277	292	120	102	98	64	3.31
1923	Cleveland	AL	13	14	.481	33	5	228	251	98	70	54	42	2.76
1924	Cleveland	AL	15	16	.484	37	2	240	286	140	108	58	73	4.05
1925	Washington	AL	20	5	.800	32	3	241	230	86	76	58	73	2.84
1926	Washington	AL	14	11	.560	36	3	245	272	112	85	50	81	3.12
1927	Washington	AL	2	1	.667	5	0	14	13	7	5	3	8	3.21
1928	New York	AL	5	1	.833	12	0	58	72	41	37	5	20	5.74
	TOTALS		215	142	.602	450	38	3,091	3,055	1,228	982	981	802	2.88

Sources: Baseball-Reference.com; National Baseball Hall of Fame and Museum

Cowens, David William "Dave" (born: October 25, 1948 in Newport, Kentucky); inducted into the Naismith Memorial Basketball Hall of Fame in 1991 as a player; Position: Center; Uniform: #18; Florida State University's all-time rebounding leader; NBA's co-Rookie of the Year (1971); NBA Most Valuable Player (1973).

Although Cowens' basketball career did not begin at Newport (Kentucky) Central Catholic High School (1962–1966) until he was a junior, he would become a two-year letter winner, and won a scholarship to Florida State University (Tallahassee, 1966–1970), where he was named to *The Sporting News* All-America Second Team as a senior.

During his collegiate career, Cowens scored 1,479 points in 78 games (19.0 points per game); ended his career among FSU's top 10 all-time scoring leaders; was FSU's all-time leading rebounder with 1,340 (17.2 per game); holds the school's record for best seasonal rebound average (17.5 in the 1968–1969 season); and his jersey number 13 was retired by the team.

After graduating from FSU, Cowens was a first-round pick (fourth overall selection) in the 1970 NBA Draft of the Boston Celtics, and went on to an 11-year NBA career with the Celtics (1970–1980) and Milwaukee Bucks (1982–1983). He was named co-Rookie of the Year in 1971 (with Portland's Geoff Petrie); league's Most Valuable Player in 1973; named to the All-NBA Second Team three times (1973, 1975, 1976); to the NBA All-Defensive First Team in 1976; to the NBA All-Defensive Second Team twice (1975, 1980); was the 1973 NBA All-Star Game Most Valuable Player; a seven-time NBA All-Star (1972–1978); named to the NBA 50th Anniversary All-Time Team (1996); and won two championships with the Boston Celtics (1974, 1976).

Relatively small for a center (6'9", 230 pounds), Cowens was known to roam the outside lanes and take jump shots instead of the more traditional role of being a back-to-the-basket pivot player. He played the entire 1970s with the Celtics, briefly retired, and returned to the NBA to play 40 games for the Milwaukee Bucks in the 1982–1983 season, before retiring for good.

Known as "Big Red," Cowens averaged 17.6 points and 13.6 rebounds per game; was the Celtics' player-coach during the 1978–1979 season; and played one year (1984–1985) with the Bay State Bombers of the Continental Basketball Association. After his playing days, he served as an assistant coach with the San Antonio Spurs (1994–1996); head coach of the Charlotte Hornets from 1996 to 1999; and was the head coach for the Golden State Warriors for 105 games (1999–2001). In May 2005, Cowens was named head coach of the newly formed Chicago Sky in the Women's National Basketball Association, and after winning only five games in the 2006 season, he left the team and joined the coaching staff of the NBA's Detroit Pistons in September 2006.

Dave Cowens' Career Statistics

SEASON	TEAM	G	MIN	FG	FT	REB	ASST	POINTS
1970–1971	Boston	81	3,076	550	273	1,216	228	1,373
1971–1972	Boston	79	3,186	657	175	1,203	245	1,489
1972–1973	Boston	82	3,425	740	204	1,329	333	1,684
1973–1974	Boston	80	3,352	645	228	1,257	354	1,518
1974–1975	Boston	65	2,632	569	191	958	296	1,329
1975–1976	Boston	78	3,101	611	257	1,246	325	1,479
1976–1977	Boston	50	1,888	328	162	697	248	818
1977–1978	Boston	77	3,215	598	239	1,078	351	1,435
1978–1979	Boston	68	2,517	488	151	652	242	1,127
1979–1980	Boston	66	2,159	422	95	534	206	940
1982–1983	Milwaukee	40	1,014	136	52	274	82	324
	TOTALS	766	29,565	5,744	2,027	10,444	2,910	13,516

Dave Cowens' NBA Coaching Record

		REGULAR SEASON			PLAYOFFS		
SEASON	TEAM	W	L	WIN%	W	L	WIN%
1978–1979	Boston Celtics	27	41	.397			
1996–1997	Charlotte Hornets	54	28	.659	0	3	.000
1997–1998	Charlotte Hornets	51	31	.622	4	5	.444
1998–1999	Charlotte Hornets	4	11	.267			
2000–2001	Golden State Warriors	17	65	.207			
2001–2002	Golden State Warriors	8	15	.348			
	TOTALS	161	191	.457	4	8	.333

Sources: Basketball-Reference.com; Naismith Memorial Basketball Hall of Fame

Cowley, William Mailes "Bill" (born: June 12, 1912 in Bristol, Quebec, Canada; died: December 31, 1993); inducted into the Hockey Hall of Fame in 1968 as a player; Position: Forward-Center; led the NHL in assists three times; only hockey hall of famer to have begun his NHL career with the St. Louis Eagles.

Cowley played 13 seasons in the National Hockey League with the St. Louis Eagles (1934–1935) and the Boston Bruins (1935–1947), and led the league in assists three times. After playing juniors and seniors for five seasons, he joined the NHL and is the only hall of fame player to have begun his career with the Eagles. When the team folded after his one year, Cowley went to the Boston Bruins in a dispersal draft.

In the 1937–1938 season, he scored 39 points and was selected to the NHL First All-Star Team. The next season, he led the league in assists (34) and helped the team to its second Stanley Cup championship, his first. In 1941, Cowley was the NHL's scoring leader and won the Hart Memorial Trophy (as the league's MVP), helping the Bruins win the team's second Stanley Cup in three years.

He again led the league in assists in 1941 and 1943, with 45 each season. His 45 assists in 1940–1941 in a 48-game schedule established a new league record. He won the Hart Memorial Trophy again in 1943; was named to the NHL First All-Star Team Center three more times (1941, 1943–1944); and was selected the Second All-Star Team Center in 1945.

On February 12, 1947, in his last season with the Bruins, Cowley surpassed Syd Howe as the NHL's career points leader, a record that would last for five years until topped by Elmer Lach. He recorded at least 30 assists in five seasons, and in 549 regular-season games he scored 548 points (195 goals, 353 assists).

After his playing days, Cowley coached in the Ottawa senior leagues and with the Vancouver Canucks of the Pacific Coast Hockey League. In 1998, he was ranked number 53 on *The Hockey News*' list of the 100 Greatest Hockey Players. The only NHL players who averaged more points per game in a season than Cowley's 1.97 in 1944 are Wayne Gretzky and Mario Lemieux.

Bill Cowley's Career Statistics

			REGULAR SEASON					PLAYOFFS				
SEASON	**TEAM**	**LEAGUE**	**GP**	**G**	**A**	**TP**	**PIM**	**GP**	**G**	**A**	**TP**	**PIM**
1929–1930	Glebe Collegiate (Ottawa)	High-ON										
1930–1931	Ottawa Primrose	OCJHL	14	10	2	12	16	4	4	1	5	8
1930–1931	Ottawa Primrose	M-Cup	9	9	3	12	4					
1931–1932	Ottawa Jr. Shamrocks	OCJHL	2	2	1	3	2	3	4	4	8	2
1931–1932	Ottawa Shamrocks	OCHL						1	0	0	0	0
1932–1933	Ottawa Shamrocks	OCHL	14	7	6	13	24	4	1	0	1	4
1933–1934	Halifax Wolverines	MSHL	38	25	25	50	42	6	2	2	4	2
1934–1935	St. Louis Eagles	NHL	41	5	7	12	10					
1934–1935	Tulsa Oilers	AHA	1	0	0	0	5					
1935–1936	Boston Bruins	NHL	48	11	10	21	17	2	2	1	3	2
1936–1937	Boston Bruins	NHL	46	13	22	35	4	3	0	3	3	0
1937–1938	Boston Bruins	NHL	48	17	22	39	8	3	2	0	2	0
1938–1939	Boston Bruins	NHL	34	8	34	42	2	12	3	11	14	2
1939–1940	Boston Bruins	NHL	48	13	27	40	24	6	0	1	1	7
1940–1941	Boston Bruins	NHL	46	17	45	62	16	2	0	0	0	0
1941–1942	Boston Bruins	NHL	28	4	23	27	6	5	0	3	3	5
1942–1943	Boston Bruins	NHL	48	27	45	72	10	9	1	7	8	4
1943–1944	Boston Bruins	NHL	36	30	41	71	12					
1944–1945	Boston Bruins	NHL	49	25	40	65	12	7	3	3	6	0
1945–1946	Boston Bruins	NHL	26	12	12	24	6	10	1	3	4	2
1946–1947	Boston Bruins	NHL	51	13	25	38	16	5	0	2	2	0
1947–1948	Ottawa Army	OHA-Sr.										
	NHL TOTALS		549	195	353	548	143	64	12	34	46	22

Sources: Hockey Hall of Fame; Hockey-Reference.com

Craddock, Robert B. (born: date unknown in England; died: date and location unknown); inducted into the National Soccer Hall of Fame and Museum in 1959 as a builder; served as president of the Greater Pittsburgh and West Penn Leagues.

Craddock arrived in the United States in 1907 and went on to become a player, official, and administrator at various soccer levels of competition in the Pittsburgh, Pennsylvania area. In the 1920s, he played in the Central League with the Pittsburgh Rovers, Thistles, and Arsenal. He later was an official in the Allegheny Valley League and served as president of the Greater Pittsburgh and West Penn leagues. Craddock also served as president of the Allegheny Valley League in the 1950s through 1963 and later served as district commissioner for the National Open Cup.

He was the father of National Soccer Hall of Fame and Museum inductee Robert W. Craddock, who was inducted in 1997 as a player.

Source: National Soccer Hall of Fame and Museum

Craddock, Robert W. (born: September 5, 1923 in Lawrenceville, Pennsylvania; died: March 28, 2003 in Myrtle Beach, South Carolina); inducted into the National Soccer Hall of Fame and Museum in 1997 as a player; Position: Forward; International Caps (1954): 1; International Goals: 0; won two U.S. Open Cup medals.

Craddock played most of his career in the Pittsburgh, Pennsylvania area for Castle Shannon and later with Harmarville, where he won an Amateur Cup medal in 1951 and two U.S. Open Cup medals (1952, 1956). While still playing for Harmarville, he was selected to the men's team for the 1950 FIFA World Cup, but never played in any games. He earned his only international cap in the National Team's 3–0 win over Haiti on April 4, 1954.

His father, Robert B. Craddock, was inducted into the National Soccer Hall of Fame and Museum in 1959 as a builder.

Source: National Soccer Hall of Fame and Museum

Craggs, Edmund (born: 1897 in Colombo, Ceylon; died: 1974 in Seattle, Washington); inducted into the National Soccer Hall of Fame and Museum in 1969 as a builder; served as commissioner of the Washington State Soccer Football Association.

After playing soccer as a boy, Craggs left school when he was 14, and eventually moved to Canada in 1914 (age 17), where he played soccer at Westmount High School (Montreal, Quebec).

He later played in Prince Rupert, British Columbia for 10 years; moved to Seattle, Washington in September 1947 and helped form the Fremont Boys Soccer Club; and by 1949, he was playing for Buchan S.C. in the first division of the State League.

While still playing, Craggs managed teams in the first division from 1958 to 1962; became a referee while still an active player in the State League; in 1962, he began refereeing senior games in the state of Washington and later refereed games in the North American Soccer League; was elected to the Washington State Soccer Football Association in 1957 and served as commissioner until 1961.

Source: National Soccer Hall of Fame and Museum

Craggs, George (born: July 8, 1929 in Calgary, Alberta, Canada); inducted into the National Soccer Hall of Fame and Museum in 1981 as a builder; served as commissioner of the Washington State Association.

Craggs was a long-time player (halfback) for amateur teams in Canada and Seattle, Washington from 1945 to 1961. He played in the Washington State League from 1949 to 1961 with first division Buchan S.C. and Germania S.C., and was also a team manager from 1958 to 1962.

He represented the Catholic Youth Organization from 1959 to 1978; was a United States Soccer Federation national referee for 23 years; and received the Barney Kempton Memorial Trophy for outstanding service to soccer in 1969.

Source: National Soccer Hall of Fame and Museum

Crawford, Joan (born: August 22, 1937 in Fort Smith, Arkansas); inducted into the Naismith Memorial Basketball Hall of Fame in 1997 as a player; won 10 AAU championships with Nashville Business College.

Crawford attended Van Buren (Arkansas) High School from 1951 to 1955 and led the team to three consecutive state championships. She was selected All-District three times; was a three-time team captain; and an All-State selection (1953) as both an offensive and defensive player. After high school, she went to Clarendon Junior College (Texas) from 1955 to 1957, where she earned All-American honors, before moving on to Nashville Business College (Tennessee, 1957–1969) as an amateur player.

At 5'11", 155 pounds, Crawford was an Amateur Athletic Union star in the late 1950s and 1960s, playing 14 AAU seasons (1955–1969), two with Clarendon and 12 with Nashville Business College. She was named to 12 consecutive AAU All-America teams and won 10 AAU championships (eight consecutively) with Nashville Business College. She was a member of the USA National Team six times (1958–1959, 1961–1962, 1965–1966) and was named Most Valuable Player in both the 1963 and 1964 National AAU Tournaments. She led the United States to a gold medal in the

1959 (Chicago, Illinois) and 1963 (São Paulo, Brazil) Pan American Games, and was a member of the 1957 USA World Championship team that defeated Russia for the gold medal.

Crawford was inducted into the AAU Hall of Fame in 1961; the Helms Women's Basketball Hall of Fame in 1967; the Arkansas Sports Hall of Fame in 1978; and the Women's Basketball Hall of Fame in 1999. She served on the National Association for Girls and Women in Sport's Rules Committee; the AAU Board of Governors; and the National AAU Executive Committee.

Sources: Arkansas Sports Hall of Fame; Naismith Memorial Basketball Hall of Fame; Women's Basketball Hall of Fame

Crawford, Samuel Earl "Sam" (born: April 18, 1880 in Wahoo, Nebraska; died: June 15, 1968 in Hollywood, California); inducted into the National Baseball Hall of Fame and Museum in 1957 as a player by the Veterans Committee; Position: Right Field; Bats: Left; Throws: Left; set the major league record for triples; set the single-season and career record for most inside-the-park home runs.

Making his debut on September 10, 1899, the 6', 190-pound Crawford played 19 major league seasons with the Cincinnati Reds (1899–1902) and the Detroit Tigers in the newly created American League (1903–1917). He played in, and lost, three consecutive World Series (1907–1909).

Nicknamed "Wahoo Sam," he used his speed on the base paths to hit triples and set the major league career record of 312 by the time he retired. He led the league in triples six times; stole 363 bases; and helped lead the Tigers (with teammate Ty Cobb) to three straight American League pennants (1907–1909). His speed helped him set the single-season record for most inside-the-park home runs (12) in 1901 and for most in a career (51). He also led the major leagues in home runs twice (1901, 1908).

He was inducted into the Cincinnati Reds Hall of Fame in 1968; in 1999, he was ranked number 84 on *The Sporting News*' list of the 100 Greatest Baseball Players; and was nominated as a finalist for the Major League Baseball All-Century Team.

After his playing days, Crawford became an umpire in the Pacific Coast League for four years.

Sam Crawford's Career Statistics

YEAR	TEAM	LG	G	AB	R	H	2B	3B	HR	BB	SO	SB	AVG	SLG
1899	Cincinnati	NL	31	127	25	39	2	8	1	2		3	.307	.472
1900	Cincinnati	NL	96	385	67	104	14	15	7	28		14	.270	.439
1901	Cincinnati	NL	124	523	89	175	22	16	16	37		13	.335	.530
1902	Cincinnati	NL	140	555	94	185	16	23	3	47		16	.333	.461
1903	Detroit	AL	137	545	93	181	23	25	4	25		18	.332	.488
1904	Detroit	AL	150	571	46	141	21	17	2	44		20	.247	.354
1905	Detroit	AL	154	575	73	171	40	10	6	50		22	.297	.433
1906	Detroit	AL	145	563	65	166	25	16	2	38		24	.295	.407
1907	Detroit	AL	144	582	102	188	34	17	4	37		18	.323	.460
1908	Detroit	AL	152	591	102	184	33	16	7	37		15	.311	.457
1909	Detroit	AL	156	589	83	185	35	14	6	47		30	.314	.452
1910	Detroit	AL	154	588	83	170	26	19	5	37		20	.289	.423
1911	Detroit	AL	146	574	109	217	36	14	7	61		37	.378	.526
1912	Detroit	AL	149	581	81	189	30	21	4	42		41	.325	.470
1913	Detroit	AL	153	610	78	193	32	23	9	52	28	13	.316	.489
1914	Detroit	AL	157	582	74	183	22	26	8	69	31	25	.314	.483
1915	Detroit	AL	156	612	81	183	31	19	4	66	29	24	.299	.431
1916	Detroit	AL	100	322	41	92	11	13	0	37	10	10	.286	.401
1917	Detroit	AL	61	104	6	18	4	0	2	4	6	0	.173	.269
	TOTALS		2,505	9,579	1,392	2,964	457	312	97	760	104	363	.309	.453

Sources: Baseball-Reference.com; Cincinnati Reds Hall of Fame; Elias Sports Bureau; National Baseball Hall of Fame and Museum

Crawford, Samuel Russell "Rusty" (born: November 7, 1885 in Cardinal, Ontario, Canada; died: December 19, 1971); inducted into the Hockey Hall of Fame in 1962 as a player; Position: Forward; won two Stanley Cup titles.

The 5'11", 165-pound Crawford played 12 professional seasons from 1912 to 1926, including two years in the National Hockey League with the Ottawa Senators (1917–1918) and the Toronto Arenas (1917–1919). Prior to the creation of the NHL, he played in the National Hockey Association, and after a brief NHL career, went on to skate in the Western Canadian Hockey League and the American Hockey Association.

After playing senior-level hockey, Crawford played five seasons in the National Hockey Association with the Quebec Bulldogs, helping lead the team to a Stanley Cup title in 1913. Prior to the inaugural NHL season (1917–1918), Crawford was selected by the Ottawa Senators in the Dispersal Draft, and later led the Toronto Arenas to the 1918 Stanley Cup championship.

Retiring from the NHL in 1919, he went on to play senior level hockey until 1930, when he coached in the Saskatchewan Senior League.

Sam Crawford's Career Statistics

			REGULAR SEASON					PLAYOFFS				
SEASON	**TEAM**	**LEAGUE**	**GP**	**G**	**A**	**TP**	**PIM**	**GP**	**G**	**A**	**TP**	**PIM**
1907–1908	Montreal Montegnards	MCHL										
1908–1909	Newington Ontarios	OHA-Sr.										
1909–1910	Prince Albert Mintos	N-SSHL	3	4	0	4						
1909–1910	Prince Albert Mintos	Sask-Pro						4	1	0	1	14
1910–1911	Prince Albert Mintos	Sask-Pro	7	26	0	26		4	4	0	4	26
1911–1912	Saskatoon Hoo-Hoos	Sask-Pro	7	7	0	7						
1911–1912	Saskatoon Wholesalers	Sask-Pro	1	2	0	2		2	2	0	2	12
1912–1913	Quebec Bulldogs	NHA	19	4	0	4	29					
1912–1913	Quebec Bulldogs	St-Cup						1	0	0	0	0
1912–1913	Quebec Bulldogs	Exhib.						3	3	0	3	19
1913–1914	Quebec Bulldogs	NHA	19	15	10	25	14					
1914–1915	Quebec Bulldogs	NHA	20	18	8	26	30					
1915–1916	Quebec Bulldogs	NHA	22	18	5	23	54					
1916–1917	Quebec Bulldogs	NHA	19	11	9	20	77					
1917–1918	Ottawa Senators	NHL	12	2	2	4	15					
1917–1918	Toronto Arenas	NHL	8	1	2	3	51	2	2	1	3	9
1918–1919	Toronto Arenas	NHL	18	7	4	11	51					
1919–1920	Saskatoon Crescents	SSHL	12	3	3	6	14					
1920–1921	Saskatoon Crescents	SSHL	14	11	7	18	12	4	2	2	4	4
1921–1922	Saskatoon Crescents / Moose Jaw	WCHL	24	8	8	16	29					
1922–1923	Saskatoon Sheiks	WCHL	19	7	6	13	10					
1922–1923	Calgary Tigers	WCHL	11	3	1	4	7					
1923–1924	Calgary Tigers	WCHL	26	4	4	8	21	2	1	0	1	2
1923–1924	Calgary Tigers	West-P						3	0	1	1	4
1923–1924	Calgary Tigers	St-Cup						2	0	0	0	0
1924–1925	Calgary Tigers	WCHL	27	12	2	14	27	2	0	0	0	4
1925–1926	Vancouver Maroons	WHL	14	0	0	0	8					
1926–1927	Minneapolis Millers	AHA	32	2	3	5	51	6	3	0	3	13
1927–1928	Minneapolis Millers	AHA	34	4	2	6	27	8	3	0	3	10
1928–1929	Minneapolis Millers	AHA	40	9	3	12	33	4	0	0	0	0
1929–1930	Minneapolis Millers	AHA	45	3	4	7	32					
1930–1931	Prince Albert Mintos	N-SSHL										
	NHL TOTALS		38	10	8	18	117	2	2	1	3	9

Sources: Hockey Hall of Fame; Hockey-Reference.com

Creekmur, Louis "Lou" (born: January 22, 1927 in Hopelawn, New Jersey; died: July 5, 2009 in Tamarac, Florida); inducted into the Pro Football Hall of Fame in 1996 as a player; Position: Tackle-Guard; won three NFL Championships.

After graduating from the College of William and Mary (Williamsburg, Virginia), Creekmur was the number two draft pick of the Detroit Lions in 1950, and spent his entire 10-year (116 games) career with the team (1950–1959). At 6'4", 246 pounds, he was an offensive lineman who was also used on the defensive line in short-yardage situations.

He was named an All-NFL guard twice (1951–1952) and an All-NFL tackle four times (1953–1954, 1956–1957); was selected to eight consecutive Pro Bowls (1950–1957; twice as a guard and six times as a tackle); and played on three Lions title teams (1952–1953, 1957).

Creekmur joined Bobby Layne and Doak Walker as only the third offensive player from the Lions' early title years to be inducted into the hall of fame.

Sources: Pro Football Hall of Fame; Pro-Football-Reference.com

Cronin, Joseph Edward "Joe" (born: October 12, 1906 in San Francisco, California; died: September 7, 1984 in Osterville, Massachusetts); inducted into the National Baseball Hall of Fame and Museum in 1956 as a player; Position: Shortstop; Bats: Right; Throws: Right; Uniform: #4; 1930 American League Most Valuable Player; served two terms as president of the American League (first former player to be selected as league president); hit two pinch-hit home runs in one day in both games of a doubleheader.

Making his major league debut on April 29, 1926, the 6', 180-pound Cronin had a 20-year career with the Pittsburgh Pirates (1926–1927), Washington Senators (1928–1934), and the Boston Red Sox (1935–1945). He was a player-manager for both the Senators (1933–1934) and the Red Sox (1935–1947); lost the 1933 World Series in five games to the New York Giants; managed in the 1946 World Series as the Red Sox lost to the St. Louis Cardinals; and was a seven-time All-Star (1933–1935, 1937–1939, 1941).

He hit better than .300 eight times; had eight 100 or more RBI seasons; won the 1933 pennant as a rookie manager with the Senators before being traded to the Red Sox; and after retiring as a player, served two terms as American League president. As a manager, Cronin compiled a 1,236–1,055 (.540) record and won two American League championships (1933, 1946).

After the 1947 season, he became the general manager of the Red Sox, a job he held until 1958. In January 1959, Cronin became the first former player to be elected president of the American League, and served until 1973, when he was replaced by Lee MacPhail.

His jersey number four was retired by the Red Sox in May 1984; in 1999, he was named as a finalist to the Major League Baseball All-Century Team; and he has been inducted into the Boston Red Sox Hall of Fame.

In 1933, Cronin was named player-manager of the Washington Senators, and he led the team to its final World Series appearance his rookie managerial year. In June 1933, he set the major league record for most hits in three games (13) and most hits in four games (15), both records have since been broken. In June 1934, Cronin and Bill Terry, managers of the 1933 pennant winners, were named to manage the All-Star teams, establishing a precedent that continues today.

Although he was married to the owner's niece, after the 1934 season, Cronin was sold to the Red Sox, where he had three seasons with a slugging percentage over .500; led the American League in doubles (51) in 1938; hit a career-high 24 home runs in 1940, while leading the league in putouts and assists; and in 1943, set a major league record with five pinch-hit home runs, including two in one day (one each in both games of a doubleheader, June 17, 1943 against the Philadelphia Athletics). After his playing career ended in 1945 when he broke his leg, Cronin stayed with the Red Sox and managed the team to the World Series in 1946, losing to the St. Louis Cardinals.

As league president for two terms, Cronin oversaw the league's expansion from eight to ten teams in 1960 (to 12 teams in 1969), and in 1970, he fired two umpires for incompetence when he learned they were trying to form a union.

Joe Cronin's Career Statistics

YEAR	TEAM	LG	G	AB	R	H	2B	3B	HR	RBI	BB	SO	SB	AVG	SLG
1926	Pittsburgh	NL	38	83	9	22	2	2	0	11	6	15	0	.265	.337
1927	Pittsburgh	NL	12	22	2	5	1	0	0	3	2	3	0	.227	.273
1928	Washington	AL	63	227	23	55	10	4	0	25	22	27	4	.242	.322
1929	Washington	AL	145	494	72	139	29	8	8	61	85	37	5	.281	.421
1930	Washington	AL	154	587	127	203	41	9	13	126	72	36	17	.346	.513
1931	Washington	AL	156	611	103	187	44	13	12	126	81	52	10	.306	.480
1932	Washington	AL	143	557	95	177	43	18	6	116	66	45	7	.318	.492

YEAR	TEAM	LG	G	AB	R	H	2B	3B	HR	RBI	BB	SO	SB	AVG	SLG
1933	Washington	AL	152	602	89	186	45	11	5	118	87	49	5	.309	.445
1934	Washington	AL	127	504	68	143	30	9	7	101	53	28	8	.284	.421
1935	Boston	AL	144	556	70	164	37	14	9	95	63	40	3	.295	.460
1936	Boston	AL	81	295	36	83	22	4	2	43	32	21	1	.281	.403
1937	Boston	AL	148	570	102	175	40	4	18	110	84	73	5	.307	.486
1938	Boston	AL	143	530	98	172	51	5	17	94	91	60	7	.325	.536
1939	Boston	AL	143	520	97	160	33	3	19	107	87	48	6	.308	.492
1940	Boston	AL	149	548	104	156	35	6	24	111	83	65	7	.285	.502
1941	Boston	AL	143	518	98	161	38	8	16	95	82	55	1	.311	.508
1942	Boston	AL	45	79	7	24	3	0	4	24	15	21	0	.304	.494
1943	Boston	AL	59	77	8	24	4	0	5	29	11	4	0	.312	.558
1944	Boston	AL	76	191	24	46	7	0	5	28	34	19	1	.241	.356
1945	Boston	AL	3	8	1	3	0	0	0	1	3	2	0	.375	.375
	TOTALS		2,124	7,579	1,233	2,285	515	118	170	1,424	1,059	700	87	.301	.468

Joe Cronin's American League Managerial Record

YEAR	TEAM	W	L	WIN%	FINISH
1933	Washington	99	53	.651	First (Player-Manager)
1934	Washington	66	86	.434	Seventh (Player-Manager)
1935	Boston	78	75	.510	Fourth (Player-Manager)
1936	Boston	74	80	.481	Sixth (Player-Manager)
1937	Boston	80	72	.526	Fifth (Player-Manager)
1938	Boston	88	61	.591	Second (Player-Manager)
1939	Boston	89	62	.589	Second (Player-Manager)
1940	Boston	82	72	.532	Fifth (Player-Manager)
1941	Boston	84	70	.545	Second (Player-Manager)
1942	Boston	93	59	.612	Second (Player-Manager)
1943	Boston	68	84	.447	Seventh (Player-Manager)
1944	Boston	77	77	.500	Fourth (Player-Manager)
1945	Boston	71	83	.461	Seventh (Player-Manager)
1946	Boston	104	50	.675	First
1947	Boston	83	71	.539	Third
	Washington	165	139	.543	
	Boston	1071	916	.539	
	TOTALS	1,236	1,055	.540	

Sources: Baseball-Reference.com; National Baseball Hall of Fame and Museum

Crum, Denzil E. "Denny" (born: March 5, 1937 in San Fernando, California); inducted into the Naismith Memorial Basketball Hall of Fame in 1994 as a coach; won two NCAA championships at Louisville.

At San Fernando (California) High School (1950–1954), Crum was a three-year letter winner in basketball and was selected All-Conference his senior year. After high school, he went to Pierce Junior College (Woodland Hills, California, 1954–1956), before finishing his college career at the University of California at Los Angeles (1956–1958).

At Pierce Junior College, he averaged 27 points a game as a freshman; earned All-Southern California Junior College honors; led the team to a conference championship as a sophomore; and was named Conference Player of the Year in 1955. He finished his college basketball career by playing for two seasons under legendary coach John Wooden at UCLA, where he averaged seven points per game; won the Irv Pohlmeyer Trophy as the team's best first-year player (1956–1957); earned the Bruin Bench Award as the team's most improved player (1957–1958); and played on teams that compiled an overall 38–14 (.731) record.

Crum began his coaching career at UCLA as a graduate assistant coach-freshman coach from 1958 to 1960. He briefly left college coaching and accepted a position as an assistant coach at Brubabe (California) High School from

He was later named secretary-treasurer of the State Association and the Peel Cup, a position he held for more than 30 years. He also served as commissioner of the Illinois Soccer Commission; treasurer of the United States Football Association from 1923 to 1931; and manager of the Chicago Bricklayers, who reached the Open Cup final in 1931.

Cummings was the manager of the U.S. World Cup team in 1930 that reached the semifinals; later wrote a soccer column for the *Chicago Daily News*; and served in the Coast Guard during World War II.

Source: National Soccer Hall of Fame and Museum

Cummings, William Arthur "Candy" (born: October 18, 1848 in Ware, Massachusetts; died: May 16, 1924 in Toledo, Ohio); inducted into the National Baseball Hall of Fame and Museum in 1939 as a pioneer-executive by the Veterans Committee; Bats: Right; Throws: Right; first major league pitcher to start, complete, and win both games of a doubleheader; president of the International Association for Professional Base Ball Players.

Cummings made his major league debut on April 22, 1872 and played for the New York Mutuals (1872), Baltimore Lord Baltimores / Canaries (1873), Philadelphia Whites (1874), Hartford Dark Blues (1875–1876), and Cincinnati Reds (1877).

At 5'9", 120 pounds, he pitched four seasons in the National Association and won 124 games, twice leading the league in shutouts, and once in innings pitched. He was the first major league pitcher to start, complete, and win both games of a doubleheader (14–4 and 8–4 over the Cincinnati Reds on September 9, 1876).

At age 17, Cummings began playing baseball with Brooklyn Excelsior of the National Association of Base Ball Players, with his first game being a 24–2 win on August 24, 1866 over the Newark Eurekas.

One of the least-known members of the hall of fame, Cummings is often credited with being the inventor-creator of the curveball, a claim that is not universally accepted.

In 1877, he left the National League after pitching only 19 games with the Cincinnati Reds to become president of the newly formed International Association for Professional Base Ball Players.

Candy Cummings' Career Statistics

YEAR	TEAM	LEAGUE	W	L	WIN%	ERA
1872	New York Mutuals	National Association	33	20	.623	2.52
1873	Baltimore Canaries	National Association	28	14	.667	2.66
1874	Philadelphia Whites	National Association	28	26	.519	2.88
1875	Hartford Dark Blues	National Association	35	12	.745	1.60
1876	Hartford Dark Blues	National League	16	8	.667	1.67
1877	Cincinnati Reds	National League	5	14	.263	4.34
			W	**L**	**WIN%**	**ERA**
	TOTALS		145	94	.607	2.49

Sources: Baseball-Reference.com; National Baseball Hall of Fame and Museum

Cunningham, William J. "Billy" (born: June 3, 1943 in Brooklyn, New York); inducted into the Naismith Memorial Basketball Hall of Fame in 1986 as a player; Position: Center; Uniform: #32; set the University of North Carolina single-game scoring record against Tulane; set the school career rebounding record; selected to the All-NBA Rookie Team; won an NBA title in 1967 as a player and a title in 1983 as a coach; named ABA Most Valuable Player in 1973; reached the 200-, 300- and 400-win mark faster than any coach in NBA history.

Cunningham attended Erasmus Hall High School (Brooklyn, New York, graduated 1961) and was named Most Valuable Player of the Brooklyn League (1961); selected First-Team All-New York City (1961), and was an All-American in 1961. After high school, he went to the University of North Carolina (Chapel Hill, 1961–1965) and played for legendary coach Dean Smith; was a three-year letter winner; selected to the All-Atlantic Coast Conference team three times (1963–1965); Atlantic Coast Conference Player of the Year (1965); selected to the All-ACC Tournament Team twice (1963–1964); ACC Academic All-Conference (1965); United States Basketball Writers Association All-American (1964–1965); Helms Foundation All-Conference (1965); United States Basketball Writers Association All-American (1964–1965); Helms Foundation All-American (1965); and named to *The Sporting News* All-American Second Team (1965).

In ACC competition, he grabbed a record 27 rebounds against Clemson (February 16, 1963); scored 48 points against Tulane (December 10, 1964), setting a single-game UNC record; scored a career total of 1,709 points (24.8 points per game); and grabbed 1,062 rebounds (15.4 per game), a UNC record.

After college, the 6'6", 210-pound Cunningham was a first-round pick (fifth selection overall) of the Philadelphia 76ers in the National Basketball Association's 1965 Draft. He played nine seasons with the team (1965–1972, 1974–1976) and two seasons with the Carolina Cougars of the American Basketball Association (1972–1974). He was selected to the All-NBA Rookie Team in 1966; All-NBA First Team three consecutive seasons (1969–1971); All-NBA Second Team (1972); a four-time NBA All-Star (1969–1972); won an NBA championship with the Philadelphia 76ers (1967); ABA MVP (1973); and selected to the ABA All-Star First Team in 1973. His jersey number 32 was retired by the Philadelphia 76ers in 1976, and he was named to the NBA 50th Anniversary All-Time Team.

After his playing career, Cunningham coached the 76ers from 1977 to 1985, leading the team to a 454–196 (.698) record and an NBA title in 1983, after losing in 1980 and 1982 to the Los Angeles Lakers. He reached the 200-, 300- and 400-win mark faster than any coach in NBA history, and led the 76ers to three Atlantic Division titles (1978, 1981, 1983). Upon his retirement, his 454 wins as a head coach were the 12th best in NBA history.

In 1987, Cunningham worked for CBS on NBA telecasts, and after one year, left CBS to become a minority owner of the NBA's Miami Heat expansion franchise, ultimately selling his interest in the team in August 1994.

Billy Cunningham's Playing Statistics

SEASON	TEAM	LG	G	MIN	FG	FT	REB	AST	PTS
1965–1966	Philadelphia 76ers	NBA	80	2,134	431	281	599	207	1,143
1966–1967	Philadelphia 76ers	NBA	81	2,168	556	383	589	205	1,495
1967–1968	Philadelphia 76ers	NBA	74	2,076	516	368	562	187	1,400
1968–1969	Philadelphia 76ers	NBA	82	3,345	739	556	1,050	287	2,034
1969–1970	Philadelphia 76ers	NBA	81	3,194	802	510	1,101	352	2,114
1970–1971	Philadelphia 76ers	NBA	81	3,090	702	455	946	395	1,859
1971–1972	Philadelphia 76ers	NBA	75	2,900	658	428	918	443	1,744
1972–1973	Carolina Cougars	ABA	84	3,248	771	472	1,012	530	2,028
1973–1974	Carolina Cougars	ABA	32	1,190	253	149	331	150	656
1974–1975	Philadelphia 76ers	NBA	80	2,859	609	345	726	442	1,563
1975–1976	Philadelphia 76ers	NBA	20	640	103	68	147	107	274
		ABA	116	4,438	1,024	2,120	1,343	680	2,684
		NBA	654	22,406	5,116	11,467	6,638	2,625	13,626
	TOTALS		770	26,844	6,140	13,587	7,981	3,305	16,310

Billy Cunningham's NBA Coaching Record

		REGULAR SEASON			PLAYOFFS		
SEASON	TEAM	W	L	WIN%	W	L	WIN%
1977–1978	Philadelphia 76ers	53	23	.697	6	4	.600
1978–1979	Philadelphia 76ers	47	35	.573	5	4	.556
1979–1980	Philadelphia 76ers	59	23	.720	12	6	.667
1980–1981	Philadelphia 76ers	62	20	.756	9	7	.563
1981–1982	Philadelphia 76ers	58	24	.707	12	9	.571
1982–1983	Philadelphia 76ers	65	17	.793	12	1	.923
1983–1984	Philadelphia 76ers	52	30	.634	2	3	.400
1984–1985	Philadelphia 76ers	58	24	.707	8	5	.615
	TOTALS	454	196	.698	66	39	.629

Sources: Basketball-Reference.com; Naismith Memorial Basketball Hall of Fame

Curry, Denise (born: August 22, 1959 in Fort Benton, Montana); inducted into the Naismith Memorial Basketball Hall of Fame in 1997 as a player; Uniform: #12; was a member of UCLA's AIAW national championship basketball team as well as the school's national championship softball team; inducted into the National High School Sports Hall of Fame; averaged a career double-double at UCLA.

Curry attended Davis (California) Senior High School from 1974 to 1977, where she was a three-year basketball letter winner; a five-sport varsity athlete; named All-Conference three times (1975–1977); *Parade* magazine All-

American (1977); Davis High School Outstanding Student-Athlete (1977); and was inducted into the National High School Sports Hall of Fame in 1991.

After high school, she went to the University of California at Los Angeles from 1977 to 1981, where she was a four-year starter; a member of the Association for Intercollegiate Athletics for Women national championship team in 1978 (the UCLA Lady Bruins defeated Maryland); a member of the school's 1978 National Championship softball team; a three-time Kodak All-American (1979–1981); an Academic All-American in 1981; averaged a career double-double (24.6 points and 10.1 rebounds per game); set 14 UCLA records and still holds school records for points scored (3,198), rebounds (1,310), most points in a game (47), season scoring average (28.5 per game), and career field goal percentage (.607); scored in double figures in all 130 games played at UCLA; was a three-time Western Collegiate Athletic Conference Most Valuable Player; inducted into the UCLA Athletic Hall of Fame in 1994; and had her jersey retired at the 25th anniversary of Pauley Pavilion.

The 6'1" Curry was a member of five U.S. national basketball teams (1979–1983); played eight professional seasons in Europe (DJK Agon 08 Dusseldorf in the German Pro League [1982–1985, led the team to three national championships, 1983–1985], Stade Francais Versailles in the French Pro League [1985–1990, led the team to national championships in 1986 and 1987 and was named French Player of the Decade], and for G.S. Ferrara in the Italian Pro League [1989–1990]); won a gold medal at the 1979 FIBA World Championships (Seoul, South Korea); a gold medal at the 1983 Pan American Games (Caracas, Venezuela); a silver medal at the 1983 World Championships (Sao Paulo, Brazil); a gold medal at the 1984 Olympics (Inglewood, California); and was named Amateur Basketball Association of the United States of America Basketball Player of the Year in 1981.

After leaving the international basketball scene as a player, Curry became an assistant coach at the University of California, Berkeley (1990–1996); an assistant coach with the San Jose Lasers of the American Basketball League (1996–1997); head coach at California State, Fullerton from 1997 to 2000; and an assistant coach at Long Beach State College (California, 2004). She is a member of the Women's Basketball (1999) and Amateur Athletic Union halls of fame.

Sources: Naismith Memorial Basketball Hall of Fame; Women's Basketball Hall of Fame

Cuyler, Hazen Shirley "Kiki" (born: August 30, 1898 in Harrisville, Michigan; died: February 11, 1950 in Ann Arbor, Michigan); inducted into the National Baseball Hall of Fame and Museum in 1968 as a player by the Veterans Committee; Position: Right Field; Bats: Right; Throws: Right; won the 1925 World Series championship.

Making his major league debut on September 29, 1921, Cuyler played 18 National League seasons with the Pittsburgh Pirates (1921–1927), Chicago Cubs (1928–1935), Cincinnati Reds (1935–1937), and Brooklyn Dodgers (1938). He played in three World Series (winning in 1925 and losing in 1929 and 1932) and was selected to the All-Star Team in 1934.

The 5'10", 180-pound Cuyler hit .300 or better in a season 10 times; led the National League in stolen bases four times; and in 1925, led the league in triples (26) and runs scored (144). On August 28, 1925, he hit two inside-the-park home runs at Philadelphia's Baker Bowl, and finished second that season in Most Valuable Player voting to triple-crown winner Rogers Hornsby.

After his professional playing days, he managed in the Southern Association and was called back to the major leagues to coach the Cubs in the early 1940s.

Kiki Cuyler's Career Statistics

YEAR	TEAM	LG	G	AB	R	H	2B	3B	HR	RBI	BB	SO	SB	AVG	SLG
1921	Pittsburgh	NL	1	3	0	0	0	0	0	0	0	1	0	.000	.000
1922	Pittsburgh	NL	1	0	0	0	0	0	0	0	0	0	0	.000	.000
1923	Pittsburgh	NL	11	40	4	10	1	1	0	2	5	3	2	.250	.325
1924	Pittsburgh	NL	117	466	94	165	27	16	9	85	30	62	32	.354	.539
1925	Pittsburgh	NL	153	617	144	220	43	26	18	102	58	56	41	.357	.598
1926	Pittsburgh	NL	157	614	113	197	31	15	8	92	50	66	35	.321	.459
1927	Pittsburgh	NL	85	285	60	88	13	7	3	31	37	36	20	.309	.435
1928	Chicago	NL	133	499	92	142	25	9	17	79	51	61	37	.285	.473
1929	Chicago	NL	139	509	111	183	29	7	15	102	66	56	43	.360	.532
1930	Chicago	NL	156	642	155	228	50	17	13	134	72	49	37	.355	.547

YEAR	TEAM	LG	G	AB	R	H	2B	3B	HR	RBI	BB	SO	SB	AVG	SLG
1931	Chicago	NL	154	613	110	202	37	12	9	88	72	54	13	.330	.473
1932	Chicago	NL	110	446	58	130	19	9	10	77	29	43	9	.291	.442
1933	Chicago	NL	70	262	37	83	13	3	5	35	21	29	4	.317	.447
1934	Chicago	NL	142	559	80	189	42	8	6	69	31	62	15	.338	.474
1935	Chicago	NL	45	157	22	42	5	1	4	18	10	16	3	.268	.389
1935	Cincinnati	NL	62	223	36	56	8	3	2	22	27	18	5	.251	.341
1936	Cincinnati	NL	144	567	96	185	29	11	7	74	47	67	16	.326	.453
1937	Cincinnati	NL	117	406	48	110	12	4	0	32	36	50	10	.271	.320
1938	Brooklyn	NL	82	253	45	69	10	8	2	23	34	23	6	.273	.399
	TOTALS		1,879	7,161	1,305	2,299	394	157	128	1,065	676	752	328	.321	.474

Sources: Baseball-Reference.com; National Baseball Hall of Fame and Museum

Chapter 4
Dalipagić to Dye

Dalipagić, Dražen (born: November 27, 1951 in Mostar, Yugoslovia [now known as Bosnia-Herzegovina]); inducted into the Naismith Memorial Basketball Hall of Fame in 2004 as a player; Position: Forward; named European Player of the Year three times.

After attending Mostar Technical School (Yugoslavia), Dalipagić continued his education at the Belgrade Teachers College in Yugoslavia. One of the most dominant players in the late 1970s and early 1980s, he played professional basketball for Partizan Belgrade (1971–1978, 1979–1980, 1981–1982), Reyer Venice (1980–1981, 1985–1988), Real Madrid (1982–1983), APU Undine (1983–1985), Verona (1988–1989), and Crvena Zvezda Belgrade (1990–1991).

He was named European Player of the Year three times (1977–1978, 1980); led Partizan to the Yugoslavian League title in 1976 and to the Fédération Internationale de Basketball Korac Cup in 1978 (scoring 50 points in the title game); averaged 33.7 points per game while playing for Partizan; led both A-1 and A-2 Italian Leagues in scoring (scoring 50 or more points in a game 15 times); set Italian League playoff career scoring record of 34.7 points per game; played 243 games for the Yugoslavian National Team (1973–1986); won an Olympic gold medal with Yugoslavia in the 1980 Games (Moscow, Russia), a World Championship gold medal in 1978 (hosted by Philippines), and was a three-time European Championships gold medal winner (1973, 1975, 1977); won a FIBA-record four World Championship medals (gold in 1978, silver in 1974, and bronze in 1982 and 1986); and won 12 total medals in international competition.

After serving in the Yugoslavian Army in 1979, he was the head coach of the professional team Gorica from 1994 to 1996.

At 6'6", 235 pounds, Dalipagić was one of the highest-scoring players in European basketball history; named the best athlete of Yugoslavia in 1978; and went on to become one of the most decorated athletes in Yugoslavian history.

Source: Naismith Memorial Basketball Hall of Fame

Daly, Charles Jerome "Chuck" (born: July 20, 1930 in St. Marys, Pennsylvania; died: May 9, 2009 in Jupiter, Florida); inducted into the Naismith Memorial Basketball Hall of Fame in 1994 as a coach; only hall of fame coach to win both an Olympic gold medal and an NBA championship.

Daly attended Kane Area (Pennsylvania) High School from 1944 to 1948, where he was a four-year letter winner and was named All-Conference twice (1947–1948). After graduating from high school, he attended St. Bonaventure University (New York, 1948–1949), where he played on the school's freshman team, before transferring to Bloomsburg State (Pennsylvania, 1949–1952), where he played basketball for two seasons.

He began his coaching career at Punxsutawney (Pennsylvania) High School (1955–1963), compiling a 111–70 (.613) record. Daly then became an assistant coach at Duke University (Durham, North Carolina, 1963–1969) and Boston College (Massachusetts, 1969–1971), before serving as head coach at the University of Pennsylvania (Philadelphia, 1971–1977). He led Penn to four consecutive Ivy League championships (1972–1975) and four NCAA Tournament appearances (1972–1975); compiled a 151–62 (.709) record; and enjoyed four straight 20-win seasons.

Daly left the college ranks to become an assistant coach for the National Basketball Association's Philadelphia 76ers (1978–1981), before becoming head coach of the Cleveland Cavaliers (1981–1982), Detroit Pistons (1983–1992), New Jersey Nets (1992–1994), and the Orlando Magic (1997–1999).

He led Philadelphia to two Division titles and four postseason appearances; led the Pistons to back-to-back NBA titles (1989–1990), to three Eastern and Central Division titles (1988–1990), to five 50-plus win seasons, and to nine straight winning seasons (1984–1992); and led New Jersey to the playoffs in both of his seasons with the team.

Daly is the only basketball hall of fame coach to win both an Olympic gold medal and an NBA championship, and is one of only seven coaches to win back-to-back NBA championships (along with Red Auerbach, Phil Jackson, John Kundla, Pat Riley, Bill Russell, and Rudy Tomjonovich). When he was enshrined into the basketball hall of fame, his 519–342 record was 15th best among all coaches and fourth best among active coaches. Daly coached the U.S. National Team to an Olympic gold medal in 1992 (Barcelona, Spain) with the first so-called "Dream Team," that ended the Olympics with a perfect 8–0 record.

The Pistons have retired jersey number 2 (representing his two NBA championships) in Daly's honor; in 1997, he was selected one of the NBA's "Ten Greatest Coaches" during the league's first 50 years; and after retiring from the NBA in 1994, Daly was a television analyst before returning to the league to coach the Orlando Magic for two seasons (1997–1999).

Chuck Daly's NBA Coaching Record

YEAR	TEAM	REG SEASON	PLAYOFFS
1981–1982	Cleveland	9–32	
1983–1984	Detroit	49–33	2–3
1984–1985	Detroit	46–36	5–4
1985–1986	Detroit	46–36	1–3
1986–1987	Detroit	52–30	10–5
1987–1988	Detroit	54–28	14–9
1988–1989	Detroit	63–19	15–2
1989–1990	Detroit	59–23	15–5
1990–1991	Detroit	50–32	7–8
1991–1992	Detroit	48–34	2–3
1992–1993	New Jersey	43–39	2–3
1993–1994	New Jersey	45–37	2–3
1997–1998	Orlando	41–41	
1998–1999	Orlando	33–17	1–3
	TOTALS	638–437	76–51

Sources: Basketball-Reference.com; Naismith Memorial Basketball Hall of Fame

D'Amico, John David (born: September 21, 1937 in Toronto, Ontario, Canada; died: May 29, 2005 in Toronto, Ontario, Canada); inducted into the Hockey Hall of Fame in 1993 as an on-ice official; retired as the last of the Original Six officials.

D'Amico officiated his first regular-season game on October 12, 1964, and when he retired in 1987, he was the last of the Original Six officials. After playing briefly as a child, he became an official and eventually worked his way up to the Ontario Hockey Association. In 1963, after signing a National Hockey League contract, he spent one season in the Central League before joining the NH full time.

He went on to officiate in four Canada Cup tournaments; the Challenge Cup; the Rendez-vous series; and appeared in 20 Stanley Cups. In 1987, he moved into the NHL head office in Toronto; joined the league's Officiating Supervisory staff in 1988; and became a supervisor of officials for the NHL, a position he held until his death.

His career included 1,689 regular season and 247 Stanley Cup playoff games.

Source: Hockey Hall of Fame

Dandridge, Raymond Emmitt (born: August 31, 1913 in Richmond, Virginia; died: February 12, 1994 in Palm Bay, Florida); inducted into the National Baseball Hall of Fame and Museum in 1987 as a Negro League Player by the Veterans Committee; Position: Third Base; Bats: Right; Throws: Right; retired with a lifetime batting average of .355.

The 5'7", 175-pound Dandridge played 10 professional seasons in the Negro Leagues with the Detroit Stars (1933), Nashville Elite Giants (1933), Newark Dodgers/Eagles (1933–1939, 1942, 1944), and as a player-manager with the New York Cubans (1949). He also played eight seasons in the Mexican League and 11 years in the Cuban Winter League.

After the major league color barrier fell, he played four years with the New York Giant's Triple-A affiliate at Minneapolis (Minnesota); hit 318; and won the American Association's Most Valuable Player award in 1950.

Often called "the best third baseman never to make the major leagues," Dandridge retired as a player in 1955 with a lifetime batting average of .355, and became a scout for the San Francisco Giants.

Source: National Baseball Hall of Fame and Museum

Dandurand, Joseph Viateur "Leo" (born: July 9, 1889 in Bourbonnais, Illinois; died: June 26, 1964); inducted into the Hockey Hall of Fame in 1963 as a builder; helped form the Canadian Amateur Hockey Association; early owner of the Montreal Canadiens and led the franchise to three Stanley Cup titles.

Born in Illinois, his family immigrated to Canada when he was 16, where Dandurand eventually worked as a referee in the National Hockey Association and assisted with the administration of the Montreal minor hockey system. He was one of the city's representatives at the meetings which formed the Canadian Amateur Hockey Association in 1914.

He later developed a business partnership with Louis Letourneau and Joseph Cattarinich that led to numerous sports deals in the local area. In November 1921, the trio purchased the Montreal Canadiens of the National Hockey League and oversaw the franchise winning the Stanley Cup three times (1924, 1930–1931).

He helped introduce the deferred penalty rule, in which no more than two players could be penalized at the same time. In 1947, he joined the Board of Governors of the International Hockey Hall of Fame.

In addition to hockey endeavors, the three partners were involved in horse racing, and at one time, owned 17 tracks, including Montreal's Dorval and Blue Bonnet facilities. Dandurand was also a director of the Montreal Royals minor league baseball team (International League); helped develop the Montreal Alouettes (of what would become the Canadian Football League); and promoted boxing and wrestling in the Montreal area. The Leo Dandurand Trophy is a CFL award presented each year to the most outstanding lineman in the East Division.

Dandurand was one of the inaugural inductees into the Nova Scotia Hockey and Sports Hall of Fame in 1963, and has been inducted into the International Hockey Hall of Fame in Kingston (Canada).

Source: Hockey Hall of Fame

Danilo, Paul (born: July 5, 1919 in Morgan, Pennsylvania); inducted into the National Soccer Hall of Fame and Museum in 1997 as a player; Position: Forward; played in two West Penn Cup Finals; scored the winning goal in the 1940 U.S. Amateur Cup final.

Danilo began his soccer career in 1937 with the Morgan Soccer Club in western Pennsylvania's Keystone League, and played in the West Penn Cup Finals in 1941 and 1945. He scored the winning goal in the 1940 U.S. Amateur Cup final for Morgan against Fall River Firestone.

He played for Heidelberg in 1937–1938, and the Pittsburgh Indians in the North American Professional Soccer League in 1946 and 1947, winning the championship in 1947. Named to numerous All-Star teams at all levels, Danilo retired as a player in 1952 after 15 seasons, before being named manager of the Morgan Soccer Club (Pennsylvania).

From 1953 to 1957, he served as first secretary, and then president, of the West Penn Soccer Association.

Source: National Soccer Hall of Fame and Museum

Dantley, Adrian Delano (born: February 28, 1956 in Washington, D.C.); inducted into the Naismith Memorial Basketball Hall of Fame in 2008 as a player; Position: Forward-Guard; Uniform: #4; won an Olympic gold medal in 1976; set a league record in the 1983–1984 season by needing the fewest field-goal attempts to average at least 30 points.

After playing basketball at DeMatha Catholic High School (Hyattsville, Maryland), the 6'4", 245-pound Dantley attended the University of Notre Dame (South Bend, Indiana). He led his teams to an overall 57–2 record and earned high school All-America honors.

Entering Notre Dame in 1973, he averaged 25.8 points per game during his three years at the school; was a two-time All-American; a two-time First Team All-American (1975–1976), named 1976 National Player of the Year; and left college after his junior year to enter the National Basketball Association draft. He ranks second on the Notre Dame career scoring list (2,223 points), and holds the school record for free throws made (615) and free throws attempted (769).

Dantley was selected in the first round (sixth choice overall) of the 1976 NBA Draft by the Buffalo Braves. Before turning professional, he played on the 1976 U.S. Olympic Team (Montreal, Quebec, Canada), and led the squad to a gold medal with a 95–74 win over Yugoslavia.

During Dantley's 15-year career, he would play for the Braves (1976–1977), Indiana Pacers (1977), Los Angeles Lakers (1977–1979), Utah Jazz (1979–1986), Detroit Pistons (1986–1989), Dallas Mavericks (1989–1990), and Milwaukee Bucks (1990–1991). He was named NBA Rookie of the Year in 1977; a two-time All-NBA Second Team selection (1981, 1984); NBA Comeback Player of the Year (1984); and was a six-time NBA All-Star (1980–1982, 1984–1986). He averaged 30 or more points per game four straight seasons (1981–1984); won two league scoring titles (1981,

1984); and set a league record in the 1983–1984 season by needing the fewest field-goal attempts (18.2 per game) to average at least 30 points.

Leaving the NBA after the 1991 season, Dantley moved to Italy and played for Breeze Milan; a year later, he became an assistant coach at Towson University (Maryland); and his uniform number four was retired by Utah in April 2007.

Adrian Dantley's NBA Career Statistics

SEASON	TEAM	G	MIN	FG	3P	FT	TRB	AST	STL	BLK	PTS
1976–1977	Buffalo	77	2,816	544		476	587	144	91	15	1,564
1977–1978	Indiana	23	948	201		207	216	65	48	17	609
1977–1978	Los Angeles	56	1,985	377		334	404	188	70	7	1,088
1978–1979	Los Angeles	60	1,775	374		292	342	138	63	12	1,040
1979–1980	Utah	68	2,674	730	0	443	516	191	96	14	1,903
1980–1981	Utah	80	3,417	909	2	632	509	322	109	18	2,452
1981–1982	Utah	81	3,222	904	1	648	514	324	95	14	2,457
1982–1983	Utah	22	887	233	0	210	140	105	20	0	676
1983–1984	Utah	79	2,984	802	1	813	448	310	61	4	2,418
1984–1985	Utah	55	1,971	512	0	438	323	186	57	8	1,462
1985–1986	Utah	76	2,744	818	1	630	395	264	64	4	2,267
1986–1987	Detroit	81	2,736	601	1	539	332	162	63	7	1,742
1987–1988	Detroit	69	2,144	444	0	492	227	171	39	10	1,380
1988–1989	Detroit	42	1,341	258	0	256	164	93	23	6	772
1988–1989	Dallas	31	1,081	212	0	204	153	78	20	7	628
1989–1990	Dallas	45	1,300	231	0	200	172	80	20	7	662
1990–1991	Milwaukee	10	126	19	1	18	13	9	5	0	57
	TOTALS	955	34,151	8,169	7	6,832	5,455	2,830	944	150	23,177

Sources: Basketball-Reference.com; Naismith Memorial Basketball Hall of Fame

Darragh, John Proctor "Jack" (born: December 4, 1890 in Ottawa, Ontario, Canada; died: June 25, 1924 in Ottawa, Ontario, Canada); inducted into the Hockey Hall of Fame in 1962 as a player; Position: Right Wing; won four Stanley Cup titles.

Darragh played 13 professional hockey seasons from 1910 to 1924, and averaged more than one goal every two games. He won four Stanley Cup championships, all with the Ottawa Senators (1911, 1920–1921 [the first NHL team to win back-to-back titles], 1923).

Unlike many players of his era, Darragh did not jump from team to team or league to league, but stayed with the Senators of the National Hockey Association, and was with the team when it joined the National Hockey League after the NHA folded in 1917. He did not play during the entire 1921–1922 season, but returned to the NHL the next year, and led the Senators to another Stanley Cup title, the team's third in four years.

Jack Darragh's Career Statistics

			REGULAR SEASON					PLAYOFFS				
SEASON	TEAM	LEAGUE	GP	G	A	TP	PIM	GP	G	A	TP	PIM
1908–1909	Ottawa Stewartons	OCHL										
1909–1910	Ottawa Stewartons	OCHL	5	11	0	11	11	1	0	0	0	3
1909–1910	Ottawa Cliffsides	OCHL						3	4	0	4	0
1910–1911	Ottawa Stewartons	OCHL	3	7	0	7	0					
1910–1911	Ottawa Senators	NHA	16	18	0	18	36					
1910–1911	Ottawa Senators	St-Cup						2	0	0	0	6
1911–1912	Ottawa Senators	NHA	17	15	0	15	10					
1911–1912	NHA All-Stars	Exhib.	3	4	0	4	8					
1912–1913	Ottawa Senators	NHA	20	15	0	15	16					
1913–1914	Ottawa Senators	NHA	20	23	5	28	69					
1914–1915	Ottawa Senators	NHA	18	11	2	13	32	5	4	0	4	9

SEASON	TEAM	LEAGUE	REGULAR SEASON GP	G	A	TP	PIM	PLAYOFFS GP	G	A	TP	PIM
1915–1916	Ottawa Senators	NHA	21	16	5	21	41					
1916–1917	Ottawa Senators	NHA	20	24	4	28	17	2	2	0	2	3
1917–1918	Ottawa Senators	NHL	18	14	5	19	26					
1918–1919	Ottawa Senators	NHL	14	11	3	14	33	5	2	0	2	3
1919–1920	Ottawa Senators	NHL	23	22	14	36	22					
1919–1920	Ottawa Senators	St-Cup						5	5	2	7	3
1920–1921	Ottawa Senators	NHL	24	11	15	26	20	2	0	0	0	2
1920–1921	Ottawa Senators	St-Cup						5	5	0	5	12
1922–1923	Ottawa Senators	NHL	24	6	9	15	10	2	1	0	1	2
1923–1924	Ottawa Senators	NHL	18	2	0	2	2	2	0	0	0	2
	NHL TOTALS		121	66	46	112	113	11	3	0	3	9

Sources: Hockey Hall of Fame; Hockey-Reference.com

Davidson, Allan M. "Scotty" (born: 1890 in Kingston, Ontario, Canada; died: June 16, 1915 in Belgium); inducted into the Hockey Hall of Fame in 1950 as a player; won the OHA title twice; won the Stanley Cup championship in 1914.

A star in hockey's early days, Davidson played pre-National Hockey League seasons with the Kingston Frontenacs (Ontario Hockey Association) and in the National Hockey Association with the Toronto Blueshirts.

Davidson led Kingston to back-to-back Ontario Hockey Association championships (1910–1911); joined Toronto in the 1912–1913 season; and led the Blueshirts to the 1914 Stanley Cup title.

He joined the military during World War I and was killed in Belgium on June 6, 1915.

Allan Davidson's Career Statistics

SEASON	TEAM	LEAGUE	REGULAR SEASON GP	G	A	TP	PIM	PLAYOFFS GP	G	A	TP	PIM
1908–1909	Kingston 14th Regiment	OHA-Sr.	4	8	0	8	11	4	4	0	4	6
1909–1910	Kingston Frontenacs	OHA-Jr.										
1910–1911	Kingston Frontenacs	OHA-Jr.										
1911–1912	Calgary Athletics	CCSHL						3	3	0	3	6
1912–1913	Toronto Blueshirts	NHA	20	19	0	19	69					
1912–1913	Toronto Tecumsehs	Exhib.	2	0	0	0	0					
1913–1914	Toronto Blueshirts	NHA	20	23	13	36	64	2	2	0	2	11
1913–1914	Toronto Blueshirts	St-Cup						2	1	0	1	7

Source: Hockey Hall of Fame

Davidson, William Morse "Bill" (born: December 5, 1923 in Detroit, Michigan); inducted into the Naismith Memorial Basketball Hall of Fame in 2008 as a contributor; oversaw three championship teams in three different sports.

Davidson served as chairman of Palace Sports and Entertainment, owner of the Detroit Pistons (National Basketball Association), Detroit Shock (Women's National Basketball Association), and the Tampa Bay Lightning (National Hockey League). His Pistons won the NBA title three times (1989–1990, 2004); the Shock won the WNBA championship twice (2003, 2006); and the Lightning won the 2004 Stanley Cup.

He graduated from the University of Michigan (Ann Arbor), majoring in business, and later from the Wayne State University Law School (Detroit, Michigan).

He purchased the Pistons in 1974, and eventually moved the team to The Palace of Auburn Hills (Michigan). Named in his honor, the William Davidson Institute at the University of Michigan (at the Ross School of Business) is a non-profit research and educational institute.

Davidson served as chairman of the NBA Board of Governors, and contributed to structuring the modern NBA salary cap and free-agency process.

Source: Naismith Memorial Basketball Hall of Fame

Davies, Robert Edris (born: January 15, 1920 in Harrisburg, Pennsylvania; died: April 22, 1990 in Hilton Head, South Carolina); inducted into the Naismith Memorial Basketball Hall of Fame in 1970 as a player; Position: Guard; Uniform: #11; led Seton Hall University to 43 consecutive wins; won an NBL championship in 1946; won an NBA title in 1951.

Davies attended John Harris High School (Harrisburg, Pennsylvania) from 1933 to 1937, where he was a three-year letter winner; named All-Conference (1937); and was the second leading scorer in Central Pennsylvania (1937). After graduation, he went to Franklin & Marshall College (Lancaster, Pennsylvania, 1937–1938), before moving on to Seton Hall University (South Orange, New Jersey) from 1938 to 1942.

While in college, Davies was a two-time All-American (1940–1941); led Seton Hall to 43 consecutive wins; scored a career total of 661 points at Seton Hall; and was named Most Valuable Player of the 1942 College All-Star game. After college, he joined the U.S. Navy during World War II, and began his professional career with the Brooklyn Indians of the American Basketball League in 1943 while finishing his military service.

After one season with the Indians, the 6'1", 175-pound Davies went on to play for the New York Gothams of the ABL (1944–1945); Rochester Royals of the National Basketball League (1945–1948); Rochester Royals of the Basketball Association of America (1948–1949); and the Rochester Royals of the National Basketball Association (1949–1955).

He led the Royals to the NBL championship in 1946; was named to the All-NBL First Team and selected NBL Most Valuable Player in 1947; named to the All-NBL Second Team in 1948; led the BAA in assists (5.4 per game) and was named to the All-BAA First Team in 1949; named to the All-NBA First Team three times (1950–1952); won an NBA championship with Rochester in 1951; and was named to the All-NBA Second Team in 1953. Davies played in four NBA All-Star games (1951–1954); set the then-NBA record for most assists (20) in a game in 1955; named to the NBA 25th Anniversary All-Time Team in 1970; and was named the "Sixth Greatest Player in the First Half-Century" by *Sport* magazine in 1970.

He was the head coach at Seton Hall from 1946 to 1947 (while still a member of the Rochester Royals), and compiled a 24–3 record. After retiring from the NBA, he coached at Gettysburg College (Pennsylvania, 1955–1957), compiling an 18–29 record.

Robert Davies' Career Statistics

SEASON	TEAM	LG	G	MIN	FG	FT	TRB	AST	PTS
1948–1949	Rochester	BAA	60		317	270		321	904
1949–1950	Rochester	NBA	64		317	261		294	895
1950–1951	Rochester	NBA	63		326	303	197	287	955
1951–1952	Rochester	NBA	65	2,394	379	294	189	390	1,052
1952–1953	Rochester	NBA	66	2,216	339	351	195	280	1,029
1953–1954	Rochester	NBA	72	2,137	288	311	194	323	887
1954–1955	Rochester	NBA	72	1,870	326	220	205	355	872
		BAA	60		317	270		321	904
		NBA	402	8,617	1,975	1,740	980	1,929	5,690
	TOTALS		462	8,617	2,292	2,010	980	2,250	6,594

Sources: Basketball-Reference.com; National Memorial Basketball Hall of Fame

Davis, Allen "Al" (born: July 4, 1929 in Brockton, Massachusetts); inducted into the Pro Football Hall of Fame in 1992 as a team and league administrator; only person in professional football to serve as a personnel assistant, scout, assistant coach, head coach, general manager, commissioner, and team owner-chief executive officer; served as commissioner of the American Football League; won three Super Bowls.

Davis, the recognized owner of the National Football League's Oakland Raiders (he is actually the president of A.D. Football, Inc.), is the only person in professional football to serve as a personnel assistant, scout, assistant coach, head coach, general manager, commissioner, and team owner-chief executive officer. As commissioner of the American Football League, he oversaw the merger of the AFL with the National Football League (a move he personally opposed); led the Raiders to the best record in professional sports from 1963 to 1991; won Super Bowl XI (1976), XV (1980), and XVIII (1983); was named AFL Coach of the Year in 1963; and compiled a career coaching record of 23–16–3.

His professional football career began in 1954 when he was a personnel assistant with the NFL's Baltimore Colts. Six years later, he was hired as the ends coach for the AFL's Los Angeles Chargers in the team's inaugural season. In 1963, at age 33, he became the head coach and general manager of the Raiders (at the time, the youngest person in the AFL to hold these positions); led the team to a 10–4 record; and was named AFL Coach of the Year.

After coaching for three seasons, Davis was named AFL Commissioner in April 1966, and within eight weeks, the league announced its merger with the NFL. Davis personally was opposed to the merger and resigned as commissioner to return to the Oakland Raiders as managing general partner in 1970.

Davis grew up in Brooklyn, New York and attended Wittenberg College (Springfield, Ohio) and Syracuse University (New York). Upon graduation, he began his coaching career as the line coach at Adelphi College (Garden City, New York) in 1950 and 1951, before becoming the head coach of the U.S. Army team at Ft. Belvoir, Virginia from 1952 to 1953. After one year with the NFL's Baltimore Colts, he served as line coach and recruiter for The Citadel (Charleston, South Carolina), before becoming the line coach for the University of Southern California (Los Angeles) for three seasons (1957–1959).

Under Davis, the Raiders became one of the most successful and profitable sports franchises. From 1967 to 1985, the team won 13 division championships, one AFL championship (1967), three Super Bowls, and made 15 playoff appearances. Even though the Raiders have not matched their early success during the past 20 years, he is known for such catchphrases as "Just win baby!," "Commitment to Excellence," and "Pride and Poise."

One of the most controversial owners in the NFL, in 1980 he attempted to move the Raiders from Oakland to Los Angeles, but was blocked by a court injunction. Davis filed an anti-trust lawsuit against the league, and in June 1982, after a federal district court ruled in his favor, he moved the team to Los Angeles for the 1982 NFL season. Although he won a Super Bowl while in Los Angeles, the Raiders were never well received by the fans, and in 1995, Davis returned the team to Oakland.

Davis was one of the first executives to provide opportunities to minority players; he often scouted and drafted from smaller schools in the South that were predominantly African-American; and in the modern era of the NFL, he was the first owner to hire a Hispanic-American (Tom Flores) and the second African-American (Art Shell) as head coach.

Davis attended Erasmus Hall High School (Brooklyn, New York) and Syracuse University, where he played baseball and football.

Al Davis' Coaching Statistics

YEAR	TEAM	LG	W	L	T	WIN%
1963	Oakland Raiders	AFL	10	4	0	.714
1964	Oakland Raiders	AFL	5	7	2	.417
1965	Oakland Raiders	AFL	8	5	1	.615
	TOTALS		23	16	3	.590

Sources: Pro Football Hall of Fame; Pro-Football-Reference.com

Davis, George Stacey (born: August 23, 1870 in Cohoes, New York; died: October 17, 1940 in Philadelphia, Pennsylvania); inducted into the National Baseball Hall of Fame and Museum in 1998 as a player by the Veterans Committee; Position: Shortstop; Bats: Both; Throws: Right; had a then-record 33-game hitting streak in 1893; won the 1906 World Series; first player in major league history to hit a home run and a triple in the same inning.

Making his major league debut on April 19, 1890, the 5'9", 180-pound Davis was a star in the early days of professional baseball, and had a 20-year career with the Cleveland Spiders (1890–1892), New York Giants (1893–1901, 1903), and Chicago White Sox (1902, 1904–1909). He was a player-manager for the Giants (1895, 1900-1901) and played in the 1906 World Series (a win over the cross-city rival Chicago Cubs).

Davis batted over .300 in nine consecutive seasons (1893–1901), and in 1893, he had a then-record 33-game hitting streak. On June 14, 1893, he became the first player in major league history to hit a home run and a triple in the same inning (fourth) in a 15-11 Giants win over the Chicago Colts.

He started his major league career in center field for his first two seasons; led the National League in outfield assists with 35 in 1890; and then moved to the infield, where he played the rest of his career. Along with most other players, his offensive numbers improved significantly when league rules moved the pitcher's mound back to 60 feet, 6 inches in 1893, and he became one of the league's stars throughout the 1890s. In 1897, he became a full-time shortstop, and eventually led the league in double plays and fielding percentage four times each.

When the American League formed, Davis played for the Chicago White Sox for one season because the league offered him more money. When he tried to return to the Giants the next season, he only played four games before it was determined that he could not play for the team under an agreement that neither league would raid each others' top talent. He sat out the remainder of the 1903 season before returning to the Sox in 1904.

On September 14, 1900 at the Polo Grounds, the Giants pulled off the first triple play of the 20th century involving Davis, Jack Doyle, and Kid Gleason.

After retiring from the major leagues, Davis served as a baseball coach, scout, and manager. He was also a professional bowler.

George Davis' Career Statistics

YEAR	TEAM	LG	G	AB	R	H	2B	3B	HR	BB	SO	SB	AVG	SLG
1890	Cleveland	NL	134	526	98	139	22	12	6	53	34	22	.264	.386
1891	Cleveland	NL	136	571	115	167	34	11	3	53	29	42	.292	.406
1892	Cleveland	NL	143	595	96	151	22	14	5	58	51	36	.254	.363
1893	New York	NL	133	533	112	199	23	26	11	42	20	54	.373	.576
1894	New York	NL	124	492	124	170	28	20	9	66	10	37	.346	.539
1895	New York	NL	110	433	106	143	32	11	5	55	12	45	.330	.490
1896	New York	NL	124	495	98	155	22	10	5	50	24	49	.313	.428
1897	New York	NL	131	525	114	188	34	11	10	41		64	.358	.522
1898	New York	NL	121	484	80	148	21	5	2	32		22	.306	.382
1899	New York	NL	111	413	69	144	25	4	1	37		38	.349	.436
1900	New York	NL	113	425	70	138	20	4	3	35		32	.325	.412
1901	New York	NL	130	495	69	153	21	6	7	40		26	.309	.418
1902	Chicago	AL	132	480	77	143	27	7	3	65		33	.298	.402
1903	New York	NL	4	15	2	4	0	0	0	1		0	.267	.267
1904	Chicago	AL	152	558	74	143	25	14	1	43		32	.256	.357
1905	Chicago	AL	157	550	74	153	29	1	1	60		31	.278	.340
1906	Chicago	AL	133	484	63	134	26	6	0	41		27	.277	.355
1907	Chicago	AL	132	466	59	111	18	2	1	47		15	.238	.292
1908	Chicago	AL	128	419	41	91	14	1	0	41		22	.217	.255
1909	Chicago	AL	28	68	5	9	1	0	0	10		4	.132	.147
	TOTALS		2,376	9,027	1,546	2,683	444	165	73	870	180	631	.297	.407

Sources: Baseball-Reference.com; National Baseball Hall of Fame and Museum

Davis, Richard Dean "Rick" (born: November 24, 1958 in Denver, Colorado); inducted into the National Soccer Hall of Fame and Museum in 2001 as a player; Position: Midfield; International Caps (1977–1988): 36; International Goals: 7; played a then-record 36 games for the U.S. National Team; won three North American Soccer League championships.

At 5'8", Davis was the most prominent American soccer player of the 1980s, at both club and National Team levels. He was a star for the U.S. National Team for more than a decade and one of the leading American players in the foreign-dominated North American Soccer League.

His soccer career began in 1965 in the American Youth Soccer Organization in Claremont, California. Forty years later, Davis now serves as the AYSO National Director of Programs.

While playing in high school, he won the McGuire Cup (National Youth Championship) with the Santa Clara (California) Broncos and, as a senior, was selected a High School All-American. He made his first appearance with the U.S. Olympic and National Teams while attending Santa Clara University (California) as a freshman. Davis played his first international game for the United States against El Salvador on September 15, 1977, and scored his first international goal six minutes into the game. He would go on to play a then-record 36 international games for the United States, scoring a total of seven goals. Beginning in 1984, he was the captain of the National Team and led the United States into the 1984 (Los Angeles, California) and 1988 (Seoul, South Korea) Summer Olympic Games, failing to win a medal at either event.

He also played for the United States in the qualifying rounds of the 1982, 1986, and 1990 World Cups. After playing in the first two 1990 qualifying games (played in the summer of 1988), Davis suffered a knee injury in January 1989 that ended his outdoor career.

Davis had joined the New York Cosmos at the start of the 1978 North American Soccer League season after playing one year in college at Santa Clara University. From 1978 to 1984, he played in a total of 154 NASL games (including post-season competition) for the Cosmos, and won three league championships (1978, 1980, 1982).

While playing for the St. Louis Steamers of the Major Indoor Soccer League in 1983, Davis was allowed to play for the Cosmos in the final NASL season in 1984. In the MISL, he played three seasons for the Steamers, one for the New York Arrows, and three for the Tacoma Stars.

During his professional playing career, he became a member of U.S. Soccer's Board of Directors as an Athlete Representative, and was also a member of the U.S. Soccer Founders Club that brought the World Cup to the United States. Davis was a television analyst during both the 1990 FIFA World Cup in Italy and the 1994 FIFA World Cup in the United States. He continues to broadcast games for Major League Soccer and the Los Angeles Galaxy, and was inducted into the AYSO Hall of Fame in 1998.

Rick Davis' NASL Statistics

YEAR	TEAM	GP	GLS	ASTS	PTS
1978	New York Cosmos	11	0	1	1
1979	New York Cosmos	29	6	13	25
1980	New York Cosmos	14	1	8	10
1981	New York Cosmos	17	1	1	3
1982	New York Cosmos	21	0	4	4
1983	New York Cosmos	29	5	12	22
1984	New York Cosmos	8	2	2	6
	TOTALS	129	15	41	71

Source: National Soccer Hall of Fame and Museum

Davis, William Delford "Willie" (born: July 24, 1934 in Lisbon, Louisiana); inducted into the Pro Football Hall of Fame in 1981 as a player; Position: Defensive End; Uniform: #87; won the first two Super Bowls.

After graduating from Grambling State University (Louisiana), Davis went on to a 12-year National Football League career with the Cleveland Browns (1958–1959) and the Green Bay Packers (1960–1969). A 15th-round NFL draft pick in 1956, instead of playing with the Browns, he joined the Army and played for the service team before turning professional with Cleveland in 1958. He was traded to the Packers in 1960 and became a defensive star under legendary coach Vince Lombardi.

The 6'3", 245-pound Davis was selected All-NFL five times; played in five Pro Bowls (1963–1967), six NFL title games, and the first two Super Bowls (beating the Kansas City Chiefs in Super Bowl I in 1967 and the Oakland Raiders in Super Bowl II in 1968); recovered 21 opponent fumbles; and did not miss a game in his 162-game career.

Davis serves on the Green Bay Packers Board of Directors, and in 1999, he was ranked number 69 on *The Sporting News*' list of the 100 Greatest Football Players. After his playing days, he worked as a color commentator on NFL games for NBC. In 1986, Davis was named the Walter Camp Man of the Year, and in 1987, he won the Career Achievement Award from the NFL Alumni.

Willie Davis' Career Statistics

			DEFENSE		
YEAR	TEAM	G	FUM REC	YDS	TD
1958	Cleveland	12	0	0	0
1959	Cleveland	12	0	0	0
1960	Green Bay	12	1	0	0
1961	Green Bay	14	3	0	0
1962	Green Bay	14	3	0	1
1963	Green Bay	14	4	10	0
1964	Green Bay	14	2	0	0
1965	Green Bay	14	2	0	0
1966	Green Bay	14	2	0	0
1967	Green Bay	14	0	0	0
1968	Green Bay	14	3	9	0
1969	Green Bay	14	2	0	0
	TOTALS	162	22	19	1

Sources: Pro Football Hall of Fame; Pro-Football-Reference.com

Dawson, Andre Nolan (born: July 10, 1954 in Miami, Florida); inducted into the National Baseball Hall of Fame and Museum in 2010 as a player; Position: Center Field; Bats: Both; Throws: Right; he and fellow hall-of-famer Willie McCovey are the only two players to hit two home runs in one inning twice.

Nicknamed the "Hawk," the 6'3", 180-pound Dawson played 21 seasons with the Montreal Expos (1976–1986), Chicago Cubs (1987–1992), Boston Red Sox (1993–1994), and the Florida Marlins (1995–1996); was an eight-time All-Star (1981–1983, 1987–1991); an eight-time Gold Glove Award winner (1980–1985, 1987–1988); 1977 National League Rookie of the Year (Expos); 1987 National League Most Valuable Player (Cubs, the first player to be named league MVP while playing for a last place team); and had his jersey number 10 retired by the Expos. His 400 home runs and 300 stolen bases have only been matched by two players: Willie Mays and Barry Bonds. He won a World Series ring in 2003 while serving as a Special Assistant to the Florida Marlins Team President.

After attending Southwest High School (Miami, Florida), he went to Florida Agricultural and Mechanical University (Tallahassee, Florida). Dawson was drafted by the Montreal Expos in the 11th round of the 1975 amateur draft (pick number 250) and made his Major League debut on September 11, 1976.

With the Expos, he set single-season team records for home runs (32, now seventh), RBI (113, now fourth), extra base hits (78, now seventh), and sacrifice flies (18, still first). He is the only player to hit 200 home runs and steal 200 bases with Montreal and he hit two home runs in the same inning twice (at Atlanta-Fulton County Stadium against the Atlanta Braves on July 30, 1978 and at Wrigley Field against the Chicago Cubs on September 24, 1985). As of this writing, he and fellow hall-of-famer Willie McCovey are the only two players to hit two home runs in one inning twice.

Andre Dawson's Career Statistics

YEAR	TEAM	G	AB	R	H	HR	RBI	SB	BA	SLG
1976	Montreal	24	85	9	20	0	7	1	.235	.306
1977	Montreal	139	525	64	148	19	65	21	.282	.474
1978	Montreal	157	609	84	154	25	72	28	.253	.442
1979	Montreal	155	639	90	176	25	92	35	.275	.468
1980	Montreal	151	577	96	178	17	87	34	.308	.492
1981	Montreal	103	394	71	119	24	64	26	.302	.553
1982	Montreal	148	608	107	183	23	83	39	.301	.498
1983	Montreal	159	633	104	189	32	113	25	.299	.539
1984	Montreal	138	533	73	132	17	86	13	.248	.409
1985	Montreal	139	529	65	135	23	91	13	.255	.444
1986	Montreal	130	496	65	141	20	78	18	.284	.478
1987	Chicago	153	621	90	178	49	137	11	.287	.568
1988	Chicago	157	591	78	179	24	79	12	.303	.504
1989	Chicago	118	416	62	105	21	77	8	.252	.476
1990	Chicago	147	529	72	164	27	100	16	.310	.535
1991	Chicago	149	563	69	153	31	104	4	.272	.488
1992	Chicago	143	542	60	150	22	90	6	.277	.456
1993	Boston	121	461	44	126	13	67	2	.273	.425
1994	Boston	75	292	34	70	16	48	2	.240	.466
1995	Florida	79	226	30	58	8	37	0	.257	.434
1996	Florida	42	58	6	16	2	14	0	.276	.414
	TOTALS	2,627	9,927	1,373	2,774	438	1,591	314	.279	.482

Sources: Baseball-Reference.com; National Baseball Hall of Fame and Museum

Dawson, Leonard Ray "Len" (born: June 20, 1935 in Alliance, Ohio); inducted into the Pro Football Hall of Fame in 1987 as a player; Position: Quarterback; Uniform: #16; played in first-ever Super Bowl and won Super Bowl IV.

The Pittsburgh Steelers' number one draft pick in 1957 (fifth pick overall), Dawson played for the team for three seasons (1957–1959). Throughout his 19-year career (1957–1975), he would also play for the Cleveland Browns (1960–1961), Dallas Texans (1962, later renamed the Kansas City Chiefs), and the Kansas City Chiefs (1963–1975). He led the Texans and the Chiefs (1969) to American Football League titles; was AFL Player of the Year in 1962; won four AFL passing titles (1962, 1964, 1966, 1968); played in the first-ever Super Bowl (1967, in a loss to the Green Bay Packers); led the Chiefs to an upset win over the Minnesota Vikings in Super Bowl IV (1970); and was named Super Bowl Most Valuable Player (1970).

One of 11 children, Dawson served as team captain for Alliance (Ohio) High School's football, baseball, and basketball teams. In football, he was named All-State twice (as a linebacker in 1951 and as a quarterback in 1952) and threw for a school-record 1,615 yards. After high school, he attended Purdue University (West Lafayette, Indiana), and in three years, threw for over 3,000 yards, leading the Big Ten Conference in that category during each season.

As a sophomore in 1954, Dawson was the NCAA leader in passing efficiency, and led Purdue to an upset win over the University of Notre Dame, ending the Irish's then-13-game winning streak.

After a very slow start in the league, Dawson's career changed significantly when he joined the Texans/Chiefs. In his first season with the team, he led the American Football League in touchdowns (29) and yards per attempt; earned AFL MVP honors; and led the team to its first of three league titles. The 6', 190-pound quarterback's mobility worked well with coach Hank Stram's "movable pocket" offense, and he would go on to win four AFL passing titles; was a league All-Star six times; and had a 10-year run as the league's highest-rated career passer. From 1962 to 1969, Dawson threw 182 touchdown passes, more than any other quarterback during the period; was selected to the Pro Bowl seven times (1962, 1964, 1966–1969, 1971); and was a five-time All-Pro selection (1962, 1964, 1966, 1968, 1971).

Representing the AFL in the first-ever Super Bowl (1967), the Chiefs were defeated 35–10 by the Green Bay Packers as Dawson completed 16 of 27 passes for 210 yards, threw one touchdown, and had one interception. During the Chief's victory in Super Bowl IV (the last game ever played by an American Football League team), Dawson completed 12 of 17 passes for 142 yards and one touchdown, rushed for 11 yards, and had one interception.

In 1979, the Chiefs retired Dawson's #16 jersey, and inducted him into the Kansas City Chiefs Hall of Fame the same year. He currently works on the Chiefs' radio games and serves as sports director for KMBC-TV in Kansas City.

Len Dawson's Career Statistics

					PASSING					RUSHING			
YEAR	TEAM	G	ATT	COMP	PCT	YDS	TD	INT	RATING	NO	YDS	AVG	TD
1957	Pittsburgh	3	4	2	50.0	25	0	0	69.8	3	31	10.3	0
1958	Pittsburgh	4	6	1	16.7	11	0	2	0.00	2	-1	-0.5	0
1959	Pittsburgh	12	7	3	42.9	60	1	0	113.1	4	20	5	0
1960	Cleveland	2	13	8	61.5	23	0	0	65.9	1	0	0	0
1961	Cleveland	7	15	7	46.7	85	1	3	47.2	1	-10	-10	0
1962	Dallas	14	310	189	61.0	2,759	29	17	98.3	38	252	6.6	3
1963	Kansas City	14	352	190	54.0	2,389	26	19	77.5	37	272	7.4	2
1964	Kansas City	14	354	199	56.2	2,879	30	18	89.9	40	89	2.2	2
1965	Kansas City	14	305	163	53.4	2,262	21	14	81.3	43	142	3.3	2
1966	Kansas City	14	284	159	56.0	2,527	26	10	101.7	24	167	7	0
1967	Kansas City	14	357	206	57.7	2,651	24	17	83.7	20	68	3.4	0
1968	Kansas City	14	224	131	58.5	2,109	17	9	98.6	20	40	2	0
1969	Kansas City	9	166	98	59.0	1,323	9	13	69.9	1	3	3	0
1970	Kansas City	14	262	141	53.8	1,876	13	14	71.0	11	46	4.2	0
1971	Kansas City	14	301	167	55.5	2,504	15	13	81.6	12	24	2	0
1972	Kansas City	14	305	175	57.4	1,835	13	12	72.8	15	75	5	0
1973	Kansas City	8	101	66	65.3	725	2	5	72.4	6	40	6.7	0
1974	Kansas City	14	235	138	58.7	1,573	7	13	65.8	11	28	2.5	0
1975	Kansas City	12	140	93	66.4	1,095	5	4	90.0	5	7	1.4	0
	TOTALS	211	3,741	2,136	57.1	28,711	239	183	82.6	294	1,293	4.4	9

Sources: Kansas City Chiefs Hall of Fame; Pro Football Hall of Fame; Pro-Football-Reference.com

Day, Clarence Henry "Happy" (born: June 1, 1901 in Owen Sound, Ontario, Canada; died: February 17, 1990 in St. Thomas, Ontario, Canada); inducted into the Hockey Hall of Fame in 1961 as a player; Position: Defenseman; Uniform: #4; won seven Stanley Cup titles (one as a player, five as a coach, and one while serving in the team's front office).

Nicknamed "Happy" (later shortened to "Hap"), Day played 14 National Hockey League seasons (1924-1938) with the Toronto St. Pats (later renamed the Toronto Maple Leafs, 1924–1927); Toronto Maple Leafs (1927–1937); and the New York Americans (1937–1938).

He had earlier played senior hockey with the Hamilton Tigers (Ontario Hockey Association, 1922–1924) and varsity hockey at the University of Toronto (Canada).

He made his professional debut on December 10, 1924 as a left wing beside future hall-of-famers Jack Adams and Babe Dye. After his rookie year, he shifted to defense, where he spent the rest of his career.

Day was the Maple Leafs' team captain from 1926 to 1936, and starting in 1931, was joined on defense by future hall-of-famer King Clancy. In the spring of 1932, the Leafs opened their new facility, Maple Leaf Gardens, with the team's first Stanley Cup championship under Conn Smythe's management.

Day played his final NHL season with the New York Americans (1937–1938) and, after retiring, became a referee for two years while coaching in the Toronto area. He won the Memorial Cup with the West Toronto juniors in 1936, and the next season, he coached the Toronto Dominions to the OHA senior title.

In 1940, Day was hired by Conn Smythe as the Leafs' coach, and over the next 10 seasons, he enjoyed more success than any other coach in the league, winning five Stanley Cup championships (1942, 1945, 1947–1949), including the first time the title had been won three seasons in a row by the same team. After retiring as a coach in 1950, he became general manager Smythe's assistant; ran the team's day-to-day operations until 1957; and won another Stanley Cup in 1951 with coach Joe Primeau.

Hap Day's Career Statistics

			REGULAR SEASON					PLAYOFFS				
SEASON	**TEAM**	**LEAGUE**	**GP**	**G**	**A**	**TP**	**PIM**	**GP**	**G**	**A**	**TP**	**PIM**
1921–1922	Collingwood Sailors	OHA-Jr.										
1922–1923	Hamilton Tigers	OHA-Sr.	11	4	11	15	4	2	0	0	0	0
1923–1924	Hamilton Tigers	OHA-Sr.	10	6	11	17		2	1	1	2	
1924–1925	Toronto St. Pats	NHL	26	10	12	22	33	2	0	0	0	0
1925–1926	Toronto St. Pats	NHL	36	14	2	16	26					
1926–1927	Toronto St. Pats/Maple Leafs	NHL	44	11	5	16	50					
1927–1928	Toronto Maple Leafs	NHL	22	9	8	17	48					
1928–1929	Toronto Maple Leafs	NHL	44	6	6	12	84	4	1	0	1	4
1929–1930	Toronto Maple Leafs	NHL	43	7	14	21	77					
1930–1931	Toronto Maple Leafs	NHL	44	1	13	14	56	2	0	3	3	7
1931–1932	Toronto Maple Leafs	NHL	47	7	8	15	33	7	3	3	6	6
1932–1933	Toronto Maple Leafs	NHL	47	6	14	20	46	9	0	1	1	21
1933–1934	Toronto Maple Leafs	NHL	48	9	10	19	35	5	0	0	0	6
1934–1935	Toronto Maple Leafs	NHL	45	2	4	6	38	7	0	0	0	4
1935–1936	Toronto Maple Leafs	NHL	44	1	13	14	41	9	0	0	0	8
1936–1937	Toronto Maple Leafs	NHL	48	3	4	7	20	2	0	0	0	0
1937–1938	New York Americans	NHL	43	0	3	3	14	6	0	0	0	0
	NHL TOTALS		581	86	116	202	601	53	4	7	11	56

Sources: Hockey Hall of Fame; Hockey-Reference.com

Day, Leon (born: October 30, 1916 in Alexandria, Virginia; died: March 13, 1995 in Baltimore, Maryland); inducted into the National Baseball Hall of Fame and Museum in 1995 as a Negro League Player by the Veterans Committee; Position: Pitcher; Bats: Right; Throws: Right; had a perfect 13–0 season in 1937; set the Negro National League record with 18 strikeouts in one game; pitched the only opening day no-hitter in Negro Leagues history; only inductee enshrined with a cap of a team outside mainland North America; his .708 winning percentage is the highest of any pitcher currently in the hall of fame.

A dominant strikeout pitcher with a blazing fastball and curve, Day played 12 Negro League seasons (1934–1950) with the Baltimore Black Sox (1934), Brooklyn Eagles (1935, later named the Newark Eagles), Newark Eagles (1936–1939, 1941–1943, 1946), and Baltimore Elite Giants (1949–1950, leading the team to the 1949 pennant).

A contact hitter with speed on the bases, Day could play in the outfield and infield when he was not pitching. He had a perfect season in 1937 (pitching to a 13–0 record while batting .320 and hitting eight home runs), and on July 23, 1942, he struck out 18 Baltimore Elite Giants (including Roy Campanella three times) to set a Negro National League record.

On September 14, 1942, in game four of the Negro League World Series, Day pitched for the Homestead Grays and struck out 12 while beating the legendary Satchel Paige and the Kansas City Monarchs 4–1. The Monarchs protested the game, contending that Day and other players were selected to play in the World Series from other teams. Day's win was eventually voided and the Monarchs went on to sweep the series in four games.

After Day spent two years pitching on integrated U.S. Army teams during World War II, in his first game back with the Eagles in 1946, he threw an opening-day no-hitter against the Philadelphia Stars, the only opening-day no-hitter in Negro Leagues history. He compiled a 9–4 record that season; led the league in strikeouts; and started two games in the Negro League World Series, helping the Eagles beat the Kansas City Monarchs.

Throwing without a windup, the 5'9", 170-pound Day appeared in a record seven East-West All-Star games from 1935 through 1946, and set an All-Star record by striking out a total of 14 batters.

In the off-season, he played winter ball in Puerto Rico and established a Puerto Rican record of 19 strikeouts in an 18-inning game that was eventually called a 1–1 tie. In 1950, he left the United States to play in Canada for a year; played in the minor leagues for the Toronto Maple Leafs (International League) in 1951 and for the Scranton Miners (Eastern League) in 1952; and returned to Canada to finish his career, retiring in 1955. Day had also played two winters in Cuba, one in Venezuela (pitching to a 12–1 record), and three summers in Mexico for the Mexico City Reds.

Day is the only hall-of-famer to be enshrined with a cap of a team outside mainland North America. His plaque identifies him as an "Aguadilla Shark" (Los Tiburones de Aguadilla), the Puerto Rican team for which he had once played. His career winning percentage of .708 is the highest of any pitcher in the hall of fame.

Source: National Baseball Hall of Fame and Museum

Dean, Everett (born: March 18, 1898 in Livonia, Indiana; died: October 26, 1993 in Caldwell, Ohio); inducted into the Naismith Memorial Basketball Hall of Fame in 1966 as a coach; led Stanford University to the school's only NCAA Men's Basketball National Championship; only coach inducted into both the Naismith Memorial Basketball Hall of Fame and the College Baseball Hall of Fame.

Dean attended Salem (Indiana) High School from 1913 to 1917, where he was a four-year letter winner. After graduating, he went to Indiana University (Bloomington, 1917–1921) and played basketball for three seasons; was named to the Helms Athletic Foundation All-America Team (1921); selected All-Big 10 (1921); and was awarded the Western Conference Medal for proficiency in Scholarship & Athletics (1921).

After finishing college, he accepted his first coaching job at Carleton College (Northfield, Minnesota) in 1921. He left in 1924 to become the head coach of his alma mater and stayed until 1938, moving on to Stanford University (Palo Alto, California), where he remained until 1955.

Dean led Carleton College to a 45–4 record; Indiana to a 163–93 record; and Stanford to a 167–120 record. He coached Indiana for 14 seasons; led the Hoosiers to the team's first Big Ten championship (1926); and tied for the championship in 1928 and 1936. He led Stanford to the 1942 national championship (a 53–38 win over Dartmouth), the university's only men's national basketball championship. In 1950, he also became Stanford's head baseball coach and led the team into the 1953 College World Series, where it was eliminated after playing three games.

In addition to coaching, Dean also wrote two basketball books, *Indiana Basketball* (1933) and *Progressive Basketball* (1949). Dean is the only coach inducted into both the Naismith Memorial Basketball Hall of Fame and the College Baseball Hall of Fame. He was also inducted into the Indiana Basketball Hall of Fame in 1965.

Sources: Indiana Basketball Hall of Fame; Naismith Memorial Basketball Hall of Fame

Dean, Frederick Rudolph "Fred" (born: February 24, 1952 in Arcadia, Louisiana); inducted into the Pro Football Hall of Fame in 2008 as a player; Position: Defensive End; won two Super Bowl championships.

A graduate from Ruston (Louisiana) High School and an All-Southland Conference linebacker at Louisiana Tech University (Ruston), Dean was a second-round pick (33rd choice overall) of the San Diego Chargers in the 1975 National Football League draft. His speed made him a great pass rusher, and he accumulated almost 100 career sacks (the exact total is unknown because when Dean played, the sack was not yet an official NFL statistic).

The 6'3", 230-pound Dean enjoyed an 11-year (141 games) NFL career with the Chargers (1975–1981) and the San Francisco 49ers (1981–1985); was twice named All-Pro (1980–1981); All-NFC twice; named to four Pro Bowls (1980–1982, 1984); and was selected NFC Defensive Player of the Year in 1981.

Early in the 1981 season, he joined the 49ers and had 12 sacks in 11 games to help the team win its first Super Bowl championship. On November 13, 1983, Dean collected a then-record six sacks in a single game in a 27–0 win over the New Orleans Saints. He played on five division winners, in three NFC championship games, and in two of San Francisco's Super Bowl victories (Super Bowls XVI and XIX).

Dean has been inducted into the Louisiana Sports Hall of Fame.

Source: Pro Football Hall of Fame

Dean, Jerome Hanna "Jay" "Dizzy" (born: January 16, 1910 in Lucas, Arkansas; died: July 17, 1974 in Reno, Nevada); inducted into the National Baseball Hall of Fame and Museum in 1953 as a player; Position: Pitcher; Bats: Right; Throws: Right; Uniform: #17; won the 1934 World Series; 1934 National League MVP; last National League pitcher to win 30 games in one season.

Making his debut on the last day of the season (September 28, 1930), Dean only played six full seasons in the major leagues during his 12-year career (1930–1947) with the St. Louis Cardinals (1930, 1932–1937), Chicago Cubs (1938–1941), and St. Louis Browns (1947). He played in the 1934 World Series (defeating the Detroit Tigers) and the 1938 World Series (losing to the New York Yankees); was named the 1934 National League Most Valuable Player; and was a four-time All-Star (1934–1937).

After his one-game appearance in 1930 (a 3–1 win over the Pittsburgh Pirates), he would not pitch in the majors again until 1932, and would go on to average 24 wins per year over his first five full seasons. Dean led the league in strikeouts four consecutive years (1932–1935); was a three-time 20-game winner; compiled a 30–7 record in 1934, the last National League pitcher to win 30 games in a single season; and won two games in the 1934 World Series as he and his brother, Paul, led the "Gashouse Gang" to the championship.

On July 30, 1933, Dean set a then-20th-century major league record with 17 strikeouts in the first game of a doubleheader against the Chicago Cubs. He later suffered a broken toe in the 1937 All-Star Game that eventually shortened his playing days. After retiring as a player, he enjoyed a long and successful broadcasting career.

After leaving military service, he played for a semi-professional team in San Antonio, Texas before joining the St. Louis Cardinals minor league farm system in 1930. He compiled a 25–10 record in the minors, before pitching his three-hitter for St. Louis on the last day of the major league season. He returned to the Houston Buffaloes (Texas League) in 1931, eventually striking out 303 batters and winning 26 games.

As a rookie in 1932, the 21-year-old Dean won 18 games and led the National League in strikeouts, shutouts, and innings pitched. From 1933 to 1936, the 6'2", 182-pound Dean won 102 games; led the league in complete games each year; and averaged 50 games started and more than 300 innings per season.

Brash and overconfident by nature, Dean often made public predictions and boasted of achievements he and his brother would accomplish (such as how many games they would win in a season), and when any one of his assertions came true, he could be heard to say, "If you can do it, it ain't braggin'."

While pitching for the National League in the 1937 All-Star Game, Dean broke his toe when he was hit by a line drive off the bat of Earl Averill of the Cleveland Indians. By many accounts, he was too eager to resume his career and came back too soon. Not fully healed, he had to change his pitching motion, which caused him to hurt his arm, eventually leading to a premature retirement.

In his four years with the Cubs, Dean only won 16 total games. While he helped the team win the pennant in 1938, he was a non-factor in the World Series as the team lost to the New York Yankees in a four-game sweep.

After retiring as a player, he was hired by the St. Louis Browns as a broadcaster and quickly became a fan favorite. After making the comment that he could "pitch better than nine of the 10 guys on this staff," the Browns (in search of publicity and in an effort to sell more tickets) activated him to pitch the last game of the 1947 season. At age 37, after not pitching for more than six years, Dean threw four innings; allowed no runs and three hits; and got a single in his only at-bat. He returned to the broadcasting booth for good after the game.

Known to regularly mangle the English language as a broadcaster, Dean was smart enough not to try to convince anyone he really was a smart guy. Instead, he promoted his image as a not-too-smart, but likeable, country bumpkin. And the fans loved it.

Once criticized by an English teacher for his regular use of the word "ain't," during a game broadcast, he responded by saying "A lot of folks who ain't sayin' ain't, ain't eatin'." His local and national broadcasting career, on both radio and television, lasted more than 20 years.

A Dizzy Dean Museum was established in Jackson, Mississippi that is now part of the Mississippi Sports Hall of Fame and Museum; his jersey number 17 was retired by the Cardinals in 1974; and he was inducted into the St. Louis Walk of Fame in 1997. In spite of playing what amounted to only half a career, in 1999 he was ranked number 85 on *The Sporting News*' list of the 100 Greatest Baseball Players, and he was nominated as a finalist for the Major League Baseball All-Century Team.

Dizzy Dean's Career Statistics

YEAR	TEAM	LG	W	L	WIN%	G	SH	IP	H	R	ER	SO	BB	ERA
1930	St. Louis	NL	1	0	1.000	1	0	9	3	1	1	5	3	1.00
1932	St. Louis	NL	18	15	.545	46	4	286	280	122	105	191	102	3.30
1933	St. Louis	NL	20	18	.526	48	3	293	279	113	99	199	64	3.04
1934	St. Louis	NL	30	7	.811	50	7	312	288	110	92	195	75	2.65
1935	St. Louis	NL	28	12	.700	50	3	325	324	126	110	190	77	3.05
1936	St. Louis	NL	24	13	.649	51	2	315	310	128	111	195	53	3.17
1937	St. Louis	NL	13	10	.565	27	4	197	200	76	59	120	33	2.70
1938	Chicago	NL	7	1	.875	13	1	75	63	20	15	22	8	1.80
1939	Chicago	NL	6	4	.600	19	2	96	98	40	36	27	17	3.38

YEAR	TEAM	LG	W	L	WIN%	G	SH	IP	H	R	ER	SO	BB	ERA
1940	Chicago	NL	3	3	.500	10	0	54	68	35	31	18	20	5.17
1941	Chicago	NL	0	0	.000	1	0	1	3	3	2	1	0	18.00
1947	St. Louis	AL	0	0	.000	1	0	4	3	0	0	0	1	0.00
	TOTALS		150	83	.644	317	26	1,967	1,919	774	661	1,163	453	3.02

Sources: Baseball-Reference.com; National Baseball Hall of Fame and Museum

DeBernardi, Forrest S. "Red" (born: February 3, 1899 in Nevada, Missouri; died: April 29, 1970); inducted into the Naismith Memorial Basketball Hall of Fame in 1961 as a player; Position: Center; won the National Basketball Tournament championship in 1921; selected as the center on the Associated Press All-Time All-American college basketball team in 1938.

DeBernardi attended Iola (Kansas) High School (1915–1916) and Northeast (Missouri) High School (1916–1919), where he was named to the All-Kansas High School team (1916) and All-City (1919). After high school, he went to the University of Kansas (Lawrence, 1920–1921) and Westminster College (Fulton, Missouri, 1921–1923), where he was named All-Conference twice (1922–1923).

As an amateur, he played for the Amateur Athletic Union Shmelzer's (1918–1919), AAU Kansas City Athletic Club (1920–1922), AAU Hillyard Shine Alls (1923–1927), AAU Cook's Painter Boys (1928–1929), and the AAU Tulsa DX Oilers (1929–1931). He won the National Basketball Tournament championship in 1921 with the Kansas City Athletic Club and finished third in 1920; led Hillyard to the AAU national title twice (1926–1927); led the Cook Paint Company to the AAU national title twice (1928–1929); named an AAU All-American seven times in 11 AAU national tournaments (at guard, forward, and center); selected as the center on the Associated Press All-Time All-American college basketball team in 1938; and won the Helms Athletic Foundation Hall of Fame Award in 1952.

While the 6'1", 172-pound DeBernardi was a two-time All-American at Westminster College (1920–1921), the school allowed him to play on the Kansas City Athletic Club basketball team that finished third in the AAU national tournament in 1920 and won the tournament in 1921.

By the time he retired in 1929, he had participated in 10 national AAU tournaments and had been named to the AAU All-American team eight times, winning five national titles.

Source: Naismith Memorial Basketball Hall of Fame

DeBusschere, David Albert "Dave" (born: October 16, 1940 in Detroit, Michigan; died: May 14, 2003 in New York, New York); inducted into the Naismith Memorial Basketball Hall of Fame in 1983 as a player; Position: Forward-Guard; Uniform: #22; youngest coach in NBA history (as a player-coach with the Detroit Pistons); named Michigan Athlete of the Year; won two NBA titles; played professional baseball with the Chicago White Sox and the Chicago Cubs.

DeBusschere attended Austin Catholic High School (Detroit, Michigan) from 1954 to 1958, where he was a three-year letter winner (1956–1958); a two-time All-State selection (1957–1958); won All-American honors in 1958; led the school to the state championship in 1958; and averaged 24.1 points per game as a senior.

After high school, he went to the University of Detroit Mercy (Michigan) from 1958 to 1962, where he was a three-year letter winner (1960–1962); a three-time All-American (1960–1962); led the school into the 1960 and 1961 National Invitation Tournament and into the NCAA Tournament in 1962; holds the school's record for most rebounds in a game (39 against Central Michigan on January 30, 1960), most rebounds in a career (1,552), and career scoring average (24.8 points per game); and was named Michigan Athlete of the Year in 1960.

After graduating from college, DeBusschere joined the National Basketball Association and played 12 years for the Detroit Pistons (1962–1968, was the team's player-coach from 1964 to 1967, making him the youngest coach in NBA history) and the New York Knicks (1969–1973). He was named to the NBA All-Rookie Team in 1963; the All-NBA Second Team in 1969; the NBA All-Defensive First Team six times (1969–1974); was an eight-time NBA All-Star (1966–1968, 1970–1974); won two NBA championships with the Knicks (1970, 1973); compiled a career average of 16.1 points and 11 rebounds per game; and was named to the NBA 50th Anniversary All-Time Team in 1996.

In addition to basketball, the 6'6", 225-pound DeBusschere played professional baseball as a pitcher with Major League Baseball's Chicago White Sox for two seasons (1962–1963, compiling a record of 3–4, with a 3.09 Earned Run Average in 1963) and in the Chicago Cubs' minor league system for two seasons (compiling a record of 25–9 with the AAA Indianapolis Indians of the International League). After four seasons in professional baseball, he retired from the game to concentrate on basketball.

After retiring as a player, he became vice-president and general manager of the New York Nets, and served as the commissioner of the American Basketball Association in the league's final season (1976). He returned to the NBA as vice-president and director of operations for the Knicks from 1982 to 1986; his jersey number 22 was retired by the Knicks; and he wrote *The Open Man*, a book that chronicled the New York Knicks' 1969–1970 championship season.

Dave DeBusschere's NBA Career Statistics

SEASON	TEAM	G	MIN	FG	FT	TRB	AST	PTS
1962–1963	Detroit	80	2,352	406	206	694	207	1,018
1963–1964	Detroit	15	304	52	25	105	23	129
1964–1965	Detroit	79	2,769	508	306	874	253	1,322
1965–1966	Detroit	79	2,696	524	249	916	209	1,297
1966–1967	Detroit	78	2,897	531	361	924	216	1,423
1967–1968	Detroit	80	3,125	573	289	1,081	181	1,435
1968–1969	Detroit	29	1,092	189	94	353	63	472
1968–1969	New York	47	1,851	317	135	535	128	769
1969–1970	New York	79	2,627	488	176	790	194	1,152
1970–1971	New York	81	2,891	523	217	901	220	1,263
1971–1972	New York	80	3,072	520	193	901	291	1,233
1972–1973	New York	77	2,827	532	194	787	259	1,258
1973–1974	New York	71	2,699	559	164	757	253	1,282
	TOTALS	875	31,202	5,722	2,609	9,618	2,497	14,053

Dave DeBusschere's NBA Coaching Career

		REG SEASON		
SEASON	TEAM	W	L	WIN%
1964–1965	Detroit	29	40	.420
1965–1966	Detroit	22	58	.275
1966–1967	Detroit	28	45	.384
	TOTALS	79	143	.356

Sources: Basketball-Reference.com; Naismith Memorial Basketball Hall of Fame

Dehnert, Henry G. "Dutch" (born: April 5, 1898 in New York, New York; died: April 20, 1979 in Far Rockaway, New York); inducted into the Naismith Memorial Basketball Hall of Fame in 1969 as a player; Position: Forward; won three consecutive championships with the Cleveland Rosenblums and two consecutive titles with the Original Celtics.

Dehnert, who did not attend high school or college, played professional basketball for the Danbury Hatters (Connecticut League, 1917–1918), Jersey City Skeeters (Connecticut League, 1917–1918), Norwalk Company K (Connecticut League, 1917–1918), Nanticoke Nans (Pennsylvania League, 1917–1920), Wilkes-Barre Barons (Pennsylvania League, 1917–1918), Bridgeport Blue Ribbons (Eastern League, 1919–1920), Philadelphia DeNeri (Eastern League, 1919–1921), Thompsonville Big Harts (Interstate League, 1919–1921), Utica Utes (Interstate League, 1919–1921), Scranton Miners (Pennsylvania League, 1920–1922), Original New York Celtics (Independent League / Eastern League / Metropolitan League / National League / American Basketball League, 1918–1919, 1921–1928, 1931–1933, 1935–1939), Cleveland Rosenblums (American Basketball League, 1928–1931), Toledo Red Men Tobaccos (American Basketball League, 1930–1931), and the New Britain Jackaways (American Basketball League, 1934–1935).

The 6', 210-pound Dehnert played or coached basketball for 35 years in more than 2,000 games; was instrumental in developing the pivot play as a member of the Original Celtics in 1925; and won three consecutive ABL championships with the Cleveland Rosenblums (1928–1930).

After retiring as a player, he became a professional coach with the Detroit Eagles (National Basketball League, 1940–1941); Harrisburg Senators (American Basketball League / Eastern League, 1942–1943); Trenton Tigers (American Basketball League, 1943–1944); Sheboygan Redskins (American Basketball League, 1940–1946); Cleveland Rebels (Basketball Association of America); and the Chattanooga Majors (Professional Basketball League of America). Dehnert led Detroit to back-to-back World Professional Championship titles (1940–1941); coached Sheboygan to a championship (1945); and led Sheboygan to two Western titles (1945–1946). When the Celtics joined the American Basketball League in 1926, Dehnert helped the team win consecutive championships in 1927 and 1928.

Source: Naismith Memorial Basketball Hall of Fame

Delach, Joseph (born: November 9, 1910 in Beadling, Pennsylvania; died: July 1975); inducted into the National Soccer Hall of Fame and Museum in 1973 as a builder; won the Honus Wagner Cup as a player and the Keystone League title as a coach.

Delach played for the Beadling Seniors from 1935 to 1946, winning the Honus Wagner Cup in 1935 and the Allegheny Valley League Championship in 1946. After retiring as a player, he managed the Beadling Seniors' 1958 team that won the Keystone League title and the West Penn Cup, before losing to the St. Louis Kutis in the National Amateur Cup final. He later served as president of the Keystone League from 1962 to 1973; commissioner of the National Amateur Cup for ten years; and was a long-time West Penn Delegate to the United States Soccer Federation annual convention.

Source: National Soccer Hall of Fame and Museum

Delahanty, Edward James "Ed" (born: October 30, 1867 in Cleveland, Ohio; died: July 2, 1903 in Niagara Falls, Ontario, Canada); inducted into the National Baseball Hall of Fame and Museum in 1945 as a player by the Veterans Committee; Position: Left Field; Bats: Right; Throws: Right; only player in major league history to hit four home runs in one game and four doubles in another game.

Delahanty made his major league debut on May 22, 1888, and went on to play 16 seasons with the Philadelphia Quakers (1888–1889), Cleveland Infants (Players' League, 1890), Philadelphia Phillies (1891–1901), and the Washington Senators (1902–1903). One of seven brothers (the oldest of five who reached the major leagues), he generated power in an era of slap hitters. He hit four home runs in one game (July 13, 1896 in a 9–8 loss to the Chicago Cubs, only the second player to do so); went 6-for-6 in a game twice (June 2, 1890 and June 16, 1894); and went 9-for-9 in a doubleheader once (July 13, 1897). On May 13, 1899, he hit four doubles in one game and is the only player in major league history to hit four home runs in one game and four doubles in another.

The 6'1", 190-pound Delahanty finished with a .346 batting average (the fourth best in major league history); hit .400 or more three times (1894–1895, 1899); and led the league in runs batted in three times.

He died when he was swept over Niagara Falls at the age of 35. According to the story, he was kicked off a train by the conductor for being drunk and disorderly and for threatening passengers with a razor. After being kicked off the train, Delahanty began crossing the International Bridge (near Niagara Falls) and fell (or jumped, depending on who is telling the story) off the bridge and died.

Ed Delahanty's Career Statistics

YEAR	TEAM	LG	G	AB	R	H	2B	3B	HR	BB	SO	SB	AVG	SLG
1888	Philadelphia	NL	74	290	40	66	11	1	1	12	26	38	.228	.283
1889	Philadelphia	NL	54	246	37	72	13	3	0	14	17	19	.293	.370
1890	Cleveland	PL	115	513	106	152	24	15	3	24	30	24	.296	.419
1891	Philadelphia	NL	128	545	92	136	19	9	5	33	50	27	.250	.345
1892	Philadelphia	NL	120	470	78	147	33	19	6	31	32	35	.313	.502
1893	Philadelphia	NL	132	588	145	218	31	20	19	47	20	36	.371	.588
1894	Philadelphia	NL	114	497	149	199	36	16	4	60	16	29	.400	.561
1895	Philadelphia	NL	116	481	148	192	47	8	11	86	31	46	.399	.599
1896	Philadelphia	NL	122	505	131	199	42	14	13	62	22	37	.394	.610
1897	Philadelphia	NL	129	530	110	200	37	15	5	60	0	28	.377	.532
1898	Philadelphia	NL	142	547	114	183	37	11	4	77	0	62	.335	.464
1899	Philadelphia	NL	145	573	133	234	56	9	9	55	0	38	.408	.585
1900	Philadelphia	NL	130	542	82	173	32	10	2	41	0	14	.319	.426
1901	Philadelphia	NL	138	538	106	192	38	16	8	65	0	29	.357	.532
1902	Washington	AL	123	474	103	178	43	14	10	62	0	16	.376	.589
1903	Washington	AL	43	154	22	52	11	1	1	12	0	3	.338	.442
	TOTALS		1,825	7,493	1,596	2,593	510	181	101	741	244	481	.346	.503

Sources: Baseball-Reference.com; National Baseball Hall of Fame and Museum

DeLamielleure, Joseph Michael "Joe" (born: March 16, 1951 in Detroit, Michigan); inducted into the Pro Football Hall of Fame in 2003 as a player; Position: Guard; Uniform: #68 (Bills), #64 (Browns); was the lead blocker for O.J.

Simpson the season that he became the NFL's first-ever 2,000-yard single-season rusher; named Offensive Lineman of the Year in 1975; first NFL player to block for a 2,000 yard rusher and a 4,000 yard passer.

After being an All-American and three-time All-Big-Ten performer at Michigan State University (East Lansing), DeLamielleure was a first-round selection (26th pick overall) of the Buffalo Bills in the 1973 National Football League draft. At 6'3", 254 pounds, he won All-Rookie honors and played in 185 consecutive games during his 13-year career with the Bills (1973–1979, 1985) and Cleveland Browns (1980–1984). He anchored the Bills' famed "Electric Company" offensive line (so-called because it "turned the Juice loose"), and was best known as the lead blocker for O. J. Simpson (the "Juice"), the NFL's first 2000-yard rusher (1973).

Eight times during his career, he was selected a First- or Second-Team All-Pro (1974–1980, 1983); named First- or Second-Team All-American Football Conference seven times (1975–1981); named to six Pro Bowls (1976–1981); selected Offensive Lineman of the Year in 1975; and was named to the NFL's 1970s All-Decade Team.

In 1980, DeLamielleure was traded to the Cleveland Browns, where he became the lead blocker for another NFL Most Valuable Player, Brian Sipe (his first being Simpson). He became the first player ever to block for a 2,000 yard rusher and a 4,000 yard passer. Of those who have done it since (Jackie Slater, Doug Smith, Irv Pankey, Kevin Glover, and Tom Nalen), only DeLamielleure's two players were NFL MVPs, and the passer (Sipe) also won the NFL passing crown.

After his NFL career, he played briefly for the Charlotte Rage of the Arena Football League, and was inducted into the East-West Shrine Game Hall of Fame in 2007.

Source: Pro Football Hall of Fame

DeLuca, Enzo (born: February 17, 1920 in Patti Messina, Italy); inducted into the National Soccer Hall of Fame and Museum in 1979 as a builder; instrumental in organizing the Italian American Soccer League of New York.

DeLuca began playing soccer in Italy in 1930, before moving to the United States. In 1949, he organized the Jersey City soccer team and the Jersey City parks team, and participated in the New Jersey State League Championships as a player and manager. He would later become a referee in New Jersey.

As a member of the New Jersey State Soccer Association and a delegate to the United States Soccer Football Association conventions in Baltimore (Maryland), Detroit (Michigan), and New York (New York), DeLuca helped organize the Italian American Soccer League of New York, and helped form the Italian American Soccer League of New Jersey in 1959–1960.

He worked as a sportswriter for *Il Progresso*, an Italian daily newspaper in the New York area, and wrote a book in Italian, *Soccer in the USA* (1962). For his contributions to the sport, the Italian government honored DeLuca with the title "Cavaliere dell'Ordine al Merito della Republica" (the Order of Merit of the Republic, which honors those who make significant contributions in the humanities, arts, sports, civil service, and military).

Source: National Soccer Hall of Fame and Museum

Delvecchio, Alexander Peter "Alex" "Fats" (born: December 4, 1931 in Fort William, Ontario, Canada); inducted into the Hockey Hall of Fame as a player in 1977; Position: Center-Left Wing; Uniform: #10; won three Stanley Cup championships; second player in NHL history to play more than 20 seasons with the same team.

Delvecchio played his entire 24-year National Hockey League career (1950–1973) with the Detroit Red Wings. When he retired, he trailed only long-time teammate Gordie Howe in games played, assists, and total points.

He helped the Red Wings win the 1952 Stanley Cup (a four-game sweep over the Montreal Canadiens); in 1953, he was named to the NHL Second All-Star Team; and he was on Red Wings teams that won the Cup in back-to-back seasons, 1954 and 1955.

He earned All-Star honors as both a center and left wing, and was only the third player (after Dit Clapper and Sid Abel) in NHL history to be so honored at two positions. In 1959, Delvecchio won his first of three Lady Byng trophies (1966, 1969) for sportsmanship and gentlemanly conduct; was a consistent 20-goal scorer; and was named team captain in 1962, a position he held until he retired.

In his last NHL season, Delvecchio won the Lester Patrick Trophy for his outstanding service to hockey in the United States, and was the second player in league history to play more than 20 seasons with the same team (Gordie Howe being the first).

After retiring as a player, he became the Red Wings' head coach intermittently from 1973 to 1977, and served as the team's general manager in 1975. In addition to winning the Stanley Cup three times, Delvecchio was named a Second Team All-Star in 1953 (at center) and 1959 (at left wing); played in 13 All-Star Games (1953–1959, 1961–1965, 1967);

and in 1998, he was ranked number 82 on *The Hockey News*' list of the 100 Greatest Hockey Players. His jersey number 10 hangs in Joe Louis Arena (home of the Red Wings).

Alex Delvecchio's Career Statistics

			REGULAR SEASON					PLAYOFFS				
SEASON	**TEAM**	**LEAGUE**	**GP**	**G**	**A**	**TP**	**PIM**	**GP**	**G**	**A**	**TP**	**PIM**
1947–1948	Fort William Rangers	TBJHL	1	0	0	0	0					
1948–1949	Fort William Rangers	TBJHL	12	16	8	24	53	1	2	0	2	0
1948–1949	Port Arthur Bruins	M-Cup	5	2	2	4	1					
1949–1950	Fort William Rangers	TBJHL	18	16	20	36	36	5	4	4	8	15
1950–1951	Oshawa Generals	OHA-Jr.	54	49	72	121	36					
1950–1951	Detroit Red Wings	NHL	1	0	0	0	0					
1951–1952	Detroit Red Wings	NHL	65	15	22	37	22	8	0	3	3	4
1951–1952	Indianapolis Capitols	AHL	6	3	6	9	4					
1952–1953	Detroit Red Wings	NHL	70	16	43	59	28	6	2	4	6	2
1953–1954	Detroit Red Wings	NHL	69	11	18	29	34	12	2	7	9	7
1954–1955	Detroit Red Wings	NHL	69	17	31	48	37	11	7	8	15	2
1955–1956	Detroit Red Wings	NHL	70	25	26	51	24	10	7	3	10	2
1956–1957	Detroit Red Wings	NHL	48	16	25	41	8	5	3	2	5	2
1957–1958	Detroit Red Wings	NHL	70	21	38	59	22	4	0	1	1	0
1958–1959	Detroit Red Wings	NHL	70	19	35	54	6					
1959–1960	Detroit Red Wings	NHL	70	19	28	47	8	6	2	6	8	0
1960–1961	Detroit Red Wings	NHL	70	27	35	62	26	11	4	5	9	0
1961–1962	Detroit Red Wings	NHL	70	26	43	69	18					
1962–1963	Detroit Red Wings	NHL	70	20	44	64	8	11	3	6	9	2
1963–1964	Detroit Red Wings	NHL	70	23	30	53	11	14	3	8	11	0
1964–1965	Detroit Red Wings	NHL	68	25	42	67	16	7	2	3	5	4
1965–1966	Detroit Red Wings	NHL	70	31	38	69	16	12	0	11	11	4
1966–1967	Detroit Red Wings	NHL	70	17	38	55	10					
1967–1968	Detroit Red Wings	NHL	74	22	48	70	14					
1968–1969	Detroit Red Wings	NHL	72	25	58	83	8					
1969–1970	Detroit Red Wings	NHL	73	21	47	68	24	4	0	2	2	0
1970–1971	Detroit Red Wings	NHL	77	21	34	55	6					
1971–1972	Detroit Red Wings	NHL	75	20	45	65	22					
1972–1973	Detroit Red Wings	NHL	77	18	53	71	13					
1973–1974	Detroit Red Wings	NHL	11	1	4	5	2					
1973–1977	Detroit Red Wings	NHLMGNT										
	NHL TOTALS		1,549	456	825	1,281	383	121	35	69	104	29

Sources: Hockey Hall of Fame; Hockey-Reference.com

Denneny, Cyril Joseph "Cy" (born: December 23, 1897 in Farran's Point, Ontario, Canada; died: September 9, 1970); inducted into the Hockey Hall of Fame in 1959 as a player; Position: Left Wing; one of the first players to use a curved stick on the ice; won five Stanley Cup titles (four as a player, one as a coach).

Denneny played 15 professional hockey seasons from 1914 to 1929, mainly with the National Hockey League's Ottawa Senators. He compiled 20 or more goals per season eight times; was one of the first players to use a curved stick on the ice; and retired as the top goal-scorer in the history of the Ottawa Senators.

In 1916, he joined the Ottawa Senators; was with the team when the franchise became one of the founding members of the National Hockey League; and won four Stanley Cups in the 1920s (1920–1921, 1923, 1927).

He was the top scorer in the NHL in the 1923–1924 season, and would finish second in scoring six times. On March 7, 1921, Denneny scored five goals in one game against the Hamilton Tigers, becoming the sixth player in NHL history to do so. He was the league's all-time top goal scorer when he retired, until surpassed by Howie Morenz in the 1933–1934 season. He also retired as the league's top point scorer (333 points), another record that was also surpassed by Morenz (1931–1932 season).

After leaving the Senators, Denneny joined the Boston Bruins as a player, coach, and assistant manager in 1928–1929; coached the team to its first Stanley Cup title (his fifth) in 1929; served as a league referee from 1929 to 1931; and in 1998, he was ranked number 62 on *The Hockey News*' list of the 100 Greatest Hockey Players.

Cy Denneny's Career Statistics

			REGULAR SEASON					PLAYOFFS				
SEASON	**TEAM**	**LEAGUE**	**GP**	**G**	**A**	**TP**	**PIM**	**GP**	**G**	**A**	**TP**	**PIM**

SEASON	TEAM	LEAGUE	REGULAR SEASON GP	G	A	TP	PIM	PLAYOFFS GP	G	A	TP	PIM
1909–1910	Cornwall Sons of England	LOVHL										
1910–1911	Cornwall Internationals	LOVHL	8	4	0	4						
1911–1912	Cornwall Internationals	LOVHL	8	9	0	9	16					
1912–1913	Russell Athletics	LOVHL										
1913–1914	Cobalt Mines	CoMHL	9	12	0	12	8					
1914–1915	Russel H.C.	LOVHL	3	3	0	3						
1914–1915	Toronto Shamrocks	NHA	8	6	0	6	43					
1915–1916	Toronto Blueshirts	NHA	24	24	4	28	57					
1916–1917	Ottawa Senators	NHA	10	3	0	3	17	2	1	0	1	8
1917–1918	Ottawa Senators	NHL	20	36	10	46	80					
1918–1919	Ottawa Senators	NHL	18	18	4	22	58	5	3	2	5	6
1919–1920	Ottawa Senators	NHL	24	16	6	22	31					
1919–1920	Ottawa Senators	St-Cup						5	0	2	2	3
1920–1921	Ottawa Senators	NHL	24	34	5	39	10	2	2	0	2	5
1920–1921	Ottawa Senators	St-Cup						5	2	2	4	13
1921–1922	Ottawa Senators	NHL	22	27	12	39	20	2	2	0	2	4
1922–1923	Ottawa Senators	NHL	24	23	11	34	28	2	2	0	2	2
1922–1923	Ottawa Senators	St-Cup						6	1	2	3	10
1923–1924	Ottawa Senators	NHL	22	22	2	24	10	2	2	0	2	2
1924–1925	Ottawa Senators	NHL	29	27	15	42	16					
1925–1926	Ottawa Senators	NHL	36	24	12	36	18	2	0	0	0	4
1926–1927	Ottawa Senators	NHL	42	17	6	23	16	6	5	0	5	0
1927–1928	Ottawa Senators	NHL	44	3	0	3	12	2	0	0	0	0
1928–1929	Boston Bruins	NHL	23	1	2	3	2	2	0	0	0	0
	NHL TOTALS		328	248	85	333	301	25	16	2	18	23

Sources: Hockey Hall of Fame; Hockey-Reference.com

Devellano, James "Jimmy" (born: January 18, 1943 in Toronto, Ontario, Canada); inducted into the Hockey Hall of Fame in 2010 as a builder; won seven Stanley Cup titles with the New York Islanders and Detroit Red Wings.

As of this writing, Devellano serves as both the senior vice-president of the Detroit Red Wings (National Hockey League) and vice-president of the Detroit Tigers (Major League Baseball). His first hockey job was as a scout for the St. Louis Blues for five seasons in the 1960s. He went on to work for the New York Islanders and the Detroit Red Wings; won three Stanley Cup titles with the Islanders (two as a scout in 1980 and 1981 and one as Assistant General Manager / Director of Scouting in 1982); and won four as the Red Wings' Senior Vice President (1997–1998, 2002, 2008). He also won a Major League Baseball American League championship ring with the Detroit Tigers in 2006 as the team's Senior Vice President.

When the expansion New York Islanders were added to the National Hockey League (1972–1973 season), Devellano was hired as a franchise scout and in 1974, he became the team's Head Scout. In 1978, he was part of Fort Worth's Adams Cup championship (Central Hockey League) and in 1979, he became General Manager of the Islanders' farm team (Indianapolis Checkers of the Central Hockey League), a job he held until 1981, and was named Minor League Executive of the Year by *The Hockey News*.

When Mike Ilitch bought the Detroit Red Wings in June 1982, he hired Devellano as the team's General Manager. Since he has been with the franchise, in addition to four Stanley Cup titles, the Red Wings has won the Presidents' Trophy (for playing to the best regular-season record) six times (1995–1996, 2002, 2004, 2006, 2008); won 15 division championships (1988–1989, 1992, 1994–1996, 1999, 2001–2004, 2006–2009); and the Western Conference championship nine times (1994–1996, 2002, 2004, 2006–2009).

Overseeing the team's minor league affiliates, he has also played a role in winning three Calder Cup championships with the American Hockey League Adirondack Red Wings (1986, 1989, 1992) and one East Coast Hockey League championship with the Toledo Storm in 1994.

He was inducted into the Michigan Sports Hall of Fame in 2006.

Source: Hockey Hall of Fame

Diaz-Miguel, Antonio (born: July 6, 1933 in Alcazar de San Juan, Ciudad Real, Spain; died: February 21, 2000 in Madrid, Spain); inducted into the Naismith Memorial Basketball Hall of Fame in 1997 as a coach; led the Spanish National Team to six Olympics, 13 European Championships, and five World Championships; named Spain's Coach of the Year twice.

Although Diaz-Miguel played soccer as a boy, his height of 6'8" eventually led him to focus on basketball. He played at the Instituto Ramiro de Maeztu Secondary School of Madrid (Spain), where he helped start the Estudiantes Club in 1950. He played two stints with the team (1950–1952, 1953–1958) and one season (1952–1953) with Cave (of the Spanish Professional League), before moving on to Real Madrid (1958–1961) and Aguilas of Bilbao (1961–1963). He played 27 games for the Spanish National Team and won the Spanish Clubs League Championship twice (1959–1960) with Real Madrid.

After retiring as a player, he became coach of Aguilas of the SPL (1963–1965), before becoming coach of the Spanish National Team from 1965 to 1992. He led the National Team to a 318–186 (.631) record; six Olympics, 13 European Championships, and four World Championships; won a silver medal in the 1984 Olympics (Los Angeles, California); two silver medals (1973, 1983) and one bronze medal (1991) in the European Championships; was named Spain's Coach of the Year twice (1981–1982); was a six-time European All-Star Team coach; and won the National Basketball Coaches Association Award in 1977.

As of this writing, he is the only Spaniard in the Naismith Memorial Basketball Hall of Fame, and in 2007, he was inducted into the Fédération Internationale de Basketball Hall of Fame.

Antonio Diaz-Miguel's International Statistics

	European Championships			World Championships	
YEAR	**SITE**	**FINISH**	**YEAR**	**SITE**	**FINISH**
1967	Helsinki, Finland	10th	1974	San Juan, Puerto Rico	5th
1969	Naples, Italy	5th	1982	Cali, Columbia	4th
1971	Essen, West Germany	7th	1986	Madrid, Spain	5th
1973	Barcelona, Spain	2nd (Silver)	1990	Buenos, Aires Argentina	10th
1975	Belgrade, Yugoslavia	4th			
1977	Liège, Belgium	9th			
1979	Turin, Italy	6th			
1981	Prague, Czechoslovakia	4th			
1983	Nantes, France	2nd (Silver)			
1985	Stuttgart, West Germany	4th			
1987	Athens, Greece	4th			
1989	Zagreb, Yugoslavia	5th			
1991	Rome, Italy	3rd (Bronze)			

Antonio Diaz-Miguel's Olympic Statistics

YEAR	SITE	FINISH
1968	Mexico City, Mexico	7th
1972	Munich, Germany	11th
1980	Moscow, Russia	4th
1984	Los Angeles, California	2nd (Silver)
1988	Seoul, South Korea	8th
1992	Barcelona, Spain	9th

Source: Naismith Memorial Basketball Hall of Fame

Dick, Walter (born: September 20, 1905 in Kirkintilloch, Scotland; died: July 24, 1989 in Lafayette, California); inducted into the National Soccer Hall of Fame and Museum in 1989 as a player; Position: Forward; International Caps (1934): 1; International Goals: 0; won five consecutive American Soccer League championships.

Dick began his professional career with Armadale F.C. in the Scottish Football League, before moving to the United States when he was 17 years old (1923) to live in Niagara Falls, New York. After a year with the Niagara Falls Rangers, he made his debut for the Providence Clamdiggers (later renamed the Providence Gold Bugs) of the American Soccer League in 1924. Between 1924 and 1930, he played 179 games in the ASL and scored 21 goals.

Moving on to the Fall River Marksmen and then to the Pawtucket Rangers (both of the ASL), Dick was a member of the Rangers' team that lost two consecutive U.S. Open Cup finals (1934–1935) to Stix, Baer and Fuller F.C. in 1934 and the same team, by now renamed St. Louis Central Breweries F.C., in 1935.

As a member of the Rangers, he was selected for the Fédération Internationale de Football Association World Cup team in 1934 and made his sole appearance in its game against Italy. In 1935, he was a guest player with the New York Americans for a series of games in Mexico; played for the Kearny Scots (also known as the Kearny Americans) during the team's run from 1937 to 1941, winning five consecutive American Soccer League championships; and also played for the American Soccer League All-Stars against the touring Scottish Football Association team in 1935.

Dick was inducted into the New England Soccer Hall of Fame in 1985.

Source: National Soccer Hall of Fame and Museum

Dickerson, Eric Demetric (born: September 2, 1960 in Sealy, Texas); inducted into the Pro Football Hall of Fame in 1999 as a player; Position: Running Back; Uniform: #29; set NFL rookie records for most rushing yards and most touchdowns; named Rookie of the Year; first player in NFL history to gain more than 1,000 yards in seven straight seasons.

After being a two-time All-American at Southern Methodist University (Dallas, Texas), Dickerson was a first-round (second selection overall) draft pick of the National Football League's Los Angeles Rams in 1983. He went on to enjoy an 11-year career with the Rams (1983–1987), Indianapolis Colts (1987–1991), Los Angeles Raiders (1992), and the Atlanta Falcons (1993). He established rookie records for most rushing attempts (390), most rushing yards (1,808), and most rushing touchdowns (18). His initial season's success earned him All-Pro, Pro Bowl, Player of the Year, and Rookie of the Year honors. In 1984, he rushed for a then NFL-record 2,105 yards and gained 1,800 or more rushing yards in three of his first four seasons. He retired as the second all-time NFL rusher with 13,259 yards on 2,996 carries; was named to six Pro Bowls (1983–1984, 1986–1989); All-Pro five times (1983–1984, 1986–1988); and led the league in rushing four times (three with the Rams and once with the Colts).

In his second season, the 6'3", 220-pound running back gained 100 or more yards in a game 12 times (breaking the record for most 100-yard games in a season previously held by O. J. Simpson), and his 2,105 total rushing yards surpassed Simpson's 1973 record of 2,003 yards.

After playing in only three games for the Rams during the strike-shortened 1987 season, Dickerson was traded to the Indianapolis Colts and rushed for 1,011 yards in only nine games with the team. In 1988, he rushed for 1,659 yards and became the first Colt to lead the league in rushing since Alan Ameche in 1955. The following season, Dickerson became the first player in NFL history to gain more than 1,000 yards in seven consecutive seasons; the seventh back to gain more than 10,000 yards; and the fastest player ever to do so, reaching the milestone in only 91 games.

In 1992, Dickerson was traded to the Los Angeles Raiders and led the team in rushing attempts and yards. The next season, he played for the Falcons in only four games, before being traded to the Green Bay Packers, where he retired after failing the team's physical.

In 1999, he was ranked number 38 on *The Sporting News*' list of the 100 Greatest Football Players, and in 2000, he worked for ABC's "Monday Night Football" as an on-field commentator.

A football star as a boy, Dickerson went to Sealy (Texas) High School; starred on the football and track teams; and won the state 100-yard dash championship. In his senior year, he ran for 2,642 yards and 37 touchdowns; led Sealy to the state high school Class AA championship; and was named a *Parade* magazine All-American in 1978.

After high school, Dickerson attended Southern Methodist University (Dallas, Texas), where he gained 4,450 yards on 790 carries (breaking Earl Campbell's Southwest Conference record for yards and attempts), and was a two-time All-American.

Eric Dickerson's Career Statistics

				RUSHING				RECEIVING		
YEAR	**TEAM**	**G**	**NO**	**YDS**	**AVG**	**TD**	**NO**	**YDS**	**AVG**	**TD**
1983	Los Angeles	16	390	1,808	4.6	18	51	404	7.9	2
1984	Los Angeles	16	379	2,105	5.6	14	21	139	6.6	0
1985	Los Angeles	14	292	1,234	4.2	12	20	126	6.3	0
1986	Los Angeles	16	404	1,821	4.5	11	26	205	7.9	0
1987	Los Angeles/Indianapolis	12	283	1,288	4.6	6	18	171	9.5	0
1988	Indianapolis	16	388	1,659	4.3	14	36	377	10.5	1
1989	Indianapolis	15	314	1,311	4.2	7	30	211	7.0	1
1990	Indianapolis	11	166	677	4.1	4	18	92	5.1	0
1991	Indianapolis	10	167	536	3.2	2	41	269	6.6	1
1992	Los Angeles	16	187	729	3.9	2	14	85	6.1	1
1993	Atlanta	4	26	91	3.5	0	6	58	9.7	0

YEAR	TEAM	G	RUSHING				RECEIVING			
			NO	YDS	AVG	TD	NO	YDS	AVG	TD
	TOTALS	146	2,996	13,259	4.4	90	281	2,137	7.6	6

Sources: Pro Football Hall of Fame; Pro-Football-Reference.com

Dickey, William Malcolm "Bill" (born: June 6, 1907 in Bastrop, Louisiana; died: November 12, 1993 in Little Rock, Arkansas); inducted into the National Baseball Hall of Fame and Museum in 1954 as a player; Position: Catcher; Bats: Left; Throws: Right; Uniform: #8; won seven World Series championships; set an American League record by catching 100 or more games 13 years in a row.

Making his major league debut on August 15, 1928, Dickey played his entire 17-year career with the New York Yankees (1928–1943, 1946); served as the team's player-manager for most of the 1946 season, finishing in third place with a 57–48 (.543) record; played in eight World Series and won seven titles (1932, 1936–1939, 1941, 1943); and was an 11-time All-Star (1933–1934, 1936–1943, 1946).

The 6'1", 185-pound Dickey hit over .300 in 10 of his first 11 full seasons; set an American League record by catching 100 or more games in a season 13 years in a row; hit over 20 home runs with 100 runs batted in four consecutive seasons (1936–1939); and his .362 batting average in 1936 is the highest single-season average ever recorded by a catcher.

After serving in the Navy during World War II, Dickey returned to the Yankees in 1946 as a player-manager, and led the team to a third-place finish, before retiring.

In 1949, he returned to the Yankees as a coach under manager Casey Stengel (from 1949 to 1957), and served as the catching instructor to help future hall-of-famer Yogi Berra, who inherited Dickey's uniform number 8. When Berra was selected to the baseball hall of fame in 1972, the Yankees retired the number in honor of both catchers. In 1999, Dickey was ranked number 57 on *The Sporting News*' list of Baseball's 100 Greatest Players, and was a nominee for the Major League Baseball All-Century Team.

Bill Dickey's Career Statistics

YEAR	TEAM	G	AB	R	H	2B	3B	HR	RBI	BB	SO	SB	AVG	SLG
1928	New York	10	15	1	3	1	1	0	2	0	2	0	.200	.400
1929	New York	130	447	60	145	30	6	10	65	14	16	4	.324	.485
1930	New York	109	366	55	124	25	7	5	65	21	14	7	.339	.486
1931	New York	130	477	65	156	17	10	6	78	39	20	2	.327	.442
1932	New York	108	423	66	131	20	4	15	84	34	13	2	.310	.482
1933	New York	130	478	58	152	24	8	14	97	47	14	3	.318	.490
1934	New York	104	395	56	127	24	4	12	72	38	18	0	.322	.494
1935	New York	120	448	54	125	26	6	14	81	35	11	1	.279	.458
1936	New York	112	423	99	153	26	8	22	107	46	16	0	.362	.617
1937	New York	140	530	87	176	35	2	29	133	73	22	3	.332	.570
1938	New York	132	454	84	142	27	4	27	115	75	22	3	.313	.568
1939	New York	128	480	98	145	23	3	24	105	77	37	5	.302	.513
1940	New York	106	372	45	92	11	1	9	54	48	32	0	.247	.355
1941	New York	109	348	35	99	15	5	7	71	45	17	2	.284	.417
1942	New York	82	268	28	79	13	1	2	37	26	11	2	.295	.373
1943	New York	85	242	29	85	18	2	4	33	41	12	2	.351	.492
1946	New York	54	134	10	35	8	0	2	10	19	12	0	.261	.366
	TOTALS	1,789	6,300	930	1,969	343	72	202	1,209	678	289	36	.313	.486

Sources: Baseball-Reference.com; National Baseball Hall of Fame and Museum

Diddle, Edgar Allen (born: March 12, 1895 in Gradyville, Kentucky; died: January 2, 1970); inducted into the Naismith Memorial Basketball Hall of Fame in 1972 as a coach; first in history to coach 1,000 games at one school.

After playing basketball for four years at Adair County (Columbia, Kentucky) High School, Diddle graduated in 1915. During World War I, he went through the Naval Aviation Program (1918–1919), before attending Centre College (Danville, Kentucky), where he was selected All-Southern (1920) and All-State twice (1919–1920). He was a member of the undefeated 1919 team that claimed the Southern championship.

After graduating from college, Diddle began his coaching career at Monticello (Kentucky) High School (1920–1921), before moving to Greenville (Kentucky) High School (1921–1922). He coached Monticello to a runner-up finish in the 1921 state finals, and led Greenville to the 1922 regional finals. In 1922, he left the high school ranks to become the head coach at Western Kentucky University (Bowling Green, Kentucky), where he stayed until 1964, compiling a .715 record (759–302) in 42 seasons.

When he was inducted into the basketball hall of fame, Diddle had the fourth most wins of any coach in history (behind Adolph Rupp, Phog Allen, and Hank Iba), and was the first in history to coach 1,000 games at one school.

In his 42 seasons with the team, the Hilltoppers won or shared 32 titles in three separate conferences (13 Kentucky Intercollegiate Athletic Conference championships; eight Southern Intercollegiate Athletic Conference championships, and won or shared 11 Ohio Valley Conference championships). The Hilltoppers ranked in the Top 10 in scoring among major colleges for seven consecutive years (1948–1955); had 18 seasons of 20 or more wins, including 10 consecutive from 1934 to 1944; and had only five losing seasons.

Diddle was named the Kentucky Press Association's Outstanding Kentuckian of the Year (1957); won the Kentucky Broadcasters Association's Kentucky Mike Award (1967); has been inducted into the Kentucky Athletic Hall of Fame and the Helms Athletic Foundation Hall of Fame; and the E.A. Diddle Arena at Western Kentucky is named in his honor.

Source: Naismith Memorial Basketball Hall of Fame

Dierdorf, Daniel Lee "Dan" (born: June 29, 1949 in Canton, Ohio); inducted into the Pro Football Hall of Fame in 1996 as a player; Position: Offensive Tackle; Uniform: #72; named NFC Offensive Lineman of the Year three straight seasons.

Born in the town that now houses the Pro Football Hall of Fame, Dierdorf went to Glenwood High School (Canton, Ohio), and after being an All-American at the University of Michigan (Ann Arbor) in 1970, he was a second-round choice (43rd overall selection) in the 1971 NFL draft of the St. Louis Cardinals, where he would play his entire 13-year career (1971–1983).

The 6'3", 275-pound Dierdorf anchored an offensive line that led the National Football League three times, and the National Football Conference five times, in fewest sacks allowed. In 1975, the Cardinals set a then-record by allowing only eight sacks in 14 games. He was selected All-Pro five times (1975–1978, 1980); played in six Pro Bowls; and was named the NFC Offensive Lineman of the Year three consecutive seasons (1976–1978) by the NFL Players Association.

After retiring as a player, he became a broadcaster and eventually worked for ABC's "Monday Night Football" and for CBS as a color commentator. Dierdorf was selected to the NFL 1970s All-Decade Team; was inducted into the College Football Hall of Fame in 2000; and in 2002, he was enshrined into the St. Louis Walk of Fame.

Sources: College Football Hall of Fame; Pro Football Hall of Fame

Dihigo, Martín Magdaleno (Llanos) (born: May 25, 1905 in Matanzas, Cuba; died: May 20, 1971 in Cienfuegos, Cuba); inducted into the National Baseball Hall of Fame and Museum in 1977 as a player by the Negro Leagues Committee; Position: Pitcher; Bats: Right; Throws: Right; Uniform: #17; only man ever inducted into the Cuban, Mexican, and National Baseball halls of fame; threw the first no-hitter in Mexican League history; won three Negro League home run titles.

Known as "El Maestro" in Mexico and "El Immortal" in Cuba, Dihigo played all nine positions in Cuba, Mexico, Puerto Rico, Venezuela, and 12 seasons in the Negro Leagues in the United States. In 1938, while playing in the Mexican League, Dihigo pitched to an 18–2 record; led the league with a 0.90 earned run average; and won the league's batting title by hitting .387. He played for the Cuban Stars East (1923–1927, 1930), Homestead Grays (1928), Hilldale Daisies (1929–1931), Baltimore Black Sox (1931), and the New York Cubans (1935–1936, 1945).

The 6'4", 195-pound Dihigo threw the first no-hitter in Mexican League history (September 16, 1937, a 4–0 win against Nogales at Veracruz); often played two different positions in the same game; and threw no-hitters in both Venezuela and Puerto Rico.

Dihigo finished his career by winning three Negro League home run titles and tying Josh Gibson for a fourth; won more than 200 games in American and Mexican leagues; was a two-time Negro League All-Star; and is the only man inducted into the Cuban, Dominican Republic, Mexican, Venezuelan, and National Baseball halls of fame.

During his 12 years in the Negro Leagues, he compiled a .307 lifetime batting average; a .511 slugging percentage; had 431 hits; 64 home runs; 61 doubles; 17 triples; 227 runs batted in; and 292 runs scored in 1,404 at bats. He also accumulated 143 walks and stole 41 bases. As a pitcher, he threw to a 26–19 record with a 2.92 earned run average, 176 strikeouts, and 80 walks in 354 innings.

In his Mexican League career, Dihigo pitched to a 119–57 record and compiled a .317 batting average, and in the Cuban League, he pitched to a 107–56 record with a .298 batting average. After retiring as a player, Dihigo managed numerous teams, and served as the Minister of Sports in Cuba until he died in 1971.

He began his American baseball career in 1923 at age 18, playing first base with the touring Cuban Stars, and played in America from 1923 until 1936. After 1936, he played summer baseball in Mexico, except in 1945, when he was the player-manager of the New York Cubans.

Source: National Baseball Hall of Fame and Museum

Dilio, Frank (born: April 12, 1912 in Montreal, Quebec, Canada; died: January 26, 1997); inducted into the Hockey Hall of Fame in 1964 as a builder; served as president of the Junior Amateur Hockey Association; served as president of the Atwater Baseball League.

Dilio attended St. Ann's Boys' School (Montreal, Quebec), and became secretary of its juvenile hockey club, which would win the Quebec Amateur Hockey Association title in his age group. In the mid-1930s, he joined the Junior Amateur Hockey Association as the group's secretary and became its president in 1939. He also served as the official scorer of the Quebec Senior Hockey League, and was president and treasurer of the Atwater Baseball League (Montreal, Quebec). In 1952, he became QAHA secretary, a position he held until 1962.

The Quebec Major Junior Hockey League named one of its divisions after him.

Source: Hockey Hall of Fame

DiMaggio, Joseph Paul "Joe" (born Giuseppe Paolo DiMaggio, Jr. on November 25, 1914 in Martinez, California; died: March 8, 1999 in Hollywood, Florida); inducted into the National Baseball Hall of Fame and Museum in 1955 as a player; Position: Center Field; Bats: Right; Throws: Right; Uniform: #5; won nine World Series titles; was a three-time American League Most Valuable Player; signed baseball's first $100,000 contract.

Making his major league debut on May 3, 1936 (getting three hits, including one triple in a New York Yankees 14–5 win over the St. Louis Browns), DiMaggio played his entire 13-year career (1936–1942, 1946–1951) with the Yankees. He played in 10 World Series and won nine titles (1936–1939, 1941, 1947, 1949–1951), losing only once, to the St. Louis Cardinals in 1942.

The 6'2", 193-pound DiMaggio was a three-time American League Most Valuable Player (1939, 1941, 1947) and made the All-Star team each year he played. Many baseball historians consider his 56-consecutive-game hitting streak in 1941 as the top baseball feat of all time. Before his major league record-setting 56-game hitting streak, DiMaggio had compiled a 61-game hitting streak in 1933 while playing with the San Francisco Seals of the Pacific Coast League. Known as "The Yankee Clipper" and "Joltin' Joe," he won two batting titles; averaged 118 runs batted in per season; and at Major League Baseball's 1969 Centennial Celebration, he was named the game's greatest living player.

DiMaggio shares the major league record for most home runs in an inning, (2 on June 24, 1936); shares the modern major league record for most triples in a game (3 on August 27, 1938); was named *The Sporting News* Major League Player of the Year (1939); and served as executive vice president-coach of the Oakland Athletics (1968–1969).

He was the eighth of nine children born to Sicilian immigrants and moved with his family to San Francisco, California when he was only one year old. As a young boy, DiMaggio turned to baseball and eventually became a star in the Pacific Coast League. His brother, Vince, was already playing for the Seals when DiMaggio joined the team as a shortstop for the last three games of the 1932 season, making his debut on October 1. He joined the team full-time the next season, and from May 28 to July 25 (1933), he hit in 61 consecutive games.

In 1935, he hit .398 with 154 runs batted in and 34 home runs; was named league Most Valuable Player; and led the team to the 1935 PCL title.

DiMaggio joined the Yankees in 1936; batted ahead of Lou Gehrig; and helped the team win four consecutive World Series titles (1936–1939), on his way to winning nine World Series titles in his 13 years with the team. Although he signed a $100,000 contract in 1949 (at the time, the largest is baseball history), DiMaggio's time away from the game during World War II combined with recurring injuries, basically forced him to retire in 1951.

When the United States entered World War II, DiMaggio enlisted in the Army Air Forces in February 1943, and was stationed at Santa Ana, California, Hawaii, and Atlantic City, New Jersey as a physical education instructor during his 31 months in the military.

During the war, in spite of their son's popularity and fame, his mother and father (Rosalia and Giuseppe) were among the thousands of immigrants classified as "enemy aliens" after the Japanese attack on Pearl Harbor (Hawaii). They were required to carry photo identification at all times and were not allowed to travel more than five miles from their home without a permit. His mother eventually became a U.S. citizen in 1944, followed by his father in 1945.

DiMaggio married actress Dorothy Arnold in November 1939, and had a son named Joseph III, before being divorced in 1944. For younger baseball fans, he is more well-known for his second marriage to legendary actress Marilyn

Monroe in January 1954 (after he had retired from baseball), and after their marriage ended nine months later, he never remarried.

DiMaggio's jersey number 5 was retired by the New York Yankees in 1952; Yankee Stadium's fifth monument was dedicated to DiMaggio in April 1999; also in 1999, he was ranked #11 on *The Sporting News*' list of the 100 Greatest Baseball Players; he was elected by fans to the Major League Baseball All-Century Team; and he was the very first inductee (1978) into the National Italian American Sports Hall of Fame.

Joe DiMaggio's Career Statistics

YEAR	TEAM	G	AB	R	H	2B	3B	HR	RBI	BB	SO	SB	AVG	SLG
1936	New York	138	637	132	206	44	15	29	125	24	39	4	.323	.576
1937	New York	151	621	151	215	35	15	46	167	64	37	3	.346	.673
1938	New York	145	599	129	194	32	13	32	140	59	21	6	.324	.581
1939	New York	120	462	108	176	32	6	30	126	52	20	3	.381	.671
1940	New York	132	508	93	179	28	9	31	133	61	30	1	.352	.626
1941	New York	139	541	122	193	43	11	30	125	76	13	4	.357	.643
1942	New York	154	610	123	186	29	13	21	114	68	36	4	.305	.498
1946	New York	132	503	81	146	20	8	25	95	59	24	1	.290	.511
1947	New York	141	534	97	168	31	10	20	97	64	32	3	.315	.522
1948	New York	153	594	110	190	26	11	39	155	67	30	1	.320	.598
1949	New York	76	272	58	94	14	6	14	67	55	18	0	.346	.596
1950	New York	139	525	114	158	33	10	32	122	80	33	0	.301	.585
1951	New York	116	415	72	109	22	4	12	71	61	36	0	.263	.422
	TOTALS	1,736	6,821	1,390	2,214	389	131	361	1,537	790	369	30	.325	.579

Sources: Baseball-Reference.com; *Joe DiMaggio: The Hero's Life* (Richard Ben Cramer); *Joe DiMaggio: The Yankee Clipper* (Beckett Publications); National Baseball Hall of Fame and Museum; National Italian American Sports Hall of Fame

Dionne, Marcel Elphege (born: August 3, 1951 in Drummondville, Quebec, Canada); inducted into the Hockey Hall of Fame in 1992 as a player; Position: Center; set an NHL rookie record with 49 assists; fastest player to score 1,000 points; last active player in the NHL who had participated in the 1972 Summit Series.

Dionne played 18 National Hockey League seasons from 1971 to 1989 with the Detroit Red Wings (1971–1975), Los Angeles Kings (1975–1987), and the New York Rangers (1987–1989). In the first round of the 1971 NHL Amateur Draft, he was selected second overall by the Red Wings; scored 77 points as a rookie (1971–1972); won the Calder Memorial Trophy as the NHL's Rookie of the Year; played for Team Canada in the 1972 Summit Series against the Soviet Union; and his 49 assists set a rookie record that was later surpassed by Bryan Trottier in 1976.

After four seasons in Detroit, the 5'8", 185-pound Dionne was traded to the Los Angeles Kings in 1975, where he would score 100 or more points in a season seven times. While playing in Los Angeles, he was a two-time winner of both the Lady Byng Trophy for sportsmanship and gentlemanly conduct (1975, 1977) and the Lester B. Pearson Award as the league's Most Valuable Player as judged by the members of the NHL Players Association (1979–1980); selected to the NHL First and Second All-Star Teams twice each; and in 1980, he won the Art Ross Trophy as the NHL's scoring leader.

Beginning with the 1979–1980 season, Dionne formed the "Triple Crown Line" with Charlie Simmer and Dave Taylor, which became one of the highest-scoring trios in NHL history. On January 7, 1981, he recorded his 1,000th point in his 740th game, the fastest player ever to reach that goal in NHL history (later surpassed by Guy Lafleur). On December 14, 1982, he scored his 500th NHL goal; scored his 700th goal on October 31, 1987; and on February 14, 1988, he passed Phil Esposito to become the second-highest goal scorer in NHL history.

He retired after playing in only 37 games of the 1988–1989 season as the third-highest scorer in NHL history, behind Wayne Gretzky and Gordie Howe. He was the last active player in the NHL who had played in the 1972 Summit Series, and in 1998, he was ranked number 38 on *The Hockey News*' list of the 100 Greatest Hockey Players, the highest-ranking player not to have played on a Stanley Cup-winning team.

Marcel Dionne's Career Statistics

			REGULAR SEASON					PLAYOFFS				
SEASON	TEAM	LEAGUE	GP	G	A	TP	PIM	GP	G	A	TP	PIM
1966–1967	Montreal L'est Cantonniers	QAAA	24	32	39	71						

SEASON	TEAM	LEAGUE	REGULAR SEASON					PLAYOFFS				
			GP	G	A	TP	PIM	GP	G	A	TP	PIM
1967–1968	Drummondville Rangers	QJHL	48	34	35	69	45	10	14	7	21	4
1967–1968	Drummondville Rangers	M-Cup	4	9	4	13	5					
1968–1969	St. Catharines Black Hawks	OHA-Jr.	48	37	63	100	38	18	15	20	35	8
1969–1970	St. Catharines Black Hawks	OHA-Jr.	54	55	77	132	46	10	12	20	32	10
1970–1971	St. Catharines Black Hawks	OHA-Jr.	46	62	81	143	20	15	29	26	55	11
1971–1972	Detroit Red Wings	NHL	78	28	49	77	14					
1972–1973	Canada	Summit-72										
1972–1973	Detroit Red Wings	NHL	77	40	50	90	21					
1973–1974	Detroit Red Wings	NHL	74	24	54	78	10					
1974–1975	Detroit Red Wings	NHL	80	47	74	121	14					
1975–1976	Los Angeles Kings	NHL	80	40	54	94	38	9	6	1	7	0
1976–1977	Canada	Can-Cup	7	1	5	6	4					
1976–1977	Los Angeles Kings	NHL	80	53	69	122	12	9	5	9	14	2
1977–1978	Los Angeles Kings	NHL	70	36	43	79	37	2	0	0	0	0
1977–1978	Canada	WEC-A	10	9	3	12	2					
1978–1979	Los Angeles Kings	NHL	80	59	71	130	30	2	0	1	1	0
1978–1979	NHL All-Stars	Ch-Cup	2	0	1	1	0					
1978–1979	Canada	WEC-A	7	2	1	3	4					
1979–1980	Los Angeles Kings	NHL	80	53	84	137	32	4	0	3	3	4
1980–1981	Los Angeles Kings	NHL	80	58	77	135	70	4	1	3	4	7
1981–1982	Canada	Can-Cup	6	4	1	5	4					
1981–1982	Los Angeles Kings	NHL	78	50	67	117	50	10	7	4	11	0
1982–1983	Los Angeles Kings	NHL	80	56	51	107	22					
1982–1983	Canada	WEC-A	10	6	3	9	2					
1983–1984	Los Angeles Kings	NHL	66	39	53	92	28					
1984–1985	Los Angeles Kings	NHL	80	46	80	126	46	3	1	2	3	2
1985–1986	Los Angeles Kings	NHL	80	36	58	94	42					
1985–1986	Canada	WEC-A	10	4	4	8	8					
1986–1987	Los Angeles Kings	NHL	67	24	50	74	54					
1986–1987	New York Rangers	NHL	14	4	6	10	6	6	1	1	2	2
1987–1988	New York Rangers	NHL	67	31	34	65	54					
1988–1989	New York Rangers	NHL	37	7	16	23	20					
1988–1989	Denver Rangers	IHL	9	0	13	13	6					
	NHL TOTALS		1,348	731	1,040	1,771	600	49	21	24	45	17

Sources: Hockey Hall of Fame; Hockey-Reference.com

DiOrio, Nicholas "Nick" (born: February 4, 1921 in Morgan, Pennsylvania; died: September 11, 2003 in Green Tree, Pennsylvania); inducted into the National Soccer Hall of Fame and Museum in 1974 as a player; Position: Forward; won the 1943 National Amateur Cup and the 1949 U.S. Open Cup; served as president of the West Penn Soccer Association.

DiOrio grew up in the Pittsburgh, Pennsylvania area; played basketball at South Fayette Township High School (McDonald, Pennsylvania), graduating in 1939; and was a member of the 1939 Avella Juniors (Pennsylvania) team that won the U-19 national junior soccer championship (the McGuire Cup).

After high school, DiOrio spent the next 22 years of his life focused on soccer, playing for the Morgan Soccer Club when the team won the U.S. Open Cup in 1949 and for Harmarville Soccer Club in 1952 and 1953. He won the National Amateur Cup in 1943 with Morgan Strasser (Pittsburgh), and played for four other Pittsburgh-area finalists for the Cup: Morgan USCO (1942), Morgan Strasser (1944), and Hamarville S.C. in 1950 and 1951.

The 5'7", 150-pound DiOrio played in the North American Professional Soccer League in 1946 and for the Pittsburgh Indians and Chicago Vikings in 1947. His teams won five Keystone Senior League championships (1943, 1951–1954); and he was a member of the U.S. National Team at the 1950 FIFA World Cup in Brazil, although he never played in a game.

After retiring as a player in 1959, he was named president of the West Penn Soccer Association in 1971.

Source: National Soccer Hall of Fame and Museum

Ditka, Michael Keller, Jr. "Mike" (born: October 18, 1939 in Carnegie, Pennsylvania); inducted into the Pro Football Hall of Fame in 1988 as a player; Position: Tight End; first tight end inducted into the hall of fame.

Ditka played football for the University of Pittsburgh (Pennsylvania) from 1958 to 1960; was an All-American selection in 1960; and was selected to the College Football All-America Team in his senior year.

After college, he was the number one pick (fifth overall selection) of the Chicago Bears in the 1961 National Football League draft; was named the league's Rookie of the Year; selected All-NFL four times (1961–1964); and played in five consecutive Pro Bowls his first five years.

He had a 12-year NFL career with the Chicago Bears (1961–1966), Philadelphia Eagles (1967–1968), and the Dallas Cowboys (1969–1972); helped the Bears win the 1963 title; and scored the Cowboys' final touchdown in the team's Super Bowl VI win (1972, 24–3 over the Miami Dolphins).

The 6'3", 225-pound Ditka was the first tight end ever inducted into the football hall of fame, and at the time of his retirement after the 1972 season, he ranked second among all tight ends in receptions.

Although a hall of fame player, Ditka is probably more well-known to younger fans as the head coach of the Chicago Bears for 11 seasons, and later as a television commentator. Known as "Iron Mike," Ditka and Tom Flores are the only two people to have won a Super Bowl ring as a player, assistant coach, and head coach; and he is the only person to participate in both of the Chicago Bears' championships in the modern era (as a player in 1963 and as head coach in 1985).

After retiring as a player, Ditka began his coaching career as an assistant with the Cowboys under head coach Tom Landry, and would stay with the team for nine seasons. During his time in Dallas, the Cowboys made the playoffs eight times, won six division titles, captured three National Football Conference Championships; and won Super Bowl XII in 1978 (a 27–10 win over the Denver Broncos).

In 1982, Chicago Bears' owner George Halas hired Ditka to be head coach of a team that had only two winning seasons in the previous 19 years. While the team's coach, he led the Bears to six NFC Central titles; three trips to the NFC Championship game; a 46–10 win over the New England Patriots in Super Bowl XX (1986); and was named NFL Coach of the Year twice (1985, 1988).

Fired after the 1992 season, Ditka became an NFL analyst for NBC, and acted in several television shows. He returned to the NFL in 1997 and coached the New Orleans Saints to three losing seasons, before leaving the NFL and returning to the broadcast booth.

As of this writing, he is one of the owners of the Chicago Rush, an Arena Football League team that won ArenaBowl XX in 2006. In 1986, he was inducted into the College Football Hall of Fame, and in 1999, he was ranked number 90 on *The Sporting News*' list of the 100 Greatest Football Players.

Mike Ditka's Career Statistics

			RECEIVING			
YEAR	**TEAM**	**G**	**NO**	**YDS**	**AVG**	**TD**
1961	Chicago	14	56	1,076	19.2	12
1962	Chicago	14	58	904	15.6	5
1963	Chicago	14	59	794	13.5	8
1964	Chicago	14	75	897	11.96	5
1965	Chicago	14	36	454	12.6	2
1966	Chicago	14	32	378	11.8	2
1967	Philadelphia	9	26	274	10.5	2
1968	Philadelphia	11	13	111	8.5	2
1969	Dallas	12	17	268	15.8	3
1970	Dallas	14	8	98	12.3	0
1971	Dallas	14	30	360	12.0	1
1972	Dallas	14	17	198	11.6	1
	TOTALS	158	427	5,812	13.6	43

Mike Ditka's Coaching Record

		REG SEASON		**PLAYOFFS**	
YEAR	**TEAM**	**W**	**L**	**W**	**L**
1982	Chicago	3	6		
1983	Chicago	8	8		
1984	Chicago	10	6	1	1
1985	Chicago	15	1	3	0
1986	Chicago	14	2	0	1
1987	Chicago	11	4	0	1

YEAR	TEAM	REG SEASON W	REG SEASON L	PLAYOFFS W	PLAYOFFS L
1988	Chicago	12	4	1	1
1989	Chicago	6	10		
1990	Chicago	11	5	1	1
1991	Chicago	11	5	0	1
1992	Chicago	5	11		
1997	New Orleans	6	10		
1998	New Orleans	6	10		
1999	New Orleans	3	13		
	TOTALS	121	95	6	6

Sources: College Football Hall of Fame; Pro Football Hall of Fame; Pro-Football-Reference.com

Doby, Lawrence Eugene "Larry" (born: December 13, 1923 in Camden, South Carolina; died: June 18, 2003 in Montclair, New Jersey); inducted into the National Baseball Hall of Fame and Museum in 1998 as a player by the Veterans Committee; Position: Center Field; Bats: Left; Throws: Right; Uniform: #14; first African-American player in the American League; first black player to hit a home run in the World Series.

Doby's professional career began with the Newark Eagles of the Negro Leagues (1942–1943, 1946–1947), and he led the team to a championship in 1946. His playing career was interrupted for two years while he served in the U.S. Navy during World War II.

Making his major league debut on July 5, 1947 (the first African-American player in the American League and the second black player in the majors, four months after Jackie Robinson had broken the color line), he had a 13-year career with the Cleveland Indians (1947–1955, 1958), Chicago White Sox (1956–1957, 1959), and the Detroit Tigers (1959). He played in two World Series (winning in 1948 over the Boston Braves and losing to the New York Giants in 1954); was a seven-time All-Star (1949–1955); and in 1962, Doby and Don Newcombe became the first former major leaguers to play for a professional Japanese team, the Chunichi Dragons. He would later manage the White Sox in 1978 to a 37–50 (.425) record, the second black manager in baseball, following Frank Robinson (1975).

The first player to go directly from the Negro Leagues to the major leagues, Doby helped Cleveland win two pennants (1948, 1954); led the American League in home runs twice; was the first black player to hit a home run in the World Series; first player to win championships in both the Negro Leagues and the major leagues; first black player to win a home run title in the major leagues; and the first black player to win an RBI title in the American League.

Larry Doby's American League Career Statistics

YEAR	TEAM	G	AB	R	H	2B	3B	HR	RBI	BB	SO	SB	AVG	SLG
1947	Cleveland	29	32	3	5	1	0	0	2	1	11	0	.156	.188
1948	Cleveland	121	439	83	132	23	9	14	66	54	77	9	.301	.490
1949	Cleveland	147	547	106	153	25	3	24	85	91	90	10	.280	.468
1950	Cleveland	142	503	110	164	25	5	25	102	98	71	8	.326	.545
1951	Cleveland	134	447	84	132	27	5	20	69	101	81	4	.295	.512
1952	Cleveland	140	519	104	143	26	8	32	104	90	111	5	.276	.541
1953	Cleveland	149	513	92	135	18	5	29	102	96	121	3	.263	.487
1954	Cleveland	153	577	94	157	18	4	32	126	85	94	3	.272	.484
1955	Cleveland	131	491	91	143	17	5	26	75	61	100	2	.291	.505
1956	Chicago	140	504	89	135	22	3	24	102	102	105	0	.268	.466
1957	Chicago	119	416	57	120	27	2	14	79	56	79	2	.288	.464
1958	Cleveland	89	247	41	70	10	1	13	45	26	49	0	.283	.490
1959	Detroit	18	55	5	12	3	1	0	4	8	9	0	.218	.309
1959	Chicago	21	58	1	14	1	1	0	9	2	13	1	.241	.293
	TOTALS	1,533	5,348	960	1,515	243	52	253	970	871	1,011	47	.283	.490

Sources: Baseball-Reference.com; National Baseball Hall of Fame and Museum

Doerr, Robert Pershing "Bobby" (born: April 7, 1918 in Los Angeles, California); inducted into the National Baseball Hall of Fame in 1986 as a player by the Veterans Committee; Position: Second Base; Bats: Right; Throws: Right; Uniform: #1; held the American League record of handling 414 chances without an error.

Making his major league debut on April 20, 1937, Doerr played his entire 14-year career with the Boston Red Sox (1937–1944, 1946–1951), with one season lost to military service during World War II. He played in the 1946 World Series (a loss to the St. Louis Cardinals) and was a nine-time All–Star (1941–1944, 1946–1948, 1950–1951).

Doerr had 100 runs batted in per season six times; once held the American League record by handling 414 chances without an error; hit 10 or more home runs for 12 consecutive seasons; and hit over .300 three times.

After retiring as a player, Doerr later served as a coach for the Red Sox and Toronto Blue Jays. His jersey number 1 was retired by the Red Sox in May 1988.

Bobby Doerr's Career Statistics

YEAR	TEAM	G	AB	R	H	2B	3B	HR	RBI	BB	SO	SB	AVG	SLG
1937	Boston	55	147	22	33	5	1	2	14	18	25	2	.224	.313
1938	Boston	145	509	70	147	26	7	5	80	59	39	5	.289	.397
1939	Boston	127	525	75	167	28	2	12	73	38	32	1	.318	.448
1940	Boston	151	595	87	173	37	10	22	105	57	53	10	.291	.497
1941	Boston	132	500	74	141	28	4	16	93	43	43	1	.282	.450
1942	Boston	144	545	71	158	35	5	15	102	67	55	4	.290	.455
1943	Boston	155	604	78	163	32	3	16	75	62	59	8	.270	.412
1944	Boston	125	468	95	152	30	10	15	81	58	31	5	.325	.528
1946	Boston	151	583	95	158	34	9	18	116	66	67	5	.271	.453
1947	Boston	146	561	79	145	23	10	17	95	59	47	3	.258	.426
1948	Boston	140	527	94	150	23	6	27	111	83	49	3	.285	.505
1949	Boston	139	541	91	167	30	9	18	109	75	33	2	.309	.497
1950	Boston	149	586	103	172	29	11	27	120	67	42	3	.294	.519
1951	Boston	106	402	60	116	21	2	13	73	57	33	2	.289	.448
	TOTALS	1,865	7,093	1,094	2,042	381	89	223	1,247	809	608	54	.288	.461

Sources: Baseball-Reference.com; National Baseball Hall of Fame and Museum

Donaghy, Edward J. (born: Cambuslang, Scotland); inducted into the National Soccer Hall of Fame and Museum in 1951 as a builder; served as president of the New York and National Referees Committees.

Donaghy played soccer in Scotland before coming to the United States in 1911, where he played for various Philadelphia, Pennsylvania-area teams until 1919. After retiring as a player, he became a referee in the western Pennsylvania area from 1920 until 1928.

He refereed the 1930 National Open Cup Final between the Fall River Marksmen and Cleveland Bruells, and the 1934 final game between St. Louis Stix, Baer and Fuller and the Pawtucket Rangers. Internationally, he refereed three World Cup elimination games in Mexico City, Mexico in 1934, before eventually serving as president of the New York and National Referees Committees.

Source: National Soccer Hall of Fame and Museum

Donelli, Aldo Teo (born: July 22, 1907 in Morgan, Pennsylvania; died: August 9, 1994 in Fort Lauderdale, Florida); inducted into the National Soccer Hall of Fame and Museum in 1954 as a player; Position: Center Forward; International Caps (1934): 2; International Goals: 5; scored five goals in the 1929 U.S. Amateur Cup title game; only man to serve as head coach of both a college football team and a National Football League team simultaneously.

Donelli joined the Morgan Strasser team at age 15, and led the local Pittsburgh, Pennsylvania-area league in scoring from 1922 to 1928. He moved on to the Heidelberg club for the 1928–1929 season, and led the team to the U.S. Amateur Cup, scoring five goals in a 9–0 finals win over the Newark First Germans.

In addition to soccer, he also played American-style football for Duquesne University (Pittsburgh, Pennsylvania) from 1926 to 1929. In the 1930s, while playing soccer in Curry, Pennsylvania, Donelli was selected to the 1934 U.S. World Cup team. In Italy, he scored four goals against Mexico in the qualifying game and the only U.S. goal against Italy in the first round.

After returning to the United States, he focused on American football and, in 1939, became the head coach at his alma mater; led the Duquesne Dukes to a 29–4–2 record; and finished in the Top 10 national poll twice in four seasons. He is the only man to serve as head coach of both a college football team and a National Football League team (Pittsburgh Steelers) simultaneously (1941). While the Dukes enjoyed an undefeated season, the Steelers were 0–5 under Donelli.

He returned to soccer in 1943 to play for Morgan Strasser in the 1944 Open Cup final against Brooklyn Hispano at the Polo Grounds; served in the U.S. Navy for a short time during the last year of World War II; and coached the NFL's Cleveland Rams (now known as the St. Louis Rams) for a single season in 1944, leading the team to a 4–6 record.

From 1947 to 1956, he coached football at Boston University (Massachusetts); compiled a 46–34–4 record; and placed a team in the Top 25 national poll. In 1957, Donelli was named the head football coach at Columbia University (New York, New York), where he would stay until 1967, compiling a 30–76–4 record. In 1961, he led Columbia to its only Ivy League Championship.

Source: National Soccer Hall of Fame and Museum

Donnelly, George F. (born: unknown); inducted into the National Soccer Hall of Fame and Museum in 1989 as a builder; served as president of the National Soccer League of New York and the Eastern New York Senior Soccer Association.

Donnelly served as a soccer administrator for 23 years, including five years as president of the National Soccer League of New York (1966–1971); president of the Eastern New York Senior Soccer Association from 1972 to 1977; and in 1977, he founded the Eastern New York Youth Soccer Association.

In 1978, he was appointed chairman of the United States Soccer Federation Appeals Committee, a position he held for nine years. From 1982 to 1985, Donnelly was president of the Cosmopolitan Soccer League and, in 1985, managed the Brooklyn College (New York) soccer team to a gold medal in the All Nepal Football Cup. He was also a member of the U.S. National Team delegation to the 1988 Olympic Games in South Korea.

The George F. Donnelly Cup is an annual amateur soccer competition organized by the United States Adult Soccer Association, and is currently held each year during the Martin Luther King, Jr. holiday weekend in January.

Source: National Soccer Hall of Fame and Museum

Donovan, Anne (born: November 1, 1961 in Ridgewood, New Jersey); inducted into the Naismith Memorial Basketball Hall of Fame in 1995 as a player; Position: Center; won two high school championships, one college national title, and two Olympic gold medals.

Donovan attended Paramus (New Jersey) Catholic High School from 1975 to 1979; was a First-Team *Parade* magazine All-American twice (1978–1979); led the school to consecutive undefeated seasons and two straight Group III state championships (1978–1979); averaged 35 points and 17 rebounds per game as a senior; and was named National High School Player of the Year by Dial Soap.

After high school, she went to Old Dominion University (Norfolk, Virginia) from 1979 to 1983, where she was a three-time All-American (1981–1983); led the Lady Monarchs to the Association for Intercollegiate Athletics for Women national title (1979); led ODU to the 1983 National Collegiate Athletic Association Final Four; and was named Naismith Player of the Year (1983). She holds ODU all-time records for points (2,719), rebounds (1,976) and blocked shots (801); holds the school's single-season records for most games played (38), most minutes played (1,159), most field goals (377), and field goal percentage (.640); was the first player in ODU history to score 2,000 points by the end of her junior season; and averaged a double-double (20 points and 14.5 rebounds per game) during her college career.

Donovan was named Street & Smith's Player of the Year (1981–1983); selected First Team All-America by the Women's Basketball Coaches Association (1981–1983); First Team All-America by the American Women's Sports Foundation (1981–1983); First Team All-America by *Basketball Weekly* (1981–1983); and First Team Academic-America by the College Sports Information Directors of America (1983).

She led the nation in rebounding (14.7 per game in 1982); pulled down 10 or more rebounds in 114 games; led the nation in blocked shots (1980–1983); is the ODU single-game scoring leader (50 points against Norfolk State on December 11, 1980); is the ODU single-game blocked shot leader (15 against San Francisco in 1980); was the Sun Belt Conference Most Valuable Player (1983); named MVP of the ODU-Optimist Classic (1980–1983); was a three-time

Olympian (1980 [boycotted by the United States to protest Russia's invasion of Afghanistan], 1984, 1988), winning a gold medal in 1984 (Los Angeles, California) and 1988 (Seoul, South Korea); was a member of the United States National Team (1979–1983); and played on the gold medal-winning World Championship team (Madrid, Spain in 1986).

After college, the 6'8" Donovan played professional basketball for Shizuoka (Japan, 1983–1988) and Modena (Italy, 1988–1989). She left the playing ranks and became an assistant coach at her alma mater from 1989 to 1995, before serving as the head coach at East Carolina University (Greenville, North Carolina) from 1995 to 1997.

Her first professional head coach position was with the Philadelphia Rage of the American Basketball League (1997–1998); she was an assistant coach for USA Basketball at the 1998 Fédération Internationale de Basketball Amateur as the team went 9–0 to win the gold medal; coached the Indiana Fever of the Women's National Basketball Association in 2000; and coached the Charlotte Sting of the WNBA in 2001–2002.

Donovan led the Sting into the 2001 WNBA Finals; coached the Eastern Conference All-Stars in the 2002 WNBA All-Star Game; was an assistant coach for USA Basketball for the 2002 FIBA World Championship team; was named coach of the WNBA's Seattle Storm in December 2002; and led the team to the WNBA title in 2004, becoming the first female coach to win a WNBA championship. On August 18, 2005, she became the fourth WNBA coach, and the first woman, to reach the 100-win mark.

Source: Naismith Memorial Basketball Hall of Fame

Donovan, Arthur James, Jr. "Art" (born: June 5, 1925 in Bronx, New York); inducted into the Pro Football Hall of Fame in 1968 as a player; Position: Defensive Tackle; first Baltimore Colt inducted into the hall of fame.

Donovan played 12 years (138 games) in the National Football League with the Baltimore Colts (1950, 1953–1961), New York Yanks (1951), and the Dallas Texans (1952); was selected All-NFL five consecutive years (1954–1958); and played in five straight Pro Bowls (1953–1957).

He played football at Mount St. Michael's High School (Bronx, New York) before joining the Marines during World War II. After his four-year military service, Donovan attended Boston College (Chestnut Hill, Massachusetts), where he was selected Second-Team All-New England, before joining the NFL as a 26-year-old rookie after graduating in 1950.

When the Colts folded after one season, he moved to the Yanks for one year, and stayed with the franchise after it moved to Dallas and became the Texans. After playing for the Texans for one season, the team moved to Baltimore and became the Baltimore Colts, where the 6'2", 263-pound Donovan would develop into one of the best defensive tackles in league history, and would eventually be named to the NFL 1950s All-Decade Team.

After his playing days, Donovan became a football analyst and published his autobiography, *Fatso*, in 1987.

Source: Pro Football Hall of Fame

Dooley, Thomas (born: May 12, 1961 in Bechhofen, Germany); inducted into the National Soccer Hall of Fame and Museum in 2010 as a player; Position: Midfielder; long-time member of the United States National Team.

One of only five players who started every game (in the modern era) in consecutive Fédération Internationale de Football Association World Cups for the United States (1994 in the United States and 1998 in France), the 6'1" Dooley captained the team in France (1998) and ended his eight-year U.S. career with 81 caps and seven goals. In 1993, he was named U.S. Soccer Male Athlete of the Year.

His very first goal for the U.S. team (after joining in May 30, 1992 in a game against Ireland) was in its famous 2–0 win against England (June 9, 1993) in the 1993 U.S. Cup. On June 13, 1993 (in the same tournament), he scored twice against his homeland (Germany, eventual cup winner) in a 4–3 loss. His other goals for Team U.S.A. occurred in a 4–0 win against Mexico (1995); a game-tying goal against Mexico in the 1996 U.S. Cup; and the game-winning score in a FIFA World Cup qualifier against Trinidad & Tobago (1996).

In 1997, he joined the Columbus Crew (of Major League Soccer) and stayed until 2000, after winning that year's Union of European Football Associations Cup with Schalke 04 (officially known as Fußball-Club Gelsenkirchen-Schalke 04), a German soccer team from the Schalke district of Gelsenkirchen, North Rhine-Westphalia. With the Crew, he was named part of the MLS Best XI although he played in only 15 games. In his second season (1998), he was again part of Best XI and played in the All-Star game. In 1999, Dooley made a second All-Star appearance with the Crew and retired at the age of 39 after playing the 2000 season with the MetroStars. While with the MLS, he continued to play for the U.S. national team and was its captain in the 1998 FIFA World Cup.

He played professionally in Germany for FC Homburg (1983–1988), FC Kaiserslautern (1988–1993, where he won the German Cup in 1990 and the Bundesliga title in 1991), Bayer Leverkusen (1994–1995), and Schalke 04 (1995–

1997). Recruited for the U.S. National Team, Dooley obtained his American passport in 1992. After MLS, he retired as a player, returned to Germany, and became the head coach of FC Saarbrücken (2002–2003).

As of this writing, he lives in Laguna Niguel, California and is the Player Development Program Manager with the South Coast Bayern Futbol Club.

Source: National Soccer Hall of Fame and Museum

Dorrance, Anson (born: April 9, 1951 in Bombay, India); inducted into the National Soccer Hall of Fame and Museum in 2008 as a builder; coached the U.S. National Team that won the first Women's World Cup.

Dorrance was the premier coach of women's soccer during the 1980s and 1990s; coached at the University of North Carolina (Chapel Hill); and guided the U.S. National Team that won the first Women's World Cup.

After serving as the UNC's men's coach for 12 years in the 1970s and 1980s, he became coach of the school's women's team in 1979, and, two years later, led the squad to a title win in the very first women's national championship tournament, held by the Association for Intercollegiate Athletics for Women. In 28 seasons (through 2009), Dorrance led teams to the championship 20 times, including nine in a row from 1986 to 1994.

During his 31 years of coaching, the Lady Tar Heels have played to a 696–36–22 (.963) record, and between 1990 and 1994, the team had a streak of 92 consecutive wins. In the 20 seasons that it has been awarded, the Hermann Trophy for the nation's outstanding college women's soccer player has been won by UNC players eight times.

In 1986, in addition to his UNC responsibilities, Dorrance became coach of the National Team; served until 1994; compiled an overall 65–22–5 record; and in 1991, he led the squad to a 2–1 win over Norway that gave the United States the championship of the first-ever Women's World Cup (hosted by Guangzhou, China). Of the 11 United States players in that game, six were from Dorrance's North Carolina team.

He had retired from coaching the North Carolina men's team in 1988 after 12 winning seasons, with an accrued record of 172–65–21, and leading the squad to the 1987 NCAA Final Four.

Dorrance was a three-time All-Atlantic Coast Conference soccer player at UNC, graduating in 1974, and has been named the NCAA Women's Soccer Coach of the Year seven times (1982, 1986, 1997, 2000–2001, 2003, 2006).

After traveling with his family through Europe and Africa, he first played soccer while living in Kenya, before graduating from Villa St. Jean International School (Fribourg, Switzerland) in 1969.

After graduating from Villa St. Jean, he moved to the United States and briefly attended community college in San Antonio, Texas, before transferring to the University of North Carolina, from where he graduated in 1974 with a B.A. in English and Philosophy.

Dorrance was named NCAA Men's Soccer Coach of the Year in 1987, and was inducted into the North Carolina Sports Hall of Fame in 2005.

Source: National Soccer Hall of Fame and Museum

Dorsett, Anthony Drew, Sr. "Tony" (born: April 7, 1954 in Rochester, Pennsylvania); inducted into the Pro Football Hall of Fame in 1994; Position: Running Back; Uniform: #33; first player to win the college football championship one year, then win the Super Bowl the next.

Dorsett attended the University of Pittsburgh (Pennsylvania), where he was a four-time All-American; led the team to a national title in 1976; won the Heisman Trophy as the country's best college football player in 1976; and finished his college career with a then-National Collegiate Athletic Association record 6,082 total rushing yards (later surpassed by Ricky Williams in 1998). Also in 1976, Dorsett won the Maxwell Award and the Walter Camp Award, both presented to the nation's top college football player.

He was the Dallas Cowboys' number one draft pick (second selection overall) in the 1977 National Football League draft, and played 12 years (173 games) with the Cowboys (1977–1987) and the Denver Broncos (1978). He played in two Super Bowls (a win over the Denver Broncos in Super Bowl XII [1978] and a loss to the Pittsburgh Steelers in Super Bowl XIII [1979]); five NFC Championship games; and four Pro Bowls (1978, 1981–1983). He was selected All-NFL in 1981 and was the National Football Conference rushing champion in 1982.

The 5'11", 192-pound Dorsett was elected to both the Pro Football and the College Football Halls of Fame in 1994, and had his name added to the Texas Stadium Ring of Honor. In 1999, he was ranked number 53 on *The Sporting News*' list of the 100 Greatest Football Players.

Dorsett is the only player in the history of football to win a national college championship, a Heisman Trophy, a place in the College Football Hall of Fame, a Super Bowl championship, and to be inducted into the Pro Football Hall of Fame. The football stadium at Hopewell High School in Aliquippa, Pennsylvania is named after him.

Tony Dorsett's Career Statistics

			RUSHING				RECEIVING			
YEAR	TEAM	G	NO	YDS	AVG	TD	NO	YDS	AVG	TD
1977	Dallas	14	208	1,007	4.8	12	29	273	9.4	1
1978	Dallas	16	290	1,325	4.6	7	37	378	10.2	2
1979	Dallas	14	250	1,107	4.4	6	45	375	8.3	1
1980	Dallas	15	278	1,185	4.3	11	34	263	7.7	0
1981	Dallas	16	342	1,646	4.8	4	32	325	10.2	2
1982	Dallas	9	177	745	4.2	5	24	179	7.5	0
1983	Dallas	16	289	1,321	4.6	8	40	287	7.2	1
1984	Dallas	16	302	1,189	3.9	6	51	459	9	1
1985	Dallas	16	305	1,307	4.3	7	46	449	9.8	3
1986	Dallas	13	184	748	4.1	5	25	267	10.7	1
1987	Dallas	12	130	456	3.5	1	19	177	9.3	1
1988	Denver	16	181	703	3.9	5	16	122	7.6	0
	TOTALS	173	2,936	12,739	4.3	77	398	3,554	8.9	13

Sources: College Football Hall of Fame; Pro Football Hall of Fame; Pro-Football-Reference.com

Douglas, James E. (born: January 12, 1898 in East Newark, New Jersey; died: March 5, 1972 in Point Pleasant, New Jersey); inducted into the National Soccer Hall of Fame and Museum in 1953 as a player; Position: Goalkeeper; International Caps (1924–1930): 9; International Goals: 0; played goal for the United States in the 1924 Olympics.

Douglas first played soccer in 1907 for Central Juniors (Newark, New Jersey), before joining the Harrison, New Jersey Soccer Club in the American Soccer League in 1922. He played in goal for the United States in the 1924 Olympics in Paris (eliminated in the second round) and for the National Team against Canada in Montreal, Quebec in 1925.

He played for numerous teams during his ASL career, including Harrison (1922–1923), Newark Skeeters (1923–1925), New York Giants (1925–1927, 1930), Fall River Marksmen (1927–1928, 1929), Philadelphia Field Club (1928), Brooklyn Wanderers (1928–1929), New York Nationals (1929–1930), and the New York Americans (1931). He was playing for the New York Nationals when he was selected for the 1930 World Cup team and, in Montevideo, Uruguay, he shut out Belgium and Paraguay. During his career, Douglas played in nine international matches between 1924 and 1930.

Although he joined the ASL in 1922, Douglas maintained his amateur status by refusing to be paid. In the 1922–1923 season, he played in 23 games, won 14, and finished the season with a 2.44 goals against average.

His first game as a member of the U.S. National Team came in the 1924 Summer Olympics. He backstopped the U.S. to a 1–0 win over Estonia on May 25, 1924, and was named the game's MVP. Although the U.S. team lost to Uruguay four days later and was eliminated from medal consideration, Douglas played the next two 1924 U.S. games. In 1925, he was at goal for a U.S. 1–0 shutout of Canada in Montreal (Quebec), and shut out Belgium and Paraguay, before losing to Argentina in the semifinals. After the World Cup, the U.S. team traveled to Rio de Janeiro, where it lost 4–3 to Brazil. Douglas finished his U.S. National Team career with four wins and three shutouts.

Source: National Soccer Hall of Fame and Museum

Douglas, Robert L. (born: November 4, 1882 in St. Kitts, British West Indies; died: July 16, 1979 in New York, New York); inducted into the Naismith Memorial Basketball Hall of Fame in 1972 as a contributor; first African-American inducted into the basketball hall of fame.

Known as the "Father of Black Professional Basketball," Douglas organized the Spartan Braves, later to be known as the New York Renaissance "Big Five," the first black salaried professional basketball team. He owned and coached the Renaissance (normally referred to as the Rens) from 1922 to 1949, and compiled an overall 2,318–381 (.859) record.

Douglas grew up in Harlem (New York City) and played amateur basketball for a number of teams in and around the area. In 1922, he decided to organize his own team (the Spartans) and the owners of the new Renaissance Casino in Harlem agreed to let the team play in the casino's second-floor ballroom, and he renamed the team the Renaissance Big Five.

He led the Rens to an 88-game winning streak (all on the road [1932–1933]); to 128 wins in 1934; compiled a 473–49 record from 1932 to 1936; and led the team to the 1939 World Professional Tournament title over the Oshkosh All-Stars (34–25) of the newly formed National Basketball League.

The Rens would play anywhere, and would play any team, black or white. Douglas and the team were inducted into the Harlem Professionals Hall of Fame in 1972, and he is the namesake of the Bob Douglas Hall of Fame in New York, New York.

By 1932, the Rens were primarily a barnstorming travelling team and would return to the Renaissance Casino to play only during the Thanksgiving and Christmas holidays. The team had 14 straight seasons of more than 100 wins; Douglas was the first African-American to be inducted into the basketball hall of fame; and the Renaissance Big Five is one of four teams elected to the hall as a unit.

Source: Naismith Memorial Basketball Hall of Fame

Drake, Bruce (born: December 5, 1905 in Gentry, Texas; died: December 4, 1983); inducted into the Naismith Memorial Basketball Hall of Fame in 1973 as a coach; each of his three NCAA tournament losses were to the eventual national championship team.

Although he never played football at Oklahoma City (Oklahoma) High School, after graduating in 1925, Drake became the University of Oklahoma's (Norman) starting quarterback for two years, and was also a pole vaulter on the school's track team. He also played basketball as a forward for three seasons at the university; switched to guard in his senior year (1928–1929); and was named to the Helms All-American team.

After graduating, he became the school's freshman basketball team coach (1929–1939), and eventually became the University of Oklahoma head coach from 1938 to 1955. As a coach, he compiled a 200–181 (.525) record; led the Sooners to three National Collegiate Athletic Association Tournaments (each time being eliminated by the eventual national champion in 1939, 1943, 1947); and won or tied for six conference championships (Big Six and Big Seven). His 1947 team made it to the NCAA finals, eventually losing to Holy Cross.

Drake served as the president of the National Association of Basketball Coaches in 1951; conducted basketball clinics throughout the world; successfully campaigned to have goaltending banned from the game; was Chairman of the NCAA Rules Committee (1951–1955); inducted into the Helms Foundation Hall of Fame as a coach in 1961; and was inducted into the Oklahoma City All-College Tournament Hall of Fame in 1969.

He coached the 1956 Air Force team to a 34–14 record and the Armed Forces Championship, which qualified the squad as one of four teams for the Olympic playoffs held in Kansas City, Missouri. In that tournament, Air Force was the only team to defeat the Amateur Athletic Union champion Phillips 66 team, which eventually won the tournament.

As a coach in the AAU, he led the National Industrial League's Wichita Vickers to a title tie in 1957.

Source: Naismith Memorial Basketball Hall of Fame

Dresmich, John W. (born: February 27, 1902 in Lithuania; died: October 1966); inducted into the National Soccer Hall of Fame and Museum in 1968 as a builder; served as chairman of the West Penn Commission.

Dresmich came to the United States as a young boy and moved to Pittsburgh, Pennsylvania. He played two years of junior soccer for Morgan and Cuddy, before graduating to the Cuddy senior team, which won the Miners League and the West Penn championship.

After retiring as a player, Dresmich managed both the Morgan and Cuddy senior teams, before being appointed a delegate to the West Council and helping to reorganize the West Penn Referees Association. Later, he helped organize the Washington County League and, in 1940, was appointed to the West Penn Commission. In 1955, he was named chairman of the West Penn Commission and served in that role until he died.

Source: National Soccer Hall of Fame and Museum

Drexler, Clyde Austin "The Glide" (born: June 22, 1962 in New Orleans, Louisiana); inducted into the Naismith Memorial Basketball Hall of Fame in 2004 as a player; Position: Guard-Forward; Uniform: #22; only player at the University of Houston to accumulate 1,000 points, 900 rebounds, and 300 steals; won an NBA championship; won an Olympic gold medal.

While playing basketball at Ross Sterling High School (Houston, Texas, 1978–1980), Drexler averaged three blocked shots and four steals per game as a senior. After graduating, he attended the University of Houston (Texas) from 1980 to 1983, where he led the team to the National Collegiate Athletic Association Final Four twice (1982–1983); was selected a First Team All-American (1983); All Southwest Conference twice (1982–1983); set the school record for steals in a single game, season, and career; and is the only player in school history to accumulate 1,000 points, 900 rebounds, and 300 steals.

Drexler was a first-round selection (14th overall pick) in the 1983 National Basketball Association draft by the Portland Trail Blazers, and went on to a 15-year career with the Trail Blazers (1983–1995) and the Houston Rockets (1995–1998). He won an NBA Championship with the Rockets (1995); was a ten-time All-Star (1986, 1988–1994, 1996–1997); one of only three players in NBA history to compile 20,000 points, 6,000 rebounds, and 6,000 assists; led the Trail Blazers to the NBA Finals twice (1990, 1992); and was selected to the NBA 50th Anniversary All-Time Team (1996). He also played on the 1992 gold medal-winning USA Olympic Team (Barcelona, Spain).

His 22,195 career points (20.4 per game) is 24th best in league history, and his jersey number 22 has been retired by both the Rockets and the Trail Blazers.

After leaving the NBA, the 6'7", 222-pound Drexler served as the head coach at the University of Houston from 1998 to 2000, before becoming an assistant coach with the NBA's Denver Nuggets (2001–2002).

Clyde Drexler's Career Statistics

SEASON	TEAM	G	MIN	FG	3P	FT	TRB	AST	STL	BLK	PF	PTS
1983–1984	Portland	82	1,408	252	1	123	235	153	107	29	209	628
1984–1985	Portland	80	2,555	573	8	223	476	441	177	68	265	1,377
1985–1986	Portland	75	2,576	542	12	293	421	600	197	46	270	1,389
1986–1987	Portland	82	3,114	707	11	357	518	566	204	71	281	1,782
1987–1988	Portland	81	3,060	849	11	476	533	467	203	52	250	2,185
1988–1989	Portland	78	3,064	829	27	438	615	450	213	54	269	2,123
1989–1990	Portland	73	2,683	670	30	333	507	432	145	51	222	1,703
1990–1991	Portland	82	2,852	645	61	416	546	493	144	60	226	1,767
1991–1992	Portland	76	2,751	694	114	401	500	512	138	70	229	1,903
1992–1993	Portland	49	1,671	350	31	245	309	278	95	37	159	976
1993–1994	Portland	68	2,334	473	71	286	445	333	98	34	202	1,303
1994–1995	Portland	41	1,428	305	87	207	234	208	74	22	117	904
1994–1995	Houston	35	1,300	266	60	157	246	154	62	23	89	749
1995–1996	Houston	52	1,997	331	78	265	373	302	105	24	153	1,005
1996–1997	Houston	62	2,271	397	119	201	373	354	119	36	151	1,114
1997–1998	Houston	70	2,473	452	106	277	346	382	126	42	193	1,287
	TOTALS	1,086	37,537	8,335	827	4,698	6,677	6,125	2,207	719	3,285	22,195

Sources: Basketball-Reference.com; Naismith Memorial Basketball Hall of Fame

Dreyfuss, Bernhard "Barney" (born: February 23, 1865 in Freiberg, Germany; died: February 5, 1932 in New York City, New York); inducted into the National Baseball Hall of Fame and Museum in 2008 as an executive by the Veterans Committee; long-time owner of the Pittsburgh Pirates; creator of the modern-day World Series.

Dreyfuss owned Major League Baseball's Pittsburgh Pirates from 1900 to 1932, and is often credited with being the creator of the modern-day World Series. He built baseball's first modern steel and concrete ballpark, Forbes Field (Pittsburgh), in 1909, and while he owned the team, the Pirates won six National League pennants (1901–1903, 1909, 1925, 1927) and two World Series titles (1909, 1925).

A successful entrepreneur in Louisville, Kentucky, Dreyfuss purchased the Louisville Colonels baseball team (American Association), and one of his most famous players was future hall-of-famer Honus Wagner. When Dreyfuss purchased the Pittsburgh Pirates in 1900, he shut down his Louisville franchise, and brought Wagner to the Pirates. When Dreyfuss died in 1932, control of the team transferred to his wife.

In 1903, he challenged the Boston Pilgrims, champions of the newly-formed American League, to a post-season tournament, which Boston won five games to three. This initial series eventually developed into the modern-day World Series.

In 1911, Dreyfuss proposed that each team in the World Series relinquish 25% of its share, to be divided among the other teams and players. This marked the beginning of league players receiving a share of World Series revenue.

He was inducted into the International Jewish Sports Hall of Fame in 1979.

Dreyfuss was also a pioneer in professional football. He co-owned and managed the Pittsburgh Athletic Club, winners of the pro football championship in 1898, recognized as professional football's fourth organized season.

Sources: International Jewish Sports Hall of Fame; National Baseball Hall of Fame and Museum

Drillon, Gordon Arthur (born: October 23, 1913 in Moncton, New Brunswick, Canada; died: September 23, 1986 in Saint John, New Brunswick, Canada); inducted into the Hockey Hall of Fame in 1975 as a player; Position: Left Wing; won the 1942 Stanley Cup championship.

Drillon played a relatively short, seven-year career in the National Hockey League with the Toronto Maple Leafs (1936–1942) and the Montreal Canadiens (1942–1943). He was a First-Team All-Star twice (1938–1939); a Second-Team All-Star in 1942; and the NHL scoring leader and Lady Byng Trophy winner (sportsmanship and gentlemanly conduct) in 1938.

He played in the 1939 Babe Siebert Memorial Game, and won a Stanley Cup championship with Toronto in 1942. After being traded to the Canadiens, he played one more season in the NHL before leaving the league to join the Royal Canadian Air Force during World War II.

After leaving the military, Drillon returned to Canada and played senior hockey, before becoming a coach and scout.
Gordon Drillon's Career Statistics

			REGULAR SEASON					PLAYOFFS				
SEASON	**TEAM**	**LEAGUE**	**GP**	**G**	**A**	**TP**	**PIM**	**GP**	**G**	**A**	**TP**	**PIM**
1926–1927	Edith Cavell School	MSBL	5	4	0	4						
1927–1928	Victoria Street School	MSBL	5	1	1	2						
1928–1929	Moncton Aberdeens	High-NB	2	0	0	0	0					
1929–1930	Moncton Chalmers Club	SNBJL	6	8	4	12	2					
1930–1931	Moncton Athletics	MJHL	6	15	4	19						
1930–1931	Moncton Aberdeens	High-NB	3	1	0	1	0	1	1	0	1	
1930–1931	Moncton Athletics	M-Cup	2	3	2	5	0					
1931–1932	Moncton Wheelers	MJHL	6	6	4	10		3	5	1	6	5
1932–1933	Moncton Hawks	MJHL	4	13	3	16	0	2	2	1	3	4
1932–1933	Moncton Swift's	MCIHL	7	11	3	14		6	13	4	17	
1933–1934	Toronto Young Rangers	OHA-Jr.	11	20	13	33	4	2	5	3	8	4
1933–1934	Toronto CCM	TMHL	2	0	1	1	0					
1933–1934	Toronto Young Rangers	M-Cup	2	0	0	0	16					
1934–1935	Toronto Lions	OHA-Jr.	11	17	9	26	2	5	2	1	3	6
1934–1935	Toronto Dominions	OHA-Sr.	11	12	6	18	2	3	2	1	3	4
1935–1936	Pittsburgh Yellowjackets	EAHL	40	22	12	34	4	8	3	2	5	0
1936–1937	Toronto Maple Leafs	NHL	41	16	17	33	2	2	0	0	0	0
1936–1937	Syracuse Stars	IAHL	7	2	3	5	2					
1937–1938	Toronto Maple Leafs	NHL	48	26	26	52	4	7	7	1	8	2
1938–1939	Toronto Maple Leafs	NHL	40	18	16	34	15	10	7	6	13	4
1939–1940	Toronto Maple Leafs	NHL	43	21	19	40	13	10	3	1	4	0
1940–1941	Toronto Maple Leafs	NHL	42	23	21	44	2	7	3	2	5	2
1941–1942	Toronto Maple Leafs	NHL	48	23	18	41	6	9	2	3	5	2
1942–1943	Montreal Canadiens	NHL	49	28	22	50	14	5	4	2	6	0
1943–1944	Toronto Army Daggers	OHA-Sr.	1	1	1	2	0					
1944–1945	Dartmouth RCAF	NSDHL	1	0	1	1	0					
1944–1945	Valleyfield Braves	QPHL	8	11	4	15	0	11	8	6	14	2
1944–1945	Valleyfield Braves	Al-Cup	3	0	0	0	0					
1945–1946	Halifax RCAF	NSDHL	3	7	8	15	4					
1946–1947	Charlottetown Legion	NSSHL	4	10	8	18	16	11	41	12	53	4
1947–1948	North Sydney Victorias	NSSHL	2	0	1	1	0					
1948–1949	Grand Falls All-Stars	Nfld-Sr.										
1948–1949	Maritime All-Stars	Exhib.	2	11	7	18	2					
1949–1950	Saint John Beavers	NBSHL	49	48	24	72	40	11	1	4	5	12
1950–1951	Moncton Hawks	MMHL										
	NHL TOTALS		311	155	139	294	56	50	26	15	41	10

Sources: Hockey Hall of Fame; Hockey-Reference.com

Drinkwater, Charles Graham (born: February 22, 1875 in Montreal, Quebec, Canada; died: September 27, 1946); inducted into the Hockey Hall of Fame in 1950 as a player; Position: Defense-Forward; won four Stanley Cup titles.

Drinkwater played six pre-National Hockey League seasons from 1892 to 1899 with the Montreal Victorias, and won four consecutive Stanley Cup titles (1895–1898). After leaving McGill University (Montreal, Quebec, Canada), he joined the Victoria Hockey Club of Montreal for the 1894–1895 season and, as a rookie, scored nine goals in eight games to help the now-named Victorias win the Amateur Hockey Association of Canada championship, which in those early days, gave the team the Stanley Cup.

Charles Drinkwater's Career Statistics

			REGULAR SEASON				PLAYOFFS			
SEASON	TEAM	LEAGUE	GP	G	A	TP	GP	G	A	TP
1892–1893	Montreal Victorias	AHAC	3	1	0	1				
1894–1895	Montreal Victorias	AHAC	8	9	0	9				
1895–1896	Montreal Victorias	AHAC	8	7	0	7				
1895–1896	Montreal Victorias	St-Cup					1	1	0	1
1896–1897	Montreal Victorias	AHAC	4	3	0	3				
1896–1897	Montreal Victorias	St-Cup					1	0	0	0
1897–1898	Montreal Victorias	AHAC	8	10	0	10				
1898–1899	Montreal Victorias	CAHL	6	0	0	0				
1898–1899	Montreal Victorias	St-Cup					2	1	0	1

Source: Hockey Hall of Fame

Driscoll, John Leo "Paddy" (born: January 11, 1896 in Evanston, Illinois; died: June 29, 1968 in Chicago, Illinois); inducted into the Pro Football Hall of Fame in 1965 as a player; Position: Quarterback-Halfback; won the 1919 Rose Bowl; was selected to the NFL 1920s All-Decade Team.

After an All-American career at Northwestern University (Evanston, Illinois), Driscoll had an 11-year (118 games) professional career with the Hammond Pros (1919, pre-NFL), Chicago Cardinals (1920–1925, was the team's head coach from 1920 to 1922), and the Chicago Bears (1926–1929). He played both offense and defense, and was also a dropkicker.

The 5'11", 160-pound Driscoll was selected All-NFL six times; scored 27 points in one game (October 7, 1923 in a 60–0 win over the Rochester Jeffersons); dropkicked a 50-yard field goal in 1924; and dropkicked a record four field goals in one game (1925). In 1926, he joined the Bears for four seasons before retiring.

He was a member of the NFL 1920s All-Decade Team, and in 1974, he was inducted into the College Football Hall of Fame. Driscoll served as head coach of the Bears for two seasons (1956–1957) and compiled a 14–10–1 record.

He also had a brief major league baseball career, playing 13 games for the Chicago Cubs in 1917.

After leaving Northwestern, Driscoll served briefly in the U.S. Navy during World War I and played football at the Great Lakes Naval Station (North Chicago, Illinois). His team won the 1919 Rose Bowl and he led the squad to a 17–0 win over Mare Island (U.S. Marine Corps).

Sources: College Football Hall of Fame; Pro Football Hall of Fame

Dryden, Kenneth Wayne "Ken" (born: August 8, 1947 in Hamilton, Ontario, Canada); inducted into the Hockey Hall of Fame in 1983 as a player; Position: Goalie; Uniform: #29; won six Stanley Cup titles in eight years.

Dryden played eight seasons in the National Hockey League, all with the Montreal Canadiens from 1970 to 1979. Although he only played six games in his first season with the team, he was added to the playoff roster; helped Montreal beat the Chicago Black Hawks in seven games to win the 1971 Stanley Cup; and won the Conn Smythe Trophy as the playoffs' most outstanding performer.

In the 1971–1972 season, he was the team's goalie and compiled a goals-against average of 2.24 in 64 games. He was named Rookie of the Year, and became the first goalie in the NHL to be awarded both the Conn Smythe and Calder Trophy (Rookie of the Year). The next season, he won the Vezina Trophy as the league's best goalie.

After winning three individual awards and two Stanley Cup championships in three partial NHL seasons, Dryden briefly retired at the end of the 1972–1973 season, before rejoining the Canadiens one year later. After Montreal won four consecutive Stanley Cup titles (1976–1979, giving him six), Dryden retired for good.

He was awarded the Vezina Trophy four more times; selected to five First All-Star Teams; and one Second All-Star Team.

Although he was chosen 14th overall by the Boston Bruins in the 1964 NHL Amateur Draft, he decided not to play in Boston and attended Cornell University (Ithaca, New York), where he played hockey until graduating in 1969. While at Cornell, he led the team to the 1967 National Collegiate Athletic Association title and three consecutive Eastern College Athletic Conference tournament championships.

Although he had a relatively brief NHL career, in 1998, Dryden was ranked number 25 on *The Hockey News*' list of the 100 Greatest Hockey Players, and the Canadiens retired his jersey number 29 in 2006.

After retiring as a player, he served as Ontario's first Youth Commissioner from 1984 to 1986, and was a sports commentator at the 1980 (Lake Placid, New York), 1984 (Sarajevo, Yugoslavia), and 1988 (Calgary, Alberta, Canada) Olympics.

In the Canadian federal election of June 2004, Dryden (a Liberal Party of Canada candidate) was elected to the Canadian House of Commons as a Member of Parliament, and was re-elected in 2006.

Ken Dryden's Career Statistics

			REGULAR SEASON						PLAYOFFS				
SEASON	**TEAM**	**LEAGUE**	**GP**	**W**	**L**	**T**	**SO**	**AVG**	**GP**	**W**	**L**	**SO**	**AVG**
1963–1964	Humber Valley Packers	THL											
1964–1965	Etobicoke Indians	OHA-B											
1965–1966	Cornell Big Red	ECAC											
1966–1967	Cornell Big Red	ECAC	27	26	0	1	4	1.46					
1967–1968	Cornell Big Red	ECAC	29	25	2	0	6	1.52					
1968–1969	Cornell Big Red	ECAC	27	25	2	0	3	1.79					
1968–1969	Canada	WEC-A	2	1	1	0	1	2.00					
1969–1970	Canada	Nat–Tm											
1970–1971	Montreal Voyageurs	AHL	33	16	7	8	3	2.68					
1970–1971	Montreal Canadiens	NHL	6	6	0	0	0	1.65	20	12	8	0	3.00
1971–1972	Montreal Canadiens	NHL	64	39	8	15	8	2.24	6	2	4	0	2.83
1972–1973	Canada	Summit-72	4	2	2	0	0	4.75					
1972–1973	Montreal Canadiens	NHL	54	33	7	13	6	2.26	17	12	5	1	2.89
1974–1975	Montreal Canadiens	NHL	56	30	9	16	4	2.69	11	6	5	2	2.53
1975–1976	Montreal Canadiens	NHL	62	42	10	8	8	2.03	13	12	1	1	1.92
1976–1977	Montreal Canadiens	NHL	56	41	6	8	10	2.14	14	12	2	4	1.55
1977–1978	Montreal Canadiens	NHL	52	37	7	7	5	2.05	15	12	3	2	1.89
1978–1979	Montreal Canadiens	NHL	47	30	10	7	5	2.30	16	12	4	0	2.48
1978–1979	NHL All-tars	Ch-Cup	2	1	1	0	0	3.50					
	NHL TOTALS		397	258	57	74	46	2.23	112	80	32	10	2.40

Sources: Hockey Hall of Fame; Hockey-Reference.com

Drysdale, Donald Scott "Don" (born: July 23, 1936 in Van Nuys, California; died: July 3, 1993 in Montreal, Quebec, Canada); inducted into the National Baseball Hall of Fame and Museum in 1984 as a player; Position: Pitcher; Bats: Right; Throws: Right; Uniform: #53; won the Cy Young Award and three World Series championships; won 20 games and hit .300 in the same season.

Making his major league debut on April 17, 1956, Drysdale had a 14-year career with the Brooklyn Dodgers (1956–1957) and Los Angeles Dodgers (1958–1969) when the team moved west. He played in five World Series (winning three times (1959, 1963, 1965) and losing twice (1956, 1966); was an eight-time All–Star (1959, 1961–1965, 1967–1968); and won the Cy Young Award in 1962 as the league's top pitcher. In his very first start (April 23, 1956), Drysdale struck out the side in the first inning, and would go on to fan nine batters in a 6–1 Brooklyn win over the Philadelphia Phillies.

His 154 career hit batsmen is still the modern-day National League record, and he set a record with 58 consecutive scoreless innings in 1968 (which has since been broken by fellow Dodger Orel Hershiser).

In 1965, Drysdale was the Dodgers' only .300 hitter, and in two separate seasons, he hit seven home runs, tying the National League record. Never missing a start in his career, Drysdale led the National League in games started four consecutive seasons (1962–1965), innings pitched twice (1962, 1964), and shutouts in 1959; led National League pitchers in home runs four times; and his career total of 29 homers ranks second behind Warren Spahn in National League history. In 1965, he hit .300 and won 20 games.

When Drysdale retired, he held the National League record for most seasons with 200 or more strikeouts (six); was the last player on the Dodgers who had played for Brooklyn, and his jersey #53 was retired in July 1984.

He won 17 games in the team's last year in Brooklyn; pitched the franchise's first West Coast game (an 8–0 loss in San Francisco to the Giants on April 15, 1958); and had the longest career played under a single manager, 13 years with Walter Alston.

He appeared as himself on several television shows, and after retiring as a player, Drysdale became a broadcaster for the Montréal Expos (1970–1971), Texas Rangers (1972), California Angels (1973–1979), Chicago White Sox (1982–1987), ABC (1978–1986), and the Los Angeles Dodgers (1988, until he died in 1993 of a heart attack after broadcasting a Dodger-Expo game). One of his most memorable calls was Kirk Gibson's dramatic walk-off home run in Game 1 of the 1988 World Series for the Dodgers Radio Network.

In 1986, he married Naismith Memorial Basketball Hall of Fame inductee Ann Meyers, marking the first time that a married couple were members of their respective sports' halls of fame.

Don Drysdale's Career Statistics

YEAR	TEAM	LG	W	L	PCT	G	SH	IP	H	R	ER	SO	BB	ERA
1956	Brooklyn	NL	5	5	.500	25	0	99	95	35	29	55	31	2.64
1957	Brooklyn	NL	17	9	.654	34	4	221	197	76	66	148	61	2.69
1958	Los Angeles	NL	12	13	.480	44	1	212	214	107	98	131	72	4.16
1959	Los Angeles	NL	17	13	.567	44	4	271	237	113	104	242	93	3.45
1960	Los Angeles	NL	15	14	.517	41	5	269	214	93	85	246	72	2.84
1961	Los Angeles	NL	13	10	.565	40	3	244	236	111	100	182	83	3.69
1962	Los Angeles	NL	25	9	.735	43	2	314	272	122	99	232	78	2.84
1963	Los Angeles	NL	19	17	.528	42	3	315	287	114	92	251	57	2.63
1964	Los Angeles	NL	18	16	.529	40	5	321	242	91	78	237	68	2.19
1965	Los Angeles	NL	23	12	.657	44	7	308	270	113	95	210	66	2.78
1966	Los Angeles	NL	13	16	.448	40	3	274	279	114	104	177	45	3.42
1967	Los Angeles	NL	13	16	.448	38	3	282	269	101	86	196	60	2.74
1968	Los Angeles	NL	14	12	.538	31	8	239	201	68	57	155	56	2.15
1969	Los Angeles	NL	5	4	.556	12	1	63	71	34	31	24	13	4.43
	TOTALS		209	166	.557	518	49	3,432	3,084	1,292	1,124	2,486	855	2.95

Sources: Baseball-Reference.com; National Baseball Hall of Fame and Museum

Dudley, George (born: April 19, 1894 in Midland, Ontario, Canada; died: May 8, 1960); inducted into the Hockey Hall of Fame in 1958 as a builder; served as secretary, vice-president, and president of both the Ontario Hockey Association and the Canadian Amateur Hockey Association.

One of the game's best administrators, after graduating from Toronto's Osgoode Hall Law School (Ontario, Canada) in 1917, he returned to Midland as an active lawyer for almost 40 years. A lifelong fan of hockey, Dudley offered his legal services to the executive offices of the Ontario Hockey Association and the Canadian Amateur Hockey Association, where he would serve as second vice-president and first vice-president, before taking over as president from 1934 to 1936. From 1936 until his death, Dudley served as OHA secretary.

After serving as second and first vice-president of the OHA, Dudley was the organization's president from 1940 to 1942, and later served as CAHA secretary and trustee of the Memorial Cup.

Internationally, he served as secretary of the International Ice Hockey Federation (1946–1947); was the North American IIHF representative from 1954 to 1960; helped organize the first exhibition tours of the Soviet National Team; and oversaw the ice hockey competition at the 1960 Winter Olympics (Squaw Valley, California).

Source: Hockey Hall of Fame

Dudley, William McGarvey "Bill" (born: December 24, 1921 in Bluefield, Virginia); inducted into the Pro Football Hall of Fame in 1966 as a player; Position: Halfback; first-ever All-American at the University of Virginia; only player in football history to receive MVP honors in college, military service, and at the professional level.

Dudley attended the University of Virginia (Charlottesville), and became the school's first All-American in 1941. He was the overall number one draft pick of the Pittsburgh Steelers in 1942 and played nine years (90 games) in the National Football League with the Steelers (1942, 1945–1946), Detroit Lions (1947–1949), and Washington Redskins (1950–1951, 1953). His career was interrupted in 1943 and 1944 when he served with the Army Air Corps during World War II.

At 5'10", 182 pounds, Dudley was named All-NFL twice (1942, 1946); NFL Most Valuable Player in 1946; and won the "triple crown" title (led the league in rushing, interceptions, punt returns). He finished his rookie season as the NFL's leading rusher (696 yards on 162 carries) and won all-league honors.

Dudley enlisted in the Army Air Corps during World War II; played for the Army football team; and in 1944, led the team to a 12–0 record, was named MVP, and selected to the All-Service squad.

After the war, he returned to the Steelers in 1945, and in 1946, he led the league in rushing, punt returns, and interceptions, winning Most Valuable Player honors. Dudley is the only player in football history to be named MVP in college, military service, and at the professional level.

After three seasons in Detroit, Dudley was traded to the Redskins; played for three seasons; and led the team in scoring each year before retiring from the NFL. In his career, he was named First- or Second-team All-NFL six times and was selected to three Pro Bowls.

Dudley first played football at Graham High School (Bluefield, Virginia) in his junior year, before attending the University of Virginia on a football scholarship.

He has been inducted into the College Football Hall of Fame (1956) and the Virginia Sports Hall of Fame (1972), and the Downtown Club of Richmond, Virginia has sponsored the Bill Dudley Award since 1990, which is presented to the state's top college football player. In June 2002, Dudley was named one of the 70 Greatest Washington Redskins.

Bill Dudley's Career Statistics

			RUSHING				RECEIVING			
YEAR	**TEAM**	**G**	**NO**	**YDS**	**AVG**	**TD**	**NO**	**YDS**	**AVG**	**TD**
1942	Pittsburgh	11	162	696	4.3	5	1	24	24	0
1945	Pittsburgh	4	57	204	3.6	3	0	0	0.0	0
1946	Pittsburgh	11	146	604	4.1	2	4	109	27.3	1
1947	Detroit	9	80	302	3.8	2	27	375	13.9	7
1948	Detroit	7	33	97	2.9	0	20	210	10.5	6
1949	Detroit	12	125	402	3.2	3	27	190	7.0	2
1950	Washington	12	66	339	5.1	1	22	172	7.8	1
1951	Washington	12	91	398	4.4	2	22	303	13.8	1
1953	Washington	12	5	15	3.0	0	0	0	0.0	0
	TOTALS	90	765	3,057	4.0	18	123	1,383	11.2	18

			PUNT RETURNS				KICKOFF RETURNS			
YEAR	**TEAM**	**G**	**NO**	**YDS**	**AVG**	**TD**	**NO**	**YDS**	**AVG**	**TD**
1942	Pittsburgh	11	20	271	13.6	0	11	298	27.1	1
1945	Pittsburgh	4	5	20	4.0	0	3	65	21.7	0
1946	Pittsburgh	11	27	385	14.3	0	14	280	20.0	0
1947	Detroit	9	11	182	16.5	1	15	359	23.9	0
1948	Detroit	7	8	67	8.4	0	10	204	20.4	0
1949	Detroit	12	11	199	18.1	1	13	246	18.9	0
1950	Washington	12	12	185	15.4	1	1	43	43.0	0
1951	Washington	12	22	172	7.8	0	11	248	22.5	0
1953	Washington	12	8	34	4.3	0	0	0	0.00	0
	TOTALS	90	124	1,515	12.2	3	78	1,743	22.3	1

			DEFENSE							PUNTING		
YEAR	**TEAM**	**G**	**INT**	**YDS**	**AVG**	**TD**	**FUMREC**	**YDS**	**TD**	**PUNT**	**YDS**	**AVG**
1942	Pittsburgh	11	3	60	20.0	0	0	0	0	18	572	31.8
1945	Pittsburgh	4	2	47	23.5	0	0	0	0	2	36	18.0
1946	Pittsburgh	11	10	242	24.2	1	7	30	0	60	2,409	40.2
1947	Detroit	9	5	104	20.8	1	2	0	0	15	657	43.8
1948	Detroit	7	1	3	3.0	0	4	28	1	23	825	35.9
1949	Detroit	12	0	0	0.0	0	1	-2	0	34	1,278	37.6
1950	Washington	12	2	3	1.5	0	1	0	0	14	585	41.8
1951	Washington	12	0	0	0.0	0	1	4	0	27	942	34.9
1953	Washington	12	0	0	0.0	0	1	0	0	0	0	0.0
	TOTALS	90	23	459	20.0	2	17	60	1	193	7,304	37.8

Sources: College Football Hall of Fame; Pro Football Hall of Fame; Pro-Football-Reference.com; Virginia Sports Hall of Fame

Duer, Alva O. (born: November 18, 1904 in Sylvia, Kansas; died: November 18, 1987); inducted into the Naismith Memorial Basketball Hall of Fame in 1982 as a contributor; led Pepperdine College to six postseason appearances; served as NAIB president.

Duer played four years of basketball at Stafford (Kansas) High School and was the team's captain from 1920 to 1923. After graduating in 1923, he attended Kansas State Teachers College (Emporia), Columbia University (New York, New York, graduating in 1929), and the University of Southern California (Los Angeles, California, graduating in 1936).

He began his coaching career at Sylvia (Kansas) High School from 1929 to 1932, before becoming the head coach at Pepperdine College (now known as Pepperdine University, Los Angeles, California) from 1939 to 1948. At Pepperdine, he compiled a 176–94 (.651) record; coached teams to 22 or more wins five times; had only one losing season; led the school to six postseason appearances (five National Association of Intercollegiate Basketball tournaments and one National Collegiate Athletic Association tournament).

During his career, Duer co-founded and directed the Los Angeles National Invitational Basketball Tournament for five years; served as NAIB president in 1947; executive secretary-treasurer of the NAIB (1949–1975); and was the director and founder of the NAIB/NAIA National Basketball Championship Tournament (1949–1975).

Duer was an Amateur Athletic Union representative to the International Basketball Federation of the United States (1960–1964); a member of the U.S. Basketball Association Ethics Committee (1960–1964); a member of the U.S. Department of State Sports Advisory Committee; served as third vice-president of the U.S. Olympic Committee (1973–1976); was awarded the Olympic Torch by the U.S. Olympic Committee; was Atlanta's Citizen of the Year in Sports (1965); Kansas City's Man of the Year in Sports (1975); and served on the Board of Directors for the AAU, U.S. Olympic Committee, Naismith Memorial Basketball Hall of Fame, and Greater Kansas City Sports Commission.

He has been inducted into the Greater Kansas City Amateur Sports Hall of Champions (1980); the National Association of Collegiate Directors of Athletics Hall of Fame (1976); and the NAIA Hall of Fame (1961).

Source: Naismith Memorial Basketball Hall of Fame

Duff, Duncan (born: December 18, 1906 in Scotland; died: April 1977 in Los Angeles, California); inducted into the National Soccer Hall of Fame and Museum in 1972 as a builder; won a league championship with Magyar A.C.; served as president of the state commission.

Duff started his soccer career in Canada and continued playing when he moved to the United States with the Los Angeles Rover Soccer Club in 1928; Pasadena-Los Angeles A.C.; and Magyar A.C.

After serving in World War II, he was twice chosen All Star right back for the Los Angeles All-Stars against San Francisco. After retiring as a player, he managed the Magyar A.C. squad and won the league championship in his first year. Later, he was elected to the state commission, becoming its secretary, treasurer, and eventually president.

Source: National Soccer Hall of Fame and Museum

Duff, Richard "Dick" (born: February 18, 1936 in Kirkland Lake, Ontario, Canada); inducted into the Hockey Hall of Fame in 2006 as a player; Position: Forward; won six Stanley Cup championships.

In his second year at St. Michael's College (Toronto, Ontario, 1953–1954), Duff led the majors in scoring with 35 goals and 75 points. During his third and final year, he again led the majors in scoring (53 points), and made his National Hockey League debut on March 10, 1955 with the Toronto Maple Leafs for the first of his three games that season.

During his NHL career, Duff played for the Toronto Maple Leafs (1954–1963), New York Rangers (1963–1964), Montreal Canadiens (1964–1969), Los Angeles Kings (1969–1970), and the Buffalo Sabres (1970–1972). He helped the Maple Leafs win the 1962 Stanley Cup in five games over the Chicago Black Hawks, and led the team to a repeat championship in 1963 with a five-game win over the Detroit Red Wings.

After playing for the Rangers for a little more than one season, Duff was sent to the Canadiens and would win four more Stanley Cup titles over the next five seasons (1965–1966, 1968–1969), before finally retiring in 1971 while with the Sabres.

Dick Duff's Career Statistics

			REGULAR SEASON					PLAYOFFS				
SEASON	**TEAM**	**LEAGUE**	**GP**	**G**	**A**	**TP**	**PIM**	**GP**	**G**	**A**	**TP**	**PIM**

SEASON	TEAM	LEAGUE	REGULAR SEASON GP	G	A	TP	PIM	PLAYOFFS GP	G	A	TP	PIM
1952–1953	St. Michael's Buzzers	OHA-B										
1952–1953	St. Michael's Majors	OHA-Jr.	16	3	2	5	2	16	6	9	15	15
1953–1954	St. Michael's Majors	OHA-Jr.	59	35	40	75	120	8	2	3	5	23
1954–1955	St. Michael's Majors	OHA-Jr.	47	33	20	53	113	5	5	2	7	22
1954–1955	Toronto Maple Leafs	NHL	3	0	0	0	2					
1955–1956	Toronto Maple Leafs	NHL	69	18	19	37	74	5	1	4	5	2
1956–1957	Toronto Maple Leafs	NHL	70	26	14	40	50					
1957–1958	Toronto Maple Leafs	NHL	65	26	23	49	79					
1958–1959	Toronto Maple Leafs	NHL	69	29	24	53	73	12	4	3	7	8
1959–1960	Toronto Maple Leafs	NHL	67	19	22	41	51	10	2	4	6	6
1960–1961	Toronto Maple Leafs	NHL	67	16	17	33	54	5	0	1	1	2
1961–1962	Toronto Maple Leafs	NHL	51	17	20	37	37	12	3	10	13	20
1962–1963	Toronto Maple Leafs	NHL	69	16	19	35	56	10	4	1	5	2
1963–1964	Toronto Maple Leafs	NHL	52	7	10	17	59					
1963–1964	New York Rangers	NHL	14	4	4	8	2					
1964–1965	New York Rangers	NHL	29	3	9	12	20					
1964–1965	Montreal Canadiens	NHL	40	9	7	16	16	13	3	6	9	17
1965–1966	Montreal Canadiens	NHL	63	21	24	45	78	10	2	5	7	2
1966–1967	Montreal Canadiens	NHL	51	12	11	23	23	10	2	3	5	4
1967–1968	Montreal Canadiens	NHL	66	25	21	46	21	13	3	4	7	4
1968–1969	Montreal Canadiens	NHL	68	19	21	40	24	14	6	8	14	11
1969–1970	Montreal Canadiens	NHL	17	1	1	2	4					
1969–1970	Los Angeles Kings	NHL	32	5	8	13	8					
1970–1971	Los Angeles Kings	NHL	7	1	0	1	0					
1970–1971	Buffalo Sabres	NHL	53	7	13	20	12					
1971–1972	Buffalo Sabres	NHL	8	2	2	4	0					
	NHL TOTALS		1,030	283	289	572	743	114	30	49	79	78

Sources: Hockey Hall of Fame; Hockey-Reference.com

Duffy, Hugh (born: November 26, 1866 in Cranston, Rhode Island; died: October 19, 1954 in Boston, Massachusetts); inducted into the National Baseball Hall of Fame and Museum in 1945 as a player by the Veterans Committee; Position: Center Field; Bats: Right; Throws: Right; first Triple Crown winner; set a record by reaching first base safely three times in one inning; his .438 average is the major league single-season record.

Making his major league debut on June 23, 1888, Duffy had a 17-year career with the Chicago White Stockings (1888–1889), Chicago Pirates (1890, Players' League), Boston Reds (1891), Boston Beaneaters/Braves (1892–1900), Milwaukee Brewers (1901, player-manager), and Philadelphia Phillies (1904–1906, player-manager). After retiring as a player, he managed the Chicago White Sox (1910–1911) and the Boston Red Sox (1921–1922).

The 5'7", 168-pound Duffy hit .300 or better 10 seasons; had 100 or more runs batted in eight times; and in 1894, he hit .438 (Major League Baseball's best-ever single season average), while leading the National League in doubles (50), hits (236), runs batted in (145), slugging percentage (.679), and home runs (18), becoming baseball's first Triple Crown winner. On June 18, 1894 against the Baltimore Orioles, Duffy reached base safely three times in one inning, a record that still stands.

Hugh Duffy's Career Statistics

YEAR	TEAM	LG	G	AB	R	H	2B	3B	HR	RBI	BB	SO	SB	AVG	SLG
1888	Chicago	NL	71	298	60	84	11	4	7	41	9	32	13	.282	.416
1889	Chicago	NL	136	584	144	182	21	7	12	89	46	30	52	.312	.433
1890	Chicago	PL	137	591	161	194	33	14	7	62	59	20	79	.328	.467
1891	Boston	AA	121	511	124	174	23	10	9	110	61	29	83	.341	.477
1892	Boston	NL	146	609	125	184	25	13	5	81	60	37	61	.302	.411
1893	Boston	NL	131	537	149	203	23	7	6	118	50	13	50	.378	.480
1894	Boston	NL	124	539	160	236	50	13	18	145	66	15	49	.438	.679
1895	Boston	NL	131	540	113	190	25	6	9	100	63	16	42	.352	.470

YEAR	TEAM	LG	G	AB	R	H	2B	3B	HR	RBI	BB	SO	SB	AVG	SLG
1896	Boston	NL	131	533	93	161	17	8	5	113	52	19	45	.302	.392
1897	Boston	NL	134	554	131	189	23	10	11	129	52		45	.341	.478
1898	Boston	NL	151	561	97	179	12	3	8	108	59		32	.319	.394
1899	Boston	NL	147	588	102	164	25	8	5	102	39		18	.279	.374
1900	Boston	NL	50	181	28	54	5	4	2	31	16		12	.298	.403
1901	Milwaukee	AL	78	286	41	88	14	8	2	45	16		13	.308	.434
1904	Philadelphia	NL	18	46	10	13	1	1	0	5	13		3	.283	.348
1905	Philadelphia	NL	15	40	7	12	2	1	0	3	1		0	.300	.400
1906	Philadelphia	NL	1	1	0	0	0	0	0	0	0		0	.000	.000
	TOTALS		1,722	6,999	1,545	2,307	310	117	106	1,282	662	211	597	.330	.453

Hugh Duffy's Managerial Record

YEAR	LG	TEAM	W	L	WIN%	FINISH
1901	AL	Milwaukee	48	89	.350	8 Player-Manager
1904	NL	Philadelphia	52	100	.342	8 Player-Manager
1905	NL	Philadelphia	83	69	.546	4 Player-Manager
1906	NL	Philadelphia	71	82	.464	4 Player-Manager
1910	AL	Chicago	68	85	.444	6
1911	AL	Chicago	77	74	.510	4
1921	AL	Boston	75	79	.487	5
1922	AL	Boston	61	93	.396	8
		Milwaukee	48	89	.350	
		Philadelphia	206	251	.451	
		Chicago	145	159	.477	
		Boston	136	172	.442	
		TOTALS	535	671	.444	

Sources: Baseball-Reference.com; National Baseball Hall of Fame and Museum

Duggan, Thomas (born: September 30, 1897 in Liverpool, England; died: November 30, 1961 in Kearny, New Jersey); inducted into the National Soccer Hall of Fame and Museum in 1955 as a player; Position: Outside Right; won the National Open Cup in 1923.

Duggan came to the United States in 1911, and three years later began playing for the Valley Boys. He then went on to play for Babcock and Wilcox of Bayonne (New Jersey, 1916); West Hudson Athletic Association (New Jersey, 1918); and Philadelphia Merchant Ship (Harriman, Pennsylvania, 1918).

When the American Soccer League was created in 1921, he joined the New York Field Club (1921–1922, 1923–1924), before moving on to play for the Paterson Silk Sox (New Jersey, 1922–1923); Indiana Flooring (New York, 1924–1925); New York Giants (1925–1926, 1929-1930); Newark Skeeters (New Jersey, 1926–1927, 1927–1928); and the New York Nationals (1927).

He was a member of the Paterson team that won the National Open Cup in 1923.

Source: National Soccer Hall of Fame and Museum

Dumars, Joe III (born: May 24, 1963 in Shreveport, Louisiana); inducted into the Naismith Memorial Basketball Hall of Fame in 2006 as a player; Position: Guard; Uniform: #4; won back-to-back NBA championships; the NBA Sportsmanship Award is named in his honor.

From his basketball start at Natchitoches (Louisiana) Central High School, Dumars would eventually go on to be drafted by the Detroit Pistons in the 1st round (18th pick overall) in the 1985 National Basketball Association Draft from McNeese State University (Lake Charles, Louisiana). He played his entire 14-year career (1985–1999) with the team and helped the Pistons win back-to-back NBA Championships in 1989 and 1990.

The 6'3", 190-pound Dumars was selected to the All-Rookie Team in 1986; named to the NBA All-Defensive First Team four times (1989–1990, 1992–1993); was a six-time NBA All-Star (1990–1993, 1995, 1997); and the Most Valuable Player of the 1989 NBA Finals. As of this writing, he is President of Basketball Operations for the Pistons.

The NBA has named its Sportsmanship Award after him (Joe Dumars Trophy), and his jersey number 4 was retired by the Pistons in 2000. After retiring as a player, he became the Pistons' President of Basketball Operations in 2000, and was voted the league's Executive of the Year in 2003.

During his four years at McNeese State University, he averaged 22.5 points per game, and finished his college career as the 11th leading scorer in NCAA history. Dumars also played for the gold medal-winning U.S. National Team in the 1994 FIBA World Championship (Toronto, Canada).

Joe Dumars' Career Statistics

SEASON	TEAM	G	MIN	FG	3P	FT	TRB	AST	STL	BLK	PF	PTS
1985–1986	Detroit	82	1,957	287	5	190	119	390	66	11	200	769
1986–1987	Detroit	79	2,439	369	9	184	167	352	83	5	194	931
1987–1988	Detroit	82	2,732	453	4	251	200	387	87	15	155	1,161
1988–1989	Detroit	69	2,408	456	14	260	172	390	63	5	103	1,186
1989–1990	Detroit	75	2,578	508	22	297	212	368	63	2	129	1,335
1990–1991	Detroit	80	3,046	622	14	371	187	443	89	7	135	1,629
1991–1992	Detroit	82	3,192	587	49	412	188	375	71	12	145	1,635
1992–1993	Detroit	77	3,094	677	112	343	148	308	78	7	141	1,809
1993–1994	Detroit	69	2,591	505	124	276	151	261	63	4	118	1,410
1994–1995	Detroit	67	2,544	417	103	277	158	368	72	7	153	1,214
1995–1996	Detroit	67	2,193	255	121	162	138	265	43	3	106	793
1996–1997	Detroit	79	2,923	385	166	222	191	318	57	1	97	1,158
1997–1998	Detroit	72	2,326	329	158	127	104	253	44	2	99	943
1998–1999	Detroit	38	1,116	144	89	51	68	134	23	2	51	428
	TOTALS	1,018	35,139	5,994	990	3,423	2,203	4,612	902	83	1,826	16,401

Sources: Basketball-Reference.com; Naismith Memorial Basketball Hall of Fame

Dumart, Woodrow Wilson Clarence "Woody" (born: December 23, 1916 in Kitchener, Ontario, Canada; died: October 19, 2001); inducted into the Hockey Hall of Fame in 1992 as a player; Position: Left Wing; won two Stanley Cup titles.

Dumart played his entire 16-year National Hockey League career with the Boston Bruins (1935–1942, 1945–1954); appeared in almost 800 NHL games; best known for his play with Milt Schmidt and Bobby Bauer as part of the "Kraut Line," so-called because of their German ancestry; and he won two Stanley Cup titles (1939, 1941).

Dumart recorded his first 20-goal season in 1939–1940, and was named to the NHL's Second All-Star Team in 1940 and 1941.

Although he started the 1941–1942 season with the Bruins, Dumart left the NHL and join the Canadian military during World War II. He played on the Ottawa Royal Canadian Air Force team and helped the squad win the Allan Cup. He served overseas in 1944 and 1945, before finally returning to the NHL for the 1945–1946 season.

He recorded four 20-goal seasons between 1946 and 1951; played in the first two annual NHL All-Star games in 1947 and 1948; and was named to the Second All-Star Team for the third time in 1947.

Woody Dumart's Career Statistics

			REGULAR SEASON					PLAYOFFS				
SEASON	TEAM	LEAGUE	GP	G	A	TP	PIM	GP	G	A	TP	PIM
1933–1934	Kitchener Empires	OHA-Jr.	12	8	3	11	12	3	1	3	4	0
1934–1935	Kitchener Greenshirts	OHA-Jr.	17	17	11	28	10	3	3	1	4	2
1935–1936	Boston Cubs	Can-Am	46	11	10	21	15					
1935–1936	Boston Bruins	NHL	1	0	0	0	0					
1936–1937	Boston Bruins	NHL	17	4	4	8	2	3	0	0	0	0
1936–1937	Providence Reds	IAHL	34	4	7	11	10					
1937–1938	Boston Bruins	NHL	48	13	14	27	6	3	0	0	0	0
1938–1939	Boston Bruins	NHL	46	14	15	29	2	12	1	3	4	6
1939–1940	Boston Bruins	NHL	48	22	21	43	16	6	1	0	1	0
1940–1941	Boston Bruins	NHL	40	18	15	33	2	11	1	3	4	9
1941–1942	Boston Bruins	NHL	35	14	15	29	8					

			REGULAR SEASON					PLAYOFFS				
SEASON	TEAM	LEAGUE	GP	G	A	TP	PIM	GP	G	A	TP	PIM
1941–1942	Ottawa RCAF Flyers	OCHL						6	7	5	12	2
1941–1942	Ottawa RCAF Flyers	Al-Cup	13	14	9	23	8					
1942–1943	Ottawa RCAF Flyers	OHA-Sr.	6	6	5	11						
1942–1943	Millward-St. George RCAF	Britain										
1945–1946	Boston Bruins	NHL	50	22	12	34	2	10	4	3	7	0
1946–1947	Boston Bruins	NHL	60	24	28	52	12	5	1	1	2	8
1947–1948	Boston Bruins	NHL	59	21	16	37	14	5	0	0	0	0
1948–1949	Boston Bruins	NHL	59	11	12	23	6	5	3	0	3	0
1949–1950	Boston Bruins	NHL	69	14	25	39	14					
1950–1951	Boston Bruins	NHL	70	20	21	41	7	6	1	2	3	0
1951–1952	Boston Bruins	NHL	39	5	8	13	0	7	0	1	1	0
1952–1953	Boston Bruins	NHL	62	5	9	14	2	11	0	2	2	0
1953–1954	Boston Bruins	NHL	69	4	3	7	6	4	0	0	0	0
1954–1955	Providence Reds	AHL	15	2	2	4	0					
	NHL TOTALS		772	211	218	429	99	88	12	15	27	23

Sources: Hockey Hall of Fame; Hockey-Reference.com

Dunderdale, Thomas (born: May 6, 1887 in Benella, Australia; died: December 15, 1960); inducted into the Hockey Hall of Fame in 1974 as a player; first Australian-born player to be inducted into the Hockey Hall of Fame.

Dunderdale played 17 professional, pre-National Hockey League seasons from 1906 to 1924, and was the first Australian-born player to be inducted into the Hockey Hall of Fame.

He moved to Ottawa, Canada in 1904, and played his first organized hockey at the Waller Street School, before joining the Manitoba Professional Hockey League in 1906. He stayed in the league until 1909, before joining the Montreal Shamrocks in the National Hockey Association.

In 1911, he played for the Victoria Aristocrats in the Pacific Coast Hockey Association, and was eventually named to the PCHA First All-Star Team six times (1912–1915, 1920, 1922).

Thomas Dunderdale's Career Statistics

			REGULAR SEASON					PLAYOFFS				
SEASON	TEAM	LEAGUE	GP	G	A	TP	PIM	GP	G	A	TP	PIM
1905–1906	Winnipeg Ramblers	MIHA										
1906–1907	Winnipeg Strathconas	MHL-Pro	10	8	0	8						
1907–1908	Winnipeg Maple Leafs	MHL-Pro	3	1	0	1						
1907–1908	Strathcona-Alberta	MHL-Pro	5	11	1	12	17	3	6	1	7	3
1908–1909	Winnipeg Shamrocks	MHL-Pro	5	12	6	18	6	3	3	0	3	6
1908–1909	Winnipeg Shamrocks	MHL-Pro	4	5	1	6	3					
1909–1910	Montreal Shamrocks	CHA	3	7	0	7	5					
1909–1910	Montreal Shamrocks	NHA	12	14	0	14	19					
1910–1911	Quebec Bulldogs	NHA	9	13	0	13	25					
1911–1912	Victoria Aristocrats	PCHA	16	24	0	24	25					
1911–1912	PCHA All-Stars	Exhib.	3	6	0	6	3					
1912–1913	Victoria Aristocrats	PCHA	15	24	5	29	36					
1912–1913	Victoria Aristocrats	Exhib.	3	3	0	3	8					
1913–1914	Victoria Aristocrats	PCHA	16	24	4	28	34					
1913–1914	Victoria Aristocrats	St-Cup						3	2	0	2	11
1914–1915	Victoria Aristocrats	PCHA	17	17	10	27	22					
1914–1915	PCHA All-Stars	Exhib.	2	0	0	0	0					
1915–1916	Portland Rosebuds	PCHA	18	14	3	17	45					
1915–1916	Portland Rosebuds	St-Cup						5	1	1	2	9
1915–1916	PCHA All-Stars	Exhib.	3	3	2	5	0					
1916–1917	Portland Rosebuds	PCHA	24	22	4	26	141					
1917–1918	Portland Rosebuds	PCHA	18	14	6	20	57					
1918–1919	Victoria Aristocrats	PCHA	20	5	4	9	28					
1919–1920	Victoria Aristocrats	PCHA	22	26	7	33	35					
1920–1921	Victoria Aristocrats	PCHA	24	9	11	20	18					
1921–1922	Victoria Cougars	PCHA	24	13	6	19	37					
1922–1923	Victoria Cougars	PCHA	27	2	0	2	16	2	0	1	1	0
1923–1924	Saskatoon Crescents	WCHL	6	1	0	1	4					

SEASON	TEAM	LEAGUE	REGULAR SEASON GP	G	A	TP	PIM	PLAYOFFS GP	G	A	TP	PIM
1923–1924	Edmonton Eskimos	WCHL	11	1	1	2	5					

Source: Hockey Hall of Fame

Dunn, James (born: March 24, 1898 in Winnipeg, Manitoba, Canada; died: January 7, 1979); inducted into the Hockey Hall of Fame in 1968 as a builder; served as president of the Manitoba Amateur Hockey Association and the Canadian Amateur Hockey Association.

Dunn played minor league hockey as a young man before enlisting in the military during World War I in 1916. After the war, he became an administrator in minor league and amateur hockey in the Winnipeg area. He served as chief secretary of the Manitoba Amateur Hockey Association from 1927 to 1941; became the association's vice-president in 1942; and in 1945, he began a six-year tenure as its president. He moved on to the Canadian Amateur Hockey Association and served as its second vice-president (1950–1952), first vice-president (1952–1954), and president (1955–1957).

Source: Hockey Hall of Fame

Dunn, James (born: August 21, 1898 in St. Louis, Missouri; died: St. Louis, Missouri); inducted into the National Soccer Hall of Fame and Museum as a player in 1974; Position: Forward; won the U.S. Open Cup in 1920.

Dunn's soccer career began in the St. Louis Municipal League with Christian Brothers College (St. Louis, Missouri) during the 1914–1915 season. He eventually joined the Ben Millers club (St. Louis, Missouri) in the St. Louis Professional Soccer League for the 1916–1917 season, and led the team to a pennant with 10 wins, two losses, and eight ties.

In 1917, Dunn enlisted in the United States Navy during World War I, and spent two years in the military before returning to the Ben Millers for the 1919–1920 season, leading the team to the U.S. Open Cup title. He stayed with the team through the 1926–1927 season, and reached the U.S. Open Cup final for the second time in 1926, eventually losing to Bethlehem Steel.

Dunn was inducted into the St. Louis Soccer Hall of Fame in 1971, and since 1986, the St. Louis Soccer Hall of Fame has awarded an annual Jimmy Dunn Memorial High School Coach of the Year Award.

Source: National Soccer Hall of Fame and Museum

Durnan, William Ronald "Bill" (born: January 22, 1916 in Toronto, Ontario, Canada; died: October 31, 1972); inducted into the Hockey Hall of Fame in 1964 as a player; Position: Goalie; won the 1940 Allan Cup; first rookie to win the Vezina Trophy as the NHL's best goalie.

Durnan played seven National Hockey League seasons from 1943 to 1950, all with the Montreal Canadiens, and won the Vezina Trophy as the league's best goalkeeper six times (1944–1947, 1949–1950).

After eight seasons of amateur hockey, Durnan moved on to the Montreal Royals of the Quebec Senior Hockey League for three seasons (1940–1943), before joining the Canadiens at the relatively old age of 28.

In his first season with the team (1943–1944), he helped the Canadiens win the Stanley Cup title; led the league in games played, wins, and goals-against average in the regular season (2.18) and in the playoffs (1.53); was the first rookie to win the Vezina Trophy as the league's best goalie; and was selected to the First All-Star Team his first year.

The 6'2", 200-pound Durnan won the Stanley Cup title twice (1944, 1946) in his first four seasons, and played in three NHL All-Star Games (1947–1949). In the 1948–1949 season, he set a then-record with a shutout streak that lasted 321 minutes, 21 seconds over four games (surpassed in 2004 by Brian Boucher of the Phoenix Coyotes).

After a relatively short NHL career, he retired in 1950, and was the last goalie to be a captain in the National Hockey League. He went on to coach the Ottawa Senators of the QSHL in 1950–1951, and the Kitchener-Waterloo Dutchmen of the Ontario Hockey Association in 1958–1959.

Despite the fact the he had a relatively short NHL career, in 1998, Durnan was ranked number 34 on *The Hockey News*' list of the 100 Greatest Hockey Players.

Bill Durnan's Career Statistics

SEASON	TEAM	LEAGUE	REGULAR SEASON GP	W	L	T	AVG	PLAYOFFS GP	W	L	T	AVG
1931–1932	North Toronto Juniors	TJrHL	8				2.12	4				2.50
1932–1933	Sudbury Wolves	NOJHA	6				1.00	2				2.00
1933–1934	Torontos	TIHL	11				1.91	1	0	1	0	5.00

SEASON	TEAM	LEAGUE	REGULAR SEASON GP	W	L	T	AVG	PLAYOFFS GP	W	L	T	AVG
1933–1934	Toronto British Consols	TMHL	15	12	2	1	2.04	5	0	2	3	3.60
1934–1935	Toronto All-Stars	TIHL	2				4.50					
1934–1935	Toronto McColl-Frontenacs	TMHL	15				4.13					
1935–1936	Toronto Dominion Bank	TIHL	1	0	1	0	6.00					
1936–1937	Kirkland Lake Blue Devils	NOHA	4	4	0	0	1.25	4	1	0	3	2.00
1937–1938	Kirkland Lake Hargreaves	NOHA	11	8	1	1	2.66	2	2	0	0	1.00
1937–1938	Kirkland Lake Blue Devils	Al-Cup	2	0	2	0	5.50					
1938–1939	Kirkland Lake Blue Devils	NOHA	7	7	0	0	1.00	2	2	0	0	1.50
1938–1939	Kirkland Lake Blue Devils	Al-Cup	5	3	2	0	2.41					
1939–1940	Kirkland Lake Blue Devils	X-Games	6				2.00					
1939–1940	Kirkland Lake Blue Devils	Al-Cup	17	14	1	2	2.02					
1940–1941	Montreal Royals	QSHL	34				3.00	8	8	0	0	3.00
1940–1941	Montreal Royals	Al-Cup	14	8	5	1	3.46					
1941–1942	Montreal Royals	QSHL	39				3.67					
1942–1943	Montreal Royals	QSHL	31				4.19	4				2.75
1943–1944	Montreal Canadiens	NHL	50	38	5	7	2.18	9	8	1		1.53
1944–1945	Montreal Canadiens	NHL	50	38	8	4	2.42	6	2	4		2.41
1945–1946	Montreal Canadiens	NHL	40	24	11	5	2.60	9	8	1		2.07
1946–1947	Montreal Canadiens	NHL	60	34	16	10	2.30	11	6	5		1.92
1947–1948	Montreal Canadiens	NHL	59	20	28	10	2.77					
1948–1949	Montreal Canadiens	NHL	60	28	23	9	2.10	7	3	4		2.18
1949–1950	Montreal Canadiens	NHL	64	26	21	17	2.20	3	0	3		3.33
1950–1951	Ottawa Senators	QMHL										
	NHL TOTALS		383	208	112	62	2.36	45	27	18		2.07

Sources: Hockey Hall of Fame; Hockey-Reference.com

Durocher, Leo Ernest (born: July 27, 1905 in West Springfield, Massachusetts; died: October 7, 1991 in Palm Springs, California); inducted into the National Baseball Hall of Fame and Museum in 1994 as a manager by the Veterans Committee; Uniform: #2; won two World Series as a player and one as a manager; first manager to win 500 games with three different teams.

Known as "The Lip," the 5'10", 160-pound Durocher had a 17-year major league playing career, beginning on October 2, 1925, with the New York Yankees (1925, 1928–1929), Cincinnati Reds (1930–1933), St. Louis Cardinals (1933–1937; was captain of the "Gashouse Gang" in 1934), and Brooklyn Dodgers (1938–1943, 1945). He was a player-manager for the Dodgers (1939–1946, 1948), and later managed the New York Giants (1948–1955), Chicago Cubs (1966–1972), and the Houston Astros (1972–1973).

Durocher appeared in five World Series (winning as a player in 1928 and 1934; won as a manager in 1954 and lost in 1941 and 1951; played in three All-Star games (1936, 1938, 1940); and was named Manager of the Year by *The Sporting News* three times (1939, 1951, 1954). As a manager, he compiled a .540 won-lost record (2,009–1,709), and won three pennants. In 1947's spring training, he personally quashed a players' rebellion protesting the presence of Jackie Robinson, who had just broken major league baseball's "color line."

He was the starting shortstop for the Brooklyn Dodgers when the team hosted the Cincinnati Reds in the first televised major league baseball game on August 26, 1939.

A rumor about Durocher stealing money and jewelry from his teammates became public after he was sold to the Reds in February 1930. It was said that the legendary Babe Ruth physically assaulted him for the transgressions. Although the rumor was never confirmed or proven, it has been charged that the Yankees convinced all American League teams to blackball Durocher. While there is no firm evidence of the team's action, he never played or managed for an American League team again.

Durocher had other problems with the game's management. He played high-stakes poker; gambled on horse races; and was friendly with known gangsters like Bugsy Siegel. In 1945, he was indicted for attacking a fan under the stands, and in 1947, he was suspended from baseball for associating with gamblers and mobsters.

Managing the Giants in 1951, Durocher led the team to a pennant, after a three-game playoff win over the Dodgers in one of baseball's most famous season comebacks, capped by Bobby Thomson's famous home run in the bottom of the ninth inning. The play is forever captured in baseball history thanks to broadcaster Russ Hodges' (on radio station WMCA-AM) famous chant, "The Giants Win the Pennant!, The Giants Win the Pennant!, The Giants Win the Pennant!"

In 1954, Durocher won his only World Series as a manager; became a television commentator after the 1955 season; and later wrote his autobiography, *Nice Guys Finish Last*, with Ed Linn.

When the Yankees began using uniform numbers in 1929, Durocher was issued number two because he batted second. He would wear number two for the rest of his career, as player, coach, and manager. On June 15, 1938, he became a part of baseball history by making the last out in Johnny Vander Meer's second no-hitter (the only pitcher to throw back-to-back no-hitters).

As a manager, Durocher had an overall winning record with each of the four teams he led, and he was the first manager to win 500 games with three different teams.

Leo Durocher's Career Statistics

YEAR	TEAM	G	AB	R	H	2B	3B	HR	RBI	BB	SO	AVG	OBP	SLG
1925	New York	2	1	1	0	0	0	0	0	0	0	.000	.000	.000
1928	New York	102	296	46	80	8	6	0	31	22	52	.270	.327	.338
1929	New York	106	341	53	84	4	5	0	32	34	33	.246	.320	.287
1930	Cincinnati	119	354	31	86	15	3	3	32	20	45	.243	.287	.328
1931	Cincinnati	121	361	26	82	11	5	1	29	18	32	.227	.264	.294
1932	Cincinnati	143	457	43	99	22	5	1	33	36	40	.217	.275	.293
1933	Cincinnati	16	51	6	11	1	0	1	3	4	5	.216	.273	.294
1933	St. Louis	123	395	45	102	18	4	2	41	26	32	.258	.306	.339
1934	St. Louis	146	500	62	130	26	5	3	70	33	40	.260	.308	.350
1935	St. Louis	143	513	62	136	23	5	8	78	29	46	.265	.304	.376
1936	St. Louis	136	510	57	146	22	3	1	58	29	47	.286	.327	.347
1937	St. Louis	135	477	46	97	11	3	1	47	38	36	.203	.262	.245
1938	Brooklyn	141	479	41	105	18	5	1	56	47	30	.219	.293	.284
1939	Brooklyn	116	390	42	108	21	6	1	34	27	24	.277	.325	.369
1940	Brooklyn	62	160	10	37	9	1	1	14	12	13	.231	.285	.319
1941	Brooklyn	18	42	2	12	1	0	0	6	1	3	.286	.302	.310
1943	Brooklyn	6	18	1	4	0	0	0	1	1	2	.222	.263	.222
1945	Brooklyn	2	5	1	1	0	0	0	2	0	0	.200	.200	.200
	TOTALS	1,637	5,350	575	1,320	210	56	24	567	377	480	.247	.299	.320

Leo Durocher's Managerial Record

YEAR	TEAM	W	L	WIN%
1939	Brooklyn	84	69	.549
1940	Brooklyn	88	65	.575
1941	Brooklyn	100	54	.649
1942	Brooklyn	104	50	.675
1943	Brooklyn	81	72	.529
1944	Brooklyn	63	91	.409
1945	Brooklyn	87	67	.565
1946	Brooklyn	96	60	.615
1948	Brooklyn	36	37	.493
1948	New York	41	38	.519
1949	New York	73	81	.474
1950	New York	86	68	.558
1951	New York	98	59	.624
1952	New York	92	62	.597
1953	New York	70	84	.455
1954	New York	97	57	.630
1955	New York	80	74	.519
1966	Chicago	59	103	.364
1967	Chicago	87	74	.540
1968	Chicago	84	78	.519
1969	Chicago	92	70	.568
1970	Chicago	84	78	.519

YEAR	TEAM	W	L	WIN%
1971	Chicago	83	79	.512
1972	Chicago	46	44	.511
1972	Houston	16	15	.516
1973	Houston	82	80	.506
	TOTALS	2,009	1,709	.540

Sources: Baseball-Reference.com; National Baseball Hall of Fame and Museum

Dutton, Mervyn "Red" (born: July 23, 1898 in Russell, Manitoba, Canada; died: March 15, 1987); inducted into the Hockey Hall of Fame in 1958 as a player; Position: Defenseman; served as president of the National Hockey League.

The 6', 185-pound Dutton played 15 professional hockey seasons from 1921 to 1936, including 10 years in the National Hockey League with the Montreal Maroons (1926–1930) and the New York Americans (1930–1936).

He attended St. John's College (Winnipeg, Manitoba), but left school in 1915 to serve during World War I. After a leg injury eventually led to his being discharged in 1919, he returned to Winnipeg and worked on rehabbing his injury by playing local hockey from 1919 to 1920.

In 1920, he turned professional with the Calgary Canadians (Big Four Hockey League); became a two-time Western Canada Hockey League First-Team All-Star; played in the NHL's Ace Bailey Benefit Game in 1934; and played for the Calgary Tigers in the 1924 Stanley Cup, eventually losing to the Montreal Canadiens.

Dutton was named manager-coach of the New York Americans in 1936, a position he held until 1941. In 1943, he was elected president of the National Hockey League, succeeding Frank Calder, and served until 1946, when he was replaced by Clarence Campbell.

He was a trustee of the Stanley Cup (1949–1987); in 1993, he was posthumously awarded the Lester Patrick Trophy for his contributions to hockey in the United States; and in 2005, he was inducted into the Alberta Sports Hall of Fame and Museum.

Outside of hockey, Dutton served as president of the Calgary Bears (a semi-professional baseball team) from 1946 to 1949; president of the Calgary Stampeders (Canadian Football League) in the early 1950s; was president of the Calgary Exhibition and Stampede from 1960 to 1961; and received the Order of Canada in 1980.

Red Dutton's Career Statistics

			REGULAR SEASON					PLAYOFFS				
SEASON	TEAM	LEAGUE	GP	G	A	TP	PIM	GP	G	A	TP	PIM
1914–1915	Winnipeg St. John's	WJrHL										
1919–1920	Winnipegs	WSrHL	8	6	7	13	10					
1919–1920	Winnipegs	Al-Cup	2	0	0	0	6					
1920–1921	Calgary Canadians	Big-4	15	5	3	8	38					
1921–1922	Calgary Tigers	WCHL	22	16	5	21	73	2	0	0	0	2
1922–1923	Calgary Tigers	WCHL	18	2	4	6	24					
1923–1924	Calgary Tigers	WCHL	30	6	7	13	54	2	0	1	1	2
1923–1924	Calgary Tigers	West-P						3	1	0	1	2
1923–1924	Calgary Tigers	St-Cup						2	0	0	0	6
1924–1925	Calgary Tigers	WCHL	23	8	4	12	72	2	0	0	0	8
1925–1926	Calgary Tigers	WHL	30	10	5	15	87					
1926–1927	Montreal Maroons	NHL	44	4	4	8	108	2	0	0	0	4
1927–1928	Montreal Maroons	NHL	42	7	6	13	94	9	1	0	1	27
1928–1929	Montreal Maroons	NHL	44	1	3	4	139					
1929–1930	Montreal Maroons	NHL	43	3	13	16	98	4	0	0	0	2
1930–1931	New York Americans	NHL	44	1	11	12	71					
1931–1932	New York Americans	NHL	47	3	5	8	107					
1932–1933	New York Americans	NHL	43	0	2	2	74					
1933–1934	New York Americans	NHL	48	2	8	10	65					
1934–1935	New York Americans	NHL	48	3	7	10	46					
1935–1936	New York Americans	NHL	46	5	8	13	69	3	0	0	0	0
	NHL TOTALS		449	29	67	96	871	18	1	0	1	33

Sources: Hockey Hall of Fame; Hockey-Reference.com

Dye, Cecil Henry "Babe" (born: May 13, 1898 in Hamilton, Ontario, Canada; died: January 2, 1962 in Chicago, Illinois); inducted into the Hockey Hall of Fame in 1970 as a player; Position: Forward; won the 1922 Stanley Cup championship; retired with the best goals-to-games ratio in the history of the NHL at the time.

Dye played 11 National Hockey League seasons with the Toronto St. Pats (Toronto Maple Leafs, 1919–1926); one game with the Hamilton Tigers; Chicago Black Hawks (1926–1928); New York Americans (1928–1929); and the Toronto Maple Leafs (1930–1931). In his first six NHL seasons, Dye scored 176 goals in 170 games, a pace that would not be equaled until Wayne Gretzky's performance in the 1980s.

An all-around athlete, the 5'8", 150-pound Dye played halfback for the Toronto Argonauts (Canadian Football League), and in the outfield for the Baltimore Orioles, Buffalo Bisons, and the Toronto Maple Leafs in the International League.

He joined the Toronto St. Pats in 1918 (Ontario Hockey Association) and led the team to a league championship. Between 1920 and 1925, he led the NHL in scoring three times; scored goals in 11 consecutive games twice; and in the 1924–1925 season, scored 38 goals, a Toronto record that stood for 35 years, until surpassed by Frank Mahovlich.

In the 1922 Stanley Cup playoffs, Dye scored two game-winning goals and nine of the team's 16 total goals (still a Stanley Cup finals record) as he led the squad to a five-game series win over the Vancouver Millionaires, his only championship.

After playing for the Black Hawks, the Americans, and the Leafs, he retired with the best goals-to-games ratio in the history of the NHL up to that time; won the Art Ross Trophy twice as the league's scoring leader (1923, 1925); and in 1998, he was ranked number 83 on *The Hockey News*' list of the 100 Greatest Hockey Players.

Following his retirement as a player, Dye became head coach of the Chicago Shamrocks (American Hockey Association) in the 1931–1932 season, and led the team to the league title.

Cecil Dye's Career Statistics

			REGULAR SEASON					PLAYOFFS				
SEASON	**TEAM**	**LEAGUE**	**GP**	**G**	**A**	**TP**	**PIM**	**GP**	**G**	**A**	**TP**	**PIM**
1916–1917	Toronto Aura Lee	OHA-Jr.	8	31	0	31						
1917–1918	Toronto De La Salle	OHA-Jr.										
1918–1919	Toronto St. Pats	OHA-Sr.	9	13	1	14		2	3	0	3	0
1919–1920	Toronto St. Pats	NHL	23	11	3	14	10					
1920–1921	Hamilton Tigers	NHL	1	2	0	2	0					
1920–1921	Toronto St. Pats	NHL	23	33	5	38	32	2	0	0	0	7
1921–1922	Toronto St. Pats	NHL	24	31	7	38	39	2	2	0	2	2
1921–1922	Toronto St. Pats	St-Cup						5	9	1	10	3
1922–1923	Toronto St. Pats	NHL	22	26	11	37	19					
1923–1924	Toronto St. Pats	NHL	19	16	3	19	23					
1924–1925	Toronto St. Pats	NHL	29	38	8	46	41	2	0	0	0	0
1925–1926	Toronto St. Pats	NHL	31	18	5	23	26					
1926–1927	Chicago Black Hawks	NHL	41	25	5	30	14	2	0	0	0	2
1927–1928	Chicago Black Hawks	NHL	10	0	0	0	0					
1928–1929	New York Americans	NHL	42	1	0	1	17	2	0	0	0	0
1929–1930	New Haven Eagles	Can-Am	34	11	4	15	16					
1930–1931	Toronto Maple Leafs	NHL	6	0	0	0	0					
1930–1931	St. Louis Flyers	AHA										
1931–1932	Chicago Shamrocks	AHA										
	NHL TOTALS		271	201	47	248	221	10	2	0	2	11

Sources: Hockey Hall of Fame; Hockey-Reference.com

Chapter 5
Eckersley to Ewing

Eckersley, Dennis Lee (born: October 3, 1954 in Oakland, California); inducted into the National Baseball Hall of Fame and Museum in 2004 as a player; Position: Pitcher; Bats: Right; Throws: Right; Uniform: #43; first of only two pitchers in major league history to have both a 20-win season and a 50-save season in a career; only pitcher with 100 saves and 100 complete games; only relief pitcher in baseball history to have more saves than base runners allowed in a single season (1990).

Making his major league debut on April 12, 1975, Eckersley (nicknamed "The Eck") played 24 seasons with the Cleveland Indians (1975–1977), Boston Red Sox (1978–1984, 1998), Chicago Cubs (1984–1986), Oakland A's (1987–1995), and the St. Louis Cardinals (1996–1997). He played in three consecutive World Series (winning in 1989 and losing in 1988 and 1990); was a six-time All-Star (1977, 1982, 1988, 1990–1992); American League Most Valuable Player in 1992; American League Cy Young winner in 1992, and a two-time winner of the Rolaids Relief Man Award (1988, 1992).

In his first major league game, Eckersley threw a three-hit shutout in a 6–0 win over the Oakland Athletics, a team for which he would later enjoy great success.

In the first half of his career, Eckersley won over 150 games, primarily as a starter, including a no-hitter in 1977 (a 1–0 win over the California Angels on May 30, 1977 with 12 strikeouts). However, he is more well-known for his last 12 seasons when he became one of major league baseball's premier relief pitchers, saving nearly 390 games. He is the only pitcher with 100 saves and 100 complete games, and in his last 10 seasons, he only walked 86 batters in more than 600 innings pitched. Eckersley was the first of only two pitchers in major league history to have both a 20-win season (1978) and a 50-save season (1992) in a career (the other being John Smoltz).

For all his success, to most baseball fans, he is probably best remembered for giving up Kirk Gibson's dramatic game-winning home run in Game 1 of the 1988 World Series, which led to the Dodgers winning the Series over a heavily-favored Athletics team.

The 6'2", 190-pound Eckersley was drafted by the Cleveland Indians out of Washington High School (Fremont, California) in the third round of the 1972 amateur draft (50th selection overall), and in his rookie year, he compiled a 13–7 record and 2.60 Earned Run Average.

After starting for the Indians, Red Sox, and the Cubs, he was traded to the Athletics in 1987, where he was converted to a closer, and became the first reliever used primarily to protect a ninth inning lead, a role that is now common in baseball.

Eckersley walked only three batters in 1989; posted a remarkable 0.61 ERA in 1990; and in that same year became the only relief pitcher in baseball history to have more saves (48) than base runners allowed (41 hits, 4 walks).

When he retired in 1998, Eckersley's 390 career saves were fifth on the all-time list.

Dennis Eckersley's Career Statistics

YEAR	TEAM	LG	W	L	PCT	G	SH	SV	IP	H	R	ER	SO	BB	ERA
1975	Cleveland	AL	13	7	.650	34	2	2	186	147	61	54	152	90	2.60
1976	Cleveland	AL	13	12	.520	36	3	1	199	155	82	76	200	78	3.43
1977	Cleveland	AL	14	13	.519	33	3	0	247	214	100	97	191	54	3.53
1978	Boston	AL	20	8	.714	35	3	0	268	258	99	89	162	71	2.99
1979	Boston	AL	17	10	.630	33	2	0	246	234	89	82	150	59	2.99

YEAR	TEAM	LG	W	L	PCT	G	SH	SV	IP	H	R	ER	SO	BB	ERA
1980	Boston	AL	12	14	.462	30	0	0	197	188	101	94	121	44	4.28
1981	Boston	AL	9	8	.529	23	2	0	154	160	82	73	79	35	4.27
1982	Boston	AL	13	13	.500	33	3	0	224	228	101	93	127	43	3.73
1983	Boston	AL	9	13	.409	28	0	0	176	223	119	110	77	39	5.61
1984	Boston/Chicago		14	12	.538	33	0	0	225	223	97	90	114	49	3.60
1984	Boston	AL	4	4	.500	4	0	0	65	71	38	36	33	13	5.01
1984	Chicago	NL	10	8	.556	24	0	0	160	152	59	54	81	36	3.05
1985	Chicago	NL	11	7	.611	25	2	0	169	145	61	58	117	19	3.08
1986	Chicago	NL	6	11	.353	33	0	0	201	226	109	102	137	43	4.57
1987	Oakland	AL	6	8	.429	54	0	16	115	99	41	39	113	17	3.03
1988	Oakland	AL	4	2	.667	60	0	45	72	52	20	19	70	11	2.35
1989	Oakland	AL	4	0	1.000	51	0	33	57	32	10	10	55	3	1.56
1990	Oakland	AL	4	2	.667	63	0	48	73	41	9	5	73	4	0.61
1991	Oakland	AL	5	4	.556	67	0	43	76	60	26	25	87	9	2.96
1992	Oakland	AL	7	1	.875	69	0	51	80	62	17	17	93	11	1.91
1993	Oakland	AL	2	4	.333	64	0	36	67	67	32	31	80	13	4.16
1994	Oakland	AL	5	4	.556	45	0	19	44	49	26	21	47	13	4.26
1995	Oakland	AL	4	6	.400	52	0	29	50	53	29	27	40	11	4.83
1996	St. Louis	NL	0	6	.000	63	0	30	60	65	26	22	49	6	3.30
1997	St. Louis	NL	1	5	.167	57	0	36	53	49	24	23	45	8	3.91
1998	St. Louis	NL	4	1	.800	50	0	1	39	46	21	21	22	8	4.76
	TOTALS		197	171	.535	1,071	20	390	3,285	3,076	1,382	1,278	2,401	738	3.50

Sources: Baseball-Reference.com; National Baseball Hall of Fame and Museum

Edwards, Albert Glen "Turk" (born: September 28, 1907 in Mold, Washington; died: January 12, 1973 in Kirkland, Washington); inducted into the Pro Football Hall of Fame in 1969 as a player; Position: Tackle; named to the NFL 1930s All-Decade Team.

After graduating from Clarkston (Washington) High School, the 6'2", 255-pound Edwards was an All-American tackle in 1930 and played in the 1931 Rose Bowl for Washington State University (Pullman). He joined the National Football League's Boston Braves in 1932 and would go on to play for the Boston Redskins (1933–1936) and the Washington Redskins (1937–1940). After the Boston Braves changed the team name to the Redskins and eventually moved to Washington, D.C. in 1937, he was named to the NFL 1930s All-Decade Team.

Although Edwards played both sides of the ball for 60 minutes and was named All-National Football League four times (1932–1933, 1936–1937), his career ended bizarrely when he suffered a freak knee injury after a pregame coin toss on September 22, 1940 against the New York Giants. Heading back to the sidelines after the coin toss, his cleats caught in the grass and his already damaged knee was injured, bringing a sudden end to his career.

After recovering from his injury, Edwards stayed with the Redskins, first as an assistant coach and then as head coach until after the 1946 season, when he retired from the game.

He was inducted into the College Football Hall of Fame in 1975.

Sources: College Football Hall of Fame; Pro Football Hall of Fame

Edwards, Gene (born: September 16, 1917 in Milwaukee, Wisconsin; died: March 28, 2000 in Milwaukee, Wisconsin); inducted into the National Soccer Hall of Fame and Museum in 1985 as a builder; served as president of the United States Soccer Football Association.

Edwards began playing soccer at age eight in Milwaukee and eventually joined a team sponsored by the Falk Corporation, which reached the 1941 national semifinals of the National Amateur Cup.

He served in the Marine Corps during World War II; was wounded at Okinawa; and when discharged from the military, he joined the Swedish-American team of the National League of Chicago, and played for the squad from 1945 to 1953, before returning to Milwaukee and playing for the Milwaukee Brewers and the Milwaukee Sport Club.

He was elected to the National Board of Directors of the United States Soccer Football Association as a third vice president in 1968, and was second and first vice president until 1974, when he assumed the presidency. He also served as president of the U.S. Soccer Federation from 1974 to 1984; was a member of the Fédération Internationale de Football Association Amateur Committee; a member of the Confederation of North, Central American and Caribbean Association Football Executive Committee; served on the Executive Committee of the United States Olympic Committee; and was manager of the United States teams at the 1971 (Cali, Colombia), the 1975 Pan American Games (Mexico City, Mexico), and the 1972 Olympic Games in Munich, Germany.

Source: National Soccer Hall of Fame and Museum

Eller, Carl Lee (born: January 25, 1942 in Winston-Salem, North Carolina); inducted into the Pro Football Hall of Fame in 2004 as a player; Position: Defensive End; won the George Halas Award.

After playing football at Atkins (Winston-Salem, North Carolina) High School, and then being a consensus All-American at the University of Minnesota (Minneapolis), Eller was a 1964 first-round draft pick (sixth overall selection) of both the National Football League's Minnesota Vikings and the American Football League's Buffalo Bills. He signed with the Vikings and played for the team from 1964 to 1978, before playing one season with the Seattle Seahawks in 1979, before retiring after 16 seasons and 225 games.

At 6'6", 247 pounds, Eller established himself as the left defensive end on the famed Vikings' "Purple People Eaters" defensive line, along with Jim Marshall, Alan Page, and Gary Larsen. He accumulated 44 sacks in three years (1975–1977); was named First- or Second-Team All-NFL seven consecutive seasons (1967–1973); played in six Pro Bowls (1969–1972, 1974–1975); and won the George Halas Award in 1971 as the NFL's leading defensive player.

While Eller was with the team, Minnesota won 10 NFL/NFC Central Division titles; the 1969 NFL championship and NFC crowns in 1973, 1974, and 1976; and played in four Super Bowls, losing them all (Super Bowl IV in 1970, Super Bowl VIII in 1974, Super Bowl IX in 1975, Super Bowl XI in 1977).

Eller recovered 23 fumbles (third best in NFL history at the time he retired), and he caused the now-famous fumble that led to teammate Jim Marshall's wrong-way run for a safety in a game against the San Francisco 49ers on October 25, 1964.

He was selected to the NFL's 1970s All-Decade Team, and in 2006, he was inducted into the College Football Hall of Fame.

As a sophomore in college, Eller helped lead the Gophers to a 21–3 Rose Bowl win over UCLA in 1962; became a two-way player as a junior; and was an All-American as a junior and senior. During his time in college, the Gophers were both National and Big Ten champions in 1960. The Carl Eller Award is presented annually to the University of Minnesota's Defensive Player of the Year.

Sources: College Football Hall of Fame; Pro Football Hall of Fame

Elliott, Edwin S. "Chaucer" (born: 1879 in Kingston, Ontario, Canada; died: March 13, 1913); inducted into the Hockey Hall of Fame in 1961 as an on-ice official; began his referee career in 1903.

Elliott began his career as a hockey referee in 1903 in the Ontario Hockey Association, where he served for 10 years before dying of cancer at age 34.

While at Queen's University (Kingston, Ontario, Canada), he was captain of the football team for two years, and played for the school's hockey team, while also playing for the Kingston Granites, winners of the Canadian championship in 1899.

Leaving school before graduating, Elliott managed a semi-professional baseball team in Kingston, and coached the Toronto Argonauts (Ontario Rugby Football Union) in 1906, before taking the Hamilton Tigers to a Canadian championship later in 1906.

In 1907, Elliott was named coach of the Montreal AAA team, where he stayed until 1911, before managing the St. Thomas Saints baseball team of the Canadian League.

Source: Hockey Hall of Fame

Elway, John Albert, Jr. (born: June 28, 1960 in Port Angeles, Washington); inducted into the Pro Football Hall of Fame in 2004; Position: Quarterback; Uniform: #7; first Denver Bronco's player to be inducted into the football hall of fame; first quarterback to start in five Super Bowls.

Elway was the first overall pick in the 1983 draft by the National Football League's Baltimore Colts. However, he refused to play for the Colts and was traded to the Denver Broncos, where he would play his entire 16-year (234 games) career (1983–1998).

He led the Broncos to an NFL-record 47 fourth-quarter comebacks; was named the NFL's Most Valuable Player in 1987; named All-Pro in 1987 and to the Second-Team All-NFL three times; was named All-AFC four times; and was selected to nine Pro Bowls (1987–1988, 1990, 1992, 1994–1995, 1997–1999).

He played in five Super Bowls (winning twice [Super Bowl XXXII in 1998 and Super Bowl XXXIII in 1999] and losing three times [Super Bowl XXI in 1987, Super Bowl XXII in 1988, Super Bowl XXIV in 1990]); and was named Most Valuable Player of Super Bowl XXXIII.

The 6'3", 215–pound Elway is the only player in NFL history to pass for more than 3,000 yards and rush for more than 200 yards in the same season seven consecutive times; was only the second quarterback in NFL history to record more than 40,000 yards passing and 3,000 yards rushing during his career; ranks second all-time in passing yards (51,475), attempts (7,250), and completions (4,123); and was selected to the NFL 1990s All-Decade Team.

At Granada Hills (California) High School, he completed 60% of his passes and threw for 5,711 yards (49 touchdowns) over his four-year career. As a senior (1979), he was recruited by college football scouts and was drafted in the 18th round by Major League Baseball's Kansas City Royals. Deciding against a professional baseball career, Elway attended Stanford University (Palo Alto, California), where he set National Collegiate Athletic Association Division I career records for passing attempts and completions; had 30 games with more than 200 yards passing; in four years, he threw for 9,349 yards and 77 touchdowns; and was named an All-American in his senior year.

In 1981, he was a first-round pick of MLB's New York Yankees, and in 1982, he played for the team's single-A farm club (Oneonta Yankees) in the New York-Penn League, before leaving the game to pursue a football career.

His last college football game will forever be known as having one of the most famous endings of all time. With Stanford just having scored and leading the California Bears (Berkeley) 20–19 with only seconds remaining, the Bears returned the kickoff and made five lateral passes to score the game-winning touchdown as time expired. The ending of the game was made famous by the fact that the Stanford band had moved onto the field and California Bears players had to maneuver around (and over) them in order to score the implausible winning touchdown. The play lives forever in the video age and is always ranked near the top of any poll as one of the greatest and most exciting finishes in college football history.

Although Elway never played in a college bowl game, his 24 touchdown passes in 1982 led the nation, and he graduated with almost every Stanford and Pacific-10 career record for passing and total offense. He won Pac-10 Player of the Year twice (1980, 1982); was a consensus All-American; and was inducted into the College Football Hall of Fame in 2000.

In addition to his college football career, Elway was also an outstanding baseball player, and in his senior year, he hit .361 with nine home runs and 50 runs batted in during 49 games, while pitching to a 5–4 record with a 4.51 earned run average.

In his rookie NFL season, Elway started 10 games and finished the year as the NFL's 17th-ranked quarterback. After losing three Super Bowls, Elway led Denver to consecutive championships before retiring (a 31–24 win over the Green Bay Packers in Super Bowl XXXII [1998] and a 34–19 win over the Atlanta Falcons in Super Bowl XXXIII).

When he retired, Elway held numerous NFL records, including most games won as a starting quarterback (148); most game-tying or game-winning drives in the fourth quarter (47); 50,000+ career passing yards; 3,000+ career rushing yards; and seven consecutive seasons with 3,000+ passing yards and 200+ rushing yards. He also holds numerous Broncos franchise records, including most total offensive yards (54,882; 51,475 passing, 3,407 rushing); most total touchdowns (334; 300 passing, 33 rushing, 1 receiving); most total plays (8,027); winning percentage (.643; 148-82-1); most career passing yards (51,475); most career completions (4,123); most career passing attempts (7,250); and most touchdown passes (300).

In 1999, his jersey number 7 was retired by the Broncos; his name was added to the Denver Broncos Ring of Fame; he was inducted into the Colorado Sports Hall of Fame; and he was ranked number 16 on *The Sporting News*' list of the 100 Greatest Football Players.

Since 2002, Elway has been a co-owner of the Colorado Crush (Arena Football League), and in 2007, he was elected chairman of the Arena Football League's executive committee.

John Elway's Career Statistics

					PASSING					RUSHING		
YEAR	**TEAM**	**G**	**ATT**	**COMP**	**YDS**	**TDS**	**INT**	**RATING**	**NO**	**YDS**	**AVG**	**TD**
1983	Denver	11	259	123	1,663	7	14	54.9	28	146	5.2	1

YEAR	TEAM	G	ATT	COMP	PASSING YDS	TDS	INT	RATING	NO	RUSHING YDS	AVG	TD
1984	Denver	15	380	214	2,598	18	15	76.8	56	237	4.2	1
1985	Denver	16	605	327	3,891	22	23	70.2	51	253	5	0
1986	Denver	16	504	280	3,485	19	13	79.0	52	257	4.9	1
1987	Denver	12	410	224	3,198	19	12	83.4	66	304	4.6	4
1988	Denver	15	496	274	3,309	17	19	71.4	54	234	4.3	1
1989	Denver	15	416	223	3,051	18	18	73.7	48	244	5.1	3
1990	Denver	16	502	294	3,526	15	14	78.5	50	258	5.2	3
1991	Denver	16	451	242	3,253	13	12	75.4	55	255	4.6	6
1992	Denver	12	316	174	2,242	10	17	65.7	34	94	2.8	2
1993	Denver	16	551	348	4,030	25	10	92.8	44	153	3.5	0
1994	Denver	14	494	307	3,490	16	10	85.7	58	235	4.1	4
1995	Denver	16	542	316	3,970	26	14	86.4	41	176	4.3	1
1996	Denver	15	466	287	3,328	26	14	89.2	50	249	5	4
1997	Denver	16	502	280	3,635	27	11	87.5	50	218	4.4	1
1998	Denver	13	356	210	2,806	22	10	93.0	37	94	2.5	1
	TOTALS	234	7,250	4,123	51,475	300	226	79.9	774	3,407	4.4	33

Sources: Bay Area Sports Hall of Fame; College Football Hall of Fame; Colorado Sports Hall of Fame; John Elway's Web Site (www.johnelway.com); Pro Football Hall of Fame; Pro-Football-Reference.com

Ely, Alexandre (born: February 9, 1938 in Sao Paulo, Brazil); inducted into the National Soccer Hall of Fame and Museum in 1997 as a player; Position: Half Back; International Caps (1960–1965): 4; International Goals: 0; won two U.S. Open titles.

Ely began his career in 1958 in the amateur Philadelphia United Soccer League, before playing with the Philadelphia Ukrainian Nationals of the American Soccer League from 1959 to 1965. While with the team, he won four league championships and two U.S. Open Cup titles. During the ASL off-seasons, he played with a variety of teams, including the New York Americans (International Soccer League, 1960); Toronto Roma (Eastern Canada League, 1961–1962); and Toronto City (Eastern Canada League, 1964–1965).

He was on the Ukrainian team that won U.S. Open Cup championships in 1960 and 1963 (lost the title game in 1964); played four World Cup qualifying-round games for the United States (all against Mexico, two in 1960 and two in 1965); and played four games for the bronze medal-winning Pan American Games (Chicago, Illinois) team in 1959.

He returned to the ASL in 1972 as a player-coach for the Philadelphia Spartans for four seasons, and retired in 1976 after one season with the Delaware Wings.

His coaching career lasted 37 years, beginning as an assistant at the University of Maryland (College Park, 1960–1965). He later coached the Philadelphia Spartans (1972); Monsignor Bonner High School (Drexel Hill, Pennsylvania, 1972–1976); Archbishop John Carroll High School (Radnor, Pennsylvania, 1981–1994); and served as the women's head coach at Swarthmore College (Pennsylvania, 1996–1997), compiling an 11–26–3 record.

He founded the America Kolping Soccer Club in 1975; served as the team's head coach for twenty years; and was inducted into the Eastern Pennsylvania Soccer Hall of Fame in 1997.

Source: National Soccer Hall of Fame and Museum

Embry, Wayne Richard (born: March 26, 1937 in Springfield, Ohio); inducted into the Naismith Memorial Basketball Hall of Fame in 1999 as a contributor; won the 1968 NBA title; first African-American NBA general manager.

Embry attended Tecumseh High School (Springfield, Ohio) from 1951 to 1954, where he was a three-year letter winner; selected All-Conference three straight years (1952–1954); and won All-State Honorable Mention honors. After graduating, he went to Miami University (Oxford, Ohio, 1954–1958), where he was a three-year letter winner; a two-time All-Mid-American Conference selection; Honorable Mention All-American (1957–1958); was the team's high scorer, captain, and Most Valuable Player twice (1957–1958); and was the fourth player in school history to have a jersey (#23) retired.

After college, Embry played 11 years in the National Basketball Association as a center-forward with the Cincinnati Royals (1958–1966), Boston Celtics (1966–1968), and Milwaukee Bucks (1968–1969). He was an NBA All-Star five consecutive years (1961–1965); team captain with the Royals (1962–1966); first captain of the Bucks (1968–1969); and won an NBA championship with the Celtics (1968).

He was the first African-American NBA general manager (with the Milwaukee Bucks from 1971 to 1979); was vice-president and general manager of the Cleveland Cavaliers (1985–1992); executive vice-president of the Cleveland Cavaliers (1992–1994); general manager of the Cavaliers (1992–1999); and was the first African-American NBA team president and chief operating officer (Cleveland Cavaliers, 1994–1999).

Embry was named *The Sporting News* NBA Executive of the Year twice (1992, 1998), and in 1998, he was inducted into the Cleveland Sports Stars Hall of Fame.

Source: Naismith Memorial Basketball Hall of Fame

Endacott, Paul (born: July 3, 1902 in Lawrence, Kansas; died: January 8, 1997); inducted into the Naismith Memorial Basketball Hall of Fame in 1972 as a player; Position: Guard; won two Helms Foundation national championships.

Endacott attended Lawrence (Kansas) High School from 1915 to 1919, where he was a three-year letter winner (1917–1919) and was selected All-State in 1919. After high school, he went to the University of Kansas (Lawrence) from 1919 to 1923, where he played three seasons under hall of fame coach Phog Allen (1921–1923); was named Helms Foundation Player of the Year (1923); led Kansas to the Helms Foundation national championship twice (1922–1923); was named First Team All-Missouri Valley Conference twice (1922–1923); Second Team All-Missouri Valley Conference (1921); member of the All-Time University of Kansas Team as selected by Dr. James Naismith (1924); and was named to Phog Allen's national All-Time College Team.

After college, Endacott played amateur basketball in the Amateur Athletic Union for the Phillips Petroleum Company Team from 1924 to 1928.

He first learned basketball directly from the game's inventor, James Naismith, at the Lawrence YMCA, and then played for the game's first full-time coach, Phog Allen, at the University of Kansas.

Source: Naismith Memorial Basketball Hall of Fame

English, Alex (born: January 5, 1954 in Columbia, South Carolina); inducted into the Naismith Memorial Basketball Hall of Fame in 1997 as a player; Position: Forward; Uniform: #2; first player in National Basketball Association history to score 2,000 points in eight straight seasons; led the NBA in scoring during the 1980s.

English attended Dreher High School (Columbia, South Carolina) from 1968 to 1972, where he was a four-year letter winner; set all-time scoring records; was a three-time All-State selection (1970–1972); and had his jersey #22 retired by the school.

After high school, he went to the University of South Carolina (Columbia) from 1972 to 1976, where he was a two-time All-American (1975–1976); ranks first in school history in scoring (1,972 points, 17.8 per game); is one of only five players in school history to score 1,000 points and grab 1,000 rebounds; played the most minutes in school history (4,113); holds team records for most field goals attempted (1,590) and most field goals made (855); and played in one National Invitation Tournament and two National Collegiate Athletic Association tournaments.

After college, the 6'8", 190-pound English played 16 professional seasons including 15 with the National Basketball Association's Milwaukee Bucks (1976–1978), Indiana Pacers (1978–1980), Denver Nuggets (1980–1990), and the Dallas Mavericks (1990–1991). After leaving the NBA, he played one more professional season in the Italian League with Depi Napoli (1991–1992). He was named to the All-NBA Second Team three times (1982–1983, 1986); was the NBA's leading scorer in the 1980s (19,682 points); his 25,613 points was seventh best in NBA history when he retired; first player in NBA history to score 2,000 points in eight straight seasons; was an eight-time NBA All-Star (1982–1989); and set numerous Denver Nuggets records, including points scored (21,645), games played (837), assists (3,679), scoring average (25.9 per game), and minutes played (29,893).

He led Denver to nine consecutive playoff appearances; two Midwest Division titles (1985, 1988); the Western Conference Finals (1985); won the NBA's 1988 J. Walter Kennedy Citizenship Award; and had his jersey number two retired by the Nuggets in 1993.

English has been inducted into the University of South Carolina Hall of Fame and the Colorado Sports Hall of Fame, and was awarded the Algernon Sydney Sullivan Award for Citizenship by the University of South Carolina.

After spending one season each as an assistant coach with the Philadelphia 76ers and Atlanta Hawks, in 2004 he was hired as the director of player development and an assistant coach for the Toronto Raptors.

Alex English's NBA Career Statistics

SEASON	TEAM	G	MIN	FG	3P	FT	TRB	AST	STL	BLK	PTS
1976–1977	Milwaukee	60	648	132		46	168	25	17	18	310

SEASON	TEAM	G	MIN	FG	3P	FT	TRB	AST	STL	BLK	PTS
1977–1978	Milwaukee	82	1,552	343		104	395	129	41	55	790
1978–1979	Indiana	81	2,696	563		173	655	271	70	78	1,299
1979–1980	Indiana	54	1,526	346	0	114	380	142	45	33	806
1979–1980	Denver	24	875	207	2	96	225	82	28	29	512
1980–1981	Denver	81	3,093	768	3	390	646	290	106	100	1,929
1981–1982	Denver	82	3,015	855	0	372	558	433	87	120	2,082
1982–1983	Denver	82	2,988	959	2	406	601	397	116	126	2,326
1983–1984	Denver	82	2,870	907	1	352	464	406	83	95	2,167
1984–1985	Denver	81	2,924	939	1	383	458	344	101	46	2,262
1985–1986	Denver	81	3,024	951	1	511	405	320	73	29	2,414
1986–1987	Denver	82	3,085	965	4	411	344	422	73	21	2,345
1987–1988	Denver	80	2,818	843	0	314	373	377	70	23	2,000
1988–1989	Denver	82	2,990	924	2	325	326	383	66	12	2,175
1989–1990	Denver	80	2,211	635	2	161	286	225	51	23	1,433
1990–1991	Dallas	79	1,748	322	0	119	254	105	40	25	763
	TOTALS	1,193	38,063	10,659	18	4,277	6,538	4,351	1,067	833	25,613

Sources: Basketball-Reference.com; Naismith Memorial Basketball Hall of Fame

Enright, James E. (born: April 3, 1910 in Sodus, Michigan; died: December 20, 1981); inducted into the Naismith Memorial Basketball Hall of Fame in 1978 as a referee; served as an official at the high school, college, professional, AAU, and Olympic levels.

Enright attended Eau Claire (Michigan) High School and graduated in 1928, where he played basketball for three years, and was a two-time captain.

Deciding not to go to college in 1930, he became a sportswriter for *The News Palladium* in Benton Harbor, Michigan, and eventually was asked to substitute for an official who was not able to make the game due to inclement weather. This opportunity led to a 30-year career, in which Enright worked at the high school, college, professional, Amateur Athletic Union, and Olympic levels. While an on-court official, he continued to work as a sportswriter for *The News Palladium* (1928–1937) and the *Chicago Evening American* (which became *Chicago Today*) from 1937 until he died.

Starting in 1944, he worked for Major League Baseball, and was the official scorer for two MLB All-Star Games (1950, 1962). He regularly officiated in the Big Ten, Big Eight, and Missouri Valley conferences, and spent one year with the National Basketball League and the National Basketball Association.

Enright officiated in two NCAA regional tournaments (1952–1953) and one Final Four (1954); two Olympic playoffs (1948, 1952); was named Referee of the Year by the Knute Rockne Club of America in Kansas City (1956); and was selected to represent the U.S. in two Air Force basketball clinics in England and Germany (1958, 1968).

After retiring in 1964, Enright continued to work as a sportswriter; was a member of the United States Basketball Writers Association; USBWA National President (1967–1968); president of the organization's Chicago chapter for three terms; and was named the Chicago Baseball Writer of the Year by the Horse Shoe Club (1970).

He received the Old Timers Official Association Award for dedication to basketball officiating (1968); was the co-author of *Ernie Banks, "Mr. Cub"*; wrote for *The Sporting News*, NCAA and Dell Publications; and served as editor of "Official Read-Easy Basketball Rules."

Source: Naismith Memorial Basketball Hall of Fame

Epperlein, Rudy (born: date unknown in Germany); inducted into the National Soccer Hall of Fame and Museum in 1951 as a builder; strong supporter of the game in the Buffalo, New York area.

Epperlein moved to the United States as a boy, and for 25 years was a strong supporter of soccer in the Buffalo, New York area. He was associated with the Buffalo Beck's (Western Division of the National Cup competitions, and in 1950, he promoted a game between the Beck's and Eintract Frankfurt (West Germany), which resulted in a 31–1 loss for Buffalo.

Source: National Soccer Hall of Fame and Museum

Ertegün, Ahmet (born: July 31, 1923 in Istanbul, Turkey; died: December 14, 2006 in New York, New York); inducted into the National Soccer Hall of Fame and Museum in 2003 as a builder; co-founder of the New York Cosmos.

Ertegün was one of the founders, with his brother, Nesuhi, of the New York Cosmos (North American Soccer League); vice-president of the team from 1971 to 1977; and president from 1978 to 1983. Under his leadership, the Cosmos appeared in the playoffs 11 times; advanced to the Soccer Bowl five times; and were NASL Champions five times (1972, 1977–1978, 1980, 1982).

The star-studded Cosmos team (with legends like Pelé playing for it) toured the world and became the most famous American professional soccer team in history.

Outside of the soccer world, Ertegün is more well-known as one of the founders of Atlantic Records in 1947 with his partner, Herb Abramson. His company was one of music's largest independent labels that attempted to challenge the more established labels of the time, including RCA, Columbia, and Decca. Under his guidance, Atlantic featured such artists as Ray Charles, the Coasters, and the Clovers; he produced or co-produced the majority of records released on the label; and wrote songs in the early days using the pseudonym "Nugetre" (Ertegün spelled backwards).

Born in Istanbul, Turkey, Ertegün and his family moved to Washington, D.C. in 1935 with his father, Münir, was appointed the Turkish Ambassador to the United States.

He graduated from St. John's College (Annapolis, Maryland) in 1944; formed Atlantic three years later; was one of the first labels to record in stereo; and in the 1960s, signed such artists as Led Zeppelin and Crosby, Stills, Nash & Young.

In 1967, the Ertegün brothers sold Atlantic to Warner Bros-Seven Arts, and four years later, used some of the money to co-found the New York Cosmos.

Ertegün was one of the co-founders of the Rock & Roll Hall of Fame (Cleveland, Ohio), and was inducted in 1987 as a pioneer-executive. He was awarded the Grammy Trustees Award for his lifetime achievements in 1993, and in 2005, the National Academy of Recording Arts and Sciences presented him with its first-ever "President's Merit Award Salute To Industry Icons."

Source: National Soccer Hall of Fame and Museum

Ertegün, Nesuhi (born: November 26, 1917 in Istanbul, Turkey; died: July 15, 1989 in New York, New York); inducted into the National Soccer Hall of Fame and Museum in 2003 as a builder; co-founder of the New York Cosmos.

Ertegün and his brother, Ahmet, were co-founders of the New York Cosmos (North American Soccer League). Under their leadership, the Cosmos appeared in the playoffs 11 times; advanced to the Soccer Bowl five times; and were NASL Champions five times (1972, 1977–1978, 1980, 1982).

The star-studded Cosmos team (with legends like Pelé playing for it) toured the world and became the most famous American professional soccer team in history.

Born in Istanbul, Turkey, Ertegün and his family moved to Washington, D.C. in 1935 when his father, Münir, was appointed the Turkish Ambassador to the United States.

When his father died in 1944, Ertegün moved to California and took over the Jazz Man Record Shop in Los Angeles; produced his own music on the Jazz Man and Crescent labels; served as the editor of *Record Changer* magazine; and from 1951 to 1954, taught at the University of California at Los Angeles, the first history of jazz course ever offered by a major American university.

In 1955, he joined his brother, Ahmet, at Atlantic Records as a partner; became vice-president in charge of the jazz and LP (album) department; built the label's catalog of jazz LPs; and produced hit records for Ray Charles, the Drifters, Bobby Darin, and Roberta Flack.

In 1971, he founded WEA International (now known as Warner Music International), which became the international distributor for all music on the Warner Brothers, Atlantic, Elektra, Geffen, and MCA labels. He was the company's chairman and chief executive from 1971 to 1987, before starting a new label, East-West Records, specializing in jazz.

Ertegün was the first president of the National Academy of Recording Arts and Sciences, which presents the Grammy awards; served as chairman of the International Federation of Phonographic Industries; was inducted into the Rock & Roll Hall of Fame in 1991; was awarded the Grammy Trustees Award for lifetime achievements in 1995; and the Nesuhi Ertegün Jazz Hall of Fame at Lincoln Center was dedicated to him in 2004.

Source: National Soccer Hall of Fame and Museum

Erving, Julius Winfield II (born: February 22, 1950 in East Meadow, New York); inducted into the Naismith Memorial Basketball Hall of Fame in 1993 as a player; Position: Forward; Uniform: #36, #32; in college, he averaged more than 20 points and 20 rebounds per game; won two ABA championships and one NBA title.

Erving played basketball at Roosevelt (New York) High School from 1964 to 1968; was selected All-Conference twice (1967–1968); and won the Outstanding Player Award. After high school, he went to the University of Massachusetts (Amherst) from 1968 to 1971, where he was one of only six players in National Collegiate Athletic Association history to average more than 20 points and 20 rebounds per game.

He was selected All-American and All-Yankee Conference twice (1970–1971); despite playing for only two varsity seasons (52 games), he holds or shares 14 university records; finished his career with 1,370 points, best in school history; ended his college career with 1,049 rebounds, best in school history; and was inducted into the University of Massachusetts Hall of Fame in 1980.

After college, Erving started his 16-year professional career in the American Basketball Association with the Virginia Squires (1971–1973) and the New York Nets (1973–1976), before entering the National Basketball Association, playing for the Philadelphia 76ers (1976–1987). During his career, he was named to the ABA All-Rookie Team; was ABA Most Valuable Player twice (1974, 1976); was a four-time ABA First Team All-Star (1973–1976); won two ABA championships with the New York Nets (1974, 1976); led the ABA in scoring three times (1973–1974, 1976); was a five-time ABA All–Star (1972–1976); and holds the career record for highest scoring average (28.7 points per game) in a minimum of 250 games.

The 6'7", 210-pound Erving was named NBA MVP in 1981; led the 76ers to an NBA championship in 1983; selected First Team All-NBA five times (1978, 1980–1983) and to the Second Team All-NBA twice (1977, 1984); appeared in 11 NBA All-Star Games (1977–1987); was a two-time All-Star Game MVP (1977, 1983); and when enshrined into the hall, was one of only three players in professional basketball history to score more than 30,000 career points.

His jersey was retired by both the Nets (#32) and the 76ers (#6); was named a member of the NBA 35th Anniversary All-Time Team (1980); a member of the NBA 50th Anniversary All-Time Team (1996); won the Walter J. Kennedy Citizenship Award in 1983; and won the Jackie Robinson Award presented by *Ebony* magazine in 1983.

He earned his nickname, "Dr. J.," while in college and was known for being able to leap in the air from behind the foul line and dunk the basketball.

After retiring, Erving became a studio analyst of NBA games on NBC, and in June 1997, he became the executive vice-president of the NBA's Orlando Magic.

He was ranked #10 on *SLAM* magazine's Top 75 NBA Players of All Time in 2003.

Julius Erving's Career Statistics

SEASON	TEAM	LG	G	MIN	FG	FT	TRB	AST	STL	BLK	PTS
1971–1972	Virginia	ABA	84	3,513	910	467	1319	335			2,290
1972–1973	Virginia	ABA	71	2,993	894	475	867	298	181	127	2,268
1973–1974	New York	ABA	84	3,398	914	454	899	434	190	204	2,299
1974–1975	New York	ABA	84	3,402	914	486	914	462	186	157	2,343
1975–1976	New York	ABA	84	3,244	949	530	925	423	207	160	2,462
1976–1977	Philadelphia	NBA	82	2,940	685	400	695	306	159	113	1,770
1977–1978	Philadelphia	NBA	74	2,429	611	306	481	279	135	97	1,528
1978–1979	Philadelphia	NBA	78	2,802	715	373	564	357	133	100	1,803
1979–1980	Philadelphia	NBA	78	2,812	838	420	576	355	170	140	2,100
1980–1981	Philadelphia	NBA	82	2,874	794	422	657	364	173	147	2,014
1981–1982	Philadelphia	NBA	81	2,789	780	411	557	319	161	141	1,974
1982–1983	Philadelphia	NBA	72	2,421	605	330	491	263	112	131	1,542
1983–1984	Philadelphia	NBA	77	2,683	678	364	532	309	141	139	1,727
1984–1985	Philadelphia	NBA	78	2,535	610	338	414	233	135	109	1,561
1985–1986	Philadelphia	NBA	74	2,474	521	289	370	248	113	82	1,340
1986–1987	Philadelphia	NBA	60	1,918	400	191	264	191	76	94	1,005
		ABA	407	16,550	4,581	2,412	4,924	1,952	764	648	11,662
		NBA	836	28,677	7,237	3,844	5,601	3,224	1,508	1,293	18,364
	TOTALS		1,243	45,227	11,818	6,256	10,525	5,176	2,272	1,941	30,026

Sources: Basketball-Reference.com; Naismith Memorial Basketball Hall of Fame

Esposito, Anthony James "Tony" (born: April 23, 1943 in Sault Ste. Marie, Ontario, Canada); inducted into the Hockey Hall of Fame in 1988 as a player; Position: Goalie; Uniform: #35; won one NCAA championship and one Stanley Cup title.

Esposito played 16 National Hockey League seasons (1968–1984) with the Montreal Canadiens (1968–1969) and the Chicago Black Hawks (1969–1984). As one-half of a hall-of-fame brother team (along with Phil), Esposito is credited with revolutionizing goalie play in the NHL with his legs-open "butterfly" style and his flop down on the ice to stop goals.

After a collegiate career with the Michigan Technological Huskies (Houghton) of the Western Collegiate Hockey Association (where he was a three-time All-American) and five seasons in the minors, he won a Stanley Cup title in 1969, although he did not appear in any playoff games.

Esposito led Michigan Tech to the National Collegiate Athletic Association championship in 1965; was named to the NCAA All-Tournament Team in 1965; and selected to the Western Collegiate Hockey Association All-Star First Team (1964–1967).

After being traded to the Chicago Black Hawks in 1969, he won the Calder Memorial Trophy (Rookie of the Year) and Vezina Trophy (league's Best Goalkeeper) with 2.17 goals-against average and a modern-era record of 15 shutouts. He was the first rookie to win the Vezina Trophy since Frank Brimsek in 1939.

The 5'11", 190-pound goalie went on to share the Vezina Trophy with Gary Smith in 1972 and with Bernie Parent in 1974. During his career, Esposito accumulated 76 regular-season shutouts and was selected to five First or Second All-Star Teams (1970, 1972–1974, 1980).

The Black Hawks made the playoffs every season that Esposito was with the team. In international competition, he played for Team Canada in the 1972 Summit Series, and played for the Canada Cup again in 1981, but for Team USA.

After retiring in 1984, he became director of hockey operations for the NHL's Pittsburgh Penguins. After leaving the team, in 1992 he joined his brother Phil in the front office of the expansion Tampa Bay Lightning. His jersey number 35 was retired by the Black Hawks in 1988, and in 1998, he was ranked number 79 on *The Hockey News*' list of the 100 Greatest Hockey Players. In 2007, both Esposito brothers were added to the Sault Ste. Marie Walk of Fame.

Tony Esposito's Career Statistics

			REGULAR SEASON					PLAYOFFS			
SEASON	**TEAM**	**LEAGUE**	**GP**	**W**	**L**	**T**	**AVG**	**GP**	**W**	**L**	**AVG**
1962–1963	Sault Ste. Marie Greyhounds	NOJHA									
1963–1964	Michigan Tech Huskies	WCHA									
1964–1965	Michigan Tech Huskies	WCHA	17				2.35				
1965–1966	Michigan Tech Huskies	WCHA	19				2.68				
1966–1967	Michigan Tech Huskies	WCHA	15				2.60				
1967–1968	Vancouver Canucks	WHL	63	25	33	4	3.20				
1968–1969	Montreal Canadiens	NHL	13	5	4	4	2.73				
1968–1969	Houston Apollos	CHL	19	10	7	2	2.42	1	0	1	3.05
1969–1970	Chicago Black Hawks	NHL	63	38	17	8	2.17	8	4	4	3.38
1970–1971	Chicago Black Hawks	NHL	57	35	14	6	2.27	18	11	7	2.19
1971–1972	Chicago Black Hawks	NHL	48	31	10	6	1.77	5	2	3	3.20
1972–1973	Canada	Summit-72	4	2	1	1	3.25				
1972–1973	Chicago Black Hawks	NHL	56	32	17	7	2.51	15	10	5	3.08
1973–1974	Chicago Black Hawks	NHL	70	34	14	21	2.04	10	6	4	2.88
1974–1975	Chicago Black Hawks	NHL	71	34	30	7	2.74	8	3	5	4.32
1975–1976	Chicago Black Hawks	NHL	68	30	23	13	2.97	4	0	4	3.25
1976–1977	Chicago Black Hawks	NHL	69	25	36	8	3.45	2	0	2	3.00
1976–1977	Canada	WEC-A	9	6	2	1	3.17				
1977–1978	Chicago Black Hawks	NHL	64	28	22	14	2.63	4	0	4	4.52
1978–1979	Chicago Black Hawks	NHL	63	24	28	11	3.27	4	0	4	3.46
1978–1979	NHL All-Stars	Ch-Cup									
1979–1980	Chicago Black Hawks	NHL	69	31	22	16	2.97	6	3	3	2.25
1980–1981	Chicago Black Hawks	NHL	66	29	23	14	3.75	3	0	3	4.19
1981–1982	United States	Can-Cup	5	2	3	0	4.00				
1981–1982	Chicago Black Hawks	NHL	52	19	25	8	4.52	7	3	3	2.52
1982–1983	Chicago Black Hawks	NHL	39	23	11	5	3.46	5	3	2	3.47
1983–1984	Chicago Black Hawks	NHL	18	5	10	3	4.82				
	NHL TOTALS		886	423	306	151	2.92	99	45	53	3.07

Sources: Hockey Hall of Fame; Hockey-Reference.com

Esposito, Philip Anthony "Phil" (born: February 20, 1942 in Sault Ste. Marie, Ontario, Canada); inducted into the Hockey Hall of Fame in 1984 as a player; Position: Center; Uniform: #7; scored 40 or more goals in seven straight seasons; led the NHL in scoring five times; won two Stanley Cup titles; was the NHL's first-ever 100 point player.

Esposito played 18 National Hockey League seasons (1963–1981) with the Chicago Black Hawks (1963–1967), Boston Bruins (1967–1975), and the New York Rangers (1975–1981).

While with the Bruins, he scored 40 or more goals in seven straight seasons, and 50 or more goals in five straight seasons. As a center, he held the record for most goals in a single season (76 in 1970–1971) until surpassed by Wayne Gretzky's 79 in 1982. He won the Art Ross Trophy (as the NHL'S regular-season scoring leader) five times (1969, 1971–1974); the Hart Memorial Trophy (NHL Most Valuable Player) twice (1969, 1974); the Lester B. Pearson Award (NHL MVP as selected by the National Hockey League Player's Association) twice (1971, 1974); and the Lester Patrick Trophy for service to hockey in the United States (1978).

The 6'1"", 205-pound Esposito was a 10-time All-Star, and represented Canada in the 1972 Summit Series, the 1976 Canada Cup, and the 1977 World Championship.

Traded to the Bruins in 1967, he went on to win two Stanley Cup championships (1970, 1972), and in his second year with the team, he became the league's first-ever 100-point player. Esposito would go on to score more than 100 points six times, including five consecutive seasons from 1971 to 1975, and in 1971, he took 550 shots on goal to set a record many believe will never be broken.

In international play, he starred for Team Canada in the 1972–1973 Summit Series as the leading individual scorer (seven goals and six assists) on the team that beat the Soviets in an eight-game series. After his performance in the Summit Series, he won the 1972 Lou Marsh Trophy as Canada's outstanding male athlete of the year, and was made an Officer of the Order of Canada.

Esposito was traded to the New York Rangers early in the 1975–1976 season, and after five years, he retired in 1981. He became one of the team's assistant coaches; worked as a television analyst for the Madison Square Garden network; and in 1986, he was named vice-president and general manager of the Rangers, a position he later accepted with the expansion Tampa Bay Lightning. His jersey number seven was retired by Boston in December 1987. In the Lightning's inaugural season, Esposito made hockey history (and generated much-needed publicity) by signing Manon Rheaume, the first woman to sign with an NHL team.

In 2007, both Esposito brothers were added to the Sault Ste. Marie Walk of Fame.

Phil Esposito's Career Statistics

			REGULAR SEASON					PLAYOFFS				
SEASON	**TEAM**	**LEAGUE**	**GP**	**G**	**A**	**TP**	**PIM**	**GP**	**G**	**A**	**TP**	**PIM**
1959–1960	Sault Ste. Marie Algoma	NOJHA										
1960–1961	Sarnia Legionnaires	OHA-B	32	47	61	108						
1961–1962	St. Catharines Teepees	OHA-Jr.	49	32	39	71	54	6	1	4	5	9
1961–1962	Sault Ste. Marie Greyhounds	EPHL	6	0	3	3	2					
1962–1963	St. Louis Braves	EPHL	71	36	54	90	51					
1963–1964	Chicago Black Hawks	NHL	27	3	2	5	2	4	0	0	0	0
1963–1964	St. Louis Braves	CPHL	43	26	54	80	65					
1964–1965	Chicago Black Hawks	NHL	70	23	32	55	44	13	3	3	6	15
1965–1966	Chicago Black Hawks	NHL	69	27	26	53	49	6	1	1	2	2
1966–1967	Chicago Black Hawks	NHL	69	21	40	61	40	6	0	0	0	7
1967–1968	Boston Bruins	NHL	74	35	49	84	21	4	0	3	3	0
1968–1969	Boston Bruins	NHL	74	49	77	126	79	10	8	10	18	8
1969–1970	Boston Bruins	NHL	76	43	56	99	50	14	13	14	27	16
1970–1971	Boston Bruins	NHL	78	76	76	152	71	7	3	7	10	6
1971–1972	Boston Bruins	NHL	76	66	67	133	76	15	9	15	24	24
1972–1973	Canada	Summit-72	8	7	6	13	15					
1972–1973	Boston Bruins	NHL	78	55	75	130	87	2	0	1	1	2
1973–1974	Boston Bruins	NHL	78	68	77	145	58	16	9	5	14	25
1974–1975	Boston Bruins	NHL	79	61	66	127	62	3	4	1	5	0
1975–1976	Boston Bruins	NHL	12	6	10	16	8					
1975–1976	New York Rangers	NHL	62	29	38	67	28					
1976–1977	Canada	Can-Cup	7	4	3	7	0					

			REGULAR SEASON					PLAYOFFS				
SEASON	TEAM	LEAGUE	GP	G	A	TP	PIM	GP	G	A	TP	PIM
1976–1977	New York Rangers	NHL	80	34	46	80	52					
1976–1977	Canada	WEC-A	10	7	3	10	14					
1977–1978	New York Rangers	NHL	79	38	43	81	53	3	0	1	1	5
1978–1979	New York Rangers	NHL	80	42	36	78	37	18	8	12	20	20
1979–1980	New York Rangers	NHL	80	34	44	78	73	9	3	3	6	8
1980–1981	New York Rangers	NHL	41	7	13	20	20					
	NHL TOTALS		1,282	717	873	1,590	910	130	61	76	137	138

Sources: Hockey Hall of Fame; Hockey-Reference.com

Evans, William George "Billy" (born: February 10, 1884 in Chicago, Illinois; died: January 23, 1956 in Miami, Florida); inducted into the National Baseball Hall of Fame and Museum in 1973 as an umpire by the Veterans Committee; served as president of the Southern Association; third umpire inducted into the baseball hall of fame; first person to hold the official title of general manager.

Evans became an American League umpire in 1906 at the age of 22, the youngest major league umpire at the time. He would go on to work in six World Series (1909, 1912, 1915, 1917, 1919, 1923) during his 22-year career, which ended in 1927. Evans wrote the book, *Umpiring from the Inside*; worked as a front office executive for various teams; and, after retiring, served as the president of the minor league Southern Association.

He served briefly as general manager of the National Football League's Cleveland (now St. Louis) Rams, and was the third umpire inducted into the hall of fame.

After being a star athlete in high school, Evans attended Cornell University (Ithaca, New York), where he played football and baseball. He left school when his father died, returned to Ohio, and worked as a reporter for the *Youngstown Daily Vindicator*. In 1904, while still a reporter, he was asked by the Youngstown team manager to work as an umpire with a short-handed crew. This appearance eventually led him to become a full-time umpire, and in 1905, he was hired by the American League, one of the very few to enter the major leagues with no prior professional experience. In the 1907 season, he single-handedly umpired seven double-headers in eight days, and he was a base umpire for Charlie Robertson's perfect game on April 30, 1922.

After retiring in 1927, Evans became the general manager of the Cleveland Indians, and is recognized as the first front office executive to have that official title. He left the Indians after eight seasons and became a scout in the Boston Red Sox's farm system, a job he held until 1940.

Evans returned to Cleveland and became general manager of the Rams for the 1941 NFL season; held the job for one year; and returned to baseball as president of the Southern Association in 1942.

In December 1946, he left the Association to become the general manager of the Detroit Tigers, and served in that position until he retired from baseball in 1951.

Source: National Baseball Hall of Fame and Museum

Evers, John Joseph "Johnny" (born: July 21, 1881 in Troy, New York; died: March 28, 1947 in Albany, New York); inducted into the National Baseball Hall of Fame and Museum in 1946 as a player by the Veterans Committee; Position: Second Base; Bats: Left; Throws: Right; won three World Series titles.

Making his major league debut on September 1, 1902, Evers played 17 complete and two one-game seasons with the Chicago Cubs (1902–1913), Boston Braves (1914–1917, 1929), Philadelphia Phillies (1917), and the Chicago White Sox (1922). He also managed the Chicago Cubs (1913, 1921) and the Chicago White Sox (1924). Evers played in four World Series (winning three times [1907–1908, 1914] and losing once [1906]), and won the 1914 National League Most Valuable Player award, then known as the Chalmers Award.

Evers was the pivot man in the Tinker-to-Evers-to-Chance infield and double-play combination made famous by the poem "Baseball's Sad Lexicon" by New York newspaper columnist Franklin Pierce Adams. Although the trio had played together since 1903, the poem was not written until 1910, the players' final season together. Although they worked well together on the field, Evers and Tinker did not speak to each other much and often traded punches in the clubhouse.

Evers' knowledge of baseball rules helped him save the National League pennant race for the Cubs as a result of the infamous Fred Merkle play (Merkle's Boner) on September 23, 1908. Merkle (of the New York Giants and the youngest player in the National League) was the runner on first who failed to touch second base after an apparent game-winning base hit by Al Bridwell had scored Moose McCormick from third in the bottom of the ninth inning. Instead of touching second base, Merkle turned back toward the dugout when he saw McCormick cross the plate.

As Polo Grounds fans rushed onto the field thinking their team had just won, Evers retrieved the ball and stepped on second base, telling the base umpire that the force-out negated the winning run. Since fan presence on the field made it impossible for the umpires to restore order, they collectively ruled that the game would be replayed, if necessary. As baseball fortune would have it, both teams were tied at the end of the season. When the game was replayed, the Cubs won the pennant and advanced to the World Series, beating the Detroit Tigers in five games.

After leading the Cubs to four National League pennants and two World Series championships, in 1914 Evers led the Braves to the World Series, and won the team's only championship with a four-game sweep of the Philadelphia Athletics (the first-ever World Series sweep).

On June 22, 1916 in a game against the New York Giants, the Braves pulled off a triple steal in the 11th inning, with Evers on the front end. It still stands as the National League's only extra-inning triple steal. The American League's only triple steal did not occur until 1941.

The 5'9", 125-pound Evers hit .300 or higher in a season twice; managed the 1913 Cubs to a third-place finish; the 1921 Cubs to a seventh-place finish; the 1924 White Sox to a sixth-place finish; and ended his career with an overall 180–192 (.484) record. Between 1912 and 1916, each member of the Tinker-Evers-Chance infield managed the Cubs.

After his playing days had apparently ended (he would play one game in 1922 and one game in 1929), Evers served in the military and was stationed in Europe during World War I. Returning from the war, he coached for the New York Giants, and was assistant manager for the Cubs in 1921. In 1923, Evers joined the Chicago White Sox as a coach and managed the team in 1924. He entered the hall of fame six months before his death, and was the last surviving member of the famed double-play combination.

Johnny Evers' Career Statistics

YEAR	TEAM	LG	G	AB	R	H	2B	3B	HR	RBI	BB	SO	SB	AVG	SLG
1902	Chicago	NL	25	89	7	20	0	0	0	2	3		1	.225	.225
1903	Chicago	NL	124	464	70	136	27	7	0	52	19		25	.293	.381
1904	Chicago	NL	152	532	49	141	14	7	0	47	28		26	.265	.318
1905	Chicago	NL	99	340	44	94	11	2	1	37	27		19	.276	.329
1906	Chicago	NL	154	533	65	136	17	6	1	51	36		49	.255	.315
1907	Chicago	NL	151	508	66	127	18	4	2	51	38		46	.250	.313
1908	Chicago	NL	126	416	83	125	19	6	0	37	66		36	.300	.375
1909	Chicago	NL	127	463	88	122	19	6	1	24	73		28	.263	.337
1910	Chicago	NL	125	433	87	114	11	7	0	28	108	18	28	.263	.321
1911	Chicago	NL	46	155	29	35	4	3	0	7	34	10	6	.226	.290
1912	Chicago	NL	143	478	73	163	23	11	1	63	74	18	16	.341	.441
1913	Chicago	NL	136	446	81	127	20	5	3	49	50	14	11	.285	.372
1914	Boston	NL	139	491	81	137	20	3	1	40	87	26	12	.279	.338
1915	Boston	NL	83	278	38	73	4	1	1	22	50	16	7	.263	.295
1916	Boston	NL	71	241	33	52	4	1	0	15	40	19	5	.216	.241
1917	Boston	NL	24	83	5	16	0	0	0	0	13	8	1	.193	.193
1917	Philadelphia	NL	56	183	20	41	5	1	1	12	30	13	8	.224	.279
1922	Chicago	AL	1	3	0	0	0	0	0	1	2	0	0	.000	.000
1929	Boston	NL	1	0	0	0	0	0	0	0	0	0	0	.000	.000
	TOTALS		1,783	6,136	919	1,659	216	70	12	538	778	142	324	.270	.334

Sources: Baseball-Reference.com; National Baseball Hall of Fame and Museum

Ewbank, Wilbur Charles "Weeb" (born: May 6, 1907 in Richmond, Indiana; died: November 17, 1998 in Oxford, Ohio); inducted into the Pro Football Hall of Fame in 1978 as a coach; only coach to win both American Football League and the National Football League championships.

Although Ewbank did not become a professional head coach until he was 47 years old, he was able to win 130 games. He led both the Baltimore Colts and New York Jets to league titles, becoming the only coach to win both AFL and NFL championships. He coached the Colts (1954–1962) and the Jets (1963–1973) with each team having a hall-of-fame quarterback, Johnny Unitas (Colts) and Joe Namath (Jets).

His Colts won back-to-back NFL titles in 1958 and 1959, and his AFL Jets won a Super Bowl III (January 1969) upset victory over his old team 16–7. The 1958 championship game (December 28 at Yankee Stadium in New York City) was the first-ever NFL game to go into sudden death overtime, and has often been called "The Greatest Game Ever Played" as Baltimore beat the New York Giants 23–17. Ewbank was selected as the head coach of the AFL All-Time Team.

After graduating from Morton High School (Richmond, Indiana) in 1924, Ewbank attended Miami University (Oxford, Ohio), where he played quarterback; was captain of the baseball team; and a forward on the basketball team. Graduating from college in 1928, he took his first football coaching job at Van Wert (Ohio) High School, before returning to Oxford to coach all sports at McGuffey High School, which was run by Miami University and separate from Oxford's public high school system. In 1939, Ewbank agreed to coach both the McGuffey High School and Miami University basketball team.

During World War II, he joined the Navy and was assigned to Great Lakes Naval Station (North Chicago, Illinois), where he worked as an assistant to Paul Brown in football and coached the basketball team.

After the war, Ewbank served as head coach at Washington University (St. Louis, Missouri, 1947–1948), compiling a 14–4 record. In 1969, he was a charter member in the Miami (Ohio) University Hall of Fame, and in 1974, he was inducted into the Indiana Football Hall of Fame.

Weeb Ewbank's Career Statistics

			REGULAR SEASON				PLAYOFFS			
YEAR	**TEAM**	**LG**	**W**	**L**	**T**	**WIN%**	**W**	**L**	**WIN%**	**NOTES**
1954	Baltimore Colts	NFL	3	9	0	.250				
1955	Baltimore Colts	NFL	5	6	1	.455				
1956	Baltimore Colts	NFL	5	7	0	.417				
1957	Baltimore Colts	NFL	7	5	0	.583				
1958	Baltimore Colts	NFL	9	3	0	.750	1	0	1.000	NFL Champions
1959	Baltimore Colts	NFL	9	3	0	.750	1	0	1.000	NFL Champions
1960	Baltimore Colts	NFL	6	6	0	.500				
1961	Baltimore Colts	NFL	8	6	0	.571				
1962	Baltimore Colts	NFL	7	7	0	.500				
1963	New York Jets	AFL	5	8	1	.385				
1964	New York Jets	AFL	5	8	1	.385				
1965	New York Jets	AFL	5	8	1	.385				
1966	New York Jets	AFL	6	6	2	.500				
1967	New York Jets	AFL	8	5	1	.615				
1968	New York Jets	AFL	11	3	0	.786	2	0	1.000	Super Bowl Champions
1969	New York Jets	AFL	10	4	0	.714	0	1	.000	
1970	New York Jets	NFL	4	10	0	.286				
1971	New York Jets	NFL	6	8	0	.429				
1972	New York Jets	NFL	7	7	0	.500				
1973	New York Jets	NFL	4	10	0	.286				
	Baltimore		59	52	1	.532	2	0	1.000	
	New York		71	77	6	.480	2	1	.667	
	TOTALS		130	129	7	.502	4	1	.800	

Sources: Pro Football Hall of Fame; Pro-Football-Reference.com

Ewing, Patrick Aloysius (born: August 5, 1962 in Kingston, Jamaica); inducted into the Naismith Memorial Basketball Hall of Fame in 2008 as a player; Position: Center; Uniform: #33; won an NCAA title; NBA Rookie of the Year in 1985.

One of the best shooting centers ever in the National Basketball Association, Ewing retired as the New York Knicks' all-time leader in almost every statistical category, and his 24,815 career points makes him the game's 13th all-time scorer. Born in Jamaica, he came to the United States when he was 11 years old, and grew to 6'10" by the time he played basketball at Cambridge (Massachusetts) Rindge & Latin School. After high school, he attended Georgetown

University (Washington, D.C.), where he played under coach John Thompson, a 6'10" former NBA backup center to Bill Russell on the Boston Celtics teams of the mid-1960s.

At Georgetown, he was named the NCAA Final Four Most Outstanding Player as both a junior and senior; was named *The Sporting News* College Player of the Year; won the Naismith Award as college basketball's best player; helped the school win its only national title (as of this writing) in 1984; and was a First Team All-American three times (1983–1985).

After graduating, the 7', 255-pound Ewing was the number one overall selection in the 1985 NBA Draft, and played for the New York Knicks (1985–2000), Seattle SuperSonics (2000–2001), and Orlando Magic (2001–2002). Never able to win a championship, he was named Rookie of the Year in 1986; selected to the All-NBA First Team (1990); All-NBA Second Team six times (1988–1989; 1991–1993; 1997); All-Defensive Second Team three times (1988–1989, 1992); an 11-time NBA All-Star (1986, 1988–1997); named to the NBA's 50th Anniversary All-Time Team (1996); and won two Olympic gold medals (1984 in Los Angeles, California, and 1992 in Barcelona, Spain).

He reached the NBA Finals twice (1994, 1999), and was on the 1998–1999 team (in the strike-shortened, 50-game season) that became the first squad to ever reach the NBA Finals from the eighth seed. After retiring from the NBA, he served as an assistant coach with the Washington Wizards; his jersey number 33 was retired by the Knicks in February 2003; and, as of this writing, he is an assistant coach with the Orlando Magic.

Patrick Ewing's NBA Career Statistics

SEASON	TEAM	G	MIN	FG	3P	FT	TRB	AST	STL	BLK	PTS
1985–1986	New York	50	1,771	386	0	226	451	102	54	103	998
1986–1987	New York	63	2,206	530	0	296	555	104	89	147	1356
1987–1988	New York	82	2,546	656	0	341	676	125	104	245	1653
1988–1989	New York	80	2,896	727	0	361	740	188	117	281	1815
1989–1990	New York	82	3,165	922	1	502	893	182	78	327	2347
1990–1991	New York	81	3,104	845	0	464	905	244	80	258	2154
1991–1992	New York	82	3,150	796	1	377	921	156	88	245	1970
1992–1993	New York	81	3,003	779	1	400	980	151	74	161	1959
1993–1994	New York	79	2,972	745	4	445	885	179	90	217	1939
1994–1995	New York	79	2,920	730	6	420	867	212	68	159	1886
1995–1996	New York	76	2,783	678	4	351	806	160	68	184	1711
1996–1997	New York	78	2,887	655	2	439	834	156	69	189	1751
1997–1998	New York	26	848	203	0	134	265	28	16	58	540
1998–1999	New York	38	1,300	247	0	163	377	43	30	100	657
1999–2000	New York	62	2,035	361	0	207	604	58	36	84	929
2000–2001	Seattle	79	2,107	294	0	172	585	92	53	91	760
2001–2002	Orlando	65	901	148	0	94	263	35	22	45	390
	TOTALS	1,183	40,594	9,702	19	5,392	11,607	2,215	1,136	2,894	24,815

Sources: Basketball-Reference.com; Naismith Memorial Basketball Hall of Fame

Ewing, William "Buck" (born: October 17, 1859 in Hoagland, Ohio; died: October 20, 1906 in Cincinnati, Ohio); inducted into the National Baseball Hall of Fame and Museum in 1939 as a player by the Veterans Committee (the year the hall of fame opened); Position: Catcher; Bats: Right; Throws: Right; first catcher inducted into the baseball hall of fame; only catcher from the 19th century inducted into the hall of fame; first major league player to hit 10 home runs in a single season.

Making his debut on September 9, 1880, Ewing had an 18-year major league career with the Troy Trojans (1880–1882), New York Gothams/Mutuals/Giants (1883–1889, 1891–1892), New York Giants (Players' League, 1890), Cleveland Spiders (1893–1894), and the Cincinnati Reds (1895–1897). He managed the New York Giants (Players' League, 1890), Cincinnati Reds (1895–1899), and the New York Giants (1900).

Considered the premier catcher of his era (although talented enough to play all the other positions) and widely regarded as one of the best and versatile players of the 19th century, Ewing was the first catcher inducted into the hall of fame; hit over .300 in 10 of his 15 full major league seasons; his strong and accurate arm allowed him to throw out base runners without rising from his crouch position behind the plate (which was practically unheard of in his time); and he led the New York Giants to the team's first world championships in 1888 and 1889.

The 5'10", 188-pound Ewing was the first major league player to hit 10 home runs in a single season (1883, a feat he was never able to repeat) and led the league with 20 triples in 1884 (which during his era of play were more common than home runs). In a game on June 9, 1883, his three triples were not enough as New York lost, 8-7, to the visiting Buffalo Bisons.

Because he was one of the leaders (and proponents) behind the formation of the short-lived Players' League, many of today's observers feel that team owner resentment limited his play in 1891 after he returned to the National League upon the demise of the Players' League.

After 1890 (due to lingering injuries and age), he rarely caught a game and played either in the outfield or at first base. He also pitched 47 innings from 1882 to 1890 with the Trojans, Gothams, and Giants, compiled a 2–3 record (.400), and a 3.45 Earned Run Average.

Buck Ewing's Career Statistics

YEAR	TEAM	LG	G	AB	R	H	2B	3B	HR	BB	SO	SB	AVG	SLG
1880	Troy	NL	13	46	1	8	1	0	0	1	3		.174	.196
1881	Troy	NL	65	267	38	65	13	6	0	7	8		.243	.337
1882	Troy	NL	72	318	65	87	16	11	2	10	15		.274	.412
1883	New York	NL	85	369	88	113	9	13	10	20	14		.306	.482
1884	New York	NL	88	374	87	104	13	18	3	28	22		.278	.433
1885	New York	NL	81	342	81	104	14	11	6	13	17		.304	.462
1886	New York	NL	70	275	59	85	10	8	4	16	17		.309	.447
1887	New York	NL	76	348	81	127	17	13	6	30	33	26	.365	.540
1888	New York	NL	103	415	83	127	17	15	6	24	28	53	.306	.463
1889	New York	NL	96	407	91	133	23	14	4	37	32	34	.327	.482
1890	New York	PL	83	349	99	122	20	15	8	39	12	36	.350	.562
1891	New York	NL	14	49	8	17	1	1	0	5	5	5	.347	.408
1892	New York	NL	97	394	58	126	12	15	8	38	26	42	.320	.487
1893	Cleveland	NL	114	477	116	177	27	17	6	41	18	47	.371	.537
1894	Cleveland	NL	53	212	32	54	12	4	2	24	9	18	.255	.377
1895	Cincinnati	NL	103	439	90	139	23	13	5	30	22	34	.317	.462
1896	Cincinnati	NL	67	266	41	75	9	5	1	29	13	41	.282	.365
1897	Cincinnati	NL	1	1	0	0	0	0	0	0	0	0	.000	.000
	TOTALS		1,281	5,348	1,118	1,663	237	179	71	362	294	336	.311	.462

Buck Ewing's Managerial Record

YEAR	LG	TEAM	W	L	WIN%	FINISH
1890	PL	New York	74	57	.565	3 (Player-Manager)
1895	NL	Cincinnati	66	64	.508	8 (Player-Manager)
1896	NL	Cincinnati	77	50	.606	3 (Player-Manager)
1897	NL	Cincinnati	76	56	.576	4 (Player-Manager)
1898	NL	Cincinnati	92	60	.605	3
1899	NL	Cincinnati	83	67	.553	6
1900	NL	New York	21	41	.339	8
		New York	74	57	.565	
		Cincinnati	394	297	.570	
		New York	21	41	.339	
		TOTALS	489	395	.553	

Sources: Baseball-Reference.com; National Baseball Hall of Fame and Museum

Chapter 6
Faber to Fulks

Faber, Urban Clarence "Red" (born: September 6, 1888 in Cascade, Iowa; died: September 25, 1976 in Chicago, Illinois); inducted into the National Baseball Hall of Fame and Museum in 1964 as a player by the Veterans Committee; Position: Pitcher; Bats: Right; Throws: Right; Uniform: #18; last legal spitballer in the American League; won three games in the 1917 World Series; holds the White Sox record for most games pitched.

Making his major league debut on April 17, 1914, Faber enjoyed a 20-year pitching career with the Chicago White Sox (1914–1933), and played in the 1917 World Series, where he won three games (2, 5, and 6) in the team's victory over the New York Giants. Although the White Sox were an underperforming team for 16 of his 20 seasons, Faber was able to win 254 games using a spitball (he was the last legal spitballer in the American League), and in 1921, he won 25 games for a team that finished in seventh place.

On August 18, 1910, while playing with the Dubuque Dubs of the Triple-I-League (Illinois-Indiana-Iowa League), the 6'2", 180-pound Faber pitched a 3–0 perfect game over the Davenport Prodigals. He developed a sore arm in his early twenties, and began throwing the spitball in 1911 to ease the pressure on his arm. In his rookie major league season, Faber started 19 games and was a reliever in 21 others; posted a 10–9 record with a 2.69 Earned Run Average; and saved a league-leading four games.

In 1915, he led the league with 50 appearances, and on May 12, 1915, Faber pitched a three-hitter, using only 67 pitches to beat the Washington Senators, 4–1. After missing most of the 1918 season while serving in the U.S. Navy during World War I, he returned to the White Sox in 1919, and immediately noticed that he was having arm problems. He finished the year with a 3.83 ERA, his only season above 3.00 in his first nine years. His arm trouble turned out to be somewhat of a blessing. Because he was sick and had a sore arm, he missed the infamous "Black Sox" scandal of the 1919 World Series, where eight of his teammates were accused of taking money to throw the Series to the Cincinnati Reds. He avoided the scandal completely and was able to continue his career unaffected.

When the spitball was banned in 1920, Faber was one of 17 pitchers allowed to use the pitch until the end of his career. He was one of only six pitchers to win 100 or more games in both the "dead ball" (through 1920) and "live ball" eras.

From 1920 to 1922, he won 69 games and led the American League in ERA twice (1921–1922), starts (1920), innings pitched (1922), and complete games twice (1921–1922). For all his personal success, the White Sox had been devastated by the "Black Sox" scandal and only had two winning seasons in his last 13 years.

To this day, he holds the franchise record for most games pitched (669), and held team records for career wins, starts, complete games, and innings pitched until they were later broken by Ted Lyons.

Faber had some unusual at bats. Although he was a career .134 switch hitter, in 1915, he walked seven times in a row and twice stole home. On July 22, 1928, playing against the New York Yankees, he came up to bat in the eighth inning with two runners on base and the game tied 4–4. After swinging and missing twice while batting right-handed against pitcher Wilcy Moore, he switched to the left side of the plate, and hit what would eventually be the game-winning single to center field.

After retiring as a player, Faber returned to the White Sox as a coach for a few seasons before leaving the game for good. He retired as the 17th winningest pitcher in major league history.

Red Faber's Career Statistics

YEAR	TEAM	LG	W	L	PCT	G	SH	IP	H	R	ER	SO	BB	ERA
1914	Chicago	AL	10	9	.526	40	2	181	154	77	54	88	64	2.69

YEAR	TEAM	LG	W	L	PCT	G	SH	IP	H	R	ER	SO	BB	ERA
1915	Chicago	AL	24	14	.632	50	2	300	264	118	85	182	99	2.55
1916	Chicago	AL	17	9	.654	35	3	205	167	67	46	87	61	2.02
1917	Chicago	AL	16	13	.552	41	3	248	224	92	53	84	85	1.92
1918	Chicago	AL	4	1	.800	11	1	81	70	23	11	26	23	1.22
1919	Chicago	AL	11	9	.550	25	0	162	185	92	69	45	45	3.83
1920	Chicago	AL	23	13	.639	40	2	319	332	136	106	108	88	2.99
1921	Chicago	AL	25	15	.625	43	4	331	293	107	91	124	87	2.47
1922	Chicago	AL	21	17	.553	43	4	352	334	128	110	148	83	2.81
1923	Chicago	AL	14	11	.560	32	2	232	233	114	88	91	62	3.41
1924	Chicago	AL	9	11	.450	21	0	161	173	78	69	47	58	3.86
1925	Chicago	AL	12	11	.522	34	1	238	266	117	100	71	59	3.78
1926	Chicago	AL	15	9	.625	27	1	185	203	84	73	65	57	3.55
1927	Chicago	AL	4	7	.364	18	0	111	131	64	56	39	41	4.54
1928	Chicago	AL	13	9	.591	27	2	201	223	98	84	43	68	3.76
1929	Chicago	AL	13	13	.500	31	1	234	241	119	101	68	61	3.88
1930	Chicago	AL	8	13	.381	29	0	169	188	101	79	62	49	4.21
1931	Chicago	AL	10	14	.417	44	1	184	210	96	78	49	57	3.82
1932	Chicago	AL	2	11	.154	42	0	106	123	61	44	26	38	3.74
1933	Chicago	AL	3	4	.429	36	0	86	92	41	33	18	28	3.45
	TOTALS		254	213	.544	669	29	4,086	4,106	1,813	1,430	1,471	1,213	3.15

Sources: Baseball-Reference.com; National Baseball Hall of Fame and Museum

Fagan, Clifford B. (born: March 3, 1911 in Mankato, Minnesota; died: January 18, 1995); inducted into the Naismith Memorial Basketball Hall of Fame in 1984 as a contributor; founder and first president of the Indianhead Officials Association.

Fagan attended Medina Township High School (Marshall, Wisconsin), where he played basketball from 1925 to 1928. After graduating in 1928, he went to Wisconsin State Teachers College (LaCrosse), graduating in 1932, and later received a master's degree from the University of Iowa (Iowa City). While at Wisconsin State, he played basketball from 1928 to 1931, and was selected All-Conference in 1928.

His coaching career began as a football coach at Fairchild (Wisconsin) High School from 1932 to 1935. He then served at Sturgeon Bay (Wisconsin) High School as the basketball, football, baseball, and wrestling coach from 1935 to 1941. He then moved on to Green Bay (Wisconsin) East High School, serving as basketball, football, and boxing coach from 1941 to 1942. Leaving the high school ranks, Fagan returned to Wisconsin State College (1942–1947) as a coach until dedicating the remainder of his career to basketball sports administration.

He conducted numerous Wisconsin rules interpretation meetings (1942–1946); officiated at regional, sectional, and state basketball tournaments; was the founder and first president of the Indianhead Officials Association of Eau Claire, Wisconsin; spent 10 years as executive secretary of the Wisconsin Interscholastic Athletic Association (1947–1957); joined the National Federation of High School Athletic Associations (1957); and served as its assistant executive secretary (1958–1959) and executive director (1959–1977).

Fagan expanded the Federation into all 50 states and implemented programs that reached 60,000 teams and more than 800,000 players (boys and girls). He served as secretary of the National Basketball Rules Committee of the United States and Canada (1958–1977); was a trustee at the Basketball Hall of Fame (1959–1976); president of the Basketball Hall of Fame (1963–1969), Basketball Federation (1967–1973) and Amateur Basketball Association of the United States of America (1974–1976); served as a member of the U.S. Olympic Committee Board of Directors (1961–1976) and Fédération Internationale de Basketball Amateur; was a FIBA Central Committee member (1976–1980); and treasurer of the Pan American Basketball Association (1975–1980).

During his career, he was honored for outstanding contributions to coaching by the National High School Coaches Association (1972); won the National Association of Basketball Coaches Appreciation Award for distinguished service to basketball (1973); won the Basketball Hall of Fame's John Bunn Award (1973); and received the "Award of Merit" from both the National Federation (1977) and National Interscholastic Athletic Administrators Association (1978).

Fagan has been inducted into the Illinois Basketball Coaches, Wisconsin State High School Football Coaches, and U.S. Track and Field halls of fame.

Source: Naismith Memorial Basketball Hall of Fame

Fairfield, Harry H. (born: March 22, 1890 in Birmingham, England; died: February 6, 1991 in Pittsburgh, Pennsylvania); inducted into the National Soccer Hall of Fame and Museum in 1951 as a builder; president of the West Penn Association and the United States Football Association.

Fairfield emigrated to the United States and played goalkeeper as a young man, before leaving the game to serve in the military during World War I. After the war, he served as a soccer referee and held various administrative positions in the Referees' Association until 1923. He served as president of the West Penn Association twice, secretary three times, and was made a life member in 1951.

He also served as vice president of the United States Football Association from 1938 to 1945, and president from 1945 to 1948. Fairfield helped organize the North American Confederation of the U.S., Canada, Cuba and Mexico in 1947, and represented the parent body at the Fédération Internationale de Football Association Congress in London, England in 1948.

Source: National Soccer Hall of Fame and Museum

Farrell, Arthur F. (born: February 8, 1877 in Montreal, Quebec, Canada; died: February 7, 1909 in Sainte-Agathe-des-Monts, Quebec, Canada); inducted into the Hockey Hall of Fame in 1965 as a player; Position: Forward; won two Stanley Cup championships.

Farrell played four pre-National Hockey League seasons from 1896 to 1901, after starting his hockey career at College Sainte-Marie (Montreal, 1895–1897).

He joined the Montreal Shamrocks (Canadian Amateur Hockey League) in 1897 and played on back-to-back Stanley Cup-winning teams (1899–1900).

After retiring, Farrell wrote what is believed to be the first book on hockey in 1899, titled *Hockey—Canada's Royal Winter Game*, which detailed the history of hockey, and explained how to play the game. Other books he wrote focused on the origins of hockey; the rules of the game in both Canada and the United States; and a guide on how to play various positions.

Source: Hockey Hall of Fame

Fawcett, Joy Lynn (born: Joy Biefield on February 8, 1968 in Inglewood, California); inducted into the National Soccer Hall of Fame and Museum in 2009 as a player; Position: Defender; International Caps (1987–2004): 239; International Goals: 0; won three Olympic medals.

Throughout the 1990s, Fawcett and fellow hall of famer Carla Overbeck anchored the U.S. women's defense. She played in four Women's World Cups (won two), and three Olympic Games (won two). She was still Joy Biefield when she played on the U.S. team that won the first-ever Women's World Cup in 1991 (hosted by China), and was Joy Fawcett when she played for the United States in the 1995 (winning a bronze medal in Sweden), 1999 (a gold medal in the United States) and 2003 (bronze medal in the United States) Women's World Cups, and the 1996 (gold medal in Atlanta, Georgia), 2000 (silver medal in Sydney, Australia), and 2004 (gold medal in Athens, Greece) Olympic Games.

Fawcett made her first appearance for the U.S. National Team against China in 1987; her 100th in the Olympic semifinal in which the United States beat Norway in 1996; her 200th against Trinidad in 2002; and her last against Mexico in 2004. In more than 20,000 minutes of play for the United States, she was never red carded and received only two yellow cards.

She was a three-time All-American (1987–1989) at the University of California in Los Angeles, and served as the women's soccer coach at UCLA from 1993 to 1997. Although more well-known for her National Team play, Fawcett also played three seasons for the San Diego Spirit (Women's United Soccer Association), and was named a WUSA First Team All Star in 2003.

Fawcett is the eighth member of the 1991 Women's World Cup championship team to be inducted into the soccer hall of fame; the sixth member of the 1996 Olympic team; the fifth member of the 1999 Women's World Cup team; and the third member of the 2004 Olympic team.

She attended Edison High School (Huntington Beach, California), before going to UCLA, where she played soccer for three seasons; holds the school record for single season scoring (23 goals in 1987); and was inducted into the UCLA Athletics Hall of Fame in October 1997.

Source: National Soccer Hall of Fame and Museum

Fears, Thomas Jesse "Tom" (born: December 3, 1922 in Guadalajara, Mexico; died: January 4, 2000 in Palm Desert, California); inducted into the Pro Football Hall of Fame in 1970 as a player; Position: End; set the NFL receiving record in 1949; caught 18 passes in one game; first wide receiver in the NFL.

The 6'2", 216-pound Fears played his entire nine-season (87 games) National Football League career with the Los Angeles Rams (1948–1956). He led the NFL in receptions his first three seasons (1948–1950); set a league record for catches (77 in 1949), and broke his own record in 1950 (with 84); caught three touchdowns in the 1950 division title game against the Chicago Bears; caught a 73-yard pass to win the 1951 NFL title game 24–17 against the Cleveland Browns (the team's first championship since moving from Cleveland after the 1945 season); caught a then-record 18 passes in one game (a 45–14 win over the Green Bay Packers on November 12, 1950); was selected All-NFL twice (1949–1950) and to the 1950 Pro Bowl; and was named to the NFL 1950s All-Decade Team.

Before joining the NFL, he had played football at Santa Clara University (California) for one year; but had his career interrupted for three years when he served in the military during World War II. After the war, Fears finished his college career at the University of California at Los Angeles with two All-American seasons. Before going to college, he had played football at Manual Arts High School (Los Angeles, California).

On October 18, 1953, Fears fractured two vertebrae against the Detroit Lions, and the injury eventually ended his career in 1956.

Staying away from the game for two seasons, he returned as an assistant coach during Vince Lombardi's first year with the NFL's Green Bay Packers, but left at mid-season. He returned to the league the next year as a coach with the Rams; stayed for two seasons, before going back to Green Bay, where he served four years as an assistant coach; and was part of two championship teams (1962, 1965). In 1966, he was an assistant coach with the Atlanta Falcons, until finally becoming a head coach with the New Orleans Saints in 1967. After four years, he left the team, having compiled a 13–34–2 (.277) record.

Fears then served as an offensive coordinator for the Philadelphia Eagles, where he stayed until after the 1972 season; was named head coach of the World Football League's newly formed Southern California Sun in January 1974; and coached the team for two seasons, until the league folded in 1975.

He was inducted into the College Football Hall of Fame in 1976; was named president of the All-Sports Council of Southern California, which helped promote amateur sports in the area; and one year later, Fears returned to coaching as an assistant at San Bernardino (California) Junior College.

In 1980, he coached the Chapman College (Orange, California) football team, before becoming part-owner of the Orange Empire Outlaws (California Football League) in 1981. In 1982, he was hired as player personnel director of the new United States Football League's Los Angeles Express, a job he kept until the league folded. His final football job came in 1990, when he was named head coach of the Milan franchise in the newly formed International League of American Football.

Fears was the first player in the NFL to line up on the line of scrimmage, away from the tackle, thus making him the first wide receiver in NFL history.

Tom Fears' Career Statistics

			RECEIVING			
YEAR	**TEAM**	**G**	**NO**	**YDS**	**AVG**	**TD**
1948	Los Angeles	12	51	698	13.7	4
1949	Los Angeles	12	77	1,013	13.2	9
1950	Los Angeles	12	84	1,116	13.3	7
1951	Los Angeles	7	32	528	16.5	3
1952	Los Angeles	12	48	600	12.5	6
1953	Los Angeles	8	23	278	12.1	4
1954	Los Angeles	10	36	546	15.2	3
1955	Los Angeles	12	44	569	12.9	2
1956	Los Angeles	2	5	49	9.8	0
	TOTALS	87	400	5,397	13.5	38

Tom Fears' NFL Coaching Record

YEAR	**TEAM**	**G**	**W**	**L**	**T**	**WIN%**
1967	New Orleans Saints	14	3	11	0	.214
1968	New Orleans Saints	14	4	9	1	.308

YEAR	TEAM	G	W	L	T	WIN%
1969	New Orleans Saints	14	5	9	0	.357
1970	New Orleans Saints	7	1	5	1	.167
	TOTALS	49	13	34	2	.277

Sources: College Football Hall of Fame; Pro Football Hall of Fame; Pro-Football-Reference.com

Federko, Bernard Allan (born: May 12, 1956 in Foam Lake, Saskatchewan, Canada); inducted into the Hockey Hall of Fame in 2002 as a player; Position: Center; Uniform: #24; first player in NHL history to record 50 or more assists in 10 consecutive seasons.

Federko played 14 National Hockey League seasons from 1976 to 1990, 13 years with the St. Louis Blues, and his last year (1989–1990) with the Detroit Red Wings.

After advancing through the amateur and junior ranks, he broke into the NHL as the seventh overall pick in the first round of the 1976 draft with the Blues. The team sent the 6', 178-pound Federko to the Blues' Central Hockey League farm club in Kansas City, where he recorded 69 points in 42 games, before being called up to the NHL in the middle of the 1976–1977 season.

Beginning in 1977–1978, he played 12 consecutive full seasons with the St. Louis Blues and was named to two All-Star teams. The next season, he led the team with 64 assists and 95 points; in 1980–1981, he recorded his first of four 100 or more points per season; and during his 13 years with the team, he led St Louis in scoring nine times.

When he left the team, Federko held 11 franchise records, including games played (927), goals (352), assists (721), and points (1,073). On March 16, 1991, his jersey number 24 was retired by the Blues, and after a brief stint as the general manager of the St. Louis Vipers (Roller Hockey International), Federko became a television color commentator for the Blues.

Bernard Federko's Career Statistics

			REGULAR SEASON						PLAYOFFS				
SEASON	TEAM	LEAGUE	GP	G	A	TP	PIM	+/–	GP	G	A	TP	PIM
1972–1973	Foam Lake Flyers	SAHA											
1973–1974	Saskatoon Blades	WCJHL	68	22	28	50	19		6	0	0	0	2
1974–1975	Saskatoon Blades	WCJHL	66	39	68	107	30		17	15	7	22	8
1975–1976	Saskatoon Blades	WCJHL	72	72	115	187	108		20	18	27	45	8
1976–1977	St. Louis Blues	NHL	31	14	9	23	15	–6	4	1	1	2	2
1976–1977	Kansas City Blues	CHL	42	30	39	69	41						
1977–1978	St. Louis Blues	NHL	72	17	24	41	27	–35					
1978–1979	St. Louis Blues	NHL	74	31	64	95	14	–15					
1979–1980	St. Louis Blues	NHL	79	38	56	94	24	+3	3	1	0	1	2
1980–1981	St. Louis Blues	NHL	78	31	73	104	47	+9	11	8	10	18	2
1981–1982	St. Louis Blues	NHL	74	30	62	92	70	–10	10	3	15	18	10
1982–1983	St. Louis Blues	NHL	75	24	60	84	24	–10	4	2	3	5	0
1983–1984	St. Louis Blues	NHL	79	41	66	107	43	–3	11	4	4	8	10
1984–1985	St. Louis Blues	NHL	76	30	73	103	27	–10	3	0	2	2	4
1985–1986	St. Louis Blues	NHL	80	34	68	102	34	+10	19	7	14	21	17
1986–1987	St. Louis Blues	NHL	64	20	52	72	32	–25	6	3	3	6	18
1987–1988	St. Louis Blues	NHL	79	20	69	89	52	–12	10	2	6	8	18
1988–1989	St. Louis Blues	NHL	66	22	45	67	54	–20	10	4	8	12	0
1989–1990	Detroit Red Wings	NHL	73	17	40	57	24	–8					
	NHL TOTALS		1,000	369	761	1,130	487		91	35	66	101	83

Sources: Hockey Hall of Fame; Hockey-Reference.com

Feibusch, Ernst (born: 1925 in Germany); inducted into the National Soccer Hall of Fame and Museum in 1984 as an administrator; won the California State Cup twice as a player; president of the San Francisco Soccer Football League.

Feibusch came to the United States at age 12 and became a player, coach, and administrator at various soccer levels in the San Francisco Bay Area from the 1940s to the 1970s. He was a star with San Francisco (California) State College (1948–1950), and was twice named to the All-American Conference team (1949–1950). He joined the San Francisco Vikings (California Youth Soccer Association-North) prior to World War II, and after the war, he returned to the team and played until 1955, winning the State Cup twice (1953–1954) and the San Francisco League title in 1953.

After his playing days, Feibusch became president of the San Francisco Soccer Football League (1955–1959), and served as the organization's secretary until 1975. He later served as director of coaching; was a longtime District 1 coaching coordinator; served as commissioner for San Francisco Schools soccer officials; and was California Youth Soccer's District 1 referee coordinator.

Feibusch served on numerous soccer committees for the National Soccer Coaches Association of America, the United States Soccer Federation, and the National Intercollegiate Soccer Officials Association. In addition to his administrative duties, he also wrote articles for *Soccer News* (New York), *National Soccer News* (Chicago), the *USSFA Guide & Newsletter*, and *Scholastic Soccer*.

He later founded the San Francisco Junior Soccer League, the oldest in Northern California, and the SF/FLAME Youth Soccer League; was inducted into the California Soccer Football Association Hall of Fame in 1968; and received the George Sundquist Youth Soccer Achievement Award in 1974.

Source: National Soccer Hall of Fame and Museum

Feller, Robert William Andrew "Bob" (born: November 3, 1918 in Van Meter, Iowa; died: December 15, 2010 in Cleveland, Ohio); inducted into the National Baseball Hall of Fame and Museum in 1962 as a player; Position: Pitcher; Bats: Right; Throws: Right; Uniform: #19; first American League pitcher to throw a complete game no-hitter on opening day; won the 1948 World Series; first pitcher to win 20 or more games before the age of 21.

Making his major league debut on July 19, 1936, Feller played his entire 18-year career (1936–1941, 1945–1956) with the Cleveland Indians. He pitched in the 1948 World Series, as the Tribe beat the Boston Braves.

Feller's fastball set the standard against which all of his successors have been judged, and his pitching statistics would have been much better than they were had he not missed four seasons in his prime while serving in the military during World War II.

In his first big-league start (August 25, 1936), Feller struck out a then-American League record 15 batters in a 4–1 win over the St. Louis Browns. In his career, he threw three no-hitters (April 16, 1940 against the Chicago White Sox; April 30, 1946 against the New York Yankees; and July 1, 1951 against the Detroit Tigers), and 12 one-hitters, while winning 20 or more games per season six times. On April 16, 1940, he became the first American League pitcher to throw a complete game no-hitter on opening day, and was the first pitcher to win 20 or more games before the age of 21.

At age 23, his major league career was interrupted when he served four years in the Navy during World War II. After the war, 6', 185-pound Feller returned to the Indians and won 46 games his first two years back in baseball. To this day, he is still the Indians' career leader in shutouts (44), strikeouts (2,581), innings pitched (3,828), and All-Star appearances (8).

He led the American League in wins six times (1939–1941, 1946–1947, 1951); in earned run average (1940); in strikeouts seven times (1938–1941, 1946–1948); named to eight All-Star teams (1938–1941, 1946–1948, 1950); in 1999, he was ranked number 36 on *The Sporting News*' list of the 100 Greatest Baseball Players; and he was nominated as a finalist for the Major League Baseball All-Century Team.

While still in high school, Feller was signed by scout Cy Slapnicka of the Cleveland Indians. When the scout became general manager of the Indians, he transferred the pitcher's contract from Fargo-Moorhead to New Orleans to the major league club without Feller visiting either team, a clear violation of baseball rules. After a three-month investigation, Commissioner Kenesaw Mountain Landis ruled that the Indians had violated established major league rules, but allowed Feller to play for the big league club anyway.

When Feller retired in 1956, he held the major league record for most walks in a career (1,764) and for most hit batsmen. He still holds the 20th century record for most walks in a season (208 in 1938).

Bob Feller's Career Statistics

YEAR	TEAM	LG	W	L	PCT	G	SH	IP	H	R	ER	SO	BB	ERA
1936	Cleveland	AL	5	3	.625	14	0	62	52	29	23	76	47	3.34
1937	Cleveland	AL	9	7	.563	26	0	149	116	68	56	150	106	3.38
1938	Cleveland	AL	17	11	.607	39	2	278	225	136	126	240	208	4.08
1939	Cleveland	AL	24	9	.727	39	4	297	227	105	94	246	142	2.85
1940	Cleveland	AL	27	11	.711	43	4	320	245	102	93	261	118	2.62
1941	Cleveland	AL	25	13	.658	44	6	343	284	129	120	260	194	3.15
1945	Cleveland	AL	5	3	.625	9	1	72	50	21	20	59	35	2.50
1946	Cleveland	AL	26	15	.634	48	10	371	277	101	90	348	153	2.18
1947	Cleveland	AL	20	11	.645	42	5	299	230	97	89	196	127	2.68

YEAR	TEAM	LG	W	L	PCT	G	SH	IP	H	R	ER	SO	BB	ERA
1948	Cleveland	AL	19	15	.559	44	2	280	255	123	111	164	116	3.57
1949	Cleveland	AL	15	14	.517	36	0	211	198	104	88	108	84	3.75
1950	Cleveland	AL	16	11	.593	35	3	247	230	105	94	119	103	3.43
1951	Cleveland	AL	22	8	.733	33	4	250	239	105	97	111	95	3.49
1952	Cleveland	AL	9	13	.409	30	0	192	219	124	101	81	83	4.73
1953	Cleveland	AL	10	7	.588	25	1	176	163	78	70	60	60	3.58
1954	Cleveland	AL	13	3	.813	19	1	140	127	53	48	59	39	3.09
1955	Cleveland	AL	4	4	.500	25	1	83	71	43	32	25	31	3.47
1956	Cleveland	AL	0	4	.000	19	0	58	63	34	32	18	23	4.97
	TOTALS		266	162	.621	570	44	3,828	3,271	1,557	1,384	2,581	1,764	3.25

Sources: Baseball-Reference.com; Bob Feller Museum (www.bobfellermuseum.org); Elias Sports Bureau; National Baseball Hall of Fame and Museum

Ferguson, John "Jack" "Jock" (born: September 17, 1887 in Dundee, Scotland; died: September 19, 1973 in Bethlehem, Pennsylvania); inducted into the National Soccer Hall of Fame and Museum in 1950 as a player; Position: Full Back; International Caps (1925): 1; International Goals: 0; played in five U.S. Open Cup Finals and five American Cup Finals.

Ferguson starred for the powerhouse Bethlehem Steel teams prior to 1920, and played in the first American Soccer League. After playing in Scotland, in 1912, he crossed the English Channel to play for Leeds City (1912), now known as Leeds United.

While with Bethlehem Steel, he played in five U.S. Open Cup finals (1915–1919) and five American Cup Finals (1915–1919), winning the title each year except for 1917. In 1917, Bethlehem Steel joined the professional National Association Football League and won three consecutive league titles (1919–1921). He traveled with the team to Sweden in 1919, and played in the first American Soccer League when it began operations in the 1921–1922 season.

In 1921, Bethlehem's owners moved the team to Philadelphia and renamed it the Philadelphia Field Club for the initial 1921–1922 ASL season, and Ferguson led the squad to the very first ASL league title. In 1922, he moved to J&P Coats and won the 1923 league title, giving him five league and four Challenge Cup titles.

On September 8, 1923, he returned to Bethlehem, and won his last league title in 1927, before retiring in 1928. Ferguson earned one international cap with the U.S. National Team in a 1–0 loss to Canada on June 27, 1925.

Source: National Soccer Hall of Fame and Museum

Fernley, John A. (born: unknown; died: November 6, 1934); inducted into the National Soccer Hall of Fame and Museum in 1951 as a builder; was an administrator in the United States Soccer Football Association.

Fernley was the first Southern New England district delegate to the newly created United States Soccer Football Association, and was elected first vice-president of the governing body in 1914. He served as the group's president from 1915 until 1917.

Source: National Soccer Hall of Fame and Museum

Ferrándiz, Pedro (González) (born: November 20, 1928 in Alicante, Spain); inducted into the Naismith Memorial Basketball Hall of Fame in 2007 as a coach; won 12 Spanish League titles; co-founder of the World Association of Basketball Coaches.

Ferrándiz was involved with basketball in his country for 15 years (1960–1975), and began coaching with Hesperia and later Real Madrid during the 1960s. From 1960 to 1975, he led Real Madrid to 12 Spanish League titles (1961–1963, 1966, 1969–1976) and 10 Spanish Cups (1961–1962, 1965–1967, 1971–1975); won four European Cup titles (1965, 1967–1968, 1974); and had three undefeated seasons in the Spanish League.

In 1976, he and fellow hall-of-famer Cesare Rubini founded the World Association of Basketball Coaches, and as of this writing, he is the only basketball coach in history to receive the Olympic Order from the International Olympic Committee (1977). He received the FIBA Order of Merit in 2000, and his overall coaching record with Real was 437–90 (.829).

During his career, Ferrándiz coached for Real Madrid (minor league teams, 1955–1957); CD Hesperia (1957–1959); Real Madrid (1959–1962, 1964–1965, 1966–1975); and the Spanish National Team (1964–1965).

The non-profit Pedro Ferrándiz Foundation works to collect information about the game and to promote the game around the world. The Foundation is supported and recognized by such entities as Fédération Internationale de Basketball Amateur, the International Olympic Committee, the National Basketball Association, and the World Association of Basketball Coaches. Since its creation in 1991, the Foundation has organized exhibitions, promoted research; organized worldwide clinics and tournaments; and issued hundreds of basketball-related publications.

Source: Naismith Memorial Basketball Hall of Fame

Ferrell, Richard Benjamin "Rick" (born: October 12, 1905 in Durham, North Carolina; died: July 27, 1995 in Bloomfield Hills, Michigan); inducted into the National Baseball Hall of Fame and Museum in 1984 as a player by the Veterans Committee; Position: Catcher; Bats: Right; Throws: Right; Uniform: #2; caught all nine innings of the first All-Star game.

One of seven brothers, Ferrell (after attending Guilford College, Greensboro, North Carolina) made his major league debut on April 19, 1929 and had an 18-year career with the St. Louis Browns (1929–1933, 1941–1943), Boston Red Sox (1933–1937), and Washington Senators (1937–1941, 1944–1945, 1947). He was an eight-time All-Star (1933–1938, 1944–1945).

A defensive star with a strong throwing arm, the 5'10", 160-pound Ferrell retired having caught more games than any other American Leaguer (1,806), a record that stood for more than 40 years until surpassed by Carlton Fisk in 1988. He hit over .300 four times, and caught all nine innings of the very first All-Star game (July 19, 1933). Ferrell and his brother Wes (playing for Cleveland) were both members of the inaugural American League All-Star team, and for the first time in baseball history, were brothers on opposing teams who hit home runs in the same game.

From 1933 to 1936, Ferrell broke Red Sox catchers' records for batting, doubles, home runs, and runs batted in, and his .302 batting average with Boston is 12th on the team's all-time list. After retiring, he served as a coach for the Senators, before joining the Detroit Tigers as a coach, scout, and general manager. In 1995, he was inducted into the Boston Red Sox Hall of Fame.

Rick Ferrell's Career Statistics

YEAR	TEAM	LG	G	AB	R	H	2B	3B	HR	RBI	BB	SO	SB	AVG	SLG
1929	St. Louis	AL	64	144	21	33	6	1	0	20	32	10	1	.229	.285
1930	St. Louis	AL	101	314	43	84	18	4	1	41	46	10	1	.268	.360
1931	St. Louis	AL	117	386	47	118	30	4	3	57	56	12	2	.306	.427
1932	St. Louis	AL	126	438	67	138	30	5	2	65	66	18	5	.315	.420
1933	St. Louis	AL	22	72	8	18	2	0	1	5	12	4	2	.250	.319
1933	Boston	AL	118	421	50	125	19	4	3	72	58	19	2	.297	.382
1934	Boston	AL	132	437	50	130	29	4	1	48	66	20	0	.297	.389
1935	Boston	AL	133	458	54	138	34	4	3	61	65	15	5	.301	.413
1936	Boston	AL	121	410	59	128	27	5	8	55	65	17	0	.312	.461
1937	Boston	AL	18	65	8	20	2	0	1	4	15	4	0	.308	.385
1937	Washington	AL	86	279	31	64	6	0	1	32	50	18	1	.229	.262
1938	Washington	AL	135	411	55	120	24	5	1	58	75	17	1	.292	.382
1939	Washington	AL	87	274	32	77	13	1	0	31	41	12	1	.281	.336
1940	Washington	AL	103	326	35	89	18	2	0	28	47	15	1	.273	.340
1941	Washington	AL	21	66	8	18	5	0	0	13	15	4	1	.273	.348
1941	St. Louis	AL	100	321	30	81	14	3	2	23	52	22	2	.252	.333
1942	St. Louis	AL	99	273	20	61	6	1	0	26	33	13	0	.223	.253
1943	St. Louis	AL	74	209	12	50	7	0	0	20	34	14	0	.239	.273
1944	Washington	AL	99	339	14	94	11	1	0	25	46	13	2	.277	.316
1945	Washington	AL	91	286	33	76	12	1	1	38	43	13	2	.266	.325
1947	Washington	AL	37	99	10	30	11	0	0	12	14	7	0	.303	.414
	TOTALS		1,884	6,028	687	1,692	324	45	28	734	931	277	29	.281	.363

Sources: Baseball-Reference.com; National Baseball Hall of Fame and Museum

Ferro, Charles (born: unknown; died: December 3, 1962); inducted into the National Soccer Hall of Fame and Museum in 1958 as a builder; soccer writer and referee.

Ferro was a goalkeeper during his playing days; a referee in the Metropolitan Soccer League of New York in the 1940s; and a well-known soccer writer for the New York Spanish-language newspaper *La Prensa*.

Source: National Soccer Hall of Fame and Museum

Fetisov, Viacheslav (Slava) Alexandrovich (born: April 20, 1958 in Moscow, Russia); inducted into the Hockey Hall of Fame in 2001 as a player; Position: Defenseman; served as captain of the Soviet National Team and of the Central Army squad; won two Stanley Cup titles as a player and one as a coach.

Fetisov captained both the National Team and the Central Army squad; named top defenseman at the European Junior Hockey Championships in 1976 and at the 1978 World Junior Championships; was a nine-time All-Star; five-time winner of the best defenseman award at the senior World Championships; and played on nine Olympic and World Championship teams during his international hockey career.

The 6'1", 215-pound Fetisov was drafted by the National Hockey League's New Jersey Devils in 1983, but could not join the team until 1989 due to the political climate in the Soviet Union and his military service obligations. He played for the Soviet National Team during the 1989 World Championships (hosted by Sweden), and was named the squad's captain. After winning the gold medal, the Soviet Union allowed him to leave the team and join New Jersey (at age 31).

Fetisov would play nine years in the NHL, his final three seasons with the Detroit Red Wings. While in Detroit, he played in the 1997 and 1998 All-Star games and won two Stanley Cup championships (1997–1998).

After retiring, he became an assistant coach with the Devils, and won his third Stanley Cup title with the team in 2000. At the 2002 Olympics, he coached the Russian National Team that won the bronze medal, and currently serves as the Minister of Sport in Russia.

Internationally, Fetisov won two Olympic gold medals: 1984 (Sarajevo, Bosnia and Herzegovina) and 1988 (Calgary, Alberta, Canada) and one Olympic silver medal in 1980 at Lake Placid, New York; won seven gold medals (1978, 1981–1983, 1986, 1989, 1990), one silver (1987), and two bronze (1985, 1991) in the World Championships; and won the Golden Hockey Stick as the top European international player three times (1984, 1986, 1990).

He was named to the Canada Cup All-Star Team in 1987; selected to the USSR First All-Star Team nine times (1979–1980, 1982–1988); was USSR Player of the Year twice (1982, 1986); and was awarded the Order of the Red Banner of Labor in 1984.

Viacheslav Fetisov's Career Statistics

			REGULAR SEASON						PLAYOFFS				
SEASON	TEAM	LEAGUE	GP	G	A	TP	PIM	+/-	GP	G	A	TP	PIM
1974–1975	CSKA Moscow	USSR	1	0	0	0	0						
1974–1975	Soviet Union	EJC-A	5	1	0	1	0						
1975–1976	CSKA Moscow Jr.	USSR-Jr.											
1975–1976	Soviet Union	WJC-A	4	0	0	0	11						
1975–1976	Soviet Union	EJC-A	4	2	0	2	0						
1976–1977	CSKA Moscow	USSR	27	3	4	7	14						
1976–1977	Soviet Union	WJC-A	7	3	2	5	4						
1976–1977	Soviet Union	WEC-A	5	3	3	6	2						
1977–1978	CSKA Moscow	USSR	35	9	18	27	46						
1977–1978	Soviet Union	WJC-A	7	3	5	8	6						
1977–1978	Soviet Union	WEC-A	10	4	6	10	11						
1978–1979	CSKA Moscow	USSR	29	10	19	29	40						
1979–1980	CSKA Moscow	USSR	37	10	14	24	46						
1979–1980	CSKA Moscow	Super-S	4	0	1	1	0						
1979–1980	Soviet Union	Olympics	7	5	4	9	10						
1980–1981	CSKA Moscow	USSR	48	13	16	29	44						
1980–1981	Soviet Union	WEC-A	8	1	4	5	6						
1981–1982	Soviet Union	Can-Cup	7	1	7	8	10						
1981–1982	CSKA Moscow	USSR	46	15	26	41	20						
1981–1982	Soviet Union	WEC-A	10	4	3	7	6						
1982–1983	CSKA Moscow	USSR	43	6	17	23	46						
1982–1983	Soviet Union	Super-S	6	1	4	5	10						
1982–1983	Soviet Union	WEC-A	10	3	7	10	8						
1983–1984	CSKA Moscow	USSR	44	19	30	49	38						
1983–1984	Soviet Union	Olympics	7	3	8	11	8						
1984–1985	CSKA Moscow	USSR	20	13	12	25	6						
1984–1985	Soviet Union	WEC-A	10	6	7	13	15						

SEASON	TEAM	LEAGUE	REGULAR SEASON GP	G	A	TP	PIM	+/-	PLAYOFFS GP	G	A	TP	PIM
1985–1986	CSKA Moscow	USSR	40	15	19	34	12						
1985–1986	CSKA Moscow	Super-S	6	3	3	6	6						
1985–1986	Soviet Union	WEC-A	10	6	9	15	10						
1986–1987	CSKA Moscow	USSR	39	13	20	33	18						
1986–1987	Soviet Union	RV-87	2	0	1	1	2						
1986–1987	Soviet Union	WEC-A	10	2	8	10	2						
1987–1988	Soviet Union	Can-Cup	9	2	5	7	9						
1987–1988	CSKA Moscow	USSR	46	18	17	35	26						
1987–1988	Soviet Union	Olympics	8	4	9	13	6						
1988–1989	CSKA Moscow	USSR	23	9	9	18	18						
1988–1989	CSKA Moscow	Super-S	7	2	3	5	7						
1988–1989	Soviet Union	WEC-A	10	2	4	6	17						
1989–1990	New Jersey Devils	NHL	72	8	34	42	52	+9	6	0	2	2	10
1989–1990	Soviet Union	WEC-A	8	2	8	10	8						
1990–1991	New Jersey Devils	NHL	67	3	16	19	62	+5	7	0	0	0	17
1990–1991	Soviet Union	WEC-A	10	3	1	4	4						
1990–1991	Utica Devils	AHL	1	1	1	2	0						
1991–1992	New Jersey Devils	NHL	70	3	23	26	108	+11	6	0	3	3	8
1992–1993	New Jersey Devils	NHL	76	4	23	27	158	+7	5	0	2	2	4
1993–1994	New Jersey Devils	NHL	52	1	14	15	30	+14	14	1	0	1	8
1994–1995	Spartak Moscow	CIS	1	0	1	1	4						
1994–1995	New Jersey Devils	NHL	4	0	1	1	0	-2					
1994–1995	Detroit Red Wings	NHL	14	3	11	14	2	+3	18	0	8	8	14
1995–1996	Detroit Red Wings	NHL	69	7	35	42	96	+37	19	1	4	5	34
1996–1997	Russia	W-Cup	4	0	2	2	12						
1996–1997	Detroit Red Wings	NHL	64	5	23	28	76	+26	20	0	4	4	42
1997–1998	Detroit Red Wings	NHL	58	2	12	14	72	+4	21	0	3	3	10
1998–2000	New Jersey Devils	NHLMGNT											
	NHL TOTALS		546	36	192	228	656		116	2	26	28	147

Sources: Hockey Hall of Fame; Hockey-Reference.com

Fingers, Roland Glen "Rollie" (born: August 25, 1946 in Steubenville, Ohio); inducted into the National Baseball Hall of Fame and Museum in 1992 as a player; Position: Pitcher; Bats: Right; Throws: Right; Uniform: #34; second relief pitcher inducted into the baseball hall of fame; pitched the last two innings of the first-ever four-pitcher, no-hitter in baseball history; first relief pitcher ever to win the American League MVP Award.

Making his major league debut on September 15, 1968, Fingers played 17 years for the Oakland A's (1968–1976), San Diego Padres (1977–1980), and Milwaukee Brewers (1981–1982, 1984–1985). He won three consecutive World Series championships with Oakland (1972–1974); was 1974 World Series Most Valuable Player; selected to seven All-Star teams (1973–1976, 1978, 1981–1982): American League Most Valuable Player and Cy Young Award winner in 1981; and won four Rolaids Relief Man Awards (1977–1978, 1980–1981).

His career focuses on the rising importance of the modern-day relief pitcher. After starting his career as a starting pitcher without much success, Fingers' career took off when the A's moved him to the bullpen. He would go on to accumulate 341 career saves and appear in 16 World Series games.

When the 6'4", 195-pound Fingers reached the major leagues, the role of relief pitchers was limited since starting pitchers rarely left games while holding a lead. However, with the rise of more productive offenses in the early 1970s, combined with the American League's introduction of the Designated Hitter in 1973, it became common practice to replace starters in the late innings in order to hold leads.

In 1980, Fingers broke Hoyt Wilhelm's record of 227 saves, and eventually finished with 341, a record that stood until Jeff Reardon surpassed it in 1992. Easily recognizable with his handlebar moustache, he is viewed as a pioneer of modern relief pitching, and defined the role of the closer for years to come. After Wilhelm, he was only the second reliever inducted into the baseball hall of fame.

On September 28, 1975, Fingers pitched the last two innings of the first-ever four-pitcher, no-hitter in baseball history, as he, Vida Blue, Glenn Abbott, and Paul Lindblad combined to beat the California Angels 5–0. On November 25, 1981, Fingers becomes the first relief pitcher ever to win the American League MVP Award.

In 1999, he ranked Number 96 on *The Sporting News*' list of Baseball's Greatest Players, and was nominated as a finalist for the Major League Baseball All-Century Team. After retiring from the major leagues, he pitched one season in the short-lived Senior Professional Baseball League; his jersey number 34 was retired by the Brewers in 1992 and by the Athletics in 1993 (one of only eight players who have had their uniform numbers retired by more than one team); and he was inducted into the Bay Area Sports Hall of Fame in 1993.

Rollie Fingers' Career Statistics

YEAR	TEAM	LG	W	L	PCT	G	SH	SV	IP	H	R	ER	SO	BB	ERA
1968	Oakland	AL	0	0	.000	1	0		1	4	4	4	0	1	36.00
1969	Oakland	AL	6	7	.462	60	1	12	119	116	60	49	61	41	3.71
1970	Oakland	AL	7	9	.438	45	0	2	148	137	65	60	79	48	3.65
1971	Oakland	AL	4	6	.400	48	1	17	129	94	46	43	98	30	3.00
1972	Oakland	AL	11	9	.550	65	0	21	111	85	35	31	113	32	2.51
1973	Oakland	AL	7	8	.467	62	0	22	127	107	41	27	110	39	1.91
1974	Oakland	AL	9	5	.643	76	0	18	119	104	41	35	95	29	2.65
1975	Oakland	AL	10	6	.625	75	0	24	127	95	43	42	115	33	2.98
1976	Oakland	AL	13	11	.542	70	0	20	135	118	40	37	113	40	2.47
1977	San Diego	NL	8	9	.471	78	0	35	132	123	47	44	113	36	3.00
1978	San Diego	NL	6	13	.316	67	0	37	107	84	33	30	72	29	2.52
1979	San Diego	NL	9	9	.500	54	0	13	84	91	47	42	65	37	4.50
1980	San Diego	NL	11	9	.550	66	0	23	103	101	35	32	69	32	2.80
1981	Milwaukee	AL	6	3	.667	47	0	28	78	55	9	9	61	13	1.04
1982	Milwaukee	AL	5	6	.455	50	0	29	79.2	63	23	23	71	20	2.60
1984	Milwaukee	AL	1	2	.333	33	0	23	46	38	13	10	40	13	1.96
1985	Milwaukee	AL	1	6	.143	47	0	17	55.1	59	33	31	24	19	5.04
	TOTALS		114	118	.491	944	2	341	1,701	1,474	615	549	1,299	492	2.90

Sources: Baseball-Reference.com; Bay Area Sports Hall of Fame; National Baseball Hall of Fame and Museum

Finks, James Edward "Jim" (born: August 31, 1927 in St. Louis, Missouri; died: May 8, 1994 in Metairie, Louisiana); inducted into the Pro Football Hall of Fame in 1995 as an administrator; long-time member of the NFL competition committee.

While Finks played seven National Football League seasons as a quarterback and defensive back with the Pittsburgh Steelers (1949–1955), his 45-year involvement with the game was primarily as a front-office official with the Minnesota Vikings (1964–1974), Chicago Bears (1974–1982), and the New Orleans Saints (1986–1992). He worked with the NFL Management Council during the 1974 league strike, and was a long-time member of the NFL competition committee.

After attending the University of Tulsa (Oklahoma), he was a 12th-round pick of the Pittsburgh Steelers in the 1949 NFL draft. Retiring after the 1955 season, he served as an assistant coach at the University of Notre Dame (South Bend, Indiana) in 1956 before moving on to the Calgary Stampeders (Canadian Football League), where he was a player, assistant coach, scout, and, eventually, general manager. He helped sign many of the players who eventually made Calgary the winningest team in the CFL during the 1960s.

Finks began his administrative career in 1964 when he was named general manager of the Vikings. Four years after he joined the franchise, the team won its first of five division titles, and played in the Super Bowl twice (SB IV, SB VIII) during his tenure, losing both times. He helped form the well-respected defensive front four, popularly known as the "Purple People Eaters" (end Jim Marshall, end Carl Eller, tackle Gary Larsen, and tackle Alan Page). When coach Norm Van Brocklin left the team in 1967, Finks hired the relatively unknown Bud Grant, who had enjoyed a successful 10-year tenure as coach of the CFL's Winnipeg Blue Bombers. After being named NFL Executive of the Year, he resigned from the Vikings in May 1974 and was hired by the Bears as general manager and executive vice-president.

He helped draft 19 of the Bears' 22 starters that would play (after Finks had left the franchise in 1982) in the team's 46–10 Super Bowl XX win (January 26, 1986) over the New England Patriots.

After leaving the Bears, Finks joined Major League Baseball's Chicago Cubs as president and chief executive officer in September 1983, but left the team after the Cubs won the 1984 National League's Eastern Division title.

He returned to the NFL with the Saints in 1986, and in his second year, the team had a winning season for the first time in its 19-season history, and would eventually win its first-ever division title in 1991. For guiding the team to a winning season, he was named the 1987 NFL Executive of the Year for the second time.

Jim Finks' Playing Statistics

			PASSING								RUSHING			
YEAR	TEAM	G	ATT	COMP	PCT	YDS	TD	INT	RATING	NO	YDS	AVG	TD
1949	Pittsburgh	11	71	24	33.8	322	2	8	19.0	35	135	3.9	1
1950	Pittsburgh	9	9	5	55.6	35	0	1	25.0	1	2	2.0	0
1951	Pittsburgh	12	24	14	58.3	201	1	1	82.1	3	27	9.0	0
1952	Pittsburgh	12	336	158	47.0	2,307	20	19	66.2	23	37	1.6	5
1953	Pittsburgh	11	292	131	44.9	1,484	8	14	49.8	12	0	0.0	2
1954	Pittsburgh	12	306	164	53.6	2,003	14	19	63.4	9	17	1.9	0
1955	Pittsburgh	12	344	165	48.0	2,270	10	26	47.7	35	76	2.2	4
	TOTALS	79	1,382	661	47.8	8,622	55	88	54.7	118	294	2.5	12

Sources: Pro Football Hall of Fame; Pro-Football-Reference.com

The First Team; inducted into the Naismith Memorial Basketball Hall of Fame in 1959 as a team; first organized basketball team.

Considered the first organized basketball team, The First Team consisted of 18 members who, at the time of the squad's creation, were training to become executive secretaries at the International YMCA Training School (now Springfield College) in Springfield, Massachusetts in 1891.

The men were all members of basketball creator Dr. James Naismith's gym class. It was with this First Team that Naismith formalized his initial 13 rules and introduced the team to a game he called Basket Ball.

Realizing that the game could not be effectively played by highlighting individual skills, Naismith introduced discipline and team play to these 18 men, who went on to form the first recognized organized basketball team, which would help spread the word about this new game.

Members of The First Team included Lyman W. Archibald (born: July 3, 1868; died: November 10, 1947); Franklin Everets Barnes (born: 1867; died: October 3, 1947); Wilbert Franklin Carey (born: October 31, 1868; died: June 16, 1940); William Richmond Chase (born: June 23, 1867; died: August 30 1951); William Henry Davis (born: July 31, 1867; died: November 1919); George Edward Day (born: September 21, 1864; died: October 31, 1919); Benjamin Snell French (born: July 14, 1871; died: 1910); Henry Gelan (born: unknown; died: March 16, 1910); Ernest Gotthold Hildner (born: October 26, 1873; died: unknown); Genzabaro Sadakni Ishikawa (born: July 21, 1870; died: June 1953); Raymond Pimlott Kaighn (born: December 8, 1869; died: July 1962); Eugene Samuel Libby (born: April 28, 1865; died: September 1, 1948); Finlay Grant MacDonald (born: April 1, 1870; died: March 29, 1951); Frank Mahan (born: October 17, 1867; died: 1905); Thomas Duncan Patton (born: May 15, 1865; died: April 1944); Edwin Pakenham Ruggles (born: January 5, 1873; died: June 19, 1940); John George Thompson (born: September 10, 1859; died: August 17, 1933); and George Radford Weller (born: unknown; died: February 11, 1956).

Source: Naismith Memorial Basketball Hall of Fame

Fisher, Harry A. (born: February 6, 1882 in Gradyville, Kentucky; died: December 29, 1967); inducted into the Naismith Memorial Basketball Hall of Fame in 1974 as a contributor; first paid full-time coach at Columbia University.

Fisher, at only 5'9", 150 pounds, attended City College High School (New York, New York) and, after graduating in 1901, went to Columbia University (New York, New York), graduating in 1905. While at Columbia, he played basketball for three years (1902–1905); was captain of the 1904 and 1905 Helms Foundation National Championship teams; was a two-time All-American (1904–1905); was selected to the All-Eastern Intercollegiate League twice (1904–1905); and led the team in scoring all three years.

After graduating from Columbia, he began his coaching career at Fordham University (Bronx, New York, 1904–1905). He returned to his alma mater as a coach from 1906 until 1916, and moved on to coach St. John's University (Queens, New York, 1909–1910), before finishing his college coaching career at the U.S. Military Academy at West Point (New York, 1921–1923, 1924–1925).

Fisher coached Fordham to a 4–2 record while still a player at Columbia, and was the first paid full-time coach at Columbia University. He led the school to a 101–39 (.721) record and three Eastern Intercollegiate League championships (1911–1912, 1914 [tied]). In the 1909–1910 season, he coached St. John's to a 15–5 record, while still coaching at Columbia.

He was personally recruited by General Douglas MacArthur, then superintendent of the U.S. Military Academy, to coach at the school after World War I. Fisher led the Academy to a 46–5 record, including an undefeated season in 1922–1923, and three wins over Navy (1922–1923, 1925).

He served on a committee that wrote the first-ever codified rules for college basketball; edited the newly formed "Collegiate Rules Committee and Collegiate Guide" (1905–1915); and served as Columbia's first graduate manager of athletics (1911–1917). He was granted Life Membership into the Eastern Intercollegiate League Basketball Association; was inducted into the Helms Athletic Foundation Hall of Fame; and was presented with the Columbia Alumni Athletic Award in 1945.

Source: Naismith Memorial Basketball Hall of Fame

Fishwick, George E. (born: July 12, 1909 in New Brighton, England; died: December 11, 1977 in Flagstaff, Arizona); inducted into the National Soccer Hall of Fame and Museum in 1954 as a builder; editor and publisher of *National Soccer News*.

Fishwick played soccer in England before immigrating to the United States in 1930. In 1939, he resumed playing soccer with Forest Park, Schwaben, and Slovaks in the Chicago, Illinois area. In 1943, he became editor and publisher of the *National Soccer News*, and then served as secretary of the Chicago National Soccer League from 1948 to 1954. He was elected president of the United States Soccer Football Association in 1963 and served two terms.

Source: National Soccer Hall of Fame and Museum

Fisk, Carlton Ernest (born: December 26, 1947 in Bellows Falls, Vermont); inducted into the National Baseball Hall of Fame and Museum in 2000 as a player; Position: Catcher; Bats: Right; Throws: Right; Uniform: #72, #27; first American League catcher to lead the league in triples; first-ever unanimous choice for American League Rookie of the Year.

Making his major league debut on September 18, 1969, Fisk enjoyed a 24-season career with the Boston Red Sox (1969, 1971–1980) and the Chicago White Sox (1981–1993). He was the first-ever unanimous choice for American League Rookie of the Year in 1972; won a Gold Glove in 1972; played on 11 All-Star teams (1972–1974, 1976–1978, 1980–1982, 1985, 1991); and played in the 1975 World Series (a loss to the Cincinnati Reds).

Nicknamed "Pudge," the 6'2", 220-pound Fisk was the most durable catcher of his time and caught more games (2,226) than any player in history. Of his 376 career home runs, 351 came as a catcher, a record that has since been surpassed by Mike Piazza. His most memorable home run came in Game Six of the 1975 World Series, a 12th-inning shot off the left field foul pole (later renamed the "Fisk Pole") at Fenway Park in Boston, giving his Red Sox a 7–6 win over Cincinnati to force a game seven, which the team ultimately lost to the Reds. The camera shot of Fisk "waving" his home run fair is one of the most-replayed moments in baseball history. For better or worse, many baseball historians point to this play as the moment when baseball cameras began focusing on player reactions to individual plays during the game.

Fisk graduated from Charlestown (New Hampshire) High School; played baseball for the American Legion team in Bellows Falls; and went to the University of New Hampshire (Durham), where he played on both the basketball and baseball teams.

Drafted in the first round (fourth overall pick) by the Red Sox in the 1967 Amateur Draft, he played intermittently for Boston in 1969 and 1971, until eventually joining the team full-time in 1972. Later, after joining the White Sox, Fisk helped the team win its first American League Western Division Title in 1983.

Fisk once held the record for most home runs after age 40 (72), and a single in the 1991 All-Star Game made him the oldest player to collect a hit in the game's history. The White Sox retired his uniform number 72 in September 1997 and the Boston Red Sox retired his uniform number 27 in September 2000 (one of only eight players to have their uniform number retired by at least two teams).

Fisk received an honorary World Series ring from the Red Sox commemorating the team's 2004 World Series victory, and on August 12, 2006, the Chicago White Sox presented him with a ring honoring the team's 2005 championship. In August 2005, the White Sox unveiled a life-sized bronze statue of Fisk, located inside U.S. Cellular Field on the main concourse in left field.

Fisk was the last active position player who had played in the 1960s; was inducted into the Boston Red Sox Hall of Fame in 1997; and in 1999, he was selected as a finalist for the Major League Baseball All-Century Team.

Carlton Fisk's Career Statistics

YEAR	TEAM	LG	G	AB	R	H	2B	3B	HR	RBI	BB	SO	SB	AVG	SLG
1969	Boston	AL	2	5	0	0	0	0	0	0	0	2	0	.000	.000
1971	Boston	AL	14	48	7	15	2	1	2	6	1	10	0	.313	.521
1972	Boston	AL	131	457	74	134	28	9	22	61	52	83	5	.293	.538
1973	Boston	AL	135	508	65	125	21	0	26	71	37	99	7	.246	.441

YEAR	TEAM	LG	G	AB	R	H	2B	3B	HR	RBI	BB	SO	SB	AVG	SLG
1974	Boston	AL	52	187	36	56	12	1	11	26	24	23	5	.299	.551
1975	Boston	AL	79	263	47	87	14	4	10	52	27	32	4	.331	.529
1976	Boston	AL	134	487	76	124	17	5	17	58	56	71	12	.255	.415
1977	Boston	AL	152	536	106	169	26	3	26	102	75	85	7	.315	.521
1978	Boston	AL	157	571	94	162	39	5	20	88	71	83	7	.284	.475
1979	Boston	AL	91	320	49	87	23	2	10	42	10	38	3	.272	.450
1980	Boston	AL	131	478	73	138	25	3	18	62	36	62	11	.289	.467
1981	Chicago	AL	96	338	44	89	12	0	7	45	38	37	3	.263	.361
1982	Chicago	AL	135	476	66	127	17	3	14	65	46	60	17	.267	.403
1983	Chicago	AL	138	488	85	141	26	4	26	86	46	88	9	.289	.518
1984	Chicago	AL	102	359	54	83	20	1	21	43	26	60	6	.231	.468
1985	Chicago	AL	153	543	85	129	23	1	37	107	52	81	17	.238	.488
1986	Chicago	AL	125	457	42	101	11	0	14	63	22	92	2	.221	.337
1987	Chicago	AL	135	454	68	116	22	1	23	71	39	72	1	.256	.460
1988	Chicago	AL	76	253	37	70	8	1	19	50	37	40	0	.277	.542
1989	Chicago	AL	103	375	47	110	25	2	13	68	36	60	1	.293	.475
1990	Chicago	AL	137	452	65	129	21	0	18	65	61	73	7	.285	.451
1991	Chicago	AL	134	460	42	111	25	0	18	74	32	86	1	.241	.413
1992	Chicago	AL	62	188	12	43	4	1	3	21	23	38	3	.229	.309
1993	Chicago	AL	25	53	2	10	0	0	1	4	2	11	0	.189	.245
	TOTALS		2,499	8,756	1,276	2,356	421	47	376	1,330	849	1,386	128	.269	.457

Sources: Baseball-Reference.com; National Baseball Hall of Fame and Museum

Flaherty, Raymond Paul "Ray" (born: September 1, 1903 in Spokane, Washington; died: July 19, 1994 in Coeur d'Alene, Idaho); inducted into the Pro Football Hall of Fame in 1976 as a coach; won two NFL titles.

Although inducted into the football hall of fame as a coach, Flaherty was also a very good player. After a college career as an end at Gonzaga University (Spokane, Washington), he played for the Los Angeles Wildcats of the American Football League in 1926. When the league folded after only one season, the 6'9", 190-pound Flaherty went to the National Football League's New York Yankees for two seasons, before joining the New York Giants in 1928. He led the NFL in receiving (21 catches for 350 yards and three touchdowns) in 1932, the first year official statistics were kept. He played until 1935, and was named All-NFL twice (1928, 1932).

After his playing days, Flaherty went on to compile a regular-season 80–37–5 (.676) coaching record with the NFL's Boston/Washington Redskins (1936–1942) and the New York Yankees of the All-America Football Conference (1946–1948). He won four Eastern Division (1936–1937, 1940, 1942) and two NFL titles (1937, 1942) with the Redskins, and two AAFC division titles with the Yankees (1946–1947). He is credited with introducing the behind-the-line screen pass (in the 1937 title game against the Chicago Bears), using quarterback Sammy Baugh. Another of his innovations was the use of the two-platoon system, one for rushing and one for passing plays.

After completing his Naval military service during World War II, Flaherty joined the New York Yankees of the newly formed All-America Football Conference and won two straight division titles, before finishing his coaching career after the 1949 season with the AAFC's Chicago Hornets.

Ray Flaherty's Coaching Record

			REGULAR SEASON				PLAYOFFS			
YEAR	TEAM	LG	W	L	T	WIN%	W	L	WIN%	NOTES
1936	Boston	NFL	7	5	0	.583	0	1	.000	
1937	Washington	NFL	8	3	0	.727	1	0	1.000	NFL Champions
1938	Washington	NFL	6	3	2	.667				
1939	Washington	NFL	8	2	1	.800				
1940	Washington	NFL	9	2	0	.818	0	1	.000	
1941	Washington	NFL	6	5	0	.545				
1942	Washington	NFL	10	1	0	.909	1	0	1.000	NFL Champions
1946	New York	AAFC	10	3	1	.769	0	1	.000	
1947	New York	AAFC	11	2	1	.846	0	1	.000	
1948	New York	AAFC	1	3	0	.250				
1949	Chicago	AAFC	4	8	0	.333				
	Washington		54	21	3	.720	2	2	.500	
	New York		22	8	2	.733	0	2	.000	

YEAR	TEAM	LG	REGULAR SEASON W	L	T	WIN%	PLAYOFFS W	L	WIN%	NOTES
	Chicago		4	8	0	.333	0	0		
	TOTALS		80	37	5	.684	2	4	.333	

Sources: Pro Football Hall of Fame; Pro-Football-Reference.com

Flaman, Ferdinand Charles "Fernie" (born: January 25, 1927 in Dysart, Saskatchewan, Canada); inducted into the Hockey Hall of Fame in 1990 as a player; Position: Defenseman; won the 1951 Stanley Cup championship; coached 19 seasons at Northeastern University.

Flaman played 17 National Hockey League seasons (1944–1961) with the Boston Bruins (1944–1950, 1954–1961) and the Toronto Maple Leafs (1950–1954). After being signed by the Bruins in 1943, he played three seasons for the minor-league Boston Olympics (Eastern Amateur Hockey League), and was named to the league's First All-Star Team twice (1945–1946). He joined the Bruins in the 1947 season, and after a little more than three years, he was traded to the Toronto Maple Leafs, where he won the 1951 Stanley Cup title his first year with the squad.

Following the 1953–1954 season, the Leafs traded Flaman back to Boston, where he captained the squad for four years, and was one of the founders of the first players' association to be recognized by the NHL, an early precursor to the union that was formed in 1967. He led the team to the Stanley Cup finals in 1957 and 1958 (losing both times to the Montreal Canadiens); was selected to the Second All-Star Team three times (1955, 1957–1958); and retired in 1961.

After leaving the NHL, Flaman joined the Rhode Island Reds of the American Hockey League in 1961, and stayed with the team until 1965. In the 1963–1964 season, he served as player, coach, and general manager. In 1965, he was elected to the Rhode Island Hockey Hall of Fame. After leaving the Reds, he moved on to become coach and general manager of the Fort Worth Red Wings of the Central Hockey League.

He returned to the NHL as a scout for Boston in 1969–1970, before becoming the head coach at Northeastern University (Boston, Massachusetts) in 1970. Flaman was named Eastern College Athletic Conference and National Collegiate Athletic Association Coach of the Year in 1982; won one ECAC title; and led his team to one NCAA Final Four appearance. In his 19 seasons with the University, he compiled a 255–301–23 record; was named United States College Coach of the Year in 1982; and led the Huskies to four Beanpot Tournament championships and a Hockey East championship in 1989. After leaving the University, he served as a scout for the NHL's New Jersey Devils from 1991 to 1995.

Ferdinand Flaman's Career Statistics

SEASON	TEAM	LEAGUE	REGULAR SEASON GP	G	A	TP	PIM	PLAYOFFS GP	G	A	TP	PIM
1942–1943	Regina Abbotts	MJHL	1	0	0	0	0					
1943–1944	Boston Olympics	EAHL	32	12	7	19	31	12	2	6	8	14
1943–1944	Brooklyn Crescents	EAHL	11	5	9	14	12					
1944–1945	Boston Bruins	NHL	1	0	0	0	0					
1944–1945	Boston Olympics	EAHL	46	16	27	43	75	10	3	5	8	13
1945–1946	Boston Bruins	NHL	1	0	0	0	0					
1945–1946	Boston Olympics	EAHL	45	11	23	34	80	12	2	7	9	11
1946–1947	Boston Bruins	NHL	23	1	4	5	41	5	0	0	0	8
1946–1947	Hershey Bears	AHL	38	4	8	12	64					
1947–1948	Boston Bruins	NHL	56	4	6	10	69	5	0	0	0	12
1948–1949	Boston Bruins	NHL	60	4	12	16	62	5	0	1	1	8
1949–1950	Boston Bruins	NHL	69	2	5	7	122					
1950–1951	Boston Bruins	NHL	14	1	1	2	37					
1950–1951	Toronto Maple Leafs	NHL	39	2	6	8	64	9	1	0	1	8
1950–1951	Pittsburgh Hornets	AHL	11	1	6	7	24					
1951–1952	Toronto Maple Leafs	NHL	61	0	7	7	110	4	0	2	2	18
1952–1953	Toronto Maple Leafs	NHL	66	2	6	8	110					
1953–1954	Toronto Maple Leafs	NHL	62	0	8	8	84	2	0	0	0	0
1954–1955	Boston Bruins	NHL	70	4	14	18	150	4	1	0	1	2
1955–1956	Boston Bruins	NHL	62	4	17	21	70					
1956–1957	Boston Bruins	NHL	68	6	25	31	108	10	0	3	3	19
1957–1958	Boston Bruins	NHL	66	0	15	15	71	12	2	2	4	10

			REGULAR SEASON					PLAYOFFS				
SEASON	TEAM	LEAGUE	GP	G	A	TP	PIM	GP	G	A	TP	PIM
1958–1959	Boston Bruins	NHL	70	0	21	21	101	7	0	0	0	8
1959–1960	Boston Bruins	NHL	60	2	18	20	112					
1960–1961	Boston Bruins	NHL	62	2	9	11	59					
1961–1962	Providence Reds	AHL	65	3	33	36	95	3	0	1	1	6
1962–1963	Providence Reds	AHL	68	4	17	21	65	6	0	2	2	0
1963–1964	Providence Reds	AHL	22	1	5	6	21	3	0	1	1	4
	NHL TOTALS		910	34	174	208	1,370	63	4	8	12	93

Sources: Hockey Hall of Fame; Hockey-Reference.com

Flamhaft, Jack (born: February 28, 1905 in New York, New York; died: June 1977 in Brooklyn, New York); inducted into the National Soccer Hall of Fame and Museum in 1964 as a builder; served as president of the American Soccer League.

Flamhaft began playing soccer in the New York high school system before attending Fordham University (Bronx, New York). Since the University did not have a soccer program at the time, he joined New York Hakoah, where he stayed for 30 years.

In 1928, while attending law school, he became a delegate to the old New York State Football Association and would eventually serve ever-higher office over the years. Starting as the Hakoah delegate to the American Soccer League, Flamhaft later served five years as president. Having been a delegate to the United States Soccer Football Association since 1935, he would later go on to serve at the national office; was a long-time vice-president for many years; and served as USSFA president for a two-year term beginning in 1959.

The Jack Flamhaft Cup is presented to the winner of the Eastern New York State Amateur Soccer Association's round-robin competition.

Source: National Soccer Hall of Fame and Museum

Fleisher, Lawrence (born: September 26, 1930 in Bronx, New York; died: May 4, 1989 in New York, New York); inducted into the Naismith Memorial Basketball Hall of Fame in 1991 as a contributor; served as general counsel for the NBA Players Association; helped implement the free agent system.

After graduating from DeWitt Clinton High School (Bronx, New York) in 1946, Fleisher attended New York University (New York, New York) and later Harvard Law School (Cambridge, Massachusetts), graduating in 1953. After finishing college, he served in the U.S. Army from 1953 to 1955.

From 1962 to 1988, he served as general counsel for the National Basketball Association Players Association (and as its president from 1962 to 1968), which over the years negotiated with the league for pensions, minimum salaries, severance pay, and disability payments. He helped create the free agent system in 1976, and represented numerous basketball players, including Bill Bradley, Dave DeBusschere, John Havlicek, Bob Lanier, Willis Reed, Jerry West, and Lenny Wilkens.

Fleisher worked with the newly created American Basketball Association in the late 1960s; was later involved with the merger of the ABA into the NBA; and organized international summer tours with NBA players competing against teams in Brazil, Yugoslavia, Italy, Greece, Israel, and the People's Republic of China.

He established the NBA Anti-Drug Agreement that provided for counseling and penalties for players involved in drug use, and negotiated the agreement that established the NBA salary cap system.

Source: Naismith Memorial Basketball Hall of Fame

Fleming, Harry G. "Pup" (born: 1900 in Scotland); inducted into the National Soccer Hall of Fame and Museum in 1967 as a builder; helped found the National Soccer Hall of Fame and Museum.

Fleming arrived in the United States in 1906 with his family and settled in the Kensington district of Philadelphia, Pennsylvania. He played soccer for Thomas Potter Public School (Philadelphia); four years with the Lighthouse Boys' Club teams; and eventually moved on to Sun Shipbuilding and then the Fairhill club from 1918 to 1920.

Beginning in 1931, and continuing after he retired as a player in 1936, Fleming was the owner-manager of the Fairhill club, and an administrator in the Allied and Pennsylvania Leagues. He helped start what is now known as the National Soccer Hall of Fame and Museum in 1950, and administered it until 1953, when it was taken over by the United States Soccer Football Association.

Source: National Soccer Hall of Fame and Museum

Fleming, Tom "Whitey" (born: January 15, 1890 in Beith, Ayrshire, Scotland; died: March 19, 1965 in Quincy, Massachusetts); inducted into the National Soccer Hall of Fame and Museum in 2005 as a player; Position: Wing-Outside Forward; won the American F.A. Cup five times, U.S. Open Cup four times, and the ASL championship three times.

One of the best wingers of his day, Fleming played soccer in Scotland for his local team in the Ayrshire Cup final (1906–1907), before coming to America in 1907. Once he settled in the Quincy, Massachusetts area, he joined the Fore River Shipyard, and helped the team win New England League and Cup in his first season. After several seasons in the New England League, Fleming returned to Scotland and joined Morton (in the First Division).

He returned to the United States before the start of World War I, and in the spring of 1914, won the American F.A. Cup playing for Bethlehem Steel. The American F.A. Cup was the championship trophy of the American Football Association, which had been formed in Newark, New Jersey in 1884, and first played in the 1884–1885 season. While playing with Bethlehem Steel, Fleming won the American F.A. Cup four more times (1916–1919) and was a member of the team that won the U.S. Open Cup four times (1915–1916, 1918–1919).

When the first American Soccer League was formed in the summer of 1921, he joined the Philadelphia Field Club, a team that was basically Bethlehem Steel, but included some players from other Philadelphia-area teams. That team won the first ASL championship, and in the summer of 1922, Fleming returned to New England and joined the J&P Coats team of Pawtucket, Rhode Island, which would go on to win the second-ever ASL championship.

He stayed with Coats for the 1923–1924 season, before moving on to the Boston Wonder Workers (1924–1925), which won the ASL championship in the 1927–1928 season.

Fleming finished his playing career in Boston having won the American F.A. Cup five times; the U.S. Open Cup four times; the ASL championship three times; the Lewis Cup once; and the American Professional Championship. While in the American Soccer League, he played 234 games (24 with Philadelphia, 49 with Coats, 161 with Boston) and scored 94 goals (15 for Philadelphia, 41 for Coats, and 38 for Boston).

After retiring as a player, he became a coach at Quincy (Massachusetts) High School.

Source: National Soccer Hall of Fame and Museum

Fletcher, George Clifford "Cliff" (born: August 16, 1935 in Montreal, Quebec, Canada); inducted into the Hockey Hall of Fame in 2004 as a builder; won a Stanley Cup title in 1989; named 1993 Executive of the Year.

Fletcher began his hockey career in 1956 with the National Hockey League's Montreal Canadiens, first as a scout and later as general manager of the Verdun Blues junior hockey team (Quebec Metropolitan Hockey League). In 1966, he joined the NHL's St. Louis Blues as a scout in eastern Canada, and later served as the team's assistant general manager. After helping the Blues reach the Stanly Cup finals the first three years of the franchise's existence (1968–1970), Fletcher was hired as the very first general manager of the Atlanta Flames, a team that joined the NHL for the 1972–1973 season.

After the team's first eight seasons, Fletcher helped move the franchise from Atlanta (Georgia) to Calgary (Alberta, Canada) in time for the 1980–1981 season. During his tenure, the Flames made the playoffs 16 straight seasons; finished first in their division three straight years (1988–1990); and won the 1989 Stanley Cup title as the Calgary Flames, the franchise's only championship as of this writing.

In 1981, Fletcher served as the general manager for Team Canada during the Canada Cup.

In 1991, after leaving the Flames, Fletcher served six seasons as chief operating officer, president, and general manager of the Toronto Maple Leafs. While he was with Toronto (1991–1997), the Leafs reached the Conference Finals in 1993 and 1994, and he was named the 1993 Executive of the Year by *The Hockey News*.

Fletcher joined the Tampa Bay Lightning in 1999, and served two seasons as a senior advisor to the general manager. In February 2001, he was hired by the NHL's Phoenix Coyotes as executive vice-president and general manager; became a senior executive vice-president of hockey operations for the team the next season; and left the team in April 2007.

In January 2008, he returned to the Toronto Maple Leafs as interim general manager.

Fletcher served seven years on the Hockey Hall of Fame Board of Directors until 2003.

Source: Hockey Hall of Fame

Flick, Elmer Harrison (born: January 11, 1876 in Bedford, Ohio; died: January 9, 1971 in Bedford, Ohio); inducted into the National Baseball Hall of Fame and Museum in 1963 as a player by the Veterans Committee; Position: Center

Field; Bats: Left; Throws: Right; won a batting title in 1905; first American League player to hit three triples in one game.

Making his major league debut on May 2, 1898, Flick played 13 seasons for the Philadelphia Phillies (1898–1901), Philadelphia Athletics (1902), and the Cleveland Naps/Indians (1902–1910). In four full years with the Phillies, Flick averaged .345 and hit a career high .378 in 1900. In nine seasons with the Cleveland Naps/Indians, he led the American League in stolen bases twice (1904, 1906); triples three times (1905–1907); and earned a batting title in 1905, hitting .308 (the lowest average to win a hitting title until Carl Yastrzemski of the Boston Red Sox hit .301 in 1968).

Following the 1901 season, the 5'9", 169-pound Flick played in the newly formed American League with the cross-town Philadelphia Athletics. However, after the Phillies took legal action to block his leaving the team, Flick moved on to the Cleveland Naps, knowing that any injunction in Pennsylvania could not be enforced in Ohio. He never visited Pennsylvania in order to avoid a subpoena, and would go on to play the rest of his career in Cleveland.

Flick hit over .300 eight times and led the league in runs batted in with 110 in 1900. On July 6, 1902, he became the first American League player to hit three triples in one game.

Elmer Flick's Career Statistics

YEAR	TEAM	LG	G	AB	R	H	2B	3B	HR	RBI	BB	SB	AVG	SLG
1898	Philadelphia	NL	133	447	84	142	16	14	8	81	86	23	.318	.470
1899	Philadelphia	NL	125	486	101	167	22	14	2	98	42	31	.344	.459
1900	Philadelphia	NL	138	547	106	207	33	16	11	110	56	35	.378	.558
1901	Philadelphia	NL	138	542	111	182	31	17	8	88	52	30	.336	.500
1902	Philadelphia	AL	11	37	15	11	2	1	0	3	6	4	.297	.405
1902	Cleveland	AL	110	427	68	126	20	11	2	61	47	20	.295	.407
1903	Cleveland	AL	142	529	84	158	23	16	2	51	51	24	.299	.414
1904	Cleveland	AL	149	575	95	174	31	18	6	56	51	42	.303	.450
1905	Cleveland	AL	132	500	72	154	29	19	4	64	53	35	.308	.466
1906	Cleveland	AL	157	624	98	194	33	22	1	62	54	39	.311	.439
1907	Cleveland	AL	147	549	80	166	15	18	3	58	64	41	.302	.412
1908	Cleveland	AL	9	35	4	8	1	1	0	2	3	0	.229	.314
1909	Cleveland	AL	66	235	28	60	10	2	0	15	22	9	.255	.315
1910	Cleveland	AL	24	68	5	18	2	1	1	7	10	1	.265	.368
	TOTALS		1,481	5,601	951	1,767	268	170	48	756	597	334	.315	.450

Sources: Baseball-Reference.com; National Baseball Hall of Fame and Museum

Florie, Thomas (born: September 6, 1897 in Harrison, New Jersey; died: April 26, 1966 in North Providence, Rhode Island); inducted into the National Soccer Hall of Fame and Museum in 1986 as a player; Position: Outside Left; International Caps (1925–1934): 8; International Goals: 2; won two U.S. Open Cup titles.

After serving in the United States Navy during World War I, Florie began his soccer career in the 1920s. He played with the Harrison Soccer Club of the American Soccer League in the 1921–1922 season, before returning to New Jersey amateur soccer for the 1922–1924 seasons in the West Hudson Amateur League.

Florie joined the Providence Clamdiggers (ASL) in 1924 and stayed with the team until early in the 1928–1929 season. He moved on to the New Bedford Whalers (ASL) and stayed until 1932, winning the U.S. Open Cup medal that season against St. Louis Stix, Bear and Fuller.

From 1924 until 1931, he scored 125 goals in the ASL, and later played for the Pawtucket Rangers (1932–1934, of the new ASL), losing the Open Cup final in 1935 against the St. Louis Central Breweries, before winning his second medal in 1941 against Detroit Chrysler.

Florie was the captain of the U.S. World Cup team in 1930 that played in Montevideo, Uruguay, eventually eliminated in the semifinal round after a 6–1 loss to Argentina. He also was a member of the 1934 World Cup team that was eliminated in the first round through a 7–1 loss to Italy in Rome.

Source: National Soccer Hall of Fame and Museum

Ford, Edward Charles "Whitey" (born: October 21, 1928 in New York, New York); inducted into the National Baseball Hall of Fame and Museum in 1974 as a player; Position: Pitcher; Bats: Left; Throws: Left; Uniform: #16; won the Cy Young Award in 1961; 1961 World Series Most Valuable Player; best winning percentage of the 20th century.

Making his major league debut on July 1, 1950, the 5'10", 181-pound Ford played his entire 16-year career with the New York Yankees (1950, 1953–1967). He played in 11 World Series (winning in 1950, 1953, 1956, 1958, 1961–1962 and losing in 1955, 1957, 1960, 1963–1964); was an eight-time All–Star (1954–1956, 1958–1961, 1964); won the Cy Young Award in 1961 as the league's top pitcher; and was the 1961 World Series Most Valuable Player.

His lifetime record of 236–106 gives him the best winning percentage (.690) of any 20th century pitcher. He led the American League in wins three times, and in earned run average and shutouts twice. He still holds numerous World Series records, including 10 wins and 94 strikeouts, while once pitching 33 consecutive scoreless innings. As of this writing, Ford still holds the Yankees record for most wins.

He was signed by the Yankees as an amateur free agent in 1947, and was nicknamed "Whitey" in the minor leagues due to his blond, almost white, hair. After one season with the Yankees, Ford served in the U.S. Army during the Korean War in 1951 and 1952, rejoining the Yankees in 1953.

In 1955, Ford led the American League in complete games and games won; in earned run average twice (1956, 1958); in winning percentage three times (1956, 1961, 1963); in games won three times (1955, 1961, 1963); and in 1961, he broke Babe Ruth's World Series record of 29-2/3 consecutive scoreless innings.

When he was inducted into the baseball hall of fame, the Yankees retired his jersey number 16, and in 1987, the team added a plaque in his honor at Yankee Stadium's Monument Park. In 1999, Ford ranked number 52 on *The Sporting News*' list of Baseball's 100 Greatest Players; was nominated for the Major League Baseball All-Century Team; and in 2003, he was inducted into the Nassau County Sports Hall of Fame.

In 11 of 16 seasons, he compiled an ERA of 3.00 or lower; allowed an average of 10.94 base runners per nine innings; and posted 45 career shutouts, including eight 1–0 wins. He was named *The Sporting News* Pitcher of the Year three times (1955, 1961, 1963), and won the Babe Ruth Award in 1961 (an annual award given to the player with the best performance in the World Series and presented by the New York chapter of the Baseball Writers Association of America). Ford set a record in 1961 by pitching 243 consecutive innings without allowing a stolen base.

Whitey Ford's Career Statistics

YEAR	TEAM	LG	W	L	PCT	G	SH	IP	H	R	ER	SO	BB	ERA
1950	New York	AL	9	1	.900	20	2	112	87	39	35	59	52	2.81
1953	New York	AL	18	6	.750	32	3	207	187	77	69	110	110	3.00
1954	New York	AL	16	8	.667	34	3	211	170	72	66	125	101	2.82
1955	New York	AL	18	7	.720	39	5	254	188	83	74	137	113	2.62
1956	New York	AL	19	6	.760	31	2	226	187	70	62	141	84	2.47
1957	New York	AL	11	5	.688	24	0	129	114	46	37	84	53	2.58
1958	New York	AL	14	7	.667	30	7	219	174	62	49	145	62	2.01
1959	New York	AL	16	10	.615	35	2	204	194	82	69	114	89	3.04
1960	New York	AL	12	9	.571	33	4	193	168	76	66	85	65	3.08
1961	New York	AL	25	4	.862	39	3	283	242	108	101	209	92	3.21
1962	New York	AL	17	8	.680	38	0	258	243	90	83	160	69	2.90
1963	New York	AL	24	7	.774	38	3	269	240	94	82	189	56	2.74
1964	New York	AL	17	6	.739	39	8	245	212	67	58	172	57	2.13
1965	New York	AL	16	13	.552	37	2	244	241	97	88	162	50	3.25
1966	New York	AL	2	5	.286	22	0	73	79	33	20	43	24	2.47
1967	New York	AL	2	4	.333	7	1	44	40	11	8	21	9	1.64
	TOTALS		236	106	.690	498	45	3,171	2,766	1,107	967	1,956	1,086	2.74

Sources: Baseball-Reference.com; National Baseball Hall of Fame and Museum

Ford, Leonard Guy, Jr. "Len" (born: February 18, 1926 in Washington, D.C.; died: March 14, 1972); inducted into the Pro Football Hall of Fame in 1976 as a player; Position: Defensive End; won three NFL championships.

After two seasons (1948–1949) with the Los Angeles Dons of the All-America Football Conference, Ford played nine years in the National Football League (99 games) with the Cleveland Browns (1950–1957) and the Green Bay Packers (1958).

The 6'4", 245-pound Ford was named All-NFL five consecutive years (1951–1955); played in four Pro Bowls (1951–1954); and recovered 20 opponent fumbles in his career (for 79 yards and one touchdown). As a member of the dominant Browns of the 1950s, he played in seven championship games (1950–1955, 1957), winning three (1950, 1954–1955).

Ford played college football for one year at Morgan State University (Baltimore, Maryland), before transferring to the University of Michigan (Ann Arbor), and after graduating, joined the Los Angeles Dons as a two-way end. As an offensive end, Ford caught 67 passes for 1,175 yards (and eight touchdowns) while with the team. When the AAFC folded in 1949, he was drafted by the Browns and became a defensive player on a unit that allowed the fewest points of any NFL team in six of seven years from 1951 to 1957.

Source: Pro Football Hall of Fame

Fortmann, Daniel John "Dan" (born: April 11, 1916 in Pearl River, New York; died: May 23, 1995 in Los Angeles, California); inducted into the Pro Football Hall of Fame in 1965 as a player; Position: Guard; drafted as the youngest player in the NFL; won three NFL championships.

After playing football at Pearl River (New York) High School, Fortmann attended Cornell University (1933–1935, Hamilton, New York), before becoming a ninth-round draft pick (78th selection overall) of the National Football League's Chicago Bears in 1936, where he played his entire career. This marked the league's first-ever draft and, at age 20, he became the youngest starter in the league. The 6', 210-pound Fortmann played on both sides of the line, and was selected First- or Second-Team All-NFL each season of his 86-game career (1936–1943). While playing football, he earned a medical degree in 1940 from the University of Chicago Medical School (Illinois), and later served as a Bears' team doctor.

The Bears were dominant during Fortmann's career and during his tenure with the team, the "Monsters of the Midway" won three NFL championships (1940–1941, 1943).

After retiring, he became a surgeon in the Los Angeles, California area, and in 1978, he was inducted into the College Football Hall of Fame.

Sources: College Football Hall of Fame; Pro Football Hall of Fame

Foster, Andrew "Rube" (born: September 17, 1879 in Calvert, Texas; died: December 9, 1930 in Kankakee, Illinois); inducted into the National Baseball Hall of Fame and Museum in 1981 as a Negro League pioneer by the Veterans Committee; often called the "Father of Black Baseball."

One of the founders and executives of the Negro Leagues, Foster played for the Chicago Union Giants (1902), Cuban X-Giants (1903), Philadelphia Giants (1904–1906), Leland Giants (1907–1910), and the Chicago American Giants (1911–1926). He also served as player-manager for the Leland Giants (1907–1910) and the Chicago American Giants (1911–1926).

Eventually serving as a player, manager, owner, commissioner, and league executive, the 6'2", 200-pound Foster started his baseball career as a star pitcher during the dead ball era (he once won 44 games in a row as a pitcher with the 1902 Cuban Giants), and in 1920, founded the first successful Negro league, the Negro National League, which prospered throughout the decade.

Known as the "Father of Black Baseball," he began his professional career with the Waco Yellow Jackets, an independent black team, in 1897, and was eventually signed by the Chicago Union Giants, a top team in black baseball, in 1902. Starting his career in a slump, later in 1902 he was released and signed with a white semi-professional team, the Bardeen's Otsego (Michigan) Independents. Toward the end of the season, he joined the Cuban X-Giants (Philadelphia) and pitched in the 1903 postseason, helping the team win the title in seven games against the Philadelphia Giants.

In 1904, playing for the Philadelphia Giants, Foster compiled a 20–6 record, including two no-hitters. In a rematch with his old team, the Cuban X-Giants, he won two games, hit .400, and led Philadelphia to the black championship. In 1905, he pitched to a 25–3 record and led the team to another championship series victory, this time over the Brooklyn Royal Giants. The following season, the Philadelphia Giants helped form the International League of Independent Professional Ball Players, made up of both all-black and all-white teams, in the Philadelphia and Wilmington, Delaware, areas. The Giants won the league's first pennant.

In 1907, Foster left the Philadelphia Giants and became player-manager of the Chicago Leland Giants, and led the team to a 110–10 record (including 48 straight wins) and the Chicago City pennant. In 1910, he became the team's owner, renamed the team the Chicago American Giants in 1911; and won the western black championship the next four seasons.

After making his last pitching appearance in 1917, Foster became a bench manager and team owner. In 1920, he and six other team owners formed the Negro National League, and he served as its president (until 1926), while remaining owner of the American Giants. The Giants won the new league's first three pennants (1920–1922), before finally losing to the Kansas City Monarchs in 1923.

His half-brother, William Foster, is also a baseball hall of fame inductee.

Source: National Baseball Hall of Fame and Museum

Foster, Harold E. "Bud" (born: May 30, 1906 in Newton, Kansas; died: July 16, 1996); inducted into the Naismith Memorial Basketball Hall of Fame in 1964 as a player; won the 1941 NCAA championship.

Foster attended Mason City (Iowa) High School from 1920 to 1924, where he played basketball for three seasons; earned a varsity letter (1924); and led the team to a third-place finish in the state championship (1924). He went on to play for Mason City Junior College (Iowa, 1924–1925) and the University of Wisconsin (Madison, 1926–1930). The 6'3", 185-pound Foster was an All-American at Wisconsin (1930); a two-time All-Big 10 Conference selection (1929–1930); helped lead the school to a share of the Big 10 title (1929); and was captain of the 1930 squad.

After graduation, and a brief professional career, he served as assistant varsity and freshman coach in 1933 at his alma mater, and became the school's head coach from 1934 to 1959. At Wisconsin, he compiled a 265–267 record; led the team to the 1941 National Collegiate Athletic Association title; and coached the Badgers to three Big 10 Conference championships (1935, 1941, 1947).

He served as president of the National Association of Basketball Coaches, and conducted more than 40 basketball clinics for the Armed Forces.

Source: Naismith Memorial Basketball Hall of Fame

Foster, William Hendrick (born: June 12, 1904 in Calvert, Texas; died: September 16, 1978 in Lorman, Mississippi); inducted into the National Baseball Hall of Fame and Museum in 1996 as a Negro League player by the Veterans Committee; Position: Pitcher; Bats: Both; Throws: Left; winning pitcher in the first-ever East-West game; won two Black World Series titles.

The half-brother of Andrew Foster, also a baseball hall of fame inductee, Foster played for the Memphis Red Sox (1923–1924, 1938), Chicago American Giants (1923–1930, 1937), Birmingham Black Barons (1925), Homestead Grays (1931), Kansas City Monarchs (1931), Cole's American Giants (1932–1935), and the Pittsburgh Crawfords (1936). He also managed the Chicago American Giants (1923–1925), and later in life (1960–1977), coached the baseball team for his alma mater, Alcorn State University (Lorman), formerly known as Alcorn Agricultural and Mechanical College.

Considered one of the best pitchers in the original Negro National League for much of its 12-year existence, he finished his career as the league's winningest pitcher. In 1926, he won 26 consecutive games, and on the last day of the season, won both games of a doubleheader to help the Chicago American Giants win the pennant. Later, in the Black World Series, he posted a 1.27 ERA to win his first championship, and was the winning pitcher in the first-ever East-West All-Star Game (1933).

In 1927, the 6'1", 195-pound pitcher posted a Negro League record of 18–3 and went 14–1 in the California Winter League. In that season's Black World Series, he helped Chicago win the title in nine games against the Bacharach Giants (Atlantic City, New Jersey). His last season in baseball was spent with a white semi-professional team in Elgin, Illinois and with a black team known as the Washington Browns (Yakima, Washington).

Source: National Baseball Hall of Fame and Museum

Foudy, Julie Maurine (born: January 23, 1971 in San Diego, California); inducted into the National Soccer Hall of Fame and Museum in 2007 as a player; Position: Center Midfield; International Caps (1987–2004): 271; International Goals: 45; first American (and woman) to win the FIFA Fair Play Award.

Playing for the U.S. Women's National Team for 17 years (1987–2004), Foudy was the captain on the team that won the silver medal in the 2000 Olympic Games (Sydney, Australia), and the gold medal-winning team in the 2004 Olympic Games (Athens, Greece). She also captained the 2002 World Cup qualifying squad and the 2003 World Cup Women's FIFA team that finished third (hosted by the United States).

During her career, she collected 271 caps (114 full-international), the third most capped player in world soccer history. Foudy was a member of U.S. teams that won the 1991 FIFA Women's World Cup (held in China); the 1999 FIFA Women's World Cup (Los Angeles, California); and won a gold medal at the 1996 Olympics Games (hosted by the United States).

At age 17, Foudy played her first international game for the United States against France in Rimini, Italy (July 29, 1988); scored her first international goal on April 3, 1991 against Hungary; played in 24 World Cup Games, 12 World Cup qualifiers, and 16 Olympic games; and played her last international game on December 8, 2004 against Mexico in Carson, California.

While attending Stanford University (Palo Alto, California), she scored 53 goals and had 32 assists; was named the 1989 Soccer America Freshman of the Year; and was named a National Soccer Coaches Association of America All-American four straight years. In 1991, Foudy was selected the Soccer America Player of the Year, and the team went to the NCAA Tournament each of her four years at Stanford. She was later selected to the Soccer America College Team of the Century.

In 1994, the 5'6", 130-pound Foudy played for the Tyreso Football Club in Sweden; for the Sacramento Storm (Women's Premier Soccer League), which won the 1993 and 1995 California State Amateur championships; played one season in the W-League; and played one season in the Japanese professional league. She played for the San Diego Spirit in the Women's United Soccer Association from 2001 to 2003, and was a Second-Team All-Star in each of her three seasons with the team. She was a founding member of the league, and played in 59 WUSA regular-season games and one WUSA playoff game.

She serves as the president of the Women's Sports Foundation, and in 1997, she became the first American, and woman, to win the FIFA Fair Play Award for her trip to Pakistan in 1997 to personally ensure that her shoe sponsor wasn't using child labor. In 2006, she launched the Julie Foudy Sports Leadership Academy.

As of this writing, she works as an in-studio analyst for ESPN on World Cups and other soccer-related events.

Foudy played soccer at Mission Viejo (California) High School, where she was a two-time First-Team All-American; named Player of the Year for Southern California three straight seasons (1987–1989); and was named the *Los Angeles Times*' soccer player of the decade. Her 2007 induction into the National Soccer Hall of Fame with Mia Hamm marked the first all-female class elected to the shrine.

Source: National Soccer Hall of Fame and Museum

Foulds, Powys, A.L. (born: October 18, 1876 in Little Hulton, Lancashire, England; died: unknown); inducted into the National Soccer Hall of Fame and Museum in 1953 as a builder; organized the first team to win the New England junior title; president of the Massachusetts state organization.

Foulds played in England with the Bolton Wanderers before moving to Canada, where he served as player-manager of the Sherbrooke team in Quebec (Ontario, Canada). Moving to the United States, he played for Trimo, Riverdale, and Walworth, and later organized the Clan Robertson team in Dorchester (Massachusetts), which won the New England title. In 1923, he helped organize the Corinthians of Revere, Massachusetts, the first team to win the New England junior title. As president of the Massachusetts state organization, Foulds organized games against teams from Quebec and New Brunswick (Canada).

His son, Samuel, is also a National Soccer Hall of Fame inductee.

Source: National Soccer Hall of Fame and Museum

Foulds, Samuel T.N. (born: August 12, 1905 in Sherbrooke, Quebec, Canada; died: January 1994 in Salem, New Hampshire); inducted into the National Soccer Hall of Fame and Museum in 1969 as a builder; president of the Bay State League; historian of the United States Soccer Federation for more than 20 years.

Foulds moved to the Boston, Massachusetts area with his parents when he was four years old, and first played soccer at O.W. Holmes Junior High School (Boston). At age 17, he signed on, as an amateur, with the Clan Robertson Club of the Boston and District League.

He was a Center Half and playing manager of the Revere Corinthians from 1924 to 1941; organized and served as president of the Bay State League from 1924 to 1936, and from 1923 to 1970, presided over the Eastern Massachusetts League, Inter-City League, Boston and District League, Massachusetts State League, and the New England League.

In later years, Foulds served as secretary, treasurer, and registration chairman of the Northern Massachusetts and New Hampshire State Association. He also coached at Revere (Massachusetts) High School and Brandeis University (Waltham, Massachusetts), and was awarded the Certificate of Merit by the National Soccer Coaches Association in 1964.

For all his achievements, Foulds will always be remembered as the historian of the United States Soccer Federation from 1972 to 1994, and who helped establish the National Soccer Hall of Fame in Oneonta, New York in 1979. He also founded the Society for American Soccer History and his father, Powys, is also a National Soccer Hall of Fame inductee.

Source: National Soccer Hall of Fame and Museum

Fouts, Daniel Francis "Dan" (born: June 10, 1951 in San Francisco, California); inducted into the Pro Football Hall of Fame in 1993 as a player; Position: Quarterback; Uniform: #14; third quarterback to pass for more than 40,000 yards;

1982 NFL Most Valuable Player; first quarterback in NFL history to throw for 4,000 or more yards in three consecutive seasons; one of only six quarterbacks in NFL history to throw 30 or more touchdowns in back-to-back seasons.

Fouts' father, Bob, was a long-time announcer for the San Francisco 49ers, and Fouts was a ball boy for the team as a young boy. After graduating from St. Ignatius High School (San Francisco), he attended the University of Oregon (Eugene), where he was an All-Pac Eight quarterback. Fouts was a third-round draft pick (84th selection overall) in 1973 of the National Football League's San Diego Chargers and would lead the team to three American Football Conference championships (1979–1981). He played his entire 15-year (1973–1987, 181 games) NFL career with the Chargers.

He was the third NFL quarterback to pass for more than 40,000 yards; was a six-time Pro Bowler (1979–1983, 1985); named All-Pro three times; AFC Player of the Year twice (1979, 1982); and named NFL Most Valuable Player in 1982.

At 6'3", 204 pounds, Fouts led the NFL in passing yardage four straight years (1979–1982) and became the first player in NFL history to throw for 4,000 yards in three consecutive seasons (1979–1981). His career got a boost when Don Coryell became head coach of the Chargers in 1978 and introduced the "Air Coryell" pass-oriented offense. Making the most of an offensive scheme to his liking, during the next eight seasons, he averaged more than 2,700 yards and 20 touchdown passes per year, and set an NFL record with 4,082 yards passing in 1979. He later surpassed his own record with 4,715 yards in 1980 and 4,802 yards in 1981. Fouts is one of only six quarterbacks in NFL history to throw 30 or more touchdowns in back-to-back seasons (1980–1981).

When he retired after the 1987 season, Fouts became a broadcaster, working for the local San Francisco television station, NBC, and briefly on ABC's "Monday Night Football." His jersey number 14 is one of two numbers retired by the San Diego Chargers, and in 1999, he was ranked number 92 on *The Sporting News*' list of the 100 Greatest Football Players. He was selected to the NFL 1980s All-Decade Team, and he holds Charger records for most passing touchdowns (254) and passing yards (43,040).

Dan Fouts' Career Statistics

						PASSING					RUSHING		
YEAR	**TEAM**	**G**	**ATT**	**COMP**	**PCT**	**YDS**	**TD**	**INT**	**RATING**	**NO**	**YDS**	**AVG**	**TD**
1973	San Diego	10	194	87	44.8	1,126	6	13	46.0	7	32	4.6	0
1974	San Diego	11	237	115	48.5	1,732	8	13	61.4	19	63	3.3	1
1975	San Diego	10	195	106	54.4	1,396	2	10	59.3	23	170	7.4	2
1976	San Diego	14	359	208	57.9	2,535	14	15	75.4	18	65	3.6	0
1977	San Diego	4	109	69	63.3	869	4	6	77.4	6	13	2.2	0
1978	San Diego	15	381	224	58.8	2,999	24	20	83.0	20	43	2.2	2
1979	San Diego	16	530	332	62.6	4,082	24	24	82.6	26	49	1.9	2
1980	San Diego	16	589	348	59.1	4,715	30	24	84.7	23	15	0.7	2
1981	San Diego	16	609	360	59.1	4,802	33	17	90.6	22	56	2.5	0
1982	San Diego	9	330	204	61.8	2,883	17	11	93.3	9	8	0.9	1
1983	San Diego	10	340	215	63.2	2,975	20	15	92.5	12	-5	-0.4	1
1984	San Diego	13	507	317	62.5	3,740	19	17	83.4	12	-29	-2.4	0
1985	San Diego	14	430	254	59.1	3,638	27	20	88.1	11	-1	-0.1	0
1986	San Diego	12	430	252	58.6	3,031	16	22	71.4	4	-3	-0.8	0
1987	San Diego	11	364	206	56.6	2,517	10	15	70.0	12	0	0.0	2
	TOTALS	181	5,604	3,297	58.8	43,040	254	242	80.2	224	476	2.1	13

Sources: Pro Football Hall of Fame; Pro-Football-Reference.com

Fowler, Daniel W. (born: July 11, 1914 in Rochester, New York; died: September 10, 1991 in Rochester, New York); inducted into the National Soccer Hall of Fame and Museum in 1970 as a builder; president of the Northwestern Inter-City League.

Fowler played high school and junior soccer before moving up to the senior level. After retiring as a player, he became both treasurer of the Northwestern Inter-City League and the first vice president of the State Association in 1946. In 1948, he became secretary of the State Association and president of the League. In 1951, Fowler became president of the State Association, a position he held for 10 years, as well as serving as president of the Northwestern Inter–City League.

His wife, Margaret, is also a soccer hall of fame inductee.

Source: National Soccer Hall of Fame and Museum

Fowler, Margaret "Peg" (born: November 9, 1916; died: February 28, 1991 in Rochester, New York); inducted into the National Soccer Hall of Fame in 1979 as a builder; second woman inducted into the soccer hall of fame.

Fowler worked with the Northwestern New York State Association and the Rochester and District Soccer League Senior Division, serving as secretary of both leagues. She was the second woman inducted into the hall of fame, and is the wife of fellow hall of fame inductee, Dan Fowler.

Source: National Soccer Hall of Fame and Museum

Fox, Jacob Nelson "Nellie" (born: December 25, 1927 in St. Thomas, Pennsylvania; died: December 1, 1975 in Baltimore, Maryland); inducted into the National Baseball Hall of Fame and Museum in 1997 as a player by the Veterans Committee; Position: Second Base; Bats: Left; Throws: Right; Uniform: #2; first Chicago White Sox player to be selected American League Most Valuable Player; set a major league record for consecutive games without striking out (98).

Making his major league debut on June 8, 1947, Fox enjoyed a 19-year career with the Philadelphia Athletics (1947–1949), Chicago White Sox (1950–1963), and the Houston Colt 45s/Astros (1964–1965). He played in the 1959 World Series (losing to the Los Angeles Dodgers); was a 12-time All-Star (1951–1961, 1963); won three Gold Gloves (1957, 1959–1960); and was named the American League Most Valuable Player in 1959 (the first White Sox player to win the award). On August 28, 1958, Fox set a major league record for consecutive games without striking out (98).

Relatively small (5'9", 150 pounds), he was part of the "Go-Go" White Sox of the 1950s, and he led the team to its first World Series in 40 years. He led the American League in hits four times and in fewest strikeouts 10 times; set the major league record for consecutive games played at second base (798, August 7, 1956 through September 3, 1960); and still holds the record for most consecutive years leading the league in singles (seven, 1954–1960).

Fox retired with a 42.7 strikeouts to at-bats ratio; led the league in most at-bats per strikeouts 13 times; and his uniform number two was retired by the Whites Sox in 1976.

Nellie Fox's Career Statistics

YEAR	TEAM	LG	G	AB	R	H	2B	3B	HR	RBI	BB	SO	SB	AVG	SLG
1947	Philadelphia	AL	7	3	2	0	0	0	0	0	1	0	0	.000	.000
1948	Philadelphia	AL	3	13	0	2	0	0	0	0	1	0	1	.154	.154
1949	Philadelphia	AL	88	247	42	63	6	2	0	21	32	9	2	.255	.296
1950	Chicago	AL	130	457	45	113	12	7	0	30	35	17	4	.247	.304
1951	Chicago	AL	147	604	93	189	32	12	4	55	43	11	9	.313	.425
1952	Chicago	AL	152	648	76	192	25	10	0	39	34	14	5	.296	.366
1953	Chicago	AL	154	624	92	178	31	8	3	72	49	18	4	.285	.375
1954	Chicago	AL	155	631	111	201	24	8	2	47	51	12	16	.319	.391
1955	Chicago	AL	154	636	100	198	28	7	6	59	38	15	7	.311	.406
1956	Chicago	AL	154	649	109	192	20	10	4	52	44	14	8	.296	.376
1957	Chicago	AL	155	619	110	196	27	8	6	61	75	13	5	.317	.415
1958	Chicago	AL	155	623	82	187	21	6	0	49	47	11	5	.300	.353
1959	Chicago	AL	156	624	84	191	34	6	2	70	71	13	5	.306	.389
1960	Chicago	AL	150	605	85	175	24	10	2	59	50	13	2	.289	.372
1961	Chicago	AL	159	606	67	152	11	5	2	51	59	12	2	.251	.295
1962	Chicago	AL	157	621	79	166	27	7	2	54	38	12	1	.267	.343
1963	Chicago	AL	137	539	54	140	19	0	2	42	24	17	0	.260	.306
1964	Houston	NL	133	442	45	117	12	6	0	28	27	13	0	.265	.319
1965	Houston	NL	21	41	3	11	2	0	0	1	0	2	0	.268	.317
	TOTALS		2,367	9,232	1,279	2,663	355	112	35	790	719	216	76	.288	.363

Sources: Baseball-Reference.com; National Baseball Hall of Fame and Museum

Foxx, James Emory "Jimmie" (born: October 22, 1907 in Sudlersville, Maryland; died: July 21, 1967 in Miami, Florida); inducted into the National Baseball Hall of Fame and Museum in 1951 as a player; Position: First Base; Bats: Right; Throws: Right; Uniform: #3; a three-time American League Most Valuable Player; holds the American League record for most walks in a game (6).

Making his major league debut on May 1, 1925 at age 17, Foxx enjoyed a 20-year career with the Philadelphia Athletics (1925–1935), Boston Red Sox (1936–1942), Chicago Cubs (1942, 1944), and the Philadelphia Phillies (1945). He played in three World Series (winning in 1929 and 1930, while losing in 1931); was named to nine All-Star teams (1933–1941); and was the American League Most Valuable Player three times (1932–1933, 1938).

Foxx was the second player in major league history to collect more than 500 home runs. The 6', 195-pound first baseman hit 30 or more home runs in 12 consecutive seasons (1929–1940) and drove in more than 100 runs 13 consecutive years (1929–1941). He won back-to-back MVP awards in 1932 and 1933; won the Triple Crown in 1933 (leading the league in home runs, runs batted in, and batting average); and holds the American League record for most walks in a game with six (June 16, 1938).

Nicknamed "Double X," he led the league in home runs four times (1932–1933, 1935, 1939); in RBI's three times (1932–1933, 1938); won two batting titles (1933, 1938); and led the league in runs scored in 1932.

After retiring as a player, Foxx worked as a minor league manager and coach, including managing the Fort Wayne Daisies of the All-American Girls Professional Baseball League. He served as the head coach for the University of Miami (Coral Gables, Florida) baseball team for two seasons, compiling an overall record of 20–20. In 1999, he was ranked number 15 on *The Sporting News*' list of the 100 Greatest Baseball Players, and was a nominee for the Major League Baseball All-Century Team.

He ended his career in style playing one season with the Philadelphia Phillies in 1945. During that year, he played first, third, catcher, pinch hit, and pitched in nine games and finished the season with a 1–0 record and a 1.59 ERA over 22-2/3 innings.

His 12 consecutive seasons with 30 or more home runs was a major league record until broken by Barry Bonds in 2004. His 534 career home runs placed him second only to Babe Ruth on the all-time list, and first among right-handed hitters.

Jimmie Foxx's Career Statistics

YEAR	TEAM	LG	G	AB	R	H	2B	3B	HR	RBI	BB	SO	SB	AVG	SLG
1925	Philadelphia	AL	10	9	2	6	1	0	0	0	0	1	0	.667	.778
1926	Philadelphia	AL	26	32	8	10	2	1	0	5	1	6	1	.313	.438
1927	Philadelphia	AL	61	130	23	42	6	5	3	20	14	11	2	.323	.515
1928	Philadelphia	AL	118	400	85	131	29	10	13	79	60	43	3	.328	.548
1929	Philadelphia	AL	149	517	123	183	23	9	33	118	103	70	10	.354	.625
1930	Philadelphia	AL	153	562	127	188	33	13	37	156	93	66	7	.335	.637
1931	Philadelphia	AL	139	515	93	150	32	10	30	120	73	84	4	.291	.567
1932	Philadelphia	AL	154	585	151	213	33	9	58	169	116	96	3	.364	.749
1933	Philadelphia	AL	149	573	125	204	37	9	48	163	96	93	2	.356	.703
1934	Philadelphia	AL	150	539	120	180	28	6	44	130	111	75	11	.334	.653
1935	Philadelphia	AL	147	535	118	185	33	7	36	115	114	99	6	.346	.636
1936	Boston	AL	155	585	130	198	32	8	41	143	105	119	13	.338	.631
1937	Boston	AL	150	569	111	162	24	6	36	127	99	96	10	.285	.538
1938	Boston	AL	149	565	139	197	33	9	50	175	119	76	5	.349	.704
1939	Boston	AL	124	467	130	168	31	10	35	105	89	72	4	.360	.694
1940	Boston	AL	144	515	106	153	30	4	36	119	101	87	4	.297	.581
1941	Boston	AL	135	487	87	146	27	8	19	105	93	103	2	.300	.505
1942	Boston	AL	30	100	18	27	4	0	5	14	18	15	0	.270	.460
1942	Chicago	NL	70	205	25	42	8	0	3	19	22	55	1	.205	.288
1944	Chicago	NL	15	20	0	1	1	0	0	2	2	5	0	.050	.100
1945	Philadelphia	NL	89	224	30	60	11	1	7	38	23	39	0	.268	.420
	TOTALS		2,317	8,134	1,751	2,646	458	125	534	1,922	1,452	1,311	88	.325	.609

Sources: Baseball-Reference.com; National Baseball Hall of Fame and Museum

Foyston, Frank Corbett (born: February 2, 1891 in Minesing, Ontario, Canada; died: January 19, 1966 in Seattle, Washington); inducted into the Hockey Hall of Fame in 1958 as a player; Position: Forward-Right Wing; one of the first players to score more than 200 goals; led the first American team to win the Stanley Cup; won three Stanley Cup titles.

Foyston played 16 professional hockey seasons from 1912 to 1928, and was one of the first players to score more than 200 career goals. He made his professional debut with the Toronto Blueshirts of the National Hockey Association in 1912–1913, and helped lead the team to the Stanley Cup title in 1914.

He joined the Seattle Metropolitans (Pacifica Coast Hockey Association) in 1915; stayed with the team for nine seasons; led the league in scoring twice; and helped the team win a Stanley Cup championship in 1917 against the Montreal Canadiens, the first time a U.S. team won the Cup. Two years later, he led Seattle to a Stanley Cup rematch with the Canadiens, but the series was eventually cancelled due to the major influenza epidemic of 1919.

During his final two seasons in the PCHA (1924–1926), Foyston played with the Victoria Cougars, and helped the team become the last non-National Hockey League squad to win the Stanley Cup (1925), again beating the Canadiens. When Victoria players were sold to the NHL's Detroit Cougars, Foyston joined the team and scored 17 goals in less than two NHL seasons, before joining the Detroit Olympics of the Canadian Professional Hockey League as a player-coach. In 1929, he retired as a player; continued to manage the Olympics before moving on to the Syracuse Stars (International Hockey League, 1930–1931); coached the Bronx Tigers of the Can-Am Hockey League (1931–1932); led the Seattle Seahawks of the North West Hockey League (1934–1935); and later served as a scout for the NHL's Detroit Red Wings.

Frank Foyston's Career Statistics

			REGULAR SEASON					PLAYOFFS				
SEASON	TEAM	LEAGUE	GP	G	A	TP	PIM	GP	G	A	TP	PIM
1908–1909	Barrie Athletic Club	OHA-Jr.	6	17	0	17	9					
1909–1910	Barrie Athletic Club	OHA-Jr.										
1910–1911	Barrie Athletic Club	OHA-Sr.	6	14	0	14						
1911–1912	Toronto Eaton's	TMHL	6	15	0	15		4	5	0	5	9
1912–1913	Toronto Blueshirts	NHA	16	8	0	8	8					
1913–1914	Toronto Blueshirts	NHA	19	16	2	18	8	2	1	0	1	0
1913–1914	Toronto Blueshirts	St-Cup						3	2	0	2	3
1914–1915	Toronto Blueshirts	NHA	20	13	9	22	11					
1915–1916	Toronto Blueshirts	NHA	1	0	0	0	0					
1915–1916	Seattle Metropolitans	PCHA	18	9	4	13	6					
1916–1917	Seattle Metropolitans	PCHA	24	36	12	48	51					
1916–1917	Seattle Metropolitans	St-Cup						4	7	3	10	3
1917–1918	Seattle Metropolitans	PCHA	13	9	5	14	9	2	0	0	0	3
1918–1919	Seattle Metropolitans	PCHA	18	15	4	19	0	2	3	0	3	0
1918–1919	Seattle Metropolitans	St-Cup						5	9	1	10	0
1919–1920	Seattle Metropolitans	PCHA	22	26	3	29	3	2	3	1	4	0
1919–1920	Seattle Metropolitans	St-Cup						5	6	1	7	7
1920–1921	Seattle Metropolitans	PCHA	23	26	4	30	10	2	1	0	1	0
1921–1922	Seattle Metropolitans	PCHA	24	16	7	23	25	2	0	0	0	3
1922–1923	Seattle Metropolitans	PCHA	30	20	8	28	21					
1923–1924	Seattle Metropolitans	PCHA	30	17	6	23	8	2	1	0	1	0
1924–1925	Victoria Cougars	WCHL	27	6	5	11	6	4	1	1	2	2
1924–1925	Victoria Cougars	St-Cup						4	1	0	1	0
1925–1926	Victoria Cougars	WHL	12	6	3	9	8	3	2	0	2	4
1925–1926	Victoria Cougars	St-Cup						4	0	0	0	2
1926–1927	Detroit Cougars	NHL	41	10	5	15	16					
1927–1928	Detroit Olympics	Can-Pro	19	3	2	5	14					
1927–1928	Detroit Cougars	NHL	23	7	2	9	16					
1928–1929	Detroit Olympics	Can-Pro	42	18	6	24	20	7	0	0	0	9
1929–1930	Detroit Olympics	IHL	31	2	1	3	6	3	0	0	0	0
1931–1932	Bronx Tigers	Can-Am										
	NHL TOTALS		64	17	7	24	32					

Sources: Hockey Hall of Fame; Hockey-Reference.com

Francis, Emile (born: September 13, 1926 in North Battleford, Saskatchewan, Canada); inducted into the Hockey Hall of Fame in 1982 as a builder; developed an early version of the present-day goalie glove; founded the New York Junior League.

Relatively small (5'6", 145 pounds), Francis had a four-decade association with hockey as a player, coach, general manager, and administrator. He started his hockey career as a goalie in the minors and juniors, before playing professionally in the Eastern Hockey League.

After serving one year in the Canadian Armed Forces during Word War II, Francis returned to the game, and in the 1945–1946 season, developed an early version of the present-day goalie glove.

He went on to play 95 regular-season games with the National Hockey League's Chicago Black Hawks and New York Rangers, and his last professional season was with the Western Hockey League's Seattle Totems (1959–1960).

After retiring as a player, Francis began a 16-year association with the Guelph Royals juniors (Ontario Hockey Association), first as the team's coach. During his tenure, he would also coach the New York Rangers intermittently, and led the team to the 1972 Stanley Cup finals, eventually losing to the Boston Bruins. He later served as the general manager of the Rangers from 1964 to 1975.

Francis coached 654 regular-season games in New York; won 342; and compiled a .602 winning percentage, all Ranger coaching records. *The Hockey News* named him NHL Coach of the Year twice (1967, 1972). He joined the NHL's St. Louis Blues in 1976; eventually served as the team's executive vice president, president, general manager, and coach; and led the squad to a franchise-record 107 points in the 1980–1981 season. During his tenure, the Blues made the playoffs in five of seven seasons and won the Smythe Division title twice (1977, 1981). In 1981, he was named NHL Executive of the Year by both *The Sporting News* and *The Hockey News*.

In 1983, Francis moved on to the Hartford Whalers as the team's president and general manager, and helped the franchise win the Adams Division title in 1987, before retiring from the NHL in 1993.

A long-time supporter of minor league hockey, Francis founded the New York Junior League; the St. Louis Metro Junior B League; was a consultant to the Amateur Hockey Association of the United States; and was awarded the Lester Patrick Trophy in 1982 for his contribution to the game in the United States.

In 2001, the American Hockey League created the Emile Francis Trophy, which is awarded to the regular-season winner of the AHL North Division.

Source: Hockey Hall of Fame

Francis, Ronald "Ron" (born: March 1, 1963 in Sault Ste. Marie, Ontario, Canada); inducted into the Hockey Hall of Fame in 2007 as a player; Position: Center-Forward; Uniform: #10 (with the Whalers/Hurricanes); won two Stanley Cup championships; scored more points than games played.

After playing less than 18 months of junior hockey, Francis joined the National Hockey League's Hartford Whalers early in the 1981–1982 season, after he had been selected fourth overall in the 1981 NHL Entry Draft. In his rookie year, Francis scored 25 goals and 43 assists (68 points).

During his 23-year NHL career, he played for the Whalers (1981–1991), Pittsburgh Penguins (1991–1998), Carolina Hurricanes (1998–2004, the name the Hartford Whalers took when the franchise relocated to Raleigh, North Carolina), and the Toronto Maple Leafs (2004). He played in four All-Star Games (1983, 1985, 1990, 1996); won the Frank J. Selke Trophy (as the league's top defensive forward); and the Lady Byng Trophy in 1995 (for sportsmanship and gentlemanly conduct). He won the Lady Byng Trophy twice more (1998, 2002) and the King Clancy Memorial Trophy (2002 for his leadership on and off the ice and for his humanitarian contributions in his community).

Midway through the 1984–1985 season, the 6'3", 200-pound Francis was made team captain, at age 22, one of the youngest captains in NHL history. In the middle of the 1990–1991 season, he was traded to the Pittsburgh Penguins, and helped the team win back-to-back Stanley Cup titles (1991–1992); and scored 100 or more points twice (1993, 1996). In 1998, he left the Penguins and joined the Carolina Hurricanes; became the team's captain; and in 2002, led the franchise to its first-ever Stanley Cup Finals, eventually losing to the Detroit Red Wings in five games.

Francis played almost six seasons in Carolina before being sent to the Toronto Maple Leafs in 2004. Following the lock-out season of 2004–2005, he retired, and in 2006, he returned to the Hurricanes as the director of player development and assistant general manager.

He retired scoring more points than games played (1,798 points in 1,731 games); one of the few players in NHL history to score 500 goals and record 1,000 assists; and in January 2006, his number 10 jersey was retired by the Hurricanes.

Ron Francis' Career Statistics

			REGULAR SEASON					PLAYOFFS				
SEASON	TEAM	LEAGUE	GP	G	A	TP	PIM	GP	G	A	TP	PIM
1979–1980	Sault Ste. Marie Legion	NOHA	45	57	92	149						
1980–1981	Sault Ste. Marie Greyhounds	OMJHL	64	26	43	69	33	19	7	8	15	34
1981–1982	Sault Ste. Marie Greyhounds	OHL	25	18	30	48	46					
1981–1982	Hartford Whalers	NHL	59	25	43	68	51					
1982–1983	Hartford Whalers	NHL	79	31	59	90	60					
1983–1984	Hartford Whalers	NHL	72	23	60	83	45					
1984–1985	Hartford Whalers	NHL	80	24	57	81	66					
1984–1985	Canada	WEC-A	10	2	5	7	2					
1985–1986	Hartford Whalers	NHL	53	24	53	77	24	10	1	2	3	4

SEASON	TEAM	LEAGUE	REGULAR SEASON GP	G	A	TP	PIM	PLAYOFFS GP	G	A	TP	PIM
1986–1987	Hartford Whalers	NHL	75	30	63	93	45	6	2	2	4	6
1987–1988	Hartford Whalers	NHL	80	25	50	75	87	6	2	5	7	2
1988–1989	Hartford Whalers	NHL	69	29	48	77	36	4	0	2	2	0
1989–1990	Hartford Whalers	NHL	80	32	69	101	73	7	3	3	6	8
1990–1991	Hartford Whalers	NHL	67	21	55	76	51					
1990–1991	Pittsburgh Penguins	NHL	14	2	9	11	21	24	7	10	17	24
1991–1992	Pittsburgh Penguins	NHL	70	21	33	54	30	21	8	19	27	6
1992–1993	Pittsburgh Penguins	NHL	84	24	76	100	68	12	6	11	17	19
1993–1994	Pittsburgh Penguins	NHL	82	27	66	93	62	6	0	2	2	6
1994–1995	Pittsburgh Penguins	NHL	44	11	48	59	18	12	6	13	19	4
1995–1996	Pittsburgh Penguins	NHL	77	27	92	119	56	11	3	6	9	4
1996–1997	Pittsburgh Penguins	NHL	81	27	63	90	20	5	1	2	3	2
1997–1998	Pittsburgh Penguins	NHL	81	25	62	87	20	6	1	5	6	2
1998–1999	Carolina Hurricanes	NHL	82	21	31	52	34	3	0	1	1	0
1999–2000	Carolina Hurricanes	NHL	78	23	50	73	18					
2000–2001	Carolina Hurricanes	NHL	82	15	50	65	32	3	0	0	0	0
2001–2002	Carolina Hurricanes	NHL	80	27	50	77	18	23	6	10	16	6
2002–2003	Carolina Hurricanes	NHL	82	22	35	57	30					
2003–2004	Carolina Hurricanes	NHL	68	10	20	30	14					
2003–2004	Toronto Maple Leafs	NHL	12	3	7	10	0	12	0	4	4	2
	NHL TOTALS		1,731	549	1,249	1,798	979	171	46	97	143	95

Sources: Hockey Hall of Fame; Hockey-Reference.com

Frazier, Walter Jr. "Walt" (born: March 29, 1945 in Atlanta, Georgia); inducted into the Naismith Memorial Basketball Hall of Fame in 1987 as a player; Position: Guard; Uniform: #10; won NIT title in 1967; won two NBA titles.

Frazier went to David Howard High School (Atlanta, Georgia) from 1959 to 1963, and was team captain his senior year before moving on to Southern Illinois University (Edwardsville) from 1963 to 1967. At SIU, he was a Division II All-American twice (1964–1965); named to *The Sporting News* All-America Second Team in 1967; averaged 17.7 points per game over 50 games; led the school to the 1965 National Collegiate Athletic Association Division II Tournament, eventually losing to Evansville in the final and being named to the All-Tournament Team; named Division I All-American in 1967; led SIU to the 1967 National Invitation Tournament title over Marquette; and was named NIT Most Valuable Player.

After college, Frazier was a 1967 first-round draft pick (fifth selection overall) of the National Basketball Association's New York Knicks. During his 13-year NBA career, he played for the Knicks (1967–1977) and the Cleveland Cavaliers (1977–1980); was named to the NBA All-Rookie Team in 1968; the All-NBA First Team four times (1970, 1972, 1974–1975); the All-NBA Second Team twice (1971, 1973); the NBA All-Defensive First Team seven times (1969–1975); was a seven-time NBA All-Star (1970–1976); and was named MVP of the 1975 All-Star Game.

He won two NBA titles with the Knicks (1970, the franchise's first, 1973) and established team records for most games played (759), minutes (28,995), field goals attempted (11,669), field goals made (5,736), free throws attempted (4,017), free throws made (3,145), assists (4,791), and points (14,617). The Knicks retired his number 10 in 1979, and in 1996, he was named to the NBA 50th Anniversary All-Time Team.

The oldest of nine children, in high school Frazier played basketball, quarterbacked the football team, and was the school's baseball catcher. Led by Frazier, SIU became the first small school to win the National Invitation Tournament.

He and teammate Phil Jackson (who would later go on to coach the Chicago Bulls and the Los Angeles Lakers) were both named to the NBA All-Rookie team. When the Knicks acquired guard Earl Monroe during the 1971–1972 season, he and Frazier combined to form the famous "Rolls-Royce backcourt." In 1972–1973, the duo's first full season together, the Knicks won the franchise's second NBA title by beating the Los Angeles Lakers in five games.

He was traded to the Cleveland Cavaliers in 1977, but only played in 66 games in three seasons with the team, and retired three games into the 1979–1980 season.

After retiring, Frazier became a player agent; invested in a team in the short-lived United States Basketball League; and moved to the U.S. Virgin Islands to become a charter-boat captain. He returned to New York in 1989 to work as an analyst on Knicks broadcasts, first on radio and eventually on television.

Walt Frazier's Career Statistics

SEASON	TEAM	LG	G	MIN	FG	FT	TRB	AST	STL	BLK	PTS
1967–1968	New York	NBA	74	1,588	256	154	313	305			666
1968–1969	New York	NBA	80	2,949	531	341	499	635			1,403
1969–1970	New York	NBA	77	3,040	600	409	465	629			1,609
1970–1971	New York	NBA	80	3,455	651	434	544	536			1,736
1971–1972	New York	NBA	77	3,126	669	450	513	446			1,788
1972–1973	New York	NBA	78	3,181	681	286	570	461			1,648
1973–1974	New York	NBA	80	3,338	674	295	536	551	161	15	1,643
1974–1975	New York	NBA	78	3,204	672	331	465	474	190	14	1,675
1975–1976	New York	NBA	59	2,427	470	186	400	351	106	9	1,126
1976–1977	New York	NBA	76	2,687	532	259	293	403	132	9	1,323
1977–1978	Cleveland	NBA	51	1,664	336	153	209	209	77	13	825
1978–1979	Cleveland	NBA	12	279	54	21	20	32	13	2	129
1979–1980	Cleveland	NBA	3	27	4	2	3	8	2	1	10
	TOTALS		825	30,965	6,130	3,321	4,830	5,040	681	63	15,581

Sources: Basketball-Reference.com; Naismith Memorial Basketball Hall of Fame

Fredrickson, Frank (born: June 11, 1895 in Winnipeg, Manitoba, Canada; died: May 28, 1979 in Vancouver, British Columbia, Canada); inducted into the Hockey Hall of Fame in 1958 as a player; Position: Center-Forward; won a gold medal at the 1920 Summer Olympics; won one Stanley Cup title.

Fredrickson played 11 professional hockey seasons from 1920 to 1931, including in the National Hockey League with the Detroit Cougars (1926–1927), Boston Bruins (1926–1928), Pittsburgh Pirates (1928–1930), and the Detroit Falcons (1930–1931). His professional career began in 1920 with the Victoria Aristocrats of the Pacific Coast Hockey Association, and in the 1922–1923 season he led the league with 39 goals and set a new record with 55 points.

Before starting his professional career, Fredrickson had enlisted in the army during World War I and helped form a military hockey team in 1916–1917 before serving overseas.

After the war, he played on the team that represented Canada in the 1920 Summer Olympics (Antwerp, Belgium), and won the gold medal. After the Olympics, Fredrickson turned professional when his Victoria Cougars joined the Western Canada Hockey League for the 1924–1925 season. He led the team to the league title; won the Stanley Cup championship over the Montreal Canadiens; and was named to the Pacific Coast Hockey Association First All-Star Team four straight years (1921–1924) and to the West Coast Hockey League First All-Star team in 1926.

In 1981, he was inducted into the Manitoba Sports Hall of Fame.

Frank Fredrickson's Career Statistics

			REGULAR SEASON					PLAYOFFS				
SEASON	TEAM	LEAGUE	GP	G	A	TP	PIM	GP	G	A	TP	PIM
1913–1914	Winnipeg Falcons	MHL-Sr.	11	13	7	20	0					
1914–1915	Winnipeg Falcons	MHL-Sr.	8	10	5	15	0	1	1	0	1	0
1915–1916	Winnipeg Falcons	MHL-Sr.	6	13	3	16	14					
1916–1917	Winnipeg 223rd Battalion	MHL-Sr.	8	17	3	20	40					
1919–1920	Winnipeg Falcons	MHL-Sr.	10	23	5	28	12					
1919–1920	Winnipeg Falcons	Allen Cup	6	22	5	27	2					
1919–1920	Canada	Olympics	3	12	0	12	7					
1920–1921	Victoria Aristocrats	PCHA	21	20	12	32	3					
1921–1922	Victoria Aristocrats	PCHA	24	15	10	25	26					
1922–1923	Victoria Cougars	PCHA	30	39	16	55	26	2	2	0	2	4
1923–1924	Victoria Cougars	PCHA	30	19	8	27	28					
1924–1925	Victoria Cougars	WCHL	28	22	8	30	43	4	3	1	4	2
1924–1925	Victoria Cougars	St-Cup						4	3	2	5	6
1925–1926	Victoria Cougars	WHL	30	16	8	24	89	4	2	1	3	6
1925–1926	Victoria Cougars	St-Cup						4	1	1	2	10
1926–1927	Detroit Cougars	NHL	16	4	6	10	12					
1926–1927	Boston Bruins	NHL	28	14	7	21	33	8	2	2	4	20
1927–1928	Boston Bruins	NHL	41	10	4	14	83	2	0	1	1	4
1928–1929	Boston Bruins	NHL	12	3	1	4	24					
1928–1929	Pittsburgh Pirates	NHL	31	3	7	10	28					

			REGULAR SEASON					PLAYOFFS				
SEASON	TEAM	LEAGUE	GP	G	A	TP	PIM	GP	G	A	TP	PIM
1929–1930	Pittsburgh Pirates	NHL	9	4	7	11	20					
1930–1931	Detroit Falcons	NHL	24	1	2	3	6					
1930–1931	Detroit Olympics	IHL	6	0	1	1	2					
1931–1932	Winnipegs	WJrHL										
	NHL TOTALS		161	39	34	73	206	10	2	3	5	24

Sources: Hockey Hall of Fame; Hockey-Reference.com; Manitoba Sports Hall of Fame

Frick, Ford Christopher (born: December 19, 1894 in Wawaka, Indiana; died: April 8, 1978 in Bronxville, New York); inducted into the National Baseball Hall of Fame and Museum in 1970 as a pioneer-executive by the Veterans Committee; first reporter to broadcast daily sports reports; National League president for 17 years; Major League Baseball commissioner for 14 years; developed the 10 Commandments of Umpiring.

A lifelong baseball fan, Frick was a graduate of DePauw University (Greencastle, Indiana); a New York City sportswriter for the *New York American*; and the first to broadcast daily sports reports, before becoming the National League's public relations director in 1934. He became league president later in 1934; served for 17 years (1934–1951); played a major role in obtaining support for the establishment of the National Baseball Hall of Fame and Museum; and later served 14 seasons (1951–1965) as Major League Baseball Commissioner.

While serving as National League president, several members of the St. Louis Cardinals planned to protest Jackie Robinson's breaking of baseball's color barrier. Hearing of the plans, Frick threatened any player involved with suspension, which basically ended the protests.

In 1949, he developed his "10 Commandments of Umpiring:" (1) keep your eye on the ball; (2) keep all your personalities out of your work, forget and forgive; (3) avoid sarcasm, don't insist on the last word; (4) never charge a player and, above all, no pointing your finger or yelling; (5) hear only the things you should hear, be deaf to others; (6) keep your temper, a decision made in anger is never sound; (7) watch your language; (8) take pride in your work at all times, remember, respect for an umpire is created off the field as well as on; (9) review your work, you will find, if you are honest, that 90% of the trouble is traceable to loafing; and (10) no matter what your opinion of another umpire, never make an adverse comment regarding him, to do so is despicable and ungentlemanly.

One of his most criticized decisions as commissioner was in convincing baseball record-keepers to list the single-season home run records of Babe Ruth and Roger Maris separately (with an "*") in 1961, based on the length of the season played. It was later revealed that Frick had been the ghostwriter of *Babe Ruth's Own Book of Baseball* and some critics charge that he had made the decision in an effort not to tarnish Ruth's reputation. Eventually, the "asterisk" was removed from the record book. As commissioner, he oversaw the growth from eight to ten teams in each league; helped negotiate more profitable national television contracts; developed a league draft and college scholarship system; and spurred the introduction of baseball on an international level (Japan, Central America, Holland, Italy, and Africa).

The first baseball commissioner not to have a legal or political background, Frick had been an English teacher at Colorado High School (Denver) after college, and was also a freelance writer for the *Colorado Springs Gazette*. After two years, he left teaching to become the supervisor of training in the rehabilitation division of the War Department for four states (Colorado, Utah, New Mexico, and Wyoming). He left his government job and worked for the *Rocky Mountain News* in Denver for a brief period, before returning to Colorado Springs to open his own advertising agency and write a weekly editorial column for the *Colorado Springs Telegraph*.

In 1922, he moved to New York City and joined the sports staff of the *New York American*, a Hearst newspaper. In 1923, he joined the *Evening Journal* and covered the New York Yankees, eventually becoming a ghostwriter for Babe Ruth. He left the newspaper business to become a sports broadcaster for WOR radio. Frick was named the first director of the National League Service Bureau, and was put in charge of all publicity for Major League Baseball, leading to his eventually becoming league president.

In 1978, Major League Baseball created the Ford C. Frick Award, presented annually to a broadcaster for "major contributions to baseball."

Source: National Baseball Hall of Fame and Museum

Fricker, Werner (born: January 24, 1936 in Karlsdotf, Yugoslavia; died: May 30, 2001 in Horsham, Pennsylvania); inducted into the National Soccer Hall of Fame and Museum in 1992 as a player; Position: Halfback; won one National Amateur Cup; president of the U.S. Soccer Federation.

Fricker and his family moved to Austria at the end of World War II, before immigrating to the United States in 1952. He was captain of the United German-Hungarians team of Philadelphia (Pennsylvania) from 1958 to 1969, including the National Amateur Cup-winning team of 1965.

He also served on the executive committee of the Confederation of North, Central American and Caribbean Association Football; was chairman of the CONCACAF Finance Committee; president of the U.S. Soccer Federation from 1984 to 1990; and led the bid to bring the 1994 World Cup to the United States.

In 2002, U.S. Soccer created the Werner Fricker Builder Award, annually presented to those who have worked to promote the sport of soccer.

Source: National Soccer Hall of Fame and Museum

Friedman, Benjamin "Benny" (born: March 18, 1905 in Cleveland, Ohio; died: November 23, 1982 in New York, New York); inducted into the Pro Football Hall of Fame in 2005 as a player; Position: Quarterback; only quarterback to lead the NFL in both rushing touchdowns and passing touchdowns in a single season.

A two-time All-American quarterback at the University of Michigan (Ann Arbor, 1924–1926), Friedman played eight seasons for the Cleveland Bulldogs (1927), Detroit Wolverines (1928), New York Giants (1929–1931), and the Brooklyn Dodgers (1932–1934). He threw a then-league record 11 touchdowns as a rookie in 1927, and set another record with 20 touchdowns in 1929; led the league in touchdown passes four consecutive seasons (1927–1930); and his 66 career touchdown passes was an NFL record for years.

In 1928, the 5'10", 183-pound Friedman became the only quarterback in NFL history to lead the league in both passing and rushing touchdowns. While playing in the NFL, he also was an assistant coach at Yale University (New Haven, Connecticut).

He was selected to the All-NFL Third-Team in 1931 and to the All-NFL Second-Team in 1933.

Friedman became the starting quarterback and placekicker midway through his sophomore year at Michigan, while also playing in the defensive backfield. In 1925 and 1926, he led the Wolverines to consecutive 7–1 seasons and first place finishes in the Big Ten. On October 10, 1925, in a game against Indiana University, Friedman accounted for 44 points (throwing for five touchdowns, kicking two field goals, and eight extra points) in a 63–0 shutout win. In 1926, he was a consensus First-Team All-American and Most Valuable Player of the Big Ten.

After retiring as a player, he coached at City College of New York (1934–1941); served in the Navy during World War II; and moved to Brandeis University (Waltham, Massachusetts) as athletic director (1949–1961) and head football coach (1951–1959) until the program was disbanded.

Friedman has been inducted into the College Football Hall of Fame (1951) and the International Jewish Sports Hall of Fame (1979).

Benny Friedman's Career Statistics

					PASSING					RUSHING		
YEAR	**TEAM**	**G**	**ATT**	**COMP**	**YDS**	**TDS**	**INT**	**RATING**	**NO**	**YDS**	**AVG**	**TDS**
1927	Cleveland	13				11						2
1928	Detroit	10				9						6
1929	New York	15				20						2
1930	New York	15				13						6
1931	New York	9				3						2
1932	Brooklyn	11	74	23	319	5	10	28.9	88	250	2.8	0
1933	Brooklyn	7	80	42	594	5	7	61.1	55	177	3.2	0
1934	Brooklyn	1	13	5	16	0	2	7.1	9	31	3.4	0
	TOTALS	81	167	70	929	66	19	60.2	152	458	3.0	18

Sources: College Football Hall of Fame; International Jewish Sports Hall of Fame; Pro Football Hall of Fame; Pro-Football-Reference.com

Friedman, Max "Marty" (born: July 12, 1889 in New York, New York; died: January 1, 1986); inducted into the Naismith Memorial Basketball Hall of Fame in 1972 as a player; Position: Guard; played 20 years of professional basketball; won eight league titles.

Friedman attended high school at Hebrew Tech Institute (New York, New York), which had no basketball team, and began his amateur playing career on University Settlement House's Amateur Athletic University team (New York). The 5'7", 138-pound guard began his 20-year professional basketball career with the New York Roosevelts in the Independent League (1908–1909). He then played for a series of teams, including the Newburgh Tenths (Hudson River Valley League, 1909–1910, 1911–1912); Hudson Company F (New York League, 1910–1911); Utica Utes (New York League, 1912–1915); Carbondale (Pennsylvania Inter-County League, 1914–1915); Philadelphia Jaspers (Eastern League, 1915–1917, 1922–1923); Brooklyn Trolley Dodgers (Interstate League, 1915–1916); New York Whirlwinds (Independent League, 1920–1921); Passaic City Athletic Association (Interstate League, 1919–1920); Turners Falls Athletics (Interstate League, 1919–1920); Trenton (Pennsylvania League, 1920–1921); New York Giants (Eastern League, 1921–1923); Brooklyn Dodgers (Metropolitan League, 1921–1923); Easthampton Hampers (Interstate League, 1920–1922); Albany Senators (New York League, 1919–1923); Bridgeport Blue Ribbons (Connecticut League, 1920–1921); Mohawk Indians (New York League, 1921–1922); Gloversville Wonder Workers (New York League, 1923–1924); and the Cleveland Rosenblums (American Basketball League, 1925–1927).

He led the New York Roosevelts to the Independent League title in 1909; Newburgh Tenths to the Hudson River Valley League title in 1912; Utica Utes to the World Championship in 1914; in 1915, his Carbondale team won 35 straight games and took the Pennsylvania Inter-County title; in 1919, he was named to the New York State League All-Star team; in the 1920–1921 season, his Easthampton Hampers won the Interstate League title while he was named to the All-Star team, and in 1921–1922, the team defeated the Original Celtics; and finished his professional career as captain of the 1926 and 1927 ABL champion Cleveland Rosenblums.

From 1925 to 1927, Friedman was a player-coach with the Rosenblums; led the team to back-to-back titles in 1926 and 1927; and coached the ABL Troy Haymakers for one season (1938–1939).

In 1994, he was inducted into the International Jewish Sports Hall of Fame.

Friedman promoted basketball internationally when World War I started by organizing a 600-team tournament in France. He also promoted the Inter-Allied games, which eventually paved the way for the creation of the World Championships and Olympic recognition.

Sources: International Jewish Sports Hall of Fame; Naismith Memorial Basketball Hall of Fame

Frisch, Frank Francis "Frankie" (born: September 9, 1898 in Bronx, New York; died: March 12, 1973 in Wilmington, Delaware); inducted into the National Baseball Hall of Fame and Museum in 1947 as a player; Position: Second Base; Bats: Both; Throws: Right; Uniform: #3; 1931 National League Most Valuable Player; retired from baseball as the game's all-time hits leader for a switch-hitter.

Making his major league debut on June 17, 1919, Frisch played 19 seasons with the New York Giants (1919–1926) and the St. Louis Cardinals (1927–1937). He was a player-manager with the Cardinals (1933–1938) and later managed the Pittsburgh Pirates (1940–1946) and Chicago Cubs (1949–1951). He played in eight World Series (winning four [1921–1922, 1931, 1934] and losing four [1923–1924, 1928, 1930]); was named to three All-Star Teams (1933–1935); and was the 1931 National League Most Valuable Player.

Frisch attended Fordham University (Bronx, New York), where he captained the baseball, basketball, and football teams, and competed in track. He was named a Second-Team All-American halfback in 1918.

After graduating in 1919, Frisch signed with the Giants and immediately entered the major leagues, bypassing the minors. Originally a shortstop, he eventually became an everyday second baseman, where his speed earned him the nickname, the "Fordham Flash."

He played on eight pennant-winners in 19 seasons; compiled 11 straight .300 seasons (1921–1931); set single-season fielding records as a second baseman for chances and assists with the Cardinals in 1927; and struck out more than 20 times in a season only twice. As a player-manager with St. Louis, he exemplified the all-out, hard-nose style of play that led the team to become known as "The Gashouse Gang."

The 5'11", 165-pound Frisch was traded to the Cardinals after the 1926 season, and helped the team win the 1928 pennant. When injuries allowed him to play only 17 games in 1937, he retired as a player. After being fired as a manager in 1938, he became a radio broadcaster for the Boston Braves for one year, before managing the Pittsburgh Pirates from 1940 through 1946.

Leaving the Pirates, he returned to broadcasting for a year; served as a coach with the Giants in 1948; and became manager of the Chicago Cubs in 1949. Fired in mid-season in 1951, Frisch left baseball for good. When he left the game, he was baseball's career leader in hits for a switch-hitter (2880), a record that stood until the Cincinnati Reds' Pete Rose collected his 2881st hit on July 25, 1977.

Frank Frisch Field in Bronx Park, New York is named in his honor.

Frank Frisch's Career Statistics

YEAR	TEAM	LG	G	AB	R	H	2B	3B	HR	RBI	BB	SO	SB	AVG	SLG
1919	New York	NL	54	190	21	43	3	2	2		4	14	15	.226	.295
1920	New York	NL	110	440	57	123	10	10	4	77	20	18	34	.280	.375
1921	New York	NL	153	618	121	211	31	17	8	100	42	28	49	.341	.485
1922	New York	NL	132	514	101	168	16	13	5	51	47	13	31	.327	.438
1923	New York	NL	151	641	116	223	32	10	12	111	46	12	29	.348	.485
1924	New York	NL	145	603	121	198	33	15	7	69	56	24	22	.328	.468
1925	New York	NL	120	502	89	166	26	6	11	48	32	14	21	.331	.472
1926	New York	NL	135	545	75	171	29	4	5	44	33	16	23	.314	.409
1927	St. Louis	NL	153	617	112	208	31	11	10	78	43	10	48	.337	.472
1928	St. Louis	NL	141	547	107	164	29	9	10	86	64	17	29	.300	.441
1929	St. Louis	NL	138	527	93	176	40	12	5	74	53	12	24	.334	.484
1930	St. Louis	NL	133	540	121	187	46	9	10	114	55	16	15	.346	.520
1931	St. Louis	NL	131	518	96	161	24	4	4	82	45	13	28	.311	.396
1932	St. Louis	NL	115	486	59	142	26	2	3	60	25	13	18	.292	.372
1933	St. Louis	NL	147	585	74	177	32	6	4	66	48	16	18	.303	.398
1934	St. Louis	NL	140	550	74	168	30	6	3	75	45	10	11	.305	.398
1935	St. Louis	NL	103	354	52	104	16	2	1	55	33	16	2	.294	.359
1936	St. Louis	NL	93	303	40	83	10	0	1	26	36	10	2	.274	.317
1937	St. Louis	NL	17	32	3	7	2	0	0	4	1	0	0	.219	.281
	TOTALS		2,311	9,112	1,532	2,880	466	138	105	1,220	728	272	419	.316	.432

Frank Frisch's Managerial Record

YEAR	LG	TEAM	W	L	WP	FINISH
1933	NL	St. Louis	36	26	.581	5 (Player-Manager)
1934	NL	St. Louis	95	58	.621	1 (WS, Player-Manager
1935	NL	St. Louis	96	58	.623	2 (Player-Manager)
1936	NL	St. Louis	87	67	.565	2 (Player-Manager)
1937	NL	St. Louis	81	73	.526	4 (Player-Manager)
1938	NL	St. Louis	63	72	.467	6
1940	NL	Pittsburgh	78	76	.506	4
1941	NL	Pittsburgh	81	73	.526	4
1942	NL	Pittsburgh	66	81	.449	5
1943	NL	Pittsburgh	80	74	.519	4
1944	NL	Pittsburgh	90	63	.588	2
1945	NL	Pittsburgh	82	72	.532	4
1946	NL	Pittsburgh	62	89	.411	7
1949	NL	Chicago	42	62	.404	8
1950	NL	Chicago	64	89	.418	7
1951	NL	Chicago	35	45	.438	8
		St. Louis	458	354	.564	
		Pittsburgh	539	528	.505	
		Chicago	141	196	.418	
		TOTALS	1,138	1,078	.514	

Sources: Baseball-Reference.com; National Baseball Hall of Fame and Museum

Fryer, William J. "Tucker" (born: July 22, 1895 in Burradon, Yorkshire, England; died: August 29, 1960 in Linden, New Jersey); inducted into the National Soccer Hall of Fame and Museum in 1951 as a player; Position: Half Back; won more than 20 league and cup championship medals.

Fryer played soccer for Barnsley F.C. from 1919 to 1921 before he moved to the United States. Once in America, he played for Tebo Yacht Basin (1921) and then Todd Shipyards (1921–1922), both in Brooklyn, New York before moving on to the Paterson Silk Sox (1922–1923) and the New York Giants (1923–1924) of the American Soccer League. While with Todd Shipyards, he lost the 1922 U.S. Open Cup final, but came back to win the Cup the next season with Paterson.

In 1924, while with the Giants, he was sold to the Fall River Marksmen, and it was as a member of the great Fall River teams from 1923 to 1927 that he made his name. After leaving Fall River, Fryer played for the Brooklyn Wanderers (1924–1927), Newark Americans (1927–1929), and eventually for the semi-professional Clan Gordon team (1930–1931) before retiring.

During his career, Fryer won more than 20 league and cup championship medals.

Source: National Soccer Hall of Fame and Museum

Fuhr, Grant S. (born: September 28, 1962 in Spruce Grove, Alberta, Canada); inducted into the Hockey Hall of Fame in 2003 as a player; Position: Goalie; second black Canadian inducted into the Hockey Hall of Fame; won five Stanley Cup championships; holds the single-season record for most points scored by a goalie.

Fuhr played 20 seasons in the National Hockey League from 1981 to 2000 with the Edmonton Oilers (1981–1991), Toronto Maple Leafs (1991–1992), Buffalo Sabres (1993–1994), Los Angeles Kings (1994–1995), St. Louis Blues (1995–1999), and the Calgary Flames (1999–2000). Before joining the NHL, he had played with the Victoria Cougars of the Western Hockey League for two seasons (1980–1981), and was a First-Team All-Star both years. He was selected in the first round (eighth overall pick) by the Edmonton Oilers in the 1981 NHL Entry Draft.

The 5'9", 188-pound goalie led the Oilers to five Stanley Cup championships (1984–1985, 1987–1988, 1990); in 1987, he accumulated a league-leading 4,304 minutes played and 40 wins; won the Vezina Trophy as the league's best goalie in 1988; was a six-time All-Star (1982, 1984–1986 [game MVP], 1988–1989); and in the 1983–1984 season, he scored 14 points, which still stands as the single-season record for most points by a goaltender.

In 1994, Fuhr and teammate Dominik Hasek shared the William Jennings Trophy for the fewest goals scored against. On October 22, he defeated the Florida Panthers for his 400th win, only the sixth goalie in league history to reach that mark. He was named to the 1984 Canada Cup team, but did not play much, and was later selected to represent Canada in the 1987 Canada Cup.

In 1998, Fuhr was ranked number 70 on *The Hockey News*' list of the 100 Greatest Hockey Players; from 2000 to 2002, he was the goaltender coach with the Calgary Flames; and in July 2004, he was hired by the Phoenix Coyotes for the same position.

Grant Fuhr's Career Statistics

			REGULAR SEASON						PLAYOFFS					
SEASON	TEAM	LEAGUE	GP	W	L	T	SO	AVG	GP	W	L	T	SO	AVG
1979–1980	Victoria Cougars	WHL	43	30	12	0	2	3.14	8	5	3		0	2.84
1980–1981	Victoria Cougars	WHL	59	48	9	1	4	2.78	15	12	3		1	3.00
1980–1981	Victoria Cougars	M-Cup	4	1	3	0	0	4.52						
1981–1982	Edmonton Oilers	NHL	48	28	5	14	0	3.31	5	2	3		0	5.05
1982–1983	Edmonton Oilers	NHL	32	13	12	5	0	4.29	1	0	0		0	0.00
1982–1983	Moncton Alpines	AHL	10	4	5	1	0	3.98						
1983–1984	Edmonton Oilers	NHL	45	30	10	4	1	3.91	16	11	4		1	2.99
1984–1985	Canada	Can-Cup	2	1	0	1	0	3.00						
1984–1985	Edmonton Oilers	NHL	46	26	8	7	1	3.87	18	15	3		0	3.10
1985–1986	Edmonton Oilers	NHL	40	29	8	0	0	3.93	9	5	4		0	3.11
1986–1987	Edmonton Oilers	NHL	44	22	13	3	0	3.44	19	14	5		0	2.46
1986–1987	NHL All-Stars	RV-87	2	1	1	0	0	4.00						
1987–1988	Canada	Can-Cup	9	6	1	2	0	3.00						
1987–1988	Edmonton Oilers	NHL	75	40	24	9	4	3.43	19	16	2		0	2.90
1988–1989	Edmonton Oilers	NHL	59	23	26	6	1	3.83	7	3	4		1	3.45
1988–1989	Canada	WEC-A	5	1	3	1	1	3.62						
1989–1990	Edmonton Oilers	NHL	21	9	7	3	1	3.89						
1989–1990	Cape Breton Oilers	AHL	2	2	0	0	0	3.01						
1990–1991	Edmonton Oilers	NHL	13	6	4	3	1	3.01	17	8	7		0	3.00
1990–1991	Cape Breton Oilers	AHL	4	2	2	0	0	4.25						
1991–1992	Toronto Maple Leafs	NHL	66	25	33	5	2	3.66						
1992–1993	Toronto Maple Leafs	NHL	29	13	9	4	1	3.14						
1992–1993	Buffalo Sabres	NHL	29	11	15	2	0	3.47	8	3	4		1	3.42
1993–1994	Buffalo Sabres	NHL	32	13	12	3	2	3.68						
1993–1994	Rochester Ameri-	AHL	5	3	0	2	0	1.94						

SEASON	TEAM	LEAGUE	REGULAR SEASON GP	W	L	T	SO	AVG	PLAYOFFS GP	W	L	T	SO	AVG
	cans													
1994–1995	Buffalo Sabres	NHL	3	1	2	0	0	4.00						
1994–1995	Los Angeles Kings	NHL	14	1	7	3	0	4.04						
1995–1996	St. Louis Blues	NHL	79	30	28	16	3	2.87	2	1	0		0	0.87
1996–1997	St. Louis Blues	NHL	73	33	27	11	3	2.72	6	2	4		2	2.18
1997–1998	St. Louis Blues	NHL	58	29	21	6	3	2.53	10	6	4		0	2.73
1998–1999	St. Louis Blues	NHL	39	16	11	8	2	2.44	13	6	6		1	2.35
1999–2000	Calgary Flames	NHL	23	5	13	2	0	3.83						
1999–2000	Saint John Flames	AHL	2	0	2	0	0	6.05						
	NHL TOTALS		868	403	295	114	25	3.37	150	92	50		6	2.92

Sources: Hockey Hall of Fame; Hockey-Reference.com

Fulks, Joseph Franklin (born: October 26, 1921 in Birmingham, Kentucky; died: March 21, 1976 in Marshall County, Kentucky); inducted into the Naismith Memorial Basketball Hall of Fame in 1978 as a player; Position: Forward; Uniform: #10; professional basketball's first scoring star; won a BAA championship.

Fulks attended Birmingham (Kentucky) High School (1936–1937) and Kuttawa (Kentucky) High School (1937–1940), where he was a four-year letter winner; named All-State in 1940; and led Kuttawa to the state tournament semifinals in 1940.

After high school, he went to Murray State University (Kentucky) from 1941 to 1943, and was a three-year letter winner before leaving school to join the Marines during World War II. Fulks was named a Helms Foundation All-American in 1939; a two-time All-Conference selection (1939–1940); team Most Valuable Player in 1940; and averaged 13.2 points per game in his college career.

After completing his military service, he turned professional with the Philadelphia Warriors of the Basketball Association of America (1946–1949), and stayed with the team when the franchise joined the National Basketball Association (1949–1953). The 6'5", 190-pound forward was considered professional basketball's first scoring star; named to the All-BAA First Team three times (1947–1949); led the BAA in scoring in 1947 (23.2 points per game) and in 1948 (22.1 points per game); selected to the All-NBA Second Team in 1951; a two-time NBA All-Star (1951–1952); won a BAA championship with the Warriors (1947); scored 63 points against the Indianapolis Jets on February 9, 1949, a single-game record that stood until surpassed by Elgin Baylor's 64 points on November 8, 1959; compiled a 16.3 points-per-game career average; and made 49 consecutive free throws twice in his career.

Fulks was named to the NBA 25th Anniversary All-Time Team in 1970; called "the greatest basketball player in the country" by *The Sporting News* in 1949; and was inducted into the National Association of Intercollegiate Athletics Basketball Hall of Fame in 1952 and the Murray State Athletic Hall of Fame in 1965.

Joseph Fulks' Career Statistics

SEASON	TEAM	LG	G	MIN	FG	FT	TRB	AST	PTS
1946–1947	Philadelphia	BAA	60		475	439		25	1,389
1947–1948	Philadelphia	BAA	43		326	297		26	949
1948–1949	Philadelphia	BAA	60		529	502		74	1,560
1949–1950	Philadelphia	NBA	68		336	293		56	965
1950–1951	Philadelphia	NBA	66		429	378	523	117	1,236
1951–1952	Philadelphia	NBA	61	1,904	336	250	368	123	922
1952–1953	Philadelphia	NBA	70	2,085	332	168	387	138	832
1953–1954	Philadelphia	NBA	61	501	61	28	101	28	150
		BAA	163		1,330	1,238		125	3,898
		NBA	326	4,490	1,494	1,117	1,379	462	4,105
	TOTALS		489	4,490	2,824	2,355	1,379	587	8,003

Sources: Basketball-Reference.com; Naismith Memorial Basketball Hall of Fame

Chapter 7
Gadsby to Gwynn

Gadsby, William Alexander "Bill" (born: August 8, 1927 in Calgary, Alberta, Canada); inducted into the Hockey Hall of Fame in 1970; Position: Defenseman; set a single-season record for assists by a defenseman.

Gadsby played 20 National Hockey League seasons with the Chicago Black Hawks (1946–1954), New York Rangers (1954–1961), and the Detroit Red Wings (1961–1966). Although he never won a Stanley Cup, he played in three Finals (losing in 1963 and 1964 to the Toronto Maple Leafs and in 1966 to the Montreal Canadiens). Gadsby was selected to the First All-Star Team three times (1956, 1958–1959) and to the Second All-Star Team four times (1953–1954, 1957, 1965).

Gadsby set a single-season record for assists by a defenseman with 46 in the 1958–1959 season. After retiring as a player, he became the head coach of the Red Wings, but was eventually fired two games into the 1969–1970 season.

In 1998, he was ranked number 99 on *The Hockey News*' list of the 100 Greatest Hockey Players.

Bill Gadsby's Career Statistics

			REGULAR SEASON					PLAYOFFS				
SEASON	**TEAM**	**LEAGUE**	**GP**	**G**	**A**	**TP**	**PIM**	**GP**	**G**	**A**	**TP**	**PIM**
1943–1944	Calgary Grills	AHA-B	9	4	1	5	4					
1944–1945	Edmonton Canadians	AJHL										
1945–1946	Edmonton Canadians	AJHL		14	12	26						
1945–1946	Edmonton Canadians	M-Cup	14	12	5	17	22					
1946–1947	Chicago Black Hawks	NHL	48	8	10	18	31					
1946–1947	Kansas City Pla–Mors	USHL	12	2	3	5	8					
1947–1948	Chicago Black Hawks	NHL	60	6	10	16	66					
1948–1949	Chicago Black Hawks	NHL	50	3	10	13	85					
1949–1950	Chicago Black Hawks	NHL	70	10	25	35	138					
1950–1951	Chicago Black Hawks	NHL	25	3	7	10	32					
1951–1952	Chicago Black Hawks	NHL	59	7	15	22	87					
1952–1953	Chicago Black Hawks	NHL	68	2	20	22	84	7	0	1	1	4
1953–1954	Chicago Black Hawks	NHL	70	12	29	41	108					
1954–1955	Chicago Black Hawks	NHL	18	3	5	8	17					
1954–1955	New York Rangers	NHL	52	8	8	16	44					
1955–1956	New York Rangers	NHL	70	9	42	51	84	5	1	3	4	4
1956–1957	New York Rangers	NHL	70	4	37	41	72	5	1	2	3	2
1957–1958	New York Rangers	NHL	65	14	32	46	48	6	0	3	3	4
1958–1959	New York Rangers	NHL	70	5	46	51	56					
1959–1960	New York Rangers	NHL	65	9	22	31	60					
1960–1961	New York Rangers	NHL	65	9	26	35	49					
1961–1962	Detroit Red Wings	NHL	70	7	30	37	88					
1962–1963	Detroit Red Wings	NHL	70	4	24	28	116	11	1	4	5	36
1963–1964	Detroit Red Wings	NHL	64	2	16	18	80	14	0	4	4	22
1964–1965	Detroit Red Wings	NHL	61	0	12	12	122	7	0	3	3	8
1965–1966	Detroit Red Wings	NHL	58	5	12	17	72	12	1	3	4	12
	NHL TOTALS		1,248	130	438	568	1,539	67	4	23	27	92

Sources: Hockey Hall of Fame; Hockey-Reference.com

Gaetjens, Joseph Eduard (born: March 19, 1924 in Port-au-Prince, Haiti; died: July 1964 in Port-au-Prince, Haiti); inducted into the National Soccer Hall of Fame and Museum in 1976 as a player; Position: Forward; International Caps (3 for the United States-1950, 1 for Haiti-1953): 4; International Goals: 1; scored the winning goal in the U.S. upset victory over England in the 1950 World Cup.

Gaetjens started playing soccer at 14 for the Haitian club L' Etoile Haitiene, and played for the team against the National Soccer League All-Star team of New York when the squad toured Haiti in 1941. In the late 1940s, he moved to the United States on a Haitian government scholarship to attend Columbia University (New York, New York), where he played for New York Brookhattan in the American Soccer League, winning the scoring title in 1950. He was a member of the 1950 World Cup team and, playing in Brazil, Gaetjens scored the famous goal that beat the heavily-favored England squad 1–0 in Belo Horizointe.

Following the World Cup, he moved to France for three years and played for second division Troyes and first division Paris Racing Club, before returning to Haiti, where he played against Mexico in a World Cup qualifying game in Port-au-Prince on December 27, 1953.

While Gaetjens did not participate in politics, his family worked for Louis Dejoie, a rival to Haitian dictator Francois "Papa Doc" Duvalier, in his 1957 run for the presidency. Gaetjens' mother and a brother were arrested after Duvalier's victory, and most of the family fled the country, although he stayed in Haiti. His family continued to campaign outside of Haiti against Duvalier, who made himself president for life in 1964.

Gaetjens was last seen on July 8, 1964, when he was arrested at work by Duvalier's secret police and supposedly sent to prison, where he later died. The kidnapping was thought to be in retaliation for his family's political activism.

Source: National Soccer Hall of Fame and Museum

Gaines, Clarence E. "Big House" (born: May 21, 1923 in Paducah, Kentucky; died: April 18, 2005 in Winston-Salem, North Carolina); inducted into the Naismith Memorial Basketball Hall of Fame in 1982 as a coach; led the first predominantly black school to win a Division II NCAA basketball title.

Gaines attended Lincoln High School (Paducah, Kentucky), graduated in 1941, played basketball for three years, and was selected All-Conference and All-State once. After high school, the 6'5", 250-pound Gaines went to Morgan State College (University) (Baltimore, Maryland) in 1941; played center on the basketball team; was a lineman on the Bears' football team (where he was named All-CIAA (Central Intercollegiate Athletic Association) as a lineman all four years); and graduated in 1945.

After graduation, Gaines became an assistant coach at Winston-Salem State University (North Carolina); took over as head basketball coach and athletic director in 1947; and continued to coach at the school for 47 years (1946–1993). He compiled an 828–447 (.649) record; won 20 or more games in a season 18 times; won 12 Central Intercollegiate Athletic Association championships; guided his 1967 team, led by future hall-of-famer Earl "The Pearl" Monroe, to a 31–1 record and became the first predominantly black school to win a Division II National Collegiate Athletic Association basketball title; and was named NCAA College Division Basketball Coach of the Year (1967), CIAA Basketball Coach of the Year five times (1961, 1963, 1970, 1975, 1980), and CIAA Outstanding Tournament Coach eight times (1957, 1960–1961, 1963, 1966, 1970, 1972, 1979).

Gaines won the Indiana Sports Foundation Lifetime Achievement Award in 1990; the Atlanta Tipoff Club Lifetime Achievement Award in 1991; and when he retired in 1993, he ranked second on the all-time wins list in NCAA history behind the legendary Adolph Rupp.

The C.E. Gaines Center at Winston-Salem State University is named in his honor. He has been inducted into the NAIA Helms Hall of Fame (1968), Morgan State College Sports Hall of Fame (1973), CIAA Sports Hall of Fame (1976), North Carolina Sports Hall of Fame (1978), Winston-Salem State University Hall of Fame (1980), Bob Douglas Hall of Fame (1985), and the National Association for Sport and Physical Education Hall of Fame (1990).

He was the first World Basketball Tournament coach (1973-Lima, Peru); served as president of the CIAA (1970–1974); CIAA Basketball Coaches president (1972–1980, 1990–1992); member of the U.S. Olympic Committee (1973–1976); board member of the Naismith Memorial Basketball Hall of Fame (1980–1990); coach of the gold medal-winning Jones Cup team (1988, Taiwan); and served as president of the National Association of Basketball Coaches (1989).

Source: Naismith Memorial Basketball Hall of Fame

Gainey, Robert Michael "Bob" (born: December 13, 1953 in Peterborough, Ontario, Canada); inducted into the Hockey Hall of Fame in 1992 as a player; Position: Left Wing; Uniform: #23; won five Stanley Cup titles as a player and one as a coach; won the first four Frank J. Selke Trophy awards.

A first-round pick (eighth overall selection) in the 1973 Amateur Draft, Gainey played his entire 16-season National Hockey League career (1973–1989) with the Montreal Canadiens; won five Stanley Cup titles (1976–1979, 1986); and represented his country in the inaugural Canada Cup (1976). He scored 16 points in the 1979 Stanley Cup series and won the Conn Smythe Trophy as the most valuable player in the playoffs.

Gainey won the first four (1978–1981) Frank J. Selke Trophies as the league's best forward. He was named team captain in the 1981–1982 season; guided Montreal to another championship in 1986; and led the team to consecutive 100-point seasons (1988–1989).

After retiring from the NHL in 1989, he was a player-coach for the Epinal Écureuil franchise in French hockey's first division, before returning to the United States in 1990 as coach and general manager of the NHL's Minnesota North Stars. In his first year with the team, he led the squad to the franchise's second Stanley Cup finals appearance in 1991, eventually losing to the Pittsburgh Penguins in six games. He stayed with the team when the franchise relocated to Dallas in 1993, and resigned as coach in 1995 to focus on being the team's general manager.

During his tenure, the Stars won the Presidents' Trophy twice for scoring the most points in the regular season (1998–1999), and in 1999, he led the franchise to its first-ever Stanley Cup. In 2003, he was hired as the general manager of the Montreal Canadiens.

In 1998, he was ranked number 86 on *The Hockey News*' list of the 100 Greatest Hockey Players and he helped select the members for Canada's men's ice hockey squad for the 1998 Winter Olympics in Nagano, Japan. In February 2008, the Canadiens retired his jersey number 23.

Bob Gainey's Career Statistics

				REGULAR SEASON						PLAYOFFS			
SEASON	**TEAM**	**LEAGUE**	**GP**	**G**	**A**	**TP**	**PIM**	**+/–**	**GP**	**G**	**A**	**TP**	**PIM**
1970–1971	Peterborough Jr. Bees	OHA-B											
1970–1971	Peterborough Petes	OHA-Jr.							4	0	0	0	4
1971–1972	Peterborough Jr. Bees	OHA-B							3	1	0	1	4
1971–1972	Peterborough Petes	OHA-Jr.	4	2	1	3	33						
1972–1973	Peterborough Petes	OHA-Jr.	52	22	21	43	99						
1973–1974	Montreal Canadiens	NHL	66	3	7	10	34	–9	6	0	0	0	6
1973–1974	Nova Scotia Voyageurs	AHL	6	2	5	7	4						
1974–1975	Montreal Canadiens	NHL	80	17	20	37	49	+23	11	2	4	6	4
1975–1976	Montreal Canadiens	NHL	78	15	13	28	57	+20	13	1	3	4	20
1976–1977	Canada	Can-Cup	5	2	0	2	2						
1976–1977	Montreal Canadiens	NHL	80	14	19	33	41	+31	14	4	1	5	25
1977–1978	Montreal Canadiens	NHL	66	15	16	31	57	+11	15	2	7	9	14
1978–1979	Montreal Canadiens	NHL	79	20	18	38	44	+11	16	6	10	16	10
1979–1980	Montreal Canadiens	NHL	64	14	19	33	32	–2	10	1	1	2	4
1980–1981	Montreal Canadiens	NHL	78	23	24	47	36	+13	3	0	0	0	2
1981–1982	Canada	Can-Cup	7	1	3	4	2						
1981–1982	Montreal Canadiens	NHL	79	21	24	45	24	+37	5	0	1	1	8
1981–1982	Canada	WEC-A	10	2	1	3	0						
1982–1983	Montreal Canadiens	NHL	80	12	18	30	43	+7	3	0	0	0	4
1982–1983	Canada	WEC-A	10	0	6	6	2						
1983–1984	Montreal Canadiens	NHL	77	17	22	39	41	+10	15	1	5	6	9
1984–1985	Montreal Canadiens	NHL	79	19	13	32	40	+13	12	1	3	4	13
1985–1986	Montreal Canadiens	NHL	80	20	23	43	20	+10	20	5	5	10	12
1986–1987	Montreal Canadiens	NHL	47	8	8	16	19	0	17	1	3	4	6
1987–1988	Montreal Canadiens	NHL	78	11	11	22	14	+8	6	0	1	1	6
1988–1989	Montreal Canadiens	NHL	49	10	7	17	34	+13	16	1	4	5	8
1989–1990	Epinal Squirrels	France-2	18	14	12	26	16		10	6	7	13	14
1990–1993	Minnesota North Stars	NHLMGNT											
1993–2000	Dallas Stars	NHLMGNT											
	NHL TOTALS		1,160	239	262	501	585		182	25	48	73	151

Sources: Hockey Hall of Fame; Hockey-Reference.com

Gale, Lauren E. "Laddie" (born: April 22, 1917 in Grants Pass, Oregon; died: July 29, 1996 in Gold Beach, Oregon); inducted into the Naismith Memorial Basketball Hall of Fame in 1977 as a player; Position: Forward; led the University of Oregon to the first-ever NCAA Division I men's championship in 1939.

Gale was a four-year letter winner in basketball at Oakridge (Oregon) High School from 1931 to 1935; selected All-State in 1935; and All-Conference twice (1934–1935). After graduation, he attended the University of Oregon (Eugene) from 1935 to 1939 and played basketball under hall-of-fame coach Howard Hobson, where he was a three-year letter winner; selected as a Helms Foundation All-American in 1939; and led the school to a national championship in the first-ever National Collegiate Athletic Association Division I men's tournament in 1939, scoring 10 points in a 46–33 finals win over Ohio State.

His 408 points as a senior broke the Pacific Coast Conference record previously set by future hall of famer Hank Luisetti; he was selected to the All-Pacific Coast Conference First Team twice (1938–1939); led the conference in scoring twice (1938–1939); led the team in scoring as a junior and senior; was named Northern Division Player of the Year in 1938; was an inaugural member of the Oregon Sports Hall of Fame and Museum in 1980; and in 1993, he was inducted into the University of Oregon Hall of Fame.

After graduation, the 6'4", 190-pound Gale played professional basketball for two years with the National Basketball League's Detroit Eagles (1939–1940). He left the NBL to serve in the military during World War II, and later was a player-coach with Amateur Athletic Union teams the Deseret Times of Salt Lake City and the Oakland Bittners. In 1948, he led the Bittners into the semi-finals of the Olympic team trials before losing to the Phillips 66ers. He left basketball in 1949 and went into the real estate business.

Source: Naismith Memorial Basketball Hall of Fame

Gallagher, James (born: June 7, 1901 in Kirkintilloch, Scotland; died: October 7, 1971 in Cleveland, Ohio); inducted into the National Soccer Hall of Fame and Museum in 1986 as a player; Position: Outside Right Half; International Caps (1928–1934): 7; International Goals: 1; won the Lewis Cup in 1929.

Gallagher came to the United States with his mother when he was 12 years old and attended school in the New York City area, and by age 17 was playing for the Tebo Yacht Basin team (Brooklyn, New York). In 1921, he joined the J&P Coats team of Pawtucket (Rhode Island) of the American Soccer League and was a member of the franchise's championship-winning team in the 1922–1923 season. He stayed in the ASL and played for the Fall River Marksmen (Massachusetts, 1923); New York Giants (1924); Fleisher Yarn (Philadelphia, Pennsylvania, 1924–1925); Indiana Flooring (New York, 1925–1927); New York Nationals (New York, 1927–1930); and the New York Giants (New York, 1930–1932), before moving to Cleveland to play for Slavia.

In 1929, Gallagher was a member of the Nationals team that won the Lewis Cup; in 1930, he was selected to play for the U.S. World Cup team; and eventually played in all three World Cup games in Montevideo, Uruguay.

In 1932, he was a member of the New York Giants team that won the American Soccer League championship over the New Bedford Whalers, and four years later, while playing with Cleveland Slavia, he was again selected for the FIFA World Cup team, and played four games in Italy.

The 5'10" Gallagher earned seven caps with the U.S. National Team between 1928 and 1934, with his first game being an 11–2 first-round loss to Argentina in the 1928 Summer Olympics (Amsterdam, Netherlands). A month later, the U.S. team played Poland to a 3–3 tie in Warsaw, with Gallagher scoring his only National Team goal. Two years later, he played in all three U.S. games at the 1930 FIFA World Cup (Uruguay), as the U.S. team made it to the semifinals, before losing 6–1 to Argentina. His last game with the National Team came in a 4–2 U.S. win over Mexico on May 24, 1934, which qualified the U.S. for the 1934 FIFA World Cup finals.

Source: National Soccer Hall of Fame and Museum

Gallatin, Harry J. (born: April 26, 1927 in Roxana, Illinois); inducted into the Naismith Memorial Basketball Hall of Fame in 1991 as a player; Position: Forward-Center; played in a then-record 682 straight professional games; first basketball player at Truman State University to have his jersey number retired.

Gallatin attended Roxana (Illinois) High School from 1940 to 1944; was a four-year letter winner; selected All-District twice (1943–1944); and was the team's co-captain for two seasons (1943–1944). He served one year in the U.S. Navy during World War II before going to Northeast Missouri State Teachers College (Kirksville, Missouri; now known as Truman State University) from 1946 to 1948; was named to the National Association of Intercollegiate Athletics First-Team twice (1947–1948); Conference Most Valuable Player in 1948 and the team's Most Valuable Player in 1947 and 1948; a Scholar Athlete in 1948; and was inducted into the NAIA Hall of Fame in 1957. In 2000, the school retired his jersey number 44, the first basketball player to have his jersey retired at the school.

After college, the 6'6", 220-pound Gallatin was a 1948 first-round draft choice of the New York Knickerbockers of the Basketball Association of America (1948–1949); stayed with the team when the franchise entered the National Basketball Association (1949–1957); and finished his career with the NBA's Detroit Pistons (1957–1958).

During his early BAA/NBA career, Gallatin also played professional baseball in the Chicago Cubs' minor league organization (1948–1949).

He was named to the All-NBA First-Team in 1954; All-NBA Second Team in 1955; was a seven-time NBA All-Star (1951–1957); played in a then-record 682 straight games; was among the league's top 10 rebounders six times and top 20 scorers six times; led the league in rebounding (1954, 15.3 rebounds per game); and never had less than 660 rebounds in any season (including a career-high 1,098 in 1954).

After retiring as a player, he became a college coach at Southern Illinois, Carbondale (1958–1962) and Southern Illinois, Edwardsville (1967–1970). Gallatin led Carbondale to a 79–35 record and Edwardsville to a 19–31 record, compiling an overall college record of 98–66 (.598). He guided Carbondale to three Interstate Intercollegiate Athletic Conference titles (1960–1962) and to a third place national finish in 1962.

In between his college stints, Gallatin coached in the NBA for the St. Louis Hawks (1962–1965) and New York Knicks (1965–1966), compiling a professional coaching record of 136–120 (.531). He was named NBA Coach of the Year in 1963.

Harry Gallatin's Career Statistics

SEASON	TEAM	LG	G	MIN	FG	FT	TRB	AST	PTS
1948–1949	New York	BAA	52		157	120		63	434
1949–1950	New York	NBA	68		263	277		56	803
1950–1951	New York	NBA	66		293	259	800	180	845
1951–1952	New York	NBA	66	1,931	233	275	661	115	741
1952–1953	New York	NBA	70	2,333	282	301	916	126	865
1953–1954	New York	NBA	72	2,690	258	433	1,098	153	949
1954–1955	New York	NBA	72	2,548	330	393	995	176	1,053
1955–1956	New York	NBA	72	2,378	322	358	740	168	1,002
1956–1957	New York	NBA	72	1,943	332	415	725	85	1,079
1957–1958	Detroit	NBA	72	1,990	340	392	749	86	1,072
		BAA	52		157	120		63	434
		NBA	630	15,813	2,653	3,103	6,684	1,145	8,409
	TOTALS		682	15,813	2,810	3,223	6,684	1,208	8,843

Harry Gallatin's NBA Coaching Record

		REGULAR SEASON			PLAYOFFS		
SEASON	TEAM	W	L	WIN%	W	L	WIN%
1962–1963	St. Louis	48	32	.600	6	5	.545
1963–1964	St. Louis	46	34	.575	6	6	.500
1964–1965	St. Louis	17	16	.515			
1964–1965	New York	19	23	.452			
1965–1966	New York	6	15	.286			
	TOTALS	136	120	.531	12	11	.522

Sources: Basketball-Reference.com; Naismith Memorial Basketball Hall of Fame

Galvin, James Francis "Pud" (born: December 25, 1856 in St. Louis (Somerville), Missouri; died: March 7, 1902 in Pittsburgh (Allegheny), Pennsylvania); inducted into the National Baseball Hall of Fame and Museum in 1965 as a player by the Veterans Committee; Position: Pitcher; Bats: Right; Throws: Right; Major League Baseball's first 300-game winner; only player in baseball history to win 20 or more games in 10 different years without winning a pennant.

Making his debut on May 22, 1875, Galvin pitched 14 major league seasons (1879–1892) with the St. Louis Brown Stockings (1875, National Association of Professional Base Ball Players), Buffalo Bisons (1879–1885, managing the team in 1885, International Association and the National League), Pittsburgh Alleghenys (1885–1889, American Association and the National League), Pittsburgh Burghers (1890, Players' League), Pittsburgh Pirates (1891–1892, National League), and the St. Louis Browns (1892, National League).

The 5'11", 180-pound Galvin was Major League Baseball's first 300-game winner, won 20 or more games per season 10 times; and in two seasons (1883–1884) won more than 40 games. When he retired in 1892, he was the all-time major league leader in wins, innings pitched, games started, games completed, and shutouts. On August 20, 1880, he became the first big league player to pitch a no-hitter on the road, a 1–0 win against the Worcester Ruby Legs. He was nicknamed "Pud" because his pitching motion supposedly turned opposing batters into "pudding."

Because he played in an era of two-man pitching staffs, Galvin was able to accumulate an incredible 6,003 innings pitched (more than 425 per season, although the total is in some dispute) and 646 complete games, both of which are second only to the legendary Cy Young. He pitched over 70 complete games in both 1883 and 1884, and 65 complete games in 1879. He is the only player in baseball history to win 20 or more games in 10 different years without winning a pennant (he never played on a team that finished better than third).

In 1883, he led the National League in games (76), starts (75), complete games (72), innings pitched (656-1/3), and shutouts (five). On August 4, 1884, he became the second pitcher in major league history with two no-hitters with an 18–0 win over the Detroit Wolverines.

On June 17, 1880, Galvin was the losing pitcher, and made the last out, in Major League Baseball's second-ever perfect game, a 5–0 loss to John Montgomery Ward of the Providence Grays. On July 21, 1892, he faced Tim Keefe in the last battle of 300-game winners until Don Sutton pitched against Phil Niekro in 1986.

James Galvin's Career Statistics

YEAR	TEAM	LG	W	L	PCT	G	SH	IP	H	R	SO	BB
1879	Buffalo	NL	37	28	.569	66	6	593	585	299	136	31
1880	Buffalo	NL	20	34	.370	58	5	459	528	279	128	32
1881	Buffalo	NL	29	24	.547	56	5	474	546	247	136	46
1882	Buffalo	NL	28	22	.560	52	3	445	476	256	162	40
1883	Buffalo	NL	46	27	.630	76	5	656	676	363	279	50
1884	Buffalo	NL	46	22	.676	72	12	636	566	255	369	63
1885	Buffalo	NL	13	19	.406	33	3	284	356	204	93	37
1885	Pittsburgh	AA	3	7	.300	11	0	88	97	64	27	7
1886	Pittsburgh	AA	29	21	.580	50	2	435	457	229	72	75
1887	Pittsburgh	NL	28	21	.571	49	3	441	490	259	76	67
1888	Pittsburgh	NL	23	25	.479	50	6	437	446	190	107	53
1889	Pittsburgh	NL	23	16	.590	41	4	341	392	230	77	78
1890	Pittsburgh	PL	12	13	.480	26	1	217	275	192	35	49
1891	Pittsburgh	NL	14	13	.519	33	2	247	256	143	46	62
1892	Pittsburgh	NL	5	5	.500	12	0	96	104	51	29	28
1892	St. Louis	NL	5	5	.500	12	0	92	102	47	27	26
	TOTALS		361	302	.544	697	57	5,941	6,352	3,308	1,799	744

Sources: Baseball-Reference.com; National Baseball Hall of Fame and Museum

Gamba, Alessandro "Sandro" (born: June 3, 1932 in Milan, Italy); inducted into the Naismith Memorial Basketball Hall of Fame in 2006 as a coach; led the Italian National Team to a silver medal in the 1980 Summer Olympics.

Gamba began playing basketball at age 13 and eventually joined the Cadet team of Borletti. After retiring as a player, he spent eight seasons as an assistant to Italy's legendary head coach, Cesare Rubini, before beginning his 30-year coaching career in Europe.

In 1973, Gamba became head coach with Ignis-Varese; led the team to back-to-back European Cup titles in 1975 and 1976; and coached the squad to Italian titles in 1974 and 1977. He was selected head coach of Italy's National Team in 1980 and led the squad to a silver medal in that year's Olympics in Moscow, Russia. He later led the National Team to a first-place finish (1983) and a second-place finish (1991) in the European Championships.

During his career, Gamba coached Italian Division I professional league teams Simmenthal (1965–1973), Ignis (1973–1977), and Turin (1977–1980); the Italian National Team (1979–1992); and four Italian Olympic teams (1980, 1984, 1988, 1992). His professional teams have won five Italian League championships, a European Championship, a Champions Cup, and a Cup of Cups title.

Source: Naismith Memorial Basketball Hall of Fame

Garcia, Prudencio "Pete" (born: October 2, 1899 in Salinas, Asturias, Spain; died: November 15, 1984 in Arlington, Virginia); inducted into the National Soccer Hall of Fame and Museum in 1964 as a builder; a referee for more than 20 years; founded the Missouri Referees' Association.

Garcia came to the United States in 1907 and played in the St. Louis Board of Education Playground League before moving on to the Sherman Park Division of the St. Louis Municipal League from 1911 to 1921. He organized a Bankers

Division in the Municipal League and managed Mercantile Trust to the championship. He played with the Garcia Football Club of East St. Louis, which was an independent club.

He promoted games in the Spanish community and ran clinics in the local schools. He joined the referee staff of the Municipal League of St. Louis in 1937, staying until 1957. He founded the Missouri Referees' Association and refereed in Public School and Police Youth leagues before moving on to the professional leagues.

Garcia refereed in the qualifying rounds of the 1950 World Cup and was later named to the panel of referees selected for the final rounds played in Brazil, where he worked as a linesman in four games.

Source: National Soccer Hall of Fame and Museum

Gard (Gardassanich), Gino (born: Gino Gardassanich on November 26, 1922 in Fiume, Italy); inducted into the National Soccer Hall of Fame and Museum in 2002 as a player; Position: Goalkeeper; won the Montgomery Trophy.

Gard played for Fiumana and Reggina in Italy; moved to the United States in 1949; in Chicago, he played for the Slovak club from 1949 to 1959; won the Montgomery Trophy as most valuable goalie in 1950; and played in the U.S. Amateur Cup final in 1953.

While with Slovak, he helped the team win the Nielsen Trophy as the Major Division Indoor champions. Gard was the goalie for the Chicago All-Star team that played against Hamburg SV of Germany in Chicago on May 10, 1950. He was selected to the 1950 World Cup team and made the trip to Brazil, but did not play in any of the three games.

Gard was inducted into the Illinois Hall of Fame in 1992.

Source: National Soccer Hall of Fame and Museum

Gardiner, Charles Robert "Chuck" (born: December 31, 1904 in Edinburgh, Scotland; died: June 13, 1934 in Winnipeg, Manitoba, Canada); inducted into the Hockey Hall of Fame in 1945 as a player; Position: Goalie; led the Chicago Black Hawks to the franchise's first Stanley Cup title.

Gardiner played all of his seven National Hockey League seasons (1927–1934) with the Chicago Black Hawks and helped the team win its first Stanley Cup title (1934). One of the few European-born players to play in the NHL during his era, before joining the Black Hawks, he had played in the Manitoba Hockey League, Canadian Hockey League, and the American Hockey Association.

In the 1930–1931 season, he recorded a league-high 12 shutouts; a goals-against mark of 1.73; and was named to the first of his three NHL First All-Star Teams. He won the Vezina Trophy the next season as the league's top goaltender, and was chosen team captain in 1933–1934.

During the 1933–1934 regular season, Gardiner led the NHL with 10 shutouts; won his second Vezina Trophy; and led Chicago to the team's first-ever Stanley Cup championship. Unfortunately, several weeks after winning the title, he died of a brain hemorrhage.

Gardiner has been inducted into Canada's Sports Hall of Fame (1975), Manitoba Sports Hall of Fame (1989), Manitoba Hockey Hall of Fame; and was a charter member of the Hockey Hall of Fame. In 1998, despite his relatively short career, he was ranked number 76 on *The Hockey News*' list of the 100 Greatest Hockey Players.

He was named to the NHL All-Star First Team twice (1932, 1934); to the All-Star Second Team in 1933; and won the Vezina Trophy three times (1931–1932, 1934). He was the first Vezina Trophy winner to catch the puck with his right hand.

Chuck Gardiner's Career Statistics

			REGULAR SEASON						PLAYOFFS					
SEASON	TEAM	LEAGUE	GP	W	L	T	SO	AVG	GP	W	L	T	SO	AVG
1921–1922	Winnipeg Tigers	MJHL	1	0	1	0	0	6.00						
1922–1923	Winnipeg Tigers	MJHL	6				0	3.08						
1923–1924	Winnipeg Tigers	MJHL							1	1	0	0	1	0.00
1924–1925	Selkirk Fishermen	MHL-Sr.	18				2	1.83	2	0	2	0	0	3.00
1925–1926	Winnipeg Maroons	CHL	38				6	2.16	5				1	2.00
1926–1927	Winnipeg Maroons	AHA	36	17	14	5	6	2.14	3	0	3	0	0	2.67
1927–1928	Chicago Black Hawks	NHL	40	6	32	2	3	2.83						
1928–1929	Chicago Black Hawks	NHL	44	7	29	8	5	1.85						
1929–1930	Chicago Black Hawks	NHL	44	21	18	5	3	2.42	2	0	1	1	0	1.05
1930–1931	Chicago Black Hawks	NHL	44	24	17	3	12	1.73	9	5	3	1	2	1.32
1931–1932	Chicago Black Hawks	NHL	48	18	19	11	4	1.85	2	1	1	0	1	3.00
1932–1933	Chicago Black Hawks	NHL	48	16	20	12	5	2.01						
1933–1934	Chicago Black Hawks	NHL	48	20	17	11	10	1.63	8	6	1	1	2	1.33

SEASON	TEAM	LEAGUE	REGULAR SEASON GP	W	L	T	SO	AVG	PLAYOFFS GP	W	L	T	SO	AVG
	NHL TOTALS		316	112	152	52	42	2.02	21	12	6	3	5	1.42

Sources: Canada's Sports Hall of Fame; Hockey Hall of Fame; Hockey-Reference.com; Manitoba Sports Hall of Fame

Gardiner, Herbert Martin "Herb" (born: May 8, 1891 in Winnipeg, Manitoba, Canada; died: January 11. 1972); inducted into the Hockey Hall of Fame in 1958 as a player; Position: Defenseman; won the Western Canada Hockey League title in 1924; won the Hart Memorial Trophy in 1927.

Gardiner played eight professional hockey seasons from 1921 to 1929. He turned professional in the 1921–1922 season with the Calgary Tigers (of the newly created Western Canada Hockey League); played for five seasons; led the team to the WCHL title in 1924. This allowed the team to compete for the Stanley Cup (under the old format), which the franchise lost 6–1 to the Montreal Canadiens.

The Montreal Canadiens signed the 5'10", 190-pound Gardiner in 1926, and he won the Hart Memorial Trophy in 1927 as the NHL's Most Valuable Player his first year with the team. In the 1929–1930 season, he was sold to the Boston Bruins and assigned to the Philadelphia Arrows (Canadian-American Hockey League) as a player-coach. He stayed with the team until the 1935–1936 season, when he joined the Philadelphia Ramblers (American Hockey League); coached the Ramblers to the Calder Cup finals in 1937 and 1939 (losing both times); and ended his coaching career with the Philadelphia Falcons (Eastern Hockey League) from 1944 to 1946.

Gardiner has been inducted into the Manitoba Hockey Hall of Fame.

Herb Gardiner's Career Statistics

SEASON	TEAM	LEAGUE	REGULAR SEASON GP	G	A	TP	PIM	PLAYOFFS GP	G	A	TP	PIM
1908–1910	Winnipeg Victorias	WSrHL										
1914–1915	Calgary Monarchs	AAHL										
1918–1919	Calgary Rotary Club	CSrHL										
1919–1920	Calgary Wanderers	Big-4	12	8	9	17	6	2	0	0	0	2
1920–1921	Calgary Tigers	Big-4	13	3	7	10	6					
1921–1922	Calgary Tigers	WCHL	24	4	1	5	6	2	0	0	0	0
1922–1923	Calgary Tigers	WCHL	29	9	3	12	9					
1923–1924	Calgary Tigers	WCHL	22	5	5	10	4	2	1	0	1	0
1923–1924	Calgary Tigers	West-P						3	1	1	2	0
1923–1924	Calgary Tigers	St-Cup						2	1	0	1	0
1924–1925	Calgary Tigers	WCHL	28	12	8	20	18	2	0	0	0	0
1925–1926	Calgary Tigers	WHL	27	3	1	4	10					
1926–1927	Montreal Canadiens	NHL	44	6	6	12	26	4	0	0	0	10
1927–1928	Montreal Canadiens	NHL	44	4	3	7	26	2	0	1	1	4
1928–1929	Chicago Black Hawks	NHL	13	0	0	0	0					
1928–1929	Montreal Canadiens	NHL	7	0	0	0	0	3	0	0	0	2
1929–1930	Philadelphia Arrows	Can-Am	1	0	0	0	0					
1930–1931	Philadelphia Arrows	Can-Am										
1931–1932	Philadelphia Arrows	Can-Am	1	0	0	0	0					
1932–1933	Philadelphia Arrows	Can-Am										
1933–1934	Philadelphia Arrows	Can-Am										
1934–1935	Philadelphia Arrows	Can-Am	12	0	0	0	0					
1935–1936	Philadelphia Ramblers	AHL										
	NHL TOTALS		108	10	9	19	52	9	0	1	1	16

Sources: Hockey Hall of Fame; Hockey-Reference.com; Manitoba Hockey Hall of Fame

Gardner, James H. "Jack" (born: March 29, 1910 in Texico, New Mexico; died: April 10, 2000 in Salt Lake City, Utah); inducted into the Naismith Memorial Basketball Hall of Fame in 1984 as a coach; only coach in history to lead two different schools to the NCAA Final Four twice each (Kansas State, Utah).

Gardner was a four-year letter winner in basketball at Redlands (California) High School, where he graduated in 1928; named All-Conference three times; and was the team's captain and leading scorer in 1928. He went on to attend the University of Southern California (Los Angeles), graduating in 1932. At USC, he was a three-year letterman in basketball; selected All-Coast once; led the team in scoring in 1931 and 1932; and was the squad's captain and Most Valuable Player in 1932.

He coached an amateur team at the AAU Los Angeles Athletic Club from 1932 to 1934 while attending graduate school at USC, and led the squad to one Southern Pacific AAU Championship. After graduate school, he became basketball coach at Alhambra (California) High School (1934–1936), where he compiled a 29–11 record and won two championships. He joined the college coaching ranks at Modesto Junior College (California, 1936–1939, 83–27 record), before moving on to Kansas State University (Manhattan, 1939–1942, 1946–1953, 147–81 record), and the University of Utah (Salt Lake City, 1953–1971, 339–154 record).

Gardner served in the U.S. Navy from 1942 to 1946 during World War II, and coached military teams at Olathe (Kansas) and San Diego (California). He served as a seven-state athletic director in the V-5 program and helped supervise the construction of numerous physical training facilities on military installations.

During his four decade career, Gardner compiled an overall 649–278 (.700) record at all levels (American Athletic Union, military, junior college, college) and a 486–235 (.674) collegiate record, which was third best in history at the time he retired. He won three state titles at Modesto Junior College; led the Kansas State Wildcats to the 1948 (fourth place) and 1951 (second place) National Collegiate Athletic Association Final Four and won three Big 7 titles; led Utah to five Skyline Conference championships in eight years (1956–1962) and tied for a sixth; and led Utah to the 1961 (fourth place) and 1966 (fourth place) NCAA Final Four. Gardner is the only coach in collegiate basketball history to lead two different schools to the NCAA Final Four twice each (Kansas State, Utah); was named National Coach of the Year in 1970; and coached the National Association of Basketball Coaches East-West All-Star Game three times (1953, 1960, 1964).

Gardner helped coach the undefeated 1964 U.S. Olympic team (Tokyo, Japan); wrote *Championship Basketball with Jack Gardner*; and has been inducted into the Helms Basketball Hall of Fame (1971), Kansas Sports Hall of Fame (2000), Southern Utah Hall of Fame, Utah All-Sports Hall of Fame, State of Utah Basketball Hall of Fame, Kansas State University Hall of Fame, Modesto Junior College Hall of Fame, and the Redlands High School Hall of Fame.

Sources: Kansas Sports Hall of Fame; Naismith Memorial Basketball Hall of Fame

Gardner, James Henry "Jimmy" (born: May 21, 1881 in Montreal, Quebec, Canada; died: November 7, 1940); inducted into the Hockey Hall of Fame in 1962 as a player; Position: Left Wing; won four Stanley Cup championships.

Gardner played 12 pre-National Hockey League seasons from 1900 to 1915, and won four Stanley Cups with the Montreal Amateur Athletic Association's club (1902–1903, Canadian Amateur Hockey League) and with the Montreal Wanderers (1909–1910, Eastern Canada Amateur Hockey Association / National Hockey Association). He was named to the International Hockey League Second All-Star Team in 1905.

He later became a player-coach with the Montreal Canadiens of the NHA (1913–1915), and stayed with the team as coach for two years after he retired as a player. Gardner officiated in the minors (1917–1918) and was an on-ice official in the Western Canada Hockey League for the 1923–1924 season. He later coached in the Canadian-American League with the Providence Reds (1928–193) and won the league title in 1930. By the late 1930s, he was coaching the Sherbrooke and Verdun teams in the Quebec League.

Jimmy Gardner's Career Statistics

			REGULAR SEASON					PLAYOFFS				
SEASON	**TEAM**	**LEAGUE**	**GP**	**G**	**A**	**TP**	**PIM**	**GP**	**G**	**A**	**TP**	**PIM**
1899–1901	Montreal AAA–2	CAIHL										
1900–1901	Montreal AAA	CAHL	1	0	0	0	0					
1901–1902	Montreal AAA	CAHL	8	1	0	1	16					
1901–1902	Montreal AAA	St-Cup						3	0	0	0	12
1902–1903	Montreal AAA	CAHL	3	3	0	3	9					
1902–1903	Montreal AAA	St-Cup						2	1	0	1	6
1903–1904	Montreal Wanderers	FAHL	6	5	0	5	12					
1903–1904	Montreal Wanderers	St-Cup						1	1	0	1	0
1904–1905	Calumet Wanderers	IHL	23	16	0	16	33					
1905–1906	Calumet Wanderers	IHL	19	3	0	3	30					

SEASON	TEAM	LEAGUE	REGULAR SEASON GP	G	A	TP	PIM	PLAYOFFS GP	G	A	TP	PIM
1906–1907	Pittsburgh Professionals	IHL	20	10	8	18	61					
1907–1908	Montreal Shamrocks	ECAHA	10	7	0	7	42					
1908–1909	Montreal Wanderers	St-Cup						2	0	0	0	13
1908–1909	Montreal Wanderers	ECHA	12	11	0	11	51					
1909–1910	Montreal Wanderers	NHA	1	3	0	3	9					
1909–1910	Montreal Wanderers	NHA	12	10	0	10	58					
1909–1910	Montreal Wanderers	St-Cup						1	0	0	0	6
1910–1911	Montreal Wanderers	NHA	14	5	0	5	35					
1911–1912	New Westminster Royals	PCHA	15	8	0	8	50					
1912–1913	New Westminster Royals	PCHA	13	3	4	7	21					
1913–1914	Montreal Canadiens	NHA	15	10	9	19	12					
1914–1915	Montreal Canadiens	NHA	2	0	0	0	0					

Sources: Hockey Hall of Fame; Hockey-Reference.com

Gartner, Michael Alfred "Mike" (born: October 29, 1959 in Ottawa, Ontario, Canada); inducted into the Hockey Hall of Fame in 2001 as a player; Position: Right Wing; won the Canadian National Wrigley Midget Championship in 1975; set a then-NHL record of scoring 30 or more goals in 14 consecutive seasons; holds the NHL record for most 30-or-more goal seasons in a career (17).

Gartner played 19 National Hockey League seasons (1979–1998) for the Washington Capitals (1979–1989), Minnesota North Stars (1989–1990), New York Rangers (1990–1994), Toronto Maple Leafs (1994–1996), and the Phoenix Coyotes (1996–1998). At age 15, while playing with the Barrie Co-Ops team (Ontario Minor Hockey Association), he won the Canadian National Wrigley Midget Championship for the 1974–1975 season.

At age 18, he signed with the Cincinnati Stingers (World Hockey Association) to start the 1978–1979 season and scored 52 points in his rookie year. After the season, the WHA merged with the NHL and the 6', 190-pound Gartner was drafted fourth overall (in the first round) during the 1979 Entry Draft by the Washington Capitals. In his first year with the team, he led the Capitals in goals (36) and points (68); over the next eight seasons with Washington, he never scored less than 35 goals; and he led the team in scoring four times.

Gartner joined the Canadian National Team and played in the World Championships four times (1981–1983, 1993) and for the Canada Cup teams twice (1984, 1987), winning one gold and two bronze medals in these six competitions.

After two partial seasons with Minnesota (1988–1990), he was traded to the New York Rangers. By the end of the 1992–1993 season, Gartner had scored 30 or more goals in 14 consecutive seasons, setting a new NHL record.

In 1994, he was traded to the Toronto Maple Leafs, and after his third season with the team, he was named a Commissioner's Selection to the 1996 All-Star team, his seventh and final appearance.

In 1996, he was traded to the Phoenix Coyotes, where he played for two seasons before retiring. In the 1997–1998 season, Gartner became just the fifth player to reach the 700-goal mark, and he holds the NHL record for most 30-or-more goal seasons in a career (17).

After retiring as a player, he served on the NHL Players' Association Negotiating Committee and as NHLPA president during the late 1990s. In spite of his hall-of-fame career, Gartner never won the Stanley Cup; never played in the Cup finals; never won an individual NHL award; and was never named to the postseason All-Star Team.

Mike Gartner's Career Statistics

SEASON	TEAM	LEAGUE	REGULAR SEASON GP	G	A	TP	PIM	PLAYOFFS GP	G	A	TP	PIM
1974–1975	Barrie Co-Op	OMHA										
1974–1975	Mississauga Reps	MTHL										
1975–1976	Toronto Young Nationals	MTHL	26	18	18	36	46					
1975–1976	St. Catharines Black Hawks	OMJHL	3	1	3	4	0	4	1	0	1	2
1976–1977	Niagara Falls Flyers	OMJHL	62	33	42	75	125					
1977–1978	Niagara Falls Flyers	OMJHL	64	41	49	90	56					
1977–1978	Canada	WJC-A	6	3	3	6	4					
1978–1979	Cincinnati Stingers	WHA	78	27	25	52	123	3	0	2	2	2
1979–1980	Washington Capitals	NHL	77	36	32	68	66					
1980–1981	Washington Capitals	NHL	80	48	46	94	100					

			REGULAR SEASON					PLAYOFFS				
SEASON	**TEAM**	**LEAGUE**	**GP**	**G**	**A**	**TP**	**PIM**	**GP**	**G**	**A**	**TP**	**PIM**
1980–1981	Canada	WEC-A	8	4	0	4	8					
1981–1982	Washington Capitals	DN-Cup	4	0	2	2						
1981–1982	Washington Capitals	NHL	80	35	45	80	121					
1981–1982	Canada	WEC-A	10	3	2	5	6					
1982–1983	Washington Capitals	NHL	73	38	38	76	54	4	0	0	0	4
1982–1983	Canada	WEC-A	10	4	1	5	12					
1983–1984	Washington Capitals	NHL	80	40	45	85	90	8	3	7	10	16
1984–1985	Canada	Can-Cup	8	3	2	5	10					
1984–1985	Washington Capitals	NHL	80	50	52	102	71	5	4	3	7	9
1985–1986	Washington Capitals	NHL	74	35	40	75	63	9	2	10	12	4
1986–1987	Washington Capitals	NHL	78	41	32	73	61	7	4	3	7	14
1987–1988	Canada	Can-Cup	9	2	2	4	6					
1987–1988	Washington Capitals	NHL	80	48	33	81	73	14	3	4	7	14
1988–1989	Washington Capitals	NHL	56	26	29	55	71					
1988–1989	Minnesota North Stars	NHL	13	7	7	14	2	5	0	0	0	6
1989–1990	Minnesota North Stars	NHL	67	34	36	70	32					
1989–1990	New York Rangers	NHL	12	11	5	16	6	10	5	3	8	12
1990–1991	New York Rangers	NHL	79	49	20	69	53	6	1	1	2	0
1991–1992	New York Rangers	NHL	76	40	41	81	55	13	8	8	16	4
1992–1993	New York Rangers	NHL	84	45	23	68	59					
1992–1993	Canada	WC-A	7	3	4	7	12					
1993–1994	New York Rangers	NHL	71	28	24	52	58					
1993–1994	Toronto Maple Leafs	NHL	10	6	6	12	4	18	5	6	11	14
1994–1995	Toronto Maple Leafs	NHL	38	12	8	20	6	5	2	2	4	2
1995–1996	Toronto Maple Leafs	NHL	82	35	19	54	52	6	4	1	5	4
1996–1997	Phoenix Coyotes	NHL	82	32	31	63	38	7	1	2	3	4
1997–1998	Phoenix Coyotes	NHL	60	12	15	27	24	5	1	0	1	18
	NHL TOTALS		1,432	708	627	1,335	1,159	122	43	50	93	125

Sources: Hockey Hall of Fame; Hockey-Reference.com

Gates, William "Pop" (born: August 30, 1917 in Decatur, Alabama; died: December 1, 1999 in New York (Harlem), New York); inducted into the Naismith Memorial Basketball Hall of Fame in 1989 as a player; only player to have appeared in all 10 World Professional Basketball Tournaments; won three ABA championships; one of the first African-Americans to play in the National Basketball League.

Gates played basketball for four years at Benjamin Franklin (New York, New York) High School from 1934 to 1938; was on the team that won the 1938 Public Schools Athletic League Basketball Championship; and was selected All-City First Team in 1938. After high school, Gates went to Clark College (Atlanta, Georgia), but only attended for one month before turning professional.

As a professional, Gates played for the New York Renaissance (Rens) (Independent League; 1938–1941, 1943–1944, 1945–1946, 1947–1948); Long Island Grumman Flyers (Independent League; 1941–1942); Washington Bears (Independent League; 1942–1943); Long Island Grumman Hellcats (Independent League; 1944–1945); Buffalo Bisons (later called the Tri-City Blackhawks; National Basketball League, 1946–1947); Dayton Rens (player-coach; National Basketball League; 1948–1949); Scranton Miners (player-coach; American Basketball League/Association; 1949–1951); and the Harlem Globetrotters (player-coach; International League; 1950–1955).

The 6'3", 196-pound Gates was an eight-time All-Pro in his 12-year professional career; led the Rens to 68 wins and the first-ever World Professional Championship in 1939; played under hall-of-fame coach Clair Bee and led the Flyers to several tournament titles; was on the Bears team that went undefeated and won the World Title in 1943; led the Miners to three consecutive ABA championships (1949–1951); only player to have appeared in all 10 World Professional Basketball Tournaments; and was one of the first African-Americans to play in the National Basketball League.

He has been inducted into the Harlem Professionals' Hall of Fame, Robert "Bob" Douglas Hall of Fame, and the Harlem YMCA Hall of Fame. He is one of the few athletes to go directly from a high school championship team to a World Professional Champion team (New York Renaissance, 1939).

Source: Naismith Memorial Basketball Hall of Fame

Gatski, Frank (born: March 18, 1919 in Farmington, West Virginia; died: November 22, 2005 in Morgantown, West Virginia); inducted into the Pro Football Hall of Fame in 1985 as a player; Position: Center; won eight league titles (four with the AAFC and four with the NFL).

Gatski anchored the offensive line during the Cleveland Browns' dominant years in both the All-America Football Conference (1946–1949) and the National Football League (1950–1956). He played one year (1957) with the Detroit Lions before retiring after 144 games. The 6'3", 233-pound Gatski played in 11 championship games in his 12-year career, with his team winning eight times (four in the AAFC and four in the NFL); was selected All-Pro four times (1951–1953, 1955); and played in the 1956 Pro Bowl.

One year after graduating from high school, Gatski played football at Marshall University (Huntington, West Virginia) until he joined the Army in 1943 during World War II. After his military service was completed in 1945, he went to Auburn University (Alabama) for one year before joining the Browns for the 1946 season.

During his tenure with the team, the Browns won all four AAFC championships and were in the title game the franchise's first six years in the NFL. The team missed the playoff in 1956, but Gatski won his eighth championship ring in 1957, when the Lions defeated his old team, 59–14, which was his last game in the NFL.

After his playing career ended, he was a scout for the NFL's Boston Patriots (now known as the New England Patriots) and a coach for the West Virginia Industrial School for Boys (Pruntytown) from 1961 to 1982. His Hall of Fame induction class included Joe Namath, O.J. Simpson, and Roger Staubach.

Marshall University retired Gatski's jersey number 72 in October 2005.

Source: Pro Football Hall of Fame

Gavitt, David (born: October 26, 1937 in Westerly, Rhode Island); inducted into the Naismith Memorial Basketball Hall of Fame in 2006 as a contributor; first native of Rhode Island to be inducted into the basketball hall of fame; helped create the Big East Conference.

Gavitt was one of the architects of the modern game of college basketball and served in a variety of roles, including coach and athletic director at Providence College (Rhode Island); founder of the Big East Conference; chairman of the National Collegiate Athletic Association Division I Men's Basketball Committee; and president of USA Basketball.

After graduating from Dartmouth College (Hanover, New Hampshire) in 1959, he was an assistant basketball coach at Worcester Academy (Massachusetts) for two years before becoming an assistant coach at Providence College in 1962. He left in 1966 to become head coach at his alma mater, and returned to Providence as the head coach in 1969.

As coach of the Friars (1969–1979), he led Providence College to 209 wins, including eight consecutive 20-win seasons (1971–1978); five NCAA tournament appearances (1972–1974, 1977–1978), including the school's first-ever Final Four in 1973; and three National Invitation Tournaments (1971, 1975–1976). He helped create the Big East Conference in 1979 and served as its first commissioner until 1990. During his tenure as commissioner, six of the conference's schools (Georgetown, Villanova, Saint John's, Providence, Seton Hall, and Syracuse) reached the NCAA Final Four. Named in his honor, the winner of the conference's basketball tournament is awarded the Dave Gavitt Trophy.

His work with the Division I Men's Basketball Committee led to the expansion of the NCAA tournament to 64 teams in order to allow smaller conferences to compete, and he helped negotiate the first television contract to broadcast the entire tournament. He left the Big East Conference to become senior executive vice-president and chief executive officer of the National Basketball Association's Boston Celtics (1990–1994); served as president of the NCAA Foundation (1995–1997); and chairman of the board of the Naismith Memorial Basketball Hall of Fame (1995–2003).

Gavitt was the head coach of the 1980 United States Olympic Team that was not able to compete due to the boycott of the Games in Moscow by the United States; was president of the U.S. Olympic governing body from 1988 to 1992; named New England Coach of the Year five times; won the John Bunn Lifetime Achievement Award in 1987; was a member of the committee that assembled the 1992 Olympic Basketball gold-medal winning "Dream Team"; and received the Naismith Outstanding Contribution to Basketball Award in 1993.

He has been inducted into the Providence College Athletic Hall of Fame (1984), National Association of Collegiate Directors of Athletics Hall of Fame (2000), International Scholar-Athlete Hall of Fame (2000); Rhode Island Heritage Hall of Fame; and the New England Basketball Hall of Fame. He is the first native of Rhode Island to be inducted into the Naismith Memorial Basketball Hall of Fame.

Source: Naismith Memorial Basketball Hall of Fame

Gehrig, Henry Louis "Lou" (born: Lugwig Heinrich Gehrig on June 19, 1903 in New York, New York; died: June 2, 1941 in Riverdale, New York); inducted into the National Baseball Hall of Fame and Museum in 1939 as a player; Position: First Base; Bats: Left; Throws: Left; Uniform: #4; first baseball player to have his uniform number retired; two-time American League Most Valuable Player; set the major league record for most consecutive games played (since broken by Cal Ripken, Jr.); set the major league record for career grand slams.

Known as "The Iron Horse" for his playing longevity, Gehrig made his Major League Baseball debut on June 15, 1923 and played his entire 17-year career (until 1939) with the New York Yankees. He played in seven World Series (winning six [1927–1928, 1932, 1936–1938] and losing one in 1926); was named to seven All-Star teams (1933–1939); and was twice selected as the American League Most Valuable Player (1927, 1936).

Ironically, considering his future professional baseball success, Gehrig attended Columbia University (New York, New York) on a football scholarship (he played fullback), and while at the school, he also played baseball, which brought him to the attention of major league scouts.

Gehrig teamed with Babe Ruth to form one of baseball's most powerful hitting duos ever. He had 13 consecutive seasons with both 100 runs scored and 100 runs batted in (1926–1938), averaging 139 runs and 148 RBIs per season; set an American League record with 184 RBI in 1931; hit a still-standing record 23 career grand slams; and won the 1934 Triple Crown (leading the league in home runs, runs batted in, and batting average). His .361 batting average in seven World Series led the Yankees to six titles. His consecutive games played streak ended at 2,130 (May 31, 1925 to May 2, 1939) when he was stopped by the disease that would later carry his name. His streak would last until broken by Cal Ripken, Jr. on September 6, 1995.

He was the son of German immigrants and was the only one of four children to survive. In 1921, Gehrig went to Columbia University and played summer professional baseball under the assumed name Henry Lewis. Once his ruse was discovered (12 games into his season with the Hartford Senators of the Eastern League), Gehrig was banned from intercollegiate sports during his freshman year at college.

Allowed to participate in sports again as a sophomore, Gehrig played fullback on the school's football team, and pitched and played first base for the Columbia Nine in 1923 as a junior. In 1923, he was signed by the Yankees, left school, and returned to the Hartford team, this time playing under his real name. When he was called up to the majors in September, he made the most of the opportunity by hitting .423 in only 26 at-bats.

Gehrig returned to Hartford for a full season, before returning to the Yankees for good in 1925. Once he replaced Wally Pipp (who is more remembered now as the answer to a trivia question) at first base, Gehrig didn't leave the playing field for more than 13 years (2,130 games). In 1926, he led the league in triples (20) and hit .348 in that season's World Series, in a losing effort to the St. Louis Cardinals in seven games.

Ruth and Gehrig began to dominate baseball in 1927 when Ruth hit 60 home runs and Gehrig hit 47; the Yankees won the World Series; and Gehrig won his first Most Valuable Player award.

On June 3, 1932, he became the first American League player to hit four home runs in a game (in a 20–13 win over the Philadelphia Athletics). While Ruth and Gehrig were formidable teammates, their personalities clashed and they rarely spoke to each other. A thaw in their relationship was evident on "Lou Gehrig Appreciation Day" at Yankee Stadium on July 4, 1939.

He accumulated more than 400 total bases in a season five times; averaged 147 RBIs per season; his 184 RBIs in 1931 remains the highest single season total in American League history; won the Triple Crown in 1934 (.363 average, 49 home runs, 165 RBI); stole home 15 times in his career; batted .361 in 34 World Series games; holds the record for career grand slams (23); and hit 73 three-run and 166 two-run homers, giving him the highest average of RBIs per home run of any player with more than 300 career homers.

As he had done earlier with Ruth, Gehrig and Joe DiMaggio dominated the league as the Yankees won four World Series in a row (1936–1939), winning a total of 16 of 19 games during this streak.

After 12 straight seasons of hitting over .300, he fell to .295 in 1938, the first sign that something was physically wrong. After collecting only four hits in the first eight games of the 1939 season, Gehrig removed himself from the lineup on May 2, 1939, ending his consecutive games played streak at 2,130. A series of medical tests at the Mayo Clinic revealed that Gehrig had a rare form of a degenerative disease called amyotrophic lateral sclerosis (ALS), which is now known as Lou Gehrig's disease. His baseball career was over.

On July 4, 1939 the Yankees held a "Lou Gehrig Appreciation Day" between games of a scheduled doubleheader with the Washington Senators. With more than 60,000 fans in attendance, he gave his famous emotional speech thanking everyone for their support and calling himself "the luckiest man on the face of the earth." When he had finished his speech, Babe Ruth put his arm around Gehrig and spoke to him, marking the first time the two legends had talked since 1934.

After retiring from the game due to poor health, New York Mayor Fiorello LaGuardia convinced Gehrig to join the Parole Board. He was sworn in for a 10-year term in June 1940, but died after serving only one year.

His 493 career home runs set a record for the most by a first baseman until Mark McGwire of the St. Louis Cardinals hit 500; he is the only player in history to drive in more than 500 runs in three seasons (174 in 1930, 184 in 1931, and 151 in 1932); his 184 RBIs in a single season (1931) are the most in American League history and second in baseball history (behind Hack Wilson's 190 with the Chicago Cubs); he was the first athlete in any sport to have his uniform number retired; and he was inducted into the National Baseball Hall of Fame early (1939) when the standard two-year waiting rule was waived.

Gehrig compiled the highest career slugging percentage of any first baseman (.632); led the league in home runs twice (1934, 1936); led the league in RBIs five times (1927–1928, 1930–1931, 1934); and led the league in times on base six times (1927, 1930–1931, 1934, 1936–1937).

Lou Gehrig's Career Statistics

YEAR	TEAM	LG	G	AB	R	H	2B	3B	HR	RBI	BB	SO	SB	AVG	SLG
1923	New York	AL	13	26	6	11	4	1	1	9	2	5	0	.423	.769
1924	New York	AL	10	12	2	6	1	0	0	5	1	3	0	.500	.583
1925	New York	AL	126	437	73	129	23	10	20	68	46	49	6	.295	.531
1926	New York	AL	155	572	135	179	47	20	16	112	105	73	6	.313	.549
1927	New York	AL	155	584	149	218	52	18	47	175	109	84	10	.373	.765
1928	New York	AL	154	562	139	210	47	13	27	142	94	69	4	.374	.648
1929	New York	AL	154	553	127	166	32	10	35	126	124	68	4	.300	.584
1930	New York	AL	154	581	143	220	42	17	41	174	101	63	12	.379	.721
1931	New York	AL	155	619	163	211	31	15	46	184	117	56	17	.341	.662
1932	New York	AL	156	596	138	208	42	9	34	151	108	38	4	.349	.621
1933	New York	AL	152	593	138	198	41	12	32	139	92	42	9	.334	.605
1934	New York	AL	154	579	128	210	40	6	49	165	109	31	9	.363	.706
1935	New York	AL	149	535	125	176	26	10	30	119	132	38	8	.329	.583
1936	New York	AL	155	579	167	205	37	7	49	152	130	46	3	.354	.696
1937	New York	AL	157	569	138	200	37	9	37	159	127	49	4	.351	.643
1938	New York	AL	157	576	115	170	32	6	29	114	107	75	6	.295	.523
1939	New York	AL	8	28	2	4	0	0	0	1	5	1	0	.143	.143
	TOTALS		2,164	8,001	1,888	2,721	534	163	493	1,995	1,509	790	102	.340	.632

Sources: Baseball-Reference.com; *Iron Horse: Lou Gehrig in His Time* (Ray Robinson); Lou Gehrig Web Site (www.lougehrig.com); National Baseball Hall of Fame and Museum

Gehringer, Charles Leonard "Charlie" (born: May 11, 1903 in Fowlerville, Michigan; died: January 21, 1993 in Bloomfield Hills, Michigan); inducted into the National Baseball Hall of Fame and Museum in 1949 as a player; Position: Second Base; Bats: Left; Throws: Right; Uniform: #2; 1937 American League Most Valuable Player; first player in major league history to hit for the cycle in order (single-double-triple-home run).

After graduating from the University of Michigan (Ann Arbor), Gehringer played second base for the Detroit Tigers during his entire 19-year major league career (1924–1942), making his debut on September 22, 1924. He played in three World Series (winning in 1935 and losing in 1934 and 1940); was named to six All-Star teams (1933–1938); and was the American League Most Valuable Player in 1937.

He hit over .300 13 times; collected 200 or more hits seven times; led the league in 1937 by batting .371; led the league in both assists and fielding percentage seven times; led the league in games played four times (1929–1930, 1933–1934), in runs twice (1929, 1934), in hits twice (1929, 1934), in doubles (1929), in triples (1929), and in stolen bases (1929); and played every inning of the first six All-Star Games as the starting second baseman for the American League.

After retiring as a player, Gehringer coached for Detroit; served as the team's general manager (1951–1959); and was a member of the National Baseball Hall of Fame and Museum Veterans Committee (1953–1990). The Tigers retired his uniform number two in 1983; in 1999, he was ranked number 46 on *The Sporting News*' list of the 100 Greatest Baseball Players; and was nominated as a finalist for the Major League Baseball All-Century Team.

At the University of Michigan, he played both basketball and baseball, but ironically, lettered only in basketball. In 1923, after only one year in college, he signed with the Tigers and was sent to the London Tecumsehs in the Class B Michigan-Ontario League. The 5'11", 180-pound Gehringer was called up to the major leagues briefly at the end of September 1924 and played five games for the Tigers. In 1925, he played in the minors with the Toronto Maple Leafs of the International League, and eight games in September with the Tigers.

Gehringer's first full season with the Tigers was 1926; in 1927, he led American League second baseman with 438 assists and 84 double plays; and in 1928, he had 507 assists, best in the league for a second baseman.

In 1929, he led the American League in hits (215), doubles (45), triples (19, including 3 in one game), runs (131), stolen bases (27), putouts (404), and fielding percentage (.975). He played in every game of the 1928, 1929, and 1930 seasons.

On August 14, 1929, the Tigers held a "Charlie Gehringer Day" and, in a 17–13 win, he collected four hits, including a home run, and stole home.

In 1934, Gehringer played in all 154 Tigers games; helped lead the team to its first American League pennant in 25 years; and led the league in runs scored (134) and hits (214). In 1935, he helped the team win the World Series; played in all six games; and hit .375. In 1937, Gehringer was named American League Most Valuable Player and won the batting title.

On May 27, 1939, in a 12–5 win over the St. Louis Browns, Gehringer became the first player in major league history to hit for the cycle in order: a single, followed by double, a triple, and then a home run.

He enlisted in the U.S. Navy after the 1942 season and served three years during World War II. Released from military service in 1945, he decided not to return to baseball and became a businessman.

Charlie Gehringer's Career Statistics

YEAR	TEAM	LG	G	AB	R	H	2B	3B	HR	RBI	BB	SO	SB	AVG	SLG
1924	Detroit	AL	5	13	2	6	0	0	0	1	0	2	1	.462	.462
1925	Detroit	AL	8	18	3	3	0	0	0	0	2	0	0	.167	.167
1926	Detroit	AL	123	459	62	127	19	17	1	48	30	42	9	.277	.399
1927	Detroit	AL	133	508	110	161	29	11	4	61	52	31	17	.317	.441
1928	Detroit	AL	154	603	108	193	29	16	6	74	69	22	15	.320	.451
1929	Detroit	AL	155	634	131	215	45	19	13	106	64	19	28	.339	.532
1930	Detroit	AL	154	610	144	201	47	15	16	98	69	17	19	.330	.534
1931	Detroit	AL	101	383	67	119	24	5	4	53	29	15	13	.311	.431
1932	Detroit	AL	152	618	112	184	44	11	19	107	68	34	9	.298	.497
1933	Detroit	AL	155	628	103	204	42	6	12	105	68	27	5	.325	.468
1934	Detroit	AL	154	601	134	214	50	7	11	127	99	25	11	.356	.517
1935	Detroit	AL	150	610	123	201	32	8	19	108	79	16	11	.330	.502
1936	Detroit	AL	154	641	144	227	60	12	15	116	83	13	4	.354	.555
1937	Detroit	AL	144	564	133	209	40	1	14	96	90	25	11	.371	.520
1938	Detroit	AL	152	568	133	174	32	5	20	107	112	21	14	.306	.486
1939	Detroit	AL	118	406	86	132	29	6	16	86	68	16	4	.325	.544
1940	Detroit	AL	139	515	108	161	33	3	10	81	101	17	10	.313	.447
1941	Detroit	AL	127	436	65	96	19	4	3	46	95	26	1	.220	.303
1942	Detroit	AL	45	45	6	12	0	0	1	7	7	4	0	.267	.333
			2,323	8,860	1,774	2,839	574	146	184	1,427	1,185	372	182	.320	.480

Sources: Baseball-Reference.com; National Baseball Hall of Fame and Museum

Gentle, James Cuthbert (born: July 21, 1904 in Brookline, Massachusetts; died: May 22, 1986 in Philadelphia, Pennsylvania); inducted into the National Soccer Hall of Fame and Museum in 1986 as a player; Position: Inside Forward; won a bronze medal with the 1932 U.S. Olympic team.

Gentle was a member of the U.S. World Cup team in 1930 that finished third at the World's Open Soccer Tournament in Uruguay, and played for the U.S. Field Hockey team at the Los Angeles Olympic Games of 1932, winning a bronze medal. In addition to playing, he acted as the team's official Spanish interpreter.

He played briefly for the Boston Wonder Workers (1925–1926) in the American Soccer League, before playing for the Philadelphia Field Club (ASL, 1926), at which time he was selected for the World Cup team.

After attending Brookline (Massachusetts) High School, Gentle entered the University of Pennsylvania (Philadelphia) in 1922, and played football as a freshman before switching to soccer and track. In his junior year, he was an All-American on Penn's intercollegiate championship varsity soccer team.

After graduation, Gentle coached soccer at Haverford College (Pennsylvania, 1935–1940), and in just over six seasons, compiled a 39-26-3 record and won two Mid-American Conference titles.

During World War II, he served in the 36th Infantry and fought in Salerno, Italy, before joining General Patton's forces in the move across Europe and into the Rhineland. After the war, Gentle served briefly as the U.S. trade and industry officer for the American zone in Germany.

Source: National Soccer Hall of Fame and Museum

Geoffrion, Bernard Joseph André "Bernie" (born: February 16, 1931 in Montreal, Quebec, Canada; died: March 11, 2006 in Atlanta, Georgia); inducted into the Hockey Hall of Fame in 1972 as a player; Position: Right Wing; Uniform: #5; second NHL player to score 50 goals in a season; won six Stanley Cup championships.

Geoffrion played 16 National Hockey League seasons (1950–1968) for the Montreal Canadiens (1950–1964) and the New York Rangers (1966–1968); won six Stanley Cup titles with the Canadiens (1953, 1956–1960); won the Art

Ross Trophy twice as the league's leading regular-season scorer (1955, 1961); and won the Hart Memorial Trophy as the NHL's Most Valuable Player in 1961.

The 5'9", 170-pound Geoffrion won the Calder Memorial Trophy in 1952 as the NHL's Rookie of the Year; was named Second All-Star Right Wing twice (1955, 1960); and First All-Star Team Right Wing once (1961).

He left the Canadiens and the NHL in 1964 to coach the Quebec Aces of the American Hockey League for two seasons. He then returned to the NHL to play two seasons for the Rangers, before retiring as a player for good in 1968 and coaching the team for less than one year.

In 1972, he coached the NHL's Atlanta Flames for just over two seasons before becoming the team's vice-president. He coached the Flames into the Stanley Cup playoffs in only his second season (1974), but they were eliminated in the first round by the Philadelphia Flyers. In 1979, he was selected as the coach of the Canadiens, but lasted only 30 games due to illness.

In the 1970s and into the 1980s, Geoffrion appeared in several television commercials for Miller Lite beer as part of the company's series of using retired athletes as spokesmen. On the day he died of stomach cancer, the Canadiens retired his jersey number five; in 1998, he was ranked number 42 on *The Hockey News*' list of the 100 Greatest Hockey Players; and he was the second player in NHL history to score 50 goals in one season (after teammate Maurice Richard).

Bernard Geoffrion's Career Statistics

			REGULAR SEASON					PLAYOFFS				
SEASON	**TEAM**	**LEAGUE**	**GP**	**G**	**A**	**TP**	**PIM**	**GP**	**G**	**A**	**TP**	**PIM**
1945–1946	Mount St-Louis College	High-QC										
1946–1947	Montreal Concordia Civics	QJHL	26	7	8	15	6					
1947–1948	Laval Nationale	QJHL	29	20	15	35	49	11	7	5	12	11
1947–1948	Laval Nationale	M-Cup	8	3	2	5	11					
1948–1949	Laval Nationale	QJHL	42	41	35	76	49	9	3	6	9	22
1949–1950	Laval Nationale	QJHL	34	52	34	86	77	3	6	0	6	8
1949–1950	Montreal Royals	QSHL	1	0	0	0	0					
1950–1951	Montreal Nationale	QJHL	36	54	44	98	80					
1950–1951	Montreal Canadiens	NHL	18	8	6	14	9	11	1	1	2	6
1951–1952	Montreal Canadiens	NHL	67	30	24	54	66	11	3	1	4	6
1952–1953	Montreal Canadiens	NHL	65	22	17	39	37	12	6	4	10	12
1953–1954	Montreal Canadiens	NHL	54	29	25	54	87	11	6	5	11	18
1954–1955	Montreal Canadiens	NHL	70	38	37	75	57	12	8	5	13	8
1955–1956	Montreal Canadiens	NHL	59	29	33	62	66	10	5	9	14	6
1956–1957	Montreal Canadiens	NHL	41	19	21	40	18	10	11	7	18	2
1957–1958	Montreal Canadiens	NHL	42	27	23	50	51	10	6	5	11	2
1958–1959	Montreal Canadiens	NHL	59	22	44	66	30	11	5	8	13	10
1959–1960	Montreal Canadiens	NHL	59	30	41	71	36	8	2	10	12	4
1960–1961	Montreal Canadiens	NHL	64	50	45	95	29	4	2	1	3	0
1961–1962	Montreal Canadiens	NHL	62	23	36	59	36	5	0	1	1	6
1962–1963	Montreal Canadiens	NHL	51	23	18	41	73	5	0	1	1	4
1963–1964	Montreal Canadiens	NHL	55	21	18	39	41	7	1	1	2	4
1964–1966	Quebec Aces	AHL										
1966–1967	New York Rangers	NHL	58	17	25	42	42	4	2	0	2	0
1967–1968	New York Rangers	NHL	59	5	16	21	11	1	0	1	1	0
	NHL TOTALS		883	393	429	822	689	132	58	60	118	88

Sources: Hockey Hall of Fame; Hockey-Reference.com

George, William J. "Bill" (born: October 27, 1929 in Waynesburg, Pennsylvania; died: September 30, 1982 in Wisconsin); inducted into the Pro Football Hall of Fame in 1974 as a player; Position: Linebacker; Uniform: #61; changed the way linebackers were positioned during pass plays.

A 1951 second-round draft choice (23rd overall pick) of the National Football League's Chicago Bears out of Wake Forest University (Winston-Salem, North Carolina), George played 15 NFL seasons for Chicago (1952–1965) and the Los Angeles Rams (1966). He called the Bears' defensive signals for eight years; was named All-NFL eight times (1955–1961, 1963); played in eight straight Pro Bowls (1955-1962); and had 18 interceptions and recovered 19 opponent fumbles. He was the leader of the powerful Bears' defensive teams of the 1950s and 1960s.

In a game against the Philadelphia Eagles in 1954, the 6'2", 237-pound George made a move that changed the way future linebackers would play the position. On passing plays, it was traditional for the linebacker to "bump" the center and then drop back into coverage. Noticing that the Eagles were successfully completing short passes over his head, he decided to simply fall back immediately into pass coverage. Two plays later, he caught the first of his 18 career interceptions. This move eventually led to the creation of the 4-3 defense.

In 1954, George scored 25 points on 13 points-after-touchdown and four field goals. In 1963, he led the Bears' defensive unit that helped beat the New York Giants 14–10 to win the NFL Championship.

He was named to the NFL 1950s All-Decade Team; the Bears retired his uniform number 61 in 1974; and in 1999, George was ranked number 49 on *The Sporting News*' list of the 100 Greatest Football Players.

Bill George's Career Statistics

YEAR	TEAM	G	INT	YDS	AVG	TD	FUMREC	YDS	TD
1952	Chicago	12	0	0	0.0	0	3	0	0
1953	Chicago	12	0	0	0.0	0	0	0	0
1954	Chicago	12	2	9	4.5	0	0	0	0
1955	Chicago	12	2	13	6.5	0	2	0	0
1956	Chicago	12	2	9	4.5	0	3	0	0
1957	Chicago	12	0	0	0.0	0	1	0	0
1958	Chicago	12	1	5	5.0	0	4	0	0
1959	Chicago	12	2	20	10.0	0	1	0	0
1960	Chicago	12	1	12	12.0	0	0	0	0
1961	Chicago	14	3	18	6.0	0	2	0	0
1962	Chicago	13	2	26	13.0	0	0	0	0
1963	Chicago	14	1	4	4.0	0	0	0	0
1964	Chicago	8	2	28	14.0	0	1	0	0
1965	Chicago	2	0	0	0.0	0	0	0	0
1966	Los Angeles	14	0	0	0.0	0	2	0	0
	TOTALS	173	18	144	8.0	0	19	0	0

Sources: Pro Football Hall of Fame; Pro-Football-Reference.com

Gerard, Eddie (born: February 22, 1890 in Ottawa, Ontario, Canada; died: December 7, 1937); inducted into the Hockey Hall of Fame in 1945 as a player; Position: Defenseman; won three Stanley Cup titles as a player and one as a coach.

Gerard was among the first 12 inductees when the Hockey Hall of Fame was founded in 1945 and played 11 professional seasons from 1907 to 1923. He was captain of three Stanley Cup-winning teams, and coached the Montreal Maroons to a Cup victory in 1926.

He signed with the Ottawa Senators (National Hockey Association/National Hockey League [1917]) for the 1913–1914 season, began his career as a forward, and switched to defense after four seasons. As the team's captain, Gerard led the franchise to three Stanley Cup titles (1920–1921, 1923), and retired immediately after the squad's last championship.

After retiring as a player, he became the coach of the Montreal Maroons at the start of the 1925–1926 season, and led the team to its first Stanley Cup title in his inaugural season.

In 1930, he coached the New York Americans before returning to the Maroons two years later. He went on to coach the St. Louis Eagles in 1934–1935, but stepped down midway through the season due to poor health.

Gerard was inducted into Canada's Sports Hall of Fame in 1975.

Eddie Gerard's Career Statistics

			REGULAR SEASON					PLAYOFFS				
SEASON	TEAM	LEAGUE	GP	G	A	TP	PIM	GP	G	A	TP	PIM
1907–1908	Ottawa Seconds	OCHL	7	8	0	8						
1908–1909	Ottawa Seconds	OCHL	5	11	0	11		2	1	0	1	5
1909–1910	Ottawa Seconds	OCHL	9	17	0	17		3	1	0	1	14
1910–1911	Ottawa New Edinburghs	OCHL	2	1	0	1	0					
1910–1911	Ottawa New Edinburghs	IPAHU	6	9	0	9	18	3	6	0	6	6
1911–1912	Ottawa New Edinburghs	IPAHU	10	12	0	12	8	4	8	0	8	6
1912–1913	Ottawa New Edinburghs	IPAHU	8	16	0	16	16	6	6	0	6	6
1913–1914	Ottawa Senators	NHA	11	6	7	13	34					
1914–1915	Ottawa Senators	NHA	20	9	10	19	39	5	1	0	1	6

SEASON	TEAM	LEAGUE	REGULAR SEASON GP	G	A	TP	PIM	PLAYOFFS GP	G	A	TP	PIM
1914–1915	East All-Stars	Exhib.	3	1	2	3	14					
1915–1916	Ottawa Senators	NHA	24	13	5	18	57					
1916–1917	Ottawa Senators	NHA	19	18	16	34	48	2	1	2	3	6
1917–1918	Ottawa Senators	NHL	20	13	7	20	26					
1918–1919	Ottawa Senators	NHL	18	4	6	10	17	5	3	0	3	3
1919–1920	Ottawa Senators	NHL	22	9	7	16	19					
1919–1920	Ottawa Senators	St-Cup						5	2	1	3	3
1920–1921	Ottawa Senators	NHL	24	11	4	15	18	2	1	0	1	6
1920–1921	Ottawa Senators	St-Cup						5	0	0	0	44
1921–1922	Ottawa Senators	NHL	21	7	11	18	16	2	0	0	0	8
1921–1922	Toronto St. Pats	St-Cup						1	0	0	0	0
1922–1923	Ottawa Senators	NHL	23	6	13	19	12	2	0	0	0	0
1922–1923	Ottawa Senators	St-Cup						6	1	0	1	4
	NHL TOTALS		128	50	48	98	108	11	4	0	4	17

Sources: Canada's Sports Hall of Fame; Hockey Hall of Fame; Hockey-Reference.com

Gervin, George (born: April 27, 1952 in Detroit, Michigan); inducted into the Naismith Memorial Basketball Hall of Fame in 1996 as a player; Position: Guard; Uniform: #44; one of seven players to score 2,000 points in six consecutive NBA seasons; one of three players to win four or more NBA scoring titles.

Gervin played basketball for four years at Martin Luther King High School (Detroit, Michigan) from 1965 to 1969; was on the varsity team for two years; and was named All-American, All-Conference, and All-State in 1969. After graduating, he attended Long Beach State University (California, 1969–1970), but after only one semester, he transferred to Eastern Michigan University (Ypsilanti, 1970–1972).

In college, Gervin scored 1,044 points (26.8 per game) and grabbed 562 rebounds (14.4 per game) in 39 total games at Eastern Michigan. He was selected First Team All-American (1972); set EMU school records in 1971–1972 for most points scored (886), most field goals (339), and most rebounds (458) in a season; and his uniform number 24 was retired by the school in January 1986. He was averaging 29.5 points-per-game in his second year at Eastern Michigan when he was suspended from the team for hitting an opposing player during a fight. After being expelled from the school, he joined the American Basketball Association.

He joined the professional ranks with the Virginia Squires (1972–1974) in the ABA, before moving on to the San Antonio Spurs (1974–1985, ABA/National Basketball Association), and the Chicago Bulls (1985–1986, NBA). After leaving the NBA, Gervin played for Banco Roma (1986–1987) of the Italian League, before returning to America and finishing his career with the Quad City Thunder (1989–1990) of the Continental Basketball Association.

He was selected to 12 consecutive ABA/NBA All-Star teams (ABA: 1974–1976; NBA: 1977–1985); named to the 1973 All-ABA Rookie team; All-ABA Second Team twice (1975–1976); NBA All-Star Most Valuable Player in 1980; All-NBA First Team five straight seasons (1978–1982); and All-NBA Second Team twice (1977, 1983).

The 6'7", 183-pound Gervin is one of seven players to score 2,000 points in six consecutive NBA seasons (1978–1983), and is one of only three players (along with Michael Jordan and Wilt Chamberlain) to win four or more NBA scoring titles (1978–1980, 1982). He scored an NBA-record 33 points in the second quarter of a game against the New Orleans Jazz (April 9, 1978); scored 50 or more points four times and 40 or more points 64 times in the NBA; and scored 1,000 points or more for 13 consecutive seasons.

In nine NBA seasons (1976–1985), he led the Spurs to five Midwest Division titles, and averaged 27.0 points-per-game in the playoffs; San Antonio retired his jersey number 44 in December 1987; was one of four charter members inducted into the San Antonio Sports Hall of Fame (1995); and founded the George Gervin Youth Center, Inc. in 1989, a non-profit organization that focuses on the development of disadvantaged youths.

Gervin was named to the NBA's 50 greatest players list and was ranked #25 on *SLAM* magazine's Top 75 NBA Players of all time in 2003.

George Gervin's Career Statistics

SEASON	TEAM	LG	G	MIN	FG	3P	FT	TRB	AST	PTS
1972–1973	Virginia	ABA	30	689	161	6	96	128	34	424
1973–1974	Virginia	ABA	49	1,728	487	8	262	418	97	1,244
1973–1974	San Antonio	ABA	25	783	185	0	116	206	45	486

SEASON	TEAM	LG	G	MIN	FG	3P	FT	TRB	AST	PTS
1974–1975	San Antonio	ABA	84	3,113	784	17	380	697	207	1,965
1975–1976	San Antonio	ABA	81	2,748	706	14	342	546	201	1,768
1976–1977	San Antonio	NBA	82	2,705	726		443	454	238	1,895
1977–1978	San Antonio	NBA	82	2,857	864		504	420	302	2,232
1978–1979	San Antonio	NBA	80	2,888	947		471	400	219	2,365
1979–1980	San Antonio	NBA	78	2,934	1,024	32	505	403	202	2,585
1980–1981	San Antonio	NBA	82	2,765	850	9	512	419	260	2,221
1981–1982	San Antonio	NBA	79	2,817	993	10	555	392	187	2,551
1982–1983	San Antonio	NBA	78	2,830	757	12	517	357	264	2,043
1983–1984	San Antonio	NBA	76	2,584	765	10	427	313	220	1,967
1984–1985	San Antonio	NBA	72	2,091	600	0	324	234	178	1,524
1985–1986	Chicago	NBA	82	2,065	519	4	283	215	144	1,325
		ABA	269	9,061	2,323	45	1,196	1,995	584	5,887
		NBA	791	26,536	8,045	77	4,541	3,607	2,214	20,708
	TOTALS		1,060	35,597	10,368	122	5,737	5,602	2,798	26,595

Sources: Basketball-Reference.com; Naismith Memorial Basketball Hall of Fame

Getzinger, Rudy (born: April 9, 1943 in Sremska-Mitrovica, Yugoslavia); inducted into the National Soccer Hall of Fame and Museum in 1991 as a player; Position: Midfield; International Caps (1964–1973): 8; International Goals: 1; won the 1964 U.S. Amateur Cup.

Getzinger began playing soccer at age six in Austria and continued playing when he moved to Chicago, Illinois in 1958. He joined the Schwaben team in Chicago's National Soccer League; won the Peel Cup his first year with the team; and was a member of the U.S. Amateur Cup-winning team in 1964.

A forward early in his career, Getzinger once led the NSL's major division with 24 goals in 21 games, before he switched to play midfield. He played for the United States in the qualifying rounds of the 1968 Olympics and was a member of the U.S. National Team during World Cup qualifiers in 1972.

When the Chicago Sting of the North American Soccer League was formed in 1975, he was one of the first players signed and stayed with the team for two seasons. He played a total of 19 NASL games and scored one goal and one assist (for a total of three points).

Getzinger earned his first cap on August 20, 1972, and scored his only international goal that game in a loss to Canada. His last cap came as a substitute for Barry Barto in a November 3, 1973 loss to Haiti.

Rudy Getzinger's North American Soccer League Statistics

YEAR	TEAM	G	GLS	ASST	PTS
1975	Chicago Sting	16	1	1	3
1976	Chicago Sting	3	0	0	0
	TOTALS	19	1	1	3

Source: National Soccer Hall of Fame and Museum

Giacomin, Edward "Eddie" (born: June 6, 1939 in Sudbury, Ontario, Canada); inducted into the Hockey Hall of Fame in 1987 as a player; Position: Goalie; Uniform #1; shared the Vezina Trophy in 1971.

Giacomin played 19 professional hockey seasons from 1959 to 1978, including with the NHL's New York Rangers (1965–1975) and the Detroit Red Wings (1975–1978). He was selected to the NHL First All-Star Team twice (1967, 1971); to the NHL Second All-Star Team three times (1968–1970); and played in six All–Star games (1967–1971, 1973).

After signing with the Providence Reds (American Hockey League) for the 1959–1960 season, he suffered second- and third-degree burns in a kitchen fire that caused him to miss an entire season. Recuperating for almost a year, Giacomin returned to the Reds at the start of the 1960–1961 season.

The 5'11", 180-pound goalie stayed with the team for five seasons until signed by the Rangers in May 1965. Appearing in only 36 games during his rookie season, he was sent to the Baltimore Clippers (American Hockey League) to gain more experience. With improved skills, Giacomin returned to New York the next season; led the NHL with nine shutouts; and was selected to the NHL First All-Star Team.

In 1970–1971, he helped the club set a franchise record with 109 points; shared the Vezina Trophy as the NHL's best goalie with Gilles Villemure; and was selected to the NHL First All-Star Team for the second time. In 1971–1972, the Rangers equaled the team's 109 points of the previous season and made it to the Stanley Cup finals for the first time since 1950, eventually losing to the Boston Bruins in six games.

Early in the 1975 season, Giacomin was claimed off waivers by the Detroit Red Wings, and stayed with the team until retiring nine games into the 1977–1978 season.

After retiring as a player, he ran a sports bar and was a broadcaster for the New York Islanders in 1979, until serving as an assistant coach with the Islanders and Red Wings. He later was the Rangers' goaltending coach, and in 1989, his uniform number one was the second to be retired by the Rangers (after Rod Gilbert).

Eddie Giacomin's Career Statistics

			REGULAR SEASON						PLAYOFFS					
SEASON	**TEAM**	**LEAGUE**	**GP**	**W**	**L**	**T**	**SO**	**AVG**	**GP**	**W**	**L**	**T**	**SO**	**AVG**
1957–1958	Commack Comets	NBHL												
1958–1959	Sudbury Bell Telephone	NBHL												
1958–1959	Washington Presidents	EHL	4	4	0	0	0	3.25						
1959–1960	Clinton Rovers	EHL	51				3	4.04						
1959–1960	Providence Reds	AHL	1	1	0	0	0	4.00						
1960–1961	Providence Reds	AHL	43	17	24	0	0	4.37						
1960–1961	New York Rovers	EHL	12	2	10	0	0	4.50						
1961–1962	Providence Reds	AHL	40	20	19	1	2	3.60						
1962–1963	Providence Reds	AHL	39	22	14	2	4	2.62	6	2	4	0	0	5.18
1963–1964	Providence Reds	AHL	69	30	34	5	6	3.37	3	1	2	0	0	4.00
1964–1965	Providence Reds	AHL	59	19	38	2	0	3.84						
1965–1966	New York Rangers	NHL	35	8	20	6	0	3.68						
1965–1966	Baltimore Clippers	AHL	7	3	4	0	0	3.00						
1966–1967	New York Rangers	NHL	68	30	27	11	9	2.61	4	0	4		0	3.41
1967–1968	New York Rangers	NHL	66	36	20	10	8	2.44	6	2	4		0	3.00
1968–1969	New York Rangers	NHL	70	37	23	7	7	2.55	3	0	3		0	3.33
1969–1970	New York Rangers	NHL	70	35	21	14	6	2.36	5	2	3		0	4.07
1970–1971	New York Rangers	NHL	45	27	10	7	8	2.16	12	7	5		0	2.21
1971–1972	New York Rangers	NHL	44	24	10	9	1	2.70	10	6	4		0	2.70
1972–1973	New York Rangers	NHL	43	26	11	6	4	2.91	10	5	4		1	2.56
1973–1974	New York Rangers	NHL	56	30	15	10	5	3.07	13	7	6		0	2.82
1974–1975	New York Rangers	NHL	37	13	12	8	1	3.48	2	0	2		0	2.79
1975–1976	New York Rangers	NHL	4	0	3	1	0	4.75						
1975–1976	Detroit Red Wings	NHL	29	12	14	3	2	3.45						
1976–1977	Detroit Red Wings	NHL	33	8	18	3	3	3.58						
1977–1978	Detroit Red Wings	NHL	9	3	5	1	0	3.14						

			REGULAR SEASON						PLAYOFFS					
SEASON	TEAM	LEAGUE	GP	W	L	T	SO	AVG	GP	W	L	T	SO	AVG
	NHL TOTALS		609	289	209	96	54	2.81	65	29	35		1	2.81

Sources: Hockey Hall of Fame; Hockey-Reference.com

Gibbs, Joe Jackson (born: November 25, 1940 in Mocksville, North Carolina); inducted into the Pro Football Hall of Fame as a coach in 1996; only active NFL coach to be inducted into the football hall of fame; won three Super Bowls.

After attending Santa Fe High School (Santa Fe Springs, California) in 1959, where he played quarterback, Gibbs went to Cerritos Junior College (Norwalk, California) and San Diego State University (California), where he played tight end, offensive guard, and linebacker on the football team that was coached by Don Coryell. He graduated from SDSU in 1964 and earned a master's degree from the university in 1966.

After college, he served as an assistant coach at San Diego State (1964–1966, under Coryell), Florida State University (Tallahassee, 1967–1968), University of Southern California (1969–1970, under John McKay), and the University of Arkansas (Fayetteville, 1971–1972, under Frank Broyles), before becoming an assistant coach in the National Football League with the St. Louis Cardinals (1973–1977, again under Coryell), Tampa Bay Buccaneers (1978, reuniting with McKay), and the San Diego Chargers (1979–1980, again with Coryell). Seventeen years after starting his coaching career, Gibbs became a head coach with the NFL's Washington Redskins in 1981. During his first stint with the team (which lasted 12 years), the Redskins won the National Football Conference title in the strike-shortened 1982 season and four NFC Eastern division championships (1983–1984, 1987, 1991). He would become the 20th and 26th head coach in the history of the Redskins.

Gibbs was named NFL Coach of the Year three times (1982–1983, 1991); compiled a 124–60–0 (.674) regular-season record and a 16–5–0 (.762) post-season mark; won three Super Bowls (XVII in 1983, XXII in 1988, and XXVI in 1992) with three different quarterbacks (Joe Theismann - XVII, Doug Williams - XXII, and Mark Rypien - XXVI); and won 10 or more games per season eight times, with only one losing season (7–9) in 1988. His combined .683 winning percentage is surpassed only by Vince Lombardi (.740) and John Madden (.731).

After retiring for the first time at the end of the 1992 season, Gibbs focused on his National Association for Stock Car Automobile Racing (NASCAR) team, Joe Gibbs Racing, which won three championships under his ownership.

In January 2004, Gibbs returned to the NFL and rejoined the Redskins as head coach and team president, eventually resigning from both positions in 2008.

Although he lost his first five games as head coach of the Redskins, Gibbs was able to finish the season at 8–8. In only his second year in Washington, he led the team to a Super Bowl XVII victory (a 27–17 win over the Miami Dolphins in January 1983) in the strike-shortened season. In the next season, he again led the Redskins into the Super Bowl, but lost to the Los Angeles Raiders 38–9.

In the 1986 season, he lost the NFC Championship game to the New York Giants. It would be the last championship game he would ever lose. In 1987, the Redskins won Super Bowl XXII (42–10 over the Denver Broncos) and in 1992 won Super Bowl XXVI (37–24 over the Buffalo Bills), giving Gibbs his third title.

His Redskins teams were known for power running (with backs like John Riggins) behind the strong offensive line, nicknamed "The Hogs," and for controlling the line of scrimmage. To complement his running game, Gibbs created a deep-threat passing game with receivers like Art Monk.

Outside of football, he created his NASCAR team, Joe Gibbs Racing, in 1991, a year before he first retired from the NFL. The first driver for his team was Dale Jarrett (1991–1992), with subsequent drivers being Bobby Labonte (1993–2005) and J.J. Yeley (2006–present). Once Gibbs returned to the NFL, his son took over day-to-day operations of the racing team.

In his first year back with the team, the Redskins finished with a record of 6–10, and in 2005, finished at 10–6, good enough to make the playoffs for the first time since 1999.

He co-wrote two books, *Joe Gibbs: Fourth and One* in 1992 and *Racing to Win* in 2003.

Joe Gibbs' NFL Head Coaching Statistics

		REGULAR SEASON				PLAYOFFS		
YEAR	TEAM	W	L	T	WIN%	W	L	WIN%
1981	Washington	8	8	0	.500			
1982	Washington	8	1	0	.889	4	0	1.000
1983	Washington	14	2	0	.875	2	1	.667

YEAR	TEAM	REGULAR SEASON W	L	T	WIN%	PLAYOFFS W	L	WIN%
1984	Washington	11	5	0	.687	0	1	.000
1985	Washington	10	6	0	.625			
1986	Washington	12	4	0	.750	2	1	.667
1987	Washington	11	4	0	.733	3	0	1.000
1988	Washington	7	9	0	.437			
1989	Washington	10	6	0	.625			
1990	Washington	10	6	0	.625	1	1	.500
1991	Washington	14	2	0	.875	3	0	1.000
1992	Washington	9	7	0	.562	1	1	.500
2004	Washington	6	10	0	.375			
2005	Washington	10	6	0	.625	1	1	.500
2006	Washington	5	11	0	.312			
2007	Washington	9	7	0	.534	0	1	.000
	TOTALS	154	94	0	.621	17	7	.708

Sources: Pro Football Hall of Fame; Pro-Football-Reference.com

Gibson, Dr. John L. "Jack" (born: September 10, 1880 in Berlin (Kitchener), Ontario, Canada; died: October 7, 1955); inducted into the Hockey Hall of Fame in 1976 as a builder; organized the very first professional hockey league.

An early hockey pioneer, Gibson organized the world's first professional hockey league in 1904, the International Hockey League. Born in Berlin (later renamed Kitchener), after graduating from Berlin High School in 1896, he was a member of the local team that won the provincial championship in 1897.

The 6', 185-pound Gibson played football at the University of Michigan (Ann Arbor), before attending the University of Detroit Dental School in Michigan. After graduation, he practiced dentistry in Houghton, Michigan, while still remaining active in hockey. He recruited players; established the Portage Lake team in 1902; and served as its captain.

In 1903–1904, the Portage Lake team (based in Houghton) posted a 24–2 record and was able to defeat the famous Montreal Wanderers twice. The success of Portage Lake convinced Gibson that northern Michigan could sustain a league, which he called the International Hockey League, the first professional circuit in the world when it began operations in the 1904–1905 season. Other teams in the league included the Calumet (Michigan) Miners, Sault Ste. Marie (Michigan) Indians, Pittsburgh (Pennsylvania) Pro Hockey Club, and Sault Ste. Marie (Ontario, Canada) Canadian Soo.

When Portage Lake challenged for the Stanley Cup in 1905 (against the Ottawa Silver Seven) and in 1906 (against the Montreal Wanderers), the professional team was refused by trustees of the Cup, who wanted only amateur clubs to compete. When many players left the league to regain their amateur status, the IHL folded after three seasons.

After retiring as a player, Gibson practiced dentistry in the area and refereed local games. Eventually, he returned to Canada and set up a dental practice in Calgary, Alberta.

Named in his honor, in 1939 the Gibson Cup was created and awarded to the champion of the Michigan-Ontario Professional Hockey League. Today, the Cup is given to the winner of an annual challenge series between the Portage Lake Pioneers and the Calumet Wolverines. The Gibson Cup is the third-oldest hockey cup in North America, behind the Stanley Cup (1893) and the MacNaughton Cup (1913).

Source: Hockey Hall of Fame

Gibson, Joshua "Josh" (born: December 21, 1911 in Buena Vista, Georgia; died: January 20, 1947 in Pittsburgh, Pennsylvania); inducted into the National Baseball Hall of Fame and Museum in 1972 as a Negro Leaguer by the Negro Leagues Committee; Position: Catcher; Bats: Right; Throws: Right; one of black baseball's best catchers and power hitters; second Negro League player inducted into the baseball hall of fame.

Gibson was the Negro Leagues' best catcher and the greatest power hitter in black baseball. During his 17-year career, he played for the Homestead Grays (1930–1931, 1937–1939, 1942–1946) and the Pittsburgh Crawfords (1932–1936). In 1937, he played for Ciudad Trujillo in the Dominican League and from 1940 to 1941, played in the Mexican League for Veracruz.

The 6'1", 210-pound Gibson hit for average and power and was a strong home run hitter, although he played in two of baseball's biggest stadiums, Forbes Field (Pittsburgh, Pennsylvania) and Griffith Stadium (Washington, D.C.).

In early 1943, Gibson fell into a coma and was diagnosed with a brain tumor. After refusing surgery, he lived the next four years of his life alternating between recurring headaches and outbursts of rage. He died in 1947, three months before Major League Baseball became integrated.

He started his professional baseball career in July 1930 with Homestead of the Negro National League and led the circuit in home runs for 10 consecutive seasons. Baseball lore has him hitting towering home runs and on June 3, 1967, *The Sporting News* credited him with a home run in a Negro League game at Yankee Stadium that was measured at 580 feet from home plate.

Because the Negro Leagues did not routinely compile season statistics or game summaries, it is difficult to separate fact from legend about Gibson's sometimes heroic accomplishments. His hall of fame plaque says he hit "almost 800" home runs in his career, although it is impossible to verify the actual figure. It is said that he retired from the Negro Leagues with a league-best .384 career batting average; and won nine home run and four batting titles.

In 1941–1942, Gibson played in the Puerto Rican Professional Baseball League for the Santurce Crabbers, winning the league batting title with an average of .480, a league record that still stands.

In 1999, he was ranked 18th on *The Sporting News*' list of the 100 Greatest Baseball Players, the highest-ranking of five players to have played all or most of their careers in the Negro Leagues (the others on the list being Satchel Paige, Buck Leonard, Cool Papa Bell, and Oscar Charleston). Also in 1999, he was nominated as a finalist for the Major League Baseball All-Century Team.

In 1923, the Gibson family moved to Pittsburgh, Pennsylvania, where he attended Allegheny Pre-Vocational School and Conroy Pre-Vocational School. He began playing organized baseball at age 16 as the third baseman for an amateur team sponsored by the Gimbels department store, where he worked as an elevator operator.

In the summer of 1930, the 18-year old Gibson was signed by Cum Posey, owner of the Homestead Grays, and on July 31, 1930, Gibson debuted with the team.

He was the second Negro League player inducted into the baseball hall of fame (after Satchel Paige).

Source: National Baseball Hall of Fame and Museum

Gibson, Pack Robert "Bob" (born: November 9, 1935 in Omaha, Nebraska; he changed his name to Robert when he turned 18); inducted into the National Baseball Hall of Fame and Museum in 1981 as a player; Position: Pitcher; Bats: Right; Throws: Right; Uniform: #45; first National League pitcher to strike out 3,000 batters; won two Cy Young Awards.

Gibson's major league debut on April 15, 1959 did not go exactly as he had hoped when the first batter he faced, Jim Baxes of the Los Angeles Dodgers, hit a home run off him. From this inauspicious start, Gibson went on to play his entire 17-year career with the St. Louis Cardinals (1959–1975); won two World Series titles (1964, 1967) and was named World Series MVP both times; an eight-time All-Star (1962, 1965–1970, 1972); named National League Most Valuable Player in 1968; won the National League Cy Young Award twice (1968, 1970); and won nine Gold Gloves (1965–1973).

The 6'1", 195-pound Gibson won 20 or more games in a season five times, and in 1968, he posted a 1.12 Earned Run Average, the lowest mark since 1914. He set World Series records for consecutive wins (seven) and most strikeouts in a game (17; Game One on October 2, 1968 against the Detroit Tigers).

Gibson played baseball and basketball at Tech High School (Omaha, Nebraska) and received a basketball scholarship to Creighton University (Omaha, Nebraska). In 1957, he received an offer to play baseball with the Cardinals, but put his career on hold for one year (1957–1958) so he could play basketball with the world-famous Harlem Globetrotters.

After leaving the Globetrotters, he joined the Cardinals' AAA farm team (Omaha Cardinals, American Association) in 1958 and, after only one year, was promoted to the major leagues. After pitching back-to-back losing seasons his first two years with the team, Gibson had his first winning season in 1961 (13–12) and had the first of his nine 200-strikeout seasons in 1962.

From 1963 to 1970, he dominated the National League, compiling a 156–81 (.658) record. On May 12, 1969, against the Los Angeles Dodgers, Gibson struck out three batters on nine pitches in the seventh inning of a 6–2 win, becoming the ninth National League pitcher, and the 15th pitcher in major league history, to accomplish this feat. On August 14, 1971, at Pittsburgh's Three Rivers Stadium, he pitched his only career no-hitter in an 11–0 win over the Pirates.

On July 17, 1974 in St. Louis' Busch Stadium, Gibson struck out the Cincinnati Reds' César Gerónimo, becoming the first National League pitcher (and the second in major league history after Walter Johnson) to strike out 3,000 batters. Coincidentally, in 1980, Gerónimo would become the Houston Astros' Nolan Ryan's 3,000th strikeout.

Gibson was one of the best-hitting pitchers in baseball history. He is one of only two pitchers (along with Bob Lemon) since World War II with a career batting average of .200 or higher (.206) with at least 20 home runs (24) and 100 RBIs (144).

His jersey number 45 was retired by the Cardinals in 1975; in 1999, he was ranked Number 31 on *The Sporting News'* list of the 100 Greatest Baseball Players, and was elected to the Major League Baseball All-Century Team; and has a star on the St. Louis Walk of Fame.

Bob Gibson's Career Statistics

YEAR	TEAM	LG	W	L	PCT	G	SH	IP	H	R	ER	SO	BB	ERA
1959	St. Louis	NL	3	5	.375	13	1	76	77	35	28	48	39	3.32
1960	St. Louis	NL	3	6	.333	27	0	87	97	61	54	69	48	5.59
1961	St. Louis	NL	13	12	.520	35	2	211	186	91	76	166	119	3.24
1962	St. Louis	NL	15	13	.536	32	5	234	174	84	74	208	95	2.85
1963	St. Louis	NL	18	9	.667	36	2	255	224	110	96	204	96	3.39
1964	St. Louis	NL	19	12	.613	40	2	287	250	106	96	245	86	3.01
1965	St. Louis	NL	20	12	.625	38	6	299	243	110	102	270	103	3.07
1966	St. Louis	NL	21	12	.636	35	5	280	210	90	76	225	78	2.44
1967	St. Louis	NL	13	7	.650	24	2	175	151	62	58	147	40	2.98
1968	St. Louis	NL	22	9	.710	34	13	305	198	49	38	268	62	1.12
1969	St. Louis	NL	20	13	.606	35	4	314	251	84	76	269	95	2.18
1970	St. Louis	NL	23	7	.767	34	3	294	262	111	102	274	88	3.12
1971	St. Louis	NL	16	13	.552	31	5	246	215	96	83	185	76	3.04
1972	St. Louis	NL	19	11	.633	34	4	278	226	83	76	208	88	2.46
1973	St. Louis	NL	12	10	.545	25	1	195	159	71	60	142	57	2.77
1974	St. Louis	NL	11	13	.458	33	1	240	236	111	102	129	104	3.83
1975	St. Louis	NL	3	10	.231	22	0	109	120	66	61	60	62	5.04
	TOTALS		251	174	.591	528	56	3,885	3,279	1,420	1,258	3,117	1,336	2.91

Sources: Baseball-Reference.com; National Baseball Hall of Fame and Museum

Giesler, Walter John (born: September 6, 1910 in St. Louis, Missouri; died: July 7, 1976 in Philadelphia, Pennsylvania); inducted into the National Soccer Hall of Fame in 1962 as a builder; served as chairman of the Missouri Soccer Commission and president of the United States Soccer Football Association.

Giesler owned a sporting goods business in St. Louis and was active in the local sports scene for more than 30 years. He played soccer for three years at McBride High School (St. Louis) and another three seasons in the Municipal League, followed by two seasons with the Ben Millers of the St. Louis Professional League.

He was a referee for five years before becoming involved in the administrative side. He served as vice president of the Municipal A.A.; vice president of the Ozark A.A.; and chairman and then secretary of the Missouri Soccer Commission. He also served as second vice-president of the United States Soccer Football Association (1945–1948) before being elected its president (1948–1949).

Giesler coached the 1948 U.S. Olympic team (games held in London, England) that was eliminated in the first round after a 9–0 loss to Italy; managed the U.S. World Cup team of 1950 (games held in Brazil); and was chairman of the 1952 USSFA Olympic Committee, and went to Helsinki, Finland with the team.

Source: National Soccer Hall of Fame and Museum

Gifford, Francis Newton "Frank" (born: August 16, 1930 in Santa Monica, California); inducted into the Pro Football Hall of Fame in 1977 as a player; Position: Halfback-Flanker; Uniform: #16; won the NFL Championship in 1956; 1956 Most Valuable Player.

After graduating from Bakersfield (California) High School, he was unable to get an athletic scholarship to the University of Southern California (Los Angeles) because of his low grades. He played one football season at Bakersfield College and was selected to the Junior College All-American team. He eventually maintained a grade point average that allowed him to transfer to USC, where he was named an All-American as a senior.

Graduating from college, he was the number one selection (11th overall pick) of the New York Giants in the 1952 National Football League Draft, and the 6'1", 197-pound Gifford played his entire 12-year NFL career (136 games) with the team (1952–1960, 1962–1964); played on both offense and defense in the 1953 season; selected All-NFL four times; named the NFL Most Valuable Player in 1956; played in seven Pro Bowls as a defensive back, halfback, and flanker

(1953–1959); and made five trips to the NFL Championship game (winning in 1956 and losing in 1958–1959, 1962–1963). He retired briefly after the 1960 season, but returned to the league in 1962 as a flanker. In 1956, he was the league's Most Valuable Player and led the Giants to a league championship, a 47–7 win over the Chicago Bears.

On November 20, 1960, Gifford suffered a head injury in a 17–10 loss against the Philadelphia Eagles when he was hit by Chuck Bednarik, which forced him to miss a season. He returned to the league after recovering and played three more years before retiring.

To younger fans, he is probably more well known as a long-time broadcaster on ABC's *Monday Night Football*, where he initially worked with Howard Cosell and Don Meredith. He replaced Keith Jackson; joined the show in its second season; and spent almost three decades with the program, retiring in 1998.

He was named to the NFL 1950s All-Decade Team; the Giants retired his jersey number 16; and he has been married since 1986 to singer and former television talk show host Kathie Lee Gifford.

Frank Gifford's Career Statistics

			RUSHING				RECEIVING			
YEAR	**TEAM**	**G**	**NO**	**YDS**	**AVG**	**TD**	**NO**	**YDS**	**AVG**	**TD**
1952	New York	10	38	116	3.1	0	5	36	7.2	0
1953	New York	12	50	157	3.1	2	18	292	16.2	4
1954	New York	9	66	368	5.6	2	14	154	11.0	1
1955	New York	11	86	351	4.1	3	33	437	13.2	4
1956	New York	12	159	819	5.2	5	51	603	11.8	4
1957	New York	12	136	528	3.9	5	41	588	14.3	4
1958	New York	10	115	468	4.1	8	29	330	11.4	2
1959	New York	11	106	540	5.1	3	42	768	18.3	4
1960	New York	8	77	232	3.0	4	24	344	14.3	3
1962	New York	14	2	18	9.0	1	39	796	20.4	7
1963	New York	14	4	10	2.5	0	42	657	15.6	7
1964	New York	13	1	2	2.0	1	29	429	14.8	3
	TOTALS	136	840	3,609	4.3	34	367	5,434	14.8	43

Sources: College Football Hall of Fame; Pro Football Hall of Fame; Pro-Football-Reference.com; *The Whole Ten Yards* (Frank Gifford and Harry Waters)

Gilbert, Rodrique Gabriel "Rod" (born: July 1, 1941 in Montreal, Quebec, Canada); inducted into the Hockey Hall of Fame in 1982 as a player; Position: Right Wing; Uniform: #7; won the 1960 OHA Memorial Cup; first 300-goal scorer in the history of the New York Rangers; first Rangers' player to have his jersey retired.

Never winning a Stanley Cup, Gilbert played his entire 18-season National Hockey League career with the New York Rangers (1960–1978). He was on the Guelph Biltmore Mad Hatters team that won the Ontario Hockey Association's 1960 Memorial Cup. At 5'9", 175 pounds, he joined the Rangers full-time for the 1962–1963 season; scored 31 points in his rookie year; and beginning in his second year, registered his first of twelve 20-goal seasons.

Slowed early in his career by a nagging back injury, after playing only 34 games of the 1965–1966 season, he underwent another operation and was able to return to the team the next season, where he scored 28 goals. One year later, Gilbert helped the Rangers advance to the playoffs for the first time in five years.

In 1970–1971, he teamed with Jean Ratelle and Vic Hadfield to help set a franchise line record of 107 points; becoming known as the GAG (Goal-A-Game) line. The following season, he helped the team reach the Stanley Cup finals, eventually losing to the Boston Bruins in six games. During the same season, the GAG line made history by becoming the first one on which all three members reached the 40-goal mark.

In 1972, he represented Canada in the Summit Series against the Soviet Union; between the 1972–1973 and 1976–1977 seasons, he scored at least 75 points per season; and on March 24, 1974, his goal against the Buffalo Sabres made him the first 300-goal scorer in the history of the New York Rangers.

In 1976, Gilbert won the Bill Masterton Memorial Trophy for his sportsmanship and dedication to hockey; on December 12, 1976, he played in his 1,000th game; and he participated in the 1977 World Championship (held in Vienna, Austria), leading Canada to a fourth-place finish.

Gilbert retired from the NHL in 1977; in October 1979, his jersey number seven was the first-ever retired by the Rangers, and he was inducted into the Nassau County Sports Hall of Fame (New York) in 2004.

He was named to the NHL First All-Star Team twice (1971–1972); to the NHL Second All-Star Team twice (1967–1968); won the Lester Patrick Trophy (1991) for outstanding service to hockey in the United States; and played in eight All-Star Games (1964–1965, 1967, 1969–1970, 1972, 1975, 1977).

When he retired, Gilbert held Rangers' team records for career goals (406) and career points (1,021).

Rod Gilbert's Career Statistics

			REGULAR SEASON					PLAYOFFS				
SEASON	**TEAM**	**LEAGUE**	**GP**	**G**	**A**	**TP**	**PIM**	**GP**	**G**	**A**	**TP**	**PIM**
1957–1958	Guelph Biltmores	OHA-Jr.	32	14	16	30	14					
1958–1959	Guelph Biltmores	OHA-Jr.	54	27	34	61	40	10	5	4	9	14
1959–1960	Guelph Biltmores	OHA-Jr.	47	39	52	91	40	5	3	3	6	4
1959–1960	Trois-Rivieres Lions	EPHL	3	4	6	10	0	5	2	2	4	2
1960–1961	Guelph Royals	OHA-B	47	54	49	103	47	6	4	4	8	6
1960–1961	New York Rangers	NHL	1	0	1	1	2					
1961–1962	New York Rangers	NHL	1	0	0	0	0	4	2	3	5	4
1961–1962	Kitchener-Waterloo Beavers	EPHL	21	12	11	23	22	4	0	0	0	4
1962–1963	New York Rangers	NHL	70	11	20	31	20					
1963–1964	New York Rangers	NHL	70	24	40	64	62					
1964–1965	New York Rangers	NHL	70	25	36	61	52					
1965–1966	New York Rangers	NHL	34	10	15	25	20					
1966–1967	New York Rangers	NHL	64	28	18	46	12	4	2	2	4	6
1967–1968	New York Rangers	NHL	73	29	48	77	12	6	5	0	5	4
1968–1969	New York Rangers	NHL	66	28	49	77	22	4	1	0	1	2
1969–1970	New York Rangers	NHL	72	16	37	53	22	6	4	5	9	0
1970–1971	New York Rangers	NHL	78	30	31	61	65	13	4	6	10	8
1971–1972	New York Rangers	NHL	73	43	54	97	64	16	7	8	15	11
1972–1973	Canada	Summit-72	6	1	3	4	9					
1972–1973	New York Rangers	NHL	76	25	59	84	25	10	5	1	6	2
1973–1974	New York Rangers	NHL	75	36	41	77	20	13	3	5	8	4
1974–1975	New York Rangers	NHL	76	36	61	97	22	3	1	3	4	2
1975–1976	New York Rangers	NHL	70	36	50	86	32					
1976–1977	New York Rangers	NHL	77	27	48	75	50					
1976–1977	Canada	WEC-A	9	2	2	4	12					
1977–1978	New York Rangers	NHL	19	2	7	9	6					
	NHL TOTALS		1,065	406	615	1,021	508	79	34	33	67	43

Sources: Hockey Hall of Fame; Hockey-Reference.com

Giles, Warren Crandall (born: May 28, 1896 in Tiskilwa, Illinois; died: February 7, 1979 in Cincinnati, Ohio); inducted into the National Baseball Hall of Fame and Museum in 1979 as a pioneer-executive by the Veterans Committee; president of the National League.

After serving in the infantry in France during World War I, Giles was elected president of the Moline (Illinois) Plowboys in the Three-I League in 1919. Officially named the Illinois-Iowa-Indiana League, the Three-I League was a Class B minor league that operated from 1901 through 1961. This began his 50-year career in baseball that culminated in his serving as president of the National League.

Leaving the Moline team, he moved to front-office positions in the farm system of Major League Baseball's St. Louis Cardinals, and eventually became the general manager of the Rochester (New York) Red Wings of the International League, at the time the Cardinals' top minor league team. In 1936, he served briefly as president of the International League, before becoming the general manager of MLB's Cincinnati Reds in 1937. He led the team to two pennants (1939–1940); a World Series Championship in 1940 over the Detroit Tigers; and was elected club president in 1948.

In 1951, Giles was elected president of the National League, and served until 1969. During his 18-year tenure, he oversaw several franchises changing locations (the Brooklyn Dodgers to Los Angeles, California; New York Giants to San Francisco, California; Boston Braves to Milwaukee, Wisconsin and then to Atlanta, Georgia) and the addition of new teams into the league (New York Mets, Houston Astros, San Diego Padres, and the Montreal Expos).

Giles was elected to the Cincinnati Reds Hall of Fame in 1969, and the Warren Giles Trophy is presented to the winner of the National League Championship Series.

Source: National Baseball Hall of Fame and Museum

Gill, Amory Tingle "Slats" (born: May 1, 1901 in Salem, Oregon; died: April 5, 1966 in Corvallis, Oregon); inducted into the Naismith Memorial Basketball Hall of Fame in 1968 as a coach; inducted into the Oregon State University Sports Hall of Fame in 1988.

Gill attended Salem (Oregon) High School from 1916 to 1920, where he played basketball for four years; won a state championship in 1919; and was selected to the All-State First Team twice (1919–1920). After high school, he went to Oregon Agricultural College (Corvallis, now known as Oregon State University) from 1920 to 1924, where he was selected All-Pacific Coast Conference twice (1922, 1924); an All-American in 1924; and was selected to the Helms Foundation All-America Team.

Graduating from college, Gill took his first coaching job at Oakland (California) High School (1924–1926). He then joined the college ranks as the freshman coach at his alma mater (1926–1928), before becoming the school's varsity coach from 1928 to 1964. He also coached the Beavers' baseball team from 1932 to 1937.

His record at OSU was 599–392 (.604); his teams won four Pacific Coast Conference titles (1933, 1947, 1949, 1955) and tied with California in 1958; and nine PCC Northern Division titles (1933, 1935, 1940, 1942, 1947–1949, 1954–1955). His 1949 and 1963 Beavers teams placed fourth in the National Collegiate Athletic Association championship. His teams won the Far West Classic championship eight consecutive seasons; he was named the National Association of Basketball Coaches West All-Star Team coach in 1964; won the Chancellor's Trophy (awarded annually to the winner of the basketball series between Oregon State and the University of Oregon) 11 out of 12 years, beginning in 1953; received the Hayward Award in 1955 as the state of Oregon's top sports personality; served as president of the NABC (1957–1958); and was an Olympic Trials Coach in 1964. After stepping down as coach, Gill served as OSU's athletic director from 1964 to 1966.

Gill has been inducted into the OSU Sports Hall of Fame (1988) and the Helms Foundation Basketball Hall of Fame. The OSU Coliseum on the school's campus is named in his honor (Gill Coliseum).

Amory Gill's Career Statistics at Oregon State University

YEAR	W	L	WIN%	YEAR	W	L	WIN%
1928–1929	12	8	.600	1946–1947	28	5	.848
1929–1930	14	13	.519	1947–1948	21	13	.618
1930–1931	19	9	.679	1948–1949	24	12	.667
1931–1932	12	12	.500	1949–1950	13	14	.481
1932–1933	21	6	.778	1950–1951	14	18	.438
1933–1934	14	20	.412	1951–1952	9	19	.321
1934–1935	19	9	.679	1952–1953	11	18	.379
1935–1936	16	9	.640	1953–1954	19	10	.655
1936–1937	11	1	.917	1954–1955	22	8	.733
1937–1938	17	16	.515	1955–1956	8	18	.308
1938–1939	13	11	.542	1956–1957	11	15	.423
1939–1940	27	11	.711	1957–1958	20	6	.769
1940–1941	19	9	.679	1958–1959	13	13	.500
1941–1942	22	7	.759	1959–1960	15	11	.577
1942–1943	22	9	.710	1960–1961	14	12	.538
1943–1944	8	16	.333	1961–1962	24	5	.828
1944–1945	20	8	.714	1962–1963	22	9	.710
1945–1946	13	11	.542	1963–1964	25	4	.862
				TOTALS	599	392	.604

Source: Naismith Memorial Basketball Hall of Fame

Gillies, Clark "Jethro" (born: April 7, 1954 in Moose Jaw, Saskatchewan, Canada); inducted into the Hockey Hall of Fame in 2002 as a player; Position: Left Wing; Uniform: #9; won the 1974 Memorial Cup; won four consecutive Stanley Cup championships.

Gillies played 14 National Hockey League seasons with the New York Islanders (1974–1986) and the Buffalo Sabres (1986–1988). As an amateur with the Regina Pats of the Western Canada Junior Hockey League, he won a Memorial Cup championship in 1974.

Later in 1974, he was drafted in the first round (fourth overall selection) by the Islanders, and made the team directly out of training camp, never playing a game in the minors.

When the 6'3", 215-pound Gillies teamed with future hall of famers Mike Bossy and Bryan Trottier, he was part of the forward line known as the "Trio Grande." He scored 30 or more goals six times in his career (1976–1979, 1981–1982) and had 30 or more assists five consecutive seasons (1978–1982).

Gillies was voted team captain in his third season; in the 1977 quarterfinal playoffs against the Buffalo Sabres, he scored three consecutive game-winning goals to tie an NHL record; and he led the team to four consecutive Stanley Cup championships (1980–1983).

Nicknamed "Jethro" (after the *Beverly Hillbillies* TV show character), he stayed with the Islanders until 1986 and was with the Sabres for two seasons before retiring. While with the Islanders, 54 of his regular-season goals were either game-winning or game-tying shots.

Gillies was a two-time NHL First Team All-Star Left Wing (1978–1979); played in the 1978 NHL All-Star Game; selected to play with the NHL All-Stars in the 1979 Challenge Cup against the Soviet Union; and the "Trio Grande" led Team Canada into the 1981 Canada Cup, finishing second.

His jersey number nine was retired by the Islanders in December 1996.

Clark Gillies' Career Statistics

			REGULAR SEASON					PLAYOFFS				
SEASON	**TEAM**	**LEAGUE**	**GP**	**G**	**A**	**TP**	**PIM**	**GP**	**G**	**A**	**TP**	**PIM**
1971–1972	Regina Pats	WCJHL	68	31	48	79	199	15	5	10	15	49
1972–1973	Regina Pats	WCJHL	68	40	52	92	192	4	0	3	3	34
1973–1974	Regina Pats	WCJHL	65	46	66	112	179	16	9	8	17	32
1973–1974	Regina Pats	M-Cup	3	1	3	4	19					
1974–1975	New York Islanders	NHL	80	25	22	47	66	17	4	2	6	36
1975–1976	New York Islanders	NHL	80	34	27	61	96	13	2	4	6	16
1976–1977	New York Islanders	NHL	70	33	22	55	93	12	4	4	8	15
1977–1978	New York Islanders	NHL	80	35	50	85	76	7	2	0	2	15
1978–1979	New York Islanders	NHL	75	35	56	91	68	10	1	2	3	11
1978–1979	NHL All-Stars	Ch-Cup	3	1	2	3	2					
1979–1980	New York Islanders	NHL	73	19	35	54	49	21	6	10	16	63
1980–1981	New York Islanders	NHL	80	33	45	78	99	18	6	9	15	28
1981–1982	Canada	Can-Cup	7	2	5	7	8					
1981–1982	New York Islanders	NHL	79	38	39	77	75	19	8	6	14	34
1982–1983	New York Islanders	NHL	70	21	20	41	76	8	0	2	2	10
1983–1984	New York Islanders	NHL	76	12	16	28	65	21	12	7	19	19
1984–1985	New York Islanders	NHL	54	15	17	32	73	10	1	0	1	9
1985–1986	New York Islanders	NHL	55	4	10	14	55	3	1	0	1	6
1986–1987	Buffalo Sabres	NHL	61	10	17	27	81					
1987–1988	Buffalo Sabres	NHL	25	5	2	7	51	5	0	1	1	25
	NHL TOTALS		958	319	378	697	1,023	164	47	47	94	287

Sources: Hockey Hall of Fame; Hockey-Reference.com

Gillman, Sidney "Sid" (born: October 26, 1911 in Minneapolis, Minnesota; died: January 3, 2003 in Carlsbad, California); inducted into the Pro Football Hall of Fame in 1983 as a coach; one of the first coaches to watch films of his opponents in order to create game plans; first coach to win division titles in both the American Football League and the National Football League; won the 1963 AFL title.

Gillman coached in the National Football League for the Los Angeles Rams (1955–1959), Los Angeles/San Diego Chargers (1960–1969, 1971), and the Houston Oilers (1973–1974). His 18-year NFL coaching record was 122-99-7 (.552) (he only coached partial seasons in 1969, 1971, and 1973); first coach to win division titles in both the American Football League and the NFL; won five AFL division titles in six seasons; and was named American Football Conference Coach of the Year in 1974.

Although he would eventually become well-known for creating innovative passing offenses, he began his coaching career when the game was dominated by powerful running teams. He believed that the running game gave a team needed first downs and allowed it to control the ball and the game's pace, but that winning, and generating fan interest required long downfield passing plays. As a coach, he was the first to study film of his opponents in order to create a game plan against the team.

Gillman played college football at Ohio State University (Columbus, graduating in 1934), and was both an All-Big Ten and an All-American end in 1932 and 1933.

After playing for the NFL's Cleveland Rams in 1936, Gillman became an assistant coach at Denison University (Granville, Ohio) and at Ohio State University. He was the head coach at Miami University (Oxford, Ohio) from 1944 to 1947, and compiled a 31–6–1 record. After four seasons, he served as an assistant coach at Army (United States Military Academy at West Point, New York in 1948), before becoming the head coach at the University of Cincinnati (Ohio). From 1949 to 1955, he compiled a record of 50–13–1 at Cincinnati, before becoming an NFL coach. It was at Cincinnati that he first gained his reputation for viewing film of upcoming opponents.

In his first NFL season (1955), he led the Rams to a division title. Five years later, when the AFL was founded, Gillman became the head coach and general manager of the Chargers, who played in Los Angeles in 1960 before moving to San Diego the next season. His high-scoring Chargers won their division in five of the league's first six seasons, and the AFL title in 1963 with a 51–10 win over the Boston Patriots. He was one of only two head coaches for the entire 10-year existence of the American Football League (the other being Hank Stram with the Dallas Texans and Kansas City Chiefs) and was the first coach to win division titles in both the AFL and NFL.

Gillman approached then-NFL Commissioner Pete Rozelle in 1963 about having the AFL and NFL champions play a single game for an overall title. The idea remained dormant until the first Super Bowl game was played in 1967.

After San Diego, he was the general manager and head coach of the Houston Oilers for two years (1973–1974) and was named NFL Coach of the Year in 1974. After recovering from health issues, Gillman was named the offensive coordinator for the Chicago Bears in 1977, the year the team made the playoffs for the first time in 14 seasons. In 1979, he moved to the Philadelphia Eagles, but poor health limited his work to developing quarterbacks. He ended his career in the 1980s as head coach of the Los Angeles Express of the now-defunct United States Football League.

Gillman devised the idea of putting players' names on the backs of their uniforms; was inducted into the College Football Hall of Fame in 1989; and into the International Jewish Sports Hall of Fame in 1991.

Sid Gillman's NFL Coaching Statistics

			REGULAR SEASON				PLAYOFFS		
YEAR	**TEAM**	**LG**	**W**	**L**	**T**	**WIN%**	**W**	**L**	**WIN%**
1955	Los Angeles Rams	NFL	8	3	1	.727	0	1	.000
1956	Los Angeles Rams	NFL	4	8	0	.333			
1957	Los Angeles Rams	NFL	6	6	0	.500			
1958	Los Angeles Rams	NFL	8	4	0	.667			
1959	Los Angeles Rams	NFL	2	10	0	.167			
1960	Los Angeles Chargers	AFL	10	4	0	.714	0	1	.000
1961	San Diego Chargers	AFL	12	2	0	.857	0	1	.000
1962	San Diego Chargers	AFL	4	10	0	.286			
1963	San Diego Chargers	AFL	11	3	0	.786	1	0	1.000
1964	San Diego Chargers	AFL	8	5	1	.615	0	1	.000
1965	San Diego Chargers	AFL	9	2	3	.818	0	1	.000
1966	San Diego Chargers	AFL	7	6	1	.538			
1967	San Diego Chargers	AFL	8	5	1	.615			
1968	San Diego Chargers	AFL	9	5	0	.643			
1969	San Diego Chargers	AFL	4	5	0	.444			
1971	San Diego Chargers	NFL	4	6	0	.400			
1973	Houston Oilers	NFL	1	8	0	.111			
1974	Houston Oilers	NFL	7	7	0	.500			
	Los Angeles Rams		28	31	1	.475	0	1	.000
	L.A./San Diego Chargers		86	53	6	.619	1	4	.200
	Houston Oilers		8	15	0	.348	0	0	
	TOTALS		122	99	7	.552	1	5	.167

Sources: Pro Football Hall of Fame; Pro-Football-Reference.com

Gilmour, Hamilton Livingstone "Billy" (born: March 21, 1885 in Ottawa, Ontario, Canada; died: March 13, 1959); inducted into the Hockey Hall of Fame in 1962 as a player; Position: Forward; won four Stanley Cup championships.

Gilmour played eight pre-National Hockey League seasons from 1902 to 1916. He was one of seven brothers (three of whom played for the Ottawa Silver Seven) and won three consecutive Stanley Cups (1903–1905) with the Ottawa Silver Seven (later known as the Senators). He won the Cup a fourth time in 1909 with Ottawa.

He was named to the Montreal City Hockey League First All-Star Team in 1907 and was an Eastern Canada Amateur Hockey Association First Team All-Star in 1908.

Hamilton Gilmour's Career Statistics

			REGULAR SEASON					PLAYOFFS				
SEASON	**TEAM**	**LEAGUE**	**GP**	**G**	**A**	**TP**	**PIM**	**GP**	**G**	**A**	**TP**	**PIM**
1900–1902	Ottawa Aberdeens	CAIHL										
1902–1903	Ottawa Silver Seven	CAHL	7	10	0	10	3	2	1	0	1	
1902–1903	Ottawa Silver Seven	St-Cup						2	4	0	4	3
1903–1904	Ottawa Silver Seven	St-Cup						3	1	0	1	0
1903–1904	McGill Redmen	MCHL	4	5	0	5	12					
1904–1905	McGill Redmen	MCHL	4	5	0	5	12					
1904–1905	Ottawa Silver Seven	FAHL	1	0	0	0	0					
1904–1905	Ottawa Silver Seven	St-Cup						2	1	0	1	8
1905–1906	Ottawa Silver Seven	ECAHA	1	0	0	0	0					
1905–1906	McGill Redmen	MCHL	4	5	0	5	21					
1906–1907	McGill Redmen	MCHL	3	2	0	2	8					
1907–1908	Montreal Victorias	ECAHA	10	5	0	5	33					
1908–1909	Ottawa Senators	ECHA	11	9	0	9	74					
1910–1911	Ottawa New Edinburghs	Exhib.										
1911–1912	Ottawa Senators	NHA	2	1	0	1	0					

Sources: Hockey Hall of Fame; Hockey-Reference.com

Glover, Charles Edward "Teddy" (born: April 7, 1902 in Bootle, Lancashire, England; died: February 8, 1993 in Pueblo, Colorado); inducted into the National Soccer Hall of Fame and Museum in 1965 as a player; Position: Full Back; won the 1931 ASL championship.

Glover played in the Football League for New Brighton, Southport (1922–1925) and Wigan Borough (1925–1927), before coming to the United States to play for the New York Giants in 1928 (Eastern Soccer League). The team had originally played in the American Soccer League and returned to the ASL after its merger with the ESL. He helped the squad win the 1931 ASL championship.

In 1932, he signed with the newly formed New York Americans of the ASL, and in 1933, he was on the team that lost the U.S. Open Cup Final to the St. Louis Stix, Bear and Fuller club. In 1934, he joined another ASL team, the New York Brookhattan, where he played for six years. Glover was a member of the ASL All-Star team that played against the Scottish F.A. touring squad in 1935.

During the early years of World War II, he played in the German American League for the Pfaelzer Soccer Club (1934–1940) and the Brooklyn Soccer Club before retiring.

Source: National Soccer Hall of Fame and Museum

Goheen, Frank Xavier "Moose" (born: February 9, 1894 in White Bear Lake, Minnesota; died: November 13, 1979 in White Baer Lake, Minnesota); inducted into the Hockey Hall of Fame in 1952 as a player; Position: Forward; won the McNaughton Trophy twice; won a silver medal at the 1920 Olympics.

Goheen began playing hockey at White Bear High School before attending the University of Indiana (Bloomington), where he was on the team that won the McNaughton Trophy in back-to-back seasons (1916–1917) as American Amateur Hockey Association champions. Missing the next two seasons, he served in the U.S. Army during World War I and, upon his return from the service, became a member and captain of the 1920 United States hockey team that played in the Olympics in Antwerp, Belgium, winning a silver medal.

He turned professional with the St. Paul (Minnesota) Hockey Club in the 1925–1926 season. The 6', 200-pound Goheen has been inducted into the Minnesota Sports Hall of Fame (1958) and the United States Hockey Hall of Fame (1973).

Frank Goheen's Career Statistics

SEASON	TEAM	LEAGUE	GP	G	A	PTS
1919–1920	United States	Olympics	4	7	0	7
1922–1923	St. Paul Saints	USAHA	20	11	0	11
1923–1924	St. Paul Saints	USAHA	20	10	4	14
1924–1925	St. Paul Saints	USAHA	32	6	0	6
1925–1926	St. Paul Saints	CHL	36	13	10	23
1926–1927	St. Paul Saints	AHA	27	2	7	9
1927–1928	St. Paul Saints	AHA	39	19	5	24
1928–1929	St. Paul Saints	AHA	28	7	4	11
1929–1930	St. Paul Saints	AHA	35	9	6	15
1930–1931	Buffalo Majors	AHA	2	0	0	0
1931–1932	St. Paul Saints	CHL	20	2	7	9

Sources: Hockey Hall of Fame; Hockey-Reference.com

Gola, Thomas Joseph (born: January 13, 1933 in Philadelphia, Pennsylvania); inducted into the Naismith Memorial Basketball Hall of Fame in 1976 as a player; Position: Guard-Forward; one of only two players to win NCAA, NIT, and NBA championships.

Gola scored 2,222 points and led his La Salle High School (Philadelphia, Pennsylvania, 1947–1951) team to a Philadelphia Catholic League Championship. After high school, he went to La Salle College (Philadelphia, Pennsylvania, 1951–1955), where he was a four-time All-District, All-State, and All-American selection.

At La Salle College, he led the team to a National Invitation Tournament Championship and was named NIT Co-Most Valuable Player (1952); selected first alternate to the U.S. Olympic Basketball Team (1952); won the 1954 National Collegiate Athletic Association Championship over Bradley in the first NCAA title game ever televised; named the NCAA Tournament MVP and College Basketball Player of the Year in 1954; selected team MVP all four years he was on the squad; led the team to a four-year record of 102–19; and when he left school, Gola was La Salle's career leader in points (2,461, 20.8 per game) and rebounds (2,201, 18.7 per game), and was the NCAA all-time rebound leader.

After graduating from La Salle, Gola played for the National Basketball Association's Philadelphia/San Francisco Warriors (1955–1962) and the New York Knicks (1962–1966). His 10-year professional career was interrupted by two years of military service (1956–1958); he was named to the All-NBA Second Team in 1958; and was a five-time NBA All-Star (1960–1964).

The 6'6", 200-pound Gola led the Warriors to an NBA championship in his rookie season (1956); was named to the All-NBA Team (1958); was a five-time NBA All-Star (1960–1964); is one of only two players to win NCAA, NIT, and NBA championships (along with C.A. "Arnie" Ferrin); and was selected to *Sport Magazine*'s All-Time All-American Team. He has been inducted into the La Salle University, Madison Square Garden, and the Helms Foundation halls of fame.

After retiring as a player, Gola became a head coach at his alma mater; in two seasons, he led his team to a 37–13 record; his 1968–1969 team was ranked second in the country; and he was named Coach of the Year by Philadelphia and New York writers in 1969. The school's Tom Gola Arena was named in his honor.

After his basketball career, he served in the Pennsylvania State Legislature; was Philadelphia City Controller; and ran an unsuccessful bid for mayor in 1983.

Thomas Gola's NBA Career Statistics

SEASON	TEAM	G	MIN	FG	FT	TRB	AST	PTS
1955–1956	Philadelphia	68	2,346	244	244	616	404	732
1957–1958	Philadelphia	59	2,126	295	223	639	327	813
1958–1959	Philadelphia	64	2,333	310	281	710	269	901
1959–1960	Philadelphia	75	2,870	426	270	779	409	1,122
1960–1961	Philadelphia	74	2,712	420	210	692	292	1,050

SEASON	TEAM	G	MIN	FG	FT	TRB	AST	PTS
1961–1962	Philadelphia	60	2,462	322	176	587	295	820
1962–1963	San Francisco	21	822	111	50	58	73	272
1962–1963	New York	52	1,848	252	120	259	225	624
1963–1964	New York	74	2,156	258	154	469	257	670
1964–1965	New York	77	1,727	204	133	319	220	541
1965–1966	New York	74	1,127	122	82	289	191	326
	TOTALS	698	22,529	2,964	1,943	5,417	2,962	7,871

Sources: Basketball-Reference.com; Naismith Memorial Basketball Hall of Fame

Gomelsky, Aleksandr "Sascha" (born: January 18, 1928 in Leningrad (Kronstadt), Russia; died: August 16, 2005 in Moscow, Russia); inducted into the Naismith Memorial Basketball Hall of Fame in 1995 as a coach; won five Soviet League titles, eight European Championships, and four Olympic medals.

Gomelsky was the team captain of the Leningrad Championship #79 High School team; played three years for the school; was selected to an equivalent All-State honor twice; and graduated in 1945. He then attended college at Coach School (Leningrad, Russia, 1945–1948), where he played for three seasons and was selected to an equivalent All-State three times.

After graduating from college, he played for SKA Leningrad (player-coach, 1948–1952), where the team became Champions of Leningrad and finished fifth in Russia. After his playing days, Gomelsky coached SKA Leningrad (1948–1952); ASK Riga (Army) (1953–1966, led the team to five Soviet League titles and three consecutive European Cups from 1957 to 1959); CSKA Moscow (Central Army Sports Club, 1966–1988); Soviet National Team (1958–1960, 1962–1970, 1976–1988); Tenerife (Spain, 1988–1989); European All-Star Team (1989–1990); and Limoges CSP (France, 1990–1991).

During his career, he compiled an overall record of 490–177 (.735) and was known as the "Father of Soviet Men's Basketball." Gomelsky won eight European Championships (1959, 1961, 1963, 1965, 1967, 1969, 1979, 1981); two World Championships (1967, 1982), led the Soviet Union to Olympic gold (1988), silver (1964), and bronze medals (1968, 1980); named Coach of the Year three times; coached the men's National Team in five Olympic Games, six Fédération Internationale de Basketball Amateur world championships, 10 FIBA European Championships, and 19 championships of the Soviet Union; and conducted more than 30 coaching clinics in Spain, France, Greece, United States, Australia, Israel, Philippines, Korea, Bulgaria, Czechoslovakia, Germany, and Russia. Gomelsky published 10 books on basketball strategy, tactics, and techniques; served as president of the Russian Basketball Federation; and was named Best European Coach by FIBA.

He was the Soviet National Team coach in 1972, but was not allowed to join the team for that year's Summer Olympics in Munich, Germany because he was Jewish and Soviet leaders felt he might defect. The Soviet team, coached by Vladimir Kondrashin, went on to win its first Olympic basketball gold medal with a 51–50 win over the United States.

In 1981, he was inducted into the International Jewish Sports Hall of Fame.

Source: Naismith Memorial Basketball Hall of Fame

Gomez, Vernon Louis "Lefty" (born: November 26, 1908 in Rodeo, California; died: February 17, 1989 in Greenbrae, California); inducted into the National Baseball Hall of Fame and Museum in 1972 as a player by the Veterans Committee; Position: Pitcher; Bats: Left; Throws: Right; Uniform: #11; as of this writing, he holds the World Series record for most wins (six) without a loss and the All-Star record for wins (three).

Gomez played 14 Major League Baseball seasons for the New York Yankees (1930–1942) and Washington Senators (1943). Making his debut on April 29, 1930, he would go on to play in, and win, five World Series (1932, 1936–1939) and was a seven-time All-Star (1933–1939). He won three All-Star games against one loss, the most wins of any pitcher.

He won 20 or more games four times (1931–1932, 1934, 1937); won the pitching equivalent of the Triple Crown (leading the league in wins, strikeouts, and earned run average) twice (1934, 1937); and set a World Series record by winning six games without a loss.

In the first-ever major league All-Star Game (July 6, 1933), Gomez drove in the first run and won the game for the American League.

The Yankees purchased the 6'2", 173-pound Gomez from his hometown San Francisco Seals in 1929, and two years later, he won 21 games with the team. As his skills began to wane with age, he compensated by becoming more of a finesse pitcher. On August 1, 1941, he pitched a 9–0 shutout against the St. Louis Browns while issuing 11 walks, at the time, the most ever allowed in a shutout. His record would stand until tied on May 21, 1970 when New York Yankee pitcher Mel Stottlemyre walked 11 batters in a 2–0 win over the Washington Senators.

Although not a run-producing pitcher, he collected the first-ever All-Star RBI, and singled home the winning run in the deciding game of the 1937 World Series.

In January 1943, the Yankees sent Gomez to the Boston Braves, and after he was released without ever playing a game, he signed with the Washington Senators on May 24th. After pitching only one game for the Senators, he retired from baseball, and was drafted into the military in 1944 during World War II. When he ended his career, his 189 wins was the third most in Yankees' history. Of the pitchers who made their major league debut from 1900 to 1950, only Lefty Grove, Christy Mathewson, and Whitey Ford have both more victories and a higher winning percentage than Gomez.

The Lefty Gomez Award is presented annually by the American Baseball Coaches Association to an individual who has distinguished himself and made significant contributions to the game locally, nationally, and internationally.

Lefty Gomez's Career Statistics

YEAR	TEAM	LG	W	L	PCT	G	SH	IP	H	R	ER	SO	BB	ERA
1930	New York	AL	2	5	.286	15	0	60	66	41	37	22	28	5.55
1931	New York	AL	21	9	.700	40	1	243	206	88	71	150	85	2.63
1932	New York	AL	24	7	.774	37	1	265	266	140	124	176	105	4.21
1933	New York	AL	16	10	.615	35	4	235	218	108	83	163	106	3.18
1934	New York	AL	26	5	.839	38	6	282	223	86	73	158	96	2.33
1935	New York	AL	12	15	.444	34	2	246	223	104	87	138	86	3.18
1936	New York	AL	13	7	.650	31	0	189	184	104	92	105	122	4.38
1937	New York	AL	21	11	.656	34	6	278	233	88	72	194	93	2.33
1938	New York	AL	18	12	.600	32	4	239	239	110	89	129	99	3.35
1939	New York	AL	12	8	.600	26	2	198	173	80	75	102	84	3.41
1940	New York	AL	3	3	.500	9	0	27	37	20	20	14	18	6.67
1941	New York	AL	15	5	.750	23	2	156	151	76	65	76	103	3.75
1942	New York	AL	6	4	.600	13	0	80	67	42	38	41	65	4.28
1943	Washington	AL	0	1	.000	1	0	5	4	4	3	0	5	5.40
	TOTALS		189	102	.649	368	28	2,503	2,290	1,091	929	1,468	1,095	3.34

Sources: Baseball-Reference.com; National Baseball Hall of Fame and Museum

Gonsalves, Adelino "Billy" (born: August 10, 1908 in Portsmouth, Rhode Island; died: July 17, 1977 in Kearny, New Jersey); inducted into the National Soccer Hall of Fame and Museum in 1950 as a player; Position: Inside Right; International Caps (1930–1934): 6; International Goals: 1; a member of the inaugural soccer hall of fame class; won two U.S. Open Cup championships.

Gonsalves began his career with the Pioneer, Charlton Mill, and Liberal youth clubs of Fall River, Massachusetts. In 1927, he moved to the Boston, Massachusetts area and led the semi-professional Lusitania Recreation club of Cambridge to the Boston and District championships. He then joined the professional Boston Wonder Workers (1927–1929) of the American Soccer League.

After two seasons, Gonsalves returned to Fall River and played on one of the greatest American soccer teams of all time, the Fall River Marksmen, also of the ASL. He played on the 1930 U.S. World Cup team and led Fall River to the U.S. Open Cup championship in back-to-back years (1930–1931).

In 1932, the 6'2" Gonsalves moved on to play for the New Bedford (Massachusetts) Whalers (ASL), then for the St. Louis (Missouri) clubs of Stix, Baer and Fuller (1933–1934) and St. Louis Central Brewery (1934–1935). He helped both St. Louis-area teams win national championships, on his way to winning six titles in a row. In 1934, he played in his second World Cup, this time as a central midfielder.

In 1936 and 1937, as a member of the St. Louis Shamrocks (St. Louis Soccer League), he reached the finals again, but lost both times, ending his streak of winning medals. In 1938, his team did not reach the final, but he returned in 1939 with Chicago Manhattan Beer, eventually losing to Brooklyn St. Mary Celtic.

After three seasons with an amateur team in White Plains, New York during World War II, Gonsalves played for Brooklyn Hispano (1942–1948) and won two more Open Cup medals in 1943 and 1944, marking a record eight titles. He spent his final seasons (1948–1952) with the German Sport Club of Newark, New Jersey and, after retiring as a player, he coached briefly.

Gannett News Service named him to the United States men's national soccer "Stars of the Century" team in 1999, and he was a member of the inaugural induction class into the National Soccer Hall of Fame and Museum in 1950.

Source: National Soccer Hall of Fame and Museum

Goodfellow, Ebenezer Robertson "Ebbie" (born: April 9, 1906 in Ottawa, Ontario, Canada; died: September 10, 1985 in Sarasota, Florida); inducted into the Hockey Hall of Fame in 1963 as a player; Position: Center-Defense-Forward; first Detroit Red Wings player to win the Hart Trophy; won three Stanley Cup titles.

Goodfellow played 14 National Hockey League seasons (1929–1943) for the Detroit Cougars (1929–1930), Detroit Falcons (1930–1932), and the Detroit Red Wings (1932–1943). He was signed by Detroit of the NHL and was sent to the Detroit Olympics of the Canadian Professional Hockey League in 1928–1929, where he was named to the league's All-Star team and led the CPHL in scoring.

He made his NHL debut in the 1929–1930 season with the Detroit Cougars and scored 17 goals; moved to defense in the 1934–1935 season; was named to the NHL's Second All-Star Team in 1936; to the First All-Star Team twice (1937, 1940); and played in two All-Star games (1937, 1939).

The 6', 180-pound Goodfellow won the Hart Trophy as the league's most valuable player in 1940 (the first player from a Detroit franchise to win the award); was the squad's captain for five years; and was a member of three Stanley Cup-winning teams (1936–1937, 1943 as a player-coach). After the team won the Cup in 1943, Goodfellow retired as a player and stayed on as a coach before becoming the head coach of the Chicago Black Hawks for two seasons (1950–1952).

Ebbie Goodfellow's Career Statistics

			REGULAR SEASON					PLAYOFFS				
SEASON	**TEAM**	**LEAGUE**	**GP**	**G**	**A**	**TP**	**PIM**	**GP**	**G**	**A**	**TP**	**PIM**
1926–1927	Ottawa Montag-nards	OCHL	4	3	1	4		2	0	0	0	0
1927–1928	Ottawa Montag-nards	OCHL	15	7	2	9		6	4	1	5	
1928–1929	Detroit Olympics	Can-Pro	42	26	8	34	45	7	3	2	5	8
1929–1930	Detroit Cougars	NHL	44	17	17	34	54					
1930–1931	Detroit Falcons	NHL	44	25	23	48	32					
1931–1932	Detroit Falcons	NHL	48	14	16	30	56	2	0	0	0	0
1932–1933	Detroit Red Wings	NHL	41	12	8	20	47	4	1	0	1	11
1933–1934	Detroit Red Wings	NHL	48	13	13	26	45	9	4	3	7	12
1934–1935	Detroit Red Wings	NHL	48	12	24	36	44					
1935–1936	Detroit Red Wings	NHL	48	5	18	23	69	7	1	0	1	4
1936–1937	Detroit Red Wings	NHL	48	9	16	25	43	9	2	2	4	12
1937–1938	Detroit Red Wings	NHL	30	0	7	7	13					
1938–1939	Detroit Red Wings	NHL	48	8	8	16	36	6	0	0	0	8
1939–1940	Detroit Red Wings	NHL	43	11	17	28	31	5	0	2	2	9
1940–1941	Detroit Red Wings	NHL	47	5	17	22	35	3	0	1	1	9
1941–1942	Detroit Red Wings	NHL	9	2	2	4	2					
1942–1943	Detroit Red Wings	NHL	11	1	4	5	4					
	NHL TOTALS		557	134	190	324	511	45	8	8	16	65

Sources: Hockey Hall of Fame; Hockey-Reference.com

Goodrich, Gail Charles, Jr. (born: April 23, 1943 in Los Angeles, California); inducted into the Naismith Memorial Basketball Hall of Fame in 1996 as a player; Position: Guard; Uniform: #25; led his UCLA freshman team to an undefeated season for the first time in the school's history; won two NCAA national titles; won one NBA championship.

Goodrich was a two-year letter winner (1960–1961) at John H. Francis Polytechnic High School (Sun Valley, California); was selected All-Conference twice (1960–1961); named both All-State and All-American in 1961; led the school to the Los Angeles City High School Championship in 1961; and was named Los Angeles Player of the Year in 1961, averaging 23.2 points per game.

After graduating in 1961, he played college basketball under hall of fame coach John Wooden at the University of California at Los Angeles, graduating in 1965. While at UCLA, Goodrich led the Bruins' freshman team to an undefeated 20–0 season for the first in UCLA history, while scoring 24.4 points per game. He was named the Bruins' Co-Rookie of the Year (1963); led the team to the Co-Championship of the Athletic Association of Western Universities (1963); and helped lead the team to an undefeated 30–0 season and the 1964 National Collegiate Athletic Association Championship, both for the first time in school history.

Goodrich was selected to the 1964 Helms Athletic Foundation All-America Team (1964); named honorable mention Associated Press and UPI All-American (1964); was a U.S. Olympic Team alternate (1964); led the Bruins to a 28–2 record and its second consecutive NCAA championship (1965); selected to the NCAA Final Four All-Tournament Team twice (1964–1965); was the Bruins' and Conference Most Valuable Player in 1965; and graduated (1965) as UCLA's all-time leading scorer (1,690 points).

After college, Goodrich joined the National Basketball Association's Los Angeles Lakers in 1964 as the team's first-round draft pick (10th overall selection) and stayed with the team until 1968. He then moved on to the Phoenix Suns (1968–1970), returned to the Lakers (1970–1976), and finished his career with the New Orleans Jazz (1976–1979).

He won an NBA championship with the Lakers in 1972, the team's first, and was the squad's leading scorer (25.9 points per game); played in a still-NBA-record 33 game winning streak in the 1971–1972 season; served as captain of the Lakers (1974–1976); was a five-time All-Star (1969, 1972–1975); named to the 1974 All-NBA First Team; led the Lakers in scoring four consecutive seasons (1972–1976); and retired as the Lakers' sixth all-time leading scorer (13,044 points).

Goodrich holds the Lakers' record for most consecutive free throws made (40); scored a career high 53 points against the Kansas City-Omaha Kings on March 28, 1975; and retired with a 1,031-game career average of 18.6 points and 4.7 assists per game.

The relatively small 6'1", 170-pound, left-handed Goodrich played for two of the greatest basketball teams in history: the undefeated 1963–1964 UCLA Bruins (winning a national championship) and the 1971–1972 Los Angeles Lakers (compiling a 69–13 record and taking the NBA title).

His Lakers' jersey #25 was retired by the team in November 1996; his UCLA jersey was retired in December 2004; and his #12 high school jersey was retired.

Gail Goodrich's NBA Career Statistics

SEASON	TEAM	G	MIN	FG	FT	TRB	AST	PTS
1965–1966	Los Angeles	65	1,008	203	103	130	103	509
1966–1967	Los Angeles	77	1,780	352	253	251	210	957
1967–1968	Los Angeles	79	2,057	395	302	199	205	1,092
1968–1969	Phoenix	81	3,236	718	495	437	518	1,931
1969–1970	Phoenix	81	3,234	568	488	340	605	1,624
1970–1971	Los Angeles	79	2,808	558	264	260	380	1,380
1971–1972	Los Angeles	82	3,040	826	475	295	365	2,127
1972–1973	Los Angeles	76	2,697	750	314	263	332	1,814
1973–1974	Los Angeles	82	3,061	784	508	250	427	2,076
1974–1975	Los Angeles	72	2,668	656	318	219	420	1,630
1975–1976	Los Angeles	75	2,646	583	293	214	421	1,459
1976–1977	New Orleans	27	609	136	68	61	74	340
1977–1978	New Orleans	81	2,553	520	264	177	388	1,304
1978–1979	New Orleans	74	2,130	382	174	183	357	938
	TOTALS	1,031	33,527	7,431	4,319	3,279	4,805	19,181

Sources: Basketball-Reference.com; Naismith Memorial Basketball Hall of Fame

Gordon, Joseph Lowell "Joe" (born: February 18, 1915 in Los Angeles, California; died: April 14, 1978 in Sacramento, California); inducted into the National Baseball Hall of Fame and Museum in 2009 by the Veterans Committee as a player; Position: Second Base; Bats: Right; Throws: Right; Uniform: #6 (New York), #4 (Cleveland); 1942 American League Most Valuable Player.

The 5'10", 180-pound Gordon played 11 seasons (1938–1943, 1946–1950) with the New York Yankees (1938–1943, 1946) and the Cleveland Indians (1947–1950); managed the Cleveland Indians (1958–1960), Detroit Tigers (1960), Kansas City Athletics (1961), and the Kansas City Royals (1969); selected to the All-Star team nine times

(1939–1943, 1946–1949); played in six World Series (winning in 1938–1939, 1941, 1943, 1948 and losing in 1942); and was voted the 1942 American League Most Valuable Player.

Nicknamed "Flash," Gordon had 25 home runs in his rookie season; hit .322 in 1942 (AL MVP); had 20 or more home runs in six seasons (the first American League second baseman to hit 20 home runs in a season); and drove in at least 100 runs four times. He also led the American League in assists four times and in double plays three times.

He attended the University of Oregon (Eugene) and helped the Ducks win the Pacific Coast Conference (Northern Division) in both 1934 and 1935.

After college, he played for the International League's Newark Bears (an affiliate of the New York Yankees located in Newark, New Jersey) in 1937, before making his Major League debut on April 18, 1938. His 25 home runs as a rookie set an American League record for second basemen, which lasted until 2006.

After his major league playing days, Gordon was a player-manager for the Pacific Coast League's Sacramento Solons in 1951 and 1952; a scout with the Detroit Tigers (1953–1956); and managed the San Francisco Seals to the 1957 PCL championship before becoming a major league manager with four different teams. In the middle of the 1960 season, he was involved in a rare trade of managers, when the Indians traded him to the Tigers for Jimmy Dykes. After he was fired from the Kansas City Athletics in the middle of the 1961 season, Gordon served as a scout and minor league instructor for the Los Angeles and California Angels from 1961 to 1968, before managing the Royals in 1969.

Joe Gordon's Career Statistics

YEAR	TEAM	G	H	HR	R	RBI	BB	SB	SO	AVG
1938	New York	127	117	25	83	97	56	11	72	.258
1939	New York	151	161	28	92	111	75	11	57	.284
1940	New York	155	173	30	112	103	52	18	57	.281
1941	New York	156	162	24	104	87	72	10	80	.276
1942	New York	147	173	18	88	103	79	12	95	.322
1943	New York	152	135	17	82	69	98	4	75	.249
1946	New York	112	79	11	35	47	49	2	72	.210
1947	Cleveland	155	153	29	89	93	62	7	49	.272
1948	Cleveland	144	154	32	96	124	77	5	68	.280
1949	Cleveland	148	136	20	74	84	83	5	33	.251
1950	Cleveland	119	87	19	59	57	56	4	44	.236
	TOTALS	1,566	1,530	253	914	975	759	89	702	.268

Joe Gordon's Managing Record

YEAR	TEAM	W	L	WIN%
1958	Cleveland	46	40	.535
1959	Cleveland	89	65	.578
1960	Cleveland	49	46	.516
1960	Detroit	26	31	.456
1961	Kansas City	26	33	.441
1969	Kansas City	69	93	.426
	TOTALS	305	308	.498

Sources: Baseball-Reference.com; National Baseball Hall of Fame and Museum

Gorman, Thomas Patrick "T.P." "Tommy" (born: June 9, 1886 in Ottawa, Ontario, Canada; died: May 15, 1961); inducted into the Hockey Hall of Fame in 1963 as a builder; won a lacrosse gold medal at the 1908 Olympics; one of the founding members of the National Hockey League; won seven Stanley Cup championships.

A lifelong hockey fan, Gorman was a journalist, player, coach, executive, and owner. As a young man, he excelled at lacrosse, and in 1908 was the youngest player on the Canadian lacrosse team that won the gold medal at the Olympic Games in London, England.

Gorman became involved in hockey for the first time when his family purchased the Ottawa Senators of the National Hockey Association during World War I. He served as the team's manager, and later was one of the founding members of the National Hockey League in 1917. Under Gorman, the Senators won three Stanley Cup titles in four years (1920–1921, 1923) and seven total.

In addition to hockey, he was an avid fan of horse racing and played a major role in reviving thoroughbred racing at Connaught Park in Ottawa after World War I. Gorman worked to keep the facility open and eventually served as a timer, racing secretary, general manager, and president of the Park. He also served as president of the Province of Quebec Racing Association. He later served as Assistant General Manager at Agua Caliente Racetrack in Tijuana, Mexico.

After the Senators' 1923 Stanley Cup win, Gorman sold his interest in the team and left the game. He returned to the NHL briefly in 1925 as owner of the Hamilton Tigers, and moved the team to New York, where it became known as the Americans. Gorman again left the NHL to focus on horse racing, but returned to the league once more to coach the Chicago Black Hawks in the middle of the 1932–1933 season. The next season, he became the team's general manager and guided the Hawks to the franchise's first Stanley Cup championship in 1934, his fourth.

He left Chicago before the 1934–1935 season to serve as coach and general manager of the Montreal Maroons, where he won his fifth Stanley Cup championship (1935). He stayed with the team until it folded in 1938, and a few years later, was hired as the general manager of the then-struggling Montreal Canadiens in the 1940–1941 season. He revived the club's fortunes and helped the team win two more Stanley Cup championships (1944, 1946), before leaving the squad in 1946.

While in the NHL, Gorman had won seven Stanley Cups and managed four different teams in five different cities. He then purchased the senior-level Ottawa Senators and led the team to the 1949 Allan Cup, and later helped bring the Ottawa Giants (International League) Triple A baseball franchise to Ottawa.

When he died at age 74, he was the last living founder of the NHL. Gorman has been inducted into the Greater Ottawa Sports Hall of Fame (1966) and the Canadian Horse Racing Hall of Fame (1977).

Sources: Canadian Horse Racing Hall of Fame; Hockey Hall of Fame

Gormley, Robert (born: August 3, 1918 in Philadelphia, Pennsylvania); inducted into the National Soccer Hall of Fame and Museum in 1989 as a player; Position: Forward-Left Wing; International Caps (1954): 1; International Goals: 0; served as a captain of the German-Americans for 12 seasons.

Gormley began his career with the McKinley Soccer Club (Philadelphia) and, as a boy, also played for the Lighthouse Boys Club in the North Philadelphia League. In 1936, he signed with the Kensington Blue Bells of the Eastern Pennsylvania League and joined the Philadelphia German-Americans of the American Soccer League the next season (1937).

In his first full year in the American Soccer League, he scored 10 goals from his left wing position and went on to play for the German-Americans for 17 years, retiring in 1954. He served as captain of the team for 12 of his 17 seasons, and represented the United States in World Cup play against Israel in 1948 and Haiti in 1954.

Gormley earned his only international cap against Haiti on April 3, 1954, after the U.S. National Team had already failed to qualify for the finals.

Source: National Soccer Hall of Fame and Museum

Goslin, Leon Allen "Goose" (born: October 16, 1900 in Salem, New Jersey; died: May 15, 1971 in Bridgeton, New Jersey); inducted into the National Baseball Hall of Fame and Museum in 1968 as a player by the Veterans Committee; Position: Left Field; Bats: Left; Throws: Right; Uniform: #4; only man to have played in each of the 19 World Series games in which the Washington Senators appeared; won two World Series titles.

Goslin enjoyed an 18-year Major League Baseball career with the Washington Senators (1921–1930, 1933, 1938), St. Louis Browns (1930–1932), and the Detroit Tigers (1934–1937). After making his debut on September 16, 1921, he went on to play in five World Series (winning in 1924 and 1935, losing in 1925, 1933–1934) and was a one-time All-Star (1936).

The 5'11", 185-pound Goslin helped lead his teams to five American League pennants, three with the Senators and two with the Tigers. He drove in 100 or more runs 11 times; hit .300 or more 11 times, led the Senators to the franchise's first-ever World Series title in 1924; won the batting title in 1928 (.379); and was the only man to have played in each of the 19 World Series games in which the Washington Senators appeared.

He is one of three players born in New Jersey to be elected into the hall of fame and in 1999, he ranked number 89 on *The Sporting News*' list of Baseball's Greatest Players and was nominated as a finalist for the Major League Baseball All-Century Team.

Goslin was responsible for the first fine ever levied against an umpire. In the 1935 World Series, he got into an argument with future hall of fame umpire Bill Klem, during which Klem lost his temper and began swearing at the player, resulting in the very first fine levied against an umpire (by Commissioner Kenesaw Landis).

On October 11, 1925, Goslin and Joe Harris hit back-to-back home runs in the fourth inning of Game Four in a 4–0 win over the Pittsburgh Pirates, the first time that had happened in World Series play. On May 26, 1930, Goslin and Joe Judge hit back-to-back home runs twice in the same game (a 10–7 win over the New York Yankees), for the first time in the 20th century. He set a new American League record by hitting the fifth pinch-hit home run of his career in a 4–3 loss to the New York Yankees on April 24, 1938.

Goslin led the American League in assists by an outfielder in 1924 and 1925, and is one of only three players (along with Edgar Renteria and Boss Schmidt) to be the last hitter of two World Series (struck out to end the 1925 World Series and won the 1935 World Series with his walk-off RBI single).

In 1939, Goslin became a player-manager for the Trenton Senators (Interstate League) before retiring as a player.

Goose Goslin's Career Statistics

YEAR	TEAM	LG	G	AB	R	H	2B	3B	HR	RBI	BB	SO	SB	AVG	SLG
1921	Washington	AL	14	50	8	13	1	1	1	6	6	5	0	.260	.380
1922	Washington	AL	101	358	44	116	19	7	3	53	25	26	4	.324	.441
1923	Washington	AL	150	600	86	180	29	18	9	99	40	53	7	.300	.453
1924	Washington	AL	154	579	100	199	30	17	12	129	68	29	16	.344	.516
1925	Washington	AL	150	601	116	201	34	20	18	113	53	50	26	.334	.547
1926	Washington	AL	147	568	105	201	26	15	17	108	63	38	8	.354	.542
1927	Washington	AL	148	581	96	194	37	15	13	120	50	28	21	.334	.516
1928	Washington	AL	135	456	80	173	36	10	17	102	48	19	16	.379	.614
1929	Washington	AL	145	553	82	159	28	7	18	91	66	33	10	.288	.461
1930	Washington	AL	47	188	34	51	11	5	7	38	19	19	3	.271	.495
1930	St. Louis	AL	101	396	81	129	25	7	30	100	48	35	14	.326	.652
1931	St. Louis	AL	151	591	114	194	42	10	24	105	80	41	9	.328	.555
1932	St. Louis	AL	150	572	88	171	28	9	17	104	92	35	12	.299	.469
1933	Washington	AL	132	549	97	163	35	10	10	64	42	32	5	.297	.452
1934	Detroit	AL	151	614	106	187	38	7	13	100	65	38	5	.305	.453
1935	Detroit	AL	147	590	88	172	34	6	9	109	56	31	5	.292	.415
1936	Detroit	AL	147	572	122	180	33	8	24	125	85	50	14	.315	.526
1937	Detroit	AL	79	181	30	43	11	1	4	35	35	18	0	.238	.376
1938	Washington	AL	38	57	6	9	3	0	2	8	8	5	0	.158	.316
	TOTALS		2,287	8,656	1,483	2,735	500	173	248	1,609	949	585	175	.316	.500

Sources: Baseball-Reference.com; National Baseball Hall of Fame and Museum

Gossage, Richard Michael "Goose" (born July 5, 1951, in Colorado Springs, Colorado); inducted into the National Baseball Hall of Fame and Museum in 2008 as a pitcher; Bats: Right; Throws: Right; won the American League Rolaids Relief Man of the Year Award; his 308th career save preserved Nolan Ryan's 308th career win.

One of Major League Baseball's most dominant closers in the late 1970s and early 1980s, Gossage played 22 seasons (1972–1994) for the Chicago White Sox (1972–1976), Pittsburgh Pirates (1977), New York Yankees (1978–1983, 1989), San Diego Padres (1984–1987), Chicago Cubs (1988), San Francisco Giants (1989), Fukuoka Daiei Hawks (1990, Pacific League [Japan]), Texas Rangers (1991), Oakland Athletics (1992–1993), and the Seattle Mariners (1994). He was a combined American-National League All-Star nine times (1975–1978, 1980–1982, 1984–1985); won the American League Rolaids Relief Man of the Year Award in 1978; played in three World Series (winning in 1978, losing in 1981 and 1984); and retired as the Yankees' career leader in earned run average (2.14) and hits allowed per nine innings pitched (6.59).

Gossage was drafted in the ninth round (198th overall selection) in the 1970 Amateur Draft out of Wasson High School (Colorado Springs, Colorado). Making his major league debut on April 16, 1972, the 6'3", 217-pound Gossage led the American League in saves three times and when he retired, ranked third in major league history in career games pitched (1,002).

He was involved in one of the more memorable home runs in major league history, forever known in baseball lore as the "Pine Tar Game/Incident." On July 24, 1983 at Yankee Stadium, Kansas City Royals' slugger George Brett hit a two-run homer off Gossage in the top of the ninth with two out to give the Royals a 5-4 lead. As Brett crossed the plate, New York manager Billy Martin demanded that Brett's bat be examined for excessive pine tar.

After reviewing the bat, the umpires ruled that it contained excess pine tar (more than 18 inches up the barrel) and called Brett out, which triggered one of the game's greatest-ever meltdowns on Brett's part as he was held back by teammates and coaches before he could attack home plate umpire Tim McClelland. With Brett being called out, the umpires ruled that the game was over with three outs in the inning. However, contrary to what many fans believe, this was not the end of the incident. The Royals protested the game, and in a rarity for the major leagues, it was upheld by the league office. League president Lee MacPhail stated that the rule only provided for the bat to be removed from the game, but not calling the player out.

On August 18, the game was resumed from the point of Brett's home run, with the Royals leading 5 to 4. Twenty-five days after the original game was played, Royals' reliever Dan Quisenberry did not allow the Yankees to score in the bottom of the ninth inning, and Kansas City finally won the game.

In one of those statistical coincidences that seemingly only happens in baseball, on July 23, 1991, Gossage (by now with the Texas Rangers) recorded his 308th career save to preserve Nolan Ryan's 308th career win. On August 4, 1994, he became the third pitcher in major league history to appear in 1,000 games.

Goose Gossage's Career Statistics

YEAR	TEAM	W	L	ERA	G	SV	IP	H	R	ER	HBP	BB	SO
1972	Chicago	7	1	4.28	36	2	80.0	72	44	38	4	44	57
1973	Chicago	0	4	7.43	20	0	49.2	57	44	41	3	37	33
1974	Chicago	4	6	4.13	39	1	89.1	92	45	41	2	47	64
1975	Chicago	9	8	1.84	62	26	141.2	99	32	29	5	70	130
1976	Chicago	9	17	3.94	31	1	224.0	214	104	98	9	90	135
1977	Pittsburgh	11	9	1.62	72	26	133.0	78	27	24	2	49	151
1978	New York	10	11	2.01	63	27	134.1	87	41	30	2	59	122
1979	New York	5	3	2.62	36	18	58.1	48	18	17	0	19	41
1980	New York	6	2	2.27	64	33	99.0	74	29	25	1	37	103
1981	New York	3	2	0.77	32	20	46.2	22	6	4	1	14	48
1982	New York	4	5	2.23	56	30	93.0	63	23	23	0	28	102
1983	New York	13	5	2.27	57	22	87.1	82	27	22	1	25	90
1984	San Diego	10	6	2.90	62	25	102.1	75	34	33	1	36	84
1985	San Diego	5	3	1.82	50	26	79.0	64	21	16	1	17	52
1986	San Diego	5	7	4.45	45	21	64.2	69	36	32	2	20	63
1987	San Diego	5	4	3.12	40	11	52.0	47	18	18	0	19	44
1988	Chicago	4	4	4.33	46	13	43.2	50	23	21	3	15	30
1989	New York	1	0	3.77	11	1	14.1	14	6	6	1	3	6
1989	San Francisco	2	1	2.68	31	4	43.2	32	16	13	0	27	24
1991	Texas	4	2	3.57	44	1	40.1	33	16	16	3	16	28
1992	Oakland	0	2	2.84	30	0	38.0	32	13	12	2	19	26
1993	Oakland	4	5	4.53	39	1	47.2	49	24	24	1	26	40
1994	Seattle	3	0	4.18	36	1	47.1	44	23	22	3	15	29
	TOTALS	124	107	3.01	1,002	310	1,809.1	1,497	670	605	47	732	1,502

Sources: Baseball-Reference.com; National Baseball Hall of Fame and Museum

Gottlieb, Edward (born: September 15, 1898 in Kiev, Ukraine, Russia; died: December 7, 1979 in Philadelphia County, Pennsylvania); inducted into the Naismith Memorial Basketball Hall of Fame in 1972 as a contributor; organized the South Philadelphia Hebrew Association team; led the Philadelphia Warriors to a BAA title.

Gottlieb played basketball for one season (1915–1916) at South Philadelphia High School (Philadelphia, Pennsylvania) before graduating in 1916 and attending college at the School of Pedagogy (Philadelphia, 1916–1918). While in college, he played basketball for two years and was the team captain in the 1917–1918 season.

After college, Gottlieb organized, played for, and coached professional basketball for the South Philadelphia Hebrew Association team from 1918 to 1925. The team won two Philadelphia League championships (1924–1925) and he served as captain of the squad for five years. The SPHAs beat the Original Celtics and New York Rens in a special showdown series in 1926; won three of four titles in the Eastern Pro League (1929–1933); and won eight of 13 titles in the American Basketball League (1933–1946), a total of 11 championships in 17 years.

Gottlieb later served as owner, general manager, and coach of the Philadelphia Warriors, one of 11 original Basketball Association of America teams (a precursor to the National Basketball Association). He coached the Warriors to a 263–318 (.453) record and led the team to the BAA title (1947) and two Eastern Division titles (1948, 1951).

He served as chairman of the NBA Rules Committee for 25 years; was the NBA's sole schedule maker for more than 30 years; organized overseas tours of the Harlem Globetrotters; and the Eddie Gottlieb Trophy is awarded annually to the NBA's top rookie. He helped in the merging of the BAA and the National Basketball League to form the NBA in 1949.

Gottlieb has been inducted into the South Philadelphia High School Sports Hall of Fame, the Pennsylvania Sports Hall of Fame, and the International Jewish Sports Hall of Fame (1980).

Source: Naismith Memorial Basketball Hall of Fame

Gould, David L. (born: 1873 Galston, Ayrshire, Scotland; died: unknown); inducted into the National Soccer Hall of Fame and Museum in 1953 as a builder; won the 1897 American Challenge Cup; coached the 1934 U.S. World Cup team.

After playing soccer in Scotland as a young boy, Gould arrived in the United States in 1891 and started playing with the Philadelphia Athletics, leading the team to the Pennsylvania League title in 1892. He later played with the Philadelphia team of the American Association and then joined the newly organized Manz Football Club, which won the American Challenge Cup in 1897.

He led Philadelphia against two touring English clubs, the Pilgrims in 1909 and the Corinthians in 1911. In 1911, he became an assistant coach at the University of Pennsylvania (Philadelphia), where he stayed for 28 years. Each year, the school honors its top men's soccer player with the David L. Gould Trophy.

For all his playing accomplishments, Gould's main claim to fame came as the head coach of the 1934 United States World Cup team that played in Italy, which was eliminated in the first round after a 7–1 loss to Italy. He later served as president of both the Referees' Examining Board and the Referees Association.

Source: National Soccer Hall of Fame and Museum

Goulet, Michel (born: April 21, 1960 in Peribonka, Quebec, Canada); inducted into the Hockey Hall of Fame in 1998 as a player; Position: Left Wing; Uniform: #16; won two Stanley Cups while serving in the front office of the Colorado Avalanche.

Goulet had a 15-year (1979–1994) National Hockey League career with the Quebec Nordiques (1979–1989) and the Chicago Black Hawks (1990–1994); scored at least 20 goals in every NHL season except his last; and scored 40 or more goals seven consecutive seasons (1981–1988).

Following the NHL/World Hockey Association merger, Goulet was the number one selection (20th overall pick) of the Quebec Nordiques in the 1979 Entry Draft, and scored 22 goals his rookie year. His 57 goals in the 1982–1983 season began a string of four consecutive 50-goal seasons, and later that spring, he represented Canada at the World Championship.

The 6'1", 185-pound Goulet represented the NHL in the Rendez–vous '87 exhibition series against the Soviet All-Stars. Held in lieu of the NHL All-Star Game, the two-game series ended in a tie as each team won one game. Later in the year, he helped Canada defend its Canada Cup title against the Soviet team.

In March 1990, Goulet was sent to Chicago, where he accumulated three straight 20-goal seasons (1991–1993). On February 23, 1991, he had a hat trick against the Minnesota North Stars to reach the 1,000-point mark. On February 16, 1992, he scored his 500th goal against the Calgary Flames.

His career ended suddenly on March 16, 1994 when he suffered a concussion in a game against the Montreal Canadiens. Goulet's jersey number 16 was retired by the Nordiques; he was selected to two Second All-Star Teams (1983, 1988); and to three First All-Star Teams (1984, 1986–1987). While never winning the Stanley Cup as a player, he did win two championships with the Colorado Avalanche: in 1996 as an assistant coach and in 2001 as the team's Director of Player Personnel.

Michel Goulet's Career Statistics

			REGULAR SEASON					PLAYOFFS				
SEASON	TEAM	LEAGUE	GP	G	A	TP	PIM	GP	G	A	TP	PIM
1976–1977	Mistasinni Majors	QAAA										
1976–1977	Quebec Remparts	QMJHL	37	17	18	35	9	14	3	8	11	19
1977–1978	Quebec Remparts	QMJHL	72	73	62	135	109	1	0	1	1	0
1978–1979	Birmingham Bulls	WHA	78	28	30	58	65					
1979–1980	Quebec Nordiques	NHL	77	22	32	54	48					
1980–1981	Quebec Nordiques	NHL	76	32	39	71	45	4	3	4	7	7

SEASON	TEAM	LEAGUE	REGULAR SEASON GP	G	A	TP	PIM	PLAYOFFS GP	G	A	TP	PIM
1981–1982	Quebec Nordiques	NHL	80	42	42	84	48	16	8	5	13	6
1982–1983	Quebec Nordiques	NHL	80	57	48	105	51	4	0	0	0	6
1982–1983	Canada	WEC-A	10	1	8	9	6					
1983–1984	Quebec Nordiques	NHL	75	56	65	121	76	9	2	4	6	17
1984–1985	Canada	Can-Cup	8	5	6	11	0					
1984–1985	Quebec Nordiques	NHL	69	55	40	95	55	17	11	10	21	17
1985–1986	Quebec Nordiques	NHL	75	53	51	104	64	3	1	2	3	10
1986–1987	Quebec Nordiques	NHL	75	49	47	96	61	13	9	5	14	35
1986–1987	NHL All-Stars	RV-87	2	0	1	1	0					
1987–1988	Canada	Can-Cup	8	2	3	5	0					
1987–1988	Quebec Nordiques	NHL	80	48	58	106	56					
1988–1989	Quebec Nordiques	NHL	69	26	38	64	67					
1989–1990	Quebec Nordiques	NHL	57	16	29	45	42					
1989–1990	Chicago Black Hawks	NHL	8	4	1	5	9	14	2	4	6	6
1990–1991	Chicago Black Hawks	NHL	74	27	38	65	65					
1991–1992	Chicago Black Hawks	NHL	75	22	41	63	69	9	3	4	7	6
1992–1993	Chicago Black Hawks	NHL	63	23	21	44	43	3	0	1	1	0
1993–1994	Chicago Black Hawks	NHL	56	16	14	30	26					
	NHL TOTALS		1,089	548	604	1,152	825	92	39	39	78	110

Sources: Hockey Hall of Fame; Hockey-Reference.com

Govier, Sheldon (born: January 11, 1883 in Coatbridge, Scotland; died: 1948 in Chicago, Illinois); inducted into the National Soccer Hall of Fame and Museum in 1950 as a player; Position: Center Halfback; won the Jackson Cup and the Peel Pennant.

Govier grew up playing for a variety of Scottish junior teams, including Cambuslang, Rutherglen, Blantyre, and Uddington. His family moved to the Chicago, Illinois area in 1891, and he played for the Pullman A.C. team. In 1895, he moved to St. Louis (Missouri) and for two years played for the St. Louis Cycling Club.

Returning to Chicago, in 1901, he became captain for the Chicago team in a Midwest professional league formed by baseball hall-of-famer Charles Comiskey. The league included teams from Chicago, St. Louis, Detroit, and Milwaukee. Midway through the season, financial support waned and the league folded.

Govier then returned to the Pullman club, where he won the Jackson Cup and the Peel Pennant. From there, he moved on to play for the Wanderers, Woodlawns, and the Buxton Red Sox, before once again returning to the Pullman team.

He was a member of the Chicago All-Star team that defeated the touring Pilgrims from England in 1905.

After his soccer career, Govier served as an alderman for the Ninth Ward in Chicago from 1918 until 1932; worked on the local Democratic Committee from 1926 until his death; was elected clerk of the Appellate Court of Cook County in 1932 (re-elected in 1938 and 1944); and was a delegate to the 1948 Democratic National Convention in Philadelphia, Pennsylvania.

Source: National Soccer Hall of Fame and Museum

Graham, Otto Everett, Jr. (born: December 6, 1921 in Waukegan, Illinois; died: December 17, 2003 in Sarasota, Florida); inducted into the Pro Football Hall of Fame in 1965 as a player; Position: Quarterback; Uniform: #14; as a senior at Northwestern University, he was an All-American selection in both football and basketball; won a National Basketball League championship.

Destined to be one of the greatest professional quarterbacks of all time, Graham played 10 professional seasons for the Cleveland Browns (1946–1955) in both the All-America Football Conference and the National Football League. He was a college tailback at Northwestern University (Evanston, Illinois), but was switched to quarterback in the professional ranks when he was the first player signed by Paul Brown as he began organizing the Cleveland Browns to play in the newly formed AAFC.

The 6'1", 195-pound Graham led the Browns to 10 division or league titles in his 10 seasons; was the top AAFC passer four times, led NFL passers twice; was named All-League in nine of his 10 years; threw four touchdown passes in the 1950 NFL title game victory (a 30–28 win over the Los Angeles Rams); and scored three running touchdowns and three passing touchdowns in the 1954 title game (a 56–10 win over the Detroit Lions).

Graham was a five-time Pro Bowl selection (1950–1954); named to the NFL 1950s All-Decade Team; selected to the NFL 75th Anniversary Team; 1950 Pro Bowl Most Valuable Player; AAFC MVP in 1947; three-time NFL MVP (1951, 1953, 1955); and his jersey number 14 was retired by the Browns.

Although Graham attended Northwestern to play basketball (he would later play briefly for the Rochester Royals in the National Basketball League), his football skills were used by Paul Brown to create the T-Formation offense with Graham at quarterback, which the Browns used to win four straight AAFC titles, while compiling a 52–4–3 record during this period.

Graham attended Waukegan (Illinois) High School before going to Northwestern on a basketball scholarship. By the time he graduated from Northwestern, he had played four years of basketball, three years of football, and two seasons of baseball. He set a Big Ten record in 1942, as a junior, by completing 89 of 182 passes for 1,092 yards; as a senior, he was an All-American selection in both football and basketball; and Graham was inducted into the College Football Hall of Fame in 1956.

In 1942, Graham served in the United States Navy during World War II. Before his service ended, Paul Brown offered him a contract to play for the Browns, which he did, after leaving the military. Before joining the Browns, however, Graham played one season (1945–1946) with the Rochester Royals of the National Basketball League and led the team to the league's title.

During his career with the team, the Browns compiled a 105–17–4 record (.861), while Graham accrued an 86.6 career passer rating. He threw 88 NFL touchdown passes in six seasons, and in his last year (1955), he won the Hickok Belt as the top professional athlete of the year. In 1999, he was ranked number seven on *The Sporting News*' list of the 100 Greatest Football Players, the highest ranking of anyone who had played in the AAFC.

After retiring as a player, Graham coached the College All-Stars to a 35–19 win in a 1958 game against the defending NFL champions, the Detroit Lions. In 1959, he became head coach at the United States Coast Guard Academy (New London, Connecticut), where he served for seven years, and led the team to an undefeated season in 1963.

Graham returned to the NFL for two seasons (1964–1965) as a radio commentator for the American Football League's New York Jets. He later coached the Washington Redskins (1966–1968), but was unable to duplicate his earlier on-field success, as the team played to a 17–22–3 (.436) record during his tenure. After being replaced by Vince Lombardi, Graham served as the athletic director at the U.S. Coast Guard Academy, retiring in 1984.

Otto Graham's Career Statistics

						PASSING					RUSHING		
YEAR	TEAM	G	ATT	COMP	PCT	YDS	TD	INT	RATING	NO	YDS	AVG	TD
1946	Cleveland	14	174	95	54.6	1,834	17	5	112.1	30	–125	–4.2	1
1947	Cleveland	14	269	163	60.6	2,753	25	11	109.2	19	72	3.8	1
1948	Cleveland	14	333	173	52.0	2,713	25	15	85.6	23	146	6.3	6
1949	Cleveland	12	285	161	56.5	2,785	19	10	97.5	27	107	4.0	3
1950	Cleveland	12	253	137	54.2	1,943	14	20	64.7	55	145	2.6	6
1951	Cleveland	12	265	147	55.5	2,205	17	16	79.2	35	29	0.8	3
1952	Cleveland	12	364	181	49.7	2,816	20	24	66.6	42	130	3.1	4
1953	Cleveland	12	258	167	64.7	2,722	11	9	99.7	43	143	3.3	6
1954	Cleveland	12	240	142	59.2	2,092	11	17	73.5	63	114	1.8	8
1955	Cleveland	12	185	98	53.0	1,721	15	8	94.0	68	121	1.8	6
	AAFC	54	1061	592	55.8	10,085	86	41	99.1	99	200	2.0	11
	NFL	72	1565	872	55.7	13,499	88	94	78.2	306	682	2.2	33
	TOTALS	126	2,626	1,464	55.8	23,584	174	135	86.6	405	882	2.2	44

Otto Graham's NFL Coaching Record

YEAR	TEAM	W	L	T	WIN%	FINISH
1966	Washington	7	7	0	.500	5
1967	Washington	5	6	3	.455	3
1968	Washington	5	9	0	.357	3
	TOTALS	17	22	3	.436	

Sources: Pro Football Hall of Fame; Pro-Football-Reference.com

Granato, Catherine "Cammi" Michelle (born: March 25, 1971 in Downers Grove, Illinois); inducted into the Hockey Hall of Fame in 2010 as a player; Position: Right Wing / Center; first woman inducted into the U.S. Hockey Hall of Fame.

The 5'7", 141-pound Granata (a right-handed shooter) played in international tournaments for 13 years (1990–2005) and was the captain of the U.S. women's hockey team that won a gold medal in the 1998 Winter Olympics (Nagano, Japan). A graduate of Providence College (Providence, Rhode Island), she also played for Concordia University (Montreal, Quebec, Canada) and for boy's/men's teams since she was a teenager.

Granato played in every world championship event for the United States women's team from the inaugural event in 1990 to 2005; was named USA Women's Player of the Year in 1996; scored the first ever Olympic goal for the U.S women's hockey team (February 8, 1998) on its way to a gold medal in Nagano, Japan (with her as team captain); was inducted into the International Ice Hockey Hall of Fame (May 2008) along with women players Geraldine Heaney and Angela James; won the 2007 Lester Patrick Trophy for her contributions to hockey in the United States; in August 2008, she was inducted into the U.S. Hockey Hall of Fame (the first woman so honored); and she and Angela James are the first two women inducted into the Hockey Hall of Fame as players.

In her first year at college (Providence), Granato was named Freshman Player of the Year; selected Eastern College Athletic Conference's Women's Hockey Player of the Year (1996); and won back-to-back titles at Providence (1992–1993). While playing at Providence, she became a founding member of the United States Women's National Team and helped lead the squad to a silver medal at the inaugural Women's World Championships in 1990 in Ottawa, Canada.

After Providence, she moved to Montreal, Quebec, Canada to attend Concordia University and to obtain her master's degree in sports administration, graduating in 1997. While playing at the school, she helped the team win three consecutive provincial championships and in 1996, she was named USA Women's Player of the Year.

In 2002, she was captain of Team USA in Salt Lake City, Utah (winning a silver medal) and won a World Championship Title in 2005 (Linkoping, Sweden).

During her career, Granato won nine medals in the International Ice Hockey Federation (eight silvers [1990, 1992, 1994, 1997, 1999–2001, 2004] and a gold [2005]); seven medals in the 4 Nations Cup (five silver [1998–2000, 2002, 2004] and two gold [1997, 2003]); and two silver medals in the International Ice Hockey Federation's Pacific Rim Championship (1995–1996).

Cammi Granato's International Playing Statistics

YEAR	TOURNAMENT	GP	G	A	TP	PIM
1990	Women's World Championship (Silver – Ottawa, Canada)	5	9	5	14	4
1992	Women's World Championship (Silver – Tampere, Finland)	5	8	2	10	2
1994	Women's World Championship (Silver - Lake Placid, New York)	5	5	7	12	6
1995	Pacific Women's Championship (Silver - San Jose, California)	5	4	7	11	4
1996	Pacific Women's Championship (Silver – Vancouver, Canada)	5	5	3	8	0
1997	Women's World Championship (Silver – Kitchener, Canada)	5	2	3	5	2
1997	Women's World Championship (Silver – Kitchener, Canada)	5	5	3	8	4
1998	Olympic Games - Women's Hockey (Gold – Nagano, Japan)	6	4	4	8	0
1999	Women's World Championship (Silver – Espoo, Finland)	5	3	5	8	0
2000	Women's World Championship (Silver – Mississauga, Canada)	5	6	1	7	0
2001	Women's World Championship (Silver – Minneapolis, Minnesota)	5	7	6	13	0
2002	Olympic Games - Women's Hockey (Silver - Salt Lake City, Utah)	5	6	4	10	0
2004	Women's World Championship (Silver – Halifax, Canada)	3	0	2	2	0
2005	Women's World Championship (Gold – Linkoping, Sweden)	5	1	3	4	2
	TOTALS	69	65	55	120	24

Source: Hockey Hall of Fame

Grange, Harold Edward "Red" (born: June 13, 1903 in Forksville, Pennsylvania; died: January 28, 1991 in Lake Wales, Florida); inducted into the Pro Football Hall of Fame in 1963 as a player; Position: Halfback-Defensive Back; Uniform: #77; a charter member of both the College Football Hall of Fame and the Pro Football Hall of Fame; won the 1923 college national title with Illinois.

A three-time All-American (1923–1925) at the University of Illinois (Urbana-Champaign), Grange would play nine years of professional football (96 games) with the Chicago Bears (National Football League: 1925, 1929–1934), New

York Yankees (American Football League, 1926), and the New York Yankees (NFL, 1927). He was selected to the first-ever official All-Pro team in 1931 and was named an All-Pro again in 1932.

In the early 1920s, George Halas, owner of the Chicago Bears, hired college legend Grange to give the newly formed NFL much needed publicity since, in the early days of the league, very few college players turned professional after graduation. On Thanksgiving Day in 1925, ten days after Grange's last college game, 36,000 fans came to Wrigley Field (Chicago, Illinois) to see his professional debut against the Chicago Cardinals (which ended in a 0–0 tie). On December 6, 70,000 fans turned out at New York's Polo Grounds to see Grange and the Bears play the New York Giants (a 19–7 Chicago win).

Realizing that the 6', 180-pound Grange, nicknamed the "Galloping Ghost," was the NFL's premier draw, the league arranged a 17-game barnstorming tour over 67 days, which attracted thousands of new fans to professional football. Leaving the NFL in 1926 over a salary dispute, Grange formed the rival American Football League and played with the New York Yankees. When the AFL folded after only one season, the Yankees were allowed to join the league in 1927 and Grange played in 13 games before a knee injury ended his season. He sat out all of 1928 rehabbing his knee and returned to the Bears in 1929 (the Yankees having folded the year before), and stayed with the team until retiring in 1934.

Because his knee injury hampered his running, Grange was converted into a defensive back. In the 1933 NFL Championship Game, Grange made a touchdown-saving tackle in the final seconds to preserve the Bears' 23–21 win over the New York Giants. A year earlier, in the 1932 Championship Game, Grange had caught the game-winning touchdown pass from Bronko Nagurski in a Bears 9–0 win over the Portsmouth Spartans.

At Wheaton (Illinois) High School, he was a four-sport letter winner (football, basketball, baseball, track), and in his junior year, Grange scored 36 touchdowns and led the school to an undefeated season, and lost only one game as a senior. He was a charter member of both the College Football Hall of Fame (1951) and the Pro Football Hall of Fame.

In his very first college football game, Grange scored three touchdowns in a 24–7 win over Nebraska, and in seven games as a sophomore, he ran for 723 yards and scored 12 touchdowns, leading Illinois to an undefeated season (8–0) and to a national championship (1923). On October 18, 1924, in a 39–14 win over Michigan, he had a 95-yard kickoff return for a touchdown and scored three more touchdowns within 12 minutes in three runs totaling 168 yards (67, 56, 45). After scoring four touchdowns in the first quarter, he sat out the second quarter, returned in the second half, and played a role in two more touchdowns, for a total of six TDs in one game.

His jersey number 77 was retired at Illinois, one of only two retired numbers in the history of the school (the other being jersey number 50 worn by Dick Butkus). Grange Field at Wheaton Warrenville South High School is named in his honor.

Grange was the only unanimous choice to the all-time college All-America team, selected in 1969 by the Football Writers Association of America to celebrate college football's 100th anniversary. In 1999, 65 years after his last professional game, Grange was ranked number 80 on *The Sporting News*' list of the 100 Greatest Football Players. On January 15, 1978 at Super Bowl XII, Grange became the first person other than the game referee to toss the opening coin at a Super Bowl. In 2008, Grange was ranked number one on ESPN's Top 25 Players in College Football History.

While an established NFL star, Grange acted in Hollywood and starred in two silent movies, *One Minute to Play* (1926) and *Racing Romeo* (1927), as well as in a 12-part serial series *The Galloping Ghost* in 1931.

Red Grange's NFL Career Statistics

					PASSING					**RUSHING**		
Year	**Team**	**G**	**ATT**	**CMP**	**PCT**	**YDS**	**TD**	**INT**	**ATT**	**YDS**	**AVG**	**TD**
1925	Chicago	5	0	0	0.0	0	1	0	0	0	0.0	2
1927	New York	13	0	0	0.0	0	0	0	0	0	0.0	1
1929	Chicago	14	0	0	0.0	0	2	0	0	0	0.0	2
1930	Chicago	14	0	0	0.0	0	3	0	0	0	0.0	6
1931	Chicago	13	0	0	0.0	0	1	0	0	0	0.0	5
1932	Chicago	12	13	5	38.5	96	0	0	57	136	2.4	3
1933	Chicago	13	33	13	39.4	169	2	3	81	277	3.4	1
1934	Chicago	12	25	6	24.0	81	1	7	32	156	4.9	1
	TOTALS	96	71	24	33.8	346	10	10	170	569	3.3	21

Sources: College Football Hall of Fame; Pro Football Hall of Fame; Pro-Football-Reference.com

Granitza, Karl-Heinz (born: November 1, 1951 in Lünen, Germany); inducted into the National Soccer Hall of Fame and Museum in 2003 as a player; Position: Forward; won two NASL championships.

Granitza was purchased by the Chicago Sting (North American Soccer League) from Hertha Berlin in 1978. He scored in his NASL debut (May 17, 1978 against the New England Tea Men) and ended the season with 19 goals in 22 games.

In seven seasons with the Sting (199 games), he scored a total of 128 goals during regular-season play and scored 13 more in the playoffs. He led Chicago to two NASL Championships (1981 over the New York Cosmos and 1984 over the Toronto Blizzard), and in the 1981 playoffs, Granitza scored seven goals in ten games.

He played for Rochling Volkingen, DJK Gutersloh, TSG Eintracht Dortmund, and VfB 08 Lünen in Germany before being signed by Hertha Berlin. Originally a central striker, he played behind the front men in the latter days of his career. Despite his legendary goal-scoring ability, he was never selected to an NASL First All-Star Team.

Granitza finished his career as the NASL's second all-time leading scorer.

Karl-Heinz Granitza's NASL Career Statistics

YEAR	TEAM	G	GLS	ASST	PTS
1978	Chicago Sting	22	19	9	47
1979	Chicago Sting	30	20	10	50
1980	Chicago Sting	31	19	26	64
1981	Chicago Sting	31	19	17	55
1982	Chicago Sting	32	20	9	49
1983	Chicago Sting	29	15	18	48
1984	Chicago Sting	24	16	12	44
	TOTALS	199	128	101	357

Source: National Soccer Hall of Fame and Museum

Grant, Harold Peter, Jr. "Bud" (born: May 20, 1927 in Superior, Wisconsin); inducted into the Pro Football Hall of Fame in 1994 as a coach; first coach to take his team to four Super Bowls; won an NBA title with the Minneapolis Lakers.

Grant served as head coach of the National Football League's Minnesota Vikings for 18 seasons (1967–1983, 1985); compiled an overall 168–108–5 (.609) career record; led the team to 11 division championships; won the 1969 NFL Championship; and won three NFC titles (1973–1974, 1976). He was the first coach to have his teams appear in four Super Bowls (IV in 1970, VIII in 1974, IX in 1975, and XI in 1977), and he lost them all. As of this writing, the Vikings have never returned to the Super Bowl since Grant's coaching tenure ended. At the time of his retirement, only George Halas, Don Shula, Tom Landry, Curly Lambeau, Chuck Noll, Chuck Knox, and Paul Brown had more professional football wins.

He was a nine-letter athlete at the University of Minnesota (Twin Cities); a two-time All-Big Ten end in football; a two-year baseball star; played basketball for three years; and went on to play in the National Basketball Association, National Football League, and the Canadian Football League before becoming head coach of the Winnipeg Blue Bombers of the CFL (1957–1966). He led the team to six Grey Cup Championship games, winning four (1958–1959, 1961–1962) and losing twice (1957, 1965). After 10 seasons with the Bombers, Grant became head coach of the Vikings in 1967.

After graduating from Superior (Wisconsin) High School in 1945, Grant enlisted in the Navy during World War II and was assigned to the Great Lakes Naval Training Station (Illinois), where he played football under legendary coach Paul Brown. After leaving the military, Grant attended the University of Minnesota.

Although a first-round draft choice (14th overall selection) of the Philadelphia Eagles in 1950, the 6'3", 195-pound Grant delayed his NFL debut to play for the Minneapolis Lakers of the National Basketball Association. He played two years with the Lakers as a backup forward; averaged 2.6 points per game; and won the NBA title with the team in 1950. In 1951, Grant turned to professional football with the Eagles; played on defense as a rookie; and became the number two pass receiver in the NFL with 56 catches for 997 yards and seven touchdowns in 1952.

In 1953, he signed with the Winnipeg Blue Bombers; played with the team until 1956 as an offensive end and defensive back; and was named a Western Division All-Star three times. As of this writing, he still holds the CFL record of five interceptions in a playoff game (Oct. 28, 1953 in a 43–5 win over the Saskatchewan Roughriders). In 1967, he became the Vikings second head coach, replacing Norm Van Brocklin.

He was inducted into the Canadian Football Hall of Fame in 1983 as a builder.

Bud Grant's NFL Career Statistics

YEAR	TEAM	REGULAR SEASON W	L	T	WIN%	PLAYOFFS W	L	WIN%
1967	Minnesota Vikings	3	8	3	.273			
1968	Minnesota Vikings	8	6	0	.571	0	1	.000
1969	Minnesota Vikings	12	2	0	.857	2	1	.667
1970	Minnesota Vikings	12	2	0	.857	0	1	.000
1971	Minnesota Vikings	11	3	0	.786	0	1	.000
1972	Minnesota Vikings	7	7	0	.500			
1973	Minnesota Vikings	12	2	0	.857	2	1	.667
1974	Minnesota Vikings	10	4	0	.714	2	1	.667
1975	Minnesota Vikings	12	2	0	.857	0	1	.000
1976	Minnesota Vikings	11	2	1	.846	2	1	.667
1977	Minnesota Vikings	9	5	0	.643	1	1	.500
1978	Minnesota Vikings	8	7	1	.533	0	1	.000
1979	Minnesota Vikings	7	9	0	.438			
1980	Minnesota Vikings	9	7	0	.563	0	1	.000
1981	Minnesota Vikings	7	9	0	.438			
1982	Minnesota Vikings	5	4	0	.556	1	1	.500
1983	Minnesota Vikings	8	8	0	.500			
1985	Minnesota Vikings	7	9	0	.438			
	TOTALS	158	96	5	.622	10	12	.455

Sources: Pro Football Hall of Fame; Pro-Football-Reference.com

Grant, Michael "Mike" (born: January 1874 in Montreal, Quebec, Canada; died: August 19, 1955); inducted into the Hockey Hall of Fame in 1950 as a player; Position: Defenseman; won five Stanley Cup titles.

Grant played nine pre-National Hockey League seasons (1893–1902) with the Montreal Victorias of the Amateur Hockey Association of Canada (Canadian Amateur Hockey League). In addition to hockey, he also played amateur lacrosse in Montreal.

He was a member of the junior champion Crystal Junior Hockey Club in 1891; won two Intermediate championships with the Crystal Intermediates (1892–1893); and with the Montreal Victorias, he won five Stanley Cup titles (1895–1898, winning the Cup twice in 1896).

He retired as a player in 1902, but returned to the game as a referee in the March 1905 Stanley Cup challenge between the Rat Portage Thistles and the Ottawa Senators.

Mike Grant's Career Statistics

SEASON	TEAM	LEAGUE	REGULAR SEASON GP	G	A	TP	PLAYOFFS GP	G	A	TP
1893–1894	Montreal Maples	MCJHL								
1893–1894	Montreal Victorias	AHAC	5	0	0	0	1	0	0	0
1894–1895	Montreal Victorias	AHAC	8	1	0	1				
1895–1896	Montreal Victorias	AHAC	8	3	0	3				
1895–1896	Montreal Victorias	St-Cup					2	0	0	0
1896–1897	Montreal Victorias	AHAC	8	3	0	3				
1896–1897	Montreal Victorias	St-Cup					1	0	0	0
1897–1898	Montreal Victorias	AHAC	8	1	0	1				
1898–1899	Montreal Victorias	CAHL	7	2	0	2				
1898–1899	Montreal Victorias	St-Cup					2	0	0	0
1899–1900	Montreal Victorias	CAHL	2	0	0	0				
1900–1901	Montreal Shamrocks	CAHL	2	0	0	0				
1900–1901	Montreal Shamrocks	St-Cup					2	0	0	0
1901–1902	Montreal Victorias	CAHL	7	0	0	0				

Sources: Hockey Hall of Fame; Hockey-Reference.com

Grant, Ulysses Franklin "Frank" (born: August 1, 1865 in Pittsfield, Massachusetts; died: May 27, 1937 in New York, New York); inducted into the National Baseball Hall of Fame and Museum in 2006 as a player by the Negro Leagues Committee; Position: Second Base; Bats: Right; Throws: Right; first black player to play on the same team in organized baseball for three consecutive seasons.

One of the greatest black players of the 19th century, Grant played six seasons in the integrated International League (minor leagues) before racism forced him to leave organized baseball and play solely with traveling black teams for the rest of his 20-year career. Primarily an infielder, the 5'7", 155-pound Grant hit .300 or more each of his years in the minors; while in the International League, twenty-five percent of his hits were for extra bases; and he played with the all-black Cuban Giants of the 1890s, before retiring in 1903.

During his career, he played for Meriden (Connecticut, Eastern League, 1886); Buffalo Bisons (International League, 1886–1888); Harrisburg Ponies (Independent, Atlantic Association); Cuban X-Giants (Independent); Genuine Cuban Giants (Independent); and the Philadelphia Giants (Independent).

In 1887, he led the International League with 11 home runs and 49 extra-base hits; led the Bisons with 40 stolen bases; and Grant was the first black player to play on the same team (Buffalo Bisons) in organized baseball for three consecutive seasons.

Source: National Baseball Hall of Fame and Museum

Green, Darrell Ray (born: February 15, 1960 in Houston, Texas); inducted into the Pro Football Hall of Fame in 2008 as a player; Position: Cornerback; Uniform: #28; set an NFL record with at least one interception for 19 straight seasons; won two Super Bowls.

The 5'8", 176-pound Green played his entire 20-year (1983–2002, 295 games) National Football League career with the Washington Redskins, after being a first-round pick (28th overall selection) of the team in the 1983 NFL Draft. As a rookie, Green scored a touchdown the very first time he touched the football, a 61-yard punt return in a preseason game against the Atlanta Falcons. He started all 16 regular-season games as a rookie; finished fourth on the team in tackles (109); and was runner-up for the Associated Press NFL Rookie of the Year Award.

He set an NFL record with at least one interception for 19 straight seasons; holds the team record for longest fumble return (78 yards in a 30–24 win against the Indianapolis Colts on November 7, 1993); was named to the NFL's 1990s All-Decade Team; selected to seven Pro Bowls (1984, 1986–1987, 1990–1991, 1996–1997); and was a four time All-Pro selection (1986–1987, 1990–1991). Three times in his career, he had five interceptions in a season (1984, 1986, 1991), and he had three interceptions in a game against the Detroit Lions on November 15, 1987.

Green played in four NFC championship games and three Super Bowls (winning SB XXII in January 1988 and SB XXVI in January 1992, while losing in SB XVIII in 1984). He won the 1996 Walter Payton Man of the Year Award (for his volunteer and charity work, as well as excellence on the field); won the 1997 Bart Starr Award (for leadership in the home, on the field, and in the community); was added to the Redskins' Ring of Fame in 2002; and was named one of the 70 Greatest Redskins in 2002.

Green's college football career (1978–1982) at Texas A&I University (now known as Texas A&M-Kingsville), earned him a 2004 induction into the College Football Hall of Fame. He left after his junior year to join the NFL. Green and former Los Angeles/St. Louis Rams offensive lineman Jackie Slater are the only players in NFL history to play for the same team for 20 seasons.

In 1999, while still active, he was ranked number 81 on *The Sporting News*' list of the 100 Greatest Football Players.

In 1988, Green created the Darrell Green Youth Life Foundation, a faith-based charitable organization to "meet the needs of children, their families, and the communities in which they live."

Darrell Green's Career Statistics

			INTERCEPTIONS			
YEAR	**TEAM**	**G**	**NO**	**YDS**	**AVG**	**TD**
1983	Washington	16	2	7	3.5	0
1984	Washington	16	5	91	18.2	1
1985	Washington	16	2	0	0.0	0
1986	Washington	16	5	9	1.8	0

			INTERCEPTIONS			
YEAR	**TEAM**	**G**	**NO**	**YDS**	**AVG**	**TD**
1987	Washington	12	3	65	21.7	0
1988	Washington	15	1	12	12.0	0
1989	Washington	7	2	0	0.0	0
1990	Washington	16	4	20	5.0	1
1991	Washington	16	5	47	9.4	0
1992	Washington	8	1	15	15.0	0
1993	Washington	16	4	10	2.5	0
1994	Washington	16	3	32	10.7	1
1995	Washington	16	3	42	14.0	1
1996	Washington	16	3	84	28.0	1
1997	Washington	16	1	83	83.0	1
1998	Washington	16	3	36	12.0	0
1999	Washington	16	3	33	11.0	0
2000	Washington	13	3	35	11.7	0
2001	Washington	16	1	0	0.0	0
2002	Washington	16	0	0	0.0	0
	TOTALS	295	54	621	11.5	6

Sources: College Football Hall of Fame; Pro Football Hall of Fame; Pro-Football-Reference.com

Green, Wilfred Thomas "Shorty" (born: July 17, 1896 in Sudbury, Ontario, Canada; died: April 19, 1960); inducted into the Hockey Hall of Fame in 1962 as a player; won the 1919 Allan Cup; scored the first-ever goal in the new Madison Square Garden.

After graduating from Sudbury High School, Green began his hockey career with the Northern Ontario senior title-winning Sudbury team in 1915; played in the 1917 Allan Cup series as a member of the 227th Battalion team (of the Ontario Hockey Association-Senior); and then served two-and-one-half years in the army during World War I.

After leaving the military in December 1918, he resumed his hockey career with the 1919 Hamilton Tigers (of the OHA-Sr.) Allan Cup-winning team, and then played four seasons with the Sudbury Wolves of the Northern Ontario Hockey Association.

Green played four National Hockey League seasons (1923–1927) with the Hamilton Tigers (1923–1925) and the New York Americans (1925–1927), when Hamilton moved to New York. He played on the "Tiger Line" with Billy Burch and brother Red Green with the Americans, and he scored the first-ever goal in the new Madison Square Garden (New York, New York).

After retiring in 1927, Green coached the Americans during the 1927–1928 season, before moving on to coach the Duluth Hornets of the American Hockey Association in 1928–1929. He returned to the game as a player intermittently from 1929 to 1932, before briefly coaching the Hamilton Tigers in the Ontario Hockey Association; and finally retired from hockey for good in 1937.

Wilfred Green's Career Statistics

			REGULAR SEASON					PLAYOFFS				
SEASON	**TEAM**	**LEAGUE**	**GP**	**G**	**A**	**TP**	**PIM**	**GP**	**G**	**A**	**TP**	**PIM**
1914–1915	Sudbury All-Stars	Exhib.	12	19	3	22						
1914–1915	Sudbury All-Stars	Al-Cup	3	6	0	6						
1915–1916	Sudbury All-Stars	Exhib.										
1916–1917	Hamilton 227th Battalion	OHA-Sr.	8	17	0	17						
1918–1919	Hamilton Tigers	OHA-Sr.	8	12	3	15		4	5	3	8	
1918–1919	Hamilton Tigers	Al-Cup	2	3	0	3						
1919–1920	Sudbury Wolves	NOHA	6	23	4	27	16	7	13	4	17	8
1920–1921	Sudbury Wolves	NOHA	4	4	2	6	7					
1921–1922	Sudbury Wolves	NOHA	9	5	4	9	9					
1922–1923	Sudbury Wolves	NOHA	7	3	1	4	16	1	0	1	1	2
1923–1924	Hamilton Tigers	NHL	22	7	6	13	31					
1924–1925	Hamilton Tigers	NHL	28	18	9	27	63					
1925–1926	New York Americans	NHL	32	6	4	10	40					

SEASON	TEAM	LEAGUE	REGULAR SEASON GP	G	A	TP	PIM	PLAYOFFS GP	G	A	TP	PIM
1926–1927	New York Americans	NHL	21	2	1	3	17					
1927–1928	New York Americans	NHLMGNT		3	0	3	69					
1928–1929	Duluth Hornets	AHA		1	1	2	47					
1929–1930	Duluth Hornets	AHA	2	0	0	0	2					
1930–1931	Duluth Hornets	AHA	1	0	0	0	8					
	NHL TOTALS		103	33	20	53	151					

Sources: Hockey Hall of Fame; Hockey-Reference.com

Greenberg, Henry Benjamin "Hank" (born: January 1, 1911 in New York, New York; died: September 4, 1986 in Beverly Hills, California); inducted into the National Baseball Hall of Fame and Museum in 1956 as a player; Position: First Base; Bats: Right; Throws: Right; Uniform: #5; first Jewish player voted Most Valuable Player in either league; first Jewish player elected into the baseball hall of fame; won two World Series; two-time American League Most Valuable Player.

Despite losing four seasons to World War II and another to a wrist injury, Greenberg was still able to hit 331 home runs and hit 40 or more in a season four times (1937–1938, 1940, 1946). Making his major league debut on September 14, 1930, he played 13 seasons with the Detroit Tigers (1930, 1933–1941, 1945–1946) and the Pittsburgh Pirates (1947); played in four World Series, winning two (1935, 1945) and losing two (1934, 1940); was a five-time All-Star (1937–1939, 1940, 1945); and was twice named American League Most Valuable Player (1935, 1940).

Baseball's first Jewish star, the 6'3", 210-pound Greenberg was a power hitter who hit for average; drove in 170 runs in his 1935 MVP season when the Tigers won the World Series; had 183 RBIs in 1937; and hit .318 in Detroit's four World Series. He is one of just three players to win the MVP award at two different positions, first base (1935) and left field (1940).

While attending James Monroe High School (Bronx, New York), he was an All-City athlete in soccer and basketball (helping the team win the City Championship), and played first base for the school's team. In 1929, Greenberg spent one semester at New York University (New York) on an athletic scholarship, before signing a contract with the Detroit Tigers.

He began his three-year minor league career in 1930 with the Hartford (Connecticut) Senators (A-Level, Eastern League), where he played 17 games and with the Raleigh (North Carolina) Capitals (C-Level, Piedmont League), where he hit .314 with 19 home runs. In 1931, he played for the Evansville (Indiana) Hubs in the Three I League (Illinois-Iowa-Indiana League), batting .318 with 15 home runs and 85 RBIs. In 1932, he played with the Beaumont Exporters (Texas League), hitting 39 home runs with 131 RBIs. After winning the MVP Award at the end of the season, he was promoted to the Tigers in 1933, where he hit .301 and drove in 87 runs as a rookie.

In 1935, he became the first Jewish player voted Most Valuable Player in either league, while helping Detroit win that season's World Series.

In May 1940, Greenberg's baseball career was interrupted when he was drafted into the Army during World War II. In August of that year, after Congress decided that men over 28 years old would not have to serve, he was discharged and returned to the Tigers. However, when the Japanese bombed Pearl Harbor in Hawaii on December 7, 1941, the U.S. declared war and Greenberg became the first major league player to enlist, even though he had already been excused. He served in the Army Air Corps in the China-Burma-India theater.

When the war ended in 1945, Greenberg returned to the Tigers and hit a home run in his first game back (July 1, 1945 against the Philadelphia Athletics), and guided the team to another World Series title. He played two more seasons (one with Detroit and his last with the Pirates) before retiring.

After retiring as a player, Greenberg became the first Jewish owner-general manager in baseball and oversaw the 1954 Cleveland Indians team that won a record 111 games. He and Bill Veeck purchased the Chicago White Sox in 1959 and led the team to the pennant for the first time in 40 years. In 1961, Greenberg sold his baseball interests and went on to a successful investment banking career on Wall Street.

As of this writing, he still has the eighth highest career slugging percentage (.605), and in 1930, he was the youngest player (age 19) in the majors.

In 1947, he was traded to the Pirates, and was one of the few opposing players to welcome Jackie Robinson into the majors. Having endured years of taunts and anti-Semitism, he prepared Robinson on what to expect.

In 1983, the Tigers retired his uniform number five; in 1999, despite playing basically half a career, Greenberg was ranked number 37 on *The Sporting News*' list of the 100 Greatest Baseball Players; and, also in 1999, he was a finalist for the Major League Baseball All-Century Team. He has been inducted into the International Jewish Sports Hall of Fame (1979); the Jewish American Hall of Fame (1991); and the National Jewish Sports Hall of Fame (1996).

Greenberg was one of the few baseball people who testified on behalf of Curt Flood in 1970, when the St. Louis Cardinal outfielder challenged the reserve clause. In 2006, he was featured on a United States postage stamp, one of a block of four honoring Baseball Sluggers (which included Mickey Mantle, Mel Ott, and Roy Campanella).

Hank Greenberg's Career Statistics

YEAR	TEAM	LG	G	AB	R	H	2B	3B	HR	RBI	BB	SO	SB	AVG	SLG
1930	Detroit	AL	1	1	0	0	0	0	0	0	0	0	0	.000	.000
1933	Detroit	AL	117	449	59	135	33	3	12	87	46	78	6	.301	.468
1934	Detroit	AL	153	593	118	201	63	7	26	139	63	93	9	.339	.600
1935	Detroit	AL	152	619	121	203	46	16	36	170	87	91	4	.328	.628
1936	Detroit	AL	12	46	10	16	6	2	1	16	9	6	1	.348	.630
1937	Detroit	AL	154	594	137	200	49	14	40	183	102	101	8	.337	.668
1938	Detroit	AL	155	556	144	175	23	4	58	146	119	92	7	.315	.683
1939	Detroit	AL	138	500	112	156	42	7	33	112	91	95	8	.312	.622
1940	Detroit	AL	148	573	129	195	50	8	41	150	93	75	6	.340	.670
1941	Detroit	AL	19	67	12	18	5	1	2	12	16	12	1	.269	.463
1945	Detroit	AL	78	270	47	84	20	2	13	60	42	40	3	.311	.544
1946	Detroit	AL	142	523	91	145	29	5	44	127	80	88	5	.277	.604
1947	Pitts-burgh	NL	125	402	71	100	13	2	25	74	104	73	0	.249	.478
	TO-TALS		1,394	5,193	1,051	1,628	379	71	331	1,276	852	844	58	.313	.605

Sources: Baseball-Reference.com; National Baseball Hall of Fame and Museum

Greene, Charles Edward "Mean Joe" (born: September 24, 1946 in Temple, Texas); inducted into the Pro Football Hall of Fame in 1987 as a player; Position: Defensive Tackle; Uniform: #75; in Super Bowl IX (1975), he became the first player ever to record an interception, a forced fumble, and a fumble recovery in a single Super Bowl; won five Super Bowl championships, four as a player.

Greene attended North Texas State University (University of North Texas, Denton) from 1966 to 1968 and led the team to a 23–5–1 record during his three seasons. After being named a consensus All-American in 1968, he was the number one choice (fourth overall selection) in the 1969 National Football League Draft of the Pittsburgh Steelers, a team he would play for his entire 13-year career (181 games, 1969–1981). With the 6'4", 275-pound Greene's size, strength, and quickness, he became a cornerstone of the defensive unit that became known as the "Steel Curtain," (which included L.C. Greenwood, Dwight White, and Ernie Holmes) that dominated the National Football League during the 1970s.

He was named NFL Defensive Rookie of the Year in 1969; NFL Defensive Player of Year twice (1972, 1974); All-Pro and/or All-American Football Conference nine times; played in six AFC title games and four Super Bowls, winning them all (Super Bowl IX in 1975, Super Bowl X in 1976, Super Bowl XIII in 1979, and Super Bowl XIV in 1980); and was selected to 10 Pro Bowls (1969–1976, 1978–1979). Greene was named to the NFL 1970s All-Decade Team and to the NFL 75th Anniversary All-Time Team. In 1999, he was ranked number 14 on *The Sporting News*' list of the 100 Greatest Football Players, the highest-ranked Steelers and second highest ranked defensive tackle behind Bob Lilly of the Dallas Cowboys.

After retiring as a player, he became an assistant under Steelers' head coach Chuck Noll in 1987, and spent the next 16 years as an assistant coach with the Steelers, Miami Dolphins, and Arizona Cardinals. In 2004, he was named the special assistant for player personnel for the Steelers, and won his fifth Super Bowl ring when the team beat the Seattle Seahawks 21–10 in Super Bowl XL (February 2006).

Greene has appeared in numerous commercials, one of which is considered one of the most famous sports commercials of all time. In the classic 1979 commercial, a young boy gives an obviously exhausted Greene a bottle of Coke as he walks into a tunnel in the stadium after a game. The gesture prompts "Mean Joe" to smile (which was in contrast to his public persona) and give the kid his game jersey. The commercial was listed as one of the top ten commercials of all time by *TV Guide*. The success of the ad prompted Coke to adapt it to other countries featuring their own local sports stars.

Greene was inducted into the College Football Hall of Fame in 1984 and into the East-West Shrine Game Hall of Fame in 2006.

Sources: College Football Hall of Fame; Pro Football Hall of Fame

Greer, Donald (born: June 12, 1927 in Geneva, New York; died: May 18, 1998 in Castro Valley, California); inducted into the National Soccer Hall of Fame and Museum in 1985 as a builder; won the San Francisco League championship in 1958; founded the California Youth Soccer Association.

Greer played soccer as a schoolboy in England and later served in the Merchant Navy during World War II. He was a player and administrator in Northern California soccer for decades after returning to the United States from England in 1946. He played for San Francisco Olympic, Hayward United, and Hermania Soccer Club in the San Francisco-Hayward area from 1946 to 1964. He won the San Francisco League championship with Hermania in 1958, and was a finalist in the California Soccer Association North Jr. Cup from 1959 to 1961.

He served as coach and team manager with Hermania (1956–1964); founded Hayward United U12-U16-U18 teams in 1958; and led the U18s to the California State Title in 1965. Greer served as an official with the California State Association-North from 1962 to 1974, and was a United States Soccer Federation vice-president from 1972 until 1984. He founded the California Youth Soccer Association in 1968 and served as its president until 1975. He also founded the United States Youth Soccer Association in 1974 and served as its chairman until 1984.

Greer launched the McGuire Cup (presented annually to the winner of the United States Youth Soccer National Championship); the Olympic Development Program; and established regional and sub-regional youth programs for the state associations during his tenure.

As chairman of the USYSA, Greer oversaw the number of players participating in soccer grow from 32,000 to over 1.3 million. He received the USYSA Founder's Award in 1992, and the Greer Cup (presented annually to the Boys U-17 National Champion), was created in 1993 and is named in his honor. He served for years as chairman of the California Old Timers Association, and was inducted into the California Youth Soccer Association Hall of Fame in 1975.

Source: National Soccer Hall of Fame and Museum

Greer, Harold Everett "Hal" (born: June 26, 1936 in Huntington, West Virginia); inducted into the Naismith Memorial Basketball Hall of Fame in 1982 as a player; Position: Guard; Uniform: #15; first African-American to play for a major college team in West Virginia; won an NBA championship.

Greer won a state championship in 1953 and was named All-Conference and All-State in 1954 while attending Douglass High School (Huntington, West Virginia). After graduating in 1954, he went to Marshall University (Huntington, West Virginia), where he was a two-time All-Conference player (1957–1958); the team's high scorer and Conference Most Valuable Player in 1958; received an Associated Press All-America Honorable Mention (1958); led the squad in 71 games as its first black scholarship athlete; and compiled a career average of 19.4 points and 10.8 rebounds per game.

When he graduated in 1959, Greer held the school's career record for field goal percentage (54.6 percent), hitting 531 of 974 attempts. After college, he was a second-round draft choice (sixth pick in the second round, 13th overall selection) of the Syracuse Nationals, and would go on to play 15 National Basketball Association seasons with the Nationals (1958–1963) and the Philadelphia 76ers (1964–1973), the new name of the Nationals when the team left Syracuse and moved to Philadelphia.

In 1967, he averaged 22 points per game and joined future hall-of-famers Wilt Chamberlain and Billy Cunningham to lead the 76ers to the NBA Championship; played in 10 consecutive NBA All-Star Games (1961–1970); was named NBA All-Star Game MVP in 1968; set the record for most points scored in a quarter (19) during the 1968 All-Star Game; selected to the All-NBA Second Team seven consecutive seasons (1963–1969); and scored 120 points in 10 All-Star Games.

Greer's jersey number 15 was retired by the 76ers; his college jersey number 16 was retired by Marshall University; and he was named to the NBA 50th Anniversary Team in 1996.

The 6'2", 175-pound Greer was one of the NBA's most durable players. When he retired in 1973, Greer had played in 1,122 games, most in league history. He is the only African-American athlete from West Virginia to be inducted into a major sports hall of fame.

Hal Greer's NBA Career Statistics

SEASON	TEAM	G	MIN	FG	FT	TRB	AST	PTS
1958–1959	Syracuse	68	1,625	308	137	196	101	753
1959–1960	Syracuse	70	1,979	388	148	303	188	924
1960–1961	Syracuse	79	2,763	623	305	455	302	1,551
1961–1962	Syracuse	71	2,705	644	331	524	313	1,619
1962–1963	Syracuse	80	2,631	600	362	457	275	1,562

SEASON	TEAM	G	MIN	FG	FT	TRB	AST	PTS
1963–1964	Philadelphia	80	3,157	715	435	484	374	1,865
1964–1965	Philadelphia	70	2,600	539	335	355	313	1,413
1965–1966	Philadelphia	80	3,326	703	413	473	384	1,819
1966–1967	Philadelphia	80	3,086	699	367	422	303	1,765
1967–1968	Philadelphia	82	3,263	777	422	444	372	1,976
1968–1969	Philadelphia	82	3,311	732	432	435	414	1,896
1969–1970	Philadelphia	80	3,024	705	352	376	405	1,762
1970–1971	Philadelphia	81	3,060	591	326	364	369	1,508
1971–1972	Philadelphia	81	2,410	389	181	271	316	959
1972–1973	Philadelphia	38	848	91	32	106	111	214
	TOTALS	1,122	39,788	8,504	4,578	5,665	4,540	21,586

Sources: Basketball-Reference.com; Naismith Memorial Basketball Hall of Fame

Gregg, Alvis Forrest (born: October 18, 1933 in Birthright, Texas); inducted into the Pro Football Hall of Fame in 1977 as a player; Position: Offensive Tackle-Guard; Uniform: #75; played in a then-record 188 consecutive games; won three Super Bowls.

After graduating from Southern Methodist University (Dallas, Texas) with a letter in football, Gregg was the number two draft pick in 1956 (20th selection overall) of the Green Bay Packers. One of the best tackles ever to play the game, he was once described by legendary coach Vince Lombardi as the "best player I ever coached."

The 6'4", 249-pound Gregg played 15 NFL seasons (193 games) with the Green Bay Packers (1956, 1958–1970) and the Dallas Cowboys (1971). He played in a then-record 188 consecutive games (1956–1971); was selected All-NFL eight straight seasons (1960–1967); played in nine Pro Bowls (1959–1964, 1966–1968); and played on five NFL championship teams with the Packers (1961–1962, 1965–1967) and three Super Bowl winners (SB I in 1967 and SB II in 1968 with the Packers and SB VI in 1972 with the Cowboys). He was named to the NFL 1960s All-Decade Team and the NFL 75th Anniversary All-Time Team. In 1965, he was selected All-NFL at both guard (by the Associated Press) and tackle (by United Press International).

After retiring as a player, Gregg served as an assistant coach with the San Diego Chargers in 1973; held the same job with the Cleveland Browns the next season; and from 1975 to 1977, he was the Browns' head coach. After sitting out the 1978 season, Gregg returned to coaching in 1979 with the Canadian Football League's Toronto Argonauts, before becoming the head coach of the Cincinnati Bengals in 1980, where he stayed until 1983. His most successful coaching season came in 1981, when he led the Bengals to a 12–4 regular-season record and defeated the San Diego Chargers 27–7 in the AFC championship game, before losing 26–21 to the San Francisco 49ers in Super Bowl XVI.

He finished his NFL coaching career with the Packers (1984–1987) and retired with an overall NFL record of 75–85–1. After leaving the NFL ranks, he coached for two years at his alma mater in 1989 and 1990, after he was brought to the university to revive a football program that had not been allowed to compete for two years due to National Collegiate Athletic Association violations, the so-called "death penalty" imposed by the NCAA in 1986. After compiling a 3–19 record, Gregg went on to serve as SMU's Athletic Director from 1990 to 1994.

He returned to the CFL with the Shreveport Pirates in 1994–1995, during the league's brief attempt to expand into the United States. His overall CFL coaching record was 13–39. In 2005, he was appointed Vice President of Football Operations for the Ottawa Renegades of the CFL, a team that suspended operations in 2006.

Forrest Gregg's NFL Coaching Statistics

		REGULAR SEASON				PLAYOFFS		
YEAR	TEAM	W	L	T	WIN%	W	L	WIN%
1975	Cleveland Browns	3	11	0	.214			
1976	Cleveland Browns	9	5	0	.643			
1977	Cleveland Browns	6	7	0	.462			
1980	Cincinnati Bengals	6	10	0	.375			
1981	Cincinnati Bengals	12	4	0	.750	2	1	.667
1982	Cincinnati Bengals	7	2	0	.778	0	1	.000
1983	Cincinnati Bengals	7	9	0	.438			
1984	Green Bay Packers	8	8	0	.500			
1985	Green Bay Packers	8	8	0	.500			

YEAR	TEAM	REGULAR SEASON W	L	T	WIN%	PLAYOFFS W	L	WIN%
1986	Green Bay Packers	4	12	0	.250			
1987	Green Bay Packers	5	9	1	.357			
	Cleveland	18	23	0	.439	0	0	
	Cincinnati	32	25	0	.561	2	2	.500
	Green Bay	25	37	1	.403	0	0	
	TOTALS	75	85	1	.469	2	2	.500

Sources: Pro Football Hall of Fame; Pro-Football-Reference.com

Gregory, Jim (born: November 4, 1935 in Port Colborne, Ontario, Canada); inducted into the Hockey Hall of Fame in 2007 as a builder; was the trainer on the 1961 Memorial Cup-winning team; won two Memorial Cups as a coach.

In 1953, while attending St. Michael's College School (Toronto, Ontario, Canada), he served as the trainer for the school's Junior "A" Majors team (Ontario Hockey Association). Eventually becoming the team's manager, in 1961, he was part of the organization that won the Memorial Cup as junior champions of Canada.

In an attempt to lower travel expenses, the Metro Junior "A" Hockey League was formed, and included St. Michaels, the Toronto Marlboros, and several Junior "B" teams from the Toronto area. Gregory maintained his position as the team's manager for the single season it played in the league before withdrawing.

Moving on, he became the manager of the Neil McNeil High School (a Catholic secondary school in Scarborough, Ontario, Canada) hockey team and led the Maroons to back-to-back league championships (1962–1963). When the short-lived league folded, players from both Neil McNeil and the Marlboros (which were both junior affiliates of the National Hockey League's Toronto Maple Leafs) were combined into one team and called the Toronto Marlboros. Gregory oversaw the merging of the two teams into one squad and coached the Marlboros to two Memorial Cup championships (1964, 1967).

Working for the Toronto Maple Leafs, he joined the Western Hockey League's Vancouver Canucks as head coach in the 1967–1968 season. After one year in the WHL, he was promoted to the NHL to run the franchise's scouting operations. In the spring of 1969, Gregory became the Leafs' General Manager, a position he held until 1979. During his tenure, the team reached the playoffs in eight of 10 seasons, but was never able to win a Stanley Cup title.

In 1979, Gregory was hired by the NHL as Director of Central Scouting, and in 1986, he was appointed Executive Director of Hockey Operations for the NHL. Currently, he operates as the Senior Vice President of Hockey Operations for the NHL, and since 1998, he has served as the chairman of the Hockey Hall of Fame's Selection Committee.

Source: Hockey Hall of Fame

Gretzky, Wayne Douglas (born: January 26, 1961 in Brantford, Ontario, Canada); inducted into the Hockey Hall of Fame as a player in 1999; Position: Center; Uniform: #99; first rookie to win the Hart Memorial Trophy; first hockey player, and the first Canadian, to be named Associated Press Male Athlete of the Year; won four Stanley Cup championships; coached the Canadian team to a 2002 Olympic gold medal; holds the record for most MVP awards of any player in North American professional sports (nine).

Nicknamed "The Great One;" seemingly born to break records; and generally recognized as the greatest player ever to play in the National Hockey League, the 6', 185-pound Gretzky enjoyed an incredible 20-year (1979–1999) career with the Edmonton Oilers (1979–1988), Los Angeles Kings (1988–1995), St. Louis Blues (1995–1996), and the New York Rangers (1996–1999).

At age 16, Gretzky represented Canada internationally for the first time in January 1978 at the World Junior Championship in Quebec City, the youngest player ever to do so. He led the tournament in scoring and was named the top center. Not yet reaching the minimum National Hockey League age of 20, in 1978, Gretzky joined the Indianapolis Racers of the World Hockey Association. When the team folded after only eight games, he was sold to the Edmonton Oilers, also of the WHA.

On Gretzky's 18th birthday, the Oilers signed him to a 20-year personal services contract, the longest in hockey history. He won the Lou Kaplan Trophy (Rookie of the Year) and finished third in league scoring with 110 points. After the league folded after his only season, the team joined the NHL.

In his first full NHL season (1979–1980), Gretzky tied Marcel Dionne for the scoring title, but lost the Art Ross Trophy because Dionne had more goals. He wasn't eligible for the Calder Trophy (NHL Rookie of the Year) because the league had ruled that players from the WHA could not be considered rookies, but he did win the Hart Memorial Trophy as the NHL's Most Valuable Player, the first time a first-year player had ever won the award. Gretzky went on to win the award eight more times.

In the 1980–1981 season, he won his first of seven consecutive scoring titles and broke Bobby Orr's assists record with 109. The next season, he surpassed Phil Esposito's record of 76 goals, by scoring 92, a mark many feel will never be surpassed. He accumulated a total of 212 points, the first of four times he would score more than 200 points in a season, an accomplishment no other player has done since.

In 1982, Gretzky became the first hockey player, and the first Canadian, to be named Associated Press Male Athlete of the Year. He was also named *Sports Illustrated* magazine's 1982 "Sportsman of the Year."

Gretzky led the Oilers to four Stanley Cup championships (1984–1985, 1987–1988), the only titles of his career. After winning the Cup in 1988, he gathered the team at center ice for a group photograph, starting a tradition that is now practiced by almost every title-winning team at every level of play.

On June 25, 1984, Gretzky was named an officer of the Order of Canada (OC) for outstanding contribution to the sport of hockey. Since the Order ceremonies are always held during the hockey season, it took 13 years before he could accept the honor, after retiring as a player.

After the 1987–1988 season, he was traded to the Los Angeles Kings and would never play for a Canadian NHL team again. The trade was a boon to the Kings as his presence guaranteed a sellout for every home game for the first time in franchise history.

Outside of hockey, Gretzky, Kings' owner Bruce McNall, and actor John Candy bought the Toronto Argonauts of the Canadian Football League, and Gretzky and McNall became more involved in other non-hockey businesses and activities.

Gretzky's arrival in California helped the NHL penetrate deeper into the United States, and during his tenure in Los Angeles, California received two more NHL franchises (the Mighty Ducks of Anaheim and the San Jose Sharks). In 1990, the Associated Press named him Male Athlete of the Decade. While with the Kings, he scored his 802nd goal to pass Gordie Howe as the all-time leading goal scorer in NHL history, and his 1,852nd point also passed Howe as the NHL's all-time scoring leader.

He was traded to the St. Louis Blues in 1996, but only played 18 regular-season games, before signing with the New York Rangers, where he stayed until retiring after the 1998–1999 season.

During his career, Gretzky set 40 regular-season records; 15 playoff records; and six All-Star records. He scored more than 100 points in a season 15 times (13 consecutively), and when he left the game, the NHL retired his jersey number 99 permanently.

Gretzky played in the NHL's All-Star Game every season he was in the league, and was the first player to be named the Game's MVP with three different teams. Internationally, he played in the World Championship in 1982 and in each Canada Cup (1981 [silver], 1984 [gold], 1987 [gold], 1991 [gold]). He also played in the 1996 World Cup (the replacement tournament for the Canada Cup), in which Canada placed second to the United States for the first time ever. He also played on the Canadian National Team at the 1998 Olympic Winter Games in Nagano, Japan, that finished a disappointing fourth, failing to medal.

When he retired, Gretzky's regular-season records included most goals in a season (92); most assists in a season (163); most points in a season (215); fastest to reach 50 goals (39 games); most goals in a 50-game period (61); and most career regular-season goals (894), assists (1,963), points (2,857), and hat tricks (50). His point total, regular-season and playoffs, is 3,239. He had more career assists than any other player has ever gained in total points.

Gretzky won the Conn Smythe Trophy (playoff MVP) twice (1985, 1988); the Lester B. Pearson Award (regular-season MVP as voted by the NHL Players Association) five times (1982–1985, 1987); the Lady Byng Memorial Trophy for sportsmanship five times (1980, 1991–1992, 1994, 1999); the NHL Plus/Minus Award for best plus-minus rating four times (1982, 1984–1985, 1987); Chrysler-Dodge/NHL Performer of the Year three times (1985–1987); the Lester Patrick Trophy for outstanding service to hockey in the United States in 1994; the Lou Marsh Trophy as Canadian Athlete of the Year four times (1982–1983, 1985, 1989); named to the NHL First All-Star Team eight times (1981–1987, 1991); and was named to the NHL Second All-Star Team seven times (1980, 1988–1990, 1994, 1997–1998).

In 1998, he was ranked number one on *The Hockey News*' list of the 100 Greatest Hockey Players, and holds the record for most MVP awards of any player in North American professional sports.

Gretzky was inducted into the Hockey Hall of Fame in November 1999, as soon as he retired, the tenth player to bypass the three-year waiting period. In 2000, he was inducted into the International Ice Hockey Federation Hall of Fame.

In 2000, he became a minority owner of the NHL's Phoenix Coyotes, and was named Executive Director of Canada's 2002 Men's Olympic Hockey team. With him making the final decision on player selections, the team won the gold medal at the XIX Olympic Winter Games (2002) in Salt Lake City, Utah for the first time in 50 years. Although he again served as Executive Director at the 2006 Winter Olympics in Turin, Italy, the team could not repeat its earlier success and was eliminated in the quarterfinals.

He created the Wayne Gretzky Foundation, which is dedicated to helping disadvantaged youngsters throughout North America play hockey. He also serves as Honorary Chairman of Ronald McDonald Children's Charities in Canada; is an Athlete Ambassador and Honorary Member of the Board of Trustees of Right to Play (a humanitarian organization that uses sports to enhance child development); and participates in "Hands That Shape Humanity," a project for the Desmond Tutu Peace Center.

Wayne Gretzky's Career Statistics

			REGULAR SEASON					PLAYOFFS				
SEASON	**TEAM**	**LEAGUE**	**GP**	**G**	**A**	**TP**	**PIM**	**GP**	**G**	**A**	**TP**	**PIM**
1974–1975	Brantford Charcon Chargers	Minor-ON										
1975–1976	Vaughan Nationals	OHA-B	28	27	33	60	7					
1976–1977	Seneca Nationals	OHA-B	32	36	36	72	35	23	40	35	75	
1976–1977	Peterborough Petes	OMJHL	3	0	3	3	0					
1977–1978	Sault Ste. Marie Greyhounds	OMJHL	63	70	112	182	14	13	6	20	26	0
1977–1978	Canada	WJC-A	6	8	9	17	2					
1978–1979	Indianapolis Racers	WHA	8	3	3	6	0					
1978–1979	Edmonton Oilers	WHA	72	43	61	104	19	13	10	10	20	2
1979–1980	Edmonton Oilers	NHL	79	51	86	137	21	3	2	1	3	0
1980–1981	Edmonton Oilers	NHL	80	55	109	164	28	9	7	14	21	4
1981–1982	Canada	Can-Cup	7	5	7	12	2					
1981–1982	Edmonton Oilers	NHL	80	92	120	212	26	5	5	7	12	8
1981–1982	Canada	WEC-A	10	6	8	14	0					
1982–1983	Edmonton Oilers	NHL	80	71	125	196	59	16	12	26	38	4
1983–1984	Edmonton Oilers	NHL	74	87	118	205	39	19	13	22	35	12
1984–1985	Canada	Can-Cup	8	5	7	12	2					
1984–1985	Edmonton Oilers	NHL	80	73	135	208	52	18	17	30	47	4
1985–1986	Edmonton Oilers	NHL	80	52	163	215	46	10	8	11	19	2
1986–1987	Edmonton Oilers	NHL	79	62	121	183	28	21	5	29	34	6
1986–1987	NHL All-Stars	RV-87	2	0	4	4	0					
1987–1988	Canada	Can-Cup	9	3	18	21	2					
1987–1988	Edmonton Oilers	NHL	64	40	109	149	24	19	12	31	43	16
1988–1989	Los Angeles Kings	NHL	78	54	114	168	26	11	5	17	22	0
1989–1990	Los Angeles Kings	NHL	73	40	102	142	42	7	3	7	10	0
1990–1991	Los Angeles Kings	NHL	78	41	122	163	16	12	4	11	15	2
1991–1992	Canada	Can-Cup	7	4	8	12	2					
1991–1992	Los Angeles Kings	NHL	74	31	90	121	34	6	2	5	7	2
1992–1993	Los Angeles Kings	NHL	45	16	49	65	6	24	15	25	40	4
1993–1994	Los Angeles Kings	NHL	81	38	92	130	20					
1994–1995	Los Angeles Kings	NHL	48	11	37	48	6					
1995–1996	Los Angeles Kings	NHL	62	15	66	81	32					
1995–1996	St. Louis Blues	NHL	18	8	13	21	2	13	2	14	16	0
1996–1997	Canada	W-Cup	8	3	4	7	2					
1996–1997	New York Rangers	NHL	82	25	72	97	28	15	10	10	20	2
1997–1998	New York Rangers	NHL	82	23	67	90	28					
1997–1998	Canada	Olympics	6	0	4	4	2					
1998–1999	New York Rangers	NHL	70	9	53	62	14					
	NHL TOTALS		1,487	894	1,963	2,857	577	208	122	260	382	66

Wayne Gretzky's Phoenix Coyotes Coaching Record

SEASON	**W**	**L**	**OTL**
2005–2006	38	39	5
2006–2007	31	46	5
2007–2008	38	37	7
TOTALS	107	122	17

Sources: *Gretzky: An Autobiography* (Wayne Gretzky with Rick Reilly); Hockey Hall of Fame; Hockey-Reference.com; Wayne Gretzky Web Site (www.waynegretzky.com)

Griese, Robert Allen "Bob" (born: February 3, 1945 in Evansville, Indiana); inducted into the Pro Football Hall of Fame in 1990 as a player; Position: Quarterback; Uniform: #12; won two Super Bowls.

A two-time All-American at Purdue University (West Lafayette, Indiana, 1964–1966), Griese led the school to the 1966 Big Ten championship and the team's first-ever appearance in the Rose Bowl (January 2, 1967, a 14–13 win over the University of Southern California). While at Purdue, Griese pitched for the baseball team, going 12–1 one season; played guard on the basketball team; and was the football team's quarterback, kicker, and punter. After graduation, he was the number one draft choice (fourth selection overall) of the National Football League's Miami Dolphins in 1967 (the team's second year in the NFL) and played his entire 14-year (161 games) career with the team (1967–1980).

Using the team's ball-control offense, he led the Dolphins to three American Football Conference titles (1971–1973) and three consecutive Super Bowl appearances (a loss in Super Bowl VI [1972] followed by back-to-back wins in Super Bowl VII [1973] and Super Bowl VIII [1974]).

The 6'1", 190-pound Griese was a six-time Dolphins Most Valuable Player; named NFL Player of the Year in 1971; was an All-Pro twice (1971, 1977); All-AFC four times (1970–1971, 1973, 1977); and played in two American Football League All-Star Games and six AFC-NFC Pro Bowls (1970–1971, 1973–1974, 1977–1978).

In the team's perfect 1972 season, he missed eight games, but returned to lead the Dolphins to wins in both the AFC title game and Super Bowl VII, finishing the season with a record of 17–0–0, the only undefeated NFL season as of this writing. In 1982, his jersey number 12 was retired by the Dolphins; in 1984, he was inducted into both the College Football Hall of Fame and the Indiana Football Hall of Fame; and in 1990, he was added to the Dolphins Honor Roll.

After retiring as a player, Griese became a television commentator for college football and NFL games.

Bob Griese's Career Statistics

						PASSING					RUSHING		
YEAR	TEAM	G	ATT	COMP	PCT	YDS	TD	INT	RATING	NO	YDS	AVG	TD
1967	Miami	12	331	166	50.2	2,005	15	18	61.6	37	157	4.2	1
1968	Miami	13	355	186	52.4	2,473	21	16	75.7	42	230	5.5	1
1969	Miami	9	252	121	48.0	1,695	10	16	56.9	21	102	4.9	0
1970	Miami	14	245	142	58.0	2,019	12	17	72.1	26	89	3.4	2
1971	Miami	14	263	145	55.1	2,089	19	9	90.9	26	82	3.2	0
1972	Miami	6	97	53	54.6	638	4	4	71.6	3	11	3.7	1
1973	Miami	13	218	116	53.2	1,422	17	8	84.3	13	20	1.5	0
1974	Miami	13	253	152	60.1	1,968	16	15	80.9	16	66	4.1	1
1975	Miami	10	191	118	61.8	1,693	14	13	86.6	17	59	3.5	1
1976	Miami	13	272	162	59.6	2,097	11	12	78.9	23	108	4.7	0
1977	Miami	14	307	180	58.6	2,252	22	13	87.8	16	30	1.9	0
1978	Miami	11	235	148	63.0	1,791	11	11	82.4	9	10	1.1	0
1979	Miami	14	310	176	56.8	2,160	14	16	72.0	11	30	2.7	0
1980	Miami	5	100	61	61.0	790	6	4	89.2	1	0	0.0	0
	TOTALS	161	3,429	1,926	56.2	25,092	192	172	77.1	261	994	3.8	7

Sources: College Football Hall of Fame; Pro Football Hall of Fame; Pro-Football-Reference.com

Griffis, Silas Seth (born: September 22, 1883 in Onaga, Kansas; died: July 9, 1950 in Vancouver, British Columbia, Canada); inducted into the Hockey Hall of Fame in 1950 as a player; won two Stanley Cup championships.

Griffis played 13 professional hockey seasons from 1902 to 1919. His speed allowed him to dominate as a rover in the seven-man game, and as a defender in the modern six-man configuration. In the mid-1890s, he moved to Rat Portage, Ontario, Canada; eventually joined the Rat Portage (name later changed to Kenora) Thistles (Manitoba Hockey League); and helped the team win the 1907 Stanley Cup. Kenora was the smallest town to ever win the Cup. In 1915, he was captain of the Vancouver Millionaires and led the squad to that year's Stanley Cup championship.

Griffis joined Rat Portage in the newly-formed Manitoba and North West Hockey League in 1902, and led the team to a league title in 1903. The circuit became known as the Manitoba Senior Hockey League in 1905, and the Rat Portage team won the league title and earned the right to challenge for the Stanley Cup, ultimately losing to the Ottawa Senators. By 1907, Rat Portage had been renamed the Kenora Thistles and finally won the Cup in a two-game challenge against the Montreal Wanderers in January 1907. The team's championship lasted only two months when the Thistles lost a challenge to the Montreal Wanderers.

Griffis would go on to join the Vancouver Millionaires of the newly formed Pacific Coast Hockey Association in 1912; scored twice with two assists in the squad's very first game (January 5, 1912); won the 1915 Stanley Cup; and scored a total of 38 goals for Vancouver before retiring in 1919.

He has been inducted into the Northwestern Ontario Sports Hall of Fame and Museum.

Silas Griffis' Career Statistics

			REGULAR SEASON					PLAYOFFS				
SEASON	TEAM	LEAGUE	GP	G	A	TP	PIM	GP	G	A	TP	PIM
1901–1902	Rat Portage Thistles	MNWHA-Int	2	0	0	0	0					
1902–1903	Rat Portage Thistles	MNWHA	5	5	0	5						
1902–1903	Rat Portage Thistles	St-Cup						2	0	0	0	
1903–1904	Rat Portage Thistles	MNWHA	12	12	2	14						
1904–1905	Rat Portage Thistles	MHL	8	15	0	15	3					
1904–1905	Rat Portage Thistles	St-Cup						3	3	0	3	3
1905–1906	Kenora Thistles	MHL	9	9	0	9						
1906–1907	Kenora Thistles	MHL-Pro	6	5	0	5						
1906–1907	Kenora Thistles	St-Cup						4	1	0	1	6
1909–1910	Nelson Hockey Club	WKHL										
1911–1912	Vancouver Millionaires	PCHA	15	8	0	8	18					
1912–1913	Vancouver Millionaires	PCHA	14	10	3	13	30					
1913–1914	Vancouver Millionaires	PCHA	13	2	3	5	21					
1914–1915	Vancouver Millionaires	PCHA	17	2	3	5	32					
1914–1915	Vancouver Millionaires	St-Cup										
1914–1915	PCHA All–Stars	Exhib.	2	0	0	0	0					
1915–1916	Vancouver Millionaires	PCHA	18	7	5	12	12					
1916–1917	Vancouver Millionaires	PCHA	23	7	4	11	34					
1917–1918	Vancouver Millionaires	PCHA	8	2	6	8	0	2	0	0	0	0
1917–1918	Vancouver Millionaires	St-Cup						5	1	0	1	9
1918–1919	Vancouver Millionaires	PCHA	2	0	2	2	0	2	1	1	2	0

Sources: Hockey Hall of Fame; Hockey-Reference.com

Griffith, Clark Calvin (born: November 20, 1869 in Clear Creek, Missouri; died: October 27, 1955 in Washington, D.C.); inducted into the National Baseball Hall of Fame and Museum in 1946 as a pioneer-executive by the Veterans Committee; first manager of the New York Highlanders, who would later be renamed the New York Yankees; his stalling actions in 1901 caused the first forfeit in American League history.

The 5'6", 155-pound Griffith enjoyed baseball as a player, manager, and owner. As a right-handed pitcher, he won 20 or more games six years in a row for the Chicago White Stockings, and finished his career with 237 wins (237–146, .619). In 1901, as a player-manager, he led Chicago to the first-ever American League pennant.

As a pitcher, he made his major league debut on April 11, 1891 and played for the St. Louis Browns (1891), Boston Reds (1891), Chicago Colts/Orphans (1893–1900), Chicago White Sox/White Stockings (1901–1902, player-manager), New York Highlanders (1903-1907, was the team's first-ever manager and stayed with the squad until 1908; team name later changed to the New York Yankees), Cincinnati Reds (1909), and Washington Senators (1912–1914). He managed the Chicago White Sox (1901–1902), New York Highlanders (1903–1908), Cincinnati Reds (1909–1911), and Washington Senators (1912–1920).

In 1901, he was one of the first stars to jump from the National League to the newly formed American League. Griffith eventually stopped participating as a player and served as a manager, before becoming a team owner of the Senators. He compiled a managerial record of 1491–1367 (.522) and, as of this writing, ranks 18th all-time in wins.

Griffith owned the Washington Senators from 1920 until his death, when control of the franchise fell to his son, Calvin, who oversaw the franchise's move to Minnesota to become the Twins.

Created in 1945, the Clark C. Griffith Collegiate Baseball League was originally known as the National Capital City Junior League. In its early years, games were played in Washington, D.C., on the Ellipse behind the White House.

Griffith served as vice president of the League Protective Players' Association, and in 1900, he led the members in baseball's first strike, demanding that the players' minimum salary be raised to $3,000 and that their uniforms be paid for by the owners. This strike was part of a master plan to establish the rival American League, and Griffith eventually became the player-manager of the Chicago White Stockings in the new league. As a manager-owner, he was the first to sign Cuban players; install a device to record pitch speed; and develop the idea of the relief pitcher.

On May 2, 1901, under cloudy skies in Chicago, the Detroit Tigers scored five runs in the top of the ninth inning to take a 7–5 lead over the White Sox. Griffith decided to slow down the game, hoping that rain would wipe out the top of the inning, and the game's score would revert to the eighth inning, resulting in a Sox win. However, umpire Tom Connolly is unhappy with the tactic and forfeits the game to Detroit, the first-ever forfeit in the American League.

Clark Griffith's Career Pitching Statistics

YEAR	TEAM	W	L	PCT	ERA	CG	SHO	SV	IP	H	ER	R	HR	BB	SO
1891	St. Louis	11	8	.579	3.33	12	0	0	186.1	195	69	122	8	58	68
1891	Boston	3	1	.750	5.63	3	0	0	40.0	47	25	33	3	15	20
1893	Chicago	1	2	.333	5.03	2	0	0	19.2	24	11	14	1	5	9
1894	Chicago	21	14	.600	4.92	28	0	0	261.1	328	143	193	12	85	71
1895	Chicago	26	14	.650	3.93	39	0	0	353.0	434	154	228	11	91	79
1896	Chicago	23	11	.676	3.54	35	0	0	317.2	370	125	189	3	70	81
1897	Chicago	21	18	.538	3.72	38	1	1	343.2	410	142	231	3	86	102
1898	Chicago	24	10	.706	1.88	36	4	0	325.2	305	68	105	1	64	97
1899	Chicago	22	14	.611	2.79	35	0	0	319.2	329	99	163	5	65	73
1900	Chicago	14	13	.519	3.05	27	4	0	248.0	245	84	126	6	51	61
1901	Chicago	24	7	.774	2.67	26	5	1	266.2	275	79	114	4	50	67
1902	Chicago	15	9	.625	4.18	20	3	0	213.0	247	99	117	11	47	51
1903	New York	14	11	.560	2.70	22	2	0	213.0	201	64	92	3	33	69
1904	New York	7	5	.583	2.87	8	1	0	100.1	91	32	40	3	16	36
1905	New York	9	6	.600	1.68	4	2	1	101.2	82	19	30	1	15	46
1906	New York	2	2	.500	3.02	1	0	2	59.2	58	20	30	0	15	16
1907	New York	0	0	.000	8.64	0	0	0	8.1	15	8	16	0	6	5
1909	Cincinnati	0	1	.000	6.00	1	0	0	6.0	11	4	8	0	2	3
1912	Washington	0	0	.000	0.00	0	0	0	0.0	1	1	1	1	0	0
1913	Washington	0	0	.000	0.00	0	0	0	1.0	1	0	0	0	0	0
1914	Washington	0	0	.000	0.00	0	0	1	1.0	1	0	0	0	0	1
	TOTALS	237	146	.619	3.31	337	22	6	3,385.2	3,670	1,246	1,852	76	774	955

Clark Griffith's American League Managerial Record

YEAR	TEAM	W	L	WIN%
1901	Chicago	83	53	.610
1902	Chicago	74	60	.552
1903	New York	72	62	.537
1904	New York	92	59	.609
1905	New York	71	78	.477
1906	New York	90	61	.596
1907	New York	70	78	.473
1908	New York	24	32	.429
1909	Cincinnati	77	76	.503
1910	Cincinnati	75	79	.487
1911	Cincinnati	70	83	.458
1912	Washington	91	61	.599
1913	Washington	90	64	.584
1914	Washington	81	73	.526
1915	Washington	85	68	.556
1916	Washington	76	77	.497
1917	Washington	74	79	.484
1918	Washington	72	56	.563
1919	Washington	56	84	.400
1920	Washington	68	84	.447
	Chicago	157	113	.581
	New York	419	370	.531
	Cincinnati	222	238	.483
	Washington	693	646	.518
	TOTALS	1,491	1,367	.522

Sources: Baseball-Reference.com; National Baseball Hall of Fame and Museum

Griffiths, Frank A., Sr. (born: December 17, 1916 in Burnaby, British Columbia, Canada; died: April 7, 1994); inducted into the Hockey Hall of Fame in 1993 as a builder; served as vice-chairman of the NHL Board of Governors.

A certified accountant and a successful businessman in the Pacific Northwest, Griffiths was a strong supporter of hockey in the Vancouver, British Columbia, Canada area, and was an active member of the National Hockey League administration.

He purchased radio station CKNW in 1956, and helped develop Western Canada International Communications Limited, which became Canada's largest publicly traded broadcasting company with interests in television, radio, and satellite services in central and western Canada.

In May 1974, he purchased Northwest Sports Enterprises, Ltd., the parent company of the NHL's Vancouver Canucks and served on the league's Audit Committee. He joined the NHL Board of Governors in 1974, and served as its vice-chairman from 1979 to 1987. As vice-chairman, Griffiths worked to stabilize teams with financial problems; participated in the merger of the World Hockey Association with the NHL; and encouraged bringing Russian hockey players to Canada to play in the NHL, a move meant to increase the international appeal of the league.

He was inducted into the British Columbia Sports Hall of Fame and Museum in 1997.

Sources: British Columbia Sports Hall of Fame and Museum; Hockey Hall of Fame

Grimes, Burleigh Arland (born: August 18, 1893 in Emerald, Wisconsin; died: December 6, 1985 in Clear Lake, Wisconsin); inducted into the National Baseball Hall of Fame and Museum in 1964 as a player by the Veterans Committee; Position: Pitcher; Bats: Right; Throws: Right; last pitcher officially permitted to throw the spitball.

Pitching for seven different teams in his 19-year career (1916–1934), the 5'10", 175-pound Grimes made his major league debut on September 10, 1916 and played for the Pittsburgh Pirates (1916–1917, 1928–1929, 1934), Brooklyn Dodgers (1918–1926), New York Giants (1927), Boston Braves (1930), St. Louis Cardinals (1930–1931, 1933–1934), Chicago Cubs (1932–1933), and the New York Yankees (1934).

He won 20 or more games five times (1920–1921, 1923–1924, 1928) and played in four World Series, winning one (1931) and losing three (1920, 1930, 1932). After his playing days, he managed the Brooklyn Dodgers for two seasons (1937–1938), compiling a 131–171 (.434) record.

Grimes was 26 years old when the spitball was banned in 1920, but he was one of 17 veteran pitchers exempted from the ban and continued using the pitch until he retired. When he left the game in 1934, he was the last of the legal spitballers. He led the league in wins twice; starts three times; and innings pitched three times.

After he retired, Grimes remained in baseball as a minor league manager and scout. He managed the Toronto Maple Leafs of the International League twice (1942–1944, 1952–1953) and won the pennant in 1943.

Burleigh Grimes' Career Statistics

YEAR	TEAM	LG	W	L	PCT	G	SH	IP	H	R	ER	SO	BB	ERA
1916	Pittsburgh	NL	2	3	.400	6	0	46	40	19	12	20	10	2.35
1917	Pittsburgh	NL	3	16	.158	37	1	194	186	101	76	72	70	3.53
1918	Brooklyn	NL	19	9	.679	41	7	270	210	94	64	113	76	2.13
1919	Brooklyn	NL	10	11	.476	25	1	181	179	97	70	82	60	3.48
1920	Brooklyn	NL	23	11	.676	40	5	304	271	101	75	131	67	2.22
1921	Brooklyn	NL	22	13	.629	37	2	302	313	120	95	136	76	2.83
1922	Brooklyn	NL	17	14	.548	36	1	259	324	159	137	99	84	4.76
1923	Brooklyn	NL	21	18	.538	39	2	327	356	165	130	119	100	3.58
1924	Brooklyn	NL	22	13	.629	38	1	311	351	161	132	135	91	3.82
1925	Brooklyn	NL	12	19	.387	33	0	247	305	164	138	73	102	5.03
1926	Brooklyn	NL	12	13	.480	30	1	225	238	114	93	64	88	3.72
1927	New York	NL	19	8	.704	39	2	260	274	116	102	102	87	3.53
1928	Pittsburgh	NL	25	14	.641	48	4	331	311	146	110	97	77	2.99
1929	Pittsburgh	NL	17	7	.708	33	2	233	245	108	81	62	70	3.13
1930	Boston	NL	3	5	.375	11	0	49	72	53	40	15	22	7.35
1930	St. Louis	NL	13	6	.684	22	1	152	174	66	51	58	43	3.02
1931	St. Louis	NL	17	9	.654	29	3	212	240	97	86	67	59	3.65
1932	Chicago	NL	6	11	.353	30	1	141	174	89	75	36	50	4.79
1933	Chicago	NL	3	6	.333	17	1	70	71	29	27	12	29	3.47
1933	St. Louis	NL	0	1	.000	4	0	14	15	13	8	4	8	5.14
1934	St. Louis	NL	2	1	.667	4	0	8	5	3	3	1	2	3.38
1934	Pittsburgh	NL	1	2	.333	8	0	27	36	24	22	9	10	7.33

YEAR	TEAM	LG	W	L	PCT	G	SH	IP	H	R	ER	SO	BB	ERA
1934	New York	AL	1	2	.333	10	0	18	22	11	11	5	14	5.50
	TOTALS		270	212	.560	617	35	4,180	4,412	2,050	1,638	1,512	1,295	3.53

Burleigh Grimes' Managerial Record

YEAR	TEAM	W	L	WP
1937	Brooklyn	62	91	.405
1938	Brooklyn	69	80	.463
	TOTALS	131	171	.434

Sources: Baseball-Reference.com; National Baseball Hall of Fame and Museum

Grimm, Russell Scott "Russ" (born: May 2, 1959 in Scottdale, Pennsylvania); inducted into the Pro Football Hall of Fame in 2010 as a player; Position: Guard; Uniform: #68; won four Super Bowl championships, three as a player

After attending Southmoreland High School (Alverton, PA) and the University of Pittsburgh (Pennsylvania, where he was an All-American center), the 6'3", 273-pound Grimm was a third-round selection (69th overall pick) of the Washington Redskins in the 1981 NFL Draft. Known as one of "The Hogs", he played his entire 11-year National Football League career (1981–1991, 140 games) for the Washington Redskins; was selected to four straight Pro Bowls (1983–1986); was All-NFC (1983–1986); played in four Super Bowls (winning SB XVII in 1983, SB XXII in 1988, and SB XXVI in 1992 while losing SBXVIII in 1984); selected to the NFL's All-Decade Team of the 1980s; and was named one of the 70 Greatest Redskins.

After his playing days, Grimm was a coach for the Washington Redskins (1992–2000), Pittsburgh Steelers (2000–2006), and the Arizona Cardinals. As an offensive line coach for the Pittsburgh Steelers, Grimm won his fourth Super Bowl ring (SB XL).

Source: Pro Football Hall of Fame

Grove, Robert Moses "Lefty" (born: March 6, 1900 in Lonaconing, Maryland; died: May 22, 1975 in Norwalk, Ohio); inducted into the National Baseball Hall of Fame and Museum in 1947 as a player; Position: Pitcher; Bats: Left; Throws: Right; Uniform: #10; won his 300th game in his last pitching appearance; American League Most Valuable Player in 1931; won two pitching triple crowns; won a record nine ERA titles; only pitcher to strike out the side on nine pitches twice in the same season.

As the ace of the Philadelphia Athletics' pitching staff, over a three-season period (1929–1931, with the team playing in the World Series each year), Grove compiled a 79–15 record (.840) and won the pitching Triple Crown (leading the league in earned run average, wins, and strikeouts) in 1930 and 1931.

Making his major league debut on April 14, 1925, Grove enjoyed a 17-year career with the Philadelphia Athletics (1925–1933) and Boston Red Sox (1934–1941). He played in three World Series (winning in 1929 and 1930, losing in 1931); was named to six All-Star teams (1933, 1935–1939); and was the American League Most Valuable Player in 1931. His MVP Award is the only one not housed in Cooperstown, but instead is located at the Georges Creek Library in Lonaconing. He led the American League in wins four times; winning percentage five times; strikeouts seven consecutive seasons; and ERA nine times.

The 6'3", 190-pound Grove joined the Baltimore Orioles in 1920 and over five seasons, compiled a 109–36 regular-season mark; led the International League in strikeouts every season; and helped his team win the league championship each year. He stayed with the team until 1924, when his contract was purchased by the Athletics.

In spite of an injury-plagued rookie season, Grove pitched to a 10–12 record and led the American League in strikeouts. Fully recovered by the next season, he won the first of a record nine earned run average titles (1926, 1929–1932, 1935–1936, 1938–1939), and in 1927, he won 20 games for the first time in his career.

After the 1933 season, Philadelphia owner Connie Mack sold Grove to the Boston Red Sox, where he led the league with a 2.70 ERA in 1935; won his eighth ERA title the next season; and in 1938, he led the league in ERA and winning percentage.

Grove's .680 lifetime winning percentage (300–141) is still eighth best all-time; in 1999, he ranked number 23 on *The Sporting News*' list of the 100 Greatest Baseball Players (the second highest-ranked left-handed pitcher behind Warren Spahn); and he was elected to the Major League Baseball All-Century Team.

In 1928, Grove twice struck out the side on nine pitches (August 23 in the second inning against the Cleveland Indians, becoming the third American League pitcher and seventh pitcher in major league history to accomplish this feat)

and on September 27, in the seventh inning against the Chicago White Sox (becoming the first pitcher in major league history to accomplish the feat twice in a career). Only Sandy Koufax and Nolan Ryan have matched this feat, although Grove remains the only pitcher to ever do it twice in the same season.

Grove was the first American League pitcher to lead the league in strikeouts and walks in the same season (1925). No batter has ever struck out as often as Grove (based on percentage). He struck out 593 times in 1,369 official at-bats, or 43% of the time. On July 25, 1941, Grove won his 300th, and final, game, in his last pitching appearance, a 10–6 win over the Cleveland Indians.

Lefty Grove's Career Statistics

YEAR	TEAM	LG	W	L	PCT	G	SH	IP	H	R	ER	SO	BB	ERA
1925	Philadelphia	AL	10	12	.455	45	0	197	207	120	104	116	131	4.75
1926	Philadelphia	AL	13	13	.500	45	1	258	227	97	72	194	101	2.51
1927	Philadelphia	AL	20	13	.606	51	1	262	251	116	93	174	79	3.19
1928	Philadelphia	AL	24	8	.750	39	4	262	228	93	75	183	64	2.58
1929	Philadelphia	AL	20	6	.769	42	2	275	278	104	86	170	81	2.81
1930	Philadelphia	AL	28	5	.848	50	2	291	273	101	82	209	60	2.54
1931	Philadelphia	AL	31	4	.886	41	4	289	249	84	66	175	62	2.06
1932	Philadelphia	AL	25	10	.714	44	4	292	269	101	92	188	79	2.84
1933	Philadelphia	AL	24	8	.750	45	2	275	280	113	98	114	83	3.21
1934	Boston	AL	8	8	.500	22	0	109	149	84	79	43	32	6.52
1935	Boston	AL	20	12	.625	35	2	273	269	105	82	121	65	2.70
1936	Boston	AL	17	12	.586	35	6	253	237	90	79	130	65	2.81
1937	Boston	AL	17	9	.654	32	3	262	269	101	88	153	83	3.02
1938	Boston	AL	14	4	.778	24	1	164	169	65	56	99	52	3.07
1939	Boston	AL	15	4	.789	23	2	191	180	63	54	81	58	2.54
1940	Boston	AL	7	6	.538	22	1	153	159	73	68	62	50	4.00
1941	Boston	AL	7	7	.500	21	0	134	155	84	65	54	42	4.37
	TOTALS		300	141	.680	616	35	3,940	3,849	1,594	1,339	2,266	1,187	3.06

Sources: Baseball-Reference.com; National Baseball Hall of Fame and Museum

Groza, Louis Roy "Lou" (born: January 25, 1924 in Martins Ferry, Ohio; died: November 29, 2000 in Middleburgh Heights, Ohio); inducted into the Pro Football Hall of Fame in 1974 as a player; Position: Offensive Tackle-Placekicker; Uniform: #76; last of the original 1946 Cleveland Browns to retire; 1954 NFL Player of the Year.

When he retired in 1967, Groza had played 21 seasons (268 games), more than any other professional player up to that time. He spent his entire career with the Cleveland Browns of the All-America Football Conference / National Football League (1946–1959, 1961–1967).

The smallest of three brothers (6'3", 240 pounds), he played one season for Ohio State University (Columbus) before being drafted into the Army during World War II. After leaving the military, he joined the Browns.

Groza began his professional career as an offensive tackle (1946–1959); sat out the entire 1960 season because of a back injury; and upon his return, converted to a kicking specialist (1961–1967). He was an All-NFL tackle for six seasons; named NFL Player of the Year in 1954; played in nine Pro Bowls; named First- or Second-Team All-League eight times; led the NFL in field goals six times (1946, 1950, 1952–1954, 1957); tied for the NFL lead in scoring in 1957; and his field goal with 30 seconds left won the 1950 NFL title game, 30–28, over the Los Angeles Rams. Nicknamed "The Toe," he scored 1,608 career points (259 in the AAFC and 1,349 in the NFL, including one receiving touchdown); helped the Browns win all four AAFC championships (1946–1949); and won four NFL titles (1950, 1954–1955, 1964).

In 1992, his uniform number 76 was retired by the Browns, and the Palm Beach County Sports Commission established the Lou Groza Award, presented annually to the best National Collegiate Athletic Association Division I kicker. In 1999, he was ranked number 99 on *The Sporting News*' list of the 100 Greatest Football Players.

He co-wrote his biography, *The Toe: The Lou Groza Story*, and in 1956, the NFL instituted the "Lou Groza Rule," prohibiting the use of artificial aids for kickers. Groza used tape and a special tee to help when kicking. The 1956 rule banned the tape.

Lou Groza's Career Statistics

YEAR	TEAM	G	GS	FGA	FGM	FG%	XPA	XPM	XP%
1946	Cleveland	14	5	29	13	.448	47	45	.957

YEAR	TEAM	G	GS	FGA	FGM	FG%	XPA	XPM	XP%
1947	Cleveland	12	5	19	7	.368	42	39	.929
1948	Cleveland	14	14	19	8	.421	52	51	.981
1949	Cleveland	12	12	9	2	.222	35	34	.971
1950	Cleveland	10	0	19	13	.684	29	29	1.00
1951	Cleveland	12	0	23	10	.435	43	43	1.00
1952	Cleveland	12	0	33	19	.576	32	32	1.00
1953	Cleveland	12	0	26	23	.885	40	39	.975
1954	Cleveland	12	0	24	16	.667	38	37	.974
1955	Cleveland	12	0	22	11	.500	45	44	.978
1956	Cleveland	12	0	20	11	.550	18	18	1.00
1957	Cleveland	12	0	22	15	.682	32	32	1.00
1958	Cleveland	12	0	19	8	.421	38	36	.947
1959	Cleveland	12	0	16	5	.313	37	33	.892
1961	Cleveland	14	0	23	16	.696	38	37	.974
1962	Cleveland	14	0	31	14	.452	35	33	.943
1963	Cleveland	14	0	23	15	.652	43	40	.930
1964	Cleveland	14	0	33	22	.667	49	49	1.00
1965	Cleveland	14	0	25	16	.640	45	45	1.00
1966	Cleveland	14	0	23	9	.391	52	51	.981
1967	Cleveland	14	0	23	11	.478	43	43	1.00
	TOTALS	268	36	481	264	.549	833	810	.972

Sources: Pro Football Hall of Fame; Pro-Football-Reference.com

Gruenig, Robert F. "Ace" (born: March 12, 1913 in Chicago, Illinois; died: August 11, 1958); inducted into the Naismith Memorial Basketball Hall of Fame in 1963 as a player; won three AAU championships.

Gruenig played basketball for four years at Crane Tech High School (Chicago, Illinois, 1927–1931); was selected All-City twice; and named All-State once. After high school, he attended Northwestern University (Evanston, Illinois), but withdrew during his freshman year without ever playing basketball at the school.

He played Amateur Athletic Union basketball for Rosenberg-Arvey (Chicago, Illinois) in 1933; Safeway Stores (Denver, Colorado, 1937–1938); Denver Nuggets (1939–1940); Denver American Legion (1942–1943); Denver Ambrose-Legion (1944–1945); Denver Ambrose Jelly Makers (1945–1946); and Denver Murphy-Mahoney Chevrolet Dealers (1948).

At 6'8", 220 pounds, Gruenig was one of basketball's first big men; named to the AAU All-America First Team 10 times (1937–1940, 1942–1946, 1948) and to the Second Team once (1933); and led Denver Safeway (1937), Denver Nuggets (1939), and Denver American Legion (1942) to AAU championships.

Source: Naismith Memorial Basketball Hall of Fame

Gryzik, Joseph (born: October 10, 1927 in Katowice, Poland); inducted into the National Soccer Hall of Fame and Museum in 1973 as a player; Position: Halfback; won the Peel Cup five times.

Gryzik immigrated to the United States in 1949; settled in the Chicago, Illinois area; and played for the Polish American Athletic Club, which changed its name to the Chicago Eagles S.A.C. the next year. He stayed with the Eagles (in the National Soccer League of Chicago) his entire playing career (1949–1965) and, as the team's captain, led the franchise to Peel Cup (Illinois State Championship) titles five times (1950, 1954–1955, 1957, 1963).

He played with the 1951 Chicago All-Stars against the touring Swedish club A.I.K. Stockholm and went on to represent various Chicago and National Soccer League teams against other touring squads, such as Eintract Frankfurt, Liverpool, Plymouth Argyle, Nuremberg, Guadalajara, Borussia Monchengladbach, Dundee, and Slovan Bratislava.

In 1955, he played for the Eagles in the U.S. Amateur Cup final, eventually losing to the Pittsburgh Heidelberg Tornados, and set a scoring record in the Peel Cup with eight goals in one game. Gryzik was a member of the United States team at the 1963 Pan-American Games in Brazil, and played in all four games. He was selected to the U.S. Olympic team in 1964 (which did not qualify for the Olympics) and to the U.S. National Team for the 1966 World Cup qualifying round.

He retired from the game in 1965 and, in 1972, he was honored by the National Soccer League of Chicago for his long-time career and sportsmanship.

Source: National Soccer Hall of Fame and Museum

Guelker, Robert (born: June 26, 1923 in St. Louis, Missouri; died: February 22, 1986); inducted into the National Soccer Hall of Fame and Museum in 1980 as a builder; won seven NCAA championships; first coach in collegiate soccer history to win both an NCAA Division II championship and an NCAA Division I championship at the same school.

Coach Guelker built St. Louis University (Missouri) into a national collegiate soccer powerhouse that won five National Collegiate Athletic Association titles (1959–1960, 1962–1963, 1965). He later coached at Southern Illinois University (Edwardsville) from 1966 to 1983, and finished his 27-year collegiate career with a coaching record of 311–76–26 (.804), and won two more NCAA titles in 1972 and 1979 with SIU.

He led his teams to 22 NCAA tournaments; served as president of the United States Soccer Football Association (1967–1969); and coached the Pan-American team in 1971 (finishing sixth in Colombia), the U.S. Olympic soccer team in Munich, Germany in 1972 (eliminated in the first round), and was the first USA Youth coach in the Confederation of North, Central American and Caribbean Association Football (U19).

Guelker served as Chair of the National Junior Cup Competition Committee; United States Soccer Federation Development Committee; Missouri Soccer Federation and Missouri Senior Soccer Association; and executive secretary for the Catholic Youth Council, Archdiocese of St. Louis (1946–1969).

He was named Soccer Coach of the Year by the Rockne Club in 1959; National Soccer Coaches Association of America Coach of the Year in 1973; won the *Sports Illustrated* Award for Merit in 1973; and was *Soccer America*'s Coach of the Year in 1980.

Guelker was the first coach in collegiate soccer history to win both an NCAA Division II championship (1972) and an NCAA Division I championship (1979) at the same school. He has been inducted into the Southern Illinois University, Edwardsville Athletics Hall of Fame.

Source: National Soccer Hall of Fame and Museum

Guennel, Dr. G. K. "Joe" (born: December 24, 1920 in Germany); inducted into the National Soccer Hall of Fame and Museum in 1980 as a builder-contributor; won the Midwest Soccer Conference title in 1955; organized the Ohio-Indiana Soccer League.

Guennel came to the United States with his family when he was eight and settled in Bangor, Pennsylvania; lettered in football, basketball, and baseball at Bangor High School; and attended Butler University (Indianapolis, Indiana).

He served in the Army in 1943 during World War II, and while being trained by the Army at the University of Missouri (Columbia), Guennel organized a soccer team, the first of many.

He organized the 7th Army team in 1945; the Indiana University (Bloomington) Soccer Club in 1949; and helped found the Midwest Soccer Conference in 1950. Guennel coached the Indiana University soccer team for eleven years and won the Midwest Soccer Conference title in 1955 and shared it in 1959. He also organized the Indianapolis Soccer Club in 1951 and started the Ohio-Indiana Soccer League.

He served as president of the Midwestern and Ohio-Indiana leagues from 1951 to 1961, and promoted the growth of collegiate and club soccer in Indiana and Colorado. In 1949, only four colleges played soccer in the Midwest, but due to his efforts, by 1963, the number had grown to 69.

Guennel served 12 years on the U.S. Olympic Committee and as president of both the National Soccer Coaches Association of America and the Colorado State Association. He was inducted into the National Soccer Coaches Association of America Hall of Fame in 1999, and wrote the book, *How to Improve Your Soccer*.

Source: National Soccer Hall of Fame and Museum

Gulick, Dr. Luther Halsey (born: December 4, 1865 in Honolulu, Hawaii; died: August 13, 1918); inducted into the Naismith Memorial Basketball Hall of Fame in 1959 as a contributor; helped convince Dr. James Naismith to invent the game of basketball; created the triangular YMCA symbol.

Gulick served as head of Physical Education at the School for Christian Workers in Springfield, Massachusetts (now known as the Young Men's Christian Association) from 1887 to 1900. He was a strong advocate of physical exercise and helped convince Dr. James Naismith to create an indoor game for off-season training, which would eventually evolve into the game of basketball. Gulick guided the new game during its formative years to national and international recognition through YMCA and Amateur Athletic Union organizations.

He attended Oberlin College (Ohio, 1880–1882, 1883–1886), Sargent Normal School of Physical Education (Cambridge, Massachusetts, 1885), and the New York University Medical College (New York, 1886–1889). He served as chairman of the AAU Basket Ball Committee (1895–1905); was a member of two Olympic Games Committees (1906-Athens, Greece; 1908-London, England); and developed the triangular YMCA symbol, signifying the physical, emotional, and intellectual.

Gulick founded the Public School Athletic League while serving as the head of physical education for the Public Schools of New York City (1903); implemented a two-minute exercise program in public schools, the first of its kind; presented a series of physical training lectures at the 1904 St. Louis (Missouri) Exposition; was a co-founder and president of the Playground and Recreation Association of America and the National Recreation Association (1906); and helped create the Boy Scouts.

Along with his wife, Gulick created the Camp Fire Girls with the goal of educating women on their changing roles outside of the home (the group's name was later changed to Camp Fire USA, as it includes both boys and girls), and led the campaign for recruiting physical education and recreation directors as soldiers in the United States and overseas.

He was superintendent of the physical training department of the International Y.M.C.A. Training School (now known as Springfield College, Springfield, Massachusetts) from 1887 to 1900; served as principal of the Pratt Institute High School (Brooklyn, New York, 1900–1903); from 1903 to 1908, he supervised physical training in the public schools of New York City; and directed the department of child hygiene at the Russell Sage Foundation (New York, New York, 1908–1913).

In addition to editing *Physical Education* (1891–1896), *Association Outlook* (1897–1900), *American Physical Education Review* (1901–1903), and the *Gulick Hygiene Series*, he wrote *Manual of Physical Measurements* (1892); *Physical Education by Muscular Exercise* (1904); *The Efficient Life* (1907); *Mind and Work* (1908); *The Healthful Art of Dancing* (1910); and *Medical Inspection of Schools*, with Leonard Ayres (1908, 1913).

He was inducted into the YMCA Hall of Fame in 1992.

Sources: Naismith Memorial Basketball Hall of Fame; YMCA Hall of Fame

Gunter, Sue (born: May 22, 1939 in Walnut Grove, Mississippi; died: August 4, 2005 in Baton Rouge, Louisiana); inducted into the Naismith Memorial Basketball Hall of Fame in 2005 as a coach; won two Association of American Universities national championships as a player; led LSU to its first-ever NCAA Final Four appearance as a coach; won an NIT title as a coach.

Before national tournaments for women, television contracts, and sellout crowds, Gunter was a basketball pioneer who helped establish the foundation for the future of the women's game. As an AAU player at Nashville Business College (Tennessee, 1958–1962), Gunter earned All-American honors in 1960, and also played two years on the United States National Team that competed against the Soviet Union. She earned a bachelor's and master's degrees from Peabody College (Nashville, Tennessee), and led the Nashville Business College to two Association of American Universities national championships.

In 1962, Gunter began her coaching career at Middle Tennessee State University (Murfreesboro) and led the Blue Raiders to undefeated seasons her two years at the school (1963–1964), before becoming the head coach of the lady's basketball program at Stephen F. Austin State University (Nacogdoches, Texas). She led the Lady Jacks to a 266–87 (.754) record in 16 seasons (1965–1980). During her time at the school, she was named an assistant coach to the 1976 U.S. Olympic team that won the silver medal in Montreal, Canada (the first time women's basketball had been a medal sport in the Olympics).

In 1980, Gunter was selected women's head basketball coach for the United States Olympic Team. However, when the United States boycotted the Games (held in Moscow, Russia) in protest of Russia's invasion of Afghanistan, she and the team lost the opportunity to compete. She would lead the U.S. National Team three times (1976, 1978, 1980).

She led SFA to top 10 rankings four times and to top-five rankings twice (1979–1980). While at the school, Gunter coached four women's sports, including basketball, softball, tennis, and track. Her basketball teams went to five Association for Intercollegiate Athletics for Women playoffs; won four state titles; and one regional championship. In 1980, she resigned as coach to become the school's Director of Women's Athletics, serving two years before returning to the coaching ranks at Louisiana State University (Baton Rouge) in 1982.

Gunter stayed at LSU for 22 seasons (until 2004); won 442 games; and led the Lady Tigers to the program's first-ever NCAA Final Four appearance (2004). She was named 1983 National Coach of the Year; led LSU to four NCAA Elite Eight appearances, two Southeastern Conference titles, and the 1985 Women's NIT title; and guided the school to fourteen 20-win seasons and one 30-win season.

While at LSU, Gunter was named the Southeastern Conference Coach of the Year twice (1997, 1999); Converse Region IV Coach of the Year in 1983; the *Basketball News* National Coach of the Year in 1983; the Louisiana Coach of the Year four times (1983, 1997, 2002–2003); won the Carol Eckman Award in 1994 (presented by the Women's Basketball Coaches Association to an active WBCA coach who best demonstrates the character of the late Carol Eckman, the mother of the collegiate women's basketball national championship); and was named WBCA Regional Coach of the Year twice (1999, 2003).

When she retired, Gunter had the third most wins (708) in women's college basketball history (behind Jody Conradt and Pat Summitt), and she was inducted into the Women's Basketball Hall of Fame in 2000.

Sue Gunter's Collegiate Coaching Career

SEASON	TEAM	W	L	WIN%
1962–1964	Middle Tennessee State (Not recognized by the NCAA)	44	0	1.000
1964–1980	Stephen F. Austin State University	266	87	.754
1982–1983	Louisiana State University	20	7	.741
1983–1984	Louisiana State University	23	7	.767
1984–1985	Louisiana State University	20	9	.690
1985–1986	Louisiana State University	27	6	.818
1986–1987	Louisiana State University	20	8	.714
1987–1988	Louisiana State University	18	11	.621
1988–1989	Louisiana State University	19	11	.633
1989–1990	Louisiana State University	21	9	.700
1990–1991	Louisiana State University	24	7	.774
1991–1992	Louisiana State University	16	13	.552
1992–1993	Louisiana State University	9	18	.333
1993–1994	Louisiana State University	11	16	.407
1994–1995	Louisiana State University	7	20	.259
1995–1996	Louisiana State University	21	11	.656
1996–1997	Louisiana State University	25	5	.833
1997–1998	Louisiana State University	19	13	.594
1998–1999	Louisiana State University	22	8	.733
1999–2000	Louisiana State University	25	7	.781
2000–2001	Louisiana State University	20	11	.645
2001–2002	Louisiana State University	18	12	.600
2002–2003	Louisiana State University	30	4	.882
2003–2004	Louisiana State University	27	8	.771
	TOTALS	708	308	.697

Sources: Naismith Memorial Basketball Hall of Fame; Women's Basketball Hall of Fame

Guyon, Joseph Napoleon "Joe" (born: November 26, 1892 at the White Earth Indian Reservation in Minnesota; died: November 27, 1971 in Louisville, Kentucky); inducted into the Pro Football Hall of Fame in 1966 as a player; Position: Halfback; won the 1927 NFL championship; one of only two American Indians to be inducted into the football hall of fame.

Guyon, an American Indian from the Chippewa Tribe, was born O-Gee-Chidah on the White Earth Indian Reservation in Minnesota. He attended the Carlisle Indian Industrial School (Carlisle, Pennsylvania), where one of his classmates and athletic teammates was the legendary Jim Thorpe, with whom he would later play on four National Football League teams (Canton, Cleveland, Oorang, and Rock Island). The 5'10", 195-pound Guyon played tackle on the team until Thorpe left in 1912, and he then replaced Thorpe at halfback. He was named to Walter Camp's Second-Team All-American team in 1913.

After leaving Carlisle, he went to the Georgia Institute of Technology (commonly referred to as Georgia Tech, in Atlanta), and played on the school's 1917 undefeated team (9–0), winning the national championship. The next season, he was selected an All-American tackle.

After college, Guyon signed a professional football contract with the Canton Bulldogs (Ohio), and played for the team in 1919 and 1920. When the National Football League was formed, he would go on to play 46 NFL games with the Cleveland Indians (1921), Oorang Indians (La Rue, Ohio; 1922–1923), Rock Island Independents (Illinois, 1924), Kansas City Cowboys (Missouri, 1924–1925), and the New York Giants (1927).

Guyon teamed up with Thorpe on the Canton Bulldogs in 1919, and was with the team when it entered the newly formed American Professional Football Association in 1920. He followed Thorpe to the Cleveland Indians, the Oorang Indians, and the Rock Island Independents. Late in the 1924 season, he left Thorpe and played for the Kansas City Cowboys. Away from the game for one season (1926), Guyon returned to play one season (1927) with the New York Giants, and helped lead the team to an 11-1-1 record (.917) and the 1927 NFL championship (prior to 1933, the champion was based on overall winning percentage).

He was inducted into the Georgia Tech Athletics Hall of Fame in 1966 and into the College Football Hall of Fame in 1971. He is one of only two American Indians to be inducted into the Pro Football Hall of Fame (along with Jim Thorpe).

Although a talented football player, his favorite sport was baseball. He hit .329 over twelve seasons, mostly with the Atlanta Crackers (Southern Association) and the Louisville Colonels (American Association) in the minor leagues, never making it to the major leagues. He stole 203 career bases, and scored 100 or more runs four times. Guyon hit .329 with a .447 slugging percentage in 1,229 minor league games; scored 900 runs; had 1,542 hits; 227 doubles; 91 triples; 49 homers; and 515 runs batted in.

He served as the head baseball coach at Clemson University (South Carolina) from 1928 to 1931. He went on to manage the Anderson Electrics (South Carolina, Palmetto League) in 1931; the Asheville Tourists in 1932 (North Carolina, Piedmont League), and the Fieldale (Virginia) Towlers (Bi-State League) in 1936.

Sources: College Football Hall of Fame; Pro Football Hall of Fame

Gwynn, Anthony Keith "Tony" (born: May 9, 1960 in Los Angeles, California); inducted into the National Baseball Hall of Fame and Museum in 2007 as a player; Position: Right Field; Bats: Left; Throws: Left; Uniform: #19; first player to collect his 3,000th hit outside the United States; first Padre to collect 200 hits in a season; first Padre to win a league batting title; at the time of his induction, he was the only member of the baseball hall of fame who was never a teammate of another baseball hall-of-famer.

The 5'11", 199-pound Gwynn was a 1981 third-round draft pick (58th overall selection) of the San Diego Padres; made his major league debut on July 19, 1982; and played his entire 20-year career (1982–2001) with the team. He was a 15-time All-Star (1984–1987, 1989–1999); compiled a .338 career batting average (20th highest in major league history), with 3,141 hits (18th all-time), and 2,378 singles (9th all-time); hit over .300 every season except his rookie year when he did not play the entire season; and his single-season best batting average of .394 in 1994 was the highest in the major leagues in the 53 years since Ted Williams was the last player to hit over .400 (.406).

The best hitter of his era, Gwynn won eight National League batting titles (1984, 1987–1989, 1994–1997), tying him with Honus Wagner of the Pittsburgh Pirates for the most in National League history; had five 200-hit seasons; led the league in hits seven times (1984, 1986–1987, 1994–1995, 1997); won five Gold Gloves (1986–1987, 1989–1991); won seven Silver Slugger Awards (1984, 1986–1987, 1989, 1994–1995, 1997); and played in two World Series (losing in 1984 and 1998).

Gwynn was nicknamed "Captain Video" because of his extensive video collection of his previous at-bats against specific teams and pitchers, which he constantly studied.

During his college days at San Diego State University (California), he was a two-sport star, playing baseball and basketball (guard). He was drafted in the third round of the Amateur Draft by the Padres on June 8, 1981, and was sent to the Walla Walla Padres (Washington) of the Northwest League (Rookie), where he won a batting title and a Most Valuable Player award.

In 1984, he became the first Padre to collect 200 hits in a season and won the franchise's first-ever batting title with a .351 average. Gwynn was voted to the All-Star team, and delivered the game-winning RBI in the fifth game of the Championship Series that sent San Diego to its first-ever World Series, where it eventually lost to the Detroit Tigers.

On September 20, 1986, he tied a major league record with five stolen bases in a 10–6 loss to the Houston Astros. On April 13, 1987, the Padres set a major league record when its first three batters (Marvell Wynne, Gwynn, and John Kruk), for the first time in history, started a major league game with consecutive home runs (off pitcher Roger Mason). The early output was not enough, however, as the Padres would suffer a 13–6 loss to the San Francisco Giants.

In 1988, he won the batting title with a .313 average, the lowest mark ever to lead the National League.

In 1998, his .321 average led the Padres to the team's second World Series, another losing effort, this time to the New York Yankees.

On August 6, 1999, Gwynn collected his 3,000th hit off pitcher Dan Smith at Montreal's Olympic Stadium, becoming the 22nd player to reach the milestone, and the first to get his 3,000th hit outside the United States. Gwynn required the third fewest number of games to reach the milestone, with only the Detroit Tigers' Ty Cobb and the Cleveland Indians' Nap Lajoie reaching 3,000 hits in fewer games.

He struck out only 434 times in 9,288 career at-bats (4.67%) and was the first National League player born during the 1960s to be inducted into the baseball hall of fame (Kirby Puckett was the first in the American League). The Padres retired his jersey #19 in 2004. In 1999, while still an active player, Gwynn was ranked number 49 on *The Sporting*

News' list of the 100 Greatest Baseball Players, and he was nominated as a finalist for the Major League Baseball All-Century Team.

His career batting average (.338) is the highest among players whose careers began after World War II, and is the fourth-highest among players whose careers took place entirely within the live-ball era (only Ted Williams, Lou Gehrig, and Bill Terry have higher averages during that time).

At the time of Gwynn's hall of fame induction, he was the only member of the baseball hall of fame who was never a teammate of another baseball hall-of-famer. This changed in 2008 with the induction of Rich "Goose" Gossage, his teammate from 1984 to 1987.

On July 21, 2007, a 10-foot statue of Gwynn was unveiled outside PETCO Park in San Diego. As of this writing, Gwynn is the head baseball coach at San Diego State University (his alma mater), and often broadcasts Padres games on local television.

Tony Gwynn's Career Statistics

YEAR	TEAM	G	AB	R	H	2B	3B	HR	RBI	BB	SO	SB	AVG	SLG
1982	San Diego	54	190	33	55	12	2	1	17	14	16	8	.289	.389
1983	San Diego	86	304	34	94	12	2	1	37	23	21	7	.309	.372
1984	San Diego	158	606	88	213	21	10	5	71	59	23	33	.351	.444
1985	San Diego	154	622	90	197	29	5	6	46	45	33	14	.317	.408
1986	San Diego	160	642	107	211	33	7	14	59	52	35	37	.329	.467
1987	San Diego	157	589	119	218	36	13	7	54	82	35	56	.370	.511
1988	San Diego	133	521	64	163	22	5	7	70	51	40	26	.313	.415
1989	San Diego	158	604	82	203	27	7	4	62	56	30	40	.336	.424
1990	San Diego	141	573	79	177	29	10	4	72	44	23	17	.309	.415
1991	San Diego	134	530	69	168	27	11	4	62	34	19	8	.317	.432
1992	San Diego	128	520	77	165	27	3	6	41	46	16	3	.317	.415
1993	San Diego	122	489	70	175	41	3	7	59	36	19	14	.358	.497
1994	San Diego	110	419	79	165	35	1	12	64	48	19	5	.394	.568
1995	San Diego	135	535	82	197	33	1	9	90	35	15	17	.368	.484
1996	San Diego	116	451	67	159	27	2	3	50	39	17	11	.353	.441
1997	San Diego	149	592	97	220	49	2	17	119	43	28	12	.372	.547
1998	San Diego	127	461	65	148	35	0	16	69	35	18	3	.321	.501
1999	San Diego	111	411	59	139	27	0	10	62	29	14	7	.338	.477
2000	San Diego	36	127	17	41	12	0	1	17	9	4	0	.323	.441
2001	San Diego	71	102	5	33	9	1	1	17	10	9	1	.324	.461
	TOTALS	2,440	9,288	1,383	3,141	543	85	135	1,138	790	434	319	.338	.459

Sources: Baseball-Reference.com; National Baseball Hall of Fame and Museum

Chapter 8
Hafey to Hynes

Hafey, Charles James "Chick" (born: February 12, 1903 in Berkeley, California; died: July 2, 1973 in Calistoga, California); inducted into the National Baseball Hall of Fame and Museum in 1971 as a player by the Veterans Committee; Position: Left Field; Bats: Right; Throws: Right; tied a then-National League record with 10 straight hits during a three-game span in 1929; collected the first-ever hit in All-Star Game history (1933).

Overcoming several beanings, Hafey developed into a reliable line-drive hitter for the St. Louis Cardinals and Cincinnati Reds. When poor vision hampered his playing career, he began wearing eyeglasses (one of the first players to do so) and hit a National League-leading .349 in 1931. He hit .329 or better six straight seasons (1927–1932) and tied a then-National League record with 10 straight hits during a three-game span in 1929 (July 7–July 9).

On July 6, 1929, he hit two grand slams in a single game (a 28–6 win over the Philadelphia Phillies in the second game of a doubleheader), and on September 9, 1929, he had four extra-base hits in one game in a 9–3 loss to the Phillies.

Making his major league debut on August 28, 1924, the 6', 185-pound Hafey had a 13-year career with the St. Louis Cardinals (1924–1931) and Cincinnati Reds (1932–1935, 1937). He played in four World Series (winning in 1926 and 1931 and losing in 1928 and 1930); won the batting title in 1931 (.349); and was named to the 1933 All-Star team.

Hafey began playing baseball as a pitcher, but switched to the outfield prior to his major league career, and was considered the second-best right-handed hitter of his day, behind Rogers Hornsby. In 1933, he hit .303; was selected to the first-ever All-Star team; and collected the first-ever hit in All-Star Game history, a single in the second inning.

In a doubleheader against the Philadelphia Phillies on July 28, 1928, Hafey set a record with six extra-base hits (two doubles, two triples, and two home runs); he set a World Series record with five doubles in 1930; and on May 24, 1935, he played in the first-ever regular-season night game, a 2–1 Cincinnati win over the Philadelphia Phillies.

Chick Hafey's Career Statistics

YEAR	TEAM	LG	G	AB	R	H	2B	3B	HR	RBI	BB	SO	SB	AVG	SLG
1924	St. Louis	NL	24	91	10	23	5	2	2	22	4	8	1	.253	.418
1925	St. Louis	NL	93	358	36	108	25	2	5	57	10	29	3	.302	.425
1926	St. Louis	NL	78	225	30	61	19	2	4	38	11	36	2	.271	.427
1927	St. Louis	NL	103	346	62	114	26	5	18	63	36	41	12	.329	.590
1928	St. Louis	NL	138	520	101	175	46	6	27	111	40	53	8	.337	.604
1929	St. Louis	NL	134	517	101	175	47	9	29	125	45	42	7	.338	.632
1930	St. Louis	NL	120	446	108	150	39	12	26	107	46	51	12	.336	.652
1931	St. Louis	NL	122	450	94	157	35	8	16	95	39	43	11	.349	.569
1932	Cincinnati	NL	83	253	34	87	19	3	2	36	22	20	4	.344	.466
1933	Cincinnati	NL	144	568	77	172	34	6	7	62	40	44	3	.303	.421
1934	Cincinnati	NL	140	535	75	157	29	6	18	67	52	63	4	.293	.471
1935	Cincinnati	NL	15	59	10	20	6	1	1	9	4	5	1	.339	.525
1937	Cincinnati	NL	89	257	39	67	11	5	9	41	23	42	2	.261	.447
	TOTALS		1,283	4,625	777	1,466	341	67	164	833	372	477	70	.317	.526

Sources: Baseball-Reference.com; National Baseball Hall of Fame and Museum

Hagan, Clifford Oldham "Cliff" (born: December 9, 1931 in Owensboro, Kentucky); inducted into the Naismith Memorial Basketball Hall of Fame in 1978 as a player; Position: Forward-Guard; won a state high school title in 1949, an NCAA title in 1951, and an NBA title in 1958; first player to play in an All-Star Game for two different leagues; first ex-University of Kentucky player to be inducted into the basketball hall of fame.

Hagan attended Owensboro Senior High School (1945–1949), where he played basketball for four years; named All-District, All-Region, All-City, All-Conference, and All-State three times (1947–1949); named Outstanding Kentucky High School Player (1949); selected All-American in 1949; led the Red Devils to the 1949 state championship; scored a then-record 41 points in the final championship game, a record that stood for 15 years; and was a member of the First Fifteen All-American High School basketball team.

After high school, he received a bachelor's degree from the University of Kentucky (Lexington, graduating in 1954) and a master's degree from Washington University (St. Louis, Missouri, graduating in 1958). While playing for hall of fame coach Adolph Rupp, Hagan led the Kentucky Wildcats to an overall 86–5 record, including an undefeated season (25–0) in 1954; led UK to the National Collegiate Athletic Association championship in 1951 as a sophomore (a 68–58 win over Kansas State; his undefeated 1954 team did not participate in the NCAA tournament); a two-time consensus All-American and All-Southeastern Conference selection (1952, 1954); averaged 24 points and 13.5 rebounds per game, and scored a school-record 51 points against Temple (1954); and was the team's Most Valuable Player in 1954. He has been inducted into the Kentucky Athletic Hall of Fame (1974) and the UK Alumni Association Hall of Distinguished Alumni. Hagan was named to the Southeastern Conference All-Time Team; *Orlando Sentinel* All-Time Southeastern Conference First Team; and All-Time collegiate player in Kentucky by *Inside Kentucky Sports* magazine (1974).

In the fall of 1952, a point-shaving scandal involving three Kentucky players (including Hagan's teammate on the 1951 championship team) over a four-year period forced Kentucky to forfeit its upcoming season. The suspension of the season made Kentucky's basketball squad the first college sports team to get the so-called NCAA "death penalty." In 1954, Hagan led the team to an undefeated regular season (25–0), finishing the year ranked number one by the Associated Press.

By the time he graduated from Kentucky, Hagan had scored 1,475 points (third in school history) and grabbed 1,035 rebounds (second in school history). His uniform number six was retired by the school.

After leaving Kentucky, he joined the U.S. Air Force and served at Andrews Air Force Base (near Washington, D.C., 1954–1956); won two Worldwide Air Force basketball championships (1954–1955); and was a two-time All-Service selection (1954–1955).

Leaving the military, the 6'4", 215-pound Hagan spent his entire 10-year National Basketball Association career (1956–1966) with the St. Louis Hawks (after he had been traded to the team by the Boston Celtics, who had originally drafted him in the third round in 1953). After finishing his NBA career, he became a player-coach with the American Basketball Association's Dallas Chaparrals (1967–1970) when the ABA began operations.

He was named to the All-NBA Second Team twice (1958–1959); a five-time All-Star (1958–1962) and a six-time All-Pro (1957–1962); and won five consecutive Western Division titles (1957–1961) and an NBA Championship in 1958 (his second year with the team).

He compiled a free-throw percentage of .790 or better seven seasons in a row; once held the NBA record for most field goals scored in a single quarter (12); played in the first-ever ABA All-Star Game; and was the first player to play in an All-Star Game for two different leagues (ABA and NBA).

In 1967, the Dallas Chaparrals of the newly formed ABA hired Hagan as a player-coach and he scored 40 points in the team's very first game. He retired as a player after playing only three games during the 1969–1970 season and remained as Dallas coach until midway into the season. Hagan played in 94 ABA games and scored 1,423 points.

In 1972, he returned to the University of Kentucky as the school's assistant athletic director and took over the top job in 1975. He resigned as athletic director in November 1988 in the midst of a recruiting scandal that would also claim the job of head basketball coach Eddie Sutton.

In 1993, the University of Kentucky renamed its baseball field Cliff Hagan Stadium.

As the player-coach in Dallas, he was named the Texas Sports Writers Association Professional Coach of the Year in 1968, and in 1978, he became the first ex-University of Kentucky player to be inducted into the Naismith Memorial Basketball Hall of Fame.

Cliff Hagan's Career Statistics

SEASON	TEAM	LG	G	MIN	FG	FT	TRB	AST	PTS
1956–1957	St. Louis	NBA	67	971	134	100	247	86	368
1957–1958	St. Louis	NBA	70	2,190	503	385	707	175	1,391
1958–1959	St. Louis	NBA	72	2,702	646	415	783	245	1,707
1959–1960	St. Louis	NBA	75	2,798	719	421	803	299	1,859
1960–1961	St. Louis	NBA	77	2,701	661	383	715	381	1,705
1961–1962	St. Louis	NBA	77	2,784	701	362	633	370	1,764
1962–1963	St. Louis	NBA	79	1,716	491	244	341	193	1,226

SEASON	TEAM	LG	G	MIN	FG	FT	TRB	AST	PTS
1963–1964	St. Louis	NBA	77	2,279	572	269	377	193	1,413
1964–1965	St. Louis	NBA	77	1,739	393	214	276	136	1,000
1965–1966	St. Louis	NBA	74	1,851	419	176	234	164	1,014
1967–1968	Dallas	ABA	56	1,737	371	277	334	276	1,019
1968–1969	Dallas	ABA	35	579	132	123	102	122	387
1969–1970	Dallas	ABA	3	27	8	1	3	6	17
		NBA	745	21,731	5,239	2,969	5,116	2,242	13,447
		ABA	94	2,343	511	401	439	404	1,423
	TOTALS		839	24,074	5,750	3,370	5,555	2,646	14,870

Sources: Basketball-Reference.com; Naismith Memorial Basketball Hall of Fame

Haines, Jesse Joseph "Pop" (born: July 22, 1893 in Clayton, Ohio; died: August 5, 1978 in Dayton, Ohio); inducted into the National Baseball Hall of Fame and Museum in 1970 as a player by the Veterans Committee; Position: Pitcher; Bats: Right; Throws: Right; threw a no-hitter in 1924.

The 6', 190-pound Haines won 210 games during his 18 years with the St. Louis Cardinals (1920–1937). Making his major league debut on July 20, 1918, he played in one game with the Cincinnati Reds before joining the Cardinals in 1920.

Haines played in four World Series (winning in 1926 and 1934, losing in 1928 and 1930); won 20 games in a season three times (1923, 1927–1928); and helped the Cardinals win five pennants between 1926 and 1934. He threw a no-hitter on July 17, 1924 against the Boston Braves, winning 5–0 (the first no-hitter by a Cardinals pitcher in the National League since 1876), and in 1926, he beat the New York Yankees twice in the World Series, throwing a shutout and winning the seventh and deciding game.

Although originally signed by the Detroit Tigers, he played his entire major league career, except for one game in 1918, with St. Louis. After his one appearance in 1918 with the Reds, Haines had been sent to the minors (Kansas City Blues of the American Association), where his contract was bought in 1920 by Cardinals president Branch Rickey, and he threw 302 innings his first year with the team.

In 1927, he led the National League with six shutouts and 25 complete games.

Jesse Haines' Career Statistics

YEAR	TEAM	LG	W	L	PCT	G	SH	IP	H	R	ER	SO	BB	ERA
1918	Cincinnati	NL	0	0	.000	1	0	5	5	1	1	2	1	1.80
1920	St. Louis	NL	13	20	.394	47	4	302	303	136	100	120	80	2.98
1921	St. Louis	NL	18	12	.600	37	2	244	261	112	95	84	56	3.50
1922	St. Louis	NL	11	9	.550	29	2	183	207	103	78	62	45	3.84
1923	St. Louis	NL	20	13	.606	37	1	266	283	125	92	73	75	3.11
1924	St. Louis	NL	8	19	.296	35	1	223	275	129	109	69	66	4.40
1925	St. Louis	NL	13	14	.481	29	0	207	234	116	105	63	52	4.57
1926	St. Louis	NL	13	4	.765	33	3	183	186	76	66	46	48	3.25
1927	St. Louis	NL	24	10	.706	38	6	301	273	114	91	89	77	2.72
1928	St. Louis	NL	20	8	.714	33	1	240	238	98	85	77	72	3.19
1929	St. Louis	NL	13	10	.565	28	0	180	230	123	114	59	73	5.70
1930	St. Louis	NL	13	8	.619	29	0	182	215	107	87	68	54	4.30
1931	St. Louis	NL	12	3	.800	19	2	122	134	48	41	27	28	3.02
1932	St. Louis	NL	3	5	.375	20	1	85	116	51	45	27	16	4.76
1933	St. Louis	NL	9	6	.600	32	0	115	113	46	32	37	37	2.50
1934	St. Louis	NL	4	4	.500	37	0	90	86	42	35	17	19	3.50
1935	St. Louis	NL	6	5	.545	30	0	115	110	49	46	24	28	3.60
1936	St. Louis	NL	7	5	.583	25	0	99	110	44	43	19	21	3.91
1937	St. Louis	NL	3	3	.500	16	0	66	81	36	33	18	23	4.50
	TOTALS		210	158	.571	555	23	3,208	3,460	1,556	1,298	981	871	3.64

Sources: Baseball-Reference.com; National Baseball Hall of Fame and Museum

Hainsworth, George (born: June 26, 1895 in Toronto, Ontario, Canada; died: October 9, 1950 near Gravenhurst, Ontario, Canada); inducted into the Hockey Hall of Fame in 1961 as a player; Position: Goalie; won an OHA championship in 1914; won the Allan Cup in 1918; won two Stanley Cup titles; set a still-standing NHL record of going 270 minutes and eight seconds without allowing a goal during the 1930 playoffs.

A dominant goalie during the 1920s and 1930s, Hainsworth played 11 National Hockey League seasons (1926–1937) with the Montreal Canadiens (1926–1933, 1937) and Toronto Maple Leafs (1933–1937). His best season was in 1928–1929, when he allowed only 43 goals in 44 games and registered 22 shutouts.

In 1911–1912 season, he led the Ontario Hockey Association in wins; won an OHA championship in 1914; and won the Allan Cup in 1918.

Hainsworth made his professional debut with the Saskatoon Crescents (1923–1926) of the Western Canada Hockey League/Western Hockey League, where he led the league in games played all three seasons.

He signed with the NHL's Montreal Canadiens on August 23, 1926; replaced the team's legendary goalie, Georges Vézina, and would win the Vézina Trophy (as the league's best goalie) the first three years it was presented (1927–1929). He led all goalies in games played nine years out of 10 (1926–1936); in 1930, he set an NHL record that still stands, going 270 minutes and eight seconds without allowing a goal during the playoffs; and led the team to back-to-back Stanley Cup titles in 1930 and 1931.

Hainsworth served as the Canadiens' captain during 1932–1933, becoming the first of only three goalies to serve as an NHL team's captain (along with Charlie Gardiner of the Chicago Black Hawks in 1933–1934 and Bill Durnan of the Canadiens during the later half of the 1947–1948 season).

In 1933, he was traded to the Toronto Maple Leafs; helped the franchise win two Canadian Division titles; and led the team to the 1935 NHL Finals, eventually losing to the Montreal Maroons. On February 14, 1934, he was the Toronto goalie in the historic Ace Bailey Benefit Game.

After leading the league twice in wins (1936–1937), the Leafs hired goalie Turk Broda, and Hainsworth was allowed to re-sign as a free agent with the Canadiens, where he played his last four NHL games.

The 5'6", 150-pound Hainsworth retired in 1937 with a 1.93 career goals-against mark, and his 94 shutouts was an NHL record until Terry Sawchuk surpassed him in the 1963–1964 season. In 1998, he was ranked number 46 on *The Hockey News*' list of the 100 Greatest Hockey Players.

After retiring from hockey, Hainsworth pursued a political career.

George Hainsworth's Career Statistics

			REGULAR SEASON						PLAYOFFS					
SEASON	TEAM	LEAGUE	GP	W	L	T	SO	AVG	GP	W	L	T	SO	AVG
1910–1911	Berlin Mavericks	Minor-ON												
1911–1912	Berlin Union Jacks	OHA-Jr.	4	3	1	0	0	3.25	6	2	3	1	0	5.00
1912–1913	Berlin City Seniors	OHA-Sr.	4	3	1	0	1	3.00	8	4	3	1	1	4.38
1913–1914	Berlin City Seniors	OHA-Sr.	7	7	0	0	0	1.57	9	7	1	1	1	3.15
1914–1915	Berlin City Seniors	OHA-Sr.	5	5	0	0	1	1.80	4	2	1	1	1	4.75
1915–1916	Berlin City Seniors	OHA-Sr.	8	8	0	0	1	2.85	4	2	2	0	0	3.86
1916–1917	Toronto Kew Beach	TIHL												
1917–1918	Kitchener Green-shirts	OHA-Sr.	9	9	0	0	0	3.44	5	3	1	1	1	2.01
1918–1919	Kitchener Green-shirts	OHA-Sr.	9	5	3	1	0	2.95						
1919–1920	Kitchener Green-shirts	OHA-Sr.	8	6	2	0	1	2.00	2	0	1	1	0	2.40
1920–1921	Kitchener Green-shirts	OHA-Sr.	10	7	3	0	3	2.20	1	0	1	0	0	6.00
1921–1922	Kitchener Green-shirts	OHA-Sr.	10	3	7	0	1	3.80						
1922–1923	Kitchener Green-shirts	OHA-Sr.	12	8	4	0	1	2.67						
1923–1924	Saskatoon Cres-cents	WCHL	30	15	12	3	4	2.34						
1924–1925	Saskatoon Cres-cents	WCHL	28	16	11	1	2	2.65	2	0	1	1	0	3.00
1925–1926	Saskatoon Cres-cents	WHL	30	17	12	1	4	2.11	2	0	1	1	0	1.86
1926–1927	Montreal Canadiens	NHL	44	28	14	2	14	1.47	4	1	1	2	1	1.43
1927–1928	Montreal Canadiens	NHL	44	26	11	7	13	1.05	2	0	1	1	0	1.41
1928–1929	Montreal Canadiens	NHL	44	22	7	15	22	0.92	3	0	3	0	0	1.67
1929–1930	Montreal Canadiens	NHL	42	20	13	9	4	2.42	6	5	0	1	3	0.75
1930–1931	Montreal Canadiens	NHL	44	26	10	8	8	1.95	10	6	4	0	2	1.75
1931–1932	Montreal Canadiens	NHL	48	25	16	7	6	2.20	4	1	3	0	0	2.60
1932–1933	Montreal Canadiens	NHL	48	18	25	5	8	2.32	2	0	1	1	0	4.00

SEASON	TEAM	LEAGUE	REGULAR SEASON GP	W	L	T	SO	AVG	PLAYOFFS GP	W	L	T	SO	AVG
1933–1934	Toronto Maple Leafs	NHL	48	26	13	9	3	2.37	5	2	3	0	0	2.19
1934–1935	Toronto Maple Leafs	NHL	48	30	14	4	8	2.25	7	3	4	0	2	1.57
1935–1936	Toronto Maple Leafs	NHL	48	23	19	6	8	2.12	9	4	5	0	0	2.99
1936–1937	Toronto Maple Leafs	NHL	3	0	2	1	0	2.84						
1936–1937	Montreal Canadiens	NHL	4	2	1	1	0	2.67						
	NHL TOTALS		465	246	145	74	94	1.93	52	22	25	5	8	1.93

Sources: Hockey Hall of Fame; Hockey-Reference.com

Halas, George Stanley, Sr. (born: February 2, 1895 in Chicago, Illinois; died: October 31, 1983 in Chicago, Illinois); inducted into the Pro Football Hall of Fame in 1963 as a founder-owner; one of the charter members of the football hall of fame; helped form the National Football League and was the only person associated with the league during all of its first 50 years; won six titles.

Halas was involved in professional football for over 60 years in a variety of roles, including player, promoter, manager, and owner. He founded the Decatur Staleys (1920) of the newly formed American Professional Football Association and represented the team at the organizational meeting in Canton, Ohio on September 17, 1920 that led to the formation of the National Football League. In 1921, the Staleys became the Chicago Staleys, and in 1922, the Chicago Bears. He was associated with the team from 1920 until his death in 1983. Halas is the only person associated with the NFL during all of its first 50 years.

Although he coached the Bears for 40 seasons, he stepped away from the coaching ranks three times (1930–1932, 1942–1945 [while he served in the military], and 1956–1957). He won six championships (1921 with the Staleys, 1933, 1940–1941, 1946, 1963) and led the team to two undefeated seasons (1934, 1942). His 318 regular-season wins and 324 total victories were long-standing NFL records until broken by Don Shula in 1993.

As a coach, Halas was the first to hold daily practice sessions; use films of opponents' games for study; schedule barnstorming tours; and have his team's games broadcast on radio. He also offered to share the Bears' television revenue with teams in smaller cities, believing that what was good for the league would ultimately benefit his own team. He used the T-formation attack to lead the Bears to a 73–0 NFL title win over the Washington Redskins in the 1940 NFL Championship Game.

Halas graduated from Crane Tech High School (Chicago, Illinois) and attended the University of Illinois (Urbana-Champaign), where he played baseball, basketball, and football, and helped the school win the 1918 Big Ten football championship.

After graduating from college in 1918, Halas served as an ensign in the Navy during World War I; played for the Great Lakes Naval Training Station team (Illinois); and was named the Most Valuable Player of the 1919 Rose Bowl by scoring two touchdowns and returning an intercepted pass 77 yards in a 17–0 win over Mare Island.

After leaving the military, he played minor league and semi-professional baseball, before being signed by Major League Baseball's New York Yankees. He played 12 games as an outfielder for the team in 1919 before a hip injury ended his baseball career.

Leaving the Yankees, he worked at Staley Starch Works (Decatur, Illinois) and played on the company-sponsored baseball team while also serving as a player-coach of the football team owned by the company's founder, A.E. Staley. He selected his alma mater's colors, orange and blue, for the team's uniforms and in 1920, represented Mr. Staley at the Canton, Ohio meeting that led to the creation of the National Football League. Halas was awarded a franchise and called the team the Decatur Staleys, in honor of the founder's financial contribution to the team. After playing to a 10–1–2 record, substantial financial losses forced the team to move to Chicago in 1921, where the team won the NFL championship its first year in its new city. The next season, 1922, the team became the Bears and played its games at Wrigley Field.

While with the team, the 6', 182-pound Halas not only played offensive end, but also conducted the franchise's business operations, and coached the team. Named to the NFL's All-Pro team throughout the 1920s, his singular playing highlight occurred on November 24, 1923 in a 26–0 win over the Oorang Indians when he stripped the legendary Jim Thorpe of the ball, recovered the fumble, and returned it 98 yards, a league record that would stand until 1972.

After nine seasons, and 104 games, Halas stepped back in 1930 and retired as a player and coach, but remained partial owner of the club, becoming sole owner in 1932. In 1933, one year after the team won the NFL championship, he returned to coach the Bears for another ten seasons. His 1934 team was undefeated until a 30–13 loss in the championship game to the New York Giants. The Bears won the NFL championship four times in the 1940s (1940–1941, 1943, 1946) and the team would later be known as the "Monsters of the Midway."

Halas again left the team during World War II and served in the U.S. Navy from 1943 to 1945, while the Bears won another title in 1943. Leaving the military, he returned to coach the Bears for a third decade, and won the title again his first year back (1946). After a brief break in 1956–1957, Halas again resumed his role as coach for a final decade (1958–1967) and won his last championship in 1963. He won his 200th game in 1950 and his 300th game in 1965, becoming the first NFL coach to reach both milestones. After the 1967 season, "Papa Bear" Halas retired as the oldest coach in league history, but continued to own the team and run its business operations.

In the 1930s, Halas played a key role in keeping the NFL segregated by refusing to sign black players for the Bears. He eventually changed his attitude and helped to integrate the league by drafting the NFL's first black player since 1933, George Taliaferro, although Taliaferro never did play for the Bears. Halas later signed Willie Thrower, who became the league's first black quarterback.

Halas was an owner for 63 years; a coach for 40 years; was a charter member of the Pro Football Hall of Fame (which is located on George Halas Drive in Canton, Ohio); the NFC championship trophy bears his name; in 1963 and 1965, he was selected NFL Coach of the Year by *The Sporting News*, Associated Press, and United Press International; in 1997, he was featured on a United States postage stamp as one of the legendary coaches of football; recognized by ESPN as one of the ten most influential people in sports in the 20th century; and to this day, the jerseys of the Chicago Bears are imprinted with "GSH" on the left sleeves in tribute to Halas.

He was named to the NFL 1920s All-Decade Team and the Chicago Bears retired his jersey number seven.

George Halas' Coaching Statistics

			REGULAR SEASON				**PLAYOFFS**			
YEAR	**TEAM**	**LG**	**W**	**L**	**T**	**WIN%**	**W**	**L**	**WIN%**	**NOTES**
1920	Decatur Staleys	APFA	10	1	2	.909				
1921	Chicago Staleys	APFA	9	1	1	.900				NFL Champions
1922	Chicago Bears	NFL	9	3	0	.750				
1923	Chicago Bears	NFL	9	2	1	.818				
1924	Chicago Bears	NFL	6	1	4	.857				
1925	Chicago Bears	NFL	9	5	3	.643				
1926	Chicago Bears	NFL	12	1	3	.923				
1927	Chicago Bears	NFL	9	3	2	.750				
1928	Chicago Bears	NFL	7	5	1	.583				
1929	Chicago Bears	NFL	4	9	2	.308				
1933	Chicago Bears	NFL	10	2	1	.833	1	0	1.000	NFL Champions
1934	Chicago Bears	NFL	13	0	0	1.000	0	1	.000	
1935	Chicago Bears	NFL	6	4	2	.600				
1936	Chicago Bears	NFL	9	3	0	.750				
1937	Chicago Bears	NFL	9	1	1	.900	0	1	.000	
1938	Chicago Bears	NFL	6	5	0	.545				
1939	Chicago Bears	NFL	8	3	0	.727				
1940	Chicago Bears	NFL	8	3	0	.727	1	0	1.000	NFL Champions
1941	Chicago Bears	NFL	10	1	0	.909	2	0	1.000	NFL Champions
1942	Chicago Bears	NFL	5	0	0	1.000				
1946	Chicago Bears	NFL	8	2	1	.800	1	0	1.000	NFL Champions
1947	Chicago Bears	NFL	8	4	0	.667				
1948	Chicago Bears	NFL	10	2	0	.833				
1949	Chicago Bears	NFL	9	3	0	.750				
1950	Chicago Bears	NFL	9	3	0	.750	0	1	.000	
1951	Chicago Bears	NFL	7	5	0	.583				
1952	Chicago Bears	NFL	5	7	0	.417				
1953	Chicago Bears	NFL	3	8	1	.273				
1954	Chicago Bears	NFL	8	4	0	.667				
1955	Chicago Bears	NFL	8	4	0	.667				
1958	Chicago Bears	NFL	8	4	0	.667				
1959	Chicago Bears	NFL	8	4	0	.667				

YEAR	TEAM	LG	REGULAR SEASON W	L	T	WIN%	PLAYOFFS W	L	WIN%	NOTES
1960	Chicago Bears	NFL	5	6	1	.455				
1961	Chicago Bears	NFL	8	6	0	.571				
1962	Chicago Bears	NFL	9	5	0	.643				
1963	Chicago Bears	NFL	11	1	2	.917	1	0	1.000	NFL Champions
1964	Chicago Bears	NFL	5	9	0	.357				
1965	Chicago Bears	NFL	9	5	0	.643				
1966	Chicago Bears	NFL	5	7	2	.417				
1967	Chicago Bears	NFL	7	6	1	.538				
	TOTALS		318	148	31	.682	6	3	.667	

Sources: *Papa Bear: The Life and Legacy of George Halas* (Jeff Davis); Pro Football Hall of Fame; Pro-Football-Reference.com

Hall, Glenn Henry (born: October 3, 1931 in Humboldt, Saskatchewan, Canada); inducted into the Hockey Hall of Fame in 1975 as a player; Position: Goalie; won the Calder Trophy as the NHL's Rookie of the Year; won two Stanley Cup championships (one before playing in a single NHL regular-season game).

Hall played 18 National Hockey League seasons (1952–1971) for the Detroit Red Wings (1952, 1954–1957), Chicago Black Hawks (1957–1967), and St. Louis Blues (1967–1971); had 84 shutouts (third all-time); and only played in four losing seasons.

Hall played briefly in the Ontario Hockey Association (1949–1951), before being signed by the NHL's Detroit Red Wings in 1951 and being sent to the team's minor league farm system for two seasons (Edmonton Flyers of the Western Hockey League and the Indianapolis Capitols of the American Hockey League).

During the 1952 playoffs, he was called up from the minor league to be the backup goalie in the finals, but did not play for Detroit. When the Red Wings won the championship, the team put Hall's name on the Stanley Cup and awarded him a ring, although he had not yet played in a single NHL game. In the 1952–1953 season, he made his first NHL appearance with Detroit, playing in six games and allowing only 1.67 goals against.

Hall was called up to Detroit full-time at the beginning of the 1955–1956 season, and the 5'11", 160-pound goalie had 12 shutouts (one shy of the then-record); allowed only 2.10 goals against; played in every game; and won the Calder Trophy as the NHL's Rookie of the Year. He played one more complete season with Detroit, before being sent to the Chicago Black Hawks.

With the Black Hawks, he played a record 502 consecutive regular-season games (and 50 more in the playoffs), a streak that ended on November 8, 1963, when he hurt his back getting dressed before a game. Hall played in Chicago 10 seasons, and was selected to the All-Star Team eight times (five First Team, three Second Team). In 1961, he led Chicago to the team's first Stanley Cup championship since 1938, and in 1963, he won his first Vezina Trophy as the league's best goalie.

He shared the Vezina Trophy with Denis DeJordy in 1967, and after the season, was signed by the expansion St. Louis Blues. He led the team to the Stanley Cup finals in its very first season in the NHL, eventually losing to the Montreal Canadiens. Hall won the Conn Smythe Trophy as the league's Most Valuable Player in the playoffs, an award rarely presented to a member of the losing team. In 1968–1969, Jacques Plante joined the team and shared goalie responsibilities with Hall, and when the season ended, both players shared the Vezina Trophy.

Hall retired in 1971, and later worked with the Blues and the Calgary Flames as a consultant and goalie coach. He won his third Stanley Cup in 1989 as the goalie coach with the Calgary Flames. In 1998, he was ranked number 16 on *The Hockey News*' list of the 100 Greatest Hockey Players.

Glenn Hall's Career Statistics

SEASON	TEAM	LEAGUE	REGULAR SEASON GP	W	L	T	SO	AVG	PLAYOFFS GP	W	L	T	SO	AVG
1947–1948	Humboldt Indians	N-SJHL	5	5	0	0	0	3.40	2	0	2	0	0	7.50
1948–1949	Humboldt Indians	N-SJHL	24	13	9	2	1	3.63	7	3	4	0	0	5.14
1949–1950	Windsor Spitfires	OHA-Jr.	43	31	11	1	0	3.53	11	6	5	0	0	3.36
1950–1951	Windsor Spitfires	OHA-Jr.	54	32	18	4	6	3.09	8				0	3.75

SEASON	TEAM	LEAGUE	REGULAR SEASON GP	W	L	T	SO	AVG	PLAYOFFS GP	W	L	T	SO	AVG
1951–1952	Indianapolis Capitols	AHL	68	22	40	6	0	3.89						
1951–1952	Detroit Red Wings	NHL												
1952–1953	Edmonton Flyers	WHL	63	27	27	9	2	3.29	15	10	5	0	0	3.51
1952–1953	Detroit Red Wings	NHL	6	4	1	1	1	1.67						
1953–1954	Edmonton Flyers	WHL	70	29	30	11	0	3.70	13	7	6	0	2	3.37
1954–1955	Edmonton Flyers	WHL	66	38	18	10	5	2.83	16	11	5	0	1	2.58
1954–1955	Detroit Red Wings	NHL	2	2	0	0	0	1.00						
1955–1956	Detroit Red Wings	NHL	70	30	24	16	12	2.10	10	5	5		0	2.78
1956–1957	Detroit Red Wings	NHL	70	38	20	12	4	2.21	5	1	4		0	3.00
1957–1958	Chicago Black Hawks	NHL	70	24	39	7	7	2.86						
1958–1959	Chicago Black Hawks	NHL	70	28	29	13	1	2.97	6	2	4		0	3.50
1959–1960	Chicago Black Hawks	NHL	70	28	29	13	6	2.56	4	0	4		0	3.37
1960–1961	Chicago Black Hawks	NHL	70	29	24	17	6	2.51	12	8	4		2	2.02
1961–1962	Chicago Black Hawks	NHL	70	31	26	13	9	2.63	12	6	6		2	2.58
1962–1963	Chicago Black Hawks	NHL	66	30	20	15	5	2.47	6	2	4		0	4.17
1963–1964	Chicago Black Hawks	NHL	65	34	19	11	7	2.30	7	3	4		0	3.24
1964–1965	Chicago Black Hawks	NHL	41	18	17	5	4	2.43	13	7	6		1	2.21
1965–1966	Chicago Black Hawks	NHL	64	34	21	7	4	2.63	6	2	4		0	3.80
1966–1967	Chicago Black Hawks	NHL	32	19	5	5	2	2.38	3	1	2		0	2.73
1967–1968	St. Louis Blues	NHL	49	19	21	9	5	2.48	18	8	10		1	2.43
1968–1969	St. Louis Blues	NHL	41	19	12	8	8	2.17	3	0	2		0	2.29
1969–1970	St. Louis Blues	NHL	18	7	8	3	1	2.91	7	4	3		0	2.99
1970–1971	St. Louis Blues	NHL	32	13	11	8	2	2.42	3	0	3		0	3.00
	NHL TOTALS		906	407	326	163	84	2.49	115	49	65		6	2.78

Sources: Hockey Hall of Fame; Hockey-Reference.com

Hall, Joseph Henry (born: May 3, 1882 in Staffordshire, England; died: April 5, 1919 in Seattle, Washington); inducted into the Hockey Hall of Fame in 1961 as a player; Position: Forward-Defenseman; won three Stanley Cup titles.

Hall and his family moved to Brandon, Manitoba, Canada in the late 1890s, where he played hockey in the Manitoba Senior League in 1902. The next year, still an amateur, he played in the Western Canada Amateur Hockey Association before turning professional in 1905–1906 with the Houghton-Portage Lakes (International Hockey League). He would go on to play 16 professional seasons from 1903 to 1919.

He was named an IHL First Team All-Star his rookie season as a forward, before becoming a defenseman. After winning a Stanley Cup title with the Kenora Thistles in 1907, the 5’10”, 175-pound Hall won two more championships with the Quebec Bulldogs (National Hockey Association) in 1912 and 1913.

When the NHA folded and the National Hockey League was created in 1917, Hall was selected by the Montreal Canadiens in the dispersal draft. In the spring of 1919, the best-of-five NHL championship series between the Canadiens and the Seattle Metropolitans was cancelled after each team had won two games because of the influenza epidemic that had spread throughout many parts of North America. Hall and most of his teammates became ill, and everyone recovered except Hall, who died in the hospital.

Joseph Hall's Career Statistics

			REGULAR SEASON					PLAYOFFS				
SEASON	**TEAM**	**LEAGUE**	**GP**	**G**	**A**	**TP**	**PIM**	**GP**	**G**	**A**	**TP**	**PIM**
1901–1902	Brandon Hockey Club	MNWHA-Int	10	11	0	11	8					
1902–1903	Brandon Elks	MNWHA	6	9	0	9						
1903–1904	Winnipeg Rowing Club	WCAHA	6	6	0	6						
1903–1904	Winnipeg Rowing Club	St-Cup						3	1	0	1	
1904–1905	Brandon Elks	MHL	8	11	0	11						
1905–1906	Portage Lakes	IHL	20	33	0	33	98					
1905–1906	Quebec Bulldogs	ECAHA	3	2	0	2	3					
1906–1907	Kenora Thistles	St-Cup										
1906–1907	Brandon Elks	MHL-Pro	10	15	1	16	32	2	5	0	5	5
1907–1908	Montreal AAA	ECAHA	4	5	0	5	11					
1907–1908	Montreal Shamrocks	ECAHA	4	4	0	4	6					
1908–1909	Edmonton Professionals	APHL	1	8	0	8	6					
1908–1909	Montreal Wanderers	ECHA	5	10	0	10	18					
1908–1909	Winnipeg Maple Leafs	MHL-Pro	2	2	1	3	0	2	2	1	3	9
1909–1910	Montreal Shamrocks	NHA	10	8	0	8	47					
1909–1910	Montreal Shamrocks	CHA	1	7	0	7	6					
1910–1911	Quebec Bulldogs	NHA	10	0	0	0	20					
1911–1912	Quebec Bulldogs	NHA	18	15	0	15	30					
1911–1912	Quebec Bulldogs	St-Cup						2	2	0	2	2
1912–1913	Quebec Bulldogs	NHA	17	8	0	8	78					
1912–1913	Quebec Bulldogs	St-Cup						2	3	0	3	0
1912–1913	Quebec Bulldogs	Exhib.	3	0	0	0	7					
1913–1914	Quebec Bulldogs	NHA	19	13	4	17	61					
1914–1915	Quebec Bulldogs	NHA	20	3	2	5	52					
1915–1916	Quebec Bulldogs	NHA	23	1	2	3	89					
1916–1917	Quebec Bulldogs	NHA	19	6	5	11	95					
1917–1918	Montreal Canadiens	NHL	21	8	7	15	100	2	0	1	1	12
1918–1919	Montreal Canadiens	NHL	17	7	1	8	89	5	0	0	0	26
1918–1919	Montreal Canadiens	St-Cup						5	0	0	0	6
	NHL TOTALS		38	15	8	23	189	7	0	1	1	38

Sources: Hockey Hall of Fame; Hockey-Reference.com

Ham, Jack Raphael, Jr. (born: December 23, 1948 in Johnstown, Pennsylvania); inducted into the Pro Football Hall of Fame in 1988 as a player; Position: Linebacker; Uniform: #59; a member of the NFL's Defensive 20/20 Club; won four Super Bowl championships.

Ham attended Bishop McCort High School (Johnstown, Pennsylvania), followed by Massanutten Military Academy (Woodstock, Virginia) for a post graduate season. He was a consensus All-American (as a senior) at Pennsylvania State University (University Park), where he played for three seasons (1968–1970). During his tenure at the school, Penn State compiled season records of 11–0, 11–0, and 7–3; he blocked three punts in 1968 (setting a school record that was not broken until 1989); and was team co-captain as a senior (1970).

After college, Ham was the 34th player taken in the 1971 National Football League Draft, a second-round selection of the Pittsburgh Steelers, and played his entire 12-year career (1971–1982, 162 games) with the team.

He became a starter as a rookie; All-American Football Conference or All-Pro seven consecutive years (1973–1979); named to eight straight Pro Bowls (1973–1980); and collected 25½ career sacks, recovered 21 opponent fumbles, and made 32 interceptions. In 1975, the *Football News* named him the Defensive Player of the Year.

The 6'3", 212-pound Ham won four Super Bowls (SB IX in 1975, SB X in 1976, SB XIII in 1979, and SB XIV in 1980, although he did not play due to injuries).

After Ham retired from the NFL, he became a radio broadcaster and sports analyst for the Penn State Radio Network, as well as working other media outlets.

He was named to the NFL 1970s All-Decade Team; selected to the NFL 75th Anniversary All-Time Team; and earned a spot in the NFL's Defensive 20/20 Club (an NFL player who accumulates at least 20 sacks and 20 interceptions in a career). In 1990, he was inducted into the College Football Hall of Fame and in 1999, he was ranked number 47 on *The Sporting News*' list of the 100 Greatest Football Players.

Jack Ham's Career Statistics

YEAR	TEAM	G	INT	YDS	AVG	TD	FUM REC	YDS
1971	Pittsburgh	14	2	4	2.0	0	1	0
1972	Pittsburgh	14	7	83	11.9	1	4	0
1973	Pittsburgh	13	2	30	15.0	0	1	0
1974	Pittsburgh	14	5	13	2.6	0	1	2
1975	Pittsburgh	14	1	2	2.0	0	1	0
1976	Pittsburgh	14	2	13	6.5	0	2	17
1977	Pittsburgh	14	4	17	4.3	0	1	0
1978	Pittsburgh	14	3	7	2.3	0	2	0
1979	Pittsburgh	15	2	8	4.0	0	1	0
1980	Pittsburgh	16	2	16	8.0	0	3	0
1981	Pittsburgh	12	1	23	23.0	0	3	0
1982	Pittsburgh	8	1	2	2.0	0	1	0
	TOTALS	162	32	218	6.81	1	22	19

Sources: College Football Hall of Fame; Pro Football Hall of Fame; Pro-Football-Reference.com

Hamilton, William Robert "Billy" (born: February 16, 1866 in Newark, New Jersey; died: December 16, 1940 in Worcester, Massachusetts); inducted into the National Baseball Hall of Fame and Museum in 1961 as a player by the Veterans Committee; Position: Center Field; Bats: Left; Throws: Right; holds major league record for most runs scored in a season (196); scored more career runs (1,691) than career games played (1,578); first New Jersey native inducted into the baseball hall of fame.

Although best remembered as a base stealer (on August 31, 1894, he tied the major league record for most stolen bases in one game with seven against the Washington Senators in an 11–5 win in the second game of a doubleheader), Hamilton was an excellent hitter and fielder. His 937 career stolen bases and single-season total of 115 in 1891 stood as National League records for almost 80 years. He hit .300 or better 12 consecutive seasons, and scored more career runs than career games played.

Making his major league debut on July 31, 1888, the 5'6", 165-pound Hamilton enjoyed a 14-year career with the Kansas City Cowboys (American Association, 1888–1889), Philadelphia Phillies (1890–1895), and the Boston Beaneaters (1896–1901). While with the Phillies, he averaged 146 runs scored and 92 stolen bases a season, while hitting as high as .404 (in 1894). In 1896, he moved to the Boston Beaneaters and scored over 100 runs in four of his six seasons with the team. He still holds the major league record for runs scored in a season, 196 (some sources indicate 192) in 1894, and is considered the game's first great leadoff hitter.

Hamilton retired after the 1901 season with a .455 career on-base percentage (fourth all-time behind Ted Williams, Babe Ruth, and John McGraw) and he was the first New Jersey native to be inducted into the baseball hall of fame.

He led the major leagues in stolen bases five times (1889–1891, 1894–1895); batting average once (1893); runs scored four times (1891, 1894–1895, 1897); and times on base three times (1894, 1896–1897).

Billy Hamilton's Career Statistics

YEAR	TEAM	LG	G	AB	R	H	2B	3B	HR	BB	SO	SB	AVG	SLG
1888	Kansas City	AA	35	128	17	32	4	4	0	4		23	.250	.344
1889	Kansas City	AA	137	532	145	160	15	15	3	87	41	117	.301	.402
1890	Philadelphia	NL	123	496	131	161	10	9	2	83	37	102	.325	.393
1891	Philadelphia	NL	133	529	142	179	21	6	2	102	28	115	.338	.412
1892	Philadelphia	NL	136	539	131	178	18	7	3	81	29	56	.330	.406
1893	Philadelphia	NL	82	349	111	138	21	7	5	63	7	41	.395	.539

YEAR	TEAM	LG	G	AB	R	H	2B	3B	HR	BB	SO	SB	AVG	SLG
1894	Philadelphia	NL	131	559	196	223	22	14	4	126	17	99	.399	.510
1895	Philadelphia	NL	121	517	166	203	19	6	7	96	30	95	.393	.493
1896	Boston	NL	131	523	153	190	26	8	3	110	29	93	.363	.461
1897	Boston	NL	125	506	153	174	17	6	3	105		70	.344	.419
1898	Boston	NL	109	417	111	153	16	4	3	87		59	.367	.446
1899	Boston	NL	81	294	62	90	6	1	1	72		19	.306	.344
1900	Boston	NL	135	524	103	174	19	5	1	107		29	.332	.393
1901	Boston	NL	99	349	70	102	11	2	3	64		19	.292	.361
	TOTALS		1,578	6,262	1,691	2,157	225	94	40	1,187	218	937	.344	.430

Sources: Baseball-Reference.com; National Baseball Hall of Fame and Museum

Hamm-Garciaparra, Mia (born: Mariel Margaret Hamm on March 17, 1972 in Selma, Alabama); inducted into the National Soccer Hall of Fame and Museum in 2007 as a player; Position: Forward; International Caps: (1987–2004): 275; International Goals: 158; scored more points in international competition than any player in history; youngest member ever on the U.S. National Team; youngest woman ever to win a World Cup; one of only two women to be placed on FIFA's list of the 125 greatest living soccer players.

Considered by many to be the greatest woman soccer player in the early years of the 21st century, Hamm scored 158 goals in international competition, more than any other player in history. A forward and midfielder for the U.S. Women's National Team, she won two FIFA World Cups (1991 in China, 1999 in California); two FIFA bronze medals (1995 in Sweden, 2003 in the United States); and three Olympic Games medals (gold in both 1996 (United States) and 2004 (Athens, Greece) and silver in 2000 (Sydney, Australia)).

She competed in 275 full international games between 1987 and 2004, and at age 15, she was the youngest person ever to be a member of the U.S. National Team. Her first international game was against China (August 1987); she made her first international goal in her 17th game on July 25, 1990 against Norway; at age 19, she became the youngest woman ever to win a World Cup (1991); and her last international game was against Mexico (in Carson City, California on December 8, 2004). On May 22, 1999, Hamm broke the all-time international record with her 108th goal in a game against Brazil in Orlando, Florida.

In 1989, Hamm attended the University of North Carolina (Chapel Hill), where she led the Tar Heels to four NCAA championships; was named an All-American and Atlantic Coast Conference Player of the Year three years in a row; won the Honda-Broderick Award as the nation's outstanding female collegiate athlete (1993–1994); led the nation in collegiate scoring three times (1990, 1992–1993); and graduated with an all-time record for most conference goals (103), assists (72), and total points (278). She was later selected to the Soccer America College Team of the Century.

The 5'5", 125-pound Hamm was a founding member of the Women's United Soccer Association; played three seasons for the Washington Freedom; won a WUSA title and was a league All-tar in 2003; and played in 49 WUSA regular-season games and four WUSA playoff games.

At the international level, she was named FIFA's Women's World Player of the Year twice (2001–2002) and the U.S. Soccer Federation Female Athlete of the Year five straight years (1994–1998). In 2004, she and teammate Michelle Akers were placed on FIFA's list of the 125 greatest living soccer players, being the only women and the only Americans to make this list.

Hamm played high school soccer at Notre Dame Catholic School (Wichita Falls, Texas), before finishing high school at Lake Braddock Secondary School (Burke, Virginia).

In 1999, she created the Mia Hamm Foundation to raise funds for bone marrow research and to empower young female athletes. The idea for the medical research came from the death of her brother, Garrett, in 1997 from a bone marrow-related disease. She is the author of the best-selling book, *Go for the Goal: A Champion's Guide to Winning in Soccer and Life*, and she is married to former Major League Baseball player Nomar Garciaparra. Her 2007 induction into the soccer hall of fame with Julie Foudy marked the first all-female class. She was inducted into the Texas Sports Hall of Fame in March 2008.

Mia Hamm-Garciaparra's Career Statistics

YEAR	TEAM	CHAMPIONSHIP/MEDAL
1989	University of North Carolina	NCAA National Champion
1990	University of North Carolina	NCAA National Champion
1991	USA Women's National Team	FIFA World Cup Champion
1992	University of North Carolina	NCAA National Champion

YEAR	TEAM	CHAMPIONSHIP/MEDAL
1993	University of North Carolina	NCAA National Champion
1995	USA Women's National Team	FIFA World Cup Third Place
1996	USA Women's National Team	Olympic Gold
1999	USA Women's National Team	FIFA World Cup Champion
2000	USA Women's National Team	Olympic Silver
2003	Washington Freedom	WUSA Founder's Cup Champion
2003	USA Women's National Team	FIFA World Cup Third Place
2004	USA Women's National Team	Olympic Gold

Source: National Soccer Hall of Fame and Museum

Hampton, Daniel Oliver "Dan" (born: September 19, 1957 in Oklahoma City, Oklahoma); inducted into the Pro Football Hall of Fame in 2002 as a player; Position: Defensive Tackle-Defensive End; Uniform: #99; won one Super Bowl; only the second Bear to play in three different decades.

After an All-American season as a senior at the University of Arkansas (Fayetteville), Hampton was a first-round draft pick of the Chicago Bears (fourth overall selection) in 1979 and played his entire 12-year National Football League career (1979–1990, 157 games) with the team. He became a starter as a rookie; named a First- or Second-Team All Pro six times (1980, 1982, 1984–1986, 1988) as either a defensive tackle or end; and was selected to four Pro Bowls (1980, 1982, 1984–1985). Hampton was selected to the NFL 1980s All-Decade Team; named the *Pro Football Weekly* 1982 NFL Defensive Player of the Year; selected NFL Players' Association 1984 NFC Defensive Lineman of the Year; and won the George S. Halas Courage Award in 1990.

As a rookie, the 6'5", 265-pound Hampton had 70 tackles (including 40 solo); two fumble recoveries, and two sacks. In 1980, he led the team with 11½ sacks and his 73 tackles were the most by a Bears lineman. In the nine-game, strike-shortened 1982 season, he played right end and led the Bears with nine sacks and was second on the team with 71 tackles.

Like most of the Bears in the 1980s, he and the team are best remembered for the 1985 season. In that year, the defense allowed only 198 points; shut out both opponents in the National Football Conference playoffs; beat the New England Patriots 46–10 in Super Bowl XX; and sacked Patriot quarterbacks seven times. To his everlasting credit, Hampton refused to participate in the infamous Bears Super Bowl Shuffle video, believing it was too cocky and showed no class.

He retired in 1990, only the second Bear to play in three different decades. As of this writing, he hosts pre- and postgame shows for the Bears on WGN Radio in Chicago.

A childhood injury prevented him from playing organized sports until his junior year at Jacksonville (Arkansas) High School, where he played football as a junior and senior, before graduating in 1975 and going to the University of Arkansas. He was a member of the Razorbacks team that beat heavily favored University of Oklahoma, 31-6, in the 1978 Orange Bowl. As a senior, Hampton was an All-American and recorded 18 quarterback sacks; named the Southwest Conference Defensive Player of the Year in 1978; a four-year letterman; a three-year starter; a two-time All-Conference selection; and was later named a member of the 1970s Razorback All-Decade Team.

In 1991, he was elected to the University of Arkansas Sports Hall of Honor; to the Arkansas Sports Hall of Fame in 1992; and in 1994, he was voted to the University of Arkansas All-Century Team.

Source: Pro Football Hall of Fame

Hanley, William "Bill" (born: February 28, 1915 in Northern Ireland; died: September 17, 1990); inducted into the Hockey Hall of Fame in 1986 as a builder; served as secretary-manager of the Ontario Hockey Association.

Nicknamed "Mr. OHA," Hanley worked for almost three decades in all phases of amateur hockey development in Ontario, Canada. He attended Ontario Agricultural College (at the University of Guelph), and after graduation, he worked on his family farm for 10 years before it was sold to open a butcher shop.

After serving in the Royal Canadian Navy during World War II, Hanley returned to work in the family butcher shop and became involved with amateur hockey, starting as a timekeeper for junior games at the Maple Leaf Gardens, a function he would later perform at National Hockey League games.

He served as an assistant to the business manager of the Ontario Hockey Association, and eventually became the league's secretary-manager, a position he held until retiring in November 1974. During his tenure, the OHA changed from a two-referee to a three-referee system.

The William Hanley Trophy is awarded annually to the most sportsmanlike player in the Ontario Hockey League.

Source: Hockey Hall of Fame

Hanlon, Edward Hugh "Ned" (born: August 22, 1857 in Montville, Connecticut; died: April 14, 1937 in Baltimore, Maryland); inducted into the National Baseball Hall of Fame and Museum in 1996 as a manager by the Veterans Committee; Position: Center Field; Bats: Left; Throws: Right; won four pre-modern-day World Series.

The leader of the dominant Baltimore Orioles teams of the 1890s, Hanlon led the franchise to three consecutive pennants (1894–1896). As with most managers, he began his baseball career as a player. Making his major league debut on May 1, 1880, he played for the Cleveland Blues (National League, 1880), Detroit Wolverines (National League, 1881–1888), Pittsburgh Alleghenys (National League, 1889, player-manager), Pittsburgh Burghers (Players' League, 1890, player-manager), Pittsburgh Pirates (National League, 1891), and the Baltimore Orioles (National League, 1892).

The 5'9", 175-pound Hanlon would go on to manage the Baltimore Orioles (1892–1898), Brooklyn Superbas (1899–1905), and Cincinnati Reds (1906–1907). He managed in six pre-modern World Series (before 1903), winning four (1896–1897, 1899–1900) and losing two (1894–1895). He played for, and was captain of, the World Champion Detroit Wolverines (1887), the first championship in Detroit baseball history, and the last until the Tigers won the World Series in 1935.

Hanlon's 1,313 wins as a manager ranks 26th all-time, and he led teams to seven consecutive .600 (or better) won-lost seasons (1894–1900).

Although more successful as a manager, he played in the major leagues for 13 seasons as a center fielder. In 1890, he was one of the players who formed the Players' League, but when the league folded, he resumed his career with the Pirates.

Ned Hanlon's Career Playing Statistics

YEAR	TEAM	G	AB	R	H	2B	3B	HR	RBI	BB	SO	AVG	OBP	SLG
1880	Cleveland	73	280	30	69	10	3	0	32	11	30	.246	.275	.304
1881	Detroit	76	305	63	85	14	8	2	28	22	11	.279	.327	.397
1882	Detroit	82	347	68	80	18	6	5	38	26		.231	.284	.360
1883	Detroit	100	413	65	100	13	2	1	40	34		.242	.300	.291
1884	Detroit	114	450	86	119	18	6	5	39	40		.264	.324	.364
1885	Detroit	105	424	93	128	18	8	1	29	47		.302	.372	.389
1886	Detroit	126	494	105	116	6	6	4	60	57		.235	.314	.296
1887	Detroit	118	471	79	129	13	7	4	69	30	24	.274	.320	.293
1888	Detroit	109	459	64	122	6	8	5	39	15	32	.266	.295	.346
1889	Pittsburgh	116	461	81	110	14	10	2	37	58	25	.239	.326	.325
1890	Pittsburgh	118	472	106	131	16	6	1	44	80	24	.278	.389	.343
1891	Pittsburgh	119	455	87	121	12	8	0	60	48	30	.266	.341	.327
1892	Baltimore	11	43	3	7	1	1	0	2	3	3	.163	.217	.233
	TOTALS	1,267	5,074	930	1,317	159	79	30	517	471	179	.260	.325	.340

Ned Hanlon's Managerial Record

YEAR	TEAM	LG	W	L	WIN%
1889	Pittsburgh	NL	26	18	.591
1890	Pittsburgh	PL	60	68	.469
1891	Pittsburgh	NL	31	47	.397
1892	Baltimore	NL	43	85	.336
1893	Baltimore	NL	60	70	.462
1894	Baltimore	NL	89	39	.695
1895	Baltimore	NL	87	43	.669
1896	Baltimore	NL	90	39	.698
1897	Baltimore	NL	90	40	.692
1898	Baltimore	NL	96	53	.644
1899	Brooklyn	NL	101	47	.682
1900	Brooklyn	NL	82	54	.603
1901	Brooklyn	NL	79	57	.581
1902	Brooklyn	NL	75	63	.543
1903	Brooklyn	NL	70	66	.515
1904	Brooklyn	NL	56	97	.366
1905	Brooklyn	NL	48	104	.316

YEAR	TEAM	LG	W	L	WIN%
1906	Cincinnati	NL	64	87	.424
1907	Cincinnati	NL	66	87	.431
	TOTALS		1,313	1,164	.530

Sources: Baseball-Reference.com; National Baseball Hall of Fame and Museum

Hannah, John Allen "Hog" (born: April 4, 1951 in Canton, Georgia); inducted into the Pro Football Hall of Fame in 1991 as a player; Position: Offensive Guard; Uniform: #73; as of this writing, he is the only hall-of-famer to have played his entire career with the New England Patriots.

While at the University of Alabama (Tuscaloosa), Hannah was an eight-letter star in football, track, and wrestling and a two-time football All-American. The 6'2", 265-pound guard was a National Football League first-round draft pick (fourth overall selection) of the New England Patriots in 1973 and played his entire 13-season career (1973–1985, 183 regular-season games) with the team.

Hannah was named All-Pro (First- or Second-Team) for 10 consecutive seasons (1976–1985); elected to nine Pro Bowls (1976, 1978–1985); selected Offensive Lineman of the Year by the NFL Players Association four straight years (1978–1981); named to the NFL 1970s All-Decade Team; to the NFL 1980s All-Decade Team; to the NFL 75th Anniversary All-Time Team; and his jersey number 73 was retired by the Patriots.

During his tenure with the team, New England had seven winning seasons; compiled a 100–91–0 (.524) record; rushed for a then-record 3,165 yards in 1978; and reached Super Bowl XX (January 1986), eventually losing 46–10 to the Chicago Bears.

Hannah excelled at football, wrestling, and track at Baylor School (Chattanooga, Tennessee), and won an individual national championship in wrestling at the National Prep Championship in 1967. He returned to Albertville, Alabama (where he had been raised) and played football in his senior year at Albertville High School, graduating in 1969.

After high school, he played tackle and guard at the University of Alabama under legendary coach Paul "Bear" Bryant from 1970 until 1972; earned All-American honors twice (1971–1972); was part of a Southeastern Conference championship-winning team; also participated in wrestling, the shot put, and the discus throw; and was inducted into the College Football Hall of Fame in 1999. Hannah was named to the University of Alabama All-Century Team and to the Alabama 1970s All-Decade team.

He was one of the few players to have been named to the NFL All-Decade Team twice (1970s and 1980s); in 1999, he was ranked number 20 on *The Sporting News*' list of the 100 Greatest Football Players, the highest-ranking Patriot, the highest-ranking guard, and the second-ranked offensive lineman behind Anthony Muñoz; and is the only hall-of-famer to have played his entire career with the Patriots. On August 3, 1981, *Sports Illustrated* named him "The Best Offensive Lineman of All Time."

After his playing days, Hannah became an assistant coach at Governor Dummer Academy (Byfield, Massachusetts), and in 2004, he became the head coach at Somerville (Massachusetts) High School. He left after one season to become a special assistant coach at Baylor School in 2005.

Sources: College Football Hall of Fame; Pro Football Hall of Fame; Pro-Football-Reference.com

Hannum, Alexander Murray "Alex" (born: July 19, 1923 in Los Angeles, California; died: January 18, 2002 in San Diego, California); inducted into the Naismith Memorial Basketball Hall of Fame in 1998 as a coach; Position: Forward-Center; first coach to win championships in both the American Basketball Association and the National Basketball Association.

Hannum played basketball for three seasons (1939–1942) at Alexander Hamilton High School (Los Angeles, California); selected All-Conference twice (1941–1942); and All-City in 1942. After graduation, he played for three seasons (1942–1943, 1945–1948) at the University of Southern California (Los Angeles); named All-Conference twice (1947–1948); and was the team's captain and Most Valuable Player in 1948.

His college career was interrupted by military service with the U.S. Army Medical Department (April 1943–March 1946) during World War II. While in the Army, he played for the Amateur Athletic Union Los Angeles Shamrocks (1943–1946), and after leaving the military, he returned to USC and finished college.

After college, the 6'7", 210-pound Hannum played in the NBA for eight seasons (1949–1957) with the Syracuse Nationals (1949–1951), Rochester Royals (1951–1954), Milwaukee Hawks (1954–1955), and the St. Louis Hawks (1955–1957, player-coach in 1957).

He began his full-time coaching career with the NBA's St. Louis Hawks in 1957, and won a league championship his very first season. He returned to coaching in 1960 with the NBA's Syracuse Nationals (1960–1963), San Francisco

Warriors (1963–1966); and Philadelphia 76ers (1966–1968, where he coached Wilt Chamberlain and won another NBA title in 1967). Leaving the NBA, Hannum coached the American Basketball Association's Oakland Oaks for one season (1968–1969), and won the league title. He returned to the NBA and coached the San Diego Rockets (1969–1971), before ending his coaching career with the ABA's Denver Rockets (1971–1974).

He was the first coach to win championships in both the NBA and the ABA, and is mostly remembered for guiding the Wilt Chamberlain-led Philadelphia 76ers to the 1967 NBA championship, ending the eight-year title streak of the Boston Celtics. In 1964, he was named NBA Coach of the Year, and in 1969, he was named ABA Coach of the Year.

Alex Hannum's Playing Statistics

SEASON	TEAM	LG	G	MIN	FG	FT	TRB	AST	PTS
1949–1950	Syracuse	NBA	64	N/A	177	128	N/A	129	482
1950–1951	Syracuse	NBA	63	N/A	182	107	301	119	471
1951–1952	Rochester	NBA	66	1,508	170	98	336	133	438
1952–1953	Rochester	NBA	68	1,288	129	88	279	81	346
1953–1954	Rochester	NBA	72	1,707	175	102	350	105	452
1954–1955	Milwaukee Hawks	NBA	53	1,088	126	61	245	105	313
1955–1956	St. Louis	NBA	71	1,480	146	93	344	157	385
1956–1957	St. Louis	NBA	59	642	77	37	158	28	191
	TOTALS	NBA	516	7,713	1,182	714	2,013	857	3,078

Alex Hannum's Coaching Record

			REGULAR SEASON			PLAYOFFS		
SEASON	TEAM	LG	W	L	WIN%	W	L	WIN%
1956–1957	St. Louis	NBA	15	16	.484	8	4	.667
1957–1958	St. Louis	NBA	41	31	.569	8	3	.727
1960–1961	Syracuse	NBA	38	41	.481	4	4	.500
1961–1962	Syracuse	NBA	41	39	.513	2	3	.400
1962–1963	Syracuse	NBA	48	32	.600	2	3	.400
1963–1964	San Francisco	NBA	48	32	.600	5	7	.417
1964–1965	San Francisco	NBA	17	63	.213			
1965–1966	San Francisco	NBA	35	45	.438			
1966–1967	Philadelphia	NBA	68	13	.840	11	4	.733
1967–1968	Philadelphia	NBA	62	20	.756	7	6	.538
1968–1969	Oakland	ABA	60	18	.769	12	4	.750
1969–1970	San Diego	NBA	18	38	.321			
1970–1971	San Diego	NBA	40	42	.488			
1971–1972	Denver	ABA	34	50	.405	3	4	.429
1972–1973	Denver	ABA	47	37	.560	1	4	.200
1973–1974	Denver	ABA	37	47	.440			
		NBA	471	412	.533	47	34	.580
		ABA	178	152	.539	16	12	.571
	TOTALS		649	564	.535	63	46	.578

Sources: Basketball-Reference.com; Naismith Memorial Basketball Hall of Fame

Hanson, Victor A. (born: July 30, 1903 in Watertown, New York; died: April 10, 1982); inducted into the Naismith Memorial Basketball Hall of Fame in 1960 as a player; Position: Forward; only player to be inducted into the Naismith Memorial Basketball Hall of Fame and the College Football Hall of Fame.

Hanson attended Central High School (Syracuse, New York, 1919–1922) and Manlius (New York) Military Academy (1922–1923). He led Central High School to the 1921 New York State High School Invitational tournament title. After high school, he went to Syracuse University (New York, 1923–1927); was the team captain in basketball, football, and baseball; earned nine varsity letters; played second base and was later signed by the New York Yankees, where he played for two years; guided the basketball team to a three-year 48–7 record; led the 1925–1926 basketball team to a 19–1 record and named by the Helms Athletic Foundation as national champions; an All-American in both basketball

(1925–1927) and football (1926); selected Helms Athletic Foundation Player of the Year twice (1926–1927); and in his senior year, he scored 280 basketball points, a single-season Syracuse record that stood until 1946.

He was inducted into the Helms Foundation Hall of Fame (1952); the Greater Syracuse Sports Hall of Fame (1987); is the only player to be inducted into both the Naismith Memorial Basketball Hall of Fame and the College Football Hall of Fame (1973); and his basketball jersey number eight was retired by Syracuse in 1981.

In 1952, sportswriter Grantland Rice selected Hanson to his All-Time All-America team, and in 1953, Hanson was named New York State's greatest amateur athlete of all time by the Helms Foundation.

After graduating in 1927, the 5'10", 175-pound Hanson played professional basketball for the Cleveland Rosenblums of the American Basketball League and won a league championship; played baseball for two seasons in the New York Yankees farm system; and returned to Syracuse to form and play in the Eastern League (semi-professional, 1927–1930) for his own team, The All-Americans of Syracuse.

He returned to his alma mater and coached football from 1930 through 1936; compiled a record of 33–21–5; and later became a high school coach and teacher.

Sources: College Football Hall of Fame; Greater Syracuse Sports Hall of Fame; Naismith Memorial Basketball Hall of Fame

Harker, Albert (born: April 11, 1910 in Philadelphia, Pennsylvania; died: April 3, 2006 in Camp Hill, Pennsylvania); inducted into the National Soccer Hall of Fame and Museum in 1979 as a player; Position: Halfback-Fullback; won two U.S. Amateur Cups, one U.S. Open Cup, four American Soccer League titles.

Harker was a left-back on the Philadelphia German-American teams that won two U.S. Amateur Cups (1933–1934) and the U.S. Open Cup in 1936, and a member of the U.S. World Cup squad in 1934 that was eliminated by host country Italy in the first round.

During his time with the German-Americans, the team won the American Soccer League title in 1935; changed its name to the Philadelphia Americans and won three more league titles (1942, 1944, 1947); and won the Lewis Cup twice (1941, 1943).

His career began at Girard College (Philadelphia, Pennsylvania), where he played on the varsity squad from 1926 to 1929. He joined the Philadelphia National League in 1929, and played for the Corinthians (1929–1930), Upper Darby (1930–1931), and the Kensington Blue Bells (1931–1932), winners of the Allied Cup. He won back-to-back Penn State League championships (1933–1934); state open and amateur championships from 1932 to 1935; and was a three-time Pennsylvania League All-Star.

He was inducted into the Girard College Athletic Hall of Fame in 2006.

Source: National Soccer Hall of Fame and Museum

Harkes, John (born: March 8, 1967 in Kearny, New Jersey); inducted into the National Soccer Hall of Fame and Museum in 2005 as a player; Position: Midfield; International Caps (1987–2000): 90; International Goals: 6; first American ever to play in England's Wembley Stadium, to ever play in the F.A. Cup final, and to play in a Union of European Football Associations Cup match; won the 1992 U.S. Cup.

Harkes received his first full international cap on May 23, 1987 against Canada, and went on to earn 90 caps and scored six goals for the United States Men's National Team. He played two games in the 1988 Olympics (held in Calgary, Canada; the team was eliminated before the Medal Round), and served as the team's captain in 1995.

He attended Kearny (New Jersey) High School, graduating in 1984, and is the only New Jersey boy's soccer player to play in four New Jersey State Interscholastic Athletic Association championship matches, including a 2–1 win over East Brunswick in the Group 4 final in 1984.

After high school, the 5'11", 165-pound Harkes played soccer at the University of Virginia (Charlottesville), before beginning his professional career with the Albany Capitals of the American Soccer League.

As a professional, he was one of the first Americans to play overseas; started all three games for the U.S. Men's National Team in the 1990 Fédération Internationale de Football Association World Cup (hosted by Italy); and was the first American ever to play in England's Wembley Stadium, when he helped Sheffield win the League Cup title over Manchester United in 1991. He was named the Most Valuable Player of the 1992 U.S. Cup, where he scored two goals and led the team to the championship.

Harkes was also the first American to ever play in the Football Association Challenge Cup final and the first to score in a League Cup final (both in 1993) while playing for the Sheffield Wednesday Football Club. He was also the first American to play in a Union of European Football Associations Cup match (1992). He played every minute of all three first-round games in the 1994 FIFA World Cup (hosted by the United States), but was suspended for the Round-of-

16 game against Brazil via a yellow card. In 1995, he was named co-MVP in the Copa America, and played two seasons with Derby County of the English First Division.

In 1996, he played his final full season in England with West Ham United of the English Premier League. Later that year, Harkes returned to the United States and played for D.C. United in the newly created Major League Soccer. He led D.C. United to the 1996 MLS Cup title and the 1996 U.S. Open Cup, the first time in U.S. Soccer history that one team won both the MLS title and the Open Cup title in the same year. He led United to back-to-back MLS Cup Titles (1996–1997), and guided the team to both the 1998 Confederation of North, Central American and Caribbean Association Football Champions' Cup and the Interamerican Cup championships.

In 1999, he was a member of the bronze medal-winning U.S. Men's National Team at the 1999 FIFA Confederations Cup (hosted by Mexico); acquired by the New England Revolution (MLS) in 1999; played two and one-half seasons with the team before being traded to the Columbus Crew in mid 2001; and ended his 13-year professional career after the 2002 season. While playing in the MLS, he scored 16 goals and 42 assists in 167 games, and played in five straight MLS All-Star Games (1996–2000).

He attended the University of Virginia from 1985 to 1987, and won the Missouri Athletic Club Award as the top Division I college soccer player. In 2003, he was awarded a star at the U.S. Soccer Star Plaza at the Home Depot Center (Carson, California).

After retiring as a player, Harkes served as D.C. United's Director of Youth Development; often worked as a color commentator for soccer broadcasts on the Fox Sports Channel; and briefly served as an assistant coach for Red Bull New York of the MLS (2006–2007).

John Harkes' U.S. National Team Statistics

YEAR	G	MIN	GLS	ASSTS	PTS	W–L–T
1987	3	270	0	0	0	1–2–0
1988	2	90	0	0	0	1–1–0
1989	12	1,080	1	0	2	6–3–3
1990	16	1,440	1	0	2	4–11–1
1992	5	438	2	0	4	2–2–1
1993	7	624	0	1	1	4–3–0
1994	3	270	0	0	0	2–0–1
1995	8	720	2	1	5	3–2–3
1996	13	1,085	0	5	5	9–3–1
1997	10	870	0	4	4	3–1–6
1998	7	630	0	0	0	4–3–0
1999	3	243	0	0	0	1–2–0
2000	1	45	0	0	0	1–0–0
TOTALS	90	7,805	6	11	23	41–33–16

John Harkes' Major League Soccer Statistics

YEAR	TEAM	G	MIN	GLS	ASSTS	PTS
1996	D.C. United	29	2,469	3	8	14
1997	D.C. United	25	2,066	5	9	19
1998	D.C. United	29	2,600	6	6	18
1999	New England	22	1,880	0	8	8
2000	New England	28	2,511	2	6	10
2001	New England	5	386	0	0	0
2001	Columbus	18	1,407	0	3	3
2002	Columbus	11	739	0	2	2
	TOTALS	167	14,058	16	42	74

Source: National Soccer Hall of Fame and Museum

Harlem Globetrotters (Team); inducted into the Naismith Memorial Basketball Hall of Fame in 2002 as a team; baseball hall of famers who have played on the Globetrotters include Bob Gibson, Ferguson Jenkins, and Lou Brock.

Considered basketball's (and America's) goodwill ambassadors, the world-famous barnstorming Harlem Globetrotters combined athleticism, comedy routines, and basketball skill to entertain millions of fans around the world. The Globetrotters were founded in 1926 by basketball hall of famer Abe Saperstein (inducted in 1971) when he was 24 years old. The team's original name was the "Savoy Big Five," named after Chicago's (Illinois) famous Savoy Ballroom. The original "Savoy Big Five" consisted of Tommy Brookings, William Grant, Inman Jackson, Lester Johnson, Joe Lillard, Randolph Ramsey, Walter Wright, and William Watson. Jackson, Johnson, and Wright would later form the nucleus of the first Globetrotters team.

The team was originally formed with players from Wendell Phillips High School (Chicago, Illinois); played in the Negro American Legion League as the "Giles Post;" and in 1927, the team turned professional as the Savoy Big Five under manager Dick Hudson. Later that year, promoter Abe Saperstein bought the team and renamed it the Harlem Globetrotters.

Saperstein's team made its debut on January 7, 1928 in Hinckley, Illinois. In 1934, the Globetrotters, an all-black team, played their 1,000th game in Iron Mountain, Michigan. In 1939, the team played in its first professional basketball championship tournament and was defeated by the New York Renaissance (also known as the Rens), another all-black team that had been formed several years before the Globetrotters, in 1922.

In 1939, for reasons that are not entirely clear, the team began clowning around on the court, in an attempt to draw laughter from the crowd. Saperstein immediately understood the value of humor to the team's success and approved this new focus, but only after the Globetrotters had secured a safe lead in the game. While humor made the team more fun to watch, winning was still the name of the game. From this moment on, the team became more of an entertainment entity than a strictly professional basketball team. Inman Jackson initiated the team's "Clown Prince" of basketball role and created the pivot position now used by all levels of basketball.

In 1940, The Globetrotters played the team's 2,000th game in Bellingham, Washington, and ended the regular season tour with a 159–8 record. Returning to Chicago, the team accepted an invitation to compete in the World Professional Basketball tournament and, in the finals, the Globetrotters beat George Halas' Chicago Bruins in overtime, 31–29, and won its first-ever World Basketball Championship.

In 1946, the Globetrotters celebrated their 20th season and played the team's 3,000th career game in Vancouver, British Columbia, Canada. On February 19, 1948 the Globetrotters (by now consisting of Ermer Robinson, Ducky Moore, Sam Wheeler, "Goose" Tatum, Marques Haynes, Babe Pressley, Ted Strong, Vertes Ziegler, and Wilbert King) defeated George Mikan and the National Basketball League champion Minneapolis Lakers, 61–59. In 1951, the 25th anniversary tour began and was highlighted by the team's 4,000th career game; on April 9, the Globetrotters beat the College All-Stars, 55–34, at the Rose Bowl (Pasadena, California); and on April 25th, the team began its first South American tour.

In 1952, the team went on a 108-game around the world tour, the first in the history of basketball, and later that year, the squad officially began using "Sweet Georgia Brown" as their theme song. In 1954, Meadowlark Lemon was signed by the team; joined the Globetrotters in 1955; played more than 1,600 games; and became the "Clown Prince" of basketball for 22 years.

On January 5, 1971, the Globetrotters lost a game in Martin, Tennessee in overtime to the New Jersey Reds 100–99, that ended a 2,495-game winning streak, one of two games the team lost over the next 8,829 games; on December 6, 1974, the Globetrotters played in their 12,000th career game at the Capital Center in Landover, Maryland; in 1977, the team celebrated its 50th season; and in 1978, the squad made the franchise's first trip to West Africa, increasing the number of countries visited to 97.

In 1982, the Globetrotters became the first and only sports team to be honored with its own star on Hollywood's famous "Walk of Fame;" in 1985, the team signed its first female player, Olympic gold medalist Lynette Woodard from Kansas; and in 1993, Mannie Jackson became the first African-American, and former player, to own a sports-entertainment organization when he bought the Harlem Globetrotters.

On September 12, 1995, the team lost 91–85 to Kareem Abdul-Jabbar's All Star Team in Vienna, Austria, ending a run of 8,829 straight victories in exhibition games going back to 1971; in June 1996, celebrating their 70th anniversary, the Harlem Globetrotters became the first professional basketball team in history to play in South Africa; and on January 12, 1998, the team played its 20,000th career game at Tri-County High School near Remington, Indiana.

Today, the team still travels the world and has played exhibition games against two intentionally bad teams over the years, the Washington Generals (1953–1995) and the New York Nationals (1995–present).

The list of players who were Globetrotters and went on to National Basketball Association success includes Wilt Chamberlain, Connie Hawkins, Nat Clifton, Marques Haynes, George "Meadowlark" Lemon, Jerome James, former Temple coach John Chaney, and Reece "Goose" Tatum. Another popular team member in the 1970s and 1980s was Fred "Curly" Neal, who was the best dribbler of his era. Baseball hall of famers Bob Gibson, Ferguson Jenkins, and Lou Brock also played for the team, and another famous former player is comedian Bill Cosby.

In its history, the Globetrotters have retired five uniform numbers: Chamberlain (13), Haynes (20), Neal (22), Lemon (36), and Tatum (50). Additionally, eight people have been officially named as honorary members by the team: Henry Kissinger (1976), Bob Hope (1977), Kareem Abdul-Jabbar (1989), Whoopi Goldberg (1990), Nelson Mandela (1996), Jackie Joyner-Kersee (1999), Pope John Paul II (2000), and Jesse Jackson (2001). Both Bill Cosby (1972) and basketball hall of famer Magic Johnson (2003) have been signed to $1-a-year lifetime contracts with the Globetrotters.

Sources: Harlem Globetrotters Web Site (www.harlemglobetrotters.com); Naismith Memorial Basketball Hall of Fame; *Spinning the Globe: The Rise, Fall, and Return to Greatness of the Harlem Globetrotters* (Ben Green)

Harridge, William "Will" (born: October 16, 1883 in Chicago, Illinois; died: April 9, 1971 in Evanston, Illinois); inducted into the National Baseball Hall of Fame and Museum in 1972 as an executive-pioneer by the Veterans Committee; third American League president; started the annual All-Star Game.

A former Wabash Railroad ticket agent who handled all American League travel arrangements, Harridge got his start in Major League Baseball when he was hired in 1911 by American League founder and president Ban Johnson as his personal secretary. When Johnson resigned as league president in 1927, Harridge became American League secretary. Four years later, in 1931, he became the third American League president and stayed in the job until he retired in 1958.

In 1933, as league president, Harridge helped convince American League team owners to play an inter-league All-Star Game, beginning the mid-summer tradition that has been played ever since. The American League Championship Series Trophy is named in his honor.

In July 1952, he and National League president Warren Giles became directors of the National Baseball Hall of Fame and Museum. After retiring as league president in 1958, he served as chairman of the board until his death in 1971.

Source: National Baseball Hall of Fame and Museum

Harris, Franco (born: March 7, 1950 in Fort Dix, New Jersey); inducted into the Pro Football Hall of Fame in 1990 as a player; Position: Running Back; first African-American and first Italian-American to be named Super Bowl Most Valuable Player; won four Super Bowl championships.

Harris went to Rancocas Valley Regional High School (Mount Holly, New Jersey) before attending Penn State University (University Park), where he was used primarily as a blocker for the Nittany Lions' All-American running back, Lydell Mitchell.

The 6'2", 230-pound Harris began his professional football career as the Pittsburgh Steelers' number one pick (13th overall selection) in the 1972 National Football League Draft. He played 13 seasons (173 games) with the Steelers (1972–1983) and the Seattle Seahawks (1984); selected All-Pro in 1977; All-American Football Conference four times (1972, 1975–1977); nine consecutive Pro Bowls (1972–1980); ran for 158 yards and was named Most Valuable Player in Super Bowl IX, a January 1975 16–6 win over the Minnesota Vikings (he was the first African-American and Italian-American to be named Super Bowl MVP); rushed for 1,000 or more yards in eight seasons and ran for 100 or more yards in a game 47 times; and played in four winning Super Bowls (SB IX in 1975, SB X in 1976, SB XIII in 1979, and SB XIV in 1980).

In his first year with the Steelers, Harris was named the NFL's Rookie of the Year by both *The Sporting News* and United Press International, and was the fourth rookie in league history to rush for 1,000 yards. Harris was the receiver of the "Immaculate Reception" pass from Terry Bradshaw that gave the Steelers the team's first-ever playoff win, 13–7, over the Oakland Raiders on December 23, 1972.

At the time of his retirement, Harris held numerous Super Bowl records, including 24 points scored and 354 yards rushing in four Super Bowls. In 1999, he was ranked number 83 on *The Sporting News*' list of the 100 Greatest Football Players.

Franco Harris' Career Statistics

			RUSHING				RECEIVING			
YEAR	**TEAM**	**G**	**NO.**	**YDS**	**AVG**	**TD**	**NO.**	**YDS**	**AVG**	**TD**
1972	Pittsburgh	14	188	1,055	5.6	10	21	180	8.6	1
1973	Pittsburgh	12	188	698	3.7	3	10	69	6.9	0
1974	Pittsburgh	12	208	1,006	4.8	5	23	200	8.7	1
1975	Pittsburgh	14	262	1,246	4.8	10	28	214	7.6	1
1976	Pittsburgh	14	289	1,128	3.9	14	23	151	6.6	0

				RUSHING				RECEIVING		
YEAR	TEAM	G	NO.	YDS	AVG	TD	NO.	YDS	AVG	TD
1977	Pittsburgh	14	300	1,162	3.9	11	11	62	5.6	0
1978	Pittsburgh	16	310	1,082	3.5	8	22	144	6.5	0
1979	Pittsburgh	15	267	1,186	4.4	11	36	291	8.1	1
1980	Pittsburgh	13	208	789	3.8	4	30	196	6.5	2
1981	Pittsburgh	16	242	987	4.1	8	37	250	6.8	1
1982	Pittsburgh	9	140	604	4.3	2	31	249	8.0	0
1983	Pittsburgh	16	279	1,007	3.6	5	34	278	8.2	2
1984	Seattle	8	68	170	2.5	0	1	3	3.0	0
	TOTALS	173	2,949	12,120	4.1	91	307	2,287	7.4	9

Sources: Pro Football Hall of Fame; Pro-Football-Reference.com

Harris, Stanley Raymond "Bucky" (born: November 8, 1896 in Port Jervis, New York; died: November 8, 1977 in Bethesda, Maryland); inducted into the National Baseball Hall of Fame and Museum in 1975 as a manager by the Veterans Committee; led American League second basemen in double plays a record five straight seasons; youngest man to lead his team to a World Series championship.

Harris spent seven decades in Major League Baseball as a player, manager, scout, and executive. Making his debut on August 28, 1919, he played as a second baseman for the Washington Senators (1919–1928) and Detroit Tigers (1929, 1931). He managed the Senators (1924–1928, 1935–1942, 1950–1954), Tigers (1929–1933, 1955–1956), Boston Red Sox (1934), Philadelphia Phillies (1943), and New York Yankees (1947–1948). He was a player-manager in two World Series with the Senators (winning in 1924 and losing in 1925), and he won the World Series in 1947 as the manager of the New York Yankees, the same season he was named Manager of the Year by *The Sporting News*.

He was only 27 years old (the youngest manager in the major leagues) when he took over as player-manager of the Senators in 1924 and won the World Series (the Senators' only title) his first year (the youngest to do so) and two pennants in a row. He hit .333 with two home runs to lead the Senators to a World Series title in 1924; won 2,159 games in 29 years as a manager; served two years (1959–1960) as general manager of the Red Sox; and was a special assistant for the expansion Washington Senators (1961–1971).

Harris led American League second basemen in putouts four times and in double plays a record five straight seasons (1921–1925); managed in both the International and Pacific Coast leagues; and in 1947, he managed the Yankees to a World Series title over the Brooklyn Dodgers in seven games.

Bucky Harris' Managerial Record

YEAR	TEAM	LG	W	L	PCT
1924	Washington	AL	92	62	.597
1925	Washington	AL	96	55	.636
1926	Washington	AL	81	69	.540
1927	Washington	AL	85	69	.552
1928	Washington	AL	75	79	.487
1929	Detroit	AL	70	84	.455
1930	Detroit	AL	75	79	.487
1931	Detroit	AL	61	93	.396
1932	Detroit	AL	76	75	.503
1933	Detroit	AL	73	79	.480
1934	Boston	AL	76	76	.500
1935	Washington	AL	67	86	.438
1936	Washington	AL	82	71	.536
1937	Washington	AL	73	80	.477
1938	Washington	AL	75	76	.497
1939	Washington	AL	65	87	.428
1940	Washington	AL	64	90	.416
1941	Washington	AL	70	84	.455
1942	Washington	AL	62	89	.411
1943	Philadelphia	NL	40	53	.430

YEAR	TEAM	LG	W	L	PCT
1947	New York	AL	97	57	.630
1948	New York	AL	94	60	.610
1950	Washington	AL	67	87	.435
1951	Washington	AL	62	92	.403
1952	Washington	AL	78	76	.506
1953	Washington	AL	76	76	.500
1954	Washington	AL	66	88	.429
1955	Detroit	AL	79	75	.513
1956	Detroit	AL	82	72	.532
	TOTALS		2,159	2,219	.493

Sources: Baseball-Reference.com; National Baseball Hall of Fame and Museum

Harris-Stewart, Lusia (born: February 10, 1955 in Minter City, Mississippi); inducted into the Naismith Memorial Basketball Hall of Fame in 1992 as a player; Position: Center; a member of the very first women's Olympic basketball team; first African-American woman inducted into the basketball hall of fame.

Harris-Stewart attended Amanda Elzy High School (Greenwood, Mississippi), graduating in 1973; named All-State twice (1972–1973); and was a three-time All-Conference and All-Region selection (1971–1973). After high school, she went to Delta State University (Cleveland, Mississippi, 1973–1977), where she was a three-time All-American; four-time All-State and All-Region selection; and the team's Most Valuable Player and high scorer.

She played for hall of fame coach Margaret Wade and led the Lady Statesmen to three consecutive Association for Intercollegiate Athletics for Women national championships (1975–1977) and a 109–6 overall record. Harris-Stewart was a member of the 1975 gold medal-winning Pan American Games team (Mexico City, Mexico) and a member of the first women's Olympic team and won an Olympic silver medal in 1976 (Montreal, Quebec, Canada).

She finished her college career with 2,981 points (25.9 per game) and 1,662 rebounds (14.4 per game), and was inducted into the Mississippi Sports Hall of Fame in 1990.

The 6'3" Harris-Stewart began her coaching career at her alma mater as an assistant women's basketball coach (1980–1984), before serving as the women's head basketball coach at Texas Southern University (Houston) from 1984 to 1986. She then joined the high school coaching ranks at her old school, Amanda Elzy High School, as head women's basketball coach (1986–1989), before becoming the ninth grade girls' basketball coach at Greenville, Mississippi Public School (1989–1990). As of this writing (1991–present), she is the girls' coach at Central High School (Ruleville, Mississippi).

She was selected in the seventh round of the 1977 National Basketball Association draft by the New Orleans Jazz, the first woman ever drafted by an NBA team, although she never played. She was the first player to win the Broderick Cup (now known as the Honda-Broderick Cup) as the top female college basketball player in the country; was one of the few women inducted into the Naismith Memorial Basketball Hall of Fame; and was in the first class inducted into the Women's Basketball Hall of Fame (Knoxville, Tennessee).

Source: Naismith Memorial Basketball Hall of Fame

Harrison, Lester (born: August 20, 1904 in Rochester, New York; died: December 23, 1997 in Rochester, New York); inducted into the Naismith Memorial Basketball Hall of Fame in 1980 as a contributor; helped merge the NBL and BAA into the NBA.

After graduating from East High School (Rochester, New York) in 1923, Harrison played, coached, organized, and promoted professional basketball in New York State for the Rochester Seagrams and the Rochester Eber Seagrams from the 1920s through the 1940s. Both teams played as independent squads as well as competed in the District Basketball League and the District Basketball Association.

In 1944, he formed a semi-professional basketball team, the Rochester Pros, with his brother Jack. The team name was later changed to the Rochester Royals when it entered the National Basketball League in 1945. In his three seasons as owner-coach, he led the Royals to a 99–43 record; three NBL finals (1946–1948); and two NBL championships (1946–1947). In 1946, he signed the first black professional player to major league basketball, Dolly King of Long Island University, and played an important role in breaking basketball's minority barrier.

Rochester jumped to the rival Basketball Association of America for the 1948–1949 season; Harrison later helped merge the NBL and the BAA to form the National Basketball Association; and the Royals won the NBA title in 1951.

In 10 seasons (1945–1955), his teams compiled a 394–220 (.642) record and won five division titles (1946–1949, 1951). The team relocated to Cincinnati, Ohio before the 1957–1958 season; he sold the team the following year; and the franchise currently exists as the Sacramento Kings.

Harrison served as a member of the Rules Committee and on the Board of Directors for the NBL, BAA, and NBA; was a major proponent of the 24-second shot clock; and in 1963, he organized the Kodak Classic Collegiate Tournament (now known as the Rochester Basketball Classic), which he directed for more than 30 years.

He has been inducted into the Rochester Jewish Sports Hall of Fame (1962), Rochester High School Athletes Hall of Fame (1975), and the International Jewish Sports Hall of Fame (1990).

Sources: International Jewish Sports Hall of Fame; Naismith Memorial Basketball Hall of Fame

Harshman, Marv K. (born: October 4, 1917 in Eau Claire, Wisconsin); inducted into the Naismith Memorial Basketball Hall of Fame in 1985 as a coach; led the United States team to a 1975 Pan American Games gold medal.

Harshman attended Lake Stevens (Washington) High School (1931–1935), where he played basketball for four years and was named All-Conference three times. After high school, he went to Pacific Lutheran University (Tacoma, Washington), graduating in 1942.

At college, he won 13 letters in four sports; was selected All-Conference (1938–1941); Little All-American (1941); and team Most Valuable Player (1939–1941). He was the team high scorer and conference MVP twice (1940–1941) and the Conference leading scorer in 1941.

During World War II, he served as a Navy Chief Specialist (1942–1945) and, after completing his military service, the 6'1", 205-pound Harshman joined the professional ranks with the Tacoma Mountaineers of the Northwest Professional Basketball League from 1945 to 1946.

He began his college coaching career at his alma mater (1945–1958), where he also coached football and track, before moving on to Washington State University (Pullman, 1958–1971), and finishing his career at the University of Washington (Seattle, 1971–1985). He coached Pacific Lutheran to a 241–121 (.666) record; won four National Association of Intercollegiate Athletics District I basketball championships; and was seven-time NAIA District I Coach of the Year. His 1957 team finished with a 28–1 record, while his 1959 club finished runner-up for the NAIA national title. He led Washington State to a 155–181 (.461) record; the University of Washington to a 246–146 (.628) record; named Pac 8 Coach of the Year in 1976; Pac 10 Coach of the Year twice (1982, 1984); and Kodak Coach of the Year for National Collegiate Athletic Association Division I in 1984. He finished his college coaching career with a 642–448 (.589) record.

Harshman was a member of the U.S. Olympic Committee (1975–1981); coached the United States to a 1975 Pan American Games gold medal (held in Mexico City, Mexico); named *Seattle Post-Intelligencer* Man of the Year in Sports (1976); served as president of the National Association of Basketball Coaches in 1981; and has been inducted into the NAIA National Hall of Fame (1972) and the Washington State Hall of Fame (1986).

Source: Naismith Memorial Basketball Hall of Fame

Hartnett, Charles Leo "Gabby" (born: December 20, 1900 in Woonsocket, Rhode Island; died: December 20, 1972 in Park Ridge, Illinois); inducted into the National Baseball Hall of Fame and Museum in 1955 as a player; Position: Catcher; Bats: Right; Throws: Right; 1935 National League Most Valuable Player; his bat and catcher's mask were the first artifacts sent to the newly created baseball hall of fame.

Hartnett made his major league debut on April 12, 1922, and played for 20 years with the Chicago Cubs (1922–1940, a player-manager from 1938 to 1940) and the New York Giants (1941). He appeared in four World Series (1929, 1932, 1935, 1938), but never won a championship; named to the first six All-Star teams ever assembled (1933–1938); and was the 1935 National League Most Valuable Player.

He caught 100 or more games per season 12 times; led the National League in putouts four times; and in assists and fielding average six times. An arm injury forced him to miss most of the 1929 season, and when the Cubs went to the World Series that year, Hartnett struck out in all three of his at-bats. He rebounded in 1930, hitting .339 with career highs of 37 home runs (a then-record for catchers) and 122 runs batted in.

Unlike most catchers, he did not slow down as he entered his 30s. After catching more than 100 games in a season only four times in his career, Hartnett would do so for the next eight consecutive years (1930–1937), and in 1939, he broke the Chicago White Sox's Ray Schalk's major league record of 1,727 career games as a catcher.

Hartnett was the 1934 All-Star Game catcher when New York Giants pitcher Carl Hubbell set a record by striking out Babe Ruth, Lou Gehrig, Jimmie Foxx, Al Simmons, and Joe Cronin in succession. He was named the National League's Most Valuable Player in 1935 after batting .344 (third in the league) and leading league catchers in assists, double plays, and fielding average. When he retired, his 236 home runs, 1,179 runs batted in, 1,912 hits, and 396 doubles were all then-records for catchers. His bat and catcher's mask were the first artifacts sent to the newly created baseball hall of fame in 1938.

After leaving the major leagues, he coached in the minors for a few seasons before retiring from the game in 1946. He later worked as a coach and scout for the Kansas City Athletics for two years in the mid-1960s, and in 1999, he was named a finalist to the Major League Baseball All-Century Team.

Gabby Hartnett's Career Statistics

YEAR	TEAM	LG	G	AB	R	H	2B	3B	HR	RBI	BB	SO	SB	AVG	SLG
1922	Chicago	NL	31	72	4	14	1	1	0	4	6	8	1	.194	.236
1923	Chicago	NL	85	231	28	62	12	2	8	39	25	22	4	.268	.442
1924	Chicago	NL	111	354	56	106	17	7	16	67	39	37	10	.299	.523
1925	Chicago	NL	117	398	61	115	28	3	24	67	36	77	1	.289	.555
1926	Chicago	NL	93	284	35	78	25	3	8	41	32	37	0	.275	.468
1927	Chicago	NL	127	449	56	132	32	5	10	80	44	42	2	.294	.454
1928	Chicago	NL	120	388	61	117	26	9	14	57	65	32	3	.302	.523
1929	Chicago	NL	25	22	2	6	2	1	1	9	5	5	1	.273	.591
1930	Chicago	NL	141	508	84	172	31	3	37	122	55	62	0	.339	.630
1931	Chicago	NL	116	380	53	107	32	1	8	70	52	48	3	.282	.434
1932	Chicago	NL	121	406	52	110	25	3	12	52	51	59	0	.271	.436
1933	Chicago	NL	140	490	55	135	21	4	16	88	37	51	1	.276	.433
1934	Chicago	NL	130	438	58	131	21	1	22	90	37	46	0	.299	.502
1935	Chicago	NL	116	413	67	142	32	6	13	91	41	46	1	.344	.545
1936	Chicago	NL	121	424	49	130	25	6	7	64	30	36	0	.307	.443
1937	Chicago	NL	110	356	47	126	21	6	12	82	43	19	0	.354	.548
1938	Chicago	NL	88	299	40	82	19	1	10	59	48	17	1	.274	.445
1939	Chicago	NL	97	306	36	85	18	2	12	59	37	32	0	.278	.467
1940	Chicago	NL	37	64	3	17	3	0	1	12	8	7	0	.266	.359
1941	New York	NL	64	150	20	45	5	0	5	26	12	14	0	.300	.433
	TOTALS		1,990	6,432	867	1,912	396	64	236	1,179	703	697	28	.297	.489

Sources: Baseball-Reference.com; National Baseball Hall of Fame and Museum

Harvey, Douglas Norman (born: December 19, 1924 in Montreal, Quebec, Canada; died: December 26, 1989 in Montreal, Quebec, Canada); inducted into the Hockey Hall of Fame in 1973 as a player; Position: Defenseman; Uniform: #2; won six Stanley Cup titles, five consecutively.

Harvey played 20 National Hockey League seasons (1947–1969) for the Montreal Canadiens (1947–1961), New York Rangers (1961–1964), Detroit Red Wings (1966–1967), and the St. Louis Blues (1967–1969). He was selected to the NHL All-Star Team 11 consecutive years, and led the Canadiens to six Stanley Cup championships, including five consecutively (1953, 1956–1960).

He won his first major hockey title in 1947 when he helped the Senior Montreal Royals of the Quebec Senior Hockey League win the Allan Cup. After playing one season with the Buffalo Bisons (American Hockey League), he joined the Canadiens for the 1947–1948 season.

He won the James Norris Memorial Trophy as the league's best defensive player seven times in eight seasons (1955–1958, 1960–1962), and after Maurice Richard retired in 1960, Harvey was named the Canadiens' captain. Despite all his on-ice success, Harvey was one of the players blacklisted by the league because of his involvement with the first attempt to form a players' association, and his jersey number two was not retired by the Canadiens until 1985.

In the 1960–1961 season, he joined the New York Rangers as a player-coach; led the team into the postseason; and won his seventh James Norris Memorial Trophy. After his first year, he became strictly a player for two more seasons before retiring from the NHL in the 1963–1964 season. After leaving the NHL, he continued to play, mainly in the American Hockey League, and made a two-game return with Detroit in 1966–1967.

Harvey began the 1967–1968 season with the Kansas City Blues of the Central Professional Hockey League, but once again returned to the NHL with the expansion St. Louis Blues for the playoffs. He helped the team make it to the Stanley Cup finals, before losing in four games to his old squad, the Canadiens. The following season, he played all 70 regular-season games with the Blues before retiring as a player for good. He stayed in hockey for one more season as the coach of the Laval Saints of the Quebec Junior Hockey League, and in 1973, he served as an assistant coach and scout with the Houston Aeros of the World Hockey Association.

In 1998, he was ranked number six on *The Hockey News*' list of the 100 Greatest Hockey Players. In 2000, the Canadian government honored him with his image being placed on a Canadian postage stamp.

Douglas Harvey's Career Statistics

			REGULAR SEASON					PLAYOFFS				
SEASON	TEAM	LEAGUE	GP	G	A	TP	PIM	GP	G	A	TP	PIM
1942–1943	Montreal Navy	MCHL	4	0	0	0	0					
1942–1943	Montreal Jr. Royals	QJHL	21	4	6	10	17	6	3	4	7	10
1942–1943	Montreal Royals	QSHL	1	0	0	0	0					
1943–1944	Montreal Jr. Royals	QJHL	13	4	6	10	34	4	2	6	8	10
1943–1944	Montreal Royals	QSHL	1	1	1	2	2					
1943–1944	Montreal Navy	MCHL	15	4	1	5	24	5	3	1	4	15
1943–1944	Montreal Jr. Royals	M-Cup	3	0	1	1	6					
1944–1945	Montreal Navy	MCHL	3	0	2	2	2	6	3	1	4	6
1944–1945	Montreal Jr. Royals	QJHL						9	2	2	4	10
1945–1946	Montreal Royals	QSHL	34	2	6	8	90	11	1	6	7	37
1946–1947	Montreal Royals	QSHL	40	2	26	28	171	11	2	4	6	62
1946–1947	Montreal Royals	Al-Cup	14	4	9	13	26					
1947–1948	Montreal Canadiens	NHL	35	4	4	8	32					
1947–1948	Buffalo Bisons	AHL	24	1	7	8	38					
1948–1949	Montreal Canadiens	NHL	55	3	13	16	87	7	0	1	1	10
1949–1950	Montreal Canadiens	NHL	70	4	20	24	76	5	0	2	2	10
1950–1951	Montreal Canadiens	NHL	70	5	24	29	93	11	0	5	5	12
1951–1952	Montreal Canadiens	NHL	68	6	23	29	82	11	0	3	3	8
1952–1953	Montreal Canadiens	NHL	69	4	30	34	67	12	0	5	5	8
1953–1954	Montreal Canadiens	NHL	68	8	29	37	110	10	0	2	2	12
1954–1955	Montreal Canadiens	NHL	70	6	43	49	58	12	0	8	8	6
1955–1956	Montreal Canadiens	NHL	62	5	39	44	60	10	2	5	7	10
1956–1957	Montreal Canadiens	NHL	70	6	44	50	92	10	0	7	7	10
1957–1958	Montreal Canadiens	NHL	68	9	32	41	131	10	2	9	11	16
1958–1959	Montreal Canadiens	NHL	61	4	16	20	61	11	1	11	12	22
1959–1960	Montreal Canadiens	NHL	66	6	21	27	45	8	3	0	3	6
1960–1961	Montreal Canadiens	NHL	58	6	33	39	48	6	0	1	1	8
1961–1962	New York Rangers	NHL	69	6	24	30	42	6	0	1	1	2
1962–1963	New York Rangers	NHL	68	4	35	39	92					
1963–1964	St. Paul Rangers	CPHL	5	2	2	4	6					
1963–1964	New York Rangers	NHL	14	0	2	2	10					
1963–1964	Quebec Aces	AHL	52	6	36	42	30	9	0	4	4	10
1964–1965	Quebec Aces	AHL	64	1	36	37	72	4	1	1	2	9
1965–1966	Baltimore Clippers	AHL	67	7	32	39	80					
1966–1967	Baltimore Clippers	AHL	24	2	9	11	10					
1966–1967	Pittsburgh Hornets	AHL	28	0	9	9	22	9	0	0	0	2
1966–1967	Detroit Red Wings	NHL	2	0	0	0	0					
1967–1968	Kansas City Blues	CPHL	59	4	16	20	12	7	0	6	6	6
1967–1968	St. Louis Blues	NHL						8	0	4	4	12
1968–1969	St. Louis Blues	NHL	70	2	20	22	30					
1969–1970	Laval Saints	QJHL										
	NHL TOTALS		1,113	88	452	540	1,216	137	8	64	72	152

Sources: Hockey Hall of Fame; Hockey-Reference.com

Harvey, Harold Douglas "Doug" (born: March 13, 1930 in South Gate, Georgia); inducted into the National Baseball Hall of Fame and Museum in 2010 as an umpire by the Veterans Committee; worked in five World Series.

The 6'2", 195-pound Harvey worked in 4,673 regular-season Major League games (third most in league history when he retired, behind Bill Klem [5,374] and Tommy Connolly [4,769]) in 31 seasons (April 10, 1962 – October 4, 1992) as a National League umpire. He worked in nine National League Championship Series (1970, 1972, 1976, 1980, 1983–1984, 1986, 1989, 1991); six All-Star Games (1963–1964, 1971, 1977, 1982, 1992); and five World Series (1968,

1974, 1981, 1984, 1988). Known for his authoritative command of baseball rules, he was among the last Major League umpires who never attended an umpiring school. Harvey was the home plate umpire for the single-game playoff to decide the National League's Western Division champion in 1980, between the Houston Astros and the Los Angeles Dodgers.

He attended San Diego State College (California) in 1955 and 1956, where he played baseball and football before becoming a full-time umpire in Major League Baseball's minor leagues. He umpired in the California League (1958–1960) and in the Pacific Coast League in 1961, before being promoted to the major leagues in 1962.

He also worked the final game of the 1972 season in which Roberto Clemente collected his 3,000th (and last) base hit; was the home plate umpire on September 10, 1963, when brothers Jesus, Matty, and Felipe Alou batted consecutively for the San Francisco Giants; and on June 3, 1987, when the Houston Astros and Chicago Cubs hit a combined three grand slams at Chicago's Wrigley Field.

Source: National Baseball Hall of Fame and Museum

Haskins, Donald Lee "Don" (born: March 14, 1930 in Enid, Oklahoma); inducted into the Naismith Memorial Basketball Hall of Fame in 1997 as a coach; won the 1966 NCAA title; started five black players in the 1966 NCAA final game.

Haskins played basketball for three years at Enid (Oklahoma) High School, graduating in 1948, and was named All-Conference three times and All-State twice. After high school, he went to Oklahoma A&M (Stillwater, now known as Oklahoma Statue University), graduating in 1953. In college, he played basketball and was team captain for three years under hall of fame coach Hank Iba; was a one-time All-Conference selection; and was selected Most Valuable Player in the All-College Tournament.

He began his coaching career at Benjamin (Texas) High School (1955–1956), before moving on to Hedley (Texas) High School (1956–1960), and finally Dumas (Texas) High School (1960–1961). He finished his high school coaching career with an overall 157–41 (.793) record.

In 1961, Haskins joined the college coaching ranks at the University of Texas at El Paso, where he stayed until 1999. At the time of his retirement, his 719–353 (.671) college record tied him for fourth place among all-time National Collegiate Athletic Association winningest coaches. He only had five losing seasons in his 38 years at UTEP; led the Miners to seventeen 20+ win seasons; won the 1966 NCAA title (after compiling a regular-season 23–1 record); seven Western Athletic Conference championships; four WAC tournament titles; and made 21 postseason trips (14 NCAA, seven National Invitation Tournament).

He is often credited with changing college basketball forever when his 1966 team (then known as Texas Western) beat Kentucky 72–65 for the NCAA title as Haskins started five black players in the championship game against coach Adolph Rupp's all-white Kentucky squad.

His 1992 team advanced to the NCAA "Sweet 16" following an upset win over number-one-ranked Kansas; he was an assistant Olympic team coach in 1972 under Iba (held in Munich, Germany); and was inducted into the Texas Sports Hall of Fame in 1987.

In 2006, the movie *Glory Road* was released by Walt Disney Pictures and featured the 1966 team, its starting of five black players in the NCAA title game, and the squad's upset win over Kentucky for the national title.

The Don Haskins Center is the home of UTEP Miners basketball.

Don Haskins' Texas Western College / University of Texas at El Paso Coaching Record

SEASON	OVERALL	CONFERENCE
1961–1962	18–6	5–3
1962–1963	19–7	N/A
1963–1964	25–3	N/A
1964–1965	16–9	N/A
1965–1966	28–1	N/A
1966–1967	22–6	N/A
1967–1968	14–9	N/A
1968–1969	16–9	N/A
1969–1970	17–8	10–4
1970–1971	16–10	9–5
1971–1972	20–7	9–5
1972–1973	16–10	6–8

SEASON	OVERALL	CONFERENCE
1973–1974	18–7	8–6
1974–1975	20–6	10–4
1975–1976	19–7	9–5
1976–1977	11–15	3–11
1977–1978	10–16	2–12
1978–1979	11–15	3–9
1979–1980	20–8	10–4
1980–1981	18–12	9–7
1981–1982	20–8	11–5
1982–1983	19–10	11–5
1983–1984	27–4	13–3
1984–1985	22–10	12–4
1985–1986	27–6	12–4
1986–1987	25–7	13–3
1987–1988	23–10	10–6
1988–1989	26–7	11–5
1989–1990	21–11	10–6
1990–1991	16–13	7–9
1991–1992	27–7	12–4
1992–1993	21–13	10–8
1993–1994	18–12	8–10
1994–1995	20–10	13–5
1995–1996	12–16	4–14
1996–1997	13–13	6–10
1997–1998	12–14	3–13
1998–1999	16–12	8–6
TOTALS	719–354	262–200

Sources: Naismith Memorial Basketball Hall of Fame; University of Texas at El Paso Athletics

Havlicek, John J. "Hondo" (born: April 8, 1940 in Lansing [Martins Ferry], Ohio); inducted into the Naismith Memorial Basketball Hall of Fame in 1984 as a player; Position: Guard-Forward; Uniform: #17; won an NCAA title in 1960; won eight NBA titles; first NBA player to score 1,000 points in 16 consecutive seasons.

Havlicek attended Bridgeport (Ohio) High School, where he played basketball for three years (1955–1958) and was named All-State in his senior year (1958). After high school, he went to Ohio State University (Columbus), where he won a National Collegiate Athletic Association championship in 1960; was named All-American and All-Big 10 in 1962; All-Conference twice (1961–1962); was the team captain in 1962; team Most Valuable Player in 1961 and co-MVP in 1962; and scored a total of 1,223 points.

After college, he joined the National Basketball Association's Boston Celtics for the 1962–1963 season and played his entire 16-year career with the team. When the 6'5", 205-pound Havlicek arrived in Boston, the team had just won its fourth consecutive championship, and he helped the Celtics win four more straight NBA titles from 1963 to 1966. He would go on to win eight NBA titles with the team (1963–1966, 1968–1969, 1974, 1976), including six in his first seven seasons; was selected to the NBA All-Rookie Team (1963); first player to score 1,000 points in 16 consecutive seasons; was a 13-time NBA All-Star (1966–1978); the Celtics retired his jersey number 17 as soon as he retired; named NBA Finals MVP in 1974; selected to 11 All-NBA Teams, First (1971–1974) and Second (1964, 1966, 1968–1970, 1975–1976); and named to the All-Defensive First Team five times (1972–1976) and to the Second Team three times (1969–1971).

Havlicek retired as the Celtics all-time leader in points scored (26,395); averaged 22.0 points per game in 172 playoff contests; and is widely regarded as the best sixth man in NBA history. He was selected to the NBA 35th Anniversary Team in 1980 and to the NBA 50th Anniversary Team in 1996.

At Bridgeport High School, Havlicek starred in basketball, baseball, and football. An All-State selection in all three sports, he was a highly-recruited quarterback, and eventually chose Ohio State, although he never played football in college. A collegiate basketball All-American, he averaged 14.6 points per game in three varsity seasons.

Nicknamed "Hondo" after the John Wayne movie of the same name, he was team captain in the 1970s and led Boston to two more NBA championships (1974, 1976). In 2003, Havlicek was ranked number 15 on *SLAM* magazine's Top

75 NBA Players of All Time. Only teammates Bill Russell and Sam Jones won more championship titles during their playing careers.

John Havlicek's NBA Career Statistics

SEASON	TEAM	G	MIN	FG	FT	TRB	AST	PTS
1962–1963	Boston	80	2,200	483	174	534	179	1,140
1963–1964	Boston	80	2,587	640	315	428	238	1,595
1964–1965	Boston	75	2,169	570	235	371	199	1,375
1965–1966	Boston	71	2,175	530	274	423	210	1,334
1966–1967	Boston	81	2,602	684	365	532	278	1,733
1967–1968	Boston	82	2,921	666	368	546	384	1,700
1968–1969	Boston	82	3,174	692	387	570	441	1,771
1969–1970	Boston	81	3,369	736	488	635	550	1,960
1970–1971	Boston	81	3,678	892	554	730	607	2,338
1971–1972	Boston	82	3,698	897	458	672	614	2,252
1972–1973	Boston	80	3,367	766	370	567	529	1,902
1973–1974	Boston	76	3,091	685	346	487	447	1,716
1974–1975	Boston	82	3,132	642	289	484	432	1,573
1975–1976	Boston	76	2,598	504	281	314	278	1,289
1976–1977	Boston	79	2,913	580	235	382	400	1,395
1977–1978	Boston	82	2,797	546	230	332	328	1,322
	TOTALS	1,270	46,471	10,513	5,369	8,007	6,114	26,395

Sources: Basketball-Reference.com; Naismith Memorial Basketball Hall of Fame

Hawerchuk, Dale (born: April 4, 1963 in Toronto, Ontario, Canada); inducted into the Hockey Hall of Fame in 2001 as a player; Position: Left Wing-Center; Uniform: #10; won the 1980 Memorial Cup; youngest NHL player to score more than 100 points in a season; youngest player to win the Calder Memorial Trophy.

During his entire career, Hawerchuk was routinely compared to the legendary Wayne Gretzky, and led his teams in scoring at every level of play. He played 16 National Hockey League seasons with the Winnipeg Jets (1981–1990), Buffalo Sabres (1990–1995), St. Louis Blues (1995), and the Philadelphia Flyers (1995–1997).

In 1979, he joined the Cornwall Royals (Quebec Major Junior Hockey League); scored 103 points his first year; and was named the league's Rookie of the Year. In the playoffs, he scored 45 points in 18 games; led the Royals to the Memorial Cup title; and was named playoffs' MVP. The next season, he scored 81 goals and 183 points; led the team to its second consecutive league title; won his second Memorial Cup MVP award; and was named Canadian Major Junior Player of the Year.

He was the number one choice (sixth overall selection) of the Winnipeg Jets in the 1981 NHL Draft and led the team, as a rookie, to the largest single-season turnaround in NHL history, a 48-point improvement (32 points in 1981 [9–57–14] to 80 points in 1982 [33–33–14]). In his first year with the team, Hawerchuk became the youngest player in NHL history to reach the 100-point plateau (103); won the Calder Memorial Trophy as the NHL's Rookie of the Year, the youngest player ever to win the award; and played in his first All-Star Game.

After being eliminated in the first round of the NHL playoffs his first season in Winnipeg, Hawerchuk played for Team Canada at the 1982 World Championships and won a bronze medal. He played for Team Canada again in 1986 (winning another bronze medal) and in 1989 (winning a silver medal).

Traded to the Buffalo Sabres in 1990, he would lead the team in scoring three times. In the summer of 1995, he signed with the St. Louis Blues and scored 41 points in 66 games, before being traded to the Philadelphia Flyers. The next season, he was selected by the Commissioner to play in his fifth, and final, All-Star Game, and scored two goals.

Hawerchuk retired after the 1996–1997 season, having recorded more than a point-per-game for 13 consecutive seasons. He was the 23rd player to reach the 500-goal plateau (1995–1996) and the 31st player to record 1,000 points (1990–1991).

Dale Hawerchuk's Career Statistics

			REGULAR SEASON						PLAYOFFS				
SEASON	TEAM	LEAGUE	GP	G	A	TP	PIM	+/–	GP	G	A	TP	PIM

SEASON	TEAM	LEAGUE	REGULAR SEASON GP	G	A	TP	PIM	+/–	PLAYOFFS GP	G	A	TP	PIM
1978–1979	Oshawa Legionnaires	OHA-B	36	32	52	84							
1979–1980	Cornwall Royals	QMJHL	72	37	66	103	21		18	20	25	45	0
1979–1980	Cornwall Royals	M-Cup	5	1	5	6	0						
1980–1981	Cornwall Royals	QMJHL	72	81	102	183	69		19	15	20	35	8
1980–1981	Canada	WJC-A	5	5	4	9	2						
1980–1981	Cornwall Royals	M-Cup	5	8	4	12	4						
1981–1982	Winnipeg Jets	NHL	80	45	58	103	47	–4	4	1	7	8	5
1981–1982	Canada	WEC-A	10	3	1	4	0						
1982–1983	Winnipeg Jets	NHL	79	40	51	91	31	–17	3	1	4	5	8
1983–1984	Winnipeg Jets	NHL	80	37	65	102	73	–14	3	1	1	2	0
1984–1985	Winnipeg Jets	NHL	80	53	77	130	74	+22	3	2	1	3	4
1985–1986	Winnipeg Jets	NHL	80	46	59	105	44	–27	3	0	3	3	0
1985–1986	Canada	WEC-A	8	2	4	6	4						
1986–1987	Winnipeg Jets	NHL	80	47	53	100	52	+3	10	5	8	13	4
1986–1987	NHL All–Stars	RV-87	2	0	1	1	2						
1987–1988	Canada	Can-Cup	9	4	2	6	0						
1987–1988	Winnipeg Jets	NHL	80	44	77	121	59	–9	5	3	4	7	16
1988–1989	Winnipeg Jets	NHL	75	41	55	96	28	–30					
1988–1989	Canada	WEC-A	10	4	8	12	6						
1989–1990	Winnipeg Jets	NHL	79	26	55	81	60	–11	7	3	5	8	2
1990–1991	Buffalo Sabres	NHL	80	31	58	89	32	+2	6	2	4	6	10
1991–1992	Canada	Can-Cup	8	2	3	5	0						
1991–1992	Buffalo Sabres	NHL	77	23	75	98	27	–22	7	2	5	7	0
1992–1993	Buffalo Sabres	NHL	81	16	80	96	52	–17	8	5	9	14	2
1993–1994	Buffalo Sabres	NHL	81	35	51	86	91	+10	7	0	7	7	4
1994–1995	Buffalo Sabres	NHL	23	5	11	16	2	–2	2	0	0	0	0
1995–1996	St. Louis Blues	NHL	66	13	28	41	22	+5					
1995–1996	Philadelphia Flyers	NHL	16	4	16	20	4	+10	12	3	6	9	12
1996–1997	Philadelphia Flyers	NHL	51	12	22	34	32	+9	17	2	5	7	0
	NHL TOTALS		1,188	518	891	1,409	730		97	30	69	99	67

Sources: Hockey Hall of Fame; Hockey-Reference.com

Hawkins, Cornelius L. "Connie" (born: July 17, 1942 in Brooklyn, New York); inducted into the Naismith Memorial Basketball Hall of Fame in 1992 as a player; Position: Forward-Center; Uniform: #42; played for the Harlem Globetrotters; first Phoenix Suns player ever named to NBA First Team; first Phoenix Sun elected to the basketball hall of fame; won the inaugural ABA championship.

Hawkins played basketball for three years at Boys' High School (Brooklyn, New York), where he was a two-time All-City, All-Conference, All-District, and All-State selection. In 1959, he led the team to an undefeated season and to the Public School Athletic League championship. In his senior year, Hawkins averaged 25.5 points per game; again led his team to an undefeated season; and won the 1960 PSAL title. Before graduating in 1960, he would be named a *Parade* magazine All-American (1960) and was a two-time team Most Valuable Player and high scorer.

After high school, he attended the University of Iowa (Iowa City), but left school during his freshman year (1960–1961) to begin playing professional basketball in the American Basketball League with the Pittsburgh Rens (1961–1963). He went on to play for the Harlem Globetrotters (1964–1966); the Pittsburgh Pipers of the American Basketball Association (1967–1968); the ABA Minnesota Pipers, after the team moved from Pittsburgh (1968–1969); the National Basketball Association's Phoenix Suns (1970–1973); NBA Los Angeles Lakers (1973–1975); and the NBA Atlanta Hawks (1975–1976).

Hawkins was named to the ABL All-Star First Team with the Rens (1962); ABL Most Valuable Player at the age of 19 (1962); named ABA MVP in the league's inaugural season, after leading the Pipers to the first-ever ABA championship (1968); a two-time ABA First Team All-Star (1968–1969); first Phoenix Suns player ever named to the NBA First Team (1970); first Phoenix Suns player elected to the basketball hall of fame; a four-time NBA All-Star (1970–1973); and Phoenix Suns Most Valuable Player (1971). When he left the game, his jersey number 42 was retired by the Phoenix Suns and, as of this writing, he works in a community relations capacity for the team.

Hawkins' college career was interrupted when, as a freshman at the University of Iowa, he became entangled in the infamous National Collegiate Athletic Association basketball point-shaving scandal because he knew many of the players involved, although it was never proven that he was involved.

In 616 professional games, the 6'8", 215-pound Hawkins scored 11,528 points (18.9 a game) and had 5,450 rebounds.

Connie Hawkins' Career Statistics

SEASON	TEAM	LG	G	MIN	FG	3P	FT	TRB	AST	STL	BLK	PTS
1967–1968	Pittsburgh	ABA	70	3,146	635	2	603	945	320			1,875
1968–1969	Minneapolis	ABA	47	1,852	496	3	425	534	184			1,420
1969–1970	Phoenix	NBA	81	3,312	709		577	846	391			1,995
1970–1971	Phoenix	NBA	71	2,662	512		457	643	322			1,481
1971–1972	Phoenix	NBA	76	2,798	571		456	633	296			1,598
1972–1973	Phoenix	NBA	75	2,768	441		322	641	304			1,204
1973–1974	Phoenix	NBA	8	223	36		18	43	28	8	3	90
1973–1974	Los Angeles	NBA	71	2,538	368		173	522	379	105	78	909
1974–1975	Los Angeles	NBA	43	1,026	139		68	198	120	51	23	346
1975–1976	Atlanta	NBA	74	1,907	237		136	445	212	80	46	610
		ABA	117	4,998	1,131	5	1,028	1,479	504			3,295
		NBA	499	17,234	3,013		2,207	3,971	2,052	244	150	8,233
	TOTALS		616	22,232	4,144	5	3,235	5,450	2,556	244	150	11,528

Sources: Basketball-Reference.com; Naismith Memorial Basketball Hall of Fame

Hay, Charles Cecil (born: June 28, 1902 in Kingston, Ontario, Canada; died: October 24, 1973); inducted into the Hockey Hall of Fame in 1974 as a builder; instrumental in the creation of Hockey Canada; helped create the 1972 Summit Series between Canada and the U.S.S.R.

A successful businessman, Hay was instrumental in promoting amateur and international hockey in Canada. He played hockey at the University of Saskatchewan (Saskatoon, Saskatchewan, Canada), and in 1921, he led the team to the Allan Cup final, losing to the Toronto Granites. After graduating with a degree in civil engineering, he worked as an executive in the petroleum industry, eventually serving as president of Hi-Way Refineries Limited and Gulf Canada Limited before retiring in 1969.

During his entire working career, Hay maintained his interest in hockey, and was a regular at the Maple Leaf Gardens in Toronto. In December 1968, he attended a meeting in Ottawa (Ontario, Canada) sponsored by the Task Force on Sport that included representatives from the National Hockey League, Canadian Amateur Hockey Association, the Canadian Government, and business leaders, all gathered to create the administrative body that became known as Hockey Canada, with the purpose of assembling the best national team possible to represent Canada in international competition. Several years later, Hay retired as a businessman and devoted most of his time to Hockey Canada, serving as the organization's president. He helped create a Certification Program for coaches; sponsored scholarships and grants to encourage students to play hockey at Canadian universities; and helped fund hockey research.

He later played a key role in the arrangement of the 1972 Summit Series between Canada and the U.S.S.R.

Source: Hockey Hall of Fame

Hay, George William (born: January 10, 1898 in Listowel, Ontario, Canada; died: July 13, 1975); inducted into the Hockey Hall of Fame in 1958 as a player; Position: Forward; played professional hockey for 12 seasons.

Hay spent his early amateur days playing hockey in Winnipeg, Manitoba (Canada), before going on to a 12-year professional career from 1921 to 1934.

Relatively small (5'6", 156 pounds), his hockey career was interrupted when he served in the military during World War I. After completing his service, he returned to Canada and played senior hockey with the Regina Victorias (Saskatchewan Senior Hockey League) for two seasons (1920–1921). Hay turned professional with the Regina Capitals of the Western Canada Hockey League (later renamed the Western Hockey League) in 1921, and played four years with the team before the franchise was transferred to Portland for the 1925–1926 season. While in the WCHL, he was named to the First All-Star Team four times (1922–1924, 1926).

When the WHL folded, he joined the National Hockey League's Chicago Black Hawks for the 1926–1927 season and played for one year before being traded to the Detroit Cougars. He retired from Detroit after playing just one game in the 1933–1934 season to become the coach of the Detroit Red Wings' farm team in London, Ontario, Canada.

George Hay's Career Statistics

	REGULAR SEASON	PLAYOFFS

SEASON	TEAM	LEAGUE	GP	G	A	TP	PIM	GP	G	A	TP	PIM
1914–1915	Winnipeg Strathconas	MHL-Sr.	7	4	0	4						
1915–1916	Winnipeg Monarchs	MHL-Sr.	7	6	4	10	10	2	2	2	4	4
1916–1917	Winnipeg Monarchs	WJrHL										
1919–1920	Regina Victorias	SSHL	12	8	3	11	5	2	1	0	1	0
1920–1921	Regina Victorias	SSHL	16	9	4	13	7	4	5	2	7	2
1921–1922	Regina Capitals	WCHL	25	21	11	32	9	4	0	0	0	4
1921–1922	Regina Capitals	West–P						2	0	1	1	0
1922–1923	Regina Capitals	WCHL	30	28	8	36	12	2	1	0	1	0
1923–1924	Regina Capitals	WCHL	25	20	11	31	8	2	1	1	2	0
1924–1925	Regina Capitals	WCHL	20	16	6	22	6					
1925–1926	Portland Rosebuds	WHL	30	19	12	31	4					
1926–1927	Chicago Black Hawks	NHL	35	14	8	22	12	2	1	2	3	2
1927–1928	Detroit Cougars	NHL	42	22	13	35	20					
1928–1929	Detroit Cougars	NHL	39	11	8	19	14	2	1	0	1	0
1929–1930	Detroit Cougars	NHL	44	18	15	33	8					
1930–1931	Detroit Falcons	NHL	44	8	10	18	24					
1931–1932	Detroit Olympics	IHL	48	10	9	19	26	6	0	0	0	2
1932–1933	Detroit Red Wings	NHL	34	1	6	7	6	4	0	1	1	0
1932–1933	Detroit Olympics	IHL	9	6	1	7	6					
1933–1934	Detroit Red Wings	NHL	1	0	0	0	0					
1933–1934	Detroit Olympics	IHL	4	0	0	0	5					
	NHL TOTALS		239	74	60	134	84	8	2	3	5	2

Sources: Hockey Hall of Fame; Hockey-Reference.com

Hayes, Elvin Ernest (born: November 17, 1945 in Rayville, Louisiana); inducted into the Naismith Memorial Basketball Hall of Fame in 1990 as a player; Position: Forward-Center; 1968 College Basketball Player of the Year; won an NBA title in 1978; his 27,313 career points was third best in NBA history when he retired.

Hayes was a three-letter winner at Eula D. Britton High School (Rayville, Louisiana), where he graduated in 1964. He was named an All-American in 1964; a two-time All-State and All-Conference selection (1963–1964); and was the team's Most Valuable Player in 1964, when he led the school to the state championship.

After high school, he went to the University of Houston (Texas, 1964–1968) and was a three-year letter winner. He was selected to *The Sporting News* All-America Second Team in 1965; *The Sporting News* All-America First Team twice (1967–1968); *The Sporting News* College Player of the Year (1968); selected All-Southwest Conference three times (1966–1968); voted Most Improved Player twice (1967–1968); served as team co-captain in 1968; won the Cougar Club Award twice as the nation's Male Athlete of the Year (1967–1968); team Most Valuable Player twice (1967–1968); played in the 1968 East-West Game; a two-time member of the National Collegiate Athletic Association District All-Star Team (1967–1968); competed in the 1968 U.S. Olympic Trials; and scored a college career total of 2,884 points (31.0 per game) in 93 varsity games.

Hayes led Houston to an overall 81–12 three-year record, including three-straight NCAA Tournament appearances, finishing third in 1967 and fourth in 1968. He scored 30 or more points 37 times in his career; scored 39 points in the team's 71–69 win over Lew Alcindor (now known as Kareem Abdul-Jabbar) and the UCLA Bruins, ending UCLA's 47-game winning streak in the Astrodome (Houston, Texas), the first-ever nationally televised college basketball game; scored 40 or more points 14 times in his career; scored 50 or more points three times in his career; led Houston in scoring three times (1966–1968); his 1,215 field goals made was an NCAA record; set school record in rebounds (1,602, 17.2 per game); and was named *The Sporting News* 1968 College Basketball Player of the Year. His jersey number 44 was retired by the school.

After college, the 6'9", 235-pound Hayes joined the professional ranks with the National Basketball Association's San Diego Rockets (1968–1971) as the team's first overall pick and the league's number one selection in the 1968 draft. He had a 16-season NBA career and went on to play for the Houston Rockets (1971–1972); Baltimore Bullets (1972–1973); Capital Bullets (1973–1974); Washington Bullets (1974–1981); and the Houston Rockets (1981–1984). He was named to the NBA All-Rookie Team in 1969; led the league in scoring (1969) with 28.4 points per game; led the NBA in minutes played with a rookie record of 3,695 minutes (45.6 per game) in 1969; selected to the All-NBA First Team three times (1975, 1977, 1979); All-NBA Second Team three times (1973–1974, 1976); All-NBA Defensive Team twice (1974–1975); and was a 12-time All-Star (1969–1980).

Nicknamed "The Big E," Hayes won an NBA title with the Washington Bullets in 1978; scored 27,313 points (21.0 per game) in 1,303 NBA games, third best in history when he retired; grabbed 16,279 rebounds (12.5 per game), third best in league history when he retired; led the league in rebounding twice (1970, 1974); and set an NBA Finals record for most offensive rebounds (11) on May 27, 1979 against the Seattle SuperSonics.

Hayes was voted to the NBA 50th Anniversary All-Time Team.

Elvin Hayes' Career Statistics

SEASON	TEAM	LG	G	MIN	FG	FT	TRB	AST	PTS
1968–1969	San Diego	NBA	82	3,695	930	467	1,406	113	2,327
1969–1970	San Diego	NBA	82	3,665	914	428	1,386	162	2,256
1970–1971	San Diego	NBA	82	3,633	948	454	1,362	186	2,350
1971–1972	Houston	NBA	82	3,461	832	399	1,197	270	2,063
1972–1973	Baltimore	NBA	81	3,347	713	291	1,177	127	1,717
1973–1974	Capital	NBA	81	3,602	689	357	1,463	163	1,735
1974–1975	Washington	NBA	82	3,465	739	409	1,004	206	1,887
1975–1976	Washington	NBA	80	2,975	649	287	878	121	1,585
1976–1977	Washington	NBA	82	3,364	760	422	1,029	158	1,942
1977–1978	Washington	NBA	81	3,246	636	326	1,075	149	1,598
1978–1979	Washington	NBA	82	3,105	720	349	994	143	1,789
1979–1980	Washington	NBA	81	3,183	761	334	896	129	1,859
1980–1981	Washington	NBA	81	2,931	584	271	789	98	1,439
1981–1982	Houston	NBA	82	3,032	519	280	747	144	1,318
1982–1983	Houston	NBA	81	2,302	424	196	616	158	1,046
1983–1984	Houston	NBA	81	994	158	86	260	71	402
	TOTALS		1,303	50,000	10,976	5,356	1,6279	2,398	27,313

Sources: Basketball-Reference.com; Naismith Memorial Basketball Hall of Fame

Hayes, George (born: June 21, 1914 in Montreal, Quebec, Canada; died: November 19, 1987); inducted into the Hockey Hall of Fame in 1988 as an on-ice official; first official to work 1,000 games.

Realizing that he did not have the skills needed to be a hockey player, Hayes turned his attention to being a referee. In 1941, after officiating local minor league games, he moved up to the Ontario Hockey Association and five years later, he began officiating in the American Hockey League.

His tenure in the AHL ended after World War II as returning officials reclaimed their former jobs and forced Hayes back to the OHA for another two years, where he refereed the 1946 Memorial Cup. National Hockey League president Red Dutton signed him to a contract in April 1946 as a referee, but a year later, he became a linesman, a position he held for the next 20 seasons. He was the first official to hand-deliver the puck to his colleagues rather than throw or slide the puck as was the habit of the time, and was famous for his scrapbooks, keeping game reports for every contest he worked. His extensive collection eventually made its way to the Hockey Hall of Fame as a special display after he retired.

Hayes was the first official to work one thousand games, and in 1959, he was part of the crew that traveled with the New York Rangers and Boston Bruins on a tour through Europe. In 1965, for reasons that have never been made clear, he refused to take an NHL-mandated eye test, and was suspended by commissioner Clarence Campbell. He then returned to Ingersoll, Ontario, Canada; wrote a column for the *Woodstock Daily Sentinel* three times a week; and never worked in the NHL again.

Source: Hockey Hall of Fame

Hayes, Robert Lee "Bob" (born: December 20, 1942 in Jacksonville, Florida; died: September 18, 2002 in Jacksonville, Florida); inducted into the Pro Football Hall of Fame in 2009 as a player; Position: Wide Receiver; Uniform: #22; won two gold medals at the 1964 Olympics.

Selected in the seventh round (88th overall pick) in the 1964 National Football League Draft out of Florida Agricultural and Mechanical (A&M) University (Tallahassee, Florida), the 5'11", 185-pound Hayes played 11 seasons (132 games) with the Dallas Cowboys (1965–1974) and the San Francisco 49ers (1975). He was also picked in the 14th round (105th overall selection) in the 1964 American Football League Draft by the Denver Broncos.

He won two gold medals (100 meters, 4 x 100 meter relay) in the 1964 Olympics (Tokyo, Japan), earning the nickname, the "World's Fastest Human."

He was named to the Pro Bowl three times (1965–1967); First-Team All Pro twice (1966, 1968); Second-Team All Pro (1967); led the Cowboys in receptions three times; appeared in two Super Bowls (winning SB VI in 1972 and losing SB V in 1971); played in two NFL Championship games (losing in both 1966 and 1967); and was added to the Dallas Cowboys Ring of Honor in 2001. Immediately answering questions some had as to whether a speedster could thrive in a contact sport, in his rookie season, Hayes caught 46 passes for 1,003 yards and 12 touchdowns.

He retired holding numerous Cowboys' regular-season records, including Most Receptions in a Career (365); Most Receiving Yards in a Career (7,295); Most Receiving Yards in a Season (1,232 in 1966); Most Points Scored in a Career (456); Highest Average Per Catch in a Season (26.1 yards in 1970); Most Punt Return Yards in a Career (1,158); Highest Punt Return Average in a Career (11.1 yards); Longest Pass Reception (95 yards from Don Meredith on November 13, 1966 against the Washington Redskins); Most Receiving Yards in a Game (246 on November 13, 1966 against the Washington Redskins); and Most Touchdowns in a Game (four on December 20, 1970 against the Houston Oilers).

He attended Matthew W. Gilbert High School (Jacksonville, Florida), where his 1958 team went undefeated (12–0) and won the Florida Interscholastic Athletic Association black school state championship. After high school, Hayes was a two-sport star at Florida A&M (football, track and field). He is the second Olympic gold medalist to be inducted into the football hall of fame (after Jim Thorpe) and is the only man to win both an Olympic gold and a Super Bowl ring. He was the Amateur Athletic Union 100-yard dash champion three consecutive years (1962–1964); in 1964, he was the NCAA 200-meter champion; and would miss part of his senior year in college to participate in the 1964 Olympics.

Bob Hayes' Career Statistics

			RECEIVING				RUSHING			
YEAR	**TEAM**	**G**	**NO**	**YDS**	**AVG**	**TD**	**ATT**	**YDS**	**AVG**	**TD**
1965	Dallas	13	46	1,003	21.8	12	4	-8	-2.0	1
1966	Dallas	14	64	1,232	19.3	13	1	-1	-1.0	0
1967	Dallas	13	49	998	20.4	10	0	0	0.0	0
1968	Dallas	14	53	909	17.2	10	4	2	0.5	0
1969	Dallas	10	40	746	18.7	4	4	17	4.3	0
1970	Dallas	13	34	889	26.1	10	4	34	8.5	1
1971	Dallas	14	35	840	24.0	8	3	18	6.0	0
1972	Dallas	12	15	200	13.3	0	2	8	4.0	0
1973	Dallas	13	22	360	16.4	3	0	0	0.0	0
1974	Dallas	12	7	118	16.9	1	0	0	0.0	0
1975	San Francisco	4	6	119	19.8	0	2	-2	-1.0	0
	TOTALS	132	371	7,414	20.0	71	24	68	2.8	2

Bob Hayes' Career Statistics (Continued)

			PUNT RETURNS				KICKOFF RTNS				SCORING	
YEAR	**TEAM**	**G**	**NO**	**YDS**	**AVG**	**TD**	**NO**	**YDS**	**AVG**	**TD**	**TD**	**PTS**
1965	Dallas	13	12	153	12.8	0	17	450	26.5	0	13	78
1966	Dallas	14	17	106	6.2	0	0	0	0.0	0	13	78
1967	Dallas	13	24	276	11.5	1	1	17	17.0	0	11	66
1968	Dallas	14	15	312	20.8	2	1	20	20.0	0	12	72
1969	Dallas	10	18	179	9.9	0	3	80	26.7	0	4	24
1970	Dallas	13	15	116	7.7	0	0	0	0.0	0	11	66
1971	Dallas	14	1	5	5.0	0	1	14	0.0	0	8	48
1972	Dallas	12	0	0	0.0	0	0	0	0.0	0	0	0
1973	Dallas	13	0	0	0.0	0	0	0	0.0	0	3	18
1974	Dallas	12	2	11	5.5	0	0	0	0.0	0	1	6
1975	San Francisco	4	0	0	0.0	0	0	0	0.0	0	0	0
	TOTALS	132	104	1,158	11.1	3	23	581	25.3	0	76	456

Sources: Pro Football Hall of Fame; Pro-Football-Reference.com

Haynes, Marques (born: October 3, 1926 in Sand Springs, Oklahoma); inducted into the Naismith Memorial Basketball Hall of Fame in 1998 as a player; Position: Guard; won a national high school championship in 1941; first Harlem Globetrotter player enshrined into the basketball hall of fame.

A two-time basketball letter winner at Booker T. Washington High School (Sand Springs, Oklahoma, 1938–1942), Haynes was twice selected All-Conference (1941–1942); Second Team All-American (1941); and won a National High School Championship in 1941. After high school, he went to Langston University (Oklahoma, 1942–1946) and led the team to an overall 112–3 record during his tenure, including a 59-game winning streak. He was named Conference Most Valuable Player three times (1944–1946) and was the team MVP and high scorer all four years at the school.

After college, the 6', 160-pound Haynes played professional basketball in the Independent League with the Harlem Globetrotters (1946–1953, 1972–1979); Harlem Magicians (1953–1972, 1983–1992); Bucketeers (1979–1981); and the Harlem Wizards (1981–1983). He was considered the "World's Greatest Dribbler"; first Harlem Globetrotter player enshrined in the basketball hall of fame; played in more than 12,000 games in his five-decade career; traveled more than four million miles and played in 97 countries around the world; and helped the Globetrotters defeat the George Mikan-led Minneapolis Lakers (National Basketball League/Basketball Association of America) in both 1948 and 1949.

In 1994, a 12-mile stretch of Oklahoma State Highway 97 was re-named Marques Haynes Highway; he owned the Harlem Magicians (Independent League, 1953–1972); and has also been inducted into the National Association of Intercollegiate Athletics Hall of Fame (1985), Oklahoma Hall of Fame (1990), East Hartford (Connecticut) Hall of Fame (1992), Jim Thorpe Hall of Fame (1993), and Langston University Hall of Fame (1995).

In 1953, due to a contract dispute with owner Abe Saperstein, Haynes left the Globetrotters and started his own team, the Harlem Magicians. He toured with the Magicians for 18 years before rejoining the Globetrotters as a player-coach in 1972. He and Meadowlark Lemon later toured with a team called the Bucketeers.

Source: Naismith Memorial Basketball Hall of Fame

Haynes, Michael James "Mike" (born: July 1, 1953 in Denison, Texas); inducted into the Pro Football Hall of Fame in 1997 as a player; Position: Cornerback; Uniform: #40; won Super Bowl XVIII.

Haynes, a two-time All-American and a three-year All-Western Athletic Conference star at Arizona State University (Tempe), was the New England Patriots' first pick in the 1976 National Football League Draft (fifth overall selection), and the first defensive back chosen. The 6'2", 192-pound Haynes played 14 seasons (177 games, 1976–1989) with the New England Patriots (1976–1982) and the Los Angeles Raiders (1983–1989). In his rookie season, he had eight interceptions and led the American Football Conference with 608 punt-return yards.

He was selected to nine Pro Bowls (1976–1980, 1982, 1984–1986); named All-AFC eight times; a five-time All-Pro choice (1977–1978, 1982, 1984–1985); intercepted a pass in Super Bowl XVIII (January 1984) in a 38–9 Raiders win over the Washington Redskins; named NFL Defensive Rookie of the Year and United Press International AFC Rookie of the Year in 1976; won the 1984 George S. Halas Trophy as the NFL's Outstanding Defensive Player; named to the NFL 1980s All-Decade Team and to the NFL 75th Anniversary All-Time Team; and had his jersey number 40 retired by the Patriots.

In 1983, Haynes was sent to the Los Angeles Raiders, where he would eventually win his only Super Bowl title. In 1999, he was ranked number 93 on *The Sporting News*' list of the 100 Greatest Football Players, and in 2001, he was inducted into the College Football Hall of Fame.

Mike Haynes' Career Defensive Statistics

YEAR	TEAM	G	INT	YDS	AVG	TD
1976	New England	14	8	90	11.3	0
1977	New England	14	5	54	10.8	0
1978	New England	16	6	123	20.5	1
1979	New England	16	3	66	22.0	0
1980	New England	13	1	31	31.0	0
1981	New England	8	1	3	3.0	0
1982	New England	9	4	26	6.5	0
1983	Los Angeles	5	1	0	0.0	0
1984	Los Angeles	16	6	220	36.7	1
1985	Los Angeles	16	4	8	2.0	0
1986	Los Angeles	13	2	28	14.0	0
1987	Los Angeles	8	2	9	4.5	0

YEAR	TEAM	G	INT	YDS	AVG	TD
1988	Los Angeles	16	3	30	10.0	0
1989	Los Angeles	13	0	0	0.0	0
	TOTALS	177	46	688	15.0	2

Sources: College Football Hall of Fame; Pro Football Hall of Fame; Pro-Football-Reference.com

Healey, Edward Francis, Jr. "Ed" (born: December 28, 1894 in Indian Orchard, Massachusetts; died: December 9, 1978 in South Bend, Indiana); inducted into the Pro Football Hall of Fame in 1964 as a player; Position: Offensive Tackle; first player sold in the NFL.

Healey attended Pomfret (Connecticut) Prep School and Springfield (Massachusetts) Classical High School before spending one year at Holy Cross (Worcester, Massachusetts) in 1914. After a single season, he moved to Dartmouth College (Hanover, New Hampshire), where he played end for the school's football team for three seasons (1916–1917, 1919). His college career was interrupted for one year in 1918 while he served overseas in the military during World War I. After the war, he returned to Dartmouth before joining the National Football League with the Rock Island Independents (Illinois) in 1920. He was inducted into the College Football Hall of Fame in 1974.

In his eight-year career (89 games), Healey played with Rock Island for three seasons (1920–1922), before joining the Chicago Bears (1922–1927). In the professional ranks, he converted from end to offensive tackle and was sold to the Bears for $100, the first player sale in the NFL.

He played on the team's barnstorming tour after the 1925 season and was named to the NFL 1920s All-Decade Team.

In 1922, with the Independents, Healey played against George Halas, the player-coach of the Chicago Bears, and was so impressive that Halas bought Healey for $100. Halas called the 6', 207-pound Healey "the most versatile tackle in history" and he was an All-League pick five times.

Healey was the first president of the Chicago Bears Alumni Association, which was founded in 1937.

Sources: College Football Hall of Fame; Pro Football Hall of Fame

Healey, George (born: Plymouth, Devon, England; died: December 16, 1960 in Kent, Ohio); inducted into the National Soccer Hall of Fame and Museum in 1951 as a builder; president of the Michigan State Association; president of the United States Soccer Football Association.

An all-around athlete, as a boy Healey played soccer, rugby, cricket, racquets, rowing, and was a swimmer. After moving to the United States, he organized a soccer league in Detroit, Michigan in the early 1900s and, in 1905, became its president. He later organized the Michigan State Association and served as its president from 1913 to 1919.

In 1916, Healey became a third vice president of the United States Soccer Football Association for two years; later served two years as second vice president; and was elected president of the organization in May 1919 and served until 1923.

Source: National Soccer Hall of Fame and Museum

Hearn, Francis Dayle "Chick" (born: November 27, 1916 in Aurora, Illinois; died: August 5, 2002 in Northridge, California); inducted into the Naismith Memorial Basketball Hall of Fame in 2003 as a contributor; broadcast 3,338 consecutive games for the NBA's Los Angeles Lakers.

Hearn attended East Aurora (Illinois) High School, graduating in 1935, where he played basketball for three seasons (1933–1935); was team captain in 1935; and was selected All-Conference.

As a professional announcer, Hearn was a broadcaster for the National Basketball Association's Los Angeles Lakers (March 27, 1961–June 12, 2002) and also served as the team's assistant general manager from 1972 to 1980.

He broadcast 3,338 consecutive games for the Lakers (November 21, 1965 to December 16, 2001); won the 1992 Naismith Memorial Basketball Hall of Fame Curt Gowdy Media Award; inducted into the American Sportscasters Hall of Fame (1995, the hall's 20th member); a two-time national Sportscaster of the Year; three-time Golden Mike Award winner; won the Academy of Television Arts and Sciences 50th Anniversary Award; inducted into the Southern California Sports Broadcasters Hall of Fame; seven-time California Sportscaster of the Year; winner of the first-ever Cable Ace Award; and was presented with a star on the Hollywood Walk of Fame in 1986.

Hearn's final broadcast was Game 4 of the 2002 NBA Finals as the Lakers defeated the New Jersey Nets to win the team's third consecutive NBA championship.

He played basketball at Bradley University (Peoria, Illinois), and in 1956, began his career in Los Angeles broadcasting University of Southern California football and basketball games. In his 50-year career, in addition to Lakers broadcasts, he also worked National Collegiate Athletic Association and National Football League football; University of Las Vegas (Nevada) basketball; Professional Golf Association tournaments; the first Muhammad Ali-Joe Frazier fight; the Rose Bowl; and was part of NBC's coverage of the 1992 gold-medal winning U.S. Olympic Basketball "Dream Team" in Barcelona, Spain.

Source: Naismith Memorial Basketball Hall of Fame

Heilmann, Harry Edwin (born: August 3, 1894 in San Francisco, California; died: July 9, 1951 in Southfield, Michigan); inducted into the National Baseball Hall of Fame and Museum in 1952 as a player; Position: Right Field; Bats: Right; Throws: Right; first player to hit a home run in every major league park used during his career.

Rogers Hornsby (St. Louis Cardinals) and Ed Delahanty (Philadelphia Phillies) are the only right-handed batters to have career batting averages higher than Heilmann's .342 mark. Making his major league debut on May 16, 1914, he played 17 seasons for the Detroit Tigers (1914, 1916–1929) and Cincinnati Reds (1930, 1932), and won four batting titles (1921, 1923, 1925, 1927).

The 6'1", 200-pound Heilmann played for the Portland Beavers and the San Francisco Seals of the Pacific Coast League, before joining Detroit full time in 1916. He hit .300 or better 12 consecutive seasons; finished in the top 10 in batting average ten times; and held the major league record of 134 hits on the road in 1925 until Ichiro Suzuki (Seattle Mariners) passed it in 2004 with 145.

He was sold to the National League's Cincinnati Reds toward the end of his career and became the first player to hit a home run in every major league park used during his career. After his 17-year playing career ended, Heilmann served as a play-by-play announcer for Tigers' games for another 17 years (1934–1950); in 1999, he was ranked number 54 on *The Sporting News*' list of the 100 Greatest Baseball Players; and he was nominated as a finalist for the Major League Baseball All-Century Team.

After leaving Sacred Heart High School (San Francisco, California), Heilmann hit .305 in 1913 for the Portland Colts (Northwest League), before his contract was purchased by the Tigers. He played briefly for Detroit in 1914; was assigned to the PCL for two seasons; and joined the Tigers as a full-time player in 1916.

An unaccomplished fielder, he was moved to first base for the 1919 and 1920 seasons, and led the American League in errors at that position both years.

Throughout the 1920s, Heilmann led all American League batters with a .364 average, and his .558 slugging percentage was fourth behind Babe Ruth, Lou Gehrig, and Al Simmons.

Harry Heilmann's Career Statistics

YEAR	TEAM	LG	G	AB	R	H	2B	3B	HR	RBI	BB	SO	SB	AVG	SLG
1914	Detroit	AL	67	182	25	41	8	1	2	18	22	29	1	.225	.313
1916	Detroit	AL	136	451	57	127	30	11	2	73	42	40	9	.282	.410
1917	Detroit	AL	150	556	57	156	22	11	5	86	41	54	11	.281	.387
1918	Detroit	AL	79	286	34	79	10	6	5	39	35	10	13	.276	.406
1919	Detroit	AL	140	537	74	172	30	15	8	93	37	41	7	.320	.477
1920	Detroit	AL	145	543	66	168	28	5	9	89	39	32	3	.309	.429
1921	Detroit	AL	149	602	114	237	43	14	19	139	53	37	2	.394	.606
1922	Detroit	AL	118	455	92	162	27	10	21	92	58	28	8	.356	.598
1923	Detroit	AL	144	524	121	211	44	11	18	115	74	40	8	.403	.632
1924	Detroit	AL	153	570	107	197	45	16	10	114	78	41	13	.346	.533
1925	Detroit	AL	150	573	97	225	40	11	13	134	67	27	6	.393	.569
1926	Detroit	AL	141	502	90	184	41	8	9	103	67	19	6	.367	.534
1927	Detroit	AL	141	505	106	201	50	9	14	120	72	16	11	.398	.616
1928	Detroit	AL	151	558	83	183	38	10	14	107	57	45	7	.328	.507
1929	Detroit	AL	125	453	86	156	41	7	15	120	50	39	5	.344	.565
1930	Cincinnati	NL	142	459	79	153	43	6	19	91	64	50	2	.333	.577
1932	Cincinnati	NL	15	31	3	8	2	0	0	6	0	2	0	.258	.323
	TOTALS		2,146	7,787	1,291	2,660	542	151	183	1,539	856	550	112	.342	.520

Sources: Baseball-Reference.com; National Baseball Hall of Fame and Museum

Heilpern, Herbert (born: March 19, 1919 in Austria; died: September 27, 1999); inducted into the National Soccer Hall of Fame and Museum in 1988 as a builder; president of the German-American Soccer League; co-founded the North American Soccer League and the New York Cosmos.

Before immigrating to the United States from Austria in 1939, Heilpern was a goalkeeper for the Hakoah club of Vienna. He later played amateur soccer in New York City's Eastern District League from 1939 to 1958 with the Bronx Jewish Soccer Club, Hakoah Soccer Club, and New World Club. He won league championships with Hakoah in 1941–1942 and New World Club in 1948–1949.

He served as president of the German-American Soccer League of New York (1969–1975) and was a co-founder of both the North American Soccer League in 1967 and the New York Cosmos in 1971.

Heilpern joined the Executive Board of the German-American Junior League in 1976 and later served as the organization's president, and was named first vice president of the Eastern New York Youth Soccer Association in 1985.

He was inducted into the Eastern New York Soccer Hall of Fame in 1997.

Source: National Soccer Hall of Fame and Museum

Hein, Melvin Jack "Mel" (born: August 22, 1909 in Redding, California; died: January 31, 1992 in San Clemente, California); inducted into the Pro Football Hall of Fame in 1963 as a player; Position: Center; Uniform: #7; only offensive lineman ever to win the NFL MVP award; a member of the initial inductee class of the football hall of fame.

Hein played both offense and defense, 60 minutes a game, for 15 seasons (170 games, 1931–1945), all for the New York Giants. During his career, he played football for a total of 25 years at Burlington High School (now known as Burlington-Edison High School, Burlington, Washington), Fairhaven High School (Bellingham, Washington), Washington State University (Pullman, 1928–1930), and the NFL. In high school, Hein played center and various positions on the defensive line, and in his senior year, he was named the Skagit County Football Most Valuable Player and was a First-Team All-State selection.

He was the first player to have his jersey number (seven) retired at Washington State University. An All-American pick following the 1930 season, he helped lead the Cougars to an undefeated record that year (8–0), before losing 24–0 to Alabama in the 1931 Rose Bowl.

After college, he joined the Giants; selected First-Team All-NFL eight straight seasons (1933–1940) and Second-Team his other five years in the league; team captain for 10 seasons; won the Joe Carr Trophy as the NFL's Most Valuable Player in 1938 (the only offensive lineman ever to win the MVP award); and led the team to the league championship that same season with a 23–17 win over the Green Bay Packers. Hein played in seven NFL Championship Games (winning twice [1934, 1938] and losing in 1933, 1935, 1939, 1941, and 1944).

The 6'2", 225-pound Hein was named to Grantland Rice's All-America team; was in the inaugural class of the Pro Football Hall of Fame; named the center on the NFL 50th Anniversary Team (1969) and was named to the 75th Anniversary Team in 1994; and in 1999, 55 years after he had retired from the NFL, Hein was ranked number 74 on *The Sporting News*' list of the 100 Greatest Football Players.

After retiring as a player, he coached at the University of Southern California (Los Angeles) during the 1950s.

During the last four years of his playing career (1942–1945), Hein coached at Union College (Schenectady, New York) during the week, then played for the Giants on Sunday without ever practicing.

He was a member of the inaugural class of the College Football Hall of Fame in 1954; the Washington State University Athletic Hall of Fame in 1978; and was the first alumni athlete inducted into the new Burlington-Edison High School Athletic Hall of Fame in 2006. He has also been elected to the Washington State Sports Hall of Fame and the Inland Empire Sports Hall of Fame. His jersey number seven has been retired by both the WSU Cougars and the New York Giants.

From 1966 to 1967, he served as the supervisor of officials for the American Football League, and in 1999, he was one of three centers named to *The Sporting News* All-Century team for college players.

Sources: College Football Hall of Fame; Pro Football Hall of Fame

Heinrichs, April (born: February 27, 1964 in Littleton, Colorado); inducted into the National Soccer Hall of Fame and Museum in 1998 as a player; Position: Forward; International Caps (1986–1991): 47; International Goals: 37; was a staff member with the U.S. team that won the first-ever Olympic gold medal in women's soccer; first woman player inducted into the soccer hall of fame.

The first woman player to be inducted into the National Soccer Hall of Fame and Museum, Heinrichs, while in the eight grade, played on a high school team that won two state championships. Despite her on-field success, she received no college scholarship offers, and briefly attended a small, local Colorado college on a basketball scholarship.

She eventually received a scholarship offer from the University of North Carolina (Chapel Hill), where she would play for head coach Anson Dorrance. She played at the school for four years; scored 87 goals in 90 games; and was named a First-Team All-American three times. While she was at UNC, the school won three National Collegiate Athletic Association championships (1983–1984, 1986) and finished runner-up to George Mason University in 1985.

Heinrichs completed her college career as the all-time NCAA leader in points scored with 225 (87 goals and 51 assists), a record that was later bested by Mia Hamm (who also attended UNC). She was captain of the United States team that won the first-ever Fédération Internationale de Football Association Women's World Cup in 1991 (played at Tianhe Stadium in Guangzhou, China). She finished her international playing career with 47 caps and 37 goals.

In 1986 and 1989, she was named U.S. Soccer Female Athlete of the Year by Soccer America; served as a full-time assistant coach to the U.S. Women's team; was head coach at the University of Virginia (Charlottesville); and was head coach of the U.S. Women's National Team (2000–2005).

After coaching briefly at Princeton University (New Jersey) in 1990 (compiling an 8–6–1 record) and at the College of William & Mary (Williamsburg, Virginia), Heinrichs coached at the University of Maryland (College Park) from 1991 to 1995; compiled an overall record of 56–4–7; and was named Atlantic Coast Conference Coach of the Year in 1995 after leading the Terrapins to their first NCAA soccer tournament berth. In 1996, she was named the head coach at the University of Virginia; compiled an overall 52–27–7 record; and led the Cavaliers to four straight NCAA playoff berths while at the school (1996–1999). During her college coaching career, she compiled an overall record of 116–73–15 (.614).

Heinrichs became a full-time assistant coach for the U.S. Women's National Team in January 1996, and was a member of the staff that led the USA to the first-ever gold medal for women's soccer at the 1996 Olympics (held in Atlanta, Georgia). In 1996, she began a four-year stint as head coach of the U.S. U-16 National Team, before being appointed head coach and technical director for the U.S. Women's National Team programs. In 1998, she became the first female player inducted into the National Soccer Hall of Fame and Museum, and she was named head coach of the National Team in January 2000, becoming the first female head coach in the 17-year history of the program.

In 2003, Heinrichs led the United States team to two major tournament championships, the Four Nations Cup in China and then the Algarve Cup in Portugal. She also led the team to a championship in the 2002 Confederation of North, Central American and Caribbean Association Football Women's Gold Cup in the Rose Bowl in Pasadena, California. After a third-place finish in the 2003 FIFA Women's World Cup (played at the Home Depot Center in Carson, California), in 2004, she led the team to the Four Nations Cup, the CONCACAF Olympic qualifying tournament, and the Algarve Cup. While coaching the National Team, she compiled an overall 87–17–20 record.

In 2005, Heinrichs coached the University of California, Irvine women's soccer team to a 3–13–1 record.

Source: National Soccer Hall of Fame and Museum

Heinsohn, Thomas William "Tommy" (born: August 26, 1934 in Jersey City, New Jersey); inducted into the Naismith Memorial Basketball Hall of Fame in 1986 as a player; Position: Forward-Center; Uniform: #15; won the 1954 NIT title; won eight NBA championships as a player and two as a coach, all for the Celtics.

A four-year letter winner, Heinsohn attended St. Michael's High School (Union City, New Jersey, 1948–1952), where he was selected All-Catholic League (1951–1952); All-State (1951–1952); All-American (1952); and starred in the North-South game in Kentucky (1952).

After high school, he went to Holy Cross College (Worcester, Massachusetts, 1952–1956), where he was a three-year letter winner, and named All-Conference (1954–1956), All-American (1956), and All-New England (1956). He graduated as the school's all-time leading scorer (1,789 points, 22.1 per game); set the single-season scoring record (740 points, 27.4 per game) in 1956; scored a school-record 51 points against Boston College (March 1, 1956); made a record 18 straight free throws against Georgetown (January 30, 1956); played on Holy Cross teams that compiled a 67–14 record; was the Most Valuable Player; and led the team to the 1954 National Invitation Tournament championship.

After college, Heinsohn played his entire National Basketball Association career (1956–1965) for the Boston Celtics, after being a first-round draft selection. He was NBA Rookie of the Year (1957); All-NBA Second Team (1961–1964); a six-time NBA All-Star (1957, 1961–1965); and won eight NBA championships (in nine seasons) with the Celtics (1957, 1959–1965).

The 6'7", 220-pound Heinsohn scored 37 points in the seventh and final game of the 1957 NBA championship against the St. Louis Hawks to help lead Boston to its first NBA title; scored his 10,000th NBA point on the same day Bob Cousy retired; led the team in scoring three times (1960–1962); and averaged 18.6 points per game in 654 regular season games and 19.8 points in 104 playoff games.

After his playing days, he coached the Celtics for nine seasons (1969–1978) and compiled a 427–263 (.619) record; led Boston to the NBA championship twice (1974, 1976), giving him 10 titles while with the team; named NBA Coach of the Year in 1973; led the team to five Atlantic Division titles (1972–1976); and led the 1973 team to a league-best 68-14 record in 1973, the team's most wins in a single season.

After retiring as a coach, in 1981, Heinsohn became a color commentator on Celtics' television broadcasts on Fox Sports New England; was inducted into the Holy Cross Varsity Club Hall of Fame (1962); and his jersey number 15 was retired by the Celtics in 1966.

Tommy Heinsohn's Career Statistics

SEASON	TEAM	G	MIN	FG	FT	TRB	AST	PTS
1956–1957	Boston	72	2,150	446	271	705	117	1,163
1957–1958	Boston	69	2,206	468	294	705	125	1,230
1958–1959	Boston	66	2,089	465	312	638	164	1,242
1959–1960	Boston	75	2,420	673	283	794	171	1,629
1960–1961	Boston	74	2,256	627	325	732	141	1,579
1961–1962	Boston	79	2,383	692	358	747	165	1,742
1962–1963	Boston	76	2,004	550	340	569	95	1,440
1963–1964	Boston	76	2,040	487	283	460	183	1,257
1964–1965	Boston	67	1,706	365	182	399	157	912
	TOTALS	654	19,254	4,773	2,648	5,749	1,318	12,194

Tommy Heinsohn's Coaching Record

		REGULAR SEASON			PLAYOFFS			
SEASON	TEAM	W	L	WIN%	W	L	WIN%	Notes
1969–1970	Boston	34	48	.415				
1970–1971	Boston	44	38	.537				
1971–1972	Boston	56	26	.683	5	6	.455	
1972–1973	Boston	68	14	.829	7	6	.538	
1973–1974	Boston	56	26	.683	12	6	.667	NBA Champions
1974–1975	Boston	60	22	.732	6	5	.545	
1975–1976	Boston	54	28	.659	12	6	.667	NBA Champions
1976–1977	Boston	44	38	.537	5	4	.556	
1977–1978	Boston	11	23	.324				
	TOTALS	427	263	.619	47	33	.588	

Sources: Basketball-Reference.com; Naismith Memorial Basketball Hall of Fame

Hemmings, William (born: 1907 in Nottingham, England; died: August 26, 1978 in Chicago, Illinois); inducted into the National Soccer Hall of Fame and Museum in 1961 as a builder; president of the National League of Chicago.

Hemmings began playing soccer in his hometown before moving to London in 1918 to play in the Wood Green League as a center halfback. He came to the United States in 1921 and played for the German-American Soccer Club in the Lehigh Valley League (Pennsylvania). He moved to Minneapolis, Minnesota in 1933 and played for local teams until 1938, when he moved to Chicago, Illinois and played for the Schwaben Soccer Club until the end of World War II.

He served two years as vice president of the National League of Chicago before becoming its president in 1947, a position he held for 24 years, until resigning in 1970. During his tenure, the league grew to 70 senior and 10 junior teams.

Source: National Soccer Hall of Fame and Museum

Henderson, Rickey Henley (born: Rickey Nelson Henley on December 25, 1958 in Chicago, Illinois); inducted into the National Baseball Hall of Fame and Museum in 2009 as a player; Position: Left Field; Bats: Right; Throws: Left; holds major league records for career stolen bases and leadoff home runs.

Drafted by the Oakland Athletics in the fourth round of the 1976 Amateur Draft (96th overall selection), the 5'10", 195-pound Henderson made his major league debut on June 24, 1979, and played 25 seasons (1979–2003) for the Oakland Athletics (1979–1984, 1989–1993, 1994–1995, 1998), New York Yankees (1985–1989), Toronto Blue Jays (1993), San Diego Padres (1996–1997, 2001), Anaheim Angels (1997), New York Mets (1999–2000), Seattle Mariners (2000), Boston Red Sox (2002), and the Los Angeles Dodgers (2003).

Widely regarded as one of the game's greatest leadoff hitters, he retired as baseball's all-time leader in walks, a record since surpassed by Barry Bonds. A member of the 3,000 hit club and a 10-time All-Star (1980, 1982–1988, 1990–1991), he holds the major league record for career stolen bases (1,406), runs scored (2,295), and leadoff home runs (81); won two World Series (1989 with the Oakland Athletics, 1993 with the Toronto Blue Jays); won the Silver Slugger Award three times (1981, 1985, 1990); won a Gold Glove Award in 1981; holds the single-season record for stolen bases (130 in 1982); only player in American League history to steal 100 bases in a season (a feat he accomplished three times); and was the American League Most Valuable Player in 1990.

A rare right-handed batter and a left-handed thrower, only two other players with more than 4,000 at bats (Hal Chase and Cleon Jones) batted right and threw left.

In 1976, Henderson graduated from Oakland (California) Technical High School, where he played baseball, basketball and football, before signing with the Athletics. In his four minor league seasons, he hit over .300, had an on-base percentage of over .400, and had more walks than strikeouts.

In 1985, while with the Yankees, he became the first player in major league history to have 80 stolen bases and 20 home runs in the same season, a mark he matched in 1986. He and Eric Davis (Cincinnati Reds) are the only players in major league history to accomplish this feat. On May 1, 1991 (while with the Athletics), Henderson stole his 939th base of his career, surpassing Lou Brock, and setting a new major league record in a 7–4 win over the New York Yankees. The feat was somewhat overshadowed by Nolan Ryan (Texas Rangers) throwing his seventh career no-hitter against the Toronto Blue Jays on the same day.

During the 2001 season (with the Padres), Henderson broke three major league career records (Babe Ruth's 2,062 career walks, Ty Cobb's 2,246 career runs, and Zack Wheat's 2,328 career games in left field), and on the last day of the season, he got his 3,000th career hit.

In 2002, he joined the Red Sox, and in one of baseball's statistical ironies, joined the team with more career stolen bases (1,395) than the Boston franchise (1,382).

Henderson played his last major league game on September 19, 2003; was hit by a pitch in his only plate appearance; and eventually scored his 2,295th run. In February 2006, he was hired as a hitting instructor by the New York Mets, and in 2007 he became the team's first base coach.

In 1999, before breaking the career records for runs scored and walks, Henderson was ranked number 51 on *The Sporting News*' list of the 100 Greatest Baseball Players, and he was a nominee for the Major League Baseball All-Century Team.

On May 28, 1980, in a 6–3 Oakland win over the Kansas City Royals, Dwayne Murphy and Henderson both stole home in the first inning, tying a major league record (last accomplished in the American League by the Minnesota Twins on May 18, 1969 and in the National League by the St. Louis Cardinals on September 19, 1925). On July 29, 1989, Henderson had no official at bats, but scored four times on four walks, while getting five stolen bases. The effort was for naught as the Seattle Mariners beat Oakland 14–6. On August 22, 1989, Nolan Ryan struck out Henderson in the fifth inning during a 2–0 loss to Oakland to become the only pitcher in major league history to strike out 5,000 batters.

On July 5, 1993, Henderson led off both games of the Athletics' doubleheader against the Cleveland Indians with home runs, the first time the feat had been accomplished since 1913. While Oakland won the first game 6–5, his home run in game two did not help the team as it lost 6–2.

Rickey Henderson's Career Statistics

YEAR	TEAM	G	R	H	2B	3B	HR	RBI	BB	SO	AVG	OBP	SLG
1979	Oakland	89	49	96	13	3	1	26	34	39	.274	.338	.336
1980	Oakland	158	111	179	22	4	9	53	117	54	.303	.420	.399
1981	Oakland	108	89	135	18	7	6	35	64	68	.319	.408	.437
1982	Oakland	149	119	143	24	4	10	51	116	94	.267	.398	.382
1983	Oakland	145	105	150	25	7	9	48	103	80	.292	.414	.421
1984	Oakland	142	113	147	27	4	16	58	86	81	.293	.399	.458
1985	New York	143	146	172	28	5	24	72	99	65	.314	.419	.516
1986	New York	153	130	160	31	5	28	74	89	81	.263	.358	.469
1987	New York	95	78	104	17	3	17	37	80	52	.291	.423	.497
1988	New York	140	118	169	30	2	6	50	82	54	.305	.394	.399
1989	New York	65	41	58	13	1	3	22	56	29	.247	.392	.349
1989	Oakland	85	72	90	13	2	9	35	70	39	.294	.425	.438
1990	Oakland	136	119	159	33	3	28	61	97	60	.325	.439	.577
1991	Oakland	134	105	126	17	1	18	57	98	73	.268	.400	.423
1992	Oakland	117	77	112	18	3	15	46	95	56	.283	.426	.457
1993	Toronto	44	37	35	3	1	4	12	35	19	.215	.356	.319
1994	Oakland	87	66	77	13	0	6	20	72	45	.260	.411	.365
1995	Oakland	112	67	122	31	1	9	54	72	66	.300	.407	.447

YEAR	TEAM	G	R	H	2B	3B	HR	RBI	BB	SO	AVG	OBP	SLG
1996	San Diego	148	110	112	17	2	9	29	125	90	.241	.410	.344
1997	San Diego	88	63	79	11	0	6	27	71	62	.274	.422	.375
1997	California	32	21	21	3	0	2	7	26	23	.183	.343	.261
1998	Oakland	152	101	128	16	1	14	57	118	114	.236	.376	.347
1999	New York	121	89	138	30	0	12	42	82	82	.315	.423	.466
2000	New York	31	17	21	1	0	0	2	25	20	.219	.387	.229
2000	Seattle	92	58	77	13	2	4	30	63	55	.238	.362	.327
2001	San Diego	123	70	86	17	3	8	42	81	84	.227	.366	.351
2002	Boston	72	40	40	6	1	5	16	38	47	.223	.369	.352
2003	Los Angeles	30	7	15	1	0	2	5	11	16	.208	.321	.306
	TOTALS	3,081	2,295	3,055	510	66	297	1,115	2,190	1,694	.279	.401	.419

Sources: Baseball-Reference.com; National Baseball Hall of Fame and Museum

Hendricks, Theodore Paul "Ted" (born: November 1, 1947 in Guatemala City, Guatemala); inducted into the Pro Football Hall of Fame in 1990 as a player; Position: Linebacker; Uniform: #83; won four Super Bowl championships.

A three-time All-American linebacker and defensive end at the University of Miami (Florida, 1966–1968), Hendricks began his 15-season, 215-game National Football League career as a second-round draft pick (33rd overall choice) of the Baltimore Colts in the 1969 NFL Draft. He would go on to play for the Colts (1969–1973); Green Bay Packers (1974); and the Oakland/Los Angeles Raiders (1975–1983). The 6'7", 220-pound Hendricks never missed a game; was selected to eight Pro Bowls (1971–1974, 1980–1983); an 11-time All-Pro selection (1971–1974, 1976–1978, 1980–1983); won four Super Bowl championships (SB V in 1971, SB XI in 1977, SB XV in 1981, SB XVIII in 1984); selected All-AFC seven times and All-NFC once; named to the NFL 1970s All-Decade Team and to the NFL 75th Anniversary All-Time Team (1994); and is a member of the 20/20 Club (20 sacks and 20 interceptions in a career).

Hendricks is the first player in NFL history to have four Super Bowl rings who never played for the San Francisco 49ers, Dallas Cowboys, or Pittsburgh Steelers.

While playing at the University of Miami, Hendricks accumulated 327 total tackles (the most ever by a UM defensive lineman); led the team with the most solo tackles by a defensive lineman (19); recovered 12 fumbles; named College Lineman of the Year by United Press International in his senior year; had his jersey retired by the team in 1997; and was inducted into the College Football Hall of Fame in 1987. In 1999, he was ranked number 64 on *The Sporting News*' list of the 100 Greatest Football Players.

After retiring, he worked on behalf of ex-players as part of the Hall of Fame Player's Association. Named in his honor, the Ted Hendricks Award is given annually to the nation's top college defensive end.

In 2007, he was named to the Florida High School Association All-Century Team, which selected the top 33 players in the 100-year history of high school football in the state of Florida's history.

Ted Hendricks' Career Statistics

						DEFENSE			
YEAR	**TEAM**	**G**	**INT**	**YDS**	**AVG**	**TD**	**FUMREC**	**YDS**	**TD**
1969	Baltimore	14	0	0	0.0	0	0	0	0
1970	Baltimore	14	1	31	31.0	0	0	0	0
1971	Baltimore	14	5	70	14.0	0	1	31	1
1972	Baltimore	14	2	13	6.5	0	0	0	0
1973	Baltimore	14	3	33	11.0	0	4	0	0
1974	Green Bay	14	5	74	14.8	0	1	0	0
1975	Oakland	14	2	40	20.0	0	0	0	0
1976	Oakland	14	1	9	9.0	0	0	0	0
1977	Oakland	14	0	0	0.0	0	1	0	0
1978	Oakland	16	3	29	9.7	0	2	0	0
1979	Oakland	16	1	23	23.0	1	0	12	0
1980	Oakland	16	3	10	3.3	0	4	4	0
1981	Oakland	16	0	0	0.0	0	1	0	0
1982	Los Angeles	9	0	0	0.0	0	1	6	0
1983	Los Angeles	16	0	0	0.0	0	1	0	0
	TOTALS	215	26	332	12.8	1	16	53	1

Sources: Pro Football Hall of Fame; Pro-Football-Reference.com

Hendy, James Cecil Valdamar (born: May 6, 1905 in Barbados, British West Indies; died: January 14, 1961); inducted into the Hockey Hall of Fame in 1968 as a builder; considered the "Father of Modern Hockey Statistics."

Hendy is considered the founder of hockey statistics and was the originator of the statistics used to track the performances of professional hockey players and teams since the 1930s.

His family immigrated to Vancouver, Canada when he was six years old, where he began playing hockey. When he got older, Hendy wrote fiction for Street & Smith's; sports articles for the *Saturday Evening Post*; and selected an annual National Hockey League All-Star team for *McCall*'s magazine. His sports-related writing eventually led him to compile records of players' statistical performances.

He published the first edition of *The Hockey Guide* in 1933, and continued to produce it annually until 1951. Throughout his career, Hendy served as president of the United States Hockey League; publicist with the National Hockey League's New York Rangers; and general manager of the Cleveland Barons (American Hockey League), which he led to four Calder Cups finals, winning three. While with the Barons, he was selected Executive of the Year twice by *The Hockey News*.

The James C. Hendy Memorial Award is presented annually to the American Hockey League's Executive of the Year.

Source: Hockey Hall of Fame

Henry, Wilbur "Pete" (born: October 31, 1897 in Mansfield, Ohio; died: February 7, 1952 in Washington, Pennsylvania); inducted into the Pro Football Hall of Fame in 1963 as a player; Position: Tackle; first player to letter in baseball, basketball, football, and track at Washington and Jefferson College; won two NFL championships.

Henry signed with the Canton Bulldogs of the National Football League the same day (September 17, 1920) that the NFL (first known as the American Professional Football Association) was being organized in Canton, Ohio. He played in the NFL for eight seasons (86 games) for the Canton Bulldogs (1920–1923, 1925–1926); New York Giants (1927); and the Pottsville Maroons (Pennsylvania, Independent, 1924, 1927–1928).

He was a three-time All-American (1917–1919) at Washington and Jefferson College (Washington, Pennsylvania) and was the first student to letter in baseball, basketball, football, and track at the school. A starting tackle when he was a 17-year-old freshman in 1915, he played for the college for five years (1915–1919), but the 1918 season did not count because he was in an Army training group on campus and the team played only four games.

At 5'10", 230 pounds, he was a two-way, 60-minute player and anchored Canton's championship lines (1922–1923). He was also a punter and kicked field goals, setting a then-NFL record for the longest field goal, a 45-yard drop-kick against the Toledo Maroons in a 19–0 win on December 10, 1922. The record stood for 12 years.

When he could not agree on salary terms with Canton, Henry left the NFL for one season and played for the independent Pottsville Maroons in 1924. In 1925, he returned to Canton as a player-coach for two seasons. He began the 1927 season with the New York Giants, but returned to Pottsville to reorganize and coach the Maroons, finishing with an NFL coaching record of 3–17–3.

Upon retiring after the 1928 season, he returned to his alma mater as line coach in 1929; served as the team's head coach in 1942; and was the school's athletic director from 1942 to 1952. Grantland Rice chose Henry for his all-time All-American team in 1952, and he was a charter member of the College Football Hall of Fame in 1951. He was named to the NFL 1920s All-Decade Team.

Sources: College Football Hall of Fame; Pro Football Hall of Fame

Hepbron, George T. (born: August 27, 1863 in Still Pond, Maryland; died: April 30, 1946); inducted into the Naismith Memorial Basketball Hall of Fame in 1960 as a referee; basketball's first official referee and rules developer.

Hepbron was a friend of basketball creator Dr. James Naismith and was the game's first official referee and rules developer. He wrote *How to Play Basketball* (1904), often cited as the first book ever written on how to play the game.

He officiated early Amateur Athletic Union and professional games and conducted the first national rules questionnaire to help codify the game. Once the game, as it was being played, became too rough, he created new rules that eliminated commonly accepted tactics, such as tackling and body blocks.

Hepbron was the first secretary of the AAU Basketball Committee (1896); a member of the AAU Rules Committee (1896–1915); edited the *AAU Basketball Guide* (1901–1914); served as secretary of the Olympic Basketball Committee (1903); chairman of the Women's National Basketball Rules Committee; secretary of the National Basketball Executive Committee; secretary of the Joint Rules Committee of the United States and Canada (from 1915 until he became a lifetime member in 1936); chairman of the National Rules Revision Committee of the Joint Rules Committee; and organized the Brooklyn Young Men's Christian Association League.

Source: Naismith Memorial Basketball Hall of Fame

Hepp, Dr. Ferenc (born: November 3, 1909 in Békés, Hungary; died: November 27, 1980 in Hungary); inducted into the Naismith Memorial Basketball Hall of Fame in 1981 as a contributor; known as the "Father of Hungarian Basketball"; served as the first director of the National School of Physical Education and Sports in Hungary.

Hepp attended Békés (Hungary) High School, graduating in 1930, before attending the Royal Hungarian College of Physical Education (Budapest), the International School of Physical Education (Geneva, Switzerland), and the University of Geneva (Switzerland).

He is known as the "Father of Hungarian Basketball" and promoted the growth of the game throughout Europe and Asia. He served as the first director of the National School of Physical Education and Sports in Hungary; founder and director of the Hungarian Scientific and Research Institute for Physical Education and Sports; president of the Hungarian Basketball Federation (1954); involved with the Fédération Internationale de Basketball Amateur for more than 40 years; member of the FIBA Technical Commission (1948–1956); member of the FIBA Central Board (1956); served as FIBA European Co-President; refereed in Hungary and throughout Europe (1937–1942, 1946–1957); member of the Hungarian Olympic Committee; president of the Hungarian National Basketball Federation; published *The Olympic Sports Dictionary* in seven languages; and was a member of the Executive Committee of the International Basketball Association.

In 2007, he was inducted as a contributor into the FIBA Hall of Fame.

Source: Naismith Memorial Basketball Hall of Fame

Herber, Arnold Charles "Arnie" (born: April 2, 1910 in Green Bay, Wisconsin; died: October 14, 1969); inducted into the Pro Football Hall of Fame in 1966 as a player; Position: Quarterback; Uniform: #38; won the NFL's first official passing title; won four NFL championships.

Herber won the National Football League passing title in 1932, the first season in which the league began compiling official statistics, and would again lead the league in 1934 and 1936. He played his 13-year (129 games) NFL career with the Green Bay Packers (1930–1940) and the New York Giants (1944–1945).

He joined the Packers as a 20-year-old rookie and threw a touchdown in his very first professional game. Teaming with Don Hutson to form the league's first great quarterback-receiver combination, he led the Packers to four NFL titles (1930–1931, 1936, 1939).

The 5'11", 203-pound Herber was a basketball and football star at Green Bay's West High School, before attending the University of Wisconsin (Madison). After one year, he transferred to Regis College (Denver, Colorado), but soon returned to Green Bay, where team coach Curly Lambeau eventually signed him.

He was named All-Pro three times (1932, 1935–1936); played in one Pro Bowl (1939); and was selected to the NFL 1930s All-Decade Team.

Arnie Herber' Career Statistics

						PASSING					RUSHING		
YEAR	TEAM	G	ATT	COMP	PCT	YDS	TD	INT	RATING	NO	YDS	AVG	TD
1930	Green Bay	10	0	0	0.0	0	3	0	0.0	0	0	0.0	0
1931	Green Bay	3	0	0	0.0	0	0	0	0.0	0	0	0.0	1
1932	Green Bay	14	101	37	36.6	639	9	9	51.5	64	149	2.3	1
1933	Green Bay	11	124	50	40.3	656	3	12	26.2	62	77	1.2	0
1934	Green Bay	11	115	42	36.5	799	8	12	45.1	37	33	0.9	0
1935	Green Bay	11	109	40	36.7	729	8	14	45.4	19	0	0.0	0
1936	Green Bay	12	173	77	44.5	1,239	11	13	58.9	20	-32	-1.6	0
1937	Green Bay	9	104	47	45.2	684	7	10	50.0	5	9	1.8	0
1938	Green Bay	8	55	22	40.0	336	3	4	48.8	6	-1	-0.2	0
1939	Green Bay	10	139	57	41.0	1,107	8	9	61.6	18	-11	-0.6	1
1940	Green Bay	10	89	38	42.7	560	6	7	53.6	6	-23	-3.8	0
1944	New York	10	86	36	41.9	651	6	8	53.0	7	-58	-8.3	0
1945	New York	10	80	35	43.8	641	9	8	69.8	6	-27	-4.5	0
	TOTALS	129	1,175	481	40.9	8,041	81	106	50.1	250	116	0.5	3

Sources: Pro Football Hall of Fame; Pro-Football-Reference.com

Herman, William Jennings Bryan "Billy" (born: July 7, 1909 in New Albany, Indiana; died: September 5, 1992 in West Palm Beach, Florida); inducted into the National Baseball Hall of Fame and Museum in 1975 as a player by the Veterans Committee; Position: Second Base; Bats: Right; Throws: Right; Uniform: #2; struck out only 428 times in 7,707 at-bats.

Making his major league debut on August 29, 1931, Herman played 15 seasons for the Chicago Cubs (1931–1941), Brooklyn Dodgers (1941–1943, 1946), Boston Braves (1946), and the Pittsburgh Pirates (1947). He played in four World Series, losing them all (1932, 1935, 1938, 1941) (although he did win a ring as a coach on the 1955 World Series champion Brooklyn Dodgers); a 10-time All-Star (1934–1943); hit .300 or better per season seven times; and scored 100 or more runs five times. In 7,707 at-bats, Herman struck out only 428 times.

He still holds the record for most putouts in a season by a National League second baseman (466); led the National League's second basemen in putouts seven times; and shares the major league record for most hits in an opening day game, with five (April 14, 1936, in a 12–7 win over the St. Louis Cardinals).

Herman missed the 1944 and 1945 seasons while serving in World War II, but returned to the major leagues in 1946 with the Brooklyn Dodgers, before being traded in mid-season to the Boston Braves. Prior to the 1947 season, he was traded to the Pittsburgh Pirates, where he was a player-manager, but only played in 15 games.

After retiring from the major leagues, Herman managed in the minors; became a major league coach with the Dodgers (1952–1957), Braves (1958–1959), and the Boston Red Sox (1960–1964); and managed the Red Sox to sub-.500 seasons in 1965 and 1966, his last job as a major league manager.

He coached the California Angels (1967); late in his career, he served in player development roles with the Oakland Athletics and San Diego Padres; and he finished with a major league managerial record of 189–274 (.408).

In 1935, he led the National League with 227 hits and 57 doubles; led the league with 18 triples in 1939; and on June 28, 1933, he tied the major league record for most second base putouts in a doubleheader (16) and tied the league record for most second base putouts in a game (11) in a sweep of the Philadelphia Phillies.

Herman was inducted into the Indiana Baseball Hall of Fame in 1979.

Billy Herman's Career Batting Statistics

YEAR	TEAM	LG	G	AB	R	H	2B	3B	HR	RBI	BB	SO	SB	AVG	SLG
1931	Chicago	NL	25	98	14	32	7	0	0	16	13	6	2	.327	.398
1932	Chicago	NL	154	656	102	206	42	7	1	51	40	33	14	.314	.404
1933	Chicago	NL	153	619	82	173	35	2	0	44	45	34	5	.279	.342
1934	Chicago	NL	113	456	79	138	21	6	3	42	34	31	6	.303	.395
1935	Chicago	NL	154	666	113	227	57	6	7	83	42	29	6	.341	.476
1936	Chicago	NL	153	632	101	211	57	7	5	93	59	30	5	.334	.470
1937	Chicago	NL	138	564	106	189	35	11	8	65	56	22	2	.335	.479
1938	Chicago	NL	152	624	86	173	34	7	1	56	59	31	3	.277	.359
1939	Chicago	NL	156	623	111	191	34	18	7	70	66	31	9	.307	.453
1940	Chicago	NL	135	558	77	163	24	4	5	57	47	30	1	.292	.376
1941	Chicago	NL	11	36	4	7	0	1	0	0	9	5	0	.194	.250
1941	Brooklyn	NL	133	536	77	156	30	4	3	41	58	38	1	.291	.379
1942	Brooklyn	NL	155	571	76	146	34	2	2	65	72	52	6	.256	.333
1943	Brooklyn	NL	153	585	76	193	41	2	2	100	66	26	4	.330	.417
1946	Brooklyn	NL	47	184	24	53	8	4	0	28	26	10	2	.288	.375
1946	Boston	NL	75	252	32	77	23	1	3	22	43	13	1	.306	.440
1947	Pittsburgh	NL	15	47	3	10	4	0	0	6	2	7	0	.213	.298
	TOTALS		1,922	7,707	1,163	2,345	486	82	47	839	737	428	67	.304	.407

Billy Herman's Managerial Record

YEAR	LG	TEAM	W	L	WIN%	FINISH
1947	NL	Pittsburgh	61	92	.399	7 (Player-Manager)
1964	AL	Boston	2	0	1.000	8
1965	AL	Boston	62	100	.383	9
1966	AL	Boston	64	82	.438	9
		Pittsburgh	61	92	.399	
		Boston	128	182	.413	
		TOTALS	189	274	.408	

Sources: Baseball-Reference.com; Indiana Baseball Hall of Fame; National Baseball Hall of Fame and Museum

Hermann, Robert R. (born: January 3, 1923 in St. Louis, Missouri); inducted into the National Soccer Hall of Fame and Museum in 2001 as a builder; president of the National Professional Soccer League.

Hermann served as president of the National Professional Soccer League when it was created in June 1966. He recruited owners, managers, and players to staff the league for a spring 1967 launch, when it became the first nationwide professional soccer league in America.

In 1967, the NPSL and the United Soccer Association, a rival professional league, merged to form the North American Soccer League, which would eventually bring the world's greatest international players to the United States, including Pelé. Hermann served as Chairman of the Executive Committee of the NASL from its founding until 1979.

He was the president and primary owner of the St. Louis Stars and the California Surf, both of the NASL, through the 1980 season. He created the first collegiate Most Valuable Player Award (the Hermann Award), which is presented annually by the Missouri Athletic Club to the top male and female National Collegiate Athletic Association Division I soccer player.

In 1999, the Robert R. Hermann Soccer Stadium (on the campus of St. Louis University in Missouri) was named in his honor.

Source: National Soccer Hall of Fame and Museum

Hern, William Milton "Riley" (born: December 5, 1880 in St. Mary's, Ontario, Canada; died: June 24, 1929); inducted into the Hockey Hall of Fame in 1962 as a player; Position: Goalie; won seven Stanley Cup titles.

Hern began playing hockey as a young boy for local school teams in St. Mary's, before turning professional with the Pittsburgh Keystones of the Western Pennsylvania Hockey League in the 1901–1902 season. He led the league with nine wins in 14 games as the Keystones took the WPHL title and he was selected a First-Team All-Star.

He played the next two seasons with Houghton-Portage Lakes of the International Hockey League; led the team to the league title in both years; selected a First-Team All-Star in 1905; and was named a Second-Team All-Star in 1906. He played the 1906–1907 season with the Montreal Wanderers (of the Eastern Canada Amateur Hockey Association) and led the team to the Stanley Cup title in four of the next five seasons (going on to win a total of seven championships) before retiring in 1911. After retiring, he served as a referee in local leagues.

Riley Hern's Career Statistics

			REGULAR SEASON						PLAYOFFS					
SEASON	TEAM	LEAGUE	GP	W	L	T	SO	AVG	GP	W	L	T	SO	AVG
1898–1901	Stratford Legionnaires	OHA-Sr.												
1901–1902	Pittsburgh Keystones	WPHL	14	9	5	0	1	2.21	1	1	0	0	1	1.00
1901–1902	Pittsburgh Keystones	WPHL	5	5	0	0	1	1.60						
1902–1903	Pittsburgh Keystones	WPHL	12	1	10	0	0	5.30						
1903–1904	Portage Lakes	Exhib.	14	13	1	0	4	1.50						
1903–1904	Portage Lakes	W-S	2	2	0	0	0	3.00						
1904–1905	Portage Lakes	IHL	24	15	7	2	2	3.54						
1905–1906	Portage Lakes	IHL	20	15	5	0	1	3.46						
1906–1907	Montreal Wanderers	ECAHA	10	10	0	0	0	3.84						
1906–1907	Montreal Wanderers	St-Cup							6	3	3	0	0	4.17
1907–1908	Montreal Wanderers	ECAHA	10	8	2	0	0	5.12						
1907–1908	Montreal Wanderers	St-Cup							5	5	0	0	0	3.20
1908–1909	Montreal Wanderers	ECHA	12	9	3	0	0	5.03						
1908–1909	Montreal Wanderers	St-Cup							2	1	1	0	0	5.00
1909–1910	Montreal Wanderers	NHA	1	1	0	0	0	6.00						
1909–1910	Montreal Wanderers	NHA	12	11	1	0	1	3.42						
1909–1910	Montreal Wanderers	St-Cup							1	1	0	0	0	3.00
1910–1911	Montreal Wanderers	NHA	16	7	9	0	0	5.43						

Sources: Hockey Hall of Fame; Hockey-Reference.com

Herzog, Dorrel Norman Elvert "Whitey" (born: November 9, 1931 in Athens, Illinois); inducted into the National Baseball Hall of Fame and Museum in 2010 as a manager; Bats: Left; Throws: Left; won 1982 World Series championship.

A former player (outfielder, pinch hitter, first baseman) with the Washington Senators (1956–1958), Kansas City Athletics (1958–1960), Baltimore Orioles (1961—1962), and Detroit Tigers (1963), the 5'11", 182-pound Herzog is best known as a manager with the Texas Rangers (1973), California Angels (1974), Kansas City Royals (1975–1979), and the St. Louis Cardinals (1980–1990). As a manager, he won the 1982 World Series, three National League Pennants, three American League West Division Championships (1976–1978), three National League East Division Championships (1982, 1985, 1987); and was named the 1985 National League Manager of the Year.

In eight seasons as a player, he batted .254 with 25 home runs, 172 runs batted in, 213 runs scored, 60 doubles, 20 triples, and 13 stolen bases in 634 games.

After leaving the game as a player, Herzog served as a scout for the Athletics (1964) and as a coach for the A's (1965) and the New York Mets (1966), before becoming the Mets' director of player development.

Whitey Herzog's Managerial Statistics

YEAR	TEAM	W	L	WIN%
1973	Texas Rangers	47	91	.341
1974	California Angels	2	2	.500
1975	Kansas City Royals	41	25	.621
1976	Kansas City Royals	90	72	.556
1977	Kansas City Royals	102	60	.630
1978	Kansas City Royals	92	70	.568
1979	Kansas City Royals	85	77	.525
1980	St. Louis Cardinals	38	35	.521
1981	St. Louis Cardinals	30	20	.600
1981	St. Louis Cardinals	29	23	.558
1982	St. Louis Cardinals	92	70	.568
1983	St. Louis Cardinals	79	83	.488
1984	St. Louis Cardinals	84	78	.519
1985	St. Louis Cardinals	101	61	.623
1986	St. Louis Cardinals	79	82	.491
1987	St. Louis Cardinals	95	67	.586
1988	St. Louis Cardinals	76	86	.469
1989	St. Louis Cardinals	86	76	.531
1990	St. Louis Cardinals	33	47	.413
	Texas Rangers	47	91	.341
	California Angels	2	2	.500
	Kansas City Royals	410	304	.574
	St. Louis Cardinals	822	728	.530
	TOTALS	1,281	1,125	.532

Sources: Baseball-Reference.com; National Baseball Hall of Fame and Museum

Hewitson, Robert W. "Bobby" (born: January 23, 1892 in Toronto, Ontario, Canada; died: January 9, 1969); inducted into the Hockey Hall of Fame in 1963 as an on-ice official; worked the very first game at Maple Leaf Gardens; first curator of the Hockey Hall of Fame.

At only 5'4", 125 pounds, Hewitson was respected for quickly breaking up on-ice fights between players. He attended the Jesse Ketchum School (Toronto, Ontario, Canada), where he played both lacrosse and football, and won championships in both sports in 1913. Realizing that his small stature would hinder any playing career, he focused on being a hockey, lacrosse, and football referee. Hewitson worked as a sports editor for the *Evening Telegram* until 1957, while refereeing local games at night.

By 1920, he was an established referee in the National Hockey League; worked the very first game played at Maple Leaf Gardens (Toronto, November 12, 1931); and retired as an official in 1934 to work on radio.

During his career, Hewitson served as secretary of the Canadian Rugby Union (1922), a position he held for 25 years; was the first curator of the Hockey Hall of Fame; and helped establish the Ontario Sportswriters and Sportscasters Association.

Source: Hockey Hall of Fame

Hewitt, Foster William, OC (born: November 21, 1902 in Toronto, Ontario, Canada; died: April 21, 1985); inducted into the Hockey Hall of Fame in 1965 as a builder; first radio announcer of the Toronto Maple Leafs.

A Canadian radio pioneer, Hewitt's voice was associated with most of the major hockey events of the 20th century and his enthusiastic play-by-play announcing became a unique promotional tool for the National Hockey League.

He attended Upper Canada College (Toronto) before transferring to the University of Toronto (Ontario), where he was the school's intercollegiate boxing champion (at 112 pounds). After graduating, he began a career in sports broadcasting with his first job at the Mutual Street Arena in Toronto on February 16, 1923 (a game between the Toronto Argonauts and the Kitchener Greenshirts).

When the NHL's Toronto Maple Leafs formed in 1927, Hewitt became the team's radio announcer and later served as the master of ceremonies when Maple Leaf Gardens opened on November 12, 1931. On November 1, 1952, he broadcast the very first televised hockey game in Canada (between the Montreal Canadiens and the Maple Leafs).

Hewitt retired in 1963, but in 1972, he came out of retirement to broadcast the Summit Series between Canada and the U.S.S.R. He was presented with the Order of Canada in 1972; inducted into the Canada's Sports Hall of Fame (1975); and the Foster Hewitt Memorial Award, named in his honor, is presented to hockey broadcasters inducted into the Hockey Hall of Fame.

After college, he worked at the Independent Telephone Company, which manufactured radios, before becoming a reporter at the *Toronto Daily Star.* On March 22, 1923, using a telephone, he made one of the earliest ice hockey broadcasts in the world from Toronto's Arena Gardens on radio station CFCA. On May 24, 1925, he and his father, William, made what is thought to be the world's first broadcast of a horse race.

For almost 40 years, Hewitt was Canada's premier hockey play-by-play broadcaster; coined the phrase "He shoots, he scores!"; and was well-known for his sign-on at the beginning of each broadcast, "Hello, Canada, and hockey fans in the United States and Newfoundland."

Source: Hockey Hall of Fame

Hewitt, William Abraham (born: May 15, 1875 in Cobourg, Ontario, Canada; died: September 8, 1966); inducted into the Hockey Hall of Fame in 1947 as a builder; worked with the Ontario Hockey Association for 60 years; organized the Canadian Amateur Hockey Association.

Hewitt's hockey career focused on the Canadian Amateur Hockey Association and the Ontario Hockey Association. He moved to Toronto as a boy and eventually became the sports editor at the *Toronto Evening News*, before moving on to the *Montreal Herald* and the *Toronto Star*.

A life-long hockey fan, in 1903, after graduating from the Jarvis Collegiate Institute (Toronto, Ontario, Canada), he began his association with the OHA as its secretary, a position he held for almost 60 years. In 1912, he helped organize the Canadian Amateur Hockey Association and served as the organization's secretary-treasurer (1915–1919), registrar (1922–1923), and registrar-treasurer (1924–1961).

In 1907, Hewitt helped establish the Big Four Football League; helped form the Interprovincial Rugby Football Union; served as president of the Canadian Rugby Union (1918–1919); and worked with the Canadian Incorporated Racing Association.

He was an honorary manager with three consecutive Olympic gold medal-winning hockey teams (Winnipeg Falcons in 1920 [Antwerp, Belgium]; Toronto Granites in 1924 [Chamonix, France]; and the Toronto Varsity Grads in 1928 [St. Moritz, Switzerland]). At the 1920 Olympics, Hewitt served as a referee in the very first Olympic hockey game (Sweden's 8–0 win over Belgium). In 1931, he was a major influence in the NHL's decision to build Maple Leaf Gardens (Toronto), and served as its Manager of Attractions.

Hewitt was named a lifetime member of the OHA, the CAHA, and the Amateur Hockey Association of the United States; served as a trustee of the Memorial Cup (Canada's annual junior hockey championship) and the Allan Cup (representing the senior hockey championship in North America); and presented the first-ever OHA Gold Stick Award in 1947.

Source: Hockey Hall of Fame

Hewitt, William Ernest "Bill" (born: October 8, 1909 in Bay City, Michigan; died: January 14, 1947); inducted into the Pro Football Hall of Fame in 1971 as a player; Position: End; first player named All-NFL with two teams (Chicago Bears, Philadelphia Eagles); won two NFL championships.

Hewitt is most often remembered for his refusal to wear a helmet, until forced to do so by changes in National Football League rules. Considered one of the best-ever two-way ends, he averaged more than 50 minutes of playing time per game.

He played his nine-year (101-game) NFL career with the Chicago Bears (1932–1936), Philadelphia Eagles (1937–1939), and the Phil-Pitt Steagles (1943), and was the first player named All-NFL with two teams (1933–1934, 1936 with the Bears and 1937 with the Eagles). After helping Chicago win the NFL championship in 1932 (by the team having the best regular-season record, 7–1–6, .875), he helped the team repeat as champions the next season with a 23–21 win over the New York Giants in the league's very first playoff.

Although not much of a football player in high school or at the University of Michigan (Ann Arbor), as a professional, the 5'9", 190-pound Hewitt would be named All-League five times (1932–1934, 1936–1938) and to the NFL 1930s All-Decade Team.

Bill Hewitt's Career Statistics

			RECEIVING			
YEAR	**Team**	**G**	**NO**	**YDS**	**AVG**	**TD**
1932	Chicago Bears	13	7	77	11.0	0
1933	Chicago Bears	13	14	273	19.5	2
1934	Chicago Bears	13	11	151	13.7	5
1935	Chicago Bears	12	5	80	16.0	0
1936	Chicago Bears	12	15	358	23.9	6
1937	Philadelphia	11	16	197	12.3	5
1938	Philadelphia	11	18	237	13.2	4
1939	Philadelphia	10	15	243	16.2	1
1943	Philadelphia-Pittsburgh	6	2	22	11.0	0
	TOTALS	101	103	1,638	15.9	23

Sources: Pro Football Hall of Fame; Pro-Football-Reference.com

Hextall, Bryan Aldwyn, Sr. (born: July 31, 1913 in Grenfell, Saskatchewan, Canada; died: July 25, 1984); inducted into the Hockey Hall of Fame in 1969 as a player; Position: Right Wing-Forward; scored the winning goal that gave the New York Rangers the 1940 Stanley Cup championship.

After playing his junior and senior hockey in Manitoba (Canada), Hextall enjoyed an 11-year National Hockey League career (1936–1948) with the New York Rangers. The 5'10", 182-pound rookie first played in the NHL in the 1936–1937 season (recording one assist in three games), before joining the team full time the next season. He led the NHL in goals scored twice (1940–1941), and won the NHL scoring title in 1942; named a First-Team All-Star three times (1940–1942); a Second-Team All-Star in 1943; and scored the wining goal that gave the team a Stanley Cup championship in 1940 (in six games over the Toronto Maple Leafs).

After a liver illness forced him to miss almost all of the 1945–1946 season, Hextall returned to the Rangers the next season; played with the team for one more year (1947–1948); and finished his career in the American Hockey League in 1949.

Bryan Hextall's Career Statistics

			REGULAR SEASON					PLAYOFFS				
SEASON	**TEAM**	**LEAGUE**	**GP**	**G**	**A**	**TP**	**PIM**	**GP**	**G**	**A**	**TP**	**PIM**
1931–1932	Winnipeg Monarchs	MJHL	4	0	0	0	0	1	2	0	2	0
1932–1933	Portage Terriers	MJHL	12	10	8	18	6	2	0	0	0	4
1933–1934	Portage Terriers	MJHL	7	6	4	10	8					
1933–1934	Vancouver Lions	NWHL	5	2	0	2	0					
1934–1935	Vancouver Lions	NWHL	32	14	10	24	27	8	0	0	0	10
1934–1935	Vancouver Lions	NWHL	5	2	0	2	2					
1935–1936	Vancouver Lions	NWHL	40	27	9	36	65	7	1	2	3	15
1936–1937	Philadelphia Ramblers	IAHL	50	27	25	52	40	6	2	4	6	6
1936–1937	New York Rangers	NHL	3	0	1	1	0					
1937–1938	New York Rangers	NHL	48	17	4	21	6	3	2	0	2	0
1938–1939	New York Rangers	NHL	48	20	15	35	18	7	0	1	1	4
1939–1940	New York Rangers	NHL	48	24	15	39	52	12	4	3	7	11
1940–1941	New York Rangers	NHL	48	26	18	44	16	3	0	1	1	0
1941–1942	New York Rangers	NHL	48	24	32	56	30	6	1	1	2	4

			REGULAR SEASON					PLAYOFFS				
SEASON	**TEAM**	**LEAGUE**	**GP**	**G**	**A**	**TP**	**PIM**	**GP**	**G**	**A**	**TP**	**PIM**
1942–1943	New York Rangers	NHL	50	27	32	59	28					
1943–1944	New York Rangers	NHL	50	21	33	54	41					
1944–1945	St. Catharines Saints	OHA-Sr.	1	0	1	1	0					
1945–1946	New York Rangers	NHL	3	0	1	1	0					
1946–1947	New York Rangers	NHL	60	20	10	30	18					
1947–1948	New York Rangers	NHL	43	8	14	22	18	6	1	3	4	0
1948–1949	Cleveland Barons	AHL	32	12	17	29	14					
1948–1949	Washington Lions	AHL	25	6	6	12	2					
	NHL TOTALS		449	187	175	362	227	37	8	9	17	19

Sources: Hockey Hall of Fame; Hockey-Reference.com

Hickerson, Robert Eugene "Gene" (born: February 15, 1935 in Trenton, Tennessee); inducted into the Pro Football Hall of Fame in 2007 as a player; Position: Offensive Guard; Uniform: #66; lead blocker for three future hall of fame running backs (Jim Brown, Bobby Mitchell, and Leroy Kelly).

While he was a fullback at Trezevant High School (Memphis, Tennessee), Hickerson became a tackle at the University of Mississippi (Oxford), where he was considered one of the best linemen in the Southeastern Conference.

He was picked by the Cleveland Browns in the seventh round (78th selection overall) of the 1957 NFL Draft; was converted from tackle to guard as a rookie; and became the lead blocker for three future hall of fame running backs: Jim Brown, Bobby Mitchell, and Leroy Kelly.

The 6'3", 248-pound Hickerson was named All-NFL five consecutive seasons (1966–1970); selected to six straight Pro Bowls (1966–1971); a seven-time All-Pro (1964–1970); named to the NFL 1960s All-Decade Team; and played his entire 16-year (202 games) NFL career with the Cleveland Browns (1958–1973).

While Hickerson was with the Browns, the team never had a losing season and played in four NFL title games (winning in 1964 and losing in 1965, 1968–1969). Before he joined the Browns, there had only been seven runners in NFL history to rush for more than 1,000 yards in a season. With him playing offensive guard, Cleveland had nine 1,000-yard rushers in his first 10 seasons, and had the league's leading rusher seven times.

Source: Pro Football Hall of Fame

Hickey, Edgar S. "Eddie" (born: December 20, 1902 in Reynolds, Nebraska; died: December 5, 1980); inducted into the Naismith Memorial Basketball Hall of Fame in 1979 as a coach; won the 1948 NIT title; president of the National Association of Basketball Coaches.

After playing basketball for four years at Trinity College Prep (Sioux City, Iowa, 1918–1922), Hickey attended Creighton University (Omaha, Nebraska), where he played basketball for two seasons before graduating in 1927.

He began his coaching career at Creighton Preparatory School (Omaha, Nebraska, 1926–1934), where he compiled an overall 115–26 (.816) record. His teams were Omaha City League champions three times (1929, 1932, 1934) and Inter-State League champions three times (1932–1934).

Hickey joined the college coaching ranks at his alma mater (1934–1943, 1946–1947). During World War II, he served in the U.S. Naval Reserve (1943–1946) and was the basketball coach for the Navy Pre-Flight (Iowa City, Iowa) and Navy Primary Flight (Ottumwa, Iowa) Stations. After completing his military service, he returned to Creighton University (1946–1947), before moving on to Saint Louis University (Missouri, 1947–1958) and ending his career at Marquette University (Milwaukee, Wisconsin, 1958–1964).

The 5'5", 147-pound Hickey led Creighton to a 132–72 (.647) record as the Bluejays won four Missouri Valley Conference titles; appeared in two National Invitation Tournaments; and played in one National Collegiate Athletic Association tournament. He coached St. Louis to an overall 212–89 (.704) record; never had a losing team at the school; led the squad to a 24–3 record and the NIT title in 1948; won three Missouri Valley Conference titles; appeared in six NITs and two NCAA tournaments; won the 1949 Cotton Bowl Tournament; and won the Sugar Bowl Tournament twice (1950, 1952).

At Marquette, he retired with a 92–70 (.568) record; led the team to one NIT appearance and two NCAA tournaments; and was named United States Basketball Writers Association Coach of the Year in 1959.

Hickey retired from coaching with an overall record of 436–231 (.654).

During his career, he served in numerous National Association of Basketball Coaches positions, including Rules Recommendation Committee (1938–1939, 1941–1944); Editorial Staff (1939–1948); Ethics Committee (1939–1941,

1954–1961); *NABC Bulletin* editor (1948–1952); second vice-president (1951–1952); first vice-president (1952–1953); president (1953–1954); chairman of the Board of Directors (1954–1955); and chairman of the All-American Selection Committee (1955–1964).

He wrote numerous basketball articles; conducted international clinics; and has been inducted into four other halls of fame (Helms Foundation, Greater St. Louis Athletic Association, Creighton Prep, and Creighton University Athletic).

Hickey played football and basketball at Creighton University and, as a senior law student in 1926–1927, coached basketball at Creighton University High School, also known as Creighton Prep.

Source: Naismith Memorial Basketball Hall of Fame

Hickox, Edward J. (born: April 10, 1878 in Cleveland, Ohio; died: January 28, 1966); inducted into the Naismith Memorial Basketball Hall of Fame in 1959 as a contributor; first-ever basketball coach at Williamsport Dickinson Seminary, Southwest State Normal School, and Colorado College; served as NABC president.

After attending Western Reserve Seminary (West Farmington, Ohio), graduating in 1899, Hickox went to Ohio Wesleyan University (Delaware, Ohio) for his Bachelor of Arts (1905), to Springfield College (Massachusetts) for his Bachelors in Physical Education (1914), and Columbia University (New York, New York) for his Master of Arts degree (1921).

He played basketball at Ohio Wesleyan, and later began his coaching career at Williamsport Dickinson Seminary (now Lycoming College, Williamsport, Pennsylvania, 1905–1906) before moving on to Southwest State Normal School (Weatherford, Oklahoma, 1907).

He left the college ranks for several years to teach in high school, first at Fort Collins (Colorado) High School (1908–1909) and then Eaton (Colorado) High School (1910–1912). While at Eaton, his teams lost only one game in his two years, and he led the squad to the championship of the Colorado, Wyoming, and Northern New Mexico district three times.

Hickox returned to the college ranks at Colorado College (Colorado Springs, 1914–1917), Springfield College (1926–1943), and American International College (Springfield, Massachusetts, 1943–1946). He was the first-ever basketball coach at Williamsport, Southwest State, and Colorado College; coached Springfield College to an overall 209–85 (.711) record; led the school to five New England Championships and two runner-up finishes; his 1936 team represented New England in the Olympic Tryouts; and his 1940 Springfield team represented New England in the National Collegiate Athletic Association Tournament. He also led American International College to a 21–3 (.875) record in 1945–1946.

He served as an intercollegiate referee (1914–1917); was a member of the National Association of Basketball Coaches (1927–1966); member of the National Basketball Rules Committee (1930–1948); vice chairman (1942–1945) and chairman (1945–1948) of the Rules Committee; NABC president (1944–1946); NABC vice president; NABC historian (1944–1966); named NABC Man of the Year in 1949; president of the New England Basketball Coaches Association; member of the Young Men's Christian Association National Basketball Committee; first executive secretary of the Naismith Memorial Basketball Hall of Fame (1949–1963); served on the Board of Directors of the Naismith Memorial Basketball Hall of Fame (1959–1966); and was inducted into the National Association of Intercollegiate Athletics Hall of Fame in 1958.

Source: Naismith Memorial Basketball Hall of Fame

Higgins-Cirovski, Shannon Danise (born: February 20, 1968 in Kent, Washington); inducted into the National Soccer Hall of Fame and Museum in 2002; Position: Midfield; International Caps (1987–1991): 51; International Goals: 4; youngest player ever inducted into the National Soccer Hall of Fame and Museum; won the 1989 women's Hermann Trophy; won the 1991 FIFA Women's Cup.

Higgins was a midfielder and a member of the United States Women's National Team that won the Fédération Internationale de Football Association Women's World Championship in 1991 (held in China).

Before winning the FIFA Cup, the 5'10" Higgins had played on four National Collegiate Athletic Association championship teams (1986–1989) at the University of North Carolina (Chapel Hill). At UNC (graduating in 1990), she played primarily as a forward and scored goals in the NCAA championship games in 1987, 1988, and 1989, including three in the school's win over North Carolina State University in the 1988 final. As a senior, she won the women's Hermann Trophy in 1989 as the top female college soccer player and, as of this writing, is the women's soccer coach at the University of Maryland (College Park). Her husband, Sasha Cirovski, is the men's head soccer coach at the University of Maryland.

Higgins is the third woman and the youngest female player ever inducted into the soccer hall of fame, and in 1999, she was named to *Soccer America*'s Team of the Century. In 2002, she was named to the Atlantic Coast Conference 50th Anniversary Team as one of the 50 greatest players in conference history, and she was inducted into the George Washington University Athletic Hall of Fame in February 2003.

The former head coach of the U.S. U-18 women's team and at George Washington University (Washington, D.C.), Higgins was named head coach of the Maryland women's soccer program in January 1999; in 2001, she led the team to the NCAA Women's Soccer College Cup; in 2002, she was named ACC Coach of the Year; and in 2004, she led the Terrapins to the NCAA Tournament's Sweet 16.

Higgins attended Mt. Rainier High School (Des Moines, Washington), graduated in 1986, and went to the University of North Carolina, where she played on the women's soccer team from 1986 to 1989. As the school won four consecutive NCAA titles, she scored the game-winning goal in her last three championship games; was a two-time First-Team All-American (1988–1989); twice named *Soccer America* Player of the Year (1988–1989); and was the 1989 Intercollegiate Soccer Association of America Player of the Year.

Source: National Soccer Hall of Fame and Museum

Hill, Joseph Preston "Pete" (born: October 12, 1880 in Pittsburgh, Pennsylvania; died: November 26, 1951 in Buffalo, New York); inducted into the National Baseball Hall of Fame and Museum in 2006 as a player by the Negro Leagues Committee; Position: Center Field; Bats: Left; Throws: Right; won two championships with the Philadelphia Giants.

Hill was one of the great line-drive hitters of his era, and from the turn of the century to the early 1920s, he played for the Pittsburgh Keystones (1899–1900), Cuban X-Giants (Independent, 1901–1902), Philadelphia Giants (Independent, 1903–1906), Leland Giants (Independent, 1907–1910), Chicago American Giants (Negro National League, 1911–1918), and the Detroit Stars (1919–1921). He led the 1910 Leland Giants to a record of 123–6 (.953).

Hill finished his career as player-manager for the Detroit Stars during the team's early days in the newly formed Negro National League. A left-handed hitter for both average and power, Hill was considered to be the best Negro League outfielder of the deadball era.

At 6'1", 215 pounds, he led the Philadelphia Giants to championships twice (1905–1906). Although hard to verify because the Negro Leagues did not maintain complete and accurate records, some sources indicate that in the 1911 season, he hit safely in 115 of 116 games and led the Giants to a 106–7 (.938) record. After retiring as a player, he managed the Milwaukee Bears in 1923 (the team's only year in the Negro National League) and the Baltimore Black Sox (Eastern Colored League) for two seasons (1924–1925), before retiring from the game.

From Negro League records, Hill was a lifetime .326 hitter and played six seasons of winter baseball in Cuba.

Source: National Baseball Hall of Fame and Museum

Hinkle, Paul D. "Tony" (born: December 19, 1899 in Logansport, Indiana; died: September 22, 1992); inducted into the Naismith Memorial Basketball Hall of Fame in 1965 as a contributor; invented the orange basketball; won a national title in 1929; won the military championship once during World War II; president of the NABC.

After attending Calumet High School (Chicago, Illinois, graduating in 1917), Hinkle went to the University of Chicago (Illinois) from 1917 to1921, where he was a Helms All-American in 1920; team captain and a two-time All-Big Ten selection; member of the 1919–1920 Big 10 Championship team; and earned three letters each in basketball and football.

After college, he was the men's basketball head coach at Butler University (Indianapolis, Indiana) from 1926 to 1970 and compiled a 560–392 (.588) record. Hinkle led the Bulldogs to the 1929 national championship (with a record of 17–2) and was an assistant coach on the team's 1924 championship squad. His only break from coaching at the school was his three years of military service in the Navy during World War II, where he coached the Great Lakes Naval Training Station (Illinois) team to 98 wins and the 1942–1943 national armed services championship.

He is often referred to as the "Dean of Indiana College Basketball Coaches;" served as president of the National Association of Basketball Coaches (1954–1955); former member of the NABC Board of Directors; former chairman of the NABC Rules Committee; compiled more than 1,000 coaching wins at Butler in baseball, basketball, and football; invented the orange basketball; and has been inducted into the Helms Foundation Basketball Hall of Fame, the Indiana Basketball Hall of Fame (1964), and the Indiana Football Hall of Fame (1974).

At Butler University, Hinkle served as a teacher, coach, and athletic administrator for almost 50 years. The Tony Hinkle Memorial Fieldhouse, where the Indiana State High School championship game is held annually, was named in his honor in 1965.

Source: Naismith Memorial Basketball Hall of Fame

Hinkle, William Clarke (born: April 10, 1909 in Toronto, Ohio; died: November 9, 1988 in Steubenville, Ohio); inducted into the Pro Football Hall of Fame in 1964 as a player; Position: Fullback-Linebacker; won two NFL titles.

Hinkle played his entire 10-year (113 games) National Football League career (1932–1941) with the Green Bay Packers. The 5'11", 202-pound fullback was selected All-NFL four times, and was the league's top scorer in 1938. A two-way player, he was named First- or Second-Team All-League each of his 10 seasons and won two league titles (1936, 1939).

While playing for Bucknell University (Lewisburg, Pennsylvania, 1929–1931), Hinkle led the team to an undefeated season in 1931. He was selected to the NFL 1930s All-Decade Team; inducted into the College Football Hall of Fame (1971) and the Green Bay Packers Hall of Fame (1972); and the Packers' west practice field across Oneida Street from Lambeau Field was named Clarke Hinkle Field in 1997.

Clarke Hinkle's Career Statistics

			RUSHING				RECEIVING			
YEAR	TEAM	G	NO	YDS	AVG	TD	NO	YDS	AVG	TD
1932	Green Bay	13	95	331	3.5	3	0	0	0.0	0
1933	Green Bay	13	139	413	3.0	4	6	38	6.3	0
1934	Green Bay	12	144	359	2.5	1	11	113	10.3	1
1935	Green Bay	9	77	273	3.5	2	1	-4	-4.0	0
1936	Green Bay	12	100	476	4.8	5	0	0	0.0	0
1937	Green Bay	11	129	552	4.3	5	8	116	14.5	2
1938	Green Bay	11	114	299	2.6	3	7	98	14.0	4
1939	Green Bay	11	135	381	2.8	5	4	70	17.5	0
1940	Green Bay	10	109	383	3.5	2	4	28	7.0	1
1941	Green Bay	11	129	393	3.0	5	8	78	9.8	1
	TOTALS	113	1,171	3,860	3.3	35	49	537	11.0	9

Sources: Pro Football Hall of Fame; Pro-Football-Reference.com

Hirsch, Elroy Leon "Crazy Legs" (born: June 17, 1923 in Wausau, Wisconsin; died: January 28, 2004 in Madison, Wisconsin); inducted into the Pro Football Hall of Fame in 1968 as a player; Position: Halfback-End; Uniform: #40; while at the University of Michigan, he was the only athlete to letter in four sports (football, basketball, track, baseball) in a single year; won the 1951 NFL title.

Hirsch was known for catching long passes and for a unique running style that earned him the nickname, "Crazy Legs." He was an All-American at both the University of Wisconsin (Madison) and the University of Michigan (Ann Arbor). After college, the 6'2", 190-pound Hirsch was a first-round draft pick (fifth overall selection) of the Chicago Rockets of the All-America Football Conference (1946–1948), and played with the team until joining the National Football League's Los Angeles Rams (1949–1957). Injuries hindered his playing time with the Rockets and his career did not go anywhere until he joined the Rams when the AAFC and NFL merged in 1949.

In 1946, while still in school, Hirsch had led the College All-Star Team to a 16–0 upset win over the Rams. While with Los Angeles, he won the 1951 NFL title by leading the Rams to a 24–17 win over the Cleveland Browns; played in three Pro Bowls (1951–1953); named to the NFL 1950s All-Decade Team; named All-Time NFL flanker in 1969; and ended his professional career having scored 405 points (60 total touchdowns, two rushing touchdowns in the AAFC, one passing touchdown in the AAFC, one punt return for a touchdown in the AAFC, one kickoff return for a touchdown in the AAFC, one rushing touchdown in the NFL, and nine extra-points kicked in the NFL).

Hirsch began his football career at Wausau (Wisconsin) High School, before playing his first college game at the University of Wisconsin in 1942. His involvement with the United States Navy V–12 program in the Marine Corps during World War II required him to transfer to the University of Michigan. He played two seasons with the Wolverines, and was the only athlete at the school to letter in four sports (football, basketball, track, baseball) in a single year.

After his playing days, Hirsch served as the athletic director at the University of Wisconsin from 1969 to 1987; the school retired his jersey number 40 in 2006; in 1999, he was ranked number 89 on *The Sporting News*' list of the 100 Greatest Football Players; and he was inducted into the College Football Hall of Fame in 1974.
Elroy Hirsch's Career Statistics

YEAR	TEAM	G	NO	RECEIVING YDS	AVG	TD
1946	Chicago	14	27	347	12.9	3
1947	Chicago	5	10	282	28.2	3
1948	Chicago	5	7	101	14.4	1
1949	Los Angeles	12	22	326	14.8	4
1950	Los Angeles	12	42	687	16.4	7
1951	Los Angeles	12	66	1,495	22.7	17
1952	Los Angeles	10	25	590	23.6	4
1953	Los Angeles	12	61	941	15.4	4
1954	Los Angeles	12	35	720	20.6	3
1955	Los Angeles	9	25	460	18.4	2
1956	Los Angeles	12	35	603	17.2	6
1957	Los Angeles	12	32	477	14.9	6
	AAFC Career Total	24	44	730	16.6	7
	NFL Career Total	103	343	6,299	18.4	53
	TOTALS	127	387	7,029	18.2	60

Sources: Pro Football Hall of Fame; Pro-Football-Reference.com

Hobson, Howard A. "Hobby" (born: July 4, 1903 in Portland, Oregon; died: June 9, 1991); inducted into the Naismith Memorial Basketball Hall of Fame in 1965 as a coach; won a high school state title as a player; first coach to win championships at the major college level on both coasts; won the first-ever NCAA basketball title; president of the NABC.

Hobson played basketball for four years at Franklin High School (Portland, Oregon), graduating in 1922; named team captain (1920–1922); All-City (1920); and All-State in 1921, the year the school won the state championship.

He went to college at the University of Oregon (Eugene), graduating in 1926 with a bachelor's degree, and Columbia University (New York, New York), graduating in 1929 with a master's degree, and in 1945 with a doctorate degree. While at Oregon, he played basketball for three seasons; team captain (1924–1926); his 1925 team tied Oregon State for the conference title, but lost in the playoffs; his 1926 team won the conference title, but lost to the University of California in the playoffs; and he was a starter on the school's baseball team.

After college, Hobson took his first coaching job at Kelso (Washington) High School (1926–1928), before moving on to Benson High School (Portland, Oregon, 1930–1932). He coached Kelso to a league championship in 1928 and Benson to a league championship in 1932.

Hobson moved up to the college coaching ranks with Southern Oregon College (Ashland, 1932–1935), before moving on to the University of Oregon (Eugene, 1935–1944, 1945–1947), and ending his career at Yale University (New Haven, Connecticut, 1947–1956). His overall 27-year college coaching record was 495–291 (.630); he led Southern Oregon to three consecutive league championships (1933–1935); led the University of Oregon to the first-ever National Collegiate Athletic Association title (1939) and three straight Pacific Coast Conference titles (1937–1939); his Yale teams won or shared five Big Three crowns (1948–1949, 1951, 1953, 1956); and his 1949 Yale team was the first NCAA entry in the school's history.

He was the first coach to win championships at the major college level on both coasts (University of Oregon, Yale); first west coast team (Oregon) to travel to the east coast for games; pioneered western travel for Yale teams and the 1948–1949 Yale team was the first to play on the Pacific Coast; served as president of the National Association of Basketball Coaches (1947); was a member of the U.S. Olympic Basketball Committee for 12 years; a member and treasurer of the National Basketball Rules Committee for four years; conducted basketball clinics in the United States and in 15 foreign countries; and was inducted into the Portland High School, Helms Foundation, Oregon State, and Portland Metro halls of fame.

Source: Naismith Memorial Basketball Hall of Fame

Holman, Nat (born: Nathan Helmanowich on October 19, 1896 in New York, New York; died: February 12, 1995 in Bronx, New York); inducted into the Naismith Memorial Basketball Hall of Fame in 1964 as a player; in 1950, he led CCNY to both the NIT and NCAA championships, becoming the only team in history to win both titles in the same year.

After being a four-year basketball letter winner at Commerce (New York) High School (1912–1916), Holman went to the Savage School for Physical Education (New York, 1916–1918), before attending graduate school at New York University (New York, 1919).

As a professional, he was considered one of the game's best shooters and ball-handlers, and played basketball for the Hoboken Gs (New Jersey) of the Interstate League (1916–1917); Bridgeport Blue Ribbons (Interstate League, 1917–1918); Jersey City Skeeters (Interstate League, 1919–1920); Albany Senators of the New York League (1919–1920); Pittsfield Hillies (NYL, 1920–1921); New York Whirlwinds (Interstate League, 1920–1921); Norwalk Company K of the Connecticut League (1920–1921); Germantown Gs of the Eastern League (1919–1921); Atlantic City Celtics (Eastern League, 1922–1923); Scranton Miners (Eastern League, 1919–1920); Original Celtics (Eastern League, 1921–1923, 1926–1927); Chicago Bruins of the American Basketball League (1929–1930); and the Syracuse All-Americans (ABL, 1929–1930).

While still playing at the professional level, he coached at City College of New York (1919–1960), making him the youngest coach at a major college at age 23, and compiled an overall 421–190 (.689) record. In 1950, Holman led CCNY to both the National Invitation Tournament and the National Collegiate Athletic Association titles, becoming the only team in history to win both titles in the same year. CCNY defeated Bradley University for both titles in Madison Square Garden (New York, New York) within a 10-day period, winning the NIT 69–61 and the NCAA 71–68.

Holman was named National Coach of the Year in 1951 by *Sport* magazine; won the Helms Foundation Award in recognition of his contributions to basketball; served as president of the National Association of Basketball Coaches in 1941; published four basketball-related books, *Scientific Basketball* (1922), *Winning Basketball* (1933), *Championship Basketball* (1942), and *Holman on Basketball* (1950); and conducted clinics in Mexico, Canada, Israel, Japan, Turkey, Korea, and Taiwan.

He was named to the First Team of the Half–Century (1900–1950) and the third greatest player of that era by American sportswriters in 1950. While coaching at CCNY, the 5'11", 165-pound Holman played professional basketball on weekends with various teams and leagues.

He was part of the group that organized the American team for the first Maccabiah Games in Palestine in 1932. In 1949, he became the first American to coach in Israel, setting up clinics to develop the sport of basketball throughout the country. In 1973, he began an eight-year term as president of the United States Committee of Sports for Israel, which sponsored the U.S. Maccabiah Games Team. He was inducted into the International Jewish Sports Hall of Fame in 1979.

Source: Naismith Memorial Basketball Hall of Fame

Holmes, Harry "Hap" (born: February 21, 1888 in Aurora, Ontario, Canada; died: June 27, 1941); inducted into the Hockey Hall of Fame in 1972 as a player; Position: Goalie; first goalie to win the Stanley Cup with four different teams; led the last non-NHL team to win the Stanley Cup.

Holmes played 16 professional seasons (1912–1928), and was the first goalie to win the Stanley Cup with four different teams (Toronto Blueshirts [1914, National Hockey Association]; Seattle Metropolitans [1917, Pacific Coast Hockey Association]; Toronto Arenas [1918, National Hockey League]; and the Victoria Cougars [1925, West Coast Hockey League]).

He debuted in the NHA with the Toronto Blueshirts in 1912–1913, and in his second year, led the league in wins and helped the squad become the first Toronto-based team to win the Stanley Cup. In the 1915–1916 season, he joined the Seattle Metropolitans and helped the team become the first U.S.–based squad to win the Stanley Cup. He was loaned to the Toronto Arenas in January 1918, and helped the team win the Stanley Cup in the very first NHL season.

Holmes returned to the Metropolitans for the 1918–1919 season and stayed with the team for six more seasons. In his first year back with the team, he was playing in the 1919 Stanley Cup finals against the Montreal Canadiens that was eventually called off due to the global influenza epidemic. He would go on to lead the PCHA in shutouts four times and in wins twice; he played two seasons with the Victoria Cougars (Western Canada Hockey League/Western Hockey League, 1924–1926); and led the WCHL/WHL in goals-against average.

In the 1924–1925 season, he led Victoria to the WCHL title and went on to defeat the Montreal Canadiens to become the last non-NHL team to win the Stanley Cup. When the Western Hockey League disbanded in 1926, Holmes joined the NHL's Detroit Cougars for his last two seasons (1926–1928) as an active player.

Named in his honor, the Hap Holmes Memorial Award (created in 1948) is presented annually to the goaltender(s) of the American Hockey League with the lowest goals-against average who have played in at least 50% of the team's regular-season games.

Hap Holmes' Career Statistics

			REGULAR SEASON						PLAYOFFS						
SEASON	TEAM	LEAGUE	GP	W	L	T	SO	AVG	GP	W	L	T	SO	AVG
1907–1908	Young Toronto	OMHA												
1908–1909	Parkdale Canoe Club	OHA-Sr.	3	0	3	0	0	7.33						

SEASON	TEAM	LEAGUE	REGULAR SEASON GP	W	L	T	SO	AVG	PLAYOFFS GP	W	L	T	SO	AVG
1909–1910	Parkdale Canoe Club	OHA-Sr.	4	2	2	0	0	6.50						
1910–1911	Parkdale Canoe Club	OHA-Sr.	4	3	1	0	0	3.00	2	0	1	1	0	4.50
1911–1912	Toronto Tecumsehs	Exhib.	1	1	0	0	0	3.00						
1912–1913	Toronto Blueshirts	NHA	15	6	7	0	1	4.47						
1913–1914	Toronto Blueshirts	NHA	20	13	7	0	1	3.24	2	1	1	0	1	1.00
1913–1914	Toronto Blueshirts	St-Cup							3	3	0	0	0	2.59
1914–1915	Toronto Blueshirts	NHA	20	8	12	0	0	4.18						
1915–1916	Seattle Metropolitans	PCHA	18	9	9	0	0	3.67						
1915–1916	PCHA All-Stars	Exhib.	1	0	1	0	0	6.00						
1916–1917	Seattle Metropolitans	PCHA	24	16	8	0	2	3.28						
1916–1917	Seattle Metropolitans	St-Cup							4	3	1	0	0	2.75
1917–1918	Toronto Arenas	NHL	16	9	7	0	0	4.73	2	1	1	0	0	3.50
1917–1918	Toronto Arenas	St-Cup							5	3	2		0	4.20
1918–1919	Toronto Arenas	NHL	2	0	2	0	0	4.50						
1918–1919	Seattle Metropolitans	PCHA	20	11	9	0	0	2.25	2	1	1	0	0	2.50
1918–1919	Seattle Metropolitans	St-Cup							5	2	2	1	2	1.79
1919–1920	Seattle Metropolitans	PCHA	22	12	10	0	4	2.46	2	1	1	0	1	1.50
1919–1920	Seattle Metropolitans	St-Cup							5	2	3	0	0	3.00
1920–1921	Seattle Metropolitans	PCHA	24	12	11	1	0	2.63	2	0	2	0	0	6.50
1921–1922	Seattle Metropolitans	PCHA	24	12	11	1	4	2.60	2	0	2	0	0	1.00
1922–1923	Seattle Metropolitans	PCHA	30	15	15	0	2	3.45						
1923–1924	Seattle Metropolitans	PCHA	30	14	16	0	2	3.26	2	0	1	1	0	1.79
1924–1925	Victoria Cougars	WCHL	28	16	12	0	3	2.25	4	2	0	2	1	1.25
1924–1925	Victoria Cougars	St-Cup							4	3	1	0	0	2.00
1925–1926	Victoria Cougars	WHL	30	15	11	4	4	1.68	4	2	0	2	1	1.45
1925–1926	Victoria Cougars	St-Cup							4	1	3	0	0	2.50
1926–1927	Detroit Cougars	NHL	41	11	26	4	6	2.23						
1927–1928	Detroit Cougars	NHL	44	19	19	6	11	1.73						
	TOTALS		103	39	54	10	17	2.43	2	1	1	0	0	3.50

Sources: Hockey Hall of Fame; Hockey-Reference.com

Holzman, William "Red" (born: August 10, 1920 in New York, New York; died: November 13, 1998 in New Hyde Park, New York); inducted into the Naismith Memorial Basketball Hall of Fame in 1986 as a coach; won an NBL and NBA title as a player; one of only 10 players to win championships as a player and coach.

Holzman played basketball for two years at Franklin K. Lane High School (Jamaica, New York) and graduated in 1938. After being selected to the All-Scholastic team in 1938, he went to the University of Baltimore (Maryland, 1938–1939), before transferring to City College of New York, where he graduated in 1942. He played two years of college basketball and was named All-Metropolitan (1940–1942) and All-American (1940–1942).

After leaving college, he joined the U.S. Navy during World War II (1942–1945) and played on the Norfolk, Virginia Naval Base team for two years (1942–1944).

Completing his military service, Holzman played nine professional seasons (1945–1954) for the Rochester Royals (National Basketball League [1945–1948] / National Basketball Association [1948–1953]) and was a player-coach for the NBA's Milwaukee Hawks (1953–1954). He was named All-Pro six times (1945–1950); won an NBL championship in 1946 and an NBA championship in 1951; one of only 10 players to win championships as a player and coach; and was selected to the NBL All-Star First Team twice (1946, 1948) and to the NBL All-Star Second Team in 1947.

During his 18-year NBA coaching career, the 5'10" Holzmann coached the Milwaukee Hawks as a player-coach (1953–1954); head coach of the Milwaukee Hawks (1954–1955) and stayed with the team when it moved to St. Louis (1955–1957); assistant coach of the New York Knicks (1957–1967); and ended his career as head coach of the New York Knicks (1967–1982). He led the Hawks to an 83–120 (.409) overall record; compiled a 613–384 (.615) record with the Knicks; led New York to two championships (1970, 1973); and was named NBA Coach of the Year in 1970.

Holzman compiled an overall career regular-season record of 696–604 (.535) and an overall playoff record of 58–48 (.547); was named NBA Coach of the Decade for the 1970s; coached two NBA All-Star Games (1970–1971); wrote numerous basketball-related books; and was the first recipient of the National Basketball Coaches Association Achievement Award in 1981. He has been inducted into the New York City Basketball Hall of Fame, City College Hall of Fame (1958), Public Schools Athletic League Hall of Fame (New York), and the International Jewish Sports Hall of Fame (1988).

Red Holzman's NBA Coaching Record

SEASON	TEAM	REGULAR SEASON W	L	WIN%	PLAYOFFS W	L	WIN%
1953–1954	Milwaukee	10	16	.385			
1954–1955	Milwaukee	26	46	.361			
1955–1956	St. Louis	33	39	.458	4	5	.444
1956–1957	St. Louis	14	19	.424			
1967–1968	New York	28	17	.622	2	4	.333
1968–1969	New York	54	28	.659	6	4	.600
1969–1970	New York	60	22	.732	12	7	.632
1970–1971	New York	52	30	.634	7	5	.583
1971–1972	New York	48	34	.585	9	7	.563
1972–1973	New York	57	25	.695	12	5	.706
1973–1974	New York	49	33	.598	5	7	.417
1974–1975	New York	40	42	.488	1	2	.333
1975–1976	New York	38	44	.463			
1976–1977	New York	40	42	.488			
1978–1979	New York	25	43	.368			
1979–1980	New York	39	43	.476			
1980–1981	New York	50	32	.610	0	2	.000
1981–1982	New York	33	49	.402			
	TOTALS	696	604	.535	58	48	.547

Sources: Basketball-Reference.com; Naismith Memorial Basketball Hall of Fame

Hooper, Charles Thomas (born: November 24, 1883 in Kenora, Ontario, Canada; died: March 23, 1960); inducted into the Hockey Hall of Fame in 1962 as a player; led the Rat Portage/Kenora Thistles to the 1907 Stanley Cup (the smallest town ever to win the championship); won two Stanley Cup titles.

Hooper played seven professional pre-National Hockey League seasons from 1902 to 1908 and scored three of the Rat Portage/Kenora Thistles goals to become the smallest town (population 4,000) to win the Stanley Cup (1907).

He first played organized hockey in 1900, at age 17, with the local high school team, and in 1902, he started his professional career with the Thistles. After the team won the league title that year, the squad traveled to Ottawa (Ontario, Canada) in March 1903 to challenge the Silver Seven Senators for the Stanley Cup, eventually losing both games. The Thistles again challenged Ottawa for the Cup in March 1905, and again lost in the best-of-three series. Finally, in January 1907, the team (now called the Kenora Thistles) beat the Montreal Wanderers, and became the smallest town ever to win the title. The squad's title claim was short-lived when only two months later (March 1907), the Wanderers challenged and reclaimed the Cup.

Shortly after losing the Stanley Cup in 1907, the Thistles disbanded and Hooper joined the Montreal AAA team of the Eastern Canada Amateur Hockey Association for the 1907–1908 season, moving to the Wanderers for the last two games of the season, where he helped the team win three Stanley Cup challenges (Ottawa Victorias in January 1908; Winnipeg Maple Leafs in March 1908; and the Edmonton Eskimos in December 1908), before retiring from the game.

Charles Hooper's Career Statistics

SEASON	TEAM	LEAGUE	REGULAR SEASON GP	G	A	TP	PIM	PLAYOFFS GP	G	A	TP	PIM
1901–1902	Rat Portage Thistles	MNWHA-Int	8	9	0	9	17					
1902–1903	Rat Portage Thistles	MNWHA	5	5	1	6						
1902–1903	Rat Portage Thistles	St-Cup						2	0	0	0	0
1903–1904	Rat Portage Thistles	MNWHA	10	2	1	3						
1904–1905	Rat Portage Thistles	MHL	8	9	0	9						
1904–1905	Rat Portage Thistles	St-Cup						3	2	0	2	12
1905–1906	Kenora Thistles	MHL	9	4	0	4						
1906–1907	Kenora Thistles	MHL-Pro	3	4	0	4		2	0	0	0	11
1906–1907	Kenora Thistles	St-Cup						3	3	0	3	0
1907–1908	Montreal AAA	ECAHA	7	9	0	9	5					
1907–1908	Pembroke Lumber Kings	UOVHL	1	0	0	0	0					
1907–1908	Montreal Wanderers	ECAHA	2	1	0	1	0					

			REGULAR SEASON					PLAYOFFS				
SEASON	TEAM	LEAGUE	GP	G	A	TP	PIM	GP	G	A	TP	PIM
1907–1908	Montreal Wanderers	St-Cup						2	0	0	0	3

Sources: Hockey Hall of Fame; Hockey-Reference.com

Hooper, Harry Bartholomew "Hoop" (born: August 24, 1887 in Bell Station, California; died: December 18, 1974 in Santa Cruz, California); inducted into the National Baseball Hall of Fame and Museum in 1971 as a player by the Veterans Committee; Position: Right Field; Bats: Left; Throws: Right; only man to play on four Boston Red Sox World Series championship teams; first player to hit two home runs in a single World Series game; first player to hit a home run to lead off both games of a doubleheader.

The 5'10", 168-pound Hooper is the only man to play on four Boston Red Sox World Series championship teams (1912, 1915–1916, 1918). Making his debut on April 16, 1909, he played his 17-year major league career for the Boston Red Sox (1909–1920) and the Chicago White Sox (1921–1925).

As of this writing, Hooper is still the Red Sox' all-time leader in triples (130) and stolen bases (300), and from 1910 to 1915, he played in one of the game's best-ever outfields with Tris Speaker (center field) and Duffy Lewis (left field), often called the "Million-Dollar Outfield." Although he never hit more than 11 home runs in a single major league season, Hooper was the first player to hit two home runs in a single World Series game (October 13, 1915).

A college graduate with an engineering degree from Saint Mary's College of California (Moraga), he scored 100 or more runs three times; batted .300 or better five times; stole 20 or more bases nine times; and finished in the top ten in triples seven times and in home runs three times.

On May 30, 1913 against the Washington Senators, Hooper became the first player in major league history to hit a home run to lead off both games of a doubleheader, a feat matched by Rickey Henderson 80 years later on July 5, 1993.

Hooper was traded to the White Sox prior to the 1921 season, and was used by team owner Charles Comiskey to restore credibility to the franchise, which had been damaged by the "Black Sox" World Series scandal of 1919.

Retiring after the 1925 season, Hooper later coached baseball at Princeton University (New Jersey) for two years (1931–1932); served as the postmaster of Capitola, California (appointed by President Franklin Roosevelt), a job he held for 24 years; and has been inducted into the Boston Red Sox Hall of Fame.

Harry Hooper's Career Statistics

YEAR	TEAM	LG	G	AB	R	H	2B	3B	HR	RBI	BB	SO	SB	AVG	SLG
1909	Boston	AL	81	255	29	72	3	4	0	12	16		15	.282	.325
1910	Boston	AL	155	584	81	156	9	10	2	27	62		40	.267	.327
1911	Boston	AL	130	524	93	163	20	6	4	45	73		38	.311	.395
1912	Boston	AL	147	590	98	143	20	12	2	53	66		29	.242	.327
1913	Boston	AL	148	586	100	169	29	12	4	40	60	51	26	.288	.399
1914	Boston	AL	141	530	85	137	23	15	1	41	58	47	19	.258	.364
1915	Boston	AL	149	566	90	133	20	13	2	51	89	36	22	.235	.327
1916	Boston	AL	151	575	75	156	20	11	1	37	78	35	27	.271	.350
1917	Boston	AL	151	559	89	143	21	11	3	45	80	40	21	.256	.349
1918	Boston	AL	126	474	81	137	26	13	1	44	70	25	24	.289	.405
1919	Boston	AL	128	491	76	131	25	6	3	49	79	28	23	.267	.360
1920	Boston	AL	139	536	91	167	30	17	7	53	88	27	16	.312	.470
1921	Chicago	AL	108	419	74	137	26	5	8	58	55	21	13	.327	.470
1922	Chicago	AL	152	602	111	183	35	8	11	80	68	33	16	.304	.444
1923	Chicago	AL	145	576	87	166	32	4	10	65	68	22	18	.288	.410
1924	Chicago	AL	130	476	107	156	27	8	10	62	65	26	16	.328	.481
1925	Chicago	AL	127	442	62	117	23	5	6	55	54	21	12	.265	.380
	TOTALS		2,308	8,785	1,429	2,466	389	160	75	817	1,129	412	375	.281	.387

Sources: Baseball-Reference.com; National Baseball Hall of Fame and Museum

Horner, George Reginald "Red" (born: May 28, 1909 in Lynden, Ontario, Canada; died: April 27, 2005 in Toronto, Ontario, Canada); inducted into the Hockey Hall of Fame in 1965 as a player; Position: Defenseman; won the 1932 Stanley Cup.

Horner played his entire 12-year National Hockey League career (1928–1940) with the Toronto Maple Leafs; won a Stanley Cup title in 1932 (the team's first); and served as the team's captain from 1938 until he retired in 1940.

After playing in only 32 Ontario Hockey Association games with the Toronto Marlboros, he was signed by the Maple Leafs in 1928 and made his league debut on December 22nd against the Pittsburgh Pirates. After breaking his hand in only his second game with the team, Horner missed most of the season and ended his rookie campaign (22 games) scoring no points and accumulating 30 penalty minutes.

His aggressive style of play caused him to lead the league in penalty minutes for eight of his 12 NHL seasons, and he retired as the league's all-time penalty minute leader, a record broken by Ted Lindsay in the late 1950s.

After retiring from the NHL as a player, Horner served as an NHL linesman for two years, before pursuing his business interests.

George Horner's Career Statistics

			REGULAR SEASON					PLAYOFFS				
SEASON	**TEAM**	**LEAGUE**	**GP**	**G**	**A**	**TP**	**PIM**	**GP**	**G**	**A**	**TP**	**PIM**
1926–1927	Toronto Marlboros	OHA-Jr.	9	5	1	6		2	0	0	0	
1927–1928	Toronto Marlboros	OHA-Jr.	9	4	5	9	2	2	0	0	0	
1927–1928	Toronto Marlboros	OHA-Sr.	1	0	0	0	0					
1927–1928	Toronto Marlboros	M-Cup	11	7	5	12						
1928–1929	Toronto Marlboros	OHA-Sr.	2	0	0	0						
1928–1929	Toronto Maple Leafs	NHL	22	0	0	0	30	4	1	0	1	2
1929–1930	Toronto Maple Leafs	NHL	33	2	7	9	96					
1930–1931	Toronto Maple Leafs	NHL	42	1	11	12	71	2	0	0	0	4
1931–1932	Toronto Maple Leafs	NHL	42	7	9	16	97	7	2	2	4	20
1932–1933	Toronto Maple Leafs	NHL	48	3	8	11	144	9	1	0	1	10
1933–1934	Toronto Maple Leafs	NHL	40	11	10	21	146	5	1	0	1	6
1934–1935	Toronto Maple Leafs	NHL	46	4	8	12	125	7	0	1	1	4
1935–1936	Toronto Maple Leafs	NHL	43	2	9	11	167	9	1	2	3	22
1936–1937	Toronto Maple Leafs	NHL	48	3	9	12	124	2	0	0	0	7
1937–1938	Toronto Maple Leafs	NHL	47	4	20	24	82	7	0	1	1	14
1938–1939	Toronto Maple Leafs	NHL	48	4	10	14	85	10	1	2	3	26
1939–1940	Toronto Maple Leafs	NHL	31	1	9	10	87	9	0	2	2	55
	TOTALS		490	42	110	152	1,254		71	10	17	170

Sources: Hockey Hall of Fame; Hockey-Reference.com

Hornsby, Rogers (born: April 27, 1896 in Winters, Texas; died: January 5, 1963 in Chicago, Illinois); inducted into the National Baseball Hall of Fame and Museum in 1942 as a player; Position: Second Base; Bats: Right; Throws: Right; his .424 batting average in 1924 is a 20th century National League record; his career batting average of .358 is the highest ever in the National League; first National League player to hit 300 home runs; only player in baseball history to win a "decade" triple crown.

Considered the game's best-ever right-handed hitter, Hornsby won seven batting titles (1920–1925, 1928); hit .400 or better three times; his .424 average in 1924 is a 20th century National League record; and his career batting average of .358 is the highest ever in the National League (second all-time to Ty Cobb's .367). Nicknamed "The Rajah," he was a two-time Most Valuable Player (1925, 1929); two-time Triple Crown winner (1922, 1925); player-manager of the St. Louis Cardinals' first-ever World Championship team in 1926; and was the first National League player to hit 300 home runs.

Making his major league debut on September 10, 1915, Hornsby played 23 years for the St. Louis Cardinals (1915–1926, 1933), New York Giants (1927), Boston Braves (1928), Chicago Cubs (1929–1932), and the St. Louis Browns (1933–1937). He managed the Cardinals (1925–1926), Giants (1927), Braves (1928), Cubs (1930–1932), Browns (1933–1937, 1952), and the Cincinnati Reds (1952–1953). He played in two World Series (winning in 1926 and losing in 1929).

The 5'11", 175-pound Hornsby was never thrown out of a game; accrued 1,011 extra-base hits (14th all-time); led his league in doubles four times; twice in triples; twice in home runs; and his 289 homers as a second baseman is an all-time record.

From 1920 to 1925, Hornsby led the National League in batting average all six years; in runs batted in four years; and in home runs twice. From 1921 through 1925, he averaged .402, and led the Cardinals to a 1926 World Series win over Babe Ruth's New York Yankees. In one of the most unusual plays in World Series history, Hornsby tagged out Babe Ruth trying to steal second for the final out of the Series, clinching the championship for St. Louis.

In 1999, he was ranked number nine on *The Sporting News*' list of Baseball's Greatest Players, the highest-ranking second baseman; later that year, he was elected to the Major League Baseball All-Century Team; and in 2000, he was honored with a star on the St. Louis Walk of Fame.

In March 1922, Hornsby signed a three-year contract with the Cardinals for $18,500 a season, making him the then-highest paid player in National League history. On September 13, 1931, he became the first player in major league history to hit an extra-inning, pinch-hit grand slam, as the Cubs defeated the Boston Braves in 11 innings, 11–7 in the first game of a doubleheader.

In 1922, Hornsby became the only player in history to hit over 40 home runs and bat over .400 in the same season, winning the first of his two triple crowns. He led the league in virtually every batting category that season, including batting average (.401), home runs (42, a National League record at the time), runs batted in (152), slugging average (.722, a record at the time), on base percentage (.459), doubles (46), hits (250, a National League record at the time), and runs scored (141). His 450 total bases is the highest for any National League player during the 20th century.

In 1925, Hornsby won his second triple crown, hitting .403 with 39 home runs and 143 RBIs. He was named the National League's Most Valuable Player and his .756 slugging percentage was the highest in the National League during the 20th century.

Early in the 1925 season, Hornsby was named player-manager of the Cardinals; led the team to its first-ever National League pennant; and to the World Series championship in 1926. In December of that year, he was traded to the New York Giants, and in the 1927 season, he led the league in runs scored (133), walks (86), and on-base percentage (.448). In the off-season, he was traded to the Boston Braves and in 1928, Hornsby won his seventh batting title (.387) and led the league in on-base percentage (.498), slugging percentage (.632), and walks (107).

Traded once again, he played for the Chicago Cubs, and in 1929, he led the league with a .679 slugging percentage and in runs scored (156, the most by a right-handed batter in the National League in the 20th century). Hornsby won his second Most Valuable Player award that season, and his second National League pennant, before losing to the Philadelphia Athletics in a five-game World Series.

An ankle injury limited his playing time in 1930, and his last full season as a player came in 1931, when he led the league in on-base percentage (.421) for the ninth and final time in his career. For the last six years of his playing career, he was primarily a pinch hitter, and played for the Cardinals and St. Louis Browns, before retiring as a player in 1937.

Hornsby's six consecutive batting titles is a major league record, and his leading the National League in slugging percentage nine times is also a record. He hit more home runs, had more RBIs, and had the highest batting average of any other National League player during the 1920's, which makes him the only player in baseball history to win a "decade" triple crown.

A remarkably consistent hitter, Hornsby's lifetime home batting average was .359, and his lifetime road batting average was .358; he had five seasons where he averaged over .400 at home, and four seasons where he averaged over .400 on the road; and he set a major league record of 13 consecutive games with two or more base hits per game (July 5 through July 18, 1923).

Rogers Hornsby's Career Statistics

YEAR	TEAM	LG	G	AB	R	H	2B	3B	HR	RBI	BB	SO	SB	AVG	SLG
1915	St. Louis	NL	18	57	5	14	2	0	0	4	2	6	0	.246	.281
1916	St. Louis	NL	139	495	63	155	17	15	6	65	40	63	17	.313	.444
1917	St. Louis	NL	145	523	86	171	24	17	8	66	45	34	17	.327	.484
1918	St. Louis	NL	115	416	51	117	19	11	5	60	40	43	8	.281	.416
1919	St. Louis	NL	138	512	68	163	15	9	8	71	48	41	17	.318	.430
1920	St. Louis	NL	149	589	96	218	44	20	9	94	60	50	12	.370	.559
1921	St. Louis	NL	154	592	131	235	44	18	21	126	60	48	13	.397	.639
1922	St. Louis	NL	154	623	141	250	46	14	42	152	65	50	17	.401	.722
1923	St. Louis	NL	107	424	89	163	32	10	17	83	55	29	3	.384	.627
1924	St. Louis	NL	143	536	121	227	43	14	25	94	89	32	5	.424	.696
1925	St. Louis	NL	138	504	133	203	41	10	39	143	83	39	5	.403	.756
1926	St. Louis	NL	134	527	96	167	34	5	11	93	61	39	3	.317	.463
1927	New York	NL	155	568	133	205	32	9	26	125	86	38	9	.361	.586
1928	Boston	NL	140	486	99	188	42	7	21	94	107	41	5	.387	.632
1929	Chicago	NL	156	602	156	229	47	8	39	149	87	65	2	.380	.679
1930	Chicago	NL	42	104	15	32	5	1	2	18	12	12	0	.308	.433
1931	Chicago	NL	100	357	64	118	37	1	16	90	56	23	1	.331	.574
1932	Chicago	NL	19	58	10	13	2	0	1	7	10	4	0	.224	.310
1933	St. Louis	NL	46	83	9	27	6	0	2	21	12	6	1	.325	.470
1933	St. Louis	AL	11	9	2	3	1	0	1	2	2	1	0	.333	.778
1934	St. Louis	AL	24	23	2	7	2	0	1	11	7	4	0	.304	.522

YEAR	TEAM	LG	G	AB	R	H	2B	3B	HR	RBI	BB	SO	SB	AVG	SLG
1935	St. Louis	AL	10	24	1	5	3	0	0	3	3	6	0	.208	.333
1936	St. Louis	AL	2	5	1	2	0	0	0	2	1	0	0	.400	.400
1937	St. Louis	AL	20	56	7	18	3	0	1	11	7	5	0	.321	.429
	TOTALS		2,259	8,173	1,579	2,930	541	169	301	1,584	1,038	679	135	.358	.577

Rogers Hornsby's Managerial Record

YEAR	TEAM	LG	W	L	WIN%	Finish
1925	St. Louis	NL	64	51	.557	4 (Player-Manager)
1926	St. Louis	NL	89	65	.578	Won World Series (Player-Manager)
1927	New York	NL	22	10	.688	3 (Player-Manager)
1928	Boston	NL	39	83	.320	7 (Player-Manager)
1930	Chicago	NL	4	0	1.000	2 (Player-Manager)
1931	Chicago	NL	84	70	.545	3 (Player-Manager)
1932	Chicago	NL	53	46	.535	1 (Player-Manager)
1933	St. Louis	AL	19	33	.365	8 (Player-Manager)
1934	St. Louis	AL	67	85	.441	6 (Player-Manager)
1935	St. Louis	AL	65	87	.428	7 (Player-Manager)
1936	St. Louis	AL	57	95	.375	7 (Player-Manager)
1937	St. Louis	AL	25	52	.325	8 (Player-Manager)
1952	St. Louis	AL	22	29	.431	7
1952	Cincinnati	NL	27	24	.529	6
1953	Cincinnati	NL	64	82	.438	6
	St. Louis		153	116	.569	
	New York		22	10	.687	
	Boston		39	83	.320	
	Chicago		141	116	.549	
	St. Louis		255	381	.401	
	Cincinnati		91	106	.462	
	TOTALS		701	812	.463	

Sources: Baseball-Reference.com; National Baseball Hall of Fame and Museum; *Rogers Hornsby* (Charles C. Alexander)

Hornung, Paul Vernon (born: December 23, 1935 in Louisville, Kentucky); inducted into the Pro Football Hall of Fame in 1986 as a player; Position: Halfback; Uniform: #5; only college player from a team with a losing record to ever win the Heisman Trophy.

A star athlete at (Bishop Benedict Joseph) Flaget High School (Louisville, Kentucky), Hornung lettered four years each in football, basketball, and baseball. After high school, he went to the University of Notre Dame (South Bend, Indiana), and in 1955, he finished fourth in the nation in total offense (1,215 yards and six touchdowns); helped Notre Dame upset number-four ranked Navy 21–7 with two offensive touchdowns and two interceptions; and in a loss to the University of Southern California, Hornung ran and threw for 354 yards, the best in the nation in 1955.

Nicknamed the "Golden Boy," he won the Heisman Trophy as a quarterback in 1956 as the year's outstanding college player, and is the only player from a team with a losing record (Notre Dame finished 2–8 that year) ever to win the trophy. He was a two-time All-American (1955–1956); considered the best all-around football player in Notre Dame history; and in the 1956 season, he led the team in passing, rushing, scoring, kickoff and punt returns, and punting.

After graduating from Notre Dame, Hornung was the number one pick (first overall selection) of the Green Bay Packers in the 1957 National Football League Draft, and would play his entire nine-year (104 games, 1957–1962, 1964–1966) career with the team. He won four league championships (1961–1962, 1965–1966) and was part of the team that won the first-ever Super Bowl in 1967, although he did not play because of a neck injury.

He was named NFL Player of the Year twice (1960–1961); led all scorers three consecutive seasons (1959–1961), including a record 176 points in 1960 (a record that stood until 2006, when San Diego Chargers running back LaDainian Tomlinson scored 180 points, playing in two more games than Hornung); played in two Pro Bowls (1959–1960); scored a record 19 points in the 1961 NFL title game (while on Christmas leave from the Army), a 37–0 Green Bay win over the New York Giants; and was named to the NFL 1960s All-Decade Team. As of this writing, he is one of only five players to have won both the Heisman Trophy and the NFL's Most Valuable Player Award (along with Marcus Allen, Earl Campbell, Barry Sanders, and O.J. Simpson).

Hornung was inducted into the Green Bay Packers Hall of Fame in 1975; into the College Football Hall of Fame in 1985; and the Paul Hornung Award, named in his honor, is presented annually to the state of Kentucky's top high school football player. He has also been inducted into the Wisconsin Hall of Fame, Kentucky Athletic Hall of Fame, and the National High School Hall of Fame.

Hornung's exuberant personality, good looks, and wealth allowed him to enjoy the partying good times off the field. He was often fined by the team for staying out past curfews, and his lifestyle caused him problems in 1963 when a major betting scandal was made public. He and Alex Karras (Detroit Lions) were suspended from the NFL for betting on games and associating with gamblers and other "undesirable persons." Instead of making up excuses or hiding behind public relations ploys (as is so common with today's players), he publically admitted his actions, served his one-year suspension, and returned to the league in 1964 with his reputation intact.

After retiring from the NFL, he was the producer and host of a nationally televised sports program, and was a commentator on college football television broadcasts. Hornung wrote two books, the autobiographical *Golden Boy* (2004) and *Lombardi and Me: Players, Coaches, and Colleagues Talk About the Man and the Myth* (2006).

Paul Hornung's Career Statistics

			RUSHING				RECEIVING			
YEAR	**TEAM**	**G**	**NO.**	**YDS.**	**AVG.**	**TD**	**NO.**	**YDS.**	**AVG.**	**TD**
1957	Green Bay	12	60	319	5.3	3	6	34	5.7	0
1958	Green Bay	12	69	310	4.5	2	15	137	9.1	0
1959	Green Bay	12	152	681	4.5	7	15	113	7.5	0
1960	Green Bay	12	160	671	4.2	13	28	257	9.2	2
1961	Green Bay	12	127	597	4.7	8	15	145	9.7	2
1962	Green Bay	9	57	219	3.8	5	9	168	18.7	2
1964	Green Bay	14	103	415	4.0	5	9	98	10.9	0
1965	Green Bay	12	89	299	3.4	5	19	336	17.7	3
1966	Green Bay	9	76	200	2.6	2	14	192	13.7	3
	TOTALS	104	893	3,711	4.2	50	130	1,480	11.4	12

Paul Hornung's Career Statistics

			KICKING				
YEAR	**TEAM**	**G**	**FG**	**FGA**	**XK**	**XKA**	**PTS**
1957	Green Bay	12	0	4	0	0	18
1958	Green Bay	12	11	21	22	23	67
1959	Green Bay	12	7	17	31	32	94
1960	Green Bay	12	15	28	41	41	176
1961	Green Bay	12	15	22	41	41	146
1962	Green Bay	9	6	10	14	14	74
1964	Green Bay	14	12	38	41	43	107
1965	Green Bay	12	0	0	0	0	48
1966	Green Bay	9	0	0	0	0	30
	TOTALS	104	66	140	190	194	760

Sources: *Golden Boy* (Paul Hornung as told to William F. Reed); Paul Hornung Web Site (www.paulhornung. com; Pro Football Hall of Fame; Pro-Football-Reference.com

Horton, Miles Gilbert "Tim" (born: January 12, 1930 in Cochrane, Ontario, Canada; died: February 21, 1974 outside St. Catharines, Ontario, Canada); inducted into the Hockey Hall of Fame in 1977 as a player; Position: Defenseman; Uniform: #2; won four Stanley Cup championships; holds the Leafs' record for most consecutive games played.

Horton played 24 National Hockey League seasons (1,446 games) from 1949 to 1974 with the Toronto Maple Leafs (1949–1950, 1951–1970), New York Rangers (1970–1971), Pittsburgh Penguins (1971–1972), and the Buffalo Sabres (1972–1974).

After several seasons in the Ontario Hockey League, he made his professional debut with the Pittsburgh Hornets of the American Hockey League in 1949, before joining the Maple Leafs full-time in the 1952–1953 season.

The 5'10", 180-pound Horton led Toronto to four Stanley Cup titles (1962–1964, 1967); was named to the First All-Star Team three times (1964, 1968–1969); and was selected to the Second All-Star Team three times (1954, 1963, 1967).

Shortly after the team's last Stanley Cup championship, Horton was traded to the New York Rangers, where he played for one season, then served two short stints with the Penguins and Sabres before being killed in a one-car accident while being chased by police for speeding.

From February 11, 1961 to February 4, 1968, Horton appeared in 486 consecutive regular-season games, still a Leafs club record; in 1996, his jersey number two was retired by the Sabres; and in 1998, he was ranked number 43 on *The Hockey News*' list of the 100 Greatest Hockey Players.

Tim Horton's Career Statistics

			REGULAR SEASON					PLAYOFFS				
SEASON	TEAM	LEAGUE	GP	G	A	TP	PIM	GP	G	A	TP	PIM
1946–1947	Copper Cliff Jr. Redmen	NOJHA	9	0	0	0	14	5	0	1	1	0
1947–1948	St. Michael's Majors	OHA–Jr.	32	6	7	13	137					
1948–1949	St. Michael's Majors	OHA–Jr.	32	9	18	27	95					
1949–1950	Toronto Maple Leafs	NHL	1	0	0	0	2	1	0	0	0	2
1949–1950	Pittsburgh Hornets	AHL	60	5	18	23	83					
1950–1951	Pittsburgh Hornets	AHL	68	8	26	34	129	13	0	9	9	16
1951–1952	Toronto Maple Leafs	NHL	4	0	0	0	8					
1951–1952	Pittsburgh Hornets	AHL	64	12	19	31	146	11	1	3	4	16
1952–1953	Toronto Maple Leafs	NHL	70	2	14	16	85					
1953–1954	Toronto Maple Leafs	NHL	70	7	24	31	94	5	1	1	2	4
1954–1955	Toronto Maple Leafs	NHL	67	5	9	14	84					
1955–1956	Toronto Maple Leafs	NHL	35	0	5	5	36	2	0	0	0	4
1956–1957	Toronto Maple Leafs	NHL	66	6	19	25	72					
1957–1958	Toronto Maple Leafs	NHL	53	6	20	26	39					
1958–1959	Toronto Maple Leafs	NHL	70	5	21	26	76	12	0	3	3	16
1959–1960	Toronto Maple Leafs	NHL	70	3	29	32	69	10	0	1	1	6
1960–1961	Toronto Maple Leafs	NHL	57	6	15	21	75	5	0	0	0	0
1961–1962	Toronto Maple Leafs	NHL	70	10	28	38	88	12	3	13	16	16
1962–1963	Toronto Maple Leafs	NHL	70	6	19	25	69	10	1	3	4	10
1963–1964	Toronto Maple Leafs	NHL	70	9	20	29	71	14	0	4	4	20
1964–1965	Toronto Maple Leafs	NHL	70	12	16	28	95	6	0	2	2	13
1965–1966	Toronto Maple Leafs	NHL	70	6	22	28	76	4	1	0	1	12
1966–1967	Toronto Maple Leafs	NHL	70	8	17	25	70	12	3	5	8	25
1967–1968	Toronto Maple Leafs	NHL	69	4	23	27	82					
1968–1969	Toronto Maple Leafs	NHL	74	11	29	40	107	4	0	0	0	7
1969–1970	Toronto Maple Leafs	NHL	59	3	19	22	91					
1969–1970	New York Rangers	NHL	15	1	5	6	16	6	1	1	2	28
1970–1971	New York Rangers	NHL	78	2	18	20	57	13	1	4	5	14
1971–1972	Pittsburgh Penguins	NHL	44	2	9	11	40	4	0	1	1	2
1972–1973	Buffalo Sabres	NHL	69	1	16	17	56	6	0	1	1	4
1973–1974	Buffalo Sabres	NHL	55	0	6	6	53					
	TOTALS		1,446	115	403	518	1,611	126	11	39	50	183

Sources: Hockey Hall of Fame; Hockey-Reference.com

Hotchkiss, Harley Norman (born: 1927 in Tillsongurg, Ontario, Canada); inducted into the Hockey Hall of Fame in 2006 as a builder; helped bring the Flames to Calgary from Atlanta.

One of the owners of the National Hockey League's Calgary Flames, Hotchkiss received a degree in geology from Michigan State University (East Lansing) after serving in World War II, and is one of Canada's leading mineral and oil explorers. He has been inducted into the Canadian Petroleum Hall of Fame (2004) and the Calgary Business Hall of Fame (2005); awarded the Officer of the Order of Canada in 1997; and the Alberta Order of Excellence in 1998.

Hotchkiss played hockey in college and later was part of the group that purchased the Flames in 1980 and moved the team to Calgary from Atlanta, Georgia. He oversaw the building of the Pengrowth Saddledome, which is used primarily by the Flames, but also served as the home of the 1988 Winter Olympic Games. While he was with the team, the Flames won the Stanley Cup in 1989.

He helped create the International Hockey Centre of Excellence for Hockey Canada; serves as the NHL Governor for the Calgary Flames; sits on the board of the Hockey Hall of Fame; and served as chairman of the National Hockey League's Board of Governors (1995–2007).

Source: Hockey Hall of Fame

Houbregs, Robert J. (born: March 12, 1932 in Vancouver, British Columbia, Canada); inducted into the Naismith Memorial Basketball Hall of Fame in 1987 as a player; Position: Center-Forward; one of only two players in the University of Washington's history to be named a consensus All-American.

After attending Queen Anne (Washington) High School (1945–1949), Houbregs was a three-year basketball letter winner at the University of Washington (Seattle, 1949–1953). He was selected National Collegiate Athletic Association Player of the Year in 1953 by the Helms Athletic Foundation; a consensus First Team All-American (1953); led UW to three Pacific Coast Conference titles; holds numerous records at Washington, including career scoring (1,774 points, 19.5 per game) and single-season scoring (25.6 points per game) in 1953; led the PCC in scoring three straight seasons; first basketball player inducted into the Husky Hall of Fame (1979); and is one of only two players in the school's history to be named a consensus All-American.

After college, the 6'8", 225-pound Houbregs was the number one draft choice (third overall selection) of the Minnesota Hawks in 1953 and played in the National Basketball Association for five seasons with the Hawks (1953), Baltimore Bullets (1954), Boston Celtics (1955), Fort Wayne Pistons (1955–1957), and the Detroit Pistons (1957–1958). Long after his playing days, he served as general manager of the Seattle SuperSonics from 1970 to 1973 and, in 2000, was inducted into the Canadian Basketball Hall of Fame.

Robert Houbregs' Career Statistics

YEAR	TEAM	G	MIN	FG	FT	TRB	ASST	PTS
1953–1954	Milwaukee-Baltimore	70	1,970	209	190	375	123	608
1954–1955	Baltimore-Boston-Fort Wayne	64	1,326	148	129	297	86	425
1955–1956	Fort Wayne	70	1,535	247	283	414	159	777
1956–1957	Fort Wayne	60	1,592	253	167	401	113	673
1957–1958	Detroit	17	302	49	30	65	19	128
	TOTALS	281	6,725	906	799	1,552	500	2,611

Sources: Basketball-Reference.com; Naismith Memorial Basketball Hall of Fame

Houston, Kenneth Ray "Ken" (born: November 12, 1944 in Lufkin, Texas); inducted into the Pro Football Hall of Fame in 1986 as a player; Position: Strong Safety; premier strong safety of the 1970s.

Houston lettered in football at Lufkin (Texas) High School before attending Prairie View A&M University (Texas). After college, he was a ninth-round pick (214th overall selection) in the 1967 National Football League Draft of the Houston Oilers and played 14 NFL seasons (196 games) for the Oilers (1967–1972) and the Washington Redskins (1973–1980).

The premier strong safety of the 1970s, Houston was named to two American Football League All-Star teams (1969, 1971); 12 Pro-Bowls (1968–1979); an All-Pro or All-American Football Conference/National Football Conference eight straight years (1971–1979); named one of the 70 Greatest Redskins; selected to the NFL 1970s All-Decade Team; and was voted to the NFL 75th Anniversary All-Time Team.

The 6'3", 197-pound Houston once held the NFL record for returning nine interceptions for touchdowns, and in 1999, he was ranked number 61 on *The Sporting News*' list of the 100 Greatest Football Players.

Ken Houston's Career Statistics

					DEFENSE				
YEAR	TEAM	G	INT	YDS	AVG	TD	FUMREC	YDS	TD
1967	Houston	14	4	151	37.8	2	1	0	0
1968	Houston	14	5	160	32.0	2	1	0	0
1969	Houston	14	4	87	21.8	1	3	7	0
1970	Houston	14	3	32	10.7	0	0	0	0
1971	Houston	14	9	220	24.4	4	2	71	1
1972	Houston	14	0	0	0.0	0	4	24	0
1973	Washington	14	6	32	5.3	0	5	8	0
1974	Washington	14	2	40	20.0	0	0	0	0

YEAR	TEAM	G	INT	YDS	AVG	DEFENSE TD	FUMREC	YDS	TD
1975	Washington	14	4	33	8.3	0	2	6	0
1976	Washington	14	4	25	6.3	0	1	0	0
1977	Washington	14	5	69	13.8	0	2	0	0
1978	Washington	16	2	29	14.5	0	0	0	0
1979	Washington	13	1	20	20.0	0	0	0	0
1980	Washington	13	0	0	0.0	0	0	0	0
	TOTALS	196	49	898	18.3	9	21	116	1

Sources: Pro Football Hall of Fame; Pro-Football-Reference.com

Howard, Ted (born: July 30, 1945); inducted into the National Soccer Hall of Fame and Museum in 2003 as a builder; served as executive director of the North American Soccer League.

A key member of the North American Soccer League administration from 1971 to 1984, Howard has served as Director of Administration (1975–1977), Director of Operations (1978–1980), and Executive Director (1981–1984). He left the NASL for an executive position with the National Basketball Association, but returned to soccer in 2000 as the Deputy Secretary for the Confederation of North, Central American and Caribbean Association Football.

He was a member of the original 1965 California State University (Chico) varsity soccer team; served as an assistant soccer coach for the team; and was the founder of the first high school soccer league in Chico, Durham, and Yuba City (all in California).

Source: National Soccer Hall of Fame and Museum

Howe, Gordon "Gordie" (born: March 31, 1928 in Floral, Saskatchewan, Canada); inducted into the Hockey Hall of Fame in 1972 as a player; Position: Right Wing; Uniform: #9; named the NHL's Most Valuable Player six times and won four Stanley Cup championships; first player to return to the National Hockey League after being inducted into the Hockey Hall of Fame (1979 with the Hartford Whalers).

Known as "Mr. Hockey," Howe played 33 professional seasons from 1945 to 1997, including 26 in the National Hockey League with the Detroit Red Wings (1946–1971) and the Hartford Whalers (1979–1980). He finished in the top five in NHL scoring 20 straight seasons; began his NHL career just as World War II ended; and played his last season as Wayne Gretzky was playing his first.

In 1946, the 6', 200-pound Howe made his professional debut with Detroit at the beginning of the 1946–1947 season, and scored in his very first game. He played on the "Production Line" with Sid Abel and Ted Lindsay; made his first All-Star appearance in 1948; and in the 1949–1950 season, the line finished 1-2-3 in the year-end scoring race, with Abel winning the Hart Trophy as the league's most valuable player.

Although he was hurt in the first game of the 1950 Stanley Cup playoffs and missed the series, when the Red Wings won the title in seven games, he had recovered enough to join the team's on-ice celebration.

Howe was selected to 21 NHL All-Star Teams (12 times to the First Team [1951–1954, 1957–1958, 1960, 1963, 1966, 1968–1970] and nine times to the Second Team [1949–1950, 1956, 1959, 1961–1962, 1964–1965, 1967]); led the league in scoring six times (winning the Art Ross Trophy in 1951–1954, 1957, 1963) and won the Hart Trophy six times (1952–1953, 1957–1958, 1960, 1963); won four Stanley Cup titles (1950, 1952, 1954–1955); and was the first player to return to the NHL (with the Hartford Whalers in 1979) after being inducted into the Hockey Hall of Fame.

Howe briefly retired in 1971, but returned to junior hockey in 1973 with the Houston Aeros (World Hockey Association) so that he could play the game with his two sons, Mark and Marty. With the Howe family in tow, the team won consecutive AVCO championships (1974–1975) and he was selected the WHA's Most Valuable Player in 1974.

All three Howe family members moved to the New England Whalers (also of the WHA) in 1977, and when the WHA merged with the NHL in 1979, Howe (at age 51), played one final season in all 80 games with the Hartford Whalers, and was selected to the 1980 NHL All-Star Game.

Howe won the Lester B. Patrick Award in 1967 for his contributions to hockey in the United States; was made an Officer of the Order of Canada in 1971; won the Gary Davidson Trophy in 1974 (awarded annually to the Most Valuable Player in the World Hockey Association; later renamed the Gordie Howe Trophy); played in two WHA All-Star Games; the last active player from the 1940s and 1950s; inducted into Canada's Sports Hall of Fame in 1975; and was inducted into Canada's Walk of Fame in 2000.

In 1998, he was ranked number three on *The Hockey News*' list of the 100 Greatest Hockey Players, the highest-ranking right wing on the list, and his jersey number nine was retired by both the Detroit Red Wings and the Hartford Whalers (later to become the Carolina Hurricanes).

Howe holds numerous records, including most NHL regular-season games played (1,767); most NHL and WHA regular-season games played (2,186); most NHL and WHA regular-season and playoff games played (2,421); most NHL seasons played (26); most NHL and WHA seasons played (32); most NHL regular-season goals by a right winger (801); most NHL regular-season assists by a right winger (1,049); and most NHL regular-season points by a right winger (1,850).

On December 26, 1917, Harry Cameron became the first player to achieve what is now called the "Gordie Howe hat trick," when a player scores a goal, gets an assist, and participates in a fight.

Gordie Howe's Career Statistics

			REGULAR SEASON					PLAYOFFS				
SEASON	**TEAM**	**LEAGUE**	**GP**	**G**	**A**	**TP**	**PIM**	**GP**	**G**	**A**	**TP**	**PIM**
1942–1943	King George High	High-SK										
1943–1944	Saskatoon Lions	SAHA	5	6	5	11	4	2	0	0	0	6
1944–1945	Galt Red Wings	OHA-Jr.										
1945–1946	Omaha Knights	USHL	51	22	26	48	53	6	2	1	3	15
1946–1947	Detroit Red Wings	NHL	58	7	15	22	52	5	0	0	0	18
1947–1948	Detroit Red Wings	NHL	60	16	28	44	63	10	1	1	2	11
1948–1949	Detroit Red Wings	NHL	40	12	25	37	57	11	8	3	11	19
1949–1950	Detroit Red Wings	NHL	70	35	33	68	69	1	0	0	0	7
1950–1951	Detroit Red Wings	NHL	70	43	43	86	74	6	4	3	7	4
1951–1952	Detroit Red Wings	NHL	70	47	39	86	78	8	2	5	7	2
1952–1953	Detroit Red Wings	NHL	70	49	46	95	57	6	2	5	7	2
1953–1954	Detroit Red Wings	NHL	70	33	48	81	109	12	4	5	9	31
1954–1955	Detroit Red Wings	NHL	64	29	33	62	68	11	9	11	20	24
1955–1956	Detroit Red Wings	NHL	70	38	41	79	100	10	3	9	12	8
1956–1957	Detroit Red Wings	NHL	70	44	45	89	72	5	2	5	7	6
1957–1958	Detroit Red Wings	NHL	64	33	44	77	40	4	1	1	2	0
1958–1959	Detroit Red Wings	NHL	70	32	46	78	57					
1959–1960	Detroit Red Wings	NHL	70	28	45	73	46	6	1	5	6	4
1960–1961	Detroit Red Wings	NHL	64	23	49	72	30	11	4	11	15	10
1961–1962	Detroit Red Wings	NHL	70	33	44	77	54					
1962–1963	Detroit Red Wings	NHL	70	38	48	86	100	11	7	9	16	22
1963–1964	Detroit Red Wings	NHL	69	26	47	73	70	14	9	10	19	16
1964–1965	Detroit Red Wings	NHL	70	29	47	76	104	7	4	2	6	20
1965–1966	Detroit Red Wings	NHL	70	29	46	75	83	12	4	6	10	12
1966–1967	Detroit Red Wings	NHL	69	25	40	65	53					
1967–1968	Detroit Red Wings	NHL	74	39	43	82	53					
1968–1969	Detroit Red Wings	NHL	76	44	59	103	58					
1969–1970	Detroit Red Wings	NHL	76	31	40	71	58	4	2	0	2	2
1970–1971	Detroit Red Wings	NHL	63	23	29	52	38					
1973–1974	Houston Aeros	WHA	70	31	69	100	46	13	3	14	17	34
1974–1975	Canada	Summit-72	7	3	4	7	2					
1974–1975	Houston Aeros	WHA	75	34	65	99	84	13	8	12	20	20
1975–1976	Houston Aeros	WHA	78	32	70	102	76	17	4	8	12	31
1976–1977	Houston Aeros	WHA	62	24	44	68	57	11	5	3	8	11
1977–1978	New England Whalers	WHA	76	34	62	96	85	14	5	5	10	15
1978–1979	New England Whalers	WHA	58	19	24	43	51	10	3	1	4	4
1979–1980	Hartford Whalers	NHL	80	15	26	41	42	3	1	1	2	2
1997–1998	Detroit Vipers	IHL	1	0	0	0	0					
	NHL TOTALS		1,767	801	1,049	1,850	1,685	157	68	92	160	220

Sources: *Gordie: A Hockey Legend* (Roy MacSkimming); Hockey Hall of Fame; Hockey-Reference.com

Howe, Sydney Harris "Syd" (born: September 28, 1911 in Ottawa, Ontario, Canada; died: May 20, 1976); inducted into the Hockey Hall of Fame in 1965 as a player; Position: Left Wing-Center-Forward; set the modern-day NHL record by scoring six goals in a single game; played in the longest game in NHL history; won three Stanley Cup titles.

Howe played hockey at the Glebe Collegiate Institute (Ottawa, Ontario, Canada) in 1926 and later played 17 National Hockey League seasons with the Ottawa Senators (1930, 1932–1934), Philadelphia Quakers (1930–1931), Toronto Maple Leafs (1931–1932), St. Louis Eagles (1934–1935), and the Detroit Red Wings (1935–1946). He set the modern-day NHL record by scoring six goals in a single game (February 3, 1944 against the New York Rangers), a record that has been tied twice but never surpassed.

Unrelated to fellow hall-of-famer Gordie Howe, he played for the Ottawa Senators for the last 12 games of the 1929–1930 NHL season, and was loaned to the NHL's Philadelphia Quakers for the 1930–1931 season, the team's only year of existence. When Ottawa ceased operations in 1931, Howe was selected by the NHL's Toronto Maple Leafs in the Dispersal Draft, but appeared in only three games, while spending most of his time with the Syracuse Stars (International Hockey League).

At 2:25 a.m. on March 25, 1936 (while with the Red Wings), he was on the ice in the Montreal Forum when Detroit scored in the sixth overtime period to win game one (1–0) of the best-of-five semi-final playoff series against the Montreal Maroons, the longest game in NHL history. The Red Wings went on to win the Stanley Cup, and Howe would win two more (1937, 1943).

On March 19, 1940, Howe scored only 25 seconds into overtime to give the Red Wings a 2–1 win over the New York Americans in game one of the quarter-finals playoff series to set the record as the fastest overtime goal scored in NHL history (stood for 29 years).

Syd Howe's Career Statistics

			REGULAR SEASON					PLAYOFFS				
SEASON	**TEAM**	**LEAGUE**	**GP**	**G**	**A**	**TP**	**PIM**	**GP**	**G**	**A**	**TP**	**PIM**
1927–1928	Ottawa Gunners	OCHL										
1927–1928	Ottawa Gunners	M-Cup	8	9	4	13	8					
1928–1929	Ottawa Rideaus	OCHL	15	7	1	8						
1929–1930	Ottawa Rideaus	OCHL	11	8	1	9	9					
1929–1930	London Panthers	IHL	5	1	0	1	0					
1929–1930	Ottawa Senators	NHL	12	1	1	2	0	2	0	0	0	0
1930–1931	Philadelphia Quakers	NHL	44	9	11	20	20					
1931–1932	Toronto Maple Leafs	NHL	3	0	0	0	0					
1931–1932	Syracuse Stars	IHL	45	9	12	21	44					
1932–1933	Ottawa Senators	NHL	48	12	12	24	17					
1933–1934	Ottawa Senators	NHL	42	13	7	20	18					
1934–1935	St. Louis Eagles	NHL	36	14	13	27	23					
1934–1935	Detroit Red Wings	NHL	14	8	12	20	11					
1935–1936	Detroit Red Wings	NHL	48	16	14	30	26	7	3	3	6	2
1936–1937	Detroit Red Wings	NHL	45	17	10	27	10	10	2	5	7	0
1937–1938	Detroit Red Wings	NHL	48	8	19	27	14					
1938–1939	Detroit Red Wings	NHL	48	16	20	36	11	6	3	1	4	4
1939–1940	Detroit Red Wings	NHL	46	14	23	37	17	5	2	2	4	2
1940–1941	Detroit Red Wings	NHL	48	20	24	44	8	9	1	7	8	0
1941–1942	Detroit Red Wings	NHL	48	16	19	35	6	12	3	5	8	0
1942–1943	Detroit Red Wings	NHL	50	20	35	55	10	7	1	2	3	0
1943–1944	Detroit Red Wings	NHL	46	32	28	60	6	5	2	2	4	0
1944–1945	Detroit Red Wings	NHL	46	17	36	53	6	7	0	0	0	2
1945–1946	Detroit Red Wings	NHL	26	4	7	11	9					
1945–1946	Indianapolis Capitols	AHL	14	6	11	17	4	5	2	0	2	0
1946–1947	Ottawa Senators	QSHL	24	19	21	40	4	11	2	1	3	0
1946–1947	Ottawa Army	OCHL	1	2	1	3	0					
1947–1948	Ottawa Army	OCHL										
1948–1949	Ottawa Army	OCHL	1	0	0	0	0					
	NHL TOTALS		698	237	291	528	212	70	17	27	44	10

Sources: Hockey Hall of Fame; Hockey-Reference.com

Howell, Bailey E. (born: January 20, 1937 in Middleton, Tennessee); inducted into the Naismith Memorial Basketball Hall of Fame in 1997 as a player; Position: Forward; first Southeastern Conference player in history to reach the 2,000-point, 1,000-rebound club; won two NBA championships.

Howell was an All-American at Middleton (Tennessee) High School (1951–1955) his senior year; was also a two-time, All-State selection (1954–1955); All-Conference (1953–1955); and set the Tennessee high school record for points (1,187 points) and points-per-game (31.2) in 38 games (1954–1955).

He was a three-year basketball letter winner at Mississippi State University (Starkville, 1955–1959); named First-Team All-American (1959) by *The Sporting News*; Second-Team All-American (1958); MSU's all-time leading scorer until 1983 (2,030 points, 27.1 per game); MSU's leading rebounder (1,277, 17.0 per game); holds MSU career scoring (27.1 points per game) and rebounding (17.0 per game) records; first Southeastern Conference player in history to reach the 2,000-point, 1,000-rebound club; a three-time All-SEC (1957–1959) selection; SEC Most Valuable Player twice (1958–1959); SEC Sophomore of the Year (1957); SEC two-time scoring champion (27.7 points per game in 1958 and 26.4 points per game in 1959); led the nation in field goal shooting (.568) in 1957; holds the school record for most points in a game (47, against Union University on December 4, 1958); led the school to an SEC title in 1959; and has been inducted into the Mississippi and MSU Halls of Fame.

After college, the 6'7", 220-pound Howell was a first round pick (second overall selection) of the Detroit Pistons in the 1959 National Basketball Association Draft, as of this writing, the highest draft pick ever chosen from Mississippi State University. During his 12-year NBA career, he played with the Detroit Pistons (1958–1964), Baltimore Bullets (1964–1966), Boston Celtics (1967–1970), and Philadelphia 76ers (1970–1971). He was named to the All-NBA Second Team in 1963; a six-time All-Star (1961–1964, 1966–1967); and won two NBA championships with the Boston Celtics (1968–1969).

Bailey Howell's Career Statistics

SEASON	TEAM	LG	G	MIN	FG	FT	TRB	AST	PTS
1959–1960	Detroit	NBA	75	2,346	510	312	790	63	1,332
1960–1961	Detroit	NBA	77	2,952	607	601	1,111	196	1,815
1961–1962	Detroit	NBA	79	2,857	553	470	996	186	1,576
1962–1963	Detroit	NBA	79	2,971	637	519	910	232	1,793
1963–1964	Detroit	NBA	77	2,700	598	470	776	205	1,666
1964–1965	Baltimore	NBA	80	2,975	515	504	869	208	1,534
1965–1966	Baltimore	NBA	79	2,328	481	402	773	155	1,364
1966–1967	Boston	NBA	81	2,503	636	349	677	103	1,621
1967–1968	Boston	NBA	82	2,801	643	335	805	133	1,621
1968–1969	Boston	NBA	78	2,527	612	313	685	137	1,537
1969–1970	Boston	NBA	82	2,078	399	235	550	120	1,033
1970–1971	Philadelphia	NBA	82	1,589	324	230	441	115	878
	TOTALS		951	30,627	6,515	4,740	9,383	1,853	17,770

Sources: Basketball-Reference.com; Naismith Memorial Basketball Hall of Fame

Howell, Henry Vernon "Harry" (born: December 28, 1932 in Hamilton, Ontario, Canada); inducted into the Hockey Hall of Fame in 1979 as a player; Position: Defenseman; Uniform: #3; last player in the pre-expansion era to win the Norris Trophy; won a Stanley Cup title as a scout for the Edmonton Oilers.

Howell played 25 professional seasons, including 22 in the National Hockey League with the New York Rangers (1952–1969), Oakland/California Seals (1969–1971), and the Los Angeles Kings (1971–1973); won the Norris Trophy in 1967 as the NHL's top defenseman; named a First-Team All-Star in 1967; and played in seven All-Star Games (1954, 1963–1965, 1967–1968, 1970). When he retired, Howell had played in more games (1,581) than any defenseman in major-league hockey history (1,411 in the NHL and 170 in the World Hockey Association).

After leaving the NHL, the 6'1", 195-pound Howell moved to the WHA, where he played for the San Diego Mariners, New Jersey Knights, and the Calgary Cowboys, before retiring as a player in 1975.

After retiring, he served as the assistant general manager with the Cleveland Barons (the new name of the Seals when the team moved to Ohio from California) of the WHA in 1976; later served as the team's general manager until the franchise merged with the Minnesota North Stars in 1978; and coached the Stars briefly in 1978–1979 (three wins, six losses, and two ties), before becoming the team's chief scout. Although never able to win a Stanley Cup title as a player, in 1990, Howell won a championship as the head scout of the Edmonton Oilers.

Henry Howell's Career Statistics

			REGULAR SEASON					PLAYOFFS				
SEASON	TEAM	LEAGUE	GP	G	A	TP	PIM	GP	G	A	TP	PIM
1949–1950	Guelph Biltmores	OHA-Jr.	3	0	1	1	2	5	0	1	1	14

			REGULAR SEASON					PLAYOFFS				
SEASON	**TEAM**	**LEAGUE**	**GP**	**G**	**A**	**TP**	**PIM**	**GP**	**G**	**A**	**TP**	**PIM**
1949–1950	Guelph Biltmores	M-Cup	5	0	1	1	14					
1950–1951	Guelph Biltmores	OHA-Jr.	50	6	16	22	77	5	1	0	1	6
1951–1952	Guelph Biltmores	OHA-Jr.	51	17	20	37	79	23	7	9	16	36
1951–1952	Cincinnati Mohawks	AHL	1	0	0	0	0					
1951–1952	Guelph Biltmores	M-Cup	12	5	5	10	24					
1952–1953	New York Rangers	NHL	67	3	8	11	46					
1953–1954	New York Rangers	NHL	67	7	9	16	58					
1954–1955	New York Rangers	NHL	70	2	14	16	87					
1955–1956	New York Rangers	NHL	70	3	15	18	77	5	0	1	1	4
1956–1957	New York Rangers	NHL	65	2	10	12	70	5	1	0	1	6
1957–1958	New York Rangers	NHL	70	4	7	11	62	6	1	0	1	8
1958–1959	New York Rangers	NHL	70	4	10	14	101					
1959–1960	New York Rangers	NHL	67	7	6	13	58					
1960–1961	New York Rangers	NHL	70	7	10	17	62					
1961–1962	New York Rangers	NHL	66	6	15	21	89	6	0	1	1	8
1962–1963	New York Rangers	NHL	70	5	20	25	55					
1963–1964	New York Rangers	NHL	70	5	31	36	75					
1964–1965	New York Rangers	NHL	68	2	20	22	63					
1965–1966	New York Rangers	NHL	70	4	29	33	92					
1966–1967	New York Rangers	NHL	70	12	28	40	54	4	0	0	0	4
1967–1968	New York Rangers	NHL	74	5	24	29	62	6	1	0	1	0
1968–1969	New York Rangers	NHL	56	4	7	11	36	2	0	0	0	0
1969–1970	Oakland Seals	NHL	55	4	16	20	52	4	0	1	1	2
1970–1971	California Seals	NHL	28	0	9	9	14					
1970–1971	Los Angeles Kings	NHL	18	3	8	11	4					
1971–1972	Los Angeles Kings	NHL	77	1	17	18	53					
1972–1973	Los Angeles Kings	NHL	73	4	11	15	28					
1973–1974	New York/New Jersey Knights	WHA	65	3	23	26	24					
1974–1975	San Diego Mariners	WHA	74	4	10	14	28	5	1	0	1	10
1975–1976	Calgary Cowboys	WHA	31	0	3	3	6	2	0	0	0	2
	NHL TOTALS		1,411	94	324	418	1,298		38	3	6	32

Sources: Hockey Hall of Fame; Hockey-Reference.com

Hoyt, George H. (born: August 9, 1883 in South Boston, Massachusetts; died: November 11, 1962); inducted into the Naismith Memorial Basketball Hall of Fame in 1961 as a referee; served as president of the Eastern Massachusetts Board of Approved Basketball Officials.

Hoyt was considered the top basketball referee in the New England area for 34 years, officiating both high school and college games. He helped create the Eastern Massachusetts Board of Approved Basketball Officials and served as its president for two years.

He helped found the New England Interscholastic Basketball Tournament; served as Chief of Officials for the Eastern Massachusetts High School Basketball Tournament; and wrote the book, *The Theory and Practice of Basketball Officiating*.

Source: Naismith Memorial Basketball Hall of Fame

Hoyt, Waite Charles (born: September 9, 1899 in Brooklyn, New York; died: August 25, 1984 in Cincinnati, Ohio); inducted into the National Baseball Hall of Fame and Museum in 1969 as a player by the Veterans Committee; Position: Pitcher; Bats: Right; Throws: Right; Uniform: #19; pitched the last game ever played by the Yankees at the Polo Grounds; retired as the winningest pitcher in World Series history.

Signed by legendary manager John McGraw, Hoyt became the premier (and winningest) pitcher on the New York Yankee teams that won six pennants (1921–1923, 1926–1928) and three World Series (1923, 1927–1928). He pitched three games in the 1921 World Series against the New York Giants, winning two of his six career World Series victories.

Making his major league debut on July 24, 1918, the 6', 180-pound Hoyt played for the New York Giants (1918, 1932), Boston Red Sox (1919–1920), New York Yankees (1921–1930), Detroit Tigers (1930–1931), Philadelphia Athletics (1931), Brooklyn Dodgers (1932, 1937–1938), and the Pittsburgh Pirates (1933–1937). He played in seven World Series (winning in 1923, 1927–1928 and losing in 1921–1922, 1926, 1931).

During his 21-year career, he won ten or more games 13 times, and retired as the winningest pitcher (6–4) in World Series history.

After his playing days, Hoyt became a broadcaster, first with the Dodgers for two seasons and with the Cincinnati Reds for 24 years, before retiring in 1965. He was one of the first professional athletes to develop a successful career in broadcasting after his playing days.

On September 10, 1922, Hoyt pitched the last game ever played by the Yankees at the Polo Grounds (a 2–1 win over the Philadelphia Athletics in the second game of a doubleheader).

Waite Hoyt's Career Statistics

YEAR	TEAM	LG	W	L	PCT	G	SH	IP	H	R	ER	SO	BB	ERA
1918	New York	NL	0	0	.000	1	0	1	0	0	0	2	0	0.00
1919	Boston	AL	4	6	.400	13	1	105	99	42	38	28	22	3.26
1920	Boston	AL	6	6	.500	22	2	121	123	72	59	45	47	4.39
1921	New York	AL	19	13	.594	43	1	282	301	121	97	102	81	3.10
1922	New York	AL	19	12	.613	37	3	265	271	114	101	95	76	3.43
1923	New York	AL	17	9	.654	37	1	239	227	97	80	60	66	3.01
1924	New York	AL	18	13	.581	46	2	247	295	117	104	71	76	3.79
1925	New York	AL	11	14	.440	46	1	243	283	124	108	86	78	4.00
1926	New York	AL	16	12	.571	40	1	218	224	112	93	79	62	3.84
1927	New York	AL	22	7	.759	36	3	256	242	90	75	86	54	2.64
1928	New York	AL	23	7	.767	42	3	273	279	118	102	67	60	3.36
1929	New York	AL	10	9	.526	30	0	202	219	115	95	57	69	4.23
1930	New York	AL	2	2	.500	8	0	48	64	27	24	10	9	4.50
1930	Detroit	AL	9	8	.529	26	1	136	176	89	72	25	47	4.76
1931	Detroit	AL	3	8	.273	16	0	92	124	70	60	10	32	5.87
1931	Philadelphia	AL	10	5	.667	16	2	111	130	60	52	30	37	4.22
1932	Brooklyn	NL	1	3	.250	8	0	27	38	27	23	7	12	7.67
1932	New York	NL	5	7	.417	18	0	97	103	43	37	29	25	3.43
1933	Pittsburgh	NL	5	7	.417	36	1	117	118	45	38	44	19	2.92
1934	Pittsburgh	NL	15	6	.714	48	3	191	184	75	62	105	43	2.92
1935	Pittsburgh	NL	7	11	.389	39	0	164	187	72	62	63	27	3.40
1936	Pittsburgh	NL	7	5	.583	22	0	117	115	44	35	37	20	2.69
1937	Pittsburgh	NL	1	2	.333	11	0	28	31	14	14	21	6	4.50
1937	Brooklyn	NL	7	7	.500	27	1	167	180	83	60	44	30	3.23
1938	Brooklyn	NL	0	3	.000	6	0	16	24	9	9	3	5	5.06
	TOTALS		237	182	.566	674	26	3,762	4,037	1,780	1,500	1,206	1,003	3.59

Sources: Baseball-Reference.com; National Baseball Hall of Fame and Museum

Hubbard, Robert Calvin "Cal" (born: October 31, 1900 in Keytesville, Missouri; died: October 17, 1977 in St. Petersburg, Florida); inducted into the Pro Football Hall of Fame in 1963 (in the inaugural class) as a player; Position: Offensive Tackle; inducted into the National Baseball Hall of Fame and Museum in 1976 as an umpire by the Veterans Committee; only man inducted into the College Football Hall of Fame, the Pro Football Hall of Fame, and the National Baseball Hall of Fame and Museum; won an NFL title as a rookie; first umpire to eject a pitcher from a game for throwing a spitball.

The 6'2", 250-pound Hubbard is the only man inducted into the College Football Hall of Fame (1962), the Pro Football Hall of Fame (1963), and the National Baseball Hall of Fame and Museum (1976). He attended Centenary College of Louisiana (Shreveport), playing football for three years (1922–1924), and played football for one season (1926) at Geneva College (Beaver Falls, Pennsylvania).

After college, he played in the National Football League for nine seasons (105 games) with the New York Giants (1927–1928, 1936), Green Bay Packers (1929–1933, 1935), and the Pittsburgh Pirates (1936, later to be renamed the Steelers). He played end with the Giants and switched to tackle with the Packers; anchored the line for the 1929–1931 Packers' title teams; named All-NFL six straight years (1928–1933); named to the NFL 1920s All-Decade Team; and was chosen the NFL's all-time offensive tackle in 1969 for the NFL's first 50 years.

Hubbard left the NFL after the 1933 season, and in 1934, served as the football line coach at Texas A&M University (College Station). After one season, he returned to the NFL for two more seasons before retiring for good. Earlier in his career, he had begun umpiring minor league baseball games during the summers in Green Bay while he was still playing professional football. The year after he retired from the NFL (1936), he became an American League umpire, and in 1944, he was the first umpire to eject a pitcher from a game for throwing a spitball (the St. Louis Browns' Nels Potter).

He umpired in the major leagues for 16 seasons (including four World Series [1938, 1942, 1946, 1949] and three All-Star games [1939, 1944, 1949]) until a hunting accident in 1951 damaged his eyesight and forced him to retire as an active umpire. He would go on to serve as supervisor of American League umpires for 15 years (1954–1969).

He developed a system of positioning which detailed each umpire's specific responsibilities for various types of plays and was instrumental in convincing the league to switch from a three-man umpiring crew to a four-man crew in 1952, which still exists in today's game.

Only the fifth umpire selected to the baseball hall of fame, Hubbard has also been inducted into the Green Bay Packers Hall of Fame (1970) and the Centenary College of Louisiana Athletic Hall of Fame (1990).

Sources: College Football Hall of Fame; National Baseball Hall of Fame and Museum; Pro Football Hall of Fame

Hubbell, Carl Owen (born: June 22, 1903 in Carthage, Missouri; died: November 21, 1988 in Scottsdale, Arizona); inducted into the National Baseball Hall of Fame and Museum in 1947 as a player; Position: Pitcher; Bats: Right; Throws: Left; Uniform: #11; first National League player to have his number retired; only peacetime pitcher ever to win two Most Valuable Player awards; won a record 24 consecutive games over two seasons (1936–1937).

Known as "The Meal Ticket" by his teammates for his ability to come through in tough situations or in big games, Hubbell anchored the New York Giants' pitching staff of the 1930s. Making his major league debut on July 26, 1928, the 6', 170-pound pitcher played his entire 16-year career (1928–1943) with the Giants and appeared in three World Series (winning in 1933 and losing in 1936 and 1937). He was a nine-time All-Star (1933–1938, 1940–1942) and was a two-time National League Most Valuable Player (1933, 1936).

Hubbell compiled a streak of 46–1/3 scoreless innings in 1933; won 16 straight games in 1936; and won a record 24 straight games over two seasons (1936–1937, July 17, 1936 [Pittsburgh Pirates] through May 27, 1937 [Cincinnati Reds]). His streak ended on May 31, 1937 with a 10–3 loss to the Brooklyn Dodgers in the first game of a doubleheader.

In the 1934 All-Star Game (at the Polo Grounds), he struck out Babe Ruth, Lou Gehrig, Jimmie Foxx, Al Simmons, and Joe Cronin in succession.

After retiring, he served as director of the Giants' minor league organization and director of player development for 35 years, and as the team's scout his last 10 years. He was the first National League player to have his number (11) retired, and in 1999, Hubbell was ranked number 45 on *The Sporting News*' list of Baseball's Greatest Players.

He led the league in wins three times (1933, 1936–1937); earned run average three times (1933–1934, 1936); innings pitched (1933); strikeouts (1937); strikeouts per nine innings pitched (1938); shutouts (1933); saves (1934); pitched a no-hitter against the Pittsburgh Pirates (an 11–0 win on May 8, 1929); and pitched 18 shutout innings against the St. Louis Cardinals in a 1–0 win on July 2, 1933.

Carl Hubbell's Career Statistics

YEAR	TEAM	LG	W	L	PCT	G	SH	IP	H	R	ER	SO	BB	ERA
1928	New York	NL	10	6	.625	20	1	124	117	49	39	37	21	2.83
1929	New York	NL	18	11	.621	39	1	268	273	128	110	106	67	3.69
1930	New York	NL	17	12	.586	37	3	242	263	120	101	117	58	3.76
1931	New York	NL	14	12	.538	36	4	247	213	92	73	156	66	2.66
1932	New York	NL	18	11	.621	40	0	284	260	96	79	137	40	2.50
1933	New York	NL	23	12	.657	45	10	309	256	69	57	156	47	1.66
1934	New York	NL	21	12	.636	49	5	313	286	100	80	118	37	2.30
1935	New York	NL	23	12	.657	42	1	303	314	125	110	150	49	3.27
1936	New York	NL	26	6	.813	42	3	304	265	81	78	123	57	2.31
1937	New York	NL	22	8	.733	39	4	262	261	108	93	159	55	3.19
1938	New York	NL	13	10	.565	24	1	179	171	70	61	104	33	3.07
1939	New York	NL	11	9	.550	29	0	154	150	60	47	62	24	2.75
1940	New York	NL	11	12	.478	31	2	214	220	102	87	86	59	3.66
1941	New York	NL	11	9	.550	26	1	164	169	73	65	75	53	3.57
1942	New York	NL	11	8	.579	24	0	157	158	75	69	61	34	3.96
1943	New York	NL	4	4	.500	12	0	66	87	36	36	31	24	4.91
	TOTALS		253	154	.622	535	36	3,590	3,463	1,384	1,185	1,678	724	2.97

Sources: Baseball-Reference.com; National Baseball Hall of Fame and Museum

Hudson, Maurice John (born: October 24, 1890 in London, England; died: November 13, 1968 in San Francisco, California); inducted into the National Soccer Hall of Fame and Museum in 1966 as a builder; served as secretary of both the California Football Association and the San Francisco League.

Hudson immigrated to the San Francisco, California Bay Area in 1907 and settled in Monterey County, where he played for the Barbarian club from 1910 until 1926. He also played on numerous San Francisco All-Star teams in intercity competition and, while with the Barbarians, won the California State Cup four times and the San Francisco League championship once.

During World War I, he served with the United States Armed Forces in Europe and played on the United States Army team in the Inter-Allied Tournament in Paris, France in 1919.

Later in life, he was appointed secretary of both the California Football Association and the San Francisco League in 1935, serving in both jobs for 15 years.

Source: National Soccer Hall of Fame and Museum

Huff, Robert E. Lee "Sam" (born: October 4, 1934 in Morgantown, West Virginia); inducted into the Pro Football Hall of Fame in 1982 as a player; Position: Linebacker; Uniform: #70; won an NFL title as a rookie; selected to the NFL 1950s All-Decade Team.

One of six children, Huff attended Farmington (West Virginia) High School, before going to West Virginia University (Morgantown, 1952–1955), where he was an All-American guard on the school's football team. After college, he was a third round pick (30th selection overall) of the New York Giants in the 1956 National Football League Draft.

The 6'1", 230-pound Huff would go on to play 13 years (168 games) in the NFL for the Giants (1956–1963) and the Washington Redskins (1964–1967, 1969). During his career, he played in six NFL title games (winning as a rookie in 1956 and losing in 1958–1959, 1961–1963); five Pro Bowls (1958–1961, 1964); was a three-time All-NFL selection; named the NFL's top linebacker in 1959; named to the NFL 1950s All-Decade Team; selected one of the 70 Greatest Redskins; added to the Redskins' Ring of Fame; and served as the Redskins' player-coach in 1969.

Huff was credited with defining the relatively new position of middle linebacker, which his play showed required a player big enough to stop power runners and fast enough to defend against the pass. He ended his career with at least one interception during each season he played.

After retiring, he became a radio broadcaster, first with the Giants and then the Washington Redskins, where he stayed for almost 30 years. In 1999, he was ranked number 76 on *The Sporting News*' list of the 100 Greatest Football Players; in November 2005, Huff's college uniform number 75 was retired by West Virginia University; and he was inducted into the College Football Hall of Fame in 1980.

Sam Huff's Career Statistics

					DEFENSE				
YEAR	**TEAM**	**G**	**INT**	**YDS**	**AVG**	**TD**	**FUMREC**	**YDS**	**TD**
1956	New York	12	3	49	16.3	0	2	0	0
1957	New York	12	1	6	6.0	0	1	3	0
1958	New York	12	2	23	11.5	0	1	0	0
1959	New York	12	1	21	21.0	0	4	5	1
1960	New York	12	3	45	15.0	0	0	0	0
1961	New York	14	3	13	4.3	0	2	12	1
1962	New York	14	1	4	4.0	0	0	0	0
1963	New York	14	4	47	11.8	1	1	0	0
1964	Washington	14	4	34	8.5	0	0	0	0
1965	Washington	14	2	49	24.5	0	1	0	0
1966	Washington	14	1	17	17.0	0	4	0	0
1967	Washington	10	2	8	4.0	0	1	0	0
1969	Washington	14	3	65	21.7	1	0	0	0
	TOTALS	168	30	381	12.7	2	17	20	2

Source: Pro Football Hall of Fame

Huggins, Miller James (born: March 27, 1879 in Cincinnati, Ohio; died: September 25, 1929 in New York, New York); inducted into the National Baseball Hall of Fame and Museum in 1964 as a manager by the Veterans Committee; first player to have no official at-bats in six plate appearances (four walks, a sacrifice fly, an infield sacrifice); won three World Series as a manager.

After a 13-year major league playing career (1904–1916) as a second baseman, the 5'6", 140-pound Huggins began his managing career as a player-manager with the St. Louis Cardinals, before joining the New York Yankees in 1918, where he stayed until his death. He led the team to six pennants (1921–1923, 1926–1928) and three World Series titles (1923, 1927–1928), and his 1927 "Murderers' Row" club, which won 110 games before sweeping the World Series over the Pittsburgh Pirates, is considered one of baseball's greatest teams ever assembled.

Making his major league debut on April 15, 1904, Huggins played for the Cincinnati Reds (1904–1909) and the St. Louis Cardinals (1910–1916), before managing the Cardinals (1913–1917) and Yankees (1918–1929). His 1,413 managerial wins ranks 20th all-time.

In his 13 years as a player, he led the National League in walks four times; scored 100 or more runs in a season three times; and led the league in putouts, assists, double plays, and fielding one season each, and twice in errors. Although he was not known as a power hitter, Huggins hit three triples on October 8, 1904 in an 8–1 win over the St. Louis Cardinals in the second game of a doubleheader.

On June 1, 1910, in a 10–5 win over the Philadelphia Phillies, Huggins became the first player in major league history to have no official at-bats in six plate appearances (four walks, a sacrifice fly, an infield sacrifice).

Miller Huggins' Playing Career Statistics

YEAR	TEAM	G	AB	R	H	2B	3B	HR	RBI	BB	SO	AVG	OBP	SLG
1904	Cincinnati	140	491	96	129	12	7	2	30	88	-	.263	.377	.328
1905	Cincinnati	149	564	117	154	11	8	1	38	103	-	.273	.392	.326
1906	Cincinnati	146	545	81	159	11	7	0	26	71	-	.292	.376	.338
1907	Cincinnati	156	561	64	139	12	4	1	31	83	-	.248	.346	.289
1908	Cincinnati	135	498	65	119	14	5	0	23	58	-	.239	.321	.287
1909	Cincinnati	57	159	18	34	3	1	0	6	28	-	.214	.335	.245
1910	St. Louis	151	547	101	145	15	6	1	36	116	46	.265	.399	.320
1911	St. Louis	138	509	106	133	19	2	1	24	96	52	.261	.385	.312
1912	St. Louis	120	431	82	131	15	4	0	29	87	31	.304	.422	.357
1913	St. Louis	121	382	74	109	12	0	0	27	92	49	.285	.432	.317
1914	St. Louis	148	509	85	134	17	4	1	24	105	63	.263	.396	.318
1915	St. Louis	107	353	57	85	5	2	2	24	74	68	.241	.377	.283
1916	St. Louis	18	9	2	3	0	0	0	0	2	3	.333	.500	.333
	TOTALS	1,586	5,558	948	1,474	146	50	9	318	1,003	312	.265	.382	.314

Miller Huggins' Managerial Record

YEAR	TEAM	LG	W	L	PCT
1913	St. Louis	NL	51	99	.340
1914	St. Louis	NL	81	72	.529
1915	St. Louis	NL	72	81	.471
1916	St. Louis	NL	60	93	.392
1917	St. Louis	NL	82	70	.539
1918	New York	AL	60	63	.488
1919	New York	AL	80	59	.576
1920	New York	AL	95	59	.617
1921	New York	AL	98	55	.641
1922	New York	AL	94	60	.610
1923	New York	AL	98	54	.645
1924	New York	AL	89	63	.586
1925	New York	AL	69	85	.448
1926	New York	AL	91	63	.591
1927	New York	AL	110	44	.714
1928	New York	AL	101	53	.656
1929	New York	AL	82	61	.573

YEAR	TEAM	LG	W	L	PCT
	TOTALS		1,413	1,134	.555

Sources: Baseball-Reference.com; National Baseball Hall of Fame and Museum

Hulbert, William Ambrose (born: October 23, 1832 in Burlington Flats, New York; died: April 10, 1882 in Chicago, Illinois); inducted into the National Baseball Hall of Fame and Museum in 1995 as a pioneer-executive by the Veterans Committee; founded the National League and served as its second president.

A successful businessman, Hulbert (part owner of the Chicago White Stockings of the National Association) and Albert Spalding founded the National League of Professional Baseball Clubs (commonly recognized as baseball's first major league) in 1876, and he served as its second president (after Morgan Bulkeley) from 1877 until his death in 1882.

As league president, he introduced the idea of regular schedules (and expelled the New York Mutuals and the Philadelphia Athletics from the league when the teams ignored the schedule); gave clubs exclusive territorial rights; banned alcoholic beverages from ballparks; hired umpires (who worked directly for the league) to instill public confidence in the integrity of the game; gave the umpires total authority; and imposed the first reserve rule to limit player salaries and to stop players moving from team to team in search of more money.

Source: National Baseball Hall of Fame and Museum

Hull, Brett Andrew (born: August 9, 1964 in Belleville, Ontario, Canada); inducted into the Hockey Hall of Fame as a player in 2009; Position: Right Wing; Uniform: #16, #17, #22; he and father Bobby are the only father and son combination in league history to each score 1,000 points.

Son of the legendary Bobby Hull and an eight-time National Hockey League All-Star (1989–1990, 1992–1994, 1996–1997, 2001), the 5'10", 200-pound Hull played in the NHL from 1986 to 2006 for the Calgary Flames (1986–1988), St. Louis Blues (1988–1998), Dallas Stars (1998–2001), Detroit Red Wings (2001–2004), and the Phoenix Coyotes (2005). After he scored his 1,000th point, Brett and Bobby became the only father and son combination in league history to each score 1,000 points.

Starting his hockey career in 1982 with the Penticton Knights (British Columbia Junior Hockey League), Hull went on to play for the University of Minnesota (Duluth) for two seasons before becoming the 117th overall selection (12th choice in the sixth round) of the Calgary Flames in the 1984 NHL Entry Draft, joining the team for the 1986 Stanley Cup playoffs.

Once signed by the Flames, he spent his early career bouncing between Calgary and its minor league affiliate, the Moncton Golden Flames, where he won the 1987 Dudley "Red" Garrett Award as the AHL's Rookie of the Year.

In 1988, the Flames traded Hull to St. Louis, and in 1990, he won the Lady Byng Memorial Trophy for his gentlemanly play and sportsmanship. In 1991, he won both the Lester B. Pearson Trophy (league's most outstanding player in the regular season as voted by the NHL Players Association) and the Hart Memorial Trophy (league Most Valuable Player).

After eleven seasons in St. Louis, Hull signed with the Dallas Stars in 1998 and helped the team win the Stanley Cup in 1999 over the Buffalo Sabres in six games, with him scoring the winning goal in triple overtime. In the 1999–2000 season, he scored his 600th goal, making him and his father, Bobby, the first and only father-son combination to do so. After three seasons in Dallas, he signed with the Detroit Red Wings and won his second Stanley Cup championship in 2002 (in five games over the Carolina Hurricanes). After three seasons in Detroit, Hull signed with the Phoenix Coyotes in 2004, sat out the lock-out year, and only played five games with the team in 2005 before retiring. After leaving the ice as a player, he was named the Executive Vice President of the Stars in 2009, after serving as a co-General Manager for the team.

In addition to his NHL on-ice accomplishments, Hull won a bronze medal at the 1986 World Championships (Moscow, Russia); a silver medal for the United States at the 1991 Canada Cup; was the top scorer (11 points) and helped the United States win a gold medal at the 1996 World Cup (Montreal, Quebec, Canada); and played in two Winter Olympics (failing to medal in 1998 in Nagano, Japan) and winning a silver medal in 2002 (held in Salt Lake City, Utah).

In 2006, his jersey numbers were retired by both the University of Minnesota, Duluth (#29 on February 3) and the St. Louis Blues (#16 on December 5). Hull was inducted into the U.S. Hockey Hall of Fame on October 29, 2008, again making him and his father, Bobby, the first father-son hockey duo to receive the honor.

In 1998, he was ranked number 64 on *The Hockey News*' list of the 100 Greatest Hockey Players.

Brett Hull's Career Statistics

SEASON	TEAM	LEAGUE	REGULAR SEASON GP	G	A	TP	PIM	+/-	PLAYOFFS GP	G	A	TP	PIM
1982–1983	Penticton Knights	BCJHL	50	48	56	104	27						
1983–1984	Penticton Knights	BCJHL	56	105	83	188	20						
1984–1985	U. of Minnesota, Duluth	WCHA	48	32	28	60	24						
1985–1986	U. of Minnesota, Duluth	WCHA	42	52	32	84	46						
1985–1986	United States	WEC-A	10	7	4	11	18						
1985–1986	Calgary Flames	NHL							2	0	0	0	0
1986–1987	Calgary Flames	NHL	5	1	0	1	0	-1	4	2	1	3	0
1986–1987	Moncton Golden Flames	AHL	67	50	42	92	16		3	2	2	4	2
1987–1988	Calgary Flames	NHL	52	26	24	50	12	+10					
1987–1988	St. Louis Blues	NHL	13	6	8	14	4	+4	10	7	2	9	4
1988–1989	St. Louis Blues	NHL	78	41	43	84	33	-17	10	5	5	10	6
1989–1990	St. Louis Blues	NHL	80	72	41	113	24	-1	12	13	8	21	17
1990–1991	St. Louis Blues	NHL	78	86	45	131	22	+23	13	11	8	19	4
1991–1992	United States	Can-Cup	8	2	7	9	0						
1991–1992	St. Louis Blues	NHL	73	70	39	109	48	-2	6	4	4	8	4
1992–1993	St. Louis Blues	NHL	80	54	47	101	41	-27	11	8	5	13	2
1993–1994	St. Louis Blues	NHL	81	57	40	97	38	-3	4	2	1	3	0
1994–1995	St. Louis Blues	NHL	48	29	21	50	10	+13	7	6	2	8	0
1995–1996	St. Louis Blues	NHL	70	43	40	83	30	+4	13	6	5	11	10
1996–1997	United States	W-Cup	7	7	4	11	4						
1996–1997	St. Louis Blues	NHL	77	42	40	82	10	-9	6	2	7	9	2
1997–1998	St. Louis Blues	NHL	66	27	45	72	26	-1	10	3	3	6	2
1997–1998	United States	Olympics	4	2	1	3	0						
1998–1999	Dallas Stars	NHL	60	32	26	58	30	+19	22	8	7	15	4
1999–2000	Dallas Stars	NHL	79	24	35	59	43	-21	23	11	13	24	4
2000–2001	Dallas Stars	NHL	79	39	40	79	18	+10	10	2	5	7	6
2001–2002	Detroit Red Wings	NHL	82	30	33	63	35	+18	23	10	8	18	4
2001–2002	United States	Olympics	6	3	5	8	6						
2002–2003	Detroit Red Wings	NHL	82	37	39	76	22	+11	4	0	1	1	0
2003–2004	Detroit Red Wings	NHL	81	25	43	68	12	-4	12	3	2	5	4
2004–2005	United States	W-Cup	2	0	0	0	2	0					
2005–2006	Phoenix Coyotes	NHL	5	0	1	1	0	-3					
	NHL TOTALS		1,269	741	650	1,391	458		202	103	87	190	73

Sources: Hockey Hall of Fame; Hockey-Reference.com

Hull, Robert Marvin "Bobby" (born: January 3, 1939 in Point Anne, Ontario, Canada); inducted into the Hockey Hall of Fame in 1983 as a player; Position: Left Wing; Uniform: #9; set the then single-season record of 58 goals (1968–1969); named top NHL player of the 1960s; won one Stanley Cup.

Hull played 23 professional hockey seasons from 1957 to 1980, including 16 years in the National Hockey League with the Chicago Black Hawks (1957–1972), Winnipeg Jets (1979–1980), and the Hartford Whalers (1979–1980). In his rookie NHL season (1957–1958), Hull scored 47 points (13 goals, 34 assists); scored 50 points in his second year; and in the 1959–1960 season, he led the league with 39 goals, while scoring 81 points. In 1960, while playing with Bill Hay and Murray Balfour (known as the "Million Dollar Line"), Hull won the Art Ross Trophy as the NHL's leading scorer and was named to the NHL's First All-Star Team.

He helped Chicago win the 1961 Stanley Cup in six games over the Detroit Red Wings, his only championship in the NHL. In 1965, he won both the Hart Memorial Trophy as the league's most valuable player and the Lady Byng Memorial Trophy for sportsmanship and gentlemanly conduct. In the 1965–1966 season, Hull set an NHL record with 54 goals (the first player ever to score more than 50 goals in a single season) and again won the Hart Memorial Trophy.

In 1968–1969, the 5'10", 208-pound Hull scored a single-season record 58 goals, a mark that would fall two seasons later when Phil Esposito of the Boston Bruins scored 76 goals. In January 1970, Hull was named by the Associated Press as the top NHL player of the 1960s.

In the February 1972 World Hockey Association General Player Draft, the league's Winnipeg Jets selected Hull and signed him to the game's first-ever $1 million contract, which immediately gave the league legitimacy. When Hull left the NHL, his 604 goals ranked him second in league history to Gordie Howe.

During the 1974–1975 WHA season, he scored 77 regular-season goals for the Jets to set a new record for a professional league. Hull led Winnipeg to win three WHA Avco Cups (1976, 1978–1979), and in 1973 and 1975, he was named the league's most valuable player. When the WHA merged with the NHL in 1979, he played 18 games before being traded to the NHL's Hartford Whalers, where he played nine games before retiring.

In 1978, he was made an Officer of the Order of Canada; his number nine jersey has been retired by both the Black Hawks and the Jets (and is still honored by the Jets' successor team, the Phoenix Coyotes); and in 1998, he was ranked number eight on *The Hockey News*' list of the 100 Greatest Hockey Players, the highest-ranking left winger.

Hull won the Lester Patrick Trophy in 1969 for his contribution to hockey in the United States; won the Art Ross Trophy three times as the league's regular-season scoring leader (1960, 1962, 1966); and was named the First All-Star Team Left Wing 10 times (1960, 1962, 1964–1970, 1972) and Second All-Star Team Left Wing twice (1963, 1971).

Bobby Hull's Career Statistics

			REGULAR SEASON					PLAYOFFS				
SEASON	**TEAM**	**LEAGUE**	**GP**	**G**	**A**	**TP**	**PIM**	**GP**	**G**	**A**	**TP**	**PIM**
1954–1955	Woodstock Athletics	OHA-B										
1954–1955	Galt Black Hawks	OHA-Jr.	6	0	0	0	0					
1955–1956	St. Catharines Teepees	OHA-Jr.	48	11	7	18	79	6	0	2	2	9
1956–1957	St. Catharines Teepees	OHA-Jr.	52	33	28	61	95	13	8	8	16	24
1957–1958	Chicago Black Hawks	NHL	70	13	34	47	62					
1958–1959	Chicago Black Hawks	NHL	70	18	32	50	50	6	1	1	2	2
1959–1960	Chicago Black Hawks	NHL	70	39	42	81	68	3	1	0	1	2
1960–1961	Chicago Black Hawks	NHL	67	31	25	56	43	12	4	10	14	4
1961–1962	Chicago Black Hawks	NHL	70	50	34	84	35	12	8	6	14	12
1962–1963	Chicago Black Hawks	NHL	65	31	31	62	27	5	8	2	10	4
1963–1964	Chicago Black Hawks	NHL	70	43	44	87	50	7	2	5	7	2
1964–1965	Chicago Black Hawks	NHL	61	39	32	71	32	14	10	7	17	27
1965–1966	Chicago Black Hawks	NHL	65	54	43	97	70	6	2	2	4	10
1966–1967	Chicago Black Hawks	NHL	66	52	28	80	52	6	4	2	6	0
1967–1968	Chicago Black Hawks	NHL	71	44	31	75	39	11	4	6	10	15
1968–1969	Chicago Black Hawks	NHL	74	58	49	107	48					
1969–1970	Chicago Black Hawks	NHL	61	38	29	67	8	8	3	8	11	2
1970–1971	Chicago Black Hawks	NHL	78	44	52	96	32	18	11	14	25	16
1971–1972	Chicago Black Hawks	NHL	78	50	43	93	24	8	4	4	8	6
1972–1973	Winnipeg Jets	WHA	63	51	52	103	37	14	9	16	25	16
1973–1974	Winnipeg Jets	WHA	75	53	42	95	38	4	1	1	2	4
1974–1975	Canada	Summit-74	8	7	2	9	0					
1974–1975	Winnipeg Jets	WHA	78	77	65	142	41					
1975–1976	Winnipeg Jets	WHA	80	53	70	123	30	13	12	8	20	4
1976–1977	Canada	Can-Cup	7	5	3	8	2					
1976–1977	Winnipeg Jets	WHA	34	21	32	53	14	20	13	9	22	2
1977–1978	Winnipeg Jets	WHA	77	46	71	117	23	9	8	3	11	12
1978–1979	Winnipeg Jets	WHA	4	2	3	5	0					
1979–1980	Winnipeg Jets	NHL	18	4	6	10	0					
1979–1980	Hartford Whalers	NHL	9	2	5	7	0	3	0	0	0	0
1981–1982	New York Rangers	DN-Cup	4	1	1	2	0					
	NHL TOTALS		1,063	610	560	1,170	640	119	62	67	129	102

Sources: Hockey Hall of Fame; Hockey-Reference.com

Hume, Frederick J. "Fred" (born: May 2, 1892 in New Westminster, British Columbia, Canada; died: February 17, 1967); inducted into the Hockey Hall of Fame in 1962 as a builder; won the Mann Cup in lacrosse; president of the New

Westminster Royals soccer team, winners of the 1928 Canadian Championships; helped found the Western Hockey League.

Hume played an integral role in the growth of amateur and professional hockey in the Pacific Northwest. Before becoming involved with hockey, he was a politician; elected alderman in New Westminster; and later served as the town's mayor (1932–1941).

Outside the political arena, Hume formed the New Westminster Salmonbelllies lacrosse team in the 1930s, and in 1937, he led the team to the Mann Cup, becoming the first British Columbia squad to win the championship. He was also the co-founder and president of the New Westminster Royals soccer team (1926 through the early 1930s), winners of the 1928 Canadian Championship.

Hume eventually moved to nearby Vancouver and served as the city's mayor from 1951 to 1958; helped found the Western Hockey League (1952–1974); and was the owner of the New Westminster Royals (1952–1959) hockey club, which eventually folded more than eight years later when the franchise was unable to sustain consistent profitability. He also owned and operated the New Westminster Royals hockey team (Pacific Coast League, 1954–1961); the Vancouver Canucks (Western Hockey League, 1962–1966); and played a major role in convincing the National Hockey League to expand into Vancouver.

Hume has been inducted into both the Canadian Lacrosse and the Canadian Hockey halls of fame.

Source: Hockey Hall of Fame

Hunt, Lamar (born: August 2, 1932 in El Dorado, Arkansas; died: December 13, 2006 in Dallas, Texas); inducted into the Pro Football Hall of Fame in 1972 as a founder-owner; first AFL person to be inducted into the Pro Football Hall of Fame; inducted into the National Soccer Hall of Fame and Museum in 1982 as a builder; helped form the North American Soccer League.

After he was unable to secure a National Football League franchise, Hunt helped form the American Football League in 1959 and founded the Dallas Texans in 1960, hiring future hall-of-famer Hank Stram as the team's first head coach. The team won the 1962 AFL Championship in 1962 and would go on to win two more titles in the league's 10-year existence.

Realizing that he could not compete with the cross-town Dallas Cowboys of the NFL, Hunt moved the team to Kansas City in 1963 and renamed the franchise the Chiefs. When the AFL became a viable competitor to the NFL, he played a major role in the NFL-AFL merger in 1966.

After being involved with professional football for only 13 years, Hunt was the first AFL figure to be inducted into the Pro Football Hall of Fame. His Chiefs participated in the very first Super Bowl (a name he created for the title event) in 1967, a 35–10 loss to Vince Lombardi's Green Bay Packers. Three years after losing the inaugural Super Bowl, the team won the city's first major sports championship by beating the heavily-favored Minnesota Vikings 23–7 in Super Bowl IV (January 11, 1970), the last Super Bowl played when the AFL was a separate league.

The Lamar Hunt Trophy, named in his honor, is presented annually to the champion of the NFL's American Football Conference.

Outside of his football interests, Hunt was also involved in the development of both the North American Soccer League and World Championship Tennis. He has been inducted into the Texas Business Hall of Fame (1977), National Soccer Hall of Fame and Museum (1982), Texas Sports Hall of Fame (1984), International Tennis Hall of Fame (1993), Missouri Sports Hall of Fame (1995), and the Kansas City Business Hall of Fame (2004).

Soccer America magazine named Hunt one of its "25 Most Influential People" in 1999; the U.S. Open Cup was renamed the "Lamar Hunt U.S. Open Cup" in 1999; he received the U.S. Soccer Federation Hall of Fame Medal of Honor in 1990; and in 2005, the U.S. Soccer Foundation honored Hunt with its Lifetime Achievement Award.

His team in the North American Soccer League, the Dallas Tornado, debuted in 1967 and won the league championship in 1971.

Hunt was one of the original founding investors of Major League Soccer, which debuted in 1996 with him owning league teams the Columbus Crew and the Kansas City Wizards. He eventually purchased the Dallas Burn (now known as FC Dallas). As of this writing, the Hunt family still owns the Crew and FC Dallas.

He was also one of the founding investors in the six-time world champion Chicago Bulls of the National Basketball Association. During his career, Hunt had 13 championship rings from five different professional sports organizations (AFL/NFL, MLS, NBA, NASL, and the U.S. Soccer "Open Cup").

Hunt was the son of oil tycoon Haroldson Lafayette (H.L.) Hunt and the younger brother of Nelson Bunker Hunt. Raised in Dallas, he graduated from The Hill School (Pottstown, Pennsylvania) in 1950 and Southern Methodist University (Dallas, Texas) in 1956, with a B.S. degree in geology.

Sources: National Soccer Hall of Fame and Museum; Pro Football Hall of Fame

Hunter, James Augustus "Catfish" (born: April 8, 1946 in Hertford, North Carolina; died: September 9, 1999 in Hertford, North Carolina); inducted into the National Baseball Hall of Fame and Museum in 1987 as a player; Position: Pitcher; Bats: Right; Throws: Right; Uniform: #27; pitched a perfect game in 1968; won the American League Cy Young Award in 1974; won five World Series championships.

Hunter pitched a 4–0 perfect game on May 8, 1968 against the Minnesota Twins; won 21 or more games five seasons in a row; and won the 1974 American League Cy Young Award. Although consistent arm trouble ended his career at the relatively young age of 33, he was able to win 224 games and five World Series rings. He died in 1999 at age 53 of amyotrophic lateral sclerosis, the same disease that killed Lou Gehrig.

Making his major league debut on May 13, 1965, the 6', 195-pound Hunter played 15 seasons with the Kansas City Athletics (1965–1967), Oakland Athletics (1968–1974), and New York Yankees (1975–1979). He played in six World Series (winning five [1972–1974, 1977–1978] and losing once in 1976); was an eight-time All–Star (1966–1967, 1970, 1972–1976); and the Oakland Athletics retired his uniform number 27.

Hunter graduated from Perquimans County High School (Hertford, North Carolina), where he played baseball; threw to a record of 26–2; and had five no-hitters. After a hunting accident sidelined him for the 1964 season, he bypassed college, did not play in the minor leagues, and signed with the Athletics in 1965.

After winning his third straight World Series championship, Hunter signed with the Yankees for $3.75 million dollars (the largest player contract ever up to that time) and helped the team reach three World Series, winning two of them.

Unable to decide which team he wanted to represent in the hall of fame, his plaque is one of the few with no insignia on the cap.

Hunter's .750 winning percentage (21–7) in 1972 and .808 (21–5) in 1973 led the league both seasons. As of this writing, he still holds Oakland's all-time record for wins (161), starts (340), innings (2,456), shutouts (31), and strikeouts (1,520).

On September 27, 1967, Hunter won the last game the Athletics played before moving to Oakland, a 4–0 win in the second game of a doubleheader against the Chicago White Sox. On May 8, 1968, he threw a perfect game against the Twins, winning 4–0, the first American League regular-season perfect game in 46 years.

Catfish Hunter's Career Statistics

YEAR	TEAM	LG	W	L	PCT	G	SH	IP	H	R	ER	SO	BB	ERA
1965	Kansas City	AL	8	8	.500	32	2	133	124	68	63	82	46	4.26
1966	Kansas City	AL	9	11	.450	30	0	177	158	87	79	103	64	4.02
1967	Kansas City	AL	13	17	.433	35	5	260	209	91	81	196	84	2.80
1968	Oakland	AL	13	13	.500	36	2	234	210	99	87	172	69	3.35
1969	Oakland	AL	12	15	.444	38	3	247	210	99	92	150	85	3.35
1970	Oakland	AL	18	14	.563	40	1	262	253	124	111	178	74	3.81
1971	Oakland	AL	21	11	.656	37	4	274	225	103	90	181	80	2.96
1972	Oakland	AL	21	7	.750	38	5	295	200	74	67	191	70	2.04
1973	Oakland	AL	21	5	.808	36	3	256	222	105	95	124	69	3.34
1974	Oakland	AL	25	12	.676	41	6	318	268	97	88	143	46	2.49
1975	New York	AL	23	14	.622	39	7	328	248	107	94	177	83	2.58
1976	New York	AL	17	15	.531	36	2	299	268	126	117	173	68	3.52
1977	New York	AL	9	9	.500	22	1	143	137	83	75	52	47	4.72
1978	New York	AL	12	6	.667	21	1	118	98	49	47	56	35	3.58
1979	New York	AL	2	9	.182	19	0	105	128	68	62	34	34	5.31
	TOTALS		224	166	.574	500	42	3,449	2,958	1,380	1,248	2,012	954	3.26

Sources: Baseball-Reference.com; National Baseball Hall of Fame and Museum

Hurley, Sr., Robert "Bob" (born: Jersey City, New Jersey in 1942); inducted into the Naismith Memorial Basketball Hall of Fame in 2010 as a coach; won 25 Parochial High School State Championships (23 as a head coach, two as an assistant coach).

After playing college basketball at St. Peter's College (Jersey City, New Jersey), Hurley became the head coach at St. Anthony's High School (Jersey City) in 1972. Since then, he has led the team to more than 900 wins and 25 State Parochial Championships. He won three *USA Today* National Championships (1989, 1996, 2008); was twice named National Coach of the Year by *USA Today* (1989, 1996); was elected to the New Jersey Sports Hall of Fame in 2000; and is only the third person elected to the Naismith Memorial Basketball Hall of Fame exclusively for his service to high school basketball (along with Morgan Wootten and Bertha Teague).

He is the father of Bobby Hurley (a former All-American point guard at Duke who won two NCAA titles) and Dan Hurley (who was hired in April 2010 to coach Wagner College after coaching at Newark, New Jersey's Saint Benedict's Preparatory School). His undefeated 1989 team (which included his son, Bobby) was ranked first in the nation by *USA Today*, three players from that team (Hurley, Terry Dehere, and Rodrick Rhodes) were first-round draft picks into the NBA; the team won New Jersey's first Tournament of Champions; amassed 50 straight victories in a two-year span; and is considered one of the best teams in New Jersey high school basketball history.

Hurley's 2007–2008 team was also undefeated; ranked number one in the United States by *USA Today*; had six seniors who received NCAA Division I scholarships; won his 10th Tournament of Champions; and won the school's 25th state championship, more than any other school in U.S. history.

Source: Naismith Memorial Basketball Hall of Fame

Hutson, Donald Montgomery "Don" (born: January 31, 1913 in Pine Bluff, Arkansas; died: June 26, 1997 in Rancho Mirage, California); inducted into the Pro Football Hall of Fame in 1963 as a player; Position: End; Uniform: #14; a charter member of the hall of fame; first receiver to catch more than 50 passes in a season (1941) and to have more than 1,000 receiving yards in a season (1942); won back-to-back Most Valuable Player awards; holds the NFL record for most points scored in a quarter (29); his jersey was the first-ever retired by the Packers.

Hutson ended his National Football League career with 99 touchdown receptions, a record that stood for more than four decades. Legendary coach Bear Bryant always described himself as the "other end" on the University of Alabama (Tuscaloosa) football team that had both Bryant and Hutson. That Crimson Tide team won the Rose Bowl in 1935 by beating Stanford University 29–13, with Hutson scoring two touchdowns.

After attending college from 1932 to 1934 (and being selected an All-American his last year), the 6'1", 183-pound Hutson played his entire 11-year (116 games) NFL career (1935–1945) with the Green Bay Packers. He led the NFL in receiving eight times; was the league's top scorer five straight seasons (1941–1945); selected All-NFL nine times; named NFL Most Valuable Player in back-to-back seasons (1941–1942); named the NFL's all-time end in 1969; won three NFL titles (1936, 1939, 1944); and still holds the record for the highest career average touchdowns per game (0.85) for a wide receiver.

Like most players in the early game, Hutson was a 60-minute player who spent most of his defensive career as a safety, and intercepted 30 passes in his last six seasons. In the first quarter of an October 7, 1945 game against the Detroit Lions in Milwaukee, he scored 29 points in 13 minutes (caught four touchdown passes and kicked five points after touchdown), still an NFL record for most points in a quarter, in a Packers 57–21 win.

He was the first receiver to catch more than 50 passes in a season (1941) and the first to collect more than 1,000 receiving yards in a season (1942).

His number 14 jersey was the first one retired by the Packers (1951); he was inducted into the College Football Hall of Fame in 1951; into the Green Bay Packers Hall of Fame in 1972; and in 1999, he was ranked number six on *The Sporting News*' list of the 100 Greatest Football Players, the highest-ranking Packer and the highest-ranking pre-World War II player. Hutson was named to the NFL 1930s All-Decade Team and to the NFL 75th Anniversary All-Time Team.

Don Hutson's Career Statistics

			RECEIVING				DEFENSE			
YEAR	**TEAM**	**G**	**NO**	**YDS**	**AVG**	**TD**	**INT**	**YDS**	**AVG**	**TD**
1935	Green Bay	9	18	420	23.3	6	0	0	0.0	0
1936	Green Bay	12	34	536	15.8	8	0	0	0.0	0
1937	Green Bay	11	41	552	13.5	7	0	0	0.0	0
1938	Green Bay	10	32	548	17.1	9	0	0	0.0	0
1939	Green Bay	11	34	846	24.9	6	0	0	0.0	0
1940	Green Bay	11	45	664	14.8	7	6	24	4.0	0
1941	Green Bay	11	58	738	12.7	10	1	32	32.0	0
1942	Green Bay	11	74	1,211	16.4	17	7	71	10.1	0
1943	Green Bay	10	47	776	16.5	11	8	197	24.6	1
1944	Green Bay	10	58	866	14.9	9	4	50	12.5	0
1945	Green Bay	10	47	834	17.7	9	4	15	3.8	0
	TOTALS	116	488	7,991	16.4	99	30	389	13	1

Source: Pro Football Hall of Fame

Hutton, John Bower "Bouse" (born: October 24, 1877 in Ottawa, Ontario, Canada; died: October 27, 1962); inducted into the Hockey Hall of Fame in 1962 as a player; Position: Goalie; won the Stanley Cup and successfully defended it three times.

Hutton was a champion lacrosse goaltender with the Ottawa Capitals; won the first Minto Cup championship (amateur junior lacrosse title in Canada); played fullback for the Canadian Football League's Ottawa Rough Riders; and played six pre-National Hockey League seasons from 1898 to 1904.

He began his hockey career with the Ottawa Hockey Club in 1898–1899, and led the team to the Stanley Cup championship in 1903 (when the team was known as the Ottawa Silver Seven). He was the squad's goalie as Ottawa successfully defended Cup challenges from the Winnipeg Rowing Club in January 1904, the Toronto Marlboros in February 1904, and the Brandon Wheat Kings in March 1904.

John Hutton's Career Statistics

			REGULAR SEASON						PLAYOFFS					
SEASON	TEAM	LEAGUE	GP	W	L	T	SO	AVG	GP	W	L	T	SO	AVG
1898–1899	Ottawa Hockey Club	CAHL	2				0	5.50						
1899–1900	Ottawa Hockey Club	CAHL	7	4	3	0	0	2.70						
1900–1901	Ottawa Hockey Club	CAHL	7	7	0	1	0	2.50						
1901–1902	Ottawa Hockey Club	CAHL	8	5	3	0	2	1.70						
1902–1903	Ottawa Silver Seven	CAHL	8	6	2	0	0	3.80	2	1	0	1	1	0.50
1902–1903	Ottawa Silver Seven	St-Cup							2	2	0	0	0	2.00
1903–1904	Ottawa Silver Seven	CAHL	4	4	0	0	0	3.82						
1903–1904	Ottawa Silver Seven	St-Cup							8	6	1	1	1	2.90
1908–1909	Ottawa Senators	FHL	5	3	2	0	1	5.20						

Sources: Hockey Hall of Fame; Hockey-Reference.com

Hyatt, Charles D. "Chuck" (born: February 28, 1908 in Syracuse, New York; died: May 8, 1978); inducted into the Naismith Memorial Basketball Hall of Fame in 1959 as a player; Position: Forward; won two national college championships; selected 1930 Helms Foundation Player of the Year; a charter member of the basketball hall of fame.

The 5'11", 160-pound Hyatt was an All-State selection in 1925 while attending Uniontown (Pennsylvania) High School (1922–1926), and earned All-American status at the National High School Tournament in Chicago (1926). After high school, he attended the University of Pittsburgh (Pennsylvania, 1926–1930), where he was a three-year letter winner; a three-time All-American (1928–1930); led Pittsburgh to two national championships (1928, 1930); led the nation in scoring (1930, 12.6 points per game); and was named the Helms Foundation Player of the Year in 1930.

Hyatt played in the Amateur Athletic Union for the Denver Ambrose Legion (1943–1944) and the Phillips 66ers, and was a nine-time AAU All-American. After leaving the game as a player, he coached the amateur Universal Pictures (1934–1935, 1943–1944) and the Phillips 66ers (1940–1942).

He joined the professional coaching ranks with the Pittsburgh Raiders of the Independent League (1944–1945), and later coached the Kansas City Blues of the Professional Basketball League of America (1947). Hyatt was a charter member of the basketball hall of fame.

Source: Naismith Memorial Basketball Hall of Fame

Hyland, Harold M. "Harry" (born: January 2, 1889 in Montreal, Quebec, Canada; died: August 8, 1969); inducted into the Hockey Hall of Fame in 1962 as a player; Position: Forward; won the 1910 Stanley Cup championship.

Hyland turned professional with the Montreal Shamrocks (Eastern Canada Hockey Association) in the 1908–1909 season, and scored two goals in his professional debut against Quebec. He went on to play 10 professional hockey seasons from 1908 to 1918, including one year in the National Hockey League (1917–1918) with the Montreal Wanderers and Ottawa Senators.

The 5'6", 156-pound Hyland joined the Montreal Wanderers (National Hockey Association) for the 1909–1910 season and helped the team win the Stanley Cup title while he was also a member of the Minto Cup champion Montreal Shamrocks lacrosse team.

In 1911–1912, he joined the New Westminster Royals (Pacific Coast Hockey Association); named to the PCHA First All-Star Team; and in 1912, he again played on another Minto Cup championship lacrosse team with the New Westminster Salmonbellies.

Hyland returned to the Wanderers the following season (1912–1913) and scored eight goals in a single game (January 27, 1913) in a 10–6 Montreal win over the Quebec Bulldogs. He remained with the Wanderers until the team folded in January 1918 when a fire destroyed its arena (Westmount Arena).

After leaving the game as a player, he coached the McGill University (Montreal, Quebec, Canada) hockey team, before coaching Columbus in the Senior Group of the Quebec Amateur Hockey Association.

1912 to 1916, while still a professional player, Hyland coached five Loyola University (Montreal, Quebec, Canada) teams, two of which won the Junior championship of Canada. He was inducted into the Loyola Sports Hall of Fame in 1969.

Harry Hyland's Career Statistics

			REGULAR SEASON					PLAYOFFS				
SEASON	**TEAM**	**LEAGUE**	**GP**	**G**	**A**	**TP**	**PIM**	**GP**	**G**	**A**	**TP**	**PIM**
1907–1908	Montreal Shamrocks	CAIHL										
1908–1909	Montreal Shamrocks	ECHA	11	19	0	19	36					
1909–1910	Montreal Wanderers	NHA	1	4	0	4	0					
1909–1910	Montreal Wanderers	NHA	11	20	0	20	23					
1909–1910	Montreal Wanderers	St-Cup						1	3	0	3	3
1910–1911	Montreal Wanderers	NHA	15	14	0	14	43					
1911–1912	New Westminster Royals	PCHA	15	26	0	26	44					
1911–1912	PCHA All-Stars	Exhib.	3	6	0	6	8					
1912–1913	Montreal Wanderers	NHA	20	27	0	27	38					
1913–1914	Montreal Wanderers	NHA	18	30	12	42	18					
1914–1915	Montreal Wanderers	NHA	19	23	6	29	49	2	0	0	0	26
1915–1916	Montreal Wanderers	NHA	20	14	0	14	69					
1916–1917	Montreal Wanderers	NHA	13	12	2	14	21					
1916–1917	Montreal St. Ann's	MCHL		3	1	4						
1917–1918	Montreal Wanderers	NHL	4	6	1	7	6					
1917–1918	Ottawa Senators	NHL	13	8	1	9	59					
1918–1919	McGill Redmen	MCHL										
	NHL TOTALS		17	14	2	16	65					

Sources: Hockey Hall of Fame; Hockey-Reference.com

Hynes, John (born: 1920 in Lochgelly, Scotland); inducted into the National Soccer Hall of Fame and Museum in 1977 as a player; Position: Outside Right; International Caps (1949): 4; International Goals: 0; 1956 American Soccer League Most Valuable Player; won two ASL titles.

When Hynes arrived in the United States at age 13, he enrolled in Curtis High School (Staten Island, New York), where he played soccer for four years and was the team's captain for two seasons. He played for Swedish F.C. (1938–1941) in the National League and three seasons, before signing with the New York Americans (a team he played for intermittently from 1941 to 1952) of the American Soccer League.

In 1943, he joined the military during World War II; was injured in the Battle of the Bulge (the Ardennes, Belgium, Luxembourg, and Germany); returned to the United States; and eventually played on various ASL All-Star teams against foreign visiting squads.

At the end of the 1952 ASL season, Hynes ended his 12-year association with the New York Americans and signed with New York Brookhattan (1952–1954), before playing for Brooklyn Hakoah (1954–1957). In 1956, he was voted the ASL Most Valuable Player and led the team to the 1957 ASL championship, before returning to Brookhattan (1957–1959).

In 1960, he played for the expansion team Colombo (Staten Island, New York; also of the ASL) and won another championship in the squad's first year in the league. He retired after the season and refereed high school and college games.

In 1997, Hynes was inducted into the Eastern New York Youth Soccer Association Hall of Fame.

Source: National Soccer Hall of Fame and Museum

Chapter 9
Iba to Ivan

Iba, Henry Payne "Hank" (born: August 6, 1904 in Easton, Missouri; died: January 15, 1993 in Stillwater, Oklahoma); inducted into the Naismith Memorial Basketball Hall of Fame in 1969 as a coach; first coach to win consecutive NCAA titles (1945–1946); as of this writing, he is the only person in history to coach three U.S. Olympic teams.

After playing basketball for four years at Easton (Missouri) High School (graduating in 1923), Iba attended Westminster College of Missouri (Fulton, 1923–1927) and Maryville Teachers College (now known as Northwest Missouri State University, graduating in 1929). He played basketball at Westminster and was selected All-Conference twice (1926–1927).

After college, Iba played amateur basketball for Sterling Milk (Oklahoma City, Oklahoma; 1928–1929) and Hillyard Shine Alls (1928–1929); started his coaching career at Classen High School (Oklahoma City, Oklahoma; 1927–1929); and led the team to an overall 51–5 record and a state championship in 1929.

He joined the college coaching ranks at his alma mater (Maryville, 1929–1933), before moving on to the University of Colorado (Boulder, 1933–1934), and Oklahoma A&M (renamed Oklahoma State University in 1957, Stillwater, 1934–1970), where he served as coach and athletic director. He coached Maryville to a 101–14 (.878) overall record, and was the 1932 National Amateur Athletic Union runner-up, losing the championship 15–14 to Henry Clothiers (Wichita, Kansas).

Iba coached the University of Colorado to an 11–8 (.579) record before coaching 36 years at Oklahoma A&M, compiling a 655–316 (.675) record. He finished his college coaching career with an overall 767–338 (.694) record, and during his tenure as athletic director, he led OSU to 19 national championships in five sports (basketball, wrestling, baseball, golf, cross country).

He was the first coach to win consecutive National Collegiate Athletic Association titles (1945–1946); named National Coach of the Year twice (1945–1946); NCAA championship runner-up in 1949; won or shared the Missouri Valley Conference title 14 times; and won the Big 8 Championship in 1965.

Iba served as president of the National Association of Basketball Coaches; won the NABC Metropolitan Award in 1947; retired as the second all-time winningest coach in NCAA history; and has been inducted into the Missouri, Oklahoma, Oklahoma Sports, Helms Foundation, Westminster Alumni, National College Basketball (2007), and the FIBA (2007) halls of fame.

As of this writing, he is the only coach in U.S. history to win two Olympic gold medals (1964 in Tokyo, 1968 in Mexico City); coached the 1972 U.S. Olympic team that lost to the Soviet Union in the infamously controversial ending (winning a silver medal); and is only person in history to coach three U.S. Olympic teams.

The Henry P. Iba Award is presented annually to the National Coach of the Year by the United States Basketball Writers Association.

Source: Naismith Memorial Basketball Hall of Fame

Iglehart, Alfredda (born: Baltimore, Maryland; died: January 3, 1960 in Govens, Maryland); inducted into the National Soccer Hall of Fame and Museum in 1951 as a builder; first woman inducted into the soccer hall of fame.

Iglehart graduated from Maryland State Normal School (Towson) and did her graduate work in Physical Education at Cornell University (Ithaca, New York). During a teaching career that lasted more than 30 years, she taught the fundamentals of soccer to more than 1,200 boys, including future hall of famer Millard Lang. From 1923 to 1934, she was goalkeeper for the Baltimore Women's Field Hockey team and became the first woman inducted into the National Soccer Hall of Fame and Museum.

Source: National Soccer Hall of Fame and Museum

Ilitch, Michael "Mike" (born: July 20, 1929 in Detroit, Michigan); inducted into the Hockey Hall of Fame in 2003 as a builder; opened the first Little Caesars pizza restaurant; won four Stanley Cup championships.

As a shortstop, Ilitch played in the minor league system of Major League Baseball's Detroit Tigers, but was never able to reach the major leagues. Abandoning his playing career, he entered the restaurant business and on May 9, 1959 opened the first "Little Caesars" pizza restaurant in Garden City, Michigan (south of Detroit), which has since grown to about 2,000 outlets.

Having succeeded in the business world, he purchased the National Hockey League's Detroit Red Wings in 1982, and 10 years later, he bought the Detroit Tigers from Tom Monaghan (founder of Domino's Pizza). Under his leadership, as of this writing, the Red Wings have won four Stanley Cup championships (1997–1998, 2002, 2008) and the Tigers won the American League pennant in 2006, before losing to the St. Louis Cardinals in the World Series.

After graduating from Cooley High School (Detroit, Michigan), Ilitch served in the U.S. Marine Corps for four years before returning home to a three-year minor league career with the Tigers.

In 2006, Ilitch was listed at number 242 on *Forbes* magazine's annual "400 Richest Americans" list, and officially joined the "billionaires club."

He was one of the early team owners in the Arena Football League with the Detroit Drive in 1988, which played in every ArenaBowl of its six-year existence, winning four championships (1988–1990, 1992) and losing twice. After Ilitch bought the Tigers in 1993, he sold the Drive, which then moved to Worcester, Massachusetts and became known as the Massachusetts Marauders.

He was inducted into the United States Hockey Hall of Fame in 2004. In Stanley Cup history, only eight women have had their names engraved on the trophy. Ilitch's wife, Marian, and their three daughters have each had their names engraved on the Cup three times.

His first experience as a sports team owner came in 1977 with the Detroit Caesars of the American Professional Slow Pitch Softball League, which won consecutive World Series titles (1977–1978) before disbanding after the 1979 season.

Source: Hockey Hall of Fame

Imlach, George "Punch" (born: March 15, 1918 in Toronto, Ontario, Canada; died: December 1, 1987); inducted into the Hockey Hall of Fame in 1984 as a builder; won four Stanley Cup titles as a coach.

Imlach played hockey as a boy, before focusing on being a coach. He attended Riverdale Collegiate Institute (Toronto, Ontario, Canada) and played junior hockey in the Ontario Hockey Association.

He enlisted in the army during World War II and began his coaching career with a military team in Cornwall, Ontario. After leaving the military, he took a job in the accounting department of Anglo-Canadian Pulp and Paper in Quebec City (Quebec, Canada) and played for (and later coached), the company-owned team, the Quebec Aces of the Quebec Senior Hockey League (1945–1949). He would stay with the Aces for 11 seasons, first as a coach and then as general manager, vice-president, and part-owner.

After the 1956–1957 season, Imlach moved to professional hockey with the National Hockey League's Boston Bruins as general manager of the team's Springfield Indians farm club (American Hockey League). The next season (1958–1959), he was hired as one of two assistant general managers, along with King Clancy, by the NHL's Toronto Maple Leafs. When Imlach became the team's general manager in November 1958, he fired coach Billy Reay; took over as the squad's coach; and in 1962, he led the Leafs to the first of three consecutive Stanley Cup championships. He won his fourth title in 1967 and was fired in 1969 after losing to the Boston Bruins in the playoffs.

In spite of his undeniable on-ice and management success, he was known to have problems with players. He would not negotiate players' contracts until training camp and tried to ban those who joined the NHL Players' Association.

He was hired by the Buffalo Sabres in 1970 as coach and general manager; took the team into the finals in just five years; and resigned as coach after having a heart attack during the 1971–1972 season. After being fired in 1979, Imlach was rehired by the Leafs as the team's coach, but could not duplicate his earlier success. His second heart attack in 1981 forced Imlach to retire from the game.

He was inducted into The Greater Buffalo Sports Hall of Fame in 1998.

Punch Imlach's Playing Statistics

		REGULAR SEASON	PLAYOFFS

SEASON	TEAM	LEAGUE	GP	G	A	TP	PIM	GP	G	A	TP	PIM
1935–1936	Toronto Young Rangers	OHA-Jr.	8	0	0	0	2	2	0	0	0	0
1936–1937	Toronto Young Rangers	OHA-Jr.	12	15	3	18	6	3	2	3	5	7
1937–1938	Toronto Young Rangers	OHA-Jr.	11	4	4	8	4	3	6	0	6	0
1938–1939	Toronto Goodyears	OHA-Sr.	17	14	13	27	8	1	2	0	2	0
1938–1939	Toronto Goodyears	Al-Cup	1	0	0	0	0					
1939–1940	Toronto Goodyears	OHA-Sr.	24	25	23	48	23	7	6	6	12	6
1939–1940	Toronto Goodyears	Al-Cup	4	1	4	5	2					
1940–1941	Toronto Marlboros	OHA-Sr.	21	5	9	14	19	11	2	2	4	2
1940–1941	Toronto Marlboros	Al-Cup	7	4	2	6	0					
1940–1941	Toronto RCAF	TMHL	3	2	1	3	0	5	3	1	4	2
1940–1941	Toronto Donnell-Mudge	TMHL						4	5	3	8	2
1941–1942	Cornwall Flyers	QSHL	37	25	17	42	11	5	4	1	5	0
1942–1943	Cornwall Army	QSHL	34	24	23	47	6	6	5	0	5	2
1945–1946	Quebec Aces	QSHL	40	19	21	40	14	6	2	2	4	2
1946–1947	Quebec Aces	QSHL	33	10	28	38	20	1	0	0	0	0
1947–1948	Quebec Aces	QSHL	42	21	20	41	44	10	2	6	8	8
1948–1949	Quebec Aces	QSHL	50	26	26	52	32	3	3	1	4	0

Punch Imlach's Coaching Record

SEASON	TEAM	W	L	T	PCT
1958–1959	Toronto	22	20	8	.520
1959–1960	Toronto	35	26	9	.564
1960–1961	Toronto	39	19	12	.643
1961–1962	Toronto	37	22	11	.607
1962–1963	Toronto	35	23	12	.586
1963–1964	Toronto	33	25	12	.557
1964–1965	Toronto	30	26	14	.529
1965–1966	Toronto	34	25	11	.564
1966–1967	Toronto	32	27	11	.536
1967–1968	Toronto	33	31	10	.514
1968–1969	Toronto	35	26	15	.559
1970–1971	Buffalo	24	39	15	.404
1971–1972	Buffalo	8	23	10	.317
1979–1980	Toronto	5	5	0	.500
	TOTALS	402	337	150	.537

Sources: Hockey Hall of Fame; Hockey-Reference.com

Ion, Fred J. "Mickey" (born: February 25, 1886 in Paris, Ontario, Canada; died: October 26, 1964); inducted into the Hockey Hall of Fame in 1961 as an on-ice official; one of the first three referees inducted into the Hockey Hall of Fame.

A multi-sport player as a boy, Ion played goalie in hockey and forward in lacrosse. After moving to Toronto (Ontario, Canada), he played professional lacrosse with the Toronto Tecumsehs in 1910 (owned by hockey entrepreneurs Frank and Lester Patrick). When the Patricks started the Pacific Coast Hockey League/Association in 1911, Ion served as a referee in the new hockey league, which started his 30-year career.

When the PCHL folded in 1924, he joined the Western Canada Hockey League as a senior official, before moving on to the National Hockey League when the WCHL folded in 1926. He was later named referee-in-chief of the NHL, a position he held until 1942.

Source: Hockey Hall of Fame

Irish, Edward S. "Ned" (born: May 6, 1905 in Lake George, New York; died: January 21, 1982); inducted into the Naismith Memorial Basketball Hall of Fame in 1964 as a contributor; served as the Basketball Director of Madison Square Garden; helped create the first National Invitation Tournament; helped found the New York Knickerbockers.

Irish attended Erasmus High School (Brooklyn, New York), graduating in 1924, before going to the University of Pennsylvania (Philadelphia, 1924–1928). He became the Basketball Director of Madison Square Garden in 1934 and brought college basketball to the Garden in the 1934–1935 season. On December 29, 1934, more than 16,000 fans attended the very first college basketball doubleheader at the Garden as New York University beat Notre Dame 25–18 and Westminster College (Pennsylvania) upset heavily-favored St. John's 37–33.

He is credited with making college basketball a popular spectator sport; helped create the first National Invitation Tournament in 1938; played a major role in the creation of the Basketball Association of America in 1946 (which eventually became the National Basketball Association); and helped form the NBA's New York Knickerbockers (serving as the team's president from 1946 to 1974).

Source: Naismith Memorial Basketball Hall of Fame

Irvin, James Dickenson "Dick" (born: July 19, 1892 in Limestone Ridge, Ontario, Canada; died: May 1957); inducted into the Hockey Hall of Fame in 1958 as a player; Position: Center; won four Stanley Cup titles as a coach.

Irvin played nine professional seasons from 1916 to 1929, including three years with the National Hockey League's Chicago Black Hawks (1926–1929). He played junior and senior amateur hockey in Winnipeg, Manitoba and won the Allan Cup in 1915 with the Winnipeg Monarchs (Manitoba Senior Hockey League).

He turned professional with the Portland Rosebuds of the Pacific Coast Hockey Association in the 1916–1917 season, but his hockey career was interrupted during World War I when he joined the Canadian Army. After his military service, the 5'9", 162-pound Irvin returned to the professional ranks in the 1921–1922 season with the Regina Capitals (Western Canada Hockey League) and helped the team win the league title his first year. In 1925, the team moved to Portland and became the Rosebuds. When the league disbanded in 1926, he joined the expansion Chicago Black Hawks of the National Hockey League.

Irvin was named the team's first captain (1926–1927); missed most of the next season due to a head injury; and returned to the league for the 1928–1929 season, eventually retiring in 1929. He began his coaching career with Chicago in the 1930–1931 season, before being named coach of the Toronto Maple Leafs for the 1931–1932 season, leading the franchise to its first Stanley Cup title. He led the Leafs to the Stanley Cup finals six more times (1933, 1935–1936, 1938–1940), but was never able to win another championship with the team.

In 1940, he was hired by the Montreal Canadiens and led the team to three Stanley Cup championships (1944, 1946, 1953), before being replaced by Toe Blake in 1955.

He was named a First All-Star Team Coach three times (1944–1946); Second All-Star Team Coach six times (1931–1935, 1941); and has been inducted into Canada's Sports Hall of Fame (1975), and the Manitoba Sports Hall of Fame (1983).

Dick Irvin's Career Statistics

			REGULAR SEASON					PLAYOFFS				
SEASON	**TEAM**	**LEAGUE**	**GP**	**G**	**A**	**TP**	**PIM**	**GP**	**G**	**A**	**TP**	**PIM**
1911–1912	Winnipeg Monarchs	MHL-Sr.	5	16	0	16	0	1	5	0	5	0
1912–1913	Winnipeg Strathconas	MHL-Sr.	7	32	0	32	12	1	0	0	0	0
1912–1913	Winnipeg Monarchs	MHL-Sr.	2	5	0	5						
1913–1914	Winnipeg Strathconas	MHL-Sr.	3	11	0	11						
1913–1914	Winnipeg Monarchs	MHL-Sr.	7	23	1	24						
1914–1915	Winnipeg Monarchs	MHL-Sr.	6	23	3	26	30	2	10	0	10	2
1914–1915	Winnipeg Monarchs	Al-Cup	6	17	3	20	20					
1915–1916	Winnipeg Monarchs	MHL-Sr.	8	17	4	21	38	2	7	1	8	2
1916–1917	Portland Rosebuds	PCHA	23	35	10	45	24					
1917–1918	Winnipeg Ypres	MHL-Sr.	9	29	8	37	26					
1919–1920	Regina Victorias	SSHL	12	32	4	36	22	2	1	0	1	4
1920–1921	Regina Victorias	SSHL	11	19	5	24	12	4	8	0	8	4
1921–1922	Regina Capitals	WCHL	20	21	7	28	17	4	3	0	3	2
1921–1922	Regina Capitals	West-P						2	1	0	1	0
1922–1923	Regina Capitals	WCHL	25	9	4	13	12	2	1	0	1	0
1923–1924	Regina Capitals	WCHL	29	15	8	23	33	2	0	0	0	4
1924–1925	Regina Capitals	WCHL	28	13	5	18	38					
1925–1926	Portland Rosebuds	WHL	30	31	5	36	29					

SEASON	TEAM	LEAGUE	REGULAR SEASON GP	G	A	TP	PIM	PLAYOFFS GP	G	A	TP	PIM
1926–1927	Chicago Black Hawks	NHL	43	18	18	36	34	2	2	0	2	4
1927–1928	Chicago Black Hawks	NHL	12	5	4	9	14					
1928–1929	Chicago Black Hawks	NHL	39	6	1	7	30					
	NHL TOTALS		94	29	23	52	78	2	2	0	2	4

Sources: Hockey Hall of Fame; Hockey-Reference.com

Irvin, Michael Jerome (born: March 5, 1966 in Ft. Lauderdale, Florida); inducted into the Pro Football Hall of Fame in 2007 as a player; Position: Wide Receiver; Uniform: #88; caught two touchdown passes in Super Bowl XXVII 18 seconds apart in the second quarter, the fastest pair of touchdowns ever scored by one player in Super Bowl history; only man to play for each of the Dallas Cowboys' first four head coaches.

A football star at St. Thomas Aquinas High School (Fort Lauderdale, Florida), Irvin attended the University of Miami (Coral Gables, Florida), and played for coach Jimmy Johnson, where he set school records for career receptions (143), receiving yards (2,423) and touchdown receptions (26), and was a member of the 1987 NCAA National Championship team. He left Miami early to join the National Football League and was a first-round selection (11th pick overall) of the Dallas Cowboys in the 1988 NFL Draft.

The 6'2", 207-pound Irvin played his entire 12-year (159 games) career with the Cowboys (1988–1999); led the NFL with 1,523 yards (93 catches) in 1991; selected to five consecutive Pro Bowls (1991–1995); a three-time All-Pro selection (1991–1993, 1992 Most Valuable Player); had 1,000 or more receiving yards in a season seven times; set an NFL record with eleven 100-yard games in 1995; won three Super Bowl championships (SB XXVII (January 1993), SB XXVIII (January 1994), SB XXX (January 1996)); added to the Dallas Cowboys Ring of Honor in 2005; and was named to the NFL 1990s All-Decade Team.

In Super Bowl XXVII, Irvin caught six passes for 114 yards and two touchdowns. His two touchdowns came 18 seconds apart in the second quarter, the fastest pair of touchdowns ever scored by one player in Super Bowl history. He was the second player to score two touchdowns in one quarter of a Super Bowl (after Ricky Sanders in Super Bowl XXII). Irvin is the only man to have played for each of the first four coaches in Cowboys' history (Tom Landry, Jimmy Johnson, Barry Switzer, Chan Gailey), and was the last former Tom Landry-coached player to retire from the NFL (1999).

Michael Irvin's Career Statistics

YEAR	TEAM	G	NO	RECEIVING YDS	AVG	TD
1988	Dallas	14	32	654	20. 4	5
1989	Dallas	6	26	378	14. 5	2
1990	Dallas	12	20	413	20. 7	5
1991	Dallas	16	93	1,523	16. 4	8
1992	Dallas	16	78	1,396	17. 9	7
1993	Dallas	16	88	1,330	15. 1	7
1994	Dallas	16	79	1,241	15. 7	6
1995	Dallas	16	111	1,603	14. 4	10
1996	Dallas	11	64	962	15. 0	2
1997	Dallas	16	75	1,180	15. 7	9
1998	Dallas	16	74	1,057	14. 3	1
1999	Dallas	4	10	167	16. 7	3
	TOTALS	159	750	11,904	15. 9	65

Sources: Pro Football Hall of Fame; Pro-Football-Reference.com

Irvin, Montford Merrill "Monte" (born: February 25, 1919 in Columbia, Alabama); inducted into the National Baseball Hall of Fame and Museum in 1973 as a Negro Leaguer by the Negro Leagues Committee; Position: Left Field; Bats: Right; Throws: Right; won a World Series title in 1954.

One of the best African-American players in professional baseball before the integration of the major leagues, Irvin was a high-average hitter. Making his major league debut on July 8, 1949, the 6'1", 195-pound Irvin played 18 seasons of professional baseball with the Negro Leagues' Newark Eagles (1937–1942, 1945–1948) and Major League Baseball's New York Giants (1949–1955) and Chicago Cubs (1956). He played in two World Series (winning in 1954 and losing in 1951), and was selected to the 1952 All-Star team.

In high school, he starred in four sports and set a state record in the javelin throw before attending Lincoln University (Chester, Pennsylvania). Irvin was one of the first black players to be signed after Major League Baseball's color line was broken by Jackie Robinson in 1947, and earlier, he had won the Triple Crown and the Most Valuable Player Award in the Mexican League.

After serving in the military during World War II (1943–1945), he returned to the Eagles and led the team to a league pennant; won his second batting title (.401); and helped Newark beat the Kansas City Monarchs in a seven-game Negro League World Series in 1946. Irvin was a five-time Negro League All-Star (1940–1941, 1946–1948).

He was named Puerto Rican Winter League Most Valuable Players twice (1945–1946) before debuting with the New York Giants in 1949. In 1951, he teamed with Hank Thompson and Willie Mays to form the first all-black outfield in the major leagues.

Years after retiring as a player, Irvin served as a scout for the New York Mets from 1967 to 1968, before working 17 years (1968–1984) in a public relations role for baseball commissioner Bowie Kuhn.

On May 18, 1950, at the Polo Grounds, Rube Walker (Chicago Cubs) hit a grand slam in the sixth inning and in the bottom of the inning, Irvin hit a grand slam for the Giants, marking the first time in major league history that each team hit a grand slam in the same inning. The game was later called because of rain after six innings, with the Giants winning, 10–4.

Monte Irvin's Career Statistics

YEAR	TEAM	LG	G	AB	R	H	2B	3B	HR	RBI	BB	SO	SB	AVG	SLG
1949	New York	NL	36	76	7	17	3	2	0	7	17	11	0	.224	.316
1950	New York	NL	110	374	61	112	19	5	15	66	52	41	3	.299	.497
1951	New York	NL	151	558	94	174	19	11	24	121	89	44	12	.312	.514
1952	New York	NL	46	126	10	39	2	1	4	21	10	11	0	.310	.437
1953	New York	NL	124	444	72	146	21	5	21	97	55	34	2	.329	.541
1954	New York	NL	135	432	62	113	13	3	19	64	70	23	7	.262	.438
1955	New York	NL	51	150	16	38	7	1	1	17	17	15	3	.253	.333
1956	Chicago	NL	111	339	44	92	13	3	15	50	41	41	1	.271	.460
	TOTALS		764	2,499	366	731	97	31	99	443	351	220	28	.293	.475

Sources: Baseball-Reference.com; National Baseball Hall of Fame and Museum

Issel, Daniel Paul "Dan" (born: October 25, 1948 in Batavia, Illinois); inducted into the Naismith Memorial Basketball Hall of Fame in 1993 as a player; Position: Center-Forward; won an American Basketball Association championship; Denver Nuggets all-time leading rebounder.

At Batavia (Illinois) High School (1962–1966), Issel was a two-year basketball letter winner; named *Parade* magazine All-American in 1966; selected both All-State and All-Conference twice (1965–1966); and was inducted into the Illinois Basketball Hall of Fame.

After high school, he attended the University of Kentucky (Lexington, 1966–1970), where he was a three-year letter winner in basketball; named *The Sporting News* Second-Team All-American (1969); *The Sporting News* First-Team All-American (1970); played for hall of fame coach Adoph Rupp; scored a career total of 2,138 points (25.8 per game, a school record); Kentucky's all-time leading rebounder (1,078, 13.0 per game); named to three Southeastern Conference championship teams (1968–1970); and played in three National Collegiate Athletic Association tournaments (1968–1970).

After college, the 6'9", 240-pound Issel was an eighth-round pick (122nd overall selection) of the American Basketball Association's Kentucky Colonels in 1970. He would go on to play professional basketball for 15 years with the Colonels (1970–1975), ABA's Denver Nuggets (1975–1976), and the National Basketball Association's Denver Nuggets (1976–1985). He was named ABA co-Rookie of the Year (1971); led the ABA in scoring (1971, 29.9 points per game); selected to the ABA All-First Team (1972) and ABA All-Second Team four times (1971, 1973–1974, 1976); won an ABA championship with the Kentucky Colonels (1975); a six-time ABA All-Star (1971–1976); ABA All-Star Game Most Valuable Player (1972); an NBA All-Star (1977); averaged 25.6 points per game in the ABA and 20.4 points per game in the NBA; and is the Nuggets' all-time leading rebounder (6,630).

Issel was awarded the NBA's J. Walter Kennedy Award for community service (1985) and has been inducted into both the Colorado and Kentucky Sports halls of fame.

After his playing days, he coached the Denver Nuggets from 1992 to 1995; compiled an overall 96–102 (.485) record; returned to the team in 1998 as vice-president and general manager; and named himself the head coach in December 1999. His second stint as coach was less successful as the team did not have a winning season before he resigned in December 2001.

Dan Issel's Career Statistics

SEASON	TEAM	LG	G	MIN	FG	3P	FT	TRB	AST	PTS
1970–1971	Kentucky	ABA	83	3,274	938	0	604	1,093	162	2,480
1971–1972	Kentucky	ABA	83	3,570	972	3	591	931	195	2,538
1972–1973	Kentucky	ABA	84	3,531	902	3	485	922	220	2,292
1973–1974	Kentucky	ABA	83	3,347	829	3	457	847	137	2,118
1974–1975	Kentucky	ABA	83	2,864	614	0	237	710	188	1,465
1975–1976	Denver	ABA	84	2,856	752	1	425	923	201	1,930
1976–1977	Denver	NBA	79	2,507	660		445	696	177	1,765
1977–1978	Denver	NBA	82	2,851	659		428	830	304	1,746
1978–1979	Denver	NBA	81	2,742	532		316	738	255	1,380
1979–1980	Denver	NBA	82	2,938	715	4	517	719	198	1,951
1980–1981	Denver	NBA	80	2,641	614	2	519	676	158	1,749
1981–1982	Denver	NBA	81	2,472	651	4	546	608	179	1,852
1982–1983	Denver	NBA	80	2,431	661	4	400	596	223	1,726
1983–1984	Denver	NBA	76	2,076	569	4	364	513	173	1,506
1984–1985	Denver	NBA	77	1,684	363	1	257	331	137	984
		ABA	500	19,442	5,007	10	2,799	5,426	1,103	12,823
		NBA	718	22,342	5,424	19	3,792	5,707	1,804	14,659
	TOTALS		1,218	41,784	10,431	29	6,591	11,133	2,907	27,482

Dan Issel's Coaching Record

			REGULAR SEASON			PLAYOFFS		
SEASON	LG	TEAM	W	L	WIN%	W	L	WIN%
1992–1993	NBA	Denver	36	46	.439			
1993–1994	NBA	Denver	42	40	.512	6	6	.500
1994–1995	NBA	Denver	18	16	.529			
1999–2000	NBA	Denver	35	47	.427			
2000–2001	NBA	Denver	40	42	.488			
2001–2002	NBA	Denver	9	17	.346			
TOTALS	NBA		180	208	.464	6	6	.500

Sources: Basketball-Reference.com; Naismith Memorial Basketball Hall of Fame

Ivan, Thomas N. (born: January 31, 1911 in Toronto, Ontario, Canada; died: June 24, 1999 in Lake Forest, Illinois); inducted into the Hockey Hall of Fame in 1974 as a builder; only one of the Original Six coaches who never played in the National Hockey League; won four Stanley Cup titles.

Ivan led the Detroit Red Wings to three Stanley Cup championships (1950, 1952, 1954).

During World War II, he joined the army and after leaving the military, was hired by the National Hockey League's Red Wings to coach its minor league affiliates, first with the Omaha Knights (United States Hockey League) and later with the Indianapolis Capitals (American Hockey League).

In 1947, he was named coach of the Red Wings, and was the only one of the Original Six coaches who never played in the NHL. After the team's third Cup title, he became the general manager of the Chicago Black Hawks and led the team to the 1961 Stanley Cup, his fourth. After leading the team to the finals four more seasons (1962, 1965, 1971, 1973) and serving as general manager for 25 years, Ivan became Chicago's vice-president and served as an alternate governor on the NHL Board of Governors.

He received the Lester Patrick Trophy in 1975 for outstanding service to hockey in the United States; served as chairman of the United States Hockey Hall of Fame and on the selection committee of the Hockey Hall of Fame; and was chairman of the organizing committee for the 1979–1980 Olympic Hockey Festival, which helped coach Herb Brooks pick the 1980 U.S. Men's Ice Hockey team that participated in the "Miracle on Ice" game against the Russians, and went on to win the gold medal at the 1980 Winter Olympics in Lake Placid, New York.

Source: Hockey Hall of Fame

Chapter 10
Jaap to Jurgensen

Jaap, John (born: August 12, 1895 in Bellshill, Scotland; died: May 1, 1974 in Pittsburgh, Pennsylvania); inducted into the National Soccer Hall of Fame and Museum in 1953 as a player; Position: Inside Right; won two American Soccer League championships.

Jaap was born in Scotland; raised in Pittsburgh; and played for Castle Shannon (Pennsylvania), Arden F.C. (Pittsburgh, Pennsylvania), Vestaburg F.C. (Pennsylvania), and Jeanette Athletic Association F.C. (Pittsburgh, Pennsylvania) from 1912 to 1920.

He later played for Philadelphia Field Club (American Soccer League) from 1921 to 1922, and in 1925, he rejoined the team after it had been renamed Bethlehem Steel (also of the ASL), and stayed until 1930. During his time with the team, the squad won the ASL championship in 1922 (as Philadelphia); repeated as ASL champions in 1927 (as Bethlehem Steel); and won the 1928 Lewis Cup. In 1926, Jaap was a member of the Bethlehem team that won the U.S. Open Cup and he scored one of the goals in the 7–2 win over St. Louis Ben Millers in the final.

In the fall of 1930, he returned to Scotland and spent one season with the Heart of Midlothian F.C. (Edinburgh, Scotland) of the Scottish Premier League. He returned to the United States in 1931 and played his last season for the Newark Americans (New Jersey) of the ASL.

After retiring as a player, Jaap coached numerous junior teams.

Source: National Soccer Hall of Fame and Museum

Jackson, Harvey "Busher" (born: January 19, 1911 in Toronto, Ontario, Canada; died: June 25, 1966); inducted into the Hockey Hall of Fame in 1971 as a player; Position: Left Wing-Forward; won the 1932 Stanley Cup title.

Jackson was a member of the "Kid Line" with Charlie Conacher and Joe Primeau as the Toronto Maple Leafs trio dominated the National Hockey League in the 1930s. He played 15 NHL seasons (1929–1944) with the Leafs (1929–1939), New York Americans (1939–1941), and the Boston Bruins (1941–1944).

He signed with the Maple Leafs in 1929, and at age 18, he was the youngest player in the league. In the 1931–1932 season, he scored 28 goals and 53 points to lead the league in scoring (winning the Art Ross Trophy) and helped the Leafs win the franchise's first Stanley Cup since their name was changed from the St. Patricks. He was named to the first of his four First All-Star Teams (1932, 1934–1935, 1937) and was selected to the Second All-Star Team in 1933.

In 1998, he was ranked number 55 on *The Hockey News*' list of the 100 Greatest Hockey Players.

Harvey Jackson's Career Statistics

			REGULAR SEASON					PLAYOFFS				
SEASON	TEAM	LEAGUE	GP	G	A	TP	PIM	GP	G	A	TP	PIM
1925–1927	Humberside Collegiate	High-ON										
1927–1928	Toronto Marlboros	OHA-Jr.	4	4	0	4	2	2	0	0	0	0
1928–1929	Toronto Marlboros	OHA-Jr.	9	10	4	14	0	3	7	2	9	
1928–1929	Toronto Marlboros	M-Cup	13	15	10	25	4					
1929–1930	Toronto Maple Leafs	NHL	31	12	6	18	29					
1930–1931	Toronto Maple Leafs	NHL	43	18	13	31	81	2	0	0	0	0
1931–1932	Toronto Maple Leafs	NHL	48	28	25	53	63	7	5	2	7	13
1932–1933	Toronto Maple Leafs	NHL	48	27	17	44	43	9	3	1	4	2
1933–1934	Toronto Maple Leafs	NHL	38	20	18	38	38	5	1	0	1	8

SEASON	TEAM	LEAGUE	REGULAR SEASON GP	G	A	TP	PIM	PLAYOFFS GP	G	A	TP	PIM
1934–1935	Toronto Maple Leafs	NHL	42	22	22	44	27	7	3	2	5	2
1935–1936	Toronto Maple Leafs	NHL	47	11	11	22	19	9	3	2	5	4
1936–1937	Toronto Maple Leafs	NHL	46	21	19	40	12	2	1	0	1	2
1937–1938	Toronto Maple Leafs	NHL	48	17	17	34	18	6	1	0	1	8
1938–1939	Toronto Maple Leafs	NHL	41	10	17	27	12	7	0	1	1	2
1939–1940	New York Americans	NHL	43	12	8	20	10	3	0	1	1	2
1940–1941	New York Americans	NHL	46	8	18	26	4					
1941–1942	Boston Bruins	NHL	26	5	7	12	18	5	0	1	1	0
1942–1943	Boston Bruins	NHL	44	19	15	34	38	9	1	2	3	10
1943–1944	Boston Bruins	NHL	42	11	21	32	25					
	NHL TOTALS		633	241	234	475	437	71	18	12	30	53

Sources: Hockey Hall of Fame; Hockey-Reference.com

Jackson, Philip Douglas "Phil" (born: September 17, 1945 in Deer Lodge, Montana); inducted into the Naismith Memorial Basketball Hall of Fame in 2007 as a coach; won an NBA title as a player; fastest coach in NBA history to reach 900 wins; first coach in NBA history to lead a team to three consecutive championships three different times.

A second-round selection (17th overall pick) in the 1967 National Basketball Association Draft, Jackson played 12 NBA seasons (1967–1980) with the New York Knicks (1967–1978) and the New Jersey Nets (1978–1980). While having a relatively long playing career, it is as a coach that the 6'8", 220-pound Jackson distinguished himself. Using the "triangle offense," he has led two of the greatest dynasties in NBA history. In nine seasons with the Chicago Bulls (1989–1998), he led the team to six NBA championships (1991–1993, 1996–1998), before moving on to the Los Angeles Lakers (1999–present) and winning five more titles (as of this writing), including three straight (2000–2002, 2009–2010). With 11 NBA titles, he has the most of any coach in NBA history.

He is the fastest coach in NBA history to reach 900 wins, and his 1996 Bulls posted the best regular-season record in NBA history (72–10), as Jackson was named NBA Coach of the Year. At the time of his hall of fame induction, he was the NBA's career leader in playoff wins (179) and playoff winning percentage (.699).

Jackson won an NBA title as a player with the Knicks in 1973; won a Continental Basketball Association title as a coach (1984); and was named CBA Coach of the Year while with the Albany Patroons in 1984.

Nicknamed the "Zen Master" for his interest in Eastern philosophy, Jackson is one of three head coaches to win an NBA championship with two different teams; first coach in NBA history to lead a team to three consecutive championships three different times; from 1996 to 2003, led his teams to an NBA-record 25 consecutive postseason series victories; and was named one of the 10 greatest head coaches in NBA history (1996).

Jackson attended Williston (North Dakota) High School, where he played varsity basketball and led the team to two state titles. He also played football, was a pitcher on the baseball team, and threw the discus on the school's track team. After high school, Jackson went to the University of North Dakota (Grand Forks), and led the Fighting Sioux to a third place finish in the NCAA Division II tournament as a sophomore (1965) and to a fourth place finish as a junior (1966).

After serving two seasons as a player-assistant coach for the New Jersey Nets, Jackson retired as a player in 1980 and began his coaching career in the Continental Basketball Association and the Baloncesto Superior Nacional (National Superior Basketball) of Puerto Rico. While in the CBA, he won his first coaching championship, leading the Albany Patroons to the franchise's first CBA title.

Jackson returned to the NBA as an assistant coach of the Chicago Bulls in 1987, and became the team's head coach in 1989, a job he held until after the 1998 season. He took a year off from coaching, and returned to the NBA in 1999 as head coach of the Los Angeles Lakers. He took off another year after the 2004 season, but returned to the team in 2005 and, as of this writing, is still the team's head coach.

On January 7, 2007, Jackson won his 900th game, currently placing him ninth on the all-time win list for NBA coaches, and making him the fastest to reach 900 career wins, doing so in only 1,264 games (surpassing Pat Riley's previous record of 900 wins in 1,278 games).

Jackson has also written several books, including *Maverick* (1975, with Charles Rosen); *Sacred Hoops: Spiritual Lessons of a Hardwood Warrior* (1995, with Hugh Delehanty); *More than a Game* (2001, with Charley Rosen); and *The Last Season: A Team in Search of Its Soul* (2004, with Michael Arkush).

Phil Jackson's Playing Career Statistics

SEASON	TEAM	LG	G	MIN	FG	FT	TRB	AST	STL	BLK	PTS
1967–1968	New York	NBA	75	1,093	182	99	338	55			463

SEASON	TEAM	LG	G	MIN	FG	FT	TRB	AST	STL	BLK	PTS
1968–1969	New York	NBA	47	924	126	80	246	43			332
1970–1971	New York	NBA	71	771	118	95	238	31			331
1971–1972	New York	NBA	80	1,273	205	167	326	72			577
1972–1973	New York	NBA	80	1,393	245	154	344	94			644
1973–1974	New York	NBA	82	2,050	361	191	478	134	42	67	913
1974–1975	New York	NBA	78	2,285	324	193	600	136	84	53	841
1975–1976	New York	NBA	80	1,461	185	110	343	105	41	20	480
1976–1977	New York	NBA	76	1,033	102	51	229	85	33	18	255
1977–1978	New York	NBA	63	654	55	43	110	46	31	15	153
1978–1979	New Jersey	NBA	59	1,070	144	86	178	85	45	22	374
1979–1980	New Jersey	NBA	16	194	29	7	24	12	5	4	65
	TOTALS		807	14,201	2,076	1,276	3,454	898	281	199	5,428

Phil Jackson's Coaching Record

			REGULAR SEASON			PLAYOFFS			
SEASON	TEAM	LG	W	L	WIN%	W	L	WIN%	NOTES
1989–1990	Chicago	NBA	55	27	.671	10	6	.625	
1990–1991	Chicago	NBA	61	21	.744	15	2	.882	NBA Champions
1991–1992	Chicago	NBA	67	15	.817	15	7	.682	NBA Champions
1992–1993	Chicago	NBA	57	25	.695	15	4	.789	NBA Champions
1993–1994	Chicago	NBA	55	27	.671	6	4	.600	
1994–1995	Chicago	NBA	47	35	.573	5	5	.500	
1995–1996	Chicago	NBA	72	10	.878	15	3	.833	NBA Champions
1996–1997	Chicago	NBA	69	13	.841	15	4	.789	NBA Champions
1997–1998	Chicago	NBA	62	20	.756	15	6	.714	NBA Champions
1999–2000	Los Angeles	NBA	67	15	.817	15	8	.652	NBA Champions
2000–2001	Los Angeles	NBA	56	26	.683	15	1	.938	NBA Champions
2001–2002	Los Angeles	NBA	58	24	.707	15	4	.789	NBA Champions
2002–2003	Los Angeles	NBA	50	32	.610	6	6	.500	
2003–2004	Los Angeles	NBA	56	26	.683	13	9	.591	
2005–2006	Los Angeles	NBA	45	37	.549	3	4	.429	
2006–2007	Los Angeles	NBA	42	40	.512	1	4	.200	
2007–2008	Los Angeles	NBA	57	25	.695	13	6	.684	
2008–2009	Los Angeles	NBA	65	17	.793	16	7	.696	NBA Champions
2009–2010	Los Angeles	NBA	57	25	.595	16	7	.696	NBA Champions
	TOTALS		1,098	460	.705	225	98	.697	

Sources: Basketball-Reference.com; Naismith Memorial Basketball Hall of Fame

Jackson, Reginald Martinez "Reggie" (born: May 18, 1946 in Wyncote, Pennsylvania); inducted into the National Baseball Hall of Fame and Museum in 1993 as a player; Position: Right Field; Bats: Left; Throws: Left; Uniform: #9, #44; first player in major league history to hit 100 or more home runs for three different teams; won four World Series; 1973 American League Most Valuable Player.

Jackson earned the nickname "Mr. October" for his clutch-hitting, World Series home runs with both the Oakland Athletics and New York Yankees. In 27 World Series games, he hit 10 home runs, including four in consecutive at-bats; accumulated 24 runs batted in; and hit for a .357 batting average.

Making his major league debut on June 9, 1967, the 6', 200-pound Jackson played 21 years (1967–1987) for the Kansas City Athletics (1967), Oakland Athletics (1968–1975, 1987), Baltimore Orioles (1976), New York Yankees (1977–1981), and the California Angels (1982–1986). He played in five World Series (winning in 1973–1974, 1977–1978 and losing in 1981) (was hurt and ineligible for the 1972 Series); named to 14 All-Star teams (1969, 1971–1975, 1977–1984); American League Most Valuable Player in 1973; two-time World Series Most Valuable Player (1973, 1977); and was the first player in major league history to hit 100 or more home runs for three different teams (Kansas City-Oakland Athletics, New York Yankees, California Angels).

Jackson graduated from Cheltenham High School (Wyncote, Pennsylvania) in 1964, where he starred in football and baseball. After high school, he went to Arizona State University (Tempe) on a football scholarship, but after his freshman year, he dropped football and concentrated on baseball.

He was a first-round pick (second overall selection) in the 1966 Major League Baseball Draft of the Kansas City Athletics. After his first season with Kansas City, he and the team moved to Oakland; he helped the squad win the 1973 American League pennant; and was named the league's Most Valuable Player. Unable to play in the 1972 World Series due to an injury, he helped Oakland win in 1973 in seven games against the New York Mets and was selected World Series Most Valuable Player. Oakland won the World Series again in 1974 in five games against the Los Angeles Dodgers, the first time that two teams from California played each other for a sport's World Championship.

In April 1976, Jackson was traded to the Baltimore Orioles, and played one season with the team before moving on to the New York Yankees, where he wore jersey number 44, in honor of Hank Aaron. His abrasive personality and showboating bothered the fans, his teammates, coaches, and manager Billy Martin. An example of the friction between Jackson and Martin showed itself early in their relationship. On June 18, 1977 (his first season with the team), in a 10–4 loss to the Boston Red Sox in a nationally-televised game at Boston's Fenway Park, Jackson appeared too lackadaisical when chasing a ball hit by Jim Rice, who would eventually reach second base with a double. Reacting to his apparent lack of effort, Martin pulled Jackson immediately from the game without waiting until the end of the inning, and began yelling at him in the dugout. The argument escalated and a national television audience watched as the two yelled at each other and had to be separated by teammates and coaches.

In spite of their relationship with each other, the team began winning and won that season's American League pennant. In the World Series against the Dodgers, Jackson hit a home run in Game Four, a home run in Game Five, and put on a show by hitting three home runs in Game Six (all on the first pitch by three different pitchers). He was named World Series MVP, making him the first player to win the award for two different teams.

In 1978, the Curtiss Candy Company released a new product, the "Reggie Bar," which made Jackson the first player to have a candy bar named after him.

In 1987, he returned to the Oakland Athletics, and in his last major league at-bat (at Chicago's Comiskey Park on October 4), he hit a single, and was the last Kansas City Athletics player to play in a major league game.

Jackson retired with a .357 lifetime World Series average (95 points higher than his career regular-season average); had the highest World Series slugging percentage (.755); and still holds the major league record for most career strikeouts (2,597).

When his relationship with Yankees owner George Steinbrenner improved after Jackson retired, he was hired by the team as a consultant. The Yankees retired his uniform number 44 in August 1993, and the Athletics retired his jersey number nine in May 2004. In 1999, Jackson ranked 48th on *The Sporting News*' list of the 100 Greatest Baseball Players, and he was a finalist for the Major League Baseball All-Century Team.

Reggie Jackson's Career Statistics

YEAR	TEAM	LG	G	AB	R	H	2B	3B	HR	RBI	BB	SO	SB	AVG	SLG
1967	Kansas City	AL	35	118	13	21	4	4	1	6	10	46	1	.178	.305
1968	Oakland	AL	154	553	82	138	13	6	29	74	50	171	14	.250	.452
1969	Oakland	AL	152	549	123	151	36	3	47	118	115	142	13	.275	.608
1970	Oakland	AL	149	426	57	101	21	2	23	66	75	135	26	.237	.458
1971	Oakland	AL	150	567	87	157	29	3	32	80	63	161	16	.277	.508
1972	Oakland	AL	135	499	72	132	25	2	25	75	59	125	9	.265	.473
1973	Oakland	AL	151	539	99	158	28	2	32	117	76	111	22	.293	.531
1974	Oakland	AL	148	506	90	146	25	1	29	93	86	105	25	.289	.514
1975	Oakland	AL	157	593	91	150	39	3	36	104	67	133	17	.253	.511
1976	Baltimore	AL	134	498	84	138	27	2	27	91	54	108	28	.277	.502
1977	New York	AL	146	525	93	150	39	2	32	110	74	129	17	.286	.550
1978	New York	AL	139	511	82	140	13	5	27	97	58	133	14	.274	.477
1979	New York	AL	131	465	78	138	24	2	29	89	65	107	9	.297	.544
1980	New York	AL	143	514	94	154	22	4	41	111	83	122	1	.300	.597
1981	New York	AL	94	334	33	79	17	1	15	54	46	82	0	.237	.428
1982	California	AL	153	530	92	146	17	1	39	101	85	156	4	.275	.532
1983	California	AL	116	397	43	77	14	1	14	49	52	140	0	.194	.340
1984	California	AL	143	525	67	117	17	2	25	81	55	141	8	.223	.406
1985	California	AL	143	460	64	116	27	0	27	85	78	138	1	.252	.487
1986	California	AL	132	419	65	101	12	2	18	58	92	115	1	.241	.408
1987	Oakland	AL	115	336	42	74	14	1	15	43	33	97	2	.220	.402
	TOTALS		2,820	9,864	1,551	2,584	463	49	563	1,702	1,376	2,597	228	.262	.490

Sources: Baseball-Reference.com; National Baseball Hall of Fame and Museum

Jackson, Rickey Anderson (born: March 20, 1958 in Pahokee, Florida); inducted into the Pro Football Hall of Fame in 2010 as a player; Position: Linebacker; Uniform: #57; first New Orleans Saints player inducted into the Pro Football Hall of Fame.

After attending Pahokee High School and the University of Pittsburgh (Pennsylvania), the 6'2", 243-pound Jackson was a second-round pick (51st selection overall) of the New Orleans Saints in the 1981 NFL Draft. He went on to play 15 years (227 games) from 1981 to 1995 with the New Orleans Saints (1981–1993) and the San Francisco 49ers (1994–1995); accumulated 128.0 career sacks; set a franchise rookie record with 8.0 sacks; and was the first Hall of Fame player who spent most of his career in New Orleans.

He was named to the All-Rookie Team in 1981; played in six Pro Bowls (1983–1986, 1992–1993); named an All-Pro (First Team) four times (1986–1987, 1992–1993); helped the Saints have the franchise's first-ever winning record in 1987 and claim the team's first-ever division title in 1991; won a Super Bowl ring (SB XXIX) in 1995 with the San Francisco 49ers in his first season with the team; had his uniform number 57 retired by the Saints; and was inducted into the New Orleans Saints Hall of Fame in 1997.

In 2007, Jackson was named to the Florida High School Association All-Century Team and in college, he was named a Second-Team All-American as a senior (1980) and a First-Team All-Big East selection (also as a senior). In the National Football League, Jackson recorded 10 or more sacks in six different seasons and led the NFL in fumble recoveries twice (1990–1991). At the time of his departure from the Saints, he held the following franchise records: Most Games (195); Most Sacks in a Career (123.0); Most Seasons Played for the Team (13, tied for first); Most Opponent Fumbles Recovered in a Career (26); and Most Opponent Fumbles Recovered in a Season (seven in 1990).

Source: Pro Football Hall of Fame

Jackson, Travis Calvin "Stonewall" (born: November 2, 1903 in Waldo, Arkansas; died: July 27, 1987 in Waldo, Arkansas); inducted into the National Baseball Hall of Fame and Museum in 1982 as a player by the Veterans Committee; Position: Shortstop; Bats: Right; Throws: Right; won the 1933 World Series.

The 5'10", 160-pound Jackson was the captain on manager John McGraw's New York Giants teams of the 1920s. He was nicknamed "Stonewall," after the Civil War general, for the wall of defense he supplied at shortstop, and during his career, he hit .300 or better six times.

Making his major league debut on September 27, 1922, Jackson played his entire 15-season career with the Giants (1922–1936); played in four World Series (winning in 1933 and losing in 1923–1924, 1936); and was selected to the All-Star team in 1934.

Although he led National League shortstops with 58 errors in 1924, he also led the league in fielding average twice, twice in double plays, and four times in assists. After his playing career, Jackson managed the Jersey City Giants (minor league affiliate of the New York Giants) in the International League.

Travis Jackson's Career Statistics

YEAR	TEAM	LG	G	AB	R	H	2B	3B	HR	RBI	BB	SO	SB	AVG	SLG
1922	New York	NL	3	8	1	0	0	0	0	0	0	2	0	.000	.000
1923	New York	NL	96	327	45	90	12	7	4	37	22	40	3	.275	.391
1924	New York	NL	151	596	81	180	26	8	11	76	21	56	6	.302	.428
1925	New York	NL	112	411	51	117	15	2	9	59	24	43	8	.285	.397
1926	New York	NL	111	385	64	126	24	8	8	51	20	26	2	.327	.494
1927	New York	NL	127	469	67	149	29	4	14	98	32	30	8	.318	.486
1928	New York	NL	150	537	73	145	35	6	14	77	56	46	8	.270	.436
1929	New York	NL	149	551	92	162	21	12	21	94	64	56	10	.294	.490
1930	New York	NL	116	431	70	146	27	8	13	82	32	25	6	.339	.529
1931	New York	NL	145	555	65	172	26	10	5	71	36	23	13	.310	.420
1932	New York	NL	52	195	23	50	17	1	4	38	13	16	1	.256	.415
1933	New York	NL	53	122	11	30	5	0	0	12	8	11	2	.246	.287
1934	New York	NL	137	523	75	140	26	7	16	101	37	71	1	.268	.436
1935	New York	NL	128	511	74	154	20	12	9	80	29	64	3	.301	.440
1936	New York	NL	126	465	41	107	8	1	7	53	18	56	0	.230	.297
	TOTALS		1,656	6,086	833	1,768	291	86	135	929	412	565	71	.291	.433

Sources: Baseball-Reference.com; National Baseball Hall of Fame and Museum

James, Angela (born: December 22, 1964 in Toronto, Ontario, Canada); inducted into the Hockey Hall of Fame in 2010 as a player; Position: Center; one of the first two women ever inducted into the Hockey Hall of Fame.

Often dubbed the "Wayne Gretzky of women's hockey," the 5'6", 155-pound James played hockey at Seneca College (Toronto, Ontario, Canada); led the team to several championships; and had her number 8 retired by the school. Beginning in the late 1970s, she played in the Ontario Women's Hockey Association (in the Central Ontario Women's Hockey League); won numerous league and provincial championships; was the leading scorer in eight seasons; and most valuable player in six.

A right-handed shooter, she won four Women's World Championships gold medals with Team Canada (1990 in Ottawa, Canada; 1992 in Tampere, Finland; 1994 in Lake Placid, New York; 1997 in Kitchener, Canada); two Three Nations Cup (Canada, United States, Finland) gold medals (1996, 1999); and a gold medal in the International Hockey Federation Pacific Rim Championship (1996) in Vancouver, Canada.

In 2009, the Hockey Hall of Fame changed its rules to allow women honorees and she (along with Cammi Granato) were the first two inducted. James was inducted into both the Black Hockey and Sports Hall of Fame and the Ontario Colleges Athletic Association Hall of Fame in 2006; she was one of three women (along with Cammi Granato and Geraldine Heaney) inducted into the International Ice Hockey Federation (the first in the organization's history) in 2008; and in 2009, she was inducted into the Canada's Sports Hall of Fame.

Since retiring from her playing career, she has worked as a sports coordinator for Seneca College and has acted as a hockey referee.

Angela James' Career Statistics

YEAR	TOURNAMENT	GP	G	A	TP	PIM
1990	Women's World Championship (Ottawa, Canada)	5	11	2	13	10
1992	Women's World Championship (Tampere, Finland)	5	5	2	7	2
1994	Women's World Championship (Lake Placid, New York)	5	4	5	9	3
1996	Pacific Women's Championship (Vancouver, Canada)	5	3	4	7	2
1997	Women's World Championship (Kitchener, Canada)	5	2	3	5	2
	TOTALS	25	25	16	41	19

Source: Hockey Hall of Fame

Jeannette, Harry Edward "Buddy" (born: September 15, 1917 in New Kensington, Pennsylvania; died: March 11, 1998 in Nashua, New Hampshire); inducted into the Naismith Memorial Basketball Hall of Fame in 1994 as a player; Position: Guard; first player-coach to win a professional championship (1947); won six championships.

After being a three-year basketball letterman and an All-Conference selection (1934) at New Kensington (Pennsylvania) High School (1930–1934), Jeannette attended Washington & Jefferson University (Washington, Pennsylvania, 1934–1938), where he averaged 12 points per game in 72 games, and was selected an All-American honorable mention in 1937.

After college, he played professional basketball with the Warren Penns (National Basketball League, 1938–1939); Detroit Eagles (NBL, 1939–1941); Sheboygan Redskins (NBL, 1942–1943); Fort Wayne Zollner Pistons (NBL, 1943–1946); Baltimore Bullets (Basketball Association of America/American Basketball League, 1946–1950); and the Baltimore Bullets (National Basketball Association, 1949–1950).

The 5'11", 175-pound Jeannette won a World Basketball Championship with Detroit (1941); was named World Basketball Champion Most Valuable Player (1940–1941); NBL MVP (1942–1943) with Sheboygan; named World Basketball Champion MVP (1944–1945); NBL MVP (1944–1945) with Fort Wayne; All-BAA Second Team (1947–1948); All-NBL First Team (1941, 1944–1946); All-NBL Second Team (1943); won three NBL championships with Fort Wayne (1943–1945); won an ABL championship with Baltimore (1947); and won a BAA championship with Baltimore (1948).

He was the first player-coach to win a professional championship (1947), a feat he repeated in 1948.

He coached at the professional level with the ABL Baltimore Bullets (1946–1947); BAA/NBA Baltimore Bullets (1947–1951); Eastern Basketball League's Baltimore Bullets (1954–1961); and the American Basketball Association's Pittsburgh Condors (1969–1970). He led the ABL's Baltimore Bullets to a league championship (1947) and coached the BAA/NBA Baltimore Bullets to the 1948 BAA title.

Jeannette also coached at the college level at Georgetown University (Washington, D.C.), and led the school to a 49–49 overall record from 1952 to 1956.

Harry Jeannette's Playing Statistics

SEASON	TEAM	LG	G	FG	FT	AST	PF	PTS
1947–1948	Baltimore	BAA	46	150	191	70	147	491
1948–1949	Baltimore	BAA	56	73	167	124	157	313
1949–1950	Baltimore	NBA	37	42	109	93	82	193
		BAA	102	223	358	194	304	804
		NBA	37	42	109	93	82	193
	TOTALS		139	265	467	287	386	997

Harry Jeannette's Coaching Statistics

			REGULAR SEASON			PLAYOFFS			NOTE
SEASON	TEAM	LG	W	L	WIN%	W	L	WIN%	
1947–1948	Baltimore	BAA	28	20	.583	9	3	.750	BAA Champions
1948–1949	Baltimore	BAA	29	31	.483	1	2	.333	
1949–1950	Baltimore	NBA	25	43	.368				
1950–1951	Baltimore	NBA	14	23	.378				
1964–1965	Baltimore	NBA	37	43	.463	5	5	.500	
1966–1967	Baltimore	NBA	3	13	.188				
1969–1970	Pittsburgh	ABA	15	30	.333				
		BAA	57	51	.528	10	5	.667	
		NBA	79	122	.393	5	5	.500	
		ABA	15	30	.333				
	TOTALS		151	203	.427	15	10	.600	

Sources: Basketball-Reference.com; Naismith Memorial Basketball Hall of Fame

Jeffrey, William "Bill" (born: August 3, 1892 in Edinburgh, Scotland; died: January 7, 1966 in Boalsburg, Pennsylvania); inducted into the National Soccer Hall of Fame and Museum in 1951 as a builder; won 10 national titles at Penn State University; served as president of the National Soccer Coaches Association of America.

Jeffrey played semi-professional soccer in Scotland before coming to the United States in 1920, where he played for Altoona, Homestead, Braddock, and Bethlehem Steel, teams all located in Pennsylvania. He served as the coach of the soccer team at Penn State University (University Park) from 1925 until the 1960s, and won 10 national college championships. He also coached the U.S. World Cup team in 1950 that beat England 1–0 in what is considered one of the greatest upsets in soccer history.

He served as president of the National Soccer Coaches Association of America in 1948 and received the organization's Honor Award in 1949. The Bill Jeffrey Award is named in his honor and is presented annually for outstanding service to, or an achievement in, intercollegiate soccer.

Source: National Soccer Hall of Fame and Museum

Jenkins, Ferguson Arthur "Fergie" (born: December 13, 1943 in Chatham, Ontario, Canada); inducted into the National Baseball Hall of Fame and Museum in 1991 as a player; Position: Pitcher; Bats: Right; Throws: Right; Uniform: #31; Canada's first player to be inducted into the baseball hall of fame; only member of the 3,000-strikeout club inducted into the hall of fame to have surrendered less than 1,000 walks; won the 1971 Cy Young Award, the first Canadian pitcher to do so.

The first Canadian player inducted into the baseball hall of fame, Jenkins is the only member of the 3,000-strikeout club inducted into the hall to have surrendered less than 1,000 walks; won 20 or more games in a season seven times; and won the National League Cy Young Award in 1971 (the first Cub pitcher and the first Canadian to do so).

Making his major league debut on September 10, 1965, Jenkins played 19 seasons (1965–1983) for the Philadelphia Phillies (1965–1966), Chicago Cubs (1966–1973, 1982–1983), Texas Rangers (1974–1975, 1978–1981), and Boston Red Sox (1976–1977). He was named to three All-Star teams (1967, 1971–1972) and was the 1974 American League Comeback Player of the Year.

The 6'5", 210-pound Jenkins led the league in wins twice; fewest walks per nine innings five times; complete games four times; and home runs allowed seven times. His streak of six consecutive seasons with 20 or more wins (1967–1972) was the longest streak in the major leagues since Warren Spahn (1956–1961).

In 1974, while with the Texas Rangers, he became the first baseball player to win the Lou Marsh Trophy, presented annually to Canada's top athlete. He was also named the Canadian Press male athlete of the year four times between 1967 and 1974.

In 1980, during a customs search in Toronto (Ontario, Canada), cocaine and marijuana were found in his possession. Commissioner Bowie Kuhn suspended him indefinitely and he missed the rest of the 1980 season. An independent arbiter later reinstated Jenkins, and he returned to the major leagues in 1981.

In 1979, he was made a Member of the Order of Canada; has been inducted into the Canadian Baseball Hall of Fame (1987), Canada's Walk of Fame (2001), and the Texas Rangers Hall of Fame (2004); and was appointed the commissioner of the now-defunct Canadian Baseball League in 2003.

For several years in the baseball off-season (1967–1969), Jenkins played basketball with the Harlem Globetrotters to keep in shape.

After retiring from the major leagues, he pitched for two seasons with the London Majors of the Intercounty Major Baseball League in Ontario, Canada.

On October 2, 1974, in the Texas Rangers' last game of the season, manager Billy Martin allowed Jenkins to hit for himself rather than use the Designated Hitter, the first time a starting pitcher hit in the American League all season. He hit a single; broke up the Minnesota Twins' Jim Hughes' bid for a no-hitter; scored the Rangers' first run; and eventually won his 25th game of the season, 2–1. On April 24, 1977, Jenkins threw the first-ever shutout in Toronto's Exhibition Stadium, as the Red Sox beat the Blue Jays, 9–0. On May 3, 1980, he beat the Baltimore Orioles 3–2 to become only the fourth pitcher to win 100 games in each league.

Ferguson Jenkins' Career Statistics

YEAR	TEAM	LG	W	L	PCT	G	SH	SV	IP	H	R	ER	SO	BB	ERA
1965	Philadelphia	NL	2	1	.667	7	0		12.0	7	3	3	10	2	2.25
1966	Philadelphia	NL	0	0	.000	1	0		2.0	3	2	1	2	1	4.50
1966	Chicago	NL	6	8	.429	60	1		182.0	147	75	67	148	51	3.31
1967	Chicago	NL	20	13	.606	38	3		289.0	230	101	90	236	83	2.80
1968	Chicago	NL	20	15	.571	40	3		308.0	255	96	90	260	65	2.63
1969	Chicago	NL	21	15	.583	43	7	1	311.0	284	122	111	273	71	3.21
1970	Chicago	NL	22	16	.579	40	3	0	313.0	265	128	118	274	60	3.39
1971	Chicago	NL	24	13	.649	39	3	0	325.0	304	114	100	263	37	2.77
1972	Chicago	NL	20	12	.625	36	5	0	289.0	253	111	103	184	62	3.21
1973	Chicago	NL	14	16	.467	38	2	0	271.0	267	133	117	170	57	3.89
1974	Texas	AL	25	12	.676	41	6	0	328.0	286	117	103	225	45	2.83
1975	Texas	AL	17	18	.486	37	4	0	270.0	261	130	118	157	56	3.93
1976	Boston	AL	12	11	.522	30	2	0	209.0	201	85	76	142	43	3.27
1977	Boston	AL	10	10	.500	28	1	0	193.0	190	91	79	105	36	3.68
1978	Texas	AL	18	8	.692	34	4	0	249.0	228	92	84	157	41	3.04
1979	Texas	AL	16	14	.533	37	3	0	259.0	252	127	117	164	81	4.07
1980	Texas	AL	12	12	.500	29	0	0	198.0	190	90	83	129	52	3.77
1981	Texas	AL	5	8	.385	19	0	0	106.0	122	55	53	63	40	4.50
1982	Chicago	NL	14	15	.483	34	1	0	217.1	221	92	76	134	68	3.15
1983	Chicago	NL	6	9	.400	33	1	0	167.1	176	89	80	96	46	4.30
	TOTALS		284	226	.557	664	49	1	4,498	4,142	1,853	1,669	3,192	997	3.34

Sources: Baseball-Reference.com; National Baseball Hall of Fame and Museum

Jennings-Gabarra, Carin (born: January 9, 1965 in East Orange, New Jersey); inducted into the National Soccer Hall of Fame and Museum in 2000 as a player; Position: Forward; International Caps (1987–1996): 117; International Goals: 53; won the first-ever FIFA World Championship for Women in 1991; led Navy to its first-ever Patriot League title in 1998; an eight-time All-American (four in high school, four in college); first U.S. player to be named MVP of the Women's World Cup; won an Olympic gold medal.

Jennings was the second female player to be inducted into the soccer hall of fame (after April Heinrichs in 1998); was on the team that won the first-ever Fédération Internationale de Football Association World Championship for Women in 1991; and was awarded the Golden Ball as the top individual player (the first U.S. player to be named Most Valuable Player of the Women's World Cup).

She won a gold medal with the U.S. team at the 1996 Summer Olympics (Atlanta, Georgia), and she and the team were inducted into the U.S. Olympic Hall of Fame in 2004.

When Jennings retired from World Cup play, her six goals and six assists were second only to Michelle Akers. In a total of 117 international appearances, she had 97 starts, scored 53 goals, and was the third all-time leading scorer.

Jennings played for the winning U.S. National Team in the 1993 and 1994 Confederation of North, Central American and Caribbean Association Football Tournaments, and was a two-time National Amateur Champion with the Ajax of Southern California club. As a college player, Jennings was a four-time National Soccer Coaches Association of America All-American at the University of California, Santa Barbara; elected Athlete of the Decade at UCSB; and was inducted into the University's Athletic Hall of Fame in 1991.

She was a four-time High School All-American; a three-time California Most Valuable Player; named U.S. Soccer's Female Athlete of the Year twice (1987, 1992); and was drafted by the L.A. United of the Continental Indoor Soccer League in 1993.

As of this writing, she serves as the women's soccer coach at the United States Naval Academy (Annapolis, Maryland), where she has been since 1993. Jennings is credited with taking the team from a club-level organization to a National Collegiate Athletic Association Tournament squad. The team began playing in the Patriot League in 1994 and won Navy's first regular-season league title in 1998. In 2002, she led the school to its first undefeated season (16–0–4), the only Division I team that went undefeated during the regular season, but was upset by American University in the Patriot League Tournament.

In 2003, Navy won its first Patriot League Tournament title and became the first Naval Academy women's team in any sport to earn a bid to the NCAA Tournament.

Before attending college, she was a star athlete at Palos Verdes (California) High School and led the nation in scoring from 1980 to 1983, while being named a high school All-American four times. At Santa Barbara, Jennings played forward and remains the record holder in almost every individual category, including most goals in a game, season, and career; most assists in a season and career; most points in a season and career; most shots in a season and career; and most games played in a career.

She began her coaching career in 1987 at Westmont College (Santa Barbara, California), before moving on to Harvard University (Cambridge, Massachusetts) in 1988 as an assistant coach.

In addition to her coaching duties at Navy, Jennings is a member of both the U.S. Soccer Athlete Advisory Council and the U.S. Olympic Committee Athlete Advisory Council.

Source: National Soccer Hall of Fame and Museum

Jennings, Hugh Ambrose "Hughie" (born: April 2, 1869 in Pittston, Pennsylvania; died: February 1, 1928 in Scranton, Pennsylvania); inducted into the National Baseball Hall of Fame and Museum in 1945 as a player by the Veterans Committee; Position: Shortstop; Bats: Right; Throws: Right; holds the career record for getting hit by pitches (287); holds the major league record for single-season batting average (.398 in 1896) for a shortstop.

The 5'8", 165-pound Jennings made his major league debut on June 1, 1891, he played 17 professional seasons (1891–1918) for the Louisville Colonels (American Association, 1891–1893), Baltimore Orioles (National League, 1893–1899), Brooklyn Superbas (National League, 1899–1900, 1903), Philadelphia Phillies (National League, 1901–1902), and the Detroit Tigers (American League, 1907, 1909, 1912, 1918). He also managed the Detroit Tigers (1907–1920) and the New York Giants for parts of 1924 and 1925.

He led the Baltimore Orioles to four straight appearances (1894–1897) in the 19th century Temple Cup world championship series; led league shortstops in fielding average three times; his .398 average in 1896 is still the major league record for shortstops; led the league in getting hit by pitches five straight seasons (1894–1898) and was hit by pitches 287 times in his career, still a major league record; managed 16 seasons in the majors; and in his first three years as manager (1907–1909), he led Detroit to three consecutive American League pennants.

In 1899, he served briefly as the baseball coach at Cornell University (Ithaca, New York).

After his baseball career, Jennings was a lawyer in Scranton, Pennsylvania.

Hugh Jennings' Playing Career Statistics

YEAR	TEAM	LG	G	AB	R	H	2B	3B	HR	BB	SO	SB	AVG	SLG
1891	Louisville	AA	81	316	46	95	10	8	1	17	36	14	.301	.392
1892	Louisville	NL	152	584	66	137	16	3	2	30	30	24	.235	.283
1893	Louisville	NL	22	80	6	12	3	0	0	3	3	1	.150	.188
1893	Baltimore	NL	16	55	6	13	0	0	1	4	3	0	.236	.291
1894	Baltimore	NL	128	505	136	168	27	20	4	37	17	36	.333	.489

YEAR	TEAM	LG	G	AB	R	H	2B	3B	HR	BB	SO	SB	AVG	SLG
1895	Baltimore	NL	131	528	159	204	40	8	4	24	17	60	.386	.515
1896	Baltimore	NL	129	523	125	208	24	9	0	19	11	73	.398	.478
1897	Baltimore	NL	115	436	131	154	22	9	2	42		60	.353	.459
1898	Baltimore	NL	143	533	136	173	24	9	1	78		31	.325	.409
1899	Baltimore	NL	2	8	2	3	0	2	0	0		0	.375	.875
1899	Brooklyn	NL	61	217	42	64	3	8	0	22		18	.295	.382
1900	Brooklyn	NL	112	440	62	119	17	7	1	31		35	.270	.348
1901	Philadelphia	NL	81	302	38	83	22	2	1	25		13	.275	.371
1902	Philadelphia	NL	78	289	31	80	16	3	1	14		8	.277	.363
1903	Brooklyn	NL	6	17	2	4	0	0	0	1		1	.235	.235
1907	Detroit	AL	1	4	0	1	1	0	0	0		0	.250	.500
1909	Detroit	AL	2	4	1	2	0	0	0	0		0	.500	.500
1912	Detroit	AL	1	1	0	0	0	0	0	0		0	.000	.000
1918	Detroit	AL	1	0	0	0	0	0	0	0		0	.000	.000
	TOTALS		1,262	4,842	989	1,520	225	88	18	347	117	374	.314	.408

Hugh Jennings' Managerial Career

YEAR	LG	TEAM	W	L	WP	FINISH
1907	AL	Detroit	92	58	.613	1
1908	AL	Detroit	90	63	.588	1
1909	AL	Detroit	98	54	.645	1
1910	AL	Detroit	86	68	.558	3
1911	AL	Detroit	89	65	.578	2
1912	AL	Detroit	69	84	.451	6
1913	AL	Detroit	66	87	.431	6
1914	AL	Detroit	80	73	.523	4
1915	AL	Detroit	100	54	.649	2
1916	AL	Detroit	87	67	.565	3
1917	AL	Detroit	78	75	.510	4
1918	AL	Detroit	55	71	.437	7
1919	AL	Detroit	80	60	.571	4
1920	AL	Detroit	61	93	.396	7
1924	NL	New York	32	12	.727	1
1925	NL	New York	21	11	.656	2
		Detroit	1,131	972	.538	
		New York	53	23	.697	
		TOTALS	1,184	995	.543	

Sources: Baseball-Reference.com; National Baseball Hall of Fame and Museum

Jennings, William M. (born: December 14, 1920 in New York, New York; died: August 7, 1981); inducted into the Hockey Hall of Fame in 1975 as a builder; the William M. Jennings Award replaced the Vezina Trophy; founded the Lester Patrick Award.

Jennings owned the National Hockey League's New York Rangers from 1959 until his death in 1981, and since he died, the William M. Jennings Trophy, named in his honor, is presented annually to the goaltender(s) having played a minimum of 25 regular-season games in the NHL and allowing the fewest goals against average. This award replaced the Vezina Trophy.

He attended Princeton University (New Jersey) as an undergraduate before graduating from Yale Law School (New Haven, Connecticut) in 1943. His ties to the National Hockey League began in 1959 when he was the legal counsel for the organization that acquired a controlling interest in the Madison Square Garden Corporation, the parent company of the New York Rangers.

Jennings was active with the team from the very start, and served as its president and representative on the NHL Board of Governors in 1962. He was appointed to the NHL Finance Committee; was chairman of the Board of Governors and Expansion Committee; and helped establish a New York office for the National Hockey League in 1964.

In 1966, he founded the Lester Patrick Award, which is presented annually for outstanding service to hockey in the United States. Jennings was named *The Hockey News* Executive of the Year in 1970; received the Lester Patrick Award in 1977; and was inducted into the U.S. Hockey Hall of Fame (1981).

Source: Hockey Hall of Fame

Johnson, Byron Bancroft "Ban" (born: January 5, 1864 in Norwalk, Ohio; died: March 28, 1931 in St. Louis, Missouri); inducted into the National Baseball Hall of Fame and Museum in 1937 (a charter member) as a pioneer-executive by the Veterans Committee; founded the American League.

A sportswriter for the *Cincinnati Commercial-Gazette* in Cincinnati, Ohio before becoming a baseball executive, Johnson founded the American League and was the game's most influential executive for almost 25 years. As president of the Western League since 1893, he changed its name to the American League in 1900 and claimed major league status the following year, with the intent of competing directly against the more established National League.

Johnson became the dominant member of the National Commission, baseball's ruling body until 1920, when the sport hired its first commissioner, Kenesaw Mountain Landis.

A long-time critic of the National League's rowdy and uncontrolled atmosphere (which was driving families and women away from the ballparks), he made his Western League more fan friendly and is credited with changing the game forever by giving umpires complete control of the on-field game. He routinely fined players and coaches who showed disrespect to them and he also fined and suspended players who used foul language on the field. With an eye toward starting a circuit that could compete with the National League, Johnson began reconfiguring the Western League by moving, adding, and dropping teams and by shoring up the league's financial strength. When complete, the Western League had been totally transformed into the American League by 1900.

An immediate success, he was given a 10-year contract as the league's president and in October 1900, he withdrew the American League from the National Agreement (the formal understanding between the National League and several minor leagues) and in January 1901, he stated that the American League would operate as a major league.

When the National League limited player salaries to $2,400 a season in 1901, Johnson seized the opportunity to expand the American League and actively pursued National League stars with a higher salary base, more than 100 of whom jumped leagues. The plan worked and in two short seasons, the American League was outdrawing its rival, forcing the National League to re-negotiate the National Agreement. Under the new deal, the junior circuit was recognized as a major league and a three-man National Commission was established, initially consisting of the presidents of both leagues and Cincinnati Reds owner Garry Herrmann. Although Herrmann was nominal president of the commission, Johnson soon dominated the governing body and basically ruled baseball for the next several years.

Johnson ruled the league with a strong hand and tried to control who could own teams. When Harry Frazee bought the Boston Red Sox in 1917, Johnson tried to force him from the league and the feud between the two men eventually led to Johnson's demise. Their battles led to teams in the league taking sides and making the relationship worse. The problems came to a head when eight members of the Chicago White Sox were accused of throwing the 1919 World Series, in what is known as the infamous "Black Sox" scandal. When Johnson ignored White Sox owner Charles Comiskey's warnings and the scandal became public after the 1920 season, the White Sox, Boston Red Sox, and the New York Yankees threatened to pull out of the American League and join the National League.

Due to Johnson's lack of action in dealing with the scandal, he lost a lot of support within the league. The scandal had badly damaged baseball's credibility and both leagues realized that a fundamental structural change had to be made. The National Commission obviously had not worked and was disbanded, and the office of the Commissioner was created, with the first "baseball czar" being Judge Kenesaw Mountain Landis. The change in structure gave most of the game's power to the Commissioner and the role of the league presidents was greatly diminished.

Landis and Johnson clashed almost from the start and it soon became clear that one of them had to go. Whenever a problem erupted between the two, Landis always threatened to resign if he did not have the game's support. Several issues came between the men over the years, until finally Johnson's contract was cancelled and he was in essence fired in 1927.

Source: National Baseball Hall of Fame and Museum

Johnson, Dennis Wayne (born: September 18, 1954 in San Pedro, California; died: February 22, 2007 in Austin, Texas); inducted into the Naismith Memorial Basketball Hall of Fame in 2010 as a player; Position: Guard; Uniform: #3, #24; won three NBA championships.

Nicknamed "DJ," the 6'4", 185-pound Johnson went to Dominguez High School (Compton, California), Los Angeles Harbor College (California, where he helped the school to a junior college state title), and Pepperdine University

(Malibu, California), before he was the 12th pick of the second round (29th overall selection) of the Seattle SuperSonics in the 1976 NBA Draft. During his tumultuous 14-year career, Johnson (who earned a reputation as a talented but difficult player to manage) played for the Seattle SuperSonics (1976–1980), Phoenix Suns (1980–1983), and Boston Celtics (1983–1990); earned nine consecutive NBA All-Defensive Team honors (First Team: 1979–1983, 1987; Second Team: 1984–1986); was a five-time All-Star (1979–1982, 1985); won three NBA championships (1979 [Seattle's only championship], 1984, 1986); was named MVP of the 1979 Finals); and had his number three jersey retired by Boston in December 1991. When he retired, Johnson was only the 11th player to have more than 15,000 points and 5,000 assists.

Dennis Johnson's NBA Player Career Statistics

SEASON	TEAM	G	MIN	FG	3P	FT	TRB	AST	STL	BLK	PTS
1976–1977	Seattle	81	1,667	285		179	302	123	123	57	749
1977–1978	Seattle	81	2,209	367		297	294	230	118	51	1,031
1978–1979	Seattle	80	2,717	482		306	374	280	100	97	1,270
1979–1980	Seattle	81	2,937	574	12	380	414	332	144	82	1,540
1980–1981	Phoenix	79	2,615	532	11	411	363	291	136	61	1,486
1981–1982	Phoenix	80	2,937	577	8	399	410	369	105	55	1,561
1982–1983	Phoenix	77	2,551	398	5	292	335	388	97	39	1,093
1983–1984	Boston	80	2,665	384	4	281	280	338	93	57	1,053
1984–1985	Boston	80	2,976	493	7	261	317	543	96	39	1,254
1985–1986	Boston	78	2,732	482	6	243	268	456	110	35	1,213
1986–1987	Boston	79	2,933	423	7	209	261	594	87	38	1,062
1987–1988	Boston	77	2,670	352	12	255	240	598	93	29	971
1988–1989	Boston	72	2,309	277	7	160	190	472	94	21	721
1989–1990	Boston	75	2,036	206	1	118	201	485	81	14	531
	TOTALS	1,100	35,954	5,832	80	3,791	4,249	5,499	1,477	675	15,535

Sources: Basketball-Reference.com; Naismith Memorial Basketball Hall of Fame

Johnson, Earvin, Jr. "Magic" (born: August 14, 1959 in Lansing, Michigan); inducted into the Naismith Memorial Basketball Hall of Fame in 2002 as a player; Position: Guard-Forward; Uniform: #32; won championships at the high school, collegiate, professional, and international levels; won the 1979 NCAA national title; won five NBA titles.

While attending Lansing Everett (Michigan) High School (1974–1977), Johnson was selected All-State three times by the Associated Press and United Press International, and was a two-time McDonald's All-American selection (1976–1977).

After high school, he went to Michigan State University (Lansing, 1977–1979) and led the school to the 1979 National Collegiate Athletic Association Championship; named NCAA Division I Tournament Most Outstanding Player (1979); selected to *The Sporting News* All-America First Team (1979); a two-time All-American (1978–1979); a two-time All-Big Ten selection (1978–1979); and was inducted into the Michigan State University Athletics Hall of Fame in 1992. He led Michigan State to the 1979 NCAA championship in a classic battle against Indiana State's Larry Bird, a rivalry that would continue throughout the 1980s in the NBA with the Los Angeles Lakers and Boston Celtics.

After college, the 6'8", 215-pound Johnson was a first-round pick (first overall selection) in the 1979 National Basketball Association Draft by the Los Angeles Lakers, where he played his entire 13-year NBA career (1979–1991, 1995–1996), with a four-year interruption due to contracting the AIDS virus. He was named to the NBA All-Rookie Team in 1980; led the Lakers to five NBA Championships (1980, 1982, 1985, 1987–1988); is the Lakers' all-time assists leader (10,141) and all-time steals leader (1,724); named NBA Most Valuable Player three times (1987, 1989–1990); a 12-time All-Star (1980, 1982–1992); All-Star Most Valuable Player twice (1990, 1992); All-NBA First Team nine times (1983–1986, 1988–1991) and Second Team once (1982); won the J. Walter Kennedy Citizenship Award (1992); and was named to the NBA 50th Anniversary All-Time Team.

As of this writing, he is the only rookie to win the NBA Finals MVP award, and is one of only four players to win NCAA and NBA championships in consecutive years.

Johnson led the NBA with 3.43 steals per game (1981) and 2.67 steals per game (1982); holds the career record for highest assists per game average (11.2); holds the career playoff record for most assists (2,346); NBA Finals single-series record for highest assist per game average (14.0 in 1985) and highest assists per game average by a rookie (8.7 in 1980); NBA Finals single-game records for most points by a rookie (42 on May 6, 1980 against the Philadelphia 76ers) and most assists in one half (14 on June 19, 1988 against the Detroit Pistons); and holds the single-series playoff record for highest assists per game average (17.0 in 1985).

He was a member of the 1992 "Dream Team" gold medal-winning U.S. Olympic squad (held in Barcelona, Spain); a broadcaster with NBC Sports (1992–1994); serves as Lakers Vice President (1994–present); and in May 2006, ESPN.com rated Johnson the greatest point guard of all time. He briefly coached the Lakers during the 1993–1994 season and compiled a 5–11 (.313) record.

In addition to his role with the Lakers, he is the Chief Executive Officer of his own business, Magic Johnson Enterprises, which is involved in numerous entities, including several Starbucks franchises; TGI Friday's franchises; 24 Hour Fitness; and more. He also created the Magic Johnson Foundation, which helps inner-city communities deal with issues surrounding HIV/AIDS and raises funds for research and prevention efforts. In 1996, he wrote the book *What You Can Do to Avoid AIDS* and proceeds from its sales were donated to the Magic Johnson Foundation.

Johnson was first nicknamed "Magic" by *Lansing State Journal* sportswriter Fred Stabley, Jr. after he watched the 15-year-old Johnson record a triple-double (36 points, 18 rebounds, 16 assists) during a high school game at Everett High School. As a senior, he led the school to a 27–1 record and went on to win the state title.

As a freshman at Michigan State, he led the team to the Big Ten Conference title and reached the Elite Eight in the 1978 NCAA tournament, before being eliminated by eventual national champion Kentucky.

In 1979, he led the team into the NCAA final game, and in what is still the highest-rated college basketball game ever broadcast, Michigan State beat Indiana State (and its star Larry Bird) 75–64. Johnson was voted Most Outstanding Player of the Final Four and the rivalry between the two players continued into the NBA.

After two years in college, Johnson left the school (finishing his career averaging 17.1 points, 7.6 rebounds, and 7.9 assists per game) to enter the 1979 NBA Draft.

In the 1981–1982 season, he led the league with 2.7 steals per game; was named to the All-NBA Second Team; and joined Wilt Chamberlain and Oscar Robertson as the only NBA players to accumulate at least 700 points, 700 rebounds, and 700 assists in the same season. The Lakers beat the Philadelphia 76ers in six games for the NBA title and Johnson won his second NBA Finals MVP award.

In 1983, Johnson was named to his first All-NBA First Team selection, and in 1984, he and Larry Bird (Boston Celtics) faced each other for the first time in the NBA Finals, eventually won by Boston in seven games. The duo (and the teams) faced each other again in the 1985 NBA Finals, with the Lakers winning the title in six games. For the entire 1985–1986 season, he averaged a double-double (18.8 points, 5.9 rebounds, 12.6 assists per game), but was unable to reach the NBA title series as the Lakers lost to the Houston Rockets in the Western Conference Finals.

In 1987, Johnson won his first regular-season MVP award; again faced Bird and the Celtics in the NBA Finals series, eventually won by Los Angeles in six games; and won his third Finals MVP Award. In the 1987–1988 season, he once again averaged a double-double (19.6 points, 6.2 rebounds, 11.9 assists per games), and won his fifth (and last) NBA championship in seven games over the Detroit Pistons.

In 1988–1989, Johnson again averaged a double-double (22.5 points, 7.9 rebounds, 12.8 assists per game); earned his second regular-season MVP award; but could not "three-peat" when the Lakers were swept in four games by the Detroit Pistons.

During a physical in 1991, Johnson tested positive for HIV and retired from the NBA. Despite retiring, the fans voted him to the 1992 NBA All-Star Game; he led the West to a 153–113 win; and was named the game's MVP (25 points, nine assists, and five rebounds).

Despite being HIV-positive, he was selected to compete in the 1992 Summer Olympics (in Barcelona, Spain) for the U.S. basketball team, which was called the "Dream Team" because of the numerous NBA stars on the roster. Knee injuries limited his playing time, but he was on the team that won the gold medal.

Johnson's jersey number 32 was retired by the Lakers in February 1992, and in the 1993–1994 season, he returned to the NBA as head coach of the Lakers. After leading Los Angeles to a 5–11 record, he quit as the team's coach, and became a minority owner when he bought five percent of the Lakers in June 1994.

In the 1995–1996 season, Johnson attempted an NBA comeback at age 36 for the last 32 games of the season. He averaged 14.6 points, 6.9 assists, and 5.7 rebounds per game, but after the Lakers were eliminated by the Houston Rockets in the first round of the playoffs, he retired for good.

Magic Johnson's Career Statistics

SEASON	TEAM	G	MIN	FG	3P	FT	TRB	AST	PTS
1979–1980	Los Angeles	77	2,795	503	7	374	596	563	1,387
1980–1981	Los Angeles	37	1,371	312	3	171	320	317	798
1981–1982	Los Angeles	78	2,991	556	6	329	751	743	1,447

SEASON	TEAM	G	MIN	FG	3P	FT	TRB	AST	PTS
1982–1983	Los Angeles	79	2,907	511	0	304	683	829	1,326
1983–1984	Los Angeles	67	2,567	441	6	290	491	875	1,178
1984–1985	Los Angeles	77	2,781	504	7	391	476	968	1,406
1985–1986	Los Angeles	72	2,578	483	10	378	426	907	1,354
1986–1987	Los Angeles	80	2,904	683	8	535	504	977	1,909
1987–1988	Los Angeles	72	2,637	490	11	417	449	858	1,408
1988–1989	Los Angeles	77	2,886	579	59	513	607	988	1,730
1989–1990	Los Angeles	79	2,937	546	106	567	522	907	1,765
1990–1991	Los Angeles	79	2,933	466	80	519	551	989	1,531
1995–1996	Los Angeles	32	958	137	22	172	183	220	468
	TOTALS	906	33,245	6,211	325	4,960	6,559	10,141	17,707

Sources: Basketball-Reference.com; Magic Johnson Web Site (www.majicjohnson.org); *My Life* (Earvin "Magic" Johnson with William Novak); Naismith Memorial Basketball Hall of Fame

Johnson, Ernest Thomas "Moose" (born: February 26, 1886 in Montreal, Quebec, Canada; died: March 25, 1963); inducted into the Hockey Hall of Fame in 1952 as a player; Position: Defenseman; one of the first five professional players allowed to compete for the Stanley Cup; won three Stanley Cup titles; used the longest stick in hockey history (with a 99-inch reach).

Johnson began playing organized hockey in the Montreal City League, and after playing two seasons in the Canadian Amateur Hockey League, he joined the Montreal Wanderers in the Eastern Canada Amateur Hockey Association's inaugural season (1905–1906). In March 1906, the Wanderers won the Stanley Cup by beating the Ottawa Silver Seven in a two-game challenge. He would go on to play 19 professional hockey seasons from 1905 to 1931, but never in the National Hockey League.

In 1906, when the ECAHA ruled that professional players could compete in the league, the Wanderers signed Johnson, Jack Marshall, Hod Stewart, Pud Glass, and Riley Hern. These five were the first professional players allowed to compete for the Stanley Cup when the Wanderers successfully won a Cup challenge from New Glasgow in December 1906. In an upset, the team was three games into the 1907 ECAHA season, when it lost the Stanley Cup challenge in a two-game series to the Kenora Thistles (the smallest town ever to win the Stanley Cup). In March 1907, the Wanderers regained the Cup by winning a two-game challenge against Kenora.

In 1908, Johnson was named to the ECAHA Second All-Star Team, and the Wanderers successfully defended the team's Stanley Cup title three times that year before losing the Cup to the Ottawa Senators in 1909. In 1910, the Wanderers won the newly formed National Hockey Association title; regained the Stanley Cup from the Senators; and successfully defended the Cup against the Berlin (now Kitchener) Union Jacks in March 1910.

Known for using the longest stick in hockey history (with a 99-inch reach), the 5'11", 185-pound Johnson played one more season with the Wanderers before moving to the New Westminster Royals of the Pacific Coast Hockey Association. His played his final year in the PCHA with the Victoria Cougars (1921–1922), and made the PCHA First All-Star Team eight times (1912–1913, 1915–1919, 1921).

Ernest Johnson's Career Statistics

			REGULAR SEASON					PLAYOFFS				
SEASON	TEAM	LEAGUE	GP	G	A	TP	PIM	GP	G	A	TP	PIM
1902–1903	Montreal St. Lawrence	MCHL										
1903–1904	Montreal AAA	CAHL	2	1	0	1						
1903–1904	Montreal AAA-2	CAIHL										
1904–1905	Montreal AAA	CAHL	9	8	0	8	9					
1905–1906	Montreal Wanderers	ECAHA	10	12	0	12	44	2	1	0	1	3
1906–1907	Montreal Wanderers	ECAHA	10	15	0	15	42					
1906–1907	Montreal Wanderers	St-Cup						6	5	0	5	8
1907–1908	Montreal Wanderers	ECAHA	10	9	0	9	33					
1907–1908	Montreal Wanderers	St-Cup						5	11	0	11	28
1908–1909	Montreal Wanderers	St-Cup						2	1	0	1	6
1908–1909	Montreal Wanderers	ECHA	10	10	0	10	34					
1909–1910	Montreal Wanderers	NHA	1	0	0	0	6					
1909–1910	Montreal Wanderers	NHA	12	7	0	7	41					

			REGULAR SEASON					PLAYOFFS				
SEASON	**TEAM**	**LEAGUE**	**GP**	**G**	**A**	**TP**	**PIM**	**GP**	**G**	**A**	**TP**	**PIM**
1909–1910	Montreal Wanderers	St-Cup						1	0	0	0	9
1910–1911	Montreal Wanderers	NHA	16	6	0	6	60					
1911–1912	New Westminster Royals	PCHA	14	9	0	9	13					
1911–1912	PCHA All-Stars	Exhib.	3	1	0	1	10					
1912–1913	New Westminster Royals	PCHA	13	7	3	10	15					
1913–1914	New Westminster Royals	PCHA	16	3	5	8	27					
1914–1915	Portland Rosebuds	PCHA	18	6	4	10	21					
1914–1915	PCHA All-Stars	Exhib.	2	0	0	0	0					
1915–1916	Portland Rosebuds	PCHA	18	6	3	9	62					
1915–1916	Portland Rosebuds	St-Cup						5	1	0	1	9
1915–1916	PCHA All-Stars	Exhib.	3	0	1	1	3					
1916–1917	Portland Rosebuds	PCHA	24	12	9	21	54					
1917–1918	Portland Rosebuds	PCHA	15	3	2	5	3					
1918–1919	Victoria Aristocrats	PCHA	15	3	3	6	0					
1919–1920	Victoria Aristocrats	PCHA	21	0	5	5	22					
1920–1921	Victoria Aristocrats	PCHA	24	5	2	7	26					
1921–1922	Victoria Cougars	PCHA	13	1	1	2	12					
1925–1926	L.A. Palais-de-Glace	Cal-Pro										
1926–1927	Minneapolis Millers	AHA	30	1	2	3	43	5	0	0	0	12
1928–1929	Portland Buckaroos	PCHL	28	1	0	1	27	1	0	0	0	0
1929–1930	Hollywood Millionaires	Cal-Pro		1	2	3						
1930–1931	San Francisco Tigers	Cal-Pro		10	6	16						

Sources: Hockey Hall of Fame; Hockey-Reference.com

Johnson, Gus (born: December 13, 1938 in Akron, Ohio; died: April 29, 1987 in Akron, Ohio); inducted into the Naismith Memorial Basketball Hall of Fame in 2010 as a player; Position: Small Forward; Uniform: #13, #25; won an ABA Championship with the Indiana Pacers.

After attending Central Hower High School (Akron, Ohio) and the University of Idaho (Moscow), the 6'6", 230-pound Johnson was a number two selection in the second-round (10th pick overall) of the Chicago Zephyrs (Baltimore Bullets) in the 1963 NBA Draft. In 10 professional seasons (1963–1973), he played for the Baltimore Bullets (1963–1972), Phoenix Suns (1972), and the Indiana Pacers of the American Basketball Association (1972–1973).

He was named to the NBA All-Rookie Team (1964); a five-time NBA All-Star (1965, 1968–1971); a two-time member of the NBA's All-Defensive team (1970–1971); helped lead the Bullets to five playoff appearances in nine seasons (including the 1971 NBA Finals); played just over nine years in the NBA and less than one full season in the ABA; won an ABA Championship with the Indiana Pacers; and had his jersey number 25 retired by the Washington Wizards (the successor team of the Baltimore Bullets).

In high school, Johnson was an All-State high school player and one of his teammates was future hall-of-famer Nate Thurmond. After high school, he went to Boise Junior College (1961–1962) before playing for one season at the Univer sity of Idaho (1962–1963), where he earned the nickname "Honeycomb." Johnson was second in the NCAA in rebounding (behind Creighton's Paul Silas) and set a school record with 31 rebounds in a game against Oregon.

In his first NBA season, he averaged 17.3 points and 13.6 rebounds, finishing second in Rookie of the Year voting to future hall-of-famer Jerry Lucas (Cincinnati Royals).

Gus Johnson's NBA/ABA Career Statistics

SEASON	**TEAM**	**LG**	**G**	**MP**	**FG**	**FT**	**TRB**	**AST**	**PTS**
1963–1964	Baltimore	NBA	78	2,847	571	210	1,064	169	1,352
1964–1965	Baltimore	NBA	76	2,899	577	261	988	270	1,415
1965–1966	Baltimore	NBA	42	1,284	273	131	546	114	677
1966–1967	Baltimore	NBA	73	2,626	620	271	855	194	1,511
1967–1968	Baltimore	NBA	60	2,271	482	180	782	159	1,144
1968–1969	Baltimore	NBA	49	1,671	359	160	568	97	878
1969–1970	Baltimore	NBA	78	2,919	578	197	1,086	264	1,353
1970–1971	Baltimore	NBA	66	2,538	494	214	1,128	192	1,202
1971–1972	Baltimore	NBA	39	668	103	43	226	51	249

SEASON	TEAM	LG	G	MP	FG	FT	TRB	AST	PTS
1972–1973	Phoenix	NBA	21	417	69	25	136	31	163
1972–1973	Indiana	ABA	50	753	132	31	245	62	299
1972–1973	Totals		71	1,170	201	56	381	93	462
		ABA	50	753	132	31	245	62	299
		NBA	582	20,140	4,126	1,692	7,379	1,541	9,944
		TOTALS	632	20,893	4,258	1,723	7,624	1,603	10,243

Sources: Basketball-Reference.com; Naismith Memorial Basketball Hall of Fame

Johnson, Ivan Wilfred "Ching" (born: December 7, 1898 in Winnipeg, Manitoba, Canada; died: June 16, 1979 in Silver Spring, Maryland); inducted into the Hockey Hall of Fame in 1958 as a player; Position: Defenseman; won two Stanley Cup titles.

The 5'11", 210-pound Johnson played 12 National Hockey League seasons with the New York Rangers (1926–1937) and the New York Americans (1937–1938). He helped the Rangers win two Stanley Cup titles (1928, 1933); was selected to the NHL First All-Star Team twice (1932–1933); to the Second All-Star Team twice (1931, 1934); and on February 14, 1934, he participated in the Ace Bailey Benefit Game to aid the former Maple Leaf star, whose career had ended prematurely after a vicious hit by Eddie Shore.

Johnson was with the New York Americans for one season (1937–1938) as a player-coach before retiring from the NHL. He later played in the minor leagues as a player-coach, and his last season in professional hockey was as the head coach of the Washington Lions (Eastern Amateur League, 1940–1941).

He was inducted into the Manitoba Sports Hall of Fame and Museum in 2004.

Ivan Johnson's Career Statistics

			REGULAR SEASON					PLAYOFFS				
SEASON	TEAM	LEAGUE	GP	G	A	TP	PIM	GP	G	A	TP	PIM
1919–1920	Winnipeg Monarchs	WSrHL	7	6	3	9	10					
1920–1922	Eveleth Rangers	USAHA										
1922–1923	Eveleth Rangers	AHA	20	4	0	4	26					
1923–1924	Minneapolis Millers	USAHA	20	9	3	12	34					
1924–1925	Minneapolis Rockets	USAHA	40	8	0	8	43					
1925–1926	Minneapolis Millers	CHL	38	14	5	19	92	3	2	0	2	6
1926–1927	New York Rangers	NHL	27	3	2	5	66	2	0	0	0	8
1927–1928	New York Rangers	NHL	42	10	6	16	146	9	1	1	2	46
1928–1929	New York Rangers	NHL	8	0	0	0	14	6	0	0	0	26
1929–1930	New York Rangers	NHL	30	3	3	6	82	4	0	0	0	14
1930–1931	New York Rangers	NHL	44	2	6	8	77	4	1	0	1	17
1931–1932	New York Rangers	NHL	47	3	10	13	106	7	2	0	2	24
1932–1933	New York Rangers	NHL	48	8	9	17	127	8	1	0	1	14
1933–1934	New York Rangers	NHL	48	2	6	8	86	2	0	0	0	4
1934–1935	New York Rangers	NHL	29	2	3	5	34	4	0	0	0	2
1935–1936	New York Rangers	NHL	47	5	3	8	58					
1936–1937	New York Rangers	NHL	35	0	0	0	2	9	0	1	1	4
1937–1938	New York Americans	NHL	31	0	0	0	10	6	0	0	0	2
1938–1939	Minneapolis Millers	AHA	47	2	9	11	60	4	0	2	2	0
1939–1940	Minneapolis Millers	AHA	48	0	4	4	26	3	0	0	0	2
1940–1941	Marquette Ironmen	NMHL										
1941–1943	Washington Lions	AHL										
1943–1944	Hollywood Wolves	PCHL										
	NHL TOTALS		436	38	48	86	808		61	2	7	161

Sources: Hockey Hall of Fame; Hockey-Reference.com

Johnson, James Earl "Jimmy" (born: March 31, 1938 in Dallas, Texas); inducted into the Pro Football Hall of Fame in 1994 as a player; Position: Cornerback; named All-Pro four straight seasons; selected to five Pro Bowls; once held the record for most games played by a San Francisco 49er.

Johnson, a 6'2", 187-pound two-way star at the University of California, Los Angeles, was the first of three first-round draft choices (sixth selection overall) of the National Football League's San Francisco 49ers in 1961, where he would play his entire 16-year (213 games) career (1961–1976). The brother of former world decathlon champion Rafer Johnson, he played wingback on offense and defensive back at UCLA.

He was named All-Pro four straight seasons (1969–1972); selected to five Pro Bowls; had 47 career interceptions for 615 yards (49ers records at the time); and played in two National Football Conference title games.

After trying him at numerous offensive and defensive positions, the 49ers eventually converted Johnson to cornerback. When he retired, his 213 career games was a 49ers record.

Johnson received the Pro Football Writers' George Halas Award for courageous play in 1971, and won the Len Eshmont Award twice (1969, 1975), given by the 49ers to team players for inspirational play.

James Johnson's Career Statistics

					DEFENSE		
YEAR	**TEAM**	**G**	**INT**	**YDS**	**AVG**	**TD**	**FUMREC**
1961	San Francisco	12	5	116	23.2	0	0
1962	San Francisco	12	0	0	0.0	0	0
1963	San Francisco	13	2	36	18.0	0	1
1964	San Francisco	14	3	65	21.7	0	0
1965	San Francisco	14	6	47	7.8	0	0
1966	San Francisco	14	4	57	14.3	1	2
1967	San Francisco	11	2	68	34.0	0	1
1968	San Francisco	13	1	25	25.0	0	0
1969	San Francisco	14	5	18	3.6	0	0
1970	San Francisco	14	2	36	18.0	1	1
1971	San Francisco	14	3	16	5.3	0	1
1972	San Francisco	14	4	18	4.5	0	0
1973	San Francisco	13	4	46	11.5	0	0
1974	San Francisco	13	3	50	16.7	0	0
1975	San Francisco	14	2	0	0.0	0	1
1976	San Francisco	14	1	17	17.0	0	0
	TOTALS	213	47	615	13.1	2	7

Sources: Pro Football Hall of Fame; Pro-Football-Reference.com

Johnson, John Henry (born: November 24, 1929 in Waterproof, Louisiana); inducted into the Pro Football Hall of Fame in 1987 as a player; Position: Fullback; part of the San Francisco 49ers "Million Dollar Backfield;" first Steeler to run for more than 1,000 yards twice in his career; won the 1957 NFL title.

Johnson was a football star at St. Mary's College of California (Moraga), until the school discontinued the program and he transferred to Arizona State University (Tempe). In the 1953 National Football League Draft, he was a second-round pick (18th overall selection) of the Pittsburgh Steelers, but decided to play for the Calgary Stampeders of the Canadian Football League. After one season in the CFL, he returned to the United States and joined the NFL's San Francisco 49ers.

For two seasons (1955–1956), he played in the "Million Dollar Backfield" that included future hall of famers Hugh McElhenny, Joe Perry, and Y. A. Tittle.

The 6'2", 210-pound fullback played in the league for 13 years (143 games) with the 49ers (1954–1956), Detroit Lions (1957–1959), Pittsburgh Steelers (1960–1965), and the Houston Oilers (1966). While in Pittsburgh, he ran for more than 1,000 yards twice (1962, 1964), the first Steeler to do so. Johnson played in four Pro Bowl games (1955, 1963–1965); was a two-time All-Pro selection (1954, 1962); and retired with 6,803 rushing yards, at the time second only to Jim Brown.

Johnson did not win a league championship until he joined the Detroit Lions, and helped the team beat the Cleveland Browns 59–14 for the 1957 NFL title.

John Henry Johnson's Career Statistics

			RUSHING				RECEIVING			
YEAR	TEAM	G	NO	YDS	AVG	TD	NO	YDS	AVG	TD
1954	San Francisco	12	129	681	5.3	9	28	183	6.5	0
1955	San Francisco	7	19	69	3.6	1	2	6	3.0	0
1956	San Francisco	12	80	301	3.8	2	8	90	11.3	0
1957	Detroit	12	129	621	4.8	5	20	141	7.1	0
1958	Detroit	9	56	254	4.5	0	7	60	8.6	0
1959	Detroit	10	82	270	3.3	2	7	34	4.9	1
1960	Pittsburgh	12	118	621	5.3	2	12	112	9.3	1
1961	Pittsburgh	14	213	787	3.7	6	24	262	10.9	1
1962	Pittsburgh	14	251	1,141	4.5	7	32	226	7.1	2
1963	Pittsburgh	12	186	773	4.2	4	21	145	6.9	1
1964	Pittsburgh	14	235	1,048	4.5	7	17	69	4.1	1
1965	Pittsburgh	1	3	11	3.7	0	0	0	0.0	0
1966	Houston	14	70	226	3.2	3	8	150	18.8	0
	TOTALS	143	1,571	6,803	4.3	48	186	1,478	7.9	7

Sources: Pro Football Hall of Fame; Pro-Football-Reference.com

Johnson, Robert "Badger Bob" (born: March 4, 1931 in Minneapolis, Minnesota; died: November 26, 1991 in Colorado Springs, Colorado); inducted into the Hockey Hall of Fame in 1992 as a builder; won two college conference championships as a player; four high school city championships as a coach; three NCAA titles as a coach; and one NHL Stanley Cup as a coach.

Johnson was an All-Star hockey player at Minneapolis (Minnesota) Central High School, and got his first taste of coaching at age 13, when he led a local midget hockey team. While playing forward for the University of North Dakota (Grand Forks) and University of Minnesota (Minneapolis) hockey teams, he often coached local high school teams. He led Minnesota to two conference championships and was the team's top scorer.

After serving in the Korean War, he became the head coach at Warroad (Minnesota) High School in 1956, and after one season, moved to Roosevelt High School (Minneapolis), where he led the team to four city championships in six seasons. In 1963, he joined the college ranks as the head coach at Colorado College (Colorado Springs), and three seasons later, moved on to the University of Wisconsin (Madison). He coached the Badgers for 15 years (1966–1981); won three national titles (1973, 1977, 1981); and was named the National Collegiate Athletic Association's Coach of the Year in 1977. Johnson also coached the U.S. National Team (1973–1975, 1981) and the Olympic team at the Innsbruck, Austria games in 1976, but failed to medal. After leaving Wisconsin, he coached the National Team at three Canada Cups: 1981 (finishing fourth), 1984 (finishing second), and 1987 (finishing fifth).

In June 1982, Johnson joined the professional coaching ranks with the National Hockey League's Calgary Flames, leading the team to the Stanley Cup finals in 1986, eventually losing to the Montreal Canadiens in five games. In 1987, he left the NHL and became executive director of USA Hockey, where he served until 1990.

In 1990, he returned to the NHL to coach the Pittsburgh Penguins and, in his first season, led the team to its first-ever Stanley Cup title (1991, beating the Minnesota North Stars in six games).

Johnson was inducted into the Wisconsin Hockey Hall of Fame in 1987 and the United States Hockey Hall of Fame in 1991.

Robert Johnson's NHL Coaching Record

YEAR	TEAM	W	L	T	PLAYOFFS
1982–1983	Calgary	30	32	14	Lost in Second Round
1983–1984	Calgary	34	32	14	Lost in Second Round
1984–1985	Calgary	41	27	12	Lost in First Round
1985–1986	Calgary	40	31	9	Lost in Cup Finals
1986–1987	Calgary	46	31	3	Lost in First Round
1990–1991	Pittsburgh	41	33	6	Won Stanley Cup
	TOTALS	232	186	58	

Sources: Hockey Hall of Fame; Hockey-Reference.com

Johnson, Thomas Christian "Tom" (born: February 18, 1928 in Baldur, Manitoba, Canada; died: November 22, 2007 in Falmouth, Massachusetts); inducted into the Hockey Hall of Fame in 1970 as a player; Position: Defenseman; won six Stanley Cup titles as a player and two championships while serving in the front office.

Johnson played 17 National Hockey League seasons (1947–1965) with the Montreal Canadiens (1947–1948, 1949–1963) and the Boston Bruins (1963–1965). After playing briefly with the Canadiens, he was sent to the minor leagues in 1948 for three seasons (Montreal Royals of the Quebec Senior League [1948] and the Buffalo Bisons of the American Hockey League [1948–1950]) to improve his skills, before rejoining the Canadiens full-time in the 1950–1951 season.

He won six Stanley Cup titles (1953, 1956–1960); was selected to the NHL Second All-Star Team in 1956; named to the First All-Star Team in 1959; won the James Norris Memorial Trophy in 1959 as the league's best defensive player; and was inducted into the Manitoba Sports Hall of Fame and Museum in 1993.

After the 1962–1963 season, he played in 121 games for the Boston Bruins before a leg injury ended his playing career. Johnson then worked for Boston as an assistant to the team's president and general manager, and helped build a team that would eventually win the Stanley Cup in 1970 (with Johnson serving as an assistant general manager) and in 1972 (with Johnson as the team's coach).

Tom Johnson's Career Statistics

			REGULAR SEASON					PLAYOFFS				
SEASON	**TEAM**	**LEAGUE**	**GP**	**G**	**A**	**TP**	**PIM**	**GP**	**G**	**A**	**TP**	**PIM**
1946–1947	Winnipeg Monarchs	MJHL	14	10	4	14	12	7	3	1	4	19
1947–1948	Montreal Canadiens	NHL	1	0	0	0	0					
1947–1948	Montreal Royals	QSHL	16	0	4	4	10					
1948–1949	Buffalo Bisons	AHL	68	4	18	22	70					
1949–1950	Buffalo Bisons	AHL	58	7	19	26	52	5	0	0	0	20
1949–1950	Montreal Canadiens	NHL						1	0	0	0	0
1950–1951	Montreal Canadiens	NHL	70	2	8	10	128	11	0	0	0	6
1951–1952	Montreal Canadiens	NHL	67	0	7	7	76	11	1	0	1	2
1952–1953	Montreal Canadiens	NHL	70	3	8	11	63	12	2	3	5	8
1953–1954	Montreal Canadiens	NHL	70	7	11	18	85	11	1	2	3	30
1954–1955	Montreal Canadiens	NHL	70	6	19	25	74	12	2	0	2	22
1955–1956	Montreal Canadiens	NHL	64	3	10	13	75	10	0	2	2	8
1956–1957	Montreal Canadiens	NHL	70	4	11	15	59	10	0	2	2	13
1957–1958	Montreal Canadiens	NHL	66	3	18	21	75	2	0	0	0	0
1958–1959	Montreal Canadiens	NHL	70	10	29	39	76	11	2	3	5	8
1959–1960	Montreal Canadiens	NHL	64	4	25	29	59	8	0	1	1	4
1960–1961	Montreal Canadiens	NHL	70	1	15	16	54	6	0	1	1	8
1961–1962	Montreal Canadiens	NHL	62	1	17	18	45	6	0	1	1	0
1962–1963	Montreal Canadiens	NHL	43	3	5	8	28					
1963–1964	Boston Bruins	NHL	70	4	21	25	33					
1964–1965	Boston Bruins	NHL	51	0	9	9	30					
	NHL TOTALS		978	51	213	264	960		111	15	23	109

Sources: Hockey Hall of Fame; Hockey-Reference.com

Johnson, Walter Perry (born: November 6, 1887 in Humboldt, Kansas; died: December 10, 1946 in Washington, D.C.); inducted into the National Baseball Hall of Fame and Museum in 1936 as a player; Position: Pitcher; Bats: Right; Throws: Right; his 110 shutouts are the most in major league history; first pitcher in baseball to win the Chalmers Award as the league's Most Valuable Player (1913); won the pitching Triple Crown three times; only pitcher in major league history to win 20 games and hit .400 in a season (1925).

Nicknamed the "Big Train," Johnson struck out 3,508 batters over his 21-year major league career (1907-1927), all with the Washington Senators, and his 110 shutouts are the most in major league history. Despite pitching for some very poor teams, he was able to win 417 games (second only to Cy Young), and won 20 or more games in a season 10 straight years (1910–1919).

The 6'1", 200-pound pitcher made his major league debut on August 2, 1907; played in two World Series (winning in 1924 and losing in 1925); was named American League Most Valuable Player twice (1913, 1924); and later managed the Senators (1929–1932) and the Cleveland Indians (1933–1935). His final major league appearance as a player came as a pinch hitter in the game where Babe Ruth hit his then-record 60th home run of the season (September 30, 1927).

The second of six children, Johnson played baseball at Fullerton (California) Union High School, graduating in 1905, and played semi-professional baseball in the Idaho State League before being signed by the Senators. He was named to the All-Star team three times (1909, 1915, 1918); first pitcher in baseball history to win the Chalmers Award as the league's Most Valuable Player (1913); won the Triple Crown as a pitcher (leading the league in wins, strikeouts, and earned run average) three times (1913, 1918, 1924); and in 1916, pitched a record 369.2 innings without giving up a single home run, a record that still stands today.

In 1924, he helped the team win its only World Series championship (in seven games against the New York Giants), and in 1925, he again led the team to the World Series, eventually losing to the Pittsburgh Pirates in seven games.

After retiring as a player in 1927 and managing in the major leagues for the Senators (1929–1932) and the Cleveland Indians (1933–1935), Johnson entered politics as a Republican and won a seat as Montgomery County Commissioner in Maryland. In 1940, he ran for the U.S. Congress, but lost to Democrat William Byron.

Johnson was in the charter class (one of the first five players) of inductees into the National Baseball Hall of Fame and Museum in 1936, along with Ty Cobb, Babe Ruth, Honus Wagner, and Christy Mathewson.

He won the Platinum Glove in 1908 for his defense; was the only pitcher in major league history to win 20 games and hit .400 in a season (1925); ranked number 60 on ESPN's top 100 athletes of the century; led the American League in earned run average five times, in strikeouts 12 times, in shutouts seven times, and in wins six times; and compiled an ERA under 2.00 eleven times.

In 1999, he ranked number four on *The Sporting News*' list of the 100 Greatest Baseball Players, the highest-ranked pitcher, and later that year, was elected to the Major League Baseball All-Century Team.

On June 9, 1907, while playing semi-professional baseball for the Weiser (Idaho) Senators, Johnson pitched the only perfect game of his career against the Emmett Prune Pickers, an 11–0 win with 14 strikeouts.

Walter Johnson's Career Statistics

YEAR	TEAM	LG	W	L	PCT	G	SH	IP	H	R	ER	SO	BB	ERA
1907	Washington	AL	5	9	.357	14	2	111	98	35	23	70	17	1.86
1908	Washington	AL	14	14	.500	36	6	257	194	75	47	160	53	1.65
1909	Washington	AL	13	25	.342	40	4	296	247	112	73	164	84	2.22
1910	Washington	AL	25	17	.595	45	8	369	262	92	56	313	76	1.37
1911	Washington	AL	25	13	.658	40	6	322	292	117	68	207	70	1.90
1912	Washington	AL	33	12	.733	50	7	369	259	89	57	303	76	1.39
1913	Washington	AL	36	7	.837	48	11	346	232	56	44	243	38	1.14
1914	Washington	AL	28	18	.609	51	9	372	287	88	71	225	74	1.72
1915	Washington	AL	27	13	.675	47	7	337	258	83	58	203	56	1.55
1916	Washington	AL	25	20	.556	48	3	371	290	105	78	228	132	1.89
1917	Washington	AL	23	16	.590	47	8	326	248	105	80	188	68	2.21
1918	Washington	AL	23	13	.639	39	8	325	241	71	46	162	70	1.27
1919	Washington	AL	20	14	.588	39	7	290	235	73	48	147	51	1.49
1920	Washington	AL	8	10	.444	21	4	144	135	68	50	78	27	3.13
1921	Washington	AL	17	14	.548	35	1	264	265	122	103	143	92	3.51
1922	Washington	AL	15	16	.484	41	4	280	283	115	93	105	99	2.99
1923	Washington	AL	17	12	.586	42	3	261	263	112	101	130	69	3.48
1924	Washington	AL	23	7	.767	38	6	278	233	97	84	158	77	2.72
1925	Washington	AL	20	7	.741	30	3	229	217	95	78	108	78	3.07
1926	Washington	AL	15	16	.484	33	2	262	259	120	105	125	73	3.61
1927	Washington	AL	5	6	.455	18	1	108	113	70	61	48	26	5.08
	TOTALS		417	279	.599	802	110	5,917	4,911	1,900	1,424	3,508	1,406	2.17

Walter Johnson's Managerial Record

YEAR	LG	TEAM	W	L	WIN%
1929	AL	Washington	71	81	.467
1930	AL	Washington	94	60	.610
1931	AL	Washington	92	62	.597

YEAR	LG	TEAM	W	L	WIN%
1932	AL	Washington	93	61	.604
1933	AL	Cleveland	48	51	.485
1934	AL	Cleveland	85	69	.552
1935	AL	Cleveland	46	48	.489
		Washington	350	264	.570
		Cleveland	179	168	.516
		TOTALS	529	432	.550

Sources: Baseball-Reference.com; Walter Johnson Web Site (www.cmgworldwide.com/baseball/johnson/index.php); National Baseball Hall of Fame and Museum

Johnson, William C. "Skinny" (born: August 16, 1911 in Oklahoma City, Oklahoma; died: February 5, 1980); inducted into the Naismith Memorial Basketball Hall of Fame in 1977 as a player; Position: Center; won three straight Big Six titles while at the University of Kansas.

Johnson was a three-year letter winner at Central (Oklahoma) High School (1925–1929), where he was named All-State twice (1928–1929); All-Oklahoma City twice (1928–1929); All-Central Conference twice (1928, 1929); and was named an All-American (1929) at the Alonzo Stagg National Interscholastic Tournament at the University of Chicago.

After high school, he attended the University of Kansas (Lawrence), where he was a three-year letter winner under legendary coach Phog Allen; named First-Team Big Six Conference twice (1932–1933); Second-Team Big Six Conference in 1931; and won three straight Big Six titles.

After college, the 6'4", 185-pound Johnson played in the Amateur Athletic Union for the Southern Kansas State Lines (1933–1934), Jones Store (1935), and Philco (1936). He led the Lines to a third-place finish in the national AAU tournament; was the Missouri Valley AAU leading scorer (1934) and All-Star Center (1934); selected Second Team AAU All-American (1934); led Jones Store to the Missouri Valley AAU championship in 1935; and led Philco to the Missouri Valley AAU championship in 1936.

Johnson joined the coaching ranks with Cleveland Chiropractic College (Kansas City, Missouri) in 1937, and led the team to a 16–2 record, the Naismith Industrial League championship, and the Kansas City Independent Tournament championship.

Source: Naismith Memorial Basketball Hall of Fame

Johnson, William Julius "Judy" (born: October 26, 1899 in Snow Hill, Maryland; died: June 15, 1989 in Wilmington, Delaware); inducted into the National Baseball Hall of Fame and Museum in 1975 as a Negro Leaguer by the Negro Leagues Committee; Position: Third Base; Bats: Right; Throws: Right; won a Negro World Series in 1935.

According to available records, Johnson was a contact hitter who consistently batted .300 or better, with a career high of .416 in 1929. He led the Hilldale Daisies (Eastern Colored League) into the inaugural Negro World Series in 1924, eventually losing to the Kansas City Monarchs (Negro National League). He was team captain with the Pittsburgh Crawfords (1932–1936), which is considered to be one of the greatest teams assembled in the Negro Leagues, with such hall of famers as Johnson, Satchel Paige, Josh Gibson, Cool Papa Bell, and Oscar Charleston.

He played 20 seasons in the Negro Leagues with the Bacharach Giants (ECL, 1918), Madison Stars (semi-professional team located in Philadelphia, Pennsylvania, 1919–1921), Hilldale Daisies (1921–1929, 1931–1932), Homestead Grays (independent, 1930, 1937), and the Pittsburgh Crawfords (independent, 1932–1936).

While a player-coach with the Grays in 1930, he is credited with discovering Negro League star and future hall of famer Josh Gibson. The 5'11", 150-pound Johnson helped the Pittsburgh Crawfords win the 1935 Negro World Series over the New York Cubans (Negro National League).

When Major League Baseball's "color line" fell, Johnson scouted and coached for the Philadelphia Athletics, and in 1954, he became the first black coach in the majors when he accompanied the Phillies to Florida for spring training. He would go on to work for the Phillies from 1959 to 1973, and was the sixth Negro Leaguer inducted into the baseball hall of fame.

Source: National Baseball Hall of Fame and Museum

Johnston, Donald Neil (born: February 4, 1929 in Chillicothe, Ohio; died: September 27, 1978 in Irving, Texas); inducted into the Naismith Memorial Basketball Hall of Fame in 1990 as a player; Position: Center; led the NBA in scoring three straight seasons (1953–1955); won an NBA title in 1956 as a player-coach; won the Eastern Basketball League title as a coach in 1966.

After being a four-year letter winner at Chillicothe (Ohio) High School (1942–1946) and named All-State in 1946, Johnston attended Ohio State University (Columbus), where he played only 27 basketball games before signing a professional baseball contract as a pitcher with the Philadelphia Phillies. He played two seasons with the team's Terre Haute (Indiana) Phillies of the Three-I-League (Illinois-Iowa-Indiana League), before turning to professional basketball after suffering an arm injury. He would go on to play with the National Basketball Association's Philadelphia Warriors from 1951 to 1959.

The 6'8", 225-pound Johnston was named to the All-NBA First Team four times (1953–1956); All-NBA Second Team in 1957; led the NBA in scoring three straight seasons (1953–1955); led the league in rebounding in 1955; was a six-time All-Star (1953–1958); led the league in minutes played (1953–1954); and won an NBA championship in 1956 against the Fort Wayne Pistons in five games.

He was a player-coach for the Warriors (1954–1961); a player-coach for the Pittsburgh Rens (American Basketball League, 1961–1963); coached the Wilmington Blue Bombers (Eastern Basketball League, 1964–1966); an assistant coach at Wake Forest University (Winston-Salem, North Carolina, 1966–1972); and was an assistant coach and scout for the NBA's Portland Trail Blazers (1976–1977).

Johnston compiled a 95–59 (.617) record at Philadelphia; a 53–50 (.515) record at Pittsburgh; and a 32–24 (.571) record at Wilmington, while leading the Blue Bombers to the 1966 EBL title.

Neil Johnston's Career Statistics

YEAR	TEAM	LG	G	MIN	FGM	FTM	TRB	AST	PTS	PPG
1951–1952	Philadelphia	NBA	64	993	141	100	342	39	382	6.0
1952–1953	Philadelphia	NBA	70	3,166	504	556	976	197	1,564	22.3
1953–1954	Philadelphia	NBA	72	3,296	591	577	797	203	1,759	24.4
1954–1955	Philadelphia	NBA	72	2,917	521	589	1,085	215	1,631	22.7
1955–1956	Philadelphia	NBA	70	2,594	499	549	872	225	1,547	22.1
1956–1957	Philadelphia	NBA	69	2,531	520	535	855	203	1,575	22.8
1957–1958	Philadelphia	NBA	71	2,408	473	442	790	166	1,388	19.5
1958–1959	Philadelphia	NBA	28	393	54	69	139	21	177	6.3
	TOTALS		516	18,298	3,303	3,417	5,856	1,269	10,023	19.4

Sources: Basketball-Reference.com; Naismith Memorial Basketball Hall of Fame

Johnston, Jack (born: 1877 in Glasgow, Scotland; died: October 1951 in Chicago, Illinois); inducted into the National Soccer Hall of Fame and Museum in 1952 as a builder; a soccer referee for 20 seasons.

Johnston immigrated to the United States in 1904 and won numerous awards as a cyclist and golf professional. In 1939, he ended his 20-year career as a soccer referee, during which time he officiated in one game of the U.S. Open Cup, the final between the Chicago Bricklayers and Fall River Marksmen in 1931 (won by Fall River in three games). He also served as a soccer reporter for the *Chicago Tribune*, where he wrote under the pen name of "Offside."

Source: National Soccer Hall of Fame and Museum

Joiner, Charles, Jr. "Charlie" (born: October 14, 1947 in Many, Louisiana); inducted into the Pro Football Hall of Fame in 1996 as a player; Position: Wide Receiver; Uniform: #18; the NFL's all-time receiver with 750 catches when he retired; last former American Football League player to retire from professional football.

Joiner played 18 seasons (239 games) in the National Football League, longer than any other wide receiver in the league's history at the time of his retirement. When he left the game, he ranked as the all-time leading receiver with 750 catches.

Never able to advance to the Super Bowl, Joiner played for the Houston Oilers (1969–1972), Cincinnati Bengals (1972–1975), and the San Diego Chargers (1976–1986). A focus of the "Air Coryell" offense (named after the offensive scheme instituted by San Diego Charger coach Don Coryell), Joiner caught 586 passes as a Charger; played in three Pro Bowls (1976, 1979–1980); and was an All-NFL selection in 1980.

Although an established receiver, the Oilers wanted the 5'11", 180-pound Joiner to play defense when the team picked the Grambling State University (Louisiana) star in the fourth round of the 1969 American Football League-NFL

Draft (93rd pick overall). Once he joined Houston, Joiner played briefly on defense and with the kickoff return team, but soon established himself as a premier pass receiver.

Although a consistent receiver for seven seasons, it was not until he joined the Chargers that he became an NFL standout performer. When he teamed with future hall of fame quarterback Dan Fouts, "Air Coryell" became a successful NFL offense. During his 11 seasons in San Diego, Joiner caught 50 or more passes in a season seven times; had 70 or more receptions in a season three times; and caught for 100 or more yards in 29 games.

Joiner was the last former American Football League player (Oilers, 1969) to retire from professional football (1986); was inducted into the Breitbard Hall of Fame in 1986; and in 1999, he was ranked number 100 on *The Sporting News*' list of the 100 Greatest Football Players.

Charlie Joiner's Career Statistics

				RECEIVING		
YEAR	**TEAM**	**G**	**NO**	**YDS**	**AVG**	**TD**
1969	Houston	7	7	77	11.0	0
1970	Houston	9	28	416	14.9	3
1971	Houston	14	31	681	22.0	7
1972	Houston/Cincinnati	12	24	439	18.3	2
1973	Cincinnati	5	13	214	16.5	0
1974	Cincinnati	14	24	390	16.3	1
1975	Cincinnati	14	37	726	19.6	5
1976	San Diego	14	50	1,056	21.1	7
1977	San Diego	14	35	542	15.5	6
1978	San Diego	16	33	607	18.4	1
1979	San Diego	16	72	1,008	14.0	4
1980	San Diego	16	71	1,132	15.9	4
1981	San Diego	16	70	1,188	17.0	7
1982	San Diego	9	36	545	15.1	0
1983	San Diego	16	65	960	14.8	3
1984	San Diego	16	61	793	13.0	6
1985	San Diego	16	59	932	15.8	7
1986	San Diego	15	34	440	12.9	2
	TOTALS	239	750	12,146	16.2	65

Sources: Pro Football Hall of Fame; Pro-Football-Reference.com

Joliat, Aurel Emile (born: August 29, 1901 in Ottawa, Ontario, Canada; died: January 2, 1986 in Ottawa, Ontario, Canada); inducted into the Hockey Hall of Fame in 1947 as a player; Position: Left Wing; Uniform: #4; won three Stanley Cup championships.

Joliat played his entire 16-year (1922–1938) National Hockey League career with the Montreal Canadiens. In the 1923–1924 season, he helped the team win the Stanley Cup and was the league's top scorer in 1924–1925. He played on his second Stanley Cup-winning team in 1930 and won his third title the next year.

After the 1930–1931 season, he was chosen as the left wing on the inaugural NHL First All-Star Team, and would go on to be named to the Second Team three times (1932, 1934–1935). In 1933–1934, the 5'7", 136-pound Joliat won the Hart Trophy as the league's Most Valuable Player.

He was inducted into the Ottawa Sports Hall of Fame in 1966; into the Canadian Sports Hall of Fame in 1975; the Canadiens named him to the team's 75th anniversary dream team in 1984; and Montreal retired his uniform number four.

In 1998, 60 years after retiring from hockey, he was ranked number 65 on *The Hockey News*' list of the 100 Greatest Hockey Players.

Aurel Joliat's Career Statistics

			REGULAR SEASON					PLAYOFFS				
SEASON	**TEAM**	**LEAGUE**	**GP**	**G**	**A**	**TP**	**PIM**	**GP**	**G**	**A**	**TP**	**PIM**
1916–1917	Ottawa New Edinburghs	OCHL	8	2	0	2		2	0	0	0	
1917–1918	Ottawa Aberdeens	OCJHL	3	2	0	2	3					

SEASON	TEAM	LEAGUE	REGULAR SEASON GP	G	A	TP	PIM	PLAYOFFS GP	G	A	TP	PIM
1918–1919	Ottawa New Edinburghs	OCHL	8	5	3	8	9					
1919–1920	Ottawa New Edinburghs	OCHL	7	12	0	12						
1920–1921	Iroquois Falls Papermakers	NOHA										
1921–1922	Iroquois Falls Flyers	NOHA										
1922–1923	Montreal Canadiens	NHL	24	12	9	21	37	2	1	0	1	11
1923–1924	Montreal Canadiens	NHL	24	15	5	20	27	2	1	1	2	0
1923–1924	Montreal Canadiens	St-Cup						4	3	1	4	6
1924–1925	Montreal Canadiens	NHL	25	30	11	41	85	1	0	0	0	5
1924–1925	Montreal Canadiens	St-Cup						4	2	0	2	16
1925–1926	Montreal Canadiens	NHL	35	17	9	26	52					
1926–1927	Montreal Canadiens	NHL	43	14	4	18	79	4	1	0	1	10
1927–1928	Montreal Canadiens	NHL	44	28	11	39	105	2	0	0	0	4
1928–1929	Montreal Canadiens	NHL	44	12	5	17	59	3	1	1	2	10
1929–1930	Montreal Canadiens	NHL	42	19	12	31	40	6	0	2	2	6
1930–1931	Montreal Canadiens	NHL	43	13	22	35	73	10	0	4	4	12
1931–1932	Montreal Canadiens	NHL	48	15	24	39	46	4	2	0	2	4
1932–1933	Montreal Canadiens	NHL	48	18	21	39	53	2	2	1	3	2
1933–1934	Montreal Canadiens	NHL	48	22	15	37	27	3	0	1	1	0
1934–1935	Montreal Canadiens	NHL	48	17	12	29	18	2	1	0	1	0
1935–1936	Montreal Canadiens	NHL	48	15	8	23	16					
1936–1937	Montreal Canadiens	NHL	47	17	15	32	30	5	0	3	3	2
1937–1938	Montreal Canadiens	NHL	44	6	7	13	24					
	NHL TOTALS		655	270	190	460	771		46	13	22	66

Sources: Hockey Hall of Fame; Hockey-Reference.com

Jones, David D. "Deacon" (born: December 9, 1938 in Eatonville, Florida); inducted into the Pro Football Hall of Fame in 1980 as a player; Position: Defensive End; Uniform: #75; coined the term "quarterback sacks;" NFL Defensive Player of the Year twice.

After a relatively obscure college career, the 6'5", 272-pound Jones was a 14th-round selection of the National Football League's Los Angeles Rams in the 1961 draft (186th overall pick). He went to college for one year at South Carolina State University (Orangeburg) in 1958, did not play football in 1959, and played a final season at Mississippi Vocational College (Itta Bena, now known as Mississippi Valley State University) in 1960. In Los Angeles, he was a member of the "Fearsome Foursome" (with Lamar Lundy, Roosevelt Grier, and Merlin Olsen), which is considered one of the best defensive lines of all time.

Jones played his 14-year (191 games) NFL career (1961–1974) with the Rams (1961–1971), San Diego Chargers (1972–1973), and Washington Redskins (1974). He coined the term "quarterback sacks;" played in eight Pro Bowls (1965–1971, 1973); was named NFL Defensive Player of Year twice (1967–1968), winning the George S. Halas Trophy; named to the NFL 1960s All-Decade Team; and to the NFL 75th Anniversary All-Time Team in 1994.

He joined San Diego in 1972; led the defensive line in tackles; was the defensive captain; and ended his career after one season in Washington.

In 1999, Jones was ranked number 13 on *The Sporting News*' list of the 100 Greatest Football Players, the highest-ranked player to have played for the Rams, highest-ranked defensive end, and second highest-ranked defensive lineman behind Bob Lilly. Also in 1999, he was named by *Sports Illustrated* as the "Defensive End of the Century."

Source: Pro Football Hall of Fame

Jones, K.C. (born: May 25, 1932 in Taylor, Texas); inducted into the Naismith Memorial Basketball Hall of Fame in 1989 as a player; Position: Guard; Uniform: #25; won two NCAA titles; won eight consecutive NBA titles as a player; won two NBA championships as a coach.

Named to the All-Northern California team as a senior (1951), Jones attended Commerce High School (San Francisco, California, 1947–1951), before going to college at the University of San Francisco (1951–1956). He was a member of back-to-back National Collegiate Athletic Association championship teams (1955–1956), but did not play in the tournament in 1956, because he was playing his fifth season of college basketball and was ineligible for postseason play; was a member of USF teams that won 60 straight games; scored 901 points in college; named All-American in 1956; and was a member of the U.S. Olympic gold medal-winning team in 1956 at Melbourne, Australia.

After college, the 6'1", 180-pound Jones served in the U.S. Army (1956–1958); played for the Fort Leonard Wood (Pulaski County, Missouri) army team; and was a two-time Amateur Athletic Union All-American (1957–1958). Leaving the military, Jones (whose given name is K.C.) rejoined Bill Russell (a former teammate at USF) and went on to play nine seasons (1958–1967) in the National Basketball Association with the Boston Celtics. Leaving the NBA, he played one season in the Eastern Basketball League (1967–1968) with the Hartford Capitols. He had been selected in the second round (eighth overall pick) of the 1956 NBA Draft, but did not join Boston until 1958, due to his military service.

He won eight consecutive NBA championships with the Celtics (1959–1966); led the team in assists three straight seasons (1964–1966); and had his jersey number 25 retired by the team.

After retiring as a player, Jones served as head coach at Brandeis University (Waltham, Massachusetts, 1967–1970), and compiled a 34–32 (.515) record, before becoming an assistant coach at Harvard University (Cambridge, Massachusetts, 1970–1971). He joined the professional ranks in the NBA as an assistant coach for the Los Angeles Lakers (1971–1972); first-ever head coach of the San Diego Conquistadors (American Basketball Association, 1972–1973); Capital Bullets (NBA, 1973–1974); Washington Bullets (NBA, 1974–1976); assistant coach with the Milwaukee Bucks (NBA, 1976–1977); assistant coach of the Boston Celtics (1978–1979, 1982–1983, 1996–1997); head coach of the Celtics (1983–1988); assistant coach of the Seattle Supersonics (NBA, 1989–1990); head coach of the Supersonics (1990–1992); assistant coach of the Detroit Pistons (NBA, 1994–1995); and head coach of the New England Blizzard of the American Basketball League (1997–1999).

He compiled a Bullets coaching record of 155–91 (.630) and led Washington to the 1975 NBA Finals, losing in four games to the Golden State Warriors. At Boston, he coached to a 308–102 (.751) record; led the Celtics to the 1984 and 1986 NBA championship (beating the Los Angeles Lakers in 1984 in seven games and beating the Houston Rockets in 1986 in six games); led Boston to four straight Eastern Conference and Atlantic Division titles (1984–1988); and coached the team to the best record in the NBA three straight seasons (1984–1986), with 60 or more wins each year.

In 1986, he was inducted into the Bay Area Sports Hall of Fame.

K.C. Jones' Playing Statistics

SEASON	TEAM	LG	G	MIN	FG	FT	TRB	AST	PTS
1958–1959	Boston	NBA	49	609	65	41	127	70	171
1959–1960	Boston	NBA	74	1,274	169	128	199	189	466
1960–1961	Boston	NBA	78	1,605	203	186	279	253	592
1961–1962	Boston	NBA	80	2,054	294	147	298	343	735
1962–1963	Boston	NBA	79	1,945	230	112	263	317	572
1963–1964	Boston	NBA	80	2,424	283	88	372	407	654
1964–1965	Boston	NBA	78	2,434	253	143	318	437	649
1965–1966	Boston	NBA	80	2,710	240	209	304	503	689
1966–1967	Boston	NBA	78	2,446	182	119	239	389	483
	TOTALS		676	17,501	1,919	1,173	2,399	2,908	5,011

K.C. Jones' Coaching Record

			REGULAR SEASON			PLAYOFFS		
SEASON	LG	TEAM	W	L	WIN%	W	L	WIN%
1972–1973	ABA	San Diego	30	54	.357	0	4	.000
1973–1974	NBA	Capital	47	35	.573	3	4	.429
1974–1975	NBA	Washington	60	22	.732	8	9	.471
1975–1976	NBA	Washington	48	34	.585	3	4	.429
1983–1984	NBA	Boston	62	20	.756	15	8	.652
1984–1985	NBA	Boston	63	19	.768	13	8	.619
1985–1986	NBA	Boston	67	15	.817	15	3	.833
1986–1987	NBA	Boston	59	23	.720	13	10	.565
1987–1988	NBA	Boston	57	25	.695	9	8	.529
1990–1991	NBA	Seattle	41	41	.500	2	3	.400
1991–1992	NBA	Seattle	18	18	.500			
	ABA		30	54	.357	0	4	.000
	NBA		522	252	.674	81	57	.587
		TOTALS	552	306	.643	81	61	.570

Sources: Basketball-Reference.com; Naismith Memorial Basketball Hall of Fame

Jones, Dr. Renato William (born: October 5, 1906 in Rome, Italy; died: April 22, 1981 in Munich, Germany); inducted into the Naismith Memorial Basketball Hall of Fame in 1964 as a contributor; first international person to be inducted into the basketball hall of fame; co-founded FIBA; helped make basketball an Olympic sport.

After graduating from Germano Someiller High School (Turin, Italy) in 1923, Jones attended Springfield College (Massachusetts), graduating in 1928; Deutsche Hochschule fuer Leibesuebungen (Berlin, Germany), graduating in 1930; and the University of Geneva (Switzerland), graduating in 1931.

He played basketball and hockey in college; introduced basketball to the University of Geneva in 1924; co-founded the Fédération Internationale de Basketball Amateur with Dr. Elmer Berry in 1932; served as FIBA secretary-general (1932–1976); organized Men's and Women's European Championships (1935–1963); organized Men's and Women's World Championships (1950–1963); helped get basketball accepted into the Olympic Games, beginning with the 11th Olympiad in Berlin, Germany in 1936; and was elected to the Board of Trustees of the Naismith Memorial Basketball Hall of Fame in 1961.

As FIBA's Secretary-General, Jones was responsible for the growth of basketball in more than 130 countries through games, tournaments, and clinics, and was the first international person to be inducted into the basketball hall of fame.

In 1958, he was named secretary-general of the International Council of Sport and Physical Education, and the William Jones Cup, named in his honor, has been presented to the winner of the annual international basketball tournament held in Taipei, Taiwan since 1977.

Jones was inducted into the FIBA Hall of Fame in 2007.

For all of his achievements, Jones is probably best remembered for one of the most controversial rulings ever made in Olympic basketball play. He was the governing official at the 1972 Olympic basketball final game (Munich, Germany) that ordered game officials to put three seconds back on the clock (due to "clock malfunction") after the United States had apparently won the gold medal in a 50–49 win over the Soviet Union. With the additional three seconds on the clock, the Soviet team scored a basket and won the game 51–50.

Source: Naismith Memorial Basketball Hall of Fame

Jones, Samuel "Sam" (born: June 24, 1933 in Laurinburg, North Carolina); inducted into the Naismith Memorial Basketball Hall of Fame in 1984 as a player; Position: Guard-Forward; Uniform: #24; won 10 NBA championships.

Jones attended Laurinburg (North Carolina) Institute (1947–1951), where he was a four-year letter winner and selected All-Conference and All-State in 1951. After high school, he went to North Central College (Durham, North Carolina, 1953–1957) and was again a four-year letter winner; scored 1,770 points; was a three-time All-Conference selection; and was inducted into the National Association of Intercollegiate Athletics Hall of Fame in 1962.

After college, the 6'4", 200-pound Jones was a first-round pick (eighth overall selection) of the National Basketball Association's Boston Celtics in 1957, where he played his entire 12-year NBA career (1957–1969). He was named to the All-NBA Second Team three times (1965–1967); a five-time NBA All-Star (1962, 1964–1966, 1968); led Boston in scoring three times (1963, 1965–1966); averaged 20 points a game or better four consecutive seasons (1965–1968); won 10 NBA championships (1959–1966, 1968–69); was named a member of both the NBA 25th Anniversary Team in 1970 and the NBA 50th Anniversary Team in 1996.

After his playing days, Jones coached college basketball at Federal City College (Washington, D.C., 1969–1973), and one year at his alma mater in 1974.

Sam Jones' Career Statistics

SEASON	TEAM	LG	G	MIN	FG	FT	TRB	AST	PTS
1957–1958	Boston	NBA	56	594	100	60	160	37	260
1958–1959	Boston	NBA	71	1,466	305	151	428	101	761
1959–1960	Boston	NBA	74	1,512	355	168	375	125	878
1960–1961	Boston	NBA	78	2,028	480	211	421	217	1,171
1961–1962	Boston	NBA	78	2,388	596	243	458	232	1,435
1962–1963	Boston	NBA	76	2,323	621	257	396	241	1,499
1963–1964	Boston	NBA	76	2,381	612	249	349	202	1,473
1964–1965	Boston	NBA	80	2,885	821	428	411	223	2,070
1965–1966	Boston	NBA	67	2,155	626	325	347	216	1,577
1966–1967	Boston	NBA	72	2,325	638	318	338	217	1,594
1967–1968	Boston	NBA	73	2,408	621	311	357	216	1,553

SEASON	TEAM	LG	G	MIN	FG	FT	TRB	AST	PTS
1968–1969	Boston	NBA	70	1,820	496	148	265	182	1,140
	TOTALS	NBA	871	24,285	6,271	2,869	4,305	2,209	15,411

Sources: Basketball-Reference.com; Naismith Memorial Basketball Hall of Fame

Jones, Stanley Paul "Stan" (born: November 24, 1931 in Altoona, Pennsylvania; died: May 21, 2010 in Broomfield, Colorado); inducted into the Pro Football Hall of Fame in 1991 as a player by the Seniors Committee; Position: Guard-Tackle; Uniform: #78; won the 1953 NCAA college championship; won an NFL title in 1963.

After playing football at Lemoyne (Pennsylvania) High School, the 6'1", 252-pound Jones was an All-American two-way tackle at the University of Maryland (College Park, 1951–1953), before playing 13 National Football League seasons (1954–1966, 157 games) with the Chicago Bears (1954–1965) and Washington Redskins (1966). He was the Bears' fifth-round draft pick (54th selection overall) in 1953 and played offensive tackle (1954), before playing offensive left guard. He was selected All-NFL four times (1955–1956, 1959–1960); played in seven straight Pro Bowls (1956–1962); and was one of the first professional players to use weight-lifting as a way to get into shape for football.

Jones helped Chicago win the 1963 NFL title with a 14–10 win over the New York Giants. After the 1965 season, he was traded to the Washington Redskins, where he played one year before retiring.

As a senior at Maryland, Jones was one of the leaders on a Terrapin team that was named by both the Associated Press and United Press International as the national collegiate champion in 1953. In 1977, he was named to the Atlantic Coast Conference's 25-year All-Star team.

After retiring as a player, Jones served as an NFL assistant coach with the Denver Broncos, Buffalo Bills, Cleveland Browns, and New England Patriots.

Source: Pro Football Hall of Fame

Jordan, Henry Wendell (born: January 26, 1935 in Emporia, Virginia; died: February 21, 1977); inducted into the Pro Football Hall of Fame in 1995 as a player; Position: Right Defensive Tackle; Uniform: #74; won the first two Super Bowls.

Jordan was the fifth player inducted into the football hall of fame from the Green Bay Packers defensive unit from the 1960s that included Willie Davis, Ray Nitschke, Herb Adderley, and Willie Wood.

After attending Warwick High School (Newport News, Virginia), he was a three-sport star at the University of Virginia (Charlottesville), where he captained the football team as a senior, and was a runner-up in the heavyweight class of the 1957 National Collegiate Athletic Association wrestling championships.

Jordan began his professional football career as a fifth-round draft pick (52nd selection overall) of the 1957 Cleveland Browns, where he played two seasons before being traded to the Packers (1959–1969).

The 6'2", 248-pound right defensive tackle was named All-NFL five straight seasons (1960–1964); played in four Pro Bowls (1960–1961, 1963, 1966) and was named the 1961 Pro Bowl Most Valuable Player; a seven-time All-Pro selection (1960–1964, 1966–1967); won five NFL titles (1961–1962, 1965–1967); and won the NFL's first two Super Bowls (1967–1968).

Jordan was inducted into the Virginia Sports Hall of Fame in 1974 and into the Green Bay Packers Hall of Fame in 1975.

Source: Pro Football Hall of Fame

Jordan, Michael Jeffrey (born: February 17, 1963 in Brooklyn, New York); inducted into the Naismith Memorial Basketball Hall of Fame in 2009 as a player; Position: Guard; Uniform: 23, 45, 9; retired from the NBA with the league's highest scoring average (30.1 points per game).

Nicknamed "Air Jordan" and considered one of the greatest basketball players of all time, Jordan was the impetus for the success of the Chicago Bulls, leading the team to a three-peat twice. During his 15-year National Basketball Association career (1984–1993, 1994–1998, 2001–2003), the 6'6", 216-pound Jordan was named Rookie of the Year in 1985 (averaging 28.2 points per game); was a six-time NBA champion (1991–1993, 1996–1998); five-time NBA MVP (1988, 1991–1992, 1996, 1998); 10-time All-NBA First Team (1987–1993, 1996–1998); named All-NBA Second Team in 1985; Defensive Player of the Year in 1988; named to the All-Defensive First Team nine times (1988–1993, 1996–1998); 14-time All-Star; All-Star MVP (1988, 1996, 1998); named one of the 50 Greatest Players in NBA History (1996); was a two-time Olympic gold medal winner (1984, 1992); and retired from the NBA with the league's highest scoring average of 30.1 points per game.

Jordan was raised in North Carolina, where he attended Emsley A. Laney High School (Wilmington, North Carolina). After high school, he went to the University of North Carolina, before being drafted in the first round (third overall) by the Bulls in the 1984 NBA draft. He would retire twice from the NBA before finally leaving the league for good as a player after the 2003 season.

In high school, his favorite sport was baseball and as a basketball player, the 5'11" sophomore was cut from the varsity team. Before his junior year, however, he grew to 6'3" and began his development into a basketball star. After being named a high school All-American, he attended UNC (Chapel Hill, North Carolina) and played for coach Dean Smith, where he first made his mark as a freshman in the 1982 National Collegiate Athletic Association Championship title game by scoring the winning basket in a 63–62 win over Georgetown and Patrick Ewing.

While playing with the Tar Heels, Jordan was named Atlantic Coast Conference Freshman of the Year by averaging 13.4 points per game and was named College Player of the Year by *The Sporting News* as a sophomore. Later, as a junior, he won the award again as well as the Naismith and Wooden awards. After his junior year, Jordan was the third overall pick in the 1984 NBA Draft by the Chicago Bulls. He returned to the school in 1986 to finish his degree.

Prior to starting his professional career, Jordan (and Ewing, among others) helped the United States win a gold medal at the 1984 Summer Olympics (Los Angeles, California). He then joined the NBA and was named Rookie of the Year.

Although he missed 64 games because of a broken foot in his second season, Jordan scored an NBA playoff-record 63 points in a first-round game against the Boston Celtics, eventually losing the game 132–131, and being swept by the team in the first round.

In the 1986–1987 season, he led the league in scoring (37.1 points per game) for the first of his seven consecutive years; was the only player other than Wilt Chamberlain to score 3,000 points in a season; and became the first player in league history to record 200 steals and 100 blocks in a season. For all his accomplishments, the Bulls were swept by the Celtics in three games in the first round of the playoffs.

In the 1987–1988 season, he won All-Star Most Valuable Player, Defensive Player of the Year, and league Most Valuable Player awards while leading his team into the second round of the playoffs. After beating the Cleveland Cavaliers in five games in the first round, the Bulls were eliminated by the Detroit Pistons in five games in the conference semifinals. Over the next two seasons, the Bulls would again lose to the Pistons, both times in the Eastern Conference Finals.

The team's fortunes improved once Phil Jackson was promoted to team coach (he had previously been a team assistant coach) when Doug Collins was fired before the 1989–1990 season. With Jackson's newly installed "Triangle Offense," the team only lost twice in the entire 1991 playoffs to win the franchise's first-ever NBA title, as Jordan won the first of his six NBA Finals MVP awards. Jordan then led the Bulls to two more consecutive NBA titles in 1992 and 1993.

After winning an Olympic gold medal in 1984, in the summer of 1992, Jordan led the so-called Dream Team (with teammates Charles Barkley, Larry Bird, Clyde Drexler, Patrick Ewing, Magic Johnson, Christian Laettner, Karl Malone, Chris Mullin, Scottie Pippen, David Robinson, and John Stockton) to the gold medal in the Olympics held in Barcelona, Spain.

After the 1994 season, Jordan retired from basketball and played minor league baseball with the Birmingham Barons, a Chicago White Sox (owned by Bulls' owner Jerry Reinsdorf) affiliate in the Class AA Southern League. Never reaching the major league, he returned to the basketball court in 1995, but the Bulls lost in six games to the Orlando Magic (led by Shaquille O'Neal) in the conference semifinals.

Jordan went on to lead the Bulls to three more consecutive NBA titles from 1996 to 1998, with such teammates as Scotty Pippen and Dennis Rodman. In the 1995–1996 season, he led the league with 30.4 points per game as the Bulls won an NBA-record 72 games in the regular season, finishing 72–10. After the team's third consecutive NBA championship in 1998, Jordan retired from the league as a player and became a part owner of the Washington Wizards in 2000.

Unhappy with the team's on-court performance, in 2001 Jordan returned to the league as a player for the Wizards for two more seasons before finally retiring for good, without making the playoffs. After leaving the game as a player, he returned as a partial team owner and executive. He is currently a part-owner and Managing Member of Basketball Operations for the Charlotte Bobcats in North Carolina.

Michael Jordan's Career Statistics

SEASON	TEAM	G	FG	FT	TRB	AST	PTS
1984–1985	Chicago	82	837	630	534	481	2,313
1985–1986	Chicago	18	150	105	64	53	408
1986–1987	Chicago	82	1,098	833	430	377	3,041
1987–1988	Chicago	82	1,069	723	449	485	2,868

SEASON	TEAM	G	FG	FT	TRB	AST	PTS
1988–1989	Chicago	81	966	674	652	650	2,633
1989–1990	Chicago	82	1,034	593	565	519	2,753
1990–1991	Chicago	82	990	571	492	453	2,580
1991–1992	Chicago	80	943	491	511	489	2,404
1992–1993	Chicago	78	992	476	522	428	2,541
1994–1995	Chicago	17	166	109	117	90	457
1995–1996	Chicago	82	916	548	543	352	2,491
1996–1997	Chicago	82	920	480	482	352	2,431
1997–1998	Chicago	82	881	565	475	283	2,357
2001–2002	Washington	60	551	263	339	310	1,375
2002–2003	Washington	82	679	266	497	311	1,640
	TOTALS	1,072	12,192	7,327	6,672	5,633	32,292

Sources: Basketball-Reference.com; Naismith Memorial Basketball Hall of Fame

Joss, Adrian "Addie" (born: April 12, 1880 in Woodland, Wisconsin; died: April 14, 1911 in Toledo, Ohio); inducted into the National Baseball Hall of Fame and Museum in 1978 as a player by the Veterans Committee; Position: Pitcher; Bats: Right; Throws: Right; only pitcher in major league history to no-hit the same team twice.

Before dying prematurely at age 31 from tubercular meningitis, Joss had played his entire nine-year Major League Baseball career with the Cleveland Bronchos / Blues / Naps / Indians (1902–1910). Making his debut on April 26, 1902, he won 20 or more games four seasons in a row (1905–1908); never had a losing season in his career; 45 of his 160 career wins were shutouts; led the American League in earned run average twice (1904, 1908); led the league in wins in 1907; and threw a perfect game on October 2, 1908 and a second no-hitter on April 20, 1910, both 1–0 wins over the Chicago White Sox. He is the only pitcher in major league history to no-hit the same team twice.

A star athlete at the Wayland Academy (Beaver Dam, Wisconsin), the 6'3", 185-pound Joss had four 20-win seasons and six sub-2.00 ERAs in his career. His 1.89 career ERA is ranked second all-time only to Ed Walsh's 1.82.

He is the only player in the hall of fame to have the 10-year rule of service waived, since he only played nine seasons.

Joss pitched a one-hitter in his 1902 major league debut against the St. Louis Browns (winning 3–0).

Addie Joss' Career Statistics

YEAR	TEAM	W	L	PCT	ERA	CG	SHO	IP	H	ER	R	HR	BB	SO
1902	Cleveland	17	13	.567	2.77	28	5	269.1	225	83	120	2	75	106
1903	Cleveland	18	13	.581	2.19	31	3	283.2	232	69	104	3	37	120
1904	Cleveland	14	10	.583	1.59	20	5	192.1	160	34	51	0	30	83
1905	Cleveland	20	12	.625	2.01	31	3	286.0	246	64	90	4	46	132
1906	Cleveland	21	9	.700	1.72	28	9	282.0	220	54	81	3	43	106
1907	Cleveland	27	11	.711	1.83	34	6	338.2	279	69	100	3	54	127
1908	Cleveland	24	11	.686	1.16	29	9	325.0	232	42	77	2	30	130
1909	Cleveland	14	13	.519	1.71	24	4	242.2	198	46	71	0	31	67
1910	Cleveland	5	5	.500	2.26	9	1	107.1	96	27	35	2	18	49
	TOTALS	160	97	.623	1.89	234	45	2,327.0	1,888	488	729	19	364	920

Sources: Baseball-Reference.com; National Baseball Hall of Fame and Museum

Juckes, Gordon W. (born: June 20, 1914 in Watrous, Saskatchewan, Canada; died: October 5, 1994 in Melville, Saskatchewan, Canada); inducted into the Hockey Hall of Fame in 1979 as a builder; served as president of both the Saskatchewan Senior League and the Canadian Amateur Hockey Association.

Juckes enlisted in the Royal Canadian Artillery during the first few months of World War II and was awarded the Order of the British Empire in 1946 for his wartime service. Leaving the military, he worked at the Melville Millionaires Hockey Club (1946–1948); was president of the Saskatchewan Senior League; worked for the Saskatchewan Amateur Hockey Association (1949–1954); and served on the executive board of the Canadian Amateur Hockey Association, serving one term as its president (1959–1960).

During his career, Juckes received the International Ice Hockey Federation Diploma of Honour (1967); the CAHA Meritorious Award (1976); and a life membership from the SAHA. The Gordon Juckes Award is presented by Hockey Canada to a person who has made exceptional contributions to the development of amateur hockey.

Source: Hockey Hall of Fame

Julian, Alvin F. "Doggie" (born: April 5, 1901 in Reading, Pennsylvania; died; July 28, 1967); inducted into the Naismith Memorial Basketball Hall of Fame in 1968 as a coach; won the 1947 NCAA title.

After playing basketball for four years at Reading (Pennsylvania) High School (1915–1919), Julian attended Bucknell University (Lewisburg, Pennsylvania, 1919–1923), where he earned 10 letters in three sports.

After college, he began his career at Schuylkill College (now known as Albright College, Reading, Pennsylvania), where he served as the team's football coach (1925–1931). He briefly left the college ranks to serve as the basketball, football, and baseball coach at Ashland (Pennsylvania) High School (1933–1935), before returning to the college level as the basketball, football, and baseball coach at Muhlenberg College (Allentown, Pennsylvania, 1936–1945).

Julian then became the head basketball and assistant football coach at Holy Cross College (Worcester, Massachusetts, 1945–1948), before coaching for two seasons in the National Basketball Association with the Boston Celtics (1948–1950), compiling a 47–81 (.367) record. He then finished his career as the head basketball coach at Dartmouth College (Hanover, New Hampshire, 1950–1967).

He led Muhlenberg to a 129–71 (.645) record and one Middle Atlantic Conference title. His record at Holy Cross was 65–10 (.867) and he led the team to become the only New England school to win the National Collegiate Athletic Association title (1947). Julian was named Boston Basketball Writers' Coach of the Year in 1947 and won that year's Sugar Bowl championship (basketball).

At Dartmouth, he coached to a 183–236 (.437) record and led the team to three Ivy League titles (1956, 1958–1959) and three NCAA tournaments. With an overall college record of 386–343 (.529), he has coached in five NCAA and two National Invitation Tournaments; served as president of the National Association of Basketball Coaches (1966–1967); and has been inducted into the Helms Athletic Foundation Hall of Fame.

Julian also played professional football with the National Football League's Pottsville Maroons (Pennsylvania) in the early to mid-1920s; professional baseball with the Reading Keystones of the International League (1923–1924); and wrote the book, *Bread and Butter Basketball*.

Alvin Julian's Basketball Association of America / NBA Coaching Record

YEAR	TEAM	LG	W	L	WIN%
1949	Boston	BAA	25	35	.417
1950	Boston	NBA	22	46	.324
	TOTALS		47	81	.367

Sources: Basketball-Reference.com; Naismith Memorial Basketball Hall of Fame

Jurgensen, Christian Adolph III "Sonny" (born: August 23, 1934 in Wilmington, North Carolina); inducted into the Pro Football Hall of Fame in 1983 as a player; Position: Quarterback; Uniform: #9; won the 1955 Orange Bowl; a member of the 1960 NFL title-winning team.

Jurgensen played his 18-year (218 games) National Football League career (1957–1974) with the Philadelphia Eagles (1957–1963) and the Washington Redskins (1964–1974). In his final season (at age 40), he won his third NFL passing title.

He retired with an 82.625 passing rating; threw for more than 3,000 yards in a season five times; passed for more than 300 yards in 25 games and for more than 400 yards in five games; played in five Pro Bowls (1961, 1964, 1966–1967, 1969); named to the NFL 1960s All-Decade Team; selected one of the 70 Greatest Redskins; and had his name added to the Redskins' Ring of Fame.

The 5'11", 202-pound Jurgensen was drafted by the Eagles in 1957 (fourth round, 43rd overall selection) out of Duke University (Durham, North Carolina), and was a member of the 1960 NFL title team (a 17–13 win over the Green Bay Packers).

With Washington, Jurgensen played in Super Bowl VII (1973), losing 14–7 to the Miami Dolphins, and after retiring, he was a radio and television sports announcer.

At New Hanover High School (Wilmington, North Carolina), he played football and baseball all four years; basketball his last three years; and was a backup quarterback on the state championship team. After graduating from high school in 1953, he attended Duke University, where he was the team's starting quarterback in 1955 and 1956; helped lead the Blue Devils to two Atlantic Coast Conference championships; and guided the squad to a 34–7 win over Nebraska to win the 1955 Orange Bowl.

Jurgensen was inducted into the North Carolina Sports Hall of Fame in 1971 and the Duke Sports Hall of Fame in 1979.

He became the Eagles' starting quarterback in 1961 and threw for 3,723 yards and 32 touchdown passes, both NFL records at the time, and was named All-Pro. He was traded to the Redskins in 1964, and in 1967, he broke his own record by passing for 3,747 yards, and set NFL single-season records for attempts (508) and completions (288).

When the legendary Vince Lombardi became Washington's head coach in 1969, Jurgensen led the NFL in passing attempts (442), completions (274), completion percentage (62%), and passing yards (3,102) as the team finished above .500 (7–5–2) for the first time since 1955.

Sonny Jurgensen's Career Statistics

			PASSING							RUSHING			
YEAR	**TEAM**	**G**	**ATT**	**COMP**	**PCT**	**YDS**	**TD**	**INT**	**RATING**	**NO**	**YDS**	**AVG**	**TD**
1957	Philadelphia	10	70	33	47.1	470	5	8	53.6	10	-3	-0.3	2
1958	Philadelphia	12	22	12	54.5	259	0	1	77.7	1	1	1.0	0
1959	Philadelphia	12	5	3	60.0	27	1	0	114.2	0	0	0.0	0
1960	Philadelphia	12	44	24	54.5	486	5	1	122	4	5	1.3	0
1961	Philadelphia	14	416	235	56.5	3,723	32	24	88.1	20	27	1.4	0
1962	Philadelphia	14	366	196	53.6	3,261	22	26	74.3	17	44	2.6	2
1963	Philadelphia	9	184	99	53.8	1,413	11	13	69.4	13	38	2.9	1
1964	Washington	14	385	207	53.8	2,934	24	13	85.4	27	57	2.1	3
1965	Washington	13	356	190	53.4	2,367	15	16	69.6	17	23	1.4	2
1966	Washington	14	436	254	58.3	3,209	28	19	84.5	12	14	1.2	0
1967	Washington	14	508	288	56.7	3,747	31	16	87.3	15	46	3.1	2
1968	Washington	12	292	167	57.2	1,980	17	11	81.7	8	21	2.6	1
1969	Washington	14	442	274	62.0	3,102	22	15	85.4	17	156	9.2	1
1970	Washington	14	337	202	59.9	2,354	23	10	91.5	6	39	6.5	1
1971	Washington	5	28	16	57.1	170	0	2	45.2	3	29	9.7	0
1972	Washington	7	59	39	66.1	633	2	4	84.9	4	-5	-1.3	0
1973	Washington	14	145	87	60.0	904	6	5	77.5	3	7	2.3	0
1974	Washington	14	167	107	64.1	1,185	11	5	94.5	4	-6	-1.5	0
	TOTALS	218	4,262	2,433	57.1	32,224	255	189	82.6	181	493	2.7	15

Sources: Pro Football Hall of Fame; Pro-Football-Reference.com

Chapter 11
Kabanica to Kurri

Kabanica, Mike (born: November 12, 1925 in Pozega-Uz, Yugoslavia; died: November 5, 1996 in Milwaukee, Wisconsin); inducted into the National Soccer Hall of Fame and Museum in 1987 as a builder; served as president of the Wisconsin State Association.

Before immigrating to the United States in 1950, Kabanica played soccer in Yugoslavia, Italy, and Austria. After settling in Milwaukee, Wisconsin, he played one season with the Hungarian Tigers and ten seasons (1951–1960) for the Milwaukee Serbians, becoming the team's manager and coach in 1960.

Kabanica served as president of the Wisconsin State Association throughout most of the 1970s and the 1980s; named coach of the Wisconsin Soccer Association All-Stars (1961); and joined the WSA Board of Directors (1962).

Annually, the Wisconsin Youth Soccer Association awards six Mike Kabanica scholarships in the amount of $500 each to three boys and three girls, all of whom must be members of a Wisconsin Youth Soccer-affiliated team.

Source: National Soccer Hall of Fame and Museum

Kaline, Albert William "Al" (born: December 19, 1934 in Baltimore, Maryland); inducted into the National Baseball Hall of Fame and Museum in 1980 as a player; Position: Right Field; Bats: Right; Throws: Right; Uniform #6; won the 1968 World Series; youngest player ever to win a batting title; first player to have his jersey number retired by the Tigers.

Making his major league debut on June 25, 1953, Kaline played his entire 22-year career with the Detroit Tigers (1953–1974). He helped the team win the 1968 World Series in seven games over the St. Louis Cardinals; was a 15-time All-Star (1955–1967, 1971, 1974); won 10 Gold Gloves (1957–1959, 1961–1967); won the 1968 Lou Gehrig Memorial Award, the 1969 Hutch Award (named after former major league pitcher and manager Fred Hutchinson), and the 1973 Roberto Clemente Award; and he was the first Tiger player to have his uniform number retired by the team.

A member of the 3,000-hit club, "Mr. Tiger" won the batting title in 1955, hitting .340 at the age of 20 (the youngest player ever to win a batting title), and his second career home run (on June 11, 1954 in a 16–5 win over the Philadelphia Athletics) was a grand slam, at the time making him the second youngest player ever to have hit one.

The 6'2", 180-pound Kaline signed with the Tigers directly out of high school for $35,000 (giving him the "Bonus Baby") tag and he never played a single game in the minor leagues. When his skills began to deteriorate with age, he was moved to first base, and in his last season, the Tigers used him as a designated hitter.

On April 17, 1955, Kaline became the 13th player in major league history to hit two home runs in the same inning (6th, in a 16-0 win over the Kansas City Athletics).

After retiring from the game, he was a color commentator on Detroit's television broadcasts (1975–2002) and later served as a consultant to the team. In 1999, he ranked number 76 on *The Sporting News*' list of the 100 Greatest Baseball Players, and was nominated as a finalist for the Major League Baseball All-Century Team.

Al Kaline's Career Statistics

YEAR	TEAM	LG	G	AB	R	H	2B	3B	HR	RBI	BB	SO	SB	AVG	SLG
1953	Detroit	AL	30	28	9	7	0	0	1	2	1	5	1	.250	.357
1954	Detroit	AL	138	504	42	139	18	3	4	43	22	45	9	.276	.347
1955	Detroit	AL	152	588	121	200	24	8	27	102	82	57	6	.340	.546
1956	Detroit	AL	153	617	96	194	32	10	27	128	70	55	7	.314	.530
1957	Detroit	AL	149	577	83	170	29	4	23	90	43	38	11	.295	.478

YEAR	TEAM	LG	G	AB	R	H	2B	3B	HR	RBI	BB	SO	SB	AVG	SLG
1958	Detroit	AL	146	543	84	170	34	7	16	85	54	47	7	.313	.490
1959	Detroit	AL	136	511	86	167	19	2	27	94	72	42	10	.327	.530
1960	Detroit	AL	147	551	77	153	29	4	15	68	65	47	19	.278	.426
1961	Detroit	AL	153	586	116	190	41	7	19	82	66	42	14	.324	.515
1962	Detroit	AL	100	398	78	121	16	6	29	94	47	39	4	.304	.593
1963	Detroit	AL	145	551	89	172	24	3	27	101	54	48	6	.312	.514
1964	Detroit	AL	146	525	77	154	31	5	17	68	75	51	4	.293	.469
1965	Detroit	AL	125	399	72	112	18	2	18	72	72	49	6	.281	.471
1966	Detroit	AL	142	479	85	138	29	1	29	88	81	66	5	.288	.534
1967	Detroit	AL	131	458	94	141	28	2	25	78	83	47	8	.308	.541
1968	Detroit	AL	102	327	49	94	14	1	10	53	55	39	6	.287	.428
1969	Detroit	AL	131	456	74	124	17	0	21	69	54	61	1	.272	.447
1970	Detroit	AL	131	467	64	130	24	4	16	71	77	49	2	.278	.450
1971	Detroit	AL	133	405	69	119	19	2	15	54	82	57	4	.294	.462
1972	Detroit	AL	106	278	46	87	11	2	10	32	28	33	1	.313	.475
1973	Detroit	AL	91	310	40	79	13	0	10	45	29	28	4	.255	.394
1974	Detroit	AL	147	558	71	146	28	2	13	64	65	75	2	.262	.389
	TOTALS		2,834	10,116	1,622	3,007	498	75	399	1,583	1,277	1,020	137	.297	.480

Sources: Baseball-Reference.com; National Baseball Hall of Fame and Museum

Keaney, Frank William (born: June 5, 1886 in Boston, Massachusetts; died: October 10, 1967); inducted into the Naismith Memorial Basketball Hall of Fame in 1960 as a coach; never had a losing season in 28 years; his 1939 squad became the first college team to average more than 50 points per game for an entire season.

After graduating from Cambridge Latin School (Boston, Massachusetts) in 1906, Keaney attended Bates College (Lewiston, Maine), graduating in 1911. He coached at Rhode Island State College (now called the University of Rhode Island, Kingston) from 1920 to 1948 and compiled a 401–124 (.764) record. When he first joined the school in 1920 as a chemistry professor, he was a one-man athletic department, coaching football, basketball, baseball, track, and cross-country.

He never had a losing season in 28 years as a basketball coach; his 1939 squad became the first college team to average more than 50 points per game for an entire season; his 1943 team averaged more than two points per minute (80.7 per game); is credited with changing the style of the game from slow and deliberate to fast breaks and high scores; and was inducted into the Helms College Basketball Hall of Fame.

The University of Rhode Island's Frank W. Keaney Gymnasium-Armory was named in his honor in 1953.

During his tenure at Rhode Island, his 84 football, basketball, and baseball teams won a total of 707 games, lost 322, and tied 14, for an overall sports department record of .687. After poor health forced him to step down as a coach, Keaney remained at the school as its athletic director until he retired in 1956. Four years later, in 1960, he was a member of the second group inducted into the Naismith Memorial Basketball Hall of Fame.

In addition to his athletic accomplishments, he also developed "Keaney Blue," the school's official color, which he created in a laboratory while teaching chemistry.

In 2000, he was inducted into the Institute for International Sport's International Scholar-Athlete Hall of Fame.

Source: Naismith Memorial Basketball Hall of Fame

Keats, Gordon Blanchard "Duke" (born: March 21, 1895 in Montreal, Quebec, Canada; died: January 16, 1971); inducted into the Hockey Hall of Fame in 1958 as a player; Position: Center; led the Big 4 Western League in scoring in back-to-back seasons; won the final WCHL playoff game that sent Edmonton to the 1923 Stanley Cup postseason.

Keats played 10 professional hockey seasons from 1915 to 1929 (including three seasons in the National Hockey League), starting with the Toronto Blueshirts of the National Hockey Association. His career was interrupted when he served in the military for two years during World War I.

In 1919, the 5'11", 195-pound Keats joined the Edmonton Eskimos of the Big 4 Western League, where he led the circuit in scoring for the next two seasons. In 1921, the Eskimos joined the Western Canada Hockey League; he was named a First-Team All-Star four times (1922–1925); and he was later selected a First-Team All-Star in the Western Hockey League in 1926.

In the 1923 WCHL final playoff game against the Regina Capitals, Keats won the game and the title with a penalty shot, which sent the team to the Stanley Cup playoffs, where it eventually lost to the Ottawa Senators.

When the WHL folded in 1926, he went on to play in the National Hockey League with the Boston Bruins (1926–1927), Detroit Cougars (1927–1928), and the Chicago Black Hawks (1928), before being traded to the Tulsa Oilers of the American Hockey Association early in 1928. Keats led the AHA in scoring his first year in the league; played until 1931; regained his amateur status; and played his finals years with the Eskimos (in the North West Hockey League).

He was inducted into the Edmonton Sports Hall of Fame in 1964.

Gordon Keats' Career Statistics

			REGULAR SEASON					PLAYOFFS				
SEASON	TEAM	LEAGUE	GP	G	A	TP	PIM	GP	G	A	TP	PIM
1912–1913	Cobalt Mines	CoMHL	9	6	0	6	18					
1913–1914	Cobalt Mines	CoMHL	8	8	0	8	8					
1913–1914	North Bay Trappers	NOHA	3	2	0	2	18	4	6	0	6	
1914–1915	Haileybury Hawks	TBSHL										
1915–1916	Toronto Blueshirts	NHA	24	22	7	29	112					
1916–1917	Toronto Blueshirts	NHA	13	15	3	18	54					
1919–1920	Edmonton Eskimos	Big-4	12	18	14	32	41	2	2	2	4	2
1920–1921	Edmonton Eskimos	Big-4	15	23	6	29	36					
1921–1922	Edmonton Eskimos	WCHL	25	31	24	55	47	2	0	1	1	6
1922–1923	Edmonton Eskimos	WCHL	25	24	13	37	72	2	2	2	4	0
1922–1923	Edmonton Eskimos	St-Cup						2	0	0	0	4
1923–1924	Edmonton Eskimos	WCHL	29	19	12	31	41					
1924–1925	Edmonton Eskimos	WCHL	28	23	9	32	63					
1925–1926	Edmonton Eskimos	WHL	30	20	9	29	134	2	0	0	0	28
1926–1927	Boston Bruins	NHL	17	4	7	11	20					
1926–1927	Detroit Cougars	NHL	25	12	1	13	32					
1927–1928	Detroit Cougars	NHL	5	0	2	2	6					
1927–1928	Chicago Black Hawks	NHL	32	14	8	22	55					
1928–1929	Chicago Black Hawks	NHL	3	0	1	1	0					
1928–1929	Tulsa Oilers	AHA	39	22	11	33	18	4	0	1	1	10
1929–1930	Tulsa Oilers	AHA	3	2	2	4	2					
1930–1931	Tulsa Oilers	AHA	43	14	10	24	44	4	0	1	1	6
1932–1933	Edmonton Eskimos	WCHL	25	8	7	15	146	8	1	4	5	0
1933–1934	Edmonton Eskimos	NWHL	25	8	6	14	8	2	0	0	0	2
	NHL TOTALS		82	30	19	49	113					

Sources: Hockey Hall of Fame; Hockey-Reference.com

Keefe, Timothy John "Tim" (born: January 1, 1857 in Cambridge, Massachusetts; died: April 23, 1933 in Cambridge, Massachusetts); inducted into the National Baseball Hall of Fame and Museum in 1964 as a player by the Veterans Committee; Position: Pitcher; Bats: Right; Throws: Right; first pitcher to have more than 300 strikeouts in three different seasons; set a then-record of 19 consecutive wins in 1888; won the Pitching Triple Crown in 1888.

Keefe won 342 games in 15 major league seasons, including his time in the Players' League. He had a then-record 19 consecutive wins during the 1888 season (which would stand for 24 years); twice won over 40 games in a season; won three pennants; first pitcher to have more than 300 strikeouts in three different seasons; and when he retired, his 2,533 career strikeouts was ranked first all-time.

Making his major league debut on August 6, 1880, the 5'10", 185-pound Keefe played for the Troy Trojans (National League, 1880–1882), New York Metropolitans (American Association, 1883–1884), New York Giants (National League, 1885–1889, 1891), New York Giants (Players' League, 1890), and the Philadelphia Phillies (National League, 1891–1893).

On July 4, 1883, Keefe pitched two complete-game wins against the Columbus Colts, and gave up a total of only three hits during the doubleheader. In 1888, he led the league with a 35–12 record, 1.74 earned run average, and 335 strikeouts, winning the Pitching Triple Crown.

Throwing in the days of two-man rotations, during most of his career, he pitched from a distance of 50 feet, after his rookie season was baseball's last at 45 feet. His final year in the game was the first of baseball's pitching distance of 60'6", today's standard.

Although one of the game's highest-paid players (reportedly earning $4,500 in the 1889 season), Keefe was a strong advocate for players' rights and helped his brother-in-law, Monte Ward, establish the Players' League, serving as its secretary-treasurer.

When the Players' League folded after its 1890 season, he played for the Phillies for three years before retiring. After retiring as a player, he was a National League umpire for two years and later coached at the college level at Harvard University (Cambridge, Massachusetts), Princeton University (New Jersey), and Tufts University (Medford, Massachusetts).

Keefe led the National League in earned run average three times (1880, 1885, 1888); in wins twice (1886, 1888); led the American Association in strikeouts in 1883 and the National League in 1888; compiled seven 20-win seasons, six 30-win seasons, and two 40-win seasons; had six 200-strikeout seasons and three 300-strikeout seasons; and compiled an ERA of under 2.00 three times.

Tim Keefe's Career Statistics

YEAR	TEAM	W	L	PCT	ERA	CG	SHO	IP	H	ER	R	HR	BB	SO
1880	Troy	6	6	.500	0.86	12	0	105.0	68	10	27	0	16	39
1881	Troy	18	27	.400	3.24	45	4	403.0	434	145	243	4	83	103
1882	Troy	17	26	.395	2.49	41	1	376.0	367	104	221	4	78	111
1883	New York	41	27	.603	2.41	68	5	619.0	488	166	244	6	108	359
1884	New York	37	17	.685	2.25	56	4	483.0	380	121	196	5	71	334
1885	New York	32	13	.711	1.58	45	7	400.0	300	70	154	6	102	227
1886	New York	42	20	.677	2.56	62	2	535.0	479	152	250	9	102	297
1887	New York	35	19	.648	3.12	54	2	476.2	428	165	260	11	108	189
1888	New York	35	12	.745	1.74	48	8	434.1	317	84	140	5	90	335
1889	New York	28	13	.683	3.31	39	3	364.0	319	134	212	9	151	225
1890	New York	17	11	.607	3.38	23	1	229.0	225	86	137	6	89	89
1891	New York	2	5	.286	5.24	4	0	55.0	70	32	57	1	27	30
1891	Philadelphia	3	6	.333	3.91	9	0	78.1	82	34	55	2	30	34
1892	Philadelphia	19	16	.543	2.36	31	2	313.1	279	82	142	4	98	136
1893	Philadelphia	10	7	.588	4.40	17	0	178.0	202	87	131	3	80	56
	TOTALS	342	225	.603	2.62	554	39	5,049.2	4,438	1,472	2,469	75	1,233	2564

Sources: Baseball-Reference.com; National Baseball Hall of Fame and Museum

Keeler, William Henry "Wee Willie" (born: March 3, 1872 in Brooklyn, New York; died: January 1, 1923 in Brooklyn, New York); inducted into the National Baseball Hall of Fame and Museum in 1939 as a player; Position: Right Field; Bats: Left; Throws: Left; set a then-major league record in 1897 with a 44-game hitting streak to start the season; his 45-game hitting streak (1896–1897) is still a National League record.

Keeler won two batting titles (1897–1898); hit .300 or better 16 times; had 200 or more hits eight straight years; and a 44-game hitting streak to start the 1897 season. The 5'4", 140-pound Keeler joined the major leagues from the Binghamton (New York) Bingoes (Eastern League), and made his debut on September 30, 1892. He played 19 seasons (1892–1910) with the New York Giants (National League, 1892–1893, 1910), Brooklyn Grooms (National League, 1893), Baltimore Orioles (National League, 1894–1898), Brooklyn Superbas (National League, 1899–1902), and the New York Highlanders/Yankees (American League, 1903–1909). Ironically, although he was one of the smallest players ever in the game, Keeler used one of the shortest, but heaviest bats, in major league history (30 inches long, weighing 46 ounces).

He hit 206 singles in 1898; had an on-base percentage of .400 or more for seven straight seasons; and when he retired in 1910, Keeler's 2,932 hits were second all-time only to Cap Anson. In 1999, he was ranked number 75 on *The Sporting News*' list of the 100 Greatest Baseball Players (the shortest person on the list), and was named a finalist to the Major League Baseball All-Century Team.

An outstanding bunter, Keeler was the cause for the rule change that made a third-strike foul bunt a strike out. He perfected the "Baltimore Chop" by hitting the ball into the ground hard enough for it to bounce so high that he could reach base before the fielder could throw the ball to first.

In 1897, Keeler set a then-National League and Major League record with a 44-game hitting streak to start the season. Since he had a hit in his last at-bat of the 1896 season, he had compiled a still-standing National League record 45-game hitting streak. His major league record would stand until surpassed by the New York Yankees' Joe DiMaggio in 1941, who had a 56-game hitting streak.

Keeler still holds the major league record with eight consecutive seasons of 200 or more hits, and in 1905, he set the Yankees team record for most sacrifice hits in a season with 42.

Willie Keeler's Career Statistics

YEAR	TEAM	G	AB	R	H	2B	3B	HR	RBI	TB	SLG	AVG
1892	New York	14	53	7	17	3	0	0	6	20	.377	.321
1893	Brooklyn	20	80	14	25	1	1	1	9	31	.388	.313
1893	New York	7	24	5	8	2	1	1	7	15	.625	.333
1894	Baltimore	129	590	165	219	27	22	5	94	305	.517	.371
1895	Baltimore	131	565	162	213	24	15	4	78	279	.494	.377
1896	Baltimore	126	544	153	210	22	13	4	82	270	.496	.386
1897	Baltimore	129	564	145	239	27	19	0	74	304	.539	.424
1898	Baltimore	129	561	126	216	7	2	1	44	230	.410	.385
1899	Brooklyn	141	570	140	216	12	13	1	61	257	.451	.379
1900	Brooklyn	136	563	106	204	13	12	4	68	253	.449	.362
1901	Brooklyn	136	595	123	202	18	12	2	43	250	.420	.339
1902	Brooklyn	133	559	86	186	20	5	0	38	216	.386	.333
1903	New York	132	512	95	160	14	7	0	32	188	.367	.313
1904	New York	143	543	78	186	14	8	2	40	222	.409	.343
1905	New York	149	560	81	169	14	4	4	38	203	.363	.302
1906	New York	152	592	96	180	8	3	2	33	200	.338	.304
1907	New York	107	423	50	99	5	2	0	17	108	.255	.234
1908	New York	91	323	38	85	3	1	1	14	93	.288	.263
1909	New York	99	360	44	95	7	5	1	32	115	.319	.264
1910	New York	19	10	5	3	0	0	0	0	3	.300	.300
	TOTALS	2,123	8,591	1,719	2,932	241	145	33	810	3,562	.415	.341

Sources: Baseball-Reference.com; National Baseball Hall of Fame and Museum

Kehoe, Robert "Bob" (born: St. Louis, Missouri); inducted into the National Soccer Hall of Fame and Museum in 1989 as a builder; International Caps (1965): 4; International Goals: 0; first American-born coach in the National American Soccer League; served as director of Soccer for the Busch Soccer Club.

Kehoe was the 1965 captain of the U.S. Men's National Team in the 1966 FIFA World Cup qualifying rounds, and coached the National Team in World Cup qualifying in 1972. His four international caps came in games with Mexico (a 2–2 tie on March 7, 1965); another game with Mexico five days later (a 2–0 loss on March 12, 1965); a 1–0 win over Honduras (March 17, 1965); and a final 1–1 tie with Honduras (March 21, 1965). With an overall 1–1–2 record, the U.S. failed to qualify for the finals.

He was the first American-born coach in the National American Soccer League with the St. Louis Stars in the 1969–1970 season, and used American players at a time when the league was dominated by international stars. Earlier, he had played on the very first St. Louis (Missouri) University High School team in 1943; was a star for many years with St. Louis Kutis, beginning in 1949; and played in the 1954 U. S. Open Cup final with the team.

Kehoe was a longtime high school and club coach, winning numerous championships. He served as the soccer head coach at Granite City (Illinois) High School (1973–1983); head coach of the Bud Light Women's Over 30 Team (and led the squad to five national finals games between 1983 and 1988); and was appointed Director of Coaching for the Busch Soccer Club in 1983.

After retiring from the game, he was a radio and television commentator for the St. Louis Steamers of the Major Indoor Soccer League (1983–1988); received the United States Soccer Federation Meritorious Service Award; and has been inducted into the St. Louis Soccer Hall of Fame (1983) and the Illinois High School Soccer Coaches Association Hall of Fame in 1989.

Source: National Soccer Hall of Fame and Museum

Kell, George Clyde (born: August 23, 1922 in Swifton, Arkansas); inducted into the National Baseball Hall of Fame and Museum in 1983 as a player by the Veterans Committee; Position: Third Base; Bats: Right; Throws; Right; Uniform: #21; won the 1949 batting title with only 13 strikeouts, the lowest ever for a batting champion in major league history.

Making his major league debut on September 28, 1943, the 5'9", 175-pound Kell played 15 seasons (1943–1957) with the Philadelphia Athletics (1943–1946), Detroit Tigers (1946–1952), Boston Red Sox (1952–1954), Chicago White Sox (1954–1956), and the Baltimore Orioles (1956–1957). He was a 10-time All-Star (1947–1954, 1956–1957); hit over .300 nine times; and led American League third basemen in fielding percentage seven times. He led the league in double plays six times, assists four times, and in putouts twice.

In 1949, Kell won the American League batting title, while having only 13 strikeouts, the lowest ever for a batting champion in major league history.

After retiring from baseball, Kell worked as a play-by-play announcer, first with the Orioles (1957) and CBS television (1958), and then with the Tigers (1959–1996).

George Kell's Career Statistics

YEAR	TEAM	LG	G	AB	R	H	2B	3B	HR	RBI	BB	SO	SB	AVG	SLG
1943	Philadelphia	AL	1	5	1	1	0	1	0	1	0	0	0	.200	.600
1944	Philadelphia	AL	139	514	51	138	15	3	0	44	22	23	5	.268	.309
1945	Philadelphia	AL	147	567	50	154	30	3	4	56	27	15	2	.272	.356
1946	Philadelphia	AL	26	87	3	26	6	1	0	11	10	6	0	.299	.391
1946	Detroit	AL	105	434	67	142	19	9	4	41	30	14	3	.327	.440
1947	Detroit	AL	152	588	75	188	29	5	5	93	61	16	9	.320	.412
1948	Detroit	AL	92	368	47	112	24	3	2	44	33	15	2	.304	.402
1949	Detroit	AL	134	522	97	179	38	9	3	59	71	13	7	.343	.467
1950	Detroit	AL	157	641	114	218	56	6	8	101	66	18	3	.340	.484
1951	Detroit	AL	147	598	92	191	36	3	2	59	61	18	10	.319	.400
1952	Detroit	AL	39	152	11	45	8	0	1	17	15	13	0	.296	.368
1952	Boston	AL	75	276	41	88	15	2	6	40	31	10	0	.319	.453
1953	Boston	AL	134	460	68	141	41	2	12	73	52	22	5	.307	.483
1954	Boston	AL	26	93	15	24	3	0	0	10	15	3	0	.258	.290
1954	Chicago	AL	71	233	25	66	10	0	5	48	18	12	1	.283	.391
1955	Chicago	AL	128	429	44	134	24	1	8	81	51	36	2	.312	.429
1956	Chicago	AL	21	80	7	25	5	0	1	11	8	6	0	.313	.413
1956	Baltimore	AL	102	345	45	90	17	2	8	37	25	31	0	.261	.391
1957	Baltimore	AL	99	310	28	92	9	0	9	44	25	16	2	.297	.413
	TOTALS		1,795	6,702	881	2,054	385	50	78	870	621	287	51	.306	.414

Sources: Baseball-Reference.com; National Baseball Hall of Fame and Museum

Kelley, Joseph James "Joe" (born: December 9, 1871 in Cambridge, Massachusetts; died: August 14, 1943 in Baltimore, Maryland); inducted into the National Baseball Hall of Fame and Museum in 1971 as a player by the Veterans Committee; Position: Left Field; Bats: Right; Throws: Right; hit a single in his very first major league at-bat.

Kelley hit over .300 in 11 consecutive seasons, and on September 3, 1894, he went a record-tying nine-for-nine in a doubleheader against the Cleveland Spiders, helping his team win both games, 13–2 and 16–3. He led the Brooklyn Superbas to the National League pennant in 1900 and later managed the Cincinnati Reds (1902–1905) and Boston Doves (1908).

The 5'11", 190-pound Kelley made his major league debut on July 27, 1891, and went on to have a 17-year career (1891–1908) with the Boston Beaneaters (National League, 1891), Pittsburgh Pirates (1892), Baltimore Orioles (National League, 1892–1898), Brooklyn Superbas (National League, 1899–1901), Baltimore Orioles (American League, 1902), Cincinnati Reds (1902–1906), and the Boston Doves (National League, 1908). In his debut, Kelley hit a single in his first at-bat against future hall of fame pitcher Mickey Welch.

In 1894, Kelley registered a .502 on-base percentage, and finished with 107 walks while batting .393.

As a major league manager, he compiled an overall record of 338–321 (.513); managed the Toronto Maple Leafs to the International League pennant in 1907; and returned to manage the team from 1909 to 1914, winning a second pennant in 1912.

Joe Kelley's Career Statistics

YEAR	TEAM	LG	G	AB	R	H	2B	3B	HR	RBI	BB	SO	SB	AVG	SLG
1891	Boston	NL	12	45	8	11	1	1	0	3	1	4	0	.244	.311
1891	Pittsburgh	NL	2	7	0	1	0	0	0	0	0	0	0	.143	.143
1892	Pittsburgh	NL	56	199	27	50	6	6	0	28	17	21	5	.251	.342
1892	Baltimore	NL	10	33	3	7	0	0	0	4	4	7	2	.212	.212
1893	Baltimore	NL	124	490	120	153	25	16	9	76	77	44	33	.312	.484

YEAR	TEAM	LG	G	AB	R	H	2B	3B	HR	RBI	BB	SO	SB	AVG	SLG
1894	Baltimore	NL	129	509	167	199	48	17	6	111	107	36	46	.391	.587
1895	Baltimore	NL	131	510	148	189	26	21	10	134	77	29	54	.371	.563
1896	Baltimore	NL	130	516	147	191	27	17	8	100	91	19	87	.370	.535
1897	Baltimore	NL	129	503	113	196	31	9	5	118	70		44	.390	.517
1898	Baltimore	NL	124	467	71	153	17	15	2	110	56		24	.328	.441
1899	Brooklyn	NL	144	540	107	178	27	12	6	93	70		31	.330	.457
1900	Brooklyn	NL	118	453	92	144	23	18	6	91	53		26	.318	.488
1901	Brooklyn	NL	120	493	77	152	21	12	4	65	40		18	.308	.424
1902	Baltimore	AL	60	222	50	69	16	7	1	34	34		12	.311	.459
1902	Cincinnati	NL	37	156	24	51	8	2	1	12	15		3	.327	.423
1903	Cincinnati	NL	105	383	85	121	22	4	3	45	51		18	.316	.418
1904	Cincinnati	NL	123	449	75	126	21	13	0	63	49		15	.281	.385
1905	Cincinnati	NL	90	321	43	89	7	6	1	37	27		8	.277	.346
1906	Cincinnati	NL	129	465	43	106	19	11	1	53	44		9	.228	.323
1908	Boston	NL	62	228	25	59	8	2	2	17	27		5	.259	.338
	TOTALS		1,835	6,989	1,425	2,245	353	189	65	1,194	910	160	440	.321	.454

Joe Kelley's Managerial Record

YEAR	TEAM	LG	W	L	WIN%	Finish
1902	Cincinnati	NL	34	26	.567	4 (Player-Manager)
1903	Cincinnati	NL	74	65	.532	4 (Player-Manager)
1904	Cincinnati	NL	88	65	.575	3 (Player-Manager)
1905	Cincinnati	NL	79	74	.516	5 (Player-Manager)
1908	Boston	NL	63	91	.409	6 (Player-Manager)
	Cincinnati		275	230	.545	
	Boston		63	91	.409	
	TOTALS		338	321	.513	

Sources: Baseball-Reference.com; National Baseball Hall of Fame and Museum

Kelly, Francis J. "Frank" (born: July 9, 1924 in Dublin, Ireland; died: December 25, 1997); inducted into the National Soccer Hall of Fame and Museum in 1994 as a builder; served as president of the South Jersey Soccer League; was a founding member of the New Jersey State Youth Soccer Association.

Kelly played Gaelic football as a young boy and then for the Bohemians Football Club in the League of Ireland from 1945 to 1948. After moving to Scotland, he played for the Eagleham Amateurs in Glasgow from 1948 to 1954.

He moved to the United States and played for the Kensington Bluebells in Philadelphia (Pennsylvania, 1956–1957), and from 1969 through 1973, he was a member, and then president, of the South Jersey Soccer League and a founding member of the New Jersey State Youth Soccer Association.

He was elected second vice-president of the New Jersey State Youth Soccer Association in June 1993; served as national chairman of the James P. McGuire Cup; was a member of the U.S. Youth Soccer Association Executive Board; and a member of the Board of Directors of U.S. Soccer. In 1981, he served as chief delegate for U.S. Soccer at an international youth tournament held in Sao Paulo, Brazil.

Source: National Soccer Hall of Fame and Museum

Kelly, George Lange (born: September 10, 1895 in San Francisco, California; died: October 13, 1984 in Burlingame, California); inducted into the National Baseball Hall of Fame and Museum in 1973 as a player by the Veterans Committee; Position: First Base; Bats: Right; Throws: Right; first player to hit a home run in three successive innings; first player to hit home runs in six consecutive games.

Kelly hit .300 or better six straight seasons (1921–1926); had 100 or more runs batted in four consecutive years (1921–1924); established single-season league records for chances, putouts, assists, and double plays by a first baseman; and helped lead the Giants to four consecutive National League pennants (1921–1924).

Making his major league debut on August 18, 1915, the 6'4", 190-pound Kelly played 16 years (1915–1932) with the New York Giants (1915–1917, 1919–1926), Pittsburgh Pirates (1917), Cincinnati Reds (1927–1930), Chicago Cubs (1930), and Brooklyn Dodgers (1932). He played in four World Series, winning two (1921–1922) and losing two (1923–1924).

On September 17, 1923, Kelly became the first player in major league history to hit a home run in three successive innings (third, fourth, and fifth), all off Vic Aldridge, in a 13–6 win over the Chicago Cubs. In 1924, he became the first player to hit home runs in six consecutive games (July 11–16).

George Kelly's Career Statistics

YEAR	TEAM	LG	G	AB	R	H	2B	3B	HR	RBI	BB	SO	SB	AVG	SLG
1915	New York	NL	17	38	2	6	0	0	1	4	1	9	0	.158	.237
1916	New York	NL	49	76	4	12	2	1	0	3	6	24	1	.158	.211
1917	New York	NL	11	7	0	0	0	0	0	0	0	3	0	.000	.000
1917	Pittsburgh	NL	8	23	2	2	0	1	0	0	1	9	0	.087	.174
1919	New York	NL	32	107	12	31	6	2	1	14	3	15	1	.290	.411
1920	New York	NL	155	590	69	157	22	11	11	94	41	92	6	.266	.397
1921	New York	NL	149	587	95	181	42	9	23	122	40	73	4	.308	.528
1922	New York	NL	151	592	96	194	33	8	17	107	30	65	12	.328	.497
1923	New York	NL	145	560	82	172	23	5	16	103	47	64	14	.307	.452
1924	New York	NL	144	571	91	185	37	9	21	136	38	52	7	.324	.531
1925	New York	NL	147	586	87	181	29	3	20	99	35	54	5	.309	.471
1926	New York	NL	136	499	70	151	24	4	13	80	36	52	4	.303	.445
1927	Cincinnati	NL	61	222	27	60	16	4	5	21	11	23	1	.270	.446
1928	Cincinnati	NL	116	402	46	119	33	7	3	58	28	35	2	.296	.435
1929	Cincinnati	NL	147	577	73	169	45	9	5	103	33	61	7	.293	.428
1930	Cincinnati	NL	51	188	18	54	10	1	5	35	7	20	1	.287	.431
1930	Chicago	NL	39	166	22	55	6	1	3	19	7	16	0	.331	.434
1932	Brooklyn	NL	64	202	23	49	9	1	4	22	22	27	0	.243	.356
	TOTALS		1,622	5,993	819	1,778	337	76	148	1,020	386	694	65	.297	.452

Sources: Baseball-Reference.com; National Baseball Hall of Fame and Museum

Kelly, James Edward "Jim" (born: February 14, 1960 in Pittsburgh, Pennsylvania); inducted into the Pro Football Hall of Fame in 2002 as a player; Position: Quarterback; Uniform: #12; played in four Super Bowls.

Selected by the Buffalo Bills in the first round (second overall pick) of the 1983 National Football League Draft out of the University of Miami (Coral Gables, Florida), the 6'3", 217-pound Kelly played his entire 11-season (160 games) NFL career with the Bills (1986–1996). He passed for more than 3,000 yards in a season eight times; passed for more than 300 yards in a game 26 times; led Buffalo to four straight Super Bowls (SB XXV in 1991, SB XXVI in 1992, SB XXVII in 1993, and SB XXVIII in 1994), losing them all; named to four Pro Bowls (1988, 1991–1993); and led the NFL with a 101.2 passer rating in 1990.

Although drafted by the Bills, Kelly actually started his professional football career playing for the Houston Gamblers of the United States Football League. In two seasons with the team (1984–1985), he threw for 9,842 yards and 83 touchdowns. When the USFL folded after the 1985 season, he signed with the Bills.

Kelly was named All-Pro in 1991; All-Pro Second Team twice (1990, 1992); All-AFC in 1991; and All-AFC Second Team in 1990. He holds numerous Super Bowl records, including most passes attempted (145); most passes attempted in a game (58 against the Washington Redskins, Super Bowl XXVI in 1992); and most passes completed in a game (31 against the Dallas Cowboys, Super Bowl XXVIII, 1994). He was the 1984 USFL Rookie of the Year; USFL Most Valuable Player in 1984; USFL Most Outstanding Quarterback in 1985; two-time USFL All-Star (1984–1985); and named to the USFL All-Time Team. He also holds USFL records for career passing touchdowns (83); singe-season passing yards (5,219 in 1984); and singe-season passing touchdowns (44 in 1984).

When he retired in 1996, Kelly owned various Buffalo Bills records, including most attempts in a career (4,779); most completions in a career (2,874); most completions in a season (304 in 1991); most passing yards in a career (35,467); most passing yards in a season (3,844 in 1991); most 300-yard games in a career (26); most touchdown passes in a career (237); most touchdown passes in a season (33 in 1991); most touchdown passes in a game (six against the Pittsburgh Steelers on September 8, 1991); most consecutive games with a touchdown pass (18); best completion percentage in a career (60.14); and best completion percentage in a season (64.14 in 1991). The Bills retired his number 12 jersey.

When his son, Hunter, died in 2005 of Krabbe Leukodystrophy (Krabbe disease), Kelly established Hunter's Hope to raise money to fight the disease.

At East Brady (Pennsylvania) High School, Kelly won all-state honors and passed for a total of 3,915 yards and 44 touchdowns. He also was a star on the school's basketball team; scored more than 1,000 points in his career; and led East Brady to the basketball state semifinals as a senior.

After high school, he attended the University of Miami and finished his career with 406 completions in 646 attempts (.628) for 5,233 yards and 32 touchdowns. He was later inducted into the University of Miami Hall of Fame in 1992.

Jim Kelly's Career Statistics

			PASSING							RUSHING			
YEAR	TEAM	G	ATT	COMP	PCT	YDS	TD	INT	RATING	NO	YDS	AVG	TD
1986	Buffalo	16	480	285	59.4	3,593	22	17	83.3	41	199	4.9	0
1987	Buffalo	12	419	250	59.7	2,798	19	11	83.8	29	133	4.6	0
1988	Buffalo	16	452	269	59.5	3,380	15	17	78.2	35	154	4.4	0
1989	Buffalo	13	391	228	58.3	3,130	25	18	86.2	29	137	4.7	2
1990	Buffalo	14	346	219	63.3	2,829	24	9	101.2	22	63	2.9	0
1991	Buffalo	15	474	304	64.1	3,844	33	17	97.6	20	45	2.3	1
1992	Buffalo	16	462	269	58.2	3,457	23	19	81.2	31	53	1.7	1
1993	Buffalo	16	470	288	61.3	3,382	18	18	79.9	36	102	2.8	0
1994	Buffalo	14	448	285	63.6	3,114	22	17	84.6	25	77	3.1	1
1995	Buffalo	15	458	255	55.7	3,130	22	13	81.1	17	20	1.2	0
1996	Buffalo	13	379	222	58.6	2,810	14	19	73.2	19	66	3.5	2
	TOTALS	160	4,779	2,874	60.1	35,467	237	175	84.4	304	1,049	3.5	7

Sources: Pro Football Hall of Fame; Pro-Football-Reference.com

Kelly, Leonard Patrick "Red" (born: July 9, 1927 in Simcoe, Ontario, Canada); inducted into the Hockey Hall of Fame in 1969 as a player; Position: Defenseman-Forward; won eight Stanley Cup championships.

Kelly was one of the National Hockey League's best-ever defensemen early in his career and developed into a high-scoring center at the end. He played 20 NHL seasons (1947–1967) for the Detroit Red Wings (1947–1960) and Toronto Maple Leafs (1960–1967); was an All-Star eight consecutive seasons (six times on the First Team [1951–1955, 1957] and twice on the Second Team [1950, 1956]); won the Lady Byng Trophy for sportsmanship and gentlemanly conduct four times (1951, 1953–1954, 1961); and the James Norris Memorial Trophy as the outstanding defenseman in the league in 1954, the first year it was presented.

He was only 20 years old when Detroit brought him up to the NHL directly from St. Michael's of the Ontario Hockey Association, and he helped lead the team to four Stanley Cup championships (1950, 1952, 1954–1955). In 1960, he left Detroit and joined the Maple Leafs, where he won another four Stanley Cup titles (1962–1964, 1967).

In 1962, while still an active NHL player, he was elected to the Canadian Parliament as a Liberal Member, where he served for three years until retiring in 1965. In 1967, after winning his last Stanley Cup, Kelly was traded to the expansion Los Angeles Kings; was named head coach; and led the team into the playoffs in back-to-back seasons. After coaching the Pittsburgh Penguins for three seasons (1969–1972), he returned to Toronto and led the Leafs to four straight quarterfinal appearances (1974–1977).

In 1998, he was ranked number 22 on *The Hockey News*' list of the 100 Greatest Hockey Players, and in 2001, he was made a Member of the Order of Canada.

Red Kelly's Career Statistics

			REGULAR SEASON					PLAYOFFS				
SEASON	TEAM	LEAGUE	GP	G	A	TP	PIM	GP	G	A	TP	PIM
1943–1944	St. Michael's Midgets	Minor-ON	8	10	5	15						
1944–1945	St. Michael's Buzzers	OHA-B	11	15	13	28	7	11	16	8	24	6
1944–1945	St. Michael's Majors	OHA-Jr.	1	0	0	0	0					
1945–1946	St. Michael's Majors	OHA-Jr.	26	13	11	24	18	11	1	0	1	7
1946–1947	St. Michael's Majors	OHA-Jr.	30	8	24	32	11	9	3	3	6	9
1946–1947	St. Michael's Majors	M-Cup	9	5	5	10	2					
1947–1948	Detroit Red Wings	NHL	60	6	14	20	13	10	3	2	5	2
1948–1949	Detroit Red Wings	NHL	59	5	11	16	10	11	1	1	2	10
1949–1950	Detroit Red Wings	NHL	70	15	25	40	9	14	1	3	4	2
1950–1951	Detroit Red Wings	NHL	70	17	37	54	24	6	0	1	1	0
1951–1952	Detroit Red Wings	NHL	67	16	31	47	16	5	1	0	1	0
1952–1953	Detroit Red Wings	NHL	70	19	27	46	8	6	0	4	4	0
1953–1954	Detroit Red Wings	NHL	62	16	33	49	18	12	5	1	6	0
1954–1955	Detroit Red Wings	NHL	70	15	30	45	28	11	2	4	6	17

			REGULAR SEASON					PLAYOFFS				
SEASON	TEAM	LEAGUE	GP	G	A	TP	PIM	GP	G	A	TP	PIM
1955–1956	Detroit Red Wings	NHL	70	16	34	50	39	10	2	4	6	2
1956–1957	Detroit Red Wings	NHL	70	10	25	35	18	5	1	0	1	0
1957–1958	Detroit Red Wings	NHL	61	13	18	31	26	4	0	1	1	2
1958–1959	Detroit Red Wings	NHL	67	8	13	21	34					
1959–1960	Detroit Red Wings	NHL	50	6	12	18	10					
1959–1960	Toronto Maple Leafs	NHL	18	6	5	11	8	10	3	8	11	2
1960–1961	Toronto Maple Leafs	NHL	64	20	50	70	12	2	1	0	1	0
1961–1962	Toronto Maple Leafs	NHL	58	22	27	49	6	12	4	6	10	0
1962–1963	Toronto Maple Leafs	NHL	66	20	40	60	8	10	2	6	8	6
1963–1964	Toronto Maple Leafs	NHL	70	11	34	45	16	14	4	9	13	4
1964–1965	Toronto Maple Leafs	NHL	70	18	28	46	8	6	3	2	5	2
1965–1966	Toronto Maple Leafs	NHL	63	8	24	32	12	4	0	2	2	0
1966–1967	Toronto Maple Leafs	NHL	61	14	24	38	4	12	0	5	5	2
1967–1968	Los Angeles Kings	NHLMGNT										
	NHL TOTALS		1,316	281	542	823	327	164	33	59	92	51

Red Kelly's Coaching Record

			REGULAR SEASON					PLAYOFFS			
SEASON	LG	TEAM	W	L	T	PTS	WIN%	W	L	T	WIN%
1967–1968	NHL	Los Angeles	31	33	10	72	.486	3	4	0	.429
1968–1969	NHL	Los Angeles	24	42	10	58	.382	4	7	0	.364
1969–1970	NHL	Pittsburgh	26	38	12	64	.421	6	4	0	.600
1970–1971	NHL	Pittsburgh	21	37	20	62	.397				
1971–1972	NHL	Pittsburgh	26	38	14	66	.423	0	4	0	.000
1972–1973	NHL	Pittsburgh	17	19	6	40	.476				
1973–1974	NHL	Toronto	35	27	16	86	.551	0	4	0	.000
1974–1975	NHL	Toronto	31	33	16	78	.488	2	5	0	.286
1975–1976	NHL	Toronto	34	31	15	83	.519	5	5	0	.500
1976–1977	NHL	Toronto	33	32	15	81	.506	4	5	0	.444
		TOTALS	278	330	134	690	.465	24	38	0	.387

Sources: Hockey Hall of Fame; Hockey-Reference.com

Kelly, Leroy (born: May 20, 1942 in Philadelphia, Pennsylvania); inducted into the Pro Football Hall of Fame in 1994 as a player; Position: Running Back; Uniform: #44; won the NFL rushing title twice.

Kelly was an eighth-round pick (110th overall selection) in the 1964 National Football League Draft by the Cleveland Browns out of Morgan State University (Baltimore, Maryland). The 6', 202-pound running back played his entire 10-year NFL career (136 games) with the Browns (1964–1973). After serving as a backup to the legendary Jim Brown for two seasons, he became a starter in 1966; gained 1,000 or more yards in a season three straight years (1966–1968); won the NFL rushing title twice (1967–1968); was a two-time punt-return leader (1965 in the NFL, 1971 in the American Football Conference); named All-NFL five times; selected to six Pro-Bowls (1966–1971); won the 1968 Bert Bell Award as the NFL's Player of the Year; and was named to the NFL 1960s All-Decade Team.

He began his football career at Simon Gratz High School (Philadelphia, Pennsylvania), before attending college at Morgan State University. After leaving the NFL in 1973, he played one season with the Chicago Fire of the World Football League in 1974, rushing for 315 yards (4.1 average per carry) and catching eight passes for 128 yards (16.0 average per catch).

Leroy Kelly's Career Statistics

			RUSHING				RECEIVING			
YEAR	TEAM	G	NO	YDS	AVG	TD	NO	YDS	AVG	TD
1964	Cleveland	14	6	12	2.0	0	0	0	---	0
1965	Cleveland	13	37	139	3.8	0	9	122	13.6	0
1966	Cleveland	14	209	1,141	5.5	15	32	366	11.4	1

YEAR	TEAM	G	RUSHING NO	YDS	AVG	TD	RECEIVING NO	YDS	AVG	TD
1967	Cleveland	14	235	1,205	5.1	11	20	282	14.1	2
1968	Cleveland	14	248	1,239	5.0	16	22	297	13.5	4
1969	Cleveland	13	196	817	4.2	9	20	267	13.4	1
1970	Cleveland	13	206	656	3.2	6	24	311	13.0	2
1971	Cleveland	14	234	865	3.7	10	25	252	10.1	2
1972	Cleveland	14	224	811	3.6	4	23	204	8.9	1
1973	Cleveland	13	132	389	2.9	3	15	180	12.00	0
	TOTALS	136	1,727	7,274	4.2	74	190	2,281	12.67	13

YEAR	TEAM	G	PUNT RETURNS NO	YDS	AVG	TD
1964	Cleveland	14	9	171	19.0	1
1965	Cleveland	13	17	265	15.6	2
1966	Cleveland	14	13	104	8.0	0
1967	Cleveland	14	9	59	6.6	0
1968	Cleveland	14	1	9	9.0	0
1969	Cleveland	13	7	28	4.0	0
1970	Cleveland	13	2	15	7.5	0
1971	Cleveland	14	30	292	9.7	0
1972	Cleveland	14	5	40	8.0	0
1973	Cleveland	13	1	7	7.0	0
	TOTALS	136	94	990	10.5	3

Sources: Pro Football Hall of Fame; Pro-Football-Reference.com

Kelly, Michael Joseph "King" (born: December 31, 1857 in Troy, New York; died: November 8, 1894 in Boston, Massachusetts); inducted into the National Baseball Hall of Fame and Museum in 1945 as a player by the Veterans Committee; Position: Right Field-Catcher; Bats: Right; Throws: Right; credited with popularizing the hit-and-run play, the hook slide, the catcher's practice of backing up first base, and the use of signs between the pitcher and the catcher; author of the first baseball autobiography; first man to popularize sports autographs.

Able to play every position, after winning the batting title in 1886, Kelly was sold to the Boston Beaneaters for a reported $10,000, a record at the time.

Making his major league debut on May 1, 1878, the 5'10", 170-pound Kelly played 16 seasons with the Cincinnati Reds (National League, 1878–1879), Chicago White Stockings (National League, 1880–1886), Boston Beaneaters (National League, 1887–1889, 1891–1892), Boston/Cincinnati Reds (Players' League / American Association, 1890–1891), Cincinnati Kelly's Killers (American Association, 1891), and the New York Giants (National League, 1893). He played in three pre-modern day World Series (1885–1886, 1892); led the league in runs scored three straight seasons (1884–1886); and in hitting twice (1884, 1886).

Kelly was the author of the first baseball autobiography, *Play Ball: Stories of the Ball Field*, published in 1888. He is also credited with popularizing the hook slide, the catcher's practice of backing up first base, and the use of signs between the pitcher and the catcher. He was the subject of the 1893 song "Slide Kelly, Slide," and a 1927 movie of the same name.

While playing for the Boston Reds in the single season of the Players' League in 1890, he led the team to the league's first and only title, before returning to the American Association in 1891 to manage Cincinnati.

Kelly was the first man to popularize sports autographs, and he was one of the first athletes to perform on the Vaudeville stage.

King Kelly's Career Statistics

YEAR	TEAM	LG	G	AB	R	H	2B	3B	HR	RBI	BB	SO	SB	AVG	SLG
1878	Cincinnati	NL	59	231	29	65	9	0	0	27	7	7		.281	.320
1879	Cincinnati	NL	76	342	78	119	22	14	2	47	8	14		.348	.512
1880	Chicago	NL	82	335	71	98	13	11	1	60	12	22		.293	.406
1881	Chicago	NL	80	353	84	114	28	3	2	55	16	14		.323	.436
1882	Chicago	NL	84	377	81	115	36	5	1	55	10	27		.305	.435

YEAR	TEAM	LG	G	AB	R	H	2B	3B	HR	RBI	BB	SO	SB	AVG	SLG
1883	Chicago	NL	98	430	92	109	27	9	3	61	16	35		.253	.379
1884	Chicago	NL	107	448	120	153	30	6	13	95	46	24		.342	.522
1885	Chicago	NL	107	438	124	126	24	7	9	75	46	24		.288	.436
1886	Chicago	NL	118	451	155	175	31	11	4	79	83	33		.388	.532
1887	Boston	NL	114	525	119	207	34	11	8	63	55	40	84	.394	.547
1888	Boston	NL	105	440	85	140	20	11	9	71	31	39	56	.318	.475
1889	Boston	NL	125	507	120	149	32	7	9	78	65	40	68	.294	.438
1890	Boston	PL	90	352	89	114	19	7	4	66	52	22	40	.324	.452
1891	Cincinnati	AA	73	249	48	69	15	7	1	5	51	28	15	.277	.406
1891	Boston	AA	4	15	2	4	0	0	1	53	0	2	1	.267	.467
1891	Boston	NL	24	96	14	23	1	0	0	4	7	13	24	.240	.250
1892	Boston	NL	72	279	40	56	9	0	2	41	39	31	24	.201	.254
1893	New York	NL	16	54	8	17	1	0	0	15	6	5	3	.315	.333
	TOTALS		1,434	5,922	1,359	1,853	351	109	69	950	550	420	315	.313	.444

King Kelly's Managerial Record

YEAR	TEAM	LG	W	L	WIN%	Finish
1887	Boston	NL	49	43	.533	5 (Player-Manager)
1890	Boston	PL	81	48	.628	1 (Player-Manager)
1891	Cincinnati	AA	43	57	.430	7 (Player-Manager)
	Boston		130	91	.588	
	Cincinnati		43	57	.430	
	TOTALS		173	148	.539	

Sources: Baseball-Reference.com; National Baseball Hall of Fame and Museum

Kempton, George P. "Barney" (born: 1890 in Belfast, Northern Ireland; died: 1959 in Seattle, Washington); inducted into the National Soccer Hall of Fame and Museum in 1950 as a builder; served as Washington State Junior Commissioner.

Kempton arrived in Los Angeles, California in 1910 from Belfast and played for the Los Angeles Rangers. Later he lived in San Francisco, California for six years and played for the Independents, the Thistles, and the Celtics. He then moved to Seattle, Washington in 1916 to play in the Northwest League, eventually going to Canada to play in Vancouver and Prince Rupert.

He retired as a player in 1934 and became secretary of the Washington State Association and then served as Junior Commissioner, before becoming a soccer writer for the *Seattle Post-Intelligencer*.

Source: National Soccer Hall of Fame and Museum

Kennedy, James Walter (born: June 8, 1912 in Stamford, Connecticut; died: June 26, 1977); inducted into the Naismith Memorial Basketball Hall of Fame in 1981 as a contributor; second NBA commissioner.

After attending St. Basil Preparatory School (Stamford, Connecticut, graduating in 1930), Kennedy attended the University of Notre Dame (South Bend, Indiana) from 1930 to 1934. He served as the public relations director of the Basketball Association of America (1946–1951) and stayed with the league when it merged with the National Basketball League to form the National Basketball Association; toured the world as the public relations director of the Harlem Globetrotters during the 1950s; and was the second NBA Commissioner (1963–1975), succeeding Maurice Podoloff.

As commissioner, he oversaw the league's expansion from nine to 18 teams; helped negotiate the NBA's first national television contract; guided the league to a 200 percent boost in income and a 300 percent increase in attendance; served as president of the Naismith Memorial Basketball Hall of Fame for two years; received the Basketball Hall of Fame's John W. Bunn Award (1975) for his contributions to the game; and served on the hall of fame's Board of Trustees for 13 years. Kennedy was elected mayor of Stamford in 1959, and the J. Walter Kennedy Sports Complex at Westhill High School (Stamford, Connecticut) was named in his honor.

After college, Kennedy was a basketball coach at various locations in the 1930s; served as the athletic director at St. Basil's Preparatory School; and in the 1940s, he returned to his alma mater as the school's sports information director.

After leaving the Globetrotters, he returned to Stamford and was elected mayor in 1959, where he served until the NBA owners elected him the league's second commissioner in 1963. Kennedy helped start the tradition of having one NBA game a year played in Springfield, Massachusetts to benefit the hall of fame.

The J. Walter Kennedy Community Service Award is presented annually by the Professional Basketball Writers Association to an NBA player or coach for outstanding service to the community.

Source: Naismith Memorial Basketball Hall of Fame

Kennedy, Matthew P. "Pat" (born: January 28, 1908 in Hoboken, New Jersey; died: June 16, 1977); inducted into the Naismith Memorial Basketball Hall of Fame in 1959 as a referee; first referee inducted into the basketball hall of fame.

After playing basketball for two years at Demarest High School (Hoboken, New Jersey, graduating in 1926), Kennedy attended Montclair State University (East Orange, New Jersey) from 1926 to 1928. Recognizing that he did not have the necessary skills to enjoy a successful playing career, he refocused his efforts and became a referee, working at the high school, college, and professional levels from 1924 to 1956.

He served in the Ivy League, American Professional League, and the National Basketball Association; officiated numerous National Collegiate Athletic Association and National Invitation Tournaments; served as NBA Supervisor of Referees and Referee-in-Chief (1946–1950); officiated for the Harlem Globetrotters (1950–1957); and worked about 4,000 games in his career.

He was the first referee inducted into the basketball hall of fame.

Source: Naismith Memorial Basketball Hall of Fame

Kennedy, Theodore Samuel "Ted" "Teeder" (born: December 12, 1925 in Humberstone, Ontario, Canada; died: August 14, 2009 in Port Colborne, Ontario, Canada); inducted into the Hockey Hall of Fame in 1966 as a player; Position: Center; won five Stanley Cup championships.

Kennedy played his entire 14-year National Hockey League career with the Toronto Maple Leafs from 1942 to 1957. Frank Selke, the Leafs' interim manager while team owner Conn Smythe was serving in the military during World War II, acquired Kennedy to play in Toronto. For reasons that have never been made clear, when Smythe returned after the war, he reportedly was so upset that the deal had been made without his approval that a feud developed between him and Selke that eventually forced Selke to leave the team and join the Montreal Canadiens in 1946. As Kennedy progressed and showed his talent, Smythe eventually changed his mind about the deal.

The 5'11", 170-pound Kennedy joined the Leafs on a full-time basis in the 1943–1944 season; was the team's top scorer the next season; and was the overall goal-scoring leader in the playoffs as the Leafs won the Stanley Cup, defeating the Montreal Canadiens in seven games. He went on to help the team win four additional Stanley Cup championships (1947–1949, 1951), with Kennedy serving as team captain for the 1949 win.

He won the Hart Memorial Trophy in 1955 as the NHL's Most Valuable Player; was selected to the Second All-Star Team three times (1950–1951, 1954); and won the inaugural J.P. Bickell Memorial Award in 1953 (and again in 1955) for on-ice excellence. After winning the Hart Memorial Trophy, Kennedy retired from the NHL, but returned briefly in 1956 to play 30 games for the team before retiring for good. In 1998, he was ranked number 57 on *The Hockey News*' list of the 100 Greatest Hockey Players.

Ted Kennedy's Career Statistics

			REGULAR SEASON					PLAYOFFS				
SEASON	**TEAM**	**LEAGUE**	**GP**	**G**	**A**	**TP**	**PIM**	**GP**	**G**	**A**	**TP**	**PIM**
1942–1943	Port Colborne Sailors	OHA-Sr.	23	23	29	52	15					
1942–1943	Toronto Maple Leafs	NHL	2	0	1	1	0					
1943–1944	Toronto Maple Leafs	NHL	49	26	23	49	2	5	1	1	2	4
1944–1945	Toronto Maple Leafs	NHL	49	29	25	54	14	13	7	2	9	2
1945–1946	Toronto Maple Leafs	NHL	21	3	2	5	4					
1946–1947	Toronto Maple Leafs	NHL	60	28	32	60	27	11	4	5	9	4
1947–1948	Toronto Maple Leafs	NHL	60	25	21	46	32	9	8	6	14	0
1948–1949	Toronto Maple Leafs	NHL	59	18	21	39	25	9	2	6	8	2
1949–1950	Toronto Maple Leafs	NHL	53	20	24	44	34	7	1	2	3	8
1950–1951	Toronto Maple Leafs	NHL	63	18	43	61	32	11	4	5	9	6
1951–1952	Toronto Maple Leafs	NHL	70	19	33	52	33	4	0	0	0	4
1952–1953	Toronto Maple Leafs	NHL	43	14	23	37	42					
1953–1954	Toronto Maple Leafs	NHL	67	15	23	38	78	5	1	1	2	2
1954–1955	Toronto Maple Leafs	NHL	70	10	42	52	74	4	1	3	4	0

SEASON	TEAM	LEAGUE	REGULAR SEASON GP	G	A	TP	PIM	PLAYOFFS GP	G	A	TP	PIM
1956–1957	Toronto Maple Leafs	NHL	30	6	16	22	35					
1957–1958	Peterborough Petes	OHA-Jr.										
	TOTALS		696	231	329	560	432	78	29	31	60	32

Sources: Hockey Hall of Fame; Hockey-Reference.com

Keogan, George E. (born: March 8, 1890 in Minnesota Lake, Minnesota; died: February 17, 1943); inducted into the Naismith Memorial Basketball Hall of Fame in 1961 as a coach; never had a losing season in 20 years at Notre Dame.

After attending Detroit Lakes (Minnesota) High School (graduating in 1909), Keogan went to the University of Minnesota (Minneapolis-St. Paul) from 1909 to 1913. He later served at the Great Lakes Naval Training Station (Illinois, 1916–1917) during World War I.

He began his coaching career at Charles City College (Iowa, 1909–1910), before moving on to Lockport (Illinois) High School (1910–1911) and then Riverside (Illinois) High School from 1911 to 1912. Keogan returned to the college coaching ranks at Superior State Teachers College (Wisconsin, 1912–1914), St. Louis University (Missouri, 1914–1915), and St. Thomas College (St. Paul, Minnesota, 1915–1916). After the war, he resumed his coaching career at Allegheny College (Meadville, Pennsylvania, 1917–1918), Valparaiso University (Indiana, 1918–1920); and at LaCrosse (Wisconsin) Central High School (1920–1923), before finally moving to the University of Notre Dame (South Bend, Indiana) from 1923 to 1943.

Keogan led Superior State to a 17–5 (.773) record; St. Louis University to 13–6 (.684); St. Thomas to 13–2 (.867); Allegheny to 10–3 (.769); and Valparaiso to 32–12 (.727), for a combined record of 85–28 (.752). At Notre Dame, he led the school to a 327–96–1 (.771) record; never had a losing season at the school; and served as head basketball coach, head baseball coach, and assistant football coach with the legendary Knute Rockne.

Source: Naismith Memorial Basketball Hall of Fame

Keon, David Michael "Dave" (born: March 22, 1940 in Noranda, Quebec, Canada); inducted into the Hockey Hall of Fame in 1986 as a player; Position: Center; named 1961 NHL Rookie of the Year; won four Stanley Cup championships.

Keon played 23 professional hockey seasons from 1960 to 1982, including 18 National Hockey League seasons with the Toronto Maple Leafs (1960–1975) and Hartford Whalers (1979–1982). After playing in the Ontario Hockey Association for several seasons, in 1960, the 5'9", 163-pound Keon turned professional with the Sudbury Wolves (Eastern Professional Hockey League) when he joined the team for four playoff games. This brief four-game stint would be his only exposure to the minor leagues before joining the Leafs in 1960.

He won the Calder Memorial Trophy as NHL Rookie of the Year, and was selected to the Second Team All-Star squad. He helped the team win four Stanley Cup championships (1962–1964, 1967); was named the playoffs Most Valuable Player in the 1967 Cup win; and won the Lady Byng Trophy for sportsmanship and gentlemanly behavior twice (1962–1963). For a brief period of time, Keon was the Leafs' all-time leading scorer; was the team's leading scorer three times (1964, 1967, 1970); and the squad's top goal scorer twice (1971, 1973).

In 1975, he left the league and played four seasons in the World Hockey Association with the Minnesota Fighting Saints, Indianapolis Racers, and the New England Whalers. In 1979, he returned to the NHL with the Hartford Whalers, and in 1982 (at age 42, the league's oldest player) ended his playing career.

In 1998, Keon was ranked number 69 on *The Hockey News*' list of the 100 Greatest Hockey Players, and The Arena Dave Keon in Rouyn-Noranda, Quebec is named in his honor.

Dave Keon's Career Statistics

SEASON	TEAM	LEAGUE	REGULAR SEASON GP	G	A	TP	PIM	PLAYOFFS GP	G	A	TP	PIM
1956–1957	St. Michael's Buzzers	OHA-B	36	20	23	43	14					
1956–1957	St. Michael's Majors	OHA-Jr.	4	1	3	4	0					
1957–1958	St. Michael's Majors	OHA-Jr.	45	23	27	50	29	9	8	5	13	10
1958–1959	St. Michael's Majors	OHA-Jr.	47	33	38	71	31	15	4	9	13	8
1959–1960	St. Michael's Majors	OHA-Jr.	46	16	29	45	8	10	8	10	18	2
1959–1960	Kitchener-Waterloo Dutchmen	OHA-Sr.	1	1	0	1	0					
1959–1960	Sudbury Wolves	EPHL						4	2	2	4	2
1960–1961	Toronto Maple Leafs	NHL	70	20	25	45	6	5	1	1	2	0
1961–1962	Toronto Maple Leafs	NHL	64	26	35	61	2	12	5	3	8	0

SEASON	TEAM	LEAGUE	REGULAR SEASON					PLAYOFFS				
			GP	G	A	TP	PIM	GP	G	A	TP	PIM
1962–1963	Toronto Maple Leafs	NHL	68	28	28	56	2	10	7	5	12	0
1963–1964	Toronto Maple Leafs	NHL	70	23	37	60	6	14	7	2	9	2
1964–1965	Toronto Maple Leafs	NHL	65	21	29	50	10	6	2	2	4	2
1965–1966	Toronto Maple Leafs	NHL	69	24	30	54	4	4	0	2	2	0
1966–1967	Toronto Maple Leafs	NHL	66	19	33	52	2	12	3	5	8	0
1967–1968	Toronto Maple Leafs	NHL	67	11	37	48	4					
1968–1969	Toronto Maple Leafs	NHL	75	27	34	61	12	4	1	3	4	2
1969–1970	Toronto Maple Leafs	NHL	72	32	30	62	6					
1970–1971	Toronto Maple Leafs	NHL	76	38	38	76	4	6	3	2	5	0
1971–1972	Toronto Maple Leafs	NHL	72	18	30	48	4	5	2	3	5	0
1972–1973	Toronto Maple Leafs	NHL	76	37	36	73	2					
1973–1974	Toronto Maple Leafs	NHL	74	25	28	53	7	4	1	2	3	0
1974–1975	Toronto Maple Leafs	NHL	78	16	43	59	4	7	0	5	5	0
1975–1976	Minnesota Fighting Saints	WHA	57	26	38	64	4					
1975–1976	Indianapolis Racers	WHA	12	3	7	10	2	7	2	2	4	2
1976–1977	Minnesota Fighting Saints	WHA	42	13	38	51	2					
1976–1977	New England Whalers	WHA	34	14	25	39	8	5	3	1	4	0
1977–1978	New England Whalers	WHA	77	24	38	62	2	14	5	11	16	4
1978–1979	New England Whalers	WHA	79	22	43	65	2	10	3	9	12	2
1979–1980	Hartford Whalers	NHL	76	10	52	62	10	3	0	1	1	0
1980–1981	Hartford Whalers	NHL	80	13	34	47	26					
1981–1982	Hartford Whalers	NHL	78	8	11	19	6					
	NHL TOTALS		1,296	396	590	986	117		92	36	68	6

Source: Hockey Hall of Fame

Keough, Harry Joseph (born: November 15, 1927 in St. Louis, Missouri); inducted into the National Soccer Hall of Fame and Museum in 1976 as a player; Position: Full Back; International Caps (1949–1957): 17; International Goals: 1; played in two Olympic Games; won five NCAA titles as a coach.

After ending his playing career, Keough became the head coach of the St. Louis University (Missouri) soccer team in 1967. He was a member of the 1950 United States World Cup team that became famous for beating England 1–0 in Brazil (South America) during qualifying rounds, considered one of the greatest soccer upsets ever. He also played in the 1952 Olympic Games (Helsinki, Finland) and the 1956 Games (Melbourne, Australia), but did not medal either time. He won U.S. Open Cup medals with St. Louis Kutis twice (1954, 1957), and U.S. Amateur Cup medals with the St. Louis Raiders in 1952 and six more times with Kutis (1956–1961).

Keough's playing career began in 1945 with the St. Louis Schumachers team that won the U.S. Junior Cup. During World War II, while serving in the Navy, he played briefly for the San Francisco (California) Barbarians in 1946. After the war, Keough was selected in 1949 to represent the United States in the qualifying competition for the 1950 World Cup (to be hosted by Brazil), where he played against Cuba twice and Mexico once, helping the team to qualify.

In 1950, as a member of the National Team, he played in all three games in Brazil and was the captain of the team in the game against Spain, but was unable to medal.

When his playing career ended, he became the head soccer coach at Florissant Valley Community College (St. Louis, Missouri). In 1967, he began coaching at St. Louis University and, in his first year, led the team to an NCAA co-championship, and eventually won four more NCAA Division I titles (1969–1970, 1972–1973) during his tenure. While at the school, he compiled a 213–50–23 (.810) overall record; was inducted into the St. Louis Soccer Hall of Fame in 1972; the St. Louis University Athletic Hall of Fame in 1995; and into the National Soccer Coaches Association of America Hall of Fame in 1996.

The Keough Award, named in his honor, is presented annually to an outstanding St. Louis-based male and female professional or college soccer player.

Source: National Soccer Hall of Fame and Museum

Kharlamov, Valeri (born: January 14, 1948 in Moscow, Russia; died: August 27, 1981); inducted into the Hockey Hall of Fame in 2005 as a player; Position: Left Wing; Uniform: #17; won three Olympic medals.

Kharlamov played 14 international seasons with the Soviet Red Army squad from 1967 to 1981; scored 507 points (293 goals, 214 assists) in 436 regular-season games; and helped his team win 11 league championships (1968, 1970–1973, 1975, 1977–1981). In eleven consecutive International Ice Hockey Federation and European Championships, Kharlamov and the Soviet team won eight gold medals, two silver, and a bronze, while he was named a tournament All-

Star four times (1972–1973, 1975–1976). He played in three Olympics, winning gold medals in 1972 (Sapporo, Japan) and 1976 (Innsbruck, Austria), and a silver medal in 1980 (Lake Placid, New York).

In 1969, at the age of 21, he was named a Merited Master of Sport, and was inducted into the IIHF Hall of Fame in 1998.

While still an active member of the Soviet team, he and his wife died in a car accident on August 27, 1981. Kharlamov is the second Soviet-trained player inducted into the Hockey Hall of Fame (teammate Vladislav Tretiak was elected in 1989 and their coach, Anatoli Tarasov, was elected in 1974).

He was a member of the Soviet Union team that lost to the "Miracle on Ice" American squad in the semifinals at the 1980 Winter Olympics in Lake Placid, New York, but went on to win the silver medal.

Source: Hockey Hall of Fame

Kiesling, Walter Andrew "Walt" (born: May 27, 1903 in St. Paul, Minnesota; died: March 2, 1962); inducted into the Pro Football Hall of Fame in 1966 as a player; won the 1936 NFL title; coached the Steelers to the team's first-ever winning season.

Kiesling had a 34-year career in professional football as a player, assistant coach, and head coach. A 6'2", 249-pound guard out of the University of St. Thomas (St. Paul, Minnesota), he played 13 seasons (1928–1938, 125 games) in the National Football League with the Duluth Eskimos (1926–1927), Pottsville Maroons (1928), Chicago Cardinals (1929–1933), Chicago Bears (1934), Green Bay Packers (1935–1936), and the Pittsburgh Pirates (1937–1938). He went on to coach the Pittsburgh Pirates/Steelers (1939–1942, 1954–1956), Philadelphia-Pittsburgh (1943), and Cardinals-Pittsburgh (1944), finishing with an overall coaching record of 30–55–5 (.353).

He was a two-way lineman for six NFL teams; named All-NFL three times (1929–1930, 1932); was a member of the unbeaten 1934 Chicago Bears; helped the 1936 Packers win an NFL title; was an assistant coach with the Steelers for 14 seasons; and led Pittsburgh to its first-ever winning season in 1942.

Walt Kiesling's Coaching Record

YEAR	TEAM	LG	W	L	T	WIN%	FINISH
1939	Pittsburgh	NFL	1	6	1	.143	4
1940	Pittsburgh	NFL	2	7	2	.222	4
1941	Pittsburgh	NFL	1	2	1	.333	5
1942	Pittsburgh	NFL	7	4	0	.636	2
1943	Philadelphia-Pittsburgh	NFL	5	4	1	.556	3
1944	Chicago-Pittsburgh	NFL	0	10	0	.000	5
1954	Pittsburgh	NFL	5	7	0	.417	4
1955	Pittsburgh	NFL	4	8	0	.333	6
1956	Pittsburgh	NFL	5	7	0	.417	4
	Pittsburgh		25	41	4	.379	
	Philadelphia-Pittsburgh		5	4	1	.556	
	Chicago-Pittsburgh		0	10	0	.000	
	TOTALS		30	55	5	.353	

Sources: Pro Football Hall of Fame; Pro-Football-Reference.com

Killebrew, Harmon Clayton (born: June 29, 1936 in Payette, Idaho); inducted into the National Baseball Hall of Fame and Museum in 1984 as a player; Position: First Base; Bats: Right; Throws: Right; Uniform: #3; first Twin inducted into the baseball hall of fame; named American League Most Valuable Player in 1969; holds the major league record for the lowest batting average by a league RBI leader (.243 in 1962); hit more home runs (393) than any other player in the 1960s.

The 5'11", 213-pound Killebrew hit 573 home runs, the most by an American League right-handed hitter, and second only to Babe Ruth among American League leaders. Over his 22-year career (1954–1975), he tied or led the league in home runs six times; hit 40 or more home runs eight seasons; and scored 100 or more runs in a season twice. Killebrew won the American League Most Valuable Player Award in 1969, when he led the league in home runs, runs batted in, walks, and on-base percentage.

Making his major league debut on June 23, 1954, he played for the Washington Senators (1954–1960), Minnesota Twins (1961–1974), and the Kansas City Royals (1975); played in the 1965 World Series (losing to the Los Angeles

Dodgers); was an 11-time All–Star (1959, 1961, 1963–1971; and in deference to his power, Killebrew was walked intentionally with no one on base three times in his career.

After being an All-State quarterback at Payette (Idaho) High School, he was signed by the Senators and for the next five seasons, split his time between Washington and the team's AA affiliate, the Chattanooga Lookouts of the Southern Association. Killebrew joined the Senators full time in 1959, and stayed with the team when it moved to Minnesota in 1961 and became the Twins.

With injuries limiting his playing time, after one year with the Royals, he retired in 1975.

He was the first Twin inducted into the baseball hall of fame, and his jersey number three was retired by the Twins.

In 1999, he was ranked number 69 on *The Sporting News*' list of the 100 Greatest Baseball Players, and was nominated as a finalist for the Major League Baseball All-Century Team. Contrary to what many fans think, he was not the model for the silhouette of a player swinging a bat that is used on the official logo of Major League Baseball.

In 1962, he won the runs batted in title while batting only .243, the lowest ever for an RBI champion, and in 1971, he again led the league in RBIs, but hit only .254, the third-lowest ever. Except for pitchers, only Killebrew, Bill Mazeroski, and Rabbit Maranville have been inducted the baseball hall of fame while never once batting .300 (over a full season) in their careers.

On July 18, 1962, Minnesota became the first 20th century team to hit two grand slams in one inning when Bob Allison and Killebrew connected in a team-record, 11-run first inning, against the Cleveland Indians, in a 14-3 win. On June 9, 1966, the Twins had the first five-home-run inning in American League history against the Kansas City Royals (Rich Rollins and Zoilo Versalles hit theirs off Catfish Hunter; Tony Oliva and Don Mincher connected off Paul Lindblad; and Killebrew hit his off John Wyatt) in the seventh inning in a 9–4 win.

Although Killebrew never hit 50 home runs in a single season, he hit the most home runs of any player in the 1960s (393).

Harmon Killebrew's Career Statistics

YEAR	TEAM	LG	G	AB	R	H	2B	3B	HR	RBI	BB	SO	SB	AVG	SLG
1954	Washington	AL	9	13	1	4	1	0	0	3	2	3	0	.308	.385
1955	Washington	AL	38	80	12	16	1	0	4	7	9	31	0	.200	.363
1956	Washington	AL	44	99	10	22	2	0	5	13	10	39	0	.222	.394
1957	Washington	AL	9	31	4	9	2	0	2	5	2	8	0	.290	.548
1958	Washington	AL	13	31	2	6	0	0	0	2	0	12	0	.194	.194
1959	Washington	AL	153	546	98	132	20	2	42	105	90	116	3	.242	.516
1960	Washington	AL	124	442	84	122	19	1	31	80	71	106	1	.276	.534
1961	Minnesota	AL	150	541	94	156	20	7	46	122	107	109	1	.288	.606
1962	Minnesota	AL	155	552	85	134	21	1	48	126	106	142	1	.243	.545
1963	Minnesota	AL	142	515	88	133	18	0	45	96	72	105	0	.258	.555
1964	Minnesota	AL	158	577	95	156	11	1	49	111	93	135	0	.270	.548
1965	Minnesota	AL	113	401	78	108	16	1	25	75	72	69	0	.269	.501
1966	Minnesota	AL	162	569	89	160	27	1	39	110	103	98	0	.281	.538
1967	Minnesota	AL	163	547	105	147	24	1	44	113	131	111	1	.269	.558
1968	Minnesota	AL	100	295	40	62	7	2	17	40	70	70	0	.210	.420
1969	Minnesota	AL	162	555	106	153	20	2	49	140	145	84	8	.276	.584
1970	Minnesota	AL	157	527	96	143	20	1	41	113	128	84	0	.271	.546
1971	Minnesota	AL	147	500	61	127	19	1	28	119	114	96	3	.254	.464
1972	Minnesota	AL	139	433	53	100	13	2	26	74	94	91	0	.231	.450
1973	Minnesota	AL	69	248	29	60	9	1	5	32	41	59	0	.242	.347
1974	Minnesota	AL	122	333	28	74	7	0	13	54	45	61	0	.222	.360
1975	Kansas City	AL	106	312	25	62	13	0	14	44	54	70	1	.199	.375
	TOTALS		2,435	8,147	1,283	2,086	290	24	573	1,584	1,559	1,699	19	.256	.509

Sources: Baseball-Reference.com; Harmon Killebrew Web Site (www.harmonkillebrew.com); National Baseball Hall of Fame and Museum

Kilpatrick, General John Reed (born: June 15, 1889 in New York, New York; died: May 7, 1960 in New York, New York); inducted into the Hockey Hall of Fame in 1960 as a builder; led the New York Rangers to two Stanley Cup championships (1933, 1940); served as Chairman of the Board of Madison Square Garden.

Kilpatrick helped make ice hockey popular in New York City, and his work with both the New York Rangers and the National Hockey League helped stabilize the NHL in the 1930s and early 1940s. A star football player at Yale University (New Haven, Connecticut), in a 1907 game against Princeton, he was credited with throwing the first overhand forward pass in college; was named to the 1910 College Football All-America Team; and was inducted into the College Football Hall of Fame in 1955.

After graduating from Yale, Kilpatrick was a businessman until serving in the Army during World War I. After his military service, he returned to New York City and became a successful businessman, finally becoming vice president of the Fuller contracting company (1923–1933). In 1933, he resigned from Fuller to become president of the Madison Square Garden Corporation, and during his tenure, the Rangers won two Stanley Cup championships (1933, 1940).

He was elected an NHL Governor in 1936; served in World War II (promoted to Brigadier General in 1942); retired from the Army in 1949, and returned to Madison Square Garden, eventually serving as Chairman of the Board from 1955 to 1959.

In 1968, after his death, Kilpatrick received the Lester Patrick Trophy for outstanding service to hockey in the United States.

Source: Hockey Hall of Fame

Kilrea, Brian Blair (born: October 21, 1934 in Ottawa, Ontario, Canada); inducted into the Hockey Hall of Fame in 2003 as a builder; won three straight Calder Cup titles as a player; scored the first-ever goal in Los Angeles Kings history; as a coach, led the Ottawa 67's to the team's first-ever Memorial Cup title.

After four junior/minor league seasons, Kilrea played for the National Hockey League's Detroit Red Wings for one game in 1958, before returning to the Troy Bruins (International Hockey League) for the 1958–1959 season, where he would be named a Second Team All–Star.

For eight seasons (1959–1968), the 5'11", 175-pound Kilrea played center with the Springfield Indians/Kings of the American Hockey League; had six 20-goal seasons; helped the team win three straight Calder Cup titles (1960–1962); and was later inducted into the Springfield Hockey Hall of Fame. In 1967, he played for the NHL's Los Angeles Kings, and scored the first goal in the history of the franchise on October 14, 1967 in a 4–2 win over the Philadelphia Flyers.

He then played four more seasons in the minors, before retiring with the Denver Spurs (World Hockey Association) in 1970. After retiring as a player, Kilrea became a coach and general manager with the Ontario Hockey League's Ottawa 67's (a job he still has as of this writing) and led the team to its first Memorial Cup title in 1984. He left the team for two years and returned in the 1986–1987 season, leading the squad to his second championship with the team in 1999. He set the Canadian junior record for coaching wins (742) on January 17, 1997, in a 6–0 win over the North Bay Centennials.

In 2002–2003, he celebrated his 1,000th win as a head coach in the Ontario Hockey League; won the Matt Leyden Trophy as OHL Coach of the Year five times (1981–1982, 1996–1997, 2003); and won the Bill Long Award in 1994 for distinguished service to the OHL. In 31 years with Ottawa, he has had only six losing seasons, and on February 2, 2007, Kilrea coached his 2000th game with the team.

Brian Kilrea's Career Playing Statistics

			REGULAR SEASON					PLAYOFFS				
SEASON	TEAM	LEAGUE	GP	G	A	PTS	PIM	GP	G	A	PTS	PIM
1954–1955	Hamilton Tiger Cubs	OHA	49	27	25	52	0					
1955–1956	Troy Bruins	IHL	60	16	36	52	22					
1956–1957	Troy Bruins	IHL	60	9	35	44	46					
1957–1958	Edmonton Flyers	WHL	3	0	0	0	0					
1957–1958	Detroit Red Wings	NHL	1	0	0	0	0					
1958–1959	Troy Bruins	IHL	54	33	60	93	44					
1959–1960	Springfield Indians	AHL	63	14	27	41	26	8	0	1	1	4
1960–1961	Springfield Indians	AHL	70	20	67	87	47	8	1	5	6	2
1961–1962	Springfield Indians	AHL	70	20	73	93	28	2	0	1	1	0
1962–1963	Springfield Indians	AHL	72	25	50	75	34					
1963–1964	Springfield Indians	AHL	72	22	61	83	28					
1964–1965	Springfield Indians	AHL	72	23	54	77	18					
1965–1966	Springfield Indians	AHL	70	13	47	60	14	6	3	1	4	0
1966–1967	Springfield Indians	AHL	63	25	38	63	29					
1967–1968	Los Angeles Kings	NHL	25	3	5	8	12					
1967–1968	Springfield Kings	AHL	38	7	25	32	14	4	0	3	3	0
1968–1969	Vancouver Canucks	WHL	1	0	1	1	0					
1968–1969	Tulsa Oilers	CHL	24	11	25	36	12	4	0	1	1	0
1968–1969	Rochester Americans	AHL	33	2	11	13	4					

SEASON	TEAM	LEAGUE	REGULAR SEASON GP	G	A	PTS	PIM	PLAYOFFS GP	G	A	PTS	PIM
1969–1970	Denver Spurs	WHL	32	5	14	19	8					
	NHL TOTALS		26	3	5	8	12					

Brian Kilrea's Coaching Record with the Ottawa 67's (Ontario Hockey League)

YEAR	REGULAR SEASON G	W	L	T	OTL	POST SEASON RESULTS
1974–1975	70	33	30	7	-	Lost in First Round
1975–1976	66	34	23	9	-	Lost in Third Round
1976–1977	66	38	23	5	-	Won J. Ross Robertson Cup
1977–1978	68	43	18	7	-	Lost in Third Round
1978–1979	68	30	38	0	-	Lost in First Round
1979–1980	68	45	20	3	-	Lost in Third Round
1980–1981	68	45	20	3	-	Lost in Second Round
1981–1982	68	47	19	2	-	Lost OHL Finals
1982–1983	70	46	21	3	-	Lost in Third Round
1983–1984	70	50	18	2	-	Won Memorial Cup
1986–1987	66	33	28	5	-	Lost in Second Round
1987–1988	66	38	26	2	-	Lost in Third Round
1988–1989	66	30	32	4	-	Lost in Second Round
1989–1990	66	38	26	2	-	Lost in First Round
1990–1991	66	39	25	2	-	Lost in Second Round
1991–1992	66	32	30	4	-	Lost in Second Round
1992–1993	66	16	42	8	-	Missed Playoffs
1993–1994	66	33	22	11	-	Lost in Third Round
1994–1995						Brief Retirement
1995–1996	66	39	22	5	-	Lost in Second Round
1996–1997	66	49	11	6	-	Lost OHL Finals
1997–1998	66	40	17	9	-	Lost OHL Finals
1998–1999	68	48	13	7	-	Lost in Second Round
1999–2000	68	43	20	4	1	Lost in Second Round
2000–2001	68	33	21	10	4	Won J. Ross Robertson Cup
2001–2002	68	36	20	10	2	Lost in Second Round
2002–2003	68	44	14	7	3	Lost OHL Finals
2003–2004	68	29	26	9	4	Lost in First Round
2004–2005	68	34	26	7	1	Lost OHL Finals
2005–2006	68	29	31	-	8	Lost in First Round
2006–2007	68	30	34	-	4	Lost in First Round
2007–2008	68	29	34	-	5	Lost in First Round
2008–2009	68	40	21	-	7	Lost in First Round
TOTALS	2,156	1,193	771	153	39	

Sources: Hockey Hall of Fame; Hockey-Reference.com

Kinard, Frank Manning, Sr. (born: October 23, 1914 in Pelahatchie, Mississippi; died: September 7, 1985); inducted into the Pro Football Hall of Fame in 1971 as a player; Position: Tackle; first player to earn both All-NFL and All-AAFC honors.

A relatively small tackle (6'1", 216 pounds), Kinard played seven seasons (73 games) with the National Football League's Brooklyn Dodgers/Tigers from 1938 to 1944. After missing the 1945 season while serving in the military during World War II, he returned to professional football for two seasons (1946–1947) with the New York Yankees of the newly formed All-America Football Conference. In 1946, he became the first player to earn both All-NFL (1940–1941, 1943–1944) and All-AAFC (1946) honors. While in the military, he was named All-Service in 1945.

After being a star at Central High School (Jackson, Mississippi), Kinard was a two-time All-American at the University of Mississippi (Oxford) and was drafted in the third round by the Dodgers in 1938.

He was inducted into the College Football Hall of Fame in 1951.

Source: Pro Football Hall of Fame

Kiner, Ralph McPherran (born: October 27, 1922 in Santa Rita, New Mexico); inducted into the National Baseball Hall of Fame and Museum in 1975 as a player; Position: Left Field; Bats: Right; Throws: Right; Uniform: #4; first National League player with two fifty-home run seasons (1947, 1949).

In a relatively short 10-year major league career, the 6'2", 195-pound Kiner hit 369 home runs, and won or shared the National League home run title in each of his first seven seasons with the Pittsburgh Pirates.

Making his debut on April 16, 1946, he played for the Pirates (1946–1953), Chicago Cubs (1953–1954), and the Cleveland Indians (1955). He was named to six straight All-Star teams (1948–1953); was the first National League player to hit more than 50 home runs in a season twice (51 in 1947 and 54 in 1949); averaged more than 100 runs batted in per season during his career; led the National League in slugging percentage three times; led the National League in home runs seven straight years (1946–1952); led the majors in home runs six consecutive seasons (1947–1952); holds the major league record of hitting a total of eight home runs in four consecutive multi-homer games (September 7–13, 1947), and his ratio of 7.1 home runs per 100 at-bats trails only Babe Ruth and Mark McGwire among retired players.

Kiner was traded to the Chicago Cubs in June 1953 and played two seasons with the team, before ending his career after one year with the Cleveland Indians in 1955. In 1961, he began a broadcasting career with the Chicago White Sox, and in 1962, he started announcing games with the expansion New York Mets. As of this writing, he is still working Mets games, making him the only broadcaster to survive through all of the team's history.

He was inducted into the New York Mets Hall of Fame in 1984; the Pirates retired his uniform number four in 1987; *The Sporting News* ranked him number 90 on its 1999 list of The 100 Greatest Baseball Players; and he was one of the finalists for the Major League Baseball All-Century Team, also in 1999.

Ralph Kiner's Career Statistics

YEAR	TEAM	LG	G	AB	R	H	2B	3B	HR	RBI	BB	SO	SB	AVG	SLG
1946	Pittsburgh	NL	144	502	63	124	17	3	23	81	74	109	3	.247	.430
1947	Pittsburgh	NL	152	565	118	177	23	4	51	127	98	81	1	.313	.639
1948	Pittsburgh	NL	156	555	104	147	19	5	40	123	112	61	1	.265	.533
1949	Pittsburgh	NL	152	549	116	170	19	5	54	127	117	61	6	.310	.658
1950	Pittsburgh	NL	150	547	112	149	21	6	47	118	122	79	2	.272	.590
1951	Pittsburgh	NL	151	531	124	164	31	6	42	109	137	57	2	.309	.627
1952	Pittsburgh	NL	149	516	90	126	17	2	37	87	110	77	3	.244	.500
1953	Pittsburgh	NL	41	148	27	40	6	1	7	29	25	21	1	.270	.466
1953	Chicago	NL	117	414	73	117	14	2	28	87	75	67	1	.283	.529
1954	Chicago	NL	147	557	88	159	36	5	22	73	76	90	2	.285	.487
1955	Cleveland	AL	113	321	56	78	13	0	18	54	65	46	0	.243	.452
	TOTALS		1,472	5,205	971	1,451	216	39	369	1,015	1,011	749	22	.279	.548

Sources: Baseball-Reference.com; National Baseball Hall of Fame and Museum

Klein, Charles Herbert "Chuck" (born: October 7, 1904 in Indianapolis, Indiana; died: March 28, 1958 in Indianapolis, Indiana); inducted into the National Baseball Hall of Fame and Museum in 1980 as a player by the Veterans Committee; Position: Right Field; Bats: Left; Throws: Right; Uniform: #1; named the 1932 National League Most Valuable Player; won the 1933 Triple Crown; first National League player in the 20th century to hit four home runs in a game.

Klein won four home run titles (1929, 1931–1933); runs batted in twice (1931, 1933); the Triple Crown in 1933 (leading the league with 28 home runs, a .368 batting average, and 120 RBIs); 1932 National League Most Valuable Player; and on July 10, 1936, became the first National League player in the 20th century to hit four home runs in a game (to help beat the Pittsburgh Pirates, 9–6). A great fielder, he still holds the modern-day, single-season record by a right fielder for assists with 44 in 1930.

Making his debut on July 30, 1928, Klein played 17 major league seasons with the Philadelphia Phillies (1928–1933, 1936–1944), Chicago Cubs (1934–1936), and the Pittsburgh Pirates (1939). He played in the 1935 World Series (losing to the Detroit Tigers), and was a two-time All-Star (1933–1934).

Klein led the league in runs scored three times (1930–1932); collected more than 200 hits in five seasons (1929–1933); twice led the league in hits (1932–1933); games played (1930, 1932); doubles (1930, 1933); stolen bases (1932); extra-base hits four times (1929–1930, 1932–1933); total bases four times (1930–1933); and hit for the cycle twice (1931, 1933).

The 6', 185-pound Klein was the last player to lead his league in home runs (38) and stolen bases (20) in the same season (1932). On July 6, 1933, he became the first Phillies player ever to bat in an All-Star Game.

In 1999, he ranked number 92 on *The Sporting News*' list of the 100 Greatest Baseball Players, and was a nominee for the Major League Baseball All-Century Team.

Chuck Klein's Career Statistics

YEAR	TEAM	LG	G	AB	R	H	2B	3B	HR	RBI	BB	SO	SB	AVG	SLG
1928	Philadelphia	NL	64	253	41	91	14	4	11	34	14	22	0	.360	.577
1929	Philadelphia	NL	149	616	126	219	45	6	43	145	54	61	5	.356	.657
1930	Philadelphia	NL	156	648	158	250	59	8	40	170	54	50	4	.386	.687
1931	Philadelphia	NL	148	594	121	200	34	10	31	121	59	49	7	.337	.584
1932	Philadelphia	NL	154	650	152	226	50	15	38	137	60	49	20	.348	.646
1933	Philadelphia	NL	152	606	101	223	44	7	28	120	56	36	15	.368	.602
1934	Chicago	NL	115	435	78	131	27	2	20	80	47	38	3	.301	.510
1935	Chicago	NL	119	434	71	127	14	4	21	73	41	42	4	.293	.488
1936	Chicago	NL	29	109	19	32	5	0	5	18	16	14	0	.294	.477
1936	Philadelphia	NL	117	492	83	152	30	7	20	86	33	45	6	.309	.520
1937	Philadelphia	NL	115	406	74	132	20	2	15	57	39	21	3	.325	.495
1938	Philadelphia	NL	129	458	53	113	22	2	8	61	38	30	7	.247	.356
1939	Philadelphia	NL	25	47	8	9	2	1	1	9	10	4	1	.191	.340
1939	Pittsburgh	NL	85	270	37	81	16	4	11	47	26	17	1	.300	.511
1940	Philadelphia	NL	116	354	39	77	16	2	7	37	44	30	2	.218	.333
1941	Philadelphia	NL	50	73	6	9	0	0	1	3	10	6	0	.123	.164
1942	Philadelphia	NL	14	14	0	1	0	0	0	0	0	2	0	.071	.071
1943	Philadelphia	NL	12	20	0	2	0	0	0	3	0	3	1	.100	.100
1944	Philadelphia	NL	4	7	1	1	0	0	0	0	0	2	0	.143	.143
	TOTALS		1,753	6,486	1,168	2,076	398	74	300	1,201	601	521	79	.320	.543

Sources: Baseball-Reference.com; National Baseball Hall of Fame and Museum

Klein, Paul (born: Alexandria, Egypt); inducted into the National Soccer Hall of Fame and Museum in 1953 as a builder; won the 1949 U.S. Amateur Cup as a manager.

Klein and his family moved to Germany in 1914, where he played junior soccer. When he eventually came to the United States in 1953, he formed teams in New Brunswick and Bloomfield (both in New Jersey).

In 1939, he joined the Elizabeth Soccer Club and two years later became manager of the team. From 1941 until he retired in 1952, Klein's teams won the U.S. Amateur Cup (1949, over St. Louis Zenthoefers); the German-American League pennant three consecutive seasons (1947–1949); and the New Jersey State Challenge Cup (1949).

Source: National Soccer Hall of Fame and Museum

Kleinaitis, Alfred (born: March 9, 1941 in Rostock, Germany); inducted into the National Soccer Hall of Fame and Museum in 1995 as a builder-official; first U.S. official to referee a full international match in Europe.

Only 11 years after starting his career as a referee, Kleinaitis became a Fédération Internationale de Football Association-level official. He refereed in the North American Soccer League, the National Collegiate Athletic Association, Olympic Games, Pan American matches, and men's and women's World Cup competitions.

He refereed NCAA Division I finals five times (1980–1983, 1989) and was the first U.S. official to referee a full international match in Europe, a game in Dublin, Ireland.

Kleinaitis worked in high school for 19 years and in college for 22 years, and was inducted into the National Intercollegiate Soccer Officials Association Hall of Fame in 1992.

Source: National Soccer Hall of Fame and Museum

Klem, William Joseph "Bill" (born: William Joseph Klimm, February 22, 1874 in Rochester, New York; died: September 1, 1951 in Miami, Florida); inducted into the National Baseball Hall of Fame and Museum in 1953 as an umpire by the Veterans Committee; first umpire to use the inside chest protector; worked the first-ever All-Star Game in 1933.

Sometimes referred to as the "Father of Baseball Umpires," Klem was considered the best umpire of his time, and was one of the first officials to use hand signals to display his calls, making it easier for fans to follow the batter's count.

He umpired from 1905 until 1941; worked 18 World Series (1908–1909, 1911–1915, 1917–1918, 1920, 1922, 1924, 1926, 1929, 1931–1932, 1934, 1940); and after retiring as an active on-field official, served as the chief of National

League umpires until his death. Klem was the first umpire to use the inside chest protector (which is now standard equipment throughout all levels of the game), and the first to stand to the side of the catcher for a better look at pitches.

When he retired, Klem had the longest career of any major league umpire (37 years, a mark tied by Bruce Froemming in 2007) and was the oldest umpire in history at age 67 (a record also later surpassed by Froemming).

Of the 16 major league teams in existence during his career, all but one (the St. Louis Browns) appeared in a World Series that he officiated. Klem was also one of the umpires who worked the first-ever All–Star Game in 1933.

He was the home plate umpire for five no-hitters (a National League record later tied by Harry Wendelstedt) and was the home plate umpire on September 16, 1924, when Jim Bottomley of the St. Louis Cardinals had a record 12 runs batted in. He and Tommy Connolly were the first two umpires inducted into the baseball hall of fame, and are also the only two to have worked in five different decades.

Source: National Baseball Hall of Fame and Museum

Knight, Robert Montgomery "Bobby" (born: October 25, 1940 in Massillon, Ohio); inducted into the Naismith Memorial Basketball Hall of Fame in 1991 as a coach; won the 1960 NCAA title as a player; won three NCAA titles as a coach at Indiana; coached the United States to an Olympic gold medal.

One of the most successful, and controversial, college basketball coaches of all time, Knight was widely respected for being able to get the most out of his players. On January 1, 2007, he won his 880th career game, passing retired North Carolina coach Dean Smith for the most career National Collegiate Athletic Association Division I men's college basketball wins, when his Texas Tech Red Raiders beat New Mexico, 70–68.

Knight played basketball for four years at Orrville (Ohio) High School, graduating in 1958. He was a two-time All-Conference selection; named All-State once; and was team captain in 1957. After high school, he attended Ohio State University (Columbus) from 1958 to 1962, where he played basketball for three years and helped the school win the 1960 NCAA championship.

After college, Knight began his coaching career as an assistant at Cuyahoga Falls (Ohio) High School (1962–1963), before joining the college ranks as an assistant at the United States Military Academy at West Point (New York, 1963–1965). He later served as the Academy's head basketball coach from 1965 to 1971, leading the school to a 102–50 (.671) record. When he took over the program at age 24, Knight was the youngest varsity coach in major college history. His Army teams led the nation in defense for three consecutive years and played in four National Invitation Tournaments in five seasons (1966, 1968–1970).

Leaving the Academy, he began a 29-year career at Indiana University (1971–2000), where he compiled a 662–239 (.735) record. His Indiana teams won 11 Big Ten Conference titles (1973–1976, 1980–1981, 1983, 1987, 1989, 1991, 1993); participated in five NCAA Final Fours (1973, 1976, 1981, 1987, 1992); had a 32–0 undefeated season in 1976; won three NCAA Championships (1976, 1981, 1987); won the 1979 NIT Championship; he was named National Coach of the Year four times (1975–1976, 1987, 1989); Big Ten Coach of the Year five times (1973, 1975–1976, 1980–1981); and coached the U.S. Pan American team to an undefeated 9–0 tournament record and the gold medal in 1979.

In 1984, he became one of only four coaches in basketball history to win an NCAA championship, NIT championship, and an Olympic gold medal (1984 in Los Angeles, California), and is one of only two coaches to both play on and coach national championship teams (the other being Dean Smith). Knight was the youngest coach to reach 200, 300, and 400 wins.

After leaving Indiana he moved to Texas Tech University (Lubbock) in 2001, where he coached until February 2008, before retiring.

For all his accomplishments, his flare-ups and controversial behavior are almost as well-known as his on-court success. He has been known to throw chairs across the floor; has been arrested for physical assault; was never afraid to be physical toward his players; and has routinely displayed a combative attitude during television interviews.

When he had one too many physical altercations in September 2000, he was asked to resign from Indiana. When he refused, the school relieved him of all his duties, basically firing him. After taking one season off, Knight became head basketball coach at Texas Tech University and took his teams to three NCAA tournaments and a Sweet 16 appearance in 2005.

Knight won the Henry Iba Award twice (1975, 1989) as the best college basketball coach of the year (as voted by the United States Basketball Writers Association); named Naismith College Coach of the Year in 1987; Clair Bee Coach of the Year Award in 2002; and was presented the Naismith Award for Men's Outstanding Contribution to Basketball in 2007.

Bobby Knight's Coaching Record

YEAR	TEAM	W	L	WIN%
1965–1966	Army	18	8	.692
1966–1967	Army	13	8	.619
1967–1968	Army	20	5	.800
1968–1969	Army	18	10	.643
1969–1970	Army	22	6	.786
1970–1971	Army	11	13	.458
1971–1972	Indiana	17	8	.680
1972–1973	Indiana	22	6	.786
1973–1974	Indiana	23	5	.822
1974–1975	Indiana	31	1	.966
1975–1976	Indiana	32	0	1.000
1976–1977	Indiana	16	11	.593
1977–1978	Indiana	21	8	.724
1978–1979	Indiana	22	12	.647
1979–1980	Indiana	21	8	.724
1980–1981	Indiana	26	9	.743
1981–1982	Indiana	19	10	.655
1982–1983	Indiana	24	6	.800
1983–1984	Indiana	22	9	.710
1984–1985	Indiana	19	14	.576
1985–1986	Indiana	21	8	.724
1986–1987	Indiana	30	4	.882
1987–1988	Indiana	19	10	.655
1988–1989	Indiana	27	8	.771
1989–1990	Indiana	18	11	.621
1990–1991	Indiana	29	5	.853
1991–1992	Indiana	27	7	.794
1992–1993	Indiana	31	4	.886
1993–1994	Indiana	21	9	.700
1994–1995	Indiana	19	12	.613
1995–1996	Indiana	20	11	.645
1996–1997	Indiana	22	11	.667
1997–1998	Indiana	20	12	.625
1998–1999	Indiana	23	11	.676
1999–2000	Indiana	20	8	.714
2001–2002	Texas Tech	23	9	.719
2002–2003	Texas Tech	22	13	.629
2003–2004	Texas Tech	23	11	.676
2004–2005	Texas Tech	22	11	.667
2005–2006	Texas Tech	15	17	.469
2006–2007	Texas Tech	21	13	.618
2007–2008	Texas Tech	12	8	.600
	Army	102	50	.671
	Indiana	662	239	.735
	Texas Tech	138	82	.627
	TOTALS	902	371	.709

Sources: *Knight: My Story* (Bob Knight with Bob Hammel); Naismith Memorial Basketball Hall of Fame

Knox, Seymour Horace III (born: March 9, 1926 in Buffalo, New York; died: May 22, 1996); inducted into the Hockey Hall of Fame in 1993 as a builder; founded the Buffalo Sabres; served on the NHL's Board of Governors for 25 years.

With his brother, Northrup, Knox brought the National Hockey League to Buffalo, New York with the Sabres. Before becoming involved with hockey, he attended Yale University (New Haven, Connecticut) and Columbia University (New York, New York); served in the United States Army during World War II; and returned to Buffalo after the war to embark on a successful banking career.

After several attempts, the Knox brothers were awarded an NHL franchise when the league expanded into both Buffalo and Vancouver, Canada for the 1970–1971 season. The brothers hired Punch Imlach as the team's first coach; oversaw a squad that qualified for postseason play in only its third year of operation (1973); and led the team into the 1975 Stanley Cup finals, losing to the Philadelphia Flyers in six games. The team's success in the 1974–1975 season led Knox to be named *The Hockey News* Executive of the Year.

He served on the NHL's Board of Governors for 25 years; was a director of the U.S. Hockey Hall of Fame; and helped establish both the Buffalo Bandits of the Major Indoor Lacrosse League (1991) and the Buffalo Blizzard of the National Professional Soccer League (1992).

He was the grandson of Seymour H. Knox (co-founder of the F.W. Woolworth Company) and the son of art historian Seymour H. Knox II. The Knox brothers built the Marine Midland Arena, now called the HSBC Arena, a 20,000-seat complex located at 1 Seymour H. Knox III Plaza in downtown Buffalo. The Arena currently houses the Buffalo Sabres and the Buffalo Bandits.

Source: Hockey Hall of Fame

Koszma, Oscar (born: November 15, 1885; died: November 1970 in Los Angeles, California); inducted into the National Soccer Hall of Fame and Museum in 1964 as a builder; longtime California administrator.

Often called the "Godfather of Soccer" in Los Angeles, Koszma was a player, coach, and administrator in various California leagues and associations.

Source: National Soccer Hall of Fame and Museum

Koufax, Sanford "Sandy" (born: Sanford Braun on December 30, 1935 in Brooklyn, New York); inducted into the National Baseball Hall of Fame and Museum in 1972 as a player; Position: Pitcher; Bats: Right; Throws: Left; Uniform: #32; first major league pitcher to throw more than three no-hitters (had a total of four no-hitters and one perfect game); first to average less than seven hits allowed per nine innings pitched over his career; first to strike out more than nine batters per nine innings pitched in his career; youngest player elected to the baseball hall of fame; 1963 Most Valuable Player; won three Cy Young Awards; won two pitcher's Triple Crowns; threw more strikeouts than innings pitched.

Although arm problems eventually ended his career after only 12 seasons (1955–1966), over a six-season stretch (1961–1966), Koufax was the most dominating pitcher the game had ever seen. Making his major league debut on June 24, 1955, he played his entire career with the Brooklyn/Los Angeles Dodgers.

He appeared in four World Series, winning three (1959, 1963, 1965) and losing one (1966); was a six-time All-Star (1961–1966); 1963 National League Most Valuable Player; won three National League Cy Young Awards (1963, 1965–1966); and was a two-time World Series MVP (1963, 1965). A devout American Jew, he refused to pitch Game 1 of the 1965 World Series because the game day fell on Yom Kippur, the Jewish High Holiday.

Koufax won 25 or more games in a season three times; captured five straight earned run average titles; pitched no-hitters in four consecutive seasons; posted a 0.95 ERA in four World Series; and threw a perfect game in 1965. In his three Cy Young Award-winning seasons, he led both leagues in wins, strikeouts, and earned run average. He was the first major league pitcher to throw more than three no-hitters; first to average fewer than seven hits allowed per nine innings pitched over his career, first to strike out more than nine batters per nine innings pitched in his career; and accumulated more strikeouts than innings pitched.

Among National League pitchers with at least 2,000 innings pitched who have debuted since 1913, he has both the highest career winning percentage (.655) and the lowest career ERA (2.76), and was the youngest player ever elected to the baseball hall of fame.

He attended Brooklyn's Lafayette High School, where he played both baseball and basketball, and also played baseball in various leagues around the city. After graduating from high school, the 6'2", 210-pound Koufax went to the University of Cincinnati (Ohio) on a basketball scholarship, and in 1954, he made the school's varsity baseball team as a pitcher.

While at Lafayette High School, he was signed by the Brooklyn Dodgers, but his major league career started slowly as he adjusted to the game. As an interesting side note, in order to make room for him on their roster, the Dodgers sent Tommy Lasorda (a current roster player who would become the team's manager in later years) to its minor league affiliate Montreal Royals of the International League.

His major league career began slowly and even though the Dodgers won the 1955 World Series for the first title in franchise history, Koufax did not play in the entire series. Already suffering arm injuries, his career seemed destined to be a short one as from 1956 to 1958, he showed no promise of having a long-term major league future.

He moved with the Dodgers to Los Angeles in 1958 and threw to an 11–11 record, and led the league in wild pitches. Seemingly out of nowhere, his potential showed itself on June 22, 1959, when he struck out 16 Philadelphia Phillies to set the record for a night game in a 6–2 win. A little over two months later, on August 31, 1959, Koufax broke his own record and tied Bob Feller's major league mark for strikeouts in one game with 18, pitching Los Angeles to a 5–2 win over the San Francisco Giants.

After six mediocre seasons, Koufax suddenly caught fire. In 1961, he set a new National League record for strikeouts in a season with 269 (surpassing Christy Mathewson's 58-year mark of 267, set in 1903); and finished the season at 18–13 with only 96 walks. This season gave him confidence as he began a six-year period of pitching dominance in the majors.

On June 30, 1962, he threw the first of his four no-hitters, against the New York Mets in a 5–0 win. In the first inning of this game, Koufax struck out three batters on nine pitches to become the sixth National League pitcher and the 11th in major league history to accomplish the feat. His other no-hitters would come on May 11, 1963 (an 8–0 win over the San Francisco Giants); June 4, 1964 (a 3–0 win over the Philadelphia Phillies); and September 9, 1965 (which was also a perfect game, a 1–0 win over the Chicago Cubs).

In 1963, he won the pitcher's Triple Crown (leading the league in wins (25), strikeouts (306), and earned run average (1.88); threw 11 shutouts; won the National League Most Valuable Player Award and the Cy Young Award (the first unanimous choice); and won the Hickok Belt as the Professional Athlete of the Year. In that season's World Series sweep against the New York Yankees, Koufax beat Whitey Ford in Game 1 with a World Series record 15 strikeouts; won Game 4 to clinch the title for the Dodgers; and was named World Series MVP.

Against the Cincinnati Reds on April 18, 1964, Koufax struck out three batters on nine pitches in the third inning to become the first, and only, pitcher to accomplish this feat twice in the National League. On June 4, he threw his third no-hitter, becoming only the second pitcher of the modern era (after Bob Feller) to pitch three no-hitters.

In 1965, he won his second pitchers' Triple Crown (1963, 1965), leading the league in wins (26), ERA (2.04), and strikeouts (382), a new record that lasted until 1973, when Nolan Ryan struck out 383 batters. On September 9, 1965, Koufax became the sixth pitcher of the modern era to throw a perfect game; helped the Dodgers win another World Series title; and won his second Cy Young Award (again by unanimous vote). He won two games in the World Series, and his second World Series MVP Award. He won the Hickok Belt a second time (the first, and only, time anyone had won the belt more than once) and was named *Sports Illustrated*'s Sportsman of the Year.

In 1966, Koufax's last season, he pitched 323 innings, threw to a 27–9 record, and had a 1.73 ERA. Although he accumulated strong pitching numbers, it was obvious that his arm troubles could not be overcome. He did not pitch well in the World Series; was the losing pitcher in Game 2; watched as the Dodgers were swept by the Baltimore Orioles; and retired after the Series was over.

After leaving the game, Koufax was a television broadcaster with NBC for five years, and in June 1972, his uniform number 32 was retired by the Dodgers. He became the team's minor league pitching coach in 1979, a job he held until 1990. In 1999, *The Sporting News* ranked Koufax number 26 on its list of The 100 Greatest Baseball Players, and in that same year, he was one of the 30 players named to the Major League Baseball All-Century Team.

He was inducted into the International Jewish Sports Hall of Fame in 1979.

Sandy Koufax's Career Statistics

YEAR	TEAM	LG	W	L	PCT	G	SH	IP	H	R	ER	SO	BB	ERA
1955	Brooklyn	NL	2	2	.500	12	2	42	33	15	14	30	28	3.00
1956	Brooklyn	NL	2	4	.333	16	0	59	66	37	32	30	29	4.88
1957	Brooklyn	NL	5	4	.556	34	0	104	83	49	45	122	51	3.89
1958	Los Angeles	NL	11	11	.500	40	0	159	132	89	79	131	105	4.47
1959	Los Angeles	NL	8	6	.571	35	1	153	136	74	69	173	92	4.06
1960	Los Angeles	NL	8	13	.381	37	2	175	133	83	76	197	100	3.91
1961	Los Angeles	NL	18	13	.581	42	2	256	212	117	100	269	96	3.52
1962	Los Angeles	NL	14	7	.667	28	2	184	134	61	52	216	57	2.54
1963	Los Angeles	NL	25	5	.833	40	11	311	214	68	65	306	58	1.88
1964	Los Angeles	NL	19	5	.792	29	7	223	154	49	43	223	53	1.74
1965	Los Angeles	NL	26	8	.765	43	8	336	216	90	76	382	71	2.04
1966	Los Angeles	NL	27	9	.750	41	5	323	241	74	62	317	77	1.73
	TOTALS		165	87	.655	397	40	2,325	1,754	806	713	2,396	817	2.76

Sources: Baseball-Reference.com; National Baseball Hall of Fame and Museum; *Sandy Koufax: A Lefty's Legacy* (Jane Leavy)

Kracher, Frank Oscar, Jr. "Sarge" (born: November 24, 1926 in Chicago, Illinois; died: January 29, 1999 in Chicago, Illinois); inducted into the National Soccer Hall of Fame and Museum in 1983 as a builder; served as an administrator in the National Soccer League of Chicago; chairman of the USSF National Soccer Hall of Fame Selection Committee.

Kracher played junior soccer with the Schwaben AC (Chicago), and stayed with the team until joining the U.S. Navy during World War II. While in the military, he played the game with the San Francisco Barbarians when he was stationed in California. After leaving the service in 1946, Kracher resumed his career with the Fiche Rams Soccer Club, playing goalie and center forward.

After playing soccer for 26 years, he retired in 1960, but stayed active in the game as an administrator within the National Soccer League of Chicago; the Illinois State Association; the United States Soccer Football Association; and with both the Chicago Mustangs and Chicago Sting of the North American Soccer League.

He joined the Chicago Police Department in 1953, and was later assigned by the department to serve on various committees handling the training sites, transportation, and entertainment for the nations competing in the Pan American Games held in the city in 1959. In 1961, he was assigned to the O'Hare International Airport (Chicago), where he stayed until retiring in 1983.

In 1995, he was named chairman of the United States Soccer Federation National Soccer Hall of Fame Selection Committee, a position he held until his death.

Source: National Soccer Hall of Fame and Museum

Kraft, Raymond B. "Granny" (born: April 28, 1919 in Baltimore, Maryland); inducted into the National Soccer Hall of Fame and Museum in 1984 as a builder; officiated in the American Soccer League, the International Soccer League, the National Professional Soccer League, the North American Soccer League, and in international competitions.

Although Kraft played soccer for 20 years for numerous teams in the Baltimore area, he is more well-known for his referee career. He officiated at local games, the American Soccer League, the International Soccer League, the National Professional Soccer League, the North American Soccer League, and international competitions.

Kraft represented the United States on the Fédération Internationale de Football Association list of referees in 1956, and from 1960 to 1966. During that time he refereed various international matches, including Germany vs. Brazil, England vs. Scotland, Switzerland vs. England, Poland vs. Yugoslavia, and England vs. the United States.

From 1943 to 1946, during World War II, he was an athletic instructor in the U.S. Navy and formed the first soccer team at Norfolk Air Station (Norfolk, Virginia).

Named in his honor, the Raymond "Granny" Kraft Referee Service Award is presented by the Old Timers Soccer Association of Maryland to honor those who have dedicated their careers as a referee or administrator in the state of Maryland.

He has been inducted into the Maryland Soccer Hall of Fame.

Source: National Soccer Hall of Fame and Museum

Kraus, Harry (born: 1908 in Vienna, Austria; died: November 18, 1966 in New York, New York); inducted into the National Soccer Hall of Fame and Museum in 1963 as a builder; secretary of the New York State Association; vice-president of the United States Football Association.

Kraus immigrated to the United States in 1922, and in 1930, he was elected to the New York State Association and became its secretary in 1932, serving for 15 years. He was elected to the board of the German-American League in 1933, and in 1937, he became a vice-president of the United States Football Association, serving on its National Commission for nine years.

He served as president of the German-American League until retiring in 1952, and was registration secretary of the Southern New York State Association in 1960.

Source: National Soccer Hall of Fame and Museum

Krause, Edward Walter "Moose" (born: Edward Walter Kriaučiūnas on February 2, 1913 in Chicago, Illinois; died: December 11, 1992); inducted into the Naismith Memorial Basketball Hall of Fame in 1976 as a player; Position: Center; won two national Catholic basketball championships in high school; second player in history to earn All-America honors three straight years (1932–1934) by the Helms Foundation; organized the first basketball team at the College of the Holy Cross; served as Notre Dame athletic director for 33 years; as a coach, led Fort Wayne Northrop High School to the 1974 state championship.

While at De La Salle (Chicago, Illinois) High School (Institute) from 1926 to 1930, Krause was an All-City selection in basketball; a captain in three sports; selected All-State in both basketball and football; and led his team to two national Catholic basketball championships.

After graduation, he attended the University of Notre Dame (South Bend, Indiana, 1930–1934), where he was a three-year basketball letter winner; starred on the school's football team; was an All-Western Conference and All-American choice in 1934; and followed Purdue University's John Wooden as the second player in history to earn consensus All-America honors three straight years (1932–1934) from the Helms Foundation.

As a sophomore, Krause scored 140 points (7.0 per game) in an 18–2 season; as a junior, he scored 213 points (9.7 per game) in a 16–6 season; and as a senior, scored 194 points (8.5 per game) in a 20–4 season, to set the three-year school record with 547 points (8.29 per game). He served as the team's captain in 1934.

After college, the 6'3", 215-pound Krause was the head coach at his alma mater from 1942 to 1947; led the school to an overall 98–46 (.671) record; organized the first basketball team at the College of the Holy Cross (Worcester, Massachusetts); and served as long-time Notre Dame athletic director (1948–1981).

While serving as athletic director, he also coached basketball at both Fort Wayne Central and Fort Wayne Northrop high schools (Fort Wayne, Indiana), and led the 1974 Northrop team to the state championship.

Krause was named Indiana Coach of the Year in 1973; won the Indiana Basketball Coaches Association Award in 1976; and was inducted into the Indiana Basketball Hall of Fame in 1989.

Source: Naismith Memorial Basketball Hall of Fame

Krause, Paul James (born: February 19, 1942 in Flint, Michigan); inducted into the Pro Football Hall of Fame in 1998 as a player; Position: Safety; Uniform: #26 (Redskins), #22 (Vikings); played in four Super Bowls; NFL's all-time interception leader (81).

Drafted in the second round (18th overall selection) in 1964 by the National Football League's Washington Redskins out of the University of Iowa (Iowa City), Krause led the league with 12 interceptions as a rookie and was named both All-NFL and All-Pro. He went on to play 16 seasons (226 games) for the Redskins (1964–1967) and the Minnesota Vikings (1968–1979).

When he retired, the 6'3", 200-pound safety was the NFL's interception leader with 81; played in eight Pro Bowls (1965–1966, 1970, 1972–1976); selected All-NFL four times (1964–1965, 1971, 1975); two-time All-Eastern Conference (1964–1965); selected All-National Football Conference seven times (1964–1965, 1970–1973, 1975); and played in four losing Super Bowls (SB IV-1970, SB VIII-1974, SB IX-1975, SB XI-1977) and five NFL/NFC championship games (1969, 1973–1974, 1976–1977). He was named one of the 70 Greatest Redskins.

He played football at Bendle (Burton, Michigan) High School, before attending the University of Iowa, and was inducted into the Iowa Sports Hall of Fame in 1985. In high school, he earned All-State honors in basketball, football, baseball, and track. At Iowa, Krause was a two-way starter as a wide receiver and defensive back. As a senior in 1963, he was selected to the East-West Shrine game; the Coaches' All-American game; and the College All-Star game.

In 2004, Krause was inducted into the Boys & Girls Clubs of Sarasota County Sports Hall of Fame.

In 1994, he was elected to the Board of County Commissioners for Dakota County, Minnesota and, as of this writing, currently serves as a Dakota County Commissioner.

Paul Krause's Career Statistics

			INTERCEPTIONS				FUMBLE RECOVERIES		
YEAR	**TEAM**	**G**	**INT**	**YDS**	**AVG**	**TD**	**NO**	**YDS**	**TD**
1964	Washington	14	12	140	11.7	1	2	0	0
1965	Washington	14	6	118	19.7	0	5	56	1
1966	Washington	13	2	0	0.0	0	0	0	0
1967	Washington	13	8	75	9.4	0	1	0	0
1968	Minnesota	14	7	82	11.7	0	3	0	0
1969	Minnesota	14	5	82	16.4	1	1	3	0
1970	Minnesota	14	6	90	15.0	0	0	0	0
1971	Minnesota	14	6	112	18.7	0	2	6	0
1972	Minnesota	14	6	109	18.2	1	1	30	1
1973	Minnesota	14	4	28	7.0	0	1	4	0
1974	Minnesota	14	2	53	26.5	0	2	0	0
1975	Minnesota	14	10	201	20.1	0	0	70	1

			INTERCEPTIONS				FUMBLE RECOVERIES		
YEAR	TEAM	G	INT	YDS	AVG	TD	NO	YDS	TD
1976	Minnesota	14	2	21	10.5	0	0	0	0
1977	Minnesota	14	2	25	12.5	0	0	0	0
1978	Minnesota	16	0	0	0.0	0	0	0	0
1979	Minnesota	16	3	49	16.3	0	1	0	0
	TOTALS	226	81	1,185	14.6	3	19	169	3

Sources: Pro Football Hall of Fame; Pro-Football-Reference.com

Kropfelder, Nicholas (born: Baltimore, Maryland); inducted into the National Soccer Hall of Fame and Museum in 1996 as a player; Position: Center Forward; won two ASL titles and three Lewis Cups.

A soccer star at Loyola College (Baltimore, Maryland), Kropfelder played for the Baltimore Americans (1942–1943, 1946–1948 [interrupted by World War II]), and helped the team win the 1946 American Soccer League championship. In 1948, he played for the Philadelphia Nationals (1948–1953), where he would win two ASL championships (1950–1951) and three Lewis Cups (1949, 1951–1952).

He led the ASL in goals scored in 1951, and retired in 1954 after playing his final season with the Baltimore Rockets (1953–1954), also of the ASL.

After retiring as a player, he served as both an NCAA and amateur referee for several decades, and in 1993, he was elected president of the Maryland Old Timers Soccer Association, serving a three-year term.

Source: National Soccer Hall of Fame and Museum

Krzyzewski, Michael William "Mike" "Coach K" (born: February 13, 1947 in Chicago, Illinois); inducted into the Naismith Memorial Basketball Hall of Fame in 2001 as a coach; won three NCAA titles at Duke; won the 2008 Olympic gold medal.

Still active as of this writing, Krzyzewski has been the head basketball coach at Duke University (Durham, North Carolina) since 1981. After playing basketball at Weber High School (Chicago, Illinois), he attended the United States Military Academy (West Point, New York), where he was a three-year letterman (1967–1969); named team captain (1968–1969); and was named to the All-National Invitation Tournament Second Team (1969).

After graduation, he served five years in the army (1969–1974), where he coached service teams for three years, and then for two years was the head coach of the U.S. Military Academy Prep School at Fort Belvoir, Virginia. After Krzyzewski resigned from the military, he began his college coaching career as a graduate assistant at Indiana University (Bloomington, 1974–1975) under legendary coach and hall of famer Bobby Knight, his former coach at Army.

Krzyzewski left Indiana to become the head coach at the U.S. Military Academy (1976–1980), where he compiled a 73–59 (.553) record and led the team to an NIT appearance in 1978, before moving on to Duke.

By the end of the 2009–2010 season, he had accumulated an overall 795–220 (.783) record at Duke; had coached the team to four National Championships (1991–1992, 2001, 2010); 11 National Collegiate Athletic Association Final Fours (1986, 1988–1992, 1994, 1999, 2001, 2004, 2010); is the winningest active coach in NCAA Tournament play and ranks first all-time in most NCAA Tournament wins (77). Krzyzewski has led Duke to 13 Atlantic Coast Conference regular-season titles (1986, 1991–1992, 1994, 1997–2001, 2004, 2006, 2008, 2010) and 12 ACC tournament titles (1986, 1988, 1992, 1999–2003, 2005–2006, 2009–2010); *Basketball Times* National Coach of the Year twice (1986, 1997); Naismith College Coach of the Year three times (1989, 1992, 1999); National Association of Basketball Coaches National Coach of the Year in 1991; ACC Coach of the Year five times (1984, 1986, 1997, 1999, 2000); and won his 800th college game on March 1, 2008 with an 87–86 win over North Carolina State.

He coached at the World University Games in 1987 (winning a silver medal in Zagreb, Yugoslavia); both the World Championship Games (winning a bronze medal in Argentina) and Goodwill Games (winning a silver medal in Seattle, Washington) (1990); was an assistant coach on the gold medal-winning team in the 1992 Olympics (Barcelona, Spain); led teams to two NIT appearances (1978 with Army, 1981 with Duke); served as president of the National Association of Basketball Coaches (1998–1999); named NABC Coach of the Decade (1990s); and in 2005, he was named head coach of the U.S. National Team through the 2008 Summer Olympics in Beijing, China (where he led the team to a gold medal).

During his tenure, Krzyzewski has maintained a 90 percent graduation rate among his players (the highest in Division I); Duke University has named its basketball floor, "Coach K Court;" and the grassy area outside the stadium has been named "Krzyzewskiville" or "K-Ville."

Mike Krzyzewski's USA Basketball Coaching Record

TEAM	POSITION	W-L	PCT	FINISH
1979 USA Pan American Games	Assistant Coach	9–0	1.000	Gold Medal
1983 U.S. Olympic Festival South	Head Coach	3–1	.775	Gold Medal
1984 U.S. Olympic Trials	Assistant Coach			
1984 U.S. Olympics	Special Assistant	8–0	1.000	Gold Medal
1987 USA World University Games	Head Coach	7–1	.875	Silver Medal
1990 USA Goodwill Games	Head Coach	3–2	.600	Silver Medal
1990 USA World Championship	Head Coach	6–2	.750	Bronze Medal
1992 U.S. Olympic Qualifying	Assistant Coach	6–0	1.000	Gold Medal
1992 U.S. Olympics	Assistant Coach	8–0	1.000	Gold Medal
2006 USA Senior National	Head Coach	5–0	1.000	
2006 USA World Championship	Head Coach	8–1	.889	Bronze Medal
2008 USA World Championship	Head Coach	8–0	1.000	Gold Medal

Mike Krzyzewski's Head Coaching Record (Army, 1975–1980)

SEASON	W-L	POSTSEASON
1975–1976	11–14	
1976–1977	20–8	
1977–1978	19–9	NIT First Round
1978–1979	14–11	
1979–1980	9–17	
TOTALS	73–59 (.553)	

Mike Krzyzewski's Head Coaching Record (Duke, 1980–present)

SEASON	REG SEASON	CONF	FINISH	POST SEASON
1980–1981	17–13	6–8	T-5th	NIT Quarterfinals
1981–1982	10–17	4–10	T-6th	
1982–1983	11–17	3–11	7th	
1983–1984	24–10	7–7	T-3rd	NCAA 2nd Round
1984–1985	23–8	8–6	T-4th	NCAA 2nd Round
1985–1986	37–3	12–2	1st	NCAA Championship Game
1986–1987	24–9	9–5	3rd	NCAA Sweet Sixteen
1987–1988	28–7	9–5	3rd	NCAA Final Four
1988–1989	28—8	9–5	T-2nd	NCAA Final Four
1989–1990	29–9	9–5	2nd	NCAA Championship Game
1990–1991	32–7	11–3	1st	NCAA Champions
1991–1992	34–2	14–2	1st	NCAA Champions
1992–1993	24–8	10–6	T-3rd	NCAA 2nd Round
1993–1994	28–6	12–4	1st	NCAA Championship Game
1994–1995	9–3	0–1		
1995–1996	18–13	8–8	T-4th	NCAA 1st Round
1996–1997	24–9	12–4	1st	NCAA 2nd Round
1997–1998	32–4	15–1	1st	NCAA Elite Eight
1998–1999	37–2	16–0	1st	NCAA Championship Game
1999–2000	29–5	15–1	1st	NCAA Sweet Sixteen
2000–2001	35–4	13–3	1st	NCAA Champions
2001–2002	31–4	13–3	2nd	NCAA Sweet Sixteen
2002–2003	26–7	11–5	T-2nd	NCAA Sweet Sixteen
2003–2004	31–6	13–3	1st	NCAA Final Four
2004–2005	27–6	11–5	3rd	NCAA Sweet Sixteen
2005–2006	32–4	14–2	1st	NCAA Sweet Sixteen

SEASON	REG SEASON	CONF	FINISH	POST SEASON
2006–2007	22–11	8–8	6th	NCAA 1st Round
2007–2008	28–6	13–3	2nd	NCAA 2nd Round
2008–2009	30–7	11–5	T-2nd	NCAA Sweet Sixteen
2009–2010	35–5	13–3	T-1st	NCAA Champions
DUKE	795–220 (.783)			
OVERALL	868-279 (.757)			

Sources: Mike Krzyzewski Web Site (www.coachk.com); Naismith Memorial Basketball Hall of Fame; USA Basketball (www.usabasketball/com)

Kuhn, Bowie Kent (born: October 28, 1926 in Takoma Park, Maryland; died: March 15, 2007 in Ponte Vedra Beach, Florida); inducted into the National Baseball Hall of Fame and Museum in 2008 as a pioneer-executive by the Veterans Committee; fifth commissioner of Major League Baseball.

Kuhn was an American lawyer and sports administrator who served as the fifth commissioner of Major League Baseball from February 4, 1969 to September 30, 1984. He had served as legal counsel for Major League Baseball owners for almost 20 years before being elected commissioner.

After graduating from Theodore Roosevelt High School (Washington, D.C.), he attended Franklin and Marshall College (Lancaster, Pennsylvania) in the V-12 Navy College Training Program before going to Princeton University (New Jersey) in 1945. He graduated from Princeton in 1947 with a bachelor of arts degree in economics and received his law degree in 1950 from the University of Virginia (Charlottesville).

After law school, Kuhn worked for the law firm of Willkie Farr & Gallagher (New York, New York), which represented the National League. He served as a counselor for the National League in a lawsuit brought against it by the city of Milwaukee when the Milwaukee Braves moved to Atlanta after the 1965 season.

During his tenure as commissioner, he oversaw the first strike in organized sports in 1981; the end of baseball's reserve clause; attendance rising from 23 million in 1968 to 45 million in 1983; and the leagues expanding from 20 to 26 teams.

Kuhn suspended numerous players for involvement with drugs and gambling and banned both Willie Mays (in 1979) and Mickey Mantle (in 1983) from the sport due to their involvement in casino promotion. In 1970, he suspended Detroit Tigers pitcher Denny McLain because of the pitcher's involvement in a bookmaking operation, and later suspended McLain for the rest of the season for carrying a gun.

On October 7, 1969, the St. Louis Cardinals traded Curt Flood to the Philadelphia Phillies, and what appeared to be a routine transaction, would change professional baseball forever. For a variety of reasons, Flood refused to report to the Phillies, and requested that Kuhn void the trade and declare him a free agent, basically challenging the validity of the game's reserve clause. When Kuhn denied the request, Flood filed a lawsuit in January 1970 against Major League Baseball, claiming a violation of anti-trust laws.

Flood's case eventually reached the U.S. Supreme Court, which ruled in favor of Major League Baseball in a 5–3 decision in 1972. While he lost his case, and ended his career, Flood's lawsuit highlighted the reserve clause and found public support in its being eliminated from the game. In 1975, players Andy Messersmith and Dave McNally both challenged the reserve clause, and the argument went to independent arbitrator Peter Seitz instead of the courts. In December 1975, Seitz basically ruled that the team could not control a player's career forever, and his decision gave rise to the sport's free agency.

On October 13, 1971, the World Series played a night game for the first time (Game 4). Kuhn's reasoning, which turned out to be correct, was that the game would attract a larger audience in prime time than was possible during the day. The increased viewership eventually led to the decision that all World Series games would be played in prime time.

Source: National Baseball Hall of Fame and Museum

Kundla, John Albert (born: July 3, 1916 in Star Junction, Pennsylvania); inducted into the Naismith Memorial Basketball Hall of Fame in 1995 as a coach; won two state championships at De La Salle High School; led the Lakers to the NBL championship (1948), BAA championship (1949), and four NBA championships (1950, 1952–1954).

After playing basketball for two years at Central High School (Minneapolis, Minnesota, graduating in 1933), Kundla attended the University of Minnesota (Minneapolis-St. Paul, graduating in 1939), where he played basketball for three seasons. He led the team to a co-Conference title with Illinois (1937); named All-Conference (1938); was the team's captain (1939); and led the squad in scoring all three seasons.

After college, Kundla began his coaching career at Ascension Elementary School (Minneapolis, 1939–1942), where he led the team to a city championship. During his tenure, he also served as an assistant coach at his alma mater (1939–1942). He then became the head coach at De La Salle High School (Minneapolis, 1942–1944), where he led the school to two state championships, before serving in the U.S. Navy during World War II (1944–1945).

After leaving the military, the 6'2", 180-pound Kundla returned to the University of Minnesota as an assistant coach (1945–1946); moved on to be the head coach at St. Thomas College (St. Paul, Minnesota, 1946–1947); and then served as head coach at his alma mater from 1959 to 1968. At St. Thomas, he compiled an 11–11 record, while coaching to a 110–105 (.512) record at the University of Minnesota.

Leaving the college ranks, he became the head coach with the Minneapolis Lakers from 1947 to 1959 (National Basketball League/Basketball Association of America/National Basketball Association). With the Lakers, he compiled an overall 466–319 (.594) record, including a 70–38 (.648) playoff record; led the team to the NBL championship (1948), BAA championship (1949), and four NBA championships (1950, 1952–54); one of only three coaches in NBA history to lead teams to three consecutive titles; coached four NBA All-Star Games (1951–1954); and in 1965, coached the U.S. All-Stars to the World University Games championship in Budapest (Hungary).

After the NBA, Kundla coached the Moroccan National Team (1983–1984).

Kundla and one of his players, Vern Mikkelson, were inducted into the basketball hall of fame in the same year, the first coach-player combination to be so honored. Kundla has also been inducted into the Minnesota and University of Minnesota halls of fame.

John Kundla's NBA Coaching Record

			REGULAR SEASON			PLAYOFFS			
SEASON	**LG**	**TEAM**	**W**	**L**	**WIN%**	**W**	**L**	**WIN%**	**NOTES**
1948–1949	BAA	Minneapolis	44	16	.733	8	2	.800	BAA Champions
1949–1950	NBA	Minneapolis	51	17	.750	10	2	.833	NBA Champions
1950–1951	NBA	Minneapolis	44	24	.647	3	4	.429	
1951–1952	NBA	Minneapolis	40	26	.606	9	4	.692	NBA Champions
1952–1953	NBA	Minneapolis	48	22	.686	9	3	.750	NBA Champions
1953–1954	NBA	Minneapolis	46	26	.639	9	4	.692	NBA Champions
1954–1955	NBA	Minneapolis	40	32	.556	3	4	.429	
1955–1956	NBA	Minneapolis	33	39	.458	1	2	.333	
1956–1957	NBA	Minneapolis	34	38	.472	2	3	.400	
1957–1958	NBA	Minneapolis	10	23	.303				
1958–1959	NBA	Minneapolis	33	39	.458	6	7	.462	
	BAA		44	16	.733	8	2	.800	
	NBA		379	286	.570	52	33	.612	
	TOTALS		423	302	.583	60	35	.632	

Sources: Basketball-Reference.com; Naismith Memorial Basketball Hall of Fame

Kuntner, Rudolph "Rudy" (born: June 10, 1908 in Vienna, Austria; died: December 16, 1982 in Rego Park, New York); inducted into the National Soccer Hall of Fame and Museum in 1963 as a player; Position: Inside Forward; International Caps (1928): 2; International Goals: 2; in 1945, he won the National Open Cup, the ASL championship, and the Lewis Cup.

Kuntner immigrated to the United States when he was seven; began playing organized soccer at age 10; and was a four-sport star (baseball, football, basketball, tennis) at Gorton High School (Yonkers, New York).

He eventually played for the United States National Team at the 1928 Summer Olympic Games (Amsterdam, Netherlands). His first international cap with the National Team came in the 1928 Olympics, where he scored in an 11–2 loss to Argentina. After the Olympics, the team traveled to Poland and tied the Polish National Team 3–3, with Kuntner again scoring.

He began his senior career with the First Vienna club of New York (1929), before advancing to the New York Giants of the American Soccer League (1930). As a member of the New York Brookhattan team of the ASL, in 1945, he won the National Open Cup, the ASL championship, and the Lewis Cup.

He originally signed with the New York Giants for the 1927–1928 season; played five games; and scored three goals, before participating in the Olympics. In 1928, he moved to the New York Hungaria team in the short-lived Eastern Soccer League, before moving on to the First Vienna (also known as Wiener Sports Club and New York Vienna F.C.) of the German American Soccer League in 1929. In 1930, he was back in the ASL with Bridgeport Hungaria, but the team moved to Newark after ten games, then folded.

Kuntner returned to the New York Giants, and when the team folded in 1932, he played for the New York Americans. By 1939, he was playing with Brooklyn St. Mary's Celtic when the team won the Open Cup final over Chicago Manhattan Beer. In the 1942–1943 season, he scored nine goals in 17 games.

Source: National Soccer Hall of Fame and Museum

Kurland, Robert Albert (born: December 23, 1924 in St. Louis, Missouri); inducted into the Naismith Memorial Basketball Hall of Fame in 1961 as a player; first player to win two Olympic basketball gold medals (1948, 1952) for the United States; won two NCAA championships; first player named Most Valuable Player in back-to-back NCAA tournaments (1945–1946); won four AAU national titles.

At Jennings (Missouri) High School (1938–1942), Kurland was a three-year letter winner; participated in two Class B state tournaments; and was a state high jump champion (in track and field) in 1942. After graduation, he attended Oklahoma State University (Stillwater, 1942–1946, then known as the Oklahoma A&M Aggies), where he was a four-year letter winner under hall of fame coach Hank Iba, and led the team to back-to-back National Collegiate Athletic Association championships in 1945 (over New York University) and 1946 (over North Carolina).

He was named First-Team Helms Foundation, Second-Team *Sporting News*, Second-Team Converse and Second-Team *Pic Magazine* All-American in 1944; was a two-time First-Team consensus All American (1945–1946); first player named Most Valuable Player in back-to-back NCAA tournaments (1945–1946); held the Oklahoma State record for most points in a career (1,669, 16.6 per game) in 118 games; scored over 500 points in a season twice (1945–1946); led the nation in scoring (1946); and has been inducted into the Helms Foundation, Oklahoma Sports, and Missouri Sports halls of fame.

After college, the 6'10", 230-pound Kurland played for the Amateur Athletic Union Phillips 66ers (1946–1952), where he was a six-time AAU All-American; was selected to the All National Industrial League (1946–1952); won four AAU national championships (1946–1948, 1950); and won two Olympic gold medals (1948 in London, England and 1952 in Helsinki, Finland) for the United States, the first player to do so.

Source: Naismith Memorial Basketball Hall of Fame

Kurri, Jari Pekka (born: May 18, 1960 in Helsinki, Finland); inducted into the Hockey Hall of Fame in 2001 as a player; Position: Right Wing; Uniform: #17; first player from Finland to be inducted into the hall of fame; led Finland to its first-ever European Junior Championship; won five Stanley Cup championships.

A future teammate of the legendary Wayne Gretzky, Kurri played hockey for the Jokerit Helsinki hockey club; played on the senior team at age 17; and spent three seasons in the Elite League.

He played for the Finnish Junior National Team for three seasons (1978–1980) and scored the winning goal at the 1978 European Junior Championship against the Soviet Union, giving Finland its first-ever gold medal. In 1980, he led Finland to its first-ever World Junior Championship medal (silver); was selected to that year's Winter Olympic team (finishing fourth at Lake Placid, New York); and later in the year, was the 69th overall pick in the National Hockey League Draft of the Edmonton Oilers.

The 6', 190-pound Kurri would go on to play 16 NHL seasons with the Oilers (1981–1990), Los Angeles Kings (1991–1995), New York Rangers (1996), Mighty Ducks of Anaheim (1996–1997), and the Colorado Avalanche (1997–1998). Teaming with Gretzky, Kurri recorded a 100-point season in 1982–1983 and a 50-goal season the following year, the first Finnish-born player to reach both marks, and he would help the Oilers win five Stanley Cup championships (1984–1985, 1987–1988, 1990). He scored 71 goals in 1984–1985 (a single-season record for a right-winger); won the Lady Byng Trophy for sportsmanship and gentlemanly conduct in 1985; and finished second to Gretzky as the league's scoring leader.

He was named to five All-Star teams (First Team in 1985 and 1987 and Second Team in 1984, 1986, and 1989), and was the 25th NHL player to score 1,000 points.

Kurri also played in four World Championships (1982, 1989, 1991, and 1994), with Finland (winning the silver medal in 1994); three Canada Cups (1981, 1987, 1991); in the 1996 World Cup; and won the bronze medal with the Finnish National Team at the 1998 Olympic Winter Games (Nagano, Japan).

After a season in Italy, Kurri returned to the NHL with the Los Angeles Kings, where he was reunited with Gretzky, and in the 1992–1993 season, the duo led Los Angeles to the team's first-ever Stanley Cup finals appearance, losing to the Montreal Canadiens in five games. He was the first European-trained player, and the 18th in NHL history, to record 500 career goals.

After playing for the Kings, New York Rangers, and the Mighty Ducks of Anaheim, he signed with the Colorado Avalanche for the 1997–1998 season; scored his 600th goal; and retired from the NHL at the end of the season, the highest scoring European-born player in NHL history. His jersey number 17 was retired by both the Oilers and the Finnish national men's ice hockey team. The Jari Kurri Trophy, named in his honor, is presented annually by the Finnish SM-Liiga to the best player in the playoffs.

He played in eight NHL All-Star games (1983, 1985–1986, 1988–1990, 1993, 1998), and in 1998, he was ranked number 50 on *The Hockey News*' list of the 100 Greatest Hockey Players, the highest-ranking Scandinavian player.

Jari Kurri's Career Statistics

				REGULAR SEASON				PLAYOFFS				
SEASON	**TEAM**	**LEAGUE**	**GP**	**G**	**A**	**TP**	**PIM**	**GP**	**G**	**A**	**TP**	**PIM**
1970–1971	Jokerit Maple Leafs	Finland-AA	9	21	6	27						
1970–1971	Jokerit Novice	Finland-AA	18	13	7	20						
1971–1972	Jokerit Atoms	Finland-AA	31	40	23	63						
1972–1973	Jokerit Atoms	Finland-AA	35	32	16	48						
1973–1974	Jokerit Atoms	Finland-AA	54	65	32	97						
1974–1975	Jokerit PeeWees	Finland-AA	18	17	9	26						
1975–1976	Jokerit PeeWees	Finland-AA	58	65	24	89						
1976–1977	Jokerit Bantams	Finland-AA	33	55	43	98						
1976–1977	Jokerit Helsinki	Finland-AA	18	4	6	10	4	5	2	2	4	6
1977–1978	Jokerit Helsinki Jr.	Fin-Jr.	5	5	4	9	2	1	1	0	1	2
1977–1978	Jokerit Helsinki	Finland	29	2	9	11	12					
1977–1978	Jokerit Helsinki	Finland–Q	6	1	7	8	2					
1977–1978	Finland	EJC-A	4	6	2	8	4					
1978–1979	Jokerit Helsinki Jr.	Fin–Jr.	2	1	1	2	2					
1978–1979	Jokerit Helsinki	Finland	33	16	14	30	12					
1978–1979	Finland	WJC-A	6	2	3	5	2					
1979–1980	Jokerit Helsinki	Finland	33	23	16	39	22					
1979–1980	Jokerit Helsinki	Finland-Q	6	7	2	9	13					
1979–1980	Finland	WJC-A	5	4	7	11	0					
1979–1980	Finland	Nat-Tm	8	3	1	4	0					
1979–1980	Finland	Olympics	7	2	1	3	6					
1980–1981	Edmonton Oilers	NHL	75	32	43	75	40	9	5	7	12	4
1981–1982	Finland	Can-Cup	5	0	1	1	0					
1981–1982	Edmonton Oilers	NHL	71	32	54	86	32	5	2	5	7	10
1981–1982	Finland	Nat-Tm	5	1	2	3	2					
1981–1982	Finland	WEC-A	7	4	3	7	2					
1982–1983	Edmonton Oilers	NHL	80	45	59	104	22	16	8	15	23	8
1983–1984	Edmonton Oilers	NHL	64	52	61	113	14	19	14	14	28	13
1984–1985	Edmonton Oilers	NHL	73	71	64	135	30	18	19	12	31	6
1985–1986	Edmonton Oilers	NHL	78	68	63	131	22	10	2	10	12	4
1986–1987	Edmonton Oilers	NHL	79	54	54	108	41	21	15	10	25	20
1986–1987	NHL All-Stars	RV-87	2	1	1	2	0					
1987–1988	Finland	Nat-Tm	6	2	2	4	2					
1987–1988	Finland	Can-Cup	5	1	1	2	4					
1987–1988	Edmonton Oilers	NHL	80	43	53	96	30	19	14	17	31	12
1988–1989	Edmonton Oilers	NHL	76	44	58	102	69	7	3	5	8	6
1988–1989	Finland	WEC-A	7	5	4	9	4					
1989–1990	Edmonton Oilers	NHL	78	33	60	93	48	22	10	15	25	18
1990–1991	HC Devils Medio. Milano	Italy	40	37	60	97	8					
1990–1991	Finland	Nat-Tm	6	4	4	8	2					
1990–1991	Finland	WEC-A	10	6	6	12	2					
1991–1992	Finland	Nat-Tm	5	0	2	2	2					
1991–1992	Finland	Can-Cup	6	2	0	2	7					
1991–1992	Los Angeles Kings	NHL	73	23	37	60	24	4	1	2	3	4
1992–1993	Los Angeles Kings	NHL	82	27	60	87	38	24	9	8	17	12
1992–1993	Finland	Nat-Tm	1	0	0	0	2					
1993–1994	Los Angeles Kings	NHL	81	31	46	77	48					
1993–1994	Finland	WC-A	8	4	6	10	2					
1994–1995	Jokerit Helsinki	Finland	20	10	9	19	10					
1994–1995	Los Angeles Kings	NHL	38	10	19	29	24					

			REGULAR SEASON					PLAYOFFS				
SEASON	**TEAM**	**LEAGUE**	**GP**	**G**	**A**	**TP**	**PIM**	**GP**	**G**	**A**	**TP**	**PIM**
1994–1995	Finland	Nat-Tm	1	0	0	0	0					
1995–1996	Los Angeles Kings	NHL	57	17	23	40	37					
1995–1996	New York Rangers	NHL	14	1	4	5	2	11	3	5	8	2
1996–1997	Finland	Nat-Tm	4	0	0	0	0					
1996–1997	Finland	W-Cup	4	1	0	1	0					
1996–1997	Mighty Ducks of Anaheim	NHL	82	13	22	35	12	11	1	2	3	4
1997–1998	Colorado Avalanche	NHL	70	5	17	22	12	4	0	0	0	0
1997–1998	Finland	Olympics	6	1	4	5	2					
	NHL TOTALS		1,251	601	797	1,398	545		200	127	233	123

Sources: Hockey Hall of Fame; Hockey-Reference.com

Chapter 12
Lach to Lyons

Lach, Elmer James (born: January 22, 1918 in Nokomis, Saskatchewan, Canada); inducted into the Hockey Hall of Fame in 1966 as a player; Position: Center; won three Stanley Cup championships.

Lach played his entire 14-year National Hockey League career with the Montreal Canadiens (1940–1954); helped the team win three Stanley Cup titles (1944, 1946, 1953); and was the center on the club's "Punch Line" with Toe Blake and Maurice Richard.

After playing in the Saskatchewan junior and senior circuits, the 5'10", 165-pound Lach joined the NHL in 1940. Throughout his career, he was injury-prone and only played a complete, injury-free season five times.

He was named to five All-Star teams (three First Teams [1945, 1948, 1952] and two Second Teams [1944, 1946]); won the Art Ross Trophy as the league's regular-season scoring leader twice (1945, 1948); and won the Hart Memorial Trophy as the NHL Most Valuable Player in 1945.

On February 23, 1952, Lach recorded his 549th point to pass Bill Cowley as the then NHL's all-time leader in scoring. He retired after the 1953–1954 season; coached the Montreal Junior Canadiens; and then retired from hockey to pursue business interests.

In 1998, he was ranked number 68 on *The Hockey News*' list of the 100 Greatest Hockey Players.

Elmer Lach's Career Statistics

			REGULAR SEASON					PLAYOFFS				
SEASON	TEAM	LEAGUE	GP	G	A	TP	PIM	GP	G	A	TP	PIM
1935–1936	Regina Abbotts	S-SJHL	2	0	1	1	2	4	3	0	3	6
1936–1937	Weyburn Beavers	S-SSHL	23	16	6	22	27	3	0	1	1	4
1937–1938	Weyburn Beavers	S-SSHL	22	12	12	24	44	3	2	1	3	0
1938–1939	Moose Jaw Millers	S-SSHL	29	17	20	37	23	10	6	4	10	8
1939–1940	Moose Jaw Millers	Al-Cup	3	1	1	2	4					
1939–1940	Moose Jaw Millers	S-SSHL	30	15	29	44	20	8	5	9	14	12
1940–1941	Montreal Canadiens	NHL	43	7	14	21	16	3	1	0	1	0
1941–1942	Montreal Canadiens	NHL	1	0	1	1	0					
1942–1943	Montreal Canadiens	NHL	45	18	40	58	14	5	2	4	6	6
1943–1944	Montreal Canadiens	NHL	48	24	48	72	23	9	2	11	13	4
1944–1945	Montreal Canadiens	NHL	50	26	54	80	37	6	4	4	8	2
1945–1946	Montreal Canadiens	NHL	50	13	34	47	34	9	5	12	17	4
1946–1947	Montreal Canadiens	NHL	31	14	16	30	22					
1947–1948	Montreal Canadiens	NHL	60	30	31	61	72					
1948–1949	Montreal Canadiens	NHL	36	11	18	29	59	1	0	0	0	4
1949–1950	Montreal Canadiens	NHL	64	15	33	48	33	5	1	2	3	4
1950–1951	Montreal Canadiens	NHL	65	21	24	45	48	11	2	2	4	2
1951–1952	Montreal Canadiens	NHL	70	15	50	65	36	11	1	2	3	4
1952–1953	Montreal Canadiens	NHL	53	16	25	41	56	12	1	6	7	6
1953–1954	Montreal Canadiens	NHL	48	5	20	25	28	4	0	2	2	0
	NHL TOTALS		664	215	408	623	478	76	19	45	64	36

Sources: Hockey Hall of Fame; Hockey-Reference.com

Lafleur, Guy Damien (OC, CQ) (born: September 20, 1951 in Thurso, Quebec, Canada); inducted into the Hockey Hall of Fame in 1988 as a player; Position: Right Wing; Uniform: #10; first player in NHL history to score at least 50 goals and 100 points in six consecutive seasons; won five Stanley Cup championships.

Lafleur played 17 National Hockey League seasons with the Montreal Canadiens (1971–1984), New York Rangers (1988–1989), and the Quebec Nordiques (1989–1991). Before joining the Canadiens, the 6', 185-pound right winger played for the Quebec Remparts (Quebec Major Junior Hockey League) and led the team to the Memorial Cup in 1971.

In the NHL, he became the first player in league history to score at least 50 goals and 100 points in six consecutive seasons (1975–1980). During this period of time, he was named a First Team All-Star all six years; won the Art Ross Trophy three consecutive seasons (1976–1978) as the league's regular-season scoring leader; won the Hart Memorial Trophy twice (1977–1978) as the league's Most Valuable Player; won the Conn Smythe Trophy in 1977 as the leading scorer in the NHL playoffs; and won the Lester B. Pearson Award three times (1976–1978) as the league's regular-season outstanding player as voted on by the members of the NHL Players Association. During his 14 years with the Canadiens, the team won the Stanley Cup five times (1973, 1976–1979).

When he retired, Lafleur had the highest career point and assist totals in Montreal history; and reached the 1,000-point mark in only 720 games, the shortest time in NHL history. When he retired the first time in 1984 (19 games into the season), he became the seventh Canadiens player to have his jersey number retired (after Jacques Plante, Doug Harvey, Jean Béliveau, Howie Morenz, Maurice Richard, and Henri Richard).

After being inducted into the Hockey Hall of Fame, Lafleur returned to the NHL in 1988 with the New York Rangers for one season, and was the second player (after Gordie Howe) to play in the NHL after being inducted into the hall of fame. He left the Rangers and played for the Quebec Nordiques for two seasons before retiring for good from the NHL.

Throughout his career, Lafleur was one of the few players who did not wear a helmet; was a member of the Canadian National Team in the 1976 and 1981 Canada Cup tournaments, winning the Cup in 1976; received the Lou Marsh Trophy in 1977 as Canada's top athlete; and was inducted into the Canadian Sports Hall of Fame in 1996. The QMJHL's Guy Lafleur Trophy, named in his honor, is presented to the league's playoff MVP and, in 1998, he was ranked number 11 on *The Hockey News*' list of the 100 Greatest Hockey Players.

In 1980, he was awarded the Officer of the Order of Canada, and in 2005, he was made a Knight of the National Order of Quebec.

Guy Lafleur's Career Statistics

			REGULAR SEASON						PLAYOFFS				
SEASON	**TEAM**	**LEAGUE**	**GP**	**G**	**A**	**TP**	**PIM**	**+/-**	**GP**	**G**	**A**	**TP**	**PIM**
1966–1967	Quebec Canadian Tire	QAHA											
1966–1967	Quebec Aces	QJHL	8	1	1	2	0						
1967–1968	Quebec Aces	QJHL	43	30	19	49							
1968–1969	Quebec Aces	QJHL	49	50	60	110	83						
1969–1970	Quebec Remparts	M-Cup	12	18	18	36	23						
1969–1970	Quebec Remparts	QJHL	56	103	67	170	105		15	25	18	43	34
1970–1971	Quebec Remparts	QMJHL	62	130	79	209	135		14	22	21	43	24
1970–1971	Quebec Remparts	M-Cup	7	9	5	14	18						
1971–1972	Montreal Canadiens	NHL	73	29	35	64	48	+27	6	1	4	5	2
1972–1973	Montreal Canadiens	NHL	69	28	27	55	51	+16	17	3	5	8	9
1973–1974	Montreal Canadiens	NHL	73	21	35	56	29	+10	6	0	1	1	4
1974–1975	Montreal Canadiens	NHL	70	53	66	119	37	+52	11	12	7	19	15
1975–1976	Montreal Canadiens	NHL	80	56	69	125	36	+68	13	7	10	17	2
1976–1977	Canada	Can-Cup	7	1	5	6	12						
1976–1977	Montreal Canadiens	NHL	80	56	80	136	20	+89	14	9	17	26	6
1977–1978	Montreal Canadiens	NHL	78	60	72	132	26	+73	15	10	11	21	16
1978–1979	Montreal Canadiens	NHL	80	52	77	129	28	+56	16	10	13	23	0
1978–1979	NHL All-Stars	Ch-Cup	3	1	2	3	0						
1979–1980	Montreal Canadiens	NHL	74	50	75	125	12	+40	3	3	1	4	0
1980–1981	Montreal Canadiens	NHL	51	27	43	70	29	+24	3	0	1	1	2
1980–1981	Canada	WEC-A	7	1	0	1	2						
1981–1982	Canada	Can-Cup	7	2	9	11	0						
1981–1982	Montreal Canadiens	NHL	66	27	57	84	24	+33	5	2	1	3	4
1982–1983	Montreal Canadiens	NHL	68	27	49	76	12	+6	3	0	2	2	2
1983–1984	Montreal Canadiens	NHL	80	30	40	70	19	-14	12	0	3	3	5
1984–1985	Montreal Canadiens	NHL	19	2	3	5	10	-3					
1988–1989	New York Rangers	NHL	67	18	27	45	12	+1	4	1	0	1	0

SEASON	TEAM	LEAGUE	REGULAR SEASON GP	G	A	TP	PIM	+/-	PLAYOFFS GP	G	A	TP	PIM
1989–1990	Quebec Nordiques	NHL	39	12	22	34	4	-15					
1990–1991	Quebec Nordiques	NHL	59	12	16	28	2	-10					
	NHL TOTALS		1,126	560	793	1,353	399		128	58	76	134	67

Sources: Hockey Hall of Fame; Hockey-Reference.com

LaFontaine, Pat (born: February 22, 1965 in St. Louis, Missouri); inducted into the Hockey Hall of Fame in 2003 as a player; Position: Center; Uniform: #16; has been inducted into the United States Hockey Hall of Fame, the Buffalo Sabres Hall of Fame, and the Nassau County Sports Hall of Fame.

The 5'10", 180-pound LaFontaine played hockey in the Canadian junior system with the Verdun Juniors (Quebec Major Junior Hockey League) for one season (1982–1983) and won the Jean Béliveau Trophy as the league's top scorer; named Canadian Major Junior player of the year; won the Michel Brière Commemorative Trophy as the regular-season Most Valuable Player; the Guy Lafleur Trophy as the playoffs MVP; and the Michel Bergeron Trophy as the Offensive Rookie of the Year.

He was the first pick (third overall selection) of the New York Islanders in the 1983 National Hockey League Draft and would go on to play 15 NHL season with all three New York-based teams, the Islanders (1983–1991), Buffalo Sabres (1991–1997), and New York Rangers (1997–1998).

Before entering the National Hockey League, he played for the U.S. National Team at the 1984 Olympics (Sarajevo, Yugoslavia) and scored eight points in six games, but failed to medal as the team finished in seventh place.

After the Olympics, LaFontaine joined the Islanders; represented the United States at the Canada Cup tournament; in 1987, registered the first of his six straight seasons with 40 or more goals; and in 1989, played for the United States at the World Championships.

In 1991, he was a member of the U.S. team that lost to Canada in the finals of the Canada Cup. In October 1991, he was traded to the Sabres, and in his second season with the team, LaFontaine scored a franchise-record 148 points (53 goals, 95 assists). At this point in his career, he began suffering a series of injuries that limited his playing time; was traded to the Rangers in 1997; and reached the 1,000-point mark on January 22, 1998, before retiring at the end of the season.

In 2003, LaFontaine was inducted into the United States Hockey Hall of Fame, and in 2006, the Sabres retired his jersey number 16 and inducted him into the Buffalo Sabres Hall of Fame. Since 2001, the Pat LaFontaine Trophy has been awarded to the winner of the Rangers-Islanders season series. In 2007, he was inducted into the Nassau County Sports Hall of Fame.

Pat LaFontaine's Career Statistics

SEASON	TEAM	LEAGUE	REGULAR SEASON GP	G	A	TP	PIM	+/-	PLAYOFFS GP	G	A	TP	PIM
1981–1982	Detroit Compuware	MNHL	79	175	149	324							
1982–1983	Verdun Juniors	QMJHL	70	104	130	234	10		15	11	24	35	4
1982–1983	Verdun Juniors	M-Cup	4	3	2	5	2						
1983–1984	United States	Nat-Tm	58	56	55	111	22						
1983–1984	United States	Olympics	6	5	3	8	0						
1983–1984	New York Islanders	NHL	15	13	6	19	6	+9	16	3	6	9	8
1984–1985	New York Islanders	NHL	67	19	35	54	32	+9	9	1	2	3	4
1985–1986	New York Islanders	NHL	65	30	23	53	43	+16	3	1	0	1	0
1986–1987	New York Islanders	NHL	80	38	32	70	70	-10	14	5	7	12	10
1987–1988	United States	Can-Cup	5	3	0	3	0						
1987–1988	New York Islanders	NHL	75	47	45	92	52	+12	6	4	5	9	8
1988–1989	New York Islanders	NHL	79	45	43	88	26	-8					
1988–1989	United States	WEC-A	10	5	3	8	8						
1989–1990	New York Islanders	NHL	74	54	51	105	38	-13	2	0	1	1	0
1990–1991	New York Islanders	NHL	75	41	44	85	42	-6					
1991–1992	United States	Can-Cup	6	3	1	4	2						
1991–1992	Buffalo Sabres	NHL	57	46	47	93	98	+10	7	8	3	11	4
1992–1993	Buffalo Sabres	NHL	84	53	95	148	63	+11	7	2	10	12	0
1993–1994	Buffalo Sabres	NHL	16	5	13	18	2	-4					
1994–1995	Buffalo Sabres	NHL	22	12	15	27	4	+2	5	2	2	4	2
1995–1996	Buffalo Sabres	NHL	76	40	51	91	36	-8					
1996–1997	United States	W-Cup	5	2	2	4	2						
1996–1997	Buffalo Sabres	NHL	13	2	6	8	4	-8					
1997–1998	New York Rangers	NHL	67	23	39	62	36	-16					

			REGULAR SEASON						PLAYOFFS				
SEASON	TEAM	LEAGUE	GP	G	A	TP	PIM	+/-	GP	G	A	TP	PIM
1997–1998	United States	Olympics	4	1	1	2	0						
	NHL TOTALS		865	468	545	1,013	552		69	26	36	62	36

Sources: Hockey Hall of Fame; Hockey-Reference.com

Lajoie, Napoleon "Nap" (born: September 5, 1874 in Woonsocket, Rhode Island; died: February 7, 1959 in Daytona Beach, Florida); inducted into the National Baseball Hall of Fame and Museum in 1937 as a player; Position: Second Base; Bats: Right; Throws: Right; won the 1901 Triple Crown; first major league player to be intentionally walked with the bases loaded; sixth player elected to the baseball hall of fame.

Lajoie hit .300 or better in 16 of his 21 major league seasons; hit .350 or better 10 times; won the Triple Crown in 1901, leading the league in home runs, runs batted in, and batting average; won three batting titles; and hit .426 in 1901, a still-standing American League record.

Making his debut on August 12, 1896, the 6'1", 195-pound Lajoie played 21 seasons for the Philadelphia Phillies (National League, 1896–1900), Philadelphia Athletics (American League, 1901–1902, 1915–1916), and the Cleveland Naps/Indians (American League, 1902–1914). He also managed the Naps/Indians from 1905 to 1909.

On May 23, 1901, in the ninth inning, Lajoie became the first major league player to be intentionally walked with the bases loaded in an 11–8 loss to the Chicago White Stockings. His batting dominance was challenged beginning in 1905 with the arrival of the legendary Ty Cobb, and the two players became rivals for years. In 1910, with Cobb having a small lead in the batting race, he sat out the last two games of the season. According to many baseball historians, Lajoie, a far more popular player than Cobb (but then again, who wasn't), was "allowed" by the St. Louis Browns to go 7-for-8 in a season-ending doubleheader. After getting a triple and a single, he had five straight bunt singles aimed at third baseman Red Corriden, who was playing in the left field grass reportedly on manager Jack O'Connor's orders. Whatever help he may have received was not enough as Cobb finished the season with a .38507 average to Lajoie's .384095. After the Browns' ploy became public, O'Connor was fired.

When he retired, his 3,242 hits was the second best in major league history behind Honus Wagner, and his 2,521 hits in the American League was the league record until Cobb surpassed it in 1918. In 1999, Lajoie ranked number 29 on *The Sporting News*' list of the 100 Greatest Baseball Players; was a nominee for the Major League Baseball All-Century Team; and was the sixth player inducted into the baseball hall of fame.

Nap Lajoie's Career Playing Statistics

YEAR	TEAM	LG	G	AB	R	H	2B	3B	HR	RBI	BB	SO	SB	AVG	SLG
1896	Philadelphia	NL	39	174	37	57	11	6	4	42	1	11	6	.328	.529
1897	Philadelphia	NL	126	545	107	197	37	25	9	127	15		22	.363	.572
1898	Philadelphia	NL	147	610	113	197	40	10	6	127	21		33	.328	.456
1899	Philadelphia	NL	72	308	70	118	17	11	6	70	12		14	.380	.565
1900	Philadelphia	NL	102	451	95	152	32	12	7	92	10		25	.346	.517
1901	Philadelphia	AL	131	543	145	232	48	13	14	125	24		27	.422	.635
1902	Philadelphia	AL	1	4	0	1	0	0	0	1	0		0	.250	.250
1902	Cleveland	AL	86	348	81	132	34	5	7	64	19		19	.368	.555
1903	Cleveland	AL	126	488	90	167	40	13	7	93	24		22	.355	.533
1904	Cleveland	AL	140	554	92	208	50	14	5	102	27		31	.381	.549
1905	Cleveland	AL	65	249	29	82	13	2	2	41	17		11	.329	.422
1906	Cleveland	AL	152	602	88	214	49	7	0	91	30		20	.355	.460
1907	Cleveland	AL	137	509	53	152	30	6	2	63	30		24	.301	.395
1908	Cleveland	AL	157	581	77	168	32	6	2	74	47		15	.289	.375
1909	Cleveland	AL	128	469	56	152	33	7	1	47	35		13	.324	.431
1910	Cleveland	AL	159	591	94	227	51	7	4	76	60		26	.384	.514
1911	Cleveland	AL	90	315	36	115	20	1	2	60	26		13	.365	.454
1912	Cleveland	AL	117	448	66	165	34	4	0	90	28		18	.368	.462
1913	Cleveland	AL	137	465	67	156	25	2	1	68	33	17	17	.335	.404
1914	Cleveland	AL	121	419	37	108	14	3	0	50	32	15	14	.258	.305
1915	Philadelphia	AL	129	490	40	137	24	5	1	61	11	16	10	.280	.355
1916	Philadelphia	AL	113	426	33	105	14	4	2	35	14	26	15	.246	.312
	TOTALS		2,475	9,589	1,506	3,242	648	163	82	1,599	516	85	395	.339	.466

Nap Lajoie's Managerial Record

YEAR	LG	TEAM	W	L	WP	FINISH

YEAR	LG	TEAM	W	L	WP	FINISH
1905	AL	Cleveland	56	57	.496	5 (Player-Manager)
1906	AL	Cleveland	89	64	.582	3 (Player-Manager)
1907	AL	Cleveland	85	67	.559	4 (Player-Manager)
1908	AL	Cleveland	90	64	.584	2 (Player-Manager)
1909	AL	Cleveland	57	57	.500	6 (Player-Manager)
		TOTALS	377	309	.550	

Sources: Baseball-Reference.com; National Baseball Hall of Fame and Museum

Lalas, Panayotis Alexander "Alexi" (born: June 1, 1970 in Birmingham, Michigan); inducted into the National Soccer Hall of Fame and Museum as a player in 2006; Position: Defender; International Caps (1991–1998): 96; International Goals: 9; won the U.S. Open Cup title in 2001; won a Major League Soccer title in 2002.

Lalas played 96 international games for the United States; was a member of the American team at the 1994 World Cup (held in the U.S., the team was eliminated in the Round of 16); played two seasons in the Italian first division; and finished his playing career with seven seasons in Major League Soccer.

The 6'3" player was not hard to see in a crowd with red hair down to his shoulders and a red goatee.

In 1991, he was a member of the United States team that played in the first round of Olympic qualifying and was a member of the team that won the United States' first-ever Pan-American Games title. In 1992, the three-time Rutgers University (New Jersey) All-American was a member of the U.S. team at the Olympics in Barcelona, Spain (1992, eliminated in the first round).

Lalas scored nine goals in his National Team career, which included the 1993 and 1995 Copa America tournaments; the 1993, 1996, and 1998 Confederation of North, Central American and Caribbean Association Football Gold Cups; and the 1994 World Cup.

After the 1994 World Cup, Lalas signed with Padova of the Italian first division, where he played for two seasons, becoming the first American in Serie A since before World War II. In 1996, he was one of many American players who returned to the United States from European clubs when Major League Soccer began operations. In the first four MLS seasons, he played for the New England Revolution (1996–1997), the MetroStars (1998), and the Kansas City Wizards (1999). He retired from the league after the 1999 season, but returned in 2001 and played three more MLS seasons, all with the Los Angeles Galaxy, winning a U.S. Open Cup title in 2001 and the MLS championship in 2002.

In 1991, he won both the Hermann and Missouri Athletic Club awards as the nation's outstanding college player. In 1995, he won the Honda Award as the outstanding National Team player; the United States Soccer Federation's Male Athlete of the Year Award; and was selected to the All-Tournament team at the Copa America in Uruguay (1995), where the United States finished fourth.

As of this writing, Lalas is the president and general manager of the Los Angeles Galaxy of Major League Soccer.

He attended Cranbrook Kingswood High School (Bloomfield Hills, Michigan), where he was named the 1987 Michigan High School Player of the Year as a senior. After high school, he went to Rutgers University, where he played on the men's soccer team from 1988 to 1991. During his four seasons at the school, he led the Scarlet Knights to the NCAA Final Four in 1989 and the National Championship Game in 1990, eventually losing to the University of California, Los Angeles. Lalas was named a Third Team All-American in 1989 and 1990, and a First Team All-American in 1991.

When he first retired from the MLS, he announced soccer matches on NBC for the 2000 Summer Olympics, and later served as an in-studio analyst for ESPN and ABC Sports coverage of the 2006 FIFA World Cup.

After retiring from the MLS as a player for good, Lalas became the general manager of the San Jose Earthquakes, and in 2005, served as the president and general manager of the MetroStars. He resigned in 2006 to become president and general manager of the Galaxy.

Source: National Soccer Hall of Fame and Museum

Lalonde, Edouard "Newsy" (born: October 31, 1887 in Cornwall, Ontario, Canada; died: November 21, 1970 in Montreal, Quebec, Canada); inducted into the Hockey Hall of Fame in 1950 as a player; Position: Center-Forward; won two NHA scoring titles; won a Stanley Cup championship.

Lalonde played 21 professional seasons from 1904 to 1927, and was involved in the early years of the National Hockey League. He earned his nickname "Newsy" because, as a young man, he had worked in a newsprint plant.

He played with the Cornwall Hockey Club (Federal Amateur Hockey League) in 1905; the Woodstock Seniors (Ontario Hockey Association Senior League) in 1905–1906; Canadian Soo (International Hockey League) in 1906–1907; and the Toronto Professionals (Ontario Professional Hockey League) in 1907.

After two seasons with Toronto, Lalonde joined the Montreal Canadiens (National Hockey Association) in 1910, and was traded to the Renfrew Millionaires in mid-season, where (on March 11, 1910), he scored nine goals in one game and won the league's inaugural scoring title. In 1911–1912, he played for the Vancouver Millionaires (Pacific Coast Hockey Association); returned to the Canadiens the next season; and won another NHA scoring title. In the 1915–1916 season, he led the team to its first Stanley Cup championship (over the Portland Rosebuds) and was with the squad when the franchise joined the National Hockey League for its inaugural 1917–1918 season. Lalonde played and scored in the first-ever NHL game on December 19, 1917, a 7–4 Canadiens win over the Ottawa Senators; led the NHL in scoring twice (1919, 1921); and on January 10, 1920, scored six goals in one game, a 14–7 win over the Toronto St. Patricks.

Lalonde was traded to the Saskatoon Sheiks (Western Canada Hockey League) in 1922 and, as a player-coach, won the scoring title his first season. He returned to the NHL as coach of the New York Americans in 1927 and went on to coach the Ottawa Senators and Montreal Canadiens, before retiring from the game in 1935.

He was also an excellent lacrosse player in the early 20th century; broke the scoring record for his Montreal team in 1910 (31 goals); in 1914, he scored 66 goals for the Montreal Nationals; and ended his lacrosse career in 1917 to focus on hockey.

In 1950, Lalonde was named athlete of the half century in lacrosse, the same year he was inducted into the Hockey Hall of Fame. He was inducted into the Canadian Lacrosse Hall of Fame in 1965 and into the Sports Hall of Fame of Canada in 1982. In 1998, he was ranked number 32 on *The Hockey News*' list of the 100 Greatest Hockey Players, making him the highest-ranking person on the list who had played in a professional league before the founding of the NHL.

Edouard Lalonde's Career Playing Statistics

			REGULAR SEASON					PLAYOFFS				
SEASON	TEAM	LEAGUE	GP	G	A	TP	PIM	GP	G	A	TP	PIM
1904–1905	Cornwall Athletics	OHA-Jr.										
1904–1905	Cornwall Hockey Club	FAHL	2	1	0	1						
1905–1906	Woodstock Seniors	OHA-Sr.	7	8	0	8						
1906–1907	Canadian Soo	IHL	18	29	4	33	27					
1907–1908	Portage-la-Prairie	MHL-Pro	1	0	0	0	0					
1907–1908	Toronto Professionals	OPHL	9	32	0	32	37					
1907–1908	Toronto Professionals	St-Cup						1	2	0	2	0
1907–1908	Haileybury Hockey Club	TPHL						1	3	0	3	0
1908–1909	Toronto Professionals	OPHL	11	29	0	29	79					
1909–1910	Montreal Canadiens	NHA	1	2	0	2	3					
1909–1910	Montreal Canadiens	NHA	6	16	0	16	40					
1909–1910	Renfrew Hockey Club	NHA	5	22	0	22	16					
1910–1911	Montreal Canadiens	NHA	16	19	0	19	63					
1911–1912	Vancouver Millionaires	PCHA	15	27	0	27	51					
1911–1912	PCHA All-Stars	Exhib.	3	5	0	5	11					
1912–1913	Montreal Canadiens	NHA	18	25	0	25	61					
1913–1914	Montreal Canadiens	NHA	14	22	5	27	23	2	0	0	0	2
1914–1915	Montreal Canadiens	NHA	7	4	3	7	17					
1915–1916	Montreal Canadiens	NHA	24	28	6	34	78					
1915–1916	Montreal Canadiens	St-Cup						4	3	0	3	41
1916–1917	Montreal Canadiens	NHA	18	28	7	35	61	1	1	0	1	23
1916–1917	Montreal Canadiens	St-Cup						4	1	0	1	24
1917–1918	Montreal Canadiens	NHL	14	23	7	30	51	2	4	2	6	17
1918–1919	Montreal Canadiens	NHL	17	22	10	32	40	5	11	2	13	15
1918–1919	Montreal Canadiens	St-Cup						5	6	0	6	3
1919–1920	Montreal Canadiens	NHL	23	37	9	46	34					
1920–1921	Montreal Canadiens	NHL	24	33	10	43	36					
1921–1922	Montreal Canadiens	NHL	20	9	5	14	20					
1922–1923	Saskatoon Sheiks	WCHL	29	30	4	34	44					
1923–1924	Saskatoon Crescents	WCHL	21	10	10	20	24					
1924–1925	Saskatoon Crescents	WCHL	22	8	6	14	42	2	0	0	0	4
1925–1926	Saskatoon Crescents	WHL	3	0	0	0	2	2	0	0	0	2
1926–1927	New York Americans	NHL	1	0	0	0	2					

SEASON	TEAM	LEAGUE	REGULAR SEASON GP	G	A	TP	PIM	PLAYOFFS GP	G	A	TP	PIM
1927–1928	Quebec Castors	Can-Am	1	0	0	0	0					
1928–1929	Niagara Falls Cataracts	Can-Pro										
	NHL TOTALS		99	124	41	165	183	7	15	4	19	32

Edouard Lalonde's Coaching Record

SEASON	TEAM	LG	W	L	T	Win%
1922–1923	Saskatoon Sheiks	WCHL	8	20	2	.300
1922–1923	Saskatoon Crescents	WCHL	8	20	2	.300
1923–1924	Saskatoon Crescents	WCHL	15	12	3	.550
1923–1924	Saskatoon Sheiks	WCHL	15	12	3	.550
1924–1925	Saskatoon Sheiks	WCHL	16	11	1	.589
1924–1925	Saskatoon Shieks	WCHL	16	11	1	.589
1924–1925	Saskatoon Crescents	WCHL	16	11	1	.589
1925–1926	Saskatoon Sheiks	WCHL	18	11	1	.617
1925–1926	Saskatoon Crescents	WCHL	18	11	1	.617
1925–1926	Saskatoon Sheiks	WHL	18	11	1	.617
1925–1926	Saskatoon Shieks	WCHL	18	11	1	.617
1926–1927	New York Americans	NHL	17	25	2	.409
1927–1928	Quebec Beavers	CAHL	18	14	8	.550
1928–1929	Niagara Falls Cataracts	CPHL	12	28	2	.310
1931–1932	Providence Reds	CAHL	23	11	6	.650
	TOTALS		236	219	35	.517

Sources: Hockey Hall of Fame; Hockey-Reference.com

Lambeau, Earl Louis "Curly" (born: April 9, 1898 in Green Bay, Wisconsin; died: June 1, 1965 in Sturgeon Bay, Wisconsin); inducted into the Pro Football Hall of Fame in 1963 as a founder-coach; founded the Green Bay Packers; won six NFL titles; an inaugural member of the football hall of fame.

Lambeau founded the Green Bay Packers in 1919, before the formation of the National Football League; played halfback for the team 11 seasons (77 games) until 1929; and was the squad's coach and general manager until 1949.

After leaving Green Bay, he coached the Chicago Cardinals (1950–1951) and the Washington Redskins (1952–1953); was the first coach to make the forward pass an integral part of the offensive game plan; retired with a 33-year overall NFL coaching record of 229–134–22 (.595); and his 229 career wins ranked second only to George Halas when he retired.

He played football (fullback) as a freshman at the University of Notre Dame (South Bend, Indiana) in 1918, but got ill and had to leave the school. He returned to Green Bay and took a job with the Indian Packing Company. In 1919, he organized a football team called the "Packers" that eventually joined the NFL in 1921, with Lambeau as a player and the team's captain. During his career, he scored three receiving touchdowns, eight rushing touchdowns, and 24 passing touchdowns.

He led the team to six NFL titles (1929–1931, 1936, 1939, 1944); left the Packers to coach the Chicago Cardinals to a 7–15 (.318) record (1950–1951); and finished his coaching career with the Washington Redskins, leading the team to a 10–13–1 (.417) record (1952–1953).

Lambeau was a member of the 1963 inaugural class of inductees to the Pro Football Hall of Fame; Lambeau Field in Green Bay is named after him; he was selected to the NFL 1920s All-Decade Team; and has been inducted into both the Green Bay Packers Hall of Fame and the Wisconsin Athletic Hall of Fame.

Curly Lambeau's Coaching Record

YEAR	TEAM	LG	REGULAR SEASON W	L	T	WIN%	PLAYOFFS W	L	WIN%	Notes
1921	Green Bay	APFA	3	2	1	.600				
1922	Green Bay	NFL	4	3	3	.571				
1923	Green Bay	NFL	7	2	1	.778				

YEAR	TEAM	LG	REGULAR SEASON W	L	T	WIN%	PLAYOFFS W	L	WIN%	Notes
1924	Green Bay	NFL	7	4	0	.636				
1925	Green Bay	NFL	8	5	0	.615				
1926	Green Bay	NFL	7	3	3	.700				
1927	Green Bay	NFL	7	2	1	.778				
1928	Green Bay	NFL	6	4	3	.600				
1929	Green Bay	NFL	12	0	1	1.000				NFL Champions
1930	Green Bay	NFL	10	3	1	.769				NFL Champions
1931	Green Bay	NFL	12	2	0	.857				NFL Champions
1932	Green Bay	NFL	10	3	1	.769				
1933	Green Bay	NFL	5	7	1	.417				
1934	Green Bay	NFL	7	6	0	.538				
1935	Green Bay	NFL	8	4	0	.667				
1936	Green Bay	NFL	10	1	1	.909	1	0	1.000	NFL Champions
1937	Green Bay	NFL	7	4	0	.636				
1938	Green Bay	NFL	8	3	0	.727	0	1	.000	
1939	Green Bay	NFL	9	2	0	.818	1	0	1.000	NFL Champions
1940	Green Bay	NFL	6	4	1	.600				
1941	Green Bay	NFL	10	1	0	.909	0	1	.000	
1942	Green Bay	NFL	8	2	1	.800				
1943	Green Bay	NFL	7	2	1	.778				
1944	Green Bay	NFL	8	2	0	.800	1	0	1.000	NFL Champions
1945	Green Bay	NFL	6	4	0	.600				
1946	Green Bay	NFL	6	5	0	.545				
1947	Green Bay	NFL	6	5	1	.545				
1948	Green Bay	NFL	3	9	0	.250				
1949	Green Bay	NFL	2	10	0	.167				
1950	Chicago	NFL	5	7	0	.417				
1951	Chicago	NFL	2	8	0	.200				
1952	Washington	NFL	4	8	0	.333				
1953	Washington	NFL	6	5	1	.545				
	Green Bay		209	104	21	.668	3	2	.600	
	Chicago		7	15	0	.318	0	0		
	Washington		10	13	1	.435	0	0		
	TOTALS		226	132	22	.631	3	2	.600	

Sources: Pro Football Hall of Fame; Pro-Football-Reference.com

Lambert, John Harold "Jack" (born: July 8, 1952 in Mantua, Ohio); inducted into the Pro Football Hall of Fame in 1990 as a player; Position: Middle Linebacker; won four Super Bowls.

After playing quarterback at Crestwood High School (Mantua), Lambert attended Kent State University (Ohio), where he was a two-time All-Mid America Conference linebacker. He was a second-round draft pick (46th overall selection) of the National Football League's Pittsburgh Steelers in 1974; became a starter as a rookie; and played with the team his entire 11-year NFL career (1974–1984, 146 games).

The 6'4", 220-pound linebacker was selected the 1974 Defensive Rookie of the Year; 1976 Defensive Player of Year; played in nine straight Pro Bowls (1976–1984); selected to both the NFL 1970s and 1980s All-Decade Teams, and the 75th Anniversary All-Time Team; and won four Super Bowls (SB IX in 1975, SB X in 1976, SB XIII in 1979, and SB XIV in 1980).

The premier linebacker of his era, Lambert was the youngest starter on the Pittsburgh defensive unit, and was part of the team's defensive "Steel Curtain." He was the team's defensive captain for eight years, and his interception late in the fourth quarter preserved Pittsburgh's fourth NFL title win in Super Bowl XIV.

Jack Lambert's Career Statistics

DEFENSE

YEAR	TEAM	G	INT	YDS	AVG	TD	FUMREC	YDS
1974	Pittsburgh	14	2	19	9.5	0	1	11
1975	Pittsburgh	14	2	35	17.5	0	1	21
1976	Pittsburgh	14	2	32	16.0	0	8	36
1977	Pittsburgh	11	1	5	5.0	0	0	0
1978	Pittsburgh	16	4	41	10.3	0	2	0
1979	Pittsburgh	16	6	29	4.8	0	0	0
1980	Pittsburgh	14	2	1	0.5	0	0	0
1981	Pittsburgh	16	6	76	12.7	0	2	38
1982	Pittsburgh	8	1	6	6.0	0	1	1
1983	Pittsburgh	15	2	–1	–0.5	0	2	0
1984	Pittsburgh	8	0	0	0.0	0	0	0
	TOTALS	146	28	243	8.7	0	17	107

Sources: Pro Football Hall of Fame; Pro-Football-Reference.com

Lambert, Ward Lewis "Piggy" (born: May 28, 1888 in Deadwood, South Dakota; died: January 20, 1958 in Lafayette, Indiana); inducted into the Naismith Memorial Basketball Hall of Fame in 1960 as a coach; won the 1932 national championship; served as commissioner of the National Professional Basketball League.

After attending Crawfordsville (Indiana) High School, where he played baseball and basketball, Lambert went on to Wabash College (Crawfordsville, Indiana), graduating in 1911. While only 5'6", he led the basketball team in scoring his sophomore year and was called "Piggy," for his tendency to hog the ball.

He began his coaching career at Lebanon (Indiana) High School (1913–1916), before joining the college ranks as the long-time head coach at Purdue University (West Lafayette, Indiana, 1916–1917, 1918–1946), where his tenure was interrupted for one year (1917–1918) while he served in the U.S. Army during World War I. At Purdue, he compiled a 371–152 (.709) record in 29 seasons; led the Boilermakers to win or share 11 Big Ten titles; and won the 1932 national championship (as determined by a panel vote rather than a National Collegiate Athletic Association tournament, which did not begin until 1939).

Lambert has been inducted into the Helms Foundation Hall of Fame and the Indiana Hall of Fame; served as commissioner of the National Professional Basketball League (1946–1949); chairman of the National Basketball Coaches Association Rules Committee for two years; a member of the Board of Directors of the National Basketball Coaches Association for two years; and wrote *Practical Basketball*, which is considered one of the game's earliest books.

After his coaching career, Lambert served as the athletic director at Richmond (Indiana) High School, as well as coaching football and track. He later went into high school administration and eventually became school superintendent.

He was inducted into the Indiana Basketball Hall of Fame in 1962.

Ward Lambert's Coaching Record

SEASON	TEAM	W	L	WIN%
1916–1917	Purdue	11	3	.786
1918–1919	Purdue	6	8	.429
1919–1920	Purdue	16	4	.800
1920–1921	Purdue	13	7	.650
1921–1922	Purdue	15	3	.833
1922–1923	Purdue	9	6	.600
1923–1924	Purdue	12	5	.706
1924–1925	Purdue	9	5	.643
1925–1926	Purdue	13	4	.765
1926–1927	Purdue	12	5	.706
1927–1928	Purdue	15	2	.882
1928–1929	Purdue	13	4	.765
1929–1930	Purdue	13	2	.867
1930–1931	Purdue	12	5	.706
1931–1932	Purdue	17	1	.944
1932–1933	Purdue	11	7	.611
1933–1934	Purdue	17	3	.850

SEASON	TEAM	W	L	WIN%
1934–1935	Purdue	17	3	.850
1935–1936	Purdue	16	4	.800
1936–1937	Purdue	15	5	.750
1937–1938	Purdue	18	2	.900
1938–1939	Purdue	12	7	.632
1939–1940	Purdue	16	4	.800
1940–1941	Purdue	13	7	.650
1941–1942	Purdue	14	7	.667
1942–1943	Purdue	9	11	.450
1943–1944	Purdue	11	10	.524
1944–1945	Purdue	9	11	.450
1945–1946	Purdue	7	7	.500
	TOTALS	371	152	.709

Source: Naismith Memorial Basketball Hall of Fame

Lamm, Kurt (born: March 10, 1919 in Salmuenster, Germany; died: January 7, 1987 in Brooklyn, New York); inducted into the National Soccer Hall of Fame and Museum in 1979 as a builder; won a U.S. Amateur Cup title as a player; served as president of the American Soccer League.

Lamm played soccer as a boy in Germany and came to the United States in 1936, where he played for the Prospect Unity Club. Later, after playing for the New York Americans, he joined Eintract (German-American League) in 1944, and won a U.S. Amateur Cup medal when the team beat Morgan Strassers. He returned to Prospect Unity in 1946 as a player-manager, and in 1952, he ended his playing career.

In 1947, Lamm became secretary of New York Hakoah, and he was with the team when it won three straight American Soccer League championships (1957–1959). He was twice named ASL Manager of the Year (1958, 1963) and coached numerous ASL All-Star teams.

In 1959, he became vice president of the ASL, and in 1963, was named its president, a job he held for five years. Lamm also served as executive secretary of the United States Soccer Football Association from 1971 to 1987.

Source: National Soccer Hall of Fame and Museum

Lamoriello, Louis "Lou" (born: October 21, 1942 in Providence, Rhode Island); inducted into the Hockey Hall of Fame as a builder in 2009; had an overall 53–34–14–5 (.642) coaching record.

Lamoriello has been with the National Hockey League's New Jersey Devils since 1987 and currently serves as the Chief Executive Officer, President, and General Manager of the team, longer than any other current general manager in the league with a single franchise. Before joining the Devils, he was a math teacher at Johnston (Rhode Island) High School and the athletic director and men's ice hockey coach at Providence College (Rhode Island).

He coached Providence College's ice hockey team from 1968 to 1987, and was named the school's athletic director in 1982. In April 1987, after then-Devils owner John McMullen named Lamoriello president of the team, he named himself general manager although he never played, coached or managed in the NHL and was unknown outside the American college hockey community.

He oversaw one of the most successful rebuilding projects of a team in North American professional sports history and in his first season as general manager, the Devils had the franchise's first-ever winning season (dating back to the team's history as the Kansas City Scouts (1974–1976) and the Colorado Rockies (1976–1982)) and reached the Wales Conference Finals. The team made the playoffs in 18 of his 20 seasons as general manager and appeared in the Stanley Cup finals four times (winning in 1995, 2000, 2003 while losing in 2001).

In 2000, Lamoriello was named the team's chairman and CEO, as well as vice-chairman and CEO of the then co-owned New Jersey Nets (National Basketball Association). In 2004, he relinquished his chairmanship of the Devils and resigned from all titles of the Nets when Jeffrey Vanderbeek bought the Devils.

In 1992, he received the Lester Patrick Trophy for his outstanding service to hockey in the United States, and in 1998, he served as the general manager of Team USA in the 1998 Winter Olympics (Nagano, Japan), leading the team to a sixth-place finish.

Lamoriello served as the interim Devils head coach starting in December 2005 when Larry Robinson suddenly resigned, and took the team to the Eastern Conference semi-finals before losing to the Carolina Hurricanes in five games.

On April 2, 2007, Lamoriello once again took over as interim head coach after he fired Claude Julien with three games left in the season. His two-time coaching record was 53–34–14–5 (.642).

The Lamoriello Trophy has been awarded annually (since 1988) to the champion of the Hockey East Men's Ice Hockey Tournament and is named in his honor of being the first-ever commissioner of Hockey East (serving from 1983 to 1987).

At Providence College he was the captain of both the hockey and baseball teams, and upon graduation, he remained at the college as an assistant coach of the men's hockey and baseball teams. Four years later, he was named head coach of the hockey team and served until 1987. Beginning in 1982, he was also the school's athletic director.

Lamoriello was inducted into the Providence College Athletic Hall of Fame in 1982, the New Jersey Sports Hall of Fame in 2002, the Rhode Island Heritage Hall of Fame in 2004, the LaSalle Academy Hall of Fame in 2004, and the Cape Cod Baseball League Hall of Fame in 2009.

Source: Hockey Hall of Fame

Landis, Kenesaw Mountain (born: November 20, 1866 in Millville, Ohio; died: November 25, 1944 in Chicago, Illinois); inducted into the National Baseball Hall of Fame and Museum in 1944 as an pioneer-executive by the Veterans Committee; baseball's first commissioner.

A high school drop-out, Landis became an attorney, a United States District Court Judge (1905–1922) and, eventually, the first commissioner of Major League Baseball (1921–1944).

While he cannot be given total credit for saving major league baseball after the infamous 1919 "Black Sox" World Series scandal, he definitely restored the credibility of the game, revived fan interest, and brought legitimacy to a business that had no oversight.

Landis enrolled in the Young Men's Christian Association Law School of Cincinnati (Ohio), and in 1891, he obtained his degree from Chicago's Union Law School (now part of Northwestern University, Evanston/Chicago, Illinois). He worked for the U.S. State Department until being appointed to the federal bench by President Theodore Roosevelt in 1905.

After the 1919 World Series scandal, baseball owners approached Landis about being the game's first commissioner, a job he accepted after being given absolute authority over all aspects of the game. He was elected by the owners on November 12, 1920, and one of his first acts as commissioner was to ban for life from baseball the eight Chicago White Sox players who had conspired to throw the 1919 World Series against the Cincinnati Reds for money. Throughout his tenure, he became known for releasing hundreds of minor league players from contracts he thought were unfair.

He was named for the Kennesaw Mountains in Georgia, where his father, a physician, had fought on the Union side in the American Civil War. The reason for the misspelling of his name is not exactly clear, but is thought to be a simple mistake made on his birth certificate.

Although involved with several high-profile trials during his career, Landis came to the attention of major league baseball in 1915, when he delayed making a decision on the Federal League's antitrust suit against Major League Baseball. He used the ploy to give both sides time to reach a negotiated settlement, in effect avoiding a legal test of baseball's monopoly status. Since he had ruled in the owners' favor, their general belief was that he could be easily controlled and used to mollify fan mistrust of the game after the World Series scandal. However, the owners had misjudged Landis and he went on to rule baseball with absolute authority.

Interestingly, Landis remained an active judge after becoming baseball's commissioner, a position that many felt was not proper. In 1922, under pressure from Congress, he resigned from the bench to focus all his efforts on baseball.

To the surprise of many (especially since Landis had no baseball administrative experience at any level), he became an active commissioner and addressed many of the game's problems, including gambling; on-field fighting among players, managers, and umpires; and widespread player resentment of their contracts. While a primarily positive influence on the game, to his discredit, he also supported baseball's color line, and his actions and decisions had the effect of delaying the integration of organized baseball. Less than one year after his death, the first modern-era black player, Jackie Robinson, was signed to a major league contract by the Brooklyn Dodgers.

Landis was inducted into the baseball hall of fame in 1944, in a special election held one month after his death, and the official name of each league's Most Valuable Player Award is the "Kenesaw Mountain Landis Award."

Source: National Baseball Hall of Fame and Museum

Landry, Thomas Wade "Tom" (born: September 11, 1924 in Mission, Texas; died: February 12, 2000 in Dallas, Texas); inducted into the Pro Football Hall of Fame in 1990 as a coach; won the 1948 Sugar Bowl and 1949 Orange Bowl as a player; won two Super Bowls as a coach.

Landry was named head coach when the Dallas Cowboys started the team's first National Football League season in 1960, and held the job for 29 seasons, until 1988. Upon his retirement, only George Halas, who coached the Chicago Bears for 40 years, surpassed his tenure with one team.

The 6'1", 195-pound Landry compiled an overall 270–178–6 (.595) record; was noted for his impassive sideline behavior; and revived the shotgun offense. He led the Cowboys to the team's first winning season and first NFL Eastern Conference championship in 1966, and never fell below .500 again until 1986. During that span, he had 20 straight winning seasons; won 13 divisional championships; won five National Football Conference titles; and coached in five Super Bowls (winning two [SB VI in 1972 and SB XII in 1978] and losing three [SB V in 1971, SB X in 1976, and SB XIII in 1979]).

Before becoming a coach, Landry was a defensive back and punter for the New York Yankees of the All-America Football Conference (1949) and the New York Giants of the NFL (1950–1955). He served as a Giants player-coach for two seasons (1954–1955) and was the team's defensive coordinator (1956–1959), before becoming the Cowboys' first coach. Landry ended his playing career with 32 interceptions in only 80 games.

He set an NFL record with 20 consecutive winning seasons (1966–1985); named NFL Coach of the Year twice (1966, 1975); developed the 4-3 defense; and popularized situational substitutions.

He attended the University of Texas (Austin), but his education was interrupted after one semester, when he served in the U.S. Army Air Forces during World War II. After the war, he returned to the university and played fullback and defensive back for the Texas Longhorns, and helped the team win the 1948 Sugar Bowl and the 1949 Orange Bowl, before joining the AAFC's Yankees.

Landry was inducted into the Cowboys "Ring of Honor" at Texas Stadium in 1993.

Tom Landry's NFL Playing Statistics

			INTERCEPTIONS				FUM REC			PUNTING		
YEAR	**TEAM**	**G**	**NO**	**YDS**	**AVG**	**TD**	**NO**	**YDS**	**TD**	**NO**	**YDS**	**AVG**
1950	New York	12	2	0	0.0	0	2	41	1	58	2,136	36.8
1951	New York	10	8	121	15.1	2	1	9	1	15	638	42.5
1952	New York	12	8	99	12.4	1	3	3	0	82	3,363	41.0
1953	New York	12	3	55	18.3	0	1	0	0	44	1,772	40.3
1954	New York	12	8	71	8.9	0	2	14	0	64	2,720	42.5
1955	New York	12	2	14	7.0	0	1	0	0	75	3,022	40.3
	TOTALS	70	31	360	11.6	3	10	67	2	338	13,651	40.4

Tom Landry's Coaching Record

			REGULAR SEASON				PLAYOFFS			
YEAR	**TEAM**	**LG**	**W**	**L**	**T**	**WIN%**	**W**	**L**	**WIN%**	**NOTES**
1960	Dallas	NFL	0	11	1	.000				
1961	Dallas	NFL	4	9	1	.308				
1962	Dallas	NFL	5	8	1	.385				
1963	Dallas	NFL	4	10	0	.286				
1964	Dallas	NFL	5	8	1	.385				
1965	Dallas	NFL	7	7	0	.500				
1966	Dallas	NFL	10	3	1	.769	0	1	.000	
1967	Dallas	NFL	9	5	0	.643	1	1	.500	
1968	Dallas	NFL	12	2	0	.857	0	1	.000	
1969	Dallas	NFL	11	2	1	.846	0	1	.000	
1970	Dallas	NFL	10	4	0	.714	2	1	.667	NFC Champions
1971	Dallas	NFL	11	3	0	.786	3	0	1.000	Super Bowl Champions
1972	Dallas	NFL	10	4	0	.714	1	1	.500	
1973	Dallas	NFL	10	4	0	.714	1	1	.500	
1974	Dallas	NFL	8	6	0	.571				
1975	Dallas	NFL	10	4	0	.714	2	1	.667	NFC Champions
1976	Dallas	NFL	11	3	0	.786	0	1	.000	
1977	Dallas	NFL	12	2	0	.857	3	0	1.000	Super Bowl Champions
1978	Dallas	NFL	12	4	0	.750	2	1	.667	NFC Champions

YEAR	TEAM	LG	REGULAR SEASON W	L	T	WIN%	PLAYOFFS W	L	WIN%	NOTES
1979	Dallas	NFL	11	5	0	.688	0	1	.000	
1980	Dallas	NFL	12	4	0	.750	2	1	.667	
1981	Dallas	NFL	12	4	0	.750	1	1	.500	
1982	Dallas	NFL	6	3	0	.667	2	1	.667	
1983	Dallas	NFL	12	4	0	.750	0	1	.000	
1984	Dallas	NFL	9	7	0	.563				
1985	Dallas	NFL	10	6	0	.625	0	1	.000	
1986	Dallas	NFL	7	9	0	.438				
1987	Dallas	NFL	7	8	0	.467				
1988	Dallas	NFL	3	13	0	.188				
	TOTALS		250	162	6	.607	20	16	.556	

Sources: Pro Football Hall of Fame; Pro-Football-Reference.com; *Tom Landry: An Autobiography* (Tom Landry with Gregg Lewis)

Lane, Richard "Dick" "Night Train" (born: April 16, 1928 in Austin, Texas; died: January 29, 2002 in Austin, Texas); inducted into the Pro Football Hall of Fame in 1974 as a player; Position: Cornerback; set the NFL record for most single-season interceptions (14) as a rookie.

After graduating from high school, Lane spent one year at Scottsbluff Junior College (Nebraska, now known as Western Nebraska Community College) before dropping out and spending the next four years serving in the United States Army.

After serving in the military, the 6'1", 200-pound Lane joined the National Football League's Los Angeles Rams in 1952 as a cornerback, and would go on to play 14 years (157 games) for the Rams (1952–1953), Chicago Cardinals (1954–1959), and the Detroit Lions (1960–1965). He set the NFL interception record (14 in 12 games) as a rookie, a record that still stands; named All-NFL six times; named to seven Pro Bowls (1954–1956, 1958, 1960–1962); was a 10-time All-Pro Selection (1954–1963); selected to the NFL 1950s All-Decade Team; named the all-time NFL cornerback in 1969 for the NFL's first 50 years; and named to the NFL 75th Anniversary All-Time Team.

He was given the nickname "Night Train" by his teammates from a popular song of the day.

In 1999, Lane was ranked number 19 on *The Sporting News*' list of the 100 Greatest Football Players, making him the highest-ranked defensive back, the highest-ranked player for the Cardinal franchise, and the second-highest ranked Lion behind Barry Sanders.

In 2001, he was inducted into the Texas Sports Hall of Fame.

Night Train Lane's Career Statistics

YEAR	TEAM	G	INTERCEPTIONS NO	YDS	AVG	TD	FUM REC NO	YDS	TD
1952	Los Angeles	12	14	298	21.3	2	0	0	0
1953	Los Angeles	11	3	9	3.0	0	3	26	1
1954	Chicago	12	10	181	18.1	0	0	0	0
1955	Chicago	12	6	69	11.5	0	0	0	0
1956	Chicago	12	7	206	29.4	1	2	11	0
1957	Chicago	8	2	47	23.5	0	2	5	0
1958	Chicago	12	2	0	0.0	0	0	0	0
1959	Chicago	12	3	125	41.7	1	0	0	0
1960	Detroit	12	5	102	20.4	1	0	0	0
1961	Detroit	14	6	73	12.2	0	0	0	0
1962	Detroit	14	4	16	4.0	0	1	15	0
1963	Detroit	12	5	70	14.0	0	2	0	0
1964	Detroit	7	1	11	11.0	0	0	0	0
1965	Detroit	7	0	0	0.0	0	1	0	0
	TOTALS	157	68	1,207	17.8	5	11	57	1

Sources: Pro Football Hall of Fame; Pro-Football-Reference.com

Lang, Millard T. (born: August 7, 1912 in Baltimore, Maryland; died: August 4, 2002 in Baltimore, Maryland); inducted into the National Soccer Hall of Fame and Museum in 1950 as a player; Position: Forward; won three national soccer championships at Johns Hopkins University; inducted into the U.S. Lacrosse Hall of Fame (1978).

An all-around athlete, Lang began playing soccer at age 13 in the Baltimore Police Athletic League, and attended Baltimore's Polytechnic High School, where he played soccer for three years and captained the team to two championships. He also played lacrosse, basketball, football, tennis, and track and field, and went on to win 12 letters in five sports.

After high school, the 5'10" Lang entered Johns Hopkins University (Baltimore) in 1930, where he played football and lacrosse; was a four-time All-American selection in lacrosse; and was on the undefeated teams (1932–1934) that won three national championships. In 1932, he was a member of the U.S. Lacrosse team at the Olympics (Los Angeles, California) when it was an exhibition sport, and defeated Canada twice.

After graduating from college, he was a member of the Baltimore Canton team when it joined the American Soccer League for the 1934–1935 season. He stayed with the team for two seasons before playing with the Cleveland Graphite Bronze (1936–1937). He then played for the Chicago Sparta team (1937–1940, 1941–1942) that won the 1938 U.S. Open Cup, although he did not play in the final.

For the 1940–1941 season, he left Sparta and joined the Chicago American Eagles, but returned to Sparta after only one season with the team. Back in Baltimore in 1942, he played for the Baltimore Americans and coached the club in the 1944–1945 season.

When he retired as a player, Lang became president of the Maryland and D.C. State Association and president, general manager, and part owner of the Baltimore Rockets of the American Soccer League.

He was inducted into the U.S. Lacrosse Hall of Fame in 1978; the Maryland Soccer Hall of Fame in 1983; the Johns Hopkins Athletic Hall of Fame in 1995; and, in December 1999, *Sports Illustrated* ranked him 44 on its list of 50 all-time great Maryland athletes.

Sources: National Soccer Hall of Fame and Museum; U.S. Lacrosse Hall of Fame

Langer, James John "Jim" (born: May 16, 1948 in Little Falls, Minnesota); inducted into the Pro Football Hall of Fame in 1987 as a player; Position: Center-Guard; Uniform: #62; won two Super Bowls.

The 6'2", 250-pound Langer played middle linebacker at South Dakota State University (Brookings), where he was a 1969 Honorable Mention All-American. After college, he signed with the National Football League's Miami Dolphins and eventually played 12 seasons (151 games) with the Dolphins (1970–1979) and the Minnesota Vikings (1980–1981).

After two seasons with limited playing time, he became a starter and played every offensive down in Miami's undefeated 1972 season. He was selected All-Pro six times (1973–1978) and All-American Football Conference five straight seasons (1973–1977); played in three AFC title games; played in six Pro Bowls (1973–1978); played in three consecutive Super Bowls (winning in SB VII in 1973 and SB VIII in 1974, and losing in SB VI in 1972); and was named to the NFL 1970s All-Decade Team.

The Jim Langer Award is presented annually to the nation's top college Division II lineman.

Source: Pro Football Hall of Fame

Langway, Rod Corry (born: May 3, 1957 in Taipei, Taiwan); inducted into the Hockey Hall of Fame in 2002 as a player; Position: Defenseman; Uniform: #5; only NHL player born in Taiwan; appeared in two NCAA tournaments in the same year (football and hockey); won the 1979 Stanley Cup championship; first American to win the James Norris Memorial Trophy.

The 6'3", 218-pound Langway played 15 National Hockey League seasons for the Montreal Canadiens (1978–1982) and the Washington Capitals (1982–1993).

He first played organized hockey at Randolph (Massachusetts) High School, where he was a three-sport athlete (hockey, baseball, football). During his high school years, he led the hockey team to the state championship twice (1973, 1975); was the school's baseball catcher; and was quarterback of the school's football team.

After high school, Langway attended the University of New Hampshire (Durham), where he played football and hockey. As a sophomore (1977), he appeared in two National Collegiate Athletic Association tournaments in the same year (football and hockey). He played linebacker for the football team that reached the NCAA Division II quarterfinals, and led the hockey team to the semifinals, before losing to the eventual champion, the University of Wisconsin.

Leaving college, he was drafted by two hockey teams in 1977: as a third-round pick (36th overall selection) of the Canadiens and as a first-round selection (sixth overall pick) of the Birmingham Bulls of the World Hockey Association.

He signed with the Bulls and split his time between Birmingham and its minor league affiliate, the Hampton Gulls (American Hockey League). After only one season, he left the WHA and joined the Canadiens in 1978.

After playing briefly with Montreal's minor league affiliate (Nova Scotia Voyageurs of the American Hockey League), Langway played for the Canadiens as the team won its fourth consecutive Stanley Cup title in 1979, the only championship he would win in his career. In 1982, he was traded to Washington, where he became the team's captain and led the team into the playoffs.

Langway was named to three All-Star teams (First All-Star Team Defense in 1983 and 1984, and Second All-Star Team Defense in 1985) and won the James Norris Memorial Trophy twice (1983–1984) as the NHL's top defenseman, the first American to win the award. He was captain of Team USA four times (1981, 1984, and 1987 Canada Cups, and the 1982 Pool "A" World Championship), but never had championship success at the international level.

After retiring from the NHL in 1993, he served as a player and/or coach for several minor league teams.

In 1997, the Capitals retired his jersey number five; in 1999, he was inducted into the United States Hockey Hall of Fame; and in 2001, he was inducted into the Massachusetts Hockey Hall of Fame.

Rod Langway's Career Statistics

			REGULAR SEASON						PLAYOFFS				
SEASON	**TEAM**	**LEAGUE**	**GP**	**G**	**A**	**TP**	**PIM**	**+/-**	**GP**	**G**	**A**	**TP**	**PIM**
1972–1973	Randolph Rockets	High-MA	16	20	19	39							
1973–1975	Randolph Rockets	High-MA											
1975–1976	U. of New Hampshire	ECAC	31	3	13	16	10						
1976–1977	U. of New Hampshire	ECAC	34	10	43	53	52						
1977–1978	Birmingham Bulls	WHA	52	3	18	21	52		4	0	0	0	9
1977–1978	Hampton Gulls	AHL	30	6	16	22	50						
1978–1979	Montreal Canadiens	NHL	45	3	4	7	30	+5	8	0	0	0	16
1978–1979	Nova Scotia Voyageurs	AHL	18	6	13	19	29						
1979–1980	Montreal Canadiens	NHL	77	7	29	36	81	+36	10	3	3	6	2
1980–1981	Montreal Canadiens	NHL	80	11	34	45	120	+53	3	0	0	0	6
1981–1982	United States	Can-Cup	6	0	1	1	8						
1981–1982	Montreal Canadiens	NHL	66	5	34	39	116	+66	5	0	3	3	18
1981–1982	United States	WEC-A	6	0	2	2	4						
1982–1983	Washington Capitals	NHL	80	3	29	32	75	0	4	0	0	0	0
1983–1984	Washington Capitals	NHL	80	9	24	33	61	+14	8	0	5	5	7
1984–1985	United States	Can-Cup	6	1	1	2	8						
1984–1985	Washington Capitals	NHL	79	4	22	26	54	+35	5	0	1	1	6
1985–1986	Washington Capitals	NHL	71	1	17	18	61	+27	9	1	2	3	6
1986–1987	Washington Capitals	NHL	78	2	25	27	53	+11	7	0	1	1	2
1986–1987	NHL All-Stars	RV-87	2	0	0	0	0						
1987–1988	United States	Can-Cup	5	0	1	1	6						
1987–1988	Washington Capitals	NHL	63	3	13	16	28	+1	6	0	0	0	8
1988–1989	Washington Capitals	NHL	76	2	19	21	65	+12	6	0	0	0	6
1989–1990	Washington Capitals	Fr-Tour	4	0	0	0	2						
1989–1990	Washington Capitals	NHL	58	0	8	8	39	+7	15	1	4	5	12
1990–1991	Washington Capitals	NHL	56	1	7	8	24	+12	11	0	2	2	6
1991–1992	Washington Capitals	NHL	64	0	13	13	22	+11	7	0	1	1	2
1992–1993	Washington Capitals	NHL	21	0	0	0	20	-13					
1993–1994	Richmond Renegades	ECHL											
1994–1995	Richmond Renegades	ECHL	6	0	0	0	2		9	1	1	2	4
1995–1996	San Francisco Spiders	IHL	46	1	5	6	38						
1996–1997	Richmond Renegades	ECHL											
1997–1998	Providence Bruins	AHL	10	0	1	1	10						
1998–2000	Richmond Renegades	ECHL											
	NHL TOTALS		994	51	278	329	849		104	5	22	27	97

Sources: Hockey Hall of Fame; Hockey-Reference.com

Lanier, Robert Jerry, Jr. "Bob" (born: September 10, 1948 in Buffalo, New York); inducted into the Naismith Memorial Basketball Hall of Fame in 1992 as a player; Position: Center; Uniform: #16; his jersey numbers have been retired at all levels of play (high school, college, professional).

During his 14-year National Basketball Association career with the Detroit Pistons (1970–1979) and Milwaukee Bucks (1980–1984), Lanier was named to the NBA All-Rookie Team (1971); was an eight-time All-Star (1972–1975, 1977–1979, 1982); Most Valuable Player of the 1974 All-Star Game; and compiled 19,248 points (20.1 per game) and 9,698 rebounds (10.1 per game), still ranking among the top 20 in NBA records as of this writing.

He attended Bennett High School (Buffalo, 1962–1966), where he was a two-year letter winner; selected All-Conference and All-City twice (1965–1966); and his jersey number 12 was retired by the school.

After high school, Lanier moved on to St. Bonaventure University (New York, 1966–1970), where he was a four-year letter winner; led the school to the National Collegiate Athletic Association Final Four in 1970; was a three-time Converse All-American selection (1968–1970); named *The Sporting News* First Team All-American (1970); National Association of Basketball Coaches First Team All-American (1970); *Coach & Athlete* magazine Player of the Year (1970); Eastern College Athletic Conference Player of the Year (1970); named to the ECAC All-Decade Team (1970–1979); a two-time ECAC All-Star; and NABC Second Team All-American (1968).

He left the school as St. Bonaventure's all-time scoring leader (2,067 points, currently ranked third); all-time scoring average leader (27.5 per game); all-time rebounding leader (1,180); all-time rebounding average leader (15.7 per game); career field goal percentage leader (57 percent); single-season rebounding leader (416, 16.2 per game in 1970); single-game scoring leader (51 points against Seton Hall on February 24, 1969); single-game rebounding leader (27 against Loyola of Maryland on December 22, 1967); and had his jersey number 31 retired by the school in 1970.

After graduation, the 6'11", 265-pound Lanier was the number one overall pick in the 1970 NBA Draft by the Pistons. He averaged more than 20 points per game in eight of his first nine professional seasons, and in his five years with the Bucks, the team won the division championship each season.

He won the J. Walter Kennedy Citizenship Award in 1978 for outstanding service and dedication to the community; the Oscar Robertson Leadership Award in 1984; served as president of the NBA Players Association (1980–1984); won the Jackie Robinson Award for service to youth, good citizenship, and leadership in 1981; chairman of the NBA Stay in School Program; and was inducted into the Michigan Sports Hall of Fame in 1990.

After retiring as a player, Lanier was an assistant coach with the NBA's Golden State Warriors (1994–1995) and was the team's head coach for 37 games in 1995, compiling a 12–25 (.324) record. When his jersey number 16 was retired by both the Pistons and the Bucks, it completed a streak of his jersey numbers being retired at all levels of play (high school, college, and professional). During his career, he had the largest feet of any player, requiring a size 22 shoe. To this day at the Naismith Memorial Basketball Hall of Fame, visitors are able to compare the size of their foot to that of Lanier's.

Bob Lanier's Career Statistics

SEASON	TEAM	LG	G	MIN	FG	FT	TRB	AST	PTS
1970–1971	Detroit	NBA	82	2,017	504	273	665	146	1,281
1971–1972	Detroit	NBA	80	3,092	834	388	1,132	248	2,056
1972–1973	Detroit	NBA	81	3,150	810	307	1,205	260	1,927
1973–1974	Detroit	NBA	81	3,047	748	326	1,074	343	1,822
1974–1975	Detroit	NBA	76	2,987	731	361	914	350	1,823
1975–1976	Detroit	NBA	64	2,363	541	284	746	217	1,366
1976–1977	Detroit	NBA	64	2,446	678	260	745	214	1,616
1977–1978	Detroit	NBA	63	2,311	622	298	715	216	1,542
1978–1979	Detroit	NBA	53	1,835	489	275	494	140	1,253
1979–1980	Detroit	NBA	37	1,392	319	164	373	122	802
1979–1980	Milwaukee	NBA	26	739	147	113	179	62	408
1980–1981	Milwaukee	NBA	67	1,753	376	208	413	179	961
1981–1982	Milwaukee	NBA	74	1,986	407	182	388	219	996
1982–1983	Milwaukee	NBA	39	978	163	91	200	105	417
1983–1984	Milwaukee	NBA	72	2,007	392	194	455	186	978
	TOTALS	NBA	959	32,103	7,761	3,724	9,698	3,007	19,248

Sources: Basketball-Reference.com; Naismith Memorial Basketball Hall of Fame

Lanier, Willie Edward (born: August 21, 1945 in Clover, Virginia); inducted into the Pro Football Hall of Fame in 1986 as a player; Position: Middle Linebacker; Uniform: #63; first African-American player to star at middle linebacker; a two-time Small College All-American; won Super Bowl IV.

Playing his entire 11-year National Football League career (1967–1977, 149 games) with the Kansas City Chiefs, Lanier was the first African-American to star at middle linebacker, and was the team's number two pick (50th overall selection) in the 1967 NFL Draft.

He helped the Chiefs win Super Bowl IV (1970); selected All American Football League/American Football Conference eight times (1968–1975); elected to the last two AFL All-Star games (1968–1969); played in the first six AFC-National Football Conference Pro Bowls; 1971 Pro Bowl Most Valuable Player; named to the NFL 75th Anniversary All-Time Team; and his uniform number 63 was retired by the Chiefs.

With the exception of his first and last years in the NFL, the 6'1", 245-pound Lanier intercepted at least two passes every season.

After graduating from Maggie L. Walker High School (Richmond, Virginia), he went to Morgan State University (Baltimore, Maryland, 1963–1966), where he was a two-time Small College All-American as a junior and senior; selected Most Valuable Player of the 1966 Tangerine Bowl; and was inducted into the College Football Hall of Fame in 2000.

Willie Lanier's Career Statistics

			DEFENSE					
YEAR	TEAM	G	INT	YDS	AVG	TD	FUM REC	YDS
1967	Kansas City	10	0	0	0.0	0	1	0
1968	Kansas City	14	4	120	30.0	1	0	0
1969	Kansas City	14	4	70	17.5	0	1	5
1970	Kansas City	14	2	2	1.0	0	2	0
1971	Kansas City	14	2	38	19.0	0	3	3
1972	Kansas City	13	2	2	1.0	0	2	0
1973	Kansas City	14	3	47	15.7	1	3	10
1974	Kansas City	14	2	28	14.0	0	2	3
1975	Kansas City	14	5	105	21.0	0	0	0
1976	Kansas City	14	3	28	9.3	0	2	0
1977	Kansas City	14	0	0	0.0	0	2	0
	TOTALS	149	27	440	16.3	2	18	21

Sources: Pro Football Hall of Fame; Pro-Football-Reference.com

Lapchick, Joseph Bohomiel "Joe" (born: April 12, 1900 in Yonkers, New York; died: August 10, 1970 in New York, New York); inducted into the Naismith Memorial Basketball Hall of Fame in 1966 as a player; Position: Center; won two world professional titles; coached St. John's University to four NIT championships; won the first-ever NBA All-Star Game.

With very little high school or college experience, Lapchick played professional basketball with the Holyoke Reds (Interstate League, 1921–1922); Schenectady Dorpians (New York League, 1920–1922); Troy Trojans (New York League, 1921–1923); Brooklyn Visitations (Metropolitan League, 1921–1923); Original Celtics (Eastern League/Independent League/National League/American Basketball League, 1923–1928, 1931–1932, 1934–1937); Toledo Red Men Tobaccos (American Basketball League, 1930–1931); and the Cleveland Rosenblums (ABL, 1928–1931).

The 6'5", 200-pound center won two world professional titles with the Cleveland Rosenblums (1929–1930) and coached the team for two seasons (1930–1931).

After retiring as a player, Lapchick became the long-time basketball head coach at St. John's University (Queens, New York) for two stints, 1936–1947 and 1957–1965. His college coaching career was interrupted from 1947 to 1956 as he coached the Basketball Association of America/National Basketball Association New York Knicks.

With St. John's, he compiled an overall 334–130 (.720) record; led the school to 12 National Invitation Tournaments and one National Collegiate Athletic Association Tournament; coached the team to four NIT championships (1943–1944, 1959, 1965); led St. John's to the first Eastern College Athletic Conference Holiday Festival title in 1958; and compiled five 20-win seasons.

While coaching the Knicks, Lapchick compiled a 326–247 (.569) record; coached the team to nine consecutive winning seasons; led the team to the Eastern Division title twice (1953–1954) and to three straight NBA Finals (1951–1953), but was unable to win a title; and coached the East All-Stars to a win in the first-ever NBA All-Star Game (March 2, 1951).

Joe Lapchick's NBA Coaching Record

			REGULAR SEASON			PLAYOFFS		
SEASON	**LG**	**TEAM**	**W**	**L**	**WIN%**	**W**	**L**	**WIN%**
1947–1948	BAA	New York	26	22	.542	1	2	.333
1948–1949	BAA	New York	32	28	.533	3	3	.500
1949–1950	NBA	New York	40	28	.588	3	2	.600
1950–1951	NBA	New York	36	30	.545	8	6	.571
1951–1952	NBA	New York	37	29	.561	8	6	.571
1952–1953	NBA	New York	47	23	.671	6	5	.545
1953–1954	NBA	New York	44	28	.611	0	4	.000
1954–1955	NBA	New York	38	34	.528	1	2	.333
1955–1956	NBA	New York	26	25	.510			
	BAA		58	50	.537	4	5	.444
	NBA		268	197	.576	26	25	.510
		TOTALS	326	247	.569	30	30	.500

Sources: Basketball-Reference.com; Naismith Memorial Basketball Hall of Fame

Laperriere, Joseph Hughes "Jacques" (born: November 22, 1941 in Rouyn-Noranda, Quebec, Canada); inducted into the Hockey Hall of Fame in 1987 as a player; Position: Defenseman; won six Stanley Cup championships as a player and two as an assistant coach.

After playing junior hockey and in the minor leagues, the 6'2", 180-pound Laperriere went on to play his entire 12-year National Hockey League career (1962–1974) with the Montreal Canadiens. He joined the team full-time in 1963, and as a rookie, scored 30 points; was selected to the NHL Second All-Star Team; and won the Calder Trophy as NHL Rookie of the Year. Although his numbers do not immediately impress the casual observer (he never scored more than seven goals in any season), he was a steady player and an integral member of the team that won six Stanley Cup championships (1965–1966, 1968–1969, 1971, 1973).

In 1966, he won the James Norris Memorial Trophy as the NHL's top defenseman; was selected to the First All-Star team twice (1965–1966); and to the Second All-Star team again in 1970.

After retiring as a player 42 games into the 1973–1974 season, Laperriere served as coach of the Montreal Junior Canadiens (Quebec Major Junior Hockey League) for the 1975–1976 season, resigning midway through the following season.

In 1980–1981, he returned to the Canadiens as an assistant, and the following season, he began his 16-year tenure as the team's assistant coach. He served under six different head coaches and won two more Stanley Cup titles (in 1986 with Jean Perron and in 1993 with Jacques Demers).

Jacques Laperriere's Career Statistics

			REGULAR SEASON					PLAYOFFS				
SEASON	**TEAM**	**LEAGUE**	**GP**	**G**	**A**	**TP**	**PIM**	**GP**	**G**	**A**	**TP**	**PIM**
1958–1959	Hull-Ottawa Canadiens	Exhib.										
1958–1959	Hull-Ottawa Canadiens	EOHL	1	1	1	2	2	2	0	0	0	0
1958–1959	Hull-Ottawa Canadiens	M-Cup	9	1	0	1	16					
1959–1960	Brockville Jr. Canadiens	OVJHL										
1959–1960	Hull-Ottawa Canadiens	EPHL	5	0	2	2	0					
1959–1960	Brockville Jr. Canadiens	M-Cup	13	0	13	13	34					
1960–1961	Hull Canadiens	IPSHL		11	29	40						
1960–1961	Hull-Ottawa Canadiens	EPHL	5	0	0	0	2	3	0	2	2	4
1960–1961	Hull Canadiens	Al-Cup	3	0	0	0	4					
1961–1962	Montreal Jr. Canadiens	OHA-Jr.	48	20	37	57	98	6	0	1	1	11
1961–1962	Hull-Ottawa Canadiens	EPHL	1	0	0	0	4	7	1	4	5	6
1962–1963	Montreal Canadiens	NHL	6	0	2	2	2	5	0	1	1	4
1962–1963	Hull-Ottawa Canadiens	EPHL	40	8	19	27	51	2	0	0	0	0
1963–1964	Montreal Canadiens	NHL	65	2	28	30	102	7	1	1	2	8
1964–1965	Montreal Canadiens	NHL	67	5	22	27	92	6	1	1	2	16
1965–1966	Montreal Canadiens	NHL	57	6	25	31	85					
1966–1967	Montreal Canadiens	NHL	61	0	20	20	48	9	0	1	1	9
1967–1968	Montreal Canadiens	NHL	72	4	21	25	84	13	1	3	4	20
1968–1969	Montreal Canadiens	NHL	69	5	26	31	45	14	1	3	4	28

SEASON	TEAM	LEAGUE	REGULAR SEASON GP	G	A	TP	PIM	PLAYOFFS GP	G	A	TP	PIM
1969–1970	Montreal Canadiens	NHL	73	6	31	37	98					
1970–1971	Montreal Canadiens	NHL	49	0	16	16	20	20	4	9	13	12
1971–1972	Montreal Canadiens	NHL	73	3	25	28	50	4	0	0	0	2
1972–1973	Montreal Canadiens	NHL	57	7	16	23	34	10	1	3	4	2
1973–1974	Montreal Canadiens	NHL	42	2	10	12	14					
1975–1977	Montreal Juniors	QMJHL										
1980–1997	Montreal Canadiens	NHLMGNT										
1997–2000	Boston Bruins	NHLMGNT										
	NHL TOTALS		691	40	242	282	674	88	9	22	31	101

Sources: Hockey Hall of Fame; Hockey-Reference.com

Lapointe, Guy Gerard (born: March 18, 1948 in Montreal, Quebec, Canada); inducted into the Hockey Hall of Fame in 1993 as a player; Position: Defenseman; won six Stanley Cup championships.

During his 16-year National Hockey League career, the 6', 185-pound Lapointe played for the Montreal Canadiens (1968–1981), St. Louis Blues (1981–1983), and the Boston Bruins (1983–1984), and helped the Canadiens win six Stanley Cup championships (1971, 1973, 1976–1979).

After playing junior hockey, Lapointe became a professional in 1968 with the Houston Apollos (Central Hockey League), before moving on to the Montreal Voyageurs of the American Hockey League the following year.

He played in the 1972 Summit Series against the Soviet team; for Canada in the 1976 Canada Cup; in the 1979 Challenge Cup against the Soviets; and was selected to the First All-Star Team Defense once (1973) and to the Second All-Star Team Defense three straight years (1975–1977).

In 1982, he was traded to St. Louis, where he played just over one season, before moving on the Boston, retiring in 1984.

After retiring as a player, Lapointe became general manager of the Longueuil Chevaliers (Quebec Major Junior Hockey League); later an assistant coach with the NHL's Quebec Nordiques; and a scout with the NHL's Calgary Flames.

Guy Lapointe's Career Statistics

SEASON	TEAM	LEAGUE	REGULAR SEASON GP	G	A	TP	PIM	+/-	PLAYOFFS GP	G	A	TP	PIM
1965–1966	Verdun Jr. Maple Leafs	QJHL	37	7	13	20	96						
1966–1967	Verdun Jr. Maple Leafs	QJHL							12	1	1	2	14
1967–1968	Montreal Jr. Canadiens	OHA-Jr.	51	11	27	38	147		11	1	6	7	40
1968–1969	Montreal Canadiens	NHL	1	0	0	0	2						
1968–1969	Houston Apollos	CHL	65	3	15	18	120		3	1	0	1	6
1969–1970	Montreal Canadiens	NHL	5	0	0	0	4						
1969–1970	Montreal Voyageurs	AHL	57	8	30	38	92		8	3	5	8	6
1970–1971	Montreal Canadiens	NHL	78	15	29	44	107	+28	20	4	5	9	34
1971–1972	Montreal Canadiens	NHL	69	11	38	49	58	+15	6	0	1	1	0
1972–1973	Canada	Summit-72	7	0	1	1	6						
1972–1973	Montreal Canadiens	NHL	76	19	35	54	117	+51	17	6	7	13	20
1973–1974	Montreal Canadiens	NHL	71	13	40	53	63	+12	6	0	2	2	4
1974–1975	Montreal Canadiens	NHL	80	28	47	75	88	+46	11	6	4	10	4
1975–1976	Montreal Canadiens	NHL	77	21	47	68	78	+64	13	3	3	6	12
1976–1977	Canada	Can-Cup	7	0	4	4	2						
1976–1977	Montreal Canadiens	NHL	77	25	51	76	53	+69	12	3	9	12	4
1977–1978	Montreal Canadiens	NHL	49	13	29	42	19	+46	14	1	6	7	16
1978–1979	Montreal Canadiens	NHL	69	13	42	55	43	+27	10	2	6	8	10
1978–1979	NHL All-Stars	Ch-Cup	1	0	0	0	0						
1979–1980	Montreal Canadiens	NHL	45	6	20	26	29	-2	2	0	0	0	0
1980–1981	Montreal Canadiens	NHL	33	1	9	10	79	-6	1	0	0	0	17
1981–1982	Montreal Canadiens	NHL	47	1	19	20	72	-3					
1981–1982	St. Louis Blues	NHL	8	0	6	6	4	-3	7	1	0	1	8
1982–1983	St. Louis Blues	NHL	54	3	23	26	43	-12	4	0	1	1	9
1983–1984	Boston Bruins	NHL	45	2	16	18	34	-3					
1984–1985	Quebec Nordiques	NHLMGNT											
1985–1987	Longueuil Chevaliers	QMJHL											
	NHL TOTALS		884	171	451	622	893		123	26	44	70	138

Sources: Hockey Hall of Fame; Hockey-Reference.com

Laprade, Edgar Louis (born: October 10, 1919 in Mine Centre, Ontario, Canada); inducted into the Hockey Hall of Fame in 1993 as a player; Position: Forward-Center; won the Calder Memorial Trophy as NHL Rookie of the Year.

The 5'8", 160-pound Laprade played his entire 10-year National Hockey League career (1945–1955) with the New York Rangers.

During World War II, he played senior hockey in the Thunder Bay Senior Hockey League; led the league in scoring twice (1941–1942); and won the Gerry Trophy as the league's Most Valuable Player twice (1939, 1941). In 1943, he joined the Canadian military and played for the Montreal Royal Canadian Air Force team.

After leaving the military, Laprade joined the Rangers in 1945; won the Calder Memorial Trophy as NHL Rookie of the Year in 1946; and won the Lady Byng Trophy in 1950 for sportsmanship and gentlemanly behavior.

He was inducted into the Northwestern Ontario Sports Hall of Fame twice: in 1982 as a player, and in 1983 as a member of the 1939 Port Arthur Bearcats Allan Cup-winning team.

Edgar Laprade's Career Statistics

			REGULAR SEASON					PLAYOFFS				
SEASON	TEAM	LEAGUE	GP	G	A	TP	PIM	GP	G	A	TP	PIM
1935–1936	Port Arthur Bruins	TBJHL	14	13	10	23	6	4	4	2	6	2
1936–1937	Port Arthur Bruins	TBJHL	18	19	14	33	2	3	6	3	9	5
1937–1938	Port Arthur Bruins	TBJHL	18	23	11	34	9	5	6	0	6	0
1938–1939	Port Arthur Bruins	TBJHL	10	7	4	11						
1938–1939	Port Arthur Bearcats	TBSHL	25	31	9	40	7	6	3	3	6	4
1938–1939	Port Arthur Bearcats	Al-Cup	13	22	4	26	6					
1939–1940	Port Arthur Bearcats	TBSHL	22	20	15	35	8	3	5	1	6	2
1939–1940	Port Arthur Bearcats	Al-Cup	12	13	10	23	6					
1940–1941	Port Arthur Bearcats	TBSHL	20	26	21	47	7	4	2	1	3	0
1941–1942	Port Arthur Bearcats	TBSHL	15	18	23	41	4					
1941–1942	Port Arthur Bearcats	Al-Cup	17	12	21	33	6					
1942–1943	Port Arthur Bearcats	TBSHL	8	7	10	17	0	3	7	4	11	4
1942–1943	Port Arthur Bearcats	Al-Cup	8	6	10	16	2					
1943–1944	Winnipeg Army	WNDHL	6	10	3	13	0					
1944–1945	Barriefield Bears	KCHL		19	28	47	2	4	5	8	13	0
1944–1945	Vimy-Kingston	Exhib.	1	2	5	7						
1945–1946	New York Rangers	NHL	49	15	19	34	0					
1946–1947	New York Rangers	NHL	58	15	25	40	9					
1947–1948	New York Rangers	NHL	59	13	34	47	7	6	1	4	5	0
1948–1949	New York Rangers	NHL	56	18	12	30	12					
1949–1950	New York Rangers	NHL	60	22	22	44	2	12	3	5	8	4
1950–1951	New York Rangers	NHL	42	10	13	23	0					
1951–1952	New York Rangers	NHL	70	9	29	38	8					
1952–1953	New York Rangers	NHL	11	2	1	3	2					
1953–1954	New York Rangers	NHL	35	1	6	7	2					
1954–1955	New York Rangers	NHL	60	3	11	14	0					
	NHL TOTALS		500	108	172	280	42	18	4	9	13	4

Sources: Hockey Hall of Fame; Hockey-Reference.com

Largent, Stephen Michael "Steve" (born: September 28, 1954 in Tulsa, Oklahoma); inducted into the Pro Football Hall of Fame in 1995 as a player; Position: Wide Receiver; Uniform: #80; holds the Seattle Seahawks career record with 819 receptions.

The 5'11", 187-pound Largent was known for his ability to run precise passing patterns. Drafted in the fourth round (117th overall selection), he played his entire 14-year (200 games) National Football League career with the Seattle Seahawks from 1976 to 1989.

Largent caught at least one pass in 177 consecutive games; had 70 or more receptions a season six times; 50 or more catches a year for 10 seasons; led the NFL in receiving yards twice (1979, 1985); selected All-Pro three times (1983, 1985, 1987); and was picked for seven Pro Bowls (1978–1979, 1981, 1984–1987).

He was named to the NFL 1980s All-Decade Team; won the 1988 Walter Payton Man of the Year award; added to the Seahawks Ring of Honor; had his uniform number 80 retired by the team; and holds the Seattle career record with 819 receptions.

After graduating in 1972 from Putnam City High School (Warr Acres, Oklahoma), Largent attended the University of Tulsa (Oklahoma), graduating in 1976.

After retiring from football, Largent entered politics and served in the United States House of Representatives as a Republican, representing the Tulsa area, and was re-elected three times (1994–2002). He resigned his seat in 2002 to run for governor of Oklahoma, but lost in a three-way race. As of this writing, he is Chief Executive Officer of the Cellular Telecommunications & Internet Association, a lobbying organization for the cellular phone industry.

In 1999, he was ranked number 46 on *The Sporting News*' list of the 100 Greatest Football Players, the only Seahawk on the list.

Steve Largent's Career Statistics

				RECEIVING		
YEAR	**TEAM**	**G**	**NO**	**YDS**	**AVG**	**TD**
1976	Seattle	14	54	705	13.1	4
1977	Seattle	14	33	643	19.5	10
1978	Seattle	16	71	1,168	16.5	8
1979	Seattle	15	66	1,237	18.7	9
1980	Seattle	16	66	1,064	16.1	6
1981	Seattle	16	75	1,224	16.3	9
1982	Seattle	8	34	493	14.5	3
1983	Seattle	15	72	1,074	14.9	11
1984	Seattle	16	74	1,164	15.7	12
1985	Seattle	16	79	1,287	16.3	6
1986	Seattle	16	70	1,070	15.3	9
1987	Seattle	13	58	912	15.7	8
1988	Seattle	15	39	645	16.5	2
1989	Seattle	10	28	403	14.4	3
	TOTALS	200	819	13,089	16.0	100

Sources: Pro Football Hall of Fame; Pro-Football-Reference.com

Larionov, Igor Nikolayevich (born: December 3, 1960 in Voskresensk, Russia); inducted into the Hockey Hall of Fame in 2008 as a player; Position: Center; won two Olympic gold medals; won three Stanley Cup championships.

The 5'9", 170-pound Larionov was already considered one of the best hockey players in the world when he made his National Hockey League debut in October 1989, eventually playing 14 NHL seasons (1989–2004) with the Vancouver Canucks (1989–1992); San Jose Sharks (1993–1995); Detroit Red Wings (1995–2000, 2001–2003); Florida Panthers (2000); and the New Jersey Devils (2003–2004). He won three Stanley Cup championships with the Detroit Red Wings (1997–1998, 2002), and was able to bring the Cup to the Soviet Union for the first time in hockey history. He left the league for one season (1992–1993) to play for HC Lugano (Switzerland), before returning to the NHL with the Sharks.

In the 2002 Stanley Cup playoffs, Larionov became the oldest player in NHL history to score a Stanley Cup Finals goal, when he did so in Game 2 against the Carolina Hurricanes.

Before entering the NHL, he was a four-time Russian First Team All-Star; won six World Championship medals (gold in 1982—Helsinki, Finland; gold in 1983—Munich, Germany; gold in 1986—Moscow, Russia; gold in 1989—Stockholm, Sweden; silver in 1987—Vienna, Austria; and bronze in 1985—Prague, Czechoslovakia); and won three Olympic medals (gold in 1984—Sarajevo, Yugoslavia; gold in 1988—Calgary, Alberta, Canada; and silver in 2002—Salt Lake City, Utah).

Larionov was a two-time World Championship All-Star; helped Russia win the 1981 Canada Cup; and was named Russian Player of the Year in 1988.

Igor Larionov's Career Statistics

SEASON	TEAM	LEAGUE	REGULAR SEASON GP	G	A	TP	PIM	PLAYOFFS GP	G	A	TP	PIM
1977–1978	Khimik Voskresensk	USSR	6	3	0	3	4					
1977–1978	Soviet Union	EJC-A	5	2	1	3	4					
1978–1979	Khimik Voskresensk	USSR	32	3	4	7	12					
1978–1979	Soviet Union	WJC-A	5	2	4	6	8					
1979–1980	Khimik Voskresensk	USSR	42	11	7	18	24					
1979–1980	Soviet Union	WJC-A	5	3	3	6	4					
1980–1981	Khimik Voskresensk	USSR	43	22	23	45	36					
1980–1981	Khimik Voskresensk	USSR-Q		4								
1981–1982	Soviet Union	Can-Cup	7	4	1	5	8					
1981–1982	CSKA Moscow	USSR	46	31	22	53	6					
1981–1982	Soviet Union	WEC-A	10	4	6	10	2					
1982–1983	CSKA Moscow	USSR	44	20	19	39	20					
1982–1983	Soviet Union	Super-S	6	4	2	6	0					
1982–1983	Soviet Union	WEC-A	9	5	7	12	4					
1983–1984	CSKA Moscow	USSR	43	15	26	41	30					
1983–1984	Soviet Union	Olympics	6	1	4	5	6					
1984–1985	Soviet Union	Can-Cup	5	1	2	3	6					
1984–1985	CSKA Moscow	USSR	40	18	28	46	20					
1984–1985	Soviet Union	WEC-A	10	2	4	6	8					
1985–1986	CSKA Moscow	USSR	40	21	31	52	33					
1985–1986	Soviet Union	WEC-A	10	7	1	8	4					
1986–1987	CSKA Moscow	USSR	39	20	26	46	34					
1986–1987	Soviet Union	RV-87	2	0	2	2	0					
1986–1987	Soviet Union	WEC-A	10	4	8	12	2					
1987–1988	Soviet Union	Can-Cup	9	1	2	3	6					
1987–1988	CSKA Moscow	USSR	51	25	32	57	54					
1987–1988	Soviet Union	Olympics	8	4	9	13	4					
1988–1989	CSKA Moscow	USSR	31	15	12	27	22					
1988–1989	CSKA Moscow	Super-S	7	0	7	7	6					
1988–1989	Soviet Union	WEC-A	8	3	0	3	11					
1989–1990	Vancouver Canucks	NHL	74	17	27	44	20					
1990–1991	Vancouver Canucks	NHL	64	13	21	34	14	6	1	0	1	6
1991–1992	Vancouver Canucks	NHL	72	21	44	65	54	13	3	7	10	4
1992–1993	HC Lugano	Swiss	23	10	21	31	40	9	3	10	13	8
1993–1994	San Jose Sharks	NHL	60	18	38	56	40	14	5	13	18	10
1994–1995	San Jose Sharks	NHL	33	4	20	24	14	11	1	8	9	2
1995–1996	San Jose Sharks	NHL	4	1	1	2	0					
1995–1996	Detroit Red Wings	NHL	69	21	50	71	34	19	6	7	13	6
1996–1997	Russia	W-Cup	5	0	4	4	2					
1996–1997	Detroit Red Wings	NHL	64	12	42	54	26	20	4	8	12	8
1997–1998	Detroit Red Wings	NHL	69	8	39	47	40	22	3	10	13	12
1998–1999	Detroit Red Wings	NHL	75	14	49	63	48	7	0	2	2	0
1999–2000	Detroit Red Wings	NHL	79	9	38	47	28	9	1	2	3	6
2000–2001	Florida Panthers	NHL	26	5	6	11	10					
2000–2001	Detroit Red Wings	NHL	39	4	25	29	28	6	1	3	4	2
2001–2002	Detroit Red Wings	NHL	70	11	32	43	50	18	5	6	11	4
2001–2002	Russia	Olympics	6	0	3	3	4					
2002–2003	Detroit Red Wings	NHL	74	10	33	43	48	4	0	1	1	0
2003–2004	New Jersey Devils	NHL	49	1	10	11	20	1	0	0	0	0
2005–2006	Brunflo IK	Sweden-3	2	1	3	4	2					
	NHL TOTALS		921	169	475	644	474	150	30	67	97	60

Sources: Hockey Hall of Fame; Hockey-References.com

Larson, Bertil (born: November 20, 1912 in Worcester, Massachusetts; died: January 9, 2003 in Hartford, Connecticut); inducted into the National Soccer Hall of Fame and Museum in 1988 as a builder; inducted into the Connecticut Soccer Hall of Fame.

Larson played soccer as a young boy and later in life played 20 years for Boston Swedish and the Providence Vikings. After World War II, he became an administrator and ran the Hartford Scandia club for several years. He later held numerous positions in the Connecticut Soccer Association and the Connecticut Youth Soccer Association, and was soccer editor at the *Hartford Courant* for more than 25 years.

Larson was inducted into the Connecticut Soccer Hall of Fame in 1999.

Source: National Soccer Hall of Fame and Museum

Lary, Robert Yale, Jr. (born: November 24, 1930 in Fort Worth, Texas); inducted into the Pro Football Hall of Fame in 1979 as a player; Position: Defensive Back; won three NFL titles.

After being a third-round draft pick in 1952 (34th overall selection), Lary played his entire 11-year (133 games) National Football League career with the Detroit Lions (1952–1953, 1956–1964), and helped the team win three NFL titles (1952–1953, 1957).

During his career, which was interrupted by military service, Lary had 50 interceptions; a 44.3-yard punting average; won three punting titles; had three touchdowns on punt returns; was selected All-NFL five times; played in nine Pro Bowls (1953, 1956–1962, 1964); and was named to the NFL 1950s All-Decade Team.

The 5'11", 185-pound defensive back was drafted out of Texas A&M University (College Station), where he had played football and baseball.

Yale Lary's Career Statistics

			DEFENSE								PUNTING		
							FUM						
YEAR	**TEAM**	**G**	**INT**	**YDS**	**AVG**	**TD**	**REC**	**YDS**	**TD**	**NO**	**YDS**	**AVG**
1952	Detroit	12	4	61	15.3	0	1	0	0	5	181	36.2
1953	Detroit	11	5	98	19.6	0	0	0	0	28	1,112	39.7
1956	Detroit	12	8	182	22.8	1	1	0	0	42	1,698	40.4
1957	Detroit	12	2	64	32.0	0	3	0	0	54	2,156	39.9
1958	Detroit	12	3	70	23.3	0	1	0	0	59	2,524	42.8
1959	Detroit	10	3	0	0.0	0	2	38	1	45	2,121	47.1
1960	Detroit	12	3	44	14.7	0	0	0	0	64	2,802	43.8
1961	Detroit	14	6	95	15.8	0	0	0	0	52	2,519	48.4
1962	Detroit	14	8	51	6.4	0	3	38	0	52	2,354	45.3
1963	Detroit	10	2	21	10.5	1	1	0	0	35	1,713	48.9
1964	Detroit	14	6	101	16.8	0	1	0	0	67	3,099	46.3
	TOTALS	133	50	787	15.7	2	13	76	1	503	22,279	44.3

			PUNT RETURNS			
YEAR	**TEAM**	**G**	**NO**	**YDS**	**AVG**	**TD**
1952	Detroit	12	16	182	11.4	1
1953	Detroit	11	13	115	8.8	1
1956	Detroit	12	22	70	3.2	0
1957	Detroit	12	25	139	5.6	0
1958	Detroit	12	27	196	7.3	1
1959	Detroit	10	21	43	2.0	0
1960	Detroit	12	1	5	5.0	0
1961	Detroit	14	1	8	8.0	0
1962	Detroit	14	0	0	0.0	0
1963	Detroit	10	0	0	0.0	0
1964	Detroit	14	0	0	0.0	0
	TOTALS	133	126	758	6.0	3

Sources: Pro Football Hall of Fame; Pro-Reference.com

Lasorda, Thomas Charles "Tommy" (born: September 22, 1927 in Norristown, Pennsylvania); inducted into the National Baseball Hall of Fame and Museum in 1997 as a manager by the Veterans Committee; won five International League titles as a player; won two World Series as a manager; led the United States to its first-ever gold medal in baseball at the 2000 Olympics in Sydney, Australia.

One of baseball's great ambassadors, Lasorda made his major league debut as a left-handed pitcher on August 5, 1954, and played for the Brooklyn Dodgers (1954–1955) and Kansas City Athletics (1956), before serving 21 seasons as the manager of the Los Angeles Dodgers (1976–1996).

On May 31, 1948, as a minor league pitcher with the Schenectady Blue Jays, Lasorda set a Class C Canadian-American League record by striking out 25 Amsterdam Rugmakers batters in a 15-inning game.

He managed the Dodgers to eight division titles; four World Series (winning in 1981 and 1988, while losing in 1977 and 1978); and was named Manager of the Year twice (1983, 1988). After retiring as a manger, Lasorda became a Dodgers executive (his association with the team has lasted seven decades and is still ongoing), and managed the United States to its first-ever gold medal in baseball at the 2000 Olympics in Sydney, Australia.

The 5'10", 175-pound Lasorda signed with the Montréal Royals of the International League in 1950; pitched a total of nine seasons; and is still the winningest pitcher in the history of the team. He led Montréal to four straight Governors' Cups (1951–1954) and a fifth championship in 1958, when he won the International League's Most Valuable Pitcher Award. He compiled a career 98–49 (.667) record with the Royals.

Despite his pitching success in the minors, for a variety of reasons, Lasorda was never given time by the Dodgers to succeed in the majors. On May 5, 1955 (in his first major league start), he tied a major league record with three wild pitches in one inning, although the team was still able to post a 4–3 win over the St. Louis Cardinals. Later in the season, Lasorda was sent back to the minor leagues (to make roster room for future hall of famer Sandy Koufax), before his contract was sold to the Kansas City Athletics in 1956.

Destined to play only in the minors from this point on, he moved to Los Angeles in 1957 (preceding the Dodgers' move west from Brooklyn by one year), and played for the Los Angeles Angels of the Pacific Coast League. He then returned to the Royals, where he ended his playing career in 1960.

After retiring as a player, Lasorda returned to the Dodgers (by now in Los Angeles) as a scout from 1961 to 1965, and in 1966, he began his long-time managing career with the Ogden (Utah) Dodgers in the rookie level Pioneer League. After spending three years managing at the rookie level, he was promoted to the AAA level with the Spokane Indians (1969–1971) and then the Albuquerque Dukes (1972), both of the Pacific Coast League. During his managing years in the minors, he won five pennants in seven seasons.

In 1973, Lasorda became the Dodgers' third-base coach for future hall of fame manager Walter Alston, and was named the team's manager when Alston retired in 1976. He retired as the team's manager in 1996, and his 1,599 wins currently rank him 16th all-time in major league history. After his health issues were resolved, Lasorda became an at-large executive with the Dodgers.

In August 1997, the Dodgers retired his jersey number two, the ninth uniform retired by the franchise. In 2006, Lasorda was inducted into both the Canadian Baseball Hall of Fame and the Pacific Coast League Hall of Fame.

Tommy Lasorda's Pitching Statistics

YEAR	TEAM	W	L	PCT	ERA	CG	SHO	SV	IP	H	ER	R	HR	BB	IBB	SO	WP	HBP
1954	Brooklyn	0	0	.000	5.00	0	0	0	9.0	8	5	5	2	5	0	5	0	0
1955	Brooklyn	0	0	.000	13.50	0	0	0	4.0	5	6	6	1	6	0	4	4	1
1956	Kansas City	0	4	.000	6.15	0	0	1	45.1	40	31	38	6	45	3	28	7	3
	TOTALS	0	4	.000	6.48	0	0	1	58.1	53	42	49	9	56	3	37	11	4

Tommy Lasorda's Managerial Record

YEAR	TEAM	LG	W	L	WIN%
1976	Los Angeles	NL	2	2	.500
1977	Los Angeles	NL	98	64	.605
1978	Los Angeles	NL	95	67	.586
1979	Los Angeles	NL	79	83	.488
1980	Los Angeles	NL	92	71	.564
1981	Los Angeles	NL	63	47	.573
1982	Los Angeles	NL	88	74	.543

YEAR	TEAM	LG	W	L	WIN%
1983	Los Angeles	NL	91	71	.562
1984	Los Angeles	NL	79	83	.488
1985	Los Angeles	NL	95	67	.586
1986	Los Angeles	NL	73	89	.451
1987	Los Angeles	NL	73	89	.451
1988	Los Angeles	NL	94	67	.584
1989	Los Angeles	NL	77	83	.481
1990	Los Angeles	NL	86	76	.531
1991	Los Angeles	NL	93	69	.574
1992	Los Angeles	NL	63	99	.389
1993	Los Angeles	NL	81	81	.500
1994	Los Angeles	NL	58	56	.509
1995	Los Angeles	NL	78	66	.542
1996	Los Angeles	NL	41	35	.539
	TOTALS		1,599	1,439	.526

Sources: Baseball-Reference.com; National Baseball Hall of Fame and Museum

Lavelli, Dante Bert Joseph (born: February 23, 1923 in Hudson, Ohio); inducted into the Pro Football Hall of Fame in 1975 as a player; Position: Offensive End; Uniform: #86; won seven titles (four in the AAFC and three in the NFL).

Lavelli, a quarterback at Hudson (Ohio) High School (graduating in 1941) and a halfback as an Ohio State University (Columbus) freshman, was moved to offensive end by Buckeye coach Paul Brown before his sophomore season.

His plans for a college football career were hindered by multiple injuries and service in the U.S. Army during World War II, limiting his playing time to only three games. After the war, he was an original member of the Cleveland Browns (All-America Football Conference/National Football League) in 1946, and played his entire 11-year career with the team (1946–1956). The 6', 190-pound Lavelli led the AAFC in receiving as a rookie and scored the winning touchdown in the 1946 title game; won four consecutive AAFC titles (1946–1949); appeared in six NFL title games (winning in 1950, 1954–1955, losing in 1951–1953); caught 11 passes in the 1950 NFL championship game (and scored two touchdowns); selected All-AAFC twice (1946–1947); selected All-NFL twice (1951, 1953); played in three of the first five Pro Bowls (1951, 1953–1954); and was named to the NFL 1940s All-Decade Team.

Dante Lavelli's Career Statistics

			RECEIVING				RUSHING			
YEAR	TEAM	G	TOT	YDS	AVG	TD	ATT	YDS	TD	AVG
1946	Cleveland	14	40	843	21.1	8	1	14	0	14.0
1947	Cleveland	13	49	799	16.3	9				
1948	Cleveland	8	25	463	18.5	5	1	9	0	9.0
1949	Cleveland	9	28	475	17.0	7				
1950	Cleveland	12	37	565	15.3	5				
1951	Cleveland	12	43	586	13.6	6				
1952	Cleveland	8	21	336	16.0	4				
1953	Cleveland	12	45	783	17.4	6				
1954	Cleveland	12	47	802	17.1	7				
1955	Cleveland	12	31	492	15.9	4				
1956	Cleveland	11	20	344	17.2	1				
	TOTALS	123	386	6,488	16.8	62	2	23	0	11.5

Sources: Pro Football Hall of Fame; Pro-Football-Reference.com

Laviolette, Jean-Baptiste "Jack" (born: July 27, 1879 in Belleville, Ontario, Canada; died: January 10, 1960 in Montreal, Quebec, Canada); inducted into the Hockey Hall of Fame in 1962 as a player; Position: Defenseman; won a Stanley Cup title in 1916.

As a young boy, Laviolette played hockey and lacrosse; participated in junior and amateur hockey; and played 12 professional seasons from 1903 to 1918.

In 1904, he joined the Michigan Soo Indians (International Hockey League), and was named to the IHL First All-Star Team twice (1905, 1907), and to the Second Team in 1906. Laviolette then played for the Montreal Shamrocks (Eastern Canadian Amateur Hockey Association) for two seasons, before joining the National Hockey Association's Montreal Canadiens in the team's inaugural season (1909–1910). With the Canadiens, he served as the team's player-manager, captain, and general manager.

With the Canadiens, he won a Stanley Cup in 1916 in a best-of-five series over the Portland Rosebuds, the first time an American-based team had played for the Cup. He played two more seasons with Montreal, including the team's first year in the National Hockey League (1917–1918), before losing his leg in a car accident in 1919.

In 1960, he was inducted into Canada's Sports Hall of Fame as a lacrosse player.

Jack Laviolette's Career Statistics

			REGULAR SEASON					PLAYOFFS				
SEASON	**TEAM**	**LEAGUE**	**GP**	**G**	**A**	**TP**	**PIM**	**GP**	**G**	**A**	**TP**	**PIM**
1902–1903	Montreal Bell Telephone	MCHL										
1903–1904	Montreal Nationals	FAHL	6	8	0	8						
1904–1905	Michigan Soo Indians	IHL	24	15	0	15	24					
1905–1906	Michigan Soo Indians	IHL	17	15	0	15	28					
1906–1907	Michigan Soo Indians	IHL	19	10	7	17	34					
1907–1908	Montreal Shamrocks	ECAHA	6	1	0	1	36					
1908–1909	Montreal Shamrocks	ECHA	9	1	0	1	36					
1909–1910	Montreal Canadiens	NHA	1	1	0	1	15					
1909–1910	Montreal Canadiens	NHA	11	3	0	3	26					
1910–1911	Montreal Canadiens	NHA	16	0	0	0	24					
1911–1912	Montreal Canadiens	NHA	17	7	0	7	10					
1912–1913	Montreal Canadiens	NHA	20	8	0	8	77					
1913–1914	Montreal Canadiens	NHA	20	7	9	16	30	2	0	1	1	0
1914–1915	Montreal Canadiens	NHA	18	6	3	9	35					
1915–1916	Montreal Canadiens	NHA	18	8	3	11	62					
1915–1916	Montreal Canadiens	St-Cup						4	0	0	0	6
1916–1917	Montreal Canadiens	NHA	17	7	3	10	24	2	0	0	0	0
1916–1917	Montreal Canadiens	St-Cup						4	1	2	3	9
1917–1918	Montreal Canadiens	NHL	18	2	1	3	6	2	0	0	0	0
	NHL TOTALS		18	2	1	3	6	2	0	0	0	0

Sources: Hockey Hall of Fame; Hockey-Reference.com

Layne, Robert Lawrence "Bobby" (born: December 19, 1926 in Santa Anna, Texas; died: December 1, 1986 in Lubbock, Texas); inducted into the Pro Football Hall of Fame in 1967 as a player; Position: Quarterback; Uniform: #22; won three NFL titles.

Layne played 15 National Football League seasons (175 games) with the Chicago Bears (1948), New York Bulldogs (1949), Detroit Lions (1950–1958), and the Pittsburgh Steelers (1958–1962).

Graduating from Highland Park High School (Dallas, Texas), he was a 1947 All-American football player at the University of Texas (Austin), and a baseball pitcher for the school. He was selected to four straight All-Southwest Conference teams (1944–1947) and was one of the first inductees into the Cotton Bowl Hall of Fame. In the 1946 Cotton Bowl game, a 40–27 Texas win over Missouri, Layne accounted for every team point (rushing for four touchdowns, throwing two touchdowns, and kicking four extra points). Layne finished his college career with a school record 3,145 passing yards.

After college, he was the third overall pick in the first round of the 1948 NFL Draft by the Chicago Bears, and was also the second overall selection in the 1948 All-America Football Conference Draft by the Baltimore Colts. Choosing the NFL, Layne played one season in Chicago, and one year in New York before being traded to the Lions in 1950, where he won three NFL titles (1952–1953, 1957). Layne was traded to the Steelers in 1958, where he played until retiring in 1962.

He was selected All-NFL twice (1952, 1956); Second-Team All-NFL four times; 1956 NFL scoring leader; selected to five Pro Bowls (1951–1953, 1956, 1959); and was named to the NFL 1950s All-Decade Team.

When he retired, Layne held career NFL records for passes attempted and completed, passing yards, and passing touchdowns.

He was voted into the Texas Longhorn Hall of Honor in 1963; inducted into the College Football Hall of Fame in 1968; and in 1999, was ranked number 52 on *The Sporting News*' list of the 100 Greatest Football Players.

Bobby Layne's Career Statistics

					PASSING						RUSHING		
YEAR	**TEAM**	**G**	**ATT**	**COMP**	**PCT**	**YDS**	**TD**	**INT**	**RATING**	**NO**	**YDS**	**AVG**	**TD**
1948	Chicago	11	52	16	30.8	232	3	2	49.5	13	80	6.2	1
1949	New York	12	299	155	51.8	1,796	9	18	55.3	54	196	3.6	3
1950	Detroit	12	336	152	45.2	2,323	16	18	62.1	56	250	4.5	4
1951	Detroit	12	332	152	45.8	2,403	26	23	67.6	61	290	4.8	1
1952	Detroit	12	287	139	48.4	1,999	19	20	64.5	94	411	4.4	1
1953	Detroit	12	273	125	45.8	2,088	16	21	59.6	87	343	3.9	0
1954	Detroit	12	246	135	54.9	1,818	14	12	77.3	30	119	4.0	2
1955	Detroit	12	270	143	53.0	1,830	11	17	61.8	31	111	3.6	0
1956	Detroit	12	244	129	52.9	1,909	9	17	62.0	46	169	3.7	5
1957	Detroit	11	179	87	48.6	1,169	6	12	53.0	24	99	4.1	0
1958	Detroit/Pittsburgh	12	294	145	49.3	2,510	14	12	77.6	40	154	3.9	3
1959	Pittsburgh	12	297	142	47.8	1,986	20	21	62.8	33	181	5.5	2
1960	Pittsburgh	12	209	103	49.3	1,814	13	17	66.2	19	12	0.6	2
1961	Pittsburgh	8	149	75	50.3	1,205	11	16	62.8	8	11	1.4	0
1962	Pittsburgh	13	233	116	49.8	1,686	9	17	56.2	15	25	1.7	1
	TOTALS	175	3,700	1,814	49.0	26,768	196	243	63.4	611	2,451	4.0	25

Sources: Pro Football Hall of Fame; Pro-Football-Reference.com

Lazzeri, Anthony Michael "Tony" (born: December 6, 1903 in San Francisco, California; died: August 6, 1946 in San Francisco, California); inducted into the National Baseball Hall of Fame and Museum in 1991 as a player by the Veterans Committee; Position: Second Base; Bats: Right; Throws: Right; Uniform: #6; first player to hit two grand slams in one game (May 24, 1936); won five World Series.

Lazzeri played on the Murderers' Row New York Yankees with Babe Ruth, Lou Gehrig, and Joe DiMaggio; won five World Series (1927–1928, 1932, 1936–1937); hit .300 or better five times; and drove in over 100 runs per season seven times. He set an American League single-game record with 11 runs batted in on May 24, 1936 (a 25–2 win over the Philadelphia Athletics) by hitting two grand slams, another home run, and a triple for 15 total bases. He became the first major league player to hit two grand slams in one game.

Making his major league debut on April 13, 1926, the 5'11", 170-pound Lazzeri played 15 seasons for the New York Yankees (1926–1937), Chicago Cubs (1938), Brooklyn Dodgers (1939), and New York Giants (1939). Along with winning the five championships in New York, he also lost two World Series (1926, 1938), and was selected to the very first American League All-Star team in 1933.

Tony Lazzeri's Career Statistics

YEAR	**TEAM**	**LG**	**G**	**AB**	**R**	**H**	**2B**	**3B**	**HR**	**RBI**	**BB**	**SO**	**SB**	**AVG**	**SLG**
1926	New York	AL	155	589	79	162	28	14	18	114	54	96	16	.275	.462
1927	New York	AL	153	570	92	176	29	8	18	102	69	82	22	.309	.482
1928	New York	AL	116	404	62	134	30	11	10	82	44	50	15	.332	.535
1929	New York	AL	147	545	101	193	37	11	18	106	70	45	9	.354	.561
1930	New York	AL	143	571	109	173	34	15	9	121	60	62	4	.303	.462
1931	New York	AL	135	484	67	129	27	7	8	83	79	80	18	.267	.401
1932	New York	AL	141	510	79	153	28	16	15	113	82	64	11	.300	.506
1933	New York	AL	139	523	94	154	22	12	18	104	73	62	15	.294	.486
1934	New York	AL	123	438	59	117	24	6	14	67	71	64	11	.267	.445
1935	New York	AL	130	477	72	130	18	6	13	83	63	75	11	.273	.417
1936	New York	AL	150	537	82	154	29	6	14	109	97	65	8	.287	.441
1937	New York	AL	126	446	56	109	21	3	14	70	71	76	7	.244	.399
1938	Chicago	NL	54	120	21	32	5	0	5	23	22	30	0	.267	.433
1939	Brooklyn	NL	14	39	6	11	2	0	3	6	10	7	1	.282	.564
1939	New York	NL	13	44	7	13	0	0	1	8	7	6	0	.295	.364
	TOTALS		1,739	6,297	986	1,840	334	115	178	1,191	872	864	148	.292	.467

Sources: Baseball-Reference.com; National Baseball Hall of Fame and Museum

Leader, George Alfred (born: December 4, 1903 in Barnsley, Manitoba, Canada; died: May 8, 1982 in Rancho Mirage, California); inducted into the Hockey Hall of Fame in 1969 as a builder; organized the Defense Hockey League; president of the Western Hockey League.

After playing junior and amateur hockey as a boy, Leader and his family moved to the United States, and he became a U.S. citizen in 1933, the same year he took his first administrative hockey position (with the Seattle City League). For the next seven years, he played, coached, and managed teams in the league, and worked as an on-ice official.

In 1940, he organized the five-team Defense Hockey League (in Seattle, Washington and Portland, Oregon), with each team being sponsored by a segment of the local defense industry.

In 1944, he was elected the secretary-manager of the Pacific Coast League. By 1952, the PCL had changed its name to the Western Hockey League; had turned professional; and named Leader its president, a job he held until retiring in 1969.

Source: Hockey Hall of Fame

LeBeau, Charles Richard "Dick" (born: September 9, 1937 in London, Ohio); inducted into the Pro Football Hall of Fame in 2010 as a player; Position: Cornerback; Uniform: #44; helped the Pittsburgh Steelers win Super Bowl XLIII in 2009 as one of the team's coaches.

The 6'1", 185-pound LeBeau played 14 seasons (185 games) in the National Football League (1959–1972) entirely with the Detroit Lions. After attending London High School (Ohio) and Ohio State University (Columbus, where he helped the team win a national title in 1957 under coach Woody Hayes), he was selected in the fifth round (58th overall pick) of the 1959 NFL Draft by the Cleveland Browns. When the team cut him in training camp, he was signed by the Lions.

In his career, LeBeau had 12 straight seasons with three or more interceptions (62 career total for 762 yards and three touchdowns); was voted to three consecutive Pro Bowls (1964–1966); was an All-NFL second-team selection four times (1964–1966, 1970); and led the National Football Conference with nine interceptions in 1970.

After his playing days, LeBeau became a coach (currently serves as the defensive coordinator of the Pittsburgh Steelers); the 2009 season marked his 37th year as a coach in the National Football League; and he helped the Steelers win Super Bowl XLIII in 2009. He was the Special Teams Coach for the Philadelphia Eagles (1973–1975); Defensive Backfield Coach for the Green Bay Packers (1976–1979); Defensive Backfield Coach for the Cincinnati Bengals (1980–1983); Defensive Coordinator for the Bengals (1984–1991); Defensive Backfield Coach for the Pittsburgh Steelers (1992–1994); Defensive Coordinator for the Pittsburgh Steelers (1995–1996); Defensive Coordinator / Assistant Head Coach for the Cincinnati Bengals (1997–2000); Head Coach for the Bengals (2000–2002); Assistant Head Coach for the Buffalo Bills (2003); and Defensive Coordinator for the Pittsburgh Steelers (2004–present).

As a head coach for the Bengals, LeBeau compiled an overall record of 12-33 (.267).

Source: Pro Football Hall of Fame

LeBel, Robert "Bob" (born: September 21, 1905 in Quebec City, Quebec, Canada; died: September 20, 1999); inducted into the Hockey Hall of Fame in 1970 as a builder; founded the Interprovincial Senior League; president of the Canadian Amateur Hockey League; president of the International Ice Hockey Federation.

A former mayor of Chambly (Quebec, Canada), LeBel played junior and minor league hockey, joined the Quebec Senior League; and several amateur hockey teams in New York State.

He founded the Interprovincial Senior League and served as its president from 1944 to 1947; led the Quebec Amateur Hockey League (Association) for two years (1955–1956); served as president of the Canadian Amateur Hockey Association from 1957 to 1969; and in 1960, was elected president of the International Ice Hockey Federation, where he served until 1962.

In 1964, LeBel was named a life member of the QAHA and CAHA, and represented the CAHA on the Governing Committee of the Hockey Hall of Fame when it opened on the Canadian National Exhibition grounds in Toronto in 1961.

He later served as president of the Quebec Junior A League; and was a trustee of both the George T. Richardson Memorial Trophy (awarded to the Eastern Canada Junior League champion) and the W.G. Hardy Trophy (presented to the Canadian Intermediate champion).

Source: Hockey Hall of Fame

Leemans, Alphonse Emil "Tuffy" (born: November 12, 1912 in Superior, Wisconsin; died: January 19, 1979); inducted into the Pro Football Hall of Fame in 1978 as a player; Position: Halfback-Fullback; won the 1938 NFL title game.

After a year at the University of Oregon (Eugene), the 6', 195-pound Leemans was a running back for George Washington University (Washington, D.C.) from 1933 to 1935; named the 1936 College All-Star Game Most Valuable Player; and ran for 2,382 yards on 490 carries during his three-year college career.

He was a second-round pick (18th overall selection) of the New York Giants in the National Football League's first-ever college draft in 1936, and would go on to play his entire eight-year (80 games) NFL career with the team (1936–1943).

He led the NFL in rushing as a rookie; selected All-NFL twice (1936, 1939); named Second-Team All-NFL five times; was a player-coach his last season; and was named to the NFL 1930s All-Decade Team.

Leemans scored New York's first touchdown and helped the team beat the Green Bay Packers 23–17 in the 1938 NFL championship game. He retired from the NFL after the 1943 season and briefly coached the George Washington University team.

Tuffy Leemans Career Statistics

					PASSING					RUSHING			
YEAR	TEAM	G	ATT	COMP	PCT	YDS	TD	INT	RATING	NO	YDS	AVG	TD
1936	New York	12	42	13	.310	258	3	6	37.7	206	830	4.0	2
1937	New York	9	20	5	.250	64	1	1	36.3	144	429	3.0	0
1938	New York	10	42	19	.452	249	3	6	48.7	121	463	3.8	4
1939	New York	10	26	12	.462	198	0	2	40.2	128	429	3.4	3
1940	New York	10	31	15	.484	159	2	3	45.7	132	474	3.6	1
1941	New York	11	66	31	.470	475	4	5	59.8	100	332	3.3	4
1942	New York	8	69	35	.507	555	7	4	87.5	51	116	2.3	3
1943	New York	10	87	37	.425	360	5	5	50.0	37	59	1.6	0
	TOTALS	80	383	167	.436	2,318	25	32	50.6	919	3,132	3.4	17

Sources: Pro Football Hall of Fame; Pro-Football-Reference.com

Leetch, Brian Joseph (born: March 3, 1968 in Corpus Christi, Texas); inducted into the Hockey Hall of Fame as a player in 2009; Position: Defenseman; Uniform: #2, #6; won the Stanley Cup title in 1994; first American-born player to win the Conn Smythe Trophy.

The 6', 185-pound Leetch was a first-round pick (ninth selection overall) of the New York Rangers in the 1986 National Hockey League Entry Draft; played 18 years for the Rangers (1987–2004), Toronto Maple Leafs (2004), and the Boston Bruins (2005–2006); and appeared in nine All-Star Games (1990–1992, 1994, 1996–1998, 2001, 2002).

Before joining the NHL, Leetch attended Cheshire (Connecticut) High School, Boston College (Chestnut Hill, Massachusetts), and played on the 1988 U.S. Olympics hockey team (finishing seventh in Canada). After the Olympics, he entered the NHL and was considered a rookie in 1989, when he won the Calder Memorial Trophy as the league's Rookie of the Year and was named to the NHL All-Rookie Team. He had his best individual season in 1991–1992 when he scored 102 points (with 22 goals and 80 assists, a team record) and won the James Norris Memorial Trophy as the league's Defensive Player of the Year.

He won his only Stanley Cup championship in 1994, the team's first since 1940, and won the Conn Smythe Trophy as the Most Valuable Player in the playoffs, the first American-born player to win the award. He again represented the United States in the 1998 Olympics (Nagano, Japan), helping his team to a sixth-place finish, and won a silver medal at the 2002 Olympics in Salt Lake City, Utah.

After playing briefly for the Maple Leafs, Leetch signed with the Bruins, and in the 2005–2006 season, he recorded his 1,000th career NHL goal before retiring on May 24, 2007.

Internationally, he represented the United States at the World Junior Championships three times (1985 [a sixth place finish in Finland)] 1986 [a bronze medal winning performance in Canada], and 1987 [a fourth-place finish in Czechoslovakia]); a sixth-place finish in the 1989 World Championships (Sweden); was a silver-medal winner as a member of Team U.S.A. at the 1991 Canada Cup (Hamilton, Ontario, Canada); a gold medal winner at the 1996 World Cup (Montreal, Quebec, Canada); and finished out of the medal running in the 2004 World Cup.

Leetch was a two-time James Norris Memorial Trophy winner as Defenseman of the Year (1992, 1997) and was inducted into the U.S. Hockey Hall of Fame in 2008.

In 1998, he was ranked number 71 on *The Hockey News*' list of the 100 Greatest Hockey Players; on September 18, 2007, he won the Lester Patrick Trophy for his contributions to hockey in the United States; and his jersey number two was retired by the Rangers on January 24, 2008.

As a sophomore at Cheshire High School, he helped the team win a baseball state championship.

Brian Leetch's Career Statistics

			REGULAR SEASON						PLAYOFFS				
SEASON	**TEAM**	**LEAGUE**	**GP**	**G**	**A**	**TP**	**PIM**	**+/-**	**GP**	**G**	**A**	**TP**	**PIM**
1983–1984	Cheshire High School	High-CT	28	52	49	101	24						
1984–1985	Avon Old Farms	High-CT	26	30	46	76	15						
1984–1985	United States	WJC-A	7	0	0	0	2						
1985–1986	Avon Old Farms	High-CT	28	40	44	84	18						
1985–1986	United States	WJC-A	7	1	4	5	2						
1986–1987	Boston College Eagles	H-East	37	9	38	47	10						
1986–1987	United States	WJC-A	7	1	2	3	8						
1986–1987	United States	WEC-A	10	4	5	9	4						
1987–1988	United States	Nat-Tm	50	13	61	74	38						
1987–1988	United States	Olympics	6	1	5	6	4						
1987–1988	New York Rangers	NHL	17	2	12	14	0	+5					
1988–1989	New York Rangers	NHL	68	23	48	71	50	+8	4	3	2	5	2
1988–1989	United States	WEC-A	10	3	4	7	4						
1989–1990	New York Rangers	NHL	72	11	45	56	26	-18					
1990–1991	New York Rangers	NHL	80	16	72	88	42	+2	6	1	3	4	0
1991–1992	United States	Can-Cup	7	1	3	4	2						
1991–1992	New York Rangers	NHL	80	22	80	102	26	+25	13	4	11	15	4
1992–1993	New York Rangers	NHL	36	6	30	36	26	+2					
1993–1994	New York Rangers	NHL	84	23	56	79	67	+28	23	11	23	34	6
1994–1995	New York Rangers	NHL	48	9	32	41	18	0	10	6	8	14	8
1995–1996	New York Rangers	NHL	82	15	70	85	30	+12	11	1	6	7	4
1996–1997	United States	W-Cup	7	0	7	7	4						
1996–1997	New York Rangers	NHL	82	20	58	78	40	+31	15	2	8	10	6
1997–1998	New York Rangers	NHL	76	17	33	50	32	-36					
1997–1998	United States	Olympics	4	1	1	2	0						
1998–1999	New York Rangers	NHL	82	13	42	55	42	-7					
1999–2000	New York Rangers	NHL	50	7	19	26	20	-16					
2000–2001	New York Rangers	NHL	82	21	58	79	34	-18					
2001–2002	New York Rangers	NHL	82	10	45	55	28	+14					
2001–2002	United States	Olympics	6	0	5	5	0						
2002–2003	New York Rangers	NHL	51	12	18	30	20	-3					
2003–2004	New York Rangers	NHL	57	13	23	36	24	-5					
2003–2004	Toronto Maple Leafs	NHL	15	2	13	15	10	+11	13	0	8	8	6
2004–2005	United States	W-Cup	5	0	1	1	6	-1					
2005–2006	Boston Bruins	NHL	61	5	27	32	36	-10					
	NHL TOTALS		1,205	247	781	1,028	571		95	28	69	97	36

Sources: Hockey Hall of Fame; Hockey-Reference.com

Lehman, Frederick Hugh "Fred" "Hughie" (born: October 27, 1885 in Pembroke, Ontario, Canada; died: April 8, 1961); inducted into the Hockey Hall of Fame in 1958 as a player; Position: Goalie; won a Stanley Cup title in 1915.

Lehman led the Ontario Professional Hockey League by posting a goals-against average of 3.00 in the 1909–1910 season.

The 5'8", 168-pound goalie played 20 professional seasons from 1908 to 1928, including two years in the National Hockey League with the Chicago Black Hawks (1926–1928). He played in the Pacific Coast Hockey Association for 13 seasons; led the league in goals-against average five times; and was named a league All-Star in ten of his 13 seasons.

He played for the Stanley Cup eight times, winning in 1915 with the Vancouver Millionaires. When the Western Hockey League disbanded after the 1925–1926 season, Lehman played for the NHL's Black Hawks in 1926; led the league in minutes played (2,797); and after playing four games the next season, he briefly coached Chicago to a 3–17–1 record.

Fred Lehman's Career Statistics

SEASON	TEAM	LEAGUE	REGULAR SEASON						PLAYOFFS					
			GP	W	L	T	SO	AVG	GP	W	L	T	SO	AVG
1903–1904	Pembroke Lumber Kings	OVHL	5	1	4	0	0							
1904–1905	Pembroke Lumber Kings	OVHL												
1905–1906	Pembroke Lumber Kings	OVHL	8	8	0	0	1	1.67	1	1	0	0	1	0.00
1906–1907	Canadian Soo	IHL	24	13	11	0	0	5.13						
1907–1908	Pembroke Lumber Kings	OVHL	4	2	2	0	0	5.50						
1908–1909	Berlin Professionals	OPHL	15	9	6	0	0	4.85						
1909–1910	Galt Professionals	St-Cup							2	0	2	0	0	7.50
1909–1910	Berlin Professionals	OPHL	6	6	0	0	0	3.00						
1909–1910	Berlin Professionals	OPHL	17	11	6	0	3	4.53						
1909–1910	Berlin Professionals	St-Cup							1	0	1	0	0	7.00
1910–1911	Berlin Professionals	OPHL	15	7	8	0	0	5.80						
1911–1912	New Westminster Royals	PCHA	15	9	6	0	0	5.07						
1911–1912	PCHA All-Stars	Exhib.	3	2	1	0	0	4.00						
1912–1913	New Westminster Royals	PCHA	12	4	8	0	0	4.14						
1913–1914	New Westminster Royals	PCHA	16	7	9	0	0	4.87						
1914–1915	Vancouver Millionaires	PCHA	17	13	4	0	1	4.08						
1914–1915	Vancouver Millionaires	St-Cup							3	3	0	0	0	2.67
1914–1915	PCHA All-Stars	Exhib.	2	2	0	0	0	4.50						
1915–1916	Vancouver Millionaires	PCHA	18	9	9	0	0	3.79						
1915–1916	PCHA All-Stars	Exhib.	2	1	1	0	0	4.50						
1916–1917	Vancouver Millionaires	PCHA	23	14	9	0	0	5.30						
1917–1918	Vancouver Millionaires	PCHA	18	9	9	0	1	3.05	2	1	0	1	1	1.00
1917–1918	Vancouver Millionaires	St-Cup							5	2	3	0	0	3.60
1918–1919	Vancouver Millionaires	PCHA	20	12	8	0	1	2.58	2	1	1	0	0	3.50
1919–1920	Vancouver Millionaires	PCHA	22	11	11	0	1	2.92	2	1	1	0	0	3.50
1920–1921	Vancouver Millionaires	PCHA	24	13	11	0	3	3.23	2	2	0	0	1	1.00
1920–1921	Vancouver Millionaires	St-Cup							5	2	3	0	0	2.40
1921–1922	Vancouver Millionaires	PCHA	22	12	10	0	4	2.82	2	2	0	0	2	0.00
1921–1922	Vancouver Millionaires	West-P							2	1	1	0	1	1.00
1921–1922	Vancouver Millionaires	St-Cup							5	2	3	0	1	3.15
1922–1923	Vancouver Maroons	PCHA	25	16	8	1	5	2.33	2	1	1	0	1	1.50
1922–1923	Vancouver Maroons	St-Cup							4	1	3	0	0	2.50
1923–1924	Vancouver Maroons	PCHA	30	13	16	1	1	2.60	2	1	1	0	0	1.34
1923–1924	Vancouver Millionaires	West-P							3	1	2	0	0	3.33
1923–1924	Vancouver Maroons	St-Cup							2	0	2	0	0	2.50
1924–1925	Vancouver Maroons	WCHL	11	7	4	0	0	2.62						
1925–1926	Vancouver Maroons	WHL	30	10	18	2	3	2.94						
1926–1927	Chicago Black Hawks	NHL	44	19	22	3	5	2.49	2	0	1	1	0	5.00
1927–1928	Chicago Black Hawks	NHL	4	1	2	1	1	4.80						
	NHL TOTALS		48	20	24	4	6	2.67	2	0	1	1	0	5.00

Sources: Hockey Hall of Fame; Hockey-Reference.com

Leith, Lloyd R. (born: December 7, 1902 in San Francisco, California; died: September 30, 1974); inducted into the Naismith Memorial Basketball Hall of Fame in 1983 as a referee; won two San Francisco city basketball championships as a coach; supervisor of officials for the Pacific Intercollegiate Athletic Conference.

Leith played basketball at Polytechnic High School (San Francisco, California, 1917–1921) and was the team's captain in 1921. After graduating, he attended the University of California (Berkeley, 1922–1926) and again served as his team's captain for two seasons (1925–1926).

After college, he played amateur basketball at the Amateur Athletic Union San Francisco Olympic Club in 1927, and eventually became a high school head basketball coach in San Francisco at Balboa High School (1931–1936); George Washington High School (1936–1942); and Mission High School (1945–1972). He compiled a 26–15 (.634) record at Balboa; a 39–12 (.765) record at George Washington; and a 162–81 (.667) record at Mission; won two city championships at George Washington (1940–1941); and was named Coach of the Year in 1940.

While coaching at the high school level, Leith also was a long-time basketball referee with the Pacific Coast Conference (1939–1955). He worked at the National AAU Championships (1930–1940); officiated in 16 National Collegiate Athletic Association Tournaments; and served as the supervisor of officials for the Pacific Intercollegiate Athletic Conference (later renamed the Pacific Coast Conference, 1955–1962).

Later, he served as a National Basketball Association scout for eight years, and in 1983, he became the tenth referee inducted into the basketball hall of fame.

Source: Naismith Memorial Basketball Hall of Fame

Lemaire, Jacques Gerard (born: September 7, 1945 in LaSalle, Quebec, Canada); inducted into the Hockey Hall of Fame in 1984 as a player; Position: Forward; won 11 Stanley Cup titles (eight as a player, two while working in the front office, and one as a coach).

Before becoming a National Hockey League coach, the 5'11", 180-pound Lemaire played his entire 12-year NHL career from 1967 to 1979 with the Montreal Canadiens, and gained a reputation for his overtime achievements in the playoffs, scoring three sudden death goals in his career.

His overtime goal on May 14, 1977 won the Cup for Montreal against the Boston Bruins, and when he made the Cup-winning goal in 1979 against the New York Rangers, he became one of only five players to have scored two Stanley Cup-winning goals. In his career, Lemaire averaged just under a point per game in the playoffs; was a member of eight Stanley Cup winning teams (1968–1969, 1971, 1973, 1976–1979); played in two All-Star games (1970, 1973); and won the Jack Adams Award twice (1994, 2003) as NHL Coach of the Year.

Lemaire left the NHL after the 1979 Stanley Cup win to begin his coaching career in Switzerland as a player-coach for HC Sierre. He returned to Canada in 1981 as the first head coach of the Quebec Major Junior Hockey League's Longueuil Chevaliers, and in his first season (1982–1983), he led the team to the QMJHL Finals.

He left the league briefly to be an assistant coach, scout, and recruiter at Plattsburgh State University (New York), before returning to the Canadiens in 1984 as the team's head coach with 17 games left in the 1983–1984 season. In 1985, Lemaire moved into the team's front office, where he worked for seven seasons, as the team won two more titles (1986, 1993).

He became head coach of the NHL's New Jersey Devils in 1993–1994, a job he held until 1998; won a Stanley Cup in 1995; and won his first Jack Adams Award as NHL Coach of the Year in 1994, his first season with the team. Lemaire returned to Montreal as assistant general manager in 1998 and stayed with the team until becoming the head coach with the NHL's expansion Minnesota Wild in 2000, where he would win his second Jack Adams Award in 2003. He announced his retirement from the NHL in April 2010.

As of this writing, he is still the team's only head coach the franchise has ever had.

Lemaire compiled a coaching record of 588–441–124–60 (.561), and in 16 National Hockey League seasons with Montreal, New Jersey, and Minnesota, he led teams into the postseason 10 times, and had a Stanley Cup playoff record of 61–56 (.521).

Jacques Lemaire's Career Playing Statistics

			REGULAR SEASON						PLAYOFFS				
SEASON	TEAM	LEAGUE	GP	G	A	TP	PIM	+/-	GP	G	A	TP	PIM
1962–1963	Lachine Maroons	QJHL	42	41	63	104							
1963–1964	Montreal Jr. Canadiens	OHA-Jr.	42	25	30	55	17		17	10	6	16	4
1964–1965	Montreal Jr. Canadiens	OHA-Jr.	56	25	47	72	52		7	1	5	6	0
1964–1965	Quebec Aces	AHL	1	0	0	0	0						
1965–1966	Montreal Jr. Canadiens	OHA-Jr.	48	41	52	93	69		10	11	2	13	14
1966–1967	Houston Apollos	CPHL	69	19	30	49	19		6	0	1	1	0
1967–1968	Montreal Canadiens	NHL	69	22	20	42	16	+15	13	7	6	13	6
1968–1969	Montreal Canadiens	NHL	75	29	34	63	29	+31	14	4	2	6	6
1969–1970	Montreal Canadiens	NHL	69	32	28	60	16	+19					
1970–1971	Montreal Canadiens	NHL	78	28	28	56	18	0	20	9	10	19	17
1971–1972	Montreal Canadiens	NHL	77	32	49	81	26	+37	6	2	1	3	2
1972–1973	Montreal Canadiens	NHL	77	44	51	95	16	+59	17	7	13	20	2
1973–1974	Montreal Canadiens	NHL	66	29	38	67	10	+4	6	0	4	4	2
1974–1975	Montreal Canadiens	NHL	80	36	56	92	20	+25	11	5	7	12	4
1975–1976	Montreal Canadiens	NHL	61	20	32	52	20	+26	13	3	3	6	2
1976–1977	Montreal Canadiens	NHL	75	34	41	75	22	+70	14	7	12	19	6
1977–1978	Montreal Canadiens	NHL	76	36	61	97	14	+54	15	6	8	14	10
1978–1979	Montreal Canadiens	NHL	50	24	31	55	10	+9	16	11	12	23	6
1979–1980	HC Sierre	Swiss-2	28	29	16	45							
1980–1981	HC Sierre	Swiss-2	12	13	13	26							
1981–1982	SUNY Plattsburgh	NCAA-2											
1983–1985	Montreal Canadiens	NHLMGNT											
1985–1993	Montreal Canadiens	NHLMGNT											
1993–1998	New Jersey Devils	NHLMGNT											
1998–2000	Montreal Canadiens	NHLMGNT											
	NHL TOTALS		853	366	469	835	217		145	61	78	139	63

Jacques Lemaire's Coaching Record

SEASON	TEAM	LEAGUE	W	L	T	OTL	WIN%	NOTES
1979–1980	Sierre	Swiss-B						
1980–1981	Sierre	Swiss-B						
1982–1983	Longueuil Chevaliers	QMJHL	37	29	4	0	.557	
1983–1984	Montreal Canadiens	NHL	7	10	0	0	.412	Lost in round 3
1984–1985	Montreal Canadiens	NHL	41	27	12	0	.588	Lost in round 2
1993–1994	New Jersey Devils	NHL	47	25	12	0	.631	Lost in round 3
1994–1995	New Jersey Devils	NHL	22	18	8	0	.542	Won Championship
1995–1996	New Jersey Devils	NHL	37	33	12	0	.524	Out of Playoffs
1996–1997	New Jersey Devils	NHL	45	23	14	0	.634	Lost in round 2
1997–1998	New Jersey Devils	NHL	48	23	11	0	.652	Lost in round 1
2000–2001	Minnesota Wild	NHL	25	39	13	5	.415	Out of Playoffs
2001–2002	Minnesota Wild	NHL	26	35	12	9	.445	Out of Playoffs
2002–2003	Minnesota Wild	NHL	42	29	10	1	.579	Lost in round 3
2003–2004	Minnesota Wild	NHL	30	29	20	3	.506	Out of Playoffs
2005–2006	Minnesota Wild	NHL	38	36	0	8	.512	Out of Playoffs
2006–2007	Minnesota Wild	NHL	48	26	0	8	.634	Lost in round 1
2007–2008	Minnesota Wild	NHL	44	28	0	10	.598	Lost in round 1
2008–2009	Minnesota Wild	NHL	40	33	0	9	.543	Out of Playoffs
2009–2010	New Jersey Devils	NHL	48	27	0	7	.628	Lost in round 1
	TOTALS		588	441	124	60	.561	

Sources: Hockey Hall of Fame; Hockey-Reference.com

Lemieux, Mario (born: October 5, 1965 in Montreal, Quebec, Canada); inducted into the Hockey Hall of Fame in 1997 as a player; Position: Forward; scored five goals in five different ways (December 31, 1988, a feat no other player has ever accomplished); won two Stanley Cup titles; first player to become an owner of his former team; won a 2002 Olympic gold medal.

The 6'4", 200-pound Lemieux played his entire 18-year National Hockey League career (1984–2006) with the Pittsburgh Penguins. He was the number one overall pick in the 1984 NHL Entry Draft, and as of this writing, he is majority owner of the team, the first NHL player to become owner of his former team.

Prior to joining the NHL, he played for the Laval Voisin (Quebec Major Junior Hockey League); was the league's top scorer in his last season (1983–1984); and in 1984, led the team to the Memorial Cup Tournament and was named the Canadian Major Junior Player of the Year.

Lemieux scored a goal in his first NHL game and became only the third rookie in league history to record 100 or more points (43 goals and 57 assists). He was selected the All-Star Game's Most Valuable Player and won the Calder Trophy as the NHL's Rookie of the Year. After his NHL rookie season, he led Canada to a silver medal in the 1985 World Championships (Prague, Czechoslovakia).

In 1987, he played for the NHL in the Rendez-vous series at the All-Star break, and later played for the home team in the Canada Cup, scoring the series-winning goal against the Soviet Union.

In the 1987–1988 season, Lemieux led the NHL with 168 points and won both the Art Ross Trophy (regular-season scoring leader) and the Hart Memorial Trophy (NHL Most Valuable Player).

On December 31, 1988, in a game against the New Jersey Devils, he made NHL history by scoring five goals in five different ways: an even-strength goal, a power-play goal, a shorthanded goal, a penalty shot goal, and an empty-net goal. No other player in league history has ever matched that feat.

In the 1988–1989 season, he again led the league in scoring (199 points), and is the only player to approach 200 points in a season, other than Wayne Gretzky, who did it four times.

Although hurt and missing most of the 1990–1991 season with back problems, he returned to the team in time for the playoffs; led the Penguins to the team's first-ever Stanley Cup title in six games over the Minnesota North Stars; and won the Conn Smythe Trophy as playoff most valuable player. In the next season, he again won the Conn Smythe Trophy as he led the team to its second Stanley Cup championship in a four-game sweep of the Chicago Black Hawks.

Continuing back problems began to diminish his playing time, but when he could return to the ice, Lemieux proved to be just as dominant as ever. Although he missed one month of the 1992–1993 season, he came back to lead the league in scoring. After missing most of the 1993–1994 and all of the 1994–1995 seasons, he returned in 1995–1996 to win both the Hart and Ross trophies in 1996, before retiring in 1997.

In 1999, he headed an ownership group that bought the Penguins, and in 2000, Lemieux announced that he would return to the league as an active player, only the third person to do so after being inducted into the Hockey Hall of Fame (the others being Gordie Howe and Guy Lafleur). In his first game back (December 27, 2000), he scored one goal and had two assists in a 5-0 win over the Toronto Maple Leafs.

As captain of Canada's Olympic team for the 2002 Winter Games (Salt Lake City, Utah), Lemieux helped the squad win the gold medal.

During his career, Lemieux won the Art Ross Trophy six times (1988–1989, 1992–1993, 1996–1997); the Bill Masterton Memorial Trophy in 1993 for perseverance, sportsmanship, and dedication to ice hockey; the Calder Memorial Trophy in 1985; the Conn Smythe Trophy twice (1991–1992); First All-Star Team five times (1988–1989, 1993, 1996–1997); Second All-Star Team four times (1986–1987, 1992, 2001); the Hart Memorial Trophy three times (1988, 1993, 1996); and the Lester B. Pearson Award (NHL MVP as voted by the National Hockey League Players' Association) four times (1986, 1988, 1993, 1996).

He was named to the NHL All-Rookie Team in 1985; NHL All-Star Game MVP three times (1985, 1988, 1990); in 1998, he was ranked number four on *The Hockey News*' list of the 100 Greatest Hockey Players, the highest-ranking French-Canadian player; and in 2004, he was inducted into Canada's Walk of Fame.

He holds numerous NHL records, including single-season record for shorthanded goals (13 in 1988–1989); only player in NHL history to score more than 30 power-play goals in two different seasons; only player in history to score more than 10 short-handed goals in two different seasons; involved in 57.3% of team's goals in the 1988–1989 season, the highest percentage in league history; and All-Star Game record for points in a single game (six in 1988).

His Penguins' records include career games played; career goals; career assists; career points; longest goal-scoring streak (12 games); single-season record for goals (85 in 1988–1989); single-season record for assists (114 in 1988–1989); and single-season record for points (199 in 1988–1989).

Mario Lemieux's Career Statistics

			REGULAR SEASON						PLAYOFFS				
SEASON	**TEAM**	**LEAGUE**	**GP**	**G**	**A**	**TP**	**PIM**	**+/–**	**GP**	**G**	**A**	**TP**	**PIM**
1979–1980	Montreal Hurricanes	QAHA											
1980–1981	Montreal-Concordia	QAAA	47	62	62	124	127		3	2	5	7	8
1981–1982	Laval Voisins	QMJHL	64	30	66	96	22		18	5	9	14	31
1982–1983	Laval Voisins	QMJHL	66	84	100	184	76		12	14	18	32	18
1982–1983	Canada	WJC-A	7	5	5	10	12						
1983–1984	Laval Voisins	QMJHL	70	133	149	282	92		14	29	23	52	29
1983–1984	Laval Voisins	M-Cup	3	1	2	3	0						
1984–1985	Pittsburgh Penguins	NHL	73	43	57	100	54	–35					
1984–1985	Canada	WEC-A	9	4	6	10	2						
1985–1986	Pittsburgh Penguins	NHL	79	48	93	141	43	–6					
1986–1987	Pittsburgh Penguins	NHL	63	54	53	107	57	+13					
1986–1987	NHL All-Stars	RV-87	2	0	3	3	0						
1987–1988	Canada	Can-Cup	9	11	7	18	8						
1987–1988	Pittsburgh Penguins	NHL	77	70	98	168	92	+23					
1988–1989	Pittsburgh Penguins	NHL	76	85	114	199	100	+41	11	12	7	19	16
1989–1990	Pittsburgh Penguins	NHL	59	45	78	123	78	–18					
1990–1991	Pittsburgh Penguins	NHL	26	19	26	45	30	+8	23	16	28	44	16
1991–1992	Pittsburgh Penguins	NHL	64	44	87	131	94	+27	15	16	18	34	2
1992–1993	Pittsburgh Penguins	NHL	60	69	91	160	38	+55	11	8	10	18	10
1993–1994	Pittsburgh Penguins	NHL	22	17	20	37	32	–2	6	4	3	7	2
1994–1995	Pittsburgh Penguins	NHL											
1995–1996	Pittsburgh Penguins	NHL	70	69	92	161	54	+10	18	11	16	27	33
1996–1997	Pittsburgh Penguins	NHL	76	50	72	122	65	+27	5	3	3	6	4
2000–2001	Pittsburgh Penguins	NHL	43	35	41	76	18	+15	18	6	11	17	4
2001–2002	Pittsburgh Penguins	NHL	24	6	25	31	14	0					
2001–2002	Canada	Olympics	5	2	4	6	0						
2002–2003	Pittsburgh Penguins	NHL	67	28	63	91	43	–25					
2003–2004	Pittsburgh Penguins	NHL	10	1	8	9	6	–2					
2004–2005	Canada	W-Cup	6	1	4	5	2	+4					
2005–2006	Pittsburgh Penguins	NHL	26	7	15	22	16	–16					
	NHL TOTALS		915	690	1,033	1,723	834		107	76	96	172	87

Sources: Hockey Hall of Fame; Hockey-Reference.com

Lemon, George "Meadowlark" (born: April 25, 1935 in Lexington County, South Carolina); inducted into the Naismith Memorial Basketball Hall of Fame in 2003 as a contributor; known as the "Clown Prince of Basketball."

An All-Conference and All-State selection for three years, Lemon attended Wiliston High School (Wilmington, North Carolina), graduating in 1952. Called the "Clown Prince of Basketball," he played professional basketball with the Harlem Globetrotters (1957–1979, returned in 1994 for 50 games); the Bucketeers (1980–1983); Shooting Stars (1984–1987); and the Meadowlark Lemon Harlem All-Stars (1988–1998).

Probably the most popular and well-known player of the Globetrotter teams, he played in more than 16,000 games; traveled to more than 70 countries in his 30-year playing career; performed three times for two popes; known for his half-court hook shot; inducted into the North Carolina Sports Hall of Fame in 1975; and received the John Bunn Award from the Naismith Memorial Basketball Hall of Fame in 2000 for his long-time contributions to the game.

The 6'6" Lemon is now a born-again Christian and an ordained minister in Scottsdale, Arizona, and earned a Doctor of Divinity degree from Vision International University (Ramona, California).

For more than five decades, he entertained fans throughout the world with his basketball skills, slapstick comedy, confetti-in-the-water-bucket routine, and his hook shots from half-court.

He started "Camp Meadowlark" in 1989, a series of co-educational sports camps to educate and offer children alternatives to the dangers of substance abuse.

Source: Naismith Memorial Basketball Hall of Fame

Lemon, Robert Granville "Bob" (born: September 22, 1920 in San Bernardino, California; died: January 11, 2000 in Long Beach, California); inducted into the National Baseball Hall of Fame and Museum in 1976 as a player; Position: Pitcher; Bats: Left; Throws: Right; Uniform: #21; won the 1948 World Series as a player and the 1978 World Series as a manager; first manager to win a World Series (with the New York Yankees) after starting the season with another team (Chicago White Sox); named American League Manager of the Year twice.

After playing professional baseball for eight years as both an infielder and outfielder, the 6', 185-pound Lemon became a pitcher at age 25. Making his major league debut on September 9, 1941 with the Cleveland Indians, he played briefly in 1942 before joining the military during World War II. After the war, in 1946, he returned to the Indians as a pitcher and would play with the team a total of 15 seasons (1941–1942, 1946–1958). On June 30, 1948, in his first full season as a pitcher, Lemon threw a no-hitter, beating the Detroit Tigers 2–0 at Briggs Stadium (Detroit).

He won 20 or more games per season seven times; appeared in two World Series (winning in 1948, losing in 1954); a seven-time All Star (1948–1954); led the American League in wins three times (1950, 1954–1955); and the Indians retired his uniform number 21.

After retiring as a player, Lemon became a manager with the Kansas City Royals (1970–1972), Chicago White Sox (1977–1978), and the New York Yankees (1978–1979, 1981–1982). As a manager, he led the Yankees to two World Series (winning in 1978, losing in 1981).

After his playing career ended, Lemon began managing in the minor leagues, and in 1966, he won the Pacific Coast League championship with the Seattle Angels. In 1970, he was promoted to the major leagues to manage the Royals in midseason, and the following year, he led the team to a winning season, earning him the American League Manager of the Year Award.

In 1976, he served as a pitching coach for the Yankees; began managing the White Sox in 1977, and led the team to 26 more wins that it had the previous season, winning his second American League Manager of the Year Award. Fired midway into the 1978 season, Lemon returned to the Yankees as a manager (replacing Billy Martin), and led the team to a World Series title, becoming the first manager in major league history to win a World Series with one team after starting the season with another.

Lemon was fired midway through the 1979 season, was replaced by Martin, and promoted to general manager. He returned as the team's manager in 1981 and led the Yankees into the World Series, eventually losing to the Los Angeles Dodgers. A few weeks into the 1982 season, he was fired for the last time by the team.

Bob Lemon's Career Pitching Statistics

YEAR	TEAM	LG	W	L	PCT	G	SH	IP	H	R	ER	SO	BB	ERA
1946	Cleveland	AL	4	5	.444	32	0	94	77	40	26	39	68	2.49
1947	Cleveland	AL	11	5	.688	37	1	167	150	68	64	65	97	3.45
1948	Cleveland	AL	20	14	.588	43	10	294	231	104	92	147	129	2.82
1949	Cleveland	AL	22	10	.688	37	2	280	211	101	93	138	137	2.99
1950	Cleveland	AL	23	11	.676	44	3	288	281	144	123	170	146	3.84
1951	Cleveland	AL	17	14	.548	42	1	263	244	119	103	132	124	3.52

YEAR	TEAM	LG	W	L	PCT	G	SH	IP	H	R	ER	SO	BB	ERA
1952	Cleveland	AL	22	11	.667	42	5	310	236	104	86	131	105	2.50
1953	Cleveland	AL	21	15	.583	41	5	287	283	119	107	98	110	3.36
1954	Cleveland	AL	23	7	.767	36	2	258	228	95	78	110	92	2.72
1955	Cleveland	AL	18	10	.643	35	0	211	218	103	91	100	74	3.88
1956	Cleveland	AL	20	14	.588	39	2	255	230	103	86	94	89	3.04
1957	Cleveland	AL	6	11	.353	21	0	117	129	70	60	45	64	4.62
1958	Cleveland	AL	0	1	.000	11	0	25	41	15	15	8	16	5.40
	TOTALS		207	128	.618	460	31	2,849	2,559	1,185	1,024	1,277	1,251	3.23

Bob Lemon's Managerial Record

YEAR	TEAM	LG	W	L	WIN%	FINISH
1970	Kansas City	AL	46	64	.418	4
1971	Kansas City	AL	85	76	.528	2
1972	Kansas City	AL	76	78	.494	4
1977	Chicago	AL	90	72	.556	3
1978	Chicago	AL	34	40	.459	5
1978	New York	AL	48	20	.706	1 (World Series)
1979	New York	AL	34	31	.523	4
1981	New York	AL	11	14	.440	6
1982	New York	AL	6	8	.429	5
	Kansas City		207	218	.487	
	Chicago		124	112	.525	
	New York		99	73	.576	
	TOTALS		430	403	.516	

Sources: Baseball-Reference.com; National Baseball Hall of Fame and Museum

Lenarduzzi, Robert "Bobby" (born: May 1, 1955 in Vancouver, British Columbia, Canada); inducted into the National Soccer Hall of Fame and Museum in 2003; Position: Defender-Midfielder; International Caps (1973–1987): 47; International Goals: 0; played in more NASL games that any other player; first Canadian player to be named NASL Player of the Year; won Soccer Bowl '79; won four straight CSL championships.

One of the best soccer players from Canada, Lenarduzzi played in more North American Soccer League games (288) than any other player. Between May 5, 1974, when he made his league debut for the Vancouver Whitecaps in the first game the team ever played, and the last game of the 1984 season, he played in 288 regular-season games and 24 playoff matches over 11 seasons. During that time, he had played all 11 positions on the field for the Whitecaps, including 45 minutes as a goalkeeper.

In 1978, he became the first Canadian player named NASL Player of the Year; in the next season, he helped the Whitecaps win Soccer Bowl '79; and would eventually play on three NASL All-Star teams (1979, 1981, 1984).

He made his international debut for Canada against Poland in Toronto in 1973, and gained his 47th (and last) cap against the Soviet Union during the 1986 World Cup Finals in Mexico.

In 1984, after the Whitecaps folded, Lenarduzzi played two seasons with the Tacoma Stars (Major Indoor Soccer League, 1984–1986); played for Canada in the 1984 Olympic Games (Los Angeles, California), but the team failed to medal; became a player-coach with the Vancouver 86ers (Canadian Soccer League) in 1987 and led the team to four consecutive CSL championships (1988–1991); named coach of Canada's National Team in 1992, a position he held until 1997; and his 86ers career record of 96–24–28 made him the winningest coach in Vancouver professional sports history.

He served as the 86ers general manager from 1988 to 1993; named the A-League's Executive of the Year in 2000; and was named CSL Coach of the Year twice (1988–1989).

Lenarduzzi was inducted into the British Columbia Sports Hall of Fame and Museum in 1992; inducted as a player into the Canadian Soccer Hall of Fame in 2001; awarded the Order of British Columbia in 2005; and was voted one of the Top 30 Players of the Century in the Confederation of North, Central America and Caribbean Association Football.

Bobby Lenarduzzi's North American Soccer League Statistics

YEAR	TEAM	G	GLS	ASST	PTS
1974	Vancouver Whitecaps	19	2	0	4
1975	Vancouver Whitecaps	20	3	3	9

YEAR	TEAM	G	GLS	ASST	PTS
1976	Vancouver Whitecaps	21	2	2	6
1977	Vancouver Whitecaps	26	0	4	4
1978	Vancouver Whitecaps	29	10	17	37
1979	Vancouver Whitecaps	28	3	3	9
1980	Vancouver Whitecaps	30	2	7	11
1981	Vancouver Whitecaps	32	5	9	19
1982	Vancouver Whitecaps	31	1	3	5
1983	Vancouver Whitecaps	28	2	5	9
1984	Vancouver Whitecaps	24	1	4	6
	TOTALS	288	31	57	119

Source: National Soccer Hall of Fame and Museum

Leonard, Walter Fenner "Buck" (born: September 8, 1907 in Rocky Mount, North Carolina; died: November 27, 1997 in Rocky Mount, North Carolina); inducted into the National Baseball Hall of Fame and Museum in 1972 as a Negro Leaguer by the Negro Leagues Committee; Position: First Base; Bats: Left; Throws: Left; played in a record 11 East-West All-Star games; his 17-year tenure with the Grays is the longest term of service with one team in Negro Leagues history; won nine consecutive Negro National League championships (1937–1945); won three Negro League World Series (1943–1944, 1948).

The 5'10", 185-pound Leonard played for the Brooklyn Royal Giants (1933) and the Homestead Grays (1934–1950); appeared in a record 11 East-West All-Star games; and his 17-year tenure with the Grays is the longest term of service with one team in Negro Leagues history.

He helped the Grays win nine consecutive Negro National League championships (1937–1945) and to five Negro League World Series (winning in 1943–1944, 1948 and losing in 1942 and 1945).

Although Negro League records are not always considered reliable, it has been documented that over a 17-year career in the Negro National League, Leonard's lifetime batting average was .341.

After retiring as a player, he worked as a truant officer, physical education instructor, and vice-president of a minor league team in his hometown.

In 1999, he ranked number 47 on *The Sporting News*' list of the 100 Greatest Baseball Players, one of five players so honored who played all or most of their careers in the Negro Leagues; was nominated for the Major League Baseball All-Century Team; and is the only Negro League first baseman inducted into the baseball hall of fame.

Source: National Baseball Hall of Fame and Museum

LeSueur, Percy (born: November 18, 1881 in Quebec City, Quebec, Canada; died: January 27, 1962); inducted into the Hockey Hall of Fame in 1961 as a player; Position: Goalie; won two Stanley Cup championships.

After playing amateur and senior hockey, LeSueur played 11 pre-National Hockey League seasons from 1905 to 1916. After the Smiths Falls Seniors (Ontario Hockey Association) lost its March 1906 Stanley Cup challenge to the Ottawa Silver Seven, the 5'7", 150-pound LeSueur switched teams and played for Ottawa in its March 1906 Cup defense, which it lost to the Montreal Wanderers, He would go on to play nine seasons in Ottawa.

LeSueur was on the Ottawa team (now called the Senators and playing in the National Hockey Association) that won two Stanley Cup championships (1910–1911). He played for the Toronto Shamrocks in 1914–1915, before ending his career with the Toronto Blueshirts in 1916.

He was the first manager of both the Windsor Arena (Ontario, Canada) and the Detroit Olympia (Michigan) stadiums; in 1927–1928, LeSueur coached the Detroit Olympics (Canadian Professional Hockey League); and later managed the Buffalo Bisons (International Hockey League).

Percy LeSeuer's Career Statistics

			REGULAR SEASON						PLAYOFFS					
SEASON	TEAM	LEAGUE	GP	W	L	T	SO	AVG	GP	W	L	T	SO	AVG
1903–1904	Smiths Falls Seniors	OHA-Sr.	6	3	3	0	2	2.11						
1904–1905	Smiths Falls Seniors	OHA-Sr.												
1905–1906	Smiths Falls Seniors	FAHL	7	7	0	0	1	2.30						
1905–1906	Smiths Falls Seniors	St-Cup							2	0	2	0	0	7.00
1905–1906	Ottawa Silver Seven	ECAHA												

SEASON	TEAM	LEAGUE	REGULAR SEASON GP	W	L	T	SO	AVG	PLAYOFFS GP	W	L	T	SO	AVG
1905–1906	Ottawa Silver Seven	St-Cup							1	1	0	0	0	3.00
1906–1907	Ottawa Senators	ECAHA	10	7	3	0	0	5.38						
1907–1908	Ottawa Senators	ECAHA	10	7	3	0	0	4.86						
1908–1909	Ottawa Senators	ECHA	12	10	2	0	0	5.19						
1909–1910	Ottawa Senators	CHA	2	2	0	0	0	4.50						
1909–1910	Ottawa Senators	NHA	12	9	3	0	0	5.41						
1909–1910	Ottawa Senators	St-Cup							4	4	0	0	0	3.75
1910–1911	Ottawa Senators	NHA	16	13	3	0	1	4.18						
1910–1911	Ottawa Senators	St-Cup							2	2	0	0	0	4.00
1911–1912	Ottawa Senators	NHA	18	9	9	0	0	4.84						
1912–1913	Ottawa Senators	NHA	18	7	10	0	0	4.18						
1913–1914	Ottawa Senators	NHA	13	6	6	0	1	3.26						
1914–1915	Toronto Shamrocks	NHA	19	8	11	0	0	5.03						
1915–1916	Toronto Blueshirts	NHA	23	9	13	0	1	3.90						

Sources: Hockey Hall of Fame; Hockey-Reference.com

Levy, Marvin Daniel "Marv" (born: August 3, 1925 in Chicago, Illinois); inducted into the Pro Football Hall of Fame in 2001 as a coach; won two Canadian Football League championships; as of this writing, he is the only coach to compete in four consecutive Super Bowls (1991–1994).

A graduate of Coe College (Cedar Rapids, Iowa), Levy coached the National Football League's Kansas City Chiefs (1978–1982) and the Buffalo Bills (1986–1997). He began his professional career in 1969 as kicking teams coach for the Philadelphia Eagles, before working for George Allen as a special teams coach for the Los Angeles Rams in 1970. After two seasons, he left the Rams to become head coach of the Montreal Alouettes (Canadian Football League) for five seasons, winning two league championships (Grey Cup, 1974, 1977).

Levy returned to the NFL in 1978 as head coach of the Kansas City Chiefs, where he would stay until 1982. After leaving the NFL for three seasons (a mini two-year retirement from coaching and serving one year as the head coach for the Chicago Blitz [1986] of the United States Football League), he returned to the NFL as head coach of the Buffalo Bills, where he would stay until 1997. He led the team to four straight Super Bowls (the only coach ever to do so), losing them all (SB XXV in 1991 through SB XXVIII [1994]); compiled an overall record of 154–120–0 (.562, tenth most wins in league history at the time of his retirement); named NFL Coach of the Year in 1988; and was selected American Football Conference Coach of the Year three times (1988, 1993, 1995).

Following his 1943 graduation from South Shore High School (Chicago, Illinois), Levy enlisted in the U.S. Army Air Forces during World War II. After leaving the military, he enrolled at Coe College and earned varsity letters in football, track, and basketball, and attended Harvard University (Cambridge, Massachusetts) for graduate studies in 1951.

His first coaching job was at St. Louis Country Day School (St. Louis, Missouri, 1951–1952), where he coached football and basketball. Two years later, Levy returned to Coe College as an assistant football coach (1953–1954), before joining the coaching staff at the University of New Mexico (Albuquerque, 1954–1958), where he became head coach in 1958. In two seasons as head coach (1958–1959), he led the Lobos to a 14–6 (.700) record and was named Skyline Conference Coach of the Year both seasons.

He became the head coach at the University of California (Berkeley) in February 1960, where he stayed until 1963, before finishing his college career as head coach at the College of William and Mary (Williamsburg, Virginia, 1964–1968), where he was twice named Southern Conference Coach of the Year.

Levy was named to the NFL 1990s All-Decade Team and was added to the Buffalo Bills Wall of Fame in 1996.

Marv Levy's Managerial Record

YEAR	TEAM	REGULAR SEASON W	L	WIN%	PLAYOFFS W	L	WIN%
1978	Kansas City	4	12	.250			
1979	Kansas City	7	9	.438			
1980	Kansas City	8	8	.500			
1981	Kansas City	9	7	.563			
1982	Kansas City	3	6	.333			
1986	Buffalo	2	5	.286			
1987	Buffalo	7	8	.467			
1988	Buffalo	12	4	.750	1	1	.500

YEAR	TEAM	REGULAR SEASON W	L	WIN%	PLAYOFFS W	L	WIN%
1989	Buffalo	9	7	.563	0	1	.000
1990	Buffalo	13	3	.813	2	1	.667
1991	Buffalo	13	3	.813	2	1	.667
1992	Buffalo	11	5	.688	3	1	.750
1993	Buffalo	12	4	.750	2	1	.667
1994	Buffalo	7	9	.438			
1995	Buffalo	10	6	.625	1	1	.500
1996	Buffalo	10	6	.625	0	1	.000
1997	Buffalo	6	10	.375			
	Kansas City	31	42	.425	0	0	.000
	Buffalo	112	70	.615	11	8	.579
	TOTALS	143	112	.561	11	8	.579

Source: Pro Football Hall of Fame; Pro-Football-Reference.com

Lewis, Herbert "Herbie" (born: April 17, 1905 in Calgary, Alberta, Canada; died: January 20, 1991 in Indianapolis, Indiana); inducted into the Hockey Hall of Fame in 1989 as a player; Position: Left Wing; played in the first-ever NHL All-Star game (1934); played in the longest NHL game in history (March 1936); won two Stanley Cup championships.

After playing city, junior, and amateur hockey, the 5'9", 163-pound Lewis played 11 National Hockey League seasons (1928–1939) with the Detroit Cougars (1928–1930), Detroit Falcons (1930–1932), and the Detroit Red Wings (1932–1939).

He played in the first-ever NHL All-Star game in 1934 (the Ace Bailey Benefit Game); participated in the longest NHL game in history on March 24–25 (1936) when his Red Wings defeated the Montreal Maroons 1–0 after six overtime periods; and helped the Red Wings win two Stanley Cup championships (1936–1937).

When Lewis left the NHL in 1939, he served as a player, coach, and general manager for the Indianapolis Capitols (International-American Hockey League), and was the team's coach when it won the Calder Cup in 1942.

Herbert Lewis' Career Statistics

SEASON	TEAM	LEAGUE	REGULAR SEASON GP	G	A	TP	PIM	PLAYOFFS GP	G	A	TP	PIM
1921–1922	Calgary Hustlers	CCJHL										
1921–1922	Calgary Hustlers	M-Cup	6	5	1	6	2					
1922–1923	Calgary Canadians	CCJHL	12	17	7	24	24					
1922–1923	Calgary Canadians	M-Cup	4	5	4	9	8					
1923–1924	Calgary Canadians	CCJHL										
1923–1924	Calgary Canadians	M-Cup	7	12	8	20	13					
1924–1925	Duluth Hornets	USAHA	40	9	0	9						
1925–1926	Duluth Hornets	CHL	39	17	11	28	52	8	3	1	4	8
1926–1927	Duluth Hornets	AHA	37	18	6	24	52	3	1	0	1	2
1927–1928	Duluth Hornets	AHA	40	14	5	19	56	5	0	0	0	8
1928–1929	Detroit Cougars	NHL	36	9	5	14	33					
1929–1930	Detroit Cougars	NHL	44	20	11	31	36					
1930–1931	Detroit Falcons	NHL	43	15	6	21	38					
1931–1932	Detroit Falcons	NHL	48	5	14	19	21	2	0	0	0	0
1932–1933	Detroit Red Wings	NHL	48	20	14	34	20	4	1	0	1	0
1933–1934	Detroit Red Wings	NHL	43	16	15	31	15	9	5	2	7	2
1934–1935	Detroit Red Wings	NHL	47	16	27	43	26					
1935–1936	Detroit Red Wings	NHL	45	14	23	37	25	7	2	3	5	0
1936–1937	Detroit Red Wings	NHL	45	14	18	32	14	10	4	3	7	4
1937–1938	Detroit Red Wings	NHL	42	13	18	31	12					
1938–1939	Detroit Red Wings	NHL	42	6	10	16	8	6	1	2	3	0
1939–1940	Indianapolis Capitols	IAHL	26	1	6	7	6	3	1	2	3	0
1940–1941	Indianapolis Capitols	AHL	2	1	0	1	0					
1941–1942	Indianapolis Capitols	AHL										
	NHL TOTALS		483	148	161	309	248	38	13	10	23	6

Sources: Hockey Hall of Fame; Hockey-Reference.com

Lewis, Horace Edgar (born: 1882 in Pontardulais, Wales; died: December 5, 1948 in Pittsburgh, Pennsylvania); inducted into the National Soccer Hall of Fame and Museum in 1950 as a builder; first president of the American Soccer League.

Lewis came to the United States at age 14, and eventually became a successful businessman with Bethlehem Steel Company (Pennsylvania), the Jeffrey Manufacturing Company (Columbus, Ohio), and Jones and Laughlin.

A lifelong soccer fan, while with Bethlehem Steel, he recruited players from Europe who would eventually go on to form one of the great teams of American soccer history. He was the driving force behind the great Bethlehem Steel teams from 1915 to 1930, and helped create the original American Soccer League, serving as its first president. His Bethlehem teams won the U.S. Open Cup five times (1915–1916, 1918–1919, 1926); the American Football Association Challenge five times (1916–1919, 1924); the ASL championship twice (1921, 1927); and the Lewis Cup in 1928.

He donated the Lewis Cup, originally presented to the winner of a special ASL cup tournament, but during the "soccer war" between the United States Football Association and the ASL in 1928, he withdrew the Cup for several seasons. In later years, the Cup was awarded to the ASL league champion, but he eventually stopped participating and withdrew the award. Deeply bothered by the entire soccer situation in the United States at the time, Lewis withdrew Bethlehem Steel from soccer competition in 1930.

Source: National Soccer Hall of Fame and Museum

Lieberman, Nancy Elizabeth (born: July 1, 1958 in Brooklyn, New York); inducted into the Naismith Memorial Basketball Hall of Fame in 1996 as a player; Position: Guard; first two-time winner of the Wade Trophy as national college basketball Player of the Year; youngest basketball player in Olympic history to win a medal (1976); first female ever inducted into the New York City Basketball Hall of Fame; first woman to play in a men's league (Springfield Flame of the United States Basketball League).

Lieberman was a three-year letter-winner in basketball at Far Rockaway (New York) High School (1972–1976), where she was a three-time All-American, All-State, and All-Conference selection (1974–1976). After graduating high school, she attended Old Dominion University (Norfolk, Virginia, 1976–1980), before playing professional basketball.

Growing up in Far Rockaway, the 5'10" guard learned and developed her basketball skills on Harlem courts. Being taller than most of the players, she played a physical and aggressive game that was unusual in women players at the time. While still in high school, she was named to the USA Women's National Team and played in the World Championships and Pan American Games, winning a gold medal in 1975 and a silver medal in 1979.

At age 18, she became the youngest basketball player in Olympic history to win a medal when the U.S. team captured a silver at the 1976 Olympics (Montreal, Canada). While at Old Dominion, she won two consecutive Association for Intercollegiate Athletics for Women National Championships (1979–1980) and one Women's National Invitation Tournament championship in 1978. She was the first two-time winner of the Wade Trophy (national college basketball Player of the Year); a two-time Broderick Cup winner for basketball as the top women's player in America (1979–1980); and was a three-time Kodak All-American (1978–1980). She finished her career at ODU with 2,430 points, 1,167 rebounds, and 961 assists.

Lieberman dropped out of college to play professional basketball and was the number one draft choice of the Dallas Diamonds of the Women's Basketball League/Women's American Basketball Association in 1980; selected WABA Most Valuable Player; and led the Diamonds to the league title in 1985. After leaving the WABA, she made history by becoming the first woman to play in a men's league when she was a member of the Springfield Flame of the United States Basketball League (1986–1987). In the 1987–1988 season, she made news again by joining the Washington Generals on a world tour with the Harlem Globetrotters.

At age 38, she briefly returned to professional basketball with the Phoenix Mercury (1997–1998) for the inaugural Women's National Basketball Association season, leaving after one year to become head coach and general manager of the WNBA's Detroit Shock (1998–2000).

In 2000, while serving as president of the Women's Sports Foundation, she returned to Old Dominion University and completed her undergraduate degree. She became a basketball analyst for ESPN's coverage of men's and women's college basketball, the WNBA, and the National Basketball Development League. On January 16, 2004, she returned to the game as the coach of the Dallas Fury (National Women's Basketball League).

Lieberman was the first female inducted into the New York City Basketball Hall of Fame; was inducted into the Women's Basketball Hall of Fame in 1999; and in 2000, she was inducted into the Nassau County Sports Hall of Fame and the Virginia Sports Hall of Fame. The annual Nancy Lieberman Award is presented to the best female point guard in Division I basketball.

Sources: Nancy Lieberman Web Site (www.nancylieberman.com); Naismith Memorial Basketball Hall of Fame

Lilly, Robert Lewis "Bob" (born: July 26, 1939 in Olney, Texas); inducted into the Pro Football Hall of Fame in 1980 as a player; Position: Defensive Tackle; Uniform: #74; first player who spent his entire career with the Dallas Cowboys to be inducted into the football hall of fame; won Super Bowl VI.

Lilly was a two-time All-Southwest Conference selection and a consensus All-American at Texas Christian University (Fort Worth, 1958–1960). After college, he was a first-round pick (13th overall selection) in the 1961 National Football League Draft by the Dallas Cowboys and played his entire 14-season (196 games) NFL career with the team (1961–1974); first player who spent his entire career with the Dallas Cowboys to be inducted into the Pro Football Hall of Fame; NFL Rookie of the Year (1961); an All-NFL/National Football Conference selection eight times (1964–1969, 1971–1972); named to 11 Pro Bowls; and played in five NFL/NFC title games and two Super Bowls (winning in SB VI [1972] and losing in SB V [1971]).

Effective as both a pass rusher and a run stopper, the 6'5", 260-pound Lilly scored four touchdowns in his career (a 17-yard interception and three fumble recoveries).

His name was the first inscribed in the "Ring of Honor" at Texas Stadium (1975); *The Sporting News* named him a member of the All-Century NFL Team; he was inducted into the College Football Hall of Fame in 1981; in 1999, was ranked number 10 on *The Sporting News*' list of the 100 Greatest Football Players, the highest-ranking defensive lineman and the highest-ranking Cowboy; and he was selected to the NFL's 75th Anniversary Team (1994) and to the AFL-NFL 25-year Anniversary Team.

Sources: Bob Lilly Web Site (www.boblilly.com); Pro Football Hall of Fame

Lindsay, Robert Blake Theodore "Ted" (born: July 29, 1925 in Renfrew, Ontario, Canada); inducted into the Hockey Hall of Fame in 1966 as a player; Position: Left Wing; Uniform: #7; won four Stanley Cup championships.

The 5'8", 160-pound Lindsay spent more time in the penalty box than any other player in his era, and played 17 National Hockey League seasons (1944–1965) with the Detroit Red Wings (1944–1957, 1964–1965) and Chicago Black Hawks (1957–1960). He won the Art Ross Trophy in 1950 as the regular-season scoring leader, a nine-time All-Star (First Team [1948, 1950–1954, 1956–1957] and Second Team [1949]); and won four Stanley Cup championships with Detroit (1950, 1952, 1954–1955).

Before joining the NHL, Lindsay played junior and minor league hockey in the Gold Belt Hockey League, St. Michael's College (Toronto, Ontario, Canada), and in the Ontario Hockey Association (junior), where he helped the Oshawa Generals win the 1944 Memorial Cup, before joining the Red Wings.

In 1957, he was traded to the Black Hawks, where he played for three seasons, before retiring in 1960. He played one more season in Detroit (1964–1965), before retiring for good. He later returned to the Red Wings as a general manager in 1977 and was named NHL Executive of the Year.

In November 1991, Detroit retired his jersey number seven, and in 1998, he was ranked number 21 on *The Hockey News*' list of the 100 Greatest Hockey Players.

Ted Lindsay's Career Statistics

			REGULAR SEASON					PLAYOFFS				
SEASON	**TEAM**	**LEAGUE**	**GP**	**G**	**A**	**TP**	**PIM**	**GP**	**G**	**A**	**TP**	**PIM**
1942–1943	Kirkland Lake Lakers	GBHL										
1943–1944	St. Michael's Majors	OHA-Jr.	22	22	7	29	24	12	13	6	19	16
1943–1944	Oshawa Generals	M-Cup	7	7	2	9	6					
1944–1945	Detroit Red Wings	NHL	45	17	6	23	43	14	2	0	2	6
1945–1946	Detroit Red Wings	NHL	47	7	10	17	14	5	0	1	1	0
1946–1947	Detroit Red Wings	NHL	59	27	15	42	57	5	2	2	4	10
1947–1948	Detroit Red Wings	NHL	60	33	19	52	95	10	3	1	4	6
1948–1949	Detroit Red Wings	NHL	50	26	28	54	97	11	2	6	8	31
1949–1950	Detroit Red Wings	NHL	69	23	55	78	141	13	4	4	8	16
1950–1951	Detroit Red Wings	NHL	67	24	35	59	110	6	0	1	1	8
1951–1952	Detroit Red Wings	NHL	70	30	39	69	123	8	5	2	7	8
1952–1953	Detroit Red Wings	NHL	70	32	39	71	111	6	4	4	8	6
1953–1954	Detroit Red Wings	NHL	70	26	36	62	110	12	4	4	8	14
1954–1955	Detroit Red Wings	NHL	49	19	19	38	85	11	7	12	19	12
1955–1956	Detroit Red Wings	NHL	67	27	23	50	161	10	6	3	9	22

SEASON	TEAM	LEAGUE	REGULAR SEASON GP	G	A	TP	PIM	PLAYOFFS GP	G	A	TP	PIM
1956–1957	Detroit Red Wings	NHL	70	30	55	85	103	5	2	4	6	8
1957–1958	Chicago Black Hawks	NHL	68	15	24	39	110					
1958–1959	Chicago Black Hawks	NHL	70	22	36	58	184	6	2	4	6	13
1959–1960	Chicago Black Hawks	NHL	68	7	19	26	91	4	1	1	2	0
1964–1965	Detroit Red Wings	NHL	69	14	14	28	173	7	3	0	3	34
	NHL TOTALS		1,068	379	472	851	1,808	133	47	49	96	194

Sources: Hockey Hall of Fame; Hockey-Reference.com

Lindstrom, Frederick Charles "Fred" "Freddie" (born: November 21, 1905 in Chicago, Illinois; died: October 4, 1981 in Chicago, Illinois); inducted into the National Baseball Hall of Fame and Museum in 1976 as a player by the Veterans Committee; Position: Third Base; Bats: Right; Throws: Right; first National League player in the 20th century to collect nine hits in a doubleheader; youngest player to appear in a World Series game.

Lindstrom dropped out of high school after his sophomore year at Loyola Academy (Chicago, Illinois) to play for the Toledo Mud Hens (American Association) in 1922, before becoming the youngest player (18 years, 10 months, 13 days) to appear in a World Series game (two years later with the New York Giants). He hit .300 or better seven times and had 231 hits in a season twice.

Making his major league debut on April 15, 1924, the 5'11", 170-pound Lindstrom played 13 National League seasons with the New York Giants (1924–1932), Pittsburgh Pirates (1933–1934), Chicago Cubs (1935), and Brooklyn Dodgers (1936), and appeared in two losing World Series (1924, 1935).

On June 25, 1928, Lindstrom became the first National League player in the 20th century to have nine hits in a doubleheader (June 25, 1928 against the Philadelphia Phillies and helped the team win both games, 12–4 and 8–2), a record that still stands.

After retiring as a player, he managed in the minor leagues in the early 1940s until serving as the baseball coach at Northwestern University (Evanston/Chicago, Illinois) from 1948 to 1962.

Freddie Lindstrom's Career Statistics

YEAR	TEAM	LG	G	AB	R	H	2B	3B	HR	RBI	BB	SO	SB	AVG	SLG
1924	New York	NL	52	79	19	20	3	1	0	4	6	10	3	.253	.316
1925	New York	NL	104	356	43	102	15	12	4	33	22	20	5	.287	.430
1926	New York	NL	140	543	90	164	19	9	9	76	39	21	11	.302	.420
1927	New York	NL	138	562	107	172	36	8	7	58	40	40	10	.306	.436
1928	New York	NL	153	646	99	231	39	9	14	107	25	21	15	.358	.511
1929	New York	NL	130	549	99	175	23	6	15	91	30	28	10	.319	.464
1930	New York	NL	148	609	127	231	39	7	22	106	48	33	15	.379	.575
1931	New York	NL	78	303	38	91	12	6	5	36	26	12	5	.300	.429
1932	New York	NL	144	595	83	161	26	5	15	92	27	28	6	.271	.407
1933	Pittsburgh	NL	138	538	70	167	39	10	5	55	33	22	1	.310	.448
1934	Pittsburgh	NL	97	383	59	111	24	4	4	49	23	21	1	.290	.405
1935	Chicago	NL	90	342	49	94	22	4	3	62	10	13	1	.275	.389
1936	Brooklyn	NL	26	106	12	28	4	0	0	10	5	7	1	.264	.302
	TOTALS		1,438	5,611	895	1,747	301	81	103	779	334	276	84	.311	.449

Sources: Baseball-Reference.com; National Baseball Hall of Fame and Museum

Liston, Emil S. (born: August 21, 1890 in Stockton, Missouri; died: October 26, 1949); inducted into the Naismith Memorial Basketball Hall of Fame in 1975 as a contributor; created the National Association of Intercollegiate Athletics Tournament; president of the Kansas Conference Coaches Association.

After graduating from the Baker Academy (Baldwin, Kansas) in 1909, Liston attended Baker University (Baldwin), where he was an All-Conference forward (1912–1913); graduated in 1913; and later went to Harvard University (Cambridge, Massachusetts), graduating in 1930.

While attending Baker University; he won 11 varsity letters and served as the basketball coach at his old high school from 1911 to 1913, where he led the school to the 1912 Kansas state title. Liston went on to coach at Fort Scott (Kansas) High School and Kemper (Missouri) Military School, leading Kemper to the Missouri Military School Championship.

He joined the college coaching ranks at Wesleyan University (Middletown, Connecticut); moved on to the Michigan College of Mines (Houghton); and finally became the long-time basketball coach at his alma mater (Baker University, 1920–1945), leading the school to two Kansas Conference Championships (1930, 1937).

Liston created the National Association of Intercollegiate Athletics Tournament in 1937 (then called the National Association of Intercollegiate Basketball) with the help of Dr. James Naismith, the first national college basketball tournament in the United States; served as NAIA Executive Secretary (1940–1949); oversaw NAIA membership growth from 40 to 300; spent 25 years at Baker University as the school's athletic director; compiled a .650 winning percentage in basketball, baseball, and football at Baker; organized the Kansas Conference Coaches Association and represented the Missouri Valley District at Amateur Athletic Union meetings; and served as president of the Kansas Conference Coaches Association (1936–1938) and the Missouri Valley AAU.

The Emil S. Liston Award is presented annually to both a male and female basketball player for their scholarship, character, and playing ability. Located inside Baker University's Charlie Richard Outdoor Sports Facility, the Liston Stadium is named in his honor.

Source: Naismith Memorial Basketball Hall of Fame

Little, Floyd Douglas (born: July 4, 1942 in New Haven, Connecticut); inducted into the Pro Football Hall of Fame in 2010 as a player; Position: Running Back; Uniform: #44; NFL rushing leader in 1971

After attending Syracuse University (Syracuse, New York) where he was a three-time All-American, the 5'10", 196-pound Little was selected by the Denver Broncos in the first round (number six pick overall) of the 1967 AFL/NFL Draft. He played for the Broncos his entire career (nine years and 117 games in the AFL from 1967 to 1969 and in the NFL from 1970 until 1975); was a two-time AFL All-Star (1968–1969); named to the Pro Bowl three times (1970–1971, 1973); was a charter member of the Denver Broncos Ring of Fame in 1984; and had his jersey number 44 retired by the team. Little was inducted into the College Football Hall of Fame in 1983.

As a rookie, he led the AFL in punt returns (16 for 270 yards); led the American Football Conference in rushing in 1970; in 1971, he became the team's first-ever 1,000-yard rusher; won the NFL rushing title in 1971; and ran for more yards than any other rusher from 1968 to 1973. He led the league in combined yards in 1967 and 1968; was the only player to return punts for TDs in both seasons; and was named "Running Back of the Year" in 1972 by the Professional Football Writers of America. In addition to his rushing duties, Little was also used as a receiver out of the backfield and caught at least 25 passes in each of his last five seasons.

When he retired, Little held the following team records: Most Yards Rushing in a Career (6,323); Most Rushing Attempts in a Career (1,641); Highest Punt Return Average in a Single Season (16.87 in 1967); and Longest Non-Scoring Kickoff Return in a Game (89 yards against the Oakland Raiders on November 10, 1968).

Floyd Little's NFL Career Statistics

			RUSHING				RECEIVING				SCORING		
Year	**Team**	**G**	**ATT**	**YDS**	**AVG**	**TD**	**NO**	**YDS**	**AVG**	**TD**	**TD**	**PTS**	**F**
1967	Denver	13	130	381	2.9	1	7	11	1.6	0	2	12	3
1968	Denver	11	158	584	3.7	3	19	331	17.4	1	5	30	6
1969	Denver	9	146	729	5.0	6	19	218	11.5	1	7	42	2
1970	Denver	14	209	901	4.3	3	17	161	9.5	0	3	18	6
1971	Denver	14	284	1,133	4.0	6	26	255	9.8	0	6	36	4
1972	Denver	14	216	859	4.0	9	28	367	13.1	4	13	78	4
1973	Denver	14	256	979	3.8	12	41	423	10.3	1	13	78	3
1974	Denver	14	117	312	2.7	1	29	344	11.9	0	1	6	2
1975	Denver	14	125	445	3.6	2	29	308	10.6	2	4	24	2
	TOTALS	117	1,641	6,323	3.9	43	215	2,418	11.2	9	54	324	32

Floyd Little's NFL Career Statistics

			PUNT RETURNS				KICKOFF RETURNS			
Year	**Team**	**G**	**NO**	**YDS**	**AVG**	**TD**	**NO**	**YDS**	**AVG**	**TD**
1967	Denver	13	16	270	16.9	1	35	942	26.9	0
1968	Denver	11	24	261	10.9	1	26	649	25.0	0
1969	Denver	9	6	70	11.7	0	3	81	27.0	0

			PUNT RETURNS				KICKOFF RETURNS			
Year	**Team**	**G**	**NO**	**YDS**	**AVG**	**TD**	**NO**	**YDS**	**AVG**	**TD**
1970	Denver	14	22	187	8.5	0	6	126	21.0	0
1971	Denver	14	0	0	0.0	0	7	199	28.4	0
1972	Denver	14	8	64	8.0	0	3	48	16.0	0
1973	Denver	14	1	7	7.0	0	0	0	0.0	0
1974	Denver	14	4	34	8.5	0	8	171	21.4	0
1975	Denver	14	0	0	0.0	0	16	307	19.2	0
	TOTALS	117	81	893	11	2	104	2,523	24.3	0

Sources: Pro Football Hall of Fame; Pro-Football-Reference.com

Little, Lawrence Chatmon "Larry" (born: November 2, 1945 in Groveland, Georgia); inducted into the Pro Football Hall of Fame in 1993 as a player; Position: Offensive Guard; Uniform: #66; won two Super Bowls.

After being a two-way tackle, team captain, and All-Conference pick at Bethune-Cookman College (Daytona Beach, Florida), Little began his National Football League career as a free agent with the San Diego Chargers in 1967, and went on to play 14 years (183 games) for the Chargers (1967–1968) and the Miami Dolphins (1969–1980).

After two seasons in San Diego, the 6'1", 265-pound Little was traded to Miami and was with the team in its undefeated 1972 season. He was named All-Pro six times (1971–1975, 1977); a five-time Pro Bowl selection (1970, 1972–1975); and played in three Super Bowls, winning in 1973 (SB VII) and 1974 (SB VIII), and losing in 1972 (SB VI).

In 1999, he was ranked number 79 on *The Sporting News*' list of the 100 Greatest Football Players.

Source: Pro Football Hall of Fame

Litwack, Harold "Harry" (born: September 20, 1907 in Galacia, Austria; died: August 7, 1999 in Huntingdon Valley, Pennsylvania); inducted into the Naismith Memorial Basketball Hall of Fame in 1976 as a coach; won four professional championships as a player; had only one losing season in 21 years at Temple University; won the NIT title in 1969.

Born in Austria but raised in Philadelphia, Pennsylvania, Litwack attended South Philadelphia High School (1921–1925), where he played basketball four years; was selected All-League three times; a two-time team Most Valuable Player; and led the team twice each in scoring and assists. He went on to Temple University (Philadelphia), where he played three years on the school's varsity team; was a two-time captain and team MVP (1928–1929); and led the squad twice in scoring and assists.

After graduating from Temple in 1930, Litwack played professional basketball for the Philadelphia SPHAs (South Philadelphia Hebrew Association) of the Eastern/American Basketball League from 1930 to 1936, and helped the team win two championships in each league (1931–1932 in the EBL and 1934, 1936 in the ABL).

While playing professional basketball, Litwack also coached at Simon Gratz High School (Philadelphia, 1930–1931) and led the team to a 15–2 record; served as the freshman basketball head coach at his alma mater from 1931 to 1947; and was the school's varsity coach from 1947 to 1973. He coached the freshman teams to a 181–32 (.850) record and the varsity squads to a 373–193 (.659) record; had only one losing season in 21 years as the school's varsity coach; won the National Invitational Tournament in 1969; named Philadelphia Basketball Writers Association Coach of the Year (1956); New York Basketball Writers Association Coach of the Year (1958); and has been inducted into the Temple University, Pennsylvania, South Philadelphia High School, and Big Five halls of fame.

He also served as an assistant coach with the Philadelphia Warriors of the Basketball Association of America/National Basketball Association from 1948 to 1951.

In 1957, Litwack coached the United States Maccabiah basketball team, and was inducted into the International Jewish Sports Hall of Fame in 1980.

Source: Naismith Memorial Basketball Hall of Fame

Lloyd, Earl Francis (born: April 3, 1928 in Alexandria, Virginia); inducted into the Naismith Memorial Basketball Hall of Fame in 2003 as a contributor; Position: Forward-Center; first African-American to play in an NBA game; won the 1955 NBA championship.

Lloyd was the first African-American to play in a National Basketball Association game (October 31, 1950 against the Rochester Royals); first African-American to win an NBA championship (1955 with the Syracuse Nationals); first African-American assistant coach, with the NBA's Detroit Pistons (1968–1970); and was the second African-American head coach and first African-American bench coach, with the Pistons (1970–1971).

He attended Parker-Gray High School (Alexandria), where he was a three-time All-South Atlantic Conference selection (1944–1946) and a two-time All-State Virginia Interscholastic Conference pick (1945–1946). After graduating in 1946, he went to West Virginia State College (Institute, West Virginia), where he graduated in 1950.

At West Virginia, Lloyd was a three-time Central Intercollegiate Athletic Association All-Conference selection (1948–1950); named a two-time All-American by the *Pittsburgh Courier* (1949–1950); led the team to back-to-back CIAA Conference and Tournament Championships (1948–1949); and helped the team become the only undefeated squad in the United States in the 1947–1948 season.

After college, the 6'6", 220-pound Lloyd was selected in the ninth-round of the 1950 NBA Draft by the Washington Capitols. He was one of three African-American players drafted that year, and only because of the league schedule, did he become the first African-American to play in an NBA game (one day ahead of Charles Cooper of the Boston Celtics (who was the first black player drafted by an NBA team) and four days ahead of Nat Clifton of the New York Knicks).

After playing in only seven games before the team folded, Lloyd then served in the Army, and joined the NBA's Syracuse Nationals in 1952 after completing his military service. He played with the team until 1958, before ending his career with the Detroit Pistons (1958–1960). He helped Syracuse win the 1955 NBA title.

After his playing career, he served as an assistant coach with the Pistons (1968–1970) and as the team's head coach (1971–1973), he led the squad to an overall 22–55 (.286) record in just over a season.

Lloyd was named to the All-Time CIAA All-Tournament team; inducted into the CIAA Hall of Fame in 1998; named to the CIAA Silver Anniversary Team; voted one of the CIAA's 50 Greatest Players; named CIAA "Player of the Decade, 1947–56"; and named to the National Association of Intercollegiate Athletics Golden Anniversary Team.

Earl Lloyd's Career Playing Statistics

SEASON	TEAM	LG	G	MIN	FG	FT	TRB	AST	PTS
1950–1951	Washington	NBA	7		16	11	47	11	43
1952–1953	Syracuse	NBA	64	1,806	156	160	444	64	472
1953–1954	Syracuse	NBA	72	2,206	249	156	529	115	654
1954–1955	Syracuse	NBA	72	2,212	286	159	553	151	731
1955–1956	Syracuse	NBA	72	1,837	213	186	492	116	612
1956–1957	Syracuse	NBA	72	1,965	256	134	435	114	646
1957–1958	Syracuse	NBA	61	1,045	119	79	287	60	317
1958–1959	Detroit	NBA	72	1,796	234	137	500	90	605
1959–1960	Detroit	NBA	68	1,610	237	128	322	89	602
	TOTALS		560	14,477	1,766	1,150	3,609	810	4,682

Sources: Basketball-Reference.com; Naismith Memorial Basketball Hall of Fame

Lloyd, John Henry "Pop" (born: April 25, 1884 in Palatka, Florida; died: March 19, 1965 in Atlantic City, New Jersey); inducted into the National Baseball Hall of Fame and Museum in 1977 as a Negro Leaguer by the Negro Leagues Committee; Position: Shortstop; Bats: Left; Throws: Right; played in the first Negro League game ever held at Yankee Stadium; won the first Eastern Colored League title as a player-manager with the Hilldale Daisies.

In a professional baseball career that lasted more than 30 years, Lloyd played for the Cuban X-Giants (Independent, 1906); Philadelphia Giants (Independent, 1907–1909); Leland Giants (Independent, 1910); New York Lincoln Giants (Independent, 1911–1915, Negro American League, 1926–1930); Chicago American Giants (Independent, 1914–1917); New York Lincoln Stars (Independent, 1915); Brooklyn Royal Giants (Independent, 1918–1920); New York Bacharach Giants (Independent, 1919); Atlantic City Bacharach Giants (Independent, 1922, 1924–1925, 1931–1932); Columbus Buckeyes (Negro National League, 1921); Hilldale Daisies (Eastern Colored League, 1923); and the Harlem Stars (Independent, 1931). He also managed the Brooklyn Royal Giants (Independent, 1918–1920); Columbus Buckeyes (Negro National League, 1921); New York Bacharachs (Independent, 1922); and the Hilldale Daisies (Eastern Colored League, 1923).

On July 5, 1930, while with the New York Lincoln Giants, he played in the first Negro League game ever held at Yankee Stadium (New York City) against the Baltimore Black Sox.

After his Negro League playing days, he moved to Atlantic City, New Jersey; was active in Little League baseball; and the city named Pop Lloyd Stadium after him.

He began his professional career in 1905 as a catcher with the Acmes of Macon, Georgia, before moving on to play second base with the Cuban X Giants of Philadelphia in 1906. The following season, he moved to the Philadelphia Giants and moved to shortstop, where he played for most of his career.

In 1921, Lloyd was hired to organize the Columbus Buckeyes in the newly-created Negro National League, but after finishing seventh in an eight-team league, the franchise folded after only one season. When the Eastern Colored League was formed in 1923, he was hired as a player-manager for the Hilldale Daisies; led the team to a 32–17 (.653) record; and won the first ECL title. In 1924, he played for the Atlantic City Bacharachs and helped the team win the 1924 ECL title.

During his career, Lloyd played 12 seasons in the Cuban League from 1908 to 1930, and won three championships (with Havana in 1912 and Almendares in 1925 and 1926).

Source: National Baseball Hall of Fame and Museum

Lockhart, Thomas F. (born: March 21, 1892 in New York, New York; died: May 18, 1979); inducted into the Hockey Hall of Fame in 1965 as a builder; formed the Eastern Amateur Hockey League; served as commissioner of the EAHL for almost 40 years; helped organize the Amateur Hockey Association of the United States.

In 1932, Lockhart began promoting amateur hockey games at Madison Square Garden (New York, New York); organized the Eastern Amateur Hockey League in 1933; in 1934, he began an 18-year term as vice-president of the Metropolitan Amateur Hockey League; was president of the EAHL in 1935; and served as commissioner of the EAHL from 1933 to 1972.

In 1937, he helped organize the Amateur Hockey Association of the United States, and served as its first president. During the 1950s, he spent six years as the business manager for the National Hockey League's New York Rangers; later served on the U.S. Olympic Committee; and in 1965, he was on the council of the International Ice Hockey Federation.

Source: Hockey Hall of Fame

Loeffler, Kenneth D. (born: April 14, 1902 in Beaver Falls, Pennsylvania; died: January 1, 1975); inducted into the Naismith Memorial Basketball Hall of Fame in 1964 as a coach; won the 1952 NIT title and the 1954 NCAA title.

Over a 20-year career, Loeffler coached at Geneva College (Beaver Falls, Pennsylvania); Yale University (New Haven, Connecticut); with the St. Louis Bombers (Basketball Association of America); Providence Steamrollers (BAA); La Salle University (Philadelphia, Pennsylvania), where he coached the team to six consecutive 20-win seasons; and Texas A&M College (University) (College Station).

The La Salle Explorers won the 1952 National Invitation Tournament title, the 1954 National Collegiate Athletic Association championship, and finished second in the 1955 NCAA tournament. Loeffler was 145–30 (.829) in six seasons at La Salle and accumulated a total of 389 wins in his career.

He played three seasons of basketball, football, and baseball at Beaver Falls High School, where he graduated in 1920. After high school, he attended Pennsylvania State University (University Park, 1920–1924) and eventually went to the University of Pittsburgh Law School (Pennsylvania), graduating in 1934. After graduating from Penn State and having a brief professional basketball career (1924–1929), Loeffler began his coaching career at Geneva College (1928–1934), before moving on to Yale University (1934–1942). After serving in the U.S. Air Force during World War II (1942–1946), he briefly coached in the BAA with the St. Louis Bombers (1946–1948, 67–42 [.615]) and the Providence Steamrollers (1948–1949, 12–48, [.200]), leaving the league with an overall coaching record of 79–90 (.467).

In 1949, Loeffler returned to the college coaching ranks at La Salle, and in 1955, he became head coach at Texas A&M College (University), a job he held until 1957. He led Geneva to a 95–55 (.633) record; Yale to a 61–82 (.427) mark; and Texas A&M to a 13–35 (.271) record.

He has been inducted into the Helms Foundation and Pittsburgh halls of fame.

Sources: Basketball-Reference.com; La Salle University 2010 Media Guide; Naismith Memorial Basketball Hall of Fame

Lofton, James David (born: July 5, 1956 in Fort Ord/Monterrey, California); inducted into the Pro Football Hall of Fame in 2003 as a player; Position: Wide Receiver; Uniform: #80; first player to score a touchdown in the 1970s, 1980s, and 1990s; oldest player in NFL history to record 1,000 receiving yards in a season; first NFL player with 14,000 receiving yards.

After graduating from George Washington High School (Los Angeles, California) and being named an All-American at Stanford University (Palo Alto, California), Lofton was the number one pick (sixth overall selection) of the Green Bay Packers in the 1978 National Football League Draft. He played 16 years (233 games) in the NFL with the

Packers (1978–1986), Los Angeles Raiders (1987–1988), Buffalo Bills (1989–1992), Los Angeles Rams (1993), and the Philadelphia Eagles (1993).

He caught 50 or more passes per season nine times; first player to score a touchdown in the 1970s, 1980s, and 1990s; National Football Conference Offensive Rookie of the Year (1978); named All-Pro four times (1980–1981, 1983–1984); All-National Football Conference three times; played in eight Pro Bowls (1979, 1981–1986, 1992); played in three consecutive Super Bowls with the Bills (SB XXV in 1991, SB XXVI in 1992, SB XXVII in 1993), losing them all; named to the NFL 1980s All-Decade Team; inducted into the Green Bay Packers Hall of Fame in 1999; and retired with 14,004 receiving yards, an NFL record at the time.

In 1991 (at age 35), Lofton became the oldest player in league history to have 1,000 receiving yards in a season.

After retiring as a player, he became a receivers coach with the San Diego Chargers in 2002.

James Lofton's Career Statistics

			RECEIVING			
YEAR	**TEAM**	**G**	**NO**	**YDS**	**AVG**	**TD**
1978	Green Bay	16	46	818	17.8	6
1979	Green Bay	16	54	968	17.9	4
1980	Green Bay	16	71	1,226	17.3	4
1981	Green Bay	16	71	1,294	18.2	8
1982	Green Bay	9	35	696	19.9	4
1983	Green Bay	16	58	1,300	22.4	8
1984	Green Bay	16	62	1,361	22.0	7
1985	Green Bay	16	69	1,153	16.7	4
1986	Green Bay	15	64	840	13.1	4
1987	Los Angeles	12	41	880	21.5	5
1988	Los Angeles	16	28	549	19.6	0
1989	Buffalo	12	8	166	20.8	3
1990	Buffalo	16	35	712	20.3	4
1991	Buffalo	15	57	1,072	18.8	8
1992	Buffalo	16	51	786	15.4	6
1993	Los Angeles / Philadelphia	10	14	183	13.1	0
	TOTALS	233	764	14,004	18.3	75

Sources: Pro Football Hall of Fame; Pro-Football-Reference.com

Loicq, Paul (born: 1890 in Brussels, Belgium; died: 1953); inducted into the Hockey Hall of Fame in 1961 as a builder; played in the 1924 Winter Olympics; president of the International Ice Hockey Federation.

After earning a law degree in Brussels and serving in World War I, Loicq played for the Belgium National Team at the 1924 Winter Olympic Games (Chamonix, France); failed to medal; and retired as a player when the Games ended.

He remained active in the game as a referee and an administrator, and served as the president of the Skaters Club of Brussels, the Belgian Federation of Skaters, and the Belgian League for Winter Sports. In 1927, Loicq was elected president of the International Ice Hockey Federation, and served in the organization for more than 20 years (1927–1947).

As a referee, his worked the Olympics, European Championships, and World Championships. He also founded the International College of Referees.

The Paul Loicq Award is presented annually by the IIHF Hall of Fame to honor an individual for his or her service to international ice hockey.

Source: Hockey Hall of Fame

Lombardi, Ernesto Natali "Ernie" (born: April 6, 1908 in Oakland, California; died: September 26, 1977 in Santa Cruz, California); inducted into the National Baseball Hall of Fame and Museum in 1986 as a player by the Veterans Committee; Position: Catcher; Bats: Right; Throws: Right; Uniform: #4; caught Johnny Vander Meer's two consecutive no-hitters in 1938; only catcher to win two batting titles (1938, 1942).

During his 17-year National League career, Lombardi hit .300 or better 10 seasons; won the National League Most Valuable Player Award in 1938; won the league batting title twice (1938, 1942), the only catcher in major league baseball history to do so; and caught Johnny Vander Meer's two consecutive no-hitters in 1938 (June 11 and June 15).

Making his major league debut on April 15, 1931, the 6'3", 230-pound Lombardi played for the Brooklyn Dodgers (1931), Cincinnati Reds (1932–1941), Boston Braves (1942), and New York Giants (1943–1947); played in two World Series (winning in 1940 and losing in 1939); and was an eight-time All-Star (1936–1940, 1942–1943, 1945).

A relatively large man and a slow runner, Lombardi grounded into 261 career double plays. In addition to leading the league in grounding into double plays four times, he holds the career record for grounding into a double play every 25.3 plate appearances. Although his slowness was well-known throughout baseball, it is ironic that he was a perfect eight-for-eight in stolen base attempts during his career.

He was inducted into the Cincinnati Reds Hall of Fame in 1958 and the Bay Area Sports Hall of Fame in 1982.

Lombardi played in the minor leagues (Pacific Coast League) for four seasons before joining the Dodgers in 1931.

On May 8, 1935, Lombardi tied a major league record with four straight doubles, all in consecutive innings (sixth, seventh, eight, ninth) and each off a different pitcher (Syl Johnson, Orville Jorgens, Euel Moore, Franklin Pearce) against the Philadelphia Phillies in a 15–4 first game win of a doubleheader. On May 9, 1937, he tied the modern major league record with six hits (five singles and a double) in six consecutive at bats, in a 21–10 win over the Phillies.

Ernie Lombardi's Career Statistics

YEAR	TEAM	LG	G	AB	R	H	2B	3B	HR	RBI	BB	SO	SB	AVG	SLG
1931	Brooklyn	NL	73	182	20	54	7	1	4	23	12	12	1	.297	.412
1932	Cincinnati	NL	118	413	43	125	22	9	11	68	41	19	0	.303	.479
1933	Cincinnati	NL	107	350	30	99	21	1	4	47	16	17	2	.283	.383
1934	Cincinnati	NL	132	417	42	127	19	4	9	62	16	22	0	.305	.434
1935	Cincinnati	NL	120	332	36	114	23	3	12	64	16	6	0	.343	.539
1936	Cincinnati	NL	121	387	42	129	23	2	12	68	19	16	1	.333	.496
1937	Cincinnati	NL	120	368	41	123	22	1	9	59	14	17	1	.334	.473
1938	Cincinnati	NL	129	489	60	167	30	1	19	95	40	14	0	.342	.524
1939	Cincinnati	NL	130	450	43	129	26	2	20	85	35	19	0	.287	.487
1940	Cincinnati	NL	109	376	50	120	22	0	14	74	31	14	0	.319	.489
1941	Cincinnati	NL	117	398	33	105	12	1	10	60	36	14	1	.264	.374
1942	Boston	NL	105	309	32	102	14	0	11	46	37	12	1	.330	.482
1943	New York	NL	104	295	19	90	7	0	10	51	16	11	1	.305	.431
1944	New York	NL	117	373	37	95	13	0	10	58	33	25	0	.255	.370
1945	New York	NL	115	368	46	113	7	1	19	70	43	11	0	.307	.486
1946	New York	NL	88	238	19	69	4	1	12	39	18	24	0	.290	.466
1947	New York	NL	48	110	8	31	5	0	4	21	7	9	0	.282	.436
	TOTALS		1,853	5,855	601	1,792	277	27	190	990	430	262	8	.306	.460

Sources: Baseball-Reference.com; National Baseball Hall of Fame and Museum

Lombardi, Vincent Thomas "Vince" (born: June 11, 1913 in Brooklyn, New York; died: September 3, 1970 in Washington, D.C.); inducted into the Pro Football Hall of Fame in 1971 as a coach; won six NFL titles; won the first two Super Bowls.

A legend in football lore, Lombardi began his head coaching career at the relatively late age of 45; was coach and general manager of the Green Bay Packers from 1959 to 1967, and coached one year (1969) with the Washington Redskins. He led Green Bay to an 89–29–4 (.754) record; five National Football League titles (1961–1962, 1965–1967); and won the first two Super Bowl titles (1967–1968). In ten years as a head coach, Lombardi never had a losing season; led the Redskins to the team's first winning record in 14 years; and ended his career with an overall record of 105–35–6 (.719).

Before becoming a head coach, Lombardi's NFL experience was only five seasons as an assistant coach with the New York Giants.

In 1968, Lombardi retired as the Packers coach but continued as the team's general manager. One season later, he became the Redskins' head coach and led the team to a 7–5–2 record, before he died.

At age 15, he entered Cathedral Preparatory Seminary (Brooklyn), with the intent of becoming a Catholic priest. Four years into the six-year program, Lombardi changed his mind about the priesthood and transferred to St. Francis Preparatory High School (Fresh Meadows, New York), where he played football.

In 1933, he attended Fordham University (Bronx, New York) on a football scholarship (graduating in 1937) and played guard for head coach Sleepy Jim Crowley, one of the legendary Four Horsemen of Notre Dame in the 1920s. Although relatively small (5'8", 185 pounds), Lombardi was part of Fordham's "Seven Blocks of Granite" offensive line.

Two years after graduating from college, he began playing semi-professional football with the Brooklyn Eagles and Wilmington Clippers, and in 1939, became an assistant coach at St. Cecilia (near Englewood, New Jersey), where he was also a classroom teacher. In 1942, he became the team's head coach; left in 1947 to be the freshman coach at his alma mater in football and basketball; and in 1948, Lombardi became an assistant coach for Fordham's varsity football team.

After the 1948 college football season, he left the school to serve as the offensive line coach at the United States Military Academy (West Point, New York) for head coach Red Blaik. After Lombardi coached at West Point for five seasons, he entered the NFL as an assistant coach with the New York Giants in 1954 (at age 41), and was with the team during its 47–7 win over the Chicago Bears in the 1956 NFL title game.

Lombardi coached in one of the most famous games in the history of football, the December 31, 1967 NFL championship contest against the Dallas Cowboys played in Green Bay, forever known as the "Ice Bowl." With sixteen seconds remaining in the game and behind by three points, Packers' quarterback Bart Starr ran a sneak play and scored, giving Green Bay a 21–17 win. Two weeks later, the Packers beat the Oakland Raiders 33–14 to win Super Bowl II, Lombardi's last game as the team's coach.

Shortly after his death, the NFL Super Bowl trophy was renamed the Lombardi Trophy.

A statue of Lombardi is located outside Lambeau Field (home of the Packers); the Rotary Lombardi Award is given annually to the best college football lineman or linebacker; and he received the Silver Buffalo Award, the highest adult award given by the Boy Scouts of America.

Lombardi was named NFL Coach of the Year in 1959; inducted into the Green Bay Packers Hall of Fame in 1975; and was named ESPN Coach of the Century in 2000.

Vince Lombardi's Career Statistics

		REGULAR SEASON				PLAYOFFS		
YEAR	**TEAM**	**W**	**L**	**T**	**WIN%**	**W**	**L**	**WIN%**
1959	Green Bay	7	5	0	.583			
1960	Green Bay	8	4	0	.667	0	1	.000
1961	Green Bay	11	3	0	.786	1	0	1.000
1962	Green Bay	13	1	0	.929	1	0	1.000
1963	Green Bay	11	2	1	.821			
1964	Green Bay	8	5	1	.607			
1965	Green Bay	10	3	1	.750	2	0	1.000
1966	Green Bay	12	2	0	.857	2	0	1.000
1967	Green Bay	9	4	1	.679	3	0	1.000
1969	Washington	7	5	2	.571			
	TOTALS	96	34	6	.738	9	1	.900

Sources: Pro Football Hall of Fame; Pro-Football-Reference.com; Vince Lombardi Web Site (www.vincelombardi.com); *Winning is the Only Thing* (Vince Lombardi, edited by Jerry Kramer)

Lombardo, Giuseppe Joseph (born: March 1, 1925 in Italy); inducted into the National Soccer Hall of Fame and Museum in 1984 as a builder; founded the Brooklyn Italians Soccer Club.

Lombardo emigrated from Italy to the United States in 1947 and joined the St. Bernadette Soccer Club as a player. In 1949, he founded the Brooklyn Italians Soccer Club and served as its secretary twice (1951–1954, 1957–1972), and as its president from 1954 to 1956.

In 1958, he helped found the Italian-American Soccer League of New York and served as Referee Assignment Chairman for the league. From 1967 through 1972, Lombardo served with the National Soccer League of New York and then as senior administrator of the Southern New York State Association from 1969 to 1984.

Source: National Soccer Hall of Fame and Museum

Lonborg, Arthur C. "Dutch" (born: March 16, 1898 in Gardner, Illinois; died: January 31, 1985); inducted into the Naismith Memorial Basketball Hall of Fame in 1973 as a coach; served as chairman of the NCAA Tournament Committee.

A coach and administrator, Lonborg's basketball career began when he played guard for two seasons for legendary coach Phog Allen at the University of Kansas (Lawrence). After graduating in 1921, he would go on to a 29-year college coaching career at McPherson College (Kansas), Washburn University (Topeka, Kansas), and Northwestern University (Evanston/Chicago, Illinois). In his 23 seasons at Northwestern, he won 237 games.

After retiring as a coach, in 1950 Lonborg served as the athletic director at his alma mater for 14 years; was chairman of the National Collegiate Athletic Association Tournament Committee (1947–1960); served as president of the National Association of Basketball Coaches in 1935; and managed the 1960 gold medal-winning U.S. Olympic basketball team under head coach Pete Newell. He led Washburn to the national Amateur Athletic Union title in 1925 and coached Northwestern to the Big Ten Championship in 1931.

After graduating from Horton (Kansas) High School, Lonborg attended the University of Kansas, where he was a three-time All-Conference football player, two-time All-Conference basketball player, and in 1920 was a basketball All-American. During his coaching career, he won 323 games (23 in two years at McPherson College, 63 in four years at Washburn University, and 237 at Northwestern University).

Lonborg has been inducted into the Washburn University Hall of Fame, KU Athletics Hall of Fame, and the Helms Foundation Hall of Fame.

Source: Naismith Memorial Basketball Hall of Fame

Long, Dennis (born: October 20, 1935 in Chicago, Illinois); inducted into the National Soccer Hall of Fame and Museum in 1993 as a builder; helped build St. Louis Soccer Park.

Long began his soccer career as a player before becoming a long-time coach and administrator. He is the former president of Anheuser Busch, Inc., and as of this writing, he is the president of Long Holdings, Inc.

He has received numerous awards and honors, including the United States Secretary of Defense Medal for Outstanding Public Service (the highest honor that can be awarded a civilian by the United States) for his work as a Worldwide Chairman of the United Service Organization.

He has been inducted into the St. Louis Hall of Fame and the Hall of Fame at St. Louis University, and received the Commissioners Award from the Major Indoor Soccer League.

Long attended St. Louis Parochial School before going to Washington University (St. Louis).

He coached more than 600 soccer games, and had more than 500 wins. As an administrator, he worked with both the North American Soccer League and the Major Indoor Soccer League. As president of Anheuser-Busch, Inc., he was chairman of the committee that built St. Louis Soccer Park.

Source: National Soccer Hall of Fame and Museum

Long, Howard Michael "Howie" (born: January 6, 1960 in Somerville, Massachusetts); inducted into the Pro Football Hall of Fame in 2000 as a player; Position: Defensive End; Uniform: #75; won Super Bowl XVIII.

Long was a second-round draft pick (48th overall selection) of the Oakland Raiders in the 1981 National Football League Draft and became a starter in his second season. He played his entire 13 seasons (1981–1993, 179 games) with the Oakland/Los Angeles Raiders; selected All-Pro three consecutive years (1983–1985); named All-American Football Conference four straight seasons (1983–1986); selected to eight Pro Bowls (1983–1987, 1989, 1992–1993); and was named to the NFL 1980s All-Decade Team.

A four-year football letterman at Villanova University (Pennsylvania), Long was named the Most Valuable Player of the 1980 Blue-Gray Game. He was a basketball and track star at Milford (Massachusetts) High School and has been inducted into the Milford Hall of Fame.

He joined the Oakland Raiders one year after the team had won Super Bowl XV (January 1981) and three years later, the 6'5", 265-pound defensive end helped the team, now in Los Angeles, win Super Bowl XVIII (January 1984). The next season, he was named NFL Defensive Lineman of the Year by the NFL Alumni Association.

Long is best known by today's younger fans for his after-football career. Leaving the NFL in 1993, he began an acting career and starred in *Firestorm*, *Broken Arrow* with John Travolta, and *3000 Miles to Graceland* with Kevin Costner and Kurt Russell. In addition to his movie career, Long and actress Teri Hatcher teamed for a series of Radio Shack commercials.

As of this writing, he is an analyst for the FOX Network's NFL coverage.

Howie Long's Career Statistics

				DEFENSE		
				FUM		
YEAR	**TEAM**	**G**	**SACK**	**REC**	**YDS**	**TD**

			DEFENSE			
				FUM		
YEAR	TEAM	G	SACK	REC	YDS	TD
1981	Oakland	16	0	0	0	0
1982	Los Angeles	9	5.5	0	0	0
1983	Los Angeles	16	13	2	0	0
1984	Los Angeles	16	12	2	4	0
1985	Los Angeles	16	10	0	0	0
1986	Los Angeles	13	7.5	2	0	0
1987	Los Angeles	14	4	2	0	0
1988	Los Angeles	7	3	0	0	0
1989	Los Angeles	14	5	1	0	0
1990	Los Angeles	12	6	1	1	0
1991	Los Angeles	14	3	0	0	0
1992	Los Angeles	16	9	0	0	0
1993	Los Angeles	16	6	0	0	0
	TOTALS	179	84	10	5	0

Source: Pro Football Hall of Fame

Looby, William (born: November 11, 1931 in St. Louis, Missouri; died: December 9, 1998 in St. Louis, Missouri); inducted into the National Soccer Hall of Fame and Museum in 2001 as a player; Position: Forward; International Caps (1954–1959): 8; International Goals: 6; won seven National Amateur Cups.

The 5’11” Looby played his first international game in a World Cup qualifier against Mexico in 1954, and his last was against England in 1959.

He played for the United States in the 1956 Olympic Games in Melbourne, Australia (but failed to medal); was a member of the U.S. National Team that won the bronze medal at the 1959 Pan-American Games in Chicago, Illinois; and played for a series of teams sponsored by the Kutis Funeral Home.

Looby won seven National Amateur Cups (one with the St. Louis Raiders in 1950 and six straight [1956–1961] with Kutis).

Source: National Soccer Hall of Fame and Museum

Lopez, Alfonso Ramon “Al” (born: August 20, 1908 in Tampa, Florida; died: October 30, 2005 in Tampa, Florida); inducted into the National Baseball Hall of Fame and Museum in 1977 as a manager by the Veterans Committee; Uniform: #42; last living player who had played in the 1920s; once held the record for most games played by a catcher.

As a major league catcher, Lopez caught 1,918 games, a record that stood for more than 40 years. As a manager, his 1954 Cleveland Indians team won 111 games, an American League record that stood for 44 years, and his 1959 Chicago White Sox won the team’s first pennant since 1919.

Making his major league debut on September 27, 1928, Lopez played 19 seasons for the Brooklyn Robins/Dodgers (1928–1935), Boston Bees/Braves (1936–1940), Pittsburgh Pirates (1940–1946), and the Cleveland Indians (1947). After retiring as a player, he would later manage the Indians (1951–1956) and the White Sox (1957–1965, 1968–1969), and managed in two World Series (1954, 1959), losing them both. He was the last living player who had played a major league game in the 1920s.

His Indians and White Sox teams were the only two clubs to interrupt the New York Yankees’ string of American League pennants from 1949 to 1964. His .581 career winning percentage ranks fourth in major league history among those who managed at least 2,000 games (after Joe McCarthy [.615], Frank Selee [.598], and John McGraw [.586]), and over his 17-year managerial career, he only had two losing seasons.

The 5’11”, 165-pound Lopez began his career with the local Tampa Smokers in 1924; broke into the major leagues briefly in 1928 with the Brooklyn Dodgers; and became the team’s starting catcher in 1930. In 1945, he surpassed Gabby Hartnett’s major league record for career games as a catcher. The record stood until 1987, when Bob Boone broke it, and his National League record was broken by Gary Carter in 1990.

In 1954, Al Lopez Field in his hometown of Tampa was named in his honor.

Al Lopez’s Career Playing Statistics

YEAR	TEAM	G	AB	R	H	2B	3B	HR	RBI	BB	SO	AVG	OBP	SLG
1928	Brooklyn	3	12	0	0	0	0	0	0	0	0	.000	.000	.000
1930	Brooklyn	128	421	60	130	20	4	6	57	33	35	.309	.362	.418
1931	Brooklyn	111	360	38	97	13	4	0	40	28	33	.269	.324	.328
1932	Brooklyn	126	404	44	111	18	6	1	43	34	35	.275	.331	.356
1933	Brooklyn	126	372	39	112	11	4	3	41	21	39	.301	.338	.376
1934	Brooklyn	140	439	58	120	23	2	7	54	49	44	.273	.349	.383
1935	Brooklyn	128	379	50	95	12	4	3	39	35	36	.251	.316	.327
1936	Boston	128	426	46	103	12	5	7	50	41	41	.242	.311	.343
1937	Boston	105	334	31	68	11	1	3	38	35	57	.204	.281	.269
1938	Boston	71	236	19	63	6	1	1	14	11	24	.267	.305	.314
1939	Boston	131	412	32	104	22	1	8	49	40	45	.252	.319	.369
1940	Boston	36	119	20	35	3	1	2	17	6	8	.294	.328	.387
1940	Pittsburgh	59	174	15	45	6	2	1	24	13	13	.259	.310	.333
1941	Pittsburgh	114	317	33	84	9	1	5	43	31	23	.265	.330	.347
1942	Pittsburgh	103	289	17	74	8	2	1	26	34	17	.256	.338	.308
1943	Pittsburgh	118	372	40	98	9	4	1	39	44	25	.263	.341	.317
1944	Pittsburgh	115	331	27	76	12	1	1	34	34	24	.230	.303	.281
1945	Pittsburgh	91	243	22	53	8	0	0	18	35	12	.218	.317	.251
1946	Pittsburgh	56	150	13	46	2	0	1	12	23	14	.307	.399	.340
1947	Cleveland	61	126	9	33	1	0	0	14	9	13	.262	.311	.270
	TOTALS	1,950	5,916	613	1,547	206	43	51	652	556	538	.261	.326	.337

Al Lopez's Managerial Record

YEAR	TEAM	LG	W	L	PCT
1951	Cleveland	AL	93	61	.604
1952	Cleveland	AL	93	61	.604
1953	Cleveland	AL	92	62	.597
1954	Cleveland	AL	111	43	.721
1955	Cleveland	AL	93	61	.604
1956	Cleveland	AL	88	66	.571
1957	Chicago	AL	90	64	.584
1958	Chicago	AL	82	72	.532
1959	Chicago	AL	94	60	.610
1960	Chicago	AL	87	67	.565
1961	Chicago	AL	86	76	.531
1962	Chicago	AL	85	77	.525
1963	Chicago	AL	94	68	.580
1964	Chicago	AL	98	64	.605
1965	Chicago	AL	95	67	.586
1968	Chicago	AL	33	48	.407
1969	Chicago	AL	8	9	.471
	TOTALS		1,422	1,026	.581

Sources: Baseball-Reference.com; National Baseball Hall of Fame and Museum

Lott, Ronald Mandel "Ronnie" (born: May 8, 1959 in Albuquerque, New Mexico); inducted into the Pro Football Hall of Fame in 2000 as a player; Position: Cornerback-Safety; Uniform: #42; won four Super Bowl titles.

An All-American at the University of Southern California (Los Angeles), Lott was a first-round draft pick (eighth overall selection) of the San Francisco 49ers in the 1981 National Football League Draft. He was a starter at left cornerback as a rookie and was moved to safety in 1985. During his 14-year career (192 games) Lott played for the 49ers (1981–1990), Los Angeles Raiders (1991–1992), and the New York Jets (1993–1994).

At 6', 203 pounds, he was a hard-hitting defender; named All-Pro at three different positions (cornerback, free safety, strong safety) nine times (1981, 1983–1984, 1986–1991); recorded more than 100 tackles per season five times; led the NFL in interceptions twice (1986, 1991); helped the 49ers win four Super Bowl championships (SB XVI in 1982, SB XIX in 1985, SB XXIII in 1989, SB XXIV in 1990); named to both the NFL 1980s All-Decade Team and the NFL

1990s All-Decade Team; selected to the NFL 75th Anniversary All-Time Team; and his jersey number 42 was retired by the 49ers in 2003.

Lott attended Eisenhower High School (Rialto, California, graduating in 1977), before moving on to USC. During his college career as a safety (1977–1980), he helped the team to a share of the 1978 national championship, and played in the 1979 and 1980 Rose Bowls, winning them both (beating the University of Michigan in 1979 and Ohio State University in 1980). He was a unanimous All-American and team captain in 1980; inducted into the USC Athletic Hall of Fame in 1995; and was inducted into the College Football Hall of Fame in 2002.

The Lott Trophy is presented annually to the college football Defensive IMPACT Player of the Year (and measures Integrity, Maturity, Performance, Academics, Community, and Tenacity); in 1999, he was ranked number 23 on *The Sporting News*' list of the 100 Greatest Football Players (making him the highest-ranked safety, the second-highest ranked defensive back behind Night Train Lane, and the highest-ranked player to have played for the New York Jets); and also in 1999, he was inducted into the Bay Area Sports Hall of Fame.

Ronnie Lott's Career Statistics

		DEFENSE						
YEAR	**TEAM**	**G**	**INT**	**YDS**	**AVG**	**TD**	**FUM REC**	**YDS**
1981	San Francisco	16	7	117	16.7	3	2	0
1982	San Francisco	9	2	95	47.5	1	0	0
1983	San Francisco	15	4	22	5.5	0	1	0
1984	San Francisco	12	4	26	6.5	0	0	0
1985	San Francisco	16	6	68	11.3	0	2	0
1986	San Francisco	14	10	134	13.4	1	0	0
1987	San Francisco	12	5	62	12.4	0	2	33
1988	San Francisco	13	5	59	11.8	0	4	3
1989	San Francisco	11	5	34	6.8	0	0	0
1990	San Francisco	11	3	26	8.7	0	1	3
1991	Los Angeles	16	8	52	6.5	0	1	4
1992	Los Angeles	16	1	0	0.0	0	1	0
1993	New York	16	3	35	11.7	0	2	0
1994	New York	15	0	0	0.0	0	1	0
	TOTALS	192	63	730	11.6	5	17	43

Sources: Pro Football Hall of Fame; Pro-Football-Reference.com; *Total Impact* (Ronnie Lott with Jill Lieber)

Lovellette, Clyde E. (born: September 7, 1929 in Petersburg, Indiana); inducted into the Naismith Memorial Basketball Hall of Fame in 1988 as a player; Position: Center-Forward; first person to play on an NCAA, Olympic, AAU, and NBA championship team; won three NBA titles; only college player to lead the nation in scoring and win the NCAA title in the same year.

Lovellette was the first person to play on a National Collegiate Athletic Association, Olympic, Amateur Athletic Union, and a National Basketball Association championship team.

He attended Garfield High School (Terre Haute, Indiana, graduating in 1948), where he was a two-time All-State selection; went to the University of Kansas (Lawrence), where he played for the legendary Phog Allen; and led the nation in scoring in his senior year.

At the professional level, the 6'9", 234-pound Lovellette was one of the game's first big men. During his 11-year National Basketball Association career, he played for the Minneapolis Lakers (1953–1957), Cincinnati Royals (1957–1958), St. Louis Hawks (1958–1962), and the Boston Celtics (1962–1964). He won a championship with Minneapolis (1954) and two with Boston (1963–1964).

He was a three-time All-American at Kansas (1950–1952); won an NCAA Championship in 1952; named Helms Foundation College Player of the Year in 1952; and won a 1952 Olympic gold medal in Helsinki, Finland. Lovellette is still the only college player to lead the nation in scoring and win the NCAA title in the same year.

He was inducted into the Indiana Basketball Hall of Fame in 1982.

Clyde Lovellette's Career Statistics

SEASON	TEAM	LG	G	MIN	FG	FT	TRB	AST	PTS
1953–1954	Minneapolis	NBA	72	1,255	237	114	419	51	588
1954–1955	Minneapolis	NBA	70	2,361	519	273	802	100	1,311
1955–1956	Minneapolis	NBA	71	2,518	594	338	992	164	1,526
1956–1957	Minneapolis	NBA	69	2,492	574	286	932	139	1,434
1957–1958	Cincinnati	NBA	71	2,589	679	301	862	134	1,659
1958–1959	St. Louis	NBA	70	1,599	402	205	605	91	1,009
1959–1960	St. Louis	NBA	68	1,953	550	316	721	127	1,416
1960–1961	St. Louis	NBA	67	2,111	599	273	677	172	1,471
1961–1962	St. Louis	NBA	40	1,192	341	155	350	68	837
1962–1963	Boston	NBA	61	568	161	73	177	95	395
1963–1964	Boston	NBA	45	437	128	45	126	24	301
	TOTALS	NBA	704	19,075	4,784	2,379	6,663	1,165	11,947

Sources: Basketball-Reference.com; Naismith Memorial Basketball Hall of Fame

Lucas, Jerry Ray (born: March 30, 1940 in Middletown, Ohio); inducted into the Naismith Memorial Basketball Hall of Fame in 1980 as a player; Position: Forward-Center; won the 1960 NCAA national title; won a gold medal at the 1960 Olympics; won the 1973 NBA championship.

Playing for hall of fame coach Fred Taylor at Ohio State University (Columbus), Lucas teamed with future hall of famers John Havlicek and Bob Knight to lead the team to a 78–6 record and three Big Ten Championships. He led the Buckeyes to three straight National Collegiate Athletic Association Finals (1960–1962), and won a national title in 1960. In 1960 and 1961, he was named the NCAA Tournament Outstanding Player. He scored 1,990 points in his college career; grabbed 1,411 rebounds; was a First-Team All-American three times (1960–1962); won an Olympic gold medal in 1960 (Rome, Italy); and was named College Player of the Year twice (1961–1962).

In 11 National Basketball Association seasons with the Cincinnati Royals (1963–1969), San Francisco Warriors (1969–1971), and New York Knicks (1971–1974), Lucas was a three-time All-NBA First-Team selection (1965–1966, 1968); named to seven NBA All-Star teams (1964–1969, 1971); selected Most Valuable Player of the 1965 All-Star game; won a title in 1973 with the Knicks; and was named to the NBA 50th Anniversary All-Time Team in 1996.

Although Lucas was not particularly big (6’8”, 230 pounds) for his era, he became one of the game’s best-ever rebounders, and his NBA career total of 12,942 (15.6 per game) is, as of this writing, the fourth best in league history (behind Wilt Chamberlain, Bill Russell, and Bob Pettit).

Lucas won championships at every level, including high school, college, and professional, and he was the youngest member (age 20) of the 1960 U.S. Olympic basketball team.

His Middletown High School teams won 76 consecutive games; claimed two state championships; and Lucas was named Ohio Player of the Year twice (1957–1958).

After college, although he was drafted by the Royals, he chose to sign with the Cleveland Pipers of the American Basketball League. When his deal with the team fell through, he sat out one season, and joined the Royals in 1963. Lucas led the league in field-goal percentage (.527); started the 1964 NBA All-Star Game; and was named NBA Rookie of the Year. In his second season, Lucas averaged 21.4 points and 20.0 rebounds per game, becoming only the third player in NBA history to average “20/20” for a season; was named that season’s All-Star Game Most Valuable Player; and was an All-NBA First Team selection.

Lucas retired in 1974; co-wrote the best-seller *The Memory Book*; and in the 1980s, he established Lucas Learning Inc., that publishes memory and learning materials for children.

In 1999, he was named to *Sports Illustrated*’s five-man College All-Century Team.

Jerry Lucas’ Career Statistics

SEASON	TEAM	LG	G	MIP	FG	FT	TRB	PTS
1963–1964	Cincinnati	NBA	79	3,273	545	310	1,375	1,400
1964–1965	Cincinnati	NBA	66	2,864	558	298	1,321	1,414
1965–1966	Cincinnati	NBA	79	3,517	690	317	1,668	1,697
1966–1967	Cincinnati	NBA	81	3,558	577	284	1,547	1,438
1967–1968	Cincinnati	NBA	82	3,619	707	346	1,560	1,760
1968–1969	Cincinnati	NBA	74	3,075	555	247	1,360	1,357
1969–1970	Cincinnati	NBA	4	118	18	5	45	41

SEASON	TEAM	LG	G	MIP	FG	FT	TRB	PTS
1969–1970	San Francisco	NBA	63	2,302	387	195	906	969
1970–1971	San Francisco	NBA	80	3,251	623	289	1,265	1,535
1971–1972	New York	NBA	77	2,926	543	197	1,011	1,283
1972–1973	New York	NBA	71	2,001	312	80	510	704
1973–1974	New York	NBA	73	1,627	194	67	374	455
	TOTALS	NBA	829	32,131	5,709	2,635	12,942	14,053

Sources: Basketball-Reference.com; Naismith Memorial Basketball Hall of Fame

Luckman, Sidney "Sid" (born: November 21, 1916 in Brooklyn, New York; died: July 5, 1998 in North Miami Beach/Aventura, Florida); inducted into the Pro Football Hall of Fame in 1965 as a player; Position: Quarterback; Uniform: #42; won four NFL titles.

A number one draft pick in 1939 (second overall selection) out of Columbia College/University (New York, New York), Luckman was a tailback in college who became the first great "T" quarterback in the National Football League (a scheme created by team owner and coach George Halas). He spent his entire 12-year career (1939–1950, 128 games) with the Chicago Bears.

Luckman was selected All-NFL (First or Second Team) nine times from 1940 to 1948; league's Most Valuable Player in 1943; threw seven touchdowns in a November 14, 1943 game against the New York Giants in a 56–7 win and had five touchdown passes in the 1943 title game against Washington in a 41–21 win; and won four NFL titles (1940–1941, 1943, 1946). He led the league in touchdown passes three times; his jersey number 42 was retired by the Bears; and he was named to the NFL 1940s All-Decade Team.

He played both baseball and football for Erasmus Hall High School (Brooklyn, New York), before moving on to Columbia University, where he completed 180 of 376 passes for 2,413 yards and 20 touchdowns.

He joined the NFL at a time when the league was dominated by the running game, with the quarterback used as a running back who would also throw a few passes. Halas, Luckman, and the scoring-oriented T-formation changed the NFL forever.

He joined the U. S. Merchant Marine during World War II after the 1943 season. While he was not allowed to practice with the team, Luckman was stationed in the United States, and received permission to fly to Bears games during the season. After the war, he returned to the Bears full-time in 1946 and led the team to its fifth championship, his fourth.

After retiring as a player in 1950, Luckman became a businessman in Chicago, and taught quarterbacks and coaches the T–formation. He was inducted into the College Football Hall of Fame in 1960 and into the International Jewish Sports Hall of Fame in 1979.

Sid Luckman's Career Statistics

						PASSING				RUSHING			
YEAR	TEAM	G	ATT.	COMP	PCT	YDS	TD	INT	RATING	NO	YDS	AVG	TD
1939	Chicago Bears	11	51	23	45.1	636	5	4	91.6	24	42	1.8	0
1940	Chicago Bears	11	105	48	45.7	941	4	9	54.5	23	-65	-2.8	0
1941	Chicago Bears	11	119	68	57.1	1,181	9	6	95.3	18	18	1.0	1
1942	Chicago Bears	11	105	57	54.3	1,024	10	13	80.1	13	-6	-0.5	0
1943	Chicago Bears	10	202	110	54.5	2,194	28	12	107.5	22	-40	-1.8	1
1944	Chicago Bears	7	143	71	49.7	1,018	11	12	63.8	20	-96	-4.8	1
1945	Chicago Bears	10	217	117	53.9	1,727	14	10	82.5	36	-118	-3.3	0
1946	Chicago Bears	11	229	110	48.0	1,826	17	16	71.0	25	-76	-3.0	0
1947	Chicago Bears	12	323	176	54.5	2,712	24	31	67.7	10	86	8.6	1
1948	Chicago Bears	12	163	89	54.6	1,047	13	14	65.1	8	11	1.4	0
1949	Chicago Bears	11	50	22	44.0	200	1	3	37.1	3	4	1.3	0
1950	Chicago Bears	11	37	13	35.1	180	1	2	38.1	2	1	0.5	0
	TOTALS	128	1,744	904	51.8	14,686	137	132	75.0	204	-239	-1.2	4

Sid Luckman's Career Statistics

			PUNTING		
YEAR	TEAM	G	PUNTS	YDS	AVG
1939	Chicago Bears	11	27	1,189	44.0
1940	Chicago Bears	11	27	1,147	42.5
1941	Chicago Bears	11	13	534	41.1

			PUNTING		
YEAR	TEAM	G	PUNTS	YDS	AVG
1942	Chicago Bears	11	24	976	40.7
1943	Chicago Bears	10	34	1,220	35.9
1944	Chicago Bears	7	20	685	34.3
1945	Chicago Bears	10	36	1,299	36.1
1946	Chicago Bears	11	33	1,235	37.4
1947	Chicago Bears	12	5	177	35.4
1948	Chicago Bears	12	10	384	38.4
1949	Chicago Bears	11	1	16	16.0
1950	Chicago Bears	11	0	0	0.0
	TOTALS	128	230	8,862	38.5

Sources: Pro Football Hall of Fame; Pro-Football-Reference.com

Luisetti, Angelo "Hank" (born: June 16, 1916 in San Francisco, California; died: December 17, 2002 in San Mateo, California); inducted into the Naismith Memorial Basketball Hall of Fame in 1959 as a player; Position: Forward; won the 1937 national championship; first college player to score 50 points in a game.

Luisetti popularized the running one-handed shot, and while playing at Stanford University (Palo Alto, California) for three years (1935–1938) under hall of fame coach John Bunn, he averaged 16.1 points per game; led the school to three consecutive Pacific Coast Conference championships (1936–1938); helped the Indians win the national championship in 1937; was a two-time All-American (1937–1938); selected Helms Foundation Player of the Year twice (1937–1938); and graduated from the school as college basketball's all-time leading scorer.

In 1936, Luisetti came to Madison Square Garden (New York, New York), scored fifteen points, and helped Stanford end Long Island University's 43-game winning streak. On January 1, 1938 in a 92–27 win over Duquesne, Luisetti became the first college player to score 50 points in a game. In 1950, he was named the second-best basketball player of the mid-century (after the legendary George Mikan) by an Associated Press poll of sportswriters and broadcasters.

A native of San Francisco, he began his basketball career at Galileo High School (San Francisco) before attending Stanford. He was inducted into the Bay Area Sports Hall of Fame in 1980.

Sources: Bay Area Sports Hall of Fame; Naismith Memorial Basketball Hall of Fame

Lumley, Harry (born: November 11, 1926 in Owen Sound, Ontario, Canada; died: September 13, 1998 in Owen Sound, Ontario, Canada); inducted into the Hockey Hall of Fame in 1980 as a player; Position: Goalie; won the 1950 Stanley Cup championship.

Lumley entered the National Hockey League as a 17-year-old goalie and played 16 NHL seasons (1943–1960) for five of the Original Six teams, including the Detroit Red Wings (1943–1950), New York Rangers (1944), Chicago Black Hawks (1950–1952), Toronto Maple Leafs (1952–1956), and the Boston Bruins (1957–1960). He won the 1950 Stanley Cup championship; was named to the First All-Star Team twice (1954–1955); and won the 1954 Vezina Trophy as the league's best goalie.

After thriving as a junior and amateur player, Lumley was signed by the Red Wings when he was only 15 years old, and was sent to the team's minor league affiliate Indianapolis Capitols (American Hockey League).

The 6', 195-pound Lumley twice led the league in wins and six times in games played, and led the NHL in shutouts during the 1947–1948 season. When Lumley won the Vezina Trophy (with a 1.86 goals-against average) in 1954, his 13 shutouts that season set a modern record that would stand until Tony Esposito registered 15 in 1970.

In 1956, Lumley left the NHL for almost two seasons to play for the Buffalo Bisons (American Hockey League), before returning to the league with the Bruins in 1957, where he played off-and-on until retiring in 1960.

Harry Lumley's Career Statistics

			REGULAR SEASON						PLAYOFFS				
SEASON	TEAM	LEAGUE	GP	W	L	T	SO	AVG	GP	W	L	SO	AVG
1942–1943	Barrie Colts	OHA-Jr.											
1943–1944	Detroit Red Wings	NHL	2	0	2	0	0	6.50					
1943–1944	Indianapolis Capitols	AHL	52	19	18	15	0	2.84	5	1	4	0	3.60
1943–1944	New York Rangers	NHL	1	0	0	0	0	0.00					
1944–1945	Detroit Red Wings	NHL	37	24	10	3	1	3.22	14	7	7	2	2.14

SEASON	TEAM	LEAGUE	REGULAR SEASON GP	W	L	T	SO	AVG	PLAYOFFS GP	W	L	SO	AVG
1944–1945	Indianapolis Capitols	AHL	21	11	5	5	2	2.14					
1945–1946	Detroit Red Wings	NHL	50	20	20	10	2	3.18	5	1	4	1	3.10
1946–1947	Detroit Red Wings	NHL	52	22	20	10	3	3.06					
1947–1948	Detroit Red Wings	NHL	60	30	18	12	7	2.46	10	4	6	0	3.00
1948–1949	Detroit Red Wings	NHL	60	34	19	7	6	2.42	11	4	7	0	2.15
1949–1950	Detroit Red Wings	NHL	63	33	16	14	7	2.35	14	8	6	3	1.85
1950–1951	Chicago Black Hawks	NHL	64	12	41	10	3	3.90					
1951–1952	Chicago Black Hawks	NHL	70	17	44	9	2	3.46					
1952–1953	Toronto Maple Leafs	NHL	70	27	30	13	10	2.39					
1953–1954	Toronto Maple Leafs	NHL	69	32	24	13	13	1.86	5	1	4	0	2.80
1954–1955	Toronto Maple Leafs	NHL	69	23	24	22	8	1.94	4	0	4	0	3.50
1955–1956	Toronto Maple Leafs	NHL	59	21	28	10	3	2.67	5	1	4	1	2.57
1956–1957	Buffalo Bisons	AHL	63	25	36	2	0	4.19					
1957–1958	Buffalo Bisons	AHL	17	7	9	1	1	3.67					
1957–1958	Boston Bruins	NHL	24	11	10	3	3	2.92	1	0	1	0	5.00
1958–1959	Boston Bruins	NHL	11	8	2	1	1	2.45	7	3	4	0	2.75
1958–1959	Providence Reds	AHL	58	27	29	2	4	3.59					
1959–1960	Boston Bruins	NHL	42	16	21	5	2	3.48					
1960–1961	Kingston Frontenacs	EPHL	2	1	1	0	0	3.50					
1960–1961	Winnipeg Warriors	WHL	61	17	40	4	0	3.49					
	NHL TOTALS		803	330	329	142	71	2.75	76	29	47	7	2.48

Sources: Hockey Hall of Fame; Hockey-Reference.com

Lyman, William Roy "Link" (born: November 30, 1898 in Table Rock, Nebraska; died: December 28, 1972); inducted into the Pro Football Hall of Fame in 1964 as a player; Position: Tackle; won four NFL titles.

After playing at the University of Nebraska (Lincoln), the 6'2", 233 Lyman had an 11-year (133 games) National Football League career with the Canton Bulldogs (1922–1923 [both undefeated seasons], 1925), Cleveland Bulldogs (1924), Frankford Yellowjackets (1925), and the Chicago Bears (1926–1928, 1930–1931, 1933–1934).

Lyman played on only one losing team in 16 seasons of high school, college, and professional football and won four NFL championships (Canton in 1922 and 1923, Cleveland in 1924, and Chicago in 1933).

Lyman did not play football at McDonald Rural Federated High School (Pawnee County, Nebraska) because only seven boys attended the school. However, his natural skills and speed helped him adapt to the game at Nebraska.

Source: Pro Football Hall of Fame

Lyons, Theodore Amar "Ted" (born: December 28, 1900 in Lake Charles, Louisiana; died: July 25, 1986 in Sulphur, Louisiana); inducted into the National Baseball Hall of Fame and Museum in 1955 as a player; Position: Pitcher; Bats: Right; Throws: Right; Uniform: #16; threw a no-hitter in only 67 minutes against the Boston Red Sox.

Making his major league debut on July 2, 1923, the 5'11", 200-pound Lyons played his entire 21-year career (1923–1942, 1946) with the Chicago White Sox; was selected to the 1939 All-Star team; and later managed the White Sox from 1946 to 1948. He led the American League in wins twice (1925, 1927) and earned run average in 1942; had three 20-win seasons; and his jersey number 16 was retired by the White Sox.

Joining the White Sox immediately after graduating from Baylor University (Waco, Texas), he managed to win 260 games for a team that was never very good. In 1942, Lyons pitched primarily on Sundays (earning the nickname "Sunday Ted"); pitched to a 14–6 record with a league-leading 2.10 earned run average; and completed all 20 of his starts.

On August 21, 1926 in a game against the Boston Red Sox, it took Lyons only 67 minutes to throw a no-hitter in a 6–0 win.

As a manager, he was not able to help the team become a winning franchise, leading Chicago to a 185–245 (.430) record. After leaving the White Sox in 1948, he served as a pitching coach for the Detroit Tigers (1949–1952) and Brooklyn Dodgers (1954).

Ted Lyons' Career Playing Statistics

YEAR	TEAM	LG	W	L	PCT	G	SH	IP	H	R	ER	SO	BB	ERA
1923	Chicago	AL	2	1	.667	9	0	23	30	21	16	6	15	6.26
1924	Chicago	AL	12	11	.522	41	0	216	279	143	117	52	72	4.88
1925	Chicago	AL	21	11	.656	43	5	263	274	111	95	45	83	3.25
1926	Chicago	AL	18	16	.529	39	3	284	268	108	95	51	106	3.01

YEAR	TEAM	LG	W	L	PCT	G	SH	IP	H	R	ER	SO	BB	ERA
1927	Chicago	AL	22	14	.611	39	2	308	291	125	97	71	67	2.83
1928	Chicago	AL	15	14	.517	39	0	240	276	133	106	60	68	3.98
1929	Chicago	AL	14	20	.412	37	1	259	276	136	118	57	76	4.10
1930	Chicago	AL	22	15	.595	42	1	298	331	160	125	69	57	3.78
1931	Chicago	AL	4	6	.400	22	0	101	117	50	45	16	33	4.01
1932	Chicago	AL	10	15	.400	33	1	231	243	104	84	58	71	3.27
1933	Chicago	AL	10	21	.323	36	2	228	260	142	111	74	74	4.38
1934	Chicago	AL	11	13	.458	30	0	205	249	138	111	53	66	4.87
1935	Chicago	AL	15	8	.652	23	3	191	194	79	64	54	56	3.02
1936	Chicago	AL	10	13	.435	26	1	182	227	115	104	48	45	5.14
1937	Chicago	AL	12	7	.632	22	0	169	182	86	78	45	45	4.15
1938	Chicago	AL	9	11	.450	23	1	195	238	93	80	54	52	3.69
1939	Chicago	AL	14	6	.700	21	0	173	162	71	53	65	26	2.76
1940	Chicago	AL	12	8	.600	22	4	186	188	85	67	72	37	3.24
1941	Chicago	AL	12	10	.545	22	2	187	199	87	77	63	37	3.71
1942	Chicago	AL	14	6	.700	20	1	180	167	52	42	50	26	2.10
1946	Chicago	AL	1	4	.200	5	0	43	38	17	11	10	9	2.30
	TOTALS		260	230	.531	594	27	4,162	4,489	2,056	1,696	1,073	1,121	3.67

Ted Lyons' Managerial Record

YEAR	TEAM	LG	W	L	WIN%
1946	Chicago	AL	64	60	.516
1947	Chicago	AL	70	84	.455
1948	Chicago	AL	51	101	.336
	TOTALS		185	245	.430

Sources: Baseball-Reference.com; National Baseball Hall of Fame and Museum